THE ROUTLEDGE HANDBOOK OF INFORMATION HISTORY

The Routledge Handbook of Information History offers a definitive, inclusive, and far-reaching study of how information practices have influenced—and have been influenced by—society, politics, culture, and technology over millennia.

Information is often considered a defining characteristic of modern society, but it is far from a modern phenomenon. In the last decades, historians have started to ask new questions about how information was understood in the past, suggesting that it has a history which is long, complex, and multifaceted. This influential volume is the first large-scale collection to use the term Information History as its titular focus, situating "information" within the historiography of the field. The book showcases a diverse assembly of over forty international contributors who explore information practices from antiquity to the contemporary world, with geographical coverage ranging across Europe, Africa, Asia, as well as North and South America.

Including overview chapters alongside a wide range of in-depth empirical studies, this ground-breaking collection will appeal to scholars and students across the arts, humanities, and social sciences, offering readers unique insights into how historical practices have influenced the understanding and role of information in our modern world.

Toni Weller is visiting research fellow in history at De Montfort University, UK. For the past twenty years she has authored numerous books, articles, and book chapters on the theory of information history, women and information, Victorian information culture, as well as the history of the surveillance state.

Alistair Black is professor emeritus in the School of Information Sciences, University of Illinois Urbana-Champaign, USA, but lives and researches in the UK. He has published extensively, over many years, on the history of information management and libraries.

Bonnie Mak is a historian of ancient, medieval, and modern information practices. She is associate professor in the School of Information Sciences at the University of Illinois Urbana-Champaign, USA, and the author of *How the Page Matters* (2011).

Laura Skouvig is associate professor in the Department of Communication at the University of Copenhagen, Denmark. She has co-edited *Histories of Surveillance from Antiquity to the Digital Era. The Eyes and Ears of Power* (2021) and has written about information and surveillance in eighteenth-century Denmark.

"Information always has a modern ring to it, but as we enter the AI revolution, we would do well to remember that many of the basic challenges we face today have roots that lead back to antiquity. This essential book shows just how deeply the origins of the modern information revolution are rooted in the past."
Jacob Soll, *University Professor and Professor of Philosophy, History, and Accounting, University of Southern California, USA*

"This is a refreshingly broad compilation, one which offers a provocative look across information-related practices, delving into cultural and historical specificities as a way to ensure that information history emerges at large as a vital area of study."
Lisa Gitelman, *Professor of English and Media, Culture, and Communication, New York University, USA*

THE ROUTLEDGE HANDBOOK OF INFORMATION HISTORY

*Edited by Toni Weller, Alistair Black,
Bonnie Mak, and Laura Skouvig*

LONDON AND NEW YORK

Designed cover image: Detail of *Auxiliary Disciplines* by Julia Pollack, in response to "quiet conversation and the cultivation of friendships." Oil pastel on paper, 11 × 7 inches (280 × 178 mm). CC BY 4.0

First published 2026
by Routledge
4 Park Square, Milton Park, Abingdon, Oxon OX14 4RN

and by Routledge
605 Third Avenue, New York, NY 10158

Routledge is an imprint of the Taylor & Francis Group, an informa business

© 2026 selection and editorial matter, Toni Weller, Alistair Black, Bonnie Mak, and Laura Skouvig; individual chapters, the contributors

The right of Toni Weller, Alistair Black, Bonnie Mak, and Laura Skouvig to be identified as the authors of the editorial material, and of the authors for their individual chapters, has been asserted in accordance with sections 77 and 78 of the Copyright, Designs and Patents Act 1988.

With the exception of Chapter 28, no part of this book may be reprinted or reproduced or utilised in any form or by any electronic, mechanical, or other means, now known or hereafter invented, including photocopying and recording, or in any information storage or retrieval system, without permission in writing from the publishers.

Chapter 28 of this book is freely available as a downloadable Open Access PDF at http://www.taylorfrancis.com under a Creative Commons Attribution-Non Commercial-No Derivatives (CC-BY) 4.0 International license.

Any third party material in this book is not included in the OA Creative Commons license, unless indicated otherwise in a credit line to the material. Please direct any permissions enquiries to the original rightsholder.

Trademark notice: Product or corporate names may be trademarks or registered trademarks, and are used only for identification and explanation without intent to infringe.

British Library Cataloguing-in-Publication Data
A catalogue record for this book is available from the British Library

Library of Congress Cataloging-in-Publication Data
Names: Weller, Toni, editor. | Black, Alistair, editor. | Mak, Bonnie, editor. | Skouvig, Laura, editor.
Title: Routledge handbook of information history / edited by Toni Weller, Alistair Black, Bonnie Mak, and Laura Skouvig.
Description: Abingdon, Oxon ; New York, NY : Routledge, 2026. | Includes bibliographical references and index.
Identifiers: LCCN 2024058536 (print) | LCCN 2024058537 (ebook) | ISBN 9781032316079 (hardback) | ISBN 9781032316178 (paperback) | ISBN 9781003310532 (ebook)
Subjects: LCSH: Information science--History. | LCGFT: Essays.
Classification: LCC Z665 .R834 2025 (print) | LCC Z665 (ebook) | DDC 020.9--dc23/eng/20250203
LC record available at https://lccn.loc.gov/2024058536
LC ebook record available at https://lccn.loc.gov/2024058537

ISBN: 978-1-032-31607-9 (hbk)
ISBN: 978-1-032-31617-8 (pbk)
ISBN: 978-1-003-31053-2 (ebk)

DOI: 10.4324/9781003310532

Typeset in Sabon
by KnowledgeWorks Global Ltd.

Access the Support Material: www.routledge.com/9781032316079

CONTENTS

List of Illustrations   *x*
List of Contributors   *xiv*
Preface and Acknowledgements   *xx*

PART I
Introduction   1

1 Situating Information History: The History and Historiography of Information and Its Practices   3
   Alistair Black, Bonnie Mak, Laura Skouvig, and Toni Weller

PART II
Visualising, Describing, Expressing   35

2 Information in the Roman Empire   37
   Andrew Riggsby

3 Information and Its Forms: Documentary Practices in the Medieval West (Mid-Ninth to Mid-Thirteenth Centuries)   52
   Brigitte Miriam Bedos-Rezak

4 The Andean Khipus: An Information System Made of String   78
   Lucrezia Milillo and Sabine Hyland

5 Racialised Language in Colonial Newspaper Advertisements During the Eighteenth and Nineteenth Centuries   95
   Natália da Silva Perez

Contents

6 "There Must be Something Vicious in the Data": Thomas
  Jefferson's Techniques of Racialisation in the Production
  of *Data*, *Facts*, and *Information*   110
  Melissa Adler

7 Encyclopaedias as Cultural Carriers of Information:
  A Scandinavian Perspective   124
  Maria Simonsen

8 Paul Otlet's Experiments with Knowledge Organisation
  and Explorations of a Future Semantic Web   139
  Charles van den Heuvel

9 Information as Instruction: A Short History of Attack
  Journalism   158
  Bethany Usher

10 The Fault Lines of Knowledge: An Examination of the History
   of Wikipedia's "Neutral Point of View" (NPOV) Information
   Policy and Its Implications for a Polarised World   173
   Brendan Luyt

11 Facial AIs and Information Systems in Historical Context   187
   Edward Higgs

PART III
Managing, Ordering, Classifying   **201**

12 "Those Who Help His Sight and Hearing Are Many":
   Information and the State in Early China   203
   Rebecca Robinson

13 Creativity in Classification: Phrasing and Presenting
   the Aristotelian Categories in the Middle Ages   215
   Irene O'Daly

14 Trading Factories as Information Factories: Aspects of Information
   Management in the Dutch East India Company's Japanese
   Factory, 1609–1623   233
   Gabor Szommer

15 The Female Body as an Object of Information: Britain during
   the Late Victorian and Edwardian Period   247
   Toni Weller

16 Information, Topography, and War: Information Management in Britain's Inter-Service Topographical Department (ISTD) in the Second World War *Alistair Black*	264
17 The Wartime Social Survey as Information History *Henry Irving*	280
18 Sensitive Information: Knowing and Preparing for Nuclear War during the Cold War *Rosanna Farbøl and Casper Sylvest*	295
19 "Men Are Engineers, Women Are Computers": Women and the Information Technology Interregnum *Antony Bryant*	308
20 Central and Local: A History of Archives in Twentieth-Century England *Elizabeth Shepherd*	324
21 Representing Information in the Western World: Classification, Cataloguing, and the Library Context since Industrialisation *Karen Attar*	338
22 The History of Computing: The Development of an Information History Field *William Aspray*	353
23 Smart Cities and Informatic Governance: The Management of Information and People in Postcolonial Singapore *Hallam Stevens and Manoj Harjani*	368

PART IV
Circulating, Networking, Controlling — 383

24 The Politics of Communication in the Early Modern City: Istanbul and Venice *Filippo de Vivo*	385
25 Recipes, Gold, and Information Exchange: Workshop Cultures in the Early Modern Metropolis *Jasmine Kilburn-Toppin*	402

26	Colonial Political Economies of Information: The East India Company and the Growth of Science in Britain *Jessica Ratcliff*	414
27	In-Between Writing and Orality: The Circulation of Information in the Black Spanish Caribbean during the Age of Revolutions, 1789–1808 *Cristina Soriano*	429
28	Information and Mobility: Migrants and Roma as Historical Cases *Eve Rosenhaft*	442
29	Emotions as Commodities: Street Ballads and the Commercialisation of Information *Laura Skouvig*	457
30	How Information Changed Between the Late Nineteenth Century and World War II *James W. Cortada*	471
31	Factual Fictions and Fictionalised Facts in the Reports of the Romanian Secret Police *Valentina Glajar and Corina L. Petrescu*	485
32	Families as Communities of Information. Or: The Importance of Knowing Your Relatives *Markus Friedrich*	501
33	Feathers and Formats: Information, Technology, and Homing Pigeons in War *Frank A. Blazich, Jr.*	516
34	Information and Communication Theories: A Global History of the (Con)fusion *Gabriele Balbi, Gianluigi Negro, Maria Rikitianskaia, Carlos A. Scolari, and Dominique Trudel*	536
35	Decolonisation and Information in Postcolonial Egypt, 1952–1967 *Zoe LeBlanc*	552

36 Dynamics of the Human Element in South Africa's Information
    History   566
    Archie L. Dick

PART V
Afterword   **581**

37 What Is Information History for?   583
    Bonnie Mak

Index   *598*

ILLUSTRATIONS

Figures

3.1 Paris, Bibliothèque nationale de France, Bourgogne 76 n° 16. Gift to the abbey of Cluny from Geoffrey, count of Nevers, 936. Top left: Chrismon. Centre: Space of subscriptions with graphic signs.   53

3.2 Orléans, Archives départementales du Loiret, Portef. n° 58. Gift to the abbey of Bonne-Nouvelle, 1037.   54

3.3 Poitiers, Archives départementales de la Vienne, PIECE RESTAUREE 57 (olim G 591 C 2 n° 8). Sale of a vine near Poitiers, 893. Contour of the animal's body is visible at bottom right.   55

3.4 Rouen, Archives départementales de la Seine-Maritime, 9 H 30/3. Gift from Roger II of Montgomery of an estate held of him to the abbey of Jumièges, 1048. "Wandering crosses" across bottom. Hole in the parchment is visible towards the end of the document's third line.   55

3.5 Paris, Archives nationales, J 168 no 6. Agreement between the abbey of Saint-Denis and Matthew, count of Beaumont, 1189. Left: Seal of the abbey of Saint-Denis. Right: Seal of the count of Beaumont. Photo by author.   56

3.6 Counterseal of Matthew of Beaumont, with coat of arms and fingerprints. Photo by author.   57

3.7 Marburg, Staatsarchiv K. Urk. Nr.54. Diploma by which Henry II, King of the Germans, gifts a forest to the abbey of Fulda, December 1012. Top left: Chrismon in the shape of the letter "C." Centre: Monogram of Henry. Bottom right: Acheiropoietic seal image. Courtesy Das Lichtbildarchiv älterer Originalurkunden (LBA).   58

3.8 Paris, Archives nationales, J 168 no 32, 1222. Fingerprints on the counterseal of Milon I, bishop of Beauvais. Photo by author.   59

3.9 Paris, Archives nationales, L//846 no 49, 1204. Details of fingerprints on the obverse of the seal of Elvise of Nangis. Photo by author.   59

3.10 Detached wax impression of the city seal of Brunswick, early thirteenth century. Obverse: A lion in a walled city. Author's collection. Photo by Ira Loeb Rezak, MD.   60

List of Illustrations

3.11 Detached wax impression of the city seal of Brunswick, early thirteenth century. Reverse: Three thumbprints amid fingerprints. Author's collection. Photo by Ira Loeb Rezak, MD. — 60

3.12 Paris, Archives nationales, AE/II/181 (J 168 no 2) and Pontoise, Archives départmentales du Val-d'Oise, 9H81. Exchange of land, rights, and revenues between Matthew III, count of Beaumont-sur-Oise (d. ca 1208) and Geoffrey, abbot of Saint-Martin of Pontoise, 1177. This piece of parchment recorded the exchange in duplicate. It was then cut through the image of Christ on the cross, to provide each party with a charter sealed by their partner in the exchange. The survival and reunion of both parts of the medieval chirograph is a relatively rare phenomenon. — 65

3.13 Angers, Archives départementales de Maine-et-Loire H 1773, fol 9vo–10. Cartulary of the abbey of Saint-Maur de Glanfeuil, ca. 1130. Visible on the left is a drawing of the seal of Peter, bishop of Poitiers (1103). At the bottom is a drawing of the Chrismon, at the beginning of the next copied charter, issued by Geoffroy, count of Anjou (ca. 1010). — 67

3.14 Angoulême, Archives départementales de la Charente, MS H(01), 1, fol. IX ro, no 43. Cartulary of Saint-Cybard. Charter copied in the cartulary; the crosses next to the names of their signatories are uniform and drawn by copyists. — 68

3.15 Angoulême, Archives départmentales de la Charente, MS H(01), 1, fol. 34vo, no 86. Cartulary of Saint-Cybard. Autograph crosses. — 69

4.1 Close up of an Inka style khipu. Primary cord is lying horizontally at the top. Groups of pendant cords are attached to the primary cord. The lowest knots on the pendant cords prevent the cord from unravelling. Above those are knots for single units, followed by those for tens. In the leftmost group of pendant cords are also knots for hundreds, visible above the knots for tens. Subsidiary cords are attached to some pendants on the right-hand side of the khipu. Both pendant and subsidiary cords are of different colours: from light, medium to dark brown as well as indigo blue. All cords are made of cotton. Berlin Ethnology Museum VA 66830. Photo by Lucrezia Milillo. — 79

4.2 Tupicocha patrimonial khipu and kayte. Nelser Ramos Romero is holding a khipu from its primary cord, coiled on itself, from which woollen pendant cords hang. In this khipu, the cords are of different colours, ranging from pale rose and beige to dark brown and dark grey. At the top is a round-shaped kayte with a bright blue and red tuft at the end. The kayte is particularly colourful, including bright blue threads together with more neutral beige and yellow-ochre threads. Photo by Lucrezia Milillo. — 88

8.1 Network of documentation in a hierarchical order of Mundaneum species. Mundaneum (Mons), D6PPP05, EUMC, 8504, @collection Mundaneum, Belgium, Mons. — 143

8.2 The Mondothèque. Mundaneum (Mons), EUMP, 8141, @collection Mundaneum, Belgium, Mons. — 144

List of Illustrations

8.3 Dimensions reduction mapping the contents of book on a line, Paul Otlet, "Théorie schématique de la classification" (detail), December 14, 1908. Mundaneum (Mons), PPPO 956, EUM farde 8, no. 42, @collection Mundaneum, Belgium, Mons. 146
8.4 Design multidimensional card system by Paul Otlet. Mundaneum (Mons), PPPO 956, EUM farde 9, no. 74–75, @collection Mundaneum, Belgium, Mons. 147
8.5 Mapping of a numerical notation by Paul Otlet. Mundaneum (Mons). "Notation" (detail), PPPO 956, EUM farde 7, no. 21, @collection Mundaneum, Belgium, Mons. 147
8.6 Comparison mappings on pyramid, cube, and octagonal cylinder by Paul Otlet, Mundaneum (Mons) "Notation, Schéma, Tableau, Ecriture" (detail), PPPO 956, farde no. 9, 105, @collection Mundaneum, Belgium, Mons. 148
8.7 Octagonal Index card by Paul Otlet, Mundaneum (Mons), PPPO 956 EUM farde 9, no. 76, @collection Mundaneum, Belgium, Mons. 148
8.8 Octagonal "Livre," by Paul Otlet, "Elements de schématique" (detail), April 1916, Mundaneum (Mons), PPPO 281, no. 7, @collection Mundaneum, Belgium, Mons. 149
8.9 Extraction of elements from multi-media documents and reassembling them into new formats by Paul Otlet, June 8, 1937, Mundaneum (Mons), "Elements et ensembles," D6PPO4, EUMC 8435, @collection Mundaneum, Belgium, Mons. 151
9.1 Anti-royalist newsbook published during the English Civil War. 160
13.1 Paris, Bibliothèque nationale de France, MS lat. 12949, fol. 27bis r. The Isidorean phrase is found above the diagram labelled *Substantia* or "Substance." 220
13.2 Detail of Göttweig, Benediktinerstift, Cod. 53b, fol. 83v. A diagram of the categories, surrounded by the words of the Isidorean phrase, with the words *Deus*, "God," and *Homo*, "Man" presented across its central axes. 226
13.3 Detail of Göttweig, Benediktinerstift, Cod. 33 (rot)/14 (schwarz), fol. III*r. A diagram of the categories with the words of the Isidorean phrase adapted to refer to Hector, not Augustine. 227
15.1 Example of one of the double-sided Newnham College Index Cards, recording the physical characteristics of Louisa Darbishire, 1898, foreside. Photograph of the cards by Toni Weller, but used with kind permission of the Principal and Fellows of Newnham College. 252
15.2 Example of one of the double-sided Newnham College Index Cards, recording the physical characteristics of Louisa Darbishire, 1898, reverse side. Photograph of the cards by Toni Weller, but used with kind permission of the Principal and Fellows of Newnham College. 252
15.3 Detail from the census return for Nellie R. Harrison, Woking, taken from 1911 Census Return for England and Wales. Image from Ancestry.com, reproduced with kind permission of The National Archives of England and Wales. 257

List of Illustrations

16.1	The ISTD female staff, probably Navy Wrens, working in the New Bodleian Library. In the interests of security, most ISTD staff were in civilian dress. Photographed by Peter Bradford (Admiralty Photographic Unit). Reproduced with permission of the Harris Manchester College, University of Oxford.	271
17.1	A member of Wartime Social Survey staff feeding punched cards into a tabulating machine in 1944 (photograph D18860), reproduced courtesy of the Imperial War Museum.	286
31.1	Cover page of Claus Stephani's informer file, code-named MOGA MIRCEA. Image from ACNSAS, Bucharest, Romania. ACNSAS, FR, File 203049.	486
31.2	First page of Franz Auerbach's report to ARIA. Image from ACNSAS, Bucharest, ACNSAS, FD, File 137, Volume 10, Page 15.	492
33.1	Pigeon post as described by Sir John Mandeville, depicted in a 1488 woodcut published by Johann Prüss.	518
33.2	Pigeon after arrival at Fort Lucy, France, carrying a message about a gas attack at Toul, October 1918. Note the aluminium message holder still attached to its leg, a refinement of Marion's original design.	521
33.3	A message transmitted by pigeon, announcing the Armistice of November 11, 1918. The message reads "All firing ceased at 11 hr. per orders." The bird with leg band number 17276 took fifteen minutes to fly the message from the post of command (PC) to the commanding officer of the Third Battalion, 112th Infantry Regiment.	522
33.4	German soldiers writing a report to be delivered by homing pigeon, March 1917.	523
33.5	Homing pigeon being released from an aircraft in flight, US Naval Air Station Anacostia, Washington, DC.	525
33.6	A refinement of Neubronner's efforts at the turn of the twentieth century, the American Central Intelligence Agency developed a miniaturised film camera for pigeons in the late 1970s which provided a remarkable resolution of less than one inch, enabling the gathering of detailed photographic information.	529

Map

14.1	Map of the trading world around Japan at the start of the seventeenth century. Drawn by the author.	236

Table

6.1	Occurrences of Jefferson's use of terms, as found among his digitised papers in *Founders Online*.	112

CONTRIBUTORS

Melissa Adler is associate professor and graduate chair in the Faculty of Information and Media Studies at the University of Western Ontario, Canada. Her book, *Cruising the Library: Perversities in the Organization of Knowledge* (2017), is a study of the history of sexuality through the lens of Library of Congress classifications and categories. Her forthcoming books are *"Peculiar Satisfaction": Thomas Jefferson and the Mastery of Subjects* (2025) and *Surveillance in the "Empire of Liberty": Why Thomas Jefferson Matters in Our Information Age* (forthcoming, 2026).

William Aspray is senior research fellow at the Charles Babbage Institute, USA. He taught for many years in information schools (Colorado, Indiana, and Texas) and also worked for nonprofit organisations (Babbage Institute, IEEE History Center, and Computing Research Association). He was formerly the editor of the journal *Information & Culture*. He is the co-author of *Computer: The History of an Information Machine* (2023) and the author of *Understanding Information History* (2023).

Karen Attar is curator of rare books and university art at Senate House Library, University of London, UK. She has published widely on library history and cataloguing. She edited the *Directory of Rare Book and Special Collections in the United Kingdom and Republic of Ireland* (3e, 2016; updated 2021).

Gabriele Balbi is full professor at USI Università della Svizzera Italiana, Switzerland, where he is also pro-rector for education and students' experience. His area of research is media and communication history. His most recent book was *The Digital Revolution. A Short History of an Ideology* (2023). His webpage is http://usi.to/cyi and his ORCID https://orcid.org/0000-0001-7752-277X.

Brigitte Miriam Bedos-Rezak is professor of history at New York University, USA. Her most recent research on documentary practices has appeared in *When Ego Was Imago. Signs of Identity in the Middle Ages* (2011); *Sign and Design and Script as Image in a Cross-Cultural Perspective* (2016); *The Faces of Charisma: Image, Text, Object in Byzantium* *and the Medieval West* (2018); and *Seals: Making and Marking Connections across the Medieval World* (2019).

Alistair Black is professor emeritus in the School of Information Sciences, University of Illinois Urbana-Champaign, USA, but lives and researches in the UK. He has authored numerous studies in information-management history, including *The Early Information Society in Britain* (2007), and has written extensively on the history of public and corporate libraries.

Frank A. Blazich, Jr., received his PhD from Ohio State University, USA, in 2013. He is curator of military history at the Smithsonian's National Museum of American History. His book publications include *Bataan Survivor* (2017) and *An Honorable Place in American Air Power* (2020).

Antony Bryant is professor of informatics at Leeds Beckett University, UK, and chief researcher at the Institute of Educational Research, Vytautas Magnus University, Lithuania. Recent articles include "Liquid Uncertainty, Chaos and Complexity: The Gig Economy and the Open Source Movement," "A Conversation between Frank Land and Antony Bryant," and "What the Web Has Wrought."

James W. Cortada is senior research fellow at the Charles Babbage Institute, University of Minnesota, USA. His most recent publications include with William Aspray, *Fake News Nation: The Long History of Lies and Misinterpretations in America* (2019), and, as solo author, *Birth of Modern Facts* (2023) and *Today's Facts: Understanding the Current Evolution of Information* (2025).

Natália da Silva Perez is assistant professor of popular culture in historical perspective at the Erasmus University Rotterdam School of History, Culture and Communication, The Netherlands. In her research, she engages in early modern history from transnational, comparative, and decolonial perspectives, focusing especially on women as they interacted with their families, communities, and authorities.

Filippo de Vivo is professor of early modern history at the University of Oxford, UK. The author of *Information and Communication in Venice: Rethinking Early Modern Politics* (2007), he has written on rhetoric, printed pamphlets, rumours, graffiti, as well as on the comparative history of archives, pharmacies, and walking.

Archie L. Dick is emeritus professor in the Department of Information Science at the University of Pretoria, South Africa. He authored *The Hidden History of South Africa's Book and Reading Cultures* (2013). His latest project investigates the exchange of medical information between the Cape and Ceylon in the early eighteenth century.

Rosanna Farbøl is associate professor of contemporary European history at the University of Oslo, Norway. Her latest works include the co-authored "Cold War Conduct: Knowledge Transfer, Psychological Defence and Media Preparedness in Denmark between Sweden, Norway and NATO, 1954–1967" in the *Scandinavian Journal of History* (2024).

Markus Friedrich is full professor of early modern European history at Hamburg University, Germany. After taking a PhD from Munich University, he held postdoctoral positions at Duke University, Boston College, University of Frankfurt, and the Max Planck Institute for the History of Science. He specialises in the history of knowledge and the history of Christianity, and is currently preparing a global history of genealogy.

Valentina Glajar is professor of German and honorary professor of International Studies at Texas State University, USA. In 2019, she received an American Council of Learned Societies Fellowship, which enabled her to complete her most recent monograph, *The Secret Police Dossier of Herta Müller* (2023).

Manoj Harjani is research fellow at the S. Rajaratnam School of International Studies (RSIS), Nanyang Technological University, Singapore, where he is also coordinator of the Military Transformations Programme. Prior to joining RSIS, Manoj worked in Singapore's civil service, holding roles in strategic foresight and digital transformation policy.

Edward Higgs is professor emeritus, School of Philosophical, Historical, and Interdisciplinary Studies at the University of Essex, UK. He is the author of *The Information State in England: The Central Collection of Information on Citizens* (2004); *Identifying the English: Personal Identification 1500 to the Present* (2011); and *Reading Faces: Facial Biometrics from Aristotle to Artificial Intelligence* (forthcoming).

Sabine Hyland is an anthropologist and professor of world religion at the University of St Andrews, UK. For the past twenty years, she has collaborated with Andean elders on preserving khipu traditions. Her work has been supported by fellowships from the Guggenheim Foundation, the British Academy, and the National Geographic Society.

Henry Irving is senior lecturer in public history at Leeds Beckett University, UK. He is an expert on British opinion monitoring in the Second World War and is the co-editor of the book *Information at War* (forthcoming). He holds a British Academy Innovation Fellowship for his work on wartime recycling.

Jasmine Kilburn-Toppin is lecturer in early modern history at Cardiff University, UK. Her research explores early modern artisanal cultures and networks of craft and "scientific" knowledge. Publications include *Crafting Identities: Artisan Culture in London, c.1550–1640* (2021), and co-authored with Rebekah Higgitt, *Metropolitan Science: London Sites and Cultures of Knowledge and Practice, c.1600–1800* (2024).

Zoe LeBlanc is assistant professor in the School of Information Sciences at the University of Illinois Urbana-Champaign, USA. She is working on a digital book, *Informing the Third World*, which explores how decolonisation transformed information networks and politics, setting the stage for many of today's debates over information sovereignty.

Brendan Luyt is associate professor at WKWSCI, Nanyang Technological University, Singapore.

Bonnie Mak is a historian of ancient, medieval, and modern information practices. She is associate professor in the School of Information Sciences at the University of Illinois

Urbana-Champaign, USA, and the author of *How the Page Matters* (2011). Other publications include a cabinet, a box, a card catalogue, some fragments, and several journal articles.

Lucrezia Milillo is a researcher in the Department of Social Anthropology at the University of St. Andrews, UK. During her doctoral research as a Wolfson Scholar, she led the Iperion-HS project, *Meaningful Materials in the Khipu Code*. Her research focuses on khipus, integrating the anthropology of technology, material culture studies, and heritage science.

Gianluigi Negro is associate professor in Chinese studies, Department of Philology and Literary Criticism, University of Siena, Italy. His research focuses on the history and the evolution of the Chinese internet as well as the relations between the history of China's media system and nationalism.

Irene O'Daly is lecturer in book studies at Leiden University, The Netherlands. Her current research explores the reception of the Latin classics in the Middle Ages, with a particular interest in how the materiality of their manuscript carriers conveys traces of their production and readership.

Corina L. Petrescu is professor of German at The University of Mississippi, USA. She is an accredited researcher with the National Council for the Study of the Securitate Archives (CNSAS) in Romania. Her research interests include secret police files as life writing, Yiddish theatre in and from Romania, transcultural literature, and subversiveness in National Socialist Germany.

Julia Pollack is creative programme manager at the Carl R. Woese Institute for Genomic Biology at the University of Illinois Urbana-Champaign, USA. She creates and curates the Art of Science Collection, which is generated from microscopy and scientific imagery that are then transformed into art. She is trained as a librarian, digital humanist, user experience designer, and artist.

Jessica Ratcliff is associate professor in the Department of Science and Technology Studies at Cornell University, USA. She works on the history of science and technology, and is especially interested in the political economy of knowledge production. Her newest book is *Monopolizing Knowledge: The East India Company and Britain's Second Scientific Revolution* (2025).

Andrew Riggsby is Lucy Shoe Meritt Professor in Classics at the University of Texas at Austin, USA. He is the author of *Mosaics of Knowledge: Representing Information in the Roman World* (2019) and a variety of articles on information and cognition in the ancient world.

Maria Rikitianskaia is course leader for BA Media and Communications and lecturer in media and communications at Regent's University London, UK. She holds a PhD in communications sciences (2018) from Università della Svizzera Italiana, Switzerland. Her research focuses on global wireless connectivity, from wireless telegraphy to Wi-Fi networks.

List of Contributors

Rebecca Robinson is assistant professor in the Department of History at the Université de Montréal, Canada. Her research is in the field of global antiquities, comparing early China with the ancient Mediterranean. Her first book, *Imperial Cults: Religion and Politics in the Early Han and Roman Empires*, was published in 2023.

Eve Rosenhaft is professor emerita of German historical studies at the University of Liverpool, UK. She has published widely on aspects of German social history since the eighteenth century. Her chapter in this volume reflects a convergence between her interest in information history, which began with studies on the origins of life insurance, and more recent research in Romani history.

Carlos A. Scolari is professor in the Department of Communication of the University Pompeu Fabra, Barcelona. His most recent book is *On the Evolution of Media. Understanding Media Change* (2023). He was the Principal Investigator of H2020 TRANSLITERACY (2015–2018) and PLATCOM (2020–2024) research projects.

Elizabeth Shepherd is professor emerita of archives and records management, Department of Information Studies, University College London, UK. She is the author of *Archives and Archivists in 20th Century England* (2009) and is currently writing a book on pioneering women archivists in England. Her research interests include rights in records for care leavers, MIRRA project (Memory-Identity-Rights in Records-Access).

Maria Simonsen is associate professor, Department of Politics and Society, Aalborg University, Denmark. Her research interests lie in the tension between media, people, institutions, and knowledge. She is particularly interested in how knowledge circulates and how it changes when circulating. Her current research focuses on the history of universities.

Laura Skouvig is associate professor in the Department of Communication at the University of Copenhagen, Denmark. She is the co-editor of *Histories of Surveillance from Antiquity to the Digital Era. The Eyes and Ears of Power* (2021), and has written about information, surveillance, and information cultures in eighteenth-century Denmark.

Cristina Soriano is associate professor of Latin American history at The University of Texas at Austin, USA. Her book, *Tides of Revolution: Information, Insurgencies, and the Crisis of Colonial Rule in* Venezuela (2018), received the 2019 Bolton-Johnson and the 2020 Fernando Coronil Awards. She co-edited the *Cambridge Companion to Latin American Independence* (2023) and is working on a project on the imperial transition in the island of Trinidad during the Age of Revolutions.

Hallam Stevens is adjunct professor at James Cook University in Queensland, Australia. His research focuses on the history of biology and the history of information technologies in the twentieth and twenty-first centuries. He is the author of *Life out of Sequence: A Data-Driven History of Bioinformatics* (2013) and *Biotechnology and Society: An Introduction* (2016).

Casper Sylvest is professor of history and head of the Saxo Institute at the University of Copenhagen, Denmark. His interdisciplinary work—combining interests in the study of politics, history, law, and technology—has in recent years primarily focused on nuclear history and environmental history.

List of Contributors

Gabor Szommer received his PhD degree in early modern history in Hungary. He works as a freelance editor and translator. His primary research interest is the early history of the Dutch and English East India Companies, and he focuses mostly on information-related details.

Dominique Trudel is associate professor in the Department of Communication and Culture of Audencia Business School, France. He specialises in media and communication history and recently co-edited the *Franklin Ford Collection* at mediastudies.press.

Bethany Usher writes for a range of regional and national publications and is senior lecturer in journalism (theory and practice) at Newcastle University, UK. She is the author of *Journalism and Celebrity* (2020) and *Journalism and Crime* (2023), and her research and advocacy can be explored further at bethanyusher.com.

Charles van den Heuvel is the former head of knowledge and art practices at the Huygens Institute for History and Culture of the Netherlands and emeritus professor for digital methods and historical disciplines, University of Amsterdam. Research interests include history of art, history of science, history of information science, and the digital humanities.

Toni Weller is visiting research fellow in history at De Montfort University, UK. She has worked in the field of information history for over twenty years, and has published extensively on the theory of information history, women and information, Victorian information culture, and the history of the surveillance state. She is also a former editor of the international journal *Library & Information History*.

PREFACE AND ACKNOWLEDGEMENTS

It has been said that we are living through a new age, an information age, characterised by revolutionary practices, from internet shopping, social media, and artificial intelligence, to digital surveillance and information warfare. However, the benefits and drawbacks of this new age should not cause us to overlook the existence of past information ages, the information practices of which have been no less important relative to the needs of the time. In recent decades, historians have begun to acknowledge that information is far from a modern phenomenon and have accordingly begun to ask questions about how information was understood in the past, thereby revealing that it has a complex and variegated history.

This volume offers a wide-ranging study of how, since antiquity, information practices have influenced, and been influenced by, society, politics, culture, and technology. It is anticipated that this *Handbook* will further energise the field of information history, which, as information practices develop further, is likely to become more deeply embedded within the historical discipline. The value of historical perspectives in throwing light on issues associated with information in our twenty-first-century world will be increasingly recognised.

As editors, we made a conscious choice in the design of this collection that it should be as inclusive and broad as possible, not just in terms of chronological, geographical, and thematic contents, but also in terms of contributing authors. Our contributors are an international and rich assemblage, composed of early career scholars as well as established names, with women in the majority. There has been an emphasis on including voices from *all* facets of the academe. This mindful selection of scholars has allowed for a unique kind of collaborative thinking about information and its historical practices.

Every contribution to the *Handbook* has been through a rigorous review process. In addition to editorial oversight, each chapter was blind reviewed. We are extremely grateful for the time and energy expended by our authors in supplying feedback in this regard. The editors would particularly like to thank Jack Andersen, James Curran, David Muddiman, Jacob Vrist Nielsen, Maria Nørby Pedersen, W. Boyd Rayward, and Allen H. Renear for additional reviews. On behalf of our authors, we also wish to thank the numerous archival collections around the world—many of them non-English language repositories—that furnished the sources and illustrations for these chapters.

Preface and Acknowledgements

We took the decision to step away from conventional cover images and instead commissioned Julia Pollack to create a piece of artwork specifically for this collection. Pollack's resultant work, *Auxiliary Disciplines*, offers an opportunity to reflect on the history and historiography of information practices. Inspired by the phrase, "quiet conversation and the cultivation of friendships," taken from the Afterword of this volume, Pollack makes manifest the important role of such activities in the visualisation of information and the production of knowledge.[1]

For us as editors, information history in various forms has been a bedrock of our academic careers, but during the creation of this volume, we have truly lived and breathed it. Fashioning such a powerful and diverse celebration of the field has been a stimulating intellectual experience, validating our longstanding collective belief that information has a history worth exploring.

The Editors
Toni Weller, UK
Alistair Black, UK
Bonnie Mak, USA
Laura Skouvig, Denmark

Note

1 Bonnie Mak, "What Is Information History For?", in this volume, 588.

PART I

Introduction

1
SITUATING INFORMATION HISTORY

The History and Historiography of Information and Its Practices

Alistair Black, Bonnie Mak, Laura Skouvig, and Toni Weller

Although the term "information history" has been in circulation since at least the mid-1980s, *The Routledge Handbook of Information History* is, we believe, by far the largest collection of studies (thirty-seven in total) to make use of it in its title.[1] We view the *Handbook* as both an endorsement of information history as a legitimate, growing sub field of history and as an opportunity to promote it further. We recognise the value and validity of employing information—*information practices*, to be specific—as a lens through which history can be viewed, researched, and explained.[2] In addition, we are convinced that this perspective will be acknowledged and adopted increasingly in the future; for if, as some claim, information has become main propellant of our (post) modern age, then its history will inevitably become ever more important and irresistible. Information history is a large, wide, and interdisciplinary field which contributes to our understanding of how information practices have determined, and been determined by, past societies.

Definition and Context

In what has become an amplified age of misinformation, disinformation, fake news, and spin, the last thing we would want to do is deceive readers of the *Handbook* by offering a title that misleads.[3] We wish to make it clear, therefore, that the word "information" in the *Handbook*'s title is mostly used by contributors to the volume as a synonym for the phrase "information practice," by which we mean the customary or repeated performance of an activity, perhaps a skill, that could variously involve the creation, collection, organisation, management, falsification, systemisation, or communication of information. However, our enthusiasm for the phrase "information practice" by no means threatens our recognition of the past and present interpretation of the meaning of information as something that is reified—a view that is closely associated with modernity.[4]

The phrase "information history" immediately raises the question of what the word "information" means.[5] The need to grapple with the matter of definition might be seen as an imperative, given any perceived novelty of the field of information history. There exists an enduring lack of consensus regarding the meaning of information. As Thomas Haigh has stated: "Information, like other concepts such as progress, freedom, or democracy, has become ubiquitous because, not in spite, of its impressive degree of flexibility."[6] Expressing a similar frustration with its slippery nature, Albert Borgman observed that information is a difficult phenomenon to analyse and discuss, not because its essence is mysterious (he views it in the tradition of "signal theory" as revolving fundamentally around a process involving a messenger, a message, and a receiver) but because "throughout human history it has been evolving in tiny steps from something simple and natural to something exceedingly complex and technical."[7]

Excavating the many definitions and perceptions of information over time and in a variety of milieux would require deep engagement in complex philosophical thinking on the nature of knowing and knowledge (the same might be said of a concept like virtue, the understanding of which obviously differs between cultures and is temporally fluid). We, therefore, offer a much simpler approach, one that allows our contributors to explore the nature of information as it was understood in the contexts about which they are writing. This is preferable to parachuting current understandings of information into different time periods and contexts; we hope thereby to avoid the dangers of presentism, which identifies phenomena in the past as relevant because they are deemed to be important in the present. This said, we are under no illusion that to disengage from presentist perspectives is no easy matter. Past and present are in perpetual dialogue. History is constantly being rewritten. This might simply be due, of course, to the discovery of new evidence. But it can also result from the appearance, as societies change, of new priorities assimilated by historians and their audiences. Therefore, without endorsing outright relativism, it might justifiably be said that history is contingent and malleable. As such, there is a danger that historians' views of what constitutes information in the past are both subjective and subject to change, thus giving rise to multiple foci. This places a premium on the information historian's ability to identify meanings attached to information in past societies and to the practices that revolved around it.[8] Given that information historians are sensitive to the temporal and cultural deviations in the definition of information, they are perhaps more aware than most of the heresy of anachronistic analysis. The analogy depicting the nineteenth-century electric telegraph as the "Victorian Internet" is a prime offender in this regard, in that the telegraph was for the most part an exclusive, elite, speciality service, whereas the World Wide Web (as opposed to the internet) was from the outset in many respects a mass, popular technology.[9]

We should remember that information history is, first and foremost, a subfield of history. As such, information history is aligned with developments in the discipline of history itself. In terms of method, this means that information historians should be expected to employ the same rigour applied by any serious historian to situate and understand their subject matter, avoiding anachronistic interpretations in the process.[10] In terms of scope, it means that information history can be, and has been, explored in an expanding variety of contexts, from colonialism and slavery to gender and class. Brendecke, Friedrich, and Friedrich situate the historical study of information pragmatically, arguing that information is always defined with reference to a given purpose.[11] Context is fundamental to the way in which we interpret that which is called "information" in any given situation. As Alistair Mutch has put it, "what is of central importance is the role of context in aiding, changing, or distorting the meaning of information."[12] This *Handbook* does exactly that. Each chapter attempts to situate information within a specific milieu. Each interpretation is inevitably differently nuanced; taken together, the overall result is a kaleidoscope of information practices—including their uses, roles, and effects—over the past two thousand years or so. There is no reason, of course, why attention could not also have been given in this volume to information in even more distant periods of history.[13]

The discussions in this *Handbook* proceed according to two basic assumptions regarding the meaning of information. The first assumption is that practices of information develop out of the sharing, or transmission, of knowledge. Knowledge resides exclusively in individuals' minds, and once communicated, it becomes information. In other words, released from the mind, knowledge takes on an informational form. The second assumption is that this sharing, or transmission, requires external representation—from sound or speech to digital encoding and more—and involves a wide range of practices.[14]

The Danger of Information History as the History of Everything

William Aspray has observed that information history has as many definitions as information itself.[15] While acknowledging the validity of this observation, we are not tempted to go further and adopt the view that information can be anything or everything. Such a position would be ahistorical, unhelpful, and opaque. We recognise that there is danger in attempting to pluck an information dimension from *any* past human activity.

A recent acute study of information in the work of the nineteenth-century realist novelist Charles Dickens illustrates the potential pitfalls in perceptions of information history becoming too broad.[16] Dickens' *Little Dorrit* (1857), for example, occasionally references certain obvious information practices and formats, including song lyrics, letters, posters, and testimonials. However, the study's main focus is the positing of realist novels of the past as part of information history because of the way they collect, interpret, and transmit information about the time and place in which they were set and created. Realist novels contain, the study explains, information about contemporary material conditions and institutions as well as social values, behaviour, perceptions, and identities. *Little Dorrit*, like other realist novels, is viewed as an "information system" because it describes how all individuals and institutions were "subject to corruption in familial, romantic, and social relations; philanthropy; investment practices; medical care; legal disputes; and government bureaucracy."[17] Arguably, however, most historians would see these attributes of the realist novel simply as primary-source evidence. Similarly, the claim that information in the realist novel includes "the way the story is told, by whom, in what order, and according to what structure or pattern" would generally be considered, it might be contended, to lie firmly within the bounds of literary criticism, a long way from the realm of information history.[18]

In some quarters, information—and, it follows, its history—has been viewed as physical, in terms of its very nature as opposed to the means of its transmission. In genetics, DNA has been viewed as information. James Gleick has reported this perception thus: "Genes encapsulate information… The body itself is an information processor. Memory resides not just in brains but in every cell … DNA is the quintessential information molecule."[19] Such a view is based on the general perception that every physical thing is "information-theoretic" in origin. As such, the universe can be seen "as a computer—a cosmic information-processing machine."[20] In astrophysics, a debate has been running over recent decades between those who on the one hand believe information, at the level of the sub-atomic particle, evaporates after entering a black hole and those who on the other hand argue that the laws of quantum physics do not allow for its disappearance.[21] Clearly, in this book, we are not concerned with matters of this kind—that is, with grand conceptualisations of information as the flywheel of the evolution of life or of the fundamental physics of the universe; and nor, it follows, of the (natural) history of the operation of this flywheel, or the history of research into it. Our interest is in the history of information practices rooted in the culture of the human species.

Some information practices are situated, it might be contended, in a grey area between information in everyday life as a legitimate historical category and information as the history of everything. Gossip is a good example in this regard. In the minds of some historians of information, gossip may not have been seen as technical enough to prompt serious historical study. However, the topic has registered a significant presence in social history in recent years.[22] Beyond being an entertaining pastime and a form of sociability, gossip has been shown to be a source of information.[23] Historically, this has been the case not only in mundane, everyday settings but also in contexts of great importance, such as in eighteenth-century revolutionary France, in which a semi-literate public sphere operating on street corners and in coffee shops—an information society of gossip—has been identified by Robert Darnton.[24]

Evidence from Norman Lewis' first-hand account of life in a remote Spanish fishing village shortly after the Spanish Civil War would arguably be of value to the information historian.[25] The inhabitants of the village had little interest in the outside world, but lively interchanges on village happenings, especially among the women mending fishing nets, were commonplace. "Net-mending was a wholly mechanical procedure, leaving the brain to create its own fancies, and to work on the raw material of speculation and known fact from which the tissue of gossip was woven," the women engaging in the activity later passing on newsworthy gossip to their husbands, thereby forming a "circuit of information" in the village.[26] Similar informal information exchanges might be identified in the practice in the homes of gentlemen in Georgian London of posting satirical prints on the walls of rooms, with the layers of innuendo, political suggestion, and social and cultural references being unpicked by those who examined them over drinks and conversation.[27]

However, there are perhaps methodological dangers inherent in pulling such everyday behaviour into the realm of information history. The risk of information history spinning out of control because of the width of perception that researchers—and readers indeed—might have of it is very real. This is where the methodological training and the sensitivities of the historian come into their own, offering structure and a framework to the vast avenues of potential information research on past societies. Attempts to excavate informational meaning from everyday technologies and social forms of the past—from architecture, design, and fashion to bodily gestures, fiction, and film—as opposed to discretely observed information practices run the risk of diluting or undermining authentic studies in information history. As Sheila Ritchie observed in citing examples of "messages" conveyed by smell and sight, it might be supposed that "anything contains information and information may relate to anything," thereby dictating, ludicrously, that the history of information can be the history of everything.[28] Yet, a field of history can only function effectively if it has recognisable boundaries. If the boundaries of information history become too elastic, it might be argued, then there will be a price to pay in terms of disciplinary coherence and legitimacy. This said, it would be remiss of information historians to ignore the move in history over recent decades towards an embracing of the "commonplace."

Content and Approach

To develop a comprehensive historical account of information and its practices as they emerged over time and in all their different contexts would be a daunting task. Our approach instead is to offer, mostly, investigations of particular instances of information practice and their contexts. These range from information in the Roman Empire, to the role of homing pigeons in military matters since classical antiquity; from information and the politics of communication in the early modern city, to the role of women in the late twentieth-century software industry. Such explorations thereby provide the reader with the opportunity to reflect on similarities that might emerge when following the trail across multiple terrains.

A number of contributions explore how historical actors across the wide scope of this *Handbook* grappled with the notion of information itself, whether or not they had yet given the concept a word. It has not been our intention to present overviews, or broad surveys, of the various aspects of information history, according to what some might consider to be the traditional role of a handbook (although a small number of chapters *do* comply with this role). Rather, illustrative of the fact that information history is a wide intellectual domain not easily sliced into predictable chronological or thematic categories, the *Handbook* generally offers in-depth "empirical" chapters that focus on specific examples and contexts. Conducive to this depth of analysis, chapters are richly referenced, including with archival sources (many of them from non-English language repositories), thus reflecting the quality of scholarship contained within the pages of the *Handbook*.

Although the study of information technologies has a place in information history, contributors have been assiduous in emphasising the conditions of the emergence and deployment of such technologies: their social milieux and their consequences, as well as the practices of which they are a part. In addition, contributions focus on *information* rather than drifting into the realm of *knowledge*, the history of which is a related but separate field. Information history shares many objects and sites of investigation with the history of knowledge—indeed, many practices of information can be also considered practices of knowledge. In addressing the overlap between information and knowledge in the context of history, Peter Burke sensibly reminds us that: "Both terms are useful, especially if we distinguish between them."[29] Regarding the distinction, it could be argued that whereas the history of knowledge emerged from the history of science and may therefore be haunted by certain kinds of canonical knowledge, information history may largely be described as domain-agnostic, being not necessarily committed to any particular subject area. Thus, even though information history and the history of knowledge take inspiration from each other and are both relatively new ways of thinking historically, they generally address different areas of research.[30]

The primary purpose of a handbook is to bring the erudition of a field together—to create an overview of the subject, although not one that is necessarily comprehensive or encyclopaedic. The co-editors of this volume have each contributed to the growing body of scholarship in information history over the years and have aspired in this *Handbook* to offer a sense of the field's grand possibilities: we highlight the field's expansive variety of themes and topics as well as the diversity of scholars working in it. We have made efforts to be inclusive of global content and to offer a healthy representation of scholars from around the world. The result is a broad narrative of information and its practices—one that is indicative of the many ways in which information can be explored as a category of historical enquiry—from antiquity to the modern day, including what can be classed as contemporary history. Contributions offer the reader numerous ways to understand the links between our information pasts, presents, and futures.

Key Episodes in the History of Information: A Historiography of Revolution and Rupture

If you think the information surge of the late twentieth and early twenty-first centuries is intrinsically something new, then you might wish to think again. In recent decades, historians have been lining up to identify critical developments, marked phases, and epoch-making watersheds in the history of information and its technologies. The slicing of the past into manageable chunks is a common practice among historians. However, periodisation can be seen as contrived and problematic. The major epochs imposed on history might be viewed as a series of cycles, not purely repetitive in their precise nature but replicating each other in terms of the grandeur of their impact, the general perception that they have moved society forward and the frequent identification of them as having been ignited by a rupture moment—moments that are generally followed by after-shocks (it is, of course, often easier to identify a departure point in a period or cycle than a point of completion).[31]

Notwithstanding these complications, in surveying the landscape of information history, it is evident that a rupture mentality—more often than not sculpted by technological change or mirroring familiar, staple eras of historical periodisation—has become a major organising principle.[32] An example of investment in this mentality is offered in the work of Judith Flanders who, in discussing alphabetical order as humanity's default method over the centuries for sifting, filing, and finding information, has observed that historians have been keen to identify "key moments" in the history of information, such as "the invention of writing, of double-entry bookkeeping, printing, the telegraph, and the computer."[33] The concept of the "information revolution"—the critical development, phase, or watershed moment—has generated a vigorous discourse of rupture.[34] "Rupture talk," as conceived by Gabrielle Hecht, Bruno Latour, and others, largely revolves around the shift from pre-modern to modern social arrangements and ways of thinking, in that we retroactively imagine a fissure in history which divides our orderly and rational modern selves from the supposed chaos of the pre-modern.[35] This might be seen as a "fabrication" which serves to convince and console ourselves that we are more organised, efficient, and progressive—essentially "better"—than our pre-modern progenitors.

Two points immediately spring to mind here. Firstly, even if one were to endorse the notion of rupture, it could be argued that there is no particular reason fractures other than that between pre-modernity and modernity—including fractures in the long history of information—should not be considered.[36] Secondly, continuities should not be overlooked. For example, the long history of capitalism, including the information practices that are woven into it, pre-dates the perceived emergence of modernity. Further, it has been observed that key elements of modernity itself, not least a belief in the efficacy of, and an investment in, sophisticated systems of information, previously non-digital, have survived into our supposedly post-modern age.[37] Even in the context of a relatively niche aspect of the history of information like information policy, an awareness of continuities is important. Today's information policy domain has its prefigurative antecedents—from surveillance, information privacy, and personal identity to intellectual property, information access, and issues of fake news.[38]

Certain events, technologies, and transitions have come to dominate the historiography of information rupture.[39] Whereas the origins of language continue to be debated, greater consensus exists concerning the origins and early history of writing.[40] Early writing devices, including writing boards and wax and clay tablets, were used not just for recordkeeping but also for scholarly activity. However, humanist scholarship, it is held, did not *take off* (as opposed to first appearing) until the broader adoption of papyrus, parchment, and paper, and the writing formats expedited by these materials. Although paper was likely first manufactured in ancient China, the papermaking techniques that were implemented in the Christian West had been refined and transmitted by the Islamicate world, a development that facilitated a wider dissemination of information from the mid-fifteenth century onwards in combination with the printing press.[41]

The growth of a more literate—and thus very early information—society in the Middle Ages, alongside an expansion of economies and trade, is said to have been one of the causes of the inception and flourishing of printing in Europe.[42] The late Middle Ages witnessed an intensification of state power, in part owing to an increase in information control by local and—eventually and increasingly—central state agencies and laws.[43] The increased information protocols and procedural formalities of governance were reflected in Baldassare Castiglione's *The Book of the Courtier* [*Il Libro del Cortegiano*], published in 1528.[44] A courtesy book (a book of manners), *The Book of the Courtier* was essentially an information protocol aimed at guiding individuals through life at court. It was a precursor to later protocols, including directives for clerical workers in a maturing capitalism; the consolidation in 1847 of the myriad of rules and regulations relating to the operation of Britain's Victorian Poor Law and its workhouses that had previously been issued sporadically; and etiquette books of the eighteenth and nineteenth centuries, designed to help citizens navigate their way through an expanding civil society and public sphere, where social friction and interaction between individuals were escalating at an unprecedented rate.[45]

In keeping with the argument that as civilisations become more sophisticated, they initiate and refine recordkeeping systems, many of them "official" in nature, some societies developed khipus (also spelled "quipus")—that is, memory, or data-storage devices, fashioned from string, with knots, twists, and colour used to communicate information. There is evidence of the existence of khipus in ancient China and Japan, but their most documented use was in Andean South America, most prolifically in the period from the twelfth century to the middle of the sixteenth century, with a continued legacy into the twentieth century.[46]

In Europe at this time, information was playing an increasingly vital role in the much-debated transition from feudalism to capitalism.[47] This was most clearly observed in the selling of information to make a profit in the context of the rise of the new print and publishing industries.[48] But it was also visible in the mechanisms and processes associated with merchant capitalism, where shippers, traders, and financiers were involved in the investment of "primitive capital" designed to create profit for further investment. Mercantile Europe, especially in the Mediterranean basin, developed a number of information innovations, from the written maritime insurance contract and partnership agreement to the bill of exchange and double-entry bookkeeping. Other information objects produced by the literate and numerate merchant cultures of the time included personal memoranda books recording business accounts and family data (such as births, marriages, and deaths) as well as, occasionally, events outside the family-household sphere. Merchant advice books recorded the ethos of the pre-modern merchant. Regarding long-distance trade, manuals of commercial practices were produced: books addressing the geography of the far-flung merchant's world, "in which information useful to merchants—trade routes; distances; local currencies, weights, and measures; lists of spices and other goods; duties and tariffs; carriage costs—was compiled directly or second-hand from correspondents."[49] Order in the realms of capitalist enterprise and state affairs was enhanced by the development from the late Middle Ages onwards of the mechanical clock, which might easily qualify as a historic information technology of universal importance.[50]

The early modern period was marked by a growing impulse to measure, classify, and collect information through observation, a development which, alongside new channels of information dissemination, such as the scientific journal and the culture of the salon, characterised the Enlightenment and the rise of a public sphere.[51] Across the sciences, the Enlightenment witnessed an upsurge of interest in taxonomy, from plants to race.[52] An initial wave of European imperial expansion took place, in which information practices played a central role.[53] The early modern period also saw the emergence of the military-fiscal state, behind which the forces of "political arithmetic"—the accounting of the wealth, strength, and trade of the nation, typified by the grandest of indirect surveillance mechanisms, the census—were conceptualised.[54] The early modern understanding of information in Europe reflected an emerging demand for an active procurement and communication of information as a justification for decision-making in state, ecclesiastical, and learned administrations. Information, in essence, became critical to processes of rationalisation and modernisation in early modern statebuilding.[55] This included the cameral sciences which emerged in Northern Europe in the eighteenth century as the means of administering state economic enterprise.[56]

However, as if to underline the importance of structuralism in human development, the period also saw the appearance of interesting and practical information storage and communication technology outside the West. The rise of the Luba kingdom in central Africa from the sixteenth century was accompanied by the introduction of "lukasa" (memory boards and other objects), under the control of "memory men" normally drawn from the tribal social elite. Lukasa were used to record and summon up the history of royal rulers, the titles and duties of courtiers, the location of royal treasuries and religious sites, and customary provers, maxims, and songs.[57]

Industrialisation, commencing in the second half of the eighteenth century, involved a significant escalation in information exchange, not least via the expansion of mail services.[58] It also brought with it a massification of culture, whereby people became more aware of the importance of, and rights to, information. In short, "information became a public cultural commodity."[59] This was a development facilitated in part by the proliferation of images in popular periodicals, such as, in Britain, *The Penny Magazine* (1832) and *The Illustrated London News* (1842), in which both fine art and contemporary illustrations were closely linked to textual information.[60] Chambers' *Information for the People* (1835) was emblematic of the desire to democratise access to information. This relatively slim encyclopaedia was published cheaply and at intervals in separate parts, the work as a whole being constituted by a "series of sheets on subjects in which distinct information is of importance among the people generally."[61] The marked fall in the price of paper from around the 1860s, as the raw-material base of its manufacture switched from rags to wood pulp, allowed scholars and others to cut and paste snippets of information from newspapers and journals into (often) appropriately indexed scrapbooks and albums for future retrieval and use, a practice that developed alongside a revival in the use of commonplace books. A large market developed in the sale of these basic information tools.[62] The middle of the nineteenth century also witnessed the arrival of a truly mass-culture information technology in the form of the photograph.[63]

This cultural commodification of information was matched by its commodification in production more broadly. This occurred at the most basic level of human need: employment. In Britain, the "tramping system" for union-organised and apprenticed workers developed into an information-reliant means of matching itinerant workers to vacancies—a decentralised system in contrast to the centralised information offices established in France and proposed in England in the seventeenth century.[64] "Tramping" from town to town, skilled workers were able to present personal documents at a designated "house of call" (often a public house) which would provide temporary lodging and food as well as act as an unofficial labour exchange in receipt of information about job openings.[65] In the United States, aside from democratising the public sphere, the expansion of the mail system—the number of post offices rose from around nine hundred in 1800 to over thirteen thousand in 1840—lubricated the wheels of business.[66] This efficient though pedestrian information system was then supplemented by one that provided near-instant delivery of messages. Aside from its social uses, the telegraph certainly had economic ramifications. For example, "throughput" in the Chicago meat packing industry was made hugely more efficient by the receipt of telegraphic messages indicating when deliveries of cattle would likely be made.[67]

In the second half of the nineteenth century, as industrialisation matured and economic activity mushroomed, the science of "systematic management," including the management of information, emerged to cope with the increasing administrative complexities that characterised the first large corporations. "To work systematically," declared an early treatise on factory management, "is to work successfully." "Method," it continued, "is the essential element on which every solid and substantial concern is based."[68] The growth of "method" in corporate performance entailed not only the rise of human-performance accounting but also planned industrial research, both of which required the efficient management of information—as did the corporate regimes of Taylorist scientific management that emerged in the early twentieth century.[69]

This second phase of industrialisation was eventually characterised by an information, or office, management revolution that was, except for the telephone and the aforementioned telegraph, manual in nature.[70] Business, as well as the state, became conscious of the heightened need to undertake and manage recordkeeping.[71] Building on the legacy of information control that abetted early colonial expansion, the era of high imperialism before the First World War was hugely facilitated by the telegraph, characterised by Standage (although perhaps illegitimately, as argued above) as the "Victorian internet."[72] Its development and global deployment was closely intertwined with the growth of European empire—"empires of cable," to invoke Mattelart's analogy.[73] Global communications were further enhanced by the standardisation of time (the establishment of international time zones) in 1884, a development which built on the standardisation of time within nations in response to the construction of extensive railway networks and the emergence of what became known as "railway time."[74] Like previous imperialist endeavours, the age of high imperialism, commencing with the "Scramble for Africa," would not have been possible without the information practices of a bureaucratic infrastructure. Because the efficiencies of this system were best exploited through direct rule as opposed to informal control, such practices thereby destabilised, and eventually destroyed, the very European empires they were meant to support.[75]

The "Belle Époque" decades around turn of the twentieth century were marked by a number of initiatives aimed at the universal control of information.[76] Following the launch in 1867 of its *Catalogue of Scientific Papers*, in 1902 the Royal Society of London inaugurated the *International Catalogue of Scientific Literature*, a large-scale, annual publishing venture aimed at tracking the circulation of print matter in the sciences, a result of the nineteenth century having seen a massive growth in scientific investigation and its dissemination, especially via the scientific journal.[77] In Belgium, in 1895, Paul Otlet established the International Institute of Bibliography and in doing so inaugurated a new discursive formation termed "documentation" (later "information science") which sought to identify and classify all manner of information objects—from books, periodicals, newspapers, and bibliographies to administrative records of government, patents, industrial catalogues, and indexes, and beyond to society's ephemera as well as new media like photographs and films—and to do this, moreover, not only at the level of the whole item but also by indexing parts, segments, or fragments of information within items.[78] To facilitate this, Otlet developed a new classification system, the Universal Decimal Classification (UDC), a granular adaptation of the Dewey Decimal Classification (DDC) which had been developed by the American librarian and library promoter and entrepreneur Melvil Dewey in 1876.[79]

Otlet's International Institute of Bibliography was restructured as a federated international association in the 1920s and renamed the International Institute for Documentation (Institut International de Documentation, IID) in 1931, subsequently renamed the International Federation for Documentation (Fédération Internationale de Documentation, FID) in 1937. Also in 1937, a World Congress of Universal Documentation was held in Paris under the sponsorship of the League of Nations. It was at this event that H.G. Wells repeated his idea of a World Brain, a new type of universal encyclopaedia, one that was exhaustive, centrally produced yet also democratic, and continually revised as a result of ongoing intellectual debate and input.[80] In line with these global information developments, in 1927 the International Federation of Library Associations (IFLA) was established.[81] Information associations also emerged at a national level. Following the inauguration of a Special Libraries Association in the United States in 1909, in Britain in 1926, the Association of Special Libraries and Information Bureaux (ASLIB) was established, aimed at representing not only specialist libraries but also the ever-growing number of intelligence and information centres in the country; meanwhile, in the United States, the American Documentation Institute (ADI) was established in 1937.[82] Together, these initiatives occurring in the decades immediately before and after 1900 represented something quite new: the need to construct robust systems, at global and national levels, for the management of information in the face of a widely acknowledged information deluge. Information was explicitly recognised as something to be *managed*.[83]

The early twentieth century saw the birth of scientific management which, due to its reliance on the introduction of new flows and analysis of information, effectively fashioned it, according to Robins and Webster, into the "original information revolution."[84] By the inter-war period, certainly in the United States, information had become deeply entrenched in commercial as well as in political and social life—to the extent that it has been possible to write an information history of the post-1918 world, to stand alongside traditional accounts of the period.[85] New public information technologies, productive of the term "mass media," began to appear. Together, the cinema, radio, television, and the gramophone, facilitated by new and efficient systems of electricity distribution, constituted a large part of what Lewis Mumford in the 1930s called the "neotechnic phase" of history, while in the commercial and state spheres, information processing was advanced by the development of punched-card and embryonic computer technologies.[86] The years to 1950 also witnessed an explosion in state intervention, driven by two world wars and the emergence of welfare states. This new level of intervention was underpinned by a massive expansion in the information capability of state agencies.[87] Information also continued to underpin the strategic and tactical concerns of *warfare* states. The world wars and the Cold War catapulted the importance of both non-digital and digital information systems in armed conflict and intelligence to new heights.[88]

By the last quarter of the twentieth century, the rhetoric of an "information age"— arising out of the mid-century development of the (ground-breaking) transistor, computers, and other technologies for signal and information processing—was becoming entrenched.[89] In 1948, Claude Shannon, widely referred to as the inventor of the information age, coined the term "bit" (a reduction of the term "binary digit") to represent a fundamental unit for measuring information quantitatively, its meaning taking no account, of course, of the quality, or value, of information. The perceived originator of information theory, Shannon also published the classical model of communication, involving sender, receiver, transmitter, and, the disrupter of the signal process, noise.[90] By the 1950s, computing technology was being accessed by the world of business, commencing in the unlikely environment of the Lyons teashop and confectionery business in the United Kingdom.[91]

In 1981, the Japanese sociologist Yoneji Masuda, labelled by some as the father of the information society, looked ahead optimistically to the eventual arrival of a "computopia," where digital technologies, underpinned by the silicon chip, would produce unprecedented levels of individual self-actualisation, education, health provision, social harmony, citizen participation, and global interdependence—in a post-materialist, post-pollution civilisation, moreover. For many, the onset of the electronic information age, where the computer made its mark on almost every aspect of human society, has trumped all previous claims to the prize of "most momentous rupture," not only in the long history of information but also history *per se*.[92]

Each of these moments in the history of information—many mapping onto perceived ruptures in history at large—has in varying degrees been badged a "revolution," heralding a subsequent "age of information," which is furthermore typified by a sense of "information overload." The long historical record is thus peppered with challenges related to the management of this information overload. The utility of alphabetic and alphabetic numeral ordering was debated throughout antiquity and in diverse geographical regions.[93] Different reference tools and finding aids were developed in universities in the twelfth century, suggesting that scholars were grappling with now-familiar information challenges, even if they did not express them in terms of an overload.[94] Ann Blair and others have noted that Conrad Gessner, although not using the term "information" explicitly, nevertheless complained about the "confusing and harmful abundance of books" in 1545.[95] Likewise, in 1685, Adrien Baillet expressed his concerns about the future of civilisation, should a plan not be developed to help identify and keep the most useful books out of the "multitude of books which grows every day in a prodigious fashion."[96] The following year, John Locke devised a "New Method" for indexing material to facilitate the practice of search and retrieval, while Leibniz still indicated that he was having difficulty keeping track of his own notes in 1693.[97] Similar anxieties were expressed in the nineteenth century. For example, the British political theorist and sociologist L. T. Hobhouse wrote in 1896 of the "deluge of specialism" and the "mass of accumulated fact" that was affecting scientific and social life.[98] Such observations on the proliferation of information indicate that there is a long history of people grappling with information-related challenges, the enduring nature of which demonstrates that they cannot be uniquely associated with digital technologies.

The discourse of rupture in the context of the history of information practices is reflected in an awareness that the meanings attached to information—to return briefly to the issue of definition—have also changed over time. For example, it has been argued that the change in the meaning of "information" in the nineteenth century represents the most significant rupture, taken to mark the beginning of a conceptual change that would ultimately help reframe the modern world.[99] The explicit use of the phrase "an age of information" in 1853 by the London *Times* suggests a shift in how the notion of information was understood.[100]

In the Victorian age, what was understood as information became increasingly abstracted from context and purpose, although this is not to say that information's semantic ground did not move according to the context in which the term was being used.[101] According to Neil Postman, in the eighteenth century, information was not thought of as a commodity to be bought and sold; rather, it was thought to have worth only if embedded in a context, thereby carrying the potential to shape political, social, and scientific concepts. What changed this perception, Postman posits speculatively, was the advent of the electric telegraph, which rendered information desirable in itself, an entity (thing) separate from its possible uses and meaning.[102] Previously considered inextricable from its particular use and context, "information" from the nineteenth century onwards began—whether or not exclusively due to the arrival of the telegraph—to be constructed increasingly as something discrete, corpuscular, and morselised, often with an immediate functional utility and value, moreover.[103]

The essence of the nineteenth-century re-orientation of the understanding of information was captured by Charles Dickens in his novel *Hard Times* (1854), a depiction of life in the imaginary industrial settlement of Coketown. In that "severely workful place," wrote Dickens, all civic institutions and public inscriptions appeared austere. In their appearance, Dickens' imagination projected, the gaol might have been the infirmary, the infirmary the town hall, the town hall the gaol. Mirroring the perceived utilitarian value and morselised nature of information that the industrial age had reinforced, everywhere in the barren landscape of Coketown and in its culture Dickens noted an evocation of the rule of "fact, fact, fact." Even the design of the local school was "all fact," he wrote.[104]

Witting and Unwitting Information History

Much can be learned about information and its practices in histories that do not wittingly set out to address either; it would be fair to say that most information history is not undertaken by scholars who would claim, in the first instance, to be an information historian.

Geoffrey Parker's analysis of the life and foreign and domestic strategies of Philip II of Spain (reign, 1556–1598), dubbed the "Paper King," provides a good example of unwitting information history.[105] Parker's account contains a sprinkling of references to the monarch's intense daily bureaucratic practices. A micro-manager, Philip attempted to govern the expanding Spanish world with his pen. The thousands of papers, which he called his "devils," that at any one time confronted him drove him to despair. To reduce the information overload he was experiencing, Philip eventually instructed secretaries, as well as a committee of senior ministers, to write summaries of long letters and reports, though to what effect is unclear. These information aspects of Philip's life appear sporadically in Parker's lengthy text. This merely occasional referencing is not surprising, as Parker did not set out to write an information history of Philip II. Evidence of information practice is overshadowed in Parker's book by much larger matters of imperial expansion and international rivalry. To retrieve an information-history perspective of Philip II's life, one would need to read between the lines and against the grain of the overall discussion, excavating an information discourse from a forensic reading of Parker's text. By contrast, Paul Dover has produced an account of Philip's life with an explicit information-history focus.[106] Philip's failures as a person and as a monarch were in some part, argues Dover, caused by a crushing, self-imposed information overload. His pre-existing obsessive personality only aggravated the overload, acting as an obstacle to optimal decision-making. Philip II's insatiable desire for information in advance of committing to a course of action meant that decisions were delayed, resulting in disadvantageous outcomes. In focusing on such issues, Dover is wittingly engaging in information history.

A similar example illustrative of unwitting and witting information history operating side by side, although in this instance in a single text as opposed to across a single subject, can be seen in the "social arithmetic" and "social knowing" connected with the Victorian city, which Martin Hewitt has explored in the context of Manchester.[107] In the new urban areas of the industrial age, against the backdrop of problems wrought by the shock of industrialisation, there was a growing interest in, and practice of, surveying the population with regard to life-chance matters like health, poverty and housing. The production of social knowledge in this respect was accomplished through a combination of the new statistical movement, the deployment of cartographic imagery, and a "visiting mode" of direct surveillance of households conducted by clerics, philanthropists, representatives of charities, and a growing cadre of experts and officials. Hewitt explores the ways in which a particular set of investigative practices structured how knowledge was collected, conceptualised, and communicated. This required analysis of observed information, out of which knowledge was produced, as well as of the information technologies deployed to record and disseminate data, including journals, surveys, and maps.[108] There is much in Hewitt's study, therefore, which speaks to the concerns of information history. Information and various of its homologues—facts, investigation, statistics—pepper the discussion. Ultimately, however, the information dimension in the study is subsidiary to the focus on "knowing." Arguably, an undisputed information-history approach to examining the production of social knowledge in the Victorian city, which was obviously not Hewitt's primary concern, would have called for the *principal* focus to have been on the details of such things as the methodologies of accumulating data; aims and parameters set in advance of investigation; methods of data collection, processing, and analysis; the possibility of bias and presumption; and avenues and tools of dissemination.

For those with a primary, self-conscious, witting interest in gathering evidence of information history from a study such as Hewitt's—a study which does not primarily set out to bolt its subject in an information-history framework but which succeeds in offering information-history evidence—it is again, as with the example of the life of Philip II above, a matter of being prepared to identify evidence at variance with the primary narrative and to dig data out at intervals from accounts that at first glance do not appear to have much of an information complexion. Information historians should, therefore, aside from conducting their own primary-source research, be sensitive to the existence of evidence in secondary sources not intentionally crafted as information history. By looking under the surface and asking relevant to their purposes, the witting information historian can also gain new insights from conventional historical narratives.

Beyond the numerous examples of unwitting information history one could cite, where information practices are embedded in historical explorations of primarily non-information themes, there has been an expanding circle of historians who consciously take up information as a particular focus or path. In this regard, our *Handbook* is testament to the maturity of the field, and a recognition of the volume and multitude of scholars around the world working on the historical study of information. There has been a steady rise of interest in information history over the past quarter of a century, while recent years have witnessed a surge in publications. Some of these witting information-history studies have been empirically specific, focusing on a particular geography or temporality.[109] Others, more comparable in structure to this *Handbook*, are the numerous edited collections which focus on specific information themes.[110] Many come under the aegis of "information and the individual," or the history of census information.[111] Specific, and eclectically themed, information history has included the study of the deliberate destruction of information repositories throughout history, the history of the filing cabinet, and differing perspectives on the information history of the First World War, while other scholars have made a strong link between information and technology.[112] This scholarship, across multiple disciplines, that has wittingly engaged in developing histories of information has led to a coalescing of interests that might now demand the formal recognition of a discrete field called information history. But what are the possible origins of this emergent field?

The Emergence of Information History

The Routledge Handbook of Information History forms part of an ongoing and dynamic exploration of the many histories of information, but untangling the complex roots of information history as a field is a challenging task. Against the backdrop of the rise of digital technology in the late twentieth century, scholars from multiple enclaves of history began to examine earlier developments in the circulation and organisation of information. Related topics were also explored by those outside the history discipline, including in sociology, media and communication studies, linguistics, and semiotics. However, none of the research in these areas has explicitly referred to the arrival of a new history of information, nor has there been a concerted effort to develop an information history "college." Such efforts *have* been evident, however, in the discipline of the information sciences, most notably in connection with history-focused scholars in the related fields of library, archival, and information science.

The history of the book is one of one of the subfields of history which has supplied useful contributions to the development of information history.[113] Any authoritative field that takes information as its focus would need to address changes in the provision of information, whether they be brought on by changes in literacy, or rhetoric and composition, or manuscript, printing, and digital technologies, each of which is of interest to historians of the book. To take the example of printing, the rise of the printer's workshop in Europe in the fifteenth century alongside the traditional copyist's desk offered a different set of possibilities for the dissemination of information.[114] Some scholars working in the history of the book have explored the effect of different communication technologies on cultural production.[115] In terms of grappling with developments relevant to information history, one of the major consequences of the adoption of the printing press in Europe was the boost it gave to scientific and technical literature, where synergies exist with the practical and applied dimensions—the tangible products—of information.[116] Printing technologies were leveraged to facilitate the development of common objects of study, accelerating the harmonisation of scientific practices that was already taking place. As historian of science Lorraine Daston notes, standardisation, another facet of information practice, "is a prerequisite for a shared world."[117] An example of a common (if not yet standardised) practice in the context of book history is the strategic use of blank space as a technique for organising information since antiquity; as a tool for segmenting text to facilitate navigation, such division chimes with the sense of information which revolves around its morselised, corpuscular nature.[118]

A feature of Daston's "shared world" of printed texts was the growth of digestible reference works, often practical and technical in nature—and therefore of great interest to those studying information history.[119] Early printed manifestations of this were medical almanacs, prognostications, calendars, practical books, devotional books of hours, and basic school texts and guides.[120] Thereafter, books for the management of daily life became popular—cheap, small-format texts for the non-specialist on matters ranging from cookery, food preservation, sewing, and gardening, to diet, general medicine, and animal husbandry.[121] By the eighteenth century, numerous compendia were in circulation, including encyclopaedias and dictionaries, as well as directories, stagecoach schedules, and a variety of other reference works.[122]

Another line of exploration that informs today's discourse in information history can be traced back through the domain of sociology.[123] Specifically, a lineage can be identified in that history-inflected segment of sociology which from the 1960s was concerned with the question of the emergence of an "information society" as a major break, or discontinuity, in history.[124] Exploring the concept of the post-industrial society, the precursor of the concept of the information society, scholars were naturally prompted to examine certain characteristics of industrial and pre-industrial history. While not delivering detailed information-history accounts of pre-information societies, there was a firm recognition of the role played by information practices throughout history. Pointing out that information had always been a factor in economic life, in the 1960s Alain Touraine argued that in post-industrial society, information had by then become much more closely bound to the realm of production, a lack of access to information forming the new basis of alienation.[125] For Daniel Bell in the 1970s, information was central to the major transformations, or new "axial principles," that had been occurring in advanced economies in the immediately preceding decades—these principles being shifts from manufacturing to services; from traditional elites to a new class of knowledge or information experts; and from technical-based production to science-based industries where the codification and testing of theoretical knowledge reigned supreme.[126] Labelling the new, post-industrial information age "The Third Wave" of civilisation, following upon the first wave of agricultural society and the second wave of industrial society, in 1980 Alvin Toffler explained that all societies have constructed an "info-sphere" of some description, for producing and distributing information.[127]

Such studies, which emphasised that the information society emerged from industrial society, laid the ground for research on the manual information-management revolution in the decades immediately preceding and following the First World War. Much of this research emanated from the worlds of management theory and organisational sociology, with historians associated with, or close to, these areas working on topics revolving around the bureaucratisation, or informatisation, of the first large-scale capitalist industrial and commercial enterprises, which began to emerge in the second half of the nineteenth century.[128]

As the digital age gained momentum and the notion of an information society became embedded in both academic and popular vocabulary, history-minded scholars in communication and media studies began to show a keen interest in the concept of concept of information.[129] In their expansive social history of the media, Asa Briggs and Peter Burke locate their work in the history of "the communication of information … by means of speech, writing, print, radio, TV and most recently the internet."[130] Such social history built on the subject matter that in 1964 Marshall McLuhan—who during the much cited communications revolution of the time had invested innovatively in the term "age of information"—had deemed worthy of research and analysis: anything from computer automation, television, radio, the movies, the telephone, and clothing as signification, to the telegraph, the typewriter, the record player, advertising, the press, the photograph, comics, clocks, and transport and trading routes as information highways.[131] Many of these topics would be prime candidates for inclusion in any expansive study of the history of information.

Although many scholars in the areas discussed above displayed an energetic involvement in the study of information, they did not concern themselves with generating a discrete field of information history. That development occurred in the information sciences, a disciplinary constellation that takes as its primary focus information and its practices and technologies. The information sciences domain is populated by a large number of fields and associated professions, from archival science, museum studies, and library science, to records management, knowledge management, information management, information systems, and computing.[132] Many of these fields developed a historical identity and college. It can be argued, in fact, that some of the deepest foundations of information history can be located in investigations revolving around the origins of the various fields that have made up the information disciplines and professions; any discipline, or profession indeed, that claims such a status must be able to summon up a history.[133]

In the popular mind, the history of computing might be understood to be synonymous with the history of information. Historians of computing have been naturally drawn to the concept of information, not least with regard to the history of information processing, of the computer as an "information machine."[134] One scholar in the history of computing has gone further, explicitly acknowledging the relevance of a "history of information."[135] Efforts have also been made to historicise information systems, these being practices associated with the adoption and operation of informational technology, as well as of soft systems, mostly in organisational and institutional settings.[136] Media archaeology has echoed the importance of information through explorations of technological devices.[137] Scholars in the archival sciences, because of their proximity to the history discipline, were attuned to historicising archives and archival practices, as well as the archival profession itself.[138] Furthermore, it is not surprising that the history of archives, being closely associated with the history of information management as well as of paperwork, scholarship, and the document as media, adopted an information vocabulary.[139] Similarly, the history of state recordkeeping activity has also been infused with the concept of information, the modern state being essentially a bureaucratic, information system, perceived reductively as an "information state."[140]

Located within a larger domain of the information sciences, history-minded scholars in the subfield of information science (termed "documentation" in Europe) became highly active in exploring the field's origins and antecedents.[141] In many ways, these scholars paved the way for the emergence of an information-history domain.[142] However, partly because they were often focused on particular technologies and techniques, their primary concern was not an engagement with the broader conceptualisation of information history, which naturally feeds heavily off social and cultural history. Nevertheless, it was a short leap from research on the history of the subfield of information science, and of the discipline of the information sciences more generally, to an acknowledgement of the historical importance of information in society generally. This was especially true with regard to the amalgamated field of library and information science (LIS), which—in the United States—frequently incorporated the field of archival studies. In the late twentieth century, the teaching of information society studies, including historical perspectives, became firmly embedded in LIS.[143] This served as a powerful catalyst in the development of information history as a discrete area of historical research. Also influential was the long tradition of research on the history of libraries and library science (or librarianship), which acted as a springboard into the history of information, as the library profession increasingly sought to modernise itself by adopting an information-focused language and identity.[144]

It was scholars attached to the relatively small and humble discipline of LIS, therefore, commencing with the work in 1986 of the American librarian Norman Stevens, an early advocate of computer technology in libraries, who began to theorise and promote information history.[145] Moreover, in developing the area, purposeful attempts were made to guide scholarship toward the robust methodologies employed in "conventional" historical investigation. Thus, whereas the emergence of information history as a distinct intellectual domain had numerous ingredients, it was in LIS that the crystallisation of the subject eventually occurred, with a small group of history-focused scholars—largely working independently of each other but sharing a commitment to the study of information—breaking new ground over the past quarter of a century.[146] We, the editors, count ourselves in that number, each of us having experienced, or continuing to experience, the world of LIS in our academic careers.

The Value of Information History

No historical field, no sub-discipline of history, can form or thrive without a recognised value being attached to its existence. So, what might be the value of information history, beyond an acceptance that it shares all the "uses" attributed to history generally?

Regarding the instrumental value of history to the present, historical approaches to the phenomenon of information can lend perspective to such matters as today's widespread digital surveillance and reliance on data science as an explanatory device. As digital information technologies continue to be promoted as the dominant driver of social change, it is all the more important that we consider how to view and understand this broader phenomenon by historicising information, especially pre-computer information practices. Given the hype associated with the notion of a digitally induced break in history, it is part of the mission of information history, with its emphasis on culture, to challenge the technological determinism that has fostered the epochal "rupture talk" enshrined in terms like the "computer age," "information age," and "information society."[147] Information history forces us to see the larger and longer trends of human social development. Information is not a phenomenon privileged to the modern period. The "information age" is not a singularly modern phenomenon. With regard to information, people have been grappling with questions of meaning, organisation, collection, protection, privacy, and access since antiquity. But in the late twentieth century, information became, as John Durham Peters has put it, the "omnipresent new idol," the concept of progress having been, as identified by John Roberts, the all-pervasive idol of the age of the Enlightenment.[148] As an antidote to digital-age idolatry, information history contributes to scepticism regarding the millenarianism and utopianism surrounding the information society proposition.[149]

This said, as time advances, digital information practices will increasingly feature as the subject of historical study, not least in terms of the emergence of a whole range of new information professions or of changes in the nature of existing professions where the presence of an information identity becomes more important. The same goes for society generally. As information practices become more ubiquitous, they will increasingly prompt historical investigation. Thus, we see that digital materials, databases, the internet, and social media have already become subjects of historical enquiry.[150]

Information history reinforces some of the exciting developments that have occurred in the world of history over the past half-century or so. Information history contributes to the study of history at the micro level, thereby enhancing the "new history," a more textured history that stresses the importance of the everyday over the history of elites and great events. Information history challenges historians to consider the diversity of their source material and to think about the (in)tangibility of information preservation, dissemination, and access, not only in terms of historical documents but also in terms of how historical contemporaries considered and managed these things day-to-day. Historians are of their own time and ask questions accordingly. Finally, linked to these fresh developments in the world of history, because all sections of society have engaged in information practice in one way or another, the opportunity arises to study groups previously hidden from history, thereby investing in the "history from below" methodology.[151]

The Value of the *Handbook*

Continuing this democratic line of thought, because information has had so much to do with authority and privilege—the recordkeeping and information systems deployed by states, businesses, and social elites being the most visible—there is a risk that explorations of information "pasts" might offer limited insight into histories that have been traditionally underrepresented. However, our focus on *practices* of information—and, by extension, the people engaging in them and their complex relationships with power—permits a wider inquisitive net to be cast. Some chapters in the *Handbook* demonstrate how practices of information are implicated in questions of gender, colonisation, and emancipation. Meanwhile, other chapters explicitly examine the contributions of, for instance, women in information work, including the role of women in the development and deployment of computer technologies and in archive work, thereby raising questions related to the gendering of certain information practices and the resultant tendency to characterise some such activities as mundane and others as revolutionary.[152]

Our *Handbook* aims to set the foundation for further reflections on the nature of information by exploring how a variety of historical actors have engaged in its practices. These practices involve the collecting, expressing, organising, and sharing of information, as well as activities related to search and retrieval. Different tools and techniques have been used to facilitate these efforts, from slips of parchment to homing pigeons to natural language processing. The dizzying array of approaches—evident across time periods, geographical regions, and context—points to enduring questions about the management of information. Although the notion of information is often taken as a ubiquitous or even defining feature of the modern world, some scholars have suggested that the activities related to it are not only learnt but also "instinctive," and therefore endure across time in all human societies.[153] Indeed, the chapters in this *Handbook* illustrate how humans have been carrying out different practices of information for millennia. The chapters in this volume not only aid an exploration of the myriad ways in which these practices were executed, but also provide a foundation for scrutinising the social, political, and economic conditions that continue to give rise to the conceiving and constituting of "information" as a particular kind of problem that is amenable to—and appropriate for—control.[154]

This collection moves across borders, communities, and time periods, but always keeps information in focus. All the chapters in the *Handbook* are connected by the idea that information is, and has been, textured in its meaning, and is therefore impossible to separate from historical context. By traversing these diverse chapters, the reader may begin to develop an enriched sense of what can "count" as information, as well as how and why some versions won out over others.

The Organisation of the *Handbook*

Acting as a grand narrative of the history and historiography of information, as well as having addressed certain methodological issues associated with information history, this *Introduction*, which forms *Part 1* of the book, situates the chapters that follow within the broader context of the field.

A large and diverse collection of chapters such as this could be organised in any number of ways. The chronological, geographical, and thematic divisions that are conventionally used to arrange historical studies were deemed unsuitable for a project that specifically sought to examine the highly variegated role of information across such categories. An alternative, less traditional organisation has thus been designed, reflecting our commitment to understanding the complex nature of information practices through time. The central three *Parts* of the book are focused on particular groupings of activities that, gathered together, provide a sense of the many recurrent ways of addressing information in human life.

The chapters that form *Part 2: Visualising, Describing, Expressing* explore ways in which information has been expressed, from antiquity to the twenty-first century. From the scratches on ceramic fragments, to the colours and twist direction of cords on a khipu, to biometric data, our contributors highlight a diversity of approaches for making information visible. Studies in *Part 3: Managing, Ordering, Classifying* investigate issues related to the handling of information, such as how it has been weaponised in times of conflict to generate intelligence, enhance communication, or monitor public attitudes. In addition, we see that information has always been used to govern urban spaces and reorder society, no matter what technologies and techniques were to hand. How sharing information can function to build networks and regulate behaviours is explored in *Part 4: Circulating, Networking, Controlling*. Chapters arranged under this rubric examine the workings of various systems of information exchange. They shed light on different political agendas that motivate practices of dissemination, as well as on important discrepancies of power, thereby enriching our understanding of what is now commonly called "access." They also raise questions about what kind of information is prepared for transmission—and in which ways. Finally, in *Part 5*, the *Afterword* offers not a conclusion but a critical mandate on why we need information history; what is it ultimately *for*?

Naturally, any single chapter can lay claim to more than one of the themes outlined above, as well as, indeed, to themes that have not been stated. This is a reflection of the ubiquity of information practices. The intrepid reader may find that there are unusual conceptual connections to be made, or threads to be followed, throughout the volume. For example, the human body appears as a site of datafication—in racialised advertisements about slavery in the eighteenth century, as well as in facial-recognition technologies. The body as an analytical category is also evident in discussions of the sensorial aspects of information exchange, in medieval documentary practices as well as the hawking of early nineteenth-century street ballads. The entwined relationship between bodies and objects—and tactility and materiality—can be observed in the handling of homing pigeons and microfilm as well as paper slips, ledgers, catalogue cards, and other paraphernalia of classification. Discussions of colonial bureaucracies, anti-colonial communications, and the operations of the Dutch and English East India Companies may foreground the idea of an information machine, with implications of standardisation and systematisation. Despite what might seem to be a shift towards mechanism, however, the human spirit retains a strong presence in many of our studies, as in the case of the use of information as a tool for liberation throughout centuries of South African history, or in the appeal to the emotions embedded in the history of attack journalism or in the instinctive drive to *remember* in researching a family lineage.

Such threads are woven across temporal, spatial, cultural, and intellectual categories, as well as the alternative themes we have identified, and tie together the different *Parts* of our volume, demonstrating the ways in which information practices are interlaced throughout history. The concepts and interpretations expressed in the themes and threads of this collection form a richly patterned tapestry that, as a whole, creates opportunities to challenge pedagogic thinking and scholarly discussions about information history itself, if not information *per se*. Thus, this *Handbook* should be read not only as a collection of discrete chapters, but also as a way of shaping crucial disciplinary conversations and the broader narrative of information history.

Notes

1. Norman Stevens, "The History of Information," *Advances in Librarianship* 14 (1986): 1–48, appears to have been the first to use the term in a scholarly context. Toni Weller, ed., *Information History in the Modern World: Histories of the Information Age* (Basingstoke: Macmillan, 2010) uses the term "information history" in its title but contains only around a quarter of the chapters presented in this volume. William Aspray, ed., *Writing Computer and Information History: Approaches, Connections and Reflections* (Lanham, MD: Rowman and Littlefield, 2024) also uses the term, the collection numbering around a half of the number of chapters presented here. Extensive collections that address the history of information but which *do not* contain the term "information history" in their title include Ann Blair et al., *Information: A Historical Companion* (Princeton, NJ: Princeton University Press, 2021); Eric Hayot, Anatoly Detwyler, and Lea Pao, eds., *Information: A Reader* (New York: Columbia University Press, 2021); Michele Kennerly, Samuel Frederick, and Jonathan Abel, eds., *Information: Keywords* (New York: Columbia University Press, 2021); Jack W. Chen et al., eds., *Literary Information in China: A History* (New York: Columbia University Press, 2021); Andreas Marklund and Laura Skouvig, eds., *Histories of Surveillance from Antiquity to the Digital Era: The Eyes and Ears of Power* (London: Routledge, 2021); Ida Nijenhuis et al., eds., *Information and Power in History. Towards a Global Approach* (London: Routledge, 2020); W. Boyd Rayward, ed., *Information Beyond Borders: International Cultural and Intellectual Exchange in the Belle Époque* (Aldershot: Ashgate, 2014); Arndt Brendecke, Markus Friedrich, and Susanne Friedrich, eds., *Information in der Frühen Neuzeit: Status, Bestände, Strategien, Pluralisierung und Autorität* 16 (Berlin: Lit, 2008); W. Boyd Rayward and Mary E. Bowden, eds., *The History and Heritage of Scientific and Technological Information Systems: Proceedings of the 2002 Conference* (Medford, NJ: Information Today, 2004); Mary Bowden, Trudi Hahn, and Robert V. Williams, eds., *Proceedings of the 1998 Conference on the History and Heritage of Science Information Systems* (Medford, NJ: Information Today, 1999); and Trudi Hahn and Michael Buckland, eds., *Historical Studies in Information Science* (Medford, NJ: Information Today, 1998).
2. Our preference is for the concept of "information practices" as opposed to "information processes," as the latter has connotations of technology, whereas the former foregrounds human agency. An earlier *Routledge Handbook*—Chris Meyns, ed., *Information and the History of Philosophy* (London: Routledge, 2021)—also uses information as a lens through which to view history. However, our collection of chapters not only employs a wider lens but also consciously aims to promote the field of information history.
3. Joseph R. Hayden, *A History of Disinformation in the U.S.* (London: Routledge, 2024); Melissa Zanders and Kembrew McLeod, eds., *Fake News: Understanding Media and Misinformation in the Digital Age* (Cambridge, MA: MIT Press, 2020); and David Miller, *A Century of Spin: How*

Public Relations Became the Cutting Edge of Corporate Power (London: Pluto Press, 2008). Yuval Harari, *Nexus: A Brief History of Information Networking from The Stone Age to AI* (New York: Random House, 2024), makes the point that human society has always experienced lies, errors, myths, delusions, and fantasies, but in today's world, where information technologies have never been more powerful and where beneficial human connectivity and networking should be at a premium, disinformation, misinformation, inaccurate information, and frictional, or even entirely obstructed, communication are increasing instead of being eroded.

4 The two strands of exploration—information history and the history of information—are complementary and both feed into the remit and scope of this collection. Moreover, irrespective of the distinction discussed here, we accept that generally scholars use the two terms interchangeably. However, a distinction might be drawn, at the risk of seeming pedantic, between the historical study of information practices and that of information. The study of past information practices could justifiably conform to the label "information history." The study of information could more fittingly be termed "the history of information," in that, aligned with conceptual history, it would focus on changes in the notion or definition of "information" over time, as has been attempted in the case of information's close cousin, data: see Daniel Rosenberg, "Data Before the Fact," in *Raw Data is an Oxymoron*, ed. Lisa Gitelman (Cambridge, MA: MIT Press, 2013), 15–40. The distinction between information history and the history of information is also discussed in Bonnie Mak and Allen Renear, "What Is Information History?," *Isis: A Journal of the History of Science Society* 114, no. 4 (December 2023): 756–757.

5 On the definition of information, see Marcia Bates, "Information and Knowledge: An Evolutionary Framework for Information Science," *Information Research* 10, no. 4 (July 2005). https://files.eric.ed.gov/fulltext/EJ1082014.pdf.

6 Thomas Haigh, "The History of Information Technology," *Annual Review of Information Science and Technology* 45, no. 1 (2011): 433.

7 Albert Borgman, "Information and Reality at the Turn of the Century," *Design Issues* 11, no. 2 (Summer 1985): 21–22.

8 For a critical discussion of these matters, see Laura Skouvig, "Present and Past: The Relevance of Information History," *Information & Culture* 58, no. 1 (2023): 1–16.

9 Richard John, "Debating the New Media: Rewriting Communications History," *Technology and Culture* 64, no. 2 (April 2023): 310. John states (313) that "It is anachronistic to study a historical phenomenon in relation to what it preceded, rather than what it followed."

10 James Cortada, "Shaping Information History as an Intellectual Discipline," *Information & Culture* 47, no. 2 (2012): 119–144.

11 Arndt Brendecke, Markus Friedrich, and Susanne Friedrich, "Information als Kategorie Historischer Forschung: Heuristik, Etymologie und Abgrenzung vom Wissensbegriff," in *Information in der Frühen Neuzeit: Status, Bestände, Strategien*, ed. Arndt Brendecke, Markus Friedrich, and Susanne Friedrich, *Pluralisierung und Autorität* 16 (Berlin: Lit, 2008), 16.

12 Alistair Mutch, "Unions and Information, Britain 1900–1960: An Essay in the History of Information," *International Review of Social History* 44 (1999): 397. The importance of context has also underpinned the work of recent advocates of information history: see, for example, Toni Weller, *Information History - An Introduction: Exploring an Emergent Field* (Oxford: Chandos, 2008); and Alistair Black, "Information and Modernity: The History of Information and the Eclipse of Library History," *Library History* 14 (May 1998): 37–43.

13 For example, Dominque Charpin, *Reading and Writing in Babylon*, trans. Jane Marie Todd (Cambridge, MA: Harvard University Press, 2011).

14 In *Dragons of Eden: Speculations on the Evolution of Human Intelligence* (New York: Random House, 1977), the astronomer Carl Sagan wrote about the concept of extrasomatic information, that is, information stored outside the body, in media, as opposed to pre-wired, genetic information or information that is extragenetic, generated by learning and experience and carried in the mind or embedded in culture: see Jeffrey Garrett, "Carl Sagan and Libraries: An Original Thinker Remembered," *IFLA Journal* 50, no. 4 (2024): 832–837.

15 William Aspray, "The Many Histories of Information," *Information & Culture* 50, no. 1 (2015): 1.

16 Carol Colatrella, "Information in the Novel and the Novel as Information System: Charles Dicken's *Little Dorrit* and Margaret Drabble's *Radiant Way* Trilogy," *Information & Culture* 50, no. 3 (2015): 339–371.

17 Colatrella, "Information in the Novel," 349.
18 Colatrella, "Information in the Novel," 343.
19 James Gleick, *The Information: A History, a Theory, a Flood* (London: Fourth Estate, 2011), 8.
20 Gleick, *The Information*, 10.
21 Gleick, *The Information*, 357–358.
22 For example, Melanie Tebbutt, *Women's Talk? A Social History of Gossip in Working Class Neighbourhoods, 1880–1960* (Aldershot: Scolar Press, 1995); and Anna Clarke, "Whores and Gossips: Sexual Reputations in London 1770–1825," in *Current Issues in Women's History*, ed. Arina Angerman et al. (London: Routledge, 1989), 231–248.
23 Elizabeth Horodowich, "Gossip," in *Information: Keywords*, ed. Michele Kennerly, Samuel Frederick, and Jonathan Abel (New York: Columbia University Press, 2021), 89–99.
24 Robert Darnton, *The Revolutionary Temper: Paris 1748–1789* (London: Allen Lane, 2023).
25 Norman Lewis, Voices of the Old Sea, rev. ed. (1984; repr., London: Eland, 2013).
26 Lewis, *Voices*, 127.
27 Vic Gatrell, *City of Laughter: Sex and Satire in Eighteenth-Century London* (New York: Walker and Co., 2006).
28 Sheila Ritchie, *Modern Library Practice* (Buckden: E.L.M. Publications, 1982), 96.
29 Peter Burke, *What is the History of Knowledge?* (Cambridge, UK: Polity Press, 2016), 6.
30 Mak and Renear, "What Is Information History?," 759; Laura Skouvig, "The Raw and the Cooked: Information and Knowledge in History," in *Forms of Knowledge: Developing the History of Knowledge*, ed. Johan Östling, David Larsson Heidenblad, and Anna Nilsson Hammar (Lund: Nordic Academic Press, 2020), 107–121; Lorraine Daston and Martin Muslow, "History of Knowledge," in *Debating New Approaches to History*, ed. Marek Tamm and Peter Burke (London: Bloomsbury Academic, 2019), 159–187; and Brendecke, Friedrich, and Friedrich, "Information als Kategorie."
31 On time cycles in history, see Penelope Corfield, *Time and the Shape of History* (New Haven, CT: Yale University Press, 2007), 248–270.
32 Alistair Black and Bonnie Mak, "Period, Theme, Event: Locating Information History in History," in *Information and Power in History. Towards a Global Approach*, ed. Ida Nijenhuis et al. (London: Routledge, 2020), 18–36.
33 Judith Flanders, *A Place for Everything: The Curious History of Alphabetical Order* (London: Picador, 2020).
34 Studies that have invoked rupture, revolution, or transformation in this regard include Paul M. Dover, *The Information Revolution in Early Modern Europe* (Cambridge, UK: Cambridge University Press, 2021); Edward Beasley, "The Nineteenth-Century Information Revolution and World Peace," in *Information and the History of Philosophy*, ed. Luciano Floridi (Abingdon: Routledge, 2016), 229–244; Aileen Fyfe, "The Information Revolution," in *The Cambridge History of the Book in Britain. Volume VI: 1830–1914*, ed. David McKitterick (Cambridge, UK: Cambridge University Press, 2009), 567–594; Leonard Dudley, *Information Revolutions in the History of the West* (Cheltenham: Edward Elgar, 2008); John McCusker, "The Demise of Distance: The Business Press and the Origins of the Information Revolution in the Early Modern Atlantic World," *The American Historical Review*, 110, no. 2 (April 2005): 295–321; Aad Blok and Greg Downey, eds., "Uncovering Labour in Information Revolutions, 1750–2000," [special issue of] *International Review of Social History*, 48, supplement 11 (2003); Jon Agar, Sarah Green, and Penny Harvey, "Cotton to Computers: From Industrial to Information Revolutions," in *Virtual Society? Technology, Cyberbole, Reality*, ed. Steve Woolgar (Oxford: Oxford University Press, 2002), 264–285; Anthony Grafton, Elizabeth Eisenstein, and Adrian Johns, "AHR Forum: How Revolutionary Was the Print Revolution?," *The American Historical Review*, 107, no. 1 (February 2002): 84–128; Thomas R. Reid, *The Chip: How Two Americans Invented the Microchip and Launched a Revolution* (New York: Random House, 2001); Jonathan Rose, "The Nineteenth-Century Information Revolution," *Nineteenth Century Studies* 13 (1999): 203–213; Kevin Robins and Frank Webster, *Times of the Technoculture: From the Information Society to the Virtual Life* (London: Routledge, 1999), 87–108 [these pages form Chapter 4, which carries the title "The Long History of the Information Revolution"]; Margaret Stieg, "The Nineteenth-Century Information Revolution," *Journal of Library History* 15, no. 1 (Winter 1980): 22–52; Michael Clanchy, *From Memory to Written Record: England, 1066–1307* (Cambridge, MA:

Harvard University Press, 1979); and Elizabeth Eisenstein, *The Printing Press as an Agent of Change: Communications and Cultural Transformations in Early-Modern Europe* (Cambridge, UK: Cambridge University Press, 1979).

35 Among others, see Gabrielle Hecht, "Rupture-talk in the Nuclear Age: Conjugating Colonial Power in Africa," *Social Studies of Science* 32, no. 6 (December 2002): 691–727; Bruno Latour, *We Have Never Been Modern*, trans. C. Porter (Cambridge, MA: Harvard University Press, 1993); and Michel Foucault, *The Archaeology of Knowledge*, trans. A. M. Sheridan Smith (New York: Pantheon, 1972).

36 For example, Philip Mirowski and Edward Nik-Khah, *The Knowledge We Have Lost in Information: The History of Information in Modern Economics* (New York: Oxford University Press, 2017), 1, highlights a particular moment of "cultural rupture," that is, the post-1945 growth in (post-modern) questioning as to whether economic analysis can ever deliver the "truth," the postmodern project being closely aligned with the move towards a digitally mediated society.

37 Anthony Giddens, *The Consequences of Modernity* (Cambridge, UK: Polity Press, 1991); David Harvey, *The Condition of Post-Modernity: An Enquiry into the Origins of Cultural Change* (Oxford: Blackwell, 1989); and Carolyn Marvin, *When Old Technologies Were New: Thinking about Electric Communication in the Late Nineteenth Century* (New York: Oxford University Press, 1988).

38 László Z. Karvalics, "Information Policy before Information Policies: Conceptual and Historical Considerations," in *Research Handbook on Information Policy*, ed. Alistair Duff (Cheltenham: Edward Elgar, 2021), 69–79.

39 David Bawden and Lyn Robinson, *Introduction to Information Science*, 2nd ed. (London: Facet, 2022), 20, outlines what have been widely seen as the defining developments in the history of information (including, and especially, the "documentary" forms that have carried it): language, recorded signs and symbols, writing and scripts, printing, mass communications, the digital computer, and the internet.

40 Steven Fischer, *A History of Language* (London: Reaktion, 1999); Stephen Houston, ed., *The First Writing: Script Invention as History and Process* (Cambridge, UK: Cambridge University Press, 2004); Steven Fischer, *A History of Writing* (London: Reaktion, 2003); and Wayne M. Senner, ed., *The Origins of Writing* (Lincoln, NE: University of Nebraska Press, 1989).

41 Jonathan Bloom, "Papermaking: The Historical Diffusion of an Ancient Technique," in *Mobilities of Knowledge*, ed. Heike Jöns, Peter Meusburger, and Michael Heffernan (Cham: Springer Open, 2017), 51–66; Fischer, *A History of Writing*; and Eisenstein, *The Printing Press*.

42 Clanchy, *From Memory to Written Record*; and James Burke, *Connections* (New York: Simon and Schuster, 2007), 127.

43 Randolph C. Head, "Records, Secretaries, and the European Information State, circa 1400–1700," in *Information: A Historical Companion*, ed. Ann Blair et al. (Princeton, NJ: Princeton University Press, 2021), 104–127; Paul Dover, *Secretaries and Statecraft in the Early Modern World* (Edinburgh: Edinburgh University Press, 2016); and Edward Higgs, *The Information State in England: The Central Collection of Information on Citizens since 1500* (Houndmills: Palgrave Macmillan, 2004).

44 Baldassare Castiglione, *The Book of the Courtier: The Singleton Translation: An Authoritative Text Criticism* (New York: W. W. Norton & Co., 2002).

45 Jacob M. Price, "Directions for the Conduct of a Merchant's Counting House, 1766," in *Business in the Age of Reason*, ed. R. T. P. Davenport-Hines and Jonathan Liebenau (London: Frank Cass, 1987), 134–150; Poor Law Commission Office, *Consolidated General Order*, July 26, 1847. https://workhouses.org.uk/gco1847.shtml. See also Toni Weller, "The Puffery and Practicality of Etiquette Books: A New Take on Victorian Information Culture," *Library Trends* 62, no. 3 (Winter 2014): 663–680.

46 Galen Brokaw, *A History of Khipus* (Cambridge, UK: Cambridge University Press, 2010).

47 Rebecca Jean Emigh, "(The) Transition(s) to Capitalism(s)? A Review Essay," *Comparative Studies in Society and History* 46, no. 1 (January 2004): 188–198.

48 Will Slauter, "Periodicals and the Commercialization of Information in the Early Modern Era," in *Information: A Historical Companion*, ed. Ann Blair et al. (Princeton, NJ: Princeton University Press, 2021), 128–151; and Alistair Black and Dan Schiller, "Systems of Information: The Long View," *Library Trends*, 62, no. 3 (Winter 2014): 632–634.

49 Sophus A. Reinhert and Robert Fredona, "Merchants and the Origins of Capitalism," Harvard Business School Working Paper No. 18-021 (2017). https://www.hbs.edu/ris/Publication%20Files/18-021_b3b67ba8-2fc9-4a9b-8955-670d5f491939.pdf.
50 Gerhard Dohrn-van Rossum, *History of the Hour: Clocks and Modern Temporal Orders* (Chicago, IL: Chicago University Press, 1996).
51 Black and Schiller, "Systems of Information," 640–644; Lorraine Daston and Elizabeth Luneburg, eds., *Histories of Scientific Observation* (Chicago, IL: Chicago University Press, 2010); and Peter M. Heimann, "The Scientific Revolutions," in *The New Cambridge Modern History. Volume 13, Companion Volume*, ed. Peter Burke (Cambridge, UK: Cambridge University Press, 1979), 248–270.
52 Devin Vartija, "Revisiting Enlightenment Racial Classification: Time and the Question of Human Diversity," *Intellectual History Review* 31, no. 4 (2021): 603–625; Anne Mariss, "A Library in the Field: The Use of Books Aboard the Ship 'Resolution' During Cook's Second Circumnavigation, 1772–1775," in *Understanding Field Science Institutions*, ed. Helena Ekerholm et al. (London: Science History Publications, 2017), 41–70; and Roger Williams, *Botonophilia in Eighteenth-Century France* (Dordrecht: Springer Science and Business Media, 2001).
53 Gabor Szommer, "Parallel Expansions: The Role of Information during the Formative Years of the English East India Company (1600–1623)," *Information & Culture* 53, nos. 3–4 (2018): 303–336; Sylvia Sellers-Garcia, *Distance and Documents at the Spanish Empire's Periphery* (Stanford, CA: Stanford University Press, 2014); and Jeremy Baskes, "Communication Breakdown: Information and Risk in Spanish Atlantic World Trade during an Era of 'Free Trade' and War," *Colonial Latin American Review* 20, no. 1 (2011): 35–60.
54 Mary Poovey, *A History of the Modern Fact: Problems of Knowledge in the Sciences of Wealth and Society* (Chicago, IL: Chicago University Press, 1998), 92–143, emphasises the late seventeenth century and Enlightenment origins and emergence of the control dynamic in the modern state, despite the growing enthusiasm for the operation of the free market and political economy. Nicholas Popper, *The Specter of the Archive: Political Practice and the Information State in Early Modern Britain* (Chicago, IL: Chicago University Press, 2024) examines the growth of the state at this time with reference to the availability of paper, the proliferation of which allowed statesmen to record drafts, memoranda and other ephemera; as original paperwork and copies alike saturated the government machine, information management was drawn to the centre of politics and state affairs in Britain. See, also, Jeremy Black, *The Power of Knowledge: How Information and Technology Made the Modern World* (New Haven, CT: Yale University Press, 2014), 135–138; Peter Burke, "Reflections on the Information State," in *Information in der Frühen Neuzeit: Status, Bestände, Strategien*, ed. Arndt Brendecke, Markus Friedrich, and Susanne Friedrich, Pluralisierung und Autorität 16 (Berlin: Lit, 2008), 51–63; Jacob Soll, *The Information Master: Jean-Baptiste Colbert's Secret State Intelligence System* (Ann Arbor, MI: University of Michigan Press, 2009).
55 Brendecke, Friedrich, and Friedrich, "Information als Kategorie," 15–18.
56 See, for example, Henry E. Lowood, "The Calculating Forester: Quantification, Cameral Science, and the Emergence of Scientific Forestry Management in Germany," in *The Quantifying Spirit in the Eighteenth Century*, ed. Tore Frängsmyr, J. L. Heilbron, and Robin E. Rider (Berkeley, CA: University of California Press, 1990), 315–343.
57 Mary N. Roberts, "The Naming Game: Ideologies of Luba Artistic Identity," *African Arts* 31, no. 4 (1998): 56–73, and 90–92.
58 Beasley, "The Nineteenth-Century Information Revolution and World Peace"; John W. Randolph, "Communication and Obligation: The Postal System of the Russian Empire," in *Information and Empire: Mechanisms of Communication in Russia, 1600–1850*, ed. Katherine Bowers and Simon Franklin (Cambridge, UK: Open Book Publishers, 2017), 155–184; and Martin Daunton, *Royal Mail: The Post Office Since 1840* (London: Athlone Press, 1985).
59 Toni Weller, *The Victorians and Information: A Social and Cultural History* (Saarbrucken: Verlag Dr. Muller, 2009), 157.
60 Weller, *The Victorians and Information*, 97–107. See also Weller, "Preserving Knowledge through Popular Victorian Periodicals: An Examination of the *Penny Magazine* and the *Illustrated London News*, 1842–1843," *Library History* 24, no. 3 (2008): 200–208.
61 William Chambers, *Memoir of Robert Chambers with Autobiographical Reminiscences of William Chambers*, 3rd ed. (New York: Scribner, Armstrong and Co., 1872), 236.

62 Jillian M. Hess, *How Romantics and Victorians Organized Information: Commonplacebooks, Scrapbooks and Albums* (Oxford: Oxford University Press, 2022).
63 Mary Warner Marien, *Photography: A Cultural History*, 5th ed. (London: Laurence King, 2021); and Robert Hirsch, *Seizing the Light: A Social and Aesthetic History of Photography*, 3rd ed. (London: Routledge, 2017).
64 W. Boyd Rayward, "Information for the Public: Information Infrastructure in the Republic of Letters," in *Information History in the Modern World*, ed. Toni Weller (Basingstoke: Palgrave Macmillan, 2011), 31–56.
65 Eric J. Hobsbawm, "The Tramping Artisan," *Economic History Review* 3, no. 3 (1951): 299–320.
66 Richard John, "Recasting the Infrastructure for the Industrial Age," in *A Nation Transformed by Information: How Information Has Shaped the United States from Colonial Times to the Present*, ed. Alfred Chandler and James Cortada (New York: Cambridge University Press, 2000), 55–105, at 60.
67 John, "Recasting the Infrastructure," 86.
68 John Tregoning, *A Treatise on Factory Management* (Lynn, MA: Thomas P. Nichols, 1891), iii. See, also, Edwin T. Freedley, *Common Sense in Business* (Philadelphia, PA: Claxton, Ramsden and Haffelfinger, 1879).
69 Alistair Black and Henry Gabb, "The Value Proposition of the Corporate Library, Past and Present," *Information & Culture* 51, no. 2 (2016): 192–225; and Frederick W. Taylor, *The Principles of Scientific Management* (New York, NY: Harper and Brothers, 1911).
70 On the history of the telephone and telegraph, see Dan Schiller, *Crossed Wires: The Conflicted History of US Telecommunications, from the Post Office to the Internet* (New York: Oxford University Press, 2023); and Laszlo Solymar, *Getting the Message: A History of Communications*, 2nd ed. (Oxford: Oxford University Press, 2021).
71 Toni Weller and David Bawden, "The Social and Technological Origins of the Information Society: An Analysis of the Crisis of Control in England, 1830–1900," *Journal of Documentation* 61, no. 6 (2005): 777–802; Gerri Flanzraich, "The Library Bureau and Office Technology," *Libraries & Culture* 28, no. 4 (Fall 1993): 403–429; John Orbell, "The Development of Office Technology," in *Managing Business Archives*, ed. Alison Turton (Oxford: British Archives Council, 1991), 60–83; JoAnne Yates, *Control Through Communication: The Rise of System in American Management* (Baltimore, MD: Johns Hopkins University Press, 1989); and James Beniger, *The Control Revolution: Technological and Economic Origins of the Information Society* (Cambridge, MA: Harvard University Press, 1986). One aspect of this manual information-management revolution was the rise of the humble memo: see JoAnne Yates, "The Emergence of the Memo as a Managerial Genre," *Management Communication Quarterly* 2, no. 4 (1989): 485–510; and from a different perspective, emphasising the decline of rhetoric rather than the rise of management, see John Guillory, "The Memo and Modernity," *Critical Inquiry* 31, no. 1 (2004): 108–132.
72 Tom Standage, *The Victorian Internet: The Remarkable Story of the Telegraph and the Nineteenth-Century's On-line Pioneers* (London: Weidenfeld and Nicolson, 1998). On the telegraph and empire generally, see Gerrit Knaap, "Communication, Information, and Power in the Dutch Colonial Empire: The Case of the Dutch East India Company, c. 1760," in *Information and Power in History: Towards a Global Approach*, ed. Ida Nijenhuis et al. (London: Routledge, 2020), 122–137; Miles Ogborn, *Indian Ink: Script and Print in the Making of the English East India Company* (Chicago, IL: Chicago University Press, 2007); Michael O'Leary, Wanda Orlikowski, and JoAnne Yates, "Distributed Work over the Centuries: Trust and Control in the Hudson Bay Company, 1670–1826," in *Distributed Work*, ed. Pamela J. Minds and Sara Kiesler (Cambridge, MA: MIT Press, 2002), 27–51; and Christopher Bayly, *Empire and Information: Intelligence-gathering and Social Communication in India, 1780–1850* (Cambridge, UK: Cambridge University Press, 1996).
73 Armand Mattelart, *The Invention of Communication* (Minneapolis, MN: University of Minnesota Press, 1996), 165–170. See, also, Nicole Starosielski, *The Undersea Network* (Durham, NC: Duke University Press, 2015).
74 Eviatar Zerubavel, "The Standardization of Time: A Sociohistorical Perspective," *American Journal of Sociology* 88, no. 1 (July 1982): 1–23. The standardisation of global time was instituted by the International Meridian Conference (Washington, DC, October 1884), which named Greenwich, in South-East London, as the site of the global meridian.
75 Peter Crooks and Timothy H. Parsons, eds., *Empires and Bureaucracy in World History: From Late Antiquity to the Twentieth Century* (Cambridge, UK: Cambridge University Press, 2016).

76 Rayward, *Information Beyond Borders*.
77 Alex Csiszar, *The Scientific Journal: Authorship and the Politics of Knowledge in the Nineteenth Century* (Chicago, IL: Chicago University Press, 2018); and Csiszar, "How Lives Became Lists and Scientific Papers Became Data: Cataloguing Authorship during the Nineteenth Century," *The British Journal for the History of Science* 50, no. 1 (March 2017): 23–60.
78 Alex Wright, *Cataloguing the World: Paul Otlet and the Birth of the Information Age* (Oxford: Oxford University Press, 2014); and Paul Otlet, *Mundaneum: Archives of Knowledge*, Occasional Paper No. 215, ed. and trans. W. Boyd Rayward (Urbana, IL: Graduate School of Library and Information Science, University of Illinois, 2010). https://www.ideals.illinois.edu/items/15485.
79 Wayne Wiegand, *Irrepressible Reformer: A Biography of Melvil Dewey* (Chicago, IL: American Library Association, 1996).
80 Dave Muddiman, "The Universal Library as Modern Utopia: The Information Society of H.G. Wells," *Library History* 14 (1998): 85–101.
81 Willem Roelf Henderikus Koops and Joachim Wieder, eds., *IFLA's First Fifty Years: Achievement and Challenge in International Librarianship* (Munich: Verlag Dokumentation, 1977).
82 David Bawden, "Aslib: A De Facto National Library/Information Organization," *Alexandria* 26, no. 1 (2016): 15–27; and Irene Farkas-Conn, *From Documentation to Information Science: The Beginnings and Early History of the American Documentation Institute – American Society for Information Science* (Westport, CT: Greenwood Press, 1990).
83 A classic example of this impulse is William H. Leffingwell, *Scientific Office Management* (New York: A.W. Shaw, 1917), which applied Frederick Taylor's scientific management methods to the information-management setting of the office. In their office operations, Leffingwell advised, companies should observe, record, standardise, set tasks, and teach (4). Filing systems should be developed "that really remember" (158). Businesses should gather information "from the outside," such as that concerning their place in the market in relation to others or that related to new techniques and products. But information should also be gathered "from the inside," with observers gathering data and recording methods in relation to work processes, including via time-and-motion behavioural studies. A further example of the internal generation of information advised by Leffingwell was the detailed data that sales staff—including salesmen in the field—should gather on the businesses they serviced (109).
84 Kevin Robins and Frank Webster, *The Technical Fix: Education, Computers and Industry* (Basingstoke: Macmillan, 1989), 39.
85 William Aspray, *Understanding Information History: The Case of America in 1920* (Cham: Springer Nature, 2023).
86 Thomas Haigh and Paul Ceruzzi, *A New History of Modern Computing* (Cambridge, MA: MIT Press, 2021); Lars Heide, *Punched-Card Systems and the Early Information Explosion, 1880–1945* (Baltimore, MD: Johns Hopkins University Press, 2009); and Lewis Mumford, *Technics and Civilization* (New York: Harcourt, Brace and Company, 1934).
87 Alistair Black, "Aspects of the History of State Information Policies in Britain before 1945," in *Research Handbook on Information Policy*, ed. Alistair Duff (Cheltenham: Edward Elgar, 2021), 80–95; Jon Agar, *The Government Machine: A Revolutionary History of the Computer* (Cambridge, MA: MIT Press, 2003); and Higgs, *The Information State*. Chris A. Williams, *Police Control Systems in Britain, 1775–1975: From Parish Constable to National Computer* (Manchester: Manchester University Press, 2014), especially 85–117, addresses information management in the police, shows that this growing capability had a long gestation.
88 Colin B. Burke, *America's Information Wars: The Untold Story of Information Systems in America's Conflicts and Politics from World War II to the Internet Age* (Lanham, MD: Rowman and Littlefield, 2018); and Alistair Black and Rodney Brunt, "Information Management in MI5 before 1945: A Research Note," *Intelligence and National Security* 16, no. 2 (Summer 2001): 158–165.
89 Some have viewed the advent of the transistor, in 1947, as the leading technical advance of the twentieth century, effectively opening the door to a digital future: see Sharon Gaudin, "The Transistor: The Most Important Invention of the Twentieth Century," *Computerworld*, December 12, 2007. https://www2.computerworld.com.au/article/202801/transistor_20th_century_most_important_invention/.
90 Jimmy Sonni and Rob Goodman, *A Mind at Play: The Brilliant Life of Claude Shannon, Inventor of the Information Age* (Stroud: Simon and Schuster, 2017); and Gleick, *The Information*, 3–4.

91 Georgina Ferry, *A Computer Called LEO: Lyons Teashop and the World's First Office Computer* (London: Fourth Estate, 2003).
92 Yoneji Masuda, *The Information Society as Post-Industrial Society* (Washington, DC: World Future Society, 1981); and Janet Abbate and Stephanie Dick, eds., *Abstractions and Embodiments: New Histories of Computing and Society* (Baltimore, MD: Johns Hopkins University Press, 2022).
93 Lionel Casson, *Libraries in the Ancient World* (New Haven, CT: Yale University Press, 2008); and Lloyd W. Daly, *Contributions of a History of Alphabetization in Antiquity and the Middle Ages* (Brussels: Latomus, 1967).
94 Richard H. Rouse and Mary A. Rouse, "*Statim Invenire*: Schools, Preachers, and New Attitudes to the Page," in *Renaissance and Renewal in the Twelfth Century*, ed. Robert L. Benson and Giles Constable with Carol Lanham (Cambridge, MA: Harvard University Press, 1982), 201–225.
95 Ann Blair, "Reading Strategies for Coping with Information Overload ca. 1550–1700," *Journal of the History of Ideas* 62, no. 1 (January 2003): 11.
96 Ann Blair, *Too Much to Know: Managing Scholarly Information Before the Modern Age* (New Haven, CT: Yale University Press, 2010), 59.
97 Michael Stolberg, "John Locke's 'New Method of Making Common-Place-Books': Tradition, Innovation and, Epistemic Effects," *Early Science and Medicine* 19, no. 5 (2014): 448–470; and Richard Yeo, "John Locke's 'New Method' of Commonplacing: Managing Memory and Information," *Eighteenth-Century Thought* 2 (2004): 1–38.
98 Leonard T. Hobhouse, *The Theory of Knowledge: A Contribution to some Problems of Logic and Metaphysics* (London: Methuen, 1896), vii.
99 Gleick, *The Information*; Weller, *Information History in the Modern World*; and Alfred D. Chandler Jr. and James Cortada, eds., *A Nation Transformed by Information: How Information Has Shaped the United States from Colonial Times to the Present* (Oxford: Oxford University Press, 2000).
100 *The Times*, December 5, 1853, 6.
101 Weller, *The Victorians and Information*, 27, and 174.
102 Neil Postman, *Building a Bridge to the 18th Century: How the Past Can Improve Our Future* (New York: Vintage Books, 2000), 86–88.
103 Geoffrey Nunberg, "Farewell to the Information Age," in The *Future of the Book*, ed. Geoffrey Nunberg (Berkeley, CA: University of California Press, 1996), 105.
104 Charles Dickens, *Hard Times: For These Times* (London: Penguin, 2003). In this context, that of equating information with facts, it is worth noting the title of the following assessment of American information history: James Cortada, *All the Facts: Information in the United States Since 1870* (Oxford: Oxford University Press, 2016).
105 Geoffrey Parker, *The Grand Strategy of Philip II* (New Haven, CT: Yale University Press, 1998).
106 Paul Dover, "Philip II, Information Overload, and the Early Modern Moment," in *The Limits of Empire: European Imperial Formations in Early Modern World History: Essays in Honor of Geoffrey Parker*, ed. Tonio Andrade and William Reger (Farnham: Ashgate, 2012), 99–120.
107 Martin Hewitt, *Making Social Knowledge in the Victorian City: The Visiting Mode in Manchester, 1832–1914* (London: Routledge, 2020).
108 Hewitt, *Making Social Knowledge*, 16–19 especially.
109 Such as Chen et al., eds., *Literary Information in China*; Cortada, *All the Facts*; Kenneth Cmiel and John Peters, *Promiscuous Knowledge: Information, Image, and Other Truth Games in History* (Chicago, IL: Chicago University Press, 2020); Brendecke, Friedrich, and Friedrich, eds., *Information in der Frühen Neuzeit*; Blair, *Too Much To Know*; Soll, *The Information Master*; Filippo De Vivo, *Information and Communication in Venice: Rethinking Early Modern Politics* (Oxford: Oxford University Press, 2007); and Higgs, *The Information State in England*.
110 For example, Nijenhuis et al., eds., *Information and Power in History*; Kate Peters et al., eds., *Archives and Information in the Early Modern World* (Oxford: Oxford University Press, 2018); Gitelman, ed., *Raw Data*; Weller, *Information History in the Modern World*. Suzanne Stauffer, *Libraries, Archives, and Museums: An Introduction to Cultural Heritage Institutions through the Ages* (Lanham, MD: Rowman and Littlefield, 2021) also offers an overview of information history specifically from a cultural heritage perspective. Rayward, *Information Beyond Borders*; and Alistair Black, Dave Muddiman, and Helen Plant, *The Early Information Society: Information*

Management in Britain Before the Computer (Aldershot: Ashgate, 2007) are further examples of the booming interest in information history.

111 On information and the individual, see Colin Koopman, *How We Became Our Data: A Genealogy of the Informational Person* (Chicago, IL: Chicago University Press, 2019); and Deborah Lupton, *Quantified Self: A Sociology of Self-Tracking* (Cambridge, UK: Polity Press, 2016). On information and the census, see Andrew Whitby, *The Sum of the People: How the Census Has Shaped Nations, from the Ancient World to the Modern Age* (New York: Basic Books, 2020); Paul Schor, *Counting Americans: How the U.S. Census Classified the Nation* (Oxford: Oxford University Press, 2017); Sarah Igo, *The Averaged American: Surveys, Citizens, the Making of a Mass Public* (Cambridge, MA: Harvard University Press, 2017); and Margo Anderson, *The American Census: A Social History* (New Haven, CT: Yale University Press, 2015).

112 Craig Robertson, *The Filing Cabinet: A Vertical History of Information* (Minneapolis, MN: University of Minnesota Press, 2021); Richard Ovendon, *Burning the Books: A History of the Deliberate Destruction of Knowledge* (Cambridge, MA: Belknap Press, 2020); and László Karvalics, ed., *Information History of the First World War* (Budapest: L'Harmattan, 2015); Agar, *The Government Machine*; and Martin Campbell-Kelly and William Aspray, *Computer: A History of the Information Machine* (New York: Basic Books, 1996).

113 James Raven, *What is the History of the Book?* (Cambridge, UK: Polity Press, 2018) offers a global perspective on the history of the book, one that, moreover, takes account of its many formats over the past 5,000 years; the history of the book is not merely about the history of the printed codex.

114 Eisenstein, *The Printing Press as an Agent of Change*, 478. Resulting in claims of a new cultural outlook in Europe, classified as "info lust," see Ann Blair and Peter Stallybrass, "Mediating Information," in *This is Enlightenment*, ed. Clifford Siskin and William Warner (Chicago, IL: Chicago University Press, 2010), 139–163.

115 Among others, Ku-ming Chang, Anthony Grafton, and Glenn W. Most, eds., *Impagination: Layout and Materiality of Writing and Publication: Interdisciplinary Approaches from East and West* (Berlin: De Gruyter, 2021); Alan Galey, "The Enkindling Reciter: E-Books in the Bibliographical Imagination," *Book History* 15 (2012): 210–247; and Bonnie Mak, *How the Page Matters* (Toronto: University of Toronto Press, 2011).

116 Eisenstein, *The Printing Press as an Agent of Change*, 520–574.

117 Lorraine Daston, "Cloud Physiognomy," *Representations* 135 (February 2016): 67.

118 Among others, Nicholas Dames, *The Chapter: A Segmented History from Antiquity to the Twenty-First Century* (Princeton, NJ: Princeton University Press, 2023); Bonnie Mak, "Manuscript," in *Cambridge Critical Concepts: Technology and Literature*, ed. Adam Hammond (Cambridge, UK: Cambridge University Press, 2023), 45–68; Rouse and Rouse, "*Statim Invenire*"; and M. B. Parkes, "The Influence of the Concepts of *Ordinatio* and *Compilatio* on the Development of the Book," in *Medieval Learning and Literature: Essays presented to Richard William Hunt*, ed. J. J. G. Alexander and M. T. Gibson (Oxford: Clarendon Press, 1976), 115–141.

119 This growth challenged attitudes to the products of the early printing industry which were seen by many, even into the sixteenth century, as "vulgar," or unrefined, because of their association with a public readership and with the evolving capitalist market: see Siobhan Keenan, *Renaissance Literature* (Edinburgh: Edinburgh University Press, 2008), 34.

120 As covered in a variety of chapters in *The Cambridge History of the Book in Britain. Volume III: 1400–1557*, ed. Lotte Hellinga and J. B. Trapp (Cambridge, UK: Cambridge University Press, 1999).

121 Lynette Hunter, "Books for Daily Life: Household, Husbandry, Behaviour," in *The Cambridge History of the Book in Britain. Volume IV: 1557–1695*, ed. John Barnard and D. F. McKenzie (Cambridge, UK: Cambridge University Press, 2002), 514–532. See, also, Blair, *Too Much to Know*.

122 Daniel Headrick, *When Information Came of Age: Technologies of Knowledge in the Age of Reason and Revolution, 1700–1850* (Oxford: Oxford University Press, 2000), 143; Fyfe, "The Information Revolution"; and Weller, "The Puffery and Practicality of Etiquette Books."

123 David Lyon, Frank Webster, and Kevin Robins are good examples of sociologists who have been keenly aware of the importance of information historically but who have not placed their work specifically in an information history framework. See, for example, David Lyon, *The Electronic*

Eye: The Rise of Surveillance Society (Cambridge, UK: Polity Press, 1994); and Kevin Robins and Frank Webster, *Information Technology: A Luddite Analysis* (Norwood: Ablex, 1986).

124 Early theorising of the "end of continuity" came from Peter Drucker, *The Age of Discontinuity* (New York: Harper and Row, 1969). On the development of the information society concept, see Alistair Duff, Davis Craig, and David McNeill, "A Note on the Origins of the Information Society," *Journal of Information Science* 22, no. 2 (1996): 117–122; David Lyon, *The Information Society: Issues and Illusions* (Cambridge, UK: Polity Press, 1988); and Susan Crawford, "The Origin and Development of a Concept: The Information Society," *Bulletin of the Medical Library Association* 71, no. 4 (October 1983): 380–385. The information society concept originated in the field of economics and later spread to other areas, including sociology and information science. The seminal work on the emergence of an information, or knowledge, economy was undertaken by Fritz Machlup, *The Production and Distribution of Knowledge in the United States* (Princeton, NJ: Princeton University, 1962). This was followed by Marc Porat, *The Information Economy* (Washington, DC: U.S. Department of Commerce, Office of Telecommunications, 1977). Both examined historical trends in knowledge/information industries and occupations.

125 Alain Touraine, *The Post-Industrial Society* (New York: Random House, 1971), 5, 19, and 61–63. The book was originally published as *La société post-industrielle* (Paris: Editions Denoël, 1969).

126 Daniel Bell, *The Coming of Post-Industrial Society: Venture in Social Forecasting* (London: Heinemann, 1974).

127 Alvin Toffler, *The Third Wave* (London: Pan Books, 1980), 46.

128 Lisa Bud-Frierman, *Information Acumen: The Understanding and Use of Knowledge in Modern Business* (London: Routledge, 1994); Yates, *Control Through Communication*; Beniger, *The Control Revolution*; and Alfred Chandler, *The Visible Hand: The Managerial Revolution in American Business* (Cambridge, MA: Harvard University Press, 1977). On the bureaucratisation of business, see Sebastian Felton and Christine von Oertzen, "Bureaucracy as Knowledge," *Journal for the History of Knowledge* 1, no. 1 (2020): 1–16; Crooks and Parsons, eds., *Empires and Bureaucracy in World History* and Christopher Dandeker, *Surveillance, Power and Modernity: Bureaucracy and Discipline from 1700 to the Present* (Cambridge, UK: Polity Press, 1990).

129 Peter Simonson et al., eds., *The Handbook of Communication History* (New York: Routledge, 2012); Dan Schiller, *How to Think about Information* (Urbana, IL: University of Illinois Press, 2007); Jorge Reina Schement, ed., *Encyclopedia of Communication and Information* (New York: Macmillan Reference U.S.A., 2002); and Dan Schiller, *Theorizing Communication: A History* (New York: Oxford University Press, 1996). Solymar, *Getting the Message*, is peppered with the word "information."

130 Asa Briggs and Peter Burke, *A Social History of the Media: From Gutenberg to Facebook*, 4th ed., with Espen Ytreberg (Cambridge, UK: Polity Press, 2020), 1.

131 Marshall McLuhan, *Understanding Media: The Extension of Man* (London: Routledge and Kegan Paul), 147, and *passim*.

132 On the definition and development of the information sciences and associated information professions, see Marcia Bates, "The Information Professions: Knowledge, Memory, Heritage," *Information Research*, 20, no. 1 (March 2015). http://informationr.net/ir/20-1/paper655.html#.Y0PnEUbMLIU. Bates does not specifically include computer science in her "definition," but it is legitimate to do so for the purpose of this discussion, the discipline having developed a strong history of itself. William Aspray, "The Many Histories of Information," *Information & Culture* 50, no. 1 (2015): 1–23, also sees the information sciences as the natural home of information history, although in addition he cites communication studies as an equally welcoming harbour.

133 As discussed by several contributors to Fritz Machlup and Una Mansfield, eds., *The Study of Information: Interdisciplinary Messages* (New York: John Wiley, 1983). See, also, Alistair Black, "Every Discipline Needs a History: Information Management and the Early Information Society in Britain," in *Aware and Responsible: Papers of the Nordic-International Colloquium on Social and Cultural Awareness and Responsibility in Library, Information and Documentation Studies (SCARLID)*, ed. W. Boyd Rayward (Lanham, MD: Scarecrow Press, 2004), 29–47.

134 Campbell-Kelly and Aspray, *Computer*. Aside from including the word "information" in their sub title, the authors explore computing's pre-electronic history, in part by deploying the concept of information processing.
135 James Cortada, "Where Did Knowledge Workers Come From?," in *The Rise of the Knowledge Worker*, ed. Cortada (Boston, MA: Butterworth Heinemann, 1998), 5, where it is argued that the literature on the "history of information" could "fill a building."
136 Anthony Bryant et al., eds., *Information Systems: Why History Matters*, [special issue of] *Journal of Information Technology* Part 1: 28, no. 1 (March 2013): 1–89; Part 2: 28, no. 2 (June 2013): 91–166.
137 For example, Markus Krajewski, *Paper Machines: About Cards & Catalogs, 1548–1929* (Cambridge, MA: MIT Press, 2011); and Friedrich A. Kittler, *Gramophone, Film, Typewriter*, trans. Geoffrey Winthrop-Young and Michael Wutz (Stanford, CA: Stanford University Press, 1999).
138 Among others, see Heather MacNeil, "From the Memory of the Act to the Act Itself. The Evolution of Written Records as Proof of Jural Acts in England, 11th to 17th Century," *Archival Science* 6, nos. 3–4 (2006): 313–328; Francis X. Blouin and William G. Rosenberg, eds., *Archives, Documentation and Institutions of Social Memory: Essays from the Sawyer Seminar* (Ann Arbor, MI: Bentley Historical Library, University of Michigan, 2006); Eric Ketelaar, *The Archival Image: Collected Essays* (Hilversum: Verloren, 1997); Luciana Duranti, "Medieval Universities and Archives," *Archivaria* 38 (1994–95): 37–44; and Ernst Posner, *Archives in the Ancient World* (Cambridge, MA: Harvard University Press, 1972).
139 Elizabeth Yale, "The History of Archives: The State of the Discipline," *Book History* 18 (2015): 332; Lisa Gitelman, *Paper Knowledge: Towards a Media History of the Document* (Durham, NC: Duke University Press, 2014); Ben Kafka, *The Demon of Writing: Powers and Failures of Paperwork* (Cambridge, MA: Zone Books, 2012); and Blair, *Too Much to Know*.
140 Randolph C. Head, *Making Archives in Early Modern Europe: Proof, Information, and Political Record-Keeping, 1400–1700* (Cambridge, UK: Cambridge University Press, 2019); Michael Mann, *The Sources of Power. Volume 2: The Rise of Classes and Nation-States, 1760–1914*, 2nd ed. (Cambridge, UK: Cambridge University Press, 2012), 444–478; Soll, *The Information Master*; and Higgs, *The Information State in England*.
141 W. Boyd Rayward, "The History and Historiography of Information Science: Some Reflections," in *Historical Studies in Information Science*, ed. Trudi Hahn and Michael Buckland (Medford, NJ: Information Today, Inc., 1998), 7–21. The American Society for Information Science and Technology is home to a historical special interest group: The History and Foundations of Information Science. The group's present name was adopted in 1995, but work on the history of information science has a much longer pedigree: see Robert V. Williams, *Bibliography of the History of Information Science and Technology*, 8th ed. (American Society for Information Science and Technology, 2012). https://www.asist.org/about/history-of-information-science/bibliography-of-the-history-of-information-science-and-technology/.
142 Such scholars include W. Boyd Rayward, Michael Buckland, Jesse Shera, Colin Burke, Irene Farkas-Conn, Thomas Hapke, and Pamela Richards. Their writings and those of other leading scholars are discussed in Michael Buckland and Ziming Liu, "The History of Information Science," *Annual Review of Information Science and Technology* 30 (1995): 385–416. See also, Thomas Haigh, "The History of Information Technology," *Annual Review of Information Science and Technology* 45, no. 1 (2011): 431–487; and Bowden, Hahn, and Williams, *Proceedings of the 1998 Conference on the History and Heritage*. The tradition of recognising the importance of historical perspective in information science has been continued, more recently, by Bawden and Robinson, *Introduction to Information Science*.
143 John Feather, *The Information Society: A Study of Continuity and Change*, 5th ed. (London: Facet, 2008); Alistair Duff, *Information Society Studies* (London: Routledge, 2000); and Geoffrey C. Bowker and Susan Leigh Star, *Sorting Things Out: Classification and Its Consequences* (Cambridge, MA: MIT Press, 1999).
144 Early seminal treatises on library history include William Munford, *Penny Rate: Aspects of British Public Library History, 1850–1950* (London: Library Association, 1951); and Sidney Ditzion, *Arsenals of a Democratic Culture: A Social History of the American Public Library Movement in New England and the Middle States from 1850–1900* (Chicago, IL: American Library Association, 1947). On librarians' adoption of an information identity, see W. Boyd Rayward, "Library

and Information Sciences: Disciplinary Differentiation, Competition, and Convergence," in *The Study of Information: Interdisciplinary Messages*, ed. Fritz Machlup and Una Mansfield (New York: Wiley, 1983), 343–363.
145 Stevens, "The History of Information."
146 In chronological order, see Pamela Richards, "The Quest for Enemy Scientific Information 1939–1945: Information History as Part of Library History," *Library History* 9, nos. 1–2 (January 1991): 5–14; László Karvalics, "The Claims, Pre-History and Programme of Historical Informatics," *Periodica Polytechnic Social and Management Sciences* 2, no. 1 (1994): 19–30; Alistair Black, "Lost Worlds of Culture: Victorian Libraries, Library History and Prospects for a History of Information," *Journal of Victorian Culture* 2, no. 1 (Spring, 1997): 124–141; Black, "Information and Modernity"; Ilkka Mäkinen, "Why Do We Need Information History?," *BOBCATSSS Symposium, Bratislava* (January 25–27, 1999). https://researchportal.tuni.fi/en/publications/why-do-we-need-information-history-paper-at-bobcatsss-symposium-b; Boris Volodin, "History of Librarianship, Library History, or Information History: A View from Russia," *Library Quarterly* 70, no. 4 (October 2000): 446–467; Ilkka Mäkinen et al., "Information and Libraries in an Historical Perspective: From Library History to Library and Information History," in *European Curriculum Reflections on Library and Information Science Education*, ed. Leif Kajberg and Leif Lørring (Copenhagen: The Royal School of Library and Information Science, 2005), 172–191; Toni Weller, "A New Approach: The Arrival of Informational History," *Proceedings of the XVI International Conference of the Association for History and Computing: Humanities, Computers and Cultural Heritage* (Amsterdam: Royal Netherlands Academy of Arts and Sciences Amsterdam, 2005), 273–278; Alistair Black, "Information History," *Annual Review of Information Science and Technology*, 40 (2006): 441–473; Toni Weller and David Bawden, "Individual Perceptions: A New Chapter on Victorian Information History," *Library History* 22, no. 2 (2006): 137–156; Laura Skouvig, "Bibliotekshistorie, død eller dristig," *Dansk Biblioteksforskning* 3, no. 1 (2007): 5–16; and Toni Weller, "Information History: Its Importance, Relevance, and Future," *ASLIB Proceedings*, 59, nos. 4–5 (2008): 437–448; and Weller, *Information History*.
147 Paul Edwards et al., "AHR Conversation: Historical Perspectives on the Circulation of Information," *American Historical Review* 116, no. 5 (December 2011): 1403–1404.
148 John Durham Peters, "Information: Notes towards a Critical History," *Journal of Communication Inquiry* 12, no. 2 (July 1988): 9; and John M. Roberts, *The Triumph of the West* (London: BBC, 1985), 236.
149 For a sceptical look at the information society proposition, see Frank Webster, *Theories of the Information Society*, 4th ed. (London: Routledge, 2014).
150 Briggs and Burke, *A Social History of the Media*, 321–354; Julienne du Toit, "Conspiring at High Speed," *Rhodes University Research Report 2021* (Makhanda [Grahamstown]: Rhodes University, 2022). https://www.ru.ac.za/media/rhodesuniversity/content/research/documents/annualresearchreports/Annual_Research_Report_2022.pdf; Niels Brügger et al., eds., *Internet Histories* (Abingdon: Routledge, 2018); Bonnie Mak, "Archaeology of a Digitization," *Journal of the Association for Information Science and Technology* 65, no. 8 (August 2014): 1515–1526; Martin Campbell-Kelly, "The History of the Internet: The Missing Narratives," *Journal of Information Technology* 28, no. 1 (March 2013): 18–33; José Van Dijck, *The Culture of Connectivity: A Critical History of Social Media* (Oxford: Oxford University Press, 2013); Johnny Ryan, *A History of the Internet and the Digital Future* (London: Reaktion Books, 2010); and Janet Abbate, *Inventing the Internet* (Cambridge, MA: MIT Press, 1999). Tom Standage, *Writing on the Wall: Social Media – The First 2000 Years* (London: Bloomsbury, 2013), demonstrates that extensive communication through social networks stretches back to antiquity.
151 See John Tosh, *The Pursuit of History: Aims, Methods and New Directions in the Study of History*, 7th ed. (London: Routledge, 2022), 55–56, and 59–60 on, respectively, the "new history" and "history from below." For an example of micro, informal, everyday information history, or information exchange, see Denice Fett, "Information, Gossip, and Rumor: The Limits of Intelligence at the Early Modern Court, 1558–1585," in *The Limits of Empire: European Imperial Formations in Early Modern World History: Essays in Honor of Geoffrey Parker*, ed. Tonio Andrade and William Reger (Farnham: Ashgate, 2012), 79–98. On informal information exchange among gentlemen scientists in the Scientific Revolution, see Steven Shapin, *A Social History of*

Truth: Civility and Science in Seventeenth-Century England (Chicago, IL: Chicago University Press, 1994).
152 Exceptions in this regard include Carla Bittel, Elaine Leong, and Christine von Oertzen, eds., *Working with Paper: Gendered Practices in the History of Knowledge* (Pittsburgh, PA: University of Pittsburgh Press, 2019); Helen Plant, "Women's Employment in Industrial Libraries and Information Bureaux in Britain, c. 1918–1960," in *The Early Information Society: Information Management in Britain Before the Computer*, ed. Alistair Black, Dave Muddiman, and Helen Plant (Aldershot: Ashgate, 2007), 219–233; and Evelyn Kerslake and Nickianne Moody, eds., *Gendering Library History* (Liverpool: Liverpool John Moores University Press, 2000).
153 Amanda Spink, *Information Behavior: An Evolutionary Instinct* (New York: Springer, 2010).
154 On surveillance as an aspect of the history of power and control, see Marklund and Skouvig, eds., *Histories of Surveillance*.

PART II
Visualising, Describing, Expressing

2
INFORMATION IN THE ROMAN EMPIRE*

Andrew Riggsby

The information landscape of the Roman Empire was a complex mix of the often alien, or seemingly "primitive," with flashes of the surprisingly modern. This chapter will survey some of the information practices of the Roman Empire—which encompassed the entire Mediterranean basin plus most of Northwestern Europe and the modern Mideast—from the accession of the first emperor (c. 30 BCE) to the official acceptance of Christianity (313 CE), and include glances earlier and later.[1]

Although a number of the particular issues discussed below have been treated individually by scholars of antiquity, they have only recently come to be seen within the field as part of a broader conversation about "information."[2] Conversely, details of the Ancient Roman world will often be unfamiliar to scholars of information in other periods. This chapter will therefore describe the broader informational environment in Rome as such. After an opening section on the basic mechanical technologies that were used to record information, the rest of the chapter is structured around a series of use contexts in which information circulated, such as the law, the economic world, "how-to" knowledge, personal identity, and way-finding.

Two important themes run through much of the discussion, as well as one that arises principally in the sections on Identity and Collections. The first has to do with the prominent role of individuals. There are perhaps a surprising number of informational transactions which depend on knowing a singular "right" person, and in many of those cases, the ultimate basis is that person's individual memory. Second, as "information" becomes a topic of study for specialists of Ancient Rome, a fundamental divide is becoming apparent between what might be described as maximalists and minimalists. Maximalism is characterised by the tendency to infer broad use or availability of information and its technologies from very limited particular instances, or even just from the existence of mechanisms that would seem to benefit from it.[3] Minimalists are more cautious in both respects, for instance, noting affirmative evidence of cases in which known technologies for managing information were used only sporadically.[4] While the position of this author is roughly minimalist, we will see the need for some nuance.

---

* I would like to thank the editors and the anonymous reviewer for valuable advice on both form and content.

The third, more specific point has to do with the accessibility of information in large collections, principally state archives. As will be described below, the Roman government collected and stored enormous amounts of information of various sorts. Some scholars have inferred that such information must have been readily accessible, at least to the state itself. I will suggest in what follows that this was not normally the case, and, in fact, the accessibility of data was highly restricted—not necessarily as a matter of policy, but one of information architecture.

Basic Modalities

Literacy in Rome was not restricted to a narrow scribal or social elite. At the same time, there was no mass literacy. Where the actual situation fell between those extremes at any given time is a matter of lively debate.[5] On the one hand, there was no system of general schooling. Nor did any obligatory interactions with the state—such as paying taxes—require the ability to read or write. On the other, literacy is directly attested among a variety of different social groups, and would have been a personally advantageous skill in a number of different contexts, among others, for craftsmen in large-scale pottery workshops or soldiers in the army. Whatever the raw level of literacy, it is widely agreed that even individually illiterate persons would have had their lives shaped by written documents that circulated around them. These documents might include state and military records or written contracts and other legal documents. Literacy was probably widespread enough that most people would have known someone who could read a modest text to them, and, for really important cases, professional scribes could be employed to read and write.

The following survey of writing media is organised in terms of a rough hierarchy of cost. Texts meant to last indefinitely were typically inscribed on bronze and stone.[6] Stone was widely used for private monuments such as tombstones (by far the most common type of inscription), religious dedications, and property markers. It was also common for public monuments (laws, more dedications). In the Western/Latin-speaking part of the empire, however, bronze was often the prestige material of choice.[7] It is striking how invested Romans were in this kind of permanent, typically public, writing. Indeed, the principal modern scholarly database lists well over five hundred thousand surviving classical Latin inscriptions.[8]

Records that were meant to be held more privately or for more limited periods of time were usually written on papyrus or inscribed onto wax tablets.[9] Papyrus is a paper-like material made from the fibres of a reed, formed into individual sheets, sometimes combined glued together into longer rolls. It is written on with ink and reed pen. This was the principal medium for literature, but was also common for letters and bookkeeping. Such papyrus documents have survived to the present day only under exceptionally dry conditions. Wax tablets were made of thin sheets of wood with a central "window" hollowed out and filled with wax. These were written on and erased with a metal stylus. Two or more such tablets were often hinged together with ties through holes in the frame as general-purpose notebooks. Moreover, the Romans also adopted a specialised diptych (later triptych) format for the preservation of important documents.[10] This involved writing an "official" text on the interior wax surfaces, binding the closed package with thread and sealing it with wax, and—where appropriate—adding an ink-on-wood external copy to make the substance of the preserved text available for easy inspection. Around four hundred of these still exist, overwhelmingly from three private business archives preserved by the eruption of Mt. Vesuvius in 79 CE.

The end of the period described in this chapter saw the rise of the codex—the modern book form—made of bound sheets of parchment. Traditional accounts have regarded this as the cause of a number of other technological advances and as something closely tied to the rise of Christianity.[11] However, more recent work has shown that neither claim holds up in simple form, but many details remain to be worked out and more nuanced versions are likely to survive.

Two other media were used almost entirely for more ephemeral records. An "ostrakon" is a ceramic fragment onto which writing was scratched with a stylus or written in ink. These would have been ubiquitously available due to breakage of storage and cooking vessels. Similarly fortuitous, at least in origin, were thin slips of wood that could be written on with ink, and even bound together into somewhat longer texts.[12] The surviving texts are mostly administrative, but also include other items such as an invitation to a birthday party.[13] The signature attached to the invitation is likely our oldest example of Latin written in the hand of a woman.

The fact of differential preservation—not just of wood slips, but of papyri and wax tablets, as well—has a couple of immediate evidentiary consequences for the historian. One is a caveat that should be kept in mind for the minimalist tendencies of the argument below. The most sophisticated information handling of which we are aware occurred disproportionately in utilitarian contexts, the material evidence of which survives only in peculiar contexts, such as being buried by lava, or in the driest part of the Egyptian desert. Thus, the extant evidence may have a pessimistic bias in terms of Roman informational capabilities. Second, while there were presumably genuine geographic disparities in the availability of information across the empire, they are hard to demonstrate. For instance, did the province of Egypt have a vastly more extensive system of state recordkeeping than the rest of the empire, as has often been maintained, or is this just an illusion created by the exceptional survival of documentary records in an especially arid region? Or how typical are a couple of incidents—known to us second-hand rather than through original documents of a type now invariably lost—in which we learn that the central government did not have reliable access to provincial records?[14]

Obviously, a substantially illiterate society must have relied considerably on non-written modalities of communication, but what may be more striking are some limits on the functions they served. For instance, there are a number of Roman occupational titles that are centred on the oral transmission of information (*praeco*, *nomenclator*). Among them, they cover much of the same ground as English "herald," "auctioneer," "spokesman," or "announcer."[15] Such titles suggest that the holders of these positions announce words that properly belong to others. In another respect, however, the names of these roles are slightly misleading. These Roman workers were not generally a substitute for mass media, addressing themselves to large and random crowds. For instance, criers did not broadly announce the time of day or calls to voting. Rather, those in such positions engaged in liaising activities, often serving as agents or go-betweens between a principal and a more limited, and likely known, counter-party.

In terms of visual or graphic communication, plans seem to have been common, at least for relatively small areas.[16] A limited number of written works, mostly technical ones, were illustrated. Two qualifications are important here. First, the information contained in these documents tends to be prescriptive (e.g. builder's plans) or declarative (e.g. setting taxation of parcels) rather than descriptive—with the exception of botanical illustrations. Second, much of the visual information only makes sense taken in combination with text; visual representations are almost never trusted as stand-alone carriers of information (contrast here, say, modern furniture assembly instructions).

Economy

To begin, the modern reader should note that the Romans lacked a number of kinds of top-down information, conventionally associated today with the notion of the "economic." The Roman state did not collect statistics such as price levels, employment, or trade balances. Nor were there systematic sales or income taxes or business licensing whose operation would incidentally have generated considerable economic information. And even in cases where the government presumably possessed informational raw material—customs duties and the census, for instance—there is no evidence that anyone ever considered aggregating the data for economic monitoring.

A fortiori, one would presume that private parties would not have had access to broad-scope information about the economy either. Nonetheless, it has been argued that professional traders had access to good information about prices of basic commodities across a great geographic range.[17] The indirect argument is based on a statistical claim that attested wheat prices across the empire vary predictably in proportion to distance from Rome. Thus, it is argued, the entire Mediterranean basin functioned as a single market, implying the existence of *some* mechanism for diffusion of knowledge of prices. Even if true, it is not clear how far one could generalise this argument beyond grain. In any case, more recent work suggests that the underlying statistical claim is faulty.[18]

There are also a number of studies of the trade in particular goods—such as real estate, labour, enslaved persons—from a "New Institutional" point of view.[19] This research has shown that the operation of all of these must have been significantly affected by information lack and asymmetry. That is, buyers would have had poor knowledge of the range of options available to them and would have known far less about any particular option than the respective sellers. Moreover, Romans themselves were broadly aware of these problems. Still, public or other formal solutions, such as professional licensing or public registers of real estate, were rare and very narrowly targeted. Private solutions typically involved repeated recourse to specific networks of personal contact, and trust or reliance on indirect signalling and proxy information. So, for instance, much long-distance trade was channelled through ethnic-based associations, with branches in multiple locations whose shared origins allowed for collective accountability. Such "solutions" thus attempted to establish secure channels for reasonably predictable trading; this avoided catastrophic failures, but left individual transactions more expensive because the segment of the market seen by any given participant was so limited.

Our best "bottom-up" evidence for the informational resources of individuals comes from fragmentary records of a few financial firms (most preserved by the eruption of Vesuvius) and of agricultural estates, mostly in Egypt. The majority of surviving financial records are copies of individual documents such as contracts or receipts for particular transactions.[20] Literary sources make it clear that there would also normally have been at least a running journal of transactions, which could then be digested into a more permanent account book and in some cases into other types of documents. In agribusiness contexts, literary sources would lead us to expect similar kinds of records, including separate accounting for different crops.[21] Some specific registers and inventory lists from a few large operations have survived.

The form of these accounts, however, was often rudimentary. Many were essentially narrative, with one entry following immediately on another.[22] When accounts were arranged in more tabular form, items such income and expenditures were not typically separated. There were no standards for accounting that were formally set by the state or non-governmental organisations, or by, say, popular instructional manuals as was the case in some later periods. It has been pointed out that in attested legal disputes, the quality of accounts is often validated on aesthetic criteria rather than expert ones.

Practices

How did people come to know "how to" perform practical tasks? Here we have two kinds of sources. On the one hand, there are surviving texts such as recipe books and apprenticeship contracts. On the other, archaeologists have begun to develop methods to examine variation in individual types of artefacts over geographical ranges as way to reconstruct the transmission of knowledge of how to construct those objects.

In a number of areas, we have manuals of practice, which have survived through the same kinds of copying traditions as more "literary" works: agricultural management, culinary and medical recipes, land surveying, architecture, oratory, law, generalship, and magic.[23] The works on grammar and law are mostly genuine textbooks, intended to be embedded into known practices of formal instruction. The texts on architecture and oratory mimic these to some extent, but are generally thought to be intended more to advertise the learning of the author than to instruct.[24] The place of the other texts listed here is less clear. It is likely that they were informational, but they would have been hard to use on their own without context or foreknowledge. For instance, the recipes for food frequently give no quantities or omit necessary steps of the preparation.[25] A number of spells for "erotic conquest" give a precise text for verbal performance but only allude to accompanying rituals that are under-specified.[26] Whether or not formal instruction was available in any of these areas, the texts would not have sufficed to replace it. So, for instance, someone who stumbled onto the text would likely still need to pay an expert to make use of it.

An important recent discovery of fragments has brought attention to what appear to be collections of information relevant for day-to-day work in commerce.[27] One preserved volume binds together metrological reference tables, algorithms to calculate the area or volume of various figures, and sample contracts for loans and a lease. The most likely hypothesis is that this composite—and similar texts—figured in an otherwise unattested form of post-primary education, aimed at non-elite persons who would become professional business agents or the like.

For craft skills, we know of at least three modes of transmission of knowledge, though all are essentially versions of on-the-job training.[28] The first is familial; professions were often handed down in families. Secondly, given that the Romans practised chattel slavery on a massive scale, it is not surprising that enslaved persons were trained in similar fashion. Finally, children could be hired out by means of formal apprenticeship contracts to learn a trade by assisting an established professional.

The evidence for the modes of transmission just described is principally textual. Archaeologists, however, have recently begun to combine those basic models with close observation of various features of material remains to infer the shape of networks of transmission of craft knowledge.[29] Several features appear to arise from this investigation. The knowledge required to establish and run a fulling or weaving operation, for instance, would not all have been in the hands of any one person, but would have been distributed among specialist communities in the craft itself and in various forms of making, such as masonry or blacksmithing. Different communities of this sort show widely differing degrees of geographic localisation. More specialised industries (say, tuna-fishing) tend to show considerably uniformity across locations; ones that were—at least at a basic level—more generic (say, cleaning clothes) developed more local pockets of modest innovation. Human mobility was the main driver of the spread of knowledge.

Law

Many surviving statutes specify that Roman laws were to be posted in readily visible form in specified places, although actual legibility may have been more problematic.[30] Nevertheless, public display is not the same as broad diffusion. The original displays were often at a single location in the city of Rome; in some cases, there was to be a single copy displayed in each of multiple locations. There is no evidence that these display copies were indexed, so finding a copy of an older statute among the many at Rome would have been a difficult task. Instead, one would presumably need a privately made copy (or descendent of a chain of copies) or one derived from archival records. As for the latter, the Roman politician Cicero complained, presumably hyperbolically, that the laws were "whatever the archival staff wanted them to be."[31] The last section of this chapter will further discuss the difficulties of archival access.

An important special case involves Imperial rulings that nominally addressed a particular case, but which could nonetheless be appealed to in subsequent disputes.[32] For instance, one emperor clarified that a rental agreement could not be rescinded if someone later offered a higher rent.[33] Individuals petitioned the emperor for intervention in their private legal disputes. His staff frequently responded by posting a copy of the petition along with an official response which clarified the legal situation. Documentary evidence shows that these clarifications ("rescripts") were sometimes used by parties in unrelated legal cases even before the very late Imperial state collected and published some of the most important examples. In a more public context, Imperial rulings might resolve disputes between whole communities. A successful party might monumentalise the text of the decision both as a way to ensure its lasting application and as a more abstract symbol of Imperial favour, but the force of these rulings could also be generalised to other cases.

The mechanisms for circulation of rescripts and other rulings are unclear, but likely include two somewhat more general phenomena. First, documentary evidence suggests that private individuals collected *ad hoc* chrestomathies of legal materials—documents, rulings, pattern formulae—sometimes only tenuously connected to one another or to any specific legal purpose.[34] For instance, a cache recently discovered near the Dead Sea mixed the personal contracts, petitions, and other documents of a second-century CE woman named Babatha with generic pattern forms that anyone could use.[35] These collections seem not to have become standardised, but elements could have been borrowed from one to another. Second, scribes and para-legal professionals may have collected documents in similar if somewhat more systematic form. The model contracts referred to above appear to have circulated in a context like this.

Private scholarship was particularly important to the Roman legal system; much of the work of legal interpretation done in Common Law systems via court decisions was done instead by individual "jurists," often operating outside of any official framework.[36] Circulation of their writings was limited by the need for individual hand copying, just as was the case for any extended text. As far as we can tell, demand for this kind of work would not have justified prepared copies taking up space in the stock of general booksellers. Rather, one would likely have had to be part of some kind of network of specialist readers who would, among other things, exchange texts.

Location

Our best information about way-finding is probably at the level of moving around within urban areas, especially Rome itself.[37] Streets could have official names, but that seems to be the exception rather than the rule. Directional signage is also nearly unattested. Small zones in which particular professions were concentrated could be named informally using phrases like "among the potters."[38] Large cities like Rome also had larger neighbourhoods or districts with names that were not semantically transparent, although there is no sign that they were marked in the urban fabric in any way. Whatever the case in those respects, there is no evidence for numeration of individual buildings either along streets or within districts, even in cities built on planned grids. Instead, locations are given with respect to individual landmarks. Some of those are named entities potentially knowable by anyone, for example, "Flumentaria Gate" or "Temple of Flora."[39] Others are *ad hoc* references that only make sense on the ground and to someone familiar with the area ("a large tree," "downhill").[40]

It is important to make explicit two things implicit in the last observation. The context for such information is (a) one person giving explicit directions to another for (b) travel between two specific points. More will be said about the role of persons below, but it is worth remarking here about the shape of the information given. The most common form is an itinerary: "go here, then here, and so on" to the eventual goal, perhaps enriched by directional markers at some points (e.g. "right," "up"). If the goal is near a genuinely major monument, we also sometimes see not so much a path chaining together multiple locations as a series of increasingly specific definitions of a single location. For instance, a judicial defendant was once required to appear for a hearing "in the Forum of Augustus, in front of the statue of Diana Lucifera, at the tenth column."[41] In either case, however, actually following the earlier directions is necessary to understanding those that follow.

For longer distances, Romans had maps.[42] However, these seem to have been rare, and they were not necessarily made to consistent scale or to follow other generalised conventions. Writers do not make much reference to their use. As a practical matter, maps probably contributed to a very general awareness of geographic orientation, but were not tools for planning specific trips in any detail. For that, the standard tool was the itinerary—a list of locations (typically cities) that one would pass along the route between some origin and destination.[43] Preserved specimens typically give the length of journey segments, but no other information. As in the intra-city case, then, one would need live informants at each intermediate point to explain which route out of town lead in the appropriate direction. Itineraries are more specialised than maps; a would-be traveller might need either to collate multiple routes or, again, rely on a live informant—presumably one who had made the trip before—to establish a path at the higher level as well.

As noted, actual maps were rare in the Roman world and their use cases were seemingly limited. A partial exception to the first point (but confirmatory of the second) are the so-called *formae* generated by land surveyors in colonial contexts.[44] In regular cases, parcels of land were often defined verbally, naming various natural and artificial landmarks and boundaries, essentially another type of itinerary. But when the Romans seized land from defeated opponents in war, they often distributed regular rectangular plots of the surrounding land to the colonists—a process known as "centuriation." These grants were characteristically recorded in multiple formats, one of which was a graphic *forma*. The surviving instances show that these were fairly minimal maps ("diagram" is possibly a better word), ignoring most terrain features and concentrating on the formal grid produced by the survey process and textual annotations about ownership, lot size, and tax liabilities. But these are not way-finding devices. Rather, someone already knowing the location of plot could use that information as an index to discover various bits of legal information about it.

Identity

What information could be gathered (especially but not exclusively by the state) around a given individual?[45] One obvious place to begin looking for evidence is the Roman "census."[46] The census in fact refers to two different if overlapping institutions. The original census dates to long before the Empire and counted only Roman citizens. It continued to be conducted sporadically over the first decades of the Empire. It was paralleled, then eventually replaced, by a system of provincial surveys which were meant to capture everyone resident within their respective areas. Both versions were periodic, although the time between iterations (five to fourteen years) varied from time to time and place to place. The basic unit of the count was the male head of household, who reported not only himself, but also his dependents (family and slaves) and an account of his property. It is not always clear how or whether orphan minor children or unmarried adult women were included in the various versions.

There is also a substantial lack of clarity over other important aspects of the census. One is the likely rate of capture. Participation was notionally mandatory, but the mechanisms of enforcing the statutory penalties are unclear. Outside the elite, who might need the census to validate their privileged status, participation would not otherwise offer particular benefits and might even incur burdens.

Another question is how readily actual people could be linked to the notional entities who populated the census entries and vice versa. On the one hand, records surviving from the Egyptian provincial census show that they sometimes contained physical descriptions.[47] On the other, this would typically be true only of the declarant himself, not the bulk of the members of the household. Moreover, descriptions are minimal: age, profession, and perhaps mention of a distinguishing scar.[48] This is of some value for confirming a suggested connection, but not as part of a search process.

A final question is the extent to which the census could have been a framework to organise data from other sources.[49] Outside of the census, the Imperial government required or allowed a number of other life events to be registered. These are diverse enough that they benefit from being reviewed individually:

Birth[50]

Citizen births could be registered in Rome or provincial capitals. This may not have been obligatory, but would have been beneficial both for the child (useful to prove status) and for the parent (evidence of parentage and conformity with pro-natal legislation). Declarations were recorded on demand, without enquiry into their correctness. Distance would have discouraged many from registering, especially among the poorer who had less to gain from compliance.

Death

At least in Egypt, we have substantial evidence of families filing notice of the death of relatives. These are almost all men of tax-paying age. This coverage—along with some anomalies in the timing of the notices—means that we do not really understand their function, though some connection with taxation remains plausible.

Military Discharge[51]

A large fraction of the Roman army was made up of non-citizens who were granted citizenship upon honourable discharge. This was documented both by publicly displayed inscriptions in Rome and by small individual bronze tablets (*diplomata*) that were kept by the former soldier.

Manumission[52]

Romans manumitted slaves, both by private mechanisms and by registration with a competent magistrate. In either case, the state collected a tax based on the market value of the slave. In principle, the magistrate's intervention could have produced a documentary record for at least some instances and the tax payment for all of them. The latter record would have been vitiated by the fact that the former owner often paid the tax. In any case, we have no instance of either kind of record being used to prove someone's free status.

Marriage[53]

Marriages often gave rise to documents called "marital tablets." Many of the surviving examples include a reference to the pro-natal legislation referred to above, but there is no evidence that they were required by that statute, much less centrally collected. Rather, these appear to have been private legal documents recording optional dowry arrangements, which only incidentally mention the broader legal context.

Grain Distribution[54]

From shortly before the beginning of the Empire, the Roman state distributed grain (and later other foodstuffs) to a significant fraction of the adult male citizen population of the city. This seems to have required some kind of administrative register containing a few hundred thousand names and corresponding tokens in the hands of the recipients, though the mechanisms to keep either lists or tokens up-to-date are not well understood.

Few if any of these systems of registration were meant to be comprehensive, deliberately excluding (for instance) women, non-citizens, citizens, or those not resident in the capital. Even beyond those formal restrictions, the nature of the survivals suggests gaps, often wide ones, between theoretical and actual capture of data. Only some of them (birth, military discharge) fed into specialised registers. Others would have existed only into the running records of officials or have been simply been private records; the different types of records all have different specific limitations and organisation. It would then seem impossible to imagine all forming part of a single meta-database built around the census.

Private forms of identification were rare and less systematic. The most broadly used are probably the combinations of signature and wax or clay impressions used to seal contracts and wills.[55] Except for the actual author of the will, however, these did not serve as stand-alone guarantors of identity. Rather, witnesses to the original act could subsequently be asked to verify their seals or signatures to guarantee the physical document had not been tampered with.

Collections

Public libraries in the city of Rome were effectively a creation of the emperors, who founded several over the course of the first three centuries CE.[56] Outside of Rome, the foundation of libraries was a prestigious form of public benefaction by local elites, and dozens of examples are known. In both cases, these libraries served as (or were embedded in) institutions with broader "high culture" functions, such as literary recitations or the display of artworks. While it is clear that the presentation of texts to the "public" was ideologically part of the mission of these institutions, there is virtually no evidence for their use by persons outside of the social elite or professional scholars (who were often associated with elite patrons). Whoever the users were, they seem to have used the books onsite.[57] The content of collections seems to have centred on literary texts, such as poetry, history, oratory, and philosophy. Some also held associated texts (say, commentaries) and in one instance an apparently scholarly collection of official documents. The largest estimate for the size of any of these collections is perhaps in the high tens of thousands of volumes.

Private libraries of the wealthy seem generally to have collected similar types of texts.[58] These private collections served as loci of both aristocratic competition and cooperation. Competition could centre on the size of collections or possession of especially prized manuscripts, but it might also have more to do with the luxury of the infrastructure. It was common for owners to allow friends and dependents of friends access to their collections. We have no real way to gauge the size of these collections, but perhaps they reached a few thousand volumes.

The contents of at least some libraries were catalogued.[59] We have (fragments of) lists of works held, identified by author and title. These lists are written continuously, so there is no straightforward way to incorporate new accessions. Nor do they contain additional information about individual texts, nor any kind of code to indicate location within the library. Some of the lists appear to be organised by genre, and at least one shows crude alphabetical order within those categories. It is possible, but not certain, that this reflects the physical organisation of books within the library. Wherever they were placed, we do know that rolls typically had end tags so a person could identify the contents of a scroll in hand without having to unroll it. All our (limited) evidence, however, suggests that those tags would not be read by individual library users. Instead, texts seem to have been fetched by permanent (enslaved) staff, relying perhaps as much on memory as on formal devices like the lists and tags. Indeed, recent scholarship has emphasised the likelihood that this use of staff was not purely mechanical, but constituted a kind of distributed authorship.[60] Bookstores—at least the ones we know of from the city of Rome—seem to have paralleled libraries in a number of respects.[61] They focused on the same kinds of texts, they were likely of similar scale, and they were sites of social interaction among elites and, especially, associated intellectuals.

The section above on identity information listed a number of kinds of information the Roman state collected about members of the population. Beyond that, organs of the state also held massive collections of internal data, including financial accounts, public contracts, and list of land-grants. Some have assumed that if the state kept this data, it must have been able to retrieve it readily.[62] I would suggest that this is far from clear. In the first instance, data appears to have been highly siloed. To some extent, different governmental offices and even individual incumbents maintained independent archives. Sometimes sets of documents were transferred from multiple locations to a more centralised collection of the same sort, but central and regional offices often did not have access to the same records. This division on the one hand imposed a certain degree of automatic order, but on the other meant that documents on a given topic might be widely scattered. Moreover, even enquiring in the right place, the only direct way to find a record in most of the collections was to know either the date of its accession or an equivalent sequential file number. This works well for verification of information already in hand; it is much worse for search or collation. To the extent that those operations would be possible, they would lean on the knowledge of permanent, enslaved staff, as in the case of libraries. It would also have been more effective in the case of the records of state actors (relatively less numerous; more likely to be of known date) than of documents about ordinary persons, much less collections thereof. And even that presupposes access would be granted in the first place.

Conclusions

We have seen numerous examples of situations where the memory of a specific person was crucial to success, such as locating texts in libraries or archives or way-finding. Whether the ultimate repository was individual memory or a document, access to the information often crucially relied on individual personal ties rather than universal or institutional structures.[63] For instance, advanced legal texts would be hard to acquire for those not already networked with the kinds of people who wrote them, and technical skills were taught through individual apprenticeship, not open schools or self-study of books. There is, however, a set of counter-examples. Recent scholarship on antiquity has identified systems of human-object interaction that are usefully described as what cognitive scientists describe as "distributed cognitive systems," which have capabilities that cannot be attributed to either the people or the objects alone.[64] For instance, I have argued that some military unit rosters were not merely tools to record assignments, but ones used interactively to establish those assignments. The reason, however, that these have not appeared before this point is that they are all restricted to very narrow use contexts, and thus are more or less invisible to a high-level survey like the one provided by this chapter. The availability of more sophisticated technologies only rarely displaced simpler ones.

Importantly, these individualised systems do not lend themselves to transfer, combination, or scaling up, which would have run up against the physical limits of memory, learning speed, or co-presence. Two libraries can be merged, for instance, but two human librarians cannot be. It would also be difficult to merge two different library catalogues, one that had been organised by author and the other by genre. In accounting, as noted above, the lack of standardised form seems to have encouraged assessment on superficial aesthetic grounds; that diversity must have obstructed detailed comparison or combination of separate records. I have argued elsewhere that Roman information systems were highly fragmented and that this would have resulted in the balkanisation of substantive knowledge as well.[65] The examples here confirm that phenomenon.

I have previously offered a very minimalist account of important information technologies, and the substantive approach offered here has been broadly along minimalist lines. Even if that is basically correct, however, it is important to recognise that irregularity is also a crucial feature of the Roman information landscape. Some Romans did use sophisticated information handling and management techniques in some situations. The distributed cognitive systems referred to above are instances. Similarly, the Roman state apparently kept track of a couple of hundred thousand people eligible for free grain (who admittedly had incentives to make themselves visible). And the fraction of Roman landed property allotted by centuriation could be identified with great precision by a combination of precise survey technology with both graphic and textual records. But the fact that these information-dense pockets were relatively scarce and relatively small would have made them harder to use as the building blocks of larger systems. Virtuous cycles of knowledge accumulation and organisation almost never took hold within the Roman Empire.

Notes

1 "Rome" will be used throughout to refer to the whole empire except where the city is explicitly specified. Following common convention among specialists, "Empire/Imperial" refer to rule by an emperor, while "empire/imperial" refer to the domination and rule of one state over others.
2 Andrew Riggsby, *Mosaics of Knowledge: Representing Information in the Roman World* (New York: Oxford University Press, 2019); and Courtney Roby, *Technical Ekphrasis in Ancient Science and Literature: The Written Machine between Alexandria and Rome* (Cambridge, UK: Cambridge University Press, 2016) plus the references in notes 3 and 4. Much of the cutting-edge work has not treated the narrowly "classical" world, but Late Antique/Early Christian contexts: see Riggsby, "Learning the Language of God," in *The Intellectual World of Late Antique Christianity*, ed. Lewis Ayres, Michael Champion, and Michael Crawford (Cambridge, UK: Cambridge University Press, 2023), 185–197 for extensive references to earlier work.
3 Examples of this tendency include Anna Dolganov, "Documenting Roman Citizenship," in *Roman and Local Citizenship in the Long Second Century CE*, ed. Myles Lavan and Clifford Ando (Oxford: Oxford University Press, 2021), 185–228; and Clifford Ando, *Imperial Ideology and Provincial Loyalty in the Roman Empire* (Berkeley, CA: University of California Press, 2000), 73–131. I should clarify that "maximalism" is a feature of the conclusions, not an assumption in its own right by these scholars. See, however, note 62.
4 John Bodel, "Documenting Identity in the Early Roman Empire," *Documentality. New Approaches to Written Documents in Imperial Life and Literature*, ed. J. Arthur-Montagne, S. J. DiGiulio, and I. N. I. Kuin (Berlin: DeGruyter, 2022), 35–56 is an excellent example. As with maximalism, Bodel's minimalism is an outcome, not a single axiom.
5 The literature is enormous, but key points are to be found in Anne Kolb, *Literacy in Ancient Everyday Life* (Berlin: De Gruyter, 2018); William Johnson and Holt N. Parker, eds., *Ancient Literacies the Culture of Reading in Greece and Rome* (Oxford: Oxford University Press, 2009); and W. V. Harris, *Ancient Literacy* (Cambridge, MA: Harvard University Press, 1989).
6 Alison Cooley, *The Cambridge Manual of Latin Epigraphy* (Cambridge, UK: Cambridge University Press, 2012).
7 Callie Williamson, "Monuments of Bronze: Roman Legal Documents on Bronze Tablets," *Classical Antiquity* 6 (1987): 160–183.
8 Epigraphik-Datenbank Clauss/Slaby (EDCS). http://www.manfredclauss.de/.
9 Anna Willi, *Manual of Roman Everyday Writing Vol. 2 Writing Equipment* (Nottingham: LatinNow ePubs, 2021).
10 Elizabeth Meyer, *Legitimacy and Law in the Roman World: Tabulae in Roman Belief and Practice* (Cambridge, UK: Cambridge University Press, 2004); and Michael Speidel, "Schreibtafeln (*tabulae ceratae*)," in *Inschriften edieren und kommentieren*, ed. Armin Eich (Berlin: de Gruyter, 2022), 99–113.
11 Colin H. Roberts and T. C. Skeat, *The Birth of the Codex* (London: Oxford University Press, 1983) is still a good general account. For some more recent perspectives, see, for instance, Sofia

Torallas Tovar, "Resisting the Codex: The Christian Use of the Roll in Late Antiquity," *Early Christianity* 12, no. 1 (2021): 61–84; Matthew Larsen and Mark Letteney, "Christians and the Codex: Generic Materiality and Early Gospel Traditions," *Journal of Early Christian Studies* 27, no. 3 (2019): 383–415; and Benjamin Harnett, "The Diffusion of the Codex," *Classical Antiquity* 36, no. 2 (2017): 183–235.

12 First set of these published in Alan K. Bowman and J. David Thomas, *Vindolanda: The Latin Writing-Tablets* (Gloucester: A. Sutton, 1984).

13 This last category was unknown until a few decades ago because of the unusual circumstances of physical preservation.

14 For the possible normalcy of Egypt, see Dolganov, "Documenting"; the second-hand accounts are in Pliny, *Letters* 10.66 and *Corpus Inscriptionum Latinarum* 10.7852.

15 Sarah E. Bond, *Trade and Taboo: Disreputable Professions in the Roman Mediterranean* (Ann Arbor, MI: University of Michigan Press, 2016), 21–58.

16 Riggsby, *Mosaics of Knowledge*, 154–172, 204–206.

17 David Kessler and Peter Temin, "Money and Prices in the Early Roman Empire," in *The Monetary Systems of the Greeks and Romans*, ed. William Harris (Oxford: Oxford University Press, 2008), 137–159; and Peter Temin, "The Economy of the Early Roman Empire," *Journal of Economic Perspectives* 20, no. 1 (2006): 133–151.

18 Giles Bransbourg, "Rome and the Economic Integration of Empire," *Institute for the Study of the Ancient World Papers* 3 (2012): n.p.

19 Giuseppe Dari-Mattiacci and Dennis P. Kehoe, eds., *Roman Law and Economics*, 2 vols. (Oxford: Oxford University Press, 2020).

20 Lance LaGroue, "Accounting and Auditing in Roman Society" (PhD diss., University of North Carolina, 2014).

21 Dominic Rathbone, *Economic Rationalism and Rural Society in Third-Century AD Egypt: The Heroninos Archive and the Appianus Estate* (Cambridge, UK: Cambridge University Press, 1991).

22 Riggsby, *Mosaics of Knowledge*, 62–66; and LaGroue, *Accounting and Auditing*.

23 Burkhard Meißner, *Die technologische Fachliteratur der Antike: Struktur, Überlieferung und Wirkung technischen Wissens in der Antike* (Boston, MA: Akademie Verlag, 2000). The manuals of generalship are all of the "armchair" variety. Perhaps interestingly, we have no trace of more mundane manuals of procedures from within the actual army.

24 John Oksanish, *Vitruvian Man: Rome under Construction* (New York: Oxford University Press, 2019).

25 Apicius, *Apicius: A Critical Edition with an Introduction and an English Translation of the Latin Recipe Text Apicius*, ed. and trans. Christopher W. Grocock and Sally Grainger (Totnes [England]: Prospect, 2006).

26 On magical knowledge systems, see Christopher Faraone and Sofía Torallas Tovar, eds., *The Greco-Egyptian Magical Formularies: Libraries, Books, and Individual Recipes* (Ann Arbor, MI: University of Michigan Press, 2022).

27 Roger Bagnall and Alexander Jones, eds., *Mathematics, Metrology and Model Contracts: A Codex from Late Antique Business Education* (New York: New York University Press, 2019).

28 Cameron Hawkins, "Contracts, Coercion, and the Boundaries of the Roman Artisanal Firm," in *Work, Labour, and Professions in the Roman World*, ed. Koenraad Verboven and Christian Laes (Leiden: Brill, 2017), 36–61.

29 Christopher Motz, "The Knowledge Networks of Workshop Construction in the Roman World" (PhD diss., University of Cincinnati, 2015).

30 The term "law" is here used in a broad sense that ignores system-internal distinctions. Williamson, "Monuments of Bronze"; and M. H. Crawford, ed., with contributions by J. D. Cloud and others, *Roman Statutes* (London: Institute of Classical Studies, School of Advanced Study, University of London, 1996), 19–20.

31 *On the Laws* 3.46.

32 Serena Connolly, *Lives Behind the Laws: The World of the Codex Hermogenianus* (Bloomington, IN: Indiana University Press, 2010).

33 *CJ* 4.65.21.

34 Ari Z. Bryen, "Reading the Citizenship Papyrus (P.Giss. I 40)," in *Citizenship and Empire in Europe 200–1900*, Potsdamer Altertumswissenschaftliche Beiträge, Bd. 54, ed. Clifford Ando

(Stuttgart: Franz Steiner, 2016), 29–44; and Bryen, "Judging Empire: Courts and Culture in Rome's Eastern Provinces," *Law and History Review* 30 (2012): 771–811.
35 The documents are published in Naphtali Lewis et al., *The Documents from the Bar Kokhba Period in the Cave of Letters* (Jerusalem: Israel Exploration Society, 1989). For more context, see Philip Esler, *Babatha's Orchard: The Yadin Papyri and an Ancient Jewish Family Tale Retold* (Oxford: Oxford University Press, 2017).
36 Bruce W. Frier, *The Rise of the Roman Jurists: Studies in Cicero's Pro Caecina* (Princeton, NJ: Princeton University Press, 2014); and Fritz Schulz, *History of Roman Legal Science* (Oxford: Clarendon Press, 1946).
37 Roger Ling, "A Stranger in Town: Finding the Way in an Ancient City," *Greece and Rome* 37, no. 2 (October 1990): 204–214. On this topic, I have also benefited greatly from conversations with Evan Jewell, who has important work forthcoming.
38 Varro, *LL* 5.154.
39 Varro, *RR* 3.2.6, Mart. *Ep.* 5.22.
40 Ter. *Adelph*. 575, 573.
41 *Tab. Herc.* 6.
42 Riggsby, *Mosaics of Knowledge*, 172–201; and Richard Talbert, "Urbs Roma to Orbs Romanus: Roman Mapping on the Grand Scale," in *Ancient Perspectives: Maps and the Place in Mesopotamia, Egypt, Greece, and Rome*, ed. Talbert (Chicago, IL: University of Chicago Press, 2012), 163–192, citing much valuable earlier work of his own.
43 Benet Salway, "The Perception and Description of Space in Roman Itineraries," in *Wahrnehmung und Erfassung geographischer Räume in der Antike*, ed. M. Rathmann (Mainz: Philipp von Zabern, 2007), 181–209.
44 Riggsby, *Mosaics of Knowledge*, 50–51, 186–188; and Oswald Dilke, *The Roman Land Surveyors: An Introduction to the Agrimensores* (Newton Abbot: David and Charles, 1971).
45 In addition to specific observations, Bodel in "Documenting Identity" raises important theoretical questions.
46 (Mostly) pre-imperial: Kaius Tuori and Juhana Heikonen, "Spaces of Citizenship," *Mélanges de l'École française de Rome. Antiquité* 134, no. 2 (2022): 335–360. Imperial: Béatrice Le Teuff, "Census: les recensements dans l'empire romain d'Auguste à Dioclétien" (PhD diss., Université Michel de Montaigne - Bordeaux III, 2012).
47 Roger S. Bagnall, *The Demography of Roman Egypt* (Cambridge, UK: Cambridge University Press, 1994), 44.
48 Minas Papakostas, Nikos Litinas, Eleni Konsolaki, and Constantinos Trompoukis, "Facial Scars in the Greek Papyri," *Archiv für Papyrusforschung und verwandte Gebiete* 68, no. 2 (2022): 325–335.
49 Possibilities are suggested by Dolganov, "Documenting," but for reasons given below, I think they are mostly mistaken.
50 Giovanni Geraci, "Le dichiarazioni di nascita e di morte a Roma e nelle province," *Mélanges de l'École française de Rome. Antiquité* 113, no. 2 (2001): 675–711.
51 M. Corbier, *Donner à voir, donner à lire. Mémoire et communication dans la Rome ancienne* (Paris: CNRS, 2006), 131–146.
52 Henrik Mouritsen, *The Freedman in the Roman World* (Cambridge, UK: Cambridge University Press, 2011), 120–205.
53 Judith Evans-Grubbs, "Marriage Contracts in the Roman Empire," in *Ancient Marriage in Myth and Reality*, ed. Lena Lovén and Agneta Strömberg (Newcastle: Cambridge Scholars, 2010), 78–101.
54 Catherine Viroulet, *Tessera Frumentaria: les procédures de distribution du blé public à Rome* (Rome: École française de Rome, 1995).
55 Meyer, *Legitimacy and Law*, 121–215; Ian Marshman, *Making Your Mark in Britannia* (PhD diss., Leicester, 2015), 16–23; and Katelijn Vandorpe, "Seals and Stamps as Identifiers in Daily Life in Greco-Roman Egypt," in *Identifiers and Identification in the Ancient World*, ed. Mark Depauw and Sandra Coussement (Leuven: Peters, 2014), 141–152.
56 Ewen Bowie, "Libraries for the Caesars," in *Ancient Libraries*, ed. Jason König, Katerina Oikonomopoulou, and Greg Woolf (Cambridge, UK: Cambridge University Press, 2013), 237–260; Matthew Nicholls, "Roman Libraries as Public Buildings in the Cities of the Empire," in *Ancient*

57 Dix and Houston, "Public Libraries," 709–710.
58 George Houston, "Papyrological Evidence for Book Collections and Libraries in the Roman Empire," in *Ancient Literacies*, ed. Johnson and Parker (New York: Oxford University Press, 2009), 233–267; and Stephanie Ann Frampton, "What to Do with Books in the 'De Finibus'," *Transactions of the American Philological Association (TAPA)* 146 (2016): 117–147.
59 Houston, "Papyrological Evidence."
60 For instance, principally on the New Testament (but with reference to the Classical authors like Cicero), Candida R. Moss, "The Secretary: Enslaved Workers, Stenography, and the Production of Early Christian Literature," *Journal of Theological Studies* 74, no. 1 (April 2023): 20–56.
61 Peter White, "Bookshops in the Literary Culture of Rome," in *Ancient Literacies*, ed. Johnson and Parker (New York: Oxford University Press, 2009), 268–287.
62 This assumption is shared by, for instance, the "maximalists" cited in note 3 and, for instance, Keith Hopkins, "Conquest by Book," in Mary Beard et al., *Literacy in the Roman World* (Ann Arbor, MI: Journal of Roman Archaeology, 1991), 133–158.
63 It is tangential to the present argument, but perhaps important more broadly to distinguish these personal cases from the restricted knowledge of, say, a priestly or political elite who hold a collective monopoly on certain kinds of knowledge (though these are not entirely unknown at Rome, especially at very early periods). By contrast, the knowers here are typically of low status, often enslaved, and their assigned sets of knowledge are often unique to their particular jobs.
64 The concept is due to Edward Hutchins, *Cognition in the Wild* (Cambridge, MA: MIT Press, 1995). For ancient examples, see Lambros Malafouris, *How Things Shape the Mind: A Theory of Material Engagement* (Cambridge, MA: MIT Press, 2013), 67–81; Courtney Roby, "Physical Sciences: Ptolemy's Extended Mind," in *Distributed Cognition in Classical Antiquity*, ed. Miranda Anderson, Douglas Cairns, and Mark Sprevak (Edinburgh: Edinburgh University Press, 2019), 37–56; and for the specific example given above, Riggsby, "Cognitive Aspects of Information Technology in the Roman World," in *Distributed Cognition*, ed. Anderson et al. (Edinburgh: Edinburgh University Press, 2019), 57–70.
65 Riggsby, *Mosaics of Knowledge*.

3
INFORMATION AND ITS FORMS

Documentary Practices in the Medieval West
(Mid-Ninth to Mid-Thirteenth Centuries)*

Brigitte Miriam Bedos-Rezak

The mediation and dissemination of information in the medieval West relied on the body and its senses, on the gestural, the oral, the haptic, and the visual in proportions that fluctuated with time and place, social status, and personal inclination. Communicated in performances and rituals, in storytelling and in graphic traces left by the hand (writing) on skins of animals (the support of writing), medieval information was tied to its human and animal creators by expressions that, partly intangible, nevertheless left retrievable impressions.[1] In the following instance of long-term oral transmission, modern historians have speculated about the origins of the cult of Saint Guinefort, a greyhound long venerated by the inhabitants of a French isolated village for his miraculous cure of sick children. The canine cult was discovered, and condemned, in the early thirteenth century by Stephen of Bourbon, an inquisitor who recorded its details in a guide for preachers as an example of folkish, indeed superstitious, behaviour from which proper Christians should abstain. No record is available to provide knowledge of the earlier years of the cult in the French peasant community.[2] This example indicates that orally transmitted information is not to be discounted because of its vocal ephemerality. Information has agency from the very moment of its formulation in transient media, immediately influencing the behaviour and environment of its recipients. Stephen's written account, however, both displaced the cult from the context that gave meaning to its practice among medieval villagers and transformed the local veneration into a representative marker of heresy. This vulnerability of the cult's oral, ritualistic, and performative framework to the translational effects of the written word raises questions about the process by which medieval written information emerged out of contemporaneous phenomena. This chapter explores the matter by examining charters (Figs. 3.1–3.6) and those

---

* The author would like to express her deepest gratitude to Bonnie Mak for her invaluable editorial assistance in sourcing the high-resolution versions of the images featured in this chapter and for her diligent efforts in obtaining the necessary permissions for their reproduction.

Figure 3.1 Paris, Bibliothèque nationale de France, Bourgogne 76 n° 16. Gift to the abbey of Cluny from Geoffrey, count of Nevers, 936. Top left: Chrismon. Centre: Space of subscriptions with graphic signs.

issued in the name of rulers, known as diplomas (Fig. 3.7), as well as the practices associated with their production, use, and preservation. As documentary records, charters constitute a specific genre of writing expected to substantiate and animate perceptions of their contents as "fact," or "truth." The documents here under consideration originated in northern regions of Europe during the Central Middle Ages (850–1250 CE), primarily in northwestern France but also encompassing Belgium, England, and the Germanic Rhineland.[3] While the focus in this chapter is on these areas, there may be occasional examinations of documents from Catalonia and Castile. No systematic rule dominated documentary production in this period and local usages frequently prevailed. Although the features analysed here are not found in all known charters, they are nevertheless representative of significant trends.[4]

The transmission and accessibility of information via lasting supports of inscription and expression between the ninth and the early thirteenth centuries in Europe was undertaken by lay professionals and churchmen, monks in particular, who could read and write, or simply read. Yet the reverberation of the written word extended well beyond the sphere of experts to reach non-literate members of "textual communities," whose lives were shaped by listening to teachings that their literate contemporaries garnered from authoritative texts.[5]

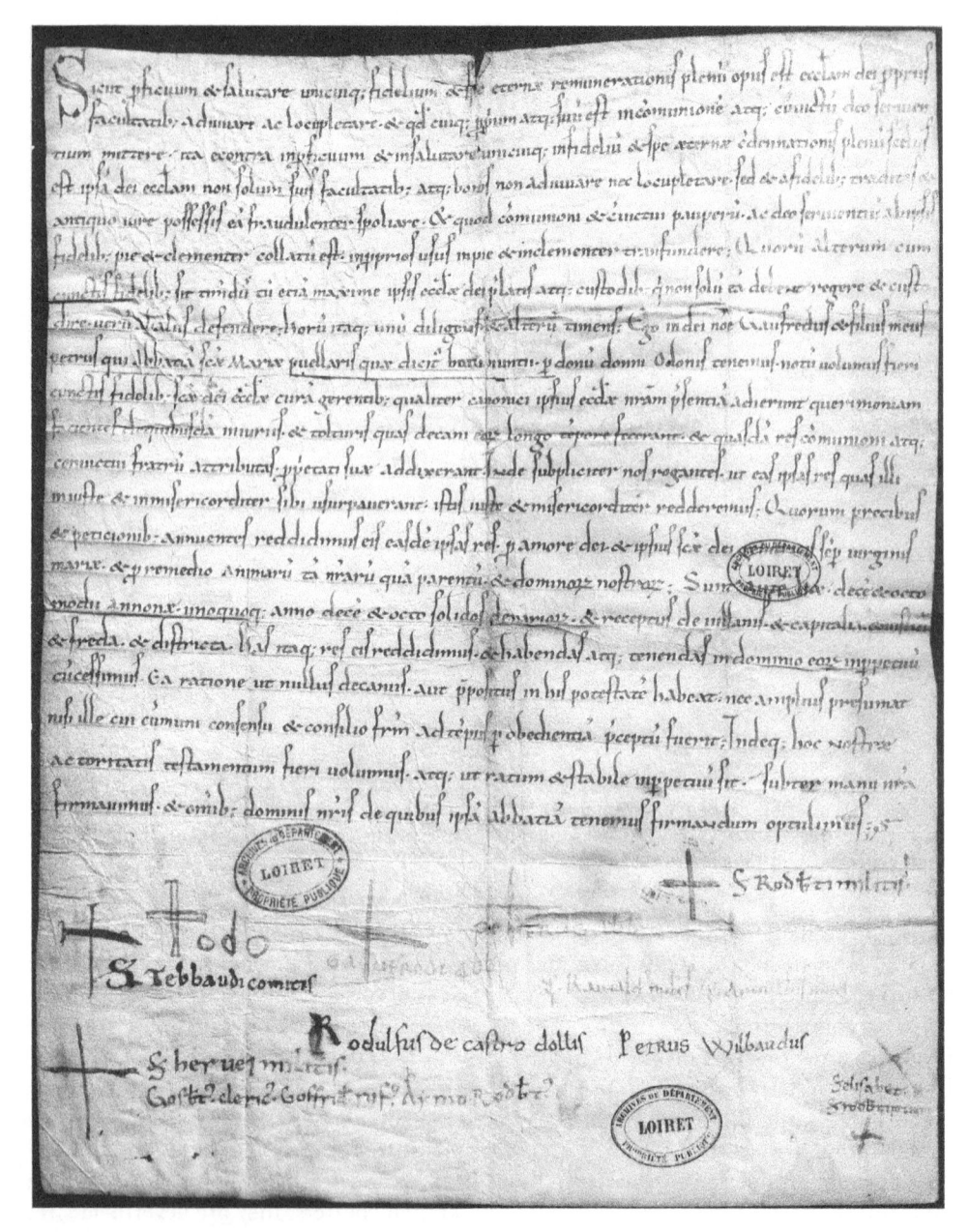

Figure 3.2 Orléans, Archives départementales du Loiret, Portef. n° 58. Gift to the abbey of Bonne-Nouvelle, 1037.

Source: Charte Artem/CMJS n°2800. http://telma.irht.cnrs.fr/outils/originaux/charte2800/.

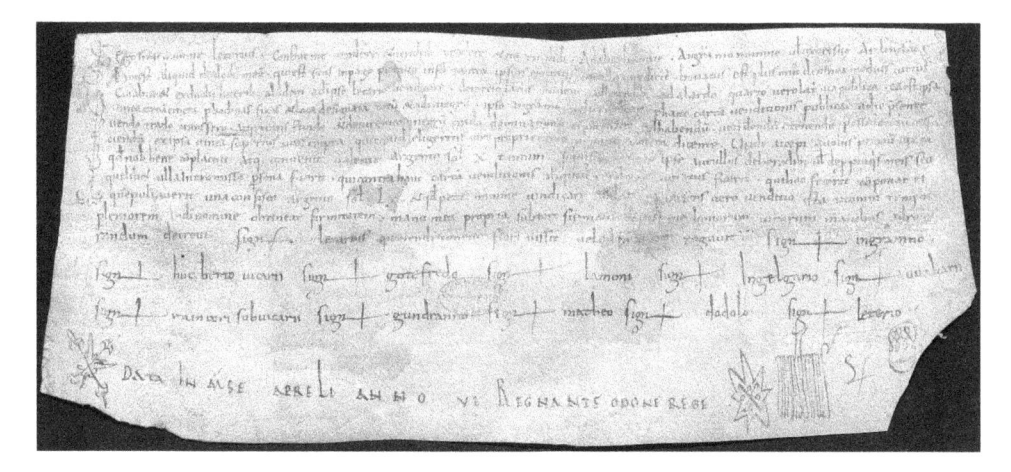

Figure 3.3 Poitiers, Archives départementales de la Vienne, PIECE RESTAUREE 57 (olim G 591 C 2 n° 8). Sale of a vine near Poitiers, 893. Contour of the animal's body is visible at bottom right.

Figure 3.4 Rouen, Archives départementales de la Seine-Maritime, 9 H 30/3. Gift from Roger II of Montgomery of an estate held of him to the abbey of Jumièges, 1048. "Wandering crosses" across bottom. Hole in the parchment is visible towards the end of the document's third line.

Figure 3.5 Paris, Archives nationales, J 168 no 6. Agreement between the abbey of Saint-Denis and Matthew, count of Beaumont, 1189. Left: Seal of the abbey of Saint-Denis. Right: Seal of the count of Beaumont. Photo by author.

Similarly, in the world of documentary practices, numbers of men and women from all social strata were actively associated with the production of deeds via modes of participation geared towards activating sensorial reactions through immediate, bodily interactions with the documentary support. These interactions involved seeing, hearing, and touching, with haptic gestures leaving direct marks and imprints in the body of the document

Figure 3.6 Counterseal of Matthew of Beaumont, with coat of arms and fingerprints. Photo by author.

(Figs. 3.1–3.6 and 3.8–3.11), suggesting that medieval charters were produced and perceived as trace-artefacts.[6]

Charters were transactional documents, written by hand on single-leaf parchments to serve as legal instruments that secured titles and privileges for their recipients. They were expected to establish facts, decisions, and actions in such a way as to prove their existence when challenged.[7] Because the transacted commodities often involved the provision of spiritual privileges in the life to come, elements of the charters' discourse had a didactic dimension, inciting recourse to writing as a way to fight oblivion, encouraging generosity to God, his saints, and his servants (the monks), and threatening divine retribution if the gift was not honoured.[8] Much was at stake in charters' authoritative agency for donors and beneficiaries alike.

Reliability, thus, was specifically expected of documentary information on several accounts.[9] Chief among them was its production and reception as the mediatic and intermedial transfer of a moment from the world of lived events onto skin, the support that received inked letters and graphic signs, and wax (Figs. 3.1–3.7), the material receptacle of seal imprints and fingerprints (Figs. 3.5 and 3.6 and 3.8–3.11). The processes for the transfer of information onto charters were not limited to a linguistic rendering of their referential contexts; they also relied on indexical operations whereby participants in the recorded moment connected physically with the charter, making and marking it with explicit traces of their presence (Figs. 3.1–3.6 and 3.8–3.11).[10] Through the metalinguistic apparatus active in their medial and mediatic formats, charters indexed the procedures that formed them, thereby producing themselves as evidence of their direct and immediate connection with the events that caused their existence. Conversely, these original events, which had themselves disappeared, achieved an enduring if partial existence in the documents whose production they prompted. From this synergy emerged the possibility that information provided

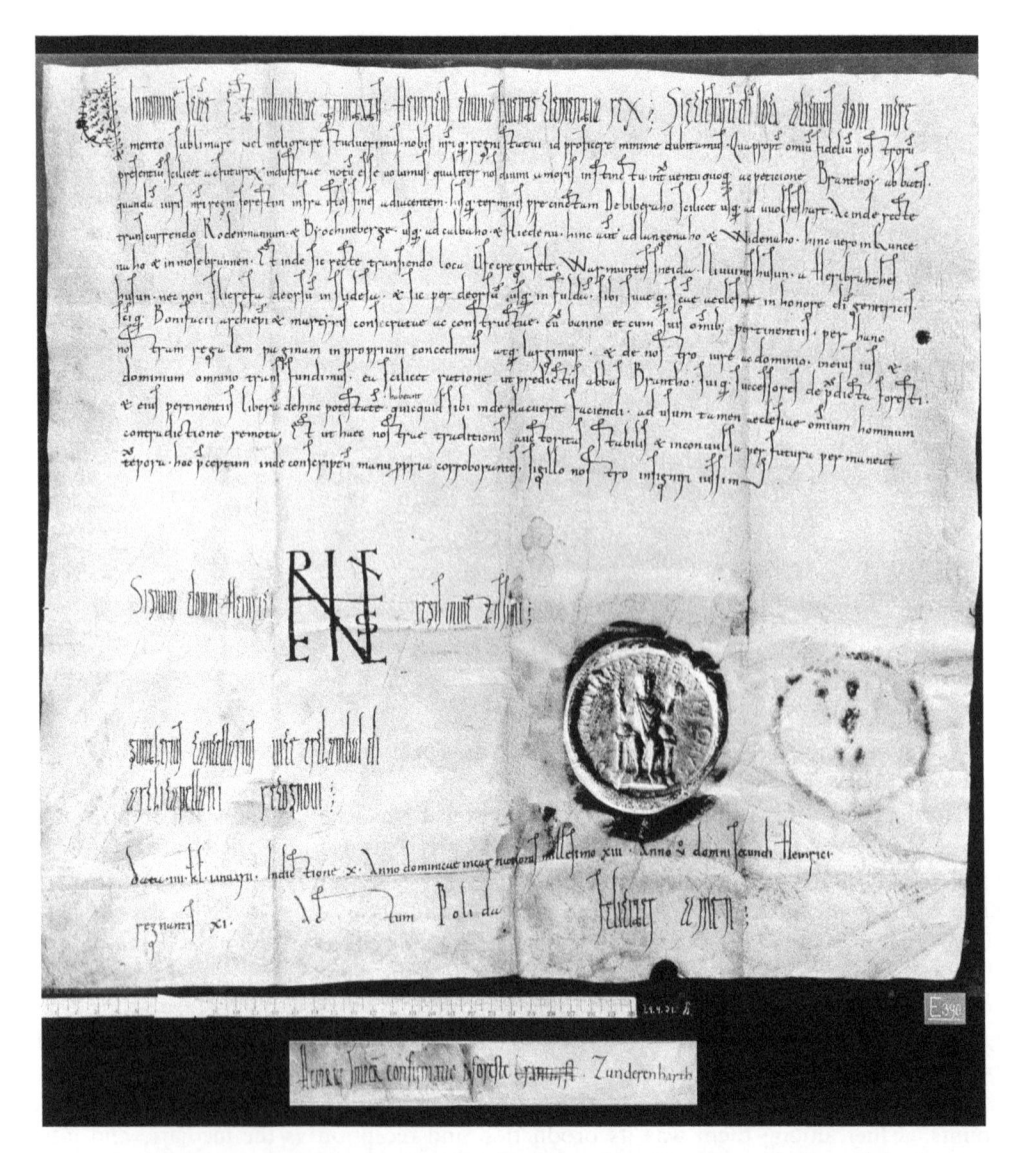

Figure 3.7 Marburg, Staatsarchiv K. Urk. Nr.54. Diploma by which Henry II, King of the Germans, gifts a forest to the abbey of Fulda, December 1012. Top left: Chrismon in the shape of the letter "C." Centre: Monogram of Henry. Bottom right: Acheiropoietic seal image. Courtesy Das Lichtbildarchiv älterer Originalurkunden (LBA).

from and about living actions and commitments was less represented than actualised. The meaning and agency of charters, thus, consisted of tracing a perceptible path from speech, gestures, and actions to their embodiment in the written medium, which then could continue to stand as the event. This is not a question of the performative nature of orality within a literate context but of the ongoing and pivotal medial operations of skin and wax in endowing documentary information with autonomy, authority, and authenticity.

Information and Its Forms

Figure 3.8 Paris, Archives nationales, J 168 no 32, 1222. Fingerprints on the counterseal of Milon I, bishop of Beauvais. Photo by author.

Figure 3.9 Paris, Archives nationales, L//846 no 49, 1204. Details of fingerprints on the obverse of the seal of Elvise of Nangis. Photo by author.

Figure 3.10 Detached wax impression of the city seal of Brunswick, early thirteenth century. Obverse: A lion in a walled city. Author's collection. Photo by Ira Loeb Rezak, MD.

Figure 3.11 Detached wax impression of the city seal of Brunswick, early thirteenth century. Reverse: Three thumbprints amid fingerprints. Author's collection. Photo by Ira Loeb Rezak, MD.

Too often, discussions of charters have focused on their texts and appearance, on their purity as originals compared to copies, and on the sacrality and symbolism that accompanied their production. In underestimating the agency of material supports and the haptic participation of those present at the time of documentary writing, these discussions have overlooked the medieval perception of the charter as both a container of omnipresent, lifelike traces that defied time by defining it as past, present, and future, and as a trace-artefact that could not be replicated because its liveliness could not be transferred.

This chapter investigates the modes of production and preservation characteristic of charters and diplomas. First, it will explain how they fulfilled the requirement expected of documentary reliability—that the information conveyed by charters carry an adequation with events recorded from life. Embedded both in textual meaning and documentary practice, whereby practice too was meaning,[11] information recorded in written documents progressively developed, requiring growing attention to its preservation, accessibility, and management.[12] Second, the chapter will analyse the various solutions that were introduced to meet the challenge posed by charters' indexical elements and by the traces they contained of immersive experiences, which resisted transfer to new administrative formats.

Living Matter. Documentary Production as Information (Ninth to Eleventh Centuries)

Whereas the writing of *codices* (books) was performed by professional scribes and illuminators in the silence of the scriptorium, the making of charters required more than just handwriting, as it also involved various other methods of manual marking. Transactions were performed, witnessed, and recorded in documents among a gathering of the parties and of those relatives, overlords, neighbours, members of the clergy, and monastic communities who had an interest in the matter. Attending scribes, parties, and witnesses were expected to confirm and strengthen the written records of transactions by marking their participation in these acts and manifesting their personal will, consent, or presence.[13] These marks of personal commitment were called subscriptions (Lat. *subscriptiones*).[14] Until the eleventh century, only imperial and royal documents, called diplomas (Fig. 3.7), received the imprint of the rulers' seals in addition to subscriptions.

In early medieval charters, subscriptions were announced formally, in textual clauses of corroboration that declared the special status of the written account of the transaction as a valid document. A typical clause would read: "In order for this charter to be reinforced and to be firmly observed in perpetuity, I strengthened it with my own hand (*manu propria*) and presented it to be touched by the hands of my loyal attendants." Clauses of corroboration made the point of mentioning the names of those who subscribed *manu propria* (with their own hand), or by touching, palpating, or imprinting the charter with their own hands (Figs. 3.1–3.4). The specific expression *manus propria* was generally though not necessarily reserved for the subscriptions of authors in whose names the documents were issued; it might suggest an autograph sign, and there is evidence that few authors marked the charter autographically with names, signs of the cross or participation in the drawing of the monogram rendering their names. Usually, the signs *manu propria* were not autographed but graphically rendered by scribes, possibly on a spot touched by the authors, who then offered the charter to the manual touch of their entourage. Such additional haptic subscriptions were also acknowledged graphically by the scribes in the charter's lower margin (Figs. 3.1–3.4).[15] Whatever their mode of inscription, subscriptions involved touch and dermal contact between written parchments and human hands. Writing was already handwork, but the work of the hand and touch was central to the joint operation of personal commitment and validation.[16] How did manual contact effectuate validation on early medieval charters? How were issuers, recipients, and users of documents convinced that they were producing trustworthy and permanent sources of information for the future?

Elements of answers to these questions are suggested by the three axes of communication at work in the charters themselves, the medial, the textual, and the graphic.[17] The first axis is formed by the lines, holes, transparencies, angles, shapes, and stains of the skin, medial characteristics that direct the gaze from the text to its support, a support that retains aspects of the animal from which it was flayed, thus displaying marks of the skin's susceptibility to treatment inflicted in the process of parchment making (Figs. 3.1 and 3.4).[18] Bi-coloured, white on the flesh side and yellow on the hair side, a parchment is less a bland surface than an organic depth, which still hosts the ghost of the living flesh that once inhabited it. Whereas the texts of the charters with their preambles, formulae, and transactional narratives were carefully laid out on the upper and middle parts of the parchment, implying a wordsmith expert at verbal and scribal composition, the subscriptions made in the lower part and the margins of the parchment were disorderly and interspersed with graphic signs (Figs. 3.1–3.4 and 3.7), two regimes that, as this chapter argues, are related, interdependent, and mutually formative.[19]

Graphic signs are neither textual nor medial although they share kinship with both modes. These graphic elements tended to cluster around the inscription of names: the monogram for the name of the king (Fig. 3.7); an inventive flourish for the name of the scribe; and the crosses and various irregular graphisms accompanying the names of the subscribing authors and witnesses (Figs. 3.1–3.4). Significantly, then, loci of authorial identification, signatory writing, and subscriptions are, on charters, spaces of graphic instability, where the letter forms have broken down, departing from a semantic notion of writing. With graphism, script is devoid of linguistic elements, marking the space of inscription not with words but with traces of gesture. Graphic shapes stress the work of the hand: the hand of the scribe, but also the hands of the subscribing authors and witnesses who, even when they did not subscribe with autographs, were nevertheless presented as having made a sign *manu propria* (Figs. 3.1–3.4) or fingered the charter with their own hands. In deconstructing letters, graphism emphasised script as a tactile phenomenon. The important thing was to render the physical and personal intervention of the parties to the act.

Tactility did not abolish the difference between letter and trace, even though both subsumed and rooted their signifying processes in bodily action and configuration. Written on a medium made of skin, a bodily organ, charters enacted the fact that bodies do not remain outside the process of signification, while also communicating that dermic mediality did not simply underpin the material aspect of letters or of graphism. The disorder characteristic of zones of subscriptions on charters includes, in addition to graphism, large white spaces and haphazard inscriptions of crosses that wander widely throughout the bottom of the document (Figs. 3.2–3.4), often obliging the scribe to contort his penmanship. The positioning of these crosses may well mimic the spontaneous placement of hands on the parchment, their shape re-enacting the gesture of crossing oneself when making a commitment. At the bottom of yet other charters, vague lines are dispersed, mimicking in their casual discontinuity the reactions of the skin to touch. Although imitation regulated the indexical relation between touch and graphic sign, it did not create a formal resemblance between them. Rather, it is posited here that the skin of charters staged graphism as a living haptic trace, enabling charters to play the role of sensitive entities, capable of receiving, reacting to, and retaining impressions, and thus remain a living memory of the actions they recorded. Graphism, then, was an attempt to mythologise the charter as a natural, presence-bearing trace, and this would in part explain the particularly turbulent presence of graphism in those parts of the charters where parties to the act were named and their physical participation mentioned.[20]

This argument, that charters from the ninth to the eleventh century show evidence that they were construed as sites sentient to manual gestures, suggests an intertwining of tactility and "textility." Manual gestures (writing, graphism, simple touch) and the dermal medium of writing (skin, parchment), came to mutually inform a notion that charters had an intrinsic capacity to be responsive to touch. Medieval perception of such enactment was made possible by the recipient of contact, the parchment, itself conceived as having the capacity for sensation and reaction because of its perceived animal and animate origin. The early medieval charter was created to capture physically haptic traces of presence during the actions recorded in writing.

This imaginative perception of the sensorial dimension of the skin was re-enforced by the spectacle that awaited scribes and monks who consulted royal charters (diplomas), the only documents to be sealed in the early medieval period: they saw the original seal of the ruler as a waxed imprint but also as a secondary detailed impression (Fig. 3.7). The secondary imprint was acheiropoietic, not made by human hands but materialised by a contact between two organic materials, the wax of the seal and the skin of the parchment. Such acheiropoietic seals demonstrated the impressionability of the skin, while also revealing the seal as both a positive and a negative, as if it were animated and capable of continuing the process of active imprinting. The charter could thus display itself as a medium capable of actively replicating some of its elements, producing an illusion that documents, by means of haptic processes, shaped themselves as living repositories of contacts and contracts.

Securing Information: Sacrifice and Divine Warranty (Ninth to Twelfth Centuries)

In a context where the informational strength and reliability of a charter resided in the presence of the consensual traces incorporated in its body at the moment of creation, there was no other option but to secure the charter itself as the very sanctuary of these traces. Thus, to ensure its permanent protection, the highest authority was summoned: God. In the medieval West, where Christianity shaped most areas of life, linking pragmatic processes with religious activities, the mundane easily integrated within the sacred sphere.[21] Moreover, the predominance of ecclesiastical documentary issuers and an even greater preponderance of clerical and monastic recipients might suggest that churchmen held a monopoly on literacy. While this assessment may be applicable to northern Europe, it does not necessarily apply to the Late Antique West or the medieval Mediterranean.[22] In this latter area, a number of extant charters demonstrate lay and especially notarial literacy.[23] Notaries were not prevalent in northern France, England, Germany, or Scandinavia, before the late thirteenth century.[24]

Be that as it may, charters issued in the central Middle Ages lost no opportunity to display signs of partnership with the divine. They typically begin with a Chrismon, Chi-Ro or Christ's monogram (Figs. 3.1 and 3.7) or a cross, followed by a religious invocation, "In the name of the Father and of the Son and the Holy Spirit, of the one, true and most high God,

Amen."[25] As noted earlier, the great majority of recorded transactions were gifts to houses of God and his saints (mostly religious and monastic communities) explicitly intended to assure the salvation of the souls of the donors and their families.[26] Both donors and beneficiaries were invested in the permanence of transactions expected to secure for them eternal life and worldly resources. Thus, charters closed with sanction clauses that, especially when papal or episcopal authorities were involved, threatened those who might contravene them with maledictions and excommunication: "If anyone presumes to contradict this charter, let him be excommunicated and cursed, as well as damned forever with Judas the traitor and with the Devil."[27] This mild example does not do justice to the extensive sanction clauses that course through many documents, often ending with the words "FIAT, FIAT (Let it be done). AMEN, AMEN." These emotional endorsements of penalisations confirm documentary narratives that specifically describe the reading of charters to all attendees before proceeding to the formalities of validation.[28] When authors and subscribers permeated charters with haptic marks of commitment to enliven their potency, they also entered a pact with the divine, an act further formalised and corroborated by ritually placing charters on an altar.[29] Charter narratives mention such ritual, using the same expression *manu propria* to describe the authors' personal act of subscribing charters (often with crosses) and of laying them on the altar.[30] Both acts were specifically said to endow charters with greater force. The placement of charters on altars could occur either once the document was fully completed, or before its authentication by touch and subscriptions.[31] In the latter case, authors, witnesses, subscribers, and scribes would all have laid hands upon and subscribed a charter, the skin of a sacrificed animal that was resting upon an altar, the very site of Christ's sacrifice enacted liturgically during daily masses. On occasions, charters were offered on the altar even during mass, at the time of the offertory when the bread and wine for use in the eucharistic service were ceremonially placed on the altar.[32]

Although exceptional, one charter issued north of Paris in 1177 deeply situates documentary practices within the sacrificial economy of Christian salvation (Fig. 3.12). This document is in the form of a bipartite chirograph, that is, a charter written in duplicate on a single piece of parchment and thereafter cut along a division marked by letters or graphic signs so that each party to an agreement or a transaction could retain a copy. Chirographic duplication, practised in England and Northern Europe from the ninth century onwards, did not originally target preservation but verification. If the need arose, the separated charters were reunited for comparison and the matching of one with the other.[33] The 1177 chirograph records an agreement between a nobleman and an abbot about an exchange of land and rights. The word *cirographum* forming the divider of the two texts was intercepted by a cross bearing the draped body of a dead Christ with a cruciform halo. After the original document was cut through Christ's body, the nobleman and the abbot each received a charter displaying the rent-image of the crucified Christ. As much as the image of the crucifixion on a chirograph is exceptional, its deliberate tearing appears positively sacrilegious were it not for the fact that Christ's Passion was lawful and necessary. Cutting through the animal skin of the parchment enfleshes the Christic body, re-enacting the sacrificial killing that provided lasting support to the written word (parchment) and confirmation of the new covenant between God and man. The division of the chirograph itself paralleled the sacramental partition of the eucharistic host on the altar. More than any of the strategies discussed earlier that were deployed to sacralise documents, the chirographic management of material, image, and technology co-implicated divine covenant and human agreements, claiming immanence of the divine

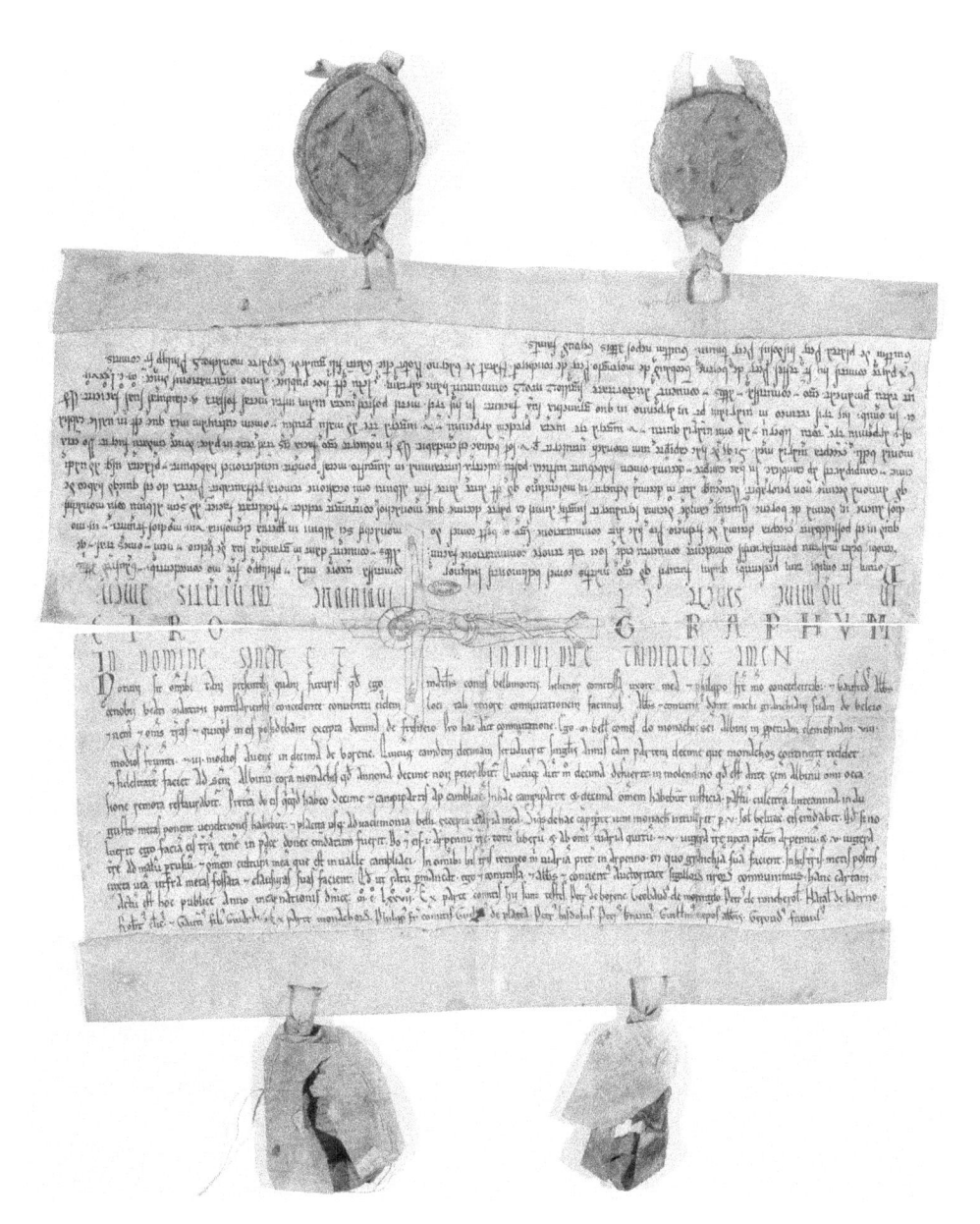

Figure 3.12 Paris, Archives nationales, AE/II/181 (J 168 no 2) and Pontoise, Archives départmentales du Val-d'Oise, 9H81. Exchange of land, rights, and revenues between Matthew III, count of Beaumont-sur-Oise (d. ca 1208) and Geoffrey, abbot of Saint-Martin of Pontoise, 1177. This piece of parchment recorded the exchange in duplicate. It was then cut through the image of Christ on the cross, to provide each party with a charter sealed by their partner in the exchange. The survival and reunion of both parts of the medieval chirograph is a relatively rare phenomenon.

in human affairs and, reciprocally, human modelling on Christ in the discharge of human business.[34]

As a record of gifts to God and his church, the chirograph or the charters placed on the altar were offerings. Inscribed on the skin of an animal, they were exposed to a liturgical osmosis that transformed the offering into a sacrifice of biblical import, initiating a transactional communication with the divine in the hope of salvific benefits. Osmosis ran in both directions, as the altar itself became suffused with the transactional tenor of the charters, and acquired a legal personality as the recipient and owner of gifts and endowments.[35] Absorbed by and circulating among multiple media, information was contagious and affected them all. The desire to provide the physical existence of documents with permanence and their textual dispositions with warranted truth, relied on their inscription within a sacred economy, on the performance of ceremonies, and on their medial capacity for indexing authorial and authorising presence. Though merging from a multimedia matrix, the charter materialised primarily as a self-referential medium. Nothing could substitute for its indexical ability to score, express, and store haptic gestures of participation and presence at the moment of its creation. To a certain extent, the semantic value of documents came second to graphic modes of expression.[36]

Early efforts at archiving charters, therefore, focused on the charters themselves, as embodiments of all the interactive systems that had produced them as authoritatively informative. They were organised geographically or chronologically, sometimes arrayed with an inventory.[37] As titles to endowments and memorabilia of the deeds and names of pious benefactors and ancestors, the charters gathered by institutions were considered to form a "holy treasury,"[38] and as such were kept with sacred books, relics of saints, and other precious mementos of past events.[39] The affinity of charters with the sacred, which had begun with their production and suffused their format, was thus initially retained in the mode of their preservation.[40] Not only were charters treasured as sacred repositories of information, but they were holy as script worthy of being in direct continuity with Holy Scripture. Documentary writing frequently entered Bibles and liturgical books.[41] At the abbey of Saint-Père of Chartres, a 1033 charter copied in a Gospel stated in its own text that its abbatial author "had confirmed it with his hand and his name and had ordered that it be written in the golden book of the holy gospel to serve as an inviolable witness for future generations."[42] This record was expected to absorb from its sacred environment the capacity for permanent and unchallengeable truth. In the mid-eleventh century, a record in English of the gifts of Bishop Leofric to the Abbey of Saint Peter at Exeter is written into a Gospel Book.[43] Even the prestigious ninth-century gospel Book of Kells received the texts of charters in Irish on its blank pages and empty spaces for eighty years during the late eleventh to early twelfth centuries.[44] In such insular cases, vernacular languages mingle with Latin. In the Book of Kells, the documentary material blends with the manuscript's sumptuous iconography; there seems to have been no concern for maintaining the stylistic integrity of the book. In all instances of charters thus enshrined, biblical narrative and documentary discourse, manuscript making and documentary additions projected multiple temporalities within a single locus of high credibility, the holy book. In both their modes of production and of preservation, documents were crucially associated with the management of time. Single-leaf charters' fusion of sensory experiences and presence endowed them with ongoing relevance in the present. Enshrined charters became part of a timeless eschatology.

Information and Its Forms

De-Signed and Consigned. From Documentary Access as Re-Mediation to the New Vitality of Seals (Eleventh to Thirteenth Centuries)

Early efforts at archiving charters had focused on the charters themselves, as natural traces of the events that brought about their creation. However, the single-leaf materiality of the charter gave it mobility and vulnerability and by the eleventh century, charters were accumulating to the point where issues of preservation and repeated access needed to be addressed.

The solution implemented by large monastic houses, ecclesiastical institutions, and major lay landowners involved copying single-leaf charters, editing and abbreviating them, and organising the transcribed texts into books, known in modern terminology as cartularies (Figs. 3.13–3.15).[45] The extent to which the arrangement of the early cartularised material followed the order in which the charters and diplomas were preserved is hard to gauge. Organised geographically, cartularies were generally expected to serve an administrative purpose. In chronological order, they favoured the historiographical goals of their compilers eager to celebrate and memorialise their institutions' illustrious past, famous patrons, and

Figure 3.13 Angers, Archives départementales de Maine-et-Loire H 1773, fol 9vo–10. Cartulary of the abbey of Saint-Maur de Glanfeuil, ca. 1130. Visible on the left is a drawing of the seal of Peter, bishop of Poitiers (1103). At the bottom is a drawing of the Chrismon, at the beginning of the next copied charter, issued by Geoffroy, count of Anjou (ca. 1010).

Source: https://arca.irht.cnrs.fr/ark:/63955/md687h14d09w.

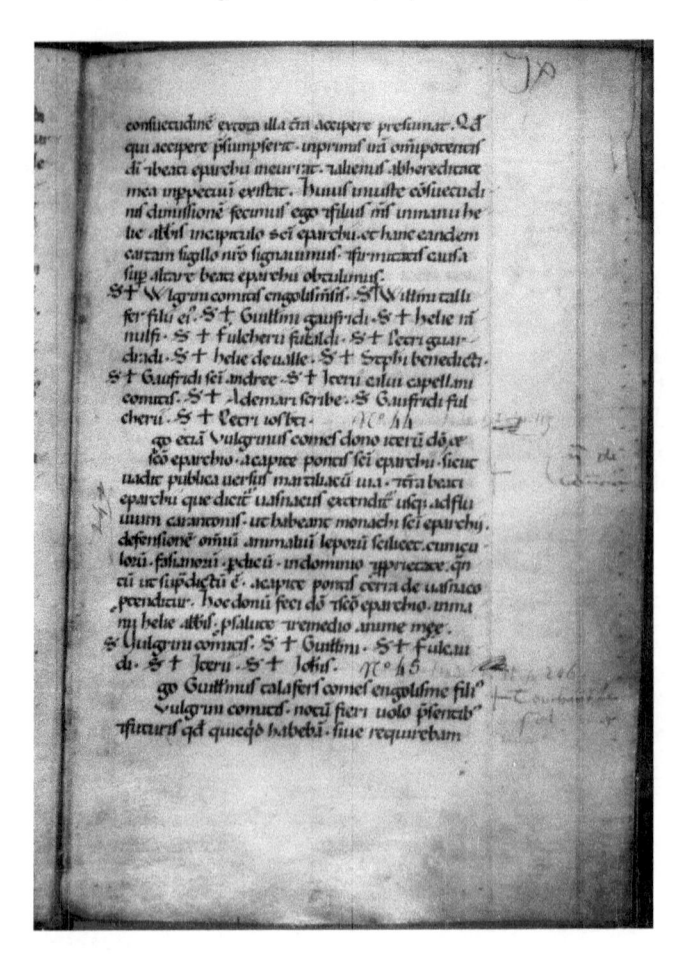

Figure 3.14 Angoulême, Archives départmentales de la Charente, MS H(01), 1, fol. IX ro, no 43. Cartulary of Saint-Cybard. Charter copied in the cartulary; the crosses next to the names of their signatories are uniform and drawn by copyists.

Source: https://arca.irht.cnrs.fr/ark:/63955/md52w3765c63.

rich endowments. Both types of arrangement, however, spanned managerial, archival, and historiographical goals, in an effort to project and protect institutional identity. Some cartularies might even be assembled to defend episcopal immunities or territorial grants against challenging claims. The utility of charters and diplomas for remembrance and settling disputes inspired some compilers to fabricate forgeries and take liberties with the documents they found in the archives.[46] Some scholars estimate that the limited number of extant early medieval original charters, as compared to the larger quantities of early medieval texts preserved in cartularies, resulted from the behaviour of postmillennial archivists bent on fitting the past into the landscape of their present by revising, casting into oblivion, or even destroying inconvenient sources.[47] Instances of such behaviour certainly occurred but were far from systematic, and many monastic institutions and cathedral chapters present situations where their medieval compilation of cartularies was not accompanied by the destruction of

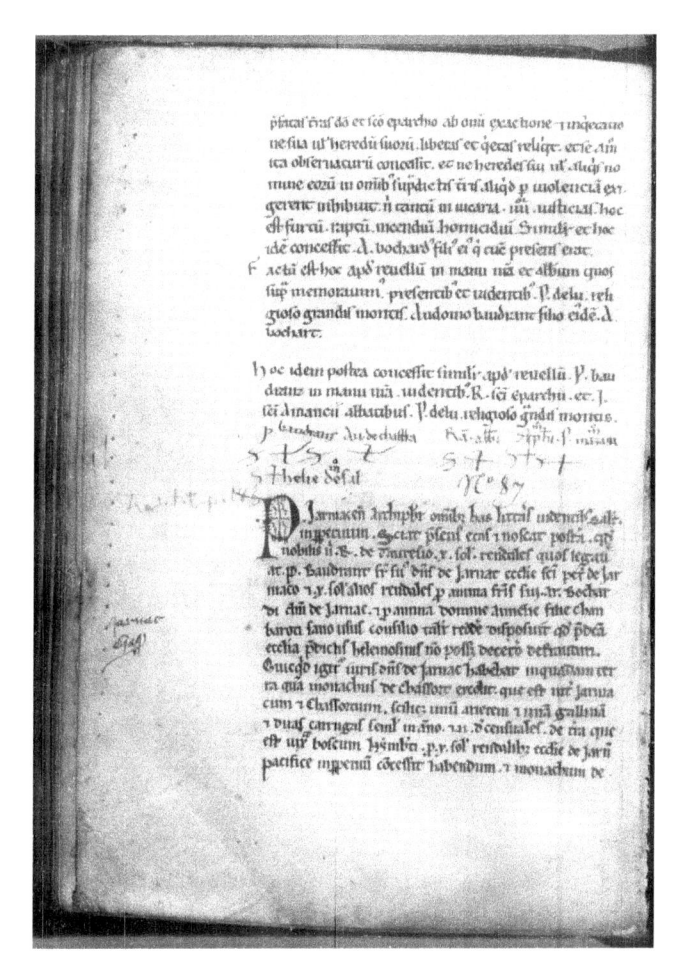

Figure 3.15 Angoulême, Archives départmentales de la Charente, MS H(01), 1, fol. 34vo, no 86. Cartulary of Saint-Cybard. Autograph crosses.
Source: https://arca.irht.cnrs.fr/ark:/63955/md52w3765c63.

original documents but by a transition during which their collection of charters became a storage of searchable documents.[48] In elegantly written prefaces, some cartularists invited readers of their compilations to verify their transcriptions against the original documents in the archives. Far from displacing an archive of charters, the cartularies derived legitimacy by reference to them. Moreover, invitations to check copies against originals explicitly addressed the distrust some "simple souls" (Lat.: *simplices*) voiced about cartularised charters (Lat.: *chartae aeditae*), which they considered to be useless novelties that ruined the value of the charters that had been originally issued (Lat.: *chartarum primae editionis respectus*).[49] Even as they encouraged a return to the sources and expressed pride in the antiquity of their charters, early cartularists were not sympathetic to the position of the *"simplices."* In prologues to their compilations, they addressed the contest between time, which erases memory, debilitates charters, and ushers oblivion, and writing, which provides an effective rampart against obliviousness. There is some dissonance between this expected ability of writing to buttress memory and the acknowledged frailty of writing whose physical support might become a casualty of time. How would the cartulary resist ageing? One of the earliest cartularies known for northwestern Europe, that of the Benedictine Cathedral Priory of Worcester (c. 1000), was copied into Worcester's Great Offa (or Ceolfrith) Bible at the end of the eleventh century, when Bishop Wulfstan II, aware of the poor conservation of the priory's original charters, had them organised and compiled into the Offa Bible, which thus housed two cartularies.[50] Early planners of archival preservation promoted and justified the cartulary using the strategy of sacred enshrinement, as had been done earlier with single-leaf charters. Bound with the great Offa Bible, the Worcester cartularies demonstrated that, in single-handedly gathering and guarding deeds integral to the Christian economy of salvation they were inscribed within universal history.[51] Sacred or mythical time might thus, possibly, be expected to overcome actual temporal decay. Prefaces of early cartularies also praise another transformative agency of cartularisation, whereby many little pieces of parchment (Lat. *membranulae*) could be formed into a single body (Lat. *unum corpus*), that is, the codex.[52] In the process, charters lost their multiplicity and their independence as three-dimensional single objects but gained a corporeal wholeness perhaps perceived to constitute a stronger weapon against time. Again, the trust placed in writing as a remedy against mental oblivion was modulated with a concern for the material fragility of writing. At any rate, there could have been no cartularies without charters, and the solution cartularies offered to relax the tension between preservation and accessibility may well have lessened the need to return to original charters. Refraining from their consultation might have also indicated a form of veneration for their status rather than disinterest.[53] In fact, old charters in a poor state of conservation inspired the desire to repair them. Moreover, damaged charters could be re-issued after proper inspection by relevant authorities, who vouched for their validity. Because of the importance of the procedure of examination preceding these new outputs, they received the name of *vidimus* or *inspeximus*.[54]

The extent to which cartularies may have "improved" and even replaced original charters remains an open and important question, which is primarily addressed currently by equating the conservation of single-leaf charters with the significance of their dispositions and the status of their issuers. Of concern here, however, is whether cartularies and other forms of copies display evidence of an understanding that early charters had information beyond lands, names, familial ties, and social and political networks; did the copying process include efforts to retrieve the metalinguistic features of patterns that challenged the full transcription of their informational content? Compilers of medieval cartularies not infrequently have prefaced their works with dubious assessments of the old charters before them, decrying their poor linguistic qualities, their dilapidated state, and their illegibility caused by the incursions of worms.[55] Were they adequately sensitive to the possibility that the visual and material aspects of documents might carry information worth preserving? Any evidence that efforts were made to transfer to copies the nonhermeneutic components of charters is local and contingent upon personal goals and skills rather than systematic, but it is nevertheless worthy of interpretation.

In a cartulary, the copied charters were ordered discretely, fixed as succeeding pages in a sequential narrative of rights and privileges. By contrast, single-leaf charters display a coexistence of past and present.[56] The systematic capture of legible texts in cartularies, typically excludes graphic signs and seals, thereby locating documentary agency uniquely in the power of logocentric writing to the detriment of the animated traces of participation discussed earlier. Cartularies evolved into repositories of disembodied texts, while the haptic and ineffable content of single-leaf charters was disregarded because transferring this inherent dynamic substance to copies was not possible. Even though rendered on skin by scribal hands, copies could not absorb the marks left by living gestures of subscription as part of the making and the make-up of original charters. The copy killed; this was not due to a lack of effort on the part of early archivists, some of whom seemed to have been aware that severing the process of documentary creation from that of documentary access transformed haptic records of dynamic practices into fixed objects. The format of a few early cartularies demonstrates concern for the effect of cartularisation. A small number contains authorial images of the individuals in whose names the copied texts were issued,[57] or drawings of graphic signs and seals suggesting the rendering of existing charters (Figs. 3.14 and 3.15).[58] These efforts at mimicking the physical traces of living events processed by charters, however, only achieved their static representations.[59] A recent study by Michael Webb has discovered evidence of a significant and previously unrecognised situation.[60] Three twelfth-century cartularies from western France (Angoumois), which are primarily made up of copied charters, also include texts subscribed with crosses made, not by cartularists, but by those who were actually party to the written transaction (Fig. 3.15). One of such texts is explicit in its final clause, which reads: "et propriis manibus una nobiscum signa sua inpresserunt in libro isto" ("and along with us, by their own hands, they impressed their signs in that book"). The reference to the book makes it clear that one of the steps taken to ratify the agreement was to sign the cartulary itself. These texts autographed with signs of the cross are contemporary with the composition of the cartularies and thus presumably coexist with copies of earlier charters, prompting a comparison between a scribal copy and a text incorporating the haptic participation of parties (Figs. 3.13–3.15). This remarkable situation suggests the likelihood of a contemporary understanding that copying charters divested them of the traceable manipulations that had been part of their creation and which had empowered them as proofs of action. It is suggested here, therefore, that autograph signing in a cartulary might have been an attempt to enliven it with immediate traces of participation by those who had a stake in the registered transaction.

Charters and cartularies remained distinct documentary genres, but the pull of the cartulary is apparent in the increased logocentrism of later charters, which seems to have paralleled the systemising modes of information management that were progressively set into place.[61] In their changing format, charters became textual, de-signed, devoid of graphic signs of subscriptions, and severed from contacts with subscribers, who surveyed the charter in the mirror of their mind. Their witnessing was devoid of all physical intervention in the written act, whose body they no longer inhabited. That bodily form of presence now emanated from the authorial wax seal.

Whereas acheiropoietic seals had manifested the impressionability of the skin, the wax seals in themselves came to epitomise impressionability. Medieval commentators noted as a fundamental quality of wax its receptive plasticity and sensitivity to touch, which enabled the transformation of the tactile into the visual, thereby providing a type of verisimilitude that not so much portrayed as it reproduced parts of a living antecedent.[62]

By the twelfth century, sealing practice presented a new landscape. Documentary sealing was no longer confined to ruling chanceries (Fig. 3.7), having extended to charters issued by numerous individuals and corporations from all strata of medieval society (Figs. 3.5 and 3.6). They were no longer pierced through to both sides of the parchment but were hung from the outer margins of documents. The production of such seals involved assemblages of imprints left by human hands and metallic seal dies coming together into contact with the wax (Figs. 3.8–3.11). In the process of its formation, the seal impression actually connected with its originating agents, entertaining with them a transient relation of contiguity. Moreover, by retaining the marks and parts of its causal agents, the seal remained in a metonymic relation with them, standing in as substitutes for them. In that context, imprints derived from human body parts took on a particular significance. For while sealers were metonymically abbreviated as their fingerprints, the fingerprints themselves were not reduced but life-size, and thus may have supported a medieval notion that seals were at least partially modelled after life. This speculative hypothesis, in turn, makes one wonder whether the ubiquitous fingerprints were not inserted as explicit signs of reproduction, so as to support the ability of seal impressions to pass on an actual, if limited, likeness of the sealers themselves. For therein lies one of the powers of verisimilitude on seals, the anatomical life-size of these marks, which intimated that the seal was imprinted directly from a person (Figs. 3.8–3.11). On seals, therefore, as on skin-charters, the decodable meaning of text and image never displaced a perception of these supports as corporeal zones where impressions were both felt and left.

Conclusion

Between the mid-ninth and the mid-thirteenth centuries, changes affected formats used for the original production of charters, and for their subsequent reproduction as multiple versions of the same information to accommodate functional (mostly historiographical, legal, and administrative) needs and archival strategies. The mutually informative relationship between text and support transformed even as it persisted, and writing's signifying modes did not escape their ties with the hand, the body, and the pictorial. Multiple versions of charters were no replicas but transformative copies made onto new mediatic supports. As artefact and text, image and script, the charter and its copies channelled information along multiple conduits, each a distinct technology with its separate valence, all claiming to convey fixed, permanent, and authoritative expressions of actual occurrences. The medieval expectation that documentary information be stable was challenged by the equally medieval documentary practice of manifold versioning. With each documentary format, and in each of its versions, a charter conjures up a set of associations that tell a different story and manifest evolving perceptions of reality. Documents *were* the things that happened.

Notes

1 Keli Rylance, "Archives and the Intangible," *Archivaria* 62 (2006): 103–120, at 104.
2 Catherine Rider, "Elite and Popular Superstitions in the Exempla of Stephen of Bourbon," *Studies in Church History* 42 (2006): 78–88; and Jean-Claude Schmidtt, *The Holy Greyhound: Guinefort, Healer of Children since the Thirteenth Century* (Cambridge, UK: Cambridge University Press, 1983).
3 The following databases have been consulted: *Chartes originales antérieures à 1121 conservées en France*, ed. Cédric Giraud, Jean-Baptiste Renault, and Benoît-Michel Tock (Nancy: Centre de Médiévistique Jean Schneider; éds électronique: Orléans: Institut de Recherche et d'Histoire des Textes, 2010), http://telma.irht.cnrs.fr/outils/originaux/index/, hereafter ARTEM; *Diplomata Belgica. Les sources diplomatiques des Pays-Bas méridionaux au Moyen Âge*, ed. Thérèse de Hemptinne et al. (Bruxelles: Commission Royale d'Histoire, depuis 2015), www.diplomata-belgica.be; Marburg. Lichtbildarchiv älterer Originalurkunden (LBA), http://lba.hist.uni-marburg.de/lba/pages; Monasterium, https://www.monasterium.net/mom/home.

4 See Matthew McHaffie, "Sources of Legal Language: The Development of Warranty Clauses in Western France, c. 1030–12.40," in *Law and Language in the Middle Ages*, ed. Jenny Benham et al. (Leiden: Brill, 2018), 196–232.

5 On "textual communities," see Brian Stock, *Implications of Literacy. Written Language and Models of Interpretation in the 11th and 12th Centuries* (Princeton, NJ: Princeton University Press, 1983).

6 I borrow the expression from Yves Janneret, "Complexité de la notion de trace. De la traque au tracé," in *Perspectives anthropologiques des traces contemporaines*, ed. Béatrice Galinon-Mélénec (Paris: CNRS, 2011), 59–86, at 59.

7 Kimberly Anderson, "The Footprint and the Stepping Foot: Archival Records, Evidence, and Time," *Archival Science* 13 (2013): 349–371, at 354. The use and consultation of charters were far from systematic during the period under consideration; see Brigitte M. Bedos-Rezak, *When Ego was Imago. Signs of Identity in the Middle Ages* (Leiden: Brill, 2010), 20–22; Karl Heidecker, "Communication by Written Texts in Court Cases: Some Charter Evidence (ca. 800–ca. 1100)" in *New Approaches to Medieval Communication*, ed. Marco Mostert (Turnhout: Brepols, 1999), 101–126; and Laurent Morelle, "*Les chartes dans la gestion des conflits* (France du nord, XIe-début XIIe siècle)," *Bibliothèque de l' École des chartes* 155, no. 1 (1997): 267–298.

8 Lay gifts and grants of land and revenues by laymen were made with the expectation of return benefits, among which were arrangements for the liturgical commemoration of the dead and the living. Arnoud-Jan A. Bijsterveld, *Do ut Des: Gift Giving, "Memoria," and Conflict Management in the Medieval Low Countries* (Hilversum: Verloren, 2007), 17–50.

9 Stanley Raffel, *Matters of Fact. A Sociological Inquiry* (London: Routledge, 1979), 16–17, discusses the difference between "'getting information' from a record" and "'learning something' from a novel."

10 The signifying mode associated with the index was theorised by Charles Sanders Peirce (1839–1914), who classified signs in three broad categories, according to their relations to their objects. A clear introduction to Peirce's sign theory is provided by Richard J. Parmentier, "Peirce Divested for Nonintimates," in his *Signs in Society: Studies in Semiotic Anthropology* (Bloomington, IN: Indiana University Press, 1994), 3–44.

11 Kobus Marais, *A (Bio)Semiotic Theory of Translation: The Emergence of Social-Cultural Reality* (London: Routledge, 2018), 169, 164–177 for a stimulating discussion of the Peircean concept of indexicality.

12 For an exemplary account of a medieval society progressively adopting the written word, see Michael T. Clanchy, *From Memory to Written Record. England, 1066–1307*, 3rd ed. (Malden, MA: Wiley-Blackwell, 2013).

13 Multilingual definitions of medieval documents and their components, and of charters in particular are given in Maria Milagros Cárcel Ortí, ed., *Vocabulaire international de la diplomatique*, 2nd ed. (Italy: Generalitat Valenciana, Conselleria de Cultura, 1997), 66, no. 254. The *Vocabulaire* is already substantially available online at https://www.cei.lmu.de/VID/#246, thanks to the work of George Voegler.

14 The fundamental work on documentary subscriptions is by Benoît-Michel Tock, *Scribes, souscripteurs et témoins dans les actes privés en France (VIIe-début du XIIe siècle)* (Brepols: Turnhout, 2005).

15 Tock, *Scribes*, 140–141, 413–417; and Benoît-Michel Tock, "La Mise en scène des actes en France au Haut Moyen Age," *Frühmittelalterliche Studien* 38, no. 1 (2004): 287–296, at 291–292.

16 Colette Sirat, *Writing as Handwork: A History of Handwriting in Mediterranean and Western Culture* (Turnhout: Brepols, 2006); and Catherine Brown, *Remember the Hand: Manuscript in Early Medieval Iberia* (New York: Fordham University Press, 2022).

17 The analysis presented in this chapter is part of the author's new research project on the sensorial aspects of charters, partially available in the following forthcoming work, Brigitte M. Bedos-Rezak, "The Original as Translation? Probing the Making and the Agency of Medieval Documents (9th–13th century)," forthcoming in *Unlikening Translation: Words, Sounds, Events, Things*, special issue of *Digital Philology*, ed. Mark Chinca and Sean Curran; and "Sensory Media. Seals and Charters in the Middle Ages," in *Das Siegel als Medium der Kommunikation und des Transfers im europäischen Mittelalter*, ed. Markus Spaeth and Andrea Stieldorf (Beihefte des Archiv für Diplomatik, forthcoming).

18 Bruce Holsinger offers a comprehensive analysis of the medial role of animal skin in shaping written cultures, *On Parchment: Animals, Archives, and the Making of Culture from Herodotus to the Digital Age* (New Haven, CT: Yale University Press, 2023).
19 On graphic signs, see Ildar H. Garipzanov, *Graphic Signs of Authority in Late Antiquity and the Early Middle Ages, 300–900* (Oxford: Oxford University Press, 2018); Garipzanov, "The Rise of Graphicacy in Late Antiquity and the Early Middle Ages," *Viator* 46, no. 2 (2015): 1–21; Andrea Stieldorf, "Die Magie der Urkunden," *Archiv für Diplomatik* 55 (2009): 1–32; Tock, *Scribes*, 147–190; Luis Casado de Otaola, "Per visibilia ad invisibilia: Representaciones figurativas en documentos altomedievales como simbolos de validaciòn y autoría," *Signo. Revista de Historia de la Cultura Escrita* 4 (1997): 39–56; and Peter Rück, ed., *Graphische Symbole in mittelalterlichen Urkunden* (Sigmaringen: Jan Thorbecke, 1996).
20 On the notion of a "presence-bearing trace," see Laura Kendrick, *Animating the Letter: The Figurative Embodiment of Writing from Late Antiquity to the Renaissance* (Columbus, OH: The Ohio State University Press, 1999), 11–35.
21 Stieldrof, "Die Magie," 5.
22 For Northern Europe, see Georges Declercq, "The Originals and Cartularies: Organization of Archival Memory (Ninth–Eleventh Centuries)," in *Charters and the Use of the Written Word in Medieval Society*, ed. Karl Heidecker (Turnhout: Brepols, 2000), 147–170, at 147. For Late Antique West and the medieval Mediterranean, see Warren Brown, Marios Costambeys, Matthew Innes, and Adam J. Kosto, eds., *Documentary Culture and the Laity in the Early Middle Ages* (Cambridge, UK: Cambridge University Press, 2012).
23 Michel Zimmermann, *Ecrire et lire en Catalogne: IXe-XIIe siècle*, 2 vols. (Madrid: Casa de Velázquez, 2003); and Adam J. Kosto, *Making Agreements in Medieval Catalonia: Power, Order, and the Written Word, 1000–1200* (Cambridge, UK: Cambridge University Press, 2001).
24 James A. Brundage, *The Medieval Origins of the Legal Profession: Canonists, Civilians, and Courts* (Chicago, IL: University of Chicago Press, 2008), 396, *passim* and at 394–406 for a good introduction to the history of medieval notaries.
25 This invocation comes from a charter issued in 1111 in the name of Lambert, bishop of Arras. Benoît-Michel Tock, *Les Chartes des évêques d'Arras (1093–1203)* (Paris: CTHS, 1991), no. 19, 29–30, ARTEM 459; the charter is edited, illustrated, analysed, and translated in French in Tock, *Scribes*, no. 7, 50–55.
26 See note 7.
27 See Lester Little, *Benedictine Maledictions. Liturgical Cursing in Romanesque France* (Ithaca: Cornell University Press, 1993), with a focus on sanction clauses in charters at 52–59.
28 Tock, "La Mise en scène," 288–290.
29 The fundamental study on the placement of gifts and charters on the altar is by Arnold Angenendt, "Cartam Offere Super Altare. Zur Liturgisierung von Rechtsvorgangen," *Frühmittelalterliche Studien* 36 (2002): 133–158. Tock, "La Mise en scène," 292–293.
30 Angenendt, "Cartam Offere Super Altare," 148, 152.
31 Angenendt, "Cartam Offere Super Altare," 148–149, 152–153.
32 Stieldorf, "Die Magie," 7–8; and Arnold Angenendt, "Das Offertorium. In liturgischer Praxis und symbolischer Kommunikation," in *Zeichen - Rituale - Werte: Internationales Kolloquium des Sonderfor Schungsbereichs 496 an der Westfälischen Wilhelms-Universität Munster*, ed. Gerd Althoff et al. (Munster: Rehma, 2004), 71–150, at 103–110.
33 Laurent Morelle and Chantal Senséby, eds., *Une mémoire partagée: recherches sur les chirographes en milieu ecclésiastique (France et Lotharingie, Xe – mi XIIIe siècle)* (Geneva: Droz, 2019); Brigitte Miriam Bedos-Rezak, "Cutting Edge. The Economy of Mediality in Twelfth Century Chirographic Writing," *Das Mittelalter*, 15 (2010): 134–161; Paul Herold, "Ein um Form bemühtes Mißtrauen. Herstellung, Gebrauch und Verbreitung von Chirographen unter besonderer Berücksichtigung von Klosterneuburg," *Jahrbuch des Stiftes Klosterneuburg* NF 17 (1999): 153–172; Kathryn A. Lowe, "Lay Literacy in Anglo-Saxon England and the Development of the Chirograph," in *Anglo-Saxon Manuscripts and their Heritage*, ed. Phillip Pulsiano and Elaine Treharne (Aldershot: Ashgate, 1998), 161–204; and Michel Parisse, "Remarques sur les chirographes et les chartes-parties antérieurs à 1120 et conservées en France," *Archiv für Diplomatik* 32 (1986): 546–567.
34 Bedos-Rezak, "Cutting Edge," for a full analysis of the chirograph as a site of mixed mediality, in which text, support, image, and technology mediate each other in the production of social communication.

35 On the legal personality acquired by the altar, Angenendt, "Cartam Offere Super Altare," 149–150.
36 John Mackenzie Owen, "Authenticity and Objectivity in Scientific Communication," in *Sign Here!: Handwriting in the Age of New Media*, ed. Sonja Neef, José van Dijck, and Eric Ketelaar (Amsterdam: Amsterdam University Press, 2006), 60–75.
37 As in the Benedictine abbey of Saint-Riquier, where the inventory of charters dates from 1098, Laurent Morelle, "Les Chartes dans la gestion des conflits," in *Pratiques de l'écrit documentaire au XIe siècle*, ed. Olivier Guyotjeannin, Morelle, and Michel Parisse, *Bibliothèque de l'Ecole des chartes* 155, no. 1 (1997): 267-298 at 268-276; and Morelle, "The Metamorphosis of Three Monastic Collections in the Eleventh Charter Century (Saint-Amand, Saint-Riquier, Montier-en-Der)," in *Charters and the Use of the Written Word*, ed. Karl Heidecker (Turnhout: Brepols, 2000), 171–204, esp. 186.
38 "*Scrinia sacra*,'" sacred chests, in the words of the eleventh-century abbot of Saint-Père of Chartres, Olivier Guyotjeannin, "'Penuria Scriptorum': le mythe de l'anarchie documentaire dans la France du Nord (Xe-première moitié du XIe siècle)," in *Pratiques de l'écrit documentaire*, 11–44, at 31.
39 Clanchy, *From Memory to Written Record*, 156, 158.
40 See Olivier Guyotjeannin and Yann Potin, "La Fabrique de la perpétuité. Le Trésor des chartes et les archives du royaume (XIIIe-XIXe siècle)," *Revue de synthèse* 125, no. 1 (2004): 15–44, at 21–26. On the association between relics and chartes in monastic contexts, Laurent Morelle, "Histoire et archives vers l'An Mil: une nouvelle 'mutation'?" *Histoire et archives* 3 (1998): 119–141, at 131.
41 Jean-Loup Lemaître, "Les Actes transcrits dans les livres liturgiques," in *Les Cartulaires: actes de la table ronde organisée par l'Ecole nationale des chartes*, ed. Olivier Guyotjeannin, Laurent Morelle, and Michel Parisse (Paris: Ecole des chartes, 1993), 59–78. The copy of documents in liturgical books was practised throughout the medieval period.
42 Guyotjeannin, "'Penuria'," 30.
43 Takako Kato, "Oxford, Bodleian Library, Auct. D. 2. 16 (2719). Donations to Exeter by Leofric and Æthelstan," in *The Production and Use of English Manuscripts 1060–1220*, ed. Orietta Da Rold, Takako Kato, Mary Swan, and Elaine Treharne (University of Leicester, 2010). https://www.le.ac.uk/english/em1060to1220/mss/EM.Ox.Auct.D.2.16.htm.
44 These Irish "charters" were records of property, grants, purchases, and settlements of disputes. See Gearóid Mac Niocaill, ed. and tr., "The Irish 'Charters,'" in *The Book of Kells: MS 58, Trinity College Library Dublin. Commentary*, ed. Peter Fox, 3 vols. (Lucerne: Fine Art Facsimile, 1990), vol. 2: 153–165, whose interpretation of the texts as copies of earlier records is revised by Máire Herbert, "Charter Material from Kells," in *The Book of Kells: Proceedings of a Conference at Trinity College Dublin, 6–9 September 1992*, ed. Felicity O'Mahony (Aldershot: Scolar Press for Trinity College Library, Dublin, 1994), 60–77, but accepted by Mary A. Valante, "'Notitiae' in the Irish Annals," *Eolas: The Journal of the American Society of Irish Medieval Studies* 1 (2006): 71–96.
45 On the "prehistory" of cartularies, which appeared in the eastern part of the Carolingian empire, Patrick Geary, *Phantoms of Remembrance. Memory and Oblivion at the End of the First Millennium* (Princeton, NJ: Princeton University Press, 1994), 87–98; Declercq, "The Originals and Cartularies," 148–149. Additional studies on Western cartularies include, Pierre Chastang, "Des Archives au codex: les cartulaires comme collections (XIe-XIVe siècle)," in *Le Moyen Âge dans le texte*, ed. Benoît Grévin and Aude Mairey (Paris: Éditions de la Sorbonne, 2016), 25–44; Jean-Baptiste Renault, ed., *Originaux et cartulaires dans la Lorraine médiévale (XIIe - XVIe siècles). Recueil d'études* (Turnhout: Brepols, 2016); Clanchy, *From Memory to Written Record*, 103–105; Chastang, "cartulaires, cartularisation et scripturalité médiévale: la structuration d'un nouveau champ de recherche," *Cahiers de civilisation médiévale* 49 (2006): 21–31; Brigitte M. Bedos-Rezak, "Towards an Archaeology of the Medieval Charter: Textual Production and Reproduction in Northern French 'Chartriers'," in *Charters, Cartularies, and Archives: The Preservation and Transmission of Documents in the Medieval West*, ed. Adam Kosto and Anders Winroth (Toronto: PIMS, 2002), 43–60, and other chapters in the same volume; and Guyotjeannin, Morelle, and Parisse, eds., *Les Cartulaires*.
46 On the role of cartularies in the production of forged documents, see most recently Robert F. Berkhofer, *Forgeries and Historical Writing in England, France, and Flanders, 900–1200* (Woodbridge:

Boydell & Brewer, 2022); and Levi Roach, *Forgery and Memory at the End of the First Millennium* (Princeton, NJ: Princeton University Press, 2021).

47 Geary, *Phantoms of Remembrance*, especially chapter III: "Archival Memory and the Destruction of the Past," 81–114.

48 Morelle, "The Metamorphosis of Three Monastic Collections," 176; Morelle, "Histoire et archives vers l'Ann Mil," 124–128, challenges Geary's conclusions (above at n. 42) about intended revisions and destructions of documents by eleventh-century archivists.

49 Could the distrust in cartularies be linked to the exclusion of graphic signs and seals? For the prefaces to cartularies, see Pascale Bourgain and Marie-Clotilde Hubert, "Latin et rhétorique dans les préfaces de cartulaires," in *Les Cartulaires*, 115–136, at 118, 124; and Benoit-Michel Tock, "Les Textes non diplomatiques dans les cartulaires de la province de Reims," in *Les Cartulaires*, 45–58, at 54.

50 Francesca Tinti, "From Episcopal Conception to Monastic Compilation: Hemming's Cartulary in Context," *Early Medieval Europe* 11.3 (2002): 189–294; and Geary, *Phantoms of Remembrance*, 100–102.

51 Bourgain and Hubert, "Latin et rhétorique," 122. G. R. C. Davis, *Medieval Cartularies of Great Britain and Ireland*, rev. by Claire Breay, Julian Harrison, and David M. Smith (London British Library, 2010), 217–218 nos. 1068–1069; and Jean-Philippe Genet, "Cartulaires anglais du Moyen Age," in *Les Cartulaires* 353, 359–360.

52 Bourgain and Hubert, "Latin et rhétorique," 134–135.

53 This respectful care of ancient documents is reminiscent of modern librarians and archivists who recommend the consultation of microfilms, facsimiles, and databases before having to expose a precious original to the touch of light and human hands.

54 For a definition of *vidimus* and *inspeximus* in particular, see Ortí et al., eds., *Vocabulaire international de la diplomatique*, no 67 at 34. On the early use of *Inspeximus* in England, See Brigitte M. Bedos-Rezak, "The English Origins of the *Sigillum Authenticum*," in *Status, Identity and Authority. Studies in Medieval and Early Modern Archives and Heraldry presented to Adrian Ailes*, ed. Sean Cunningham, Anne Curry, and Paul Dryburgh, 97–124 (London: The Heraldry Society, 2021), 108–112; on late medieval *Inspeximus*, Jessica Berenbeim, *The Art of Documentation: Documents and Visual Culture in Medieval England* (Toronto: PIMS, 2015), 161–185.

55 Bourgain and Hubert, "Latin et rhétorique," 118–119.

56 K. Patrick Fazioli, *The Mirror of the Medieval: An Anthropology of the Western Historical Imagination* (Oxford: Berghahn Books), 147–148.

57 A selective bibliography devoted to illuminated cartularies includes Auguste de Loisne, "Les miniatures du cartulaire de Marchiennes," *Bulletin archéologique du Comité des travaux historiques et scientifiques* (1903): 476–489; Casado de Otaola, "Per visibilia ad invisibilia," 44–52; Robert A. Maxwell, "Sealing Signs and the Art of Transcribing in the Vierzon Cartulary," *The Art Bulletin* 81 (1999): 576–597; Markus Späth, *Verflechtung von Erinnerung: Bildproduktion und Geschichtsschreibung im Kloster San Clemente a Casauria während des 12. Jahrhunderts* (Berlin: Akademie Verlag, 2007); Jessica Berenbeim, *Art of Documentation*, 45–69; Laura Cleaver, *Illuminated History Books in the Anglo-Norman World, 1066–1272* (Oxford: Oxford University Press, 2018), 114–155. Perhaps the most celebrated illustrated cartulary is the twelfth-century Catalonian *Liber Feudorum*: Adam J. Kosto, "The Liber Feudorum Maior of the Counts of Barcelona: The Cartulary as an Expression of Power," *Journal of Medieval History* 27, no. 1 (2001): 1–22; Shannon L. Wearing, "Power and Style: The 'Liber Feudorum Maior' and the Court of Alfonso II, King of Aragon and Count of Barcelona (r. 1162–1196)" (PhD dissertation, New York University, 2015); and Susanne Wittekind, "Visuelle Rechtsordnung und Herrschaftslegitimation in katalanischen 'Libri Feudorum' und 'Capbreus'," in *Die Urkunde: Text – Bild – Objekt*. ed. Andrea Stieldorf (Berlin: de Gruyter, 2019), 383–417.

58 On the suggestion of the rendering of existing charters, see Jean-Luc Chassel, "Dessins et mentions de sceaux dans les cartulaires médiévaux," in *Les Cartulaires*, 91–104; Mathias Auclair, "Dessins d'armoiries et de sceaux dans le cartulaire de Sainte-Glossinde de Metz," *Revue française d'héraldique et de sigillographie* 66 (1996), 53–59; and Cleaver, *Illuminated History Books*, 130. See note 43 for the relationship between cartularisation and documentary forgery.

59 This is not to say that such representations were ineffective. See Cleaver, *Illuminated History Books*, 138–146.

60 Michael F. Webb, "They Impressed their Signs in that Book: Original Charters in the Cartularies of Angoumois," *Manuscripta* 65, no. 1 (2021): 71–138.
61 Paul Bertrand, *Documenting the Everyday in Medieval Europe: The Social Dimensions of a Writing Revolution, 1250–1350* (Turnhout: Brepols, 2019), who, in claiming a "documentary revolution" between 1200 and 1330, tends to ignore earlier cultural literacies and pragmatic writing.
62 Ann-Sophie Lehmann, "Taking Fingerprints: The Indexical Affordance of Artworks' Material Surfaces," in *Spur der Arbeit: Oberfläche und Werkprozess*, ed. Magdalena Bushart and Henrike Haug (Cologne: Böhlau, 2018), 199–218; and Brigitte M. Bedos-Rezak, "Status. An Impression," in *Seals and Status: The Power of Objects*, ed. John Cherry, Jessica Berenbeim, and Lloyd De Beer (London: The British Museum, 2018), 45–53, at 51–52.

4
THE ANDEAN KHIPUS
An Information System Made of String

Lucrezia Milillo and Sabine Hyland

Introduction

One of the most mysterious and least understood means for storing data was the "khipu": a system of knotted, twisted, and coloured cords that were used in the Andes for over a millennium to record information. How could this three-dimensional device, so unlike two-dimensional scripts and signs, encode data? Khipus are most closely associated with the Inka Empire, the largest pre-European state in the Americas, which extended nearly five thousand kilometres from modern-day Ecuador to Chile. During the Inka Empire, which lasted roughly from 1400 to 1572 CE, khipus served as the basis for imperial governance, recording data on population, labour tribute, religious rituals, laws, and military conquests, among others. Spanish chroniclers tell us that khipus could also record narrative information, such as the biographies of kings and even poetry. How could a state as powerful and complex as that of the Inkas have relied on an information device that was so unlike any other kind of writing?

Khipu structures have varied greatly throughout their millennium of use. The most common type of khipu is that which specialists refer to as the "standard Inka khipu." This consists of a horizontal primary cord from which hang multiple pendant cords. Other cords, called "subsidiary cords," may be attached to the pendant cords. "Top cords" are pendants that are oriented upwards from the primary cord, sometimes summarising the content of the pendants that come before them. Khipus often, but not always, have a hierarchical branching structure (Fig. 4.1).

Made of plant or animal fibres, khipus represent a unique system for storing, managing, and sharing information. In Quechua, the word "khipu" (or "quipu") means "knot on one single cord," and knots indeed play an important role in most khipus. In contrast to other cord-based information systems found around the world, khipus are remarkable for their structural complexity, the range of subjects that could be recorded on them, the level of standardisation that they reached under the Inka rule, and the extensiveness of the territory in which they were used. There are, however, considerable gaps in our ability to interpret khipus. Khipu research is a field which involves ongoing collaborations among experts in different disciplines and a profound knowledge of ancient Andean culture and cosmology.

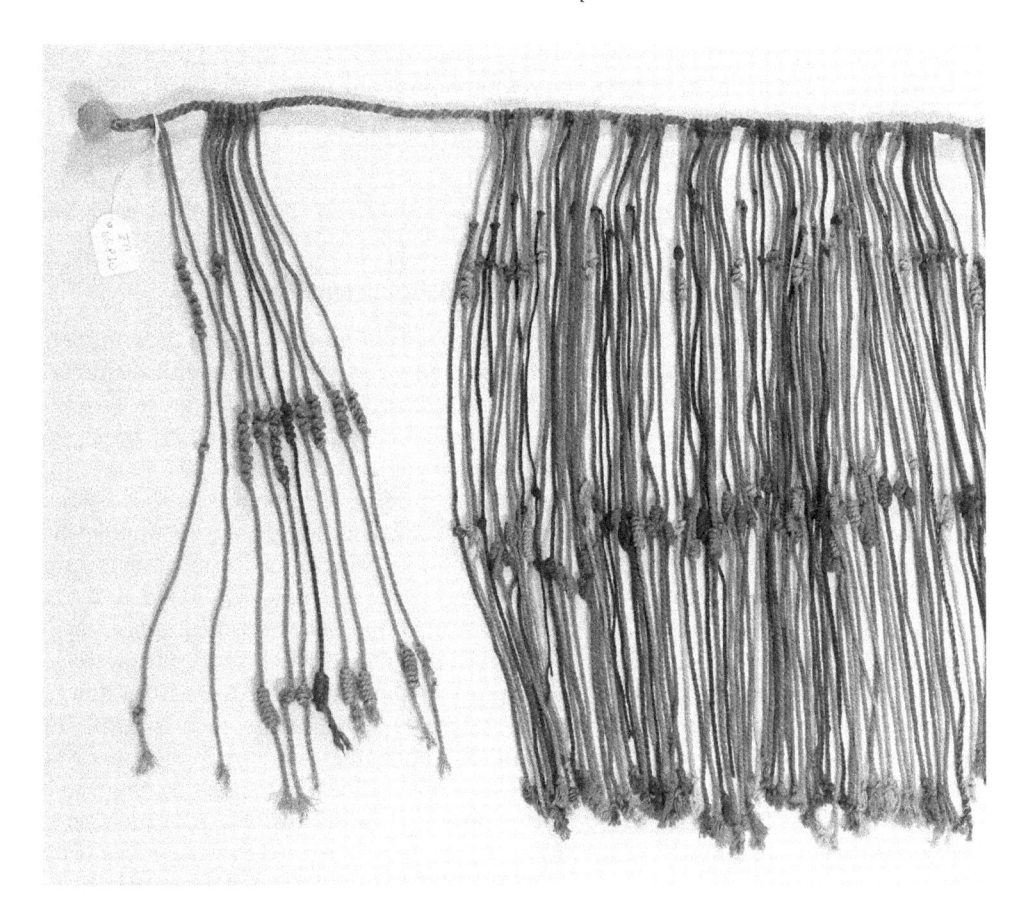

Figure 4.1 Close up of an Inka style khipu. Primary cord is lying horizontally at the top. Groups of pendant cords are attached to the primary cord. The lowest knots on the pendant cords prevent the cord from unravelling. Above those are knots for single units, followed by those for tens. In the leftmost group of pendant cords are also knots for hundreds, visible above the knots for tens. Subsidiary cords are attached to some pendants on the right-hand side of the khipu. Both pendant and subsidiary cords are of different colours: from light, medium to dark brown as well as indigo blue. All cords are made of cotton. Berlin Ethnology Museum VA 66830. Photo by Lucrezia Milillo.

Understanding the history, functions, and evolution of khipus is a challenging task that requires expertise in multiple areas, including ethnography, ethnohistory, archaeology, linguistics, semiotics, heritage science, and statistics.

This chapter will survey the complexity of the khipu as a medium for the transmission of information and the difficulties of understanding its nature, beginning with the Europeans' initial impressions of this technology and ending with the place of contemporary khipus today. Because early modern accounts have played such an outsized role in shaping subsequent khipu research, we first review the descriptions of khipus provided by European observers of the Andes. This will be followed by a survey of the development of khipu from pre-Columbian times, examining how this medium changed from the Wari Empire to the twentieth century. The section on Inka khipus will focus on five topics of particular salience: radiocarbon dating and chronology; morphology and meaning; numerical information; colour, colour grouping, and materiality; and subject markers and flow chart theory. The chapter concludes by discussing the value of ethnographic khipus for both research and contemporary Andean peoples. Khipus remain of great importance in many rural Andean communities, yet their continued existence is under threat by the forces of modernisation.

From Early Modern to Modern Encounters

In the early sixteenth century, when the Spaniards arrived on the western coast of South America and as they headed inland, they encountered a complex socio-political situation. A vast and still-expanding empire, the Inka *Tawantinsuyu*, ruled over a great variety of cultural groups. While these groups shared many common Andean cultural traits, they also had specific and unique customs, material culture, and languages. The first written testimony of a khipu comes from Hernan Pizarro, brother of the more famous conquistador Francisco. In a 1533 letter, Hernan describes a khipu being used for double-entry bookkeeping. He provides eyewitness accounts of knots being untied from some pendant cords of the khipu and tied onto others to account for changes as sheep, wood, and other goods were taken by the Spaniards from a local storehouse.[1] After this first appearance in Pizarro's report, khipus are subsequently described in many other chronicles from the late sixteenth to the seventeenth century. The authors of these accounts were from different social and ethnic backgrounds. While many were born in Spain, others, such as Felipe Guaman Poma de Ayala and Diego de Castro Titu Cusi Yupanqui, were born in the Viceroyalty of Peru to indigenous parents. Garcilaso de la Vega, instead, was the son of a conquistador and an Inka noblewoman. The individual factors of personal history, education, intentions, social background, and the era in which these authors penned their accounts played a significant role in influencing how they depicted Inka cosmology and the capabilities of khipu technology. Their views on this aspect of Inka technology were also in dialogue with wider debates about the nature of the Indians' humanity, including whether they could be Christianised or enslaved.[2] Affirming whether Andean people had a form of writing was a very strong political statement in this context, and made a difference in whether they could be used as sources in official trials, which eventually they were. Some early modern authors suggested that khipus were the Inka form of writing; meanwhile, others maintained that the *"indios"* did not have any sort of writing and that khipus were merely a mnemonic device. Yet others stated that although ancient Peruvians did not have writing, they used khipus to serve the exact same purposes. Despite these differences in understanding, there are some commonalities in the chroniclers' claims about the purpose of the knotted cords and the range of topics they documented. Most chroniclers wrote that the Inkas used khipus in accounting for goods and people.[3] The chronicles also indicate that knots served as numbers and that colours were used to distinguish different classes of items.[4] Early modern authors also mentioned the use of khipus as calendars and as supports for narrating their history and the histories of their kings.[5] For example, the Mercedarian chronicler, Martín de Murúa, wrote:

> These quipus were a type of knots, made in somewhat thick cords of wool and different colours. With these they counted, and referred to the days, weeks, months, and years, and for this they made units, tens, hundreds, thousands, and millions.

To differentiate them for the things they wanted to say, they made some knots bigger than the others, and [they] included different colours, so that for one thing they had a red knot, and for another yellow or green or blue or black. The knot was thicker or thinner depending on the quality and number [of the thing]. By these knots they recounted the events of history and when each Inka reigned, how many children he had, if he was good or bad, brave or cowardly, who he married, which lands he conquered, the buildings he constructed, the servants and wealth that he possessed, how many years he lived, when he died, and what things he cared about a lot. In short, everything that our books teach us and show us were taken from [those khipus].[6]

Numerous Spanish chroniclers claimed that the historical information that they were presenting had been derived from khipu records.

Spanish chroniclers also indicate that khipu-makers or khipu-keepers were called *khipukamayuq*, a Quechua term that goes beyond the idea of crafting and managing. *Kamay* is often translated as the verb "create," but this term expresses a much more complex concept than "creating." It has to do with animating and can better be translated with "to charge with being," or "to infuse with power."[7] It implies an energy dynamic involving the infusion of life into something. Considering this, the khipukamayuq is more than a khipu-maker, socially regarded as a powerful being who could infuse life and energy into khipus. Khipus, in turn, were probably regarded as agency-charged objects, possibly capable of having effects on the real world.[8]

Although Spanish chroniclers of Peru provided descriptions of khipus in their published works, khipus did not take hold of the European imagination until the eighteenth century. In 1747, inspired by the veritable "Inka-mania" that was then sweeping France, Françoise de Graffigny published her epistolary novel, *Lettres d'une Péruvienne* (*Letters of a Peruvian Woman*).[9] The letters that comprised the novel, purportedly written by an Inka princess in France to her Peruvian lover, were supposedly sent as khipus. As the princess explained, "I ran to my quipus ... and hastened to knot them in hopes that by their assistance I might render immortal the history of our love."[10] The enormous success of Graffigny's novel solidified the belief that khipus were as expressive a form of writing as alphabetic texts; this led to a new interest in the knotted cords.[11] In 1751, for example, Raimondo di Sangro, inspired by Graffigny's fiction, published a volume containing an imaginative phonetic rendering of a poetic khipu.[12] His khipu symbols, however, bore little resemblance to any pre-Columbian cords.

Decades later, an English ship's carpenter named Alexander Strong publicly displayed seven "quipolas" of knotted strings which he claimed were genuine khipus from Chile. Strong also prepared a "Prospectus" containing the complex narrative histories that he said were recorded on the quipolas.[13] An eccentric Irish peer, Lord Kingsborough, purchased the quipolas and published a coloured print of one of them in his monumental *Antiquities of Mexico*.[14] Today, Strong's quipolas and their respective histories are regarded as fake, but throughout the nineteenth century they were widely viewed as legitimate South American khipus with their accompanying texts. It was only with the advent of scientific excavations in Peru in the twentieth century, and the discovery of genuine Inka khipus in archaeological contexts, that scholars began to recognise the basic structures of ancient Andean khipus. As additional archaeological, ethnohistoric, and ethnographic evidence comes to light, our understanding of khipus continues to evolve and become more refined.

Ancient Khipus in Context

While khipu technology is predominantly associated with the Inka Empire, its roots extend further back in time. Understanding how khipus changed in history and how Andean people adapted them to respond to their needs is important to better grasp how they functioned. Archaeological context provides important insights into the cultural context and value of pre-Columbian khipus, as well as into their possible content. Archaeological data are also fundamental to interpret the understandings that early modern chroniclers provided about khipus. In this section, a chronological description of khipu technology according to archaeological context will be offered. The importance and limitations of radiocarbon dating will be also presented.

Wari Khipus

According to scholars, the Wari, dating from the sixth to tenth centuries CE, is the first coastal-Andean civilisation universally recognised to have produced khipus. Wari khipus are relatively small in size, with knots that appear to have functioned according to a base-ten system.[15] Wari khipus are notable for the presence of colourful thread wrappings that are often found on the upper part of the pendant cords and at the beginning of the primary cord. Only about forty examples of Wari khipus are known to date, and for most of them, we do not know the context in which they were found. Those found *in situ* have always been recovered from Middle Horizon tombs with Middle Horizon material culture.[16] One significant discovery of Wari khipus was made at the site of Castillo de Huarmey in northern Peru, where a cache of khipus was found in a Wari-era tomb in 2013. These complex khipus include a variety of colours and materials, indicating that they were used for a range of purposes beyond simple accounting.[17]

It remains unclear precisely how the recordkeeping technology using knotted cords was acquired by the Inkas, but, despite the visible differences between Wari and Inka khipus, it is widely acknowledged that the Inkas assimilated and transformed the earlier khipu information system to enable them to manage a vast centralised empire.

Inka Khipus

Despite precursors developed by the Wari, khipu technology has been predominantly associated with Inka culture. Although the Inkas utilised woven graphic icons called *tokapus*, the symbolic functions of which are not fully understood today, they did not possess any kind of inscription that used graphic signs comparable to our contemporary conception of writing. Instead, the Inkas adopted the khipu from the abovementioned Wari culture and developed it according to their needs. The reason for this can be found in the challenges that the Inkas faced when expanding and becoming a hegemonic empire. Nonetheless, as Galen Brokaw has highlighted, the imperial standardisation of khipu technology might not have affected local agropastoral use of khipus. Different domains could have had different degrees of standardisation of khipu use: from a highly regulated khipu-making practice (with access to a wider variety of materials), to more local pastoral use.[18] Indeed, spinning yarns and making threads, as well as dyeing and knotting, were part of common and basic knowledge of Andean agropastoral people where camelid wool was abundantly available. For this reason, Frank Salomon has highlighted the demotic potential of the khipu as a medium.[19] This potential was still utilised in some twentieth-century Andean farming contexts, as will be discussed below. Despite what is commonly believed, khipu technology had a long-lasting legacy throughout the Spanish colonial era and into the twentieth century.

The height of the Inka political power ran from the first half of 1400 to 1572 when the last Inka resistance against the Conquistadors-led army was defeated. Biological evidence suggests that the Inkas' ancestors originally came from the Titicaca highland region and were therefore more related to Aymara- or Puquina-speaking peoples, adopting Quechua as an official language at a later time.[20] The territory over which they extended their political control was vast and included many different cultural and ecological areas, from the pre-Amazonian *selva* to the Andean mountain ridge to the arid coastal desert. An intricate road system, including the well-known rope bridges, was finely tuned to the diverse landscape to provide connection among all areas of the *Tawantinsuyu*, or "the four interconnected parts" as the Inkas called their vast empire. The mastery of hydraulic engineering manifested in extensive irrigation canals. Storage facilities were strategically located to ensure the successful and efficient interconnectedness of the territories. Agricultural terraces, shaped like mathematical arches, were utilised to maximise arable land and minimise erosion. These terraces, sometimes incorporating soil from different regions of the *Tawantinsuyu*, were also employed for experimenting with crop cultivation in various climatic spheres within a single location. Without the use of any mortar, the Inka skilfully fitted stones together, shaping them into imposing, often anti-seismic, structures, fortresses, and palaces. The landscape of the Inka Empire was a meaningful territory organised through the intricate ceremonial and spatial *siq'i* system, where powerful and agentive beings known as *wak'as* were located.[21] This system also played a crucial role in numerous annual rituals and ceremonies. Census-taking was a systematic practice under Inka rule, and groups of people were redistributed across the territory based on labour needs through a system called *mit'a*. The socio-economic structure through which the Inka managed their empire was a non-monetary and redistributive economy where practices way more complex than what we describe as "barter" ensured the repartition and reallocation of goods across the many climatic regions. In other words, the population contributed to the functioning of the empire with labour contributions, while state officials ensured that natural resources (like food), raw materials (for example, cotton), and processed, manufactured objects (such as textiles) were redistributed throughout different climatic areas and regions of the *Tawantinsuyu*. The Inkas scaled up to empire-level what John V. Murra called "vertical archipelago," a local Andean strategy that was used to distribute access to resources available in different climatic zones.[22] This non-monetary system, based on reciprocity and labour exchange, required precise statal control of the contributors, and of the work and goods they provided. Both material goods and *mit'a* labour contribution were meticulously recorded. Remarkably, all that is mentioned above was accomplished without the use of writing in the conventional sense, but instead with the use of khipus.

Most of the approximately thirteen hundred khipus we know today, which are generally assumed to be Inka, lack precise provenance.[23] This is largely due to the looting of archaeological sites and the smuggling of artefacts for the Western and South American *curiosa*, ethnographic, and art markets.[24] While in some cases it is the archaeological context that helps researchers generate more informed questions regarding the use and social value of khipus, it can also be the other way around. For instance, in the great ceremonial complex of Pachacamac, a monumental site on the southern outskirts of Lima, khipus have been found in a variety of archaeological contexts. In the case of those from burial contexts, there is little to say apart from recognising them as funerary paraphernalia since the tombs almost always have been already looted before the excavation.[25] Pachacamac khipus have also been found hidden in a pit covered by adobes, earth, and archaeological residues which might suggest a deliberate action of hiding or protecting the information encoded onto them from theft or destruction.[26] Highly degraded khipus have also been found spread out on the floor of an Inka platform at Pachacamac. Thanks to this discovery, the platform was able to be identified as a working place, with an adjacent storehouse, of a functionary who controlled the exchange of goods at the border of the monumental area.[27]

At Inkawasi, an Inka military outpost in the Cañete Valley, the archaeologist Alejandro Chu found numerical khipus close to or covered by different heaps of edible products like chili pepper, black beans, and peanuts. This archaeological context is preserved well enough to allow archaeologists to conclude that these khipus were used to record quantities of the products with which they were associated. At Inkawasi, khipus were also found in pairs; an analysis of their numerical values suggests that they may have been used for checks-and-balance accounting, similar to the one that Pizarro had witnessed.[28] Another example of khipus used for data management comes from the administrative centre of Puruchuco, on the central coast of Peru. Here, Carrie Brezine found that khipus were used at multiple hierarchical levels of data administration, with some khipus synthesising data that had been recorded in more detail at lower accounting levels of the administrative process.[29]

From the site of Laguna de Los Condores in northern Peru, where human activity is attested from Middle Horizon, c. 500–1000 CE, through the early colonial period, comes an exemplary case of multiple Inka-style khipus found together in one funerary context. As previously mentioned, burials are the sites most likely to have been plundered. In this case, looters themselves reported to have found khipus on top of groups of mummies and hanging from the ceiling above them. Repeated lootings have irreversibly compromised the finding context and the integrity of these khipus.[30]

A recent archaeological discovery of a workbasket with ready-made khipu cords in Inkawasi suggests that the construction of khipus in Inka times possibly required multiple human actors, perhaps operating at different stages of the production line.[31] However, the precise practicalities of khipu-making (that is, *how* ancient Andeans aggregated and transformed the raw materials into a meaningful record-keeping artefact) are not yet fully understood.

Radiocarbon Dating and Chronology

As mentioned above, most khipus lack precise provenance. Therefore, AMS-Radiocarbon Dating (AMS C-14) can be a crucial tool for understanding khipus as information systems because it allows us to attribute the origin of a khipu to specific cultural periods. This is of great importance for determining whether specific features of a khipu are related to specific historical contexts. For example, while twenty-four khipus with colourful thread wrapping have been found in Wari sites, five other Wari-style khipus without precise provenance were radiocarbon dated to 779–1024 CE, the expansionist period of the Wari culture.[32] This dating confirms that the technique of thread wrapping is a dominant and specific (although not exclusive) characteristic of Wari khipus.[33] It also suggests that the emergence and use of khipus responded to the needs of an expanding polity.

For later periods that are closer to the Spanish invasion, AMS C-14 dating often requires supporting data, such as provenance, as well as contextual and ethnohistorical details.[34] This is because the measurement of C-14 quantity results in a calibrated curve that covers the possible timespan in which the organic material (fibre in this case) was acquired from its living source (plant or animal). If the khipu was made during the Inka expansion *or* the early colonial period, the calibrated curve may present two peaks, one of which falls exactly before the Spanish invasion and one which falls afterwards. This can make accurate cultural attribution of Inka or early colonial khipus complicated if one relies upon radiocarbon dating exclusively. When a radiocarbon date includes both the Inka and the early colonial eras, it is essential to corroborate the attribution with details gathered through archaeological, archival, and/or ethnohistorical methods.

So far, fewer than one hundred khipus have been radiocarbon dated. When used in conjunction with other information, this technique can shed new light on how the structural variation in khipus relates to different historical periods and socio-cultural circumstances. Radiocarbon dating of small groups of museum khipus has revealed that some khipus that had been assumed to be "Inka" date, in fact, to the colonial period.

Inka Khipu Morphology: Structure and Meaning

The preceding section delineated the notable shifts in khipu morphology as they evolved from their application within the Wari cultural sphere to subsequent usage in the Inka cultural sphere. This exploration elucidated both the potentials and constraints of archaeological methodologies employed in khipu studies, highlighting distinctions and opportunities for collaboration with early modern perceptions of khipus. The preservation of a relatively consistent Inka khipu morphology during the early colonial period was also briefly addressed. This prompts questions regarding the symbolic significance of khipu morphology, the nature of information encoded in khipu signs, and the methodologies for comprehending their potential as information system.

The first step in understanding what a khipu means is carrying out a meticulous morphological study. Early (as well as more recent) descriptions of khipus continue to be of great value for helping us to appreciate the sophisticated nuances of khipu morphology. These reports and drawings that detail the relational perception of colour and the presence or absence of objects like tassels or needlework bundles, along with the number of cords and knots, can help us to assess how deterioration and other contingencies have affected the data we are able to access today. Written, schematic, and photographic representations of khipus are essential to identify the possible relations of morphological features within the structure.[35] Today, the digital representations of khipus, such as those featured in Ashok Kohsla's *The Khipu Field Guide*, expedite the two-dimensional visualisation of khipus, a crucial step in understanding their morphology.[36] Once the details of khipu morphology have been established, which is nevertheless an ongoing process, a comparative analysis of khipus with each other and with other Andean cultural artefacts, such as textiles, can help identify common elements and potential meanings.[37]

On an even larger scale, statistical analyses that identify and analyse patterns in khipus can shed light on the nature of khipu signs and, possibly, on their relational value as well as, perhaps, their meaning. This has been demonstrated, for example, by Jon Clindaniel, who found statistically relevant occurrences of khipu signs (such as ply direction and knot directionality) that had been previously identified as meaningful and relevant through ethnographic research.[38] Clindaniel currently oversees the open-access Online Khipu Repository (OKR), the largest database of khipu descriptions in the world which is facilitating new avenues of research using computational methods and data science.

Numerical Information

In 1912, an American mathematician, Leland Locke, demonstrated for the first time how quantitative information was recorded on knots through a base-ten system on Inka khipus.[39] In the "Lockean" decimal organisation, knots occur in vertically spaced zones on pendant cords; the knots' decimal value depends on which zone they pertain to. At the lowest level, knots stand for single units; on the upper level there are the tens. Above the zone for the tens is the zone for the hundreds and so on as illustrated in Fig. 4.1. Simple knots are used for powers of ten and above. Numbers from two to nine are indicated by long knots located in the lowest zone on the pendant. The number one is represented by a figure-eight knot. Generally, knots are the last step in khipu-making. However, it is not rare to find marks of unravelled knots on Inka khipus of various dimensions and complexity, that is, on khipus pertaining to both lower and higher levels of centralised information management. This means that information could be untied and possibly retied on the same khipu, or that khipus could be reused according to specific cycles, such as in the case of the more recent Anchucaya khipus.[40]

Knots in surviving khipus occasionally diverge from the Lockean decimal organisational system. It has been argued that khipus with non-Lockean knots might not register quantities. Such khipus, it has been suggested, might be the narrative khipus described by the chroniclers. However, it has become clear that at least some of the so-called "non-Lockean" knots are, in fact, numerical. For example, some khipus that contain an extra knot below the unit level in an area of the pendant that should be free of any knots, according to Locke's scheme. These "nether knots," as they have been termed, appear to indicate a second number on a pendant, one that should usually be subtracted from the pendant total. Sabine Hyland's research shows that rather than indicating a non-numerical narrative khipu, the presence of anomalous "nether knots" reveals that the numerical system is more complex than has previously been understood.[41]

The meaning of other anomalies in or related to the knots, such as when the cord colour changes within the knot, or when long knots occur in all the decimal positions, or when there are knots that fall outside of Locke's tri-partite classification, is yet to be understood. Although such anomalous knots usually have been disregarded as individual idiosyncrasies, there have been recent efforts to examine these apparent "anomalies" as intentional and as possible bearers of a shared meaning.[42] Although scholars have now gained a relatively solid understanding of how most numerical information was encoded in khipus, much more remains to be learned about how qualitative and even narrative information was recorded. What do khipu numbers count? How can we determine the topic of any particular khipu?

Colour, Colour Grouping, and Materiality

The pendant cords on Inka khipus are frequently organised into groups. These cord groupings may or may not match other features like cord colour and/or material. In some cases, uniformly spaced cords are grouped only by colour; they are arranged either in groups of cords of the same colour (a pattern called "colour banding") or in sequences of repeating cycles of colours (a pattern called "seriation"). Hyland has deciphered the meaning of these two patterns in ethnographic contexts, in which colour banding represents individual and lower-level information in a khipu hierarchy, while seriation signifies aggregate information summarised from multiple lower-level khipus.[43] Clindaniel found correlation among khipus in the OKR between their colour pattern and the magnitude of the numbers they encoded, which was consistent with Hyland's finding. With some exceptions, most colour-banded khipus encoded lower numbers than seriated khipus, as one would expect if colour banding indicated individual information, while seriation denoted aggregate quantities. These findings reveal a high degree of continuity between Inka and modern khipus.[44] The importance of these two colour patterns highlights the centrality of colour to the khipu code, especially when viewed in light of the chronicler's consistent emphasis on the relevance of colour.

The determination of cord colour is one of the first choices the khipu-maker will make, in some cases even before spinning the cord (that means, even before deciding the final twist direction). The raw material already has its own colour: camelid wool can be of different shades of brown, white, or black. Wool types used in khipu-making could also include viscacha and, in post-Inka times, sheep wool was also utilised to make khipus. Andean cotton, on the other hand, can be not only naturally white but also medium brown, dark brown, or brown with slightly purple shades. Other plant fibres, such as leaf fibres from plants of the *Agavoideae* subfamily (informally referred to as "*maguey*"), have a natural ivory-beige colour.

While all these materials possess a natural colour that was utilised for organising colour combinations, dyes could also be applied. In the dyeing process, the final results are influenced not only by temperature, immersion time, acidity of the dyebath, and mordanting materials and techniques, but also by the original colour of the fibre.[45] The relevance of colour in the khipu information system emerges from aggregated cord colour patterns, like the aforementioned colour banding and seriation, as well as from colour combinations within the individual cords. Besides cords with solid colours (either natural or dyed), cords can be barber pole (two or more different coloured threads are combined in the final plying stage), mottled (a speckled pattern obtained by mixing threads of two colours in the early plying stage), or segmented (the cord appears as vertically bipartite: it presents one colour in the upper segment and another in the lower segment). A typical Wari-style segmentation presents a solid colour on the upper segment and a barber pole cord on the lower segment.[46] Cords might also present colourful threads running through the cord just for a reduced section. These have been named by the Aschers as "thread run through," abbreviated as "(td rt)."[47] It is still unclear how the threads running through affect the semantic quality of the cord as a whole, leaving aside the issue of threads running through only specific knots.

We know from the accounts of early modern chroniclers that colour played a key role in storing information in khipus.[48] Various chroniclers have stated that colour would stand for a specific meaning or referent in a one-to-one relation, such as yellow to indicate gold, white to represent silver, and red for soldiers.[49] The straightforward application of this explanation has been widely rejected by contemporary scholars because, despite colours being the most variable feature among khipu constitutional elements, there is not enough colour variation to cover the variety of topics that are said to be encoded in khipus. However, Mariano Eduardo de Rivero's "flow chart" theory of khipu signification, described in the section below, presents a solution to this conundrum. If the meaning of colour and other indicators vary according to the subject of a khipu, then the range of possible meaning is greatly expanded.

Subject Markers and the "Flow Chart" Theory

One of the most pressing issues in khipu studies is how to understand what a khipu is talking about, that is, what kind of information has been organised and stored in its strings. In practice, this means understanding the relationship between morphology (of either the entire khipu or its parts) and meaning. For example, the presence of decimal Lockean knots is considered an indicator that the khipu is giving an account of quantifiable items, material or not.

In the nineteenth century, a Peruvian scientist, Mariano Eduardo de Rivero, who conducted ethnographic fieldwork among Andean herders, discovered that special threads or needlework bundles at the beginning of the primary cord could signify a khipu's subject matter.[50] Rivero's insights had been largely forgotten, but recent investigations into modern accounting khipus have confirmed that special markers on the primary cord indicated the khipus's subject; the structure of the primary cord probably did as well.[51] From the ethnographic context, the terms *pachacamanta* and *kayte* have been identified as referring to these bundles. *Pachacamanta* is Quechua for "related to a hundred," while *kayte* is Quechua for "wool thread, spool of wool, bundle of wool."[52] Although kaytes usually comprise tufts or needlework bundles, they can also appear on some occasions as thread wrappings.[53] These add-ons are mostly attached to one extremity of the primary cord, although occasionally they occur on both ends, or even along the primary cord. Kaytes are one of the khipu components with the highest degree of representational capacity, as they can exhibit both abstract patterns and realistic images in their needlework (Fig. 4.2).

Figure 4.2 Tupicocha patrimonial khipu and kayte. Nelser Ramos Romero is holding a khipu from its primary cord, coiled on itself, from which woollen pendant cords hang. In this khipu, the cords are of different colours, ranging from pale rose and beige to dark brown and dark grey. At the top is a round-shaped kayte with a bright blue and red tuft at the end. The kayte is particularly colourful, including bright blue threads together with more neutral beige and yellow-ochre threads. Photo by Lucrezia Milillo.

Rivero also theorised that the meaning of other signs on a khipu varied according to the particular topic.[54] According to this theory, known as the "flow chart" theory of khipu signification, the meaning of secondary symbols, such as colour, final twist direction, and knot direction, depended upon the type of khipu. The meaning of a crimson pendant, for example, would vary according to whether the khipu was a record of tribute labour, an inventory of goods, or another type of record. Dyadic markers, like the difference in the final twist direction (whether cords were twisted to the right or the left) and in knot direction, signified dichotomous contrasts, such as the distinction between male and female. The exact meanings of such dyadic features depended upon the type of khipu and on the where the cord or knot was placed.

For khipus that possess kaytes, these unique woven objects may provide an entry point for interpreting the khipu. Present both in ethnographic and in Inka khipus, kaytes worked as subject matter, indicators of the khipu's topic and therefore tools to distinguish between khipu types and genres. This would imply that khipu signs at different hierarchical levels would consequently stand for different meanings according to the kayte.[55] For khipus without kaytes, the colours, fibres, and other features of the primary cord may indicate the subject matter.

Colonial and Republican Khipus

Until recently, scholars believed that, except for the supposedly simple knotted cords used to account for herds and pastoral activities in the countryside (discussed in further detail below), khipu usage came to an end in the sixteenth century. Carmen Beatriz Loza has argued that after an initial period between 1550 and 1581 when the viceregal government incorporated khipu data into colonial administrative accounts, the Peruvian Catholic Church banned khipus and carried out a campaign to destroy them. She asserted that episcopal legislation in 1583 directed Catholic missionaries to eradicate khipus, leading to their eventual disappearance from the Andes.[56] However, Galen Brokaw successfully challenged Loza's thesis, demonstrating that, except for a few isolated instances, neither the Catholic Church nor the colonial government attempted to suppress the use of khipus among Andean peoples.[57]

We now know that khipus continued to be created and preserved by Andean peoples throughout the Spanish colonial era. During legal trials in the sixteenth and seventeenth centuries, Andean witnesses entered evidence from their khipus into the court record, indicating that khipu usage persisted among the rural population of this time.[58] The khipu testimony from colonial legal cases, often referred to as "paper khipus," has provided insights into the ongoing role of khipus in the colonial Andes.[59] Catholic missionaries often encouraged parishioners to make catechetical khipus for prayers, confessions, and other ecclesiastical purposes, although no examples of such Catholic khipus survive, other than the khipu boards described below.

Khipu use continued in rural areas despite the fact that by the seventeenth century, Andean elites in the countryside were well acquainted with alphabetic literacy and urban scribal culture. Andean leaders consistently relied upon the "delegated writing" of colonial scribes to pursue legal claims in viceregal courtrooms.[60] Village archives today, such as the one found in San Juan de Collata, Peru, contain colonial legal petitions signed by local leaders who appear to have possessed at least some level of alphabetic literacy. Nonetheless, khipus persisted in a situation of "graphic pluralism" in which two radically different systems of inscription co-existed.[61] There are multiple reasons for the perpetuation of this Andean corded technology. The haptic qualities of khipus, which encompass the feel of distinctive materials and knots, are better suited to Andean epistemologies whereby greater authority is accorded to knowledge gained through multiple senses.[62] In certain ritual contexts, khipus are believed to embody connections with ancestors and with powerful mountain beings; this is particularly true for khipus made of animal fibres.[63] Because outsiders were unable to interpret the cords, maintaining accounts and other types of data on khipus allowed information to be kept secret, out of the sight of colonial officials. In the eighteenth century, for example, rebel forces employed khipus as secret missives during indigenous rebellions in Huarochiri province.[64]

Ethnographic Khipus

A number of indigenous villages in the Andes have retained their own khipus into the modern era as either a treasured artefact from their ancestors, or as an active recording technology. Such "ethnographic khipus," as they are called, have provided researchers with invaluable insights into the ritual roles of khipus and how khipus fit into community life. Ethnographic khipus fall into one of four types: (1) patrimonial, (2) khipu boards, (3) funerary, and (4) herding. "Patrimonial khipus" are cords that are treasured by the descendants of their makers, but that can no longer be read.[65] Such rare khipus exist throughout the Central Andes in San Juan de Collata, San Cristobal de Rapaz, San Andrés de Tupicocha, and Santiago de Anchucaya, and in at least one site in Bolivia.[66] The earliest known patrimonial khipus are those of Collata, which have been radiocarbon dated to the mid-sixteenth century. Village elders affirm that the khipus of Collata are missives (*cartas*) created by local leaders to exchange with other regional authorities about their wars on behalf of the Inka. These animal fibre khipus appear to be logosyllabic; however, it is unclear whether their logosyllabism is strictly a regional invention.[67]

Catholic missionaries developed "khipu boards" in the sixteenth century to keep track of how their Andean parishioners participated in church events, such as Mass, catechesis, and other festivals, and paid the tithes that they owed to the church. Khipu boards consist of a rectangular wooden board covered with paper upon which are written the names of the villagers. Next to each name is a hole from whence hangs a multicoloured khipu cord indicating the nature of the associated person's contributions and necessary ritual items for particular ceremonies. The use of khipu boards survived until the 1950s in some villages in the Central Andes, including Mangas, San Pedro de Pari, and San Pedro de Casta.[68] Khipu boards have also been found in Ayacucho and Arica, Chile as well, indicating the wide geographic reach of these hybrid khipu/alphabetic texts.

Many communities in the Central Andes preserve the tradition of funerary khipus: special knotted cords wrapped around the waist of the deceased and buried with the dead. The meaning and composition of the knots vary among the different communities where funerary khipus continue to be made. In some cases, the knots signify Roman Catholic prayers. The knots can also represent incidents in the life of the deceased, while on other occasions they indicate the syllables of ancient Quechua prayers. It is believed that the funerary khipus allow the deceased to walk in the afterlife, enabling them to pass through various trials that occur after death, so they can arrive at the land of the *machus*, or "ancestors." The custom of making funerary khipus witnessed a resurgence in the Central Peruvian Andes during the COVID-19 epidemic.[69]

Additionally, herders throughout the Andes maintained knotted cord records of their flocks, including numerical information on animal type, gender, age, grazing lands, milking status, and so forth. First documented by ethnographers in the nineteenth century, modern woollen herding khipus have simpler structures than Inka cotton khipus.[70] Although herding and produce khipus can vary significantly throughout the Andes, a number of features appear frequently as signifying elements: cord thickness, knot placement, knot type, colour, ply and knot direction, material (such as wool from sheep or llama), and objects (dried potatoes or dried beans, for example) tied to the cords.[71] It is thought that modern herding khipus descend from pre-Columbian herding khipu predecessors.[72]

Although previous generations of khipu researchers assumed that modern cords were supposedly "degenerated" forms that held little interest for scholars, more recent ethnographic investigation has revealed considerable continuity between Inka and post-Inka khipus. Aspects of khipu semiosis such as the meaning of colour banding and seriation; the significance of knot direction; and the importance of subject markers have been uncovered through the study of modern khipu traditions. In the communities that continue to possess khipus, they are a cherished symbol of village identity.

However, modern khipu traditions are greatly endangered. In many villages where Hyland has conducted research, only a few elderly individuals have any recollection of when khipus were an active recording mechanism. In other communities, such as those that maintain the tradition of funerary khipus, the more secretive and esoteric meanings of these cords are slowly being forgotten. As the *Cambridge University Endangered Writing Network* has shown, across the globe today, "there are many writing system whose usage and existence are under threat … [L]anguage and writing are both important elements of culture that can suffer as local traditions compete with global means of communication, including supra-regionally popular languages and technologies such as the internet."[73] Researching and disseminating information about endangered khipu traditions is a vital step towards preserving this valuable cultural heritage.

The continued presence of khipus in remote parts of the Andes today do not merely represent a quaint curiosity. The modern khipu traditions of the Central Peruvian Andes are remnants of one of the most sophisticated and complex intellectual and information systems of the Western hemisphere, that of the khipus of the ancient Inka Empire, which spanned half the South American continent and was equal in size and complexity to the Western Roman Empire at its height. Knowing how Andean peoples use khipus not only to express, organise, and preserve information, but also to communicate knowledge and cultural heritage serves as a powerful testament to the intellectual capacity as well as the creative and technological achievements of indigenous South American peoples.

Notes

1 Hernando Pizarro, "A los Señores Oydores de la Audiencia Real de Su Magestad," in *Colección de libros y documentos referentes a la historia del Perú*, vols. 2–3, ed. Horacio H. Urteaga (Lima: Libreria Sanmarti, 1920), 165–180.

2 Lewis Hanke, *All Mankind Is One: A Study of the Disputation between Bartolomé De Las Casas and Juan Ginés De Sepúlveda in 1550 on the Intellectual and Religious Capacity of the American Indians* (Dekalb, IL: Northern Illinois University Press, 1974).

3 For example, Pedro de Cieza de León, *Parte primera de la Cronica del Peru* (Seville: Martin de Montesdoca, 1553), 99.

4 See, for instance, Pedro Sarmiento de Gamboa, *Historia de los Incas* (1572; repr., Buenos Aires: Emecé, 1943). See also Garcilaso de la Vega, *Los comentarios reales de los Incas*, vol. 2, ed. Horacio H. Urtega (1609; repr., Lima: Libreria Sanmarti, 1919), 152.
5 Pedro de Cieza de León, *Segunda parte de la Cronica del Peru* (Madrid: Imprenda de Manuel Gines Hernandez, 1880), 34–36; 39–41. On khipus as calendars, see José Puente de la Luna, "Calendars in Knotted Cords: New Evidence on How Khipus Captured Time in the Andes," *Ethnohistory* 66, no. 3 (2019): 437–464; and Sabine Hyland, "Festival Threads: Khipu Calendars and Mercedarian Missions in Rapaz, Peru (c. 1565–1825)," *Catholic Historical Review* 107, no. 1 (2021): 119–147.
6 Martin de Murúa, *Historia general del Peru* (1613; repr., Madrid: Historia 16, 1987), 372–373. Translated from the Spanish by Sabine Hyland.
7 Frank Salomon, Jorge Urioste, and Francisco de Avila, *The Huarochiri Manuscript: A Testament of Ancient and Colonial Andean Religion* (Austin, TX: University of Texas Press, 1991); and Gerald Taylor, "*Camay, Camac* et *Camasca* dans le manuscrit quechua de Huarochiri," *Journal de la Société des américanistes* 63 (1974): 231–244.
8 On khipus as agentive or divinatory object, see Sabine Hyland, Sarah Bennison, and William P. Hyland, "Khipus, Khipu Boards, and Sacred Texts: Toward a Philology of Andean Knotted Cords," *Latin American Research Review* 56, no. 2 (2021): 400–416; and Frank Salomon, *The Cord Keepers: Khipus and Cultural Life in a Peruvian Village* (Durham, NC: Duke University Press, 2004).
9 Fernanda Macchi, *Incas ilustrados: reconstrucciones imperiales en la segunda mitad del siglo XVIII* (Madrid-Frankfurt, Vervuert-Iberoamericana, 2009).
10 Françoise de Grafigny, *Letters of a Peruvian Princess: With the Sequel*, vol. 1 (London: J. Aspin, 1798), 2.
11 Joan DeJean and Nancy K. Miller, "Introduction," in *Letters from a Peruvian Woman by François de Graffigny*, ed. DeJean and Miller (New York: Modern Language Association of America, 1993), xx.
12 Raimondo di Sangro Sansevero, *Lettera apologetica dell'Esercitato accademico della Crusca: contenente la difesa del libro intitolato Lettere d'una Peruana* (Naples, 1750).
13 Alexander Strong, *A Prospect of the Quipola, or an Explanation of Quipoes, now open for Public Opinion* (London: J. Phair, 1827).
14 Edward King Kingsborough, *Antiquities of Mexico*, vol. 4 (London: Robert Havell, 1841).
15 Jeffrey C. Splitstoser, "Los Khipus Wari," in *Khipus*, ed. Cecilia Pardo (Lima: Museo de Arte de Lima, 2020), 28–35.
16 Splitstoser, "Los Khipus Wari."
17 Jeffrey C. Splitstoser and Miłosz Giersz, "Wari-Style Khipus from El Castillo de Huarmey," (conference presentation, 81st Annual Meeting of the Society for American Archaeology, Vancouver, British Columbia, 2017).
18 Galen Brokaw, *A History of the Khipu* (New York: Cambridge University Press, 2010).
19 Frank Salomon, "The Twisting Paths of Recall: Khipu (Andean Cord Notation) as Artifact," in *Writing as Material Practice: Substance, Surface and Medium*, ed. Kathryn E. Piquette and Ruth D. Whitehouse (London: Ubiquity Press, 2013), 15–44.
20 For an extensive discussion of the rise and development of the Inkas, see Terence N. D'Altroy, *The Incas*, 2nd ed. (Chichester: Wiley-Blackwell, 2015).
21 On the former, see R. Tom Zuidema, *The Ceque System of Cuzco: The Social Organization of the Capital of the Inca* (Leiden: Brill, 1964). On the latter, Tamara L. Bray, ed., *The Archaeology of Wak'as: Explorations of the Sacred in the pre-Columbian Andes* (Boulder, CO: University Press of Colorado, 2015).
22 John V. Murra, *formaciones económicas y políticas del mundo andino* (Lima: IEP Editiones, 1975).
23 For the most up-to-date inventory of khipus known to date, see the "anexo" in Manuel Medrano, *Quipus: mil años de historia anudada en los Andes y su futuro digital* (Lima: Planeta, 2021).
24 Stefanie Ganger, "The Khipu," chap. 2 in *Relics of the Past: The Collecting and Study of Pre Columbian Antiquities in Peru and Chile, 1837–1911* (Oxford: Oxford University Press, 2014).
25 Peter Eeckhout and Carlos Farfán, *Proyecto Ychsma, Temporada 2000–2001* (Final report to the Peruvian Instituto Nacional de Cultura, Lima, 2001).

26 Alberto Bueno Mendoza, "Hallazgo de un kipu en Pachacamac," in *Quipu y yupana: colección de escritos*, ed. Carol J. Mackey, Hugo Pereyra, Carlos Radicati, Humberto Rodríguez, and Oscar Valverde (Lima: CONCYTEC, 1990), 97–104.
27 Peter Eeckhout, "Inca Storage and Accounting Facilities at Pachacamac," *Andean Past* 10, no. 1 (2012): 213–239.
28 Gary Urton and Alejandro Chu, "Accounting in the King's Storehouse: The Inkawasi Khipu Archive," *Latin American Antiquity* 26, no. 4 (2015): 512–529.
29 Gary Urton and Carrie J. Brezine, "Khipu Accounting in Ancient Peru," *Science* 309, no. 5737 (2005): 1065–1067.
30 Gary Urton, *The Khipus of Laguna de los Cóndores* (Lima: Nuevas Imágenes, 2007).
31 Jon Clindaniel, "Toward a Grammar of the Inka Khipu: Investigating the Production of Non-numerical Signs" (PhD diss., Harvard University, Graduate School of Arts & Sciences, 2019).
32 Splitstoser, "Wari Khipus."
33 Lucrezia Milillo, "Inka Khipus, Thread Wrappings and Subject Markers," *IX Jornadas Internacionales de Textiles Precolombinos y Amerindianos/9th International Conference on Pre-Columbian and Amerindian Textiles, Museo delle Culture, Milan 2022* (Lincoln, NE: Zea Books, 2024), 146–161.
34 Elmo León Canales, "Los quipus y la calibración radiocarbónica," in *Atando cabos*, ed. Carmen Arellano Hoffmann and Gary Urton (Lima: Ministerio de Cultura, 2011), 229–237.
35 Marcia Ascher, "How Can Spin, Ply, and Knot Direction Contribute to Understanding the Quipu Code?" *Latin American Antiquity* 16, no. 1 (2005): 99–111.
36 Ashok Kohsla, "The Khipu Field Guide," https://www.khipufieldguide.com/index.html.
37 Jeffrey C. Splitstoser, "Practice and Meaning in Spiral-Wrapped Batons and Cords from Cerrillos, a Late Paracas Site in the Ica Valley, Peru," in *Textiles, Technical Practice, and Power in the Andes*, ed. Denise Y. Arnold with Penelope Dransart (London: Archetype, 2014), 46–80; and Denise Y. Arnold and Elvira Espejo, "Andean Weaving Instruments for Textile Planning: The Waraña Coloured Thread-Wrapped Rods and their Pendant Cords," *Indiana* 29 (2012): 173–200. See also Rebecca R. Stone, "Dialogues in Thread: The Quechua Concepts of *Ayni*, *Uhku*, *Tinku*, *Q'iwa*, and *Ushay*," *Threads of Time: Tradition and Change in Indigenous American Textiles*, Michael C. Carlos Museum, Emory University 2017. http://threads-of-time.carlos.emory.edu/exhibits/show/essays/dialoguesinthread.
38 Clindaniel, "Toward a Grammar"; Sabine Hyland, "Writing With Twisted Cords, The Inscriptive Capacity Of Andean Khipus," *Current Anthropology* 58, no. 3 (June 2017): 412–419; Hyland, "Ply, Markedness, and Redundancy: New Evidence for How Andean Khipus Encoded Information," *American Anthropologist* 116, no. 3 (September 2014): 643–648; Hyland, "How Khipus Indicated Labour Contributions in an Andean Village: An Explanation of Colour Banding, Seriation, and Ethnocategories," *Journal of Material Culture* 21, no. 4 (December 2016): 490–509; and Hyland, Gene A. Ware, and Madison Clark, "Knot Direction in a Khipu/Alphabetic Text from the Central Andes," *Latin American Antiquity* 25, no. 2 (June 2014): 189–197.
39 Leland Locke, "The Ancient Quipu, a Peruvian Knot Record," *American Anthropologist* 14, no. 2 (1912): 325–332.
40 Hyland, "How Khipus Indicated Labour Contributions."
41 Sabine Hyland, "Knot Anomalies on Inka Khipus: Revising Locke's Knot Typology," *IX Jornadas Internacionales de Textiles Precolombinos y Amerindianos/9th International Conference on Pre-Columbian and Amerindian Textiles, Museo delle Culture, Milan, 2022* (Lincoln, NE: Zea Books 2024): 162–180.
42 Hyland, "Knot Anomalies"; and Kylie E. Quave, "Confronting Anomaly in the Khipu Structure: Cultural and Individual Variations from Two Museum Collections," *Actas de las IV Jornadas Internacionales sobre Textiles Precolombinos* (2009): 241–251.
43 Hyland, "How Khipus Indicated Labour Contributions."
44 Clindaniel, "Toward a Grammar."
45 Lucrezia Milillo et al., "Heritage Science Contribution to the Understanding of Meaningful Khipu Colours," *Heritage* 6, no. 3 (2023): 2355–2378, esp. 2375.
46 Splitstoser, "Wari Khipus."
47 Salomon, *The Cord Keepers*, 156.

48 See, for instance: Antonio de la Calancha, *Cronica moralizada del Orden de San Augustin en el Peru* (Barcelona: Pedro Lacavalleria, 1638); Murúa, *Historia general* (1613; repr. 1987); Vega, *Los comentarios* (1609; repr. 1919); and Jose de Acosta, *Historia natural y moral de las Indias* (Barcelona: Iayme Cendrat, 1591).
49 Vega, *Los comentarios*, 152.
50 Mariano Eduardo de Rivero and Johann Jakob von Tschudi, *Peruvian Antiquities*, trans. Francis J. Hawks (New York: Putnam 1853), 111.
51 Hyland, "How Khipus Indicated Labour Contributions."
52 Jorge A Lira, *Diccionario Kkechuwa-Español*, 2nd ed. (Bogotá: Secretaría Ejecutiva del Convenio Andrés Bello, 1982), 127, *s.v.* kayte.
53 Milillo, "Inka Khipus."
54 Rivero and Tschudi, *Peruvian Antiquities*, 111.
55 Sabine Hyland, "Subject Indicators and the Decipherment of Genre on Andean Khipus," *Anthropological Linguistics* 62, no. 2 (November 2021): 137–158.
56 Carmen Beatriz Loza, "Du bon usage des quipus face à l'administration colonial espagnole (1550–1600)," *Population* 53, nos. 1–2 (1998): 139–159.
57 Brokaw, *A History of the Khipu*, 198–219.
58 A seminal publication for the study of colonial khipus is Marco Curatola Petrocchi and José Carlos de la Puente Luna, "Contar concertando: quipus, piedritas, y escritura en los Andes coloniales," in *el quipu colonial: estudios y materiales*, ed. M. Curatola Petrocchi and J. C. de la Puente Luna (Lima: PUCP, 2013), 193–244.
59 Manuel Medrano, "Khipu Transcription Typologies: A Corpus-Based Study of the *Textos Andinos*," *Ethnohistory* 68, no. 2 (2021): 311–341; Medrano, "Toward a Khipu Transcription 'Insistence': A Corpus-Based Study of the *Textos Andinos*" (Bachelor's thesis, Harvard College, 2020); and Martti Pärssinen and Jukka Kiviharju, *Textos Andinos: Corpus de textos "khipu" incaicos y coloniales*, vol. 1 (Madrid: Instituto Iberoamericano de Finlandia, Universidad Complutense de Madrid, 2004).
60 Kathryn Burns, *Into the Archive: Writing and Power in Colonial Peru* (Durham, NC: Duke University Press, 2010), 124–145.
61 Frank Salomon and Sabine Hyland, "Graphic Pluralism: Native American Systems of Inscription and the Colonial Situation: Guest Editors Introduction," *Ethnohistory* 57, no. 1 (2010): 1–9.
62 Hyland et al., "Khipus, Khipu Boards, and Sacred Texts."
63 Sabine Hyland, "Festival Threads: Khipu Calendars and Mercedarian Missions in Rapaz, Peru (c. 1565–1825)," *The Catholic Historical Review* 107, no. 1 (Winter 2021): 119–147.
64 Hyland, "Writing with Twisted Cords"; and Salomon, *The Cord Keepers*.
65 Salomon, *The Cord Keepers*.
66 Respectively, see Hyland, "Writing with Twisted Cords"; Salomon, "The Twisting Paths of Recall"; Salomon, *The Cord Keepers*; Hyland, "How Khipus Indicated Labour Contributions"; and Nelson D. Pimentel H., *Amarrando colores: la producción del sentido en quipus aymaras* (Oruro: CEPA, 2005).
67 Hyland, "Writing with Twisted Cords."
68 Hyland et al., "Khipus, Khipu Boards, and Sacred Texts"; and Hyland et al., "Knot Direction."
69 Sabine Hyland, Christine Lee, and Roberto Aldave Palacios, "*Khipus* to Keep Away the Living Dead: Andean Funerary Khipus Resurge during the COVID-19 Pandemic," *Anthropology News* 64 (October 22, 2021): n.p.
70 Carol Mackey, "The Continuing Khipu Tradition: Principles and Practices," in *Narrative Threads: Accounting and Recounting in Andean Khipu*, ed. Jeffrey Quilter and Gary Urton (Austin, TX: University of Texas Press, 2002), 321–347.
71 Hyland et al., "*Khipus* to Keep Away"; and Hyland, "Ply."
72 Brokaw, *A History of the Khipu*.
73 Visual Interactions in Early Writing Systems, The VIEWS Project, Faculty of Classics, University of Cambridge. https://viewsproject.wordpress.com/endangered-writing-network/.

5
RACIALISED LANGUAGE IN COLONIAL NEWSPAPER ADVERTISEMENTS DURING THE EIGHTEENTH AND NINETEENTH CENTURIES*

Natália da Silva Perez

Introduction

On both sides of the Atlantic, throughout the eighteenth and nineteenth centuries, newspapers abounded with advertisements mentioning enslaved people.[1] The content was varied. Some offered for hire the services of skilled enslaved workers and could include the price of the rent charged for their labour. There were advertisements reporting on auctions and sales of enslaved people, sometimes including the price and the conditions of purchase. There were others about enslaved people who had escaped, where enslavers offered rewards for the recapture of the person. Yet others reported on fugitives who had been recaptured and kept in local jails, serving to alert the enslavers that they could come and reclaim the enslaved person. Sometimes the advertisements conveyed detailed descriptions of the enslaved person as individuals. Other times they were written in language that objectified them as chattel. Interestingly, when descriptions focused on individuals, they could include many clues about the life, family, skills, ethnicity, geographical origin, and even desires of the people whose bodies were being offered for hire or for sale. Details were especially plentiful in the advertisements that reported on people—whether recaptured or at large—who sought their freedom by escaping. Due to this wealth of details, this chapter focuses on this latter type of advertisement.

In terms of information history, these advertisements are interesting because they conveyed ideas—from the perspective of the oppressor—about who the enslaved person was, how to recognise this person, or how to know their place in society. The advertisements helped newspaper readers—mostly "free" people, many who were members of the enslaver

---

* Research for this chapter was funded by a Sapere Aude grant from the Independent Research Fund Denmark under Grant ID 10.46540/2063-00035B, by the European Research Council (ERC) under the Horizon 2020 research and innovation programme grant agreement number ERC-2019-COG 863671, and by the University of Copenhagen under a Data Plus 2021 grant for the research project Privacy Black & White.

class—to form an opinion about the enslaved person who had escaped, and if necessary, to take action.[2] The advertisements were an attempt to minimise uncertainty about that fugitive individual amidst the chaos of colonial social. As short texts that sought to convey actionable information, the advertisements described people who escaped from enslavement, but whose descriptions were formulated from the perspective of the enslaver. As with any historical source, they are partial, potentially biased. Thus, this chapter considers advertisements about enslaved people as emphasising the entanglement between information and meaning.[3] In other words, the focus is on information as semantic, raising questions about whether signs of the body are natural, independent of human perceptions, and about how precisely these signs can be formed by language.

Regardless of whether the descriptions in the advertisements were individualising or objectifying, when we read them today, they seem derisive and overtly racist. Racialised language travelled across imperial and colonial borders from very early on, in both oral and written forms, influencing how enslaved Africans came to be portrayed in writing throughout history.[4] What information in these obsolete advertisements conveys racialising ideas? How did this information ultimately help to spread the socially constructed reality of racial difference in informationally connected colonial settings?

This chapter examines a selection of five advertisements in five different languages—Dutch, Danish, Portuguese, French, and English—from a trans-imperial perspective, using examples published between the eighteenth and nineteenth centuries from the newspapers *De Curaçaosche Courant*, *Sanct Thomæ Tidende*, *Jornal do Commercio*, *Gazette de la Guadeloupe*, and *The Quebec Gazette*.[5] The first criterion used to select these examples were the descriptions about the enslaved person being as detailed as possible. A second criterion was representing as many colonial languages beyond English as possible. The advertisements from *De Curaçaosche Courant*, *Sanct Thomæ Tidende*, *Jornal do Commercio*, and *Gazette de la Guadeloupe*—newspapers which have been digitised and made available online in open access—were found by manual search performed by myself and colleagues in the context of the research project *In the Same Sea*.[6] The advertisement from *The Quebec Gazette* came from the database *Marronage dans le Monde Atlantique*.[7] This chapter surveys information about enslaved people contained within these advertisements to investigate how the formulations used in public discourse about people of colour contributed to spreading and ingraining racist ideas across colonial and imperial societies. The chapter argues that this happened through interlinked colonial-metropolitan informational networks that helped to influence the spread of racialising—and ultimately racist—global discourses. Newspapers were one of the technologies that enabled connections between nodes of this network; by their use of language, they contributed to connecting historical processes of racialisation.

Thus, the goal is to showcase trans-imperial evidence—even if non-exhaustive—of discursive processes by which enslaved Africans came to be widely perceived as racialised, and European colonisers came to be perceived as racially neutral. Here, the trajectory of the word *negro* will serve as a representative—but not exhaustive—example for discussion. This analysis of advertisements from historical newspapers taken from different geographical locations and languages will help us understand the role that early print media played in the long, trans-imperial process of racialisation. Though this chapter focuses on discussing the word *negro*—and its equivalent in the languages discussed—it considers it alongside information represented along other axes, such as gender, ethno-racial identifiers, and socio-economic skills (such as professional knowledge and language skills), which the enslavers considered relevant. However, it is important to keep in mind that the experience of racial differentiation that Africans have endured since the early modern period cannot be fully explained by focusing on written language use alone; thus, future work focusing on historical primary sources from the African and Afro-diasporic perspectives needs to follow. Likewise, not all racialising experiences were the same; this study offers a window onto just a few examples. Nonetheless, studying racialising discourse from the perspective of the oppressor can serve as a useful gauge to examine the sociolinguistic dissemination of oppressive ideas about racial difference.[8] In other words, through the example of the use of the word *negro* in the selected advertisements, it is possible for us to understand how written information was operationalised by enslavers to wield power in colonial settings. Moreover, the legacy of this word, as well as its diverse reappropriations by members of the African diaspora in the Americas, allows us to glimpse at the struggles around racialising connotations that started during the Atlantic trade in enslaved people and continue to this day.

Describing Enslaved People

European colonisers of the new world were very concerned with categorising. Laurent Dubois and Richard Turits, in their discussion of early colonisation in the Caribbean islands, argue that the process of colonisation was "from the beginning, partly a struggle over categories and their meanings. European colonialism always combined colonialism in its rawest forms—of killing, enslavement, control—with the work of categorisation and description (...)."[9] Colonial legal systems, along with governance institutions, tended to be initiating vehicles for categorisation, the symbolic aspect of colonialism invoked by Dubois and Turits.[10]

The Danish West Indies provide a clear example of the role legal institutions played in imposing definitions onto signs produced by enslaved people during the eighteenth and nineteenth centuries. We can witness this in the book *Slaves Stories*, where Gunvor Simonsen engaged with testimonies given by enslaved people in the jurisdiction of Christiansted, St. Croix. Their statements were meticulously registered through the legal apparatus of the Danish West Indies and kept for posterity. For Simonsen, the 190 volumes of colonial judicial records that survive today in Denmark's *Rigsarkiv* are evidence of "the important role that slaves' words played in the Danish Atlantic legal institutions during the eighteenth and nineteenth centuries." But as she emphasises, the words of enslaved people themselves only acquired meaning "through the ingenious interpretations of schooled jurists."[11]

In Brazil, the situation was similar. Aldair Rodrigues shows that, amidst the gold and diamond rush of eighteenth-century Brazil, the bureaucratic and legal apparatuses in service of the colonial government shaped the meaning of information that came from enslaved people, imposing interpretations onto signs that might originally have meant something completely different. Consider the category of "nation," for example. Rodrigues argues that, though this word might have intended to document a straight-forward piece of information about an enslaved person who worked in the Brazilian mines, the word "nation" was a far cry from providing clarity about the person. The word "nation," referring to something about the origin of enslaved Africans, went through a complex process of polysemic transformation in the Brazilian official archives, something that eventually also spilled over into language used in newspapers advertisements. Rodrigues explains that:

> nation could designate toponyms in macro areas of the slave trade, slave shipping ports, kingdoms and empires, micro-political affiliations, linguistic classifications at various levels, ethnonyms closer to specific ethnic identities, and even self-ascription.[12]

Categorisation of enslaved colonial subjects was also a concern in Europe. In the Dutch Republic, similar processes of semantic shift also took place in efforts at categorising African people. Dienke Hondius, reporting on research about the presence of Africans in the Dutch Republic and in Amsterdam during the seventeenth century, notes that the word for slave was avoided in legal writing, probably due to the explicit legal prohibition against slavery present in several cities of the Dutch Republic. According to Hondius, "Black Africans are called *swart* or *neger* (both meaning black), or *moor* in Dutch sources."[13] Their legal status as enslaved or free often remained unclear or ambiguous. Additional evidence comes from the work of Lydia Hagoort, who also reports that the word for slave was omitted from the Sephardic Jewish cemetery's records after the second half of the seventeenth century.[14]

Nonetheless, Marc Ponte traced the presence of a thriving community of people of African descent in seventeenth-century Amsterdam. Many of these "Afro-Atlantic" Amsterdamers were free, working, marrying among the members of the community, and baptising their friends' children.[15] It is notable that, according to Ponte, marriage banns that attested to their presence were "the only source in which the origin of suitors is consistently recorded."[16] These documents are among the rare historical sources where geographical information about people of African origin came closer to being self-ascribed.

The depictions of enslaved people in the newspaper advertisements that are discussed below also reflect efforts of categorisation. Newspapers seem to have been part of a network of information vehicles that contributed performatively to disseminating categories originating in colonial legal discourse. The nature of information in newspaper advertisements varied; by reading them we can sometimes detect that this variation had something to do with the aim of the individual advertisement. An advertisement announcing an auction would often include only general information about the people being sold, while one presenting an enslaved person for hire might mention specific skills. But it is the advertisements about people who escaped captivity that tend to include the most detailed descriptions of individuals. These advertisements demonstrate how enslavers operationalised language to propel their efforts of subjugation in the face of resistance from enslaved people.

Advertisements in Different Languages

The advertisements selected are analysed and discussed below in chronological order of their publication.

The Quebec Gazette/La Gazette de Quebec, Published March 8, 1787

At the time of publication of this advertisement, *The Quebec Gazette* was a bilingual newspaper printed by Brown & Gilmore. It was published between 1764 and 1874. English language texts appeared on the left-hand column and French language texts appeared on the right-hand column.[17] This advertisement, however, only appears on the left side in English.

Racialised Language in Colonial Newspaper Advertisements

It reports on a woman named Bett who ran away in Quebec. The advertisement includes her age (eighteen years old), the clothes she was wearing, the fact that she was pregnant, and the three languages she spoke fluently: English, French, and German:

Quebec, 6th March, 1787.

RAN-AWAY From the Subscribers, between the hours of seven and eight o'clock yesterday evening, a NEGRO WENCH named BETT, about eighteen years old, middle stature, speaks the English, French and German languages well; had on when she went away, a blue Kersey Jacket and Pettycoat, a dark cotton Cap with yellow strings, and an Indian Shawl round her neck, was big with child, and within a few days of her time. Whoever will apprehend said Negress, and secure her return, shall be paid A REWARD of TWENTY DOLLARS, and all reasonable expences [sic]. Any person who may harbour or conceal the said Negress, will be prosecuted to the rigour of the law, by JOHNSTON & PURSS.

Advertisements that report on women running away from their enslavers tend to appear less frequently than those reporting on men.[18] In the advertisements that do report on women, however, it is relatively common for them to mention that the woman brought children with her, or as in the case of Bett, that she was pregnant. The information about Bett's age, her stature, and her clothes could be helpful in identifying Bett physically. The advertisement emphasises that Bett was very close to her due date, which would also make it easier to identify her.

The people reporting on Bett's escape offered a reward of twenty dollars, sizable at the time, for her recapture, indicating that she was valuable for those who owned her. The advertisement ends with a threat of legal persecution for anyone "who may harbour or conceal the said Negress."[19] Though such offers of reward and threats of persecution were common formulations in advertisements about fugitive enslaved people, they were not always both present in the same advertisement. The person who placed the advertisement would mix and match the formulations according to their needs. In this case, the presence of a reward coupled with the threat suggests the urgency of finding Bett for her enslaver, possibly because she was pregnant and close to delivering the child. The repeated use of the feminine inflected word "negress" suggests the importance of Bett being gendered as a woman, pregnant with a potentially enslavable child. In combination with information about her language skills, Bett is presented as a valuable slave.

Gazette de la Guadeloupe, Published May 29, 1788

Published in French at "l'Imprimerie de la Ve. Bénard, Imprimeur du Roi," the advertisement below, though also reporting on an enslaved person who escaped, is different from the one from *The Quebec Gazette*.[20] In the extant issues of *Gazette de la Guadaloupe*, the most common type of advertisements found reporting on enslaved people are those where a representative of the local government or of the police alerts the readers of fugitives who were caught and detained in the local jail:

Il est détenu à la Géole de la Basse-Terre, un negre nouveau, dont on ne peut connoître la nation, taille de 5 pieds 4 pouces, jolie figure, l'air riant, les yeux cavés, sourcils peu garnis, bouche moyenne, grosses levres, belles dents, ayant des marques de son pays en grin de Chapelet, qui lui descendent du front, lui partage le nez, ainsi que le menton, en ayant aussi qui lui descendent des sourcils, & s'étendent en forme de Croix jusqu'à ses oreilles, la poitrine serrée, & deux marques en lignes qui vont d'un sein à l'autre, en ayant aussi qui montent des deux poignets jusqu'à la jointure du coude, âgé d'environ 20 ans.

[Detained at the Basse-Terre jail, a newcomer negro whose nation we cannot determine, height of 5 feet 4 inches, good appearance, smiling demeanour, sunken eyes, sparse eyebrows, medium-sized mouth, big lips, beautiful teeth, having marks of his country in the shape of beads of a rosary which descend from his forehead, through his nose as well as his chin, also some that descend from his eyebrows, and extend in the form of a cross up to his ears, tight chest and two lines which go from one breast to the other, also some that go up from the two wrists to the elbow, approximately 20 years old.][21]

The advertisement describes a man without mentioning his name. The fact that he is referred to as "un negre nouveau" suggests that he had recently arrived in Guadeloupe from his unknown African place of origin. Interestingly, the advertisement explains that his nation cannot be determined. The lack of description of his clothing shows how language could be used to categorise the man with a description heavily focused on his bodily and physical characteristics. This raises the question of how such categorisation affects those being categorised, as racialised physical descriptions continued to permeate society into the nineteenth and twentieth centuries.[22]

The frequency of advertisements in *Gazette de la Guadeloupe* indicates that local newspapers were valuable sources for enslavers whose slaves had recently run away in Guadeloupe. An advertisement like this one which contained detailed physical descriptions was an attempt to provide enough basis to allow the fugitive person to be recognised. The advertisement does not mention any deadline for the enslaver to reclaim this detained man, suggesting that he could remain in prison for an indeterminate amount of time until someone came to claim him.

Sanct Thomæ Tidende, Published May 29, 1815

This advertisement about a man named William does not contain a great deal of detail. Danish and English versions with the same information appeared in sequence, in the same region of the page. Unlike the previous advertisement, there is very little information enabling a reader to physically recognise William:

EN Neger navnlig William, tilhörende Hr. Dix paa Tortola, er som Maroon optagen og arresteret i Stedets Fort, og Baaden, hvori han hertil ankom ligger i Politiekammerets Plads. Dersom besagde Neger og Baad ikke reklameres inden 6 Uger fra Dato, vil de blive solgte pa offentlig Auction. Sc. Thomae Politiekammer, den 26de Maii 1816. PORTH.

A NEGRO by name William belonging to Mr. Dix of Tortola, has been apprehended as a Maroon and arrested in the local Fort and the boat wherein he was detected is laying in the yard of the Police Station. If the said Negro and Boat are not claimed within 6 weeks from this date, they will be sold at public Auction. St. Thomas Police Station, 26th May 1815. PORTH.

The text contains William's name and the name of his alleged enslaver, Mr. Dix, who is said to be from the island of Tortola. It states that William was caught in a boat and reports that both William and the boat were being kept in the police office. For an experienced canoe rider, the distance of about 25 km from Tortola to St. Thomas would have been manageable by canoe, given that the path would skirt the island of St. John, providing some shelter.[23] The main goal of the advertisement was, ostensibly, to alert any person who might want to reclaim William as their property to act swiftly, otherwise he and the boat would be sold at a public auction. The advertisement is dated and signed "St. Thomas Police Station." It is questionable whether this information would reach a potential claimant in another island in time to claim William as property. Nonetheless, by making William's arrest public information, the police authority could prevent any accusation of illegally harbouring a fugitive enslaved person. As a historical source, the advertisement points to the inter-island movement across imperial borders in Caribbean colonies, providing corroborating evidence of knowledge among enslaved people about maritime routes used for escaping.[24]

De Curaçaosche Courant, Published October 18, 1834

The advertisement below is bilingual, appearing in English and Dutch on the top left side of an inside page:

RUN AWAY from Mayaguez, Porto Rico, a Negro Woman, (Slave) named CHARLOTTE, of a tall slender figure, about forty years of age, speaks Curaçao, Creole French, and broken Spanish, understands housework, is a native of Curaçao, and it is said now calls herself CATHARINE; her being a native of this Islands, causes suspicion she may be here. Any person giving sufficient information to cause her apprehension, will be rewarded by O. M. DACOSTA. October 17, 1834.

WEGGELOOPEN. Van Mayaguez, Porto Rico, eene Negerin (Slavin) met name CHARLOTTE. Zy is omtrent 40 jaren oud en van eene hooge en ranke gestalte, zy spreekt de Curaçaosche taal, Creool Fransch en gebroken Spaansch, zy verstaat huiswerk en is eene inboorling van Curaçao; thans zegt men, noemt zy zich CATHARINA; en daar zy hier geboren is, ontstaat het vermoeden, dat zy zich hier bevindt; zoo wordt hierby eene belooning aan den gene, die genoegzaam narigt ter harer opvatting kan geven, uitgeloofd door O. M. DACOSTA. Den 17 October 1834.

This advertisement also demonstrates inter-island movement of enslaved people seeking freedom. It reports on a woman named either Charlotte or Catharine, who is said to have escaped from her enslaver in Porto Rico, but whose enslaver suspected that she went to Curaçao, which explains the advertisement in *De Curaçaosche Courant*.[25] This advertisement also included details about her characteristics: she spoke two Caribbean languages fluently, Curaçao (perhaps meaning Papiamentu) and Creole French, as well as some level of Spanish, and had some knowledge of housework. These skills would potentially indicate why she was considered valuable enough to be searched in another island.

Jornal do Commercio, Published in the First Issue of 1870

Published in Rio de Janeiro, Brazil, in Portuguese this last advertisement reports on the escape of José. He is described as "de nação" [of nation], perhaps meaning that he was born somewhere in Africa as opposed to in Brazil. José is said to be fifty years old:

ATTENÇAO

Acha-se fugido desde 9 de Dezembro do anno passado o escravo José, de nação, de 50 annos de idade, pouco mais ou menos, tendo sido escravo do Sr. João Vieira Rangel, suppõe-se que se intitula forro, e desconfia-se que anda pelos lados do Rio Secco ou Barra Mansa, onde tem alguns filhos; quem o apprehender ou der notícias certas a seu senhor o capitão João da Silveira Dutra, em Retiro de Maricá, será gratificado.

[ATTENTION Runaway since the 9th of December of last year, the slave José, of nation, 50 years old more or less, having been the slave of Mr. João Vieira Rangel, it is assumed that he calls himself freed, and it is suspected that he is around the vicinities of Rio Secco or Barra Mansa, where he has some children; whoever captures him or gives accurate news to his master, Captain João da Silveira Dutra, in Retiro de Maricá, will be rewarded.]

Unlike some of the other advertisements above, this one does not provide any clues about José's appearance or his skills. It names José's former enslaver, João Vieira Rangel, and the person who claims to be his new enslaver, João da Silveira Dutra. The advertisement also indicates that José is suspected to be claiming the title of *forro* [freed].[26] No threat of persecution was made to anyone giving shelter to José, instead, a reward was offered for either capturing him, or even for simply providing information that could lead to his recapture. The most interesting part is that José had children in the region of Rio Secco or Barra Mansa, who could have given him refuge when he escaped. This advertisement presents a different type of information from those above where enslaved people were characterised by their physical appearance.

What all these advertisements have in common is the way in which their language carried information with a socio-political or cultural loading that differentiated the people described based on social hierarchy. Through iteration over time, this language helped inculcate, even normalise, the idea that enslaved Africans were inferior. Because of the visible difference in skin colour between enslaved Africans and their European enslavers, this visibility came to be associated with different placements in the social hierarchy of the colonies. This sociolinguistic process of racialisation is particularly evident in the trajectory of the word "negro."

Racialisation as a Sociolinguistic Process

Historians Linda Heywood and John Thornton explain that, in the early stages of incursions in Central Africa during the fifteenth century, Portuguese invaders started to use the word *negro* as an ethnic marker to refer to the inhabitants of that region.[27] By the seventeenth century, this word, which originally referred to the colour black, had already started to go through a semantic shift acquiring also a connotation of *slave* or *enslaved servant*.[28]

Heywood and Thornton highlight that, in the Portuguese language used for trade in the colonial encounters in West Central Africa:

> The meaning of *negro* and slave also became linked in the minds of Africans, for by the middle of the seventeenth century, Kongolese were insulted to be referred to as *negros*, a term only used for slaves, insisting that foreigners, when referring to skin color, use the alternate Portuguese term for black, *pretos*.[29]

The fact that Kongolese people were insulted by being referred to as *negros* indicates that sometime during the period of Portuguese colonial incursions, this word started to carry information beyond just skin colour and to include also the connotation of a marker of forced servitude. From the seventeenth century onwards, as this use spread to other languages of the Northern and Western European empires involved in the Atlantic trade in enslaved people, the conflation of meanings between *negro* and slave also spread and became gradually ingrained.[30]

Indeed, most of the advertisements discussed above—printed in the eighteenth and nineteenth centuries—referred to the enslaved person by the language specific term for *negro*. In Quebec, Bett was referred to as *negro wench*; in Guadeloupe, the unnamed man was referred to as *negre nouveau*; in Saint Thomas, William was referred to as *neger* in Danish and as *negro* in English; and in Curaçao, Charlotte/Catharine was referred to in English as *negro woman* and *slave*, and in Dutch as *negerin* and *slavin*. Only José, in Rio de Janeiro, was referred to just as *escravo*, without any mention of his skin colour. In fact, the word for slave appears only in two of the above advertisements, the one in *Jornal do Commercio* and in the one in *De Curaçaosche Courant*. In the adverts that use a language's equivalent of *negro*, this word carries information that the person in question was both enslaved and had a dark skin colour. In other words, in the way this word was used in the advertisements, the word *negro* connotes the socioeconomic legal status together with the appearance of the person, conflating both types of information about the person being described.

This historical sociolinguistic conflation of two meanings in one word—*negro* meaning dark skin colour and forced servitude—is a representative example of how linguistic formulations contributed to the historical development of global racist discourses. At every iteration formulated from the perspective of enslavers, this employment of *negro* (and its derivatives in other languages) contributed to ingraining and naturalising the idea that people with darker skin colour were servants, and enslaved ones at that. Echoes of this sociolinguistic process of conflation can still be seen today, as people of African descent with darker skin colour are often met with negative assumptions or presumed to occupy positions of subservience rather than higher positions in society.[31]

In Brazilian Portuguese, since the 1970s, through the work of civil rights organisations, the words *negro/negra*, in their ethnic sense, have gone through a process of positive resignification.[32] According to philosopher Djamila Ribeiro, the act of using the words *negro/negra* to mark one's own belonging serves to remember and resist the colonial violence of slavery as well as the country's subsequent eugenicist policies that tried to render invisible the African roots of the Brazilian population.[33] Moreover, it also serves to remember the social and economic contribution from the enslaved workers that helped to develop the country throughout its history. In Brazil, the shade of a person's skin colour can connote the level of belonging to a racialised social group, also indicating socioeconomic position.[34] This colourism, which has permeated the country's history, jeopardises social and economic opportunities for people of African descent. In this context, the words *preto/preta* have more recently also been reclaimed as an ethnic marker of belonging by Brazilians of darker skin tone. The political information implied in self-ascribing the ethnic marker *preto/preta* in Brazil is to bring attention, explicitly and proudly, to one's dark skin as something desirable.[35]

In French, African and Antillean anticolonial activists of the early twentieth century have also reclaimed the word *nègre* in a similar way as described above by Djamila Ribeiro. Within the intellectual movement *Négritude*, the term *nègre* was reclaimed with emphasis on its political connotation of remembering slavery as a crime and of standing against colonial violence.[36] Martinican author and politician Aimé Césaire employed the word with this goal throughout his acclaimed *Discours sur le colonialisme*.[37] However, French language dictionaries *Le Robert* and *Larousse* both recommend using the word *noire* to refer to people of dark skin colour in French.[38] Unlike the case of Brazilian Portuguese, the political reclamation of the term *nègre* in French has been reserved for contexts of anticolonial or antiracist activism when used by Black people, and has not spread to other linguistic registers.[39] If used outside of acceptable registers, the word *nègre* in French has a racist connotation.

In Dutch, the word *neger* has been reclaimed, for example, by youth of Suriname descent in Rotterdam. In interviews conducted in 2004, young men who self-identify as Surinamese are reported as using the term *neger* to refer to themselves and to those they consider as belonging to the same social group, in a process the researchers call "selfing."[40] The information contained in the word *neger*, used in these contexts, indicates belonging considered authentic. In addition, derivations of the word—such as *nepneger* [noun: fake *neger*] or *vernegerd* [verb: to turn *neger*]—serve as a means of "othering," that is, to mark other identities in opposition to one's own, as in the example below:

Martin: sommigen willen vernegerd doen.
Fieldworker: hoe doe je dan vernegerd?
Martin: ik weet niet hoe ze doen je ziet het dan ook hoe ze zich kleden. Ik weet niet, gewoon nepneger zo.[41]
Martin: some want to act vernegerd [neger-ized].
Fieldworker: what does it mean to act vernegerd?
Martin: I don't know how they act, you can tell also by the way they dress. I don't know, just "nepneger" [fake neger].

What is worth highlighting here is that reclaiming racialised terms is not the prerogative only of activists and intellectuals engaged in antiracism. Young people in Rotterdam whose migration background is in former Dutch colonies reappropriate the term in their day-to-day language as a form of identifying their own ethnic belonging, attaching new information to a term that was once considered racist.

In Danish, it is very difficult to find any evidence of reclaiming of the Danish word *neger* on the part of Afro-Danes. From the perspective of Danish people of African descent who participated in a study by the *Institut for Menneskerettigheder* [Institute for Human Rights], the word *neger* is pejorative and a racial slur. Adham (pseudonym) reports on an incident from when he was a child in school:

Jeg kan huske helt tilbage i 0. klasse, hvor jeg blev kaldt neger, og jeg græd, og så var der en eller anden, det kunne sagtens været en pædagogmedhjælper, der sagde: "Nej men altså, du skal bare sige til ham: "Ja det er jeg, og hvad er der galt med det."[42]

[I remember way back in preschool, when I was called *neger* and I cried, and then someone, it could easily have been a teaching assistant, said: "No, but then, you just have to tell him: "Yes, I am, and what is wrong with that."]

Adham's example demonstrates that the teaching assistant who tried to sooth him did not fully understand how hurt he felt as a boy being referred to by the word *neger*. The word conveyed a different informational meaning for each of them. The problem, in other words, was not the boy's relationship with his own skin colour, as the teaching assistant presumed. It was the fact that the boy was called by a word he perceived as a racial slur. Indeed, we have evidence that some members of the white Danish majority still believe that the word *neger* can be used in a neutral sense. Though it has been falling out of use, as recently as 1995, Copenhagen Director of Police, Poul Eefsen, defended the use of the word to refer to a person of African origin. He argued that if the word *neger* was offensive, a recognised and official Danish term should replace it. Otherwise, Eefsen argued, people with an African background would also have to recognise that a Black or dark Brown person in Danish—in contrast to, for example, in American English—could be referred to as *neger*.[43]

More recently, in 2016, right-wing politician Søren Espersen referred to President Barack Obama as "første neger i USA's præsidentembede" [first *neger* in the US presidency]. Espersen also employed the word *neger* when defending against criticism to a publicity campaign by his party Dansk Folkeparti. In the publicity campaign in question, a white family was portrayed with the slogan "Vores Danmark – der er så meget vi skal passe på" [Our Denmark, there is so much we must care for]. Responding to complaints on the lack of diversity portrayed in the picture, Espersen claimed to be colour-blind and thus indifferent to the colour of the people portrayed[44]:

Sådan tænker vi ikke. Vi kunne da sagtens have sat en neger ind, og hvad så? Hvad havde det ændret på noget som helst?[45]

[We don't think like that. We could easily have put in a *neger*, and so what? What would it have changed at all?]

Like Copenhagen police director Poul Eefsen, many users of Danish who insist on the neutrality of the Danish word *neger* perceive its pejorative sense to be an import from American English.

Indeed, for people of African descent in the United States, the act of renaming themselves has historically been part of their struggles to improve their social position and to resignify their cultural belonging. In a country where people of African descent were also historically oppressed through slavery and segregation—much like the Brazilian, Martinican, and Surinamese cases mentioned above—language has been a site of political struggle for Black people who want to claim a just place for themselves in society.

In American English, the term *African-American* started to gain traction in the late 1980s in an effort to move the focus away from skin colour and towards ethnocultural heritage. According to Geneva Smitherman, using the term *African-American* "constructs an identity of unified global struggle against race domination, linking Africans in North America with Continental Africans and with other Diasporic African groups."[46] During the 1960s, users of American English had adopted *Black* as their preferred term to convey information about their political striving for belonging. The words *Coloured* and *Negro*, which today sound archaic and pejorative, were once the terms of self-ascription used by people of colour in the United States.[47]

In all languages represented in the advertisements discussed above—English, French, Danish, Dutch and Portuguese—people of African descent can also be referred to by terms for the colour black. In English, there is *Black*; in French, *noir/noire*; in Danish, *sort/sorte*; in Dutch, *zwart/zwarte*; in Portuguese, *preto/preta*. These terms have local connotations that can convey information ranging from positive, to neutral, to negative. In addition, as an attempt to indicate the African roots of a person while eschewing racist connotations, the practice of appending the prefixes *Afro* or *African-* to a demonym—as in the case of African-American—giving less emphasis to a person's skin colour, has also gained traction in languages with a colonial past of involvement with the Atlantic trade in enslaved people.

Conclusion

The long historical process of racialisation of Africans—since the establishment of the Atlantic trade in enslaved people and of colonialism in the new world—was in great part sociolinguistic. Colonisers and enslavers controlled the means of communication and of the spread of information much like they controlled the means of production and of subjugation of enslaved workers. Early mass-produced newspapers are among the means of communication that helped, if not to create racialisation, then to spread and ingrain it in societies that were dominated by European imperialism. Importantly, this process did not happen in each national empire in isolation. Colonial empires exchanged information with each other through early mass print media, and this information was produced and circulated across colonial and imperial borders.

As we have seen above with the trans-imperial examples of the newspaper advertisements from the eighteenth and nineteenth century reporting on enslaved people who escaped captivity, enslavers deployed linguistic formulations to assert their power over the human beings that they sought to control. The example of the word *negro*, as an indicator of socioeconomic legal status coupled with skin colour, is representative of these dynamics. For Alim and Smitherman, "repeated use of particular words by particular people in particular contexts over time is how words come to take on socially charged meanings."[48] Indeed, this is the process by which information conveyed by a given word can change over time. The word *negro* acquired its conflated meaning as it was iterated and as it travelled across languages over the course of four centuries in the context of the colonial exploitation of slavery. Nonetheless, as Cornips and De Rooij remind us:

> Taking a dynamic perspective on word meaning should not blind us to the fact that certain words evoke strong feelings and emotions regardless of the contexts in which they are used … the language user is always in some sense a prisoner of past usage. And yet, he is also free to use words in unexpected, unconventional ways.[49]

Despite resignification, the informational past of a word also stays with it. We can see this with the word *negro*, which is now a site of political articulation, albeit with localised connotations ranging from positive to negative in the different places of the world where it has reached. In some cases, it is experienced as a racial slur by Afro-descendants who feel that they cannot have much influence on the majority's discourse. In other cases, it has been reclaimed by people of colour who identify as descendants of those who were enslaved as an icon of recognition of their plight.

Notes

1 Tamara Extian-Babiuk, *"To Be Sold, a Negro Wench." Slave Ads of the Montreal Gazette, 1785–1805* (Ottawa: Library and Archives Canada: Bibliothèque et Archives Canada, 2007); Jean-Pierre Le Glaunec and Léon Robichaud, "Le Marronnage Dans Le Monde Atlantique, 1760–1848," http://www.marronnage.info/fr/corpus.php. Renato P. Colistete, "Predicting Skills of Runaway Slaves in São Paulo, 1854–1887" (Department of Economics-FEA/USP: Working Paper Series no. 2021-15), 27; and Simon Newman, *Freedom Seekers: Escaping from Slavery in Restoration London* (London: University of London, 2022).

2 Jordan E. Taylor, "Enquire of the Printer: Newspaper Advertising and the Moral Economy of the North American Slave Trade, 1704–1807," *Early American Studies: An Interdisciplinary Journal* 18, no. 3 (2020): 291–292.

3 Fred I. Dretske argues that we ought to make a distinction between information and meaning: "Once this distinction is clearly understood, one is free to think about information (though not meaning) as an objective commodity, something whose generation, transmission, and reception do not require or in any way presuppose interpretive processes." When dealing with information about human beings entangled in uneven power relations—as in the case of enslaved people and their enslavers—Dretske's emphasis on the distinction between information and meaning helps to erase the skewed nature of information generated from the point of view of those more powerful. In other words, this chapter argues that information about enslaved people produced by enslavers does, indeed, "presuppose interpretive processes." Fred I. Dretske, *Knowledge & the Flow of Information* (Cambridge, MA: MIT Press, 1981).

4 Carmen Espejo, "European Communication Networks in the Early Modern Age," *Media History* 17, no. 2 (May 1, 2011): 189–202; Michiel van Groesen and Helmer Helmers, "Managing the News in Early Modern Europe, 1550–1800," *Media History* 22, nos. 3–4 (October 1, 2016): 261–266.

5 For the databases used see *De Curaçaosche Courant*, 1816 (Delpher, KB Nationale Bibliotheek) https://www.delpher.nl/nl/kranten/results?coll=dddtitel&facets%5BtitleString%5D%5B%5D=De+Curac%CC%A7aosche+courant&sortfield=date; *Sanct Thomæ Tidende*, May 29, 1815 (Mediestream, Det Kgl. Bibliotek), http://hdl.handle.net/109.3.1/uuid:44ec975c-f228-4cfe-a35a-3533068ec773; *Jornal Do Commercio*, 1827 (Hemeroteca Digital, Fundação Biblioteca Nacional), http://memoria.bn.br/DocReader/docmulti.aspx?bib=364568; *Gazette de La Guadeloupe*, May 28, 1788, (Gallica, Bibliothèque Nationale de France), https://gallica.bnf.fr/ark:/12148/bpt6k895969f; The *Quebec Gazette/La Gazette de Québec*, March 8, 1787, Bibliothèque National du Québec, https://collections.banq.qc.ca/ark:/52327/4267091.

6 Gunvor Simonsen, "In the Same Sea," University of Copenhagen, https://inthesamesea.ku.dk/.

7 Le Glaunec and Robichaud, "Le Marronnage," see note 1.

8 H. Samy Alim, "Introducing Raciolinguistics: Racing Language and Languaging Race in Hyperracial Times," in *Raciolinguistics,* ed. H. Samy Alim, John R. Rickford, and Arnetha F. Ball (New York: Oxford University Press, 2016), 1–30.

9 Laurent Dubois and Richard Lee Turits, *Freedom Roots: Histories from the Caribbean* (Chapel Hill, NC: University of North Carolina Press, 2019), 53–92.

10 For an example of the impetus to categorise taken to its extreme, see the discussion of Apartheid by Geoffrey C. Bowker and Susan Leigh Star in the chapter "The Case of Race Classification and Reclassification under Apartheid," *Sorting Things Out: Classification and Its Consequences*, Inside Technology, Geoffrey C. Bowker and Susan Leigh Star (Cambridge, MA: MIT Press, 1999), 195–225.

11 Gunvor Simonsen, *Slave Stories: Law, Representation, and Gender in the Danish West Indies* (Aarhus: Aarhus University Press, 2017), 13.

12 Aldair Rodrigues, "African Body Marks, Stereotypes and Racialisation in Eighteenth-Century Brazil," *Slavery & Abolition* 42, no. 2 (April 3, 2021), 317.

13 Dienke Hondius, "Black Africans in Seventeenth-Century Amsterdam," *Renaissance & Reformation/Renaissance et Reforme* 31, no. 2 (Spring 2008), 89.

14 Lydia Hagoort, *Het Beth Haim in Ouderkerk aan de Amstel: de begraafplaats van de Portugese Joden in Amsterdam 1614–1945* (Hilversum: Verloren, 2005).

15 "AfroAtlantisch, omdat zij afkomstig waren uit de hele 'Atlantic', van het vaste land in Afrika, zoals Angola en Congo, van eilanden als Sint Jago (Cabo Verde) en Sao Tomé, uit Brazilië en het Caribisch gebied." Mark Ponte, "'Al de Swarten Die Hier Ter Stede Comen'. Een Afro-Atlantische Gemeenschap in Zeventiende-Eeuws Amsterdam," *TSEG/ Low Countries Journal of Social and Economic History* 15, no. 4 (March 2019), 38.
16 Ponte, "Al de Swarten," 40.
17 *The Quebec Gazette/La Gazette de Québec*. See note 6.
18 Newman reports of a striking gender disparity in advertisements published in London between 1655 and 1704. Only 6 per cent were about women, but 94% about men, Newman, *Freedom Seekers*. Provisional results from the projects *In the Same Sea*, led by Gunvor Simonsen, and *Privacy Black and White*, at the University of Copenhagen, also indicate a gender disparity in the Caribbean region. These findings are supported by advertisements from the corpus within the database *Marronage dans le Monde Atlantique*. See note 1.
19 All quotations are taken directly from the advertisements being discussed, unless stated otherwise.
20 On "l'Imprimerie de la Ve. Bénard, Imprimeur du Roi," see Anne Pérotin-Dumon, *La Ville Aux Iles, La Ville Dans l'île: Basse-Terre et Pointe-à-Pitre, Guadeloupe, 1650–1820* (Paris: Karthala, 2000), 609–620.
21 Translation by Natália da Silva Perez.
22 Michael Omi and Howard Winant, *Racial Formation in the United States: From the 1960s to 1990s* (New York: Routledge, 1994).
23 For a thorough discussion of the use of small boats in escaping from slavery, see Gunvor Simonsen and Rasmus Christensen, "Together in a Small Boat: Slavery's Fugitives in the Lesser Antilles," *The William and Mary Quarterly* 80, no. 4 (2023): 611–646; See also Neville A. T. Hall, "Maritime Maroons: 'Grand Marronage' from the Danish West Indies," *The William and Mary Quarterly* 42, no. 4 (1985): 482.
24 Simonsen and Christensen, "Together in a Small Boat."
25 Though Charlotte/Catharina is described as a "negro woman" and "negerin," she might have also had partly indigenous background. For further discussion, see Anjali DasSarma and Linford D. Fisher, "The Persistence of Indigenous Unfreedom in Early American Newspaper Advertisements, 1704–1804," *Slavery & Abolition* 44, no. 2 (April 3, 2023): 267–291.
26 This change of ownership might have been contentious from José's perspective if, for example, his former enslaver had promised to free José, but instead sold him. Escaping could have been a form of resistance to an undesired sale.
27 Heywood and Thornton, *Central Africans, Atlantic Creoles, and the Foundation of the Americas, 1585–1660* (New York: Cambridge University Press, 2007), 317.
28 Linda M. Heywood and John K. Thornton, *Central Africans*, 294–332; James H. Sweet, "The Iberian Roots of American Racist Thought," *The William and Mary Quarterly* 54, no. 1 (1997): 143–166.
29 Heywood and Thornton, *Central Africans*, 318.
30 "Censo Demografico, 2022," Instituto Brasileiro de Geografia e Estatística, https://www.ibge.gov.br/estatisticas/sociais/populacao/22827-censo-demografico-2022.html?t=conceitos-e-metodos.
31 Consider the example of Lakisha (pseudonym), an Afro-Danish woman who grew up in Denmark, who reported that she was met with negative expectations during her school years where a teacher was highly surprised that she did well in school: "… Og en lærer, der var sådan 'Okay, det havde jeg ikke regnet med fra dig.'" [… And a teacher who said 'Okay, I didn't expect that from you'] "Afro-Danskeres Oplevelse Af Diskrimination i Danmark," Institut for Menneskerettigheder, 19, https://menneskeret.dk/files/media/dokumenter/udgivelser/afrodanskere_web.pdf. See also H. Samy Alim and Geneva Smitherman, "Raciolinguistic Exceptionalism: How Racialized 'Compliments' Reproduce White Supremacy," in *The Oxford Handbook of Language and Race*, ed. H. Samy Alim, Angela Reyes, and Paul V. Kroskrity (Oxford University Press, 2020), 472–496.
32 Gevanilda Santos and José Adão de Oliveira, *Movimento Negro Unificado: A Resistência nas Ruas* (SESC, 2020); Verena Alberti and Amilcar Araujo Pereira, *Histórias do Movimento Negro no Brasil: Depoimentos ao CPDOC* (Pallas Editora, 2016).
33 *Termo Negro Foi Ressignificado No Brasil, Explica Djamila Ribeiro*, 2020, https://www.youtube.com/watch?v=dfzwtPFEbDQ; Djamila Ribeiro, *Quem tem Medo do Feminismo Negro?* (Editora Companhia das Letras, 2018); Alberti and Pereira, *Histórias*.
34 The Instituto Brasileiro de Geografia e Estatística (IBGE) [Brazilian Institute of Geography and Statistics], which is responsible for the national census, collects ethno-racial information on the

population by referring to colour and race at the same time. In the 2022 census, we see the question 'Qual a sua cor ou raça?' [What is your color or race?]. The options for answers are branca [white], preta [black], amarela [yellow], parda [a contested word meaning afro-descendants of lighter skin tone], and indígena [indigenous]. See "Censo Demografico," 2022.

35 A discussion of the terms *pardo/parda* and *mulato/mulata* is relevant for understanding how colourism manifests in Brazil, but is beyond the scope of this chapter. For discussions of these terms (including their reclaiming or abandonment), see Eliane Silvia Costa and Lia Vainer Schucman, "Identidades, Identificações e Classificações Raciais no Brasil: O Pardo e as Ações Afirmativas," *Estudos e Pesquisas em Psicologia* 22, no. 2 (June 2022): 466–484; Aloysio de França, Leonardo Gomes Ribeiro, and Marcela Ignácio, "Sobre a Invenção da Mulata: A importância da Reflexão Teórica Sobre a Análise Histórica," no. 15 (2021); Márcia Regina de Souza and Joelma Aparecida Bressanin, "Quem é Pardo no Brasil? Uma Análise dos Sentidos de Pardo nos Modos de Definir cor ou Raça," *Revista de Estudos Acadêmicos de Letras* 12, no. 2 (October 2019): 75–88; Lauro Felipe Eusébio Gomes, "Ser Pardo: O Limbo Identitário-Racial Brasileiro e a Reivindicação da Identidade," *Cadernos de Gênero e Diversidade* 5, no. 1 (May 2019): 66–78; Djamila Ribeiro, "A Mulata Globeleza: Um Manifesto," in *Quem tem Medo do Feminismo Negro?* (Editora Companhia das Letras, 2018); and Angela Gilliam and Onik'a Gilliam, "Negociando a Subjetividade de Mulata no Brasil," *Estudos Feministas* 3, no. 2 (1995): 525.

36 Brian J. Reilly, "Negritude's Contretemps: The Coining and Reception of Aime Cesaire's Neologism," *Philological Quarterly* 99, no. 4 (September 2020): 377–399; Reiland Rabaka, *The Negritude Movement: W.E.B. Du Bois, Leon Damas, Aime Cesaire, Leopold Senghor, Frantz Fanon, and the Evolution of an Insurgent Idea*, Critical Africana Studies (Lanham, MD: Lexington Books, 2015).

37 Aimé Césaire, *Discours sur le Colonialisme* (Paris: Éditions Présence Africaine, 1955); Gregson Davis, *Aimé Césaire* (Cambridge, UK: Cambridge University Press, 1997), 35.

38 'nègre', in *Le Robert*, https://dictionnaire.lerobert.com/definition/negre; 'nègre', in *Larousse*, https://www.larousse.fr/dictionnaires/francais/nègre.

39 In Raphaël Confiant's *Dictionnaire Créole Martiniquais-Français*, the word *neg* is listed with six different neutral meanings, including that of "man," "friend," "Black man," "person from…" Raphaël Confiant, *Dictionnaire Créole Martiniquais-Français: L-Z* (Ibis Rouge, 2007).

40 Leonie M. E. A. Cornips and Vincent A. De Rooij, "Selfing and Othering through Categories of Race, Place, and Language among Minority Youths in Rotterdam, The Netherlands," in *Multilingualism and Language Diversity in Urban Areas: Acquisition, Identities, Space, Education*, ed. Peter Siemund et al., vol. 1 (Amsterdam: John Benjamins Publishing Company, 2013), 129–164. See also Merlien Hardenberg, "Streetlanguage" (master's thesis, Haagse Hogeschool and Meertens Instituut, 2003).

41 Cornips and De Rooij, "Selfing and Othering," 146–147.

42 "Afro-Danskeres Oplevelse Af Diskrimination i Danmark," 20.

43 Jørgen Schack, "Om Ordet Neger," *Nyt Fra Sprognævnet*, no. 4 (December 1995), https://dsn.dk/wp-content/uploads/2021/01/december-1995-pdf.pdf.

44 "Modtræk til 'løjerlig' DF-Kampagne Stormer frem på Facebook," *Berlingske.dk*, May 17, 2016, https://www.berlingske.dk/content/item/47218.

45 Mathias Mosskov, "Søren Espersen vil Ikke Undskylde: 'Neger' Ligger Dybt i mit Vokabularium," *nyheder.tv2.dk*, May 18, 2016, https://nyheder.tv2.dk/politik/2016-05-18-soeren-espersen-vil-ikke-undskylde-neger-ligger-dybt-i-mit-vokabularium. The entry *neger* in Den Danske Ordbog is marked as "oftest nedsættende" [most often derogatory]. "Neger," in *Den Danske Ordbog*, accessed August 4, 2023, https://ordnet.dk/ddo/ordbog?query=neger.

46 Geneva Smitherman, "'What Is Africa to Me?' Language, Ideology, and African American," *American Speech* 66, no. 2 (1991): 123.

47 Smitherman, "'What is Africa to Me?'" 118–122; See also Tom W. Smith, "Changing Racial Labels: From 'Colored' to 'Negro' to 'Black' to 'African American,'" *Public Opinion Quarterly* 56, no. 4 (1992): 496.

48 Alim and Smitherman, "Raciolinguistic Exceptionalism," 489.

49 Cornips and De Rooij, "Selfing and Othering," 142.

6
"THERE MUST BE SOMETHING VICIOUS IN THE DATA"

Thomas Jefferson's Techniques of Racialisation in the Production of *Data, Facts*, and *Information*

Melissa Adler

Thomas Jefferson's various positions as lawyer, governor, Secretary of State, US President, and President of the American Philosophical Society all place him simultaneously as a central figure in state power and scholarly scientific circles. This chapter offers a close reading of Thomas Jefferson's use of the terms "data," "information," "fact," and "evidence," to intervene in the conversations regarding the meaning and use of the words by which information professionals live and work. Of particular interest are the processes of abstraction in the history of what we now call datafication and the development of information management techniques, particularly in the overlapping contexts of the plantation and the formation of liberal government in the early United States.[1]

The aim of this analysis is to draw connections between the discourses inscribed in the *Declaration of Independence*, Jefferson's classified book catalogue, and his *Notes on the State of Virginia*, to show how Jefferson organised information according to a universalised white male subject. Patrick Wolfe tells us that "the great taxonomies of natural science with the political rhetoric of the rights of man" merged in the construct of race in the late eighteenth century. He identifies this as a "Jeffersonian fusion of bourgeois political ideology with classificatory natural science, of power with knowledge" that "gave race its epistemic purchase on post-Enlightenment thought."[2] Deciphering the code and understanding the processes by which datafication of human life has occurred are important for unpacking the relationship between information and processes of racialisation.

The universalisation of the white male propertied subject as he who stands for what it means to be human is inscribed within the systems that store and retrieve information; by placing racialised and gendered others in "special topics" in library classifications, for example. This practice is rooted in old racial taxonomic projects that promoted white supremacy by upholding slavery, the removal and assimilation of Indigenous peoples, and the withholding of rights for women. Hope Olson stands out among the scholars who have critiqued the Dewey Decimal Classification and the Library of Congress's subject headings and shelf classification. Olson places an emphasis on the universalising assumptions in these systems that simultaneously impose sameness identity on the Other in order to uphold patriarchal ideals. She calls for making space within these systems, not simply to add more categories, but to leave them open "for the Other to fill should she desire to do so."[3] The history of racialisation and colonialism in the history of information has become increasingly relevant with the rise of datafication in the twentieth century. Safiya Umoja Noble explains that "library classification projects undergird the invention of search engines such as Google, and [library and information studies] is implicated in the algorithmic process of sorting and classifying information and records."[4]

The concept of "datafication" was first introduced in 2013 by Viktor Mayer Schonberger and Kenneth Cukier, framed by the assertion that "Big Data" was ushering in a revolutionary infrastructural change:

> We fail to appreciate this because today's project is so new, because we are in the middle of it, and because unlike the water that flows on the aqueducts the product of our labours is intangible. The project is datafication … With the help of big data, we will no longer regard our world as a string of happenings that we explain as natural or social phenomena, but as a universe comprised essentially of information.[5]

We know, however, that datafication has material effects on our lives.[6] Following Dencik, Hintz, Redden, and Treré, this chapter is based in the belief that a "grounded understanding of datafication" is essential to discussions of social justice because "the expanding generation, the collection and use of data across areas of social and public life is increasingly seen as substantively and qualitatively transforming economic, political, social, and cultural practices in such a way that entrenches and introduces power dynamics in need of scrutiny and critique."[7] Understanding the history of racialisation in datafication may bring clarity to this conversation. Wolfe writes, "in addition to noting race's development as an organised narrative or doctrine, we need to observe it in operation, as a set of classificatory regimes that seek to order subject populations differentially in pursuit of particular historical agendas."[8] Jefferson's archive shows that datafication is not entirely new. The racialising taxonomies that supported early American nation-building and expansion are embedded in systems today. As Lisa Lowe writes, "what we might identify as residual within the histories of settler or colonial capitalism does not disappear. To the contrary, it persists and endures, even if less legible with the obfuscations of a new dominant."[9] Examining the history of data, facts, and information assists in understanding how datafication reified and amplified relations of power through racialising categories and hierarchies.

Looking for *Data, Facts,* and *Information*

Daniel Rosenberg has discerned the relationship between data and modernity by examining the rhetorical use of the term "data" in the eighteenth century. He writes that "it is tempting to want to give data an essence, to define what exact kind of fact data is. But this misses the most important aspect of the term, and it obscures why the term became so useful in the mid-twentieth century. Data has no truth."[10] This chapter places Rosenberg's analysis into dialogue with Thomas Jefferson's data management practices in his personal and political lives. It argues that datafication and nation-building were intimately connected in the early United States, and focuses on Jefferson because of his extensive use of the terms "data," "facts," "truth," "evidence" (including self-evidence), "information," and "knowledge" and because of his political and intellectual influence. As Toni Weller notes, differentiating between these terms is a difficult task, partly because it was not until the nineteenth century that these distinctions were regarded as important.[11] We can gain insights into the rhetorical and definitional significance of these terms by examining their use during and after the American Revolution. Their emergence in that context provides historical specificity regarding their use. These terms were meaningful for the expansion of empire and liberal democracy, which required the collection and organisation of vast and diverse informational resources. This analysis also shows that we have inherited some principles from this era in which datafication was particularly essential for settler colonial knowledge production.

Rosenberg points to some of the challenges of performing queries to quantify instances of terminologies on the existing databases that contain the full text of eighteenth-century documents. He used *Eighteenth-Century Collections Online* (ECCO) and the *Google Books* NGram feature, noting that imperfections in scanning and metadata introduce a margin of error, but he nevertheless viewed these databases to be highly effective tools for analysis.[12] Fortunately, *Founders Online*, an online full-text database that contains the papers of George Washington, Benjamin Franklin, Alexander Hamilton, John Jay, John Adams, Thomas Jefferson, and James Madison, has highly effective advanced search options that allow users to find occurrences of specific words across documents.[13] The search strategy was to isolate terms within certain collections and written by Jefferson, leaving out any results that occur in editors' notes. For example, it is possible to look for Jefferson's use of the word "data" by using the following query: "Documents: 'data' Author: 'Jefferson, Thomas' Project: 'Jefferson Papers.'" Related searches for other terms were also performed and the results were quantified (Table 6.1):

Table 6.1 Occurrences of Jefferson's use of terms, as found among his digitised papers in *Founders Online*

Information	2,669
Fact	1,565
Truth	860
Evidence	643
Document	276
Knowledge	148
Data	30
Statistics	14
Datum	3

This is an imperfect, and certainly not an exhaustive search, as it does not include texts like his classified book catalogue, his Garden Book, or his Farm Book, the ledger in which he recorded information about the people he enslaved and tabulated the plantation's expenses and income.[14] *Founders Online* does include many of his public and private papers, such as bills that he authored, his autobiography, his memorandum books, and his personal letters to friends, family, and colleagues. The infrequent occurrence of "data" suggests that the term is emergent. In total, the number of documents in which the term appears in all of *Founders Online* is only 398 out of a total of more than 185,000.[15]

A similar search was performed of the only book he published, *Notes on the State of Virginia*, to see how Jefferson put the terms "data," "fact," and "information" to use in that text. He uses the word "fact" twenty-seven times, "information" seventeen times, and "data" just three. Close contextual readings were conducted of each of those instances as they appear in *Notes on the State of Virginia*, as well as each use of "data" in the Jefferson Papers that are digitally transcribed in *Founders Online*.

Rosenberg observed that Joseph Priestley put "data" into discourse in the context of historical data in 1788. As Rosenberg points out, the term "data" was not in common usage at the time, but when it was used, it referred to quantitative data. For it to be deployed to describe historical "data" was different, and in Rosenberg's assessment, "it is crucial to observe that the term 'data' serves a different rhetorical and conceptual function than do sister terms such as 'facts' and 'evidence.' To put it more precisely, in contrast to these other terms, the semantic function of data is specifically rhetorical."[16] Jefferson's first documented use of the term, according to the search of *Founders Online*, occurred in a letter dated November 2, 1780. Did he use it in the way that Rosenberg has described?—As a rhetorical technique or in contexts other than mathematical and statistical sciences? Can examining the emergence of the term in one man's papers tell us something about the age?

Data

In the 1780 letter cited above, Jefferson wrote to Maryland Governor and planter Thomas Sim Lee to communicate military intelligence information that he had obtained about British troops in Virginia during the Revolutionary War. Jefferson wrote of a British deserter, "some information was given interesting to the state over which your Excellency presides and which therefore I think it my duty to communicate."[17] Jefferson provided enough information to establish the person's credibility, and although he observed him to be trustworthy, he suggested that the British reports were likely to complicate things: "The man appears credible and affectionate to his country as far as we can judge from his appearance; but how far we are to credit the reports prevailing in their army, or what his Colo. might say in his presence is a very different question. Your Excellency will judge in this for yourself."[18] The British troops' contradictory movements had "induced an opinion with some that they are about to embark," whereas the "settlement of the refugees in their own houses" suggested otherwise.[19] Jefferson stated he was of the opinion that Lord Cornwallis had planned to join his troops in Virginia by that time, but was delayed, and his troops were waiting for him to give them further orders. I "rather believe," wrote Jefferson, but "we have not data enough to confide in any opinion."[20] In other words, Jefferson did not have enough evidence to confirm the truth of any given intelligence that he'd received pertaining to Lord Cornwallis's whereabouts and plans for his troops. He had access to different beliefs, opinions, and contradictory evidence. His use of data here appears to be synonymous with facts.

Subsequently, Jefferson used "data" in several types of communications. In November 1782 he explained his travel plans to James Madison and that he wished to meet the Chevalier de la Luzerne to discuss negotiations. He was not sure if he'd make it in time to have had an adequate debriefing for such a meeting: "From these data you will be enabled to judge of the chance of availing myself of his Excy. The Chev. de la Luzerne's kind offer."[21] Most often he used the term in the context of calculating mathematical data. Congress had asked him to supply information about how much money would be required to retrieve American sailors who were being held captive in Algeria. Rather than providing a simple sum total, Jefferson wrote, "it is proper to state to you some data whereby you may judge what sum is necessary."[22] He provided dollar figures for the ransom, cost of feeding, clothing, and transporting the prisoners, and suggested that $10,000 would be the minimum expense, but that more than that should be allocated.

He also used data in letters about engineering and mathematical calculations. In his notes on his tour through Holland and the Rhine Valley, he calculated the length of a bridge needed to accommodate boats passing through: "From these data the length of the bridge should be 9f.-8I+18f-10i×40=1140 feet."[23] Similarly, when he was Secretary of State, he assigned Andrew Ellicott the task of surveying the federal territory that would become Washington, DC. "This is intended as the first rough essay to furnish data for the last accurate survey."[24] In other words, this was meant as an initial inquiry in ongoing measurements of the land, and further studies will improve the accuracy. This use of "data" seems to signal work in progress, that gathering data was an iterative process, and that more data would lead to more certainty. Indeed, Jefferson used "data" this way relatively frequently, writing "there are not yet sufficient data to ground a judgment" regarding the possibility of peace following the Russo-Turkish War of 1768–1774.[25] He opposed data to conjecture, or qualified incomplete information as "conjectural data," very often to refute claims that he viewed to be based on faulty data. In 1786, when he was attempting to calculate the US financial debt owed to England, he wrote, "I am of opinion (conjecturing from loose data of my memory only as to the amount and true worth of the sums emitted by Congress and by the several states)."[26] He suggested that the large sum of money owed could easily be paid off by selling lands. Here "loose data" was something that was stored in his memory, but the unreliable retrieval of such data meant that he could only provide an opinion, not facts. When he was trying to estimate the size of classrooms at the University of Virginia, he resorted to estimation: "having no data on which we could act with precision, we were obliged to assume some numbers conjecturally."[27] And in a trigonometry exercise in which he had written down different approaches to solving spherical triangles, he wrote at the bottom of the page, "there must be something vicious in the data."[28]

Jefferson also used the Latin *datum* three times in his letters, first in one of his earliest surviving letters. Writing to his college friend John Page in 1763 at the age of nineteen, he placed the word it in a Latin sentence, which roughly translates as "but it is not meant to be" or more literally, "it is not what is given as fact." In what can only be read as a lament, Jefferson wrote:

> Why cannot you and I be married too, Page, when and to whom we would chuse? Do you think it would cause any such mighty disorders among the planets? Or do you imagine it would be attended with such very bad consequences in this bit of a world, this clod of dirt, which I insist is the vilest of the whole system? No body knows how much I wish to be with you, 'sed non ita facto datum.'"[29]

The Latin is most likely borrowed from Livy, but it is mistranslated. The original reads, "*si hoc ita fato datum erat.*" The proper translation suggests that it is "fated" to be. Jefferson makes two adjustments to this passage, adding the negative "non" and changing "fato" to "facto." A reference to facts—"*facto datum*" is typical of Jefferson the scientist, as is thinking about the order of human relationships with respect to the cosmos—the notion that the laws of human relations are written in nature. He is of a moment in-between, when science has become established as a set of practices of observation, testing, and fact-checking, but while there is still so much that remains a mystery. It is before objectivity became an "epistemic virtue."[30] Jefferson read the ancients widely and based much of his thinking on their works, from the formulation of an ideal republic to models of ideal friendship. But he was not a person who would grant that the course of events on earth could be explained by the fates. He was avidly opposed to metaphysics and resisted belief in anything that could not be based in matters of fact, supported by evidence. He is playing with this in-betweenness, it seems, by invoking the notion that a union on earth might have the power to disrupt the cosmos, while at the same time, correcting Livy and insisting that it is not the fates that have determined their situation, but that it is a fact that Page and Jefferson cannot live together.

A half-century later, well into his retirement, he wrote a curiously similar sentence, but this time lamenting the realisation that he will not live to see an end to slavery, but this time referring to fate, rather than fact:

> I am grown old, go little from home, and am desirous to retire from every thing public and to give to repose and tranquility the feeble existence which remains to me. the discoveries daily made, and vast amelioration of the condition of man resulting from them, might i[n]spire a curiosity to live to see them in action. *Sed hoc non fatum datum est.* to this necessity I resign myself willingly, and to the guardianship of my younger fellow citizens, for whom, in the day of weakness I have endeavored to perform the same good offices.[31]

Jefferson's Latin is suggestive of long-held ideas about what data means. The distinction between whether it is given by fate or facts is interesting from a philosophical standpoint, but both cases point to the concept of data. Rosenberg's explanation is useful:

> Data means—and has meant for a very long time—that which is given prior to argument. As a consequence, the meaning of data must always shift with argumentative strategy and context—and with the history of both. The rise of modern economics and empirical natural science created new conditions of argument and new assumptions about facts and evidence. And the histories of those terms and new assumptions about facts and evidence.[32]

The interesting point about data is the way that it is seen to be something that is accumulated, and the more data one gathers, the closer one gets to certainty. Sometimes data is synonymous with information and fact, but the specificity of its emergence in context reveals its significance as a rhetorical device. This is peculiarly evident in his *Notes on the State of Virginia*, which he wrote in response to a set of queries from the French diplomat, François Marbois about Virginia's landscape, inhabitants, commerce, manufacturing, plants, and animals. *Notes on the State of Virginia* is a fascinating result of quantitative and qualitative analyses. It is thick with description, tables, measurements, statistics, and figures. Jefferson submitted his initial responses to Marbois in 1781 but significantly revised the manuscript, adding more details before submitting it to printers in 1785.[33] Most of the writing was occurring just after he first used the term "data" in his 1780 letter described above. The word only appears three times in the *Notes on the State of Virginia*, and each instance is strangely compelling.

In the response to the first query, which asks about the boundaries of Virginia, Jefferson provides information about the distance from the Atlantic Ocean to the Mississippi River: "By admeasurements through nearly the whole of this last line, and supplying the unmeasured parts from *good data*, the Atlantic and Missisipi [sic], are found in this latitude to be 758 miles distant, equal to 13°. 38'. of longitude, reckoning 55 miles and 3144 feet to the degree."[34] It is a rather convoluted sentence, but what stands out is his reference to "good data." Apparently, some of the territory has been measured, and what has not been adequately measured has been calculated based on data that readers are meant to trust is "good." He does not cite his sources or tell us how he came to the data.

"Data" next appears in query four, on Virginia's mountains: "From data, which may found a tolerable conjecture, we suppose the highest peak to be about 4000 feet perpendicular, which is not a fifth part of the height of the mountains of South America, nor one third of the height which would be necessary in our latitude to preserve ice in the open air unmelted through the year."[35] Again, he presents data with no reference, but that data is meant to provide the grounds for a "tolerable conjecture" about the height of the mountain, which he then invokes as a point of comparison with mountains of South America.

Query seven is a curiosity. Marbois asked Jefferson to supply "a notice of all that can increase the progress of human knowledge." Jefferson's response begins, "Under the latitude of this query, I will presume it not improper nor unacceptable to furnish some data for estimating the climate of Virginia."[36] Indeed, the entire response is about climate, with little to no explicit connection to the progress of human knowledge. He does not describe his intention, but it appears that he used this query to establish evidence about the climate in Virginia so that he can defend his responses to other queries, in which he refutes European natural historians' claims that the climate of North America is poor in comparison with European climate and contributes to biologically inferior plant, animal, and human life. Fundamentally, his aim is to prove that the climate of North America supports and sustains healthy life forms and that the Indigenous peoples are equal to whites in intelligence. He also uses related queries to support his claim that Indigenous communities should adapt Euro-American agricultural practices, family structures, language, and cultural norms. This is a roundabout way of connecting climate to the progress of human knowledge.

Facts

One of Jefferson's most oft-cited quotes appears in *Notes in the State of Virginia*: "A patient pursuit of facts, and cautious combination and comparison of them, is the drudgery to which man is subjected by his Maker, if he wishes to attain sure knowledge."[37] Facts are pursued; data is that which is given. Jefferson uses the term "fact" twenty-seven times in the *Notes on the State of Virginia*. Over half of these instances appear in the phrase, "in fact," which one might generally regard as a rhetorical flourish intended to emphasise the truth of the assertion to which the phrase is attached.

He also puts "facts" to use in the *Declaration of Independence*, which is, in form and substance, a well-reasoned argument. The *Declaration* articulates several premises, beginning with the "self-evident" *truth* that people are endowed with unalienable rights. Governments are instituted to secure those rights; the power of the government is derived from the people; and if/when the government becomes despotic, then it is the right and duty of the people to abolish said government. "The history of the present King of Great Britain is a history of repeated injuries and usurpations, all having in direct object the establishment of an absolute Tyranny over these States," wrote Jefferson in the *Declaration of Independence*. "To prove this let Facts be submitted to a candid world."[38]

What follows in the next section of the *Declaration* is a catalogue of offences against the people living in the British colonies. Based on the historical facts and the truth of the premises, the conclusion must be drawn that it has become "necessary for one people to dissolve the political bands which have connected them with another."[39]

Bruno Latour has shown how the truth of facts becomes established in processes of inscription in networks of scientists: "A fact only becomes such when it loses all temporal qualifications and becomes incorporated into a large body of knowledge drawn upon by others."[40] For Jefferson, facts can be doubted or affirmed: "but they are either so loosely mentioned as to leave a doubt of the fact;"[41] "And though, till it be decided, we are as free to deny, as others are to affirm the fact, yet for a moment let it be supposed …"[42] When facts are beyond a doubt they gain collective truth value, as in, "it is a fact well known with us."[43] Facts can even be events: "we may venture to say further, that no fact has taken place, either in our own days, or in the thousands of years recorded in history, which proves the existence of any natural agents, within or without the bowels of the earth, of force sufficient to heave, to the height of 15,000 feet, such masses as the Andes."[44] In other words, never has a fact presented itself to indicate that mountains form by rupturing from the earth.

Ultimately, the important thing about facts is that they are the basis of human knowledge in Jefferson's view. They form the foundation upon which more knowledge is built. Scientists can use known facts as variables in experimentation, or to advance knowledge based on philosophical reasoning. Facts are to be taught to children in school. Jefferson uses "facts" twice in explaining his views about education. First, to make a case for a public education and libraries for all citizens, regardless of wealth: "But that time is not lost which is employed in providing tools for future operation: more especially as in this case the books put into the hands of the youth for this purpose may be such as will at the same time impress their minds with useful facts and good principles."[45] He also discusses the type of books that should be made available. Jefferson famously edited his own copy of the Bible, removing any passages that referred to the supernatural and keeping only material that could be regarded as historic fact. He believed that religious teachings should not be included in schools: "Instead therefore of putting the Bible and Testament into the hands of the children, at an age when their judgments are not sufficiently matured for religious inquiries, *their memories may here be stored with the most useful facts* from Grecian, Roman, European and American history."[46] In this extraordinary sentence, Jefferson regards the minds of children as memory storage spaces for useful facts.

Information

While it is clear that data is something that accumulates, and facts are to be pursued, *information* is something that one can possess, collect, own, and claim. Several fragments from Jefferson's *Notes* demonstrate this usage: "From all the information I have been able to collect;"[47] "would require information of which no one individual is possessed;"[48] "from the information of others;"[49] "the most precise information we have;" "which have come within my information;"[50] "I infer from Scheffer's information"[51]: "the best information I can get."[52] By contrast, Jefferson was much more likely to refer to "these data" or he would refer to the negative if using the possessive, "I have no data," "I possess no data," or "having no data on which we could act with precision." Not having data forces one to resort to conjecture. But when data are put to use, they become "these data"—detached, rather than data that belongs to someone. As with data and facts, the more information, the closer one gets to the truth: "Further information will, doubtless, produce further corrections."[53]

Reaching farther back into Jefferson's archive, before he wrote the Declaration of Independence, we find another use of "information." He was writing to Ebenezer Hazard, in regard to his massive project towards archiving and assembling colonial documents for posterity. Jefferson stated that the proposed project was "an undertaking of great utility" for its potential to contribute "to *the information* of all those concerned in the administration of government," as well as any historian that would benefit from materials that he "would otherwise acquire with great difficulty and perhaps not acquire at all."[54] His use of the word "information" was in accord with the now obsolete eighteenth-century definition: "formation or moulding of the mind or character, instruction."[55] Jefferson is using the word more like a verb than a noun.

Geoffrey Nunberg explains that the meaning ascribed to "information" today is actually derived from this usage. He observes a shift in meaning that contributed to the commodification of information based on a (mis)reading of the term that is "particularly easy to make when the context involves talk of 'having,' 'acquiring,' or 'receiving' information."[56] Nunberg suggests that this conceptualisation of information was highly strategic: "On the one hand, it resituated the agency of instruction in the text and its producers, and reduced the reader to the role of a passive consumer of content."[57] The shift in the meaning of information from effect to cause was useful insofar as it served the aim of producing an informed public, through the production of information—"that is, on whose free exchange the functioning of democratic society, the free marketplace, and the rest are routinely held to depend."[58] Jefferson was keenly aware of the importance of education, access to books, a free press, and delivery of the news which were essential to the formation and success of the early republic. Each of these required the transmission of information.

Data, Facts, and Information in Jefferson's Taxonomic Racial Science

Jefferson's uses of *information, facts, and data* were intentional and specific. Rosenberg makes distinctions among these and related concepts. He writes:

> facts are ontological, evidence is epistemological, data is rhetorical. A datum may also be a fact, just as a fact may be evidence. But, from its first vernacular formulation, the existence of a datum has been independent of any consideration of corresponding ontological truth. When a fact is proven false, it ceases to be a fact. False data is data nonetheless.[59]

Isolating the occurrences of terms in context provides interesting documentary evidence, which may not be conclusive, but is at least compelling. The project cannot end there, though. We must also look at Jefferson's statements that assert the findings of fact. Some facts are presented in tables in the *Notes on the State of Virginia*. He performed an early census, which counted "free men" and "slaves" as "tithable persons" (people that could be taxed), but not white male minors or women. Indigenous tribes are listed and described in the chapter he called "Aborigines." Indeed, Thomas Dikant regards Jefferson's tables as early forms of "settler colonial statistics" that serve as an indication of how people were counted and for what purposes.[60]

In some cases, Jefferson seems to expect readers of *Notes on the State of Virginia* to take for granted that his statements are true, or that we should trust his research methods. This is particularly evident in Query 14, titled "Laws" which begins with an explanation of the criminal justice system and a history and list of the existing laws in Virginia. It continues with a comparison of racial differences between Indigenous, Black, and white peoples. Some of these differences are presented as matters of fact, some as questions or conjectures. But his overarching conclusion is unequivocal. The most egregious example is his conclusion that people of African descent are improved by mixing with whites. "The improvement of the blacks in body and mind, in the first instance of their mixture with the whites, has been observed by every one, and proves that their inferiority is not the effect merely of their condition of life."[61] To say that this has been observed by everyone is to present an appearance of "good data" by way of a citation that is not a citation at all. The authority with which he states that all scientists are in agreement on this "fact" proffers an extra degree of truth. Ideas about racial difference that placed whites at the top of a hierarchy in body and mind were circulating widely among natural historians and taxonomists, from Carolus Linnaeus to the Compte de Buffon, and Jefferson took such writings to have established matters of fact. Jefferson referenced Linnaeus's taxonomic project in the *Notes on the State of Virginia*, and in letters he noted his admiration for the Linnaean system. Linnaeus is widely cited by historians as a progenitor of nineteenth-century scientific racism, and his outline of human variety was among the most important eighteenth-century classificatory projects.

Jefferson used the works of Ignatius Sancho and Phillis Wheatley (Peters) to demonstrate what he believed to be an imaginative and intellectual defect of Black people in his *Notes on the State of Virginia*. In his book catalogue, he placed their works at the bottom of the columns of the "Epistolary" and "Pastorals, Odes, Elegies" chapters, respectively. Ignatius Sancho was an incredibly important figure in his day. His book, *Letters of the Late Ignatius Sancho*, was one of the earliest accounts of African slavery written in English by a formerly enslaved person. Of Sancho's letters, Jefferson wrote:

> Whether they will be equal to the composition of a more extensive run of melody, or of complicated harmony, is yet to be proved. Misery is often the parent of the most affecting touches in poetry.—Among the blacks is misery enough, God knows, but no poetry. Love is the peculiar œstrum of the poet. Their love is ardent, but it kindles the senses only, not the imagination. Religion indeed has produced a Phyllis Whately; but it could not produce a poet. The compositions published under her name are below the dignity of criticism.
>
> Ignatius Sancho has approached nearer to merit in composition; yet his letters do more honour to the heart than the head ....
>
> Upon the whole, though we admit him to the first place among those of his own colour who have presented themselves to the public judgment, yet when we compare him with the writers of the race among whom he lived, and particularly with the epistolary class, in which he has taken his own stand, we are compelled to enroll him *at the bottom of the column.*

In fact, this is precisely what Jefferson did in his book classification, placing Sancho's letters at the bottom of the Epistolary chapter.[62] Jefferson is showing us that his cataloguing decisions are intentional and reasoned. Sancho's letters are placed at the bottom of the "Epistolary" class in the original classification and remained in that position until 1815, when he sold his collection and classified catalogue to the Library of Congress.[63] Arguably, Sancho's work would be better placed in a history section, as it featured actual letters sent and received by Sancho, not fictional ones. To classify is to make a statement—or in fact, a series of statements—a declaration, so to speak. Jefferson's classificatory decisions in Ignatius Sancho's work demonstrate this point.[64]

Although Jefferson's affirmation of existing theories about the biological inferiority of people of African descent elevated such ideas to the status of fact, he challenged beliefs based in the idea that different climates and landscapes might lead to degeneration. Buffon had espoused the notion that the Americas were inherently less fertile places and that human and non-human animals were less likely to thrive. Jefferson used the *Notes on the State of Virginia* to refute that theory, using Indigenous and non-human animal bodies and the size and quantity of wild animals as evidence. He even shipped the remains of a moose to France to show that animals grew large on the American landscape. Information historians will recall Suzanne Briet's 1951 description of how an antelope in the wild becomes a document when it is captured, studied, and displayed, demonstrates how an animal becomes an information resource to be used by humans.[65] Rendering life as evidence for science is part of the same processes of rendering information a thing.

Ronald E. Day refers to the philosophy of evidence, or "how something becomes evident and is taken as evidence of what is," as "documentarity." In Jefferson's writings, we see how documentation is the foundation for much of what we call information. Day's recent work helps enormously in thinking about the ways in which "documentarity and today, 'information,' have not only epistemic, but also political and aesthetic, qualities that should be taken account of."[66] He continues that "the philosophy of evidence not only governs knowledge institutions, but has also governed political institutions and has managed the role of knowledge in colonialism and the spread of 'the West' and its notions of literacy and their importance." Relatedly, Michael Buckland writes, in his article "Information as Thing," that "evidence" implies passiveness. "Evidence, like information-as-thing, does not do anything actively. Human beings do things with it or to it. They examine it, describe it, and categorise it."[67] If human or non-human bodies become informational, then, they become passive. Buckland points out that "document" is derived from the Latin *docére*, which means "to teach." But we can take this connection even farther, noting that *docére* is also the root of "docile." The Oxford English Dictionary's definition of docile is fascinating for the way that it indicates teaching and teachability, submission, and that this can be *"transferred* of things":

1 a apt to be taught; ready and willing to receive instruction; teachable
   b Submissive to training; tractable, manageable

2 *transferred* of things: Yielding readily to treatment; easily managed or dealt with; tractable (emphasis in source)

When something or someone becomes a document, they also become informational—an object of inquiry that is submitted to the ordering techniques of taxonomies, catalogues, tables, and statistics, according to the design principles of the systems' makers. The information is meant to instruct. When considered alongside Nunberg's assessment that the commodification of information occurred in processes that rendered the consumer of information a passive receiver of content, it becomes clear that people in power controlled the content and circulation of information. In the early United States, information was being produced for the purpose of shaping the minds of citizens. Indeed, the mastery of subjects included the position of master in relation to others, as well as academic subjects. The master was in a position of power and produced the information that would inform the citizenry, and mastered processes of rendering information from the humans he enslaved, studied, or governed.

These techniques cannot be thought without considering the contexts from which they arose. Jefferson was cataloguing his books and writing the *Notes on the State of Virginia* at his home at Monticello, where he owned a large plantation and enslaved over six hundred people during the course of his adult life. His writings demonstrate the ways in which coloniality was inscribed in different types of documents that circulated among various scholarly and official communities. The *Declaration of Independence*, *Notes on the State of Virginia*, and his classified book catalogue, along with all of his other censuses, ledgers, maps, policies, and scientific documents inscribed racial difference through discourses and classificatory techniques that universalised whiteness. Jefferson's use of data, facts, and information show how he viewed racialised others and put his scientific research into discourse. Rather than being regarded as humans, Indigenous and Black lives were used as evidence that supported claims that upheld that universalising discourse by using them as information in comparison with idealised citizen. Data, facts, and information were instrumental to early American statecraft and westward expansion. Life can be datafied and dehumanised when data are regarded as something out there. The emergence of the term "data" as detached from the human, at the same time that information was shifting in meaning towards commodification, were integral to early scientific racism in eighteenth-century processes of datafication.

Notes

1 This chapter is part of an ongoing project on Jefferson's information management strategies, tentatively titled *Thomas Jefferson and the In-formation of Empire*.
2 Patrick Wolfe, *Traces of History: Elementary Structures of Race* (London: Verso, 2016), 8–9.
3 Hope Olson, "The Feminist and the Emperor's New Clothes," *Library & Information Science Research* 19, no. 2 (1997), 194.
4 Safiya Umoja Noble, *Algorithms of Oppression: How Search Engines Reinforce Racism* (New York: NYU Press, 2018), 12.
5 Viktor Mayer-Schönberger and Kenneth Cukier, *Big Data: A Revolution That Will Transform How We Live, Work, and Think* (Boston, MA: Houghton Mifflin Harcourt, 2013), 96.
6 See, for example, Sasha Costanza-Chock, *Design Justice: Community-led Practices to Build the Worlds We Need* (Cambridge, MA: MIT Press, 2020); Virginia Eubanks, *Automating Inequality: How High-tech Tools Profile, Police, and Punish the Poor* (New York: St. Martin's Press, 2018); and Noble, *Algorithms of Oppression*.
7 Lina Dencik, Arne Hintz, Joanna Redden, and Emiliano Treré, *Data Justice* (London: Sage, 2022), 1.
8 Wolfe, *Traces of History*, 9–10.
9 Lisa Lowe, *The Intimacies of Four Continents* (Durham, NC: Duke University Press, 2015), 20.
10 Daniel Rosenberg, "Data before the Fact," in *"Raw Data" is an Oxymoron,* ed. Lisa Gitelman (Cambridge, MA: MIT Press, 2013), 15–41, at 37.

11 Toni Weller, *Information History - An Introduction: Exploring an Emergent Field* (Oxford, UK: Chandos, 2008), 16.
12 Rosenberg, "Data before the Fact," 27–28.
13 *Founders Online,* National Archives, https://founders.archives.gov/.
14 Occasionally the search turns up results if the main body of the document is an editor's note, but the influence on the total results is negligible.
15 The earliest occurrence appears in a letter from John Mitchell to Benjamin Franklin, probably in 1745. It is a fascinating passage in its own right, with "data" appearing in italics and used in the context of both induction and deduction to find a cure for yellow fever: "In the short account of the yellow fever, which I left with you at Philadelphia, I have not endeavoured to establish any theory, or even to make any deductions from any established theory of that, or like diseases ... nor have I either health or leisure at present, to deduce any theory or particular applications of it, from these *data*." John Mitchell to Benjamin Franklin, [March 1745?]," *Founders Online* (emphasis in original). The transcriptions are mostly derived from the published volumes of Thomas Jefferson's papers. Most have been verified as correct. The Retirement Papers are still in production.
16 Rosenberg, "Data before the Fact," 18.
17 Letter from TJ to Thomas Sim Lee, November 2, 1780, *Founders Online*.
18 Letter from TJ to Thomas Sim Lee, November 2, 1780, *Founders Online*.
19 Letter from TJ to Thomas Sim Lee, November 2, 1780, *Founders Online*.
20 Letter from TJ to Thomas Sim Lee, November 2, 1780, *Founders Online*.
21 TJ to James Madison, November 26, 1782, *Founders Online*.
22 TJ to the Commissioners of the Treasury, September 18, 1787, *Founders Online*.
23 "Notes of a Tour through Holland and the Rhine Valley," March 3–April 23, 1788, *Founders Online*.
24 TJ to Andrew Ellicott, February 2, 1791, *Founders Online*.
25 TJ to William Short, February 28, 1789, *Founders Online*.
26 "I. Answers to DéMeunier's First Queries," January 24, 1786, *Founders Online*.
27 TJ to James Madison, April 30, 1823, *Founders Online*.
28 TJ, "Trigonometry Exercise," December 4, 1815, *Founders Online*.
29 TJ to John Page, January 20, 1763, *Founders Online*.
30 Lorraine Daston and Peter Galison, *Objectivity* (New York: Zone Books, 2007), 39.
31 TJ to John L. Sullivan, February 8, 1817, *Founders Online*. Indeed, this is a bit of a conjecture, since the available data are unreliable. The original manuscript is apparently illegible, and the editors of Jefferson's papers transcribed it as *Sed hoc non f[atum?] datum est, which they translated to,* "but this is not a fate given to me." It is possible that he wrote "factum."
32 Rosenberg, "Data before the Fact," 36.
33 For a history of the drafts and editions, see Douglas L. Wilson, "The Evolution of Jefferson's 'Notes on the State of Virginia,'" *Virginia Magazine of History and Biography* 112, no. 2 (2004): 98–133.
34 Jefferson, *Notes on the State of Virginia*, in *Writings,* ed. Merrill Peterson (New York: Library of America, 1984), 127, emphasis added.
35 Jefferson, *Notes*, 144.
36 Notes on the State of Virginia, 200.
37 Jefferson, *Notes*, 192.
38 All quotes from the *Declaration* are from Thomas Jefferson, "The Autobiography," in *Writings*, ed. Merrill Peterson (New York: Library of America, 1984), 19.
39 Thomas Jefferson, "The Autobiography," 19.
40 Latour, *Laboratory Life* (Princeton, NJ: Princeton University Press, 1986), 106.
41 Jefferson, *Notes*, 166.
42 Jefferson, *Notes*, 170.
43 Jefferson, *Notes*, 187.
44 Jefferson, *Notes*, 155.
45 Jefferson, *Notes*, 274.
46 Jefferson, *Notes*, 274, emphasis added.
47 Jefferson, *Notes*, 179.
48 Jefferson, *Notes*, 182.

49 Jefferson, *Notes*, 184.
50 Jefferson, *Notes*, 198.
51 Jefferson, *Notes*, 199.
52 Jefferson, *Notes*, 292.
53 Jefferson, *Notes*, 178.
54 TJ to Ebenezer Hazard, April 30, 1775, *Founders Online*, National Archives, https://founders.archives.gov/documents/Jefferson/01-01-02-0102, emphasis added.
55 The *Oxford English Dictionary* cites a letter from TJ to John Melish as an example of this usage of "information," "information, n.," *OED Online* (March 2023), https://www.oed.com/view/Entry/95568?redirectedFrom=information.
56 Geoffrey Nunberg, "Farewell to the Information Age," in *The Future of the Book*, ed. Geoffrey Nunberg (Los Angeles, CA: University of California Press, 1996), 103–138, 113.
57 Nunberg, "Farewell to the Information Age,"
58 Nunberg, "Farewell to the Information Age," 114.
59 Rosenberg, "Data Before the Fact," 18.
60 Thomas Dikant, "Settler Colonial Statistics: Jefferson, Biopolitics, and Notes on the State of Virginia," *Early American Literature*, 54, no. 1 (2019): 69–96.
61 Jefferson, *Notes*, 267.
62 This passage about Sancho was added to the original as an attachment to the *Notes*. 1783 Catalog of Books [circa 1775–1812], page 224, by Thomas Jefferson [electronic edition]. *Thomas Jefferson Papers: An Electronic Archive* (Boston, MA: Massachusetts Historical Society, 2003), http://www.thomasjeffersonpapers.org/ *Letters of the Late Ignatius Sancho, an African* was first published in London in 1782.
63 James Gilreath and Douglas L. Wilson, eds., *Thomas Jefferson's Library: A Catalog with the Entries in His Own Order* (Washington, DC: Library of Congress, 1989), 123.
64 Jefferson modelled his book classification on the method that Diderot used to organise the *Encyclopedie*, following Francis Bacon's division of knowledge into three faculties—Memory, Reason, and Imagination. Jefferson first applied the Baconian framework in the catalogue commonly referred to as his "1783 Catalogue." The faculties are translated into categories for knowledge: Memory is what is known – or what can be considered facts. Reason is *Philosophy* or science, that is, the advancement of knowledge. And imagination is *Fine Arts* and literature. His book catalogue was essential to his own political and scientific practices, and his classification method is in direct conversation with other Enlightenment era natural historians.
65 Suzanne Briet, *What is Documentation?* trans. Ronald E. Day, Laurent Martinet and Hermina G. B. Anghelescu (Lanham, MD: Scarecrow Press, 2006).
66 Ronald E. Day, *Documentarity* (Cambridge, MA: MIT Press, 2019), 2.
67 Michael K. Buckland, "Information as Thing," *Journal of the American Society for Information Science* 42, no 5 (1991), 353. For an expanded analysis of antelope as document see Melissa Adler, "Mounting the Antelope: How the Early American Wild Became a Document," *The Canadian Journal of Information and Library Science* 47, no. 3 (2024): 59–69.

7
ENCYCLOPAEDIAS AS CULTURAL CARRIERS OF INFORMATION
A Scandinavian Perspective*

Maria Simonsen

Introduction

Several times each day, people turn to Google in their search for answers to questions big and small that come up at work, in school, or just when they need to find a recipe for the evening meal. Searching for information on the internet has become such an integrated part of our daily routines—regardless of age—that it is almost unthinkable to understand that less than a generation ago, we found and conveyed information and knowledge in completely different ways than we do today. Nevertheless, there was a time, not so many years ago, when the book was considered the absolute authority when it came to the storing and dissemination of information.

For hundreds of years, the physical book has enjoyed a particular status. As a carrier of religious, political, and philosophical thoughts, ideas, and ideals, it had a unique position of power in ever-changing society.[1] Also, beyond the circles of the elite, physical books have had essential functions. Books have enabled the crossing of boundaries in imagination and society, and have thus opened new worlds for great and small. In its capacity as an authority, the physical book was, for a long time, not in competition with other media, as it is today. It was during the digital era that the physical book's position as the authority of information and knowledge gradually changed.

The encyclopaedia is one genre in particular that stands out when it comes to information, knowledge, and authority. Masterpieces of erudition or compendia of information such as the French *Encyclopédie, ou Dictionnaire Raisonné des Sciences, des Arts et des Métiers* (1751–1772), the English *Encyclopaedia Britannica* (1st ed., 1768–1771) or the German *Brockhaus Enzyklopädie* (1st ed., 1809–1811) are all examples of works that came to play an essential role in the development of the genre.[2] For centuries, these works have enjoyed enormous respect—and with good reason. Collecting, organising, and disseminating information to the extent that these large encyclopaedias did was a major challenge

---

* The author is grateful to Laura Skouvig, Barnaby Cullen, and Alistair Black for the helpful advice and comments during the work with the chapter. This chapter has been written with support from the Department of Politics and Sciences at Aalborg University.

on several parameters, not least in terms of financial and technical printing conditions.[3] It is easy to understand why many of the publishers, editors, authors, and others involved in their publication are remembered to the present day.

However, there are numerous other explanations for the extraordinary respect that surrounds this genre. Encyclopaedias have been seen as an important symbol of political ideals—perhaps the most famous example of this being the interconnection between the Enlightenment and the *Encyclopédie*.[4] The role of encyclopaedias as mediators of history and culture in national contexts is another reason why they have been given a special prestige throughout the ages. From the end of the nineteenth century and up to our new millennium, newspapers, publishers, and even politicians have described the importance of having a national carrier of culture and history in the form of an encyclopaedia.[5] Furthermore, the idea of an encyclopaedia as a source of information and education has always been present in various ways in the history.

This chapter deals with the broad and complex history of the encyclopaedia from the end of the eighteenth century to the present day. The focus of the study is Northern Europe since the Scandinavian countries have a rich, but not well-known, tradition of publishing encyclopaedias. Nonetheless, this tradition illustrates very well the prominent tendencies in the history of encyclopaedias in the Western world. Based on examples from Sweden, Denmark, and Norway, this chapter gives insight into the development and use of the encyclopaedia and its changing societal role from printed to digitised forms and, thereby, its role as cultural carrier of information.[6]

Masterpieces of Erudition

Through the ages, encyclopaedias have had many different titles: lexicon, conversations-lexicon, reference work, or even dictionary were often-used names for encyclopaedias up until the last decades of the eighteenth century. It can be difficult to draw a sharp line between the definition and use of the diverse titles. As Daniel Headrick states regarding one of the early synonyms: "In theory, it is easy to distinguish between dictionaries and encyclopaedias, but in practice there is no clear way to differentiate them."[7] Many encyclopaedias contained a variety of labels in their titles. *Encyclopédie, ou Dictionnaire Raisonné*, *Encyclopaedia Britannica; or a Dictionary of Arts and Sciences* or the Danish publication *Salmonsens Store Illustrerede Konversationsleksikon. En Nordisk Encyklopædi* (*Salmonsen's Major Illustrated Conversations-Lexicon. A Nordic Encyclopaedia*) are just three examples.[8]

It was due to the fame of the *Encyclopédie* that the word "encyclopaedia" became more widespread.[9] The word *encyclopaedia* (encyclopedia in the more modern, American-inspired spelling) originates from the neo-Latin *encyclopaedia* and the Greek *enkyklios paideia*. *En-* and *kyklos* means circle or ring, while *paideia* can be translated as education or teaching. Together, the two words have given their name to the encyclopaedia as a way of managing or handling information.[10] Literally translated, an encyclopaedia becomes "everything contained in the circle of knowledge" or "general knowledge." Conversations-lexicons, on the other hand, "were no masterpieces of erudition or compendia of all knowledge."[11] As more simple reference works, they were considered suppliers of practical and up-to-date information.[12]

Regardless of their title, in the history of the modern encyclopaedia, the meanings of the different titles often fused together. Ultimately, the titles in many of the publications fundamentally covered the same matter: an alphabetically organised reference work that, in a precise language, described and explained such things as ground-breaking historical events, biological phenomena, influential personalities, or the development of countries or cities, as well as different kinds of concepts, terms, or trends.[13] Today the term encyclopaedia is the most used. In contrast, the term conversations-lexicon is considered old-fashioned and is closely connected with the German encyclopaedic tradition of the nineteenth and twentieth centuries.

The idea behind the encyclopaedia was (and still is) that it as genre, in principle, should include a complete collection of all human knowledge—regardless of the fact that this has never been possible in practice. Although the purposes of the encyclopaedia have changed over time, the modern, Enlightenment-created encyclopaedia stretches back even further historically. They have roots in ancient and medieval efforts to scientise and categorise the world. These compendiums of information constituted an attempt to understand the natural (or divine) order of things and to reproduce this understanding systematically.[14]

The oldest forerunners of the modern encyclopaedia are found in Antiquity and the Middle Ages. In *Naturalis Historia* (AD 77–79), Pliny the Elder, who lived in the first century AD, "collected information on 20,000 things, taken from 2000 volumes and written by 100 authors," as he emphasises in the first chapter.[15] *Naturalis Historia* can be said to be encyclopaedic in its content, but it was far from what we would today call an encyclopaedia.

During the Middle Ages, there was a marked growth in the number of encyclopaedias. Among the most important (and impressive) was the *Etymologia* (c. 600–625) compiled by the Christian bishop Isidore of Seville. The work was considered "a compendium of all worthwhile knowledge, based on the Roman circle of the liberal arts," but it also contained Latin grammar and practical information about, among other things, shipbuilding and architecture, as well as a dictionary section.[16] About five hundred years after the *Etymologia*, the *Speculum Majus* was published by the French Dominican friar, Vincent of Beauvais. The *Speculum Majus* was a mammoth work of almost ten thousand chapters.[17] For centuries, it stood as a mastodon of knowledge, and it was not until the Renaissance that its importance declined.

During the early modern period, the content of the encyclopaedias was expanded significantly, as the different entries were no longer only about things and phenomena but also people. This change was an offshoot of the Renaissance's emphasis on the importance of the individual. In the eighty-volume work *Grosses Vollständiges Universal-Lexicon* (1732–1754) by the Leipzig bookseller, publisher, and self-made businessman Johann Heinrich Zedler, there was an enormous gallery of people—both living and dead.[18] Zedler's *Universal-Lexicon* challenged the existing genre in several ways. As Jeff Loveland writes, "two-thirds of its entries were on history and geography. Yet the remaining third were the longest, and they were mainly on the arts and sciences."[19] Furthermore, it had entries on everyday language.[20] Another aspect of Zedler's *Universal-Lexicon* that prefigures the modern encyclopaedia is "the idea of a collective work," as different topics were assigned to several specialists.[21] According to Zedler, the identity of the participating experts would be announced when the work was completed. Ultimately, however, this never came to pass.[22]

Encyclopaedias for Social Conversations

From the eighteenth century onwards, there are three main avenues in the history of the encyclopaedia: the English, the French, and the German tradition. Although all three traditions are rooted in the works of the Middle Ages and Renaissance, it was in the Age of

Reason that the genre evolved from lists of words "into the fact-filled, up-to-date ready reference works we know today."[23] A milestone in that connection is *Cyclopaedia; Or an Universal Dictionary of Arts and Sciences* (1728–1788), prepared by the English writer Ephraim Chambers. *Cyclopaedia* is considered one of the first general encyclopaedias in English and was of great importance in the development of the genre, not least because it was alphabetically organised and was the first encyclopaedia "to have a network of explicit cross-references."[24] Subsequently, cross-references became "an expected component of the modern encyclopaedia."[25]

The system of cross-references was imitated by the most important encyclopaedia of the eighteenth century—the *Encyclopédie*. The publication of *Cyclopaedia* had attracted great attention in France. Soon the publisher André Le Breton decided to translate the work. The story is well-known: the two friends, the philosopher Denis Diderot and the mathematician Jean le Rond d'Alembert, organised and edited the ambitious project, and the *Encyclopédie* ended up being the most important work of the French Enlightenment. Its publication became a unifying event for the entire Enlightenment movement, far beyond the French borders.[26]

The *Encyclopédie* made publishers and booksellers dream of imitating the success of the Encyclopédistes. Under the name "A Society of Gentlemen in Scotland," a trio consisting of the bookseller and printer Colin Macfarquhar, the engraver Andrew Bell, and the reputedly unemployed scholar William Smellie, decided to exceed the French and publish an even better and more comprehensive encyclopaedia. With only three volumes, the first edition of *Encyclopædia Britannica* ended up being far smaller than its French role model, which consisted of twenty-eight volumes. Despite its somewhat inaccurate content, *Britannica* became a resounding success and new editions soon followed.[27]

Although both the French and English traditions are central to the history of the encyclopaedia, the German tradition plays a special role regarding the development of the genre. The far-sighted publisher Friedrich Arnold Brockhaus (1772–1893) helped create a type of encyclopaedia which, with its different approach to content and form, became particularly widespread and influenced the development of the genre in a completely new direction.[28]

In the early 1800s, F. A. Brockhaus bought an unfinished (and unsuccessful) work entitled *Conversationslexicon mit Vorzüglicher Rücksicht auf die Gegenwärtigen Zeiten* and out of it he created a reference work "aimed at a popular, not a scholarly, audience, and its short, up-to-date articles were tightly packed with information dealing with topics in the arts and sciences that might arise 'in social conversation'"[29]—all of which helped make the *Brockhaus* a comprehensive sales success. The sold-out listings said it all. A new encyclopaedic bestseller, that was in many ways contrary to the nature of the *Encyclopédie*, had seen the light of day. *Brockhaus* created the foundation for a new generation of encyclopaedias, including the Scandinavian ones.

Both *Britannica* and *Brockhaus* share responsibility for the development and spread of the content, language, and communication of modern encyclopaedias. The addition of biographies of living people became characteristic—especially for the conversations-lexicon. Most importantly, the publishers behind *Britannica* and *Brockhaus* understood the need for updating. While the *Encyclopédie* stood as a symbol of a certain culture of knowledge, the later works, *Britannica* and *Brockhaus* demonstrated understanding of the changeability of information. F. A. Brockhaus started a process in which editions constantly overlapped each other.[30]

Much has happened since the publication of *Britannica*, *Brockhaus* and other later, similar encyclopaedia. Like many other media, the encyclopaedia has changed its form and content in line with the developments in printing technology, increased reading skills, changing political affairs, and a multitude of other circumstances that have influenced the media landscape over the last several hundred years. After this short, guided tour through the history of the European encyclopaedia, we will turn our gaze towards the development and use of encyclopaedias in Scandinavia.

The Scandinavian Tradition

The Scandinavian countries have a long history of publishing encyclopaedias.[31] It is a tradition which reflects key aspects of the history of modern encyclopaedias in the Western world. As in many other countries, Scandinavian publishers were inspired by the French and German encyclopaedias in particular. There were several unsuccessful attempts throughout the eighteenth century to translate both the *Encyclopédie*, *Brockhaus Enzyklopädie* and *Meyers Konversations-Lexikon* (1st ed., 1857–1860/61).[32] In an effort to make French encyclopaedias accessible to a Danish audience, the priest Laurits Michael Frølund undertook a comprehensive project in trying to translate not just one but two French encyclopaedias. It was, however, too large a task, and he only reached the letter G.[33]

The same was true even for the energetic and enterprising Swedish librarian and publisher Carl Christopher Gjörwell. Like Frølund, he was strongly inspired by the French tradition, and his mission was to publish a Swedish summary of the *Encyclopédie*.[34] Even though Gjörwell was an experienced publisher with good connections in the Swedish book industry, his ambitions exceeded his abilities.[35] As Jakob Christensson describes in his extensive study of the publishing project, Görwell failed to become a Swedish Diderot.[36] Görwell was not the type to give up. Instead of translating the French work, he decided to publish a Swedish-language encyclopaedia, *Encyclopedie, eller Fransyskt och Svenskt Real- och Nominal-Lexicon*, but even this attempt floundered. The encyclopaedia never got further than the entry "améne."[37] To top it all, the failed publishing project left Gjörwell bankrupt.[38] After Gjörwell's unsuccessful publication attempts, the information-hungry Swedes had to turn to the updated foreign works, and more than thirty years would pass before a new major Swedish encyclopaedia could see the light of day.[39]

In the history of the Scandinavian encyclopaedias, there are many broken dreams and lost destinies due to abortive projects. Fortunately, there are also several success stories.[40] One such example is the German conversations-lexicon. As in many other countries, *Brockhaus* as well as *Meyers* laid the foundation for the publications in Scandinavian languages. The first to succeed was the eighteenth-century history and geography teacher Hans Ancher Kofod, who taught at The Metropolitan School in Copenhagen. In the period 1816–1828, he finished a Danish translation of *Brockhaus*.[41] Kofod not only translated; he also added new articles about Danish personalities who had not found their way into, or were poorly described, in the German original. Kofod's work thus became much more than a translation and gained great popularity in both Denmark and Norway.[42]

The translations of especially the German encyclopaedias continued to dominate the Scandinavian book market well into the nineteenth century. However, in the last part of the century, Swedish, Norwegian, and Danish publishers began to support original works, and the publication of Scandinavian encyclopaedias entered a new phase.

Entering the International League of Encyclopaedias

For both practical and ideological reasons, there was great interest in making the French- and German-language encyclopaedias available in the Scandinavian languages.[43] However, the strong German influence and inspiration on the Scandinavian book markets was not wholly embraced. On the one hand, the German works were in every way central to the production and dissemination of encyclopaedias, but on the other, there was a desire to dispose of and outcompete the German legacy and influence. Denmark's wars and confrontations with Germany in the Schleswig Wars in the middle of the nineteenth century created a wish to distance itself from all that was German, and at the same time, a strong sense of national pride was growing across Scandinavia.

The currents of nationalism showed themselves in several ways in society, and thus also in the cultural scene: among other things, in the establishment of national museums in Stockholm and Copenhagen in 1866 and 1892, respectively. Periodical publications such as *Svenska Familj-Journalen* (1864–1887) and the Danish equivalent *Illustreret Familie Journal* (1877–present) likewise reflected the increased focus on the national elements, given that the content was prepared by and for Swedes and Danes, respectively.[44] In the same period, the first Norwegian encyclopaedia which did not consist of translations of foreign works was published: the three-volume *Norwegian Handlexikon (Norsk Haandlexikon)* (1881–1888).[45] The content of the Norwegian work left much to be desired, however. There were no illustrations, and the academic depth of the articles was not impressive. As was the case with many encyclopaedias of the time, some articles were even quite subjective in their tone.[46]

One example of a publication that was both inspired by the German tradition and part of the strong nationalistic trends was the Danish *Salmonsen (Salmonsens store Illustrerede Konversationsleksikon*, (1st ed., 1893–1911). *Salmonsen* was published in several different editions from 1893 to 1956.[47] Throughout the years of its publication *Salmonsen* changed, both in terms of layout and content, and in relation to the readers and users. Due to the publication's longevity, the history of *Salmonsen* in many ways represents the development of the genre.[48]

Thanks to the enterprising nineteenth-century publisher Frederik Hostrup Schultz, who managed the renowned family company J. H. Schultz, *Salmonsen* became a cultural institution of the Danish and Norwegian book markets. In the late nineteenth century, F. H. Schultz decided to initiate a translation of the German *Meyers Konversations-Lexikon*,[49] together with the bookseller Isac Salmonsen, another well-known figure in the Danish publishing industry at the time, who also lent his name to the publication.[50]

However, as had happened so many times before in the history of encyclopaedias, the translation project turned out to be much more extensive and, not least, expensive, than first expected. After the publication of a few installments, the decision was made to prepare an original Danish encyclopaedia.[51] The length of the entries, the use of cross-references and the overall organisation of *Salmonsen* was identical to the German conversationslexicon, but the content of the encyclopaedia was adapted to Danish and Norwegian culture and history.[52] Many entries could be translated from the German original without major changes, but as the editors explained in the preface

> a careful investigation had shown that a replantation as intended could not, in reality, be carried out, but that, in order for anyone consulting the work everywhere to get a definite impression of being on Nordic soil, it was necessary to let the individual

author decide whether he could use the foreign text as a basis for his independent development of the entry or not (...).[53]

Salmonsen's first edition was a resounding success. The reviewers were enthusiastic. Among other things they praised the entries on Danish history and culture.[54] "We particularly recommend this encyclopaedia, which promises to be an exceptionally good handbook of useful knowledge for Danes," a reviewer noted in the newspaper *Politiken*.[55] There is no doubt that the reviews helped to establish the encyclopaedia's status as national and cultural repository of knowledge.[56] Sales went well; the first edition was initially set at a print run of five thousand but was soon doubled and sold-out.[57] Shortly after the final publication of the first edition, the publishing house decided to start work on a new, more extensive edition. Compared to its predecessor, the second edition was significantly expanded. The old entries had been updated, new entries were added and, above all, the number of illustrations was increased significantly.

The intended readers and users of *Salmonsen* were first and foremost Danes. In advertisements for the text, the publisher stated that the encyclopaedia was for *all* Danes. For obvious reasons this was a qualified truth. Few Danes could afford to acquire a copy of the extensive encyclopaedia, and the size of the print run showed that the publisher knew this very well. The first edition, as noted above, was published in a print run of around ten thousand, while the second edition was close to thirty thousand.[58] *Salmonsen* was very likely available in certain libraries and schools, but how many copies were to be found outside the larger cities is another question altogether.

Another aspect is the content: how accessible was it for *all* Danes in the context of literacy? The school reform from 1814 meant that the proportion of Danes who could read rose steadily throughout the nineteenth century.[59] But long entries written by the foremost scientists of the day hardly appealed to everyone. Many probably turned to more accessible literature such as the weekly and monthly magazines, book series, and handbooks in all guises that swarmed forth through the twentieth century.[60] We do not know much about its readers, but an educated guess is that *Salmonsen* particularly appealed to the intellectual elite and, to some extent, the bourgeoisie, while others turned to the cheaper and simpler works such as *Allers Illustrerede Konversationsleksikon* (1st ed., 1892–1899). The price difference between the instalments was considerable: fifteen øre for *Allers* and fifty øre for *Salmonsen*.[61]

Salmonsen was not only a success in Denmark. Due to their shared history Norway was an important market for the Danish publishers and *Salmonsen's* editor had a special focus on incorporating Norwegian material and perspectives. During the writing of the first edition a Norwegian editorial board was established, and although it disappeared in the preparation of the second edition, several Norwegian experts wrote entries. Both editions were widely distributed in Norway, where it also obtained a special status as a repository of information. As in Denmark, other lexical publications were compared to *Salmonsen*.

Although the Swedes already had a "national" encyclopaedia—the comprehensive *Nordisk Familjebok*—started by the publisher Christian Gernandt in the 1870s, *Salmonsen* also received attention in neighbouring Sweden. This was much to the chagrin of the publishing house behind *Nordisk Familjebok*, who anonymously issued advertisements in which the editors described the superior quality of the Swedish encyclopaedia compared to the Danish one.[62]

After the publication of the comprehensive second edition, which was completed with a supplement in 1920, *Salmonsen* was published in three more editions: *Den lille Salmonsen (The Small Salmonsen)* (1937–1940) in twelve volumes; *Den nye Salmonsen (The New Salmonsen)* (1949) first published in a single volume weighing 3.7 kg, later in two volumes; and finally, the lexicon periodical *Salmonsens Leksikon-Tidsskrift (Salmonsen's Lexicon-Magazine)* (1941–1957).[63] The three publications shared the common characteristic that they all differed significantly from their predecessors in scope, layout, and content. According to Palle Raunkjær, the editor-in-chief for *Den lille Salmonsen* and a strong advocate of public education, the new edition was prepared according to completely new principles and with particular emphasis on the so-called "practical issues of current interest."[64] In the preface, a thorough argument was made for the new editing principles. The articles had become shorter and clearer, while at the same time containing many facts, exhaustive definitions, and in-depth explanations. Furthermore, *Den lille Salmonsen* was far more illustrated and had a larger font than that used in other encyclopaedias.

In the adverts, the publisher explained why the new edition did not need to have the same large-scale scope as the previous editions to cover all knowledge of the world:

In our time with the fast pace and the strong demands about being up to date, the residents of both the countryside and the cities, have felt the need to get a smaller lexicon that could unify the objectivity of the old *Salmonsen* and the sterling worth of a smaller lexicon that could provide quick information and completely up-to-date organisation of information and knowledge.[65]

The longing for faster updates soon made a twelve-volume encyclopaedia seem heavy and slow to use. The time of the great multi-volume encyclopaedias seemed to have come to an end. Together with other encyclopaedias in the first half of the twentieth century, *Salmonsen* was one of the most important gateways for the Scandinavians when it came to information.[66] There were, of course, other paths to information: newspapers, journals and books, conversations, and education. But the encyclopaedia had a special authority, which its publishers were eager to highlight in any advertisement for encyclopaedic publications. Regardless of whether the publication was in one or fifteen volumes, every opportunity to highlight the different encyclopaedias' ability to cover all knowledge was emphasised.[67] From time to time, the publishers ended up in a paradox in the marketing of the new encyclopaedias: on the one hand, they wanted to give authority to the new editions by establishing a straight line to the earlier editions, while on the other, they wished to develop the genre in relation to the book market's demands for change.

With the first and second editions of *Salmonsen*, Denmark was finally entering the group of nations that had their very own encyclopaedia. The same pattern manifested itself in Sweden and Norway. The publishers managed to establish an incredibly strong brand around their publications—so strong that even today, encyclopaedias are compared to the *Salmonsen* or *Nordisk Familjebok*. At the end of the 1950s, however, several of the great works disappeared from the book market, but with their digitisation at the beginning of the new millennium both *Salmonsen* and *Nordisk Familjebok* gained new relevance despite their outdated content. Before digitalisation took hold, however, another type of encyclopaedia set the agenda: the book club encyclopaedia presented the publishing industry with a new direction for the encyclopaedia to take.

Between the Cultural and Commercial

Despite its position as an institution of culture and knowledge, the encyclopaedia has always been a commercial product, albeit rarely a successful one, produced and distributed by publishers with financial interests. This duality is also an important part of a larger cultural historical narrative about the encyclopaedia as a cultural carrier of information. At the same time, this helps to explain the many different forms of encyclopaedia-publishing throughout the ages: encyclopaedias in the form of serial magazines, one-volume encyclopaedias, or children's or worker's encyclopaedias. But perhaps more than any other publications within this genre, the book club publication renders the commercial aspect of the encyclopaedia most visible.

An example of a successful book club encyclopaedia was the Danish *Lademanns Leksikon* (1st ed., 1971–1978), published by the enterprising Jørgen Lademann. Through his company, he sold all kind of things, from bikes and coffee to car radios—anything, in fact, from which he could make money. He advertised his company in large-scale cinema advertisements. To that extent, Lademann stood in great contrast to the traditional Scandinavian book market and its publishers. *Lademanns Leksikon* stood out by prioritising breadth of appeal and popularity on all parameters, including content, price, and material.[68] The articles were short, in simple, easy-to-read language, and peppered with a wealth of photographs, maps, and graphics. This was all in stark contrast to the more traditional encyclopaedias, giving *Lademanns Leksikon* a completely different appeal to the readers of the time.[69] This new way of disseminating encyclopaedic content was met with scepticism in certain academic circles, but the encyclopaedia's sales figures and positive reviews spoke for themselves. The book club encyclopaedia was a great success, and *Lademanns Leksikon* even won an award for "the best book craft of the year" in 1972.[70]

The book club encyclopaedia gained influence in Sweden and Norway also. The Swedish publishing house Bra Böcker borrowed the idea, as well as entries and illustrations, from the Danish book club innovation when they prepared the first edition of *Bra Böckers Lexikon* (1st ed., 1973–1981).[71] Like its Danish counterpart, the publication became a great success. It had a popular appeal, and although some from the intellectual elite, as in Denmark, expressed displeasure with the publication, it found its way into many homes that would not necessarily have bought an encyclopaedia otherwise. In several ways, the book club publications heralded new times for the genre that digitalisation was to bring.

Book club encyclopaedias have often been overlooked in the history of the encyclopaedia, where the focus has been on the great and (academically) respected works. However, the book club encyclopaedias are interesting for several reasons. They played an important role in the democratisation of information, addressing as they did a broader audience than the classic publications. At the same time, they were central to a new type of information dissemination. By using a wide array of pictures, graphs, and other illustrations, the new encyclopaedia spoke a completely different language of information than was otherwise found in the genre.

Before digitisation's public breakthrough, printed encyclopaedias took one last deep breath. From the beginning of the 1970s until the 1990s, the traditional publishing houses had prepared several smaller encyclopaedias, while attempts at more extensive publications had failed. At the end of the 1970s, the Swedish government decided to set up a committee to investigate the question of publishing a major Swedish encyclopaedia.[72] The committee ended up recommending the publication of a new multi-volume encyclopaedia. To the surprise of many, it ended up being the book club publisher Bra Böcker, and not a more traditional publisher, who had to publish the new national encyclopaedia named *Nationalencyklopedin* (1989–1996). In contrast to the book club publication, *Nationalencyklopedien* included the more classic features of an encyclopaedia: lengthy entries signed by a recognised expert in the field. Of course, there were illustrations—in colour, moreover—but the text was its central feature, not the illustrations.

Inspired by the Swedish project, a large new encyclopaedia was also launched in Denmark – *Den Store Danske Encyklopædi* (*The Great Danish Encyclopaedia*). Both the Danish and Swedish projects were financially supported by the state with the argument of the need to ensure that up-to-date, objective information was available to the citizens of the countries. Both encyclopaedias became great successes. However, technological changes in media occurred quickly: the printed works became obsolete even before their last volume was published.

The Rebirth of the Encyclopaedia

The digital era became decisively important for the entire book industry and affected all book genres, but it was particularly important for the development of encyclopaedias. When the different digital encyclopaedias began to appear around the turn of the millennium, it demonstrated that another shift in the dissemination of encyclopaedic information was on its way – the shift from printed to the digitised.[73] Several genres, especially the fiction genre, found their way through this transformation and today the same title is published in audio, electronic, and printed formats. Publishers of the printed encyclopaedias, however, had a hard time figuring out which path to choose in the digital universe.

When Wikipedia was established by the Americans Jimmy Wales and Larry Sanger in January 2001, it was driven by a philosophy of a user-controlled, non-profit internet encyclopaedia that could be edited by anyone anywhere in the word.[74] The ambitions were exactly the same as in previous printed encyclopaedias: gather all the world's knowledge on a single platform. Wikipedia was a game changer on all fronts for the encyclopaedia as a genre. Even though Wikipedia provided traditional publishers with tools and suggestions for how an encyclopaedia could be built and function in the digital age, it also posed the genre a challenging question: How many online encyclopaedias could the internet make room for?

It came as no surprise that the rise of the digital era subsequently caused the disappearance of most encyclopaedias. Printed works simply could not keep up with the rapid information flow of the digital world. At the same time, digital solutions appeared, which created entirely new possibilities for the genre. Several significant works, such as *Brockhaus* and *Britannica*, adjusted to the new reality and thus have survived as knowledge authorities, even though they now operate in the new digital medium.

This was also the case in the Scandinavian countries, where several initiatives to create digital information platforms were launched. *Nationalencyklopedin* and *Den Store Danske Encyklopædi* were converted to online encyclopaedias, on a subscription basis, in 2001 and 2006, respectively. However, the outcome for the publishers was very different: *Nationalencyklopedin* found a working business model, while its Danish counterpart, Den Store Danske—as the platform was named—after several (failed) attempts at funding its operation through advertising, ended up gathering dust on the digital bookshelf.[75]

The Norwegian Solution

The Norwegians, however, found a model that proved to be sustainable both in relation to a digital continuation of the former printed national encyclopaedias and the open access possibilities of the genre introduced by Wikipedia. The history of *Store Norske Leksikon* (*The Great Norwegian Lexicon*) goes back to the early twentieth century, when Aschehoug, the traditional Norwegian publishing house founded in 1872, published *Illustreret Norsk Konversationsleksikon* (1907–1913). Throughout the twentieth century, several major Norwegian encyclopaedias were published. However, in 1975, the two most prominent publishing houses, Aschehoug and Gyldendal, decided to merge several of their different encyclopaedias and dictionaries and founded a new publishing house Kunnskapsforlaget. In 1978, the new company published the first edition of *Store Norske Leksikon*.

From 1978 to 2007, Kunnskapsforlaget published four different editions of the Norwegian encyclopaedia, establishing itself as a giant of information in Norway. Obviously, a digital solution had to be found. In 2000, the website snl.no was launched, behind a paywall. In 2009, the paywall was removed, and snl.no became a free, advertising-funded service. Only one year later, in 2010, Kunnskapsforlaget withdrew from *Store Norske Leksikon* and left the content and websites to the two foundations Fritt Ord and Sparebankstiftelsen DNB. The path towards a comprehensive space for digital information was paved. After several years of planning work, the Norwegian Parliament established a public-support scheme for an online encyclopaedia with the aim of supporting "professionally edited and professionally quality-assured online encyclopaedias in Norwegian."[76] In 2014 the association *Store Norske Leksikon* was founded. The members were a mix of various Norwegian foundations, science academies and Norwegian universities.[77]

The Norwegian ambitions paved the way for a similar model in Denmark. In April 2019, the statutory general meeting for the association Lex.dk was held, and a new Danish information platform was born. Den Store Danske may have been abandoned, but a new online encyclopaedia was born.[78]

The Encyclopaedia in the Changing Information Societies

Books move across borders far more quietly than wars, epidemics, or climate crises. Nevertheless, for centuries, the encyclopaedia has had a significant role in developing and accessing information. In many ways, the encyclopaedia has been capable of adapting itself to the changing information societies of recent centuries.

A simple but telling way to visualise these changes is by comparing book pages and their layout in encyclopaedias through the ages. The function of the book page is to carry the text that communicates and transmits thoughts and ideas from author to reader, and thereby it is "the most significant site for displaying information, and in the process, it has determined what counts as intellectual authority, logical argument, and useful information."[79] In the layout of the Scandinavian encyclopaedias it is clear how the dissemination of information has changed.[80] Graphically, the text has gradually become slightly larger and the illustrations more numerous. The language has likewise changed, becoming more inclusive. All this testifies to how the readers and users of the encyclopaedia have changed also. Broadly speaking, these changes can be described as a movement away from addressing the intellectual elite towards wanting to reach a wider audience—if not anybody with an internet connection.

From an information-historical perspective, there have been—and still are—several different purposes for the publication of this genre. Some purposes have remained the same over extended periods, while others have arisen in connection with changes in the book market, including the different readers and users, or due to changes in media technology. There is no doubt that many encyclopaedias have a strong connection to both cultural and national values. The press's laudatory mentions and comprehensive reviews of the various publications, and the political interference in, and financing of, the works and their digital platforms are all examples of the cultural significance of the encyclopaedias.[81] Encyclopaedias were considered essential: something to be mentioned in newspapers and a topic that, at least in the Scandinavian countries, has reached the political agenda repeatedly.

This chapter demonstrates the potential of the history of encyclopaedias as a means of examining our modern information culture, from the end of the eighteenth century to the present day, a generation after the turn of the millennium. Several times in the history of the encyclopaedia, it has looked as if the time of the great encyclopaedias was over, and that they would disappear, and the encyclopaedia has done just that—in terms of the traditional book. However, the digital age has meant a new beginning for the encyclopaedia. New ways of creating and sharing information have meant that the genre remains an essential knowledge authority. With both the distant and recent past in mind, there is no reason to believe that enterprising, imaginative, and ambitious publishers, as well as far-sighted information nerds, will not continue to develop the genre.

Notes

1 Irene Vallejo, *Evigheden i Et Siv. Historien om Bogen* (Copenhagen: Gutkind Forlag, 2021); Joel Halldorf, *Bokens Folk. En Civilisationshistoria Från Papyrus till Pixlar* (Stockholm: Fri Tanke, 2023).
2 Maria Simonsen, *Det store leksikon* (Aarhus: Aarhus University Press, 2021), 44–60.
3 Siv Frøydis Berg, Øivind Berg, Sine Halkjelsvik Bjordal and Helge Jordheim, eds., *All Verdens Kunnskap. Leksikon gjennom To Tusen år* (Oslo: Forlaget Press, 2012).
4 Daniel Headrick, *When Information Came of Age: Technologies of Knowledge in the Age of Reason and Revolution, 1700–1850* (New York: Oxford University Press, 2000), 143.
5 Maria Simonsen, "Encyclopedias and Nationalism in Denmark: A Study of the Reception of Three Encyclopedias, from Print to Digital," *Mémoire du Livre/Studies in Book Culture* 13, no 1 (Spring 2022): 1–31.
6 Each Scandinavian country has its unique story about the development of the encyclopaedic genre. However, it is impossible to go through the entire history of each country in this chapter. The individual sections go in-depth by giving examples from one country. However, this does not mean there are no other central histories from the other Scandinavian countries.
7 Headrick, *When Information Came of Age*, 143.
8 Headrick, *When Information Came of Age*, 144; Maria Simonsen, *Den Skandinaviske Encyklopædi. Udgivelse og Udformning af Nordisk Familjebok og Salmonsens Konversationsleksikon* (Lund: Makadam Förlag, 2016), 49–50.
9 Robert L. Collison, "Encyclopaedias," Britannica Online (May 24, 2023), https://www.britannica.com/topic/encyclopaedia.
10 Simonsen, *Det store leksikon*; Collison, "Encyclopaedias," Britannica Online (May 24, 2023), https://www.britannica.com/topic/encyclopaedia.
11 Headrick, *When Information Came of Age*, 143.
12 For a well-developed discussion of encyclopaedia titles through the ages, see Headrick, *When Information Came of Age*, 143.
13 Simonsen, *Det store leksikon*, 8.
14 Simonsen, *Det store leksikon*, 8.

15 "han har samlet informasjon om 20,000 'ting', hentet fra 2000 bind og skrevet av 1000 forfattere." Tone Bratteteig and Anne Beate Maurseth, "Kart, Trær, Labyrinter," in *All Verdens Kunnskap. Leksikon gjennom To Tusen år*, ed. Berg et al. (Oslo: Forlaget Press, 2012), 17–78, at 28.
16 Yeo, *Encyclopaedic Visions. Scientific Dictionaries and Enlightenment Culture* (Cambridge, UK: Cambridge University Press, 2001), 5; Simonsen, *Det store leksikon*, 46.
17 Yeo, *Encyclopaedic Visions*, 5.
18 Simonsen, *Det store leksikon*, 48.
19 Loveland, *The European Encyclopedia*, 24.
20 Loveland, *The European Encyclopedia*, 24.
21 Øivind Berg, "Encycklopedien, Biblioteket og Drømmen om Fullstendighed," in *All Verdens Kunnskap. Leksikon gjennom To Tusen år*, ed. Berg et al. (Oslo: Forlaget Press, 2012), 242–268, at 258.
22 Berg, "Encycklopedien," 258.
23 Headrick, *When Information Came of Age*, 144.
24 Loveland, *The European Encyclopedia*, 191.
25 Loveland, *The European Encyclopedia*, 192.
26 Frank Beck Lassen, "Oplysningens Bibel," in *Den Franske Encyklopædi - Et Udvalg*, ed. Denis Diderot og Jean le Rond d'Alembert (Aarhus: Forlaget Klim, 2014), 301–357.
27 Simonsen, *Det store leksikon*, 50.
28 Simonsen, *Det store leksikon*, 57.
29 Headrick, *When Information Came of Age*, 152.
30 Anders Fagerjord and Helge Jordheim, "Oppdatert Eller Utdatert. Encyclopedisjangeren og Tiden," in *All Verdens Kunnskap. Leksikon gjennom To Tusen år*, ed. Berg et al. (Oslo: Forlaget Press, 2012), 70–116, at 82.
31 An essential reason why the history of Scandinavian encyclopaedias (and other Nordic book history) is not so widespread is connected to the fact that Nordic book historians only until recently have begun to publish more in English. As Henning Hansen and Maria Simonsen have emphasised, "most Scandinavians, as well as a great number of Finns, can read and understand the other Scandinavian languages (except for Icelandic and Faroese), which to some extent explains why a large part of Nordic book history is only available in the Scandinavian languages. Another important reason for this is that Nordic book history has arguably addressed chiefly Nordic issues and targeted primarily a domestic audience." Henning Hansen and Maria Simonsen, "Book History in the Nordic Countries," *Mémoire du Livre/Studies in Book Culture*, 13, no 1 (Spring 2022): 2; Simonsen, "Enylopedias and Nationalism," 1–31.
32 Maria Simonsen, "The Rise and Fall of Danish Encyclopedias, 1891–2017," in *Stranded Encyclopedias, c. 1700–2000. Exploring Unfinished, Unpublished, Unsuccessful Encyclopedic Projects*, ed. Linn Holmberg and Maria Simonsen (London: Palgrave Macmillan, 2021).
33 Simonsen, *Det store leksikon*, 60.
34 Jakob Christensson, "En Upplysningstida Encyklopedists Uppgång och Fall," *Lychnos. Årsbok för idé och Lärdomshistoria* (1993), 111.
35 Simonsen, *Den Skandinaviske Encyklopædi*, 79–82.
36 Jakob Christensson, *Lyckoriket. Studier i Svensk Upplysning* (Stockholm: Atlantis, 1996), 87.
37 Simonsen, *Det store leksikon*, 16.
38 Christensson, "En Upplysningstida Encyclopedist."
39 Christensson, "En Lyckoriket," 100; Sven Lidman, "Den Svenska Uppslagsboken," in *Den Svenska Bogen 500 år*, ed. Harry Järv (Stockholm: Liber Förlag, 1983), 338.
40 The same applies to the history of encyclopaedias in other parts of the world. In the anthology *Stranded Encyclopedias, c. 1700–2000*, there are many examples of failed and abandoned publishing projects from around the eighteenth century until today. Holmberg and Simonsen, *Stranded Encyclopedias*.
41 Simonsen, *Den Skandinaviske Encyklopædi*, 57.
42 Simonsen, *Det store leksikon*, 63.
43 Simonsen, *Det store leksikon*, 64.
44 Simonsen, *Den Skandinaviske Encyklopædi*, 67.
45 Sine Halkjelsvik Bjordal and Johan L. Tønnesson, "Kunnskap og Ideologi," in Berg, *All Verdens kunnskap*, ed. Berg et al., 118–185, at 152.
46 Bjordal and Tønnesson, "Kunnskap og Ideologi," 152.

47 Robert Collison, *Encyclopaedias: Their History Throughout the Ages* (New York & London: Hafner Publishing Company, 1964), 195–196.
48 The Danish work is not alone in representing the development of the genre. The Swedish encyclopaedia *Nordisk Familjebok* (1876–1993) was also published in several editions in the same period and underwent a similar transformation in terms of material and content. The publication history of the *Nordisk Familjebok* is described in detail in Simonsen, *Den Skandinaviske Encyklopædi*.
49 André Nicolet, *Encyklopædier og Konversationslexika Gennem Tiderne* (Copenhagen: J.H. Schultz, 1946), 80.
50 Simonsen, *Det store leksikon*, 29; Hans Hertel, *Den Daglige Bog. Bøger, Formidlere og Læsere i Danmark Gennem 500 år* (Copenhagen: Christian Ejlers' Forlag, 1983), 44–45.
51 Simonsen, *Den Skandinaviske Encyklopædi*, 96–97; Simonsen, "The Rise and Fall," 296.
52 "Forord," *Salmonsens Store Illustrerede Konversationsleksikon – En Nordisk Encyklopædi* (Copenhagen: Brødrene Salmonsen, 1893).
53 "[E]n omhyggelig Undersøgelse [viste], at en Omplantning som den paatænkte i Virkeligheden ikke lod sig udføre, men at det, for enhver ved at slaa op i Værket overalt maatte faa et bestemt Indtryk af at befinde sig paa nordisk Grund, var nødvendigt at lade den enkelte Forfatter afgøre, om han kunde benytte den fremmede Tekst som Grundlag for sin selvstændige Udvikling af Æmnet eller ej (…)." "Forord," *Salmonsens Store Illustrerede Konversationsleksikon*.
54 Simonsen, "Encyclopedias and Nationalism," 13.
55 "Vi anbefaler særdeles dette Leksikon, der tegner til at blive en enestaaende god Haandbog i nyttig Viden for Danske," *Politiken*, February 12, 1892.
56 Simonsen, *Den Skandinaviske Encyklopædi*, 270.
57 Jørgen Bang, "Den Store Salmonsen," in *Danske Opslagsværker* ed. Axel Andersen (Copenhagen: G.E.C. Gad, 1970), 10.
58 Simonsen, *Den Skandinaviske Encyklopædi*, 148; Bang, "Den Store Salmonsen," 5–35.
59 Christian Larsen, Erik Nørr and Pernille Sonne, "Da Skolen tog Form, 1780–1850," in *Dansk Skolehistorie: Hverdag, Vilkår og Visioner Gennem 500 år*, vol. 2. ed. Charlotte Appel and Ning de Coninck-Smith (Aarhus: Aarhus University Press, 2013), 127–114.
60 Simonsen, *Det store leksikon*, 33.
61 Hertel, *Den daglige bog*, 44–47.
62 Simonsen, *Den Skandinaviske Encyklopædi*, 104.
63 Simonsen, "The Rise and Fall," 301.
64 See, for example, *Thisted Amts Tidende*, November 20, 1940 or *Kolding Folkeblad*, November 20, 1940.
65 "I vor tid med det hastige tempo og de stærke krav om at være up to date har både landets og byens beboere imidlertid følt nødvendigheden af at få et mindre leksikon, der kunne forene den store Salmonsens saglighed og lødighed med det lille leksikons hurtige oplysning og helt tidssvarende stoftilrettelæggelse." The quote is in "Prøvehæfte for Den Lille Salmonsen" [undated] Bogvæsen og Boghandel, Schultz, Småtrykssamlingen, The Royal Danish Library, 36.
66 Simonsen, *Det store leksikon*, 31.
67 Simonsen, *Den Skandinaviske Encyklopædi*, 192.
68 Henrik Sejerkilde, *Dansk Bogdesign i det 20. århundrede* (Odense: University Press of Southern Denmark, 2017), 371.
69 Simonsen, "The Rise and Fall of Danish Encyclopedias," 312.
70 Sejerkilde, *Dansk Bogdesign,* 371.
71 Lidman, "Den Svenska Uppslagsboken," 359.
72 Lars Tynell, "Mot Bättre Vetande. Förslag från Uppslagsverkskommittén," *Statens Offentliga Utredningar,* 26 (Stockholm: Norstedts, 1980).
73 Simonsen, *Det store leksikon*, 7.
74 Loveland, *The European Encyclopedia,* 374–382; Thomas Leitch, *Wikipedia U: Knowledge, Authority, and Liberal Education in the Digital Age* (Baltimore, MD: Johns Hopkins University Press, 2014).
75 Simonsen, *Det store leksikon*, 97.
76 "Store Norske Leksikon," snl.no, February 4, 2024, https://snl.no/Store_norske_leksikon.
77 "Store Norske Leksikon."

78 Simonsen, "The Rise and Fall of Danish Encyclopedias," 316–317.
79 Peter Stoicheff and Andrew Taylor, eds., *The Future of the Page* (Toronto: University of Toronto Press, 2003), 5; Maria Simonsen, "(Bog)sidens Manifestationer. Et Boghistorisk Studie af Informations- og Kundskabsidealer i Tre Danske Encyklopædier," *Temp – tidsskrift for historie* 17, no. 14 (2017), 129.
80 Simonsen, "(Bog)sidens," 127–151.
81 Simonsen, "Encyclopedias and Nationalism," 3.

8
PAUL OTLET'S EXPERIMENTS WITH KNOWLEDGE ORGANISATION AND EXPLORATIONS OF A FUTURE SEMANTIC WEB*

Charles van den Heuvel

Introduction

Paul Otlet (1868–1944) has been viewed by some as the forgotten forefather of the World Wide Web (WWW).[1] Others, however, have warned against such teleological readings of Otlet's work, explaining that his notion of the network of, and relations between and within, documents was different from the internet and hypertext.[2] Otlet explored the organisation and distribution of information in a classification of the sciences and via substitutes for the books to produce fundamental knowledge that could serve society. In doing so, he mobilised a large number of metaphors, including the "tree of knowledge," to illuminate his project. However, it will be explained that despite claims in historical studies of Otlet, the role of the tree structure in classifying the multidimensionality and dynamics of information is ultimately rather limited.[3] This chapter discusses the difficulties that Otlet (and his close colleague Henri La Fontaine) faced in his experiments to find the most effective ways of representing the dynamics of information transfer by means of the schematic use of multidimensional notations and visualisations of the Universal Decimal Classification (UDC). In particular, the chapter focuses on Otlet's ontological visualisations or schemas of information organisation to create essential knowledge from the masses of information available, "les schèmes fondamentaux," and argues that a comparison of Otlet's experiments with creating multidimensional notations and visualisations with his notion of the "document-instrument"—whereby the document becomes one with the instrument that registers and analyses the document's information—can help to illuminate ongoing processes in the WWW, such as the restructuring of its extension, the Semantic Web.

---

* All figures are reproduced with the permission of the Mundaneum (Mons). I would like to thank Stéphanie Manfroid, Responsable des Archives, Mundaneum for her assistance in my archival research as well as the editor and the reviewer of this chapter for their valuable comments.

Paul Otlet: A Man with a Mission

Paul Otlet must be understood in his time rather than putting him forward as a precursor of the WWW. The life and works of Paul Otlet have been described at length by W. Boyd Rayward. Rayward sketches the upbringing of a young boy, son of a rich entrepreneur and politician, who grew up in the wealthy residential areas of Brussels. From Otlet's diary, we get the impression of a well-protected, but also solitary, youngster reading and writing texts, collecting objects, and making drawings in his bedroom. From the age of fifteen, he started classifying rigorously his own notes. In 1888, at twenty years old, Otlet left for Paris to study sociology and law and a year later he took a degree in the latter discipline in Brussels. In those formative years, Otlet showed a great interest in the works of such positivist sociologists and philosophers as Herbert Spencer, August Comte, and Alfred Fouillée. They shaped his positivist and utilitarian views of society and his belief in the necessity of synthesis of the sciences to support mankind.[4]

In 1890, after graduating in law from the Free University of Brussels, Otlet became an intern of Edmond Picard, a friend of the family, an influential Brussels lawyer and major figure in the cultural and intellectual life of Belgium. Otlet may have met his lifelong friend and collaborator in Picard's office, Henri La Fontaine, who had been an intern there a decade before. Both men were involved in compiling bibliographies of law, in Otlet's case, and of sociology, in La Fontaine's. They shared the vision of creating a "Universal and International" library which could be coordinated by learned societies and others interested in bibliographical matters.

In 1895, Otlet and La Fontaine organised an International Conference on Bibliography to discuss and ultimately to recommend the creation of an International Institute of Bibliography and the compilation within it of the Répertoire Bibliographique Universel, a universal catalogue of knowledge representations. This was to be organised for subject access, via the Dewey Decimal Classification (DDC), which Otlet had become acquainted with in the same year.

The bibliographical and classificatory enterprise in Brussels received more and more visibility through a series of conferences in the first decade of the twentieth century that paved the way for a further international institutionalisation of documentary work with a wider scope. Otlet introduced and discussed extensively the idea of documentation to refer to all that was involved in the creation and use of recorded information, and as time progressed, in whatever format it was recorded, expressed, or transferred. In 1907, a Central Office of International Institutions was set up, aiming at: "The study of everything which contributes to proper organisation and documentation, such as the preparation of collections, repertories, publications and services on a co-operative basis."[5]

Following a World Congress in 1910, the Belgian Government agreed to provide a centralised location in which all the elements that Otlet and his colleagues had elaborated could be consolidated. This was the huge left wing of the Palais du Cinquantenaire in Brussels. A new component occupying a major part of the location was an international museum, the entire enterprise given the name Palais Mondial (World Palace) or Mundaneum. After a long history, the Mundaneum has been recreated in Mons (Belgium) as an archive and exhibitions centre concerned with historical and contemporary developments in the world of information.[6]

Interrelated Strategies for Information as Action

Otlet wrote many, sometimes repetitive, texts with his views on the organisation of documentation and of the world, as conceptualised, and in part initiated, by the Mundaneum. His most important publications on these subjects were *Traité de Documentation* (1934) and *Monde: Essai d'Universalisme* (1935).[7] He ultimately conceptualised the Mundaneum as "an idea, an institution, a method, a material body of works and collections, a building and a network."[8] Metaphor and materialisation mixed in Otlet's mind. In his view, the Mundaneum was as much an architecture of knowledge as a knowledge architecture. Otlet developed interrelated strategies which combined documentation, the study of the forms and representation of information, and institutionalisation involving concrete plans for buildings. Otlet's actions to organise information were initially successful. To give an example, since the first ideas for its creation in 1895, the Répertoire Bibliographique Universel grew in four years from almost half to more than three million entries from memory (the original experimental file for the 1895 conference was four hundred thousand cards); in 1903, it contained over six million entries, in 1912 over nine million entries, and by the outbreak of World War I no less than eleven million cards were classified by author and subject. To the Répertoire Bibliographique Universel, a bibliographical catalogue was added a repertory of files or dossiers of substantive information, the Universal Documentary Repertory, which by 1912 counted a quarter of a million documents in various textual and non-textual media "relative to all the objects and all the facts which constitute human activity in its widest extension."[9]

As his work developed, Otlet became aware of the problems that had to be grappled with. First was the problem of the enormous increase of information, already observed since Antiquity but which with the introduction of the printing press increased to such an extent that by the turn of the twentieth century, libraries across the world counted millions upon millions of publications in their collections. A second problem was the introduction of new publication formats and media. Otlet's early texts and drawings reveal a preoccupation with the organisation and distribution not only of printed matter but of photographs and films also. Later, they reveal a deep concern for the newer broadcast media such as radio and television. A third problem was the dynamic growth and diversification of the sciences and the voluminous fragmentation of information produced. To meet these problems, Otlet employed interrelated strategies designed to help in the analysis and synthesis of information.

The approach to handling the first problem, that of the information deluge, was a combination of old and new ways of information reduction to enable the creation of essential knowledge. The old method—dating back to late Antiquity and the Middle Ages—was Otlet's aim to summarise fundamental information privately and collectively in encyclopaedic formats.[10] The new method, inspired by the latest developments in physics and chemistry, was an atomist approach to fragmenting information into the tiniest, most essential particles of knowledge, called "faits" (facts) and to regroup these in a synthesis based on collaborative research.[11] In a material sense, this information reduction implied summarising the contents of books on cards or microfilming them.[12]

Otlet was in fact conceptualising the need for what he called "substitutes for the book" to present re-worked information no longer in the linear text format of the traditional book: "For written works a re-arrangement of their contents not along the lines of the special plan of a particular book, but according to the genus and species appropriate does not make for any loss of substance."[13]

Otlet experimented with all sorts of substitutes for the book both in ephemeral media, such as radio, and in mechanical devices, such as rotating card systems, what he called "machine à lire." In a published lecture of 1908 with the title *"La Function et les Transformation du Livre,"* Otlet not only stated that the book might be substituted by radio, but also envisioned the development of immense centres for "irradiation on demand" of documents kept in a world library: "Multiple places for reading and listening around the world, all linked to the same universal network, would permit henceforth the diffusion of knowledge without any sort of limitation."[14] Shortly before his death in 1944, Otlet visualised his Mundaneum as an active knowledge building transmitting audio and visual information by radio and television.

These ideas were part of Otlet's vision of a world-wide hierarchical network ("reseau universel") (see Fig. 8.1). From what he conceived a world city of universal knowledge (Civitates Mundaneum), information in multiple formats would eventually be transmitted in such a way that it arrived at an interactive multimedia desk (Mondothèque) for personal use; a desk that would contain new systems and technologies based on mechanical devices such as a film projector, gramophone, telephone, radio, and television, as well as posters, charts, and printed volumes (Fig. 8.2).

Thus, Otlet's strategies of knowledge organisation focused on information reduction and distribution by multimedia mechanical devices networked in an international arrangement of documentation centres. These devices were envisioned to support qualitative processes of analysis and synthesis of information. The main tool for achieving this—turning now to the third of Otlet's strategies—was a system of classification that could keep up with the dynamic changes occurring in the sciences, the diversification in their contents and the continuous interactions of multiple points of view. Otlet stated: "While a classification always involves the abstract point of view and deals with the objects in their relationships with each other, it is nevertheless necessary to be aware that the two points of view constantly interact."[15]

The classification Otlet and La Fontaine used for this purpose was based on the DDC: "It provided first of all a nomenclature of human knowledge, fixed, universal, and able to be expressed in an international language-that of numbers [....] It is a kind of agglutinative language: its numerals are its roots, predicative and attributive roots [...] They are placed above and outside any grammatical categories, in that they express abstractions, pure scientific categories."[16] However, they soon realised the limitations of the DDC, which was designed primarily as a classification system for use in libraries. They proposed changes to make it more suitable for organising and disseminating the dynamic production of scientific information.

The challenges to be overcome were to abstract scientific information in a such way that (1) the most essential knowledge could be captured, synthesised, and disseminated using a logical notation; (2) the growth of the sciences could be captured in classes and subclasses; (3) the dynamics within the sciences could be captured within this notation by keeping the fundamental structure in place but allowing to express changes in classes as well; (4) multiple points of view could be added. To achieve these objectives, Otlet and his colleagues introduced special features and coding practices into the system, such that their UDC ultimately diverged very considerably from the original DDC.[17]

In 1951, a Dutch chemical engineer, Frits Donker Duyvis, who since 1920 had joined Otlet and La Fontaine in their mission to develop the UDC, described in an article entitled

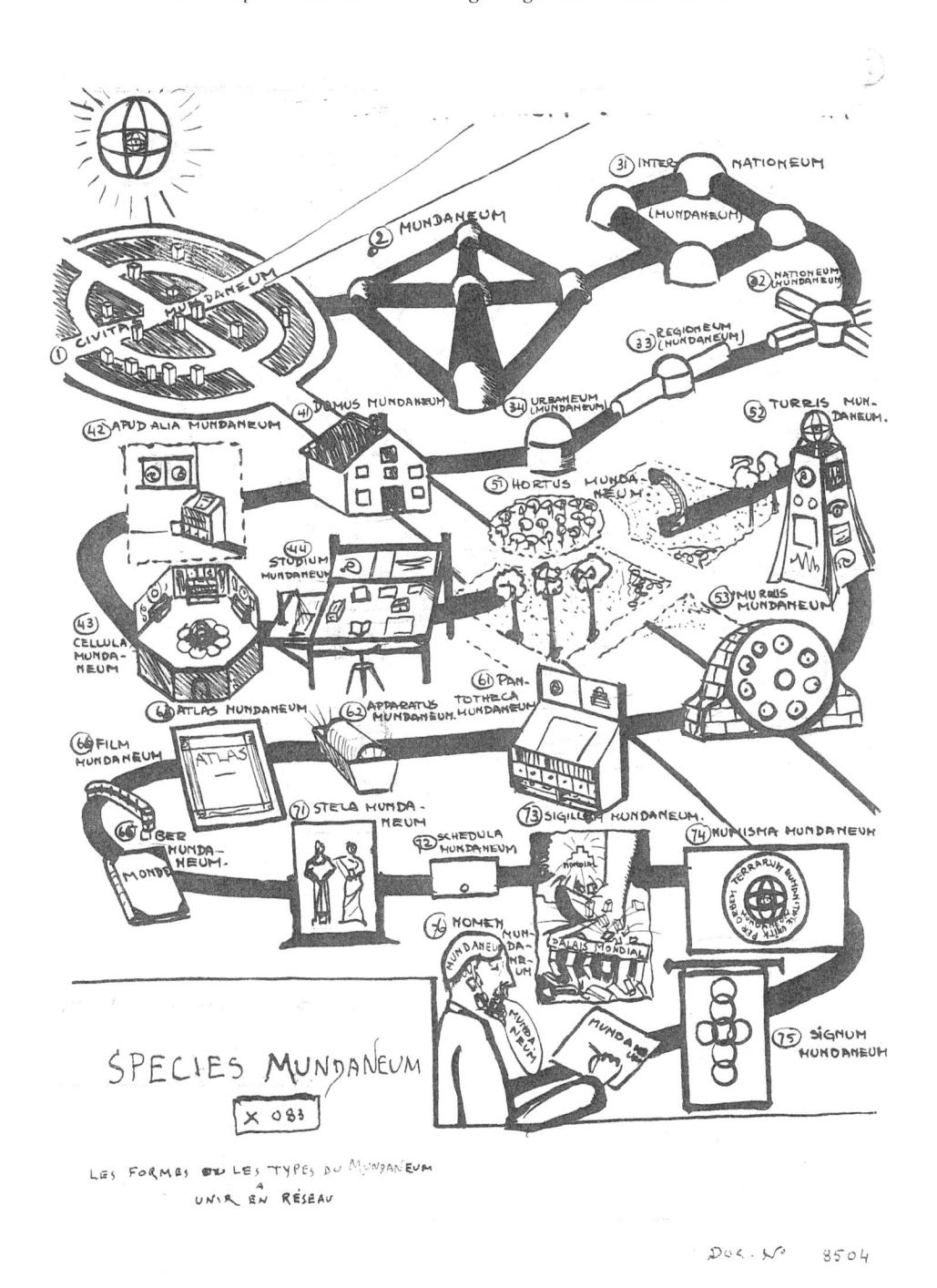

Figure 8.1 Network of documentation in a hierarchical order of Mundaneum species. Mundaneum (Mons), D6PPP05, EUMC, 8504, @collection Mundaneum, Belgium, Mons.

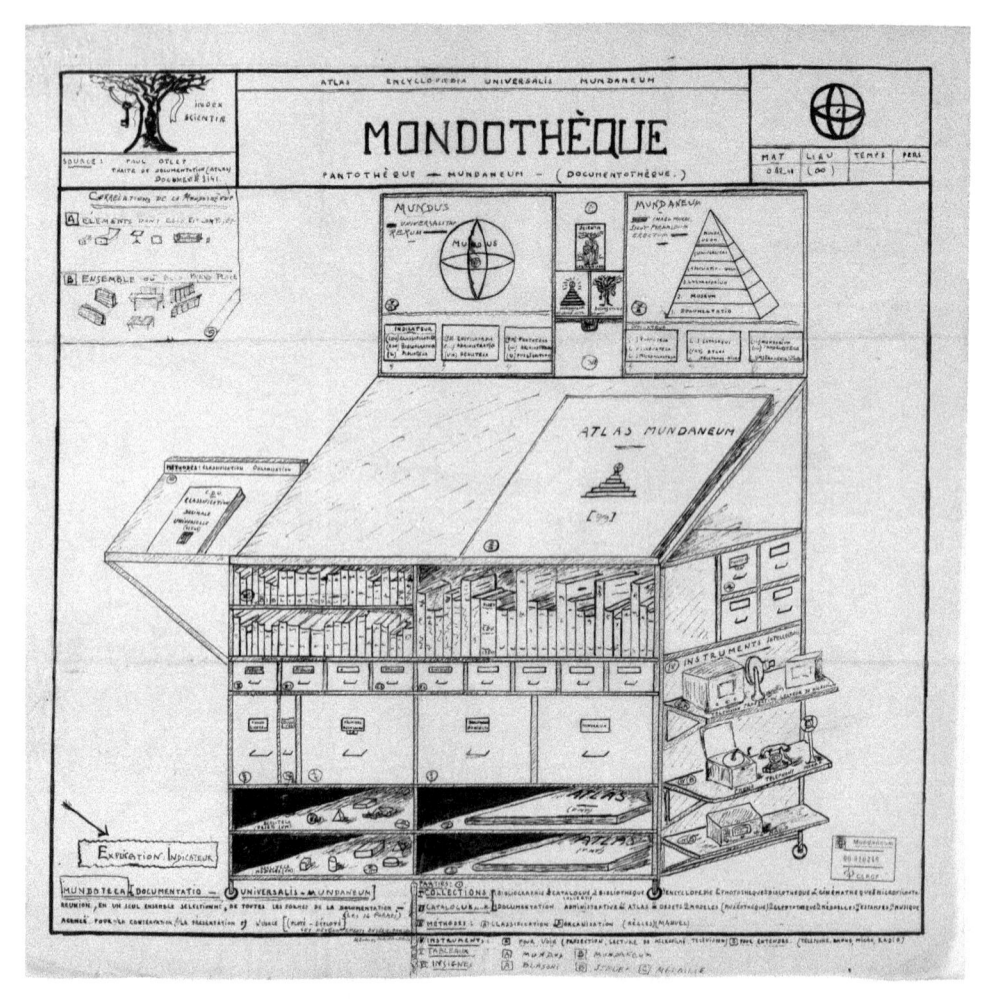

Figure 8.2 The Mondothèque. Mundaneum (Mons), EUMP, 8141, @collection Mundaneum, Belgium, Mons.

"The UDC: What It Is And What It Is Not" the fundamental differences that had grown between "Dewey's philosophical conception of the classification of knowledge," and the "practical UDC."[18] Fundamental to Donker Duyvis' analysis of the UDC is the idea that: "The word 'decimal' is not quite accurate since the UDC is not only decimal. The word 'classification' in itself is right, but it is not sufficiently limited by the word 'universal' and 'decimal.' It should certainly be added that the classification is 'multidimensional' (which is more characteristic than the feature 'decimal' [....]."[19]

Although it took more than fifty years to recognise multidimensionality as one of the main characteristics of the UDC, it played a fundamental role in Otlet's conceptualisations of knowledge structures from the start. It became apparent in his earlier publications on the structure of classifications, in his designs for substitutes for the book and in his sketches of knowledge objects, which he called: "les schèmes fondamentaux."[20] In the latter sketches or schemas, Otlet tried to visualise his thoughts on the notation of information in multiple dimensions to capture the essential expressions of knowledge and to arrive at an elementary theory of classification.[21]

Fundamental Schemas of Knowledge: Multidimensional Notation and Visualisation

Even before Otlet became acquainted with the DDC, he became aware of the need of multidimensionality to deal with the growth and dynamics in the classification of the sciences. Otlet was a passionate reader of the works of Herbert Spencer who as early as 1864 had stressed the limitations of the classificatory representations of the sciences in tables: "that [.] their relations cannot be truly shown on a plane, but only in a space of three dimensions."[22] Otlet was aware of the problem of multidimensionality when for the UDC he introduced a system that made a distinction between number codes expressing "permanent meaning" that recur regularly throughout the classification and those expressing changing characteristics or aspects that related to these basic concepts. He designed a special notation that could be used to link to the basic classificatory structure, codes drawn from a set of what he called "auxiliary tables" expressing "facets" of knowledge such as language, geography, chronology, and points of view.[23] This provided more flexibility in the subclasses, but the organisation in the main classes could not keep up with the dynamic disciplinary developments in the sciences.

Otlet would not only seek a further elaboration and systematisation of the tables of the UDC as a kind of universal language, efforts that would be continued long after his death by Donker Duyvis and others, but he also explored the possibilities of another strategy: visualisation. In 1912, Otlet and the Scottish sociologist and town planner Patrick Geddes proposed the preparation of an *Encyclopedia Synthetica Schematica* by an international group of collaborating scientists under their direction. They would create schemas and diagrams that would constitute a "graphical language that would permit the expression of general or more abstract ideas more completely and definitely" than could words.[24] In this respect, Otlet was building on a long tradition, stretching back to the Middle Ages.[25]

The Mundaneum in Mons preserves in its archives thousands of visualisations either drawn or commissioned by Otlet.[26] In his autobiographical "Carnet Bleu" (1916), Otlet explains that since his youth drawings had helped him to order his thoughts: "I find that I must draw certain ideas, certain graphics. And the movements that I draw: a circle, a triangle, a line come directly from my mind."[27] In short, these sketches can be best understood as visual thought experiments. Otlet tried to use them to capture his basic ideas on the organisation of elements in the information processes of abstraction and synthesis and the development of substitutes for the book sometimes in mechanical form. What most of Otlet's sketches of elements of information organisation or alternatives for the traditional book format have in common is that the representations are multidimensional. What he called "schemes fondamentaux" must be understood as instrumental in the development of a new classification theory that went beyond the scheme devised by Dewey.

In his manuscript "Théorie Schématique de la Classification" (December 14, 1908), Otlet describes and visualises schematically the multidimensional reduction of the content of various formats to one line and the reassembly of these elements in multidimensional knowledge constructions (Fig. 8.3).[28]

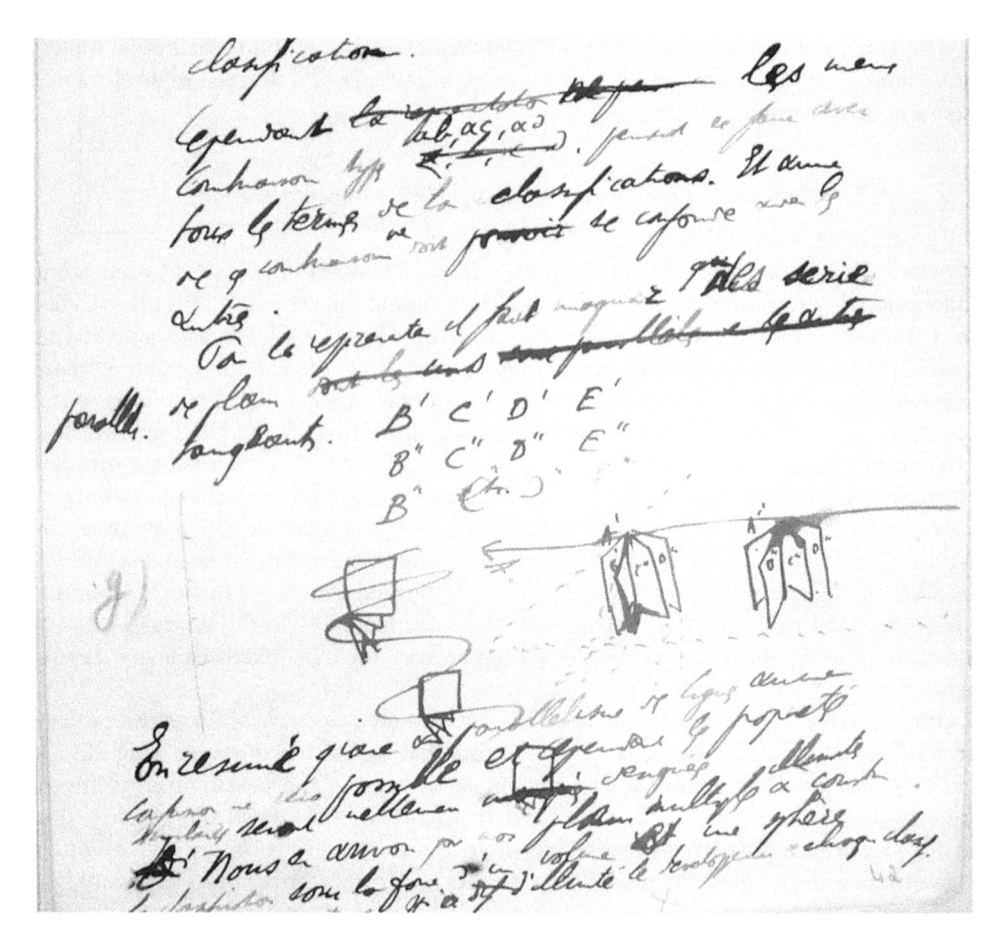

Figure 8.3 Dimensions reduction mapping the contents of book on a line, Paul Otlet, "Théorie schématique de la classification" (detail), December 14, 1908. Mundaneum (Mons), PPPO 956, EUM farde 8, no. 42, @collection Mundaneum, Belgium, Mons.

In successive pages, he translates these dimensions into the numerical notation of the UDC and includes sketches of multidimensional knowledge objects in which these various classes meet. Examples of exploring multidimensional substitutes of the book are sketches for various card systems of such as a physical structure from which to hang cards allowing perception of multiple subjects from different angles and points of view, new card formats, and the use of different colour codes to visualise the relations between the extracted content of the various cards (Fig. 8.4).

Through his sketches, Otlet also became aware of conflicts that could occur between notations of the UDC and their multidimensional representations. For instance, one of the most common multidimensional forms of Otlet's visual experiments, the cube, has six faces. These six faces do not easily map onto the ten classes of the UDC (Fig. 8.5). For that reason, apart from the obvious choice of the sphere, which allows for unlimited projections of points, Otlet also visualised combinations of spheres and cubes and created octagonal forms with a total ten faces (Fig. 8.6). To translate these visualisations of multidimensional

Figure 8.4 Design multidimensional card system by Paul Otlet. Mundaneum (Mons), PPPO 956, EUM farde 9, no. 74–75, @collection Mundaneum, Belgium, Mons.

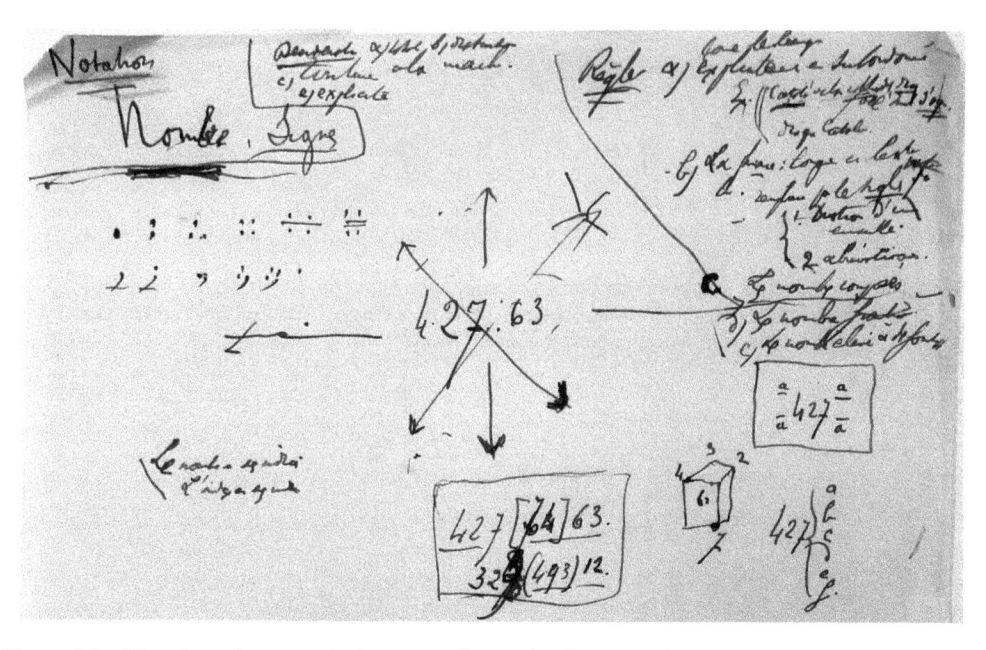

Figure 8.5 Mapping of a numerical notation by Paul Otlet. Mundaneum (Mons). "Notation" (detail), PPPO 956, EUM farde 7, no. 21, @collection Mundaneum, Belgium, Mons.

knowledge objects that might substitute for the book, Otlet experimented with octagonal system cards and oblong octagonal "books" (Figs. 8.7 and 8.8). Through these visual experiments with multidimensional representations of knowledge objects, Otlet must have become aware of the limitation of the tree of knowledge as an organisational structure to capture the growth and the dynamics of the sciences and its consequences for classification that would become a recurrent theme in information history.

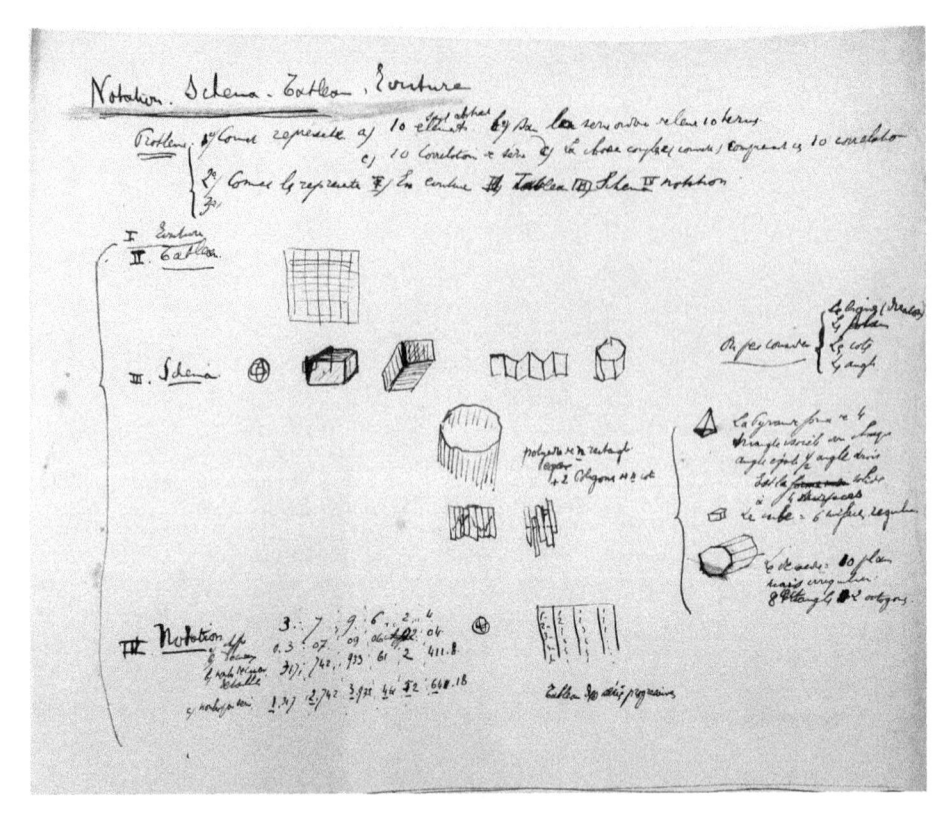

Figure 8.6 Comparison mappings on pyramid, cube, and octagonal cylinder by Paul Otlet, Mundaneum (Mons) "Notation, Schéma, Tableau, Ecriture" (detail), PPPO 956, farde no. 9, 105, @collection Mundaneum, Belgium, Mons.

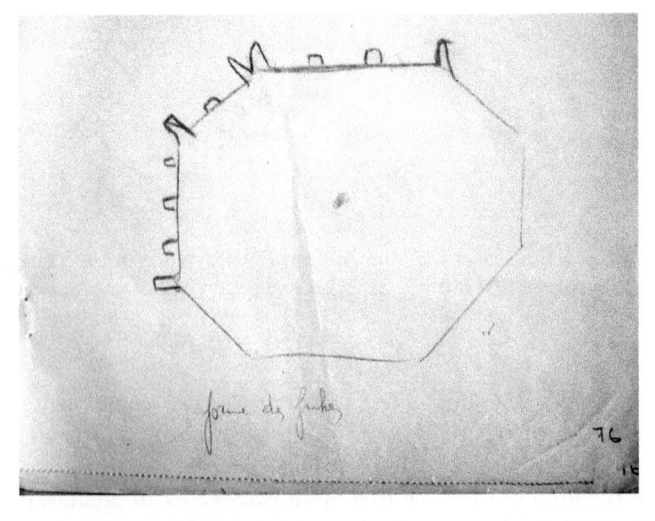

Figure 8.7 Octagonal Index card by Paul Otlet, Mundaneum (Mons), PPPO 956 EUM farde 9, no. 76, @collection Mundaneum, Belgium, Mons.

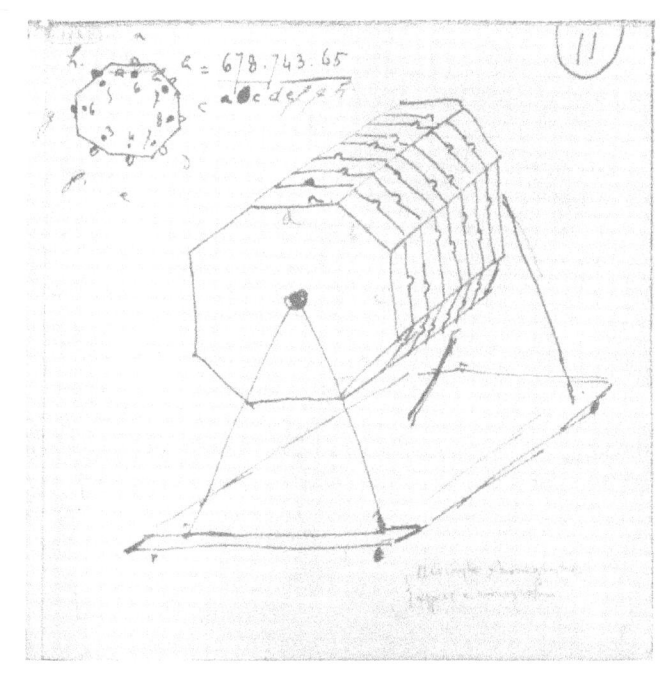

Figure 8.8 Octagonal "Livre," by Paul Otlet, "Elements de schématique" (detail), April 1916, Mundaneum (Mons), PPPO 281, no. 7, @collection Mundaneum, Belgium, Mons.

Ramifications in Trees of Knowledge and Limits in Classifications

It is hardly surprising that Otlet chose the very old metaphor of the tree of knowledge to symbolise the growth of human knowledge. It was figured with a golden key dangling from its branches mirrored by the description "index scientia," which appeared in the logo of almost every publication of the Institut International de Bibliographie to express its role in providing access to the sciences.[29] Without pursuing the philosophical issues that the idea of the tree of knowledge engendered its practical use in classification to capture the increasing complexity and dynamics of the sciences was more and more questioned.[30]

The main problem was, as Spencer already had observed, the linear growth of branches. The original notation of the UDC allowed for expressing multiple points of view on a particular branch of the sciences or subject by changing the order of its particular parts (later described as facets). However, to capture the dynamic interactions between the branches required an organisational structure of the classification which allowed for exchanges of facets between multiple branches.[31] This requirement came to light in critical comments on the UDC by classification theorists with a mathematical background, such as Shiyali Ramamrita Ranganthan, developer of the Colon Classification (CC), and Gérard Cordonnier, designer of a classification as "an arborescent intellectual space." Both chose a different "tree of knowledge" form to express the limitations of the UDC in capturing the growth in the sciences. Ranganthan stated: "It is well known that in the Decimal Classification the class number can only grow at its end. A decimal number is like a coconut palm tree. It can only grow at the top. But the Colon Number is like the banyan tree which can grow in all directions simultaneously."[32] Cordonnier praised the work of Ranganathan but also recognised illogical orders in certain classes and notation of the CC to accommodate the growth and dynamics of the sciences. Therefore, he proposed that his "arborescent" classification would have "ramifications forming a coordinate system of an indefinite number from which the branches project without a unique order."[33]

In short, there was a growing awareness that the hierarchical order in the tree of knowledge and variations of it were of limited use in capturing the dynamics required in modern classifications. The result was proposals for universal classifications in which an object or idea should not have a unique place in a hierarchical order anymore. Cordonnier stated: "A universal classification should be a collection ordered by points of view. An object will be found in more rubrics [classes under more subject headings] of which the whole defines its place in the intellectual domain, similar to a point in space being defined by its coordinates or projections according to more points of view."[34] Others, like Jesse Shera and Jason Farradane, stressed the limits of universal classifications. Shera stated: "The fallacy, of course, lay in the fact that a hierarchical structure is but one pattern of thought in a universe of infinite patterns [...] what is a rational or logical association for one can be quite irrational and illogical for another."[35]

It is important for the following discussion about hypertext and the internet that Shera and Farradane did not focus merely on the position of the knowledge units, but rather on the relations between them. Shera argues that any single unit of knowledge may be meaningful in any number of different relationships depending upon the immediate purpose. Likewise, Farradane formulated this as follows: "Owing to the difficulties of representing all possible relational series in any fixed form, printed form, each classification, shows only a limited selection, which imposes a rigid network which is mostly neither adaptable nor logically true throughout."[36] To free oneself of such limitations was an important starting point of the WWW. In his description of the first experiments at CERN of the computer program Enquire that anticipated the design of the WWW, Tim Berner-Lee writes: "I liked Enquire and made good use of it because it stored information without using structures like matrices and trees. [...] The human mind uses these organising structures all the time but can also break out of them [...]."[37]

Hypertext, Internet, and the Broken Dream of the World Wide Web

Tim Berners-Lee described the WWW as a marriage between hypertext and the internet, not as an invention but rather as the outcome of a gradual design process. This process is part of a long evolution in information organisation, but at the same it tends to break with hierarchical classification systems.[38] The point not to confuse the multidimensional notational system of the UDC with hypertext and the "reseau de documentation" with the internet is therefore well-taken.[39] Nevertheless, Boyd Rayward has made clear that despite the differences in philosophical background between the UDC and hypertext, their languages have characteristics in common.[40] They share the flexibility to change the order of particular parts, and both have a non-linear, multidimensional structure (Fig. 8.9).

Although there are, as mentioned above, differences between Otlet's network of documentation and the internet, it is important to realise that in the early experiments of developers of the internet, hypertext, and the WWW, the relevance of documentation and hierarchical structures in the organisation of information remained apparent. Ted Nelson coined the term hypertext in 1975 in a publication with the telling title "A File Structure for

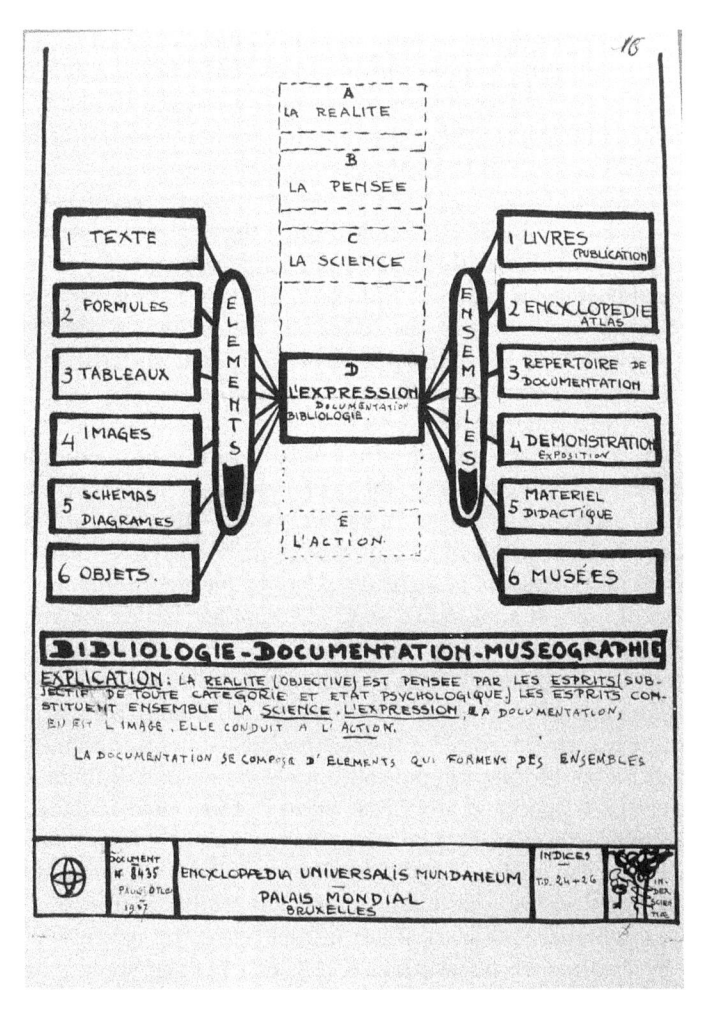

Figure 8.9 Extraction of elements from multi-media documents and reassembling them into new formats by Paul Otlet, June 8, 1937, Mundaneum (Mons), "Elements et ensembles," D6PPO4, EUMC 8435, @collection Mundaneum, Belgium, Mons.

the Complex, the Changing and the Indeterminate" that reveals his preoccupation to get a grip on all sorts of documentation in flux.[41] In his later announcement of an alternative for the WWW, XanaduSpace, he stated: "We are not just building a different kind of hypertext, but seeking the most general form of document. The issue is *how to represent all possible documents*."[42]

The WWW as a happy marriage between the internet and hypertext has changed considerably since its origins. In *Weaving the Web*, Berners-Lee set out his "dream of the web" in two parts. In the first part, the web becomes a more powerful means for collaboration between people. In the second part of the dream, the collaboration extends to computers capable of analysing all data and all transactions between people and computers—resulting in a Semantic Web.[43]

However, after the early development of the WWW, this twofold dream seemed to gradually fall apart, under pressure from two main threats.[44] The first threat is that people tend to lose more and more the control of their own data to governments and to large tech companies and therefore will be less able to collaborate. The Stanford law professor Lawrence Lessig stated that cyberspace, left to itself, will not fulfil its promise of freedom. The main argument in his *Code and Other Laws of Cyberspace* is the threat "that the invisible hand of cyberspace is building an architecture that is quite the opposite of what it was at cyberspace's birth. The invisible hand, through commerce is constructing an architecture that makes possible highly efficient control […] in an axis between commerce and the state."[45] Lessig advocates more regulation of the code, but the computer scientist Albert-László Barabási in his seminal work *Linked. How Everything is Connected to Everything Else and What It Means for Business, Science, and Everyday Life* pointed to an even more serious threat that requires a different strategy.

This second threat is that the growth of the WWW can be less controlled by code and that the development of its architecture, the evolution of its topological structure, will be more and more dependent on collective human behaviour—that is to say, the mouse clicks of millions of users.[46] This collective human behaviour is shaped by blatant distortions of information such as fake news, but to a greater extent by the algorithms and "bots" that manipulate the clicks of users in an invisible way. The outcome is a seemingly self-organising, fragmented WWW in which the transactions between people and computers on the Semantic Web become controlled by manipulations of what Lessig called the invisible hand.

Both threats—the loss of control over our own data and more control over data by the invisible hand of large tech companies and governments—reinforce each other and require interventions not only in information policies but also in existing technologies. Such interventions, as Berner-Lee's colleague at CERN, Brian E. Carpenter, stated as early as 1996, should follow architectural principles based on change and evolution that had been found useful in the past: "A good analogy for the development of the internet is that of constantly renewing the individual streets and buildings of a city, rather than razing and rebuilding it."[47] In recent years, Berners-Lee himself has started restructuring the WWW to deal with the first threat by creating an infrastructure in which people would gain control again over their own data in so-called "pods" (personal online data stores).[48] Solving the second threat of the invisible deformations of the original architecture of the WWW entails perhaps an even bigger endeavour. Following Carpenter's advice, we will investigate the past and explore how the work of Paul Otlet can be inspirational in finding solutions for this second threat that the WWW and its extension the Semantic Web of collaborating computers evolve further with less means of control by its users.

Document-Instrument and the Semantic Web

The previous section described two threats to the WWW which reinforce each other and shape its extension, the Semantic Web, that is imagined as have the potential to add more meaning to the hyperlinked information on the internet. The WWW Consortium (W3C) promotes the so-called Resource Description Framework (RDF) to optimise the exchange of machine-readable (meta-) data formats and protocols. The RDF model is based on the idea of making statements about resources in expressions of the form: subject-predicate-object, so-called triples. Although the aim is to let computers talk to computers as much as possible, enormous amounts of information need to be organised properly and in a transparent way. Only then can the Semantic Web become not just a web of data but also a meaningful web of knowledge where information can be used as evidence and proof.

If the collective behaviour of people that shapes the WWW is under threat from a combination of visible and invisible manipulations, it is crucial to know where that information is coming from before it is incorporated in the Semantic Web. Trust and proof make part of the framework of the Semantic Web. However, they not only require regulations as to who has access, but also guarantees that added information can be checked. To create trustworthy, meaningful information it is important to (co-)create ontological models based on domain knowledge and expertise. To get insight in the quality of those models and added data, we need documentation of provenance—that is, information that provides insight into both the resources underpinning the information and who added or changed the information.[49]

A re-examination of historical explorations to create a universe of knowledge based on the sciences can be inspirational and instrumental in order to realise this future dream of the Semantic Web as a meaningful and trustworthy web of knowledge. Such explorations have a long tradition within the history of information organisation. Nevertheless, there are two reasons to focus our attention on the experiments and visions of Paul Otlet.

Firstly, there is the potential of the classificatory language of the UDC to add information with points of view through its auxiliary tables. Above we quoted Otlet's statement on the interactions within classification between the objects in their relationships with each other on the one hand and abstract points of view on the other.[50] However, it is important to note that Otlet's notion of "point of view" is completely different from what we nowadays call "social tags." Otlet was not interested in users expressing opinions on information. For him, it was important how they could contribute to the processes of abstraction and synthesis of the sciences. Before they could be used such contributions and suggestions for change needed to be scientifically checked by domain experts. In the end, this could result in exchanges between institutions and people for which Otlet experimented with concordances. The reality was that contributions for changes to classifications were set aside in temporary shadow classifications and seldom resulted in updates.[51] Nevertheless, later Donker Duyvis would stress the role the UDC could play as a flexible scientific system, that would even allot space for scientific error, "as long as publications on such error are available."[52] This flexibility is crucial because it allows the inclusion of conflicting points of view as long their provenance is traceable.

The potential to add annotations that could refer to publications and other sources and that reveal by whom they are added could also provide the necessary provenance of information on the Semantic Web. Adding provenance to the Semantic Web is not new. The W3C consortium developed a Provenance Ontology (PROV-O) based on a Provenance Data Model that also includes links to derivations of information such as revisions, quotations, or primary sources.[53] However, examples of the latter are interpreted mainly as publications and no attributes are defined to primary sources. For that reason, experiments have been set up with additional ontologies for provenance of primary sources, such archival resources and interpretations thereof.[54] Based on the assumption that no database is neutral, others have suggested an interesting alternative approach to capturing multiple, often conflicting and contested, historical arguments. This approach entails expanding the Linked Open Data triple (that is subject-predicate-object) with two extra nodes: the "authority" (that is, the person that made a historical assertion) and the source (that supports the claim), to create so-called Structured Assertion Records (STARs).[55] This fundamental intervention in the

Semantic Web, by replacing its fundamental building block the triple by a STAR, brings us to the second reason why the visions of Otlet could be a source of inspiration.

Paul Otlet envisioned a future documentation system, which he labelled "Hyperdocumentation." It was a utopian dream in which documents of all the five senses come together. Recently, potential relations between Hyperdocumentation and the WWW have been discussed in all sorts of dimensions.[56] However, it is noteworthy that Otlet mentions this concept only once in all his works and even describes it as "irrational." Nevertheless, one of the six stages leading to Hyperdocumentation is of interest for its similarities with the Semantic Web. Otlet called the fifth stage "le Document-Instrument."[57] As the name suggests, the document and instrument are herein no longer distinct entities but are merged to allow the document directly to be registered and analysed as an instrument. The Semantic Web combines meta-data and data, ontologies to structure this information, and algorithms to reason over this structured information for further analysis. In short, the Semantic Web can be seen as a complex document-instrument. Moreover, by adding two extra extensions to the triple (subject-predicate-object) to contextualise it with essential information about who is responsible for which assertions based on which sources, the complexity of the Semantic Web structure would increase even more.

Since the information added to the Semantic Web by people is interwoven with invisible computer interactions, we need to develop visualisations and interfaces that provide more insight into changes to the topological structure of the Semantic Web. Despite some attempts to create multidimensional visualisations of clusters of information, knowledge representations of the Semantic Web are still very flat.[58] We need experimentations with multidimensional notation and visualisation. Otlet's visual thought experiments were described above, concluding that they were not only intended as knowledge representations, but also as critical instruments to assess inconsistencies in mappings between notations and visualisations of the classification system. Such experiments with critical assessments of the ways in which information is organised can be easily set up as well in a digital context to contribute to greater transparency and trust in knowledge systems.[59] They are particularly important when fundamental changes are proposed such as extending triples to STARs in the Semantic Web. However, to enable the validation of such experiments, we need to be able to see the impact of human and computer interactions on the increasing complexity of its topological structure. To bring this about it is of interest to investigate historical creations of multidimensional knowledge spaces and past dreams of the concept of the "document-instrument." Creating a transparent memory of such creations might contribute to a better understanding of the threats to our current global information systems, the WWW, and the Semantic Web. The creation of such a memory requires the engagement of information history.

Notes

1 Alex Wright, *Cataloging the World: Paul Otlet and the Birth of the Information Age* (Oxford: Oxford University Press, 2014), 14–15.
2 Wouter Van Acker, "Seeing the Networks for the Trees of Knowledge: Paul Otlet's (1868–1944) Universal Network of Documentation," in *Networks of Design: Proceedings of the 2008 Annual International Conference of the Design History Society* (London: Design History Society, 2009), 402, https://research-repository.griffith.edu.au/handle/10072/61716, cites, as examples, the following: Alex Wright, "The Web Time Forgot," *The New York Times*, June 17, 2008; Charles van den Heuvel, "Architectures of Global Knowledge: The Mundaneum and the World Wide

Web," *Destination Library* 15, no. 1 (2008): 48–53; and W. Boyd Rayward, "Visions of Xanadu: Paul Otlet (1868–1944) and Hypertext," *Journal of the American Society for Information Science* 45, no. 4 (1994): 235–250. However, the latter two studies point to differences rather than to similarities and make comparisons but do not suggest causal or historical relationships.

3 Van Acker, "Seeing the Networks for the Trees of Knowledge," 369, claims that for Otlet's universe of knowledge "the traditional 'tree of knowledge' rather than the network, served as the structural model."

4 W. Boyd Rayward, *The Universe of Information: The Work of Paul Otlet for Documentation and International Organisation*, FID 520 (Moscow: VINITI, 1975). For a translation and discussion of some of Otlet's important works, see Paul Otlet, *International Organisation and Dissemination of Knowledge: Selected Essays of Paul Otlet*, ed. and trans. W. Boyd Rayward, FID 684 (Amsterdam: Elsevier, 1990). An accessible discussion of Otlet's project can be found in Paul Otlet, *Mundaneum: Archives of Knowledge*, ed. and trans. W. Boyd Rayward (Urbana, IL: Graduate School of Library and Information Science, University of Illinois, Occasional Paper 215, May 2010), https://www.ideals.illinois.edu/items/15485.

5 Rayward, *The Universe of Information*, 175; Paul Otlet, "Sur la Structure des Nombres Classificateurs," *IIB Bulletin I* (1895–1896): 230–243, in Paul Otlet, *International Organisation*, 51–62.

6 W. Boyd Rayward, "Creating the UIA: Henri La Fontaine, Cyrille van Overbergh and Paul Otlet," in *International Organisations and Global Civil Society: Histories of the Union of International Associations*, ed. Danial Laqua, Wouter Van Acker, and Christopher Verbruggen (London: Bloomsbury, 2019), 17–35; and Wouter Van Acker, "Sociology in Brussels: Organicism and the Idea of a World Society in the Period before the First World War," in *Information Beyond Borders: International Cultural and Intellectual Exchange on the Belle Epoque*, ed. W. Boyd Rayward (Farnham: Ashgate, 2014), 143–168.

7 Paul Otlet, *Traité de Documentation: Le Livre sur le Livre* (Bruxelles: Editiones Mundaneum, 1934); and Paul Otlet, *Monde: Essai d'Universalisme* (Bruxelles: Editiones Mundaneum, 1935).

8 Otlet, *Monde*, 448.

9 Louis Masure, *Rapport sur la Situation et les Travaux pour l'Année 1912* (Bruxelles: IIB, 1913), 31; Cf. Rayward, *The Universe of Information*, 154, n. 75.

10 For collaborative initiatives in the Late Antiquity and the Middle Ages, see Ann M. Blair, *Too Much to Know: Managing Scholarly Information before the Modern Age* (New Haven, CT: Yale University Press, 2010).

11 Paul Otlet, "Un Peu de Bibliographie," *Palais* (Bruxelles: Vromant, 1891–1892), 254–271, in Otlet, *International Organisation*, 12.

12 Robert Goldschmidt and Paul Otlet, *Sur une Forme Nouvelle du Livre: Le Livre Microphotographique* (Bruxelles: IIB, 1906), in Otlet, *International Organisation*, 87–95; and Otlet, "Un Peu de Bibliographie," in Otlet, *International Organisation*, 17.

13 Otlet, "Un Peu de Bibliographie," in Otlet, *International Organisation*, 17.

14 Paul Otlet, *La Function et les Transformations du Livre. Résumé de la conference Faite à la Maison du Livre 14 November 1908* (Bruxelles: Musée du Livre, 1909), 29.

15 Paul Otlet, *Règles pour les Développements à Apporter à la Classification Décimale* (Bruxelles: OIB, 1896), in Otlet, *International Organisation*, 64.

16 Henri La Fontaine and Paul Otlet, *Création d'un Repertoire Bibliographique Universel* (Bruxelles 1895), in Otlet, *International Organisation*, 26, and 34.

17 Charles van den Heuvel "Dynamics of Networks and of Decimal Classification Systems 1905–1935," in *Information Beyond Borders: International Cultural and Intellectual Exchange in the Belle Époque*, ed. W. Boyd Rayward (Farnham: Ashgate, 2014), 221–241.

18 Charles van den Heuvel, "The Dutch Connection: Donker Duyvis and Perceptions of American and European Decimal Classification Systems in the History of Information Science and Technology," in *Proceedings of ASIS&T 2012: 75th Pre-Conference on the History of ASIS&T and Information Science and Technology, Baltimore 27 October 2012, Asist Monograph Series, Inc.*, ed. Toni Carbo and Trudi Bellardo Hahn (Medford, NJ: Information Today, 2012), 174–186.

19 Frits Donker Duyvis, "The UDC: What It Is and What It Is Not," *Revue de la Documentation* 18, no. 2 (1951): 99.

20 Fundamental early texts that deal with the multidimensionality in classification and the creation of non-linear book formats are: "Un Peu de Bibliographie" and "Sur la structure des Nombres

Classificateurs" et "La function." For the "fundamental schemas," see Charles van den Heuvel "Multidimensional Classifications: Past and Future Conceptualizations and Visualizations," *Knowledge Organization* 39 (2012): 446–460; and Wouter Van Acker, "Universalism as Utopia: A Historical Study of the Schemes and Schemas of Paul Otlet (1868–1944)" (PhD diss., University of Ghent, 2011), 50–51.

21 Mundaneum (Mons), PPPO 955 -EUM, I Généralités Fardes 1–6, and PPPO 956 – EUM: II Thèmes 1 Méthodologie Fardes 7–13. Otlet formulated outlines of such a theory in manuscript and in typescript, with the titles, respectively: Théorie Schématique de la Classification (December 14, 1908) PPP0 956—EUM—Farde 8 no. 42, and Notions et Conceptions Fondamentales en Matière de Classification—(December 4, 1922) PPPO 42/1/8/1.

22 Herbert Spencer, *The Classification of the Sciences: Which Are Added Reasons for Dissenting from the Philosophy of M. Comte* (New York: D. Appleton and Co., 1864), 25–26. Spencer refers to two-dimensional tables in the form of dichotomies.

23 Paul Otlet, "Sur la Structure," 230–243. See, W. Boyd Rayward, "On the Structure of Classification Numbers," in Otlet, *International Organisation*, 51–53.

24 Mundaneum (Mons), PPPO 955—EUM, I Généralités -Farde 4—Orbis Encyclopedia Synthetica: printed title page and an introductory note in typescript dated September 17, 1912, 1.

25 Ayelet Even-Ezra, *Lines of Thought: Branching Diagrams and the Medieval Mind* (Chicago, IL: Chicago University Press, 2021).

26 Although most visualisations indeed are preparatory drawings in various stages for the Encyclopedia Universalis Mundaneum, the boxes labelled "EUM" also contain many sketches that are not directly related to this encyclopaedic enterprise of visualisations. For the various stages in the making of visualisations for the EUM, see Charles van den Heuvel, "Building Society," 139; and Van Acker, *Universalism as Utopia*, 50–55.

27 Francoise Levie, *L'Homme qui Voulait Classer de Monde: Paul Otlet et le Mundaneum* (Bruxelles: Les Impressions Nouvelles, 2006), 281.

28 Otlet, "Théorie Schématique de la Classification."

29 Van Acker, *Universalism as Utopia*, 88.

30 See for a general discussion: Scott Weingart, "From Trees to Webs Uprooting Knowledge through Visualization," in *Classification & Visualization: Interfaces to Knowledge*, ed. Aida Slavic, Almila Akdag Salah and Sylvie Davies (Würzburg: Ergon Verlag 2013), 43–57.

31 On the limitations of the knowledge tree in the work of Ranganathan, see Charles van den Heuvel "Multidimensional Classifications," 452–454; and Charles van den Heuvel and Almila Akdag Salah, "Knowledge Space Lab, Visualizing Universes of Knowledge: Design and Visual Analysis of the UDC," in *Proceedings of the International UDC Seminar Classification and Ontology, Formal Approaches and Access to Knowledge, The Hague, 19–20 September 2011*, ed. Aida Slavic and Edgardo Civallero (Würzburg: Ergon Verlag 2011), 283–294.

32 Shiyali Ramamrita Ranganthan, "Colon Classification and its Approach to Documentation," in *Bibliographic Organization: Papers presented before the Fifteenth Annual Conference of the Graduate Library School July 24–29, 1950*, ed. Jesse H. Shera and Margaret E. Egan (Chicago, IL: The University of Chicago Press 1951), 100. See also Joseph Tennis, "Fringe types and KOS Systematics: Examining the Limits of the Population Perspective of Knowledge Organization Systems," *Advances in Classification Research Online* 20, no. 1 (2009).

33 On the banyan tree order, see Shiyali Ramamrita Ranganthan, *Prolegomena to Library Classification* (New York: Asia Publishing House, 1951), 368; and Gérard Cordonnier, *Classification et Classement. Extrait du Bulletin d'Information Scienifique et Technique* 6 (1944).

34 Cordonnier, *Classification et Classement*, 7.

35 Jesse H. Shera "Pattern, Structure, and Conceptualization in Classification," in *Proceedings of the International Study Conference on Classification for Information Retrieval held at Beatrice Webb House, Dorking, England 13–17 May 1957*, ASLIB 4, ed. Jesse H. Shera and Margaret E. Egan (London: Pergamon Press, 1957), 15–27, 22.

36 Jason E. L. Farradane, "A Scientific Theory of Classification and Indexing: Further Considerations," *Journal of Documentation* 8, no. 2 (1952): 75; and Jesse H. Shera, "Classification as the Basis of Bibliographic Organization," in *Bibliographic Organization*, 84.

37 Tim Berners-Lee, *Weaving the Web: The Past, Present and Future of the World Wide Web by Its Inventor* (London: Harper Business, 2000), 10.

38 Berners-Lee, *Weaving the Web*, 6.
39 Van Acker, "Seeing the Networks for the Trees of Knowledge," 396, and 402.
40 Rayward, "Visions of Xanadu," 239–240.
41 Theodor H. Nelson, "A File Structure for the Complex, the Changing and the Indeterminate," in *Proceedings of the ACM 20th National Conference* (New York: ACM, 1965), 84–100.
42 Theodor H. Nelson and Robert Adamson Smith, *Back to the Future: Hypertext the Way It Used to Be* (2007), http://xanadu.com/XanaduSpace/btf.htm. Italics in the quote are those of the authors.
43 Berners-Lee, *Weaving the Web*, 157–158.
44 This paragraph is based on a more elaborate, non-published paper: Charles van den Heuvel, "Urban Grids, Computer Grids and Global Grids: A Historical Exploration of Analogous Architectures of the Information Society," presented at the colloquium *Analogous Spaces Architecture and the Space of Information, Intellect and Action* at the University of Ghent, 2008, https://www.academia.edu/7342034/UrbanGridsComputerGridsGlobalGrids.
45 Lawrence Lessig, *Code and other Laws of Cyberspace* (New York: Basic Books 1999), 6.
46 Barabási, *Linked*, 174–175.
47 Brian E. Carpenter was a group leader of the Communications Systems Computing and Networks Division at CERN. He formulated his vision in: "Architectural Principles of the Internet" (1996) RFC 1958 IAB, 1, https://www.ietf.org/rfc/rfc1958.txt.
48 See, the Solid Project, https://www.inrupt.com/solid.
49 The ISO 20579-4:2018(en) definition of provenance information covers both meanings. For provenance and data quality: ISO 8000-120:2016(en).
50 Otlet, *Règles*, in Otlet, *International Organisation*, 64.
51 See, Kathryn La Barre et al., "The Other as A Research Agenda for Information Science," in *Proceedings of the American Society for Information Science and Technology* 49, no. 1 (2012): 1–3. Donker Duyvis developed the "P.E. system" to allow suggestions by users for changes to the UDC to be assessed by the Classification Committee: see Van den Heuvel, "The Dutch Connection," 185. For a discussion of the illustration, see Van den Heuvel, "Urban Grid," fig. 8.7.
52 Donker Duyvis, "The UDC," 101. See further Van den Heuvel, "Dynamics," 232.
53 W3C, "PROV-O: The PROV Ontology," https://www.w3.org/TR/prov-o/.
54 See, for instance, the ROAR++ model: Leon van Wissen, Veruska Zamborlini, and Charles van den Heuvel: "Toward an Ontology for Archival Resources. Modelling Persons, Objects, and Places in the Golden Agents Research Infrastructure," in *Digital History Berlin (Blog)*, January 11, 2021, https://dhistory.hypotheses.org/361.
55 James Baillie et al. "Modelling Historical Information with Structured Assertion Records," in *Digital History Berlin (Blog)*, February 22, 2021, https://dhistory.hypotheses.org/518.
56 Olivier Le Deuff, *Hyperdocumentation* (London: ISTE; Hoboken, NJ: Wiley, 2021); Olivier Le Deuff and Arthur Perret, "Hyperdocumentation: Origin and Evolution of a Concept," *Journal of Documentation* 75, no. 6 (2019): 1463–1474; and Otlet, *Traité de Documentation*, 419.
57 Charles van den Heuvel and Richard Smiraglia "Visualizing Knowledge Interaction in the Multiverse of Knowledge," in *Classification & Visualization*, 63; and Heuvel and Rayward, "Facing Interfaces," 2322.
58 Frank van Harmelen et al. "Ontology-based Information Visualisation," in *Proceedings of the Workshop on Visualisation in Conjunction with the 5th International Conference on Information Visualisation* (London: VSW-01, 2001), 36–48. For a general overview of recent visualisations of the sciences, see Katy Börner, *Atlas of Science* (Cambridge, MA: MIT Press, 2010); and Katy Börner, *Atlas of Knowledge* (Cambridge, MA: MIT Press, 2015).
59 See, for instance, Charles van den Heuvel and Richard P. Smiraglia, "Knowledge Spaces: Visualizing and Interacting with Dimensionality," in *Linking Knowledge. Linked Open Data for Knowledge Organization and Visualization*, ed. Richard P. Smiraglia and Andrea Scharnhorst (Baden-Baden: Ergon Verlag, 2021), 199–217, in which such an experiment revealed inconsistencies in the Information Coding Classification.

9
INFORMATION AS INSTRUCTION
A Short History of Attack Journalism

Bethany Usher

Attack journalism is more visible than ever. Via algorithmic feeding loops fed by clicks, shares, and likes, it snakes across digital timelines, is perpetuated by word-of-mouth and can encourage moments of mass and participatory public shaming on social media. It facilitates the display of opinion, allegiance, morality, and emotion, often in direct opposition to others and "fuses cause and effect," which increases the "synoptic" and "panoptic" functions of information itself.[1] But attack journalism—the vilification (whether justified or not) of an individual by the media—is also one of the first representational cultures of news and there is much to learn about its current political power from examining its development as part of information history. Few industries-of-information have a "pack mentality" like journalism. If a story garners attention on one platform, it often piques the interest of others and is republished again without further verification. Potential news stories pass through a series of value judgements, including those of journalists, editors, and owners, which can lead to the "symbolic annihilation" of social groups by "omission, trivialisation or condemnation."[2] When an individual is perceived to be a *direct threat* to their commercial or socio-political power, an attack can become part of editorial strategy.[3] Attack journalism is therefore a process of celebrification whereby a person's visibility is raised, while simultaneously there is an attempt to limit public engagement with what they have to say. This chapter offers a short historical sweep through attack journalism's complex history in relation to key changes in technology, platforms, people, and purposes. It highlights how bringing together the informational and instructional as part of an ongoing story of daily news shaped languages and temporal and geographic dimensions of journalism itself.

While there is broad acceptance that "modern societies ... have been information societies from their inception," there are few examinations of the micro-meso-macro relationships that explain *how and why* news developed as a tool of information and instruction together.[4] Seminal research into the constructs of news identified how (post) modern forms shape our understanding of reality, others and ourselves and the political, commercial, and cultural institutions that govern our lives.[5] Attack journalism first developed in early modern newsbooks and was subsequently transformed by press popularisation, modernisation, multi-media technologies and most recently convergence in digital spaces. Unpicking cause and effect can often seem contradictory. On the one hand, journalists use attacks to maintain audience interest when exposing complex issues of corruption or holding governments to account, as normative expectations of their role. This is an example of how the "architecture of informational cultures" has facilitated "empowerment of citizens through an enhancement of their rights; for the satisfaction of such rights—legal, political, economic, and social."[6] On the other hand, individualised attacks can fuel political polarisation and limit public debate.[7] News shapes our opinion of "us" and "other" and made visible versions of identity that best perpetuated the symbols, values, and beliefs that facilitate the governance of capitalist democracies. This chapter explores the development of attack journalism in relation to three key shifts in production and dissemination in seventeenth- and eighteenth-century daily newspapers, then the early nineteenth-century popular press and finally multi-media tabloid news cultures of the twentieth and early twenty-first centuries. Through a transdisciplinary approach to information history that looks to structure, agency, and societal cause together, it defines the characteristics of attack journalism so that we might spot and counter its very worst tendencies.

Attack Journalism, the Rise of Daily News and the Debates of Public Spheres (1640–1790)

Between 1640 and the 1780s, London daily news publications developed an (un)holy trinity for content focused on politics, crime, and celebrity culture.[8] Changes in monarchical and aristocratic power, associated advances of democracy, arguments of Enlightenment, and revolutions in individualised consumer cultures, all intertwined with the advancement of daily news and helped to form its political place. Attacks rely on repetition and momentum, with news both informational and instructional about individuals who often *embody* politicised issues. Three shifts provided key characteristics of the type of attack journalism with which we are familiar today. The first responded to the iterative and reiterative nature of daily news and drew on older print popular cultures to create representational and political tools of *rhetorical criminalisation*. The second was the *inclusion of gossip* about private immorality of public figures that was evident in both news and spilled into the debates of bourgeois public spheres. The third was *radicalised othering*—first appearing in relation to class—aimed squarely at limiting engagement with voices from outside those of established power and linguistically shaped by the use of descriptive adjectives inserted into informational news.

The first royal patent for the "publishing of all matter of History or News … in the English tongue" in 1640 is often hailed as the opening gambit in a "heroic" but highly mythologised "struggle" for press freedom over the next two hundred or so years.[9] Within months, several newsbooks hit London's streets and by 1644 there were at least a dozen titles printed six days a week (Fig. 9.1). Expansions and speed ups of information had its most marked effects in the capital, but even though print runs were fewer than one thousand copies, newsbooks soon became part of established information networks in towns and cities across England, read aloud and sold alongside pamphlets and royal proclamations in alehouses and market squares.[10] Joad Raymond describes newsbooks during the English Civil War (1641–1649) as a first step towards the invention of the newspaper containing the first continuous communication and commentary on political events as daily news.[11] Martin Conboy summarises their significance against political cut and thrust and argues they created the first "identifiable features of journalism" as both news culture and site of argumentation, which addressed readers as a community or audience.[12] This community was viewed as starchily protestant, staunchly pro-parliamentarian, and was often urged to direct action, with newsbooks and

A COPIE OF THE

10

Kings Meſſage ſent by the Duke of *Lenox*.

Alſo the Copie of a Petition to the KING from the Inhabitants of *Somerſetſhire*, to come with him to the Parliament.

A Declaration by the Committee of Dorſetſhire, againſt the Cavaliers in thoſe parts; declaring how ſixe French Papiſts raviſhed a woman one after another: She having been but three dayes before delivered out of Child-bed.

Alſo, how a Gentleman at Oxford was cruelly tortured in Irons, and for what they were ſo cruell towards him.

And how they would have burnt down an Ale-houſe at the Briil, becauſe the woman refuſed Farthing tokens; And other cruelties of the Cavaliers, manifeſted to the Kingdome.

Publiſhed according to Order of Parliament.
LONDON, Printed by *Iane Coe*. 1644.

Figure 9.1 Anti-royalist newsbook published during the English Civil War.
Source: The Thomason Tracts, The British Library.

pamphlets acknowledged as "Principal Engines of Battery" during the civil war, where "not any one thing ... hurt the late King more than the paper bullets of the Press."[13]

Early Modern Newsbooks and the "Rhetorical Criminalisation" of the Cavaliers and the King

Shorter news forms irrevocably shifted the temporal dimensions of information. Usually written by the "grubs" of London's Grub Street and published around Tower Bridge, newsbooks also drew from older traditions and particularly the languages and styles of popular crime pamphlets and ballads.[14] They repurposed their "strategies transformed and condensed, shaping their tropes and offering new voices and kenspeckled characters" from murder, witchcraft and highwaymen pamphlets to "make sense of chaos" of the Civil War.[15] The Thomason Tracts—the earliest archive of English-language daily news—was collected contemporaneously and first referenced by the British Library in date order.[16] Engaging with material in the same way highlights how attacks gain momentum and develop longer narratives across daily news. This first sustained attack focused on the King as the embodiment of tyranny and established some existing thematic and linguistic patterns. Grubs and their publishers rhetorically criminalised by upping the ante of anti-Catholic propaganda before applying it to both the cavaliers and the King, and some of their claims led directly to charges, trial, and execution.[17] There were constant links with "barbarous" and "bloody" violence at the hands of Catholics, such as in a "true relation of all those cruell Rapes and Murders that have lately been committed by the Papists." Accounts of "bloody massacre by the Papists," "Bloody News from Norwich ... a relation of a bloody attempt of the Papists to consume the city by fire" and "A bloodie massacre upon live Protestants by a company of Papists," sat alongside opinion pieces that outlined the "Lineage of Locusts ... or the Popes pedigree, beginning with his prime ancestor the Divell" and ending with King Charles and his French Catholic wife, Henrietta Maria. It proved powerful propaganda. From 1641 onwards, newsbooks told of reports to the authorities for "Popish" beliefs, confessions extracted under torture or mob-violence, mass conversions and many towns and cities took their advice to shut out the King after he fled the capital. Attack journalism as a culture of daily news *dismantled* what Roland Barthes described as the mythology of "God-King" and replaced it with the "King-Object" as *constructed* by the media and answerable to his people rather than divine justice.[18] In his indictment, Charles was guilty of "wicked designs, wars, and evil practices ... for the advancement and upholding of a personal interest of will, power ... against the public interest, common right, liberty, justice, and peace of the people of this nation."[19] Puritan parliamentarian pamphlets and newsbooks *made* the King a criminal through strategic use of the structural and representational languages of crime and in doing so, revealed the potential powers of a press who claimed to speak to, and for, the public.

This was a step towards the type of systematic attack journalism that solidified in the eighteenth-century press following the lapse of the Licensing Act in 1695 and the resulting newspaper boom. Discussions of the idealised functions of journalism often build from Jürgen Habermas' concept of bourgeois public spheres (including eighteenth-century London coffee houses) to consider how newspapers negotiated citizenship within new nations as political communities.[20] Philosophical liberalism "insist[s] on common language and nations as prerequisites for effective citizenship" and once these things formed, public spheres aided the advancement of deliberative democracy[21]. Coffee house counters were so full of publications that they resembled pamphlet shops,[22] and Habermas argued that newspapers generally "levelled up" in the interest of self-education and cultivation. Our focus on attack journalism also evidences how gossip was part of political argumentation. While some anonymous politicos certainly reflected ideals of rational debate and the public interest,[23] and many became popular and influential without royal favour and beyond the demands of the ballot box,[24] Junius, a writer or writers working between 1769 and 1772, stands out in terms of popularity. He is a familiar figure in histories of the press and universally viewed in heroic terms. His letters "raised journalism to a much more important position than ever before"[25] and he "stood forth in unchallenged mastery" of the field of early political comment because of "ruthless sarcasm, keen invective, and political daring."[26] The trials of his publishers proved a significant step in freedom of press, resulting in numerous high-profile acquittals over the next fifty or so years.[27] But for Junius "public conduct" was "the counterpart of ... private history,"[28] which highlights limitations in arguments that "public" and "private" were separate realms in newspapers or public spheres at this time.

Junius made attack journalism "a ritual of celebrification, through which public and private life were brought together through gossip,"[29] and it was this that resulted in the circulation of the *Public Advertiser* almost doubling to forty-eight hundred.[30] He particularly condemned those who placed personal gratification over public propriety and linked this to shaming of body with even lewd descriptions of genitalia. The Duke of Grafton may have "recovered from the errors of his youth, the distraction of play and the bewitching smiles of burgundy" but was still somewhat prey to the "heat of midnight excesses." He "frequently led his mistress into public," burying "shame and decency" under the ruins of "an ancient temple of Venus" and even parading her "in front of the Queen." The Duke of Bedford was advised not to "Take back [his] mistress, attend Newmarket" or engage in the same "busy agitations, in which your youth and manhood were exhausted." When Junius turned his attention to the Crown,[31] his work was "destined to make publishing history" as the criminal trials of his publishers established the first legal public interest balance with privacy. He urged King George not to adopt "Stuart principles" of opulent spending and political dictatorship and warned that "while [the crown] was acquired by one revolution, it may be lost by another." Prosecution promptly followed for his publisher and six others who reprinted the letters and when the first trial resulted in a guilty verdict, there was outcry, both in print and on the streets of London. All other publishers were subsequently cleared, which "prepared the way for a broader, a higher, consideration of press law and the press in politics."[32] While Junius is celebrated in many histories of the press, some responses to his work in readers' letters evidence fascinating similarities with contemporary criticisms of tabloid cultures. His loudest critics described him as the "high priest of envy, malice and uncharitableness" were dismayed that "political questions" could focus on "the most odious personalities" and claimed he had "no reluctance to attack the character of any man, the throne is not too high, nor the cottage too low."[33] There is some irony that this moment of using gossip as part of political argumentation is celebrated by scholars of journalism, when contemporary use of such methods is usually not. It was the purpose and impact, rather than his journalistic methods, from which such contradictions stem.[34] Like pro-parliamentarian newsbooks during the civil war, Junius aimed to dismantle inherited political privilege and used gossip and innuendo in a similar way to the rhetorical criminalisation of the King. He is therefore viewed as on the right side of the history of a democratic and free press.

Over the next fifty or so years, many newspapers that launched during the eighteenth-century print boom became intertwined with systems of establishment economic and political power. As a result, attack journalism increasingly became a tool to limit the agency and voice of people from outside these spheres of influence. By the time of "Revolution Controversy"—from France's "new dawn" in 1789 to December 1795 when "Pitt's Government introduced measures to stop the spread of radicalism by the printed and spoken word"[35]—newspapers such as *The Times* often linked "revelations" of personal impropriety to political argument. Dynamics of celebrity news such as gossip, innuendo and the banal became part of the debate of ideas.[36]

Surviving material from numerous newspapers demonstrates that working-class politico and journalist Thomas Paine (arguably the most significant journalist of the age in terms of influence on European and American democracy) was perceived as one of the greatest individualised threats to the power of the establishment and its bourgeois press. He "arrived to much celebrity by his political writings,"[37] particularly because of the vast popular and commercial success of *Rights of Man*,[38] which was cheaply produced, written in everyday vernacular, and banned in 1792. Paine's exile to France ahead of his trial (where he was convicted and sentenced to execution) was described as the "Principal Occurrence of 1792" in the New Year newspaper lists across the political spectrum. During the revolution controversy more than a fifth (21%) of surviving news content in British Library archives about Paine during this period *only* offered details of his private life and a further third linked his personal life to political argument.[39] Some newspapers, including *The Times*, and pamphlet publishers who advertised in it, produced fake and scurrilous biographies to coincide with trials for booksellers caught with copies of *Rights of Man*.[40] In this attack emerged the use of belittling adjectives linked to elements of social difference (a spectacular and vitriolic ritual of "celebrification" and "othering") and cross publication feeding frenzies. Karin Wahl-Jorgensen and Bob Franklin discuss the "heavy ideological baggage" of journalism's languages, which can linguistically exclude based on class, race, gender, or sexuality.[41] Paine had a "mind not disciplined by early education" and was part of the "greasy multitude."[42] He was an outcast and traitor who was "hissed and hooted" at by crowds when making his escape into exile, and his effigy was burnt nationwide.[43] He was a devil—a "Beelzebub,"[44] a "Traitor,"[45] and a "public pest" who was "envious" of the wealthy.[46] He was "seditious," "scandalous," and belittled as "Mad Tom" or "Poor Tommy."[47] The *Public Advertiser* claimed they had accessed his military records from the American Revolution, which "reveal[ed] he was a thief,"[48] and *The Times* questioned his sexuality by suggesting his breeches were often found in the "water closet."[49] From this point, representational "othering" became an ever more prevalent tool to diminish the voices of a range of people who challenged social or political norms and for women, this had gendered dynamics that perpetuated their symbolic annihilation from public spheres.[50] Attack journalism as part of news was a means by which newspapers shaped public opinion while claiming to only reflect it. It was the press' stake to the claim that inspired both a new generation of popular radical journalists and at the same time offered rhetorical tools for the bourgeois establishment press to argue against their equal freedom of press.

Rhetorical Wars: Attack Journalism and the Rise and Fall of the Nineteenth-Century Radical Popular Press

In the eighteenth century, daily newspapers and pamphlets had helped establish the "expressive conception of man" and "made us who we are."[51] In the early nineteenth century, information became part of how modern states built and "pacified their territories [and] subjects," and fostered an increasingly common language.[52] At the same time, they brought individuals together in relation to issues of national identity and visions of citizenship towards more (albeit still limited) members of the general population.[53] Establishment bourgeois and radical popular newspapers alike—the latter often claiming descent from Painite radical journalism—explored their own moral obligations, the "idea of universal benevolence" and the "imperative to reduce suffering" as principles of "universal justice."[54] Each argued their place as rightful custodians of public opinion and expanded the languages and purposes of attack journalism to diminish engagement with the arguments of others.

The concept of public opinion tentatively solidified in Jeremy Bentham's 1820 collection of letters *On the Liberty of the Press and Public Discussion* and was then popularised by second-wave Enlightenment philosopher John Stuart Mill in *On Liberty* in 1859. Bentham also penned a popular pamphlet outlining the model of the panopticon prison, which later became the metaphor for Michel Foucault's discussions of panopticism, and both broadly considered societal control via the carceral and/or the instructional.[55] Attack journalism became a component of the press' self-claimed justifies "place in the sun as the arbitrators of democracy" and these "grandiose visions" of "Fourth Estate" were seized upon with righteous zeal by bourgeois establishment newspapers.[56] For example, on February 6, 1852, *The Times* declared that in its pages "daily" news was "for ever appealing to the enlightened force of public opinion" and brought together "the present and the future ... extending its survey to the horizon of the world." This vision for their own political power sat amidst constant attacks on freedom of press for others and forever shaped our understanding of what counts as journalism. Mill argued that the bourgeois press was too servile to government and had limited perspectives on press freedom, "not seeing that unless the reasons are good for an extreme case, they are not good for any case."[57]

By contrast, the radical press built from models of journalism-as-activism popularised by eighteenth-century pamphleteers and direct and inventive written and representational tools of grubs. They turned patterns of rhetorical criminalisation squarely on the government and agents of authority, including courts, police, and the bourgeois establishment press. Many became popular by experimenting with popular forms and languages, including illustrations and direct newsgathering from courts, watchmen, political clubs, and workingmen institutes. Because they overtly rejected mythologies of objectivity and balance as existing in fact or as unquestionable forces for good, bourgeois establishment newspapers dismissed their passionate and inventive style and even some recent, but rather Whiggish histories-of-press, argue that this group were "publicists" for political ideologies rather than journalists.[58] Many were belittled and condemned, but the rhetorical war between *The Times* and William Cobbett offers a particularly pertinent example of the macro-micro-meso informational, social, and political interplays of attack journalism. Cobbett is one of the most divisive figures in histories of the press and critics at the time and since argued that his "unsystematic" and "personalized" approach limited the value of his work.[59] This too builds from an uncritical acceptance that the "balanced" and "rational" ideals of the establishment press and their self-congratulating claims of Fourth Estate. Cobbett's alternative vision for journalism was one of passion, activism, romanticised, emotive language, and radical left ideology.[60] In his *Weekly Political Register* (1802–1836), he highlighted the "crimes" of political and governmental tyranny at home and abroad and made claims of corruption, brutality, and injustice, linked to personal immorality.

Cobbett was prosecuted eight times, more often acquitted than not, but a two-year stint in Newgate Gaol for "treasonous libel" after condemning the flogging of soldiers only intensified his desire to expose the social and legal inequalities that caused the misfortunes of those he met. From his cell, he devised the weekly *Two-Penny Trash* (1812–1817; 1830–1835), named as a two-fingered salute to critics, and declared that the propertied were the real "idlers in society" whose "food, all the drink, all the clothing, all the houses, all the horses and carriages" relied on exploitation of working people.[61] *Two-Penny Trash* relaunched during the rural Swing Riots of 1830 and this time he was directly blamed for inciting "the mob" and criminalised, first rhetorically by pockets of the establishment press and then by the authorities. In a series of inflammatory articles, *The Times* attacked Cobbett as a "notorious demagogue" and claimed that it was a "singular fact" that during a lecture tour he had encouraged riot.[62] It published three increasingly more sensational versions of what turned out to be a fictitious confession of a "labourer" to a local Tory parson. They declared Cobbett had led "a deluded multitude to their ruin" and suggested that before "the mob" engage in "destruction of machinery, to tumult, to arson, to murder," each "poor wretch" among them "should ask himself, 'Will this writer be hanged or transported for me, or with me?'"[63] Cobbett quickly proved the account false—"a mere invention if not of the *Bloody Old Times* [original emphasis] then of someone else"[64]—and *The Times* later admitted there was "no truth" in some of their reports. But he was charged with seditious treason at the Old Bailey for the special edition of the *Political Register* that accounted the "Rural War," despite his stress on peaceful resolution.[65] In the wake of the Whig government's brutal crackdown—more than 2,000 trials across 90 courts ordered 19 executions, 694 long-term imprisonments and 481 transportations to Australia—there was no guarantee that this might not have proven fatal. *The Times* suggested two years imprisonment in Newgate would suffice,[66] and Cobbett declared that "double vengeance ought to fall on [their] heads" for making up claims so that he was put out of business and thrown in prison.[67] He was subsequently cleared.

When Cobbett died four years later, by then an elected Member of Parliament after the second Reform Bill finally allowed representation for some urban areas, a *Times* obituary summed up the establishment press' complaints.[68] Cobbett's working-class "origin and progress" from "a self-taught peasant to an MP" might have made him in "some respects the most extraordinary Englishman of his time" and demonstrated new opportunities to "burst through the barrier which separates the English gentleman from all those beneath him." His "birth, station, employment, ignorance, temper" had not prevented his rise or his "masculine force of genius." But his "faults" of "coarseness, brutality and tedious repetition" when fighting for working-class rights were, nonetheless, grave. They could not let his death pass without condemning his "habits and character ... his errors, contradictions, prejudices, hatreds, shameless disregard for the truth for its own sake, and matchless power of illustrating or confounding it, as might suit his temper at that moment." Ironically, even in this piece, *The Times* claimed that Cobbett's declarations that they wished to destroy his reputation were the paranoid ramblings of an uneducated man. Cobbett's vision for a radical press was finally defeated—or reconciled with the priorities of the establishment press depending on your perspective—by weekender (Saturday and Sunday) popular newspapers from the 1840s and while these commercial publications took much from the populist content of the radicals, they emphasised social advancement via leisure activities and education rather than systemic political change.[69] While this neutralised radical journalism, the characteristic of attack journalism as reflecting the press' place as rightful arbitrators of public opinion through popular power was perfectly primed for the vast expansion of multi-media tabloidism that characterised how information was mediatised in the twentieth century.

Attack Journalism and Tabloidism (1870–2020s)

Twentieth-century tabloidism was defined by shifts in informational news because of relatively rapid advancement in multi-media technologies, first of cinema (newsreels from 1908), then radio (news bulletins in audio form from the 1920s), television (visual and audio forms together from the 1930s), and finally the beginnings of digital production (from the 1990s). These took from and influenced traditions of printed news and intertwined with its own developments in illustrations and photographs. There is some critical slippage between the terminologies of "tabloids" (print newspapers, magazines, and later their associated digital brands), tabloidisation (a process that happened to news), tabloid cultures (spanning broadcast and then digital media forms), and tabloidism, defined here as a multi-platform and then multi-media media culture of news, that developed primarily in Britain and America because of ties between cultural spheres of journalism and celebrity. These were expanded by technologies of information sharing such as the transatlantic cables from the 1860s with newspapers often referring to "this hemisphere" of news or indicating when it was gathered "via the transatlantic cable." The speed up of information sharing and easier transatlantic travel for journalists themselves, ploughed much ground for the modernisation of the press and "New" or "Yellow" journalism that emerged from the 1870s onwards.[70]

With changes in platform and people the number of publicly visible individuals and associated cultures-of-fame expanded. Attack journalism increasingly focused on the image with candid shots and later on-screen confrontation and discussion of physicality. Political functions broadened too from a primary focus on the cut and thrust of democratic governance to greater focus on people who often *embodied* socio-political change and shifts-in understanding and performance of identity. Some individuals became axis for debate in public spheres and when they challenged the socio-political values of journalists, editors, and owners, subject to vicious systematic attacks. The greater visibility of bodies, faces, emotions, and immoralities of those in the public eye also created a boom of gossip-as-news from the most trivial and banal details of everyday life to vitriolic rumours, conjecture, and innuendo. The popularity of such content tied into commercial priorities and became so intertwined with the development of tabloidism that many scholarly examinations focus primarily on worst tendencies.

Attacks now happened simultaneously across different production timelines, which further collapsed boundaries of informational time and space. But newspapers still often led the charge and across the twentieth century, a handful of news barons on both sides of the Atlantic became representative figureheads for tabloidism. Alfred Harmsworth's (later Lord Northcliffe), who dominated British tabloid news at the beginning of the century, and Rupert Murdoch, who held similar power over British and US news at the end, are most associated with tabloid cultures-of-attack and both were also pioneers of corporatised news media. They brought together the establishment power of the bourgeois press (both purchased *The Times*) with the popular linguistic and visual tools of the radical working-class press who claimed to speak "for the people" and in doing so solidified and extended elements of attack journalism. Their publications usually focused on those who opposed their own narrow, conservative social and political views, ranging from union leaders, suffragettes and later feminists, celebrities, and other ordinary people made famous through mediatised visibility. Their biggest successes in the United Kingdom—Harmsworth's *Daily Mail* (1896–present) and Murdoch's *The Sun* (relaunched 1969)—influenced many rivals, with newspapers of different partisanship adopting layout styles, increased focus on celebrity culture and linguistic plays with adjectives and puns. Tabloid attacks became more prevalent in the United States after Murdoch's purchase of the *New York Post* (in 1976) and the *Fox News* (1996), which shared elements of his characteristic style.

Three intertwined strands of celebrity culture dominated twentieth-century tabloid news—stardom (for example, Hollywood, European dictatorships, and later popular music), "celebrification" of politicians, and ordinary people "made famous" through the application of news media constructs.[71] Attack journalism, characteristically a political discourse from origin, focused more on the first two, although there were also increases in individualised public shaming around morality and the body that also impacted significantly on the last. Stardom is a discourse of consecration where individuals are lifted by media discourses even to the point of deity and tabloid attacks became tools of desecration by which they might be brought crashing back down from the heavens.[72] Richard deCordova best articulates how magazine journalism helped to establish "the star" as a symbolic identity and a site for attention.[73] The image and later voices of individuals—from paparazzi, publicity events, and interviews—became part of daily informational news and increasingly focused on appearances and morality.[74] For female stars, celebrities and politicians particularly, there were incessant questions of worthiness, linked to overt sexualisation, and suggestions of how public roles impacted on roles of wife, mother, and daughter and this became a focus of second-wave feminism scholarship that evidenced how the personal was political and misogynistic news(room) cultures.[75] Such dynamics broadened the wider socio-political dimensions of attack journalism and how it shaped public debate.

Some standout, spectacular moments demonstrate how key characteristics of attack journalism responded to new cultures of stardom, tabloidism, advances in equality in relation to sex, sexuality, gender fluidity, and identity play. David Bowie strategically used imagery and discourses from stardoms of Hollywood and European Dictators as part of the building of the entirely fictional self-branded Ziggy Stardust.[76] Bowie was already a popular figure in the British popular music press such as *Melody Maker*, who declared 1972 the "year of the transvestite" and the Ziggy publicity campaign launched less than a year after London's first gay rights marches. The character, and by extension Bowie himself, embodied potent societal changes and for many fans this offered opportunities to explore their own sexuality and gender-identities.[77] *Melody Maker's* tabloid sister paper *The Daily Mirror*[78] initially declared that the "camp" stage persona was just an act—Bowie was really "plain David Jones back home in Beckenham, Kent" living happily with "wife Angie and baby son Zowie."[79] But as lines between Bowie and "gay" Ziggy blurred, they became increasingly hostile. In "Has the Star Gone Too Far" they declared he "behaves more like a Soho stripper than a top pop-star" as he "bumps [...] grinds [...] waggles his hips." The word "bizarre" appeared in almost every piece, usually in the lead paragraph. Bowie was also "camp," "odd," a "weirdo," and "dangerous." Headmasters suspended schoolchildren for copying his sexually ambiguous hairstyle and a mum's letter became a news story because she feared Bowie was sexualising and corrupting her pre-teen daughter. "Clean cut" Cliff Richard even penned "This Rotten Pop" where he questioned what Bowie was "trying to prove" and why he is "effeminate" despite having a "wife and child."[80] Such attacks stemmed from the homophobia that was rampant in newsrooms dominated by white, heteronormative men, as evident during debates leading to the decriminalisation of homosexuality in 1967. Throughout the 1950s and 1960s, many newspapers countered demands for gay rights by rhetorically criminalising gay men as sinful reflections of social decline.

The *Mirror* sister paper the *Sunday Pictorial* (later the *Sunday Mirror*) had published an infamous three-part series on "Evil Men" that linked homosexuality to paedophilia, argued for detention and medical intervention, and declared almost all frequented "male prostitutes."[81] A similar hit job in the *NotW* dismissed gay men as an invisible "evil in our midst" and called for far harsher prosecution.[82] In the seminal *Coming Out*, published in 1977, Jeffrey Weeks highlighted how such pieces sustained beliefs in the evils of the gay community that had circulated in the press since the nineteenth century and slowed their fight for civil rights by influencing public opinion and parliamentary decisions.[83]

The tensions between mainstream celebrity cultures, tabloid news, and politics fed back into systems of democracy which also interplayed with visual cultures of celebrity and tabloidism in new ways. Larry Sabato offered a range of examples from the advancement of television news bulletins and later rolling twenty-four-hour TV in the United States to evidence the purposes and patterns of "Attack Journalism and Feeding Frenzies," which he declared a uniquely "American Style" Inquisition. Sabato argued they reflected a "new world of omnipresent journalism" which was "far more interested in finding sleaze and achieving fame and fortune than in serving as ... honest broker between citizens and government" and had contributed to "decline in citizen's confidence in, and respect for, the news media."[84] The amplification, acceleration, and appetite for attack mean that uncovering misdemeanour and private impropriety is now key to holding audience (and therefore voter) attention as part of party-political cut and thrust. While the visuality of tabloidism certainly extended the frenzy and spectacle-of-attack, key characteristics such as rhetorical criminalisation, gossip about the personal as part of political argumentation and the self-claimed place of the press as the voice of public opinion were constants. Television news, as a culture of tabloidism, expanded rather than invented the frenzy, making it more present and prescient for audiences.

In the first two decades of the twenty-first century, attack journalism expanded again with digital informational technology. Greater public place of audiences as part of an all-encompassing "viewer society" fused panopticism with synopticism,[85] whereby the many contemplated and commented on politicians and celebrities whose visibility expanded across intercommunicative representational mainstream news and presentational social media.[86] But once more the press staked their claim as leaders of attack and when in 2015 Britain had what was declared as its first "social media election," amidst greater volumes of publicly and visible public debate, the Tory tabloid press led a charge against Labour leader Ed Miliband. There were startling similarities in tone, language, and purpose as the attack on Thomas Paine almost 250 years before, particularly in Murdochian newspapers. The reason for both attacks was similar, with each perceived as a direct threat to the commercial and political power of tabloid news media and political orders. Paine radically disrupted models of print production by offering pamphlets that were affordable, easier to digest, informational, and instructional that argued for wide-scale political and social change to include working-class people in democratic systems. Miliband criticised the ethics of tabloid media and monopolies and suggested governments work together to dismantle Rupert Murdoch's empire.[87] A News Corporation executive allegedly threatened that this meant that they were "going to make it personal."[88] The representational parameters and languages were remarkably similar too. *The Sun* unimaginatively labelled Miliband as "Red Ed," whereas *The Times* had dubbed Paine "Mad Tommy."[89] Both were falsely accused of criminality, with suggestions that Miliband used "slave labour" and that Paine was a thief. They were both portrayed as stupid and bent on class division—in Miliband's case a "grisly mix of left and lefter" and in Paine's a "public pest" who was "envious" of the wealthy because he was working class and uneducated. There were references to mental health ("barmy" or "lunacy") and suggestions that each of them would "defile" the political and social order. Perhaps the most curious similarity were questions of masculinity linked to attire. Miliband would "not wear the trousers" while Paine's "breeches" were found in the "water closet." In a time when so many of the mechanisms of electioneering were transformed by the changes in digital technology and how it expanded the cultures of tabloidism—creating spectacles of attack journalism of magnitude and complexity that far outstripped all that had gone before—much of the discourse was very old news.

What Is to Be Done?

We have all witnessed a press attack. Suddenly, the public visibility of an individual increases and, at the same time, the information and instruction about them guide audiences to cast them from respectable social spheres. Willingly or unwittingly, we may have joined in by clicking on content, comments and subtweets, shares, and likes. In stat-driven newsrooms, popularity means that more of the same is produced and other publications follow suit. Attack journalism is the oldest representational culture that brings together information and instruction for specific purpose. Now it sits among a never-ending stream of similar content with primarily commercial purposes, including shaming of body and gossip that reveals personal impropriety. As such how can we spot and counter those moments that perpetuate division to maintain the commercial, social, and political powers of the press?

Looking back at key moments brings into focus that attack journalism has a clear methodology. It is sustained, usually across multiple publications and platforms and while with hindsight this is often for a relatively condensed in time, there is no visible end in sight for audiences watching and/or participating in the spectacle. It often refers to, or hints at, characteristics of difference such as class, race, gender or sex, religion and claims to simply reflect public opinion, when its purpose is really to shape it. The dominance of white men in public spheres meant that the examples included here to evidence methodological development were often from this social group. But broader media representation of people from the twentieth century onwards means those that are most often attacked have other characteristics of difference. From young black sports stars claiming a political voice, to politicians who argue substantive social change, to celebrities declared as "woke" for highlighting issues of environmental, racial or LGBTQ injustice, attacks relate identity to opinion in complex ways. Expansions in digital space, including what is often referred to as "cancel culture," might be politically driven too, but attack journalism is one way the news industry maintains its gatekeeping and place as arbitrator of public opinion.

As we approach four hundred years since the first systematic attack journalism, and in the wake of numerous legal battles and ongoing campaigns against news media's cultures of attack, it seems incredible that no press codes of conduct address it directly. In the United Kingdom, the IPSO Code (print press and their digital brands) and OFCOM (broadcast and new online powers) codes of practice define public interest and issues of harassment and/or fairness. But while both IPSO and Ofcom address *persistent pursuit*, neither consider how *persistent publication* can also be harassment or unfair. In text, image, or audiovisual form, persistent publication can include references to sex or gender, sexuality, class, race, religion, nationality, or disability and publication of falsehood, rumour, or conjecture. Codes of practice should address such inequalities of representation and repetition directly.

Imbalances between understanding the realities of news as both informational and instructional allow attack journalism—and broader cultures of public shaming—to germinate, perpetuate, and grow. Popularity of information that might already be in the public domain becomes justification for repeating or extending it. By understanding the methodology, we might better moderate such expansions and extend media literacy among journalists and their audiences alike about attack journalism's purposes and power.

Notes

1 Aaron Doyle, "Revisiting the Synopticon: Reconsidering Mathiesen's 'The Viewer Society' in the Age of Web 2:0," *Theoretical Criminology* 15, no. 3 (August 2011): 283–299; and Thomas Mathiesen, "The Viewer Society: Michael Foucault's 'Panopticon' Revisited," *Theoretical Criminology* 1, no. 2 (May 1997): 215–234.
2 Gaye Tuchman, "Introduction: The Symbolic Annihilation of Women by the Mass Media," in *Hearth and Home: Images of Women in the Mass Media*, ed. Gaye Tuchman, Arlene Kaplan Daniels, and James Benét (New York: Oxford University Press, 1978), 3–38.
3 Bethany Usher, *Journalism and Celebrity* (London and New York: Routledge, 2020), 38.
4 For quote, see Anthony Giddens, *The Nation State and Violence: Volume Two of a Contemporary Critique of Historical Materialism* (Cambridge, UK: Polity, 1985), 177–178.
5 Michael Schudson, *Discovering the News* (New York: Basic Books, 1978); and Gaye Tuchman, *Making News: A Study in the Construction of Reality* (New York: The Free Press, 1978).
6 Alistair Black and Bonnie Mak, "Period, Theme, Event: Locating Information History in History," in *Information and Power in History towards a Global Approach*, ed. Ida Nijenhuis et al. (London: Routledge, 2021), 18–36.
7 James Fallows, *Breaking the News: How the Media Undermine American Democracy* (New York: Vintage, 1997).
8 Bethany Usher, *Journalism and Crime* (London and New York: Routledge, 2023).
9 James Curran and Jean Seaton, *Power without Responsibility*, 8th ed. (London: Routledge, 2018), 3.
10 Chris Kyle, "Monarch and Marketplace: Proclamations as News in Early Modern England," *Huntington Library Quarterly*, 78, no. 4 (2015): 771–787; and Jason Peacey, *Print and Public Politics in the English Revolution* (Cambridge, UK: Cambridge University Press, 2013).
11 Joad Raymond, *The Invention of the Newspaper: English Newsbooks 1641–1649*, 2nd ed. (Oxford: Oxford University Press, 2005).
12 Martin Conboy, *Journalism: A Critical History* (London: Sage, 2004), 26–43.
13 John Nalson, *An Impartial Collection of the Great Affairs of State* (London: 1682), 807.
14 Usher, *Journalism and Crime*, 49.
15 Raymond, *Invention of the Newspaper*, 185.
16 George K. Fortescue, *The Catalogue of the Pamphlets, Books, Newspapers, and Manuscripts Relating to the Civil War, the Commonwealth, and Restoration, Collected by George Thomason, 1640–1661* (London: British Library, 1908). References from 1641.
17 Usher, *Journalism and Crime*, 51.
18 Roland Barthes, *Mythologies* (London: Jonathan Cape, 1972 [1957]), 45.
19 Samuel R. Gardiner, *The Constitutional Documents of the Puritan Revolution 1625–1660* (Oxford: Oxford University Press, 1906), 282–283.
20 Jürgen Habermas, *The Structural Transformation of the Public Sphere* (Cambridge, MA: MIT Press).
21 Toby Miller, "Journalism and the Question of Citizenship," in *The Routledge Companion to News and Journalism*, ed. Stuart Allan (Abingdon: Routledge, 2012), 397–406.
22 Jeremy Black, *The English Press in the 18th Century* (London: Routledge, 1987).
23 Kevin Barnhurst and John Nerone, "Journalism History," in *The Handbook of Journalism Studies*, ed. Karin Wahl-Jorgensen and Thomas Hanitzsch (New York: Taylor and Francis, 2009), 18.
24 Robert Rea, *The English Press in Politics, 1760–1774* (Lincoln, NE: University of Nebraska Press, 1963), 3.

25 Henry Richard Fox-Bourne, *English Newspapers* (London: Routledge, 1998), 190.
26 Rea, *The English Press*, 175.
27 Rea, *The English Press*, 174–185.
28 Junius' letters were first published in the *Public Advertiser* between January 21, 1769 and January, 1772. Available at the British Library Newspaper Archive, https://www.britishnewspaperarchive.co.uk/.
29 Usher, *Journalism and Celebrity*, 32.
30 Rea, *The English Press*, 176.
31 *Public Advertiser*, December 19, 1769.
32 Rea, *The English Press*, 187.
33 William Draper, *Public Advertiser*, January 26, 1769.
34 Usher, *Journalism and Celebrity*, 33.
35 Marilyn Butler, *Burke, Paine, Godwin and the Revolution Controversy* (Cambridge, UK: Cambridge University Press, 1984).
36 Usher, *Journalism and Celebrity*, 34–39.
37 *The Whitehall Evening Post*, August 16, 1791. All subsequent references to Paine are from the British Library Newspaper Archive 1791–1792, https://www.britishnewspaperarchive.co.uk/.
38 Butler, *The Revolution Controversy*, 108.
39 Usher, *Journalism and Celebrity*, 36.
40 *The Times,* July 30, 1791.
41 Karin Wahl-Jorgensen and Bob Franklin, "Journalism Research in Great Britain," in *Global Journalism Research: Theories, Methods, Findings, Future*, ed. Martin Löffelholz and David Weaver (New York: Blackwell, 2008), 172–184.
42 *Oracle*, October 3, 1792.
43 *Public Advertiser*, September 19, 1792.
44 *The Times,* July 14, 1792; and *Morning Herald*, June 15, 1792.
45 *Morning Herald,* December 22, 1792.
46 *The Times*, May 7, 1792; and *Oracle*, October 3, 1792.
47 *Oracle*, July 14, 1792; and *Morning Herald,* January 22, 1793.
48 *Public Advertiser*, December 28, 1792.
49 *The Times,* May 11, 1792.
50 Gaye Tuchman, "The Symbolic Annihilation of Women."
51 Charles Taylor, *Sources of the Self: The Making of the Modern Identity* (Cambridge, UK: Cambridge University Press, 1985), 393.
52 Giddens, *The Nation State*, 177–178.
53 Taylor, *Sources of the Self*, 415.
54 Taylor, *Sources of the Self*, 394–395.
55 Jeremy Bentham, *Panopticon; or, the Inspection-house* (London: 1787). See also Michel Foucault, *Discipline and Punish* (New York: Random House, 1975).
56 George Boyce, "The Fourth Estate: A Reappraisal of a Concept," in *Newspaper History from the 17th Century to the Present Day*, ed. George Boyce, James Curran, and Peter Wingate (London: Sage, 1978), 19–40.
57 John Stuart Mill, *On Liberty* (Kitchener: Batoche Books, 2001 [1859]), 23.
58 Jean K. Chalaby, *The Invention of Journalism* (Basingstoke: Palgrave Macmillan, 1998).
59 See Conboy, *Journalism: A Critical History*, 86–93.
60 Roger Wells, "Mr William Cobbett, Captain Swing and King William IV," *The Agricultural History Review*, 45, no. 1 (1997): 34–48.
61 Usher, *Journalism and Crime*, 108.
62 *The Times*, December 24, 1830.
63 *The Times*, January 2, 1831.
64 *Political Register*, February 19, 1831.
65 *Political Register*, December 11, 1830.
66 *Political Register*, February 9, 1831.
67 *Political Register*, February 19, 1831.
68 *The Times*, June 20, 1835.

69 Usher, *Journalism and Crime*, 121–128.
70 Usher, *Journalism and Crime*, 175.
71 Usher, *Journalism and Celebrity*, 81–170.
72 Usher, *Journalism and Celebrity*, 81–109.
73 Richard deCordova, *Picture Personalities: The Emergence of the Star System in America* (Urbana, IL: University of Illinois Press, 1990).
74 Graeme Turner, *Understanding Celebrity*, 2nd ed. (London: Sage, 2014)
75 Patricia Holland, "The Page Three Girl Speaks to Women, Too," *Screen* 24, no 3 (May–June 1983), 84–102.
76 Andrew Lindridge and Toni Eagar, "'And Ziggy Played Guitar': Bowie, the Market, and the Emancipation and Resurrection of Ziggy Stardust," *Journal of Marketing Management* 31, nos. 5–6 (March 2015), 546–576.
77 Sean Redmond and Tojia Cinque, *The Fandom of David Bowie: Everyone Says "Hi"* (Cham: Palgrave Macmillan, 2019).
78 Owned by IPC media, whose director, Cecil Harmsworth King, was Alfred Harmsworth's nephew and purchased the title from the family business.
79 All references from British Library *Daily Mirror* archive, January to October 1973, https://www.britishnewspaperarchive.co.uk/.
80 *Daily Mirror*, June 19, 1973.
81 *Sunday Pictorial*, June 4, 1952.
82 *News of the World*, November 1, 1953.
83 Jeffrey Weeks, *Coming Out* (London: Quartet Books, 1977), 162–163.
84 Larry Sabato, *Feeding Frenzy: Attack Journalism and American Politics* (New York: Lanahan, 2000 [1991]), 2–3, 34.
85 Aaron Doyle, "Revisiting the Synopticon," 283–299.
86 P. David Marshall, "Persona Studies: Mapping the Proliferation of the Public Self," *Journalism*, 15, no. 2 (2014): 153–170.
87 Ed Miliband, "Rupert Murdoch's Empire Must Be Dismantled," *The Guardian*, July 16, 2011, https://www.theguardian.com/politics/2011/jul/16/rupert-murdoch-ed-miliband-phone-hacking.
88 Ed Miliband, "We Are at a Crossroads. Will we be Scared, or Will we Stand up?" *The Guardian*, March 16, 2013, https://www.theguardian.com/politics/2011/jul/16/rupert-murdoch-ed-miliband-phone-hacking.
89 All references from the British Library Newspaper Archive. For Paine see *The Times* 1791–1792; for Ed Miliband, see *The Sun*, 2014–2015, https://www.bl.uk/collection-guides/british-newspaper-archive.

10
THE FAULT LINES OF KNOWLEDGE

An Examination of the History of Wikipedia's "Neutral Point of View" (NPOV) Information Policy and Its Implications for a Polarised World

Brendan Luyt

Wikipedia is the newest manifestation of an old dream—the encapsulation of the world's knowledge within a readily available space, all done for the good of humanity. Joseph Reagle traces this dream back to the European Enlightenment of the eighteenth century and the iconic *Encyclopédie* (1751–1772), compiled by Dennis Diderot.[1] Reagle and others also direct our attention to twentieth-century versions of the dream, including Paul Otlet's concept of the Universal Decimal Classification (UDC) and the monographic principle that underpinned his vision of the Mundaneum, a vast information infrastructure that he believed capable of achieving that most elusive of targets, world peace.[2] Vannevar Bush's Memex is also part of this tradition. Bush, writing at the end of the Second World War, considered that the management of information was a key post-war task. For him, new electro-mechanical technologies would allow for the development of a device that could put on the desk entire libraries of documents.[3] A few decades later, inspired by the rapid development of digital computing technology, Ted Nelson had a similar dream. In the 1970s, he envisaged a distributed information system that he called Xanadu. It embodied within an electronic document system the intertextuality of literary theorists and was a precursor to the much more primitive hypertext of today's internet.[4]

Wikipedia has been much more successful than any of these previous visions of a universal encyclopaedia. In the space of two decades it has become an integral component of much of the world's information infrastructure. The success it has enjoyed derives from its relatively low barriers to participation and an ethos, encouraged by its founders Jimmy Wales and Larry Sanger, that encouraged people with different belief systems to edit, if not entirely peacefully then at least with a set of rules to guide and resolve their disputes. Chief among these was (and remains) the "Neutral Point of View" (NPOV) information policy (hereafter simply referred to as "policy").

NPOV: A Foundation Stone for Wikipedia

In theory, NPOV seeks to make Wikipedia not an arbiter of truth, but rather a repository of descriptions of what knowledgeable people (variously defined but sharing the characteristic of having been published) have claimed truth to be. Wales and Sanger believed that this style of writing would allow for the inclusion of all important points of view on any particular topic. Certainly, it allowed for Wikipedia's rapid growth, although it is also clear that large gaps in coverage still exist.

There have been several studies that focus on the nature of Wikipedia's NPOV policy.[5] Two stand out. Matei and Dobrescu examined the policy in terms of its function within the community. They argue that although NPOV advocates a universal approach to the encyclopaedia's content, it is undermined by a culture of "personalized interpretations," a tension which is only relieved by a certain tolerance for "systemic ambiguity."[6] Matei and Dobrescu note that the NPOV talk page is filled with "repeated requests for clarification" but that debates over the policy merely "end up reinforcing the status quo." NPOV, they conclude "is unenforceable in its letter" becoming instead "a term that is used to beat one's adversaries over the head and justify forcible impositions of meaning on specific topics."[7]

Jens-Erik Mai provides us with a more prescriptive analysis. His work aims to highlight the problems associated with Wikipedia's homogeneous community of editors, but also to demonstrate the need for Wikipedia to reconsider its epistemological foundation. He argues that Wikipedia's NPOV policy maintains a "position that is absolutistic at the center, but relative at the edges. Wikipedia assumes that the centre exists in a space that is 'uncontested and uncontroversial,' whereas there is only room for 'conflicting opinions' at the edges."[8] Mai argues that Wikipedia would be better to see knowledge as a rhizomatic network which has the property of including "multiple interpretations."[9]

An examination of the history of the NPOV policy suggests that there has been a hardening of the epistemological positions observed in Wikipedia by these two studies. Although there existed from the beginning fault lines in the project over what information was worthy of inclusion, the gulf has only grown wider over time. It is this development, as manifested in the changes, additions, and deletions to the NPOV policy page, as well as their implications for the future of Wikipedia's stated dream to encapsulate all the world's knowledge, that form the focus of this chapter, a partial history of NPOV policy.

Writing Histories of Wikipedia

There are two challenges to writing histories of Wikipedia. The first is the sheer size of the encyclopaedia. The second is its dynamic and ever-changing nature. The two challenges are related in so far as Wikipedia's size is a product not just of the number of articles it hosts, but also due to its recording even the smallest of changes to these articles in the form of edit histories. These edit histories are available for each article, adding considerably to the total available text that could potentially be examined. This chapter narrows the scope of investigation in two ways. The first is to look only at the various versions of the Wikipedia page that outlines and explains the NPOV policy. Looking at the changes to this page is extremely revealing as it in effect documents the issues seen as important to some of the encyclopaedia's most senior editors who make sure to monitor and revert the page when they feel it necessary to do so. The scope has also been narrowed by selecting from the multitude of edits and hence versions of the page, only the first edit/version of each year. This provides an annual snapshot of the development of the policy. The earliest version of NPOV dates to 2001. Both that year and the subsequent six years, up to 2007, are examined here. Certain major trends may be seen to have developed over this period of time, trends that have continued into the present, as attested to by the further examination of the most recent version as of the writing of this chapter. The links to each of these archived versions are provided at the end of this chapter and all quotations are taken directly from these policy documents.

First Drafts of NPOV Policy (2001–2002)

Like many new articles, the NPOV policy page ("WP: NPOV") was relatively short at the beginning of its life in 2001, being only a few paragraphs long. Unlike other Wikipedia articles, however, it was signed by Jimbo Wales, Wikipedia's primus inter pares. In the article, NPOV was defined in terms of its motivation, as an attempt "to present ideas and facts in such a fashion that both supporters and opponents can agree." Caveats were in order though, as Wales noted that full agreement was "not possible" rather the target for agreement was "essentially rational people who may differ on particular points." Wales drew two short examples to illustrate how NPOV would work in practice and then a general strategy editors could use to create NPOV articles: "… write about what people believe, rather than what is so." He ended by asking editors who felt this would be too "subjectivist or collectivist or imperialist" to discuss with him "because I think that you are just mistaken."

This article, and especially its call for discussion at the end, was in keeping with the culture of Wikipedia at the time: small, idealistic, articulate, a little naive, and adhering to certain shared epistemological foundations seen to be universal in scope. Hence, it is not surprising that the article was short on specifics (it was assumed to be easily understandable) and that those not willing to engage with it could be dismissed as irrational.

Some discussion did follow and reading it today we can clearly see the beginnings of an epistemological fault line taking shape as some editors began to create hierarchies of knowledge that other editors contested. Among these was a distinction between scientific and non-scientific information. One editor argued that "the practice of including other points of view" with the implication "that an article should treat them equally" should not always be followed. Instead, "it is within the obligation of an encyclopedia to emphasise the lack of scientific basis for some beliefs, and to clearly state that belief in such things is not justified by apparent facts." In response, a second nameless editor counselled caution, suggesting that "science is not the be-all and end-all of human inquiry, and its supposed infallibility has at times delayed recognition of valid observations or procedures because they were 'unscientific'." This editor suggested that "a clear mention of lack of scientific basis without additional emphasis is adequate to place anomalous or pseudoscientific positions in context … it is not necessary to exhibit antagonism for these ideas beyond that."

However, even at this early date antagonism was already present with another editor proceeding to claim the high ground for science as being just another term for "methodical honesty," with everything else reduced to "a crackpot's speculation" that occasionally was correct. Still another editor took this antagonism to the level of a crusade, suggesting a new rule that would allow editors to "forget about NPOV for a moment" if it "would make a single reader believe that some utter bullshit is as legitimate as other theories about the same subject." Candidates for this treatment were "all science vs. religious fanaticism debates, like creationism vs. evolutionism." Larry Sanger, co-founder of Wikipedia, weighed in on this comment, sharply declaring that "I could not disagree more strongly. I'm sorry, but you are not the final arbiter of what is and what is not utter bullshit." But the attitude would persist and alter the balance of NPOV in the future.

Towards the very end of 2001, a much-expanded version of the NPOV policy page was uploaded to Wikipedia by user Cunctator and then edited by Sanger. The new page attempted to flesh out in more detail what exactly was meant by NPOV and how it could be achieved. It included an executive summary, an introduction to the idea of neutrality and why it was necessary for Wikipedia to be neutral, followed by sections on the policy itself, an example, and a list of objections and clarifications. The new page acknowledged that the meaning of NPOV "isn't obvious, and is easily misunderstood" noting especially that NPOV was not a POV at all, but rather neutral writing in which "one is very careful not to state (or imply or insinuate or carefully but subtly massage the reader into believing) that any particular view at all is correct" and that this could be achieved by "representing disputes by characterizing them, rather than engaging in them." But the editors of the new policy page clarified that presenting views rather than debating them did not go so far as to giving each view equal space in which to be represented: "We should not attempt to represent a dispute as if a view held by only a small minority of people deserved as much attention as a very popular view." Such a position would, it was claimed "be misleading as to the shape of the dispute." In adopting this stance, the Wikipedia editors were taking a page out of the guidebook to traditional encyclopaedia writing where balance was carefully apportioned between subjects depending on their assessed importance to the scope of the work or the field in which it was a part.

This was not the only way that Wikipedia could have been organised. Sanger tells us that very early in the history of Nupedia/WP, there had been proposals to allow for more than one article per subject, meaning that various points of view would be allowed to compete equally. But it was not adopted.[10] Instead, like many technologies, the new was patterned on the old. But it also made the life of the average Wikipedia editor more difficult because somehow, they had to allocate space for POVs based on the number of "experts on the subject, or among the concerned parties." There were two issues here. The first was that most editors probably did not have a thorough enough knowledge of a subject area to know who its experts were. This gap was compounded by the tendency to rely on easily available online sources of dubious quality instead of solid academic works harder to access and harder to read. I have argued elsewhere that many Wikipedia editors lack what I call "bibliographic imagination" — a desire to explore a wide variety of sources on a subject in favour of a shallow and piecemeal approach.[11] The result is that the information maps Wikipedia editors develop around subjects tend to be incomplete and inaccurate, making a true NPOV writing style close to impossible, if POVs were to be weighted as the new policy document ordained.

A second issue stemming from the new policy document concerned the notion that not only were subject experts to be considered in allocating space between POVs, but also "concerned parties." This would allow for the entire universe of Wikipedia information to fall under the NPOV policy (while there were no certified "experts" on Pokémon characters, one could probably find "concerned parties"), but it also meant that just about anyone could be given an equivalent status to expert. Clearly, although the aim of the new policy article was to reduce confusion, in both instances, new questions were raised just as quickly.

Furthermore, the new policy enshrined the notion of hierarchies of information — some information was better than others and deserved favoured treatment, although it tried to guard against abuse of this hierarchy. It argued, for example, that the policy did not mean "that minority views cannot receive as much attention as we can possibly give them on pages specifically devoted to those views" as "there is no size limit to Wikipedia." It also, in a separate section entitled "Fairness and sympathetic tone," declared that "we should present competing views with a consistently positive, sympathetic tone" so that "all positions presented are at least plausible." Despite these caveats, editors who believed they could distinguish "utter bullshit" from legitimate information could exploit the notion of a hierarchy of information to exclude whenever possible views they considered beyond the pale.

The new policy also, unwittingly to be sure, clouded the murky waters of NPOV still further by presenting an "alternative formulation of NPOV" in which editors were told to "assert the facts, including facts about opinions – but don't assert the opinions themselves." A fact in turn was defined as "a piece of information about which there is no serious dispute." Examples followed. We are told that "'Mars is a planet' is a fact" and "that Socrates was a philosopher" was also a fact. The idea behind the introduction of the concept of a "fact" was to again argue for a neutral writing style in which expressions of ideas by sources could be inserted into articles without editors committing to the truth of those expressions. Instead of saying "God exists," editors could say "Thomas Aquinas believed that God exists"—a statement which was undoubtedly true. The problem of course is that by including examples such as "Mars is a planet" the article created a category of statements that, if an editor could persuade his/her fellow editors that any particular claim was "a fact," would allow its inclusion in the article without attribution. As a result, editors not only had to contend with establishing how much weight to give to particular points of view without a clear understanding of the intellectual terrain they were mapping, they also needed to evaluate who was to be allowed to pronounce on any given subject, and decide what statements about the subject were facts or opinion. A tall order indeed.

The last section of the NPOV article was a set of answers to what was described as "common objections, or questions" regarding the policy. It provides an indication of the problems facing Wikipedia's editorial community at the time as it tried to implement NPOV. At the top of the list was the notion that taking a truly objective stance on any issue was impossible, hence NPOV was a futile exercise. The mismatch between the name of the policy and its directive was clear. People read the name and naturally concluded that each article was to exhibit a kind of middle ground between perspectives. This was not the case at all, but despite repeated attempts at explanation over the years the confusion remained. The vexed question of pseudoscience was next on the list. The article made it clear that Wikipedia's editors did not have to "describe pseudoscience as if [it] were on a par with science" but that it was not necessary to adopt what some editors referred to as the Scientific Point of View (SPOV). Instead, "the task is to represent the majority view and the minority (sometimes pseudoscientific) view as the minority and, moreover, to explain how scientists have received pseudoscientific theories." In other words, the yardstick for establishing majority and minority views was to be a community of scientists. This ran counter to the notion that either "concerned parties" as well as experts could be used to establish the proportionality of representation of various viewpoints. And while SPOV was explicitly rejected, a further entry point for similar views had been opened up as an abstract notion of science as universal truth was to be the de facto arbiter of much Wikipedia content.

Tackling Religion and Verifiable Sources (2005)

The years 2003 and 2004 saw little change to the NPOV policy page, but the following year ended the page's stability as a number of additions were made. Religion was the focus of many of the more substantial changes—an entire sub-section was added specifically to address the issue in the objection and clarifications section, suggesting that editorial battles were being fought on the subject. The sub-section noted that many adherents to a religion "would prefer that the article describe their faith as they see it, which is often from a non-historical perspective." Unlike the case of pseudoscience, these points of view were to be handled without the creation of an information hierarchy. History and the science of archaeology were not allowed to trump religion. Instead, the religious POV "must be mentioned" but, editors were told, "there is no contradiction" in so doing as "NPOV policy means that we say something like this: 'Many adherents of the faith believe X, which they believe that members of their group have always believed; however, due to the acceptance of some findings by modern historians and archaeologists other adherents of this faith now believe Z.'" Scientists were not privileged here as information arbiters. Furthermore, and again unlike the case of "pseudoscience," describing religious beliefs in a "pejorative" way was forbidden; hence, the term "fundamentalism" was to be used only in a "technical" sense.

The other major addition to the page was the insertion of a section entitled "An important component: good research." Around this time, NPOV was increasingly complemented with another policy, Verifiability with Reliable Sources (V/RS). The new policy required editors to back up their claims with references to published sources deemed "reliable." Likely the research section of the NPOV reflects the growing awareness of V/RS among the Wikipedia community. The 2005 version of the policy page informs us that POV battles "would be made much easier through the practice of good research. Facts are not points of view in and of themselves. So an easy way to avoid making a statement that promotes a point of view is to find a reputable source for a fact and cite the source." The rest of the section provided the rather banal advice that one should find "the best and most reputable" source, including "the most reliable online resource." Readers were also pointed to the library as a source of "good books and journal articles." While a step in the right direction, such advice was hardly going to overcome a lack of bibliographic imagination. However, the wording of the section was certainly likely to contribute to confusion over what the NPOV was supposed to be about. It used the phrase "POV battles" to describe the efforts required to make sure that each article was neutrally written and in so doing re-iterated the double-meaning POV had come to take on in the Wikipedia community. As an acronym it referred to "Point of View"—a good thing, as NPOV was premised on providing access to all points of view on a subject. But POV had also come to be used as an adjective, describing the opposite of NPOV—a bad thing and also likely to further the mistaken notion that NPOV was itself a POV, rather than a writing style. The inaccurate implication was that NPOV was meant to create articles having no apparent perspective on any given subject.

Narrowing the Focus: "Undue" Weight and "Minority" Views (2006)

The year 2006 saw further major changes to the NPOV policy page. The first and most important of these was the introduction of the concept of "undue weight." As in previous versions, the policy page continued to tell editors that views needed to be represented proportionally to the number of people holding those views (be it experts or "concerned parties"), only now a label was attached to perspectives that Wikipedia editors over-emphasised in their articles.

At the same time, another clause was added to the same section, exhorting editors that articles did not need to "include tiny-minority views at all" as well as providing the "Flat Earth" theory as an example of such a view. The flat earth theory example went on to be a commonly used example of both a fringe, and hence unworthy theory, and a poster child for how well Wikipedia was doing in accommodating even these outliers. Intended to add authority to the enforcement of undue weight was a direct quote from the co-founder of the Wikipedia project, Jimmy Wales who declared, in September 2003 mailing list post, that: "if a viewpoint is held by an extremely small (or vastly limited) minority it doesn't belong in Wikipedia (except perhaps in some ancillary article)." Undue weight received attention at other points on the page as well. The section on "fairness and sympathetic tone" had added to it the clause "bearing in mind the important qualifications about extreme minority views" and the next sentence qualified still further by adding the adjective "significant" to the phrase "competing views."

Signs of Conflict (2006)

Another term was introduced for the first time in the 2006 version of the NPOV policy page: "POV fork." In computer science, a fork occurs when the code of one version of an open-source project is split off from a parent project and used to develop a different project. Forking usually takes place when members of a project cannot agree on how the project is to be further developed and decide as a result to go their separate ways. A POV fork was defined by the policy page as "an attempt to evade POV guidelines by creating a new article about a certain subject that is already treated in an article often to avoid or highlight negative or positive viewpoints or facts" and was declared "unacceptable." The creation of the term and its inclusion on the policy page was a sign of the struggles taking place on Wikipedia over what NPOV really meant in practice, as well as an indicator that people either did not accept the validity of NPOV as a guide or, more likely, did not understand what it was all about. The former would suggest that the community/universe of rational, like-minded editors envisaged in earlier years had disappeared. The later suggests that the policy was confusing and beyond the capabilities of many editors to implement. Likely both factors were at work.

A further sign of conflict over the interpretation of NPOV policy was the increasing use of bold highlighting. The undue weight section had its first sentence in bold: "Now an important qualification." In the following section readers were told to convert opinions into facts by attributing them to a person or group. But evidently some editors had been attributing claims more generally to "some people" because now the policy informed that this was unacceptable: "The reference requires an identifiable and subjectively quantifiable population or, better still, a name." The phrase "an identifiable population" and "a name" were both in bold. Yet another example of highlighting problematic areas of the policy is found in the sub-section on pseudoscience, where the phrase, "represent the majority (scientific) view as the majority view and the minority (sometimes pseudoscientific) view as the minority view" was bolded—again, emphasising Wikipedia's hierarchy of information.

The section on pseudoscience also included the following sentence: "pseudoscience can be seen as a social phenomenon and therefore significant. However, pseudoscience should not obfuscate the description of the main views, and any mention should be proportional to the rest of the article." The need to specifically make allowance for the inclusion of "pseudoscience as a social phenomenon" suggests the lack of bibliographical imagination of some editors, but also that other editors were contesting this state of affairs, but having to do so in a circumspect way by constantly reminding readers (and more extreme editors who likely would have wanted to banish any talk about these topics) that pseudoscience, social phenomenon or not, was not a "main view."

At the same time accounts of pseudoscience were authorised, but hedged with preconditions, the special status of religious beliefs was further entrenched, again suggesting conflict within the ranks of Wikipedia editors. It seemed necessary to add a further qualification to the use of the term fundamentalism. Editors were told that they "should remember that it is not a synonym for 'opposition to science' nor 'deeply held beliefs' and it should not be used to refer to religious or political conservatism when those do not meet the word's technical senses."

A final, small, but extremely important change needs to be noted before ending this account of 2006. Ironically enough, in the sub-section entitled "Lack of neutrality as an excuse to delete" an injunction not to delete text that contained "valid information" was removed. This may have been an attempt to tidy up the language as the previous sentence still read "many of us believe that the fact that some text is biased is not enough, in itself, to delete it outright," but this sentence, in its various qualifications was not as powerful as the phrase that was removed. That phrase had unambiguously stated that text containing "valid information ... should simply be edited accordingly and certainly not deleted."

Radically Changing NPOV (2007)

The year 2007 saw major changes introduced to the NPOV policy page, changes that in some cases overturned and dramatically altered the nature of the policy. Others, such as the removal of the common questions and objections section to a series of separate articles reflected a struggle to make the policy document less cumbersome. Nevertheless, when compared to the "original" of 2002, this newest version of the page was a rambling and contradictory text. It also continued to be a text obsessed with the idea of "undue weight." The very first paragraph after the introduction sums up this obsession. We are told that conflicting views should be presented fairly, meaning that "none of the views should be given undue weight, or asserted as being the truth, and all significant published points of view are to be presented not just the most popular one." But while "undue weight" is italicised for emphasis, the equally important injunction "asserted as being the truth" is not. Clearly the editors responsible for the introduction of this text were primarily concerned with proportionality, rather than neutral writing in the strict sense of the term. Buttressing this concern was the use of the adjective "significant" and "published" to qualify just what perspectives deserved mention. This was the first time that the criterion of being a published source was included, a stipulation that would have repercussions in the future as at least some Wikipedia editors realised that a great deal of the world's information was not written down, but remembered and accessed orally.[12]

The need to watch for "undue weight" was not only repeated in the dedicated section on undue weight that followed the introduction, but expanded. Editors were told that "giving undue weight to other verifiable and sourced statements" was also a misdemeanour. In fact, there were many ways of giving undue weight, "including, but not limited to, depth of detail, quantity of text, prominence of placement, and juxtaposition of statements." Wales' quote was kept and a sentence just after it hammered home the point again, if the reader had not been paying attention: "views held only by a tiny minority of people should not be represented as though they are significant minority views, and perhaps should not be represented at all."

But the most astonishing change in the page, and the clearest evidence the most editors had never understood the policy in the first place, came in the second paragraph where it was declared that "as the name suggests, the neutral point of view is a point of view, not the absence or elimination of viewpoints. It is a point of view that is neutral – that is neither sympathetic nor in opposition to its subject." In describing NPOV as itself a POV, Wikipedia was jettisoning, probably unconsciously, the original conception of NPOV. In the 2003 version, we are told specifically that "the prevailing Wikipedia understanding is that the neutral point of view is not a point of view at all"; rather, it was a style of writing. The 2007 change was clearly not thought through carefully enough. One of the reasons why the initial formulation of NPOV declared that NPOV was not a POV was that it made possible the refutation of one of the key objections to neutrality—that it was impossible because there was really no true neutral point of view available. Every perspective was a view from somewhere. Now that editors were being told that NPOV was a view, that objection was bound to rise again.

The same sentence also made it more difficult to maintain the previously held notion that editors were supposed to write about differing viewpoints as sympathetically as possible. What had been meant by this was the realisation that one cannot write in a neutral way without trying to, at least temporarily, adopt the position of someone actually believing in the position to be described. Now, editors were told that "a point of view" was neutral if it was "neither sympathetic nor in opposition to its subject" without also being told that a certain level of empathy was required in order to write in this fashion. In fact, it appeared that the opposite of empathy was required as the proper stance was a "cold" and "rational" one. Clearly, the editors responsible for these changes wrongly conflated the need to be sympathetic while presenting a particular viewpoint with the notion of being biased toward that viewpoint. Once again, the epistemological complexity of the concepts involved created a great deal of confusion and a dilution of the original goal of Wikipedia to represent all the world's knowledge.

The 2007 version contained a number of other changes, not as important as the ones so far discussed. A list of biases was added, including the common ones such as gender and racial bias, but also bias based on commercial considerations and sensationalism. The last was defined as "bias in favor of the exceptional over the ordinary." Also added was a section entitled "History of NPOV" which informed that "NPOV is one of the oldest policies on Wikipedia" followed by a list of briefly annotated links.

NPOV Policy Today (2022)

The emphasis on the need for an information hierarchy along with the requirement to establish levels of significance and the fact/opinion divide continued unabated in versions of the NPOV policy page after 2007. The most recent page is no exception. In the first section readers are told that NPOV "means including all verifiable points of view" before providing a series of bulleted guidelines that highlight the different treatment to be accorded facts versus opinions. "Uncontested and uncontroversial factual assertions made by reliable sources should normally be directly stated in Wikipedia's voice" and "there is no need for specific attribution for the assertion ...." However, editors are warned not to state opinions as facts, that is, not to use Wikipedia's voice to express opinions, rather they "should be attributed in the text to particular sources."

More detailed advice was provided in the following section, "Achieving neutrality," which opened with an injunction to "remove material only where you have a good reason to believe it misinforms or misleads readers in ways that cannot be addressed by rewriting the passage." Afterwards, attention turns to specific problems editors are likely to encounter. Under "Article Structure" we find a discussion about POV forking and undue weight, but undue weight appears again in a sub-section of its own where it is given the most comprehensive treatment of all the problems taken up. On three occasions in this sub-section readers are reminded that the views of small minorities "should not be included" except as a separate article dealing specifically with those views, but even then "these pages should still appropriately reference the majority viewpoint wherever relevant and must not represent content strictly from the minority view perspective."

As well as being sufficiently significant or not, views were also to be scrutinised for being pseudoscience or fringe theories (both categories are lumped together in the same sub-section). Previous to this version, pseudoscience had never been defined. Now it was, as "'theories' [that] are presented by proponents as science but characteristically fail to adhere to scientific standards and methods." The policy declared that pseudoscience should not be given undue weight and that articles devoted to such subjects required an "explanation of how scientists have reacted" to them to be prominently placed in the text. Pseudoscience slides without distinction into a more catch-all term of "fringe theories" which are not explicitly defined, but which are identified as such by "more reliable sources to either lack evidence or actively ignore evidence." On the other hand, religion, in the most recent NPOV page version, retains its special status with "mythology" and "critical" joining "fundamentalism" as words to be used only in a technical sense "to avoid causing unnecessary offense or misleading the reader."

Further adding to the hierarchy of information is the concept of bias, an idea that although appearing in earlier versions is given emphasis now. This notion introduced further complexity to the intellectual labour to be performed by Wikipedia's editors as now sources could be challenged for being biased. The policy was rather vague, however, in explaining what was to be done with them. On the one hand, "biased sources are not inherently disallowed based on bias alone ..." but on the other hand, "this does not mean any biased source *must* be used; it may well serve an article better to exclude the material altogether" (italics in original). Strengthening the hold of the concept of bias on the imagination of Wikipedia's editors was a further sub-section, "attributing and specifying biased statements" where we are told that "biased statements of opinion can be presented only with in-text attribution." This is an entirely unnecessary injunction as any opinion was to be treated in this fashion!

The notion that some sources could, potentially, be excluded, muddies the NPOV waters to an even greater extent than before, as it suggests that there are sources that are somehow above bias, in other words, objective. This strikes at the core of the original formulation of the policy that saw NPOV as not a God-like view of a subject, but a style of writing that attempted to include as many perspectives (points of view) as possible. Now a source, and hence perspective, arguing for a particular point of view too firmly for the taste of one or more editors could be eliminated from consideration by being labelled as "biased." Such a development fits well with the overall trend of the development of NPOV policy we have been charting. There are serious implications for this trend.

Implications for an Increasingly Polarized World

The first of these has already been noted—the increase in the intellectual work required of the editors if they are to be responsible members of the Wikipedia community. Whether or not many are up to the task is a debatable question and much of the unevenness of coverage in Wikipedia may be due to the calibre of editors attracted to certain articles over others. Certainly, it raises issues about research practice among Wikipedia editors. Here the policy clearly falls flat. The best advice it offers in the current version is "try the library for reputable books and journal articles, and look online for the most reliable resources." Wikipedia needs to do a better job of encouraging, what is referred to in this chapter as, "bibliographic imagination" among its editors.

But there are deeper implications to the hierarchy of information that NPOV establishes relating to the online encyclopaedia's place in the world's information infrastructure. Since 2016, the issue of "fake news" and more generally mis- and dis-information have been on the minds of opinion leaders both in and out of governments around the world. The dominant response has been to fall back on the notion of demarcation, in other words, the establishment and policing of boundaries between good and bad users and sources of information.[13] The prescriptive idea behind demarcation is that "citizens" need to be protected against certain ideas and that this is to be achieved by either strategies of shielding or inoculation.[14] Wikipedia is, currently, firmly in the demarcation camp. In the past, demarcation may have been possible as an epistemological strategy. It is not so easy today. The sieve-like nature of digital communication technologies and the financial interests of giant capitalist social media firms conspire against such a course of action. But equally important is the collective memory of society, which over the course of the post-war decades has seen experts and authorities more generally lose the trust built up during the 1930s and 1940s as they are revealed to be caught up in the power (social and economic) games of our contemporary elite, in many cases, to end up embroiled in scandal and hypocrisy. In the United States, a turning point in this regard was the publication of the Pentagon Papers in 1971, an exposé of the mismatch between the reality of the Vietnam War and the image of that conflict portrayed by a cynical government and establishment. Since then, there has been a polarisation of views on a range of controversial topics behind which lies a segment of the public that no longer implicitly believes in the truth offered by traditional forms of expertise. The recent debate over the efficacy and side effects of COVID vaccination is only the latest of these debates.

It is important not to characterise these debates as Manichean in nature. As Harambam notes, for most people, science and expert advice is still considered valuable, just not on the terms it has traditionally been presented in. Instead, he argues that people want expert advice, rather than expert domination. They also want a greater degree of transparency in the work of experts.[15]

When we reflect on the sorry track record of science and engineering, as well as the social sciences, working within the broader political economy of late capitalism, this does not appear too much to ask. But this presents a conundrum for Wikipedia. From its earliest days, its core community of editors has wanted to achieve respectability for their product, not just in terms of the quantity of articles, but for their "quality" as well. Conscious or not, they have held up the ideal of the encyclopaedia as a storehouse of positivist and authoritative facts, making them natural allies of those who wish to somehow contain or reverse the erosion of traditional expert authority. At the same time, their "brand" is a product of a "simpler" more naive time when digital networking technologies promised radical new ways of producing and organising information that could bypass traditional expertise, allowing "the people" to participate in the process to a degree never possible before. But what Wikipedia's founders really wanted was a select version of "the people"—people that shared certain basic epistemological assumptions.

This ideal demographic has become harder to sustain with the growth of the NPOV page standing as eloquent witness to the work required to discipline unruly Wikipedians to recognise as natural a hierarchy of information claims and be willing to perform the cognitive work to maintain it. Is this effort the ideal strategy for Wikipedia to take? It is really possible to continue it in the long run? Does it take full advantage of the capabilities of Wikipedia technology? And perhaps most important of all, does it contribute constructively to de-escalate the polarisation facing our societies in what is shaping up to be a rocky and perilous twenty-first century?

While the dominant response to the erosion of the authority of the expert and the proliferation of conspiracy theories and "fake news" is to return to the past, there are some scholars who suggest that there is a better alternative, given that to strictly demarcate today invites further polarisation and is hypocritical given the abuses of expertise in the past.[16] What is needed rather are new spaces for citizens to debate information claims. Harambam points to novel institutions in both Ireland and Taiwan that successfully demonstrate that such spaces can be created, maintained, and work to produce new forms of consensus among large numbers of heterogeneous people.[17] The need for new forms of democratic space is a point also raised by Jasonoff and Simmet who argue, contra the demarcationists, that "reality should be up for debate, if indeed that debate is about whose reality counts and by what measures." In the view of these authors, truth claims need to be linked to publicly held values and purposes, and the only means to achieve this is through conversations among diverse groups taking place in democratic conditions of access.[18]

It seems to me that Wikipedia could be one of these democratic spaces, if NPOV was to return more to its early roots. Whether that is possible or not is another issue. Sanger claims that Wikipedia "has been transformed into a thuggish defender of the epistemic prerogatives of the powerful ... its operations [are now] a black box, an enigma thriving on anonymity and dark arts of dishonest social games and back-room deals. It is a mockery of an 'encyclopedia anybody can edit.'"[19] To be sure, this is an exaggeration made to promote his vision of an "encyclosphere," a decentralised networked of encyclopaedia articles, but it does have an element of truth, in that Wikipedia now has vested interests in its current structure and much to lose if that structure was unduly changed. What is clearer is that Wikipedia does have a choice to make—to follow the dominant epistemological tradition and embrace a system of demarcation or move towards pluralism as a truly key principle of its operation.

It is not an easy choice. If there is little likelihood that a demarcation approach will work to put the "genie" back in its epistemological bottle, there is a risk too in opening up to new forms of pluralism. Arguments against providing spaces for information considered beyond the pale are common—the idea being that it would only encourage their spread. But is hiding them away a better solution? Since when has prohibition ever really worked—perhaps outside a totalitarian state? Might it not be better to open up this despised information to the light by not only giving their proponents a space for their views but making them present their arguments as best they can (which often will not amount to much) and with as much evidence as they can (likely to be little). And allow (and trust) readers to decide. Of course, not all will make the choices "we" want them to make. But then the onus is on "us" to develop better or clearer arguments for why "we" are right, and "they" are wrong. Or better still to synthesise from these choices experimental facts that reveal something deeper about the needs and concerns of the communities making up our societies and why they chose to believe the things they do.[20]

Appendix: Archived NPOV Policy Pages Consulted

2001: https://en.wikipedia.org/w/index.php?title=Wikipedia:Neutral_point_of_view&oldid=334854039.

2002: https://en.wikipedia.org/w/index.php?title=Wikipedia:Neutral_point_of_view&oldid=270461.

2003: https://en.wikipedia.org/w/index.php?title=Wikipedia:Neutral_point_of_view&oldid=656009.

2004: https://en.wikipedia.org/w/index.php?title=Wikipedia:Neutral_point_of_view&oldid=2323839.

2005: https://en.wikipedia.org/w/index.php?title=Wikipedia:Neutral_point_of_view&oldid=9353495.

2006: https://en.wikipedia.org/w/index.php?title=Wikipedia:Neutral_point_of_view&oldid=33571151.

2007: https://en.wikipedia.org/w/index.php?title=Wikipedia:Neutral_point_of_view&oldid=97833709.

2022: https://en.wikipedia.org/w/index.php?title=Wikipedia:Neutral_point_of_view&oldid=1104199660.

Notes

1 Joseph Reagle, *Good Faith Collaboration: The Culture of Wikipedia* (Boston, MA: MIT Press, 2010), 18.
2 Alex Wright, *Cataloging the World: Paul Otlet and the Birth of the Information Age* (Oxford: Oxford University Press, 2014).
3 E. Pascal Zachary, *Endless Frontier: Vannevar Bush Engineer of the American Century* (New York: Free Press, 2018).
4 Ken Knowlton, "Ted Nelson's Xanadu," in *Intertwingled: The Work and Influence of Ted Nelson*, ed. Douglas R. Dechow and Daniele Struppa (New York: Springer, 2015), 25–28.
5 Erinc Salor, "Neutrality in the Face of Reckless Hate: Wikipedia and Gamergate," *Nordisk Tidsskrift for Informationsvidenskab og Kulturformidling* 5, no. 1 (2016): 23–29; Shane Greenstein and Feng Zhu, "Open Content, Linus' Law, and Neutral Point of View," *Information Systems Research* 27, no. 3 (2016): 618–635; Nathaniel Tkacz, *Wikipedia and the Politics of Openness* (Chicago, IL: University of Chicago Press, 2014); and Linsay Fullerton and James Ettema, "Ways of World-Making: Reality, Legitimacy and Collaborative Knowledge Making," *Media, Culture and Society* 36, no. 2 (2014): 183–199.
6 Sorin Adam Matei and Caius Dobrescu, "Wikipedia's 'Neutral Point of View': Settling Conflict through Ambiguity," *The Information Society* 27, no. 1 (2011): 41.
7 Matei and Dobrescu, "Wikipedia's 'Neutral Point of View'," 48.
8 Jens-Erik Mai, "Wikipedians' Knowledge and Moral Duties," *Nordisk Tidsskrift for Informationsvidenskab og Kulturformidling* 5, no. 1 (2016): 20.
9 Mai, "Wikipedians' Knowledge and Moral Duties," 18.
10 Larry Sanger, *Essays on Free Knowledge: The Origins of Wikipedia and the New Politics of Knowledge* (Canal Winchester, OH: Sanger Press, 2020), 12.
11 Brendan Luyt, "Representation and the Problem of Bibliographic Imagination on Wikipedia," *Journal of Documentation* 78, no. 5 (2022): 1075–1091.

12 Heather Ford, "Fact Factories: Wikipedia and the Power to Represent," (Oxford University, 2018), https://ora.ox.ac.uk/objects/uuid:b34fdd6c-ec15-4bcd-acba-66a777739b4d/download_file?safe_filename=thesishford_thesis.pdf&file_format=application%2Fpdf&type_of_work=Thesis.
13 Noortje Marres, "Why We Can't Have Our Facts Back," *Engaging Science, Technology, and Society* 4 (2018): 423–443.
14 Jaron Harambam, "Against Modernist Illusions: Why We Need More Democratic and Constructivist Alternatives to Debunking Conspiracy Theories," *Journal for Cultural Research* 25, no. 1 (2021): 104–122.
15 Jaron Harambam, Kamile Grusauskaite, and Lars de Wildt, "Poly-truth, or the Limits of Pluralism: Popular Debates on Conspiracy Theories in a Post-truth Era," *Public Understanding of Science* 31, no. 6 (2022): 784–798.
16 Marres, "Why," 423–443.
17 Harambam, "Against," 104–122.
18 Sheila Jasanoff and Hilton R. Simmet, "No Funeral Bells: Public Reason in a 'Post-truth' Age," *Social Studies of Science* 47, no. 5 (2017): 751–770.
19 Larry Sanger, *Essays on Free Knowledge: The Origins of Wikipedia and the New Politics of Knowledge* (Canal Winchester, OH: Sanger Press, 2020), 219.
20 Marres, "Why," 423–443.

11
FACIAL AIs AND INFORMATION SYSTEMS IN HISTORICAL CONTEXT

Edward Higgs

Introduction

Faces have always been about information, in terms of signs or utterances that convey meaning to others. This is a very broad concept of "information," which allows us to consider forms of communication and its storage that are often overlooked. It also enables us to consider flows in the opposite direction, from meaning embedded in prior discourses to the perception of phenomenon in the external world. This is, of course, a well-known anthropological theme, in which beliefs can be projected onto external reality.[1] The concept of a reading of the world based on a projection of systems of thoughts to create an external reality also recalls the Renaissance *episteme* posited by Michel Foucault. Here the universe was replete with information in the form of signs and signatures to be read, as in astrology or the correspondence between the appearance of medicinal plants and the diseases they were supposed to treat. Foucault believed that this structure of thought gave way to later *epistemes* based on classification and measurement from the eighteenth century onwards, the basis of modern information flows.[2] However, much of the present chapter relates to the continuation of this Renaissance *episteme* into the modern world.

In the case of the human face, the concept of communication/information flows applies most obviously to the speech that proceeds from the mouth, but faces have also always provided information to allow others to recognise individuals and to have access to their emotions through reading expressions. At various times and places, faces have, in addition, been used to ascribe characteristics to individuals and groups of people. Hence the "face of the savage" or the "face of the criminal" in Western discourses. Artificial Intelligence (AI) systems are now being deployed to mimic these human processes, based on measuring, classifying, and comparing data. Such systems include facial recognition; emotion, or affect, technologies; and digital physiognomy. In these systems, the face and the body more generally are turned into stored information in datasets of measurements, which can be mapped onto pre-existing templates of emotions or characteristics, or onto later presentations of a face, as in facial recognition systems. The face becomes a source, and archive, of its own data. Of course, such technologies are often only supplements to the inter-personal practices that have existed throughout human history, although they have increasing salience in important contexts. They also build on the long development of the information collecting and surveillance capacities of the state and commercial companies.[3]

The creation of such AI systems is a multibillion-dollar business, and they are being used by immigration officials, police forces, recruiters, marketing businesses, and so on. The affect/emotion recognition industry, for example, is undergoing a period of significant growth. One report claims that the market for such technology was worth $12 billion in 2018 and estimates that the industry will grow to over $90 billion by 2024.[4] Similarly, the global facial recognition market was valued at $3.86 billion in 2020 and is expected to expand at a compound annual growth rate (CAGR) of 15.4% from 2021 to 2028.[5] These figures may well be underestimated, especially given the vast expansion of the deployment of such technologies in China. This innovative technology and other forms of biometrics have raised great hopes in quarters such as the United Nations and World Bank as means of providing the benefits of identification in developing countries, in terms of easier access to welfare benefits and voting rights, and the ability to make commercial transactions. This is seen as a means of achieving the United Nations' Sustainable Development Goal 16.9— that everyone should have a verifiable identity.[6] For others, the spread of such biometric AI systems is a threat because of their inherent biases, the invasion of privacy they entail, and the lack of democratic control over their deployment and use.[7]

Although the creation of such biometric systems is the work of technologists and scientists, there has been a dialogue with the Humanities community about such systems in the realms of philosophy and ethics. This has been institutionalised in bodies such as Oxford University's Institute for Ethics in AI, the Centre for Technological Futures at the University of Edinburgh, and the Montreal AI Ethics Institute, among others.[8] Given the futuristic and utopian (or dystopian) potential of such technologies, it might be asked what a study of the past has to add to such debates around their nature, introduction, and utility? This chapter argues that historical analysis is relevant because modern AI research has made direct reference to past discourses or sits within the context these have created. Past histories can also predispose people to accept the decisions made by AIs as "common sense." Similarly, some phenomenological issues with regard to AI systems can be considered in terms of past attempts to do similar things. In addition, some of the problems with contemporary applications, and the reasons for their implementation, can be brought into focus by examining similar issues with past analogue approaches. This is especially true of facial recognition, where present attempts to introduce such systems, whether or not they are effective, in order to "modernise" police work have echoes of nineteenth-century policing innovations. This contribution to the present collection explores some examples of these processes.

Historical Discourses and Facial AIs

We might start by examining recent attempts to use AIs to impute characteristics to individuals based on their facial features, which can be seen within the context of the long history of physiognomy. Such technologies are becoming commercial applications. For example, Faception, a company based in Tel Aviv, has claimed that it can:

> analyze faces from video streams (recorded and live), cameras, or online/offline databases, encode the faces in proprietary image descriptors and match an individual with various personality traits and types with a high level of accuracy. We develop

proprietary classifiers, each describing a certain personality type or trait such as an Extrovert, a person with High IQ, Professional Poker Player or a Terrorist.[9]

Other personality types they claimed their systems could detect included bingo players, brand promoters, white-collar offenders, paedophiles, and academic researchers.[10] The company bases these assertions on the conflation of two arguments: that personality is genetically determined and that genetics plays a large role in face shape.[11] The fallacy here is that even if both personality and faces are genetically determined, itself a contentious argument, there is no reason why the two sets of genes should be linked.

An example of a somewhat more rigorous research approach is that of Michal Kosinski and Yilun Wang, who claim to have developed an AI system that can tell from information derived from photographs if people are homosexual or heterosexual. This is based on an analysis of the faces of people stating their sexual preferences on dating websites. Among other features, they place emphasis on the size of the jaw (gracile in gay men, robust in lesbians) in identifying homosexuality. They explain this in terms of the differential exposure of male and female foetuses to certain prenatal androgens in the womb responsible for the sexual differentiation of faces, preferences, and behaviour.[12] These conclusions chime to some extent with the results of psychometric testing that showed that people find that strong jaws denote dominant males, while narrow jaws denote submissive men.[13] Gracile chins also appear to be associated with "babyfacedness," which is positively correlated with perceptions of naiveté, honesty, kindness, and warmth.[14]

However, this belief in these supposed characteristics based on differences in the jawline could also be seen as reflecting the long historical association of the "masculine" jaw with dominance and aggression found in racist anthropology.[15] The greater development of the "negro" jaw has been a standard trope since the publication in the late eighteenth century of Petrus Camper's *Dissertation sur les Varieties Naturelles qui Caracterisent la Physiognomie des Hommes*.[16] However, it was immaterial to Camper whether Adam and Eve had been white-skinned or black, and he saw the differences between the skulls of the races as being due to the effects of differing climate, food, manners, and claims on the physique.[17] Nevertheless, the association between this enlarged jaw, ancient humans and apes, and the latter's presumed savagery became a recurrent theme of racist ideology in the nineteenth-century works of Western authors such as Baron Cuvier, Josiah Clark Nott, Joseph Arthur de Gobineau, and Paul Broca.[18] This is a vast and important field of research, requiring a discussion of genetics, imperial ideology, taxonomy, anthropology, photography, race theory, and so on, and is, regrettably, beyond the scope of this chapter.[19]

An even more striking example of the link between historical models of physiognomy and contemporary AI research can be seen in the attempts by Indonesian researchers to use artificial neural networks for predicting four fundamental temperaments (sanguine, choleric, melancholic, and phlegmatic) from information derived from a set of facial features. These include the dimension of the eyes, the distance between two opposite corners of the eyes, the width of the nose, mouth, and eyes, and the thickness of the lower lip.[20] The overall predictive accuracy of their system was not very impressive, but what is interesting is the attempt to use the ancient medical model of the four humours to identify character types. Humouralism, associated with the followers of Hippocrates in the fifth century BC, and the physician Galen in the second century AD, posited that illness was due to imbalances of blood, yellow bile, black bile, and phlegm in the body caused by external factors such as diet, temperature, wet or dry conditions, and so on.[21] Such ideas still appear to influence popular attitudes to health in the West, although they have long been abandoned by the medical profession.[22]

These, and other examples of the use of AI to identify character, may be seen as merely esoteric exercises but there are other forms of facial AIs which have much more impact.[23] An example of this are "affect AIs" which are, as already noted, AI systems that purport to be able to detect underlying human emotions from information based on measuring facial expressions. Commercial affect systems are often based on the Facial Action Coding System (FACS) developed by the US psychologist Paul Ekman in the 1970s, which describes the facial expressions said to be linked to six underlying emotions – happiness, sadness, fear, disgust, anger, and surprise. It has been suggested that affect AIs can pick up subtle "micro-expressions" that can reveal if a person is lying and attempts have been made to introduce them at airports in the United States and the EU to determine if people are telling the truth to immigration officials.[24]

In very crude terms, the dominant model underlying affect AIs, the Basic Emotion Theory (BET), hold that there is a unitary person who has a series of simple emotions, or feelings, that lead automatically to a set of universal facial expressions, the dimensions of which can be measured, and that are understood by all other human beings. Ekman followed earlier psychologists in seeing expressions as automatic reflexes to situations which trigger emotions.[25] This implies that you would not have an expression in one context, which meant something in another—a face contorted in a cry would not mean joy in one context but anger in another. There are, of course, a whole suite of issues that arise here. Are there "unitary persons," one might ask? Are there simple emotions? Do emotions lead automatically to expressions? Are expressions understood universally? Is context irrelevant?

Given these problems, what is the origin of the BET model? Its central concepts can actually be traced back to *Aristotle's Physiognomonica* of the early third century BC. For Aristotle and his followers, the nutritive Soul was the immanent potential of the human body. Since the Aristotelian Soul was the form and organising principle of the human body, there was no conceptual, or physical, gap between the Soul, the person, the emotion, and the facial expression. What affected the Soul would naturally affect the Body, and vice versa. The understanding of facial expressions was also universal among human beings, since the human Soul was also universal. Those who could not understand the emotions of other human beings were simply not human because it was the *telos*, the inherent purpose or end, of human beings to be sociable.[26]

This formulation could be problematic in Christian thought, when the Body and the Soul were seen as distinct entities, could exist independently, and could be understood as in opposition. This duality was taken to its ultimate conclusion by the seventeenth-century philosopher René Descartes, for whom the physical world and the human Soul were completely, and conceptually, distinct. How then could human beings exist both as spiritual and material beings, and how could states of the Soul be communicated? Descartes answered these questions by replacing the Aristotelian identity of the Soul/Body with the movements of the muscles of face and body as signifying the hidden motions of the Soul. He posited that God had so designed Creation that external objects had "dispositions" that made them set up various kinds of motions in the body's nerves, which set up sensations in the Soul via the pineal gland in the brain. Similarly, the Soul's act of willing set up motions in the pineal gland, which, in turn, moved "animal spirits" to the nerves, which moved the limbs and facial muscles. The pineal gland was a unitary organ, like the Soul, in the dichotomous brain.[27]

This way of thinking was swept aside by Charles Darwin in his *Expression of the Emotions in Man and Animals*, published 1872.[28] For Darwin, expressions could be explained in purely physical terms. Nor were they unique to human beings but had evolved from our animal ancestors. Nevertheless, expressions were universal because human beings were a single species. But the contexts within which expressions were made and understood were important to Darwin—he did not see them as automatic but part of social interaction. Ekman saw himself as following Darwin in believing that expressions were universal and universally understood, although he also saw them as automatic in the same way that computer programmes can act as feedback loops from "triggers."[29] In some ways, Ekman returned to Aristotle, in the sense that expressions do not involve human volition, a conscious exchange of information or context.

The Phenomenological Limitations of Facial AI Systems and Their Analogue Precursors

The previous section looked at the link between expressions/features of faces and character/dispositions, and how these sat in the context of past scientific and pseudo-scientific discourses. This section will look at these issues and also attempts to delineate types of faces, in terms of phenomenology. The later can be understood as "the study of 'phenomena': appearances of things, or things as they appear in our experience, or the ways we experience things, thus the meanings things have in our experience."[30] This is a useful context in which to interrogate the problem of affect systems' inability to understand context. Alexander Todorov shows in his *Face Value: The Irresistible Influence of First Impressions* how a photograph of a man with an apparent expression of anger can be turned into one showing disgust simply by putting a soiled nappy into the man's hand.[31] Why would an AI system have difficulty understanding the effect of context here? The answer is that AI systems are not (currently?) embodied entities that interact with what the German philosopher Edmund Husserl described in the 1930s as the "lifeworld"—the universe of what is self-evident, or given, that human subjects may experience together.[32] An affect AI is not a conscious being that understands what a nappy is, what goes into it, and how this might affect a middle-aged man. The information it analyses has no meaning to it.

Problems related to the status of phenomena also arise when attempting to create typologies via which the army of piece workers apply predetermined labels to images to create training datasets for AIs. Such labels may exist more in biased human perception than in actual sensuous reality. An example of this can be found in the racist classifications that Safiya Umoja Noble found in results produced by the Google search engine. When Noble searched for the term "black girls" in 2009, the results page was mainly about pornography, and in 2015, it was reported that Google's auto-tagging and facial recognition software had automatically tagged photos of African Americans as "apes" and "animals."[33] The "simianisation" of supposedly inferior racial groups, such as the Irish, has, of course, been a staple of British pictorial "humour" since the Victorian period.[34] Similarly, before they were removed, some of the classifications on ImageNet, a large image database used in visual object recognition software research, included the terms: Bad Person, Call Girl, Crazy, Failure, Fucker, Loser, Pervert, Slut, Spastic, Tosser, Wimp, and so on.[35]

Phenomenological problems can also be found in the work of Chinese scholars Xiaolin Wu and Xi Zhang on the "automated inference on criminality using face images," based on analysing information from photographs of 730 Chinese criminals.[36] Wu and Zhang claimed that these were not mugshots but normal ID photos, although 330 of the ID photos were provided "by the ministry of public security of China," and others by a city police department.[37] These were then compared to the faces of "non-criminals" taken from the Web. They claimed that their system was able to identify criminals with 90% accuracy from such photographs. When looking at the specific features that distinguished criminals from non-criminals, they pointed to the curvature of the upper lip, the distance between the two inner eye corners, and the angle enclosed between lines from the nose tip to the two corners of the mouth. The distance between the two eye corners was also shorter in criminals. The underlying assumption here was that murderers and thieves share a common quality, "criminality," which can be seen in the architecture of their faces, and sets them apart from law-abiding citizens. However, US computer scientists argued that Wu and Zhang had merely developed a "smile detector," since they were comparing sombre official portraits with jollier promotional photographs.[38] The phenomena they thought they were deducing from the evidence were actually created by a process of imputing a biased meaning to information.

Wu and Zhang's basic assumptions can be critiqued through a study of past attempts to identify the "criminal face." One of the most famous examples is the work of the nineteenth-century Italian criminologist Cesare Lombroso. Lombroso, whose work still has resonance with some contemporary criminal psychologists, rejected the established classical school of criminology, which held that crime was a characteristic trait of human nature.[39] Criminology revolved, therefore, around the best forms of law and punishment to control "natural" human impulses. Instead, although Lombroso recognised social and environmental causes of crime, his theory of anthropological criminology was based on the belief that criminality could be inherited.[40] This concept of the "residuum" was widely held in the period.[41] In addition, someone "born criminal" could be identified by the information contained in physical features, especially in the face, which confirmed them as savage or atavistic throwbacks. In this model of criminology, the calculus of punishment was less relevant, since "born" criminals would commit crimes whatever the judicial system did.[42]

In the various editions of his *L'uomo Delinquent* (*Criminal Man*), published from 1876 onwards, Lombroso argued that after compiling information from skulls and photographs of criminals, he could identify certain physical traits they had in common, which set them apart from "normal" people. In much the same way as the modern AI analysis of facial features is quantitative, Lombroso claimed that, "Anthropology requires numbers rather than isolated and isolated generic descriptions to prove its theories."[43] Thus, the first edition of *Criminal Man* began with a description of sixty-six criminal crania, while in the fifth edition of 1896–1897, Lombroso claimed to have statistical proof of the "abnormalities" of criminals based on information derived from an examination of twenty-five hundred criminals and twelve hundred "honest individuals." However, he merely stated the percentage of the twenty-five hundred criminals having jug ears, crooked noses, over-developed canine teeth, and large jaws, without any attempt to compare this data to his supposed control group.[44] His claims came down in the end to equating ugly, or unusual, features with "abnormality" and this, in turn, with criminality. He did not indicate how "abnormal" such faces were, or how far they reflected environmental effects, such as poverty or regional variations, rather than some inherent criminality. In many ways, Lombroso's arguments reflected the ancient Greek idea of *kalokagathia*, that the beautiful are virtuous and the ugly evil.[45]

A more rigorous attempt to delineate the "criminal face," and one that engaged directly with phenomenological issues, were the experiments by Francis Galton, the Victorian English polymath, to produce photographic "composite portraits" of criminals. These were based on over three hundred photographs of the inmates of Pentonville and Millbank prisons. Galton understood his composite portraits as creating a mean image of a particular human type. Deviations around the centre of the distribution formed a haze around the central features, like the tails on either end of a bell curve.[46] As he explained the process in the *Fortnightly Review* in 1880:

> I threw magic-lantern portraits of different persons on the top of one another, on the same screen, and elicited a resultant face which resembled no one of the components in particular, but included all. Whatever was common to all the portraits became intensified by combination; whatever was peculiar to each portrait was relatively too faint to attract attention, and virtually disappeared.[47]

In many ways, Galton's ideas for composite photographs were an extension of his statistical work on correlation, regression, and the standard deviation, itself an outcome of his research on human and animal inheritance. Galton wished to measure how characteristics, such as "intelligence" or "genius," were shared by members of the same family.[48] The latter led, in turn, to his foundation of the pseudo-science of eugenics, in which various forms of selective breeding were envisaged as a means of improving the racial stock.[49] However, unlike Lombroso, Galton regarded his attempts to identify individual types of criminal—the murderer, the thief, men convicted of manslaughter, and so on—as a failure.[50] Instead, he went on to develop the modern theory of fingerprinting to identify individual criminals.[51]

For Galton, his composite photographs mimicked how he believed people grasped phenomena more generally. Humans, he argued, formed conceptions of specific entities in the outside world by the repetition of similar stimuli forming "blended memories," to which a linguistic label was then given. He argued that:

> Whenever any group of brain elements has been excited through an impression of one of the senses, it becomes, so to speak, tender and liable to become again excited, under the influence of other kinds of stimuli. Whatever may be the cause of any new excitation, the result of its reproduction is to create an imaginary sense-impression, similar to that by which the first excitation had been caused, and this we call memory.[52]

Hence, if people saw enough dogs, they would form a pure blended memory of dogs ("dogness"), which would be different to that of the "catness" of cats, and would call this to mind whenever they saw a dog. The linguistic label "dog" would also call to mind this blended memory.[53]

However, this theory of phenomenology assumed at the outset that there were specific things called dogs. "Dogness" could not be ascribed to dogs if the images combined in the blended memory of dogs included those of cats, trees, and so on. Some ability to recognise what was a dog was assumed at the outset.[54] This is a fundamental problem with the inductive reasoning championed by Galton, in which one is supposed to be able to move from independent observations to general principles based on this information. In his composite photographs, he assumed from the outset, therefore, that a criminal type existed. This meant that he assumed the existence of what he wanted to reveal, and led him to fall back on torturous arguments when his composites showed nothing of the sort. As he himself admitted, when the faces of criminals were combined, the "special villainous regularities in the [composites] have disappeared and the common humanity that underlies them has prevailed."[55] Thus, the composite face of the criminal was "the type of face that is apt to accompany criminal tendencies *before* (if I may be allowed the expression) the features have been brutalised by crime."[56] However, if it is a life of crime that leads to the creation of a criminal face, then why did Galton need to assume an original criminal character in the first place? Such problems underlie many forms of AI and related research based on physiognomy, which assume the existence at the outset of what they seek to analyse, and other technologies based on labelling phenomena.

The Politics of Facial Recognition in Historical Context

As already noted, facial recognition systems have expanded across the world, having multiple uses from passport control at borders to tracing missing persons.[57] They work by comparing information gathered on the dimensions of the facial features of individuals with pre-existing profiles stored on databases. These profiles are not measurements of all dimensions but enough information to allow matches within certain tolerances—hence the possibility of false negatives and positives. However, their indiscriminate use, especially in identifying people moving in public places, has also raised issues of biases, unreliability, and the infringement of human rights.[58] The effectiveness of such systems is often taken for granted but a closer analysis of their use has raised some issues. For example, Pete Fussey, Bethan Davies, and Martin Innes examined the outcomes of six deployments of facial recognition systems by the Metropolitan Police in London streets in 2018–2019. They found that of the forty-three alerts flagged by the technology of targets whose facial dimensions matched those of "persons of interest" on a police database, only twenty-seven were deemed "credible" by human police monitors. Of these matches, only 9 (21%) were proved correct after police officers physically checked the IDs of the persons targeted. The question Fussey, Davies, and Innes raise is whether the cost of these operations and their intrusion into the personal privacy of large numbers of members of the public are proportional to the result of identifying just over one "person of interest" per deployment.[59] The London police are continuing, nevertheless, to evaluate the use of live facial recognition "to prevent and detect crime, find wanted criminals, safeguard vulnerable people, and to protect people from harm ...."[60]

Information gathering by the state to protect the rights of citizens in these respects has, of course, a long, and laudable, history.[61] However, the British police appear to be getting worse at clearing up crimes, something which has caused public disquiet.[62] It is perhaps understandable that in this situation the police should publicly put their faith in technology to reverse this trend. However, this can be seen as part of what James C. Scott has referred to as "high modernism."[63] Such a belief in the power of technology and its creators to solve all problems can also be found in developing countries, where, for good or ill, biometrics have been seen as the solution to poor governance, electoral exclusion, and a lack of civil identity. However, the "fetishization" of technology can sometimes fail to deliver the expected benefits. In the 2016 elections in Chad, for example, the government and opposition were encouraged by outside donors to use facial biometric voter registration as a technical means of preventing fraud. Both sides accepted new technology as a feature of modernity. However, despite an expenditure of 24.5 million Euros, the lack of card readers at polling stations undermined the system's utility. In addition, the technology failed to prevent voter intimidation, inequality in the resources available to government and the opposition, lack of observers in polling stations, and a social media blackout that prevented the opposition sharing local results.[64] Similarly, in Cameroon, the length of time required to obtain new biometric identity cards, up to two years, has left many citizens undocumented, and theoretically outside of the law.[65]

The debates around such issues can be contextualised by looking at a historical example of another biometric form of identification in police work, that of Alphonse Bertillon's anthropometrics. The technique that Bertillon developed as a clerk in the Paris Prefecture of Police in the late nineteenth century involved the use of complex apparatus by trained police officers to take elaborate measurements of parts of the body of criminals, including the face. This information was recorded on a card along with a photograph and carefully controlled discursive descriptions of facial features and distinctive marks, based on standard classifications of types of ears, noses, eyes, and so on. The measurements were used to index individuals in a card database and to allow for easy retrieval of information on individuals when they were re-measured at a later date.[66] This has been linked to the mania for the scientific classification of knowledge in the same period.[67]

Standardised abbreviations referring to these precise descriptions formed the basis of a "*portrait parlé*," via which a trained telegraph operator could transmit to another operator a usable physical description of a criminal entirely in words, numbers, and coded abbreviations.[68] The identification of the deviant was reduced to standardised information which could be stored in an information system, retrieved at a later date and transmitted over distances. In this manner, identification ceased to require "co-presence" between the authenticating identifier and the identified, who could now be widely separated in time and space.[69] The workings of this system have, of course, many striking similarities to modern facial recognition technologies.

Bertillon's anthropometrics spread widely across Europe and America, North and South, but was soon replaced by fingerprinting. The latter did not require costly instruments, the length of time needed to take measurements, and avoided the necessity of transcribing measurements where errors could be made.[70] Yet in 1931, *Pietr the Latvian*, the first novel by Georges Simenon featuring his redoubtable detective Inspector Maigret, could still open with the Inspector receiving a *portrait parlé* from the "International Identification Bureau" in Copenhagen:

> This 'word-picture' of Pietr was as clear as a photograph to Inspector Maigret. The principal features were the first to emerge: the man was short, slim, young and fair-haired, with sparse blond eyebrows, greenish eyes and a long neck.[71]

However, the whole book actually revolves around the fact that this was a case of mistaken identity—the "Pietr" that Maigret pursues is actually Pietr's twin Hans, who had killed his brother at the outset of the novel. Bertillon's system could be found just as wanting in the real world. In Argentina in 1906, two medical doctors, Berta and Nogueira, undertook an experiment to test the accuracy of Betillionage by measuring the heads of more than two hundred docile subjects in the national mental asylum. The measurements were taken twice on each subject with an interval of one and a half months, using several different methods. Differences of a millimetre in measurements were very common, those of two millimetres frequent, and those of three or more, which Bertillon saw as proof of non-identity, were not rare. The inference was that if trained medical professionals could not measure docile subjects accurately, poorly trained police would make larger errors.[72] This led, in part, to the shift in South America to the system of fingerprinting developed locally by Juan Vucetich in Argentina.[73] Similarly, when anthropometrics was applied to the corpses in the Paris morgue, it proved to be of little use. The processes of decomposition may have created problems but the bodies involved were hardly uncooperative.[74]

In recent works, it has been suggested that rather than being primarily designed to catch criminals, "Bertillionage" was actually a means of giving the police in several countries the means of appearing modern and scientific. Professionalisation was a means of raising the status of the police, rather than of catching criminals. The "portrait parlé," for example, was part of the higher training of Parisian police officers wishing for advancement but was comparatively little used in practice.[75] Similarly, anthropometrics and fingerprinting in New York in the late nineteenth and early twentieth centuries were seldom used by the police to catch criminals. Their real purpose was to give the police an air of professionalism and scientific worth to improve their thuggish reputation.[76] In addition, in Latin America, anthropometrics could be an openly scientific project in the hands of medics to identify criminal types in the manner of Lombroso and Galton, rather than a tool of practical policing.[77]

The relationship between policing, public faith in the police, and AI technology is a complex one, and it could be argued that recourse to facial recognition systems has actually undermined the relationship between the police and some members of the public. However, a historical perspective on the matter gives the opportunity to pose questions that have relevance today.

Conclusions

It would, of course, be wrong to try to shoehorn all discussions of AI technologies into a historical framework. History does not always repeat itself, as is often claimed, although it does frequently echo. It is sometimes useful, however, to take debates about AI information systems out of the technical fog in which they are often conducted, and to place them into broader historical contexts. This allows general issues of phenomenology, bias, and the ulterior motives of actors, to be brought into a sharper focus for a broader audience. It may also help to avoid such debates reinventing the wheel. Historical figures, such as Petrus Camper, Charles Darwin, Francis Galton, Cesare Lombroso, and Alphonse Bertillon, were all trying to do similar things with faces to some modern AI systems, and met similar problems. It is unfortunate if such precedents are ignored, especially since some of them had direct impacts on subsequent theoretical work underpinning such technology.

These arguments can, of course, be turned on their head. The differences between the implications of modern facial AI systems and earlier analogues are also important. The facial recognition systems that Fussey and others examined were not exactly like the earlier police practice of searching crowds for people on wanted posters because everybody passing within their purview was analysed. Nine persons turned out to be "persons of interest" when their ID was checked but what of the other eighteen who were checked as "creditable" matches but turned out not to be so? Equally problematic is when past phenomena are used to justify the introduction of AI technology, as in the argument used by the International Civil Aviation Organization that the use of facial recognition systems at borders was merely an extension of the widely accepted use of photographs on passports.[78] In short, technology and the politics of modernity are historical phenomena and need to be treated as such.

Notes

1 Alfred Gell, *Art and Agency: An Anthropological Theory* (Oxford: Clarendon Press, 1998).
2 Michel Foucault, *Les Mots et les Choses* (Paris: Gallimard, 1966), translated as Michel Foucault, *The Order of Things*, trans. Alan Sheridan (London: Routledge, 1970).
3 Andreas Marklund and Laura Skouvig, eds., *Histories of Surveillance from Antiquity to the Digital Era: The Eyes and Ears of Power* (London: Routledge, 2021); Shoshana Zuboff, *The Age of Surveillance Capitalism: The Fight for a Human Future at the New Frontier of Power* (London: Profile Books, 2019); Ilsen About, James Brown, and Gayle Lonergan, eds., *People, Papers, and Practices: Identification and Registration in Transnational Perspective, 1500–2010* (London: Palgrave, 2013); Keith Breckenridge and Simon Szreter, eds., *Registration and Recognition. Documenting the Person in World History* (Oxford: Oxford University Press, 2012); Toni Weller, "The Information State: An Historical Perspective on Surveillance," in *Routledge Handbook of Surveillance Studies*, ed. Kirstie Ball, Kevin D. Haggerty, and David Lyon (London: Routledge, 2012), 57–63; Edward Higgs, *Identifying the English: Personal Identification 1500 to the Present* (London: Continuum, 2011); Edward Higgs, *The Information State in England: The Central Collection of Information on Citizens since 1500* (London: Palgrave, 2004); David Lyon, *The Electronic Eye: The Rise of the Surveillance Society* (Cambridge, UK: Polity, 1994).
4 Paul Sawers, "Realeyes Raises $12.4 Million to Help Brands Detect Emotion Using AI on Facial Expressions," VentureBeat, June 2019, Realeyes raises $12.4 million to help brands detect emotion using AI on facial expressions | VentureBeat.
5 Grand View Research, Facial Recognition Market Size, Share & Trends Analysis Report, Report ID: 978-1-68038-311-9, https://www.grandviewresearch.com/industry-analysis/facial-recognition-market.
6 The World Bank, ID4D, https://id4d.worldbank.org/.
7 Center for Human Rights & Global Justice, *Paving a Digital Road to Hell: A Primer on the Role of the World Bank and Global Networks in Promoting Digital ID* (New York: Center for Human Rights & Global Justice, 2022); Privacy International, "Have a Biometric ID Information Coming Your Way? Key Questions to Ask and Arguments to Make," July 2019, https://www.privacyinternational.org/long-read/3067/have-biometric-id-system-coming-your-way-key-questions-ask-and-arguments-make.
8 Oxford University's Institute for Ethics in AI, https://www.oxford-aiethics.ox.ac.uk; The Centre for Technological Futures at the University of Edinburgh, https://efi.ed.ac.uk/centre-technomoral-futures/; The Montreal AI Ethics Institute, https://montrealethics.ai/.
9 Faception, "Facial Personality Analytics," https://www.faception.com.
10 Faception, "Facial Personality Analytics."
11 Faception website, "About us," https://www.faception.com/about-us.
12 Yilun Wang and Michal Kosinski, "Deep Neural Networks Are More Accurate than Humans at Detecting Sexual Orientation from Facial Images," *Journal of Personality and Social Psychology* 114, no. 2 (2018): 246–257.
13 Nancy Etcoff, *The Survival of the Prettiest: The Science of Beauty* (New York: Anchor Books, 2000), 155–156; Diane S. Berry and L. Z. McArthur, "Some Components and Consequences of a Babyface," *Journal of Personality and Social Psychology* 48 (1985): 312–323.
14 Berry and McArthur, "Consequences of a Babyface."
15 Edward Higgs, "A Short History of the Modern Western Jaw: From Aristotle's Physiognomy to Facial Biometrics," *Research Gate*, July 2019, https://www.academia.edu/40012766/A_short_history_of_the_modern_western_jaw_from_Aristotles_physiognomy_to_facial_biometrics.
16 Petrus Camper, *Dissertation sur les Varieties Naturalles qui Caracterisent la Physionomie des Hommes des Divers Climats et des Differens Ages* (Paris: H. J. Jansen, 1791). See also Higgs, "A Short History of the Modern Western Jaw."

17 Camper, *Dissertation*, 17–18, 49.
18 Paul Broca, *Memoires sur l'Hybridite* in *Mémoires d'Anthropologie* (Paris: C. Reinwald, 1977), 397; J. D. Nott, "Appendix" to Joseph Arthur de Gobineau, *The Moral and Intellectual Diversity of Races* (Philadelphia, PA: J. B. Lippincott & Co., 1856), 480–481; Joseph Arthur de Gobineau, *The Moral and Intellectual Diversity of Races* (Philadelphia, PA: J. B. Lippincott & Co., 1856), 312–330; Jean Léopold Nicolas Frédéric and Baron Cuvier, *Le Règne Animal Distribué d'Après son Organisation, le Règne Animal Distribué d'Après son Organisation*, vol. I (Paris: Belin, 1817), 95.
19 However, for a discussion along these lines, see Chapter 6, "The Face of Race," in Edward Higgs, *Reading Faces: Facial Biometrics from Aristotle to Artificial Intelligence* (forthcoming). See also John P. Jackson and Nadine M. Weidman, *Race, Racism and Science* (London: Rutgers University Press, 2006); Kenan Malik, *The Meaning of Race: Race, History and Culture in Western Society* (Basingstoke: Macmillan, 1996); and John S. Haller, *Outcasts from Evolution: Scientific Attitudes of Racial Inferiority, 1859–1900* (Urbana, IL: University of Illinois Press, 1971).
20 Ardinintya Diva Setyadi, Tri Harsano and Sigit Wasista, "Human Character Recognition Application Based on Facial Features Using Face Detection," *2015 International Electronics Symposium (IES), IEEE* (September 2015), 263–267.
21 Vivian Nutton, "Humoralism," in *Companion Encyclopaedia of the History of Medicine*, vol. 1, ed. W. F. Bynum and Roy Porter (London and New York: Routledge, 1993), 281–291.
22 Vicky Rippere, "The Survival of Traditional Medicine in Lay Medical Views: An Empirical Approach to the History of Medicine," *Medical History* 25 (1981): 411–414.
23 For examples of the use of AI to identify character, see Lou Safra, Coralie Chevallier, Julie Grèzes and Nicholas Baumard, "Tracking Historical Changes in Trustworthiness Using Machine Learning Analyses of Facial Cues in Paintings," *Nature Communications* 11, no. 4728 (2020): 1–7; Ting Zhang, Ri-Zhen Qin, Qiu-Lei Dong, Wei Gao, Hua-Rong Xu, and Zhan-Yi Hu, "Physiognomy: Personality Traits Prediction by Learning," *International Journal of Automation and Computing* 14 (June 2017): 386–395.
24 European Commission, "Smart Lie-Detection System to Tighten EU's busy Borders," October 2018, https://ec.europa.eu/research-and-innovation/en/projects/success-stories/all/smart-lie-detection-system-tighten-eus-busy-borders; US Government Accountability Office, "Aviation Security: TSA Should Limit Future Funding for Behavior Detection Activities," (November 2013), GAO-14-159. For a related technology based on the analysis of head movements, see James Wright, "Suspect AI: Vibraimage, Emotion Recognition Technology and Algorithmic Opacity," *Science, Technology and Society* 28, no. 3 (2021): 468–487.
25 Silvan S. Tomkins, *Affect Imagery Consciousness: Volume I, The Positive Affects* (London: Tavistock, 1962), 1–7.
26 Armand Marie Leroi, *The Lagoon: How Aristotle Invented Science* (London: Bloomsbury, 2015), 162, 177.
27 Stewart Goetz and Charles Taliaferro, *A Brief History of the Soul* (Chichester: Wiley-Blackwell, 2011), 76–78; Charles Taylor, *Sources of the Self: The Making of Modern Identity* (Cambridge, UK: Cambridge University Press, 1989), 143–158.
28 Charles Darwin, *The Expression of the Emotions in Man and Animals* (London: John Murray, 1872).
29 Paul Ekman, "Introduction," in *Darwin and Facial Expression: A Century of Research in Review*, ed. Paul Eckman (Cambridge, MA: Malor Books, 2014), 2–6.
30 David Woodruff Smith, "Phenomenology," in *The Stanford Encyclopedia of Philosophy*, ed. Edward N. Zalta (Summer 2018 Online Edition). https://plato.stanford.edu/archives/sum2018/entries/phenomenology/.
31 Alexander Todorov, *Face Value: The Irresistible Influence of First Impressions* (Oxford: Princeton University Press, 2017), 248–249.
32 Edmund Husserl, *The Crisis of European Sciences and Transcendental Phenomenology*, trans. D. Carr (Evanston, IL: Northwestern University Press, 1970).
33 Safiya Umoja Noble, *Algorithms of Oppression: How Search Engines Reinforce Racism* (New York: New York University Press, 2018), 6, 17–19.
34 Lewis Perry Curtis, *Apes and Angels: The Irishman in Victorian Caricature* (London: Smithsonian Institution, 1997); Mary Cowling, *The Artist as Anthropologist: The Representation of Type and Character in Victorian Art* (Cambridge, UK: Cambridge University Press, 1989), 121–181.

35 Kate Crawford, *Atlas of AI: Power, Politics, and the Planetary Costs of Artificial Intelligence* (London: Yale University Press, 2021), 141.
36 Xiaolin Wu and Xi Zhang, "Automated Inference on Criminality Using Face Images," *arXiv preprint arXiv:1611.04135* (2016): 4038–4052.
37 Wu and Zhang, "Automated Inference."
38 Carl T. Bergstrom and Jevin West, "Calling Bullshit in the Age of Big Data," Lecture 5.5 Critical Learning Machine (Information School, University of Washington), https://www.youtube.com/watch?v=rga2-d1oi30.
39 On the overlap with contemporary criminal psychologists, see Aman Amrit Cheema and Ashish Virk, "Reinventing Lombroso in the Era of Genetic Revolution: Whether [the] Criminal Justice System Actually Imparts Justice or Is Based on 'Convenience of Assumption'," *International Journal of Criminology and Sociological Theory* 5, no. 2 (2012): 936–946.
40 Pasquale Pasquino, "Criminology: The Birth of a Special Knowledge," in *The Foucault Effect: Studies in Governmentality with Two Lectures by and an Interview with Michel Foucault*, ed. Graham Burchell, Colin Gordon, and Peter Miller (London: Harvester Wheatsheaf, 1991), 235–250.
41 Higgs, *Identifying the English*, 122–125.
42 David G. Horn, "This Norm Which Is Not One: Reading the Female Body in Lombroso's Anthropology," in *Deviant Bodies: Critical Perspectives on Difference in Science and Popular Culture*, ed. Jennifer Terry and Jacqueline Urla (Bloomington, IN: Indiana University Press, 1995), 111.
43 Cesare Lombroso, *Criminal Man*, trans. Mary Gibson and Nicole Hahn Rafter (London: Duke University Press, 2006), 310.
44 Lombroso, *Criminal Man*, 46–49, 310–311.
45 Anthony Synnott, *The Body Social: Symbolism, Self and Society* (London: Routledge, 1993), 79.
46 Josh Ellenbogen, *Reasoned and Unreasoned Images: The Photography of Bertillon, Galton, and Marey* (University Park, PA: Pennsylvania State University Press, 2012), 133; Allan Sekula, "The Body and the Archive," *October* 39 (1986): 48.
47 Francis Galton, "Mental Imagery," *Fortnightly Review* 28 (1880): 320.
48 Francis Galton, *Hereditary Genius: An Inquiry into Its Laws and Consequences* (London: Macmillan and Co., 1869).
49 Ruth Schwartz Cowan, "Galton, Sir Francis," *Online Oxford Dictionary of National Biography* (September 2005).
50 Francis Galton, "Generic Images," *Nineteenth Century* 6 (July 1879): 161–162.
51 Higgs, *Identifying the English*, 132–138.
52 Galton, "Generic Images," 158.
53 George Pavlich, "The Subjects of Criminal Identification," *Punishment & Society* 11, no. 2 (2009): 180.
54 Ellenbogen, *Reasoned and Unreasoned Images*, 78–79, 84.
55 Francis Galton, "Composite Portraits," *Nature* 18 (May 23, 1878): 97–98.
56 Galton, "Generic Images," 161.
57 David Lyon, "Surveillance as Social Sorting: Computer Codes and Mobile Bodies," in *Surveillance as Social Sorting: Privacy, Risk, and Digital Discrimination*, ed. David Lyon (Abingdon: Routledge, 2003), 13–30.
58 Kashmir Hill, "Wrongfully Accused by an Algorithm," *The New York Times*, June 24, 2020, https://www.nytimes.com/2020/06/24/technology/facial-recognition-arrest.html; Paul Mozur, "One Month, 500,000 Face Scans: How China Is Using A.I. to Profile a Minority," *The New York Times*, April 14, 2019, www.nytimes.com/2019/04/14/technology/china-surveillance-artificial-intelligence-racial-profiling.html; Clare Garvie, Alvaro Bedoya, and Jonathan Frankle, *The Perpetual Line-Up: Unregulated Police Face Recognition in America* (Georgetown, WA: Center on Privacy & Technology, Georgetown Law, 2016).
59 Pete Fussey, Bethan Davies, and Martin Innes, "'Assisted' Facial Recognition and the Reinvention of Suspicion and Discretion in Digital Policing," *British Journal of Criminology* 61 (2021): 325–344. See also Clare Garvie, *A Forensic without the Science: Face Recognition in U.S. Criminal Investigations* (Georgetown, WA: Center on Privacy & Technology at Georgetown Law, 2022). For a more positive report on the accuracy of ambient facial recognition, see Tony Mansfield, *Facial Recognition Technology in Law Enforcement, Equitability Study, Final Report*, NPL Report MS 43 (Teddington: National Physical Laboratory, 2023).

60 Metropolitan Police website, "Facial Recognition," https://www.met.police.uk/advice/advice-and-information/fr/facial-recognition.
61 Higgs, *The Information State*.
62 See Home Office, *Crime Outcomes in England and Wales 2018 to 2019* (Statistical Bulletin HOSB 12/19: July 2019); Home Office, *Crime Outcomes in England and Wales: Year Ending March 2018* (Statistical Bulletin HOSB 10/18: July 2018). Later versions of these reports are not comparable because of the effects of the Coronavirus epidemic. See also BBC News website, "Crimes Solved by Police in England and Wales at New Low," July 18, 2019. https://www.bbc.co.uk/news/uk-49029545.
63 James C. Scott, *Seeing Like a State: How Certain Schemes to Improve the Human Condition Have Failed* (New Haven, CT: Yale University Press, 1999). See also Nic Cheeseman, Gabrielle Lynch, and Justin Willis, "Digital Dilemmas: The Unintended Consequences of Election Technology," *Democratization* 25, no. 8 (2018): 1397–1418.
64 Marielle Debos, "Biometrics and the Disciplining of Democracy: Technology, Electoral Politics, and Liberal Interventionism in Chad," *Democratization* 28, no. 8 (2021): 1406–1422.
65 Georges Macaire Eyenga, Gaetan Omgba Mimboe and Joseph Fabrice Bindzi, "Être Sans-Papiers Chez Soi? Les Mésaventures de l'Encartement Biométrique au Cameroun," *Critique Internationale* 97 (2022): 113–134.
66 Simon A. Cole, *Suspect Identities. A History of Fingerprinting and Criminal Identification* (London: Harvard University Press, 2001), 45.
67 Alex Csiszar, "Bibliography as Anthropometry: Dreaming Scientific Order at the Fin de Siècle," *Library Trends* 62, no. 2 (2013): 442–455.
68 Alphonse Bertillon, *Identification Anthropometrique: Instructions Signaletiques* (Melun: Imprimerie Administrative, 1893), 137–144. See also Cole, *Suspect Identities*, 46–47.
69 Anthony Giddens, *The Constitution of Society* (Cambridge, UK: Polity Press, 1986), 64–73, 123–124.
70 Higgs, *Identifying the English*, 130–138.
71 George Simenon, *Pietr the Latvian*, trans. David Bellos (London: Penguin, 2013), 11.
72 Mercedes Garcia Ferrari, *Marcas de Identidad; Juan Vucetich y el Surgimeninto Transnacional de la Dactiloscopia* (Rosario: Prohistoria Ediciones, 2015), 179.
73 Mercedes Garcia Ferrari, "Una Aproximacion a las Relaciones Entre Identificación y Justicia en Argentina (1886–1933)," *Estudios Sociales* 48 (2015): 39–58.
74 Bruno Bertherat, "L'identification sans Bertillon? Le Cas de la Morgue de Paris," in *Aux Origines de la Police Scientifique: Alphonse Bertillon, Precurseur de la Science du Crime*, ed. Pierre Piazza (Paris: Editions Karthala, 2011), 224–225.
75 Laurent Lopez, "Alphonse Bertillon dans l'Ombre des Recidivists et le Bertillionnage dans l'Oeil des Force de l'Ordre de la Belle Epoque," in *Aux Origines de la Police Scientifique*, ed. Piazza, 99, 105–107.
76 Yan Philippe, "Alphonse Bertillon a New York," in *Aux Origines de la Police Scientifique*, ed. Piazza, 332–345.
77 Ferrari, *Marcas de Identidad*, 125; Diego Galeano and Mercedes Garcia Ferrari, "Cartographie du Bertillionage. Le Systeme Anthropometrique en Amerique Latine: Circuits de Diffusion, Usages at Resistances," in *Aux Origines de la Police Scientifique*, ed. Piazza, 320.
78 Liv Hausken, "The Face in the Biometric Passport," in *The Art of Identification: Forensics, Surveillance, Identity*, ed. Rex Ferguson, Melissa M. Littlefield, and James Purdon (University Park, PA: Pennsylvania State University Press, 2021), 159–181.

PART III

Managing, Ordering, Classifying

12

"THOSE WHO HELP HIS SIGHT AND HEARING ARE MANY"

Information and the State in Early China*

Rebecca Robinson

Introduction

Information is ubiquitous in today's society. We are bombarded by information in our daily lives and are constantly providing information about ourselves to various stakeholders, whether we know it or not. Due to the importance of digital technologies in gathering information, as well as the prevalent discourse about the "information age," it is commonplace to assume that the collection and creation of information, particularly by state agents, is a modern phenomenon. However, as scholars of information history have rightly argued, information is as old as society itself.[1] Taking early China as a case study, this chapter will explore ideas about information, particularly regarding the state's collection of information about the people. Ideas about information from early China will be considered using contemporary theory, in order to contextualise them for a modern audience and to situate them within the history of information studies. What becomes clear from a reading of the early Chinese texts is that, despite having limited technological means, scholars and statesmen from early China were largely of the opinion that information about the people and their actions should be gathered, organised, and transmitted to the ruler in a timely fashion, and that such information was necessary to the governing of the state.

The Warring States period (475–221 BCE) was a period of intense internecine warfare between rival states that emerged following the breakup of the Zhou state. While the warring states competed with each other for land and hegemony, peripatetic scholars, referred to as the *shi* 士, debated questions related to state and society, hoping to find employment at one of the courts.[2] Many of these scholars, or their schools, produced treatises that discuss questions related to human nature, interpersonal relationships, the cosmos, and social organisation, leading to the period, roughly corresponding temporally with that of ancient Greece, being dubbed the "golden age of Chinese philosophy." However, as most of these scholars were seeking employment by rulers of the warring states, much of their attention

---

* The work described in this chapter was supported by a grant from the Research Grants Council of the Hong Kong Special Administrative Region, China (Project No. HKBU 12620422).

was focused on the best ways to govern. Many of the thinkers, "schools," and texts from this period went on to have an enormous impact in later periods, particularly those related to Confucianism and Daoism. While a number of texts that were produced during this period have survived, we must assume that these represent only a handful and that there were many more scholars whose ideas were never recorded, or that have been lost to us. Some of the works that survive directly address governance, and central to most of these theories of governance was the idea, either implicit or explicit, that the ruler needed to know what was going on in his state in order to rule effectively. Effective rule could mean various things, from maintaining a defensive, peaceful society, to an aggressive programme of expansion. But no matter what the ruler's goals, information was necessary to achieve them.

In this chapter, ideas about information and the state in early China will be discussed through reading two very different texts from this period. The first, the *Mozi* 墨子, espoused a theory of pacifism. The text contains ideas from the school of Mohists, who were followers of the master Mo Di 墨翟 (fl. ca. fifth century BCE). Shocked by the large-scale devastation that was wrought by warfare, the author(s) advocated a principle of "universal love" (*jian ai* 兼愛) envisioning a society where people treated each other as equals without regard to wealth or status.[3] In order to ensure that a state based on universal love could survive during this period of intense warfare, the text is also well known for its sections on defensive warfare.[4] As we shall see, in this text, the ruler was expected to be all-knowing, so that he could bring beneficial treatment to all people of his realm, regardless of their social rank. In contrast, the second text, the *Book of Lord Shang* (*shangjun shu* 商君書), was focused on aggressive expansion and the need to develop a strong military and agricultural base to bring about state expansion. The primary author of this text, the statesman Shang Yang 商鞅 (d. 338 BCE), believed that all should be treated equally under the law, and that everyone should know their place within the highly stratified society.[5] He, too, believed that the ruler required large amounts of information about the people in order to maintain a highly organised bureaucracy that could direct resources to where they were needed the most. The authors of the *Mozi* and the *Book of Lord Shang* held very different opinions of how states should be governed, and the role of the ruler in governing. However, despite these differences, both texts agree that the ruler ought to have unimpeded access to information about his population and their activities. Through a comparison of these two texts, we will see how the role of information was envisioned in early Chinese thought.

These two texts will be the focal points of the chapter, supplemented towards the end by relevant legal documents from the period, which show how statesmen attempted to gather and organise information about the population. The chapter focuses on the state's interest in information about the population rather than information in a more general sense. Due to the relative paucity of sources from this period in comparison to later times, we lack the documentation to talk about information more generally. Population information, however, was central to governments' operations, and, therefore, is dealt with both in theoretical treatises and in administrative documents, allowing us to consider the idea of information in a restricted dimension.

The chapter will consider how information was thought about and organised in these two texts using Michael Buckland's three uses of the term information as a point of departure. Buckland's thesis was constructed during debates about information related to the information age and the large-scale collection and creation of data using computers. While his definitions are developed within the context of his own time, Buckland's analysis of different uses of the word "information" is general enough to be useful in other contexts. He argued for the growing need to consider the meaning of information as a "thing"—information as an object—however, this meaning of information was by no means new or unique to the information age. Buckland argues that it is this meaning that has now come to dominate discourses of information, and that it was therefore worthy of more careful consideration.[6] In his 1991 article, "Information as Thing," Buckland offered "principal uses of the word 'information'" which can help us think through the different ways "information" can be viewed in society. They are as follows:

1 Information-as-process: When someone is informed, what they know is changed. In this sense "information" is "The act of informing …; communication of the knowledge or 'news' of some fact or occurrence; the action of telling or fact of being told of something" (Oxford English Dictionary, 1989, vol. 7, p. 944).
2 Information-as-knowledge: "Information" is also used to denote that which is perceived in "information-as-process:" the "knowledge communicated concerning some particular fact, subject, or event; that of which one is apprised or told; intelligence, news" (Oxford English Dictionary, 1989, vol. 7, p. 944). The notion of information as that which reduces uncertainty could be viewed as a special case of "information-as-knowledge." Sometimes information increases uncertainty.
3 Information-as-thing: The term "information" is also used attributively for objects, such as data and documents, that are referred to as "information" because they are regarded as being informative, as "having the quality of imparting knowledge or communicating information; instructive" (Oxford English Dictionary, 1989, vol. 7, p. 946).[7]

In 1991, the use of "information" to denote a tangible thing was only starting to become commonplace, although this is perhaps now the most familiar usage.[8] The term "information" is now commonly used to denote physical objects or bits of data, almost to the extent that in everyday circumstances, it has come to eclipse the other two uses. The growing usage of information-as-thing has come about in large part due to the rise of the information society and to theorisations about its rise. The emergence of information history as a field has also been largely tied to discussions about information in a modern context, and far less attention has been paid to information and information history in the pre-modern world.[9] However, information itself, whether it be as process, meaning, or thing, is not new. This is not to suggest that any definition of information must transcend spatiotemporal boundaries, but that information, as difficult as it is to define, existed in all societies and played an important role in how societies organised themselves. Without arguing for the universality of "information," this chapter will make use of Buckland's definitions, particularly his division between intangible types of information, definitions one and two, and information which is tangible, definition three. By reading the two texts from pre-imperial China with these definitions in mind, we can see that not only did similar conceptions of information exist, but that there was likewise a shift during the Warring States period to viewing information as something beneficial but intangible, to something that was tangible, manipulatable, and necessary for governing. While the texts discussed here were separated by several hundred years, this chapter does not argue that this was necessarily a linear progression, from intangible to tangible, but that different ideas about information, and how it should be used by the state, existed in these early times, and that, over time, states made more attempts to organise it.

The All-Knowing Ruler of the *Mozi*

The *Mozi* insists that the easy transmission about the deeds of the people to the Son of Heaven is essential to create a unified people and empire. In particular, the text emphasises the need to "unify the principles of the state"—that this is the only way to eliminate disorder in the state. According to the text, when there was no government, the people followed different principles, and this resulted in disorder. As a result, a worthy and good man was selected as a leader and charged with establishing the unified principles of the state, in line with those of Heaven.[10] In order to rule effectively, the Son of Heaven had to determine the unified principles and then ensure that they were being followed. A system of rewards and punishments would encourage people to follow these principles, but ultimately these rewards and punishments was to be meted out by the Son of Heaven, who needed to know about the behaviours of the people in order to do so.

In an idealised golden age of the past, the *Mozi* argues that the Son of Heaven's information about the events in his state was so extensive that he was believed by the people to be omniscient—to have the sight and hearing of a god. He was able to reward those who had done good deeds and punish those who had done bad almost immediately after those actions had taken place, even if they were thousands of *li* away.[11] But the Son of Heaven only had such god-like powers due to his management of information networks:

> Thus the people of the world were all fearful, agitated and awe-struck, and did not dare act in a depraved or evil manner, saying that the Son of Heaven's sight and hearing were those of a god. [But] the former kings' words said: 'He is not a god. It is only that he is able to use the ears and eyes of the people to help his own speech, to use the minds of the people to help his own plans, and to use the limbs of the people to help his own actions.' If those who help his sight and hearing are many, then what he hears and sees is far distant. If those who help his speech are many, then the comfort given by his wise words is far-reaching. If those who help his plans are many, then his schemes and devices are swiftly accomplished. If those who help him in his activities are many, then the matters he embarks upon will be swiftly brought to completion.[12]

By relying on the ears and eyes of the people, the Son of Heaven could be informed of events before even the perpetrator's family members knew of them:

> So it was that, if there was someone who had done good several thousand or even ten thousand *li* away, although family members were completely unaware of it and district and village had not heard of it at all, the Son of Heaven learned of it and rewarded him. And if there was someone who had done evil several thousand or even ten thousand *li* away, although family members were completely unaware of it and district and village had not heard of it at all, the Son of Heaven learned of it and punished him.[13]

The text envisions information flowing freely from all parts of the state directly to the Son of Heaven, and an equally easy transmission of rewards and punishments in response to the information received, but of course this was all quite idealistic. The *Mozi* offers some suggestions as to how it might work in practice: responsibility for monitoring compliance with the unified principles was to be distributed across various levels of social organisation. At the lowest level, the family head would regulate the actions of his family. Next the village head (*li zhang* 里長), who was the most benevolent man of the village, "brought administrative order to the people of the village" and extolled them to inform the district head (*xiang zhang* 鄉長) of any good or evil deeds that took place.[14] The people of the village were to model themselves on the district head: "What the district head takes to be right, all must take to be right. What the district head takes to be wrong, all must take to be wrong. Do away with bad words and study the good words of the district head. Do away with bad actions and study the good actions of the district head."[15] Above the district head was the ruler of the state (*guo jun* 國君), who, like the village head and the district head, was chosen for being the most benevolent person at that level. The district head was to inform the ruler of the state and to model himself on what the ruler of the state took to be right and wrong.[16] Above the ruler of the state was the Son of Heaven (*tianzi* 天子) himself, who received reports from the ruler of the state, and who established the unified principles on which his subordinates were to model themselves. The Son of Heaven's principles should be in alignment with Heaven, and so any transgressions against these principles were transgressions against Heaven itself, which could respond by sending calamities such as floods and famines.[17] It was for this reason that the sage kings of antiquity established the five punishments (*wuxing* 五刑) in order to "bring into line the ordinary people of the world who did not respect, and make themselves like, those above."[18]

Punishments existed to deter wrongdoing, but rewards were also issued to those who did good, and this system of rewards and punishments,[19] along with the benefits of living in a well-ordered society, was considered to be enough for people to actively share information, reporting on the transgressions of their family members and neighbours:

> And it is the case that everywhere the people of the state all wish to get the rewards and praise of their leaders and avoid their censure and punishment. This is why, if the people see someone who is good, they will speak of it, and, if they see someone who is not good, they will speak of it, so the ruler of the state will learn of the good people and reward them, and will learn of the bad people and punish them. If the good people are rewarded and the bad people are punished, then the state will certainly be well ordered. So what is it that determines that a state is well ordered? It is nothing more than being able to exalt unity of principles as a basis for administration.[20]

The information we see circulating in the *Mozi* is quite simplistic. The Son of Heaven is expected to know the good and bad deeds of the people so that he can mete out corresponding rewards and punishments. The text does not elaborate on specifics, such as the types of rewards and punishments to be issued for specific good or bad deeds, nor on how the information should be organised.[21] Following Buckland's definitions, the information in the *Mozi* can be read as "information-as-knowledge," information that exists simply to inform the Son of Heaven so that he can make decisions based on it. In the text, it is treated as something intangible—information about good and bad deeds simply appears before the Son of Heaven almost as soon as it happens. The chains of transmission outlined in the text are so vague, and there is no mention of any form of written records that would contain this information that, despite the authors' claims that information was passed through a hierarchy, it seems as though they do believe that it would effortlessly arrive to the Son of Heaven's eyes and ears. After receiving that information, the Son of Heaven, equally effortlessly, could distribute appropriate rewards and punishments, and uphold the unified principles of the state.

This freely flowing information was necessary to the Son of Heaven, who, according to the *Mozi*, should have an almost limitless amount of information about his population, without himself being omniscient. However, the types of information he received and the methods for obtaining it were left unexplained and under-theorised. To see the development of theories about information and the state, we must turn to a later text.

Lord Shang's Data-Driven State

Like the *Mozi*, the *Book of Lord Shang* envisioned a world in which the ruler would have access to an abundance of information about his people. Unlike the *Mozi*, the *Book of Lord Shang* lays out clear means for gathering and using said information, and by so doing, articulates a form of information that we would regard more familiarly as data—in Buckland's schema, information-as-thing. Also unlike the *Mozi*, we know that attempts were made to implement this system—the Qin rulers gathered extensive information about their population and used it as a tool to strengthen their state. The *Book of Lord Shang* was a highly polemical treatise that laid out the visions of Shang Yang and his school in short, repetitive statements. While little in the text itself can be considered actionable, it outlined the conditions and measures that Shang Yang and his school believed were necessary for successful governance.[22] We have more information about Shang Yang and his influence in other texts and documents which allow us to see the application and impact of these ideas.

Collecting information about the population was central to the Qin project of expansion and was quite successful. Many of the bureaucratic systems of the Qin remained in place during the Han dynasty and continued with various modifications into later imperial times. The imperial system established by the Qin was successful because of its documentation—information, usually written on bamboo slips or wooden boards, was collected and stored by the government in large quantities.[23] There were two facets to the state-information gathering. The first was the collection of data about the people and the land. The second was the use of the population as informants to ensure that no one was breaking the laws, including laws about registration and place of residence.

According to the text, the state should know thirteen numbers:

> A strong state should know thirteen numbers within its borders: the number of granaries and residents; the number of adult men and women; the number of the old and infirm; the number of officials and men-of-service; the number of those who obtain emoluments by talking; the number of beneficial people; the number of horses, oxen, hay, and straw. If one wants to strengthen one's state but does not know these thirteen numbers, then even if the state's soil is advantageous and residents are numerous, it will be increasingly weakened to the point of dismemberment.[24]

Extant records from the Qin reveal that, while the state may not have monitored these specific thirteen numbers, the government did keep track of the land and people. Having this information was central to Lord Shang's programme. It enabled the state to correctly allocate resources, to maintain a balance between those in military service and those engaged in agriculture, to ensure that fertile agricultural land was not left untilled, and to carefully monitor the number of "those who obtain emoluments by talking" in order to stave off the possibility of rebellion. Lord Shang was himself one who obtained his emoluments by talking, as was Master Mo. Lord Shang was concerned that rival thinkers, being allowed too much freedom, might foment rebellion. This was closely related to his primary objective in keeping the people primarily engaged in agriculture, rather than other professions:

> In registering the number of the people, record the living and erase the dead. When the people do not abscond from [producing] grain, fields will not be covered by wild grasses. Then the state is rich. He whose state is rich is strong.[25]

In the *Book of Lord Shang*, the reason given for this is to prevent people from engaging in professions other than agriculture; by prohibiting people from moving around the state, they would not have any other means by which to make a living, and would remain docile, farming the land.[26] As such, the gathering of information about the population was also an attempt to shape the behaviour of the population, both by keeping them engaged in agriculture and, as we shall see below, in adhering to the law.

Maintaining sufficient land under cultivation was necessary to support the army, and Lord Shang saw the expansion of farmland as a necessary partner to the expansion of the state through warfare. The ruler needed to know the above thirteen numbers in order to divide his territory in the most efficient way possible, ensuring that there was enough land under cultivation, but also land that remained fallow, forests, mountains, and rivers that could provide natural resources, and infrastructure built to facilitate the movement of people and goods throughout the state.[27] Up-to-date information also allowed the state to provide relief in times of environmental disasters, and to provide support to the elderly and the infirm, as we know from some of the legal documents from this time.[28] While Lord Shang's ideas about population surveillance seem on the surface to be wholly draconian, it was not entirely without concern for the welfare of the people, even if that concern was only intended to further strengthen the state.

As we have seen from his description of the thirteen numbers, Lord Shang's system of government required the accumulation of vast amounts of information about the population, and, more importantly, the handling of that information as data. Unlike the system envisioned by the *Mozi*, where bits of information made their way to the ruler in an unsystematic and unspecified way, Lord Shang required that information be classified into groups: information about the number of farmers, merchants, and officials; information about land and resources; information about the comings and goings of the people. These pieces of information were written down, organised, filed, and checked by the relevant authorities, and, in the case of the population registries, updated on an annual basis.[29] While surely a rather cumbersome system involving the storage and organisation of bamboo slips and wooden boards, this organisation of information into data would have, theoretically at least, allowed the ruler to be able to access information about any of his subjects at a given time. In part due to the desire to maintain such oversight of the population, movement of the people was highly regulated. A person was tied to their place of registration and required permission to move to a different county. If they moved from one area to another, they were required to register in their new county. The officials in their previous place of residence were also required to transfer the registration document to the new county. Anyone who failed to report themselves to their new county or to transfer the documents would be fined.[30] Of course, many people tried to evade the state and leave their place of residence, perhaps registering themselves anew in a different county. The state was very concerned with this crime of abscondence, and created many legal statutes to deal with it, though the Qin remained relatively ineffective at preventing it.[31] It was not only the moving of a residence that was regulated under the Qin state and empire, but the travel of the population between regions, particularly into the capital region. Extant legal records show that passports (*zhuan* 傳) were required to travel, and these passports included information not only about the bearer's physical description and rank, but also the types of treatment he was permitted to receive on his journey, such as accommodation, transportation, or other.[32] These passports were checked and sealed by officials and innkeepers, who would be penalised for providing accommodation to someone without the correct documentation. Ironically, according to the biography of Lord Shang in the *Shiji* 史記, Lord Shang met his own downfall when fleeing punishment from the new King of Qin, because he did not have the correct documentation to enter an inn.[33]

The requirement that people, even regular people, check documents and verify the identities and actions of others was central to the Qin information system. Lord Shang envisioned, and largely implemented, a system whereby the state was able to track information about its population and relay this to the central government rapidly—not quite as rapidly as the *Mozi* imagined, but, nonetheless, rather quickly for the ancient world. This was accomplished by engaging members of the population in the creation and dissemination of information, by making it a punishable offence not to do so. This is the second component of Lord Shang's system, which attempted to put into action the free flow of information described by the *Mozi*, and, like the *Mozi*, used the people's eyes and ears to inform the ruler.

The state of Qin implemented a system of "linked liability" (*lian zuo* 連坐) whereby members of the population were held mutually responsible for the behavior of others. In practical terms, this required the organisation of the population into groups of five households, each of whose members could be punished for the crimes of other households within the group unless they reported their crimes to the relevant officials. If your neighbour, for example, stole a sheep, you would be punished as if you had yourself stolen the sheep, unless you reported it. Linked liability extended into the marketplace, where merchants were also grouped into fives, and to the household, where members were expected to report on any transgressions committed by their family members.[34] The organisation of the population into these groups of linked liability was intended to prevent crime by having one's immediate neighbours, who were often members of the same kinship group, keep the other members on the straight and narrow.[35] While we do not have direct information about the effectiveness of the system in deterring crime, evidence suggests that the state was relatively safe, and the system continued on into subsequent dynasties, in modified forms.[36]

The authorities were particularly concerned with the crime of abscondence—leaving one's place of registration without authorisation and slipping through the net of government surveillance and taxation.[37] The systems of registration discussed above outline the desire to record the location of the population and organise that information into data which could be handled by central authorities. The linked liability system ensured that, once registered, no one would be able to leave their place of registration without being caught by their old or new neighbours.[38] This concern over abscondence may have been linked to the state's capabilities to monitor the population. In modern societies, it is of course relatively simple to maintain and update databases of addresses. For the Qin, such changes of registration were more complicated, requiring scribes and other officials to personally verify and register relevant information. Rather than allowing the population to migrate at will, it was far simpler, from a data-management perspective, to deter people from relocating. The annual updating of the population registries became a much more straightforward task when the population remained fixed in place, and the job of the government officials in ensuring that the people remained in their place of registration was facilitated by the use of the population as informants.

The systems envisioned by Lord Shang and implemented by the state and empire of Qin illustrate the desire that the ruler should know everything about his population, including not only their places of residence and landholdings, but to whether or not they followed the laws of the state. Like the author of the *Mozi*, the Qin believed that this information was necessary to create a harmonious state, and that only through knowing what was happening in the state could the ruler make necessary corrections. The systems developed by Lord Shang and the Qin officials transformed this information into data that could be collected and maintained by government officials, and ensured that any changes to that information—be it the change of registration of a household or a crime committed within a community—would be observed and reported in a timely fashion, ensuring that the state's data was always up to date.

Conclusion

Information was of great concern to the state in early China, and as we have seen, it was not only the opinion of scholars that the ruler should have unfettered flows of information to his desk, but that the state also attempted to create systems for the collection, organisation, and transmission of information about the people. Thinkers such as Lord Shang would have been delighted with contemporary information systems and the ability of the state to collect information about the movements and habits of people in real time.[39] While these practices bear some resemblance to modern information collection, they differ from them in some important ways. The main distinction that must be drawn is that the Qin state and empire were not creating *statistics*. John Durham Peters has written of the emergence of statistics with regard to the idea of information: statistics is "a new kind of knowledge - knowledge that absolves individuals from the claims of deixis, of existing at one place and at one moment."[40] While the rulers of the Qin and Han may have shared similar goals of the modern states of the nineteenth century, in that they wanted to have information about their states that would be all-encompassing, the Qin and Han did not analyse this information in quite such abstract ways. The information they gathered was, or was intended to be, deictic—the information tied to the individual at a particular place, at a particular moment. Summaries were made to be forwarded to the central government, but there is no evidence, as yet, that these summaries were used as statistics. This difference is significant but does not change the fact that these early states shared with our modern world similar desires to gather and organise information about the population, and that people millennia ago attempted to develop information societies with the technologies available to them.

This brief discussion of two texts from the Warring States period along with some of the relevant administrative policies only begins to scrape the surface of the vast topic of information in the ancient world. As Toni Weller has remarked, "information has always been part of human society, right back to ancient times; indeed, a society cannot exist without information,"[41] and in this chapter, we have only been able to scrape the surface of one particular dimension of information in early China—that which related to the ruler's information about the population. These two texts, the *Mozi* and the *Book of Lord Shang*, furthermore, only represent two viewpoints on information from the period. While they both agree that the ruler should have unrestricted and up-to-date information about the people, other texts expressed the opinion that the ruler should not actively create data about his population, and that doing so could bring about calamity.[42] These ideas about information in early China, like in other times and places, were culturally specific and are reflective of the authors' political views, demonstrating that there was a plurality of opinion about the uses (and abuses) of the state's collection of information. Exploration of other facets of information in this time period will surely reveal a similarly rich landscape of opinions.

Notes

1. Toni Weller, "Information History: Its Importance, Relevance and Future," *Aslib Proceedings* 59, nos. 4/5 (July 12, 2007): 440.
2. For a general discussion of the *shi* and social mobility for political advisors, see Yuri Pines, *Envisioning Eternal Empire: Chinese Political Thought of the Warring States Era* (Honolulu, HI: University of Hawai'i Press, 2009), 115–184.
3. The texts from this period of Chinese history were usually named after the scholar whose views they espouse but were rarely written by a single author. The textual history of these works is complex, but, generally speaking, the texts were compiled based on writings that reflected the views of the schools of thought. As they are generally composite works, it is also very difficult to provide accurate dates for the production of the texts. Kenneth Brashier has compared some early Chinese texts to a loose-leaf binder, where pages can be added and subtracted with ease. Kenneth E. Brashier, *Ancestral Memory in Early China* (Cambridge, MA: Harvard University Asia Center, 2011), 48–49. For more detailed information on the *Mozi* and the *Book of Lord Shang*, see the respective entries in *Early Chinese Texts: A Bibliographical Guide*, ed. Michael Loewe (Berkeley, CA: Society for the Study of Early China and Institute of East Asian Studies, 1993), 336–341 and 368–375. See also the translators' introductions in *The Book of Lord Shang: Apologetics of State Power in Early China*, ed. and trans. Yuri Pines (New York: Columbia University Press, 2017) and Ian Johnston, *The Mozi: A Complete Translation* (Hong Kong: The Chinese University of Hong Kong Press, 2010) which discuss the major findings about the compilation and authorship of these two texts. For references to Chinese texts, the chapter and section numbers are given prior to the page numbers.
4. See Robin D. S. Yates, "The Mohists on Warfare; Technology, Technique, and Justification," *Journal of the American Academy of Religion* 47, no. 35 (1979), Thematic Issue: 549–603.
5. Lord Shang's belief that all, including the royal family, should be treated equally under the law brought about his downfall when the prince of Qin disagreed.
6. Michael K. Buckland, "Information as Thing," *Journal of the American Society for Information Science* 42, no. 5 (1991): 351.
7. Buckland, "Information as Thing," 351.
8. For 1991 usage, see Buckland, "Information as Thing," 352.
9. Toni Weller, *Information History–An Introduction: Exploring an Emergent Field* (Oxford: Chandos, 2008), 4–5.
10. Johnston, *The Mozi*, 12.1–12.2, 99–101. Heaven (*tian* 天) was a non-anthropomorphised nature deity which many believed to set the patterns which created order. The Son of Heaven (*tianzi* 天子), the earthly ruler, was expected to rule in such a way that Heavenly patterns were reproduced on earth. Failure to do so could result in disruptions in the form of natural disasters or phenomena.
11. A *li* 里 was a measurement of distance, which, during the Han period, was equal to 415.8 m. A.F.P. Hulsewé, "Han measures," *T'oung pao* 49, no. 3 (1961): 206–207.
12. Johnston, *The Mozi*, 12.11, 113.
13. Johnston, *The Mozi*, 12.11, 113.
14. Johnston, *The Mozi*, 11.3, 95.
15. Johnston, *The Mozi*, 11.3, 95.
16. Johnston, *The Mozi*, 11.4, 95.
17. Johnston, *The Mozi*, 11.4, 95; 97. Of course, it was also theoretically possible that the Son of Heaven failed to establish principles that followed Heaven and would therefore receive punishment

"Those Who Help his Sight and Hearing Are Many"

from Heaven. However, in the idealised golden age expressed in the *Mozi*, this possibility is not introduced.
18 Johnston, *The Mozi*, 11.5, 97. The five (mutilating) punishments were, in order of increasing severity, tattooing of the forehead, amputation of the nose, amputation of the foot, castration, and death. Although these five became well known as a "set" of punishments, the penal system was more complicated, and involved various grades of punishments, not all of them involving bodily mutilation.
19 Another thinker and statesman from later in this period, Han Feizi, later wrote in great detail about the importance of both rewards and punishments, which he described as the "two handles" of government.
20 Johnston, *The Mozi*, 13.6, 123.
21 Several hundred years later, the state of Qin did establish a system which required neighbours to inform on each other, modelled on the reforms of Shang Yang, discussed below. See also the discussion in Rebecca Robinson, "Big Data in Early China: Population Surveillance in the Early Chinese Empires," in *Histories of Surveillance from Antiquity to the Digital Age: The Eyes and Ears of Power*, ed. Andreas Marklund and Laura Skouvig (London: Routledge, 2021), 20–36.
22 For an overview of Lord Shang's school and the text, see the discussion in Pines, *The Book of Lord Shang*.
23 Tsang Wing Ma has provided a discussion about the scribes who were charged with producing these documents, and the difficult effort that it was. Ma, "Scribes in Early Imperial China" (PhD diss., UC Berkeley, 2017).
24 Pines, *The Book of Lord Shang*, 4.10, 154.
25 Pines, *The Book of Lord Shang*, 4.7, 153.
26 Discoveries of administrative and legal documents have revealed that the Qin state was not as opposed to commerce as the *Book of Lord Shang* would have us believe. See the chapters in Elisa Sabattini and Christian Schwermann, eds., *Between Command and Market: Economic Thought and Practice in Early China*, Sinica Leidensia, vol. 154 (Leiden; Boston, MA: Brill, 2022) for in-depth discussions on new understandings of economic thought and practice in early China.
27 Pines, *The Book of Lord Shang*, 6.2, 159. See Charles Sanft, "Environment and Law in Early Imperial China (third century BCE–first century CE): Qin and Han Statutes Concerning Natural Resources," *Environmental History* 15, no. 4 (2010): 701–721 for a discussion of the Qin's regulation of the environment.
28 Anthony J. Barbieri-Low and Robin D. S. Yates, *Law, State, and Society in Early Imperial China: A Study with Critical Edition and Translation of the Legal Texts from Zhangjiashan Tomb No. 247*, Sinica Leidensia, vol. 126/1 and 126/2 (Leiden; Boston, MA: Brill, 2015), 785.
29 Barbieri-Low and Yates, *Law, State, and Society*, 792–793.
30 Barbieri-Low and Yates, *Law, State, and Society*, 792–793.
31 Barbieri-Low and Yates, *Law, State, and Society*, 574.
32 Pines, *The Book of Lord Shang*, 2.8; 2.11, 127; 128. On the legal statutes related to the fords and passes, see Ōba Osamu et al., "The Ordinances on Fords and Passes Excavated from Han Tomb Number 247, Zhangjiashan," *Asia Major, THIRD SERIES* 14, no. 2 (2001): 119–141.
33 Sima Qian 司馬遷 (145? – 86? BCE). *Shiji* (Beijing: Zhonghua shuju, 1959), 68.2232–2233 (Hereafter, *Shiji*). There are different versions of the events that led to Lord Shang's execution, but the *Shiji* tale is that which captured popular imagination. See the discussion in Pines, *The Book of Lord Shang*, 23.
34 Barbieri-Low and Yates, *Law, State, and Society*, 138. The law placed restrictions on who could denounce whom; for example, wives could not denounce their parents-in-law, and elders over the age of seventy had to make the denunciation on three consecutive days. False accusations were treated very severely under Qin law.
35 Charles Sanft has suggested that the linked households could have also been grounds for collusion among members. Charles Sanft, "Shang Yang Was a Cooperator: Applying Axelrod's Analysis of Cooperation in Early China," *Philosophy East and West* 64, no. 1 (2014): 174–191.
36 Barbieri-Low and Yates, *Law, State, and Society*, 216. For a brief discussion of the continuation and metamorphoses of the linked liability system, see Robinson, "Big Data," 31–33.
37 See the discussion in Barbieri-Low and Yates, along with the translation of the Barbieri-Low and Yates, "Statutes on Abscondence," *Law, State, and Society*, 574–593.

38 Here the state relied on the fact that most communities were small and comprised members of kinship groups. An outsider entering a community would be immediately noticed and deemed suspicious.
39 Though one might suspect he would have been less enthused about the abilities of private corporations to do the same.
40 John Durham Peters, "Information: Notes toward a Critical History," *Journal of Communication Inquiry* 12, no. 2 (July 1988): 15.
41 Weller, "Information History," 440.
42 This view is taken by the authors of the *Huainanzi*, who may have been trying to limit the central government's oversight into the Kingdom of Huainan. Liu An and John S. Major, *The Huainanzi: A Guide to the Theory and Practice of Government in Early Han China*, Translations from the Asian Classics (New York: Columbia University Press, 2010). 8.1, 270.

13
CREATIVITY IN CLASSIFICATION
Phrasing and Presenting the Aristotelian Categories in the Middle Ages

Irene O'Daly

Introduction

This chapter investigates the long life of a short sentence attributed to Isidore of Seville, who lived c. 560–636 CE and was the author of the monumental medieval encyclopaedic work, *Etymologiae* [the *Etymologies*]. The sentence, which reads as follows—"Augustine, the great orator, the son of that man, standing, in the temple, today, wearing a priest's fillet, is worn out from arguing"—may at first reading appear to be flatly descriptive.[1] Who is this Augustine, why should we be concerned with what he is doing and wearing, to whom he is related, with how he is feeling? In posing this selection of questions, however, the purpose of the sentence comes into focus: the phrase offered a reader a set of classifications to describe all words, concepts, or things. These classifications were derived from those introduced by Aristotle (384–322 BCE) in his fundamental logical study, the *Categories*. Isidore's phrase, although initially unassuming, captured Aristotle's categories into one expression, and in so doing became a powerful heuristic for gathering, organising, and classifying information about the known world.

In this present study, we explore how medieval scholars used this simplest of devices—a single phrase—to understand the most complex of questions: what is reality? Focusing on the pre-scholastic period (prior to the fuller recovery of the Aristotelian corpus in the Latin West in the thirteenth century), the discussion will show how the sentence's use in various textual contexts suggests a chameleonic capacity to blend to a variety of purposes. The particular ways in which the sentence was presented in various manuscript carriers suggest its utility as a mnemonic. Meanwhile, modifications to its wording indicate that it was used as a ludic device, capable of stimulating pedagogic play and generating new combinations. Delving into its transmission, we investigate the various levels on which the sentence functioned as a tool for textual and informational management.[2] It facilitated storage of information (through description), its retrieval (by permitting ordered recollection), and its generation (through its application to different texts and its use in different contexts). Further, as we shall see, the sentence functioned not only as a signifier of information, a shorthand to refer to the categories, but also as a referent, more generally speaking, to a tradition of Greek learning.

The Significance of the Categories

In his *Categories*, Aristotle described the ten categories as follows: "Of things said without any combination, each signifies either substance or quantity or qualification or a relative or where or when or being-in-a-position or having or doing or being affected."[3] These are (using the Latin term) the *predicamenta*, or predicaments—that is, what can be said of something. As Michael Griffin has pithily observed, early commentators on Aristotle's works quickly established the fundamental nature of the categories: "A student who grasps the *Categories*' lessons will be equipped to distinguish the features that mark a thing out for *what it is*, and so properly belong in its definition, from those incidental features that merely describe *how* it is that way."[4] The beauty of Aristotle's categorical classification, however, lay in its inherent ambiguity. Did it just concern words (what can be said of something) or also an ontological reality (what something is)? This question of what precisely Aristotle was categorising (words, concepts, things) motivated continued interest in his text, intriguing scholars from William of Ockham in the thirteenth century to Immanuel Kant in the eighteenth, throughout the medieval and early modern periods, and up to the present day.[5]

For much of the Middle Ages, the original Greek of Aristotle's *Categories* was accessed indirectly via Latin translations and paraphrases. Moreover, important works of Aristotle's oeuvre which contextualised his discussion of being, such as his *Metaphysics*, were only translated into Latin and became known to Western European scholars from the twelfth century onwards. Various commentaries were written on the *Categories* throughout the Middle Ages, including a significant one by the Roman senator and philosopher, Boethius (c. 480–524 CE); these commentaries played an important role in explicating and influencing interpretations of Aristotle's work. The *Categories* circulated in three Latin versions: a translation of Aristotle's text made by Boethius; a version which combined the *lemmata* from Boethius's *Commentary on the Categories* with various passages supplied by an anonymous translator; and a paraphrase known as the *Categoriae decem* [*Ten Categories*], composed in the late fourth century, and attributed during the medieval period to the church father Augustine (354–430 CE).[6] Boethius's translation circulated in medieval schools from the eleventh century onwards (as part of the corpus of the *logica vetus*) and would become the translation of reference.[7] These translations—and particularly the paraphrase, *Categoriae decem*, which was highly influential in the early Middle Ages—transmitted Aristotle's way of thinking. His discussion of the categories appealed to medieval Christian writers who were curious to understand the fundaments of the world: how could the products of God's creative acts be described and explained? More significantly, if these categories of being applied to all things, did they also apply to God Himself?[8]

The Isidorean Phrase

Aristotle had offered a sample of each type of category to the reader: "To give a rough idea, examples of substance are man, horse; of quantity: four-foot, five-foot; of qualification: white, grammatical; of a relative: double, half, larger; of where: in the Lyceum, in the market-place; of when: yesterday, last-year; of being-in-a-position: is-lying, is sitting; of having: has-shoes-on, has-armour-on; of doing: cutting, burning; of being-affected: being-cut, being-burned."[9] These examples seem to have served as the inspiration for the sample sentence found in Isidore's *Etymologiae*, a sixth-century encyclopaedia oriented by subject matter. The *Etymologiae* was divided into twenty books, each treating a different aspect of knowledge, from grammar to medicine, angels to war. This work became an essential reference volume for scholars in the medieval period, as well as an important vehicle for the transmission of classical ideas.[10]

The first two books of the *Etymologiae* treat the traditional liberal arts of the medieval trivium: grammar, rhetoric, and dialectic. Dialectic—also termed "logic"—is described as "the discipline devised for investigating the causes of things."[11] After situating logic within the context of the various parts of philosophy, Isidore turns to summarising some of the principal works of relevance, starting with the *Isagoge* of Porphyry, an introduction to the categories (which was also translated by Boethius). Book II.XXVI then introduces Aristotle's categories one by one.

> Countless things are classified in these nine types, of which we have presented some as examples, or in the type 'substance' itself, which is οὐσία ("essential being"). It is also the case with whatever we perceive with the intellect: we present them in speech with one or another of these ten predicates. A sentence full of these runs like this: "Augustine, the great orator, the son of that man, standing, in the temple, today, wearing a priest's fillet, is worn out from arguing."[12]

Here "Augustine" connotes substance (*substantia*); "great," quantity (*quantitas*); "orator," quality (*qualitas*); "the son of that man," relation (*relatio*); "standing," situation (*situs*); "in the temple," place (*locus*); "today," time (*tempus*); "wearing a priest's fillet," habit (*habitus*); "is worn out," activity (*agere*); "from arguing," passivity (*pati*).

Isidore's sample sentence is an effective linguistic mnemonic: it supplies examples of each of the categories in turn, while offering a prompt for recalling them in their appropriate order by organising them into a cogent grammatical phrase. Isidore's choice to employ the figure of Augustine, a familiar one for the medieval reader, may have been prompted by his acquaintance with the *Categoriae decem*, a text supposedly authored by the church father.[13] In any case, by transposing Aristotle's categories into a Christian context, expressed by the disputing Augustine, Isidore renders the classification into a form immediately accessible to his readers: novel, but also familiar. The success of his transposition is apparent in the ready excerption of the phrase from the *Etymologiae*; it comes to circulate in other texts and contexts. The appeal of the sentence seems to lie in its scope: it is reductive—substituting each category with a specific example—but also all-encompassing: a shorthand for classifying everything, distilled into a few memorable words.

An example of how the sentence travelled into new textual contexts is found in its inclusion in the dialogic *De dialectica [On dialectic]*, a text composed by Alcuin of York (c. 735–804), famous scholar at the court of Charlemagne.[14] Alcuin's *De dialectica* borrowed heavily from Isidore's *Etymologiae*, and directly from the *Categoriae decem* for its treatment of the categories.[15] Alcuin's respect for the latter text and its way of thinking is demonstrated by the fact that he even gifted a copy of it to his famous imperial pupil, Charlemagne, referring in an accompanying verse directly to the list of categories: "this little book contains ten words of nature, amazing words which by their power represent every property of things, which can be perceived by our minds."[16] In *De dialectica*, the categories are discussed one by one. The pupil, Charlemagne, then asks his teacher to: "Combine a single sentence for me out of all of these ten predicaments." Alcuin duly obliges, providing the Isidorean phrase and then supplying an explanation of how each element of the sentence relates to a particular category.[17] Alcuin played a fundamental role in reintroducing the *Categoriae decem* to the medieval curriculum, and it would seem that the Isidorean phrase, perhaps particularly palatable on account of its association with Augustine, was communicated into the Carolingian curriculum as part of this philosophical inheritance.[18]

Paratextual Functions of the Phrase

The attraction of the phrase is demonstrated by its appearance in a variety of textual contexts. One intriguing instance is its presence in the Laon Greek-Latin glossary (Laon, Bibliothèque municipale [BM], MS 444) associated with an Irish teacher at the cathedral school, Martin of Laon (819–875 CE).[19] In this manuscript, the phrase is presented subsequent to a series of Greek terms (given with their Latin equivalents), derived from the grammatical writings of Priscian (fl. 500 CE) (fols 276r–287v), on a page that also contains a Graeco-Latin wordlist concerning the human body and a Latin note on the origin of the alphabet (fol. 289v).[20] The Isidorean phrase is preceded by a title, "*Ista sunt decem predicamenta quibus constat uniuersitas*," "These are the ten predicaments which constitute all things." The phrase is then provided, written in large rounded letters and presented in two columns of text, with one word per line. Each word is annotated by the name of the categories, which are added in smaller letters in the interlinear space.

The script of both phrase and annotation is distinctive in comparison to the other writings on the page, which suggests that they were added in a second scribal campaign.[21] The larger size of the letter-forms relative to the rest of the writing on the page, coupled with their lighter colour of ink, emphasises the sentence. Meanwhile, the aerated graphic expression of the words in two columns gives the phrase a quasi-tabular appearance. These visual aspects could have enhanced the mnemonic function of the phrase. While its presence in the context of this Graeco-Latin vocabulary seems initially anomalous, its addition was likely prompted by the list of Greek words which follows (fols 290r–291r), all of which were drawn from the *Categoriae decem*.[22] Here the Isidorean phrase takes its place in a deliberately informational context—among word lists and glossaries. But it also acquires an important paratextual function; it introduces and contextualises the philosophical information that follows, signposting further content.[23]

Martin's attention to the phrase is also illustrated by its presence in another teaching manual copied under his direction (Laon, BM, MS 468).[24] This manuscript, an important witness to Virgilian reception in this period, also includes a short treatise on the liberal arts attributed to Martin, which has been regarded as reflective of his teaching programme.[25] Following a discussion of the divisions of philosophy, this treatise concludes with a brief treatment of the arts of rhetoric and dialectic. Here Martin refers to the categories, lists them all, and then provides an "*exemplum*," that of the disputing Augustine (borrowing, as he does in many instances in this treatise, from Isidore's *Etymologiae*).[26] In the manuscript, the sentence is accompanied by an interlinear commentary (a gloss) which repeats the Latin names of the categories above the relevant words, explaining its terms (fol. 10v).[27] Significantly, Martin's discussion of the categories in this context ends with a phrase almost identical in wording to that used to introduce the Isidorean phrase in Laon, BM, MS 444: "*Istis decem praedicamentis universitas constat.*"[28]

The echo in wording of the phrase and clarificatory rubric across these two manuscripts suggests that these two instances work in tandem. Given that these manuscripts were produced for use within the same learning environment, the Isidorean phrase would seem to suggest and invite a practice of consultative multi-codex reference, encouraging one to look from Martin's treatise on the arts to the glossary, and perhaps beyond these summaries to the *Categoriae decem* itself. The repetition of these elements across the two codices designed by Martin elevates the phrase from the status of a handy mnemonic hook (particularly when enhanced by other presentational techniques, such as the enlarged script used for the phrase in the Graeco-Latin glossary), to prompting information retrieval both within the context of a single book and across multiple books of a school collection. The phrase is intrinsic to the content of each manuscript: it is a means for efficiently storing key elements of information while it simultaneously acquires a paratextual referential function. In this way, the phrase can be interpreted as evidence for practices of the retrieval of related information, and even as a prompt for cross-reference.

Glossing the *Categoriae Decem*

Martin's interest in the *Categoriae decem* was typical of this period. The *Categoriae decem* was heavily glossed, or annotated, with many of the surviving manuscripts of the text dating from the ninth to twelfth centuries containing additional notes in the margins and between its lines, intended to aid reader comprehension. This is not the place for a detailed discussion of the range, authorship, or content of these glosses, save to reiterate John Marenbon's conclusion that they "give a picture of the development of logical studies from the ninth to the twelfth century."[29] These annotations, added by scholars in the Middle Ages to their manuscripts, are relatively fluid in form, varying from copy to copy in terms of their placement and presentation. They are also textually variable, influenced by production contexts, the nature of the exemplar from which the scribe was copying, and the projected audience by which the manuscript would be used.[30] These glosses shaped interpretations and understandings of the *Categoriae decem* and, by extension, of Aristotle's categories. The inclusion of the Isidorean phrase in a number of the glossed manuscripts of the *Categoriae decem* suggests its perceived utility as an aid for understanding the text and its ideas.[31] As the analysis of the following examples will show, however, through the flexible medium of the gloss the sentence was elevated from a commonplace phrase to a consultative informational device permitting the storage and retrieval of information.

An instructive example may be found in Paris, Bibliothèque nationale de France [BnF], MS lat. 12949, an early tenth-century manuscript which contains glosses to the *Categoriae decem* attributed to various scholars, including Heiric of Auxerre (841–876 CE) (Fig. 13.1).[32] Annotated by several hands, the manuscript contains a number of small slips of parchment throughout, inserted to provide additional room for the notes to the text. On the recto of one of these parchment slips (fol. 27 bis) is a diagram portraying *"substantia,"* substance (the Greek word *"οὐσία"* is also given), described as the *"genus generalissimum,"* and reflecting the scholarly interest of readers of the *Categoriae decem* in its discussion of "being."[33] Examples of different types of substance—precious stones, trees, animals—are provided. A variant of the Isidorean sentence, with some biographical updates, is placed directly above the diagram (Augustine is described here as *"filius Monicae,"* the son of Monica; he is disputing not *"in templo"* but *"in ecclesia,"* in a church). The elements are accompanied by both the Latin and Greek names of the categories. The wording of the sentence is somewhat disordered, perhaps reflecting the rather small dimensions of the leaf; alternate Latin terms are linked to the Greek names of the categories by small symbols, placed sometimes at a distance from the Greek to which they are relevant. The graphic expression of the sentence is notable: the words (*"Augustinus - essentia - οὐσία,"* etc.) are

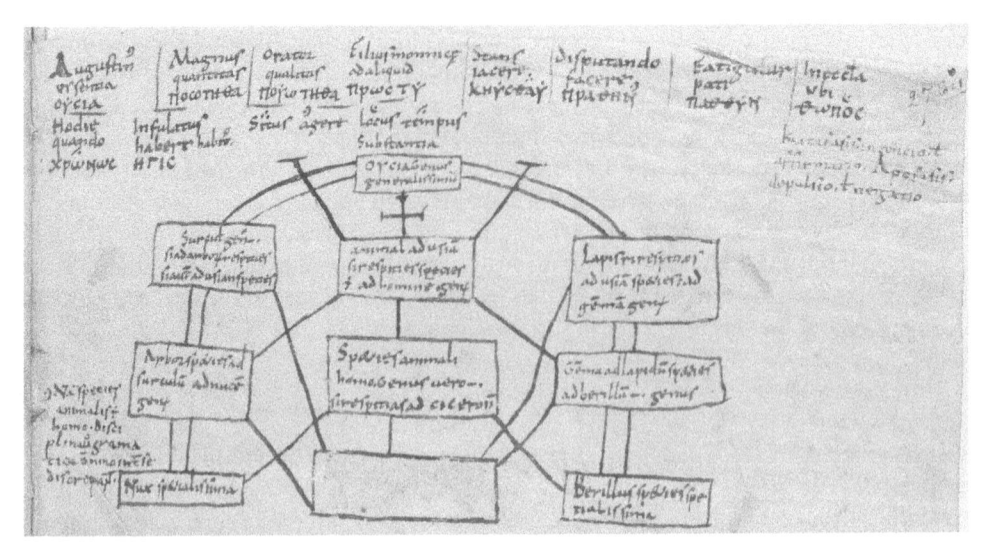

Figure 13.1 Paris, Bibliothèque nationale de France, MS lat. 12949, fol. 27bis r. The Isidorean phrase is found above the diagram labelled *Substantia* or "Substance."

Source: Gallica/Bibliothèque nationale de France.

stacked on top of each other, and each constituent element—or category—is separated by a line. The result is a quasi-tabular presentation; the sentence is deliberately broken into its constituent parts, no longer intended to be read only in fluid prose. Instead, the information storage function of the sentence is emphasised. In listing different iterations of its key elements in a distinctive graphic manner, the presentation prompts reference and recollection.

This tendency to break down the phrase into its constituent elements is also reflected in two other glossed manuscripts of the *Categoriae decem*. In Munich, Bayerische Staatsbibliothek [BSB], Clm 6367, a tenth-century manuscript produced in the monastery of Freising, the phrase is squeezed into the inner margin of a folio (6r).[34] Here its components are intercalculated with the Latin names of the categories and then stacked on top of each other. Although space was clearly a factor here, with the scribe obliged to squeeze the gloss into the narrow margin, the list-like presentation of the phrase seems again to emphasise its information storage and retrieval capacities. Finally, in Orléans, BM, MS 263, a ninth-century manuscript also produced in a monastic context (this time in Fleury), the phrase, added in a tenth-century hand, is placed in the upper margin of the page (p. 46), with the Latin names of the categories provided below each element—here Augustine is described as "*predicator*," preacher, and tires not from disputing, but from preaching, "*predicando*," a further update to the content of the phrase.[35] The words are distanced from each other, and further separated by punctuating dots which add grammatical clarity as well as emphasis. As was the case in Paris, BnF, MS lat. 12949, the resulting presentation is quasi-tabular; the sentence can be read not only as prose, but also as a series of disjunctive elements. The later annotator, who added the phrase to the extensive ninth-century commentary that already surrounded the text, clearly felt it would be a handy additional aid to the reader.

The inclusion of the phrase in each of these three manuscripts was likely self-referential, prompted by Augustine's alleged authorship of the accompanying *Categoriae decem*.[36]

Creativity in Classification

Variability in the phrase's wording demonstrates the inherent heterogeneity of the glossing tradition. It is notable that the sentence is distinguished from other explanatory elements in these manuscripts through its presentation. These aspects visually highlighted the gloss on the page, inviting the reader to refer back to this basic phrase while reading the accompanying text. Its simplicity offered a moment of mental grounding, a foundation upon which a more abstract philosophical discourse around the categories could be built. The visual deconstruction of the phrase, manifested in the separation of its elements from each other, along with the explicit inclusion of the terminology of the categories in each case, prompts us to query its multiple functions as an informational tool. The phrase stores information, by providing a summary (and hence serving a consultative function), while its unusual presentation prompts recollection of its elements (a retrieval function). Moreover, the seemingly deliberate fracturing of the prose of the sentence, evident in its quasi-tabular or list-like features, emphasises the generic quality of the categories. This aspect seems to invite the extrapolation of the phrase's elements to other contexts, encouraging experimentation in categorical thinking, and perhaps even the generation of further sample classifications.

Teaching the Categories at St Gall

To understand the significance of the phrase within the broader context of the study of the categories in the medieval period, it is worth turning to its use in a single intellectual centre. The medieval school at the monastery of St Gall was famous for its extensive library, already numbering 264 codices (containing 395 separate works) by the mid-ninth century, as recorded in its first library catalogue.[37] Here the phrase gathered traction, appearing among a cluster of other textual elements in several manuscripts dating from the ninth and tenth centuries. The oldest manuscript in which the phrase is found is St Gallen, Stiftsbibliothek (SB), Cod. Sang. 397, the so-called *vademecum* or handbook of Grimald, abbot of St Gall from 841–872 CE.[38] This manuscript contains a variety of liturgical, theological, computistic, and other miscellaneous texts.[39] The Isidorean sentence is found in a highly miscellaneous quire of the volume.[40] This quire opens with several definitions taken from Boethius's *Liber contra Eutychen et Nestorium*.[41] This text was an important conduit for logical terminology in the medieval period.[42] Here, along with the Latin equivalents for Greek terms such as essence and substance, we also find Boethius's definitions of nature ("the specific differentia which informs a thing") and person ("an individual substance of a nature endowed with reason"), definitions which presuppose knowledge of important aspects of the Aristotelian logical tradition, notably the system of genera and species.[43]

Turning the page, we find a short glossary containing various Greek terms for Byzantine charitable institutions, accompanied by their Latin definitions (p. 38).[44] As Bernice Kaczynski established, this "philanthropic nomenclature," which originally derived from Justinian's *Novellae*, seems to have appealed to medieval scribes as a "lexicographical curiosity," although it is likely that it travelled into Cod. Sang. 397 on account of its use in a collection of capitularies regarding ecclesiastical property.[45] The Isidorean phrase directly follows this "philanthropic nomenclature." It is preceded by a title reading "*CATAGORIE*" [sic], and followed by Isidore's definition of "*definitio*" (definition) as "a brief statement determining the nature of each thing as it is distinguished by what it has in common with other things by an individual, proper signification."[46] While its presentation directly following the "philanthropic nomenclature" may suggest that the phrase was also regarded as a "lexicographical curiosity," it is more accurately seen to be in conversation with the other textual elements here relating to the nature of being and philosophical definition. As was the case with its inclusion in the Laon Graeco-Latin glossary, the Isidorean phrase seems to be of interest here not only as a heuristic for memorising the categories but also on account of its connection with a broader tradition of Greek learning. Significantly, title aside, in this instance the phrase contains no reference to the individual Aristotelian categories themselves. It bypasses, even conceals, its connection with that terminology and in so doing, assumes the function of a proxy, substituting for—and thereby implying knowledge of—that terminology.

A second manuscript from the late ninth century, St Gallen, SB, Cod. Sang. 899, contains passages copied directly from Cod. Sang. 397, and includes a similar constellation of texts, but offers a more explicit couching of the phrase within its logical context.[47] Page 59 opens with definitions of *"isagoga"* (introduction), *"periermeniae"* (interpretation), and a definition of the epichireme (as *"genus syllogismi"*), before describing the categories and providing a list of all ten. Subsequent to the list, we find the Isidorean phrase, presented, as was the case in Cod. Sang. 397, directly following a majuscule title (*"CATEGORIAE"*) and followed by Isidore's definition of *"definitio."*[48] The commonplace status of the phrase is reinforced by its presence in one further manuscript associated with St Gall: the tenth-century manuscript, Munich, BSB, Clm 19413 (from the German monastery of Tegernsee), which contains, among other texts, a copy of Notker Balbulus's (c. 840–912 CE) *Compendium*, a teaching text used at St Gall.[49]

BSB, Clm 19413 also contains the "philanthropic nomenclature," Boethius's definitions of nature and person (fol. 118r), followed by a summary of the categories highly similar to that found in Cod. Sang. 899, and then the Isidorean phrase (fol. 118v).[50] Unlike the other two instances, the phrase was not preceded here by a title. The fact that no explicit link is made between the phrase and the categories seems to have confused at least one later reader. Red lines were added to this section to separate out the various miscellaneous items, including a line bifurcating the summary of the categories from the Isidorean phrase, suggesting that the two were not seen as specifically related. Moreover, another hand, writing in green, has added alongside the phrase the single word *"Augustinus."* For this reader, at least, the sentence seemingly acquired significance not on account of its association with the logical tradition of the categories, but due to its mention of the church father, Augustine. As this example shows, the value of the phrase as an information-management device depended on some pre-existing knowledge of the categories of Aristotle. In the absence of this, it risked being read as an empty encomium.

The Phrase as a Grammatical Aid

As we have seen, the circulation of ideas about the categories is attested to in manuscripts associated with St Gall. Divorced from its original context in the *Etymologiae*, a key ingredient in this intellectual ferment was the Isidorean phrase. It is unsurprising, therefore, to find the phrase also integrated into the works of one of St Gall's most famous teachers, Notker Labeo (c. 950–1022 CE). Dialectic, the art of logical reasoning, was a fundamental element of the St Gall curriculum.[51] Writing in his treatise, *Distributio omnium specierum*, which concerns the connection between grammar and dialectic and in which Notker explores the relationships between Aristotle's ten categories and Priscian's twenty-seven classes of the common noun, Notker described how dialectic held an "epistemologically prior position" compared to grammar[52]:

> The eight parts of speech in grammar show clearly what words are in themselves. Aristotle's ten categories, which pertain to logic, show first what those parts of speech signify beyond themselves, and then what they are in themselves. Nature shows us this same sequence in children, for they learn to understand what the word "man" is predicated of before they learn the inflection of the form.[53]

Notker proceeds to provide the Isidorean phrase, describing it as a "line" (*versus*) used by "our predecessors" (*priores nostri*).[54] Here Notker refers to Augustine as a "preacher" (*pr[a]edicator*), "son of Monica" (*filius munic[a]e* [sic]), linking (as we have seen various commentators on the *Categoriae decem* do) the phrase securely to its patristic heritage.[55] Notker's reference to "our predecessors," while they remain unspecified, serves to add authority to the phrase, while he describes the function of the phrase as "*ad agnoscenda decem categoriae*," with the verb *agnoscere* meaning in this context either to understand or to learn the ten categories.[56] That is, Notker specifically situates the example within a pedagogical context: its function as information device is to permit comprehension and recollection.

Notker's positioning of the phrase in *Distributio omnium specierum*, a work that sought to identify the commonalities and differences between grammar and dialectic, reflects the fact that the phrase was also employed within grammatical contexts.[57] Sedulius Scotus, for example, had already used it in the ninth century in his grammatical commentary on Donatus, exploring, as Anneli Luhtala describes, "the Priscianic doctrine of the pre-eminence of the noun and the verb as components of the clause."[58] Elke Krotz has examined the occurrence of the phrase in a set of ninth-century glosses to the *Ars Prisciani* (Oxford, MS Bodl. Libr., Auct. T.1.26, from the Auxerre area) where the phrase is introduced with the words "*Hec sunt decem categorie id est decem praedicamenta in quibus continentur omnes res*" ("Here are the ten categories, that is the ten predicaments, in which are contained all things"), with the elements of the sentence then intercalculated with the names of the categories. She compares this presentation to that found in Laon, BM, MS 444, suggesting, in turn, that the glossator may have depended, perhaps indirectly, on material from the circle of Martin of Laon.[59] These examples show, as Luhtala identified, an interest in relating the categories to grammatical material—particularly to the writings of Priscian, an important figure in the medieval grammar curriculum—even if such engagement remained at a fairly elementary level.[60] In each case, the Isidorean phrase seems to function as an exercise in scholarly shorthand, "flagging" the categories and perhaps substituting for a full exposition on that subject.

Anna Grotans, in turn, cites an instance of the use of the phrase from a later pedagogic context in BSB, Clm 18375, a ninth-century copy of Priscian's *Institutiones* from Tegernsee that contains eleventh-century marginal and interlinear glossing.[61] On fol. 10v, the glossator introduces the categories, continuing (in translation): "To better understand these accidents, or ten categories, let's use this example: 'Because Augustine, the son of his mother Monica, is a great teacher, he, while he is standing in the temple today and wearing a headband, teaches until he can teach no more.'"[62] Aside from the fact that we find here a further elaboration of Augustine's biography (he is now "teacher," "doctor," as well as "the son of his mother Monica"), the quotation is again a useful demonstration of the function of the phrase as an explanatory device ("to better understand"), an informational function further emphasised by the fact that there is a gloss-to-the-gloss provided in the manuscript, with the various categories annotated in the interlinear space by words from the phrase ("*in templo,*" "*docendo,*" "*fatigatur*"), thus easing cross-reference.[63]

The Isidorean phrase seemingly had a long life within the context of the relationship between grammar, dialectic, and the other liberal arts. Writing in his *Metalogicon* in 1159, John of Salisbury (late 1110s–1180 CE), one of the first authors to engage with the rediscovered Aristotelian *Organon* (the corpus of logical translations), referred to both Isidore and Alcuin in his extensive discussion of Aristotle's ten categories, noting that they "give the following very full [complete] sentence" "to illustrate their point." John praises the sentence: "The foregoing is [indeed] a full sentence, and indicates the substance, quality, quantity, and other predicables of the subject concerning whom it speaks, although perhaps its [proposed] example of quantity is not quite accurate."[64] John notes that the sentence is not without ambiguity: is Augustine, "*magnus orator,*" "great" in terms of his stature, or is "great" intended as a qualifier of "orator"? For the sentence to succeed as an example only the former works, although both are grammatically viable interpretations. John's attention to the phrasing of the sentence shows that it continued to hold intellectual currency and prompt debate on the categories, even in a period where more translations of Aristotle's logical works were coming into circulation. Indeed, aside from its function as a mnemonic clause, its presence in this twelfth-century educational treatise alludes to a new context of interest in the study of the Aristotelian categories, namely their relevance for the ongoing debate surrounding the ontological status of "universals."[65] In this debate, which centred on the nature of words and what they signify, understanding the categories would continue to be of essential importance.

Playing with the Phrase

Writing in his *Confessions*, Augustine described how many of his compatriots struggled with reading Aristotle's *Categories* even "after the most erudite teachers had not only given oral explanations but had drawn numerous diagrams in the dust."[66] We do not know what these tracings of Augustine's compatriots looked like, but the study of the categories continued to prompt visualisations throughout the Middle Ages. We have seen, with reference to the glossing tradition of the *Categoriae decem*, that the Isidorean phrase was presented in quasi-tabular fashion or as a list in certain contexts, deconstructing its components, thereby facilitating recollection and perhaps inviting extrapolation. It could also be rendered into diagrammatic form, as two manuscripts, now Göttweig, Benediktinerstift, Cod. 33 (rot)/14 (schwarz) and Göttweig, Benediktinerstift, Cod. 53b (rot) illustrate.[67]

The first of these manuscripts, Cod. 33/14, contains a twelfth-century list of books that a certain "Frater Heinricus" gave to an unidentified "*ecclesia*" (with Lambach, Göttweig, and Prüfening suggested as destinations of the "*donatio*"), a time-capsule of titles which were accessible to this particular scholar.[68] A single parchment leaf has been bound into this manuscript, originally adjacent to the booklist.[69] Smaller in size than the other leaves of the manuscript, and seemingly cut from an inferior section of parchment, this leaf contains a number of diagrams, attesting to the presence and use of such devices in twelfth-century contexts of learning.[70] These include a Porphyrian tree (perhaps echoing contemporary interests in universals), and a hierarchically structured diagram of Porphyry's five predicates on the verso. On the recto, we find a circular diagram, subdivided into sections and

Creativity in Classification

accompanied by alphabetic notation, attributing musical octaves to voices of various ages, along with a scheme outlining the categories (on which more anon). Although blind ruling is visible on the leaf, suggesting that it was prepared to receive text, its inferior parchment and heterogeneous content may suggest that it was a "crib-sheet" or ephemeral note, perhaps never intended to be preserved in this context (the manuscript contains unrelated works of Augustine, Jerome, and Claudianus Mamertus on the soul).[71]

Interest in this particular cluster of diagrams is attested by their inclusion in yet another manuscript, Göttweig, Benediktinerstift, Cod. 53b. The manuscript, which was probably produced at Göttweig in the early twelfth century, has a later Lambach provenance and contains an incomplete copy of the *Consuetudines Fructuarienses*, the customary of the eleventh-century Fruttuarian reform movement.[72] Towards the end of the manuscript, a hand active in copying the principal text left an uninscribed opening (fols 83v–84r) at the conclusion of the customary, before copying a further short text (fols 84v–85v), and leaving an additional blank sheet at its conclusion (the last of a six-leaf quire completing the manuscript). Later in the twelfth century, these blank spaces were filled in in at least two scribal campaigns, with one hand adding Marian texts (on fols 85v, 86v), and another supplying a diagram series on fols 83v–84r, 86r.[73] The scribes used the formerly empty parchment spaces within this book in an inventive way; although these logical and musical schemata have no relationship to the *Consuetudines*, parchment was clearly a valued resource and the bounds of a codex provided a seemingly secure space to store short texts and notations. Evidence of the continued consultation of this codex for logical study is provided by the work of another twelfth-century hand who, writing in a darker ink, squeezed a "square of opposition," a common logical diagram, into the corner of fol. 83v, alongside the diagram of the categories.

The two sets of diagrams in Cod. 33/14 and Cod. 53b are not wholly identical, a fact that raises questions about their relationship.[74] It is possible that they were derived from a common, perhaps ephemeral, resource, or even from an oral teaching tradition. In any case, the clustering of visual devices in these manuscripts implies both an appetite for a diagrammatic mode of learning and a common approach underlying their compilation. A closer examination of the diagrammatic representation of the categories found in both manuscripts illuminates its potential pedagogic appeal.[75] At its heart is a square containing lines in a cruciform arrangement. Both squares contain the letters *DEUS* (God) at the terminals or centre-point of the cruciform lines; in Cod. 53b, further radial lines are added with the letters *HOMO* (man) at their ends, while in Cod. 33/14, the letters *HOMO* are arranged at the corners of the square, linked by a free-form sketched frame (Figs. 13.2 and 13.3). In both manuscripts, the ten categories are listed around the square; in Cod. 53b, they are placed around its bounds, while in Cod. 33/14, they are presented in circular nodes, radiating from the edges of the square. The implication (or perhaps invitation to debate) of the schematic formulation is clear: the categories, placed outside the bounds of the square, represent the perceptible reality of being, while simultaneously referring inwards to "man" as both an example of substance and the observer of the perceptible world, and to God as the creator of all things, independent of and yet intrinsic to that world.

In Cod. 53b, each category is accompanied by the words of the Isidorean phrase, with the elements deconstructed and placed alongside their relevant category. In Cod. 33/14, however, the elements have been drastically modified to read: "*Hector magnus pugnator filius priami steti in campo heri armatus pugnans occiditur*": "Hector, a great man, a fighter, the son of Priam, who stood armed in the battlefield yesterday, was killed while fighting."

225

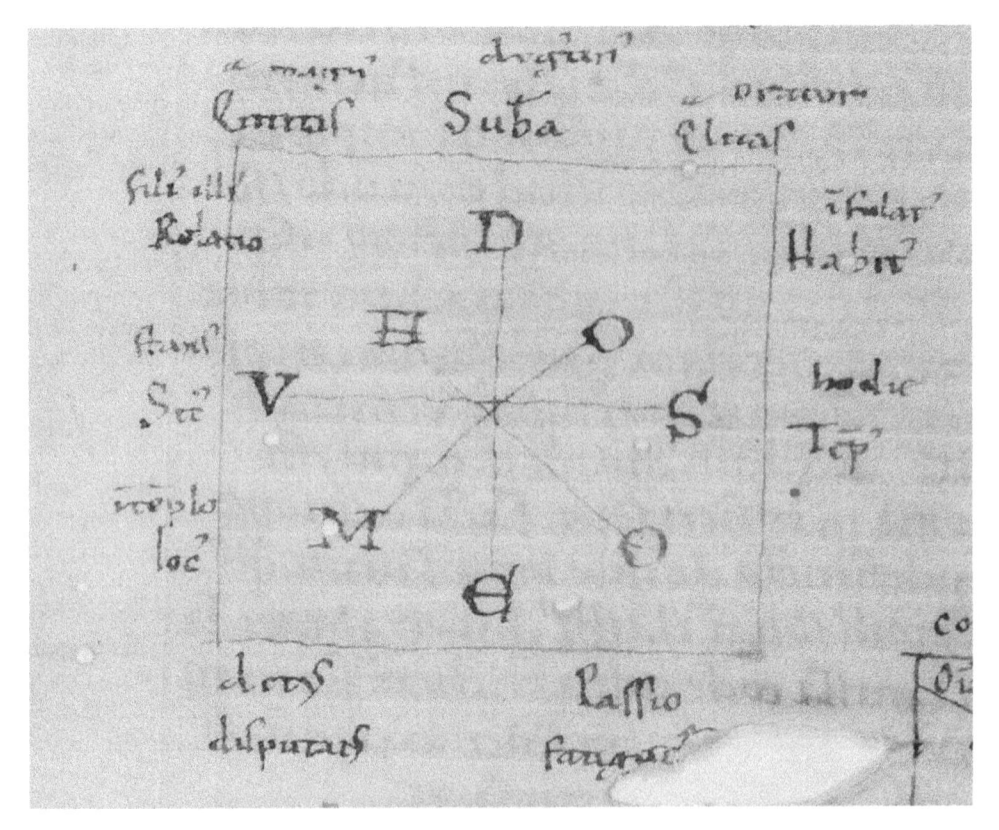

Figure 13.2 Detail of Göttweig, Benediktinerstift, Cod. 53b, fol. 83v. A diagram of the categories, surrounded by the words of the Isidorean phrase, with the words *Deus*, "God," and *Homo*, "Man" presented across its central axes.

Source: https://manuscripta.at/diglit/AT2000-53b/0168. Copyright: Göttweig, Benediktinerstift.

The transposition of the Isidorean phrase is striking: Hector, the hero of Troy, is the subject, not Augustine the patristic father; the context is pagan, not religious; and the tense has shifted from present to past. A link may be drawn here with the content of "Frater Heinricus'" booklist, which referred to two rolls, one including a representation of the seven liberal arts, another with scenes of the Trojan War.[76] Although we cannot be sure when this parchment leaf was bound into Cod. 33/14, both this diagram and the booklist suggest an interest in visual pedagogic devices, along with a contemporary curiosity about the epic tradition.

The repurposing of the Isidorean phrase to refer to a classical rather than a patristic context invites speculation regarding the pedagogic potential of this diagram. As we have seen, Isidore's words could be augmented or clarified (with Augustine alternately teacher or preacher, identified as the son of Monica, teaching in the church, not the temple), with the elements of the phrase changing to appeal to a particular readership. Its extension here to a classical context (Hector rather than Augustine) does not affect the principal function of the phrase, namely its capacity to connote the categories. The form of the diagram, however,

Creativity in Classification

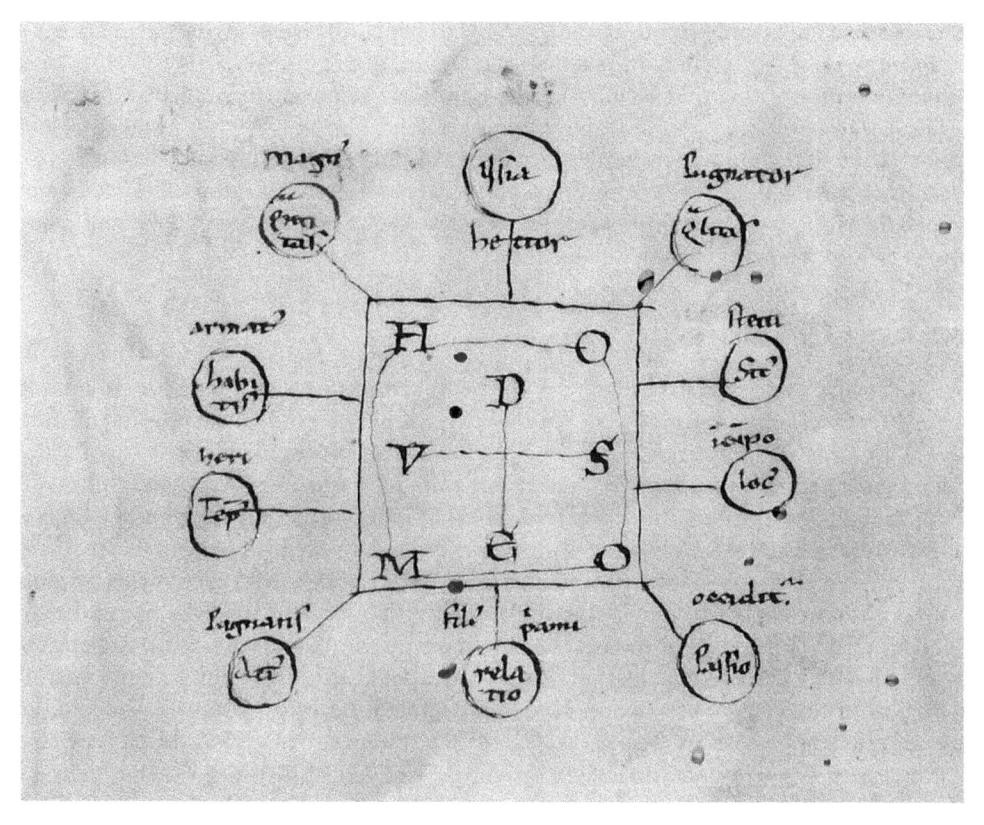

Figure 13.3 Detail of Göttweig, Benediktinerstift, Cod. 33 (rot)/14 (schwarz), fol. III*r. A diagram of the categories with the words of the Isidorean phrase adapted to refer to Hector, not Augustine.

Source: https://manuscripta.at/diglit/AT2000-33/0303. Copyright: Göttweig, Benediktinerstift.

may have enhanced not only recollection, but also the extrapolative quality of the phrase, its capacity to generate information. Substance (here Augustine or Hector) is placed at the north-point of its imagined radial compass but it is flanked by *qualitas* (quality) and *quantitas* (quantity), interrupting the natural reading order of the phrase. Here its deconstruction is complete, with manipulation of the phrase taking on an almost ludic quality. Pedagogic play of the type we seem to see in action here may have reinforced learning and memorisation, but could also prompt invention.

A parallel to the classicising reworking of the phrase in Göttweig, Cod. 33/14 is found in a much later collection of the humanist Marsilio Ficino (1433–1499 CE), now Florence, Bibliotheca Moreniana, Cod. Palagi 199. As recorded by Paul Oskar Kristeller, the manuscript contains at its opening "a table of Aristotelian categories, then a short encomium of Aristotle and a few memorial verses and logical examples."[77] The so-called encomium reads, *Aristoteles magne scientie Platonis discipulus disputando fatigatus hodie in scolis sedet coronatus*. ["Aristotle, [man] of great knowledge, student of Plato, worn out from disputation, today, sits in schools, adorned with a crown."][78] As Anna Corrias has established,

227

"this sentence looks more like a logical example in which the list of Aristotelian categories is applied to linguistic expression" than an encomium, noting its similarity to the Isidorean tradition and suggesting that Ficino "rephrased it [the Augustine example] by adapting it to the character of Aristotle."[79] In fact, we could read this as a further instance of ludic manipulation of the phrase: inspired by Aristotle, Isidore's phrase is repurposed to *apply* to Aristotle, perhaps in an (even ironic?) acknowledgement by Ficino of its ultimate source. Despite the reductive nature of the sentence, it continued to offer potential for experimentation, even into the period of the Renaissance.

Conclusion

As the examples surveyed here illustrate, the Isidorean phrase had a long life. In a period where direct access to Aristotle's texts was limited, the phrase offered a handy and memorable way to facilitate memorisation of the Aristotelian categories, the ultimate classificatory system, which could potentially be used to organise all words, concepts, and things. The phrase's simplicity eased its transition into multiple contexts, perhaps belying the inherent complexity of categorical classification, which remained a vexed subject in medieval ontological debates about the nature of God and being. The phrase itself functioned in multiple ways as an information device. It stored information about the categories, permitting retrieval from one's memory of their terms. Its frequent paratextual presentation permitted (cross-)reference, and even navigation. It could also serve as a proxy for a more expansive discussion of the categories (as apparent in its integration into grammatical texts), and through implicit allusion suggest knowledge of the tradition of Greek learning writ large, even in a period where such learning was limited. The text of the phrase could be broken down and recombined, with graphic features added to enhance its message, facilitating recollection and perhaps opening up the possibility of extrapolation or the production of information. This tendency seems to come to fruition in its visual expression in diagrammatic form, along with an associated variant, in the Göttweig examples, where the simplicity of the mnemonic permits pedagogic play and reworkings. Although only twelve words long, its varied presentations show the potential this simple phrase held as a tool of information storage, retrieval, and even generation. Intended as an explanatory mnemonic for accessing Aristotle's classifications of being, the phrase in fact became a tool for generating new understandings of these classifications.

Notes

1 Isidore of Seville, *The Etymologies of Isidore of Seville*, trans. Stephen A. Barney et al. (Cambridge, UK: Cambridge University Press, 2009), Book II.xxvi.11, 82; Isidore, *Isidori Hispalensis Episcopi Etymologiarum Sive Originvm Libri XX*, ed. W. M. Lindsay, vol. 1 (Oxford: Oxford University Press, 1911), Book II.xxvi,11: *Augustinus, Magnus Orator, Filius Illius, Stans in Templo, Hodie, Infulatus, Disputando Fatigatur*. The infula, according to the Oxford English Dictionary, was a woollen headband worn by a priest, also known as a "fillet."
2 By referring to "information management" here, I acknowledge the inspiration of Ann Blair's concept of "the 4 S's of text management": "storing, sorting, selecting, and summarising." See Ann Blair, *Too Much to Know: Managing Scholarly Information Before the Modern Age* (New Haven, CT: Yale University Press, 2010), 3.
3 Aristotle, *Categories and De Interpretatione*, trans. J. L. Ackrill (Oxford: Oxford University Press, 1975), 1b25, 5.

4 Michael Griffin, *Aristotle's Categories in the Early Roman Empire* (Oxford: Oxford University Press, 2015), 10.
5 Amie Thomasson, "Categories," *The Stanford Encyclopedia of Philosophy*, ed. Edward N. Zalta and Uri Nodelman (Winter 2022 Edition), https://plato.stanford.edu/archives/win2022/entries/categories/.
6 On the translations, see John Marenbon, *From the Circle of Alcuin to the School of Auxerre* (Cambridge, UK: Cambridge University Press, 1981), 16–17. See also Marenbon, "The Tradition of Studying the Categories in the Early Middle Ages (until c. 1200): A Revised Working Catalogue of Glosses, Commentaries and Treatises," in *Aristotle's Categories in the Byzantine, Arabic and Latin Traditions. Scientia Danica: Series H, Humanistica 8*, vol. 5, ed. Sten Ebbesen, John Marenbon, and Paul Thom (Copenhagen: The Royal Danish Academy of Sciences and Letters 2013), 139–173, esp. 152–153 for considerations of the authorship of the *Categoriae decem*.
7 Bernard G. Dod, "Aristoteles Latinus," in *The Cambridge History of Later Medieval Philosophy: From the Rediscovery of Aristotle to the Disintegration of Scholasticism, 1000–1600*, ed. Norman Kretzmann, Anthony Kenny, Jan Pinborg, and Eleonore Stump (Cambridge, UK: Cambridge University Press, 1982), 43–79, 64, 74. William of Moerbeke translated the *Categories* again in 1266, along with Simplicius's sixth-century commentary on the text.
8 Rosamond McKitterick, *The Frankish Kingdoms under the Carolingians, 751–987* (London: Routledge, 1983), 287. For example, see Marenbon, *From the Circle*, 72–73.
9 Aristotle, *Categories and De Interpretatione*, 1b25–2a1.
10 Isidore, *Etymologies*, 24–26.
11 Isidore, *Etymologies*, Book II.xxii.1, 79.
12 Isidore, *Etymologies*, Book II.xxvi.10–11, 82.
13 Marenbon notes that in the glossing tradition on *Categoriae decem*, "little capital is made of the great Father's supposed authorship." See Marenbon, *From the Circle*, 17.
14 Alcuin, "De Dialectica," in *Patrologia Latina*, vol. 101, ed. J. P. Migne (Paris, 1863).
15 John Marenbon, *Medieval Philosophy: A Historical and Philosophical Introduction* (London: Routledge, 2007), 71.
16 Eva Rädler-Bohn, "Re-Dating Alcuin's De Dialectica," *Anglo-Saxon England* 45 (2017): 81–83. Anna Dorofeeva, trans., *Reading Nature in the Early Middle Ages: Writing, Language and Creation in the Latin Physiologus, ca. 700–1000* (Leeds: Arc Humanities Press, 2023), 28.
17 Alcuin, "De Dialectica," 0962 C-D.: *K. Ex his omnibus decem praedicamentis unam mihi coniunge orationem. A. Plena enim oratio de his ita coniungi potest*: "Augustinus magnus orator, filius illius, stans in templo hodie infulatus disputando fatigatur."
18 McKitterick, *Frankish Kingdoms*, 288. For its use by scholars such as Heiric of Auxerre and Ratramnus of Corbie, see Marenbon, *From the Circle*, 16–17, 67–87.
19 Laon, BM, Suzanne Martinet, MS 444, https://gallica.bnf.fr/ark:/12148/btv1b84921401. John Contreni, "The Irish 'Colony' at Laon during the Time of John Scottus," in *Jean Scot Erigène et l'histoire de la philosophie, Laon 7–12 juillet 1975*, ed. René Roques (Paris: CNRS, 1977), 59–67, esp. 63–66. On its Greek content, see A. C. Dionisotti, "Greek Grammars and Dictionaries in Carolingian Europe," in *The Sacred Nectar of the Greeks: The Study of Greek in the West in the Early Middle Ages*, ed. Michael Herren and Shirley Ann Brown (London: University of London, King's College, 1988), 1–56, 45–54.
20 Laon, BM, Suzanne Martinet, MS 444, fol. 289v, https://gallica.bnf.fr/ark:/12148/btv1b84921401/f583.item.
21 On scribal collaboration in the manuscript, see John Contreni, "The Formation of Laon's Cathedral Library in the Ninth Century," *Studi Medievali* 3, no. 13 (1972): 919–939.
22 Dionisotti, "Greek Grammars," 51.
23 Note that the note is also in the contents list of Laon, BM MS 444, fol. 1v, where it is described as *Item decem predicamenta quibus constat universitas*.
24 Laon, BM Suzanne Martinet, MS 468, https://gallica.bnf.fr/ark:/12148/btv1b8492139c.
25 John Contreni, "John Scottus, Martin Hiberniensis, the Liberal Arts and Teaching," in *Insular Latin Studies: Papers on Latin Texts and Manuscripts of the British Isles, 550–1066*, ed. Michael Herren (Toronto: Pontifical Institute of Medieval Studies, 1981), 23–44, esp. 13–22.
26 Contreni, "John Scottus," 14, 20.

27 Laon, BM Suzanne Martinet, MS 468, fol. 10v, https://gallica.bnf.fr/ark:/12148/btv1b8492139c/f26.item.
28 Contreni, "John Scottus," 20.
29 Marenbon, *From the Circle*, 175. See 173–206 for a study of some of these glossed manuscripts.
30 Marenbon, "The Tradition," 142.
31 See Édouard Jeauneau, "Pour le dossier d'Israël Scot," *Archives d'histoire doctrinale et littéraire du Moyen Age* 52 (1985): 7–72, esp. 71 for a further example of the use of the sentence in a gloss to the *Categoriae decem* in a manuscript now in St Petersburg, which I have been unable to consult.
32 Paris, Bibliothèque nationale de France [BnF], MS lat. 12949, https://gallica.bnf.fr/ark:/12148/btv1b10542356v. Marenbon, *From the Circle*, 176–177. See also Veronika Von Büren, "Auxerre, lieu de production de manuscrits?," in *Études d'exégèse carolingienne: autour d'Haymon d'Auxerre*, ed. Sumi Shimahara (Turnhout: Brepols, 2007), 167–186, esp. 174–175; and Irene van Renswoude, "Paris, BnF, lat. 12949," *The Art of Reasoning in Medieval Manuscripts* (December 2020), https://art-of-reasoning.huygens.knaw.nl/lat12949.
33 Paris, Bibliothèque nationale de France [BnF], lat. MS 12949, fol. 27bis r, https://gallica.bnf.fr/ark:/12148/btv1b10542356v/f75.item. The scheme is also present in Munich, BSB, Clm 6367, see Jeauneau, "Pour le dossier d'Israël Scot," 71.
34 Munich, BSB, Clm 6367, fol. 6r, https://www.digitale-sammlungen.de/en/view/bsb00115089?page=15.
35 Orléans, BM, MS 263, https://mediatheques.orleans.fr/recherche/viewnotice/id/746903.
36 Jeauneau, "Pour le dossier d'Israël Scot," 71.
37 Rosamond McKitterick, *The Carolingians and the Written Word* (Cambridge, UK: Cambridge University Press, 1989), 182–183.
38 St Gallen, SB, Cod. Sang. 397, https://www.e-codices.unifr.ch/en/list/one/csg/0397. Uwe Grupp, "Der Codex Sangallensis 397 - Ein Persönliches Handbuch Grimalds von St. Gallen?" *Deutsches Archiv für Erforschung des Mittelalters* 70 (2014): 425–463; and Bernhard Bischoff, "Bücher am Hofe Ludwigs des Deutschen und die Privatbibliothek des Kanzlers Grimalt," in *Mittelalterliche Studien. Ausgewählte Aufsätze zur Schriftkunde und Literaturgeschichte*, vol. 3 (Stuttgart: Hiersemann, 1981), 187–212.
39 Grupp, "Der Codex Sangallensis 397," 453–463.
40 St Gallen, SB, Cod. Sang. 397, 37–52.
41 St Gallen, SB, Cod. Sang. 397, 37.
42 Christophe Erismann, "The Medieval Fortunes of the Opuscula Sacra," in *The Cambridge Companion to Boethius*, ed. John Marenbon (Cambridge, UK: Cambridge University Press, 2009), 155–178, 164–165.
43 Trans. in Erismann, "The Medieval Fortunes," 165.
44 St Gallen, SB, Cod. Sang. 397, 38.
45 Bernice M. Kaczynski, "Some St. Gall Glosses on Greek Philanthropic Nomenclature," *Speculum* 58 (1983): 1008–1017.
46 St Gallen, SB, Cod. Sang. 397, p. 38, https://www.e-codices.unifr.ch/en/csg/0397/38. Isidore, trans., *Etymologies*, Book II.xxix.1 84.
47 St Gallen SB, Cod. Sang. 899. https://www.e-codices.unifr.ch/en/list/one/csg/0899. Note that its leaves are now disordered, but the leaf containing the Isidorean phrase (59–60) was originally part of a (now incomplete) section of the manuscript (103–108, 59–64) that also contained the Boethian definitions of essence, substance, etc. (107). See Franz Dolveck, "Le Manuscrit Saint-Gall 899: réintégration des feuillets épars et essai de restitution," *Bibliothèque de l'Ecole des chartes* 174 (2018–2019 [2020]): 297–313.
48 St Gallen SB, Cod. Sang. 899, 59, https://www.e-codices.unifr.ch/en/csg/0899/59.
49 Munich, BSB, Clm 19413, https://www.digitale-sammlungen.de/en/details/bsb00105014. As Till Hennings notes, Notker's *Compendium* was "augmented" in this manuscript "by small texts found in Saint Gall at this time," with Cod. Sang. 397 serving as one of the antigraphs of its various "text ensembles." See Hennings, "Notker the Stammerer's Compendium for His Pupils," in *Education Materialised: Reconstructing Teaching and Learning Contexts through Manuscripts*,

ed. Stefanie Brinkmann, Giovanni Ciotti, and Stefano Valente (Berlin: De Gruyter, 2021), 34–47, 39.
50 Munich, BSB, Clm 19413, fol. 118v, https://www.digitale-sammlungen.de/en/view/bsb00105014?page=240.
51 Anna S. Grotans, *Reading in Medieval St. Gall* (Cambridge, UK: Cambridge University Press, 2006); and L. M. De Rijk, "On the Curriculum of the Arts of the Trivium at St. Gall from c. 850-c. 1000," *Vivarium* 4 (1966): 1–57.
52 Vivien Law, "Carolingian Grammarians and Theoretical Innovation," in *Diversions of Galway: Papers on the History of Linguistics from ICHoLS V, Galway, Ireland, 1–6 September 1990*, ed. Anders Ahlqvist (Amsterdam: John Benjamins, 1992), 27–37, 34. *Distributio Omnium Specierum* is edited in Notker, *Notker latinus zu den kleineren Schriften*, ed. James C. King and Petrus W. Tax, *Die Werke Notkers des Deutschen* 7 (Tübingen: Max Niemeyer Verlag, 1996), 3–45.
53 Grotans, *Reading*, 86; and Law, "Carolingian Grammarians," 33–34.
54 Notker, *Notker* (1996), 3, 16–19: *ut in illo uersu apparet. quem priores nostri. ad agnoscenda decem pr[a]edicamenta. exemplum dederunt. Augustinus magnus pr[a]edicator filius munic[a]e stans in templo hodie. infulatus disputando fatigatur.*
55 Notker, *Notker latinus zu den kleineren Schriften*, ed. James C. King and Petrus W. Tax, *Die Werke Notkers des Deutschen* 7A (Tübingen: Max Niemeyer Verlag, 2003), 5–6. Here King and Tax suggest that Notker referred to Augustine as "preacher" on account of his acquaintance with the *Enarrationes in Psalmos*.
56 Notker, *Notker* (1996), 3, 16–17.
57 Anneli Luhtala, "Syntax and Dialectic in Carolingian Commentaries on Priscian's *Institutiones Grammaticae*," in *History of Linguistic Thought in the Early Middle Ages*, ed. Vivien Law (Amsterdam: John Benjamins, 1993), 145–192, esp. 150–151. See McKitterick, *Frankish Kingdoms*, 287: "It [the categories] was a way of discussing being which gave prominence to the relationship between things, other things and their properties, and in which the function of particular words within a sentence assumed great importance."
58 Sedulius Scottus, *In Donati Artem maiorem*, ed. Bengt Löfstedt (Turnhout: Brepols, 1977) (*CCCM*, 40 B), 62, 50–61: *Verbi gratia:* "*Augustinus magnus orator, filius Monicae, stans hodie in templo infulatus disputando fatigatur*"; "*Augustinus*" *substantia,* "*magnus*" *quantitas,* "*orator*" *qualitas,* "*filius Monicae*" *ad aliquid, id est ad matrem,* "*stans*" *situs,* "*hodie*" *tempus,* "*in templo*" *locus,* "*infulatus*" *habitus,* "*disputando*" *agere,* "*fatigatur*" *pati*. See Luhtala, "Syntax and Dialectic," 150.
59 Elke Krotz, "Remigius von Auxerre und die *Ars Prisciani*," *Archivum Latinitatis Medii Aevi* 72 (2014): 21–82, esp. 40–41.
60 Luhtala, "Syntax and Dialectic," 151.
61 Munich, BSB, Clm 18375, https://www.digitale-sammlungen.de/en/view/bsb00045761?page=,1. Grotans, *Reading*, 87.
62 Quoted in Grotans, *Reading*, 87. Note that the gloss is found on fol. 10v, not 11v, as cited in Grotans.
63 Munich, BSB, Clm 18375, fol. 10v, https://www.digitale-sammlungen.de/en/view/bsb00045761?page=26.
64 John of Salisbury, *The Metalogicon of John of Salisbury*, trans. Daniel D. McGarry (Berkeley; Los Angeles, CA: University of California Press, 1955), Book III.3, 160–161. See John of Salisbury, *Metalogicon*, ed. J. B. Hall and K. S. B. Keats-Rohan (Turnhout: Brepols, 1991), Book III.3, 112: *Isidorus, Alcuinus, et quidam alii sapientum, omnia alia de primis substantiis, asserunt praedicari, et sententiam plenissimam decem praedicamentorum absolutione perficiunt, ut in hoc eorum patet exemplo. Augustinus magnus orator filius illius stans in templo hodie infulatus disputando fatigatur. Perfecta enim sententia est et subiecti, id est illius de quo agitur substantiam, qualitatem, et quantitatem, cum ceteris indicat, et si forte minus proprium dederit quantitatis exemplum.*
65 For a general introduction, see Gyula Klima, "The Medieval Problem of Universals," in *The Stanford Encyclopedia of Philosophy*, ed. Edward N. Zalta (Spring 2022 Edition), https://plato.stanford.edu/archives/spr2022/entries/universals-medieval/.
66 Augustine, *Confessions*, trans. Henry Chadwick (Oxford: Oxford University Press, 2008), IV.XVI.28, 69.
67 Göttweig, Benediktinerstift, Cod. 33, https://manuscripta.at/diglit/AT2000-33/0001; Göttweig, Benediktinerstift, Cod. 53b, https://manuscripta.at/diglit/AT2000-53b/0001.

68 Göttweig, Benediktinerstift, Cod. 33, fol. 148v. For a summary of discussion on its provenance, see Nikolaus Czifra, "Die Bibliothek des Benediktinerstiftes Göttweig - Aspekte der Bestandsgeschichte," in *Vom Schreiben und Sammeln: Einblicke in die Göttweiger Bibliotheksgeschichte*, ed. Astrid Breith (St. Pölten: NÖ Institut für Landeskunde, 2021), 13–62, 14–18.

69 Göttweig, Benediktinerstift, Cod. 33, fol. III. This folio was originally bound adjacent to the booklist, but the two items are now separated by an eighteenth-century transcription of the booklist. See codicological description, https://manuscripta.at/hs_detail.php?ID=36485.

70 For examples of visual devices from the logical and rhetorical traditions, see various entries by Irene O'Daly, in *The Art of Reasoning in Medieval Manuscripts* (December 2020), notably: "Diagrams in the Rhetorical Tradition," https://art-of-reasoning.huygens.knaw.nl/schemes.html; "Squares and Trees," https://art-of-reasoning.huygens.knaw.nl/trees.html; and "Reasoning through Syllogisms," https://art-of-reasoning.huygens.knaw.nl/syllogism.html.

71 For a comparable "crib sheet" in Leiden, Universiteitsbibliotheek, BPL 88, see O'Daly, "Reasoning through Syllogisms," *The Art of Reasoning*, https://art-of-reasoning.huygens.knaw.nl/syllogism.html.

72 On its provenance and contents, see Benjamin Pohl, "Two Downside Manuscripts and the Liturgical Culture of Lambach in the 12th Century," *The Downside Review* 136, no. 1 (January 2018): 41–79, esp. 65–66; and Lisa Fagin Davis, *The Gottschalk Antiphonary: Music and Liturgy at Twelfth-Century Lambach* (Cambridge, UK: Cambridge University Press, 2000), 12.

73 Given their distribution, it is likely that the addition of the schematic series preceded the addition of the Marian texts, which appear to be written in two distinct hands.

74 Göttweig, Benediktinerstift, Cod. 59b, fol. 83v contains the diagram of octaves, with its accompanying note found on fol. 84r. Fol. 83v contains the scheme of the categories, along with that of the five predicables. The Porphyrian tree is found on fol. 86r, although note that the examples of "*homo*" used here (Cato, Plato, Cicero) are different from those found in Cod. 33/14. Cod. 59b also includes a Guidonian hand (a device used in singing for memorising and teaching notes) on fol. 84r.

75 See Göttweig, Benediktinerstift, Cod. 33/14, fol. III*r, https://manuscripta.at/diglit/AT2000-33/0303; Göttweig, Benediktinerstift, Cod. 53b, fol. 83v, https://manuscripta.at/diglit/AT2000-53b/0168.

76 Göttweig, Benediktinerstift, Cod. 33/14, fol. 148v: *Rodale in quo vii liberales artes depicte. Item rodale in quo Troianum bellum depictum.*

77 Paul Oskar Kristeller, "The Scholastic Background of Marsilio Ficino with an Edition of Unpublished Texts," *Traditio* 2 (1944): 257–318, esp. 264.

78 Kristeller, "The Scholastic Background," 274; Anna Corrias, trans., *The Renaissance of Plotinus: The Soul and Human Nature in Marsilio Ficino's Commentary on the Enneads* (London: Routledge, 2020), 55.

79 Corrias, *The Renaissance of Plotinus*, 55.

14

TRADING FACTORIES AS INFORMATION FACTORIES

Aspects of Information Management in the Dutch East India Company's Japanese Factory, 1609–1623

Gabor Szommer

Introduction

It is a commonplace that the complex nature of commerce requires sophisticated information use. This was no different in the early seventeenth-century European trade conducted by trading companies in maritime Asia, although these ventures certainly had their own specifics. An important organisational unit of this trade was the factory or trading outpost (compound), located in significant commercial hubs of the region. The companies left behind agents who bought and sold products, and provided the return cargo for ships destined for home. These agents, however, did not only conduct trade. The factories were also the most important information gateways of the companies to the outside world. Their personnel played a vital role in managing information and were active in each segment of information cycles: they gathered information, interpreted and reflected on it, used it for actions, generated feedback regarding it, created copies of it in various formats, and disseminated data both within the company and to/from the outside world. Furthermore, the factors (agents employed by the Company undertaking transactions for the business) collected not only commercial information, but also, for instance, cultural, geographical, and scientific knowledge. Such "other" types could also play a fundamental role in trade. These information actions were an absolute necessity for success, and many of them will be examined below, in the context of the Dutch East India Company—officially Vereenigde Oost-Indische Compagnie or United East India Company; hereinafter VOC—established in 1602 as one of the world's first joint-stock companies, with an initial monopoly of trade for a period lasting twenty-one years.[1]

The aforementioned copying of documents offers an important insight into the information-related aspects of trading companies' operations. Company agents noted down information in a wide spectrum of document types.[2] Many will be referenced below. Not surprisingly, the bulk of documents created in Asia were letters written by merchants. Diaries, both private and official, were also kept by many VOC employees. Unfortunately, they are not particularly useful for Japanese matters in these early years as the official journal (*dagh-register*) kept by the head of Japanese factory is available only from 1633, and just fragments of the Bantam/Batavia journals survived from the years covered. Another type of document that is often referenced below is the company's "minutes and resolutions." For reconstructing in-depth commercial details many non-narrative sources are—and for the VOC merchants were—useful. Lists may be considered as the most popular genre. For this chapter, price lists and cargo lists are the most important types, but many lists, for instance, those of employees, soldiers, or ships were created in these years. The earliest price list for the Japanese factory of the VOC was assembled as early as 1610. Interestingly, it was soon acquired and translated by English East India Company officials, and it was probably used by the English when they decided on settling a factory in Japan in 1613. Furthermore, both factories and ships had their own trade journals (*journaal*) that recorded day-to-day transactions and general ledgers (*grootboek*). Besides, for each departing ship, a cargo list (*factura*) was composed. Finally, it should be noted that non-written information also played a huge role in these years, although sources rarely offer direct insight into this type of communication. Regarding oral information, there are only a few direct references—for instance, to interviews. It is safe to assume that extensive conciliations preceded the making of resolutions, but little evidence is available regarding this. Finally, sending merchants to potential partner regions to examine circumstances there and circulate samples of products to survey commercial opportunities were both used extensively.[3]

The general scope of this chapter is information management, which has a long premodern history that is often considered to be marginal.[4] The major aim of the chapter, therefore, is to help remedy this oversight through an examination of a number of related topics in a specific case: that of the history of the early years of the VOC's settlement in Japan.[5] The main emphasis will be on the actors, and this requires a micro-level approach.[6] This level of granularity is useful because it allows for unearthing many specific particulars. An insight into the minute details of the everyday work of the merchants in the field shows perfectly how they contributed to the information-management routines of their organisation. The strict limitation of the chosen time frame is also important. The chapter examines the formative years of the factory, when virtually no prior information was available regarding the country or the trade there. The VOC merchants had to create an information pool almost from scratch as no previous patterns and practices were available; thus, the years in focus were a period of experimentation and constant change. Accordingly, the most important question posed in this chapter is: How did the company adapt to the unexpected challenges arising from its environment?

Adaptation will be examined through three interlinked supplementary examples. Each relates to a different segment of Japanese VOC trade. They illustrate, respectively, the early optimisation of decision-making and finding the proper organisation level for it; the adjustment of regional VOC trade to the monsoon wind system; and surveying markets and finding the best one for the most important Japanese export commodity, silver. The three cases, in various ways, all relate to information. They have similarities, the most significant being that difficulties in question were completely unexpected, and accordingly, no prior preparations were made. In each case, gathering new information helped in finding a solution, but often this alone was not enough: proper evaluation and setting this new information within the specific context were also necessary. Extensive communication was also a must. The parties not only shared basic data with each other, but also made their perspectives explicit or circulated their related calculations. This constant dialogue contributed a great deal to finding a correct solution.

Nonetheless, the three cases have significant differences, the most important being the nature of the challenge. In the first example, the difficulty originated from the organisational structure of the company, which allowed more room for manoeuvre for the interested actors. In the second, although the organisational structure made finding a solution difficult, the dilemma related to the outside physical environment, a fixed condition. Finally, in the third example, the commercial and social environment posed a problem, and in this case the VOC had some, albeit seriously limited, influence upon the events. The difference in the character of the challenges required different adaptative strategies, the examination of which is an important goal of this chapter. Finally, some answers chosen by the actors sometimes had unexpected results, and could even unearth new problems. One of these is described below, namely an emerging disagreement and uncertainty regarding accounting practices, which will be useful because it highlights how different challenges intertwined to become a complex information environment.

The Early History of the VOC in the Far East

At the turn of the sixteenth and seventeenth centuries, the Low Countries, deeply involved in a war of independence against Spain, made serious efforts to participate in Asian trade.[7] The first smaller companies were merged into the VOC, in 1602. Its charter granted the new company a monopoly of Dutch trade in Asia, and altogether made it an important tool for extending the war against Spain and Portugal into Asia. Indeed, the VOC acted as both a commercial and a military agent. It conducted intensive, albeit somewhat chaotic and basically fruitless, attacks on Spanish and Portuguese ships and settlements. At the same time, it established several trading posts in Asia, including its centre of operations in Asia (in the early years in Bantam; this central compound was later relocated to Batavia, today Jacarta) and a number of smaller factories, including those at Patani and Ayutthaya, in present-day Thailand, and in Japan (Map 14.1).

The first Dutch ship that reached Japan was not a ship of the VOC. It was the *Liefde*, a vessel of a Dutch predecessor company, which was shipwrecked there in 1600.[8] Although this could have been a valuable opportunity, the Dutch were not able to exploit it because no survivor was allowed to leave the country for years. Thus, the Dutchmen in Japan could not accumulate much information about the regional trade in the South China Sea, and what little was gathered could not be communicated effectively to the outside world. At the same time, the VOC tapped into other sources. As early as 1603, one of its merchants in Patani gathered some information from Japanese merchants about trade opportunities in Japan. His letter may be the earliest extant VOC record about Japanese trade, but the details in it were vague.[9] Finally, in 1605, the captain of the *Liefde*, Jacob Quaeckernaeck, and a merchant, Melchior van Santvoort, were allowed to travel to Patani. The latter started a private trading career and made several trips between the two regions in subsequent years. Despite these early developments, information regarding Japan trickled only very slowly into the VOC pool.

Japanese foreign commerce saw an expansion in the second half of the sixteenth century.[10] Japanese diasporas were settled in several cities of the region—for example, Manila, Hoi An (often mentioned as Quinam or Cochinchina in the VOC records), and Ayutthaya (often referred to as Siam)—and a solid regional trade network evolved, with Southern Kyushu as its Japanese centre. At the turn of the century, not only Japanese but also Chinese, Portuguese, and Spanish merchants were intricately involved in this trade. Although

Map 14.1 Map of the trading world around Japan at the start of the seventeenth century. Drawn by the author.

many products enabled high profits to be made in Japan, the most rewarding was the import of Chinese silk and silk products. However, the supply in the regions mentioned was limited, so finding a source with a more consistent output was necessary. Certainly, port towns of China would have been the best option, but the imperial court of China banned its subjects from trading directly with Japan, which created a perfect opportunity for middlemen. The Portuguese, based on their settlement in Macau, could exploit this situation, and from the second half of the sixteenth century carried huge amounts of silk to Japan. Another important feature of Japanese commerce was the steady silver output of the country. The exported silver had a ready market in China, allowing huge profits to be made. The Portuguese, who exported the silver they received as a payment, could not hide their success for long, and more and more reports disclosed various aspects of this venture. From a Dutch perspective, Lucas Janszoon Waghenaer's *Thresoor der Zeevaert* and Jan Huyghen van Linschoten's *Itinerario* were the most influential works, effectively communicating both general and specific (such as navigational) information.[11]

A presence in Japan would put pressure on the Portuguese and could allow the VOC a fair profit; thus, the company's arrival in the country was only a matter of time. The first two VOC ships in the country in 1609 settled a factory in the town of Hirado, and the VOC merchants were finally able to gather first-hand information about Japanese commerce.[12] The head of the factory, who is frequently mentioned below, was Jacques Specx. He left Japan in 1613, but his contract was renewed, and he returned in 1614 and stayed until 1621. In the short interval of Specx's absence, Hendrik Brouwer managed the factory. Another prominent person who had an impact on the Japanese trade of the VOC was Jan Pieterszoon Coen. He arrived in Bantam in 1613. In 1617, he was promoted to Governor-general, the highest-ranking official of the VOC in Asia, and acted in this capacity until 1622. His term saw the relocation of the VOC headquarters from Bantam to Batavia (today Jacarta) in 1619.

Overall, the first decade of the VOC trade in Japan was not particularly successful. The factory was seriously under-supported. Despite an adequate Dutch involvement in the regional trade, and fair loot obtained through piracy against Chinese and Portuguese vessels, the commercial numbers were not impressive.[13] In the 1610s, the Japanese VOC factory can be considered as much a logistics centre and a navy support base for the anti-Iberian War as a commercial depot. Dutch vessels were able to retreat there to finish necessary careening and repair works. A significant part of the export was provisions and military equipment, and many Japanese mercenaries also left the country on VOC vessels to serve under the Dutch flag. This situation started to change only in the early 1620s, when the role of the Hirado factory changed, as a result of several factors, and the outpost turned into a fundamental part of the Dutch intra-Asian commercial system.

Initial Decision-Making in Europe and the First Feedback of Information

The ships that settled the VOC factory in Japan left the country in October 1609. One proceeded home, arriving in the Netherlands on July 21, 1610. The enthusiastic managers immediately started to organise a new expedition to Japan. They were relatively optimistic because the first accounts judged Japanese commerce to be profitable and presented the country as a fair market for European products. This impression was gathered primarily via interviews with persons, who had first-hand knowledge about Japan. Their main source of information was Abraham van den Broeck. Given his former position as a chief merchant of the expedition visiting Japan and his having been one of the envoys to the shogunal court, he was no doubt the best-informed person around.[14] At the same time, decision-makers also tapped other information sources. VOC correspondence mentions that a "young man" who had lived long in Japan was interviewed by the Amsterdam chamber. Although the reference does not mention his name, it is safe to assume that he was a survivor of the *Liefde*, who left Japan on board a VOC vessel.[15]

Based on the above information, in late August, the primary management body of the VOC, the Heren Zeventien (HZ) judged that the Japanese trade was promising enough. The plan for the next Japanese voyage was developed quickly and was debated at the next meeting of the HZ.[16] This first strategy was of variable quality, but it already considered many details that were later regarded as important cornerstones of the VOC presence in Japan: the abundance of foodstuff, the steady supply of silver, and the possibility of vending European products. The end of this stage of decision-making, which took place entirely in Europe, is marked by the dispatch in December 1610 of a ship carrying products intended specifically for Japan. She finally reached Japan in August 1612 in good order.

The cargo disappointed the VOC factors in Japan, and the first feedback was not at all positive. Overall, the demand for European products was overestimated and selling the stock finally took several years.[17] The fundamental problem, which both Specx and Brouwer highlighted, was that the information used in Europe was inadequate:

> Unfortunately such an important cargo has come so badly sorted, thus it is to be feared that my Honourable Masters, for the time being, will not achieve the great results that they, based on some reports, hoped for. I find it strange that so much goods of one type was sent, based on the report of a person who attended the country only for a short while. More consideration should have been taken to examine the state and the commerce of such a wonderful country, not in such a hurry, as, in my opinion, it would require not 3 or 4 months, but even years to get properly informed.[18]

This European decision based on deficient information resulted in a further unexpected problem. Coen, at that time director in Bantam, alerted the European management in a letter sent home in early 1614 that the Asian factories did not have enough ready money, and the Bantam factory had problems with paying even the tolls for the pepper laded into the VOC ships.[19] The European managers were surprised, "because we had hoped that enough silver could have been sent there from Japan, therefore we sent only little ready money in the last year and before that," and finally had to make the necessary corrections.[20]

The arrival in Japan of the first cargo that was assembled in Europe and the feedback sent home mark the end of the first period of laying the information basis of the VOC trade in Japan. This period saw many changes that had a fundamental impact on later commerce. It became apparent that due to the length of time involved in communication, the involvement of the European headquarters in decision-making should be limited. In fact, it is interesting that the managers in the Netherlands confidently, without any hesitation, hoped to control this venture by themselves, but the ill-fated cargo showed that this was not a practice to be followed subsequently, and the decision-making structure adapted to this situation instinctively. Meanwhile, the factors in Japan spent years testing, extending, and updating initial information, and this new stock overwrote the initial data available via van den Broeck. By the end of 1614, the respective head merchants, Specx and Brouwer, became the new primary references, and the control of Japanese trade took place *in loco* and regionally. European managers subsequently provided Japan only with the products that the merchants in Asia requested, and, seeing the lack of profit, continuously suggested closing down the Japanese factory—a suggestion that was promptly ignored by Coen and the decision-makers in Bantam/Batavia.[21]

Information and the Shipping Schedules

Long before the products sent from Europe reached Japan, the VOC factories in the region started to coordinate their actions. This effort was completely independent of the European headquarters and resulted from the proactive attitude of the merchants of the regional factories, who did not wait for the instructions of their superiors, but gathered local information, shared it with each other, debated relevant details, and made their knowledge available for decisions (or made decisions themselves).

It soon turned out that the South China Sea region should be the primary direction for commerce, especially because several VOC factories had been settled there. Patani was considered as an evident partner. Ayutthaya (Siam) provided the best-quality deer skins, a product in high demand in Japan. A Dutch presence at Camboja was explicitly justified for Japanese trade, and attempts were also made in Quinam. Finally, Bantam, the Asian centre of the VOC, and the primary transshipment centre for products arriving from Europe, played a role in this trade framework. Altogether, Japan and the regions mentioned were considered as an interconnected structure, and, as such, this trade should have worked without issues.[22]

However, it soon emerged that adding new nodes to an existing factory network was not as simple as the merchants thought, but required many details to be adjusted and amended. It was evident that basic commercial data, most notably prices, supply and demand specifics, and details regarding products, should be gathered and shared regularly. Such information, often with detailed explanations, was regularly mentioned in the merchants' correspondence. Price lists were also circulated regularly, and the cargo manifests of ships also included the prices of products sent, and occasionally even explanatory notes regarding them. At the same time, other preconditions had received less attention until related difficulties surfaced. Two of these are examined below, namely organising ship movements and scanning regional markets in order to make the best of silver export.

Maritime traffic in the region was determined by monsoon winds, with southwestern winds blowing between May and September, and northeastern winds blowing between November and March.[23] The first VOC schemes considered Japanese trade an unproblematic round trip. A ship loaded with European products had to leave Bantam for Japan in early spring. On her way, she was to visit Patani and/or Siam, and load products vendible in Japan. If everything went smoothly, she arrived in Japan in early summer. During the winter monsoon, she left for Bantam, either directly or via Siam/Patani. The vessel could thus reach Bantam before the homeward-bound fleet left for Europe, and all necessary products could be transshipped. At the same time, the return cargo from Japan, mainly silver, would create the financial background for a new round trip.

Specx suggested a shipping plan along similar lines as early as November 1610, and he later elaborated this further. He proposed that products from Siam should be sent to Japan not directly, but via Patani. This required two vessels. A smaller one had to be used for round trips between Siam and Patani, departing from Siam around March. At the same time, a ship with cargo for Japan had to be dispatched from Bantam in April. Her first destination was Patani, where products received via the Siam "round trip" mentioned could be transshipped. According to Specx's calculations, there was not enough time to load the cargo in Siam, so using Patani as a transshipment station was a must. The ship could finally leave Patani for Japan around May.[24]

The merchants in Siam were not particularly enthusiastic about this framework. In their opinion, the very foundation of the scheme was shaky, as timing and shipping schedule obstacles compromised it, and they suggested direct traffic between Siam and Japan. They highlighted several details that made Specx's concept impossible to implement. Skins and hides could be bought only between August and October, and if they were sent via Patani, the time they spent in the ship's hold could easily deteriorate their quality. Furthermore, the hold of a Japanese junk was better ventilated than that of a Patanese junk (which was supposed to be used for the round trip), and thus there would be fewer worms to damage the skins. Besides, Japanese sailors, unlike "foolhardy" Patanese ones, were experienced in handling deerskins; this was of paramount importance, because "if a bundle got even a bit wet, it could ruin all other skins." Transportation of sapan wood, the other important product for Japan, was also held to be problematic. It arrived in Ayutthaya from the neighbouring regions no sooner than early May, which was weeks too late for a departure for Patani. To all this was added the increased costs and the double risk of the two voyages (to Patani, then to Japan), and the fact that there was always a risk that the VOC ship sent from Bantam could not reach Patani in time. In that case, merchandise from Siam would have had to be stored in the warehouses in Patani for a whole year, resulting in huge extra costs. As a solution, the merchants in Siam recommended regular direct travels between Siam and Japan.[25]

It seemed that Specx's leaving Japan would resolve the situation. The new head merchant, Brouwer, purchased a junk to use for direct traffic to Siam. However, in 1614, Specx returned to Japan. On his way back, he touched Patani and discussed the issue with the factors there. They promptly ignored the doubts of the personnel in Siam. Direct traffic between Siam and Japan would have required Japanese mariners, a solution deemed too expensive, while sending a VOC ship from Bantam directly to Siam and from there to Japan was also argued to be inappropriate. To support their case, Specx and his fellow merchants even attached a detailed cost calculation to the resolution.[26]

A stalemate developed which had no solution in the given circumstances. None of the three factories concerned was superior to the others, so none of the parties could issue a direct order. Meanwhile, the Bantam managers, who had the administrative power to settle the matter, felt underinformed, and were thus not confident enough to get involved in this debate. They simply directed the parties to solve the problem themselves.

Finally, reality broke the deadlock. The trip from Siam to Patani proved to be a problem as early as 1615. The vessel could be dispatched only in mid-May, resulting in her late arrival in Patani, ten days after the ship from Bantam had left for Japan. However, the news of her final safe arrival did not reach Japan. As a fallback solution, despite all his reluctance, Specx dispatched a vessel to Siam to fetch the products there—the bulk of which had already been in Patani.[27] To make matters worse, a third of the skins that finally arrived in Patani were rotten. Factors in Patani also realised that expenses such as wages, and repair and living costs were much higher than expected.[28] This blunder convinced the parties that using Patani as a transshipment centre was untenable. By mid-1616, direct ventures between Siam and Japan were accepted as the best solution, and in subsequent years, this was the preferred option.[29]

This coordination process was rather short; yet it features a few points that are worthy of mention. Specx's original idea, shared with his fellow merchants in his letters, was a purely theoretical design, simply because only a few VOC vessels had travelled these waters before, and practical knowledge was thus scarce. Although he had spent a few weeks in Patani, Specx lacked (or ignored) information regarding local procedures, circumstances, and customs that was necessary to draft an effective shipping schedule. At the same time, the reasoning of the factors in Siam showed an awareness of the relevant technicalities. Specx and the factors in Patani emphasised the costs and overlooked the fact that the primary issue was not the expenses, but the timing, as factors in Siam correctly recognised. As a consequence of these different approaches, Specx and the Patani factors ignored all the doubts shared with them by the factors in Siam, resulting in a decision that finally proved inadequate in practice.

Market Research and the Sharing of Information for Silver Export

At first glance, export from Japan was a straightforward matter. The country produced a significant amount of silver, a product that was in great demand in the region. The Portuguese silk–silver trade and its profitability was a generally well-known fact and was thus readily available as an example to be followed.[30] However, the Dutch merchants quickly realised that exporting Japanese silver was not as straightforward as descriptions of Portuguese trade had reported.

The main difficulty arose from the fact that several types of silver were available in Japan, and even more circulated in the broader region of the South China Sea. The term "Japanese silver" used in the historical records was more of a category than a single product. *Keichō chōgin*, referred to as *schuitsilver* by Dutch traders, had approximately 80% silver content and was less requested; thus, its exchange outside of Japan could produce a loss.[31] Uncast silver with significantly higher content, generally referred to as *haifuki*, was more popular in the region. It had different types that were of somewhat different quality, named after the mines from which they originated. The VOC records mentioned *seda* and *soma* or *somo* most often.[32] There was also a type named *berchsilver* by the Dutch, which, in these years, had fine and unrefined versions in at least three degrees of purity.[33] To this already complex picture came several "non-Japanese" types that circulated in the region. The most important was the Spanish silver currency, the real, but Siam or Phatthalung also had its own silver output. Needless to say, the quality, silver content, and price of these different sorts differed significantly, and thus their exchange rates were different. However, it was not at all certain that higher-quality silver yielded a better price, and requests often depended on the destination region. Therefore, in order to be successful in the Japanese trade, the Dutch had the enormous task of surveying this field.

The first VOC reference to silver, in 1610, mentions only "refined" and "ordinary common" silver with no more details, which shows that the Dutch did not realise the depth of the issue.[34] The first sign of a developing awareness of the complexity appears in 1612. Specx wanted a fellow merchant to check if *haifuki* silver, "that is *sado*," could be acquired in Kyoto. The reference shows a gradual extension of Dutch knowledge. Specx had an exact name; he realised that it might offer more profit, and he wanted to keep the whole transaction secret, so he probably knew that exporting this silver type was officially illegal.[35] The VOC vessel departing in the same year carried three samples of silver to Patani, which was considered the main partner for Japanese VOC commerce. Using these samples to obtain more exact information, the agents there asked to survey the attitude of the local merchants towards Japanese silver. The first "commercial quantity" of silver soon followed the samples, in 1615. The cargo included several types, the bulk being refined silver cast in plates, "similar to the sort carried out by the Portuguese from the country."[36] The result, however, was disappointing. Asian merchants generally preferred the Spanish real to any Japanese silver. Although the finest sort had better silver content, Malay merchants stubbornly refused to take it even at the weight of the Spanish currency. Other merchants did not reject *haifuki* outright, but the price they offered did not cover the costs of refinement. These first tests showed that sending Japanese silver to Patani was a waste. However, later investigations nuanced this conclusion and showed that it was valid only for the city of Patani, but not the whole region. Nonetheless, finding other markets for Japanese silver seemed a wise move.[37]

As the first news started to trickle in from Patani, the next year's attempt was made in Bantam.[38] Initial attempts showed that the Bantamese market was better. Uncast and unrefined *berchsilver* was the most popular with Chinese merchants there. Selling better alloys was less profitable, and, as a specific detail, no Japanese marks should have been stamped into the silver bars or plates.[39] However, the silver trade of Bantam was judged to be unpredictable, and even in 1618 Coen was not able to provide precise insight into the situation, other than favouring *berchsilver*. As a bottom line, Coen discouraged refining silver into the purity of reals and suggested supplying the smaller factories in the region—Siam, Quinam—with Japanese silver first.[40] These smaller VOC factories in the region also surveyed their markets for Japanese silver. *Haifuki* was well received in Siam. Although later scrutiny showed some loss at the exchange, Siam still offered the best market for this alloy.[41] Finally, Quinam did not meet the Dutch expectations either, as local merchants there also preferred reals to Japanese silver.

These surveys offered several conclusions. As a general lesson, it became apparent that sending the right sort of silver to the right region was of primary importance, and that the silver should be sorted accordingly. It was also learned that refining Japanese silver resulted in a loss. This unexpected information was a disappointment for Coen, who wrote to the European managers in 1618 that minting change in Asia would be the only profitable way of using Japanese silver.[42] Although the situation was not as grim as this suggests, silver export certainly required more sophisticated trade coordination, as refinement costs had to be compared against respective sales prices. Dutch difficulties with finding a proper market finally eased significantly in the early 1620s, when the VOC secured a solid trade in Taiwan, where *soma* silver gave a steady 9% more income than reals.[43]

This more sophisticated coordination also resulted in improving organisational processes. Soon after the first significant export of silver, two unexpected questions arose regarding that trade: Who should bear the costs of the refinement and how should the relevant numbers be recorded in the accounts? In 1615, when he sent out the first significant silver cargo, Specx accounted the costs of refining to the Patani factory. The head merchant there immediately disputed this and appealed to the Bantam managers. Coen took the side of the Patani factors, thus answering the first question.[44] Regarding the second, the constant inter-factory communication via reports, letters, and various lists not only allowed respective markets to be evaluated, but also provided Specx with all the necessary data to calculate exact comparative prices.[45] After a few years, he was able to share the exchange rates of the most important types of silver, which allowed both making minute calculations and fine-tuning the accounting, and thus the final closing down of the coordination of silver commerce. Interestingly, these details were put in a cargo manifest. However, the same information could also be sent via a letter. Specx's numbers were made available to the Batavian managers, who informed the head merchant about the exact exchange rates he had to use for his account books in the future.[46]

Conclusion

This chapter highlights a number of information-management functions that a trading compound in Asia fulfilled in early modern trade. The scope and time frame were admittedly limited; yet some general conclusions can be drawn. The most general one is that information should be considered essential in this given context, which requires close attention from historians. This dimension is a highly complex one. It was not only commercial information that had an impact on trade, for other areas of knowledge—cultural, political, or navigational—were also important, and many adaptive processes were required by the actors. Although this study has paid more attention to communication and information gathering, the above examples also make clear that collecting information was not, in itself, sufficient for success. The problem of shipping schedules clearly shows that having all the necessary information could be useless if the circumstances, priorities, or other aspects made the interpretations by the parties inadequate or contradictory. This leads us to consider administrative structure, which improved continuously in the examined years. The unwillingness (and thus, finally, the inability) to handle a conflict that could cripple the movement of products turned into a framework that effectively controlled the minutiae of accounting silver exchange costs. This certainly required a proper survey of the field, analysing the data and disseminating the necessary information so that it could finally be used by the decision-makers. Adaptation via individual learning (which might even be considered as organisational learning) certainly played a role in this structural improvement.

However, it would be a mistake to judge the VOC information-managing architecture a completely rational and sophisticated one. Little effort was invested in forecasting, in predicting possible trajectories or in systematically monitoring the environment, so each of the problems described came out of the blue. Certainly, the fact that the VOC was a newcomer meant that having little and often low-quality information in these years made its situation difficult, and problem solving could not be planned in advance. The factors were often only reacting and improvising, giving the impression that the Japanese factory was drifting along with events. Solving the problems highlighted in this chapter took many years, for a variety of reasons. The slow pace of communication at that time was an important circumstance, but information gathering was also somewhat *ad hoc*. This all resulted in a limited information pool and through that, as a bottom line, a decision-making pattern that could appear to a modern eye as deficient.

Finally, the above cases show that this early period of the Japanese factory was not as insignificant as it is often considered in the literature. It is certainly the case that commercial results were not impressive, and the factory also played a role as a naval base providing war supplies for the VOC. However, it acted as an information gate, and much of the information that was gathered, organised, and processed in these years created a foundation that was absolutely vital in making later Japanese VOC trade a success story.

Notes

1 The English (later British) East India Company, also a joint-stock corporation, had been founded two years earlier.
2 The best general overview for the many types of available Dutch sources is Joyce Pennings and Remco Raben, *Nationaal Archief Manual: Introduction to the Archives of the Verenigde Oostindsche Compagnie* (The Hague, 1992), 40–61, https://www.nationaalarchief.nl/sites/default/files/afbeeldingen/toegangen/NL-HaNA_1.04.02_introduction-VOC.pdf.

3 On the examination of the role of unwritten navigational information regarding Japan, see Gábor Szommer, "Dutch Navigational Knowledge on Japan, 1608–1641," *Bulletin of Portuguese/Japanese Studies* 13 (2017): 9–30.
4 Alistair Black, "Information Management in the Intelligence Branch of Britain's War Office, 1873–1914: 'All Information Flows Toward it, or Returns to it, in a Form Worked up into Shape'," *Open Information Science* 4 (2020): 91–92. https://www.degruyter.com/document/doi/10.1515/opis-2020-0008/html.
5 The most detailed overview of the Hirado years of the VOC is: W. Z. Mulder, *Hollanders in Hirado, 1597–1641* (Haarlem: Fibula-Van Dishoeck, s.d.).
   It is not novel to examine the importance of information to early modern overseas trade, or even to the specific case of the VOC. See, for example, Ida Nijenhuis et al., eds., *Information and Power in History: Towards a Global Approach* (New York: Routledge, 2020); Karel Davids, "Dutch and Spanish Global Networks of Knowledge in the Early Modern Period," in *Centres and Cycles of Accumulation in and Around the Netherlands During the Early Modern Period*, ed. Lissa Roberts (Berlin: LIT Verlag, 2011), 29–52; Siegfried Huigen et al., eds., *The Dutch Trading Companies as Knowledge Networks* (Leiden: Brill, 2010); and Ann Carlos and Santhi Hejeebu, "Specific Information and the English Chartered Companies, 1650–1750," in *Information Flows: New Approaches in the Historical Study of Business Information*, ed. Leos Müller and Jari Ojala (Helsinki: Finnish Literature Society, 2007), 139–166.
6 Focusing on information-related aspects within the framework of microhistory may prove a less-researched, yet fruitful, approach. See, for instance, Laura Skouvig, "Present and Past: The Relevance of Information History," *Information & Culture* 58, no. 1 (January 2023): 1–16; and Filippo de Vivo, "Microhistories of Long-Distance Information: Space, Movement and Agency in the Early Modern News," *Past & Present* 242, no. 14 (November 2019): 179–214. For a more theoretical and general approach, see László Z. Karvalics, "A Hétköznapi Információs Viselkedés Helye az Információ Mikrotörténetében," in *Az Információ Mikrotörténetéhez*, ed. Gulyás László Szabolcs (Budapest: Gondolat, 2014), 7–36; and László Z. Karvalics, "Hírforgalom és Információáramlás – új Elméleti és Történeti Narratívák Felé," *Jel-Kép* 34, no. 3 (October 2014), https://real-j.mtak.hu/18019/9/Jel-kép_2014_3.pdf.
7 Femme Gaastra, *The Dutch East India Company: Expansion and Decline* (Zutphen: Walburg Pers, 2003); Jurrien van Goor, *Prelude to Colonialism: The Dutch in Asia* (Dordrecht: Hilversum, 2004), 7–83; and Leonard Blussé and George Winius, "The Origin and Rhythm of Dutch Aggression against the Estado da India, 1601–1661," in *Indo Portuguese History. Old issues, New Questions*, ed. Teotonio R. de Souza (New Delhi: Concept Publishing, 1985), 73–83.
8 Anthony Farrington and Derek Massarella, "William Adams and Early English Enterprise in Japan," *LSE STICERD Research Paper No. IS394* (July 2000). For the voyage of the *Liefde*, see, for instance, William Corr, *Adams the Pilot* (London and New York: Routledge, 1995), 18–42.
9 Paulo van Sold to the directors [bewindhebbers], n.d. [cca 1603], 1.11.01.01: 35–38, Nationaal Archief [hereafter: NA].
10 Geoffrey C. Gunn, *World Trade Systems of the East and West* (Leiden: Brill, 2018); Adam Clulow, "From Global Entrepôt to Early Modern Domain: Hirado, 1609–1641," *Monumenta Nipponica* 65, no. 1 (Spring 2010): 1–35; Michael Laver, *Japan's Economy by Proxy* (New York: Cambria Press, 2008); and Bhawan Ruangsilp, *Dutch East India Company Merchants at the Court of Ayutthaya* (Leiden: Brill, 2007).
11 Lucas Waghenaer, *Thresoor der Zeevaert* (Amsterdam: Theatrum Orbis Terrarum Ltd, 1965), 197–199; and Jan Huygen van Linschoten, *Itinerario* (Amsterdam, 1595–1596). The English translation of the first volume of *Itinerario* was republished: see Arthur Coke Burnell and P. A. Tiele, *The Voyage of John Huyghen van Linschoten to the East Indies* (London: Hakluyt Society, 1885).
12 Adam Clulow, *The Company and the Shogun: The Dutch Encounter with Tokugawa Japan* (New York: Columbia University Press, 2013), 43–45.
13 Jurre Knoest, "Company Privateers in Asian Waters: The VOC-Trading Post at Hirado and the Logistics of Privateering, ca. 1614–1624," *Leidschrift. Historisch Tijdschrift* 26, no. 3 (2011): 43–57; and Adam Clulow, "Pirating in the Shogun's Waters: The Dutch East India Company and the Santo Antonio Incident," *Bulletin of Portuguese/Japanese Studies* 13 (2006): 65–80.
14 "Resolutions," Heren XVII, August 30, 1610, 1.04.02 100: 76, 86, NA.

15 Letter of Zeeland Chamber to Amsterdam Chamber, August 15, 1610, 1.04.02 7291: 25, NA. A letter sent from Hirado, August 25, 1612, 1.04.02 1054, Katern: Japan: 17, NA. The exact identity of this survivor is unclear. I assumed that he was Pieter Adriaensz Blanckert: see Szommer Gábor, "Pieter Adriaensz Blanckert: Another Survivor of the Liefde's Voyage to Japan," *The Mariner's Mirror* 107, no. 4 (October 2021): 478–479, while Keiko Cryns assumed that he was Adrijaen Cornelissen: see Keiko Cryns, "アドリアーン・コルネーリセン—忘れられたリーフデ号の元乗組員—" [Adrijaen Cornelissen – Former Crew Member of the Forgotten *Liefde*], https://kutsukake.nichibun.ac.jp/obunsiryo/wp-content/uploads/dadb86efaa7c7a18766f68b54a0be461.pdf. Both versions have supporting sources. Nevertheless, regarding information transfer, it is not his name that is the interesting detail, but his impact.

16 "Resolutions," Heren XVII, September 16, 1610, 1.04.02 100: 108, NA.

17 Elbert Woutersz in Japan to Patani, November 4, 1612, 1.04.02 1054, Katern: Japan: 23, NA. Fragment of a letter sent from Hirado, November 2, 1612, 1.04.02 1054, Katern: Japan: 18v, NA. Jacques Specx, Hirado to Cornelis Nijenroode and Martin Houtman, Ayutthaya, November 3, 1612, 1.04.02 1054, Katern: Japan: 20v, NA.

18 Jacques Specx, Tidore to the directors in Amsterdam, August 2, 1613, 1.04.02 1056, Katern: Ternate: 87v, NA. Brouwer even suggested that Specx, who had been gathering experience about Japan for three years, should return to the Netherlands and personally inform the decision-makers there, so they could have "proper instructions and information." Hendrik Brouwer, Kawachi [in Japan] to Pieter Both, February 11, 1613, 1.04.02 1054, Katern: Japan: 33v, NA. Much of this first cargo was still unsold in the factory warehouse as late as 1616. Leonard Camps, Hirado to the Chamber of Amsterdam, October 10, 1616, 1.04.02 1063: 102v, NA.

19 Herman Theodoor Colenbrander, ed., *Jan Pietersz Coen. Bescheiden Omtrent zijn Bedrijf in Indie*, vol. 1 (Gravenhage: Martinus Nijhoff, 1919), 36–37, 97–100.

20 Letter sent from Amsterdam to Governor-general Gerard Reijnst, April 30, 1614, 1.04.02 312: 159, NA; and Colenbrander, *Jan Pietersz Coen*, vol. 4, 305, and 320. Another aspect of this shortage of silver was a funding difficulty in Europe, as highlighted by Oscar Gelderblom. This difficulty may also have played an important role in the VOC directors' decision to cut the amount of silver destined for Asia: see Oscar Gelderblom, Abe de Jong, and Joost Jonker, "Learning How to Manage Risk by Hedging: the VOC insurance contract of 1613," *European Review of Economic History* 24, no. 2 (May 2019): 1–24.

21 Letter sent to Governor-general Reijnst, November 21, 1614, 1.04.02 312: 62, 64, NA.

22 Mihoko Oka, "The Nanban and Shuinsen Trade in Sixteenth and Seventeenth-Century Japan," in *Global History and New Polycentric Approaches*, ed. Lucio De Sousa and Manuel Pérez García (Singapore: Springer, 2017), 163–182; Gunn, *World Trade Systems*, 19–45; Geoffrey C. Gunn, *History Without Borders: The Making of an Asian World Region (1000–1800)* (Hong Kong: Hong Kong University Press, 2011), 211–237; Hoang Anh Tuan, *Silk for Silver: Dutch-Vietnamese Relations, 1637–1700* (Leiden: Brill, 2007), 26–57; and Ruangsilp, *Dutch East India Company Merchants*, 35–53.

23 P. J. Rivers, "Monsoon Rhythms and Trade Patterns: Ancient Times East of Suez," *Journal of the Malaysian Branch of the Royal Asiatic Society* 77, no. 2 (2004): 75–91. See, also, Sea Conditions Guide: South China Sea and Southeast Asia (DTN, 2019), https://www.dtn.com/wp-content/uploads/2020/03/wp_offshore_south-china-sea_1019.pdf.

24 Letter sent to Lambert Jacobsz Heijn in Siam from Hirado, Japan, November 7, 1610, 1.04.02 1054, Katern: Japan: 6, NA. Jacques Specx, Hirado to Cornelis van Nijenroode and Marten Houtman, Ayutthaya, November 3, 1612, 1.04.02 1054, Katern: Japan: 20, NA.

25 Letter of Lambert Jacobsz Heijn [to Japan], March 28, 1610, 1.04.02 1054, Katern: Siam 3: 15, NA. Suggestions taken out from a letter of senior merchant Houtman, not dated, 1.04.02 1054, Katern: Siam 2: 41, NA. Maarten Houtman, Ayuthia to Hendrik Janszoon, Patani, March 18, 1613, 1.04.02 1056, Katern: Siam: 96r, NA. Maarten Houtman, Siam to Hirado, June 8, 1616, 1.04.21 276, NA.

26 "Resolutions," Patani, July 1, 1614, 1.04.02 1063: 363–365, NA. Colenbrander, *Jan Pietersz Coen*, vol. 7, 14–15.

27 "Resolutions," Hirado, November 7, 1615, 1.04.02 1061: 253r, NA.

28 Letter of Hendrik Janszoon sent to Bantam, November 15, 1615, 1.04.02 1059: 244v, NA.

29 "Resolutions," Patani, July 21, 1616, 1.04.02 1063: 366r, NA. Hendrik Janszoon to the Chamber of Amsterdam, October 25, 1616, 1.04.02 1063: 77r, NA.

30 The author is much indebted to many members of the Historical Metallurgy Society, who helped with information regarding the several different types of silver mentioned in this section. Regarding regional silver trade, see Dong Shaoxin, "Portuguese–Dutch Conflicts and the Macao–Nagasaki Trade in the Early Seventeenth Century," *Itinerario* 37, no. 3 (December 2013): 70–74; João Paulo Costa Oliveira, "A Route under Pressure: Communication between Nagasaki and Macao (1597–1617)," *Bulletin of Portuguese/Japanese Studies* 1, no. 1 (December 2000): 75–95; and Dennis O. Flynn and Arturo Giraldez, "Silk for Silver: Manila-Macao Trade in the 17th Century," *Philippine Studies* 44, no. 1 (First Quarter, 1996): 52–68.

31 *Schuitzilver* meant silver in the form of a metal bar, often used for payment. The word comes up in several entries in VOC Glossarium, https://resources.huygens.knaw.nl/pdf/vocglossarium/VOC-Glossarium.pdf. For trade-related details, see Takekoshi Yosoburo, *The Economic Aspects of the History of the Civilization of Japan*, vol. 2 (London: Allen & Unwin, 1930), 401.

32 Kozo Yamamura and Tetsuo Kamiki, "Silver Mines and Sung Coins," in *Precious Metals in the Later Medieval and Early Modern Worlds*, ed. J. F. Richards (Durham: Carolina Academic Press, 1983), fn 51, 349. The name *haifuki* originated from the technology used for refinement. VOC records sometimes treated *haifuki* as a separate sort instead of a category and highlighted a separate exchange rate of it.

33 Cargo List [of cash and products laden in Japan on the last day of January 1619], 1.04.02 1070: 358r, NA.

34 A letter sent from Nagasaki, November 3, 1610, 1.04.02 1054, Katern: Japan: 5r, NA.

35 Fragment of a letter sent from Hirado [probably to Patani], November 2, 1612, 1.04.02 1054, Katern: Japan: 19r, NA.

36 Hendrik Janszoon to the Chamber of Amsterdam, October 20, 1614, 1.04.02 1063: 71v, NA. Cargo List, Products sent from Hirado to Patani, March 6, 1615, 1.04.02 1063: 444v, NA.

37 Hendrik Janszoon, Patani to Jacques Specx, Hirado, July 12, 1615, 1.04.21 276: 39r, 44r, NA. Colenbrander, *Jan Pietersz Coen*, vol. 7, 59–60, 208, 525.

38 Cargo List, Products sent from Hirado to Bantam, February 28, 1616, 1.04.02 1070: 358r, NA.

39 Colenbrander, *Jan Pietersz Coen*, vol. 2, 108–109. Memorandum for Jacques Specx in Hirado, regarding what he should and should not send here, May 14, 1616, 1.04.21 276: 81v, NA. Japanese silver bars often bore the marks of the respective refiners. This is probably what Coen referred to.

40 Colenbrander, *Jan Pietersz Coen*, vol. 2, 370–371.

41 Martin Houtman, Siam to Jacques Specx, Japan, June 8, 1616, 1.04.21 276: 88r, NA. Cornelis van Nijenroode, Siam to the Chamber of Amsterdam, September 20, 1617, 1.04.02 1067: 121r, NA. Cornelis van Nijenroode, Ayuthia to Jacques Specx, Hirado, May 31 and June 7, 1619, 1.04.02 1070: 519–524, NA.

42 Colenbrander, *Jan Pietersz Coen*, vol. 1, 394.

43 Leonard Camps, Hirado to the Governor-general, January 12 and October 5, 1623, 1.04.02 1080: 377–383, NA.

44 Colenbrander, *Jan Pietersz Coen*, vol. 7, 59–60. Cornelis van Nijenroode, Ayuthia to Jacques Specx, Hirado, May 31 and June 7, 1619, 1.04.02 1070: 519–524, NA.

45 Cornelis van Nijenroode, Siam to the Chamber of Amsterdam, September 20, 1617, 1.04.02 1067: 121r, NA.

46 Colenbrander, *Jan Pietersz Coen*, vol. 7, 195–196, 307. Cargo List [of cash and products laden in Japan on the last day of January 1619], 1.04.02 1070: 358r, NA. Letter sent to Cornelis Nijenroode in Japan from Batavia, June 11, 1623, 1.04.02 1082: 263r, NA. A letter sent from Hirado to Governor-general Pieter de Carpentier, January 12, 1624, 1.04.02 1083: 262r, NA.

15
THE FEMALE BODY AS AN OBJECT OF INFORMATION
Britain during the Late Victorian and Edwardian Period*

Toni Weller

Introduction

Objectification is an idea central to contemporary feminist theory which occurs, in its simplest form, when a woman is treated as an object.[1] This chapter focuses on the end of the nineteenth century in Britain and explores how the female body became an object of *information*, where her physical measurements, attributes, reproductive organs, and mental abilities became objects of discussion and assessment, by both men and other women.[2] The last decades of the nineteenth century, and into the early twentieth, witnessed complex and profound challenges to the existing social and cultural norms, exacerbated by industrialisation, urbanisation, imperial tensions, and the growth of the women's movement. Western science, reason, and rational thought perpetuated the idea that women's bodies needed to be observed, monitored, and controlled in order to shield the inherent dangers and fragilities of the female form. In so doing, it was argued, the Empire and health of the nation would be protected by ensuring strong mothers with robust reproductive health.

One might view physical differences and sexual objectification as a Foucauldian power paradigm, in which networks of practices sustain the established positions of dominance, or where "potential resistance is not merely undercut but utilized in the maintenance and reproduction of existing power relations."[3] With late Victorian society in upheaval from the impact of industrialisation, and traditional norms and roles beginning to be challenged, "creating categories and propagating certain stereotypes was a way of reacting to all of these new developments."[4] The collection of information on women objectified them in two significant ways. First, that they were considered suitable entities for information collection placed them into what can be understood as a broader diagnostic category of "Victorian things" (the idea of "collecting" a wife was even embedded into Henry James' 1881 novel *A Portrait of a Lady*).[5] Second, where women were viewed as reproductive vessels, their bodies became objectified as part of the wider "ideological mapping of gender roles."[6]

---

* Thanks to Alistair Black, Bonnie Mak, Laura Skouvig, and Helen Yallop-Emmott, for their insightful suggestions on earlier drafts of this chapter.

This chapter shows how information about women and their bodies could be utilised to perpetuate ideas of them as inherently fragile, where child bearing and domestication were considered to be better suited to natural female abilities than pursuing the vote, paid work, or higher education. Feminists might argue that this was a way "for men to try and regain control over women, who suddenly challenged their assigned roles and tried to break free of the restrictions that society imposed on them."[7] Yet this chapter also challenges the traditional feminist interpretation, suggesting that women themselves could also collect and use their personal and physical information as a way of operating within the changing social contexts of the late nineteenth century.[8] The focus throughout are the bodies of white women in Britain, but from the outset this is also to acknowledge the inherent privilege of this group.[9] The chapter touches on themes of class and race which may sit uncomfortably with a modern reader, given contemporary feminist rhetoric. Yet the female perspective acts as a powerful counterweight to both the dominance of the Victorian male voice of this period and the hitherto historiographical focus on male information collection and discourse.

Information collection on women's bodies and minds fed into, and was influenced by, the broader social and scientific discourses of the period. The chapter explores four key themes of this era: the mind/body connection, anthropometrics, eugenics, and the information state. The first section of the chapter explores the context for women in the late nineteenth century in which their physical and mental health were seen as irrevocably linked. Information collected about their physical self was used to perpetuate, justify, or challenge ideas of women's mental frailty, and their consequent ability to attend higher education, vote, or work. This is developed upon in the section on anthropometrics, a technique most well-known for helping to classify Victorian criminals, but which was also utilised to categorise the intellect of, in particular, middle-class women in relation to their reproductive health. The third section of the chapter explores the national debate over the health and security of the nation at the end of the century, which used the emergent pseudo-science of eugenics to justify information collection on women as a national concern. The final section discusses how the nascent information state legitimised the bodies of women as objects for discussion, often in terms of perpetuating the British race. Information collection on birth control, standards of working-class mothering, knowledge of hygiene and food, as well as the continuing accumulation of information by head teachers regarding their female student's physical health were a critical part of early 1900s discourse. However, women were not just passive subjects of information collection; as this chapter argues, they also pro-actively collected corporeal information themselves, used it for different purposes, or resisted demands to provide it. Viewing women as "information objects" allows us to challenge the conventional narrative of late nineteenth-century information discourse and potentially offers a feminist revision of existing information historiography.

The Mind/Body Connection

The relationship between women's bodies and their physical and mental health was not new to the late nineteenth century. The connection between the womb and the mind was first made in the ancient world where it was believed that a woman was vulnerable to mental disorders if she failed to have children, or had them too late in life.[10] The notion of a "wandering womb," which was believed to, literally, wander or move about the female body causing multiple pathologies, ultimately evolved into the notion of hysteria, with its entomological roots in the Greek word for womb, *hystera*. Women's bodies, argued medical and philosophical thinkers from Hippocrates to Freud, needed to be confined and controlled in order to protect a woman's mental and physical health.[11] During the long eighteenth century, hysteria and the associations between female mind and body became "a powerful cultural metaphor" to explain "everything that was wrong with women."[12] Feminist discourses have interpreted "hysteria" as the way American and European cultures made sense of women's changing roles during the nineteenth century, with both industrialisation and the movement for women's rights challenging established gender and cultural norms.[13] Feminist historians began to ask whether "the diagnostic category of hysteria was simply a way of keeping women in the home."[14] Hysteria and the links between women's bodies and minds were particularly noticeable in the debate over women in higher education, which, during the Victorian period, became increasingly prominent. Such ideology erected social and cultural barriers to women's access to opportunities within the "public" sphere.[15]

The notion of "separate spheres," the structuring of society into two distinct gendered domains, the private (female) and the public (male), was a social construction dating back to Aristotle's *Politics*.[16] It was during the ages of Enlightenment and industrialisation, however, that the modern ideology of separate spheres really took hold. Industrialisation encouraged a new distinction between work and home, while the Enlightenment values of liberty and equality (largely denied in practice to women until the late nineteenth and early twentieth centuries) fuelled discussion about whether these principles should apply to women who were seen to belong to a different social sphere and gendered space than men. Such debates were perpetuated throughout the nineteenth century by Marxist theorists who argued, in crude terms, that capitalism meant the home was no longer recognised as a means of production as it traditionally had been and instead should be recognised as a private, separate, sphere in which women operated while men went out to work (in the public sphere).[17] The idea of the "Victorian angel in the house" retained enormous power even by the latter decades of the nineteenth century.[18] Arguably, this stereotype not only reinforced, even venerated, established social norms, but also appeared as a reaction against the fictional Victorian "New Woman" of the 1890s who represented associations of female independence and suffrage. As Sarah Kühl has shown, "these terms, or labels, as well as the ideas behind them were an important part of Victorian life and were not just reflected but also actively propagated in the arts and literature of the time."[19] As the century progressed, these feminine ideals and associations began to be justified not only within culture, but by Victorian science itself.

Concurrent to these developments were nascent moves towards a more centralised form of information state, which saw its role as increasingly interventionist compared to the more laissez-faire approach of the early Victorian government.[20] At the same time, the Victorian obsession with facts and statistical information collection that had underpinned parliamentary commissions and reports during the mid-century began to undergo a shift. Statisticians moved from using information to support social change, towards a more eugenical interest in what were believed to be inherited mental or physical characteristics or qualities.[21] Of course, Victorian interest in eugenics was in no way the same as the philosophies developed in the twentieth century under Nazi ideology, nor were any of the actors in this chapter thinking in the terms that would come later.[22] Yet there was an interest, led by Francis Galton, to collect information on human populations, or what became known as anthropometrics.

Anthropometrics and the Female Body

The Victorians had long loved collecting information on all kinds of things; yet "is it an ocean into which scholars have not yet dipped more than a toe."[23] By the end of the century, women's bodies had become just another facet on which to collect information, most notably to reinforce the idea that intellectual effort could lead to physical frailty, consequently impacting fertility and marriageability. Whereas local and central government had collected information on citizens more generally since at least the early modern period, it was not until the nineteenth century that techniques, such as those of Adolphe Quetelet and Francis Galton, were created for its retrieval and analysis.[24] As Fara has argued in her study of science and suffrage, during the Victorian period, "biological and medical ideas continued to reinforce the inferior status of women."[25]

By the latter decades of the century, Charles Darwin's evolutionary theories were being adopted and revised by anthropometrics, most notably by Darwin's half-cousin, Francis Galton. Galton was a notable polymath of the era, the first to use questionnaires and surveys for collecting information on human groups, and the first to apply statistical methods to human biological differences and questions of inherited intelligence. His studies in anthropometrics required a vast amount of corporeal information collection. In order facilitate this, Galton established the Anthropometric Laboratory at the London International Health Exhibition of 1885, at which over nine thousand visitors not only consented to be measured but also paid a small fee to be so – they were even given a copy of their data as a souvenir.[26] Galton wrote of the popularity of the exhibit and described in detail the devices used to measure "keenness of sight; colour sense; judgment of eye; hearing; highest audible note; breathing power; strength of pull and squeeze; swiftness of blow; span of arms; height, standing and sitting; and weight."[27] One area that he omitted to measure was the head, since he "feared it would be troublesome to perform on most women on account of their bonnets and the bulk of their hair, and that it would lead to objections and difficulties."[28] Women had their measurements taken in all other categories. While Galton's academic work was predominately based in London at University College, in 1885 he was appointed the Rede Lecturer at the University of Cambridge and set up in the library of the Philosophical Society to record the physical measurements of male students.[29] Between 1887 and 1888, Galton managed to record details on 1,450 men and claimed the results of most interest to him were the conclusions drawn "about the intellectual characteristics and the correlation of these with the physical."[30] While the experiment was somewhat skewed to start with, he concluded, in essence and in the most simplistic terms, that the cleverest men had the largest heads.

Galton used his physical information collections to demonstrate that white male dominance was legitimately based on mental superiority.[31] Rosalind Miles argues that Victorian craniology—the science of the brain and brain size—linked intelligence to brain size and "proved" that the brains of white males were larger than any minority group, including women.[32] Even Darwin, in a different context, wrote of the less highly evolved female brain.[33] While some argued for education as a way to avoid the unhealthy impact of "an exceedingly dull life," much of the literature on the frailness of the female brain during the nineteenth century suggested that anything more taxing than gentle reading could encourage nervous disorders.[34] There was a clear link perceived between girls who had been educated at university, their fertility and their ability to go on to have successful marriages. As Marland has shown, class differences were reflected in the medical literature of the period;

the strain of intellectual work on middle-class girls versus more physical damage to the body faced by working-class women.[35]

A decade later, the collection of anthropometric information remained topical in Cambridge. Previous research on material from the all-female Newnham College at Cambridge University shows how, for a short window of time under the Principality of Eleanor Sidgwick, the College recorded bodily measurements of its female students to enable Sidgwick's call to support higher education for women.[36] Established in 1871, at a time when women faced immense challenges in attending higher education, it is a useful focus for the debates on how intellectual study could detrimentally impact a women's biology. The Newnham Roll Letter for 1898 featured a handwritten note by Eleanor Sidgwick discussing the information collected by Galton. She wrote that his measurements had "yielded results of considerable interest ... But there has been a difficulty in getting enough statistics to be of use in the case of women."[37] This comment was prescient of an issue that would continue into the modern day.[38] Sidgwick continued that it was not convenient for women to be measured at the Philosophical Library because, echoing Galton's comments from the International Health Exhibition in 1885, the "most important" head measurements "involve, as a rule, the taking down of the hair."[39] As a consequence of this, the College received a donation of a set of measuring apparatus.[40] The donation was given "in the hope that we shall gradually be able to accumulate a valuable amount of information, in the first instance among our own students, and perhaps also among other women." The College, led by Sidgwick, rallied to the call; for a period of two years between 1898 and 1900, there was a systematic collection of personal physical information on the girls at Newnham.

The archives at the College hold 150 unpublished index cards containing anthropometric data very similar to that collected by Galton at the 1885 Health Exhibition in London almost fifteen years previously (see Figs. 15.1 and 15.2):

skin (pale, ruddy, dark, freckled); hair (red, fair, brown, dark, jet-black, straight, wavy, curly); eyes (light, medium, dark); face (long/narrow, medium, short/broad); cheekbones (inconspicuous, prominent); ears (flat, outstanding); and lobes (absent, present). Following this, there is room for the actual measurements for each individual's head (length, breadth, and height measurements); nose (length, breadth, profile measurements); face (length, upper face length, breadth, inter ocular breadth, bigonial breadth measurements); height, span, weight, breathing power, strength (pull as archer, squeeze of right and left hand); eyesight (right and left eye measurements), colour sense (i.e. normal or colour blind). In addition to this, there is space for (although few are completed) Cephalic Index, Nasal Index, Total Facial Index, and Upper Facial Index.[41]

Unusual as these metrics appear to a modern eye, Galton considered his own similar list to be "the chief physical characteristics of man."[42] The point was to duplicate what had already been collected on men to "prove" that higher education did not necessarily lead to frailty and infertility. Using Galton's methodology, Sidgwick attempted to demonstrate, statistically, that women could study at higher education and still go on to fulfil their roles as wives and mothers, preparing for the health and security of the nation, a subject which was of national importance at the turn of the century. In pursuing this agenda, Sidgwick objectified the Newnham women on her own terms. Her collection of information on the

Figure 15.1 Example of one of the double-sided Newnham College Index Cards, recording the physical characteristics of Louisa Darbishire, 1898, foreside. Photograph of the cards by Toni Weller, but used with kind permission of the Principal and Fellows of Newnham College.

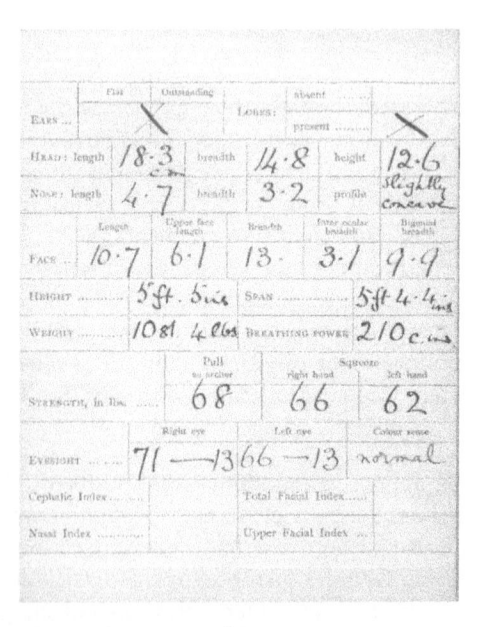

Figure 15.2 Example of one of the double-sided Newnham College Index Cards, recording the physical characteristics of Louisa Darbishire, 1898, reverse side. Photograph of the cards by Toni Weller, but used with kind permission of the Principal and Fellows of Newnham College.

girls' physical health and strength showed how women could pro-actively use masculine dominated information practices for their own ends.

Unlike Galton's, the Newnham measurements did include those of the head. Within the privacy of College walls, as opposed to the more public environment of Galton's laboratory at the male-dominated Philosophical Society, it was socially acceptable for a woman to loosen her hair in order to be measured; an upholding of the Victorian separate spheres ideology. The measurements were also undertaken by a woman, Alice Jonson, private secretary to the Principal at this time and a former Newnham student herself. According to figures for College attendance for these years, it seems evident that the majority of the girls were measured, with Eleanor Sidgwick herself listed among those who had their corporeal information collected.

Prior to the index cards, Sidgwick had published *Health Statistics of Women Students of Cambridge and Oxford and of Their Sisters* in 1890.[43] In this, she tried to assess the long-term impact upon health for those women who had studied at Oxford or Cambridge (colloquially known as "Oxbridge"), compared to any siblings who had not studied there. The unpublished underlying questionnaire and letter, on which the published statistics were based, was sent to Newnham students and featured a high level of detail in the questions. The questionnaire was separated into two parts for comparative purposes: one for former students of female colleges at Oxbridge, and one for their female relatives who had not attended university. The questions were the same for both and included detailed queries as to the individual's health before, during, and after college, as well as at certain ages, any hereditary illnesses of disorders, and the health of the individual's mother and father, brothers, and sisters. The response rate was high–85% of women across the four female Oxbridge colleges sent replies.[44] As Sidgwick had noted, "authentic and detailed information" on the health of women in higher education, "can scarcely be said to have existed hitherto in England," although there had been efforts to collect health statistics of women at university in North America in 1885, as well as similar collections at Trinity College Dublin in the early 1890s.[45]

Mary Beard has suggested that Eleanor Sidgwick used "some elaborate statistical manoeuvring" in order to make the statistics support her case that women who studied at Oxbridge retained their biological potency for marriage and fertility despite being exposed to an intellectual education.[46] Yet, arguably, the significance of this collection was not whether or not there was any "elaborate manoeuvring"–Galton also can be said to have been guilty of this–but more that it allowed women a platform to objectify their own physical information.

Perhaps, in collecting information about themselves in this way, "they came in part to judge each other according to the discriminatory agenda they wished to contest."[47] In response to Sigwick's questionnaire of 1890, Francis Galton wrote to her husband, Henry, one of the founders of Newnham, offering to set up a fund for rewarding physically strong graduate women and encouraging their marriage. Galton anecdotally proposed a financial prize to Newnham graduates on the event of their marriage, with a second instalment paid on the birth of their first child. Such a scheme, he suggested, would show young men "that marriage with such girls was *safe*" as well as ensuring the perpetuation of the race by "hereditarily gifted" women.[48] No such scheme was ever adopted by the College. Yet, during the Victorian period, hysteria became so irrevocably linked with the middle-class female body, that the "latest scientific theories of evolution and physiology worked hand-in-hand with long established social convictions."[49] Undoubtedly, Victorian women had to operate within the reality of their own social confines; yet as Margaret Sanger, the controversial birth control advocate, wrote in 1920, "no woman can call herself free who does not own and control her own body."[50] By the turn of the nineteenth century, this objectification of the female form through information collection became linked into the ideas of the health of the nation and the eugenics movement.

Eugenics, Statistics, and the Health of the Nation

It was not unconventional, for men or indeed some women, to believe that allowing women to participate in higher education would leave them either physically unable, or mentally unwilling, to "do their duty" and have children.[51] By the 1870s, these arguments had become part of the national rhetoric and those arguing against had science and statistics to support their arguments.[52] In 1874, Henry Maudsley published an article in the *Fortnightly Review* which shared with a more general audience the scientific evidence, and physiological impact, that intellectual study could cause to a women's body and mind. Academic studies, he argued, could cause "excessive mental drain as well as the natural physical drain" which he believed most women were unable to bear. Such stresses would lead to mental, moral, and intellectual weaknesses as well as a poorly developed reproductive system.[53] It was arguments such as these that Eleanor Sidgwick attempted to repute through her own information collection on female bodies at Cambridge. Maudsley's arguments were influential, however, with others taking up his position. Some, such as Robert Lawson Tait, a leading Victorian gynaecologist, advocated himself as a supporter of women's rights while tempering this with a warning that too much female freedom could be detrimental to the human race. If those who made themselves ill through too greater liberty, only what he termed, "inferior women," would be left to "perpetuate the species" which would ultimately lead to a decline in civilisation.[54] Civilised society required healthy progeny to maintain the British race. Women's reproductive health had become not only a national issue but an imperial concern.

Such concerns were exacerbated by the Anglo-Boer War of 1899–1902 which had generated shock at the inadequate state of the British army. Large numbers of men had been rejected from army recruitment drives due to poor health. According to one contemporary, men were "physically unfit to carry a rifle or to stand the fatigues of discipline."[55] This led to a government interdepartmental committee of enquiry to investigate the declining health of the nation, part of which concluded that women, particularly working-class women, showed an ignorance of nutrition and hygiene, along with a poor maternal instinct, which had contributed to a generation of weak British men.[56] While middle-class women had been the focus of corporeal information collection relating to emancipation and education, now working-class women became subject to information collection on their maternal proficiency. The "health and happiness" of the individual woman was of secondary importance given that her ovaries, as one medical doctor wrote in 1890, were so important that "the future of the world's population rests upon them."[57] This idea of planned reproduction for racial improvement to "improve the inborn qualities of a race" became known by contemporaries as the "science" of eugenics.[58] Women's bodies, as mothers to the future British race, were seen by many as legitimate targets of information collection for the greater good, in order to ensure their ability to bear healthy children for a strong nation and army.[59]

Eugenics was a fundamental part of the world view of many women at the turn of the nineteenth century, and even some of the most vocal advocates of bodily autonomy and birth control also used eugenic rhetoric, a paradox that sits uncomfortably with modern-day feminism.[60] Francis Galton was the first, in 1884, to use the term "eugenics," although the concept far predated the word.[61] While eugenics reached its cultural and mainstream peak in the early twentieth century, including the foundation of the Eugenics Education Society in 1907, there was also much contemporary intellectual and moral opposition to many of its ideas.[62]

Angelique Richardson has argued that the most sustained discussions of eugenics in late nineteenth-century Britain was within fiction, particularly feminist or "New Woman" fiction of this period.[63] During the 1890s, British novelists were still associating nervous disorders with high achievers and the "New Woman"; yet by the end of the decade, this had evolved towards increasingly "biologically deterministic" medical writings on girls and their health.[64] Debates were not a neat dichotomy between feminists and male doctors; there were advocates and critics from both sexes.[65] Some continued to argue that the smaller female brain and intellectual over exertion would lead to, among other things, anaemia, short-sightedness, and loss of the hair and teeth.[66] Elizabeth Garrett Anderson, England's first female physician, believed that many girls at independent schools were "seriously injured" by overpressure.[67] Others still believed the undernourished brains of working-class children could not cope with the intellectual demands of education—an argument that continues to be evidenced today.[68] Many of these discussions continued to use the terminology of race. The eugenicist Havelock Ellis was one of several scientists who interpreted Darwin's theories as placing women as inherently biologically inferior to men. In his 1897 book, *Man and Woman*, Ellis used Darwinian concepts to liken women's physiology with that of the "lower" and "savage" races in a racial polemic typical of the period.[69]

The early twentieth century "was marked by a major shift in ideas about what constituted a healthy female body, a process dovetailing with the increased visibility of girls."[70] At Cambridge, where women were increasingly visible, it was often stressed that women should be as inconspicuous as possible to avoid attracting unwanted comments about their physical potency or intellectual ability. Evolutionary theories implied a natural hierarchy, with specific characteristics biologically determined. Gender could be, and was, racialised.[71] Briggs argues that "the whiteness of hysteria signaled [sic] the specifically reproductive and sexual failings of white women; it was a language of 'race suicide'."[72] More specifically, reproduction could be perceived as a single issue with two facets: the "social body" from which women's health could be used as a political strategy to maintain the status quo of sexual division, and increasingly, the "health of the physical body of the nation."[73] Information collection became critical to both of these facets.

By the 1880s, the emergent information state saw a marked difference in the purpose behind Victorian information collection, especially in its use of statistics. Lawrence Goldman has shown how, prior to the 1880s, Victorian statistics used numerical information to create arguments towards advancing social change, such as the numerous commissions on factory conditions or the work of Florence Nightingale towards sanitation reform in the army. What changed, post-1880, argues Goldman, was that the growing body of eugenicists used statistics not to advocate for liberal change to improve social and economic conditions, but instead to argue that certain groups of people (such as the poor, the ill, or minority groups such as women) had physical characteristics which they were biologically and inherently unable to change, no matter what the legislative intervention.[74] Statistical surveys such as Charles Booth's investigation of the London poor looked for environmental factors which led to certain behaviours.[75] If these factors could be changed, then behaviour, and thus society, could be improved; this followed the classic pre-1880 model of Victorian statistical information collection. Yet the last decades of the nineteenth century saw a shift towards eugenically modelled social categories fixed by inherent biologies, in which statistical information could be used to justify actions that were ideological in origin, not least the maintaining of the status quo. Not all eugenicists had "malignant intent," but many "used numbers for malign purposes" as Goldman has argued.[76] Collections of information could, in Foucauldian terms, be used to manage a population through reform or control.[77]

As Victorian women began to challenge the established order, they often became the subjects of criticism about the "rejection of their natural femininity."[78] Angelique Richardson argues that "eugenics, the 'natural' solution to the 'population question,' was figured as kind and feminine."[79] Eugenics itself was essentially gendered. While Marland has questioned how far women were actually seen as "victims of biological vulnerability," there was little doubt that by the latter decades of the nineteenth century, alongside a potent mix of eugenics and empire, anxieties about the female role as mothers became representative of the "health of the physical body of the nation."[80] Many of the leading figures of birth control movements were women (such as Annie Besant and Marie Stopes) but, as Jane Carey shows, "birth control gained support largely through its representation as a tool for (white) racial progress and population control, rather than as an issue of women's rights."[81] While feminists all over the world "enthusiastically produced and incorporated eugenics in their campaigns," in most basic terms, "eugenicists saw women's social role as determined by their reproductive function."[82]

The eugenics ideals varied according to national concerns; in Germany on mental health, in the United States on race, but in Britain it was class that dominated the eugenics rhetoric.[83] Information about women's bodies could, therefore, be used to perpetuate existing ideas of women as the Other. Statistician Karl Pearson, protégé of Galton, compared women with the labouring classes in their role as mothers. "Sexual rather than natural selection," he argued, "must invariably be the means by which woman will seek to make her maternal activity of the highest social value."[84] Such polemic was used as an attack on female demands for political equality, but by the early decades of the twentieth century, many contemporary middle-class British women did feel that they could "best serve the race, the country and their own interests" through the selection of a sound reproductive partner.[85] This was reinforced by a national narrative led by the British government and an increasingly, if gradually, centralised information state.

The Information State

As women became more visible, by the early decades of the twentieth century, their information gathering profile in terms of the state also increased. Edward Higgs has argued that the early information state in England up to the late nineteenth century was notable because it was *not* enforced by the central state.[86] Instead, information collection tended to be at a local level until the welfare/warfare dichotomy of the twentieth century.[87] Amid fears of the deterioration of the physical health of the British people plans were drafted in 1904 to measure thousands of individuals in order to gather information on the condition of the population. The British Association's Anthropometric Committee submitted their proposals to the Interdepartmental Committee on Physical Deterioration but medical, moral, and political objections meant that only school children were measured.[88] As Higgs has shown, "increasingly the central state was seen as the answer to the problems of society and Empire," where action and solutions were required via state intervention, although there continued to be laissez-faire resistance to central information collection.[89] Moreover, "the masculine basis of the state was also being challenged" by the growth of the women's movement.[90]

While women could be complicit in the information gathering tools used against them, or pro-actively use information collected about their bodies for different purposes, they could also choose to actively withhold information about themselves. In 1911, suffragists from the Women's Social and Political Union (WSPU) encouraged their members to boycott the census of that year, arguing that if the state refused to allow women the vote, women should not, as Fara has summarised, "let themselves be counted as if they were mere pieces of data."[91] The census was to include questions about the fertility of married women; since women had no vote, and therefore no say in legislation that would affect their bodies, why, it was asked, should they provide detailed information about their marital status and fertility? Some women deliberately defaced or wrote comments on their census returns, in one example refusing "to give any information about herself because she wishes in this way to protest against women not having the vote" (see Fig. 15.3).[92] Not all agreed with the withholding of information in this way. A letter to the editor of *The Times* from April of the same year argued that refusing to provide personal information to the government for the census was counterproductive, since the state could not improve the situation of women without it.[93] This fed into the broader twentieth-century debates about the right and role of the state to collect information on individuals for the dual purposes of welfare and warfare. In order to offer citizens social and protective legislation, those governing needed to know details of who they governed.[94]

After 1918, there were a huge number of government reports into health and mortality, particularly following the creation of the Ministry of Health in 1919. These increasingly focused on collection of women's corporeal information. For working-class women, these official reports by the state were often "measured exclusively in terms of mortality statistics," as Jane Lewis has argued.[95] Judy Giles has said that working-class women in this period

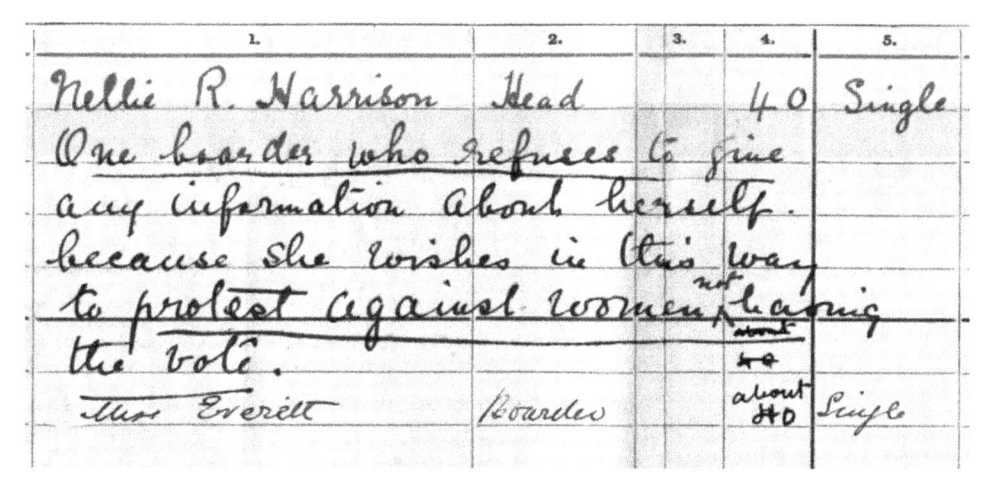

Figure 15.3 Detail from the census return for Nellie R. Harrison, Woking, taken from 1911 Census Return for England and Wales. Image from Ancestry.com, reproduced with kind permission of The National Archives of England and Wales.

"frequently entered the public discourse ... and her 'private' life were surveilled and probed by an increasing number of educationalists, social reformers, health visitors and housing officials," as the modern information state began to emerge.[96] Such were the consequences of female objectification in information collecting. Working-class women in their roles as housewives and mothers became "objects of detailed scrutiny," while high child mortality rates were cited as an example of the urban degeneration of the British race.[97] In 1903 a quarter of all deaths in England and Wales were those of children. Statistics such as these helped feed the contemporary narrative, justifying the necessity for state-driven information collection on working-class women.[98]

Those contemporaries who argued in favour of a more diverse curriculum for girls often linked back to the idea of reproduction and the health of the nation. The journal *Nature* had suggested in 1870 that an education in science, especially that of chemistry, would provide "enormous gain" to the human race, not least because such knowledge would afford an awareness "into the wholesomeness or unwholesomeness of different articles of food!"[99] In other words, chemistry could be useful for girls to study in order to understand the nutritional value of what to feed their families, rather than for scientific merit in its own right. In 1885, Galton had noted that the use of information collection on "school boys and girls" could be of great value with the aim of keeping check on the "physical well-being by a judicious serious of physical measurements."[100] By the early twentieth century, it was commonplace for medical officers at schools to carry out regular medical examinations which recorded in detail the growth, health, and medical history of each child.[101] Not all girls were simply passive recipients of information though; as with the Newnham and 1911 census examples, some schools did encourage girls to take an active role in negotiating their female identity.[102] For most though, the rhetoric of the period was of a woman's moral duty to the nation state, or, as Lynn Abrams has argued, what had been deemed a woman's natural role in the eighteenth century became a cultural one by the end of the nineteenth.[103] Corporeal information collection on women had moved from gendered hysteria to national responsibility, facilitated by the techniques and processes of the nascent information state.

Conclusion

The objectification of women that occurred during this period can be seen as an attempt at a move towards a conscious feminist information narrative. Traditional discourses of class, race, and gender at the turn of the nineteenth century can sit uncomfortably for a modern reader but perhaps they also allow us to view contemporary discourses about women's bodies and personal information collection through a historic lens, particularly important when the notion of women's bodies as objects of information remains highly topical.[104]

Historically, women's bodies had long been objectified as vessels for motherhood, marriage, and the domestic angel. During the late nineteenth and early twentieth centuries, women also began to be objectified through information collected about their bodies and physical form. Victorian debates about female health became intrinsically linked to feminine biological potency and corporal information: women literally embodied the information that became used and collated for social and political agendas about the role of women and the growth of the emancipation movement more broadly. As women began to challenge established social and political norms, Victorian medical science, and the era's fascination with using statistics and information collection for change, legitimised calls to preserve the established gender order. The growth of the eugenics movement and fears over the decline of the Empire and future race of Britons occurred alongside the emergence of the more centralised information state, with women—specifically their bodies—caught in the middle.

Notes

1 See Lina Papadaki, "What Is Objectification?" *Journal of Moral Philosophy* 7 (2010): 16–36. See also Nathan Heflick and Jamie Goldenberg, "Seeing Eye to Body: The Literal Objectification of Women," *Current Directions in Psychological Science* 23, no. 3 (2014): 225–229; Barbara Fredrickson et al., "Bringing Back the Body: A Retrospective on the Development of Objectification Theory," *Psychology of Women Quarterly* 35, no. 4 (2011): 689–696. There are, of course, many feminist perspectives; this chapter does not embrace a reductive or universalist concept of feminism.

2 The idea of women as "information objects" is first discussed in Toni Weller, "The Racialisation of British Women During the Long Nineteenth Century: How White Women's Bodies Became Tools For Control and Surveillance," in *The Cambridge Handbook of Race and Surveillance*, ed. Michael Kwet (Cambridge, UK: Cambridge University Press, 2023), 57–75. See also Toni Weller, *The Racialization of British Women during the Long Nineteenth Century*; a podcast (University of Erasmus: The Time Traveller's Almanac, S2E4, June, 2024). https://almanac.transistor.fm/s2/4. The idea of an "informational person" is discussed in Colin Koopman, *How We Became Our Data. A Genealogy of the Informational Person* (Chicago, IL: University of Chicago, 2019) but his focus is more on data-tracking technologies and their impacts on the self, rather than the body *itself* as an object. Koopman also only begins his study in 1913, at roughly the point at which this chapter ends, although he acknowledges the precedents set by Victorian pseudo-sciences.

3 Susan R. Bordo, "The Body and the Reproduction of Feminity: A Feminist Appropriation of Foucault," in *The Body; Critical Concepts in Sociology*, ed. Andrew Blaikie, Mike Hepworth, and Mary Holmes (Essex: Psychology Press, 2003), 239. See also Michel Foucault, *The History of Sexuality: An Introduction* (New York: Pantheon Books, 1978).

4 Sarah Kühl, *The Angel in the House and Fallen Women: Assigning Women Their Places in Victorian Society* (Oxford: Open Educational Resources, University of Oxford, 2016), 172.

5 See Asa Briggs, *Victorian Things* (London: Batsford, 1998) on Victorian love of collecting and classifying.

6 Barbara Harrison, "Women and Health," in *Women's History: Britain, 1850–1945. An Introduction*, ed. Jane Purvis (Abingdon: Routledge, 1995), 171.

7 Kühl, *The Angel in the House*, 172.

8 See also Toni Weller, *The Victorians and Information: A Social and Cultural History* (Saarbrücker: VDM Verlag, 2009), 47–53.

9 This focus is not to ignore or negate the impact of objectification on women of colour or different social class. Discussing race and class can be a fraught practice since terminology can be loaded and sensitive, but there is a growing and significant body of literature on the history of women of colour in particular during this period; see, for example, Ruby Hamad, *White Tears/Brown Scars: How White Feminism Betrays Women of Colour* (Paris: Hachette, 2020); Zine Magubane, "Which Bodies Matter? Feminism, Poststructuralism, Race, and the Curious Theoretical Odyssey of the 'Hottentot Venus'," *Gender & Society* 15, no. 6 (2001): 816–834.

10 Cecilia Tasca et al., "Women and Hysteria in the History of Mental Health," *Clinical Practice and Epidemiology in Mental Health* 8 (2012): 110–119; Henry Sigerist, *A History of Medicine. Primitive and Archaic Medicine* (Oxford: Oxford University Press, 1951).

11 See, for example, M. Trimble and E. H. Reynolds, "A Brief History of Hysteria: From the Ancient to the Modern," in *Handbook of Clinical Neurology*, ed. Mark Hallett, Jon Stone, and Alan Carson (Amsterdam: Elsevier, 2016), vol. 139, 3–10.

12 Heather Meek, "Of Wandering Wombs and Wrongs of Women: Evolving Conceptions of Hysteria in the Age of Reason," *ESC: English Studies in Canada* 35, no. 2 (2009): 106.

13 Omella Moscucci, *The Science of Woman: Gynaecology and Gender in England, 1800–1929* (Cambridge, UK: Cambridge University Press, 1990); Elaine Showalter, *The Female Malady: Women, Madness, and English Culture, 1830–1980* (New York: Pantheon, 1985).

14 Laura Briggs, "The Race of Hysteria: 'Overcivilization' and the 'Savage' Woman in Late Nineteenth-Century Obstetrics and Gynecology," *American Quarterly* 52, no. 2 (June 2000): 246.
15 Jeanne M. Peterson, "No Angels in the House: The Victorian Myth and the Paget Women," *The American Historical Review* 89, no. 3 (1984): 677–708.
16 Aristotle discussed the two areas of Greek society, the *oikos* (home) and the *polis* (city), which have been interpreted as confining women to a domestic role, although many argue this was not the reality of ancient Greek society, nor Aristotle's intended position. See Mika Ojakangas, "Polis and Oikos: The Art of Politics in the Greek City-State," *The European Legacy* 25, no. 2 (2020): 1–17.
17 Friedrich Engels, *The Origin of the Family, Private Property, and the State* (Chicago, IL: Charles H. Kerr & Co., 1902); see also Linda K. Kerber, "Separate Spheres, Female Worlds, Woman's Place: The Rhetoric of Women's History," *The Journal of American History* 75, no. 1 (1988): 9–39.
18 Kühl, *The Angel in the House*, 171–178; Amanda Vickery, "Golden Age to Separate Spheres? A Review of the Categories and Chronology of English Women's History," *The Historical Journal* 36 (1993): 383–414.
19 Kühl, *The Angel in the House*, 171.
20 See Alistair Black, "Aspects of the History of State Information Policies in Britain before the Digital Age," in *Research Handbook on Information Policy*, ed. Alistair Duff (Cheltenham: Edward Elgar Publishing, 2021), 80–95; Toni Weller, "The Information State: An Historical Perspective on Surveillance," in *Routledge Handbook of Surveillance Studies*, ed. Kirstie Ball, Kevin D. Haggerty, and David Lyn (Abingdon: Routledge, 2012), 57–63; Edward Higgs, *The Information State in England: The Central Collection of Information on Citizens Since 1500* (Basingstoke: Palgrave, 2004).
21 See Lawrence Goldman, *Victorians and Numbers: Statistics and Society in Nineteenth Century Britain* (Oxford: Oxford University Press, 2002).
22 See Alison Bashford and Philippa Levine, eds. *The Oxford Handbook of the History of Eugenics* (Oxford: Oxford University Press, 2010).
23 Aileen Fyfe "The Information Revolution," in *The Cambridge History of the Book in Britain, Vol. VI: 1830–1914*, ed. David McKitterick (Cambridge, UK: Cambridge University Press, 2009), 568.
24 See also Paul Csiszar's discussion of Alphonse Bertillon and measuring the body; Bertillon was a competitor of Francis Galton and an interesting connection to Paul Otlet: Alex Csiszar, "Bibliography as Anthropometry: Dreaming Scientific Order at the Fin de Siècle," *Library Trends* 62, no. 2 (2013): 442–455.
25 Patricia Fara, *A Lab of One's Own: Science and Suffrage in the First World War* (Oxford: Oxford University Press, 2018), 32.
26 Some of the measuring devices from the Galton Laboratory, including head spanners, craniometers, hair and eye colour reference samples, and a hand dynamometer, form part of the Galton archive collection at University College, London. The Galton Collection was a subject of much discussion during the UCL Eugenics Inquiry of 2018–2020. Its visibility has been an issue of some philosophical and moral controversy over the nature of its collection and the ethics of historical representation. See, for example, Robert Langkjær-Bain, "The Troubling Legacy of Francis Galton," *Significance* 16, no. 3 (2019): 16–21.
27 Francis Galton, "On the Anthropometric Laboratory at the Late International Health Exhibition," *The Journal of the Anthropological Institute of Great Britain and Ireland* 14 (1885): 205.
28 Galton, "Anthropometric Laboratory," 210.
29 John Venn, "Cambridge Anthropometry," *The Journal of the Anthropological Institute of Great Britain and Ireland* 18 (1889): 141.
30 Venn, "Cambridge Anthropometry," 143.
31 Penny Hubbard and Ruth Lowe, eds. *Women's Nature: Rationalizations of Inequality* (Oxford: Pergamon Press, 1983), 48.
32 Rosalind Miles, *The Women's History of the World* (Boulder, CO: Paladin, 1989), 226–227.
33 Charles Darwin, *The Descent of Man, and Selection in Relation to Sex* (London: John Murray, 1871).
34 Quote from Emily Davies, *On Secondary Instruction as Relation to Girls* (London: William Ridgway, 1864), 9.

35 Hilary Marland, *Health and Girlhood in Britain, 1874–1920* (Basingstoke: Palgrave, 2013), 5.
36 See Toni Weller and David Bawden, "Individual Perceptions: A New Chapter on Victorian Information History," *Library History* 22, no. 2 (July 2006): 137–156; Weller, *Victorians and Information*.
37 Eleanor Sidgwick, handwritten note in the *Newnham College Club Cambridge Roll Letter* (1898), 22–23. Newnham College Archives.
38 In 2013, the legal case of the prescription sleep drug zolpidem (Ambien) was recognised as part of "long history of inattention to biological sex differences" in science and medicine in which information collection and research based upon male bodies is used to inform medicines subsequently used on women. Quote from Helen Zhao et al., "Making a 'Sex-Difference Fact': Ambien Dosing at the Interface of Policy, Regulation, Women's Health, and Biology," *Social Studies of Science* 53, no. 4 (2023): 475.
39 Sidgwick, *handwritten note*, 22–23.
40 These were donated by Mary Ewart (a friend of Galton and benefactor of the early College). The College also had a measuring instrument given by Horace Darwin (son of Charles and a Fellow of Trinity College, Cambridge). Margaret Birney Vickery, *Buildings for Bluestockings: The Architecture and Social History of Women's Colleges in Late Victorian England* (Newark, DE: University of Delaware Press, 1999), 43, 45; Alice Gardener, *A Short History of Newnham College, Cambridge* (Cambridge, UK: Bowes & Bowes, 1921), 28.
41 Newnham College Archives, EC/2/6/3. Very little scholarly work has hitherto discussed the Index Cards or set them within their broader context. See Mary Beard, "Pull as an Archer, in Lbs," *London Review of Books* 18, no. 17 (September 5, 1996). Notably, although the Newnham Index cards are mentioned, the article is actually a review of two unrelated books. For other discussion of the cards, see Toni Weller and David Bawden, "Individual Perceptions," 137–156; Weller, *Victorians and Information*, 51–52.
42 Galton, "Anthropometric Laboratory," 205.
43 Mrs Henry Sidgwick, *Health Statistics of Women Students of Cambridge and Oxford and of Their Sisters* (Cambridge, UK: Cambridge University Press, 1890).
44 *The Girton Review*, 26 (August 1890), 4–5; Sidgwick, *Health Statistics*, 11.
45 Sidgwick, *Health Statistics*, 5.
46 Beard, "Pull as an Archer," 23.
47 Beard, "Pull as an Archer," 23.
48 *Letter from Francis Galton to Henry Sidgwick* (August 25, 1890). Wren Library, Trinity College, Cambridge – Add Mss c 94 (1).
49 Fara, *A Lab of One's Own*, 32.
50 Margaret Sanger, *Woman and the New Race* (Elkhart, IN: Truth Publishing Company, 1920), 94. One might also pose the rather more modern question, who "owned" the information collected about these women?
51 Geoffrey Rayner-Canham and Marelene Rayner-Canham, *Chemistry Was Their Life: Pioneering British Women Chemists, 1880–1949* (London: Imperial College Press, 2008).
52 Joan N. Burstyn, "Education and Sex: The Medical Case against Higher Education for Women in England, 1870–1900," *Proceedings of the American Philosophical Society* 117, no. 2 (1973): 79–89.
53 Henry Maudsley, "Sex in Mind and in Education," *The Fortnightly Review*, 21, no. 15 (April 1874): 467. See also the counter-response to Maudsley's article in Elizabeth Garrett Anderson, "Sex in Mind and Education: A Reply," *The Fortnightly Review*, 21, no. 15 (May 1874): 582–594.
54 Joan Burstyn, "Educators' Response to Scientific and Medical Studies of Women in England, 1860–1900," in *Is Higher Education Fair to Women?* ed. Sandra Acker and David Warren Piper (Guildford: SRHE & NFER-Nelson, 1984), 70.
55 Arnold White, *Efficiency and Empire* (London: Methuen, 1901), 102–103.
56 *Report of the Inter-Departmental Committee on Physical Deterioration*, vol. I (London: London Parliamentary Papers, 1904), 47, 53–54, 57.
57 Robert Reid Rentoul, *Dignity of Woman's Health and the Nemesis of Its Neglect (A Pamphlet for Women and Girls)* (London: J. & A. Churchill, 1890), xvi.
58 Francis Galton, "Eugenics: Its Definition, Scope and Aims," *The American Journal of Sociology* X, no. 1 (July 1904): 1. See also Richard Allen Soloway, "Feminism, Fertility, and Eugenics

in Victorian and Edwardian England," in *Political Symbolism in Modern Europe*, ed. Seymour Drescher (Abingdon: Routledge, 1982), 114–139.
59 Weller, "Racialisation of British Women," 57–75.
60 Women were prominent in many of the eugenics movements of Britain, the United States, and Australia. Women's relationship to eugenics was complicated by the fact that involvement in these movements could provide varying degrees of empowerment.
61 The concept of selective breeding was suggested by philosophers as early as 400 BCE. See Plato, *The Republic*, trans. Desmond Lee (London: Penguin Classics, 1987), Book IV.
62 See, for example, Emel Aileen Gökyiğit, "The Reception of Francis Galton's 'Hereditary Genius' in the Victorian Periodical Press," *Journal of the History of Biology* 27, no. 2 (1994): 215–240; F. C. Constable, *Poverty and Hereditary Genius; A Criticism of Mr Francis Galton's Theory of Hereditary Genius* (London: Arthur C. Fifield, 1906). Galton also recognised the need to convince the public of the value of his work; see Elise Smith, "'Why do we Measure Mankind?' Marketing Anthropometry in Late-Victorian Britain," *History of Science* 58, no. 2 (2020): 142–165.
63 See, for example, the writings of Sarah Grand, Grant Allen, Mona Caird, George Egerton, Emma Frances Brooke, and Ménie Muriel Dowie.
64 Jane Wood, *Passion and Pathology in Victorian Fiction* (Oxford: Oxford University Press, 2001).
65 See Gillian Sutherland, *Ability, Merit and Measurement: Mental Testing and English Education, 1880–1940* (Oxford: Oxford University Press, 1984).
66 See the medical papers of James Crichton-Browne as well as "An Oration on Sex in Education," *The Lancet* 1 (7 May, 1892), 1011–1018 by the same author.
67 Elizabeth Garrett Anderson, "Educational Pressure," *The Times* (15 April, 1880), 11.
68 Robert Farquharson, "Brain Exhaustion," *The Times* (19 April, 1880), 12. For a more contemporary study, see Uma Chitra and C. Radha Reddy, "The Role of Breakfast in Nutrient Intake of Urban Schoolchildren," *Public Health Nutrition* 10, no. 1 (2007): 55–58.
69 Havelock Ellis, *Man and Woman: A Study of Human Secondary Sexual Characters* (Newcastle: Walter Scott, 1897), 56–60.
70 Marland, *Health and Girlhood*, 2. Interestingly, Beth Linker explores a similar phenomenon occurring in the United States during the same period, where information on female posture and menstruation were measured and observed in order to "map the female body" in the interests of good health. See Beth Linker, "Tracing Paper, the Posture Sciences, and the Mapping of the Female Body," in *Working with Paper: Gendered Practices in the History of Knowledge*, ed. Carla Bittel, Elaine Leong, and Christine von Oertzen (Pittsburgh, PA: University of Pittsburgh Press, 2019), 124–139.
71 See Weller, "Racialisation of British Women," 57–75.
72 Briggs, "Race of Hysteria," 266. See also Annie Besant, *The Law of Population* (Freethought Publishing Company, 1877).
73 Harrison, "Women and Health," 182.
74 Goldman, *Victorians and Numbers*.
75 Charles Booth, *The Life and Labour of the People of London* (17 volumes in 3 series: Poverty, Industry and Religion) (London: 1889–1903).
76 Lawrence Goldman, *Victorians and Numbers*, 295.
77 Michel Foucault, *Power: Essential Works of Foucault, 1954–1984*, vol. 3 (London: Penguin, 2001).
78 Marland, *Health and Girlhood*, 2.
79 Angelique Richardson, "The Life Sciences: 'Everybody Nowadays Talks about Evolution'," in *A Concise Companion to Modernism*, ed. David Bradshaw (Hoboken, NJ: Wiley-Blackwell, 2002), 20.
80 Marland, *Health and Girlhood*, 6–7; Harrison, "Women and Health," 182.
81 Jane Carey, "The Racial Imperatives of Sex: Birth Control and Eugenics in Britain, the United States and Australia in the Interwar Years," *Women's History Review* 21, no. 5 (2012): 733. This also feeds into a bigger debate on race and reproduction than is covered in the scope of this chapter—see Richard Soloway, *Birth Control and the Population Question in England, 1877–1930* (Chapel Hill, NC: University of North Carolina Press, 1982).
82 Susanne Klausen and Alison Bashford, "Fertility Control: Eugenics, Neo- Malthusianism, and Feminism," in *The Oxford Handbook of the History of Eugenics*, ed. Alison Bashford and Philippa Levine (Oxford: Oxford University Press, 2010), 109–10.

83 Dan Stone, "Race in British Eugenics," *European History Quarterly* 31, no. 3 (2001): 397–425.
84 Karl Pearson, "Woman and Labour," *Fortnightly Review* 55, no. 329 (1894): 577.
85 Angelique Richardson, *Love and Eugenics in the Late Nineteenth Century: Rational Reproduction and the New Woman* (Oxford: Oxford University Press, 2003), 215.
86 Higgs, *Information State in England*.
87 Jon Agar, *The Government Machine. A Revolutionary History of the Computer* (Cambridge, MA: MIT Press, 2003).
88 Elise Juzda Smith, "Class, Health and the Proposed British Anthropometric Survey of 1904," *Social History of Medicine* 28, no. 2 (2015): 308–329.
89 Higgs, *Information State in England*, 99, 101.
90 Higgs, *Information State in England*, 102.
91 Fara, *A Lab of One's Own*, 31.
92 See Fig. 15.3. The example is taken from the census return of Nellie R. Harrison, who completed her own census return but noted on it that her boarder, Miss Everett, refused. Census return for Nellie R. Harrison. Census ref. RG14; Piece; 3017; Schedule Number: 266. *Census Returns of England and Wales, 1911*. Kew, Survey, England. The National Archives of the UK (Ancestry.com).
93 The Registrar, "Suffragists and the Census," *The Times* (1 April, 1911), 7.
94 Weller, "The Information State," 57–63.
95 Jane Lewis, *The Politics of Motherhood: Child and Maternal Welfare in England, 1900–1950* (Kent: Croom Helm, 1980), 16.
96 Judy Giles, *Women, Identity and Private Life in Britain, 1900–1950* (New York: Macmillan, 1995), 18.
97 Giles, *Women, Identity and Private Life*, 100. For contemporary comment on child mortality rates and degeneration of the race, see George Newman, *Infant Mortality: A Social Problem* (New York: Menthuen, 1906), v–vi.
98 John Walker-Smith, "Sir George Newman, Infant Diarrhoeal Mortality and the Paradox of Urbanism," *Medical History* 42 (1998): 349.
99 Anon, "The Scientific Education of Women," *Nature* 2 (16 June, 1870), 117–118.
100 Galton, "Anthropometric Laboratory," 207. This idea is somewhat echoed through the modern National Child Measurement Programme in English primary schools in which children are weighed and measured by the NHS. See B. E. Kovacs, F. B. Gillison and J. C. Barnett, "Is Children's Weight a Public Health or a Private Family Issue? A Qualitative Analysis of Online Discussion About National Child Measurement Programme Feedback in England," *BMC Public Health* 18 (2018): 1295.
101 Paul Atkinson, "Fitness, Feminism and Schooling" in *The Nineteenth Century Woman: Her Cultural and Physical World*, ed. S. Delamont et al. (Kent: Croom Helm, 1978), 107–117.
102 Lauren O'Hagan, "'Clean Nails Are the Mark of a Well Brought-Up Girl': Exploring Gender in a Post Edwardian Girls' School Exercise Book," *Women's Studies* 47, no. 8 (2018): 765–790.
103 Lynn Abrams, *The Making of a Modern Woman: Europe, 1789–1918* (Harlow: Longman, 2002), 41.
104 Bryndl Hohmann-Marriott, "Periods as Powerful Data: User Understandings of Menstrual App Data and Information," *New Media & Society* 25, no. 11 (2023): 3028–3046; Michele Estrin Gilman, "Periods for Profit and the Rise of Menstrual Surveillance," *Columbia Journal of Gender & Law* 41, no. 1 (2021): 100–113.

16
INFORMATION, TOPOGRAPHY, AND WAR

Information Management in Britain's Inter-Service Topographical Department (ISTD) in the Second World War

Alistair Black

Topographical intelligence—derived from the collection, processing, organisation, analysis, and dissemination of information related to the study of land-surface features, whether natural or artificial—has been a key variable in the determination of success or failure in organised warfare. At the Battle of Culloden in 1746, the last full-scale pitched battle to take place in the British Isles, poor topographical intelligence proved critical in the rout of the Scottish Jacobites (those seeking the restoration of the Stuart dynasty) at the hands of the British Army. Advancing into unobserved boggy terrain, the Jacobite troops were unable to exploit their most potent tactic, the blood-curdling Highland Charge. Culloden was a turning point in British history. It had profound consequences for the future of the countries of the British Isles as well as the rest of the world, creating over the next century and a half a largely uncontested and centralised fiscal-military state (funded by a national debt) and leading to the rise of Great Britain to a position of imperial and international economic hegemony.[1]

Deficiencies in Topographical Intelligence at the Start of the Second World War

Almost exactly two centuries after Culloden, Britain and its empire emerged triumphant from a world war that nonetheless underlined its fall from supremacy. That fall had been signalled in the Spring of 1940 with the failure of the military expeditions to both Norway and northern France. In both the short-lived Norway campaign commencing in early April and the Dunkirk evacuation in late May, British forces were hampered by inadequate geographical intelligence.[2]

The experiences of Norway and Dunkirk shocked the government into improving topographical intelligence. With British land forces confined to their island home, and discounting bombing raids by the Royal Air Force, the only military operations in the foreseeable future that could be mounted against Nazi-occupied mainland Europe would be amphibious as well as, crucially, multi-service in nature. Topographical intelligence is at a premium where terrain conditions play a big part in military action.[3] Nowhere are such conditions

Information, Topography, and War

more shifting and unpredictable than in coastal areas. Not surprisingly, therefore, topographical intelligence would contribute much to the work of the Combined Operations Command which was formed in the Spring of 1940 to coordinate commando raids along the German-occupied coast of Europe, with support from the Navy and Air Force.

Tri-service warfare requires integrated intellectual support.[4] The combined, amphibious operations envisaged after the withdrawals from Norway and northern France emphasised the importance of sharing information and pooling its management, whereas over the decades—stretching back even into the nineteenth century with regard to army-navy relations—the intelligence units in the three services had got used to working in silos.[5] However, during the crisis of 1940, it was soon realised that topography as a research subject was "single, coherent and indivisible" and, as such, it was "far more economical in effect, and reliable in results, that one organisation should be made responsible for all topographical facts about a given area."[6] The duplication of effort in the area of topographical intelligence had to end if operations were to achieve success. What was needed was a centralised "clearing house" for information, one that would cut across partisan rivalries between the services.[7] As Rear-Admiral John Godfrey, Director of Naval Intelligence (DNI), put it at the time: "Total war deserves total intelligence."[8]

Good intentions regarding inter-service collaboration in topographical intelligence would come to nothing if the infrastructure for the management of information was not well resourced. Just as between the wars there had been little or no intelligence cooperation between the three services, the same period witnessed a severe retrenchment in intelligence operations across the board, including in matters of topography. Cost-cutting in the 1920s and 1930s "had practically sterilised all intelligence work."[9] After 1918, a reassessment of national priorities in favour of social and industrial reconstruction meant a diversion of spending away from the military, while the slump of the 1930s affected virtually all government programmes and departments, including military intelligence which was forced to exist on a shoestring.[10] In topographical intelligence, little or no effort was made to build on the advances made in the First World War, so that by 1939 it was wholly justifiable to refer to "twenty years of [topographical] intelligence starvation between the wars."[11]

The recognition and intended satisfaction of urgent topographical needs early in the war led to the genesis in the Spring of 1940 of the Inter-Service Topographical Department (ISTD), whose charter—marking it out like other areas of military intelligence as a genuine information institution—called for the "collection, collation and publication in suitable form of topographical information."[12]

The Formation, Infrastructure, and Development of the ISTD

The military applications of scientific topography can be traced back to operations conducted by Napoleon's armies. In Britain, episodes of active military topography can be identified in the nineteenth century. However, its formal development did not occur until the First World War. The Second World War witnessed a large escalation in military topography, as this chapter will outline, although this did not happen until the second year of the war, under the direction of the ISTD.[13]

The failures in topographical intelligence early in the war became common knowledge at the highest level. Churchill was made aware of the poor topographical information provided in support of the Norway campaign. It was perhaps Churchill's memory of the failure of the landings at Gallipoli in 1915, a plan which as First Lord of the Admiralty (the Navy's political head) he had enthusiastically spearheaded, which ignited his interest in topographical intelligence—specifically, the importance of good information on the nature of the terrain over which one would be fighting, something which was conspicuously absent in the Gallipoli campaign.[14] Whether or not this *was* Churchill's motivation, his engagement and support certainly accelerated the growth of the ISTD.[15]

Efforts to create a single topographical intelligence agency were led by the Naval Intelligence Division (NID). The origins of NID can be traced back to the establishment of the Foreign Intelligence Committee of the Admiralty in 1882. Aiming to "classify, collate and index information which would be required for naval operations," five years later, the Committee was upgraded to the Naval Intelligence Department, which was further elevated to the status of a Division in 1912.[16] Early in 1940 the idea of an ISTD began to germinate in the mind of the aforementioned DNI, John Godfrey. On February 12, 1940, Godfrey, accompanied by his assistant, Lieutenant-Commander Ian Fleming (the future creator of James Bond), approached the renowned geographer Kenneth Mason.[17] Mason was asked to prepare three critical reports, a task which he accomplished within the tight deadlines set.[18] Godfrey realised a more permanent, formal arrangement was required, so in late April, Colonel Sam Bassett, a long-serving naval intelligence officer, was approached to build a topographical section in NID. In the three-month period to the end of May 1940, Mason and Bassett between them oversaw the production of thirty brief topographical reports.[19]

These reports were on a wide variety of geographical areas but what they had in common was the immediacy of the reporting required. Responsibility for them gravitated towards Bassett's team, later designated NID6.[20] The reports produced by this team were wholly different to the heavyweight geographical assessments—the Naval Intelligence (Geographical) Handbooks—which required extensive research and which were prepared over a long period of time. Preparation of these assessments was under Mason's direction. His geographical unit within the ISTD was later designated NID5 and went on to contain a Geological Section, formally established in November 1943. Sections for Engineering, Economics (Resources), Railways, and Fire Susceptibility (regarding air raids on Germany) were also established in the ISTD at various points.[21]

It is important to emphasise, therefore, that administratively, the ISTD comprised two main units with different fundamental briefs, but it is also important to stress that the two did not operate in isolation: NID6 constantly drew on NID5's long-term work as well as its personnel.[22] Despite the links between the two units and their existence under the ISTD panoply, this chapter concentrates on the work of NID6, for which the ISTD *per se* serves as a convenient synonym.

On October 1, 1940, the ISTD moved from London to Oxford, which was largely free from bombing and, in Bassett's words, "away from the seemingly lunatic confusion of Whitehall."[23] The move to Oxford marked the effective inauguration of the ISTD, even if it had been working as an embryonic unit for several months by that time. It first set up shop in the School of Geography, opposite Manchester College. A year later, the latter was requisitioned "in the national interest."[24] Huts were also built in the gardens of the School of Geography and on the Balliol cricket ground nearby, a collection of temporary structures which became known as the "Admiralty Village."[25] The ISTD also took over parts of the Ashmolean Museum, the upper and lower libraries of New College, the Isis Hotel, and, most prominently, virtually the whole of the New Bodleian Library, which was used to house, among other materials, the Department's large collection of photographs.[26]

Commencing with a skeleton staff of just six, thereafter the ISTD grew significantly: 72 members at the end of 1941, increasing to 541 at the start of 1944.[27] The ISTD became truly inter-service in March 1941, the Directors of Intelligence in the Army and RAF having finally warmed to a project that had been initiated in the Admiralty.[28] Increasingly, the ISTD's personnel were drawn from all three armed services, augmented by civilian members of staff, from clerks to academics.[29] By 1943, the ISTD had also become inter-Allied, bringing American, Dutch, Norwegian, and French experts and military personnel under its wing. The ISTD worked closely with operatives in US intelligence, eventually establishing its own section in Washington, DC.[30] In the summer of 1944, shortly after D-Day, ISTD staffing reached its peak, with 750 personnel, military, and civilian.[31] Thus, although "tiny and insignificant" to begin with, the ISTD eventually grew into a "colossus," as Bassett put it.[32] Godfrey described it as an "inter-service monster."[33]

The ISTD's staff frequently found themselves hard pressed, having to prepare reports at very short notice, with staff occasionally working both day and night shifts.[34] Often, information was gathered for plans that were not executed, placing great strain on ISTD staff. In one ninety-day period straddling late 1941 and early 1942, the ISTD created thirty reports in response to special operations, the vast majority of which never materialised.[35] The performance of the ISTD had attracted considerable praise in higher military circles and efforts were made to ensure the continuation of its good work and core remit.[36] Following an enquiry into the work of the Department, in August 1943, a memorandum on the ISTD's staff requirements and workload was issued by the Joint Intelligence Committee (JIC), the ISTD's supervisory body. It concluded that the ISTD's contribution was highly valuable but that its "customers" were at fault in making too many unnecessary demands on the organisation.[37] The JIC endeavoured to ease the pressure on the ISTD by allowing an increase in staffing and by rationing the amount of non-topographical and low-grade intelligence work it needed to undertake.[38] Regarding the second of these initiatives, a special committee, with links to high-level planners, was established to formulate a list of operational priorities and, in accordance with the list, to scrutinise and filter requests for ISTD assistance.[39]

For reasons of security, most ISTD personnel wore civilian dress to avoid attracting attention. Their inconspicuous appearance at once chimed with the sober intellectual tasks they were required to accomplish and contrasted starkly with the daring operations they underpinned with their intelligence work. These operations would not have been successful without the systematic and steady application of information-management skills by ISTD personnel—ranging from basic clerical, administrative, and organisational work to searching, analytical, and academic expertise—whose unsung contributions were in many ways no less heroic than those who took part in the intrepid military actions the ISTD supported.

The ISTD's Information-Management System

The purpose of the ISTD was to act as a "central collecting, collating and compilation department for all the topographical knowledge bearing on a proposed site for amphibious assault."[40] More practically and reductively, the work, as Bassett saw it, was a matter of "searching for information, reducing this information to its military value, and then producing books [mostly reports] complete with every graphic and technical aid."[41] Such information-management practices pre-date the computer and have been studied in a variety of "early information society" contexts, including the history of military intelligence and communications.[42] Like these other pre-computer contexts, the presence of a rational system of information management in military intelligence—in this case that of the ISTD—becomes visible when examined in terms of a system's planned phases for the collection, processing, organisation, analysis, and dissemination of information.

Collection

Once the ISTD had been informed of a planned operation, a pro-forma, known as the "ISTD Questionnaire and Layout," was sent to the participating services to ascertain their requirements.[43] Such direct contact between those producing topographical intelligence and the end user was encouraged.[44] The type of information the ISTD collected to meet planners' requirements was wide ranging. Fully fledged topographical intelligence meant, in Bassett's view, "drawing up a detailed picture of any area, city, town, manor, parish, or what-have-you" and recording "everything that exists in that area ... natural or artificial."[45] Initially conceptualised as essentially a geographical unit, with a responsibility for collecting geological and soil information also, the ISTD soon began to gather and publish information on wider matters, such as communications, transport, military and economic installations, climate, medical resources, and power supplies—that is, not only information on the natural environment but on man-made features also. The ISTD was not expected to confine its work to matters of natural geography and geology, although there is evidence that the zeal it displayed in broadening its brief was curbed slightly by the JIC.[46]

Sources of information ranged from surveillance activities of various kinds, including what is known today as "human intelligence" (HUMINT) and "imagery intelligence" (IMINT), to traditional, pre-existing intellectual materials in the public domain. Resistance movements in Europe were a good source, as in the case of reports from the French resistance prior to D-Day. Also valuable was information disclosed by those who had escaped Nazi occupation, such as the refugees who were able to pass on information about the geography around Kaa Fjord in northern Norway where the battleship Tirpitz, head of the German Naval Battle Group and a severe threat to Allied shipping in the northern Atlantic, had sought shelter in 1943. An ISTD-supported air raid in April 1944 crippled the battleship. The raid had been partly informed by a reconnaissance flight with a landscape artist on board.[47]

During and shortly after the Dunkirk evacuation, in-person reconnaissance was undertaken of as many beaches as possible in northern France before the Germans arrived. The detailed information obtained was added to the embryonic topographical database for later operations, including the return of British forces *en masse* to France.[48] The ultimate example of human topographical intelligence was provided by Bassett himself. A few days before the D-Day landings were due to take place, Bassett volunteered to be dropped by submarine at a prospective landing area that was believed could prove difficult for armoured vehicles to negotiate due to possible deposits of peat under the sand (peat under wet sand was problematic, but under dry sand not so).[49] Similar "on the ground" investigations had been performed by Combined Operations Pilotage Parties (COPPs), which had made stealth landings in the middle of the night to assess the beaches under the noses of German sentries.

In late 1941, the ISTD began approaching refugee aliens systematically as a source of topographical intelligence. Their names were initially contained in a Refugee Register which was later absorbed into a larger Contacts Register, also a card index, housed in the New Bodleian Library.[50] Listed in the Contacts Register were the names of British and Colonial citizens in commerce (such as shipping and insurance), industry, mining, and engineering, as well as experienced travellers and explorers, who might have information on terrain, infrastructure, and military installations in foreign countries.[51] By the end of 1943, fifteen staff were working on the Contacts Register.[52] Information gathered from private firms was said to be particularly valuable.[53] Photographs from the Royal Mail Steamship Company proved valuable, as did information from the travel firm Thomas Cook and from Lloyd's Insurance.[54]

The most famous information gathering exercise conducted by the ISTD was the radio appeal (conducted in the name of the Admiralty) it made as plans for D-Day began to take shape. Following a successful appeal broadcast on the BBC in 1941 by the Ministry of Economic Warfare for foreign phone directories and guidebooks, in 1942 the ISTD mounted a similar appeal, for images of the coast and immediate interior of northern France. The appeal explained how a recent commando raid had succeeded because planners were able to draw on the very kind of material being requested. The appeal was for postcards, maps, holiday snaps, Michelin guidebooks, magazine illustrations, and any other information relating to the French coast (the entire coast in order not to reveal the location of any planned landings).[55] Within thirty-six hours, around thirty thousand letters and packages (some containing whole albums of family snaps) had been received from a generous public. Eventually, over sixty thousand correspondences were received, resulting in an accumulated four million photographs. Later, the appeal was taken up by the national press, pushing the total collection of images to ten million. Many of these were images extracted from amateur cine films.[56] Photographs were also collected from a variety of institutional sources, including the Royal Geographical Society and commercial photographic news agencies, although some of the latter, such as the Exclusive News Agency, were destroyed in the Blitz.[57]

To supplement these sources, detailed, up-to-date aerial photographs were required. To avoid giving away the exact location of the landings, the photographic reconnaissance sorties were flown over the entire length of the northern French coast. Aircraft flew along the coast at a high altitude but also, daringly, at very low levels. the ISTD commissioned a special squadron of Spitfires fitted with cameras to fly at "zero elevation" (essentially a few metres above the waves) at 90° to the coast to photograph beaches, defensive installations, and buildings. Such was the excellence of these "low oblique" photographs that sometimes one could see right through the windows of buildings and into the rooms that overlooked the coast.[58] These photos were added to the ISTD's stock of over one million photographs housed in the New Bodleian Library.[59] Such topographical imagery was critical to the planning of D-Day.

The ISTD's base in Oxford proved invaluable for accessing public domain information deposited in the city's impressive libraries and learned societies. The ISTD collected thousands of reference books from these sources, as well as from the private collections of individuals (after the war a determined effort was made to return these to their owners).[60] The New Bodleian Library (virtually finished by the start of the war, though not officially opened until 1946) served as a place of safe keeping for many collections of books, journals, and archival papers deposited there by libraries and learned societies from around the country. One of these deposits was the collection of forty thousand volumes from the Natural History Museum, from which loans to the ISTD were authorised from July 1942 onwards.[61] The ISTD made heavy use of pre-war technical journals and by 1943 it was receiving over eighty technical publications each month.[62]

Processing and Organisation

Much of the ISTD's information-management activity was accounted for by processing and organising photographs. Useful technology was received from the United States. This included a machine which could increase or reduce the size of photographs to produce standard-sized copies suitable for filing. The machine had the added advantage of reproducing images from books and albums without damaging their spines.[63] Other sophisticated reproduction machines were also deployed. In preparation for D-Day—including the production of coastal recognition silhouettes (more about these below)—the ISTD commandeered the only (three) Graber photographic reproduction machines in the country. Graber machines were famous for reproducing glossy postcards, the copies they made being detailed and vivid. They could also reproduce thousands of copies in a single print run, for inclusion in the multiple reports and other outputs produced by the ISTD.[64]

Sorting through the photographs and other materials bearing images of northern France that resulted from the BBC and press appeals was a monumental task. Replies were initially handled by a commercial firm, before their contents were deposited in the New Bodleian. Bassett estimated that from the time of receiving an image to the moment it was filed away systematically in the New Bodleian, some sixty separate operations were involved. Naturally, few people had captioned the photographs they had sent in. Those photographs that were captioned may have contained inaccuracies or used a very broad and thus less-than-helpful descriptive term, such as "Out in the Country" or "John's Yacht."[65]

Large numbers of additional handling, as opposed to analytical, staff were needed to sort, caption, and file the photographic collection. The local labour exchange in Oxford was helpful in sending good numbers of young women to the ISTD. However, it was observed that "their standard of intelligence was not the highest," too much reliance having to be made, unfortunately, on the girls' own, limited knowledge of geography because gazetteers were in short supply. The situation was eased when fifty high-quality American service women arrived directly from the United States to help with the handling.[66] These American service women were later replaced by British Wrens (Fig. 16.1).[67]

An ISTD Central Index helped staff prepare reports and answer enquiries. This was an index to in-house sources as well as sources available in the nation's libraries, societies, and commercial firms. The index covered literature, maps, photographs, and the records of private enterprises. It also included interviews with individuals recorded in the Contacts Register.[68] Staff were too few in number to undertake any kind of significant classification work.[69] It does not appear that any deep indexing system was adopted or devised for photographs or other materials, although perhaps in order to facilitate retrieval the ISTD did produce what it regarded as the first dictionary of nautical terms.[70] In the end, the ISTD abandoned the idea of filing its vast collection of photographs housed in the New Bodleian according to a grid-reference (latitude-longitude) indexing system. A "geographical system" was adopted instead, with the result that "it became the proud boast of the library that no matter what place was asked for, it [an image] could be produced within a matter of minutes."[71] Home-grown methods of organising materials were also in evidence: a member of staff recalled that one room in the ISTD had its walls plastered with postcards of Normandy.[72] After the war, regret was expressed that in the interests of on-going or future

Figure 16.1 The ISTD female staff, probably Navy Wrens, working in the New Bodleian Library. In the interests of security, most ISTD staff were in civilian dress. Photographed by Peter Bradford (Admiralty Photographic Unit). Reproduced with permission of the Harris Manchester College, University of Oxford.

procurement, no attempt had been made to catalogue sources that were not visible in printed reports.[73]

Although highly sophisticated indexing protocols are difficult to detect, the general impression is of a highly organised system in operation in the ISTD. Once located in Oxford, the character of the ISTD changed from a unit answering *ad hoc* questions and collecting piecemeal scraps of information for "rushed" reports and almost immediate (sometimes verbal) replies to enquiries (termed "special tasks"), to an organised department with a programme of work and outputs (termed "routine tasks").[74] Bassett was described by his close colleague Mason as "a first-class organizer."[75] In the settled environment of Oxford, Bassett and his colleagues were, in Bassett's own words, "able to really organise our work; to decide which operations were likely to be urgent; to schedule certain jobs and fulfill them by a stated date. There was [both] system and method in our work."[76] An example of this systematic method is the ISTD questionnaires sent to the various service units once the broad plan of an operation had been assigned. These not only helped identify material to be collected, they also served as the main method of organising the work plan for researching the operation's topographical elements—research which often required high-level analytical skills, to which our attention is now turned.[77]

Analysis

At the start of the war, intelligence analysis was not seen as something that readily resided in naval intelligence. Historically, the naval officer had been seen as "a prisoner of his narrow technical education" and pre-occupied with the contemporary revolution in ship design and naval technology.[78] Contradicting this stereotype, the genesis of the ISTD, at its core an analytical body, was in naval intelligence circles, specifically NID.

Military intelligence depends initially on the prior acquisition of information that is relevant, accurate and adequate, but thereafter its value is determined by effective interpretation and evaluation.[79] The ISTD's efficiency in analysing information was founded first and foremost on the focused way it collected it. It is true that in the early period of the ISTD's existence, there were some concerns regarding the ability of the many staff to identify and search sources effectively.[80] The quality of staff in NID at the start of the war was noted by Bassett.[81] However, generally speaking, an "indiscriminate and haphazard" approach to collecting topographical information was avoided.[82] "Snowballing"—potentially useful information being subjected to intelligent analysis leading to the uncovering of further caches of productive information—was seen as a key feature of the analytical process.[83]

To produce a ten-page illustrated report for even a modest operation, an ISTD team would have to consult and analyse dozens of maps and charts, hundreds of books, magazines, and technical journals, and thousands of photographs, both aerial and ground. Elements of this labour could be vastly reduced, of course, by extracting information from an appropriate expert.[84] Analysis in the ISTD was driven forward by the high-quality experts it recruited. The ISTD tapped expertise in the fields of geology, geography, hydrography, economics, and engineering. British geologists added significantly to topographical military intelligence. None of the geologists in the Geological Section had experience in military applied geology prior to joining the ISTD.[85] However, they soon made an impact, members of the Geological Section contributing extensively to the Department's reports.[86] Royal Engineers were brought into the team in order to assess the significance of such infrastructure as piers, jetties, wharf cranes, lifting gear, beaches, bridges, rail gauges, tunnel clearance, and railway systems generally.[87] The ISTD drew on technical competence in Britain's own, as well as Allied, armed forces, and across all three services. By 1941, officers from the War Office and a geographer and geologist from the Air Ministry had joined ISTD.[88] In the summer of 1943, Dutch nationals added to the ISTD's establishment partly because of their knowledge of the Far East, and after Bassett's visit to the United States that same year, several American officers, including geographers and photographic experts, were seconded to the ISTD. The American additions were highly valued, described as they were as "men with objective research minds."[89] Norwegian officers and experts were also recruited.[90]

A good deal of the work in NID5 on the Naval Intelligence Handbooks was undertaken by a little-known cohort of around a hundred academic geographers, a fifth of them women, working on a part-time basis while undertaking teaching at various universities around the country. The women geographers were particularly skilled at producing maps and images for the Handbooks, and also performed this work for NID6.[91]

In Oxford, the ISTD was able to tap some of the country's brightest academic minds, notwithstanding that work on the Handbooks was also shared with Cambridge. Moreover, it was not just academics in the earth and applied sciences that made a telling contribution. The ISTD made extensive use of non-specialist academics, who proved "invaluable when it came to the complicated job of editing material."[92] These non-specialists were not qualified to comment on scientific content. However, they were able to make suggestions regarding clarity, in addition to correcting style, standardising layout and names and welding a narrative into a coherent whole.[93] Some classical scholars were thought suitable for the research because they were used to "collating defective scraps of evidence, their pedantic exactitude was seen to be worthwhile when lives were at stake, and they had a reputation ... for writing concisely and clearly."[94] One such scholar was Bassett's assistant, A.F. (Freddy) Wells, from University College, who was considered to be a brilliant classical academic.[95] People of this ilk were deemed "to possess clarity of thought combined with dispassionate and yet penetrating judgement and brilliant intuition, that enables them to turn their minds to any problem and to bring their painstaking research to a successful conclusion."[96] Regarding one ISTD report produced by the classicist William Watt, the DNI commented: "I doubt if a commander of an operation has ever before been given his intelligence in so complete and so legible a form."[97] Bassett praised Watt, who spoke French, German, and Italian, for his "deadly accurate and quick mind."[98] Such eminent minds, including those skilled in languages and editing, were hard to recruit. Bassett found himself constantly negotiating for salaries equivalent to those found in the commercial sphere (adequate salaries were certainly important for those ISTD personnel who were having to fund two homes). Good quality lower-grade information workers, such as clerks and typists, were also hard to find on the salaries that the ISTD were allowed to offer.[99]

Both library and museum workers contributed to ISTD at an intellectual level. Staff of the Geological Museum and Library in London participated extensively in the activities of the ISTD. Not only was raw information provided, but staff in the Museum and Library also helped write ISTD reports, as well as a small number of chapters in the Naval Intelligence Handbooks (staff also edited and checked chapters in the Handbooks).[100] Library workers in the New Bodleian and in other Oxford libraries also lent intellectual support. This said, after the war, it was reflected that more subject-specialist library assistance would have been beneficial.[101]

Dissemination

When word got out that a special topographical intelligence unit had been established, ISTD began to receive a large number and variety of requests for information from the services, which it did its best to satisfy within the boundaries of the slim resources it had at its disposal.[102] Throughout, the ISTD disseminated packets of information in response to enquiries from various government departments and other military intelligence units.[103]

However, the ISTD's main avenue of dissemination was through its commissioned reports—each badged an Inter-Service Intelligence Study (ISIS)—which initially formed the basis for joint-service high echelon planning.[104] The dissemination of these was assisted by Oxford University Press (OUP). The ISTD's earliest reports were crude, being produced in typescript, illustrated by photographs stuck onto brown paper by hand and loosely bound in filing folders. Intended only for higher officials and military operatives, these took a long time to produce, even in small quantities. However, following its move to Oxford, the ISTD was able to capitalise on the long-standing relationship between the Navy and OUP, which was already printing the former's codes, cyphers, and signal books.[105] Eventually, OUP was doing so much work for the ISTD (at one point, it accounted for two-thirds of the output of the Press), that some printing had to be outsourced to other printers around the country.[106] Security in the printing phase of the ISTD's production of reports was a priority. It was said that the plates for each print run of a sensitive report, if it extended beyond one day, were kept overnight by the Director of OUP, John Johnson, under a bed he slept on in his office.[107] The most secret parts of reports would be printed at the Press at night, after the "day staff" had gone home.[108] Special allocations of paper to facilitate printing such vast quantities of reports and booklets had to be arranged with the Stationery Office, while the Mines Department was brought onside to secure the fuel needed to drive the paper mills.[109]

The quality of ISTD reports became widely admired.[110] One of the ISTD's most innovative outputs were coastline silhouettes—concertina panoramas comprising continuous, horizontal strip images printed in booklets or albums, to facilitate beach recognition during the D-Day landings. The images were taken by the adapted low-flying Spitfires mentioned above. The silhouettes—a kind of modern, military Bayeux Tapestry—were studied by those charged with creating highly detailed maps and three-dimensional models of the D-Day landing zones, as well as by operational officers to enhance for geographical and installation recognition. However, they were also required lower down the hierarchy.[111] Originally, the ISTD understood that only forty silhouettes were needed. Actually, D-Day's planners required forty *thousand*. Copies were needed not just for the higher authorities but also for ships' gun crews and for landing craft operators.[112] The aforementioned Graber photographic reproduction machines were found to be too slow to accomplish this enormous task, so a new prototype reproduction machine was commandeered from RAF Farnborough, while the massive extra stocks of photographic paper and chemicals required were brought in from the United States on emergency flights.[113] For the invasion, the ISTD produced not only the forty thousand silhouette booklets requested, but also thousands of reports and brochures. In addition to information on coastal geography, these included intelligence on possible landing areas for gliders and parachutists and on targets for demolition by the French resistance.[114]

A great deal of time and effort was taken up by the continual updating of intelligence outputs. Last-minute amendments, additions, and improvements came as part of the intelligence territory.[115] A good example of this was the many iterations of the maps of the beaches of northern France, especially those in Normandy identified as probable landing areas for D-Day. From the middle of 1942, German coastal defences multiplied and shifted rapidly. This required an on-going revision of maps and narrative reports. Regarding mapping, a new method was introduced whereby charts were overlaid by traces on which symbols representing such elements as new gun emplacements, pill boxes, communication posts, or damaged roads were marked. Stretches of coast were color-coded on traces according to the strength of defences calculated using a formula combining the number and calibre of guns. On another trace, the suitability of beach exits for landing troops might be recorded. These several traces were photo-stated and distributed with the original "base" charts, accompanied by revised textual reports.[116] Other colour-coded mapping included zonal maps for prospective air raids, produced by the ISTD's Fire Susceptibility Section. These identified areas in Germany that offered a higher fire risk, thereby maximising the effectiveness of incendiary bombs which would otherwise have been wasted on low-risk districts.[117]

Models, manufactured by the ISTD's in-house model-making unit, were used to disseminate information in a way that was digestible, vivid, and memorable. One of the earliest models produced was for the amphibious attack on Dieppe in 1942. Photographs of the model taken at appropriate angles were used to produce hundreds of silhouette booklets for the raiding forces. The raid was considered a failure, for many and various reasons, although valuable lessons were also learned in advance of the full-scale invasion of France that was still to come. However, failure at Dieppe had nothing to do with any deficiencies in the model or the silhouettes that it generated.[118] Models proved highly valuable in the aforementioned raid on the Tirpitz. Models of the fjord in which the aforementioned Tirpitz was hiding were produced for the air crews tasked with attacking the ship, the artist on board the reconnaissance flight being able to advise the model makers on the precise colouring of the topography to improve navigation of the fjord.[119]

Finally, although the work of NID5 is not the focus of this study, brief mention is required of its production of the Naval Intelligence Handbook series, described in an ISTD source after the war as "geographically the greatest event of the century."[120] Between 1941 and 1946, thirty-one Naval Intelligence Handbook titles were produced, in fifty-eight volumes, containing over five thousand maps and diagrams and over six thousand photographs, by geographers and geologists in the School of Geography (Oxford) and the Scott Polar Institute (Cambridge). The series built significantly on the handbook series produced in the First World War, released into the public domain in 1921. The Handbooks produced by NID5 were to be used not only by the armed services but also by government departments and embassies and became a major resource for dealing with post-war problems.[121]

Conclusion

The wartime activities of the ISTD's back-room, desk-bound personnel, including the information-management systems they developed and followed, although not as historically visible, heroic, or iconic as the Spitfire, Turing's codebreaking computer or the D-Day landings, nonetheless contributed markedly to the Allied victory in Europe (as well as later in the Far East).[122] ISTD became "an active clearing-house for the collection of, and research into, every kind of information" about the terrain over which Allied forces would operate.[123] According to a self-reflective, post-war report recording and evaluating the ISTD's work (in itself an information-management practice), the "organisation of victory, from Africa, Sicily and Italy to the beaches of Normandy was in every case preceded by long hours of concentrated research, writing and editing at [ISTD] Oxford."[124] A "great organisation of incalculable value" was how Rear-Admiral Edmund Rushbrooke, successor to John Godfrey as DNI, described the ISTD in 1946.[125]

This study has highlighted the undertakings involved in wartime topographical military intelligence, a potent information milieu *per se*. Moreover, it has drilled down into the rational and systematic information-management practices deployed in that milieu. However, there is a broader implication for the history of information to be drawn from the story related in this chapter, one that is linked to the proposition that information societies before the *digital* information society are readily identifiable. The information-management history of the ISTD supports the argument that in the half-century or so before the arrival of the computer, during the legacy phase of what Landes termed the "Second Industrial Revolution" and what Barraclough theorised as the rise of the contemporary era of history, mechanical- and paper-based information systems—whether in business, government administration or, the focus of this chapter, military intelligence—contributed to an information revolution as impactful relative to the needs of the time as that which has occurred in the digital realm over the past half-century.[126]

Notes

1 Murray Pittock, *Culloden* (Oxford: Oxford University Press, 2016). Trevor Royle, *Culloden: Scotland's Last Battle and the Forging of the British Empire* (London: Abacus, 2017), 88–94, argues that several factors contributed to the debacle at Culloden, but one of the major causes was the lack of topographical information. Although the Jacobite rebels chose the battlefield, they failed before they did so to inspect adequately the nature of its topography.
2 David O'Keefe, *One Day in August: Ian Fleming, Enigma and the Deadly Raid on Dieppe* (London: Icon Books, 2020), 158; and Christine Jennings, *Robbie: The Life of Sir Robert Jennings* (Kibworth Beauchamp: Matador, 2019), 55.
3 F. H. Hinsley, *British Intelligence in the Second World War. Volume 1* (London: HMSO, 1979), 40. The other volumes in the series *British Intelligence in the Second World War*, each also written by Hinsley and published in London by HMSO, are: volume 2 (1981); Vol 3, Part 1 (1984); Vol 3, Part 2 (1988); Vol 4 (1990).
4 Michael Herman, "Assessment Machinery: British and American Models," in *Intelligence Analysis and Assessment*, ed. David Charters, Stuart Farson, and Glenn Hastedt (London: Frank Cass, 1996), 16.
5 Kenneth Mason, Memoir [typescript], c. 1965, 508, World War II Geographers Collection, Royal Geographical Society Archive. The historic lack of sharing of intelligence mirrored poor army-navy relations in the Victorian period when "co-operation between the services was almost non-existent," according to John Gooch, *The Plans of War: The General Staff and British Military Strategy, c. 1900–1916* (London: Routledge and Kegan Paul, 1974), 11. The mistrust between the two services revolved around the prioritisation of the navy in military strategy in relation to the continent, as explained by Steven Ross, "Blue Water Strategy Revisited," *Naval War College Review* 30, no. 4 (Spring 1978): 58–66. From the late 1880s, huge amounts of money were spent, relative to that received by the army, building up naval strength. This was part of the adoption of a "Blue Water" strategy, whereby an enlarged navy was tasked with protecting not only the Empire (to help Britain maintain its industrial supremacy) but also the homeland (the perceived threat of invasion from the continent being never far away). It was only after the vicissitudes of the Boer War and the subsequent establishment, in 1906, of a General Staff for the army that the latter became involved in this essentially navy-led strategy by shifting its focus from being an imperial police force to forming, in the absence of any serious amphibious, dual-service alternative, a well-trained expeditionary force that could fight alongside the French in answer to any German aggression. This reversal of military isolationism on the part of the army was backed up politically by alliances forged by Britain with both France and Russia. On the issue of acrimony in relation to the air force in the inter-war period, see David Hall, "From Khaki and Light Blue to Purple: The Long and Troubled Development of Army/Air Co-operation in Britain, 1914–1945," *The RUSI Journal* 147, no. 5 (2002): 78–83.
6 Sam Bassett and A. Frederick Wells, Inter-Service Topographical Department, 1946, paragraph 40, ADM/223/90, National Archives.
7 Bassett and Wells, Inter-Service Topographical Department, paragraph 43.
8 O'Keefe, *One Day in August*, 157.
9 Mason, Memoir, 505.
10 Kevin Quinlan, *The Secret War Between the Wars: MI5 in the 1920s and 1930s* (Woodbridge: The Boydell Press, 2014), 15; Keith Jeffery, *MI6: The History of the Secret Intelligence Service, 1909–1945* (London: Bloomsbury, 2010), 155–157 and 245–282.
11 Sam Bassett, *Royal Marine: The Autobiography of Colonel Sam Bassett* (London: Peter Davies, 1962), 157.
12 History of ISTD, SEAC [South-East Asia Command], Singapore, 1946, 9, ADM/223/90, National Archives.
13 Edward Rose, Judy Ehlen, and Ursula Lawrence, "Military Use of Geologists and Geology: A Historical Overview and Introduction," in *Military Aspects of Geology, Fortification, Excavation and Terrain Evaluation*, Geological Society Special Publication 473, ed. Edward Rose, Julie Ehlen, and Ursula Lawrence (London: Geological Society), 1, 5–7, and 12.
14 Peter Doyle and Matthew Bennett, "Military Geography: The Influence of Terrain in the Outcome of the Gallipoli Campaign, 1915," *The Geographical Journal* 165, no. 1 (March 1999): 12–36.

15 O'Keefe, *One Day in August*, 156.
16 Matthew Allen, "The Foreign Intelligence Committee and the Origins of the Naval Intelligence Committee of the Admiralty," *The Mariner's Mirror* 81, no. 1 (February 1995): 65–78.
17 Mason, Memoir, 519.
18 Mason, Memoir, 505; O'Keefe, *One Day in August*, 156.
19 Mason, Memoir, 507. The range of reports produced can be found in List of Reports: ISTD, WO/252/1462, National Archives.
20 Mason, Memoir, 522 states that official recognition of the ISTD as Admiralty unit NID6 occurred in February 1941.
21 Edward Rose and Jonathan Clatworthy, "Terrain Evaluation for Allied Military Operations in Europe and the Far East during World War II: 'Secret' British Reports and Specialist Maps Generated by the Geological Section, Inter-Service Topographical Department," *Quarterly Journal of Engineering Geology and Hydrogeology* 41, no. 2 (2008): 238; Mason, Memoir, 518; Bassett and Wells, Inter-Service Topographical Department, paragraph 72; History of the Geological Section, ISTD, 1943–1946, WO/402/378, National Archives. Both NID5 and NID6, which together formed the ISTD, were under the supervision of the Joint Intelligence Committee (JIC). After the war, the ISTD became the nucleus of the Joint Intelligence Board (JIB) under the Ministry of Defence.
22 Mason, Memoir, 519.
23 Bassett, *Royal Marine*, 174.
24 B. Kilner (Ministry of Works and Buildings) to R. Nicol Cross (Principal of Manchester College, Oxford), October 17, 1941, Harris Manchester College Archives.
25 Mason, Memoir, 529.
26 Bassett, *Royal Marine*, 175; Rose and Clatworthy, "Terrain Evaluation," 238.
27 Mason, Memoir, 515; O'Keefe, *One Day in August*, 158.
28 History of ISTD, SEAC, 9. The prototype of non-departmental intelligence was the Industrial Intelligence Centre (IIC), established in 1931 to study the German economy: Herman, "Assessment Machinery," 15.
29 Rose and Clatworthy, "Terrain Evaluation," 238.
30 Hinsley, *British Intelligence in the Second World War*, Vol 2, 51. In 1944, ISTD (SEAC [South East Asia Command]) was created, founded on ISTD (India), which had been established in August 1943: History of ISTD, SEAC.
31 History of ISTD, SEAC, 9.
32 Bassett, *Royal Marine*, 165.
33 Quoted in Bassett and Wells, Inter-Service Topographical Department, paragraph 1.
34 Hinsley, *British Intelligence*, Vol 2, 483; Bassett and Wells, Inter-Service Topographical Department, paragraph 39.
35 Robin Nisbet, "William Smith Watt, 1913–2002," Biographical Memoirs of Fellows, *Proceedings of the British Academy* 124 (2004): 363; O'Keefe, *One Day in August*, 158.
36 Hinsley, *British Intelligence in the Second World War*, Vol 2, 192 and 482.
37 War Cabinet, Chiefs of Staff Committee, Minutes, August 5, 1943, CAB/79/27/34, National Archives.
38 Hinsley, *British Intelligence*, Vol 3, Part 1, 474.
39 War Cabinet, Chiefs of Staff Committee, Demands on the ISTD: Note by the Secretary, CAB/84/56/48, National Archives.
40 O'Keefe, *One Day in August*, 155.
41 Bassett, *Royal Marine*, 180.
42 See, for example, Ann Blair et al., *Information: A Historical Companion* (Princeton, NJ; Oxford, UK: Princeton University Press, 2021). On information management in military intelligence specifically, see Alistair Black, "Information Management in the Intelligence Branch of the British War Office, 1873–1914," *Open Information Science* 4 (2020): 91–105; Jos Gabriëls, "Mapping Out Future Victories: Information Management by Napoleon's Depot General de la Guerre, 1800–1914," *European Review of History* 26, no. 2 (2019): 258–283; Brian Hall, "The British Army, Information Management and the First World War Revolution in Military Affairs," *Journal of Strategic Studies* 41, no. 7 (2018): 1001–1030; Rodney Brunt, "Special Documentation Systems at the Government Code and Cypher School, Bletchley Park during the Second World War,"

Intelligence & National Security 21, no. 1 (2006): 129–149; and Alistair Black and Rodney Brunt, "MI5, 1909–1945: An Information Management Perspective," *Journal of Information Science* 26, no. 3 (2000): 185–197.
43 History of ISTD, SEAC, 9.
44 Bassett and Wells, Inter-Service Topographical Department, paragraph 64.
45 Bassett, *Royal Marine*, 166.
46 Hinsley, *British Intelligence*, Vol 2, 9–10.
47 Hinsley, *British Intelligence*, Vol 3, Part 1, 258, and 274.
48 Bassett and Wells, Inter-Service Topographical Department, paragraph 28.
49 Bassett, *Royal Marine*, 222.
50 Bassett and Wells, Inter-Service Topographical Department, paragraph 82.
51 Bassett, *Royal Marine*, 175; Hinsley, *British Intelligence*, Vol 2, 9.
52 Bassett and Wells, Inter-Service Topographical Department, paragraph 87.
53 Bassett, *Royal Marine*, 157. In the days and weeks after the invasion, ISTD "target parties" were sent to northern France to retrieve vital information (and equipment) from commercial enterprises as well as research establishments: Bassett, 222.
54 Bassett and Wells, Inter-Service Topographical Department, paragraphs 10, 55.
55 Peter Caddick-Adams, *Sand and Steel: A New History of D-Day* (London: Arrow Books, 2019), 120–121.
56 Bassett, *Royal Marine*, 186; "Inter-Services Topographical Department (ISTD), Oxford," *The D-Day Story: D-Day on Your Doorstep* (2022). https://theddaystory.com/markers/inter-services-topographical-department-istd-oxford/.
57 Mason, Memoir, 536; Bassett and Wells, Inter-Service Topographical Department, paragraph 76.
58 Bassett, *Royal Marine*, 208.
59 Hinsley, *British Intelligence*, Vol 3, Part 2, 90.
60 Bassett, *Royal Marine*, 214.
61 Robert Bruce, "Deposits in the New Bodleian during the Second World War," *Bodleian Library Record* 26, no. 1 (April 2013): 68.
62 Hinsley, *British Intelligence*, Vol 2, 192; Bassett, *Royal Marine*, 175.
63 Bassett, *Royal Marine*, 188.
64 Bassett, *Royal Marine*, 207.
65 Bassett, *Royal Marine*, 187.
66 Bassett, *Royal Marine*, 187.
67 Bassett, *Royal Marine*, 188.
68 History of the Geological Section, 12.
69 Mason, Memoir, 505.
70 Bassett, *Royal Marine*, 172.
71 Bassett, *Royal Marine*, 188.
72 Caddick-Adams, *Sand and Steel*, 121.
73 History of Geological Section, Appendix, 4.
74 Bassett and Wells, Inter-Service Topographical Department, paragraph 39. History of the Geological Section, 10.
75 Mason, Memoir, 516.
76 Bassett, *Royal Marine*, 175.
77 History of ISTD, SEAC, 9.
78 Allen, "The Foreign Intelligence Committee," 65.
79 Hinsley, *British Intelligence*, Vol 1, vii.
80 Mason, Memoir, 505.
81 Bassett, *Royal Marine*, 158.
82 Bassett, *Royal Marine*, 164.
83 Bassett, *Royal Marine*, 163.
84 Bassett, *Royal Marine*, 166.
85 Ludford, "Discussion," 134.
86 Edward Rose and Jonathan Clatworthy, "Specialist Maps of the Geological Section, Inter-Service Topographical Department: Aids to British Military Planning during World War II," *The Cartography Journal* 44, no. 1 (February 2007): 14.

87 Bassett, *Royal Marine*, 166.
88 Bassett, *Royal Marine*, 172.
89 Bassett and Wells, Inter-Service Topographical Department, paragraph 88.
90 Hinsley, *British Intelligence*, Vol 3, Part 1, 474.
91 Avril Maddrell, "The 'Map Girls': British Women Geographers' War Work, Shifting Gender Boundaries and Reflections on the History of Geography," *Transactions of the Institute of British Geographers* 33, no. 1 (January 2008): 133.
92 Bassett, *Royal Marine*, 177.
93 History of the Geological Section, 15.
94 Nisbet, "William Smith Watt," 363.
95 Mason, Memoir, 506 and 508.
96 NID5 and NID6, 3.
97 Nisbet, "William Smith Watt," 364.
98 Bassett and Wells, Inter-Service Topographical Department, paragraphs 97, 98.
99 Bassett and Wells, Inter-Service Topographical Department, paragraphs 89–100.
100 Department of Scientific and Industrial Research, *Report of the Geological Survey Board for the Year 1945* (London: HMSO, 1947), 20.
101 History of the Geological Section, Appendix, 4.
102 Bassett and Wells, Inter-Service Topographical Department, paragraph 24.
103 Department of Scientific and Industrial Research, *Report of the Geological Survey Board*, 20.
104 Leonard Wilson, "Some Observations on Wartime Geography in England," *Geographical Review* 36, no. 4 (October 1946): 602.
105 Bassett and Wells, Inter-Service Topographical Department, paragraph 40; Bassett, *Royal Marine*, 175.
106 O'Keefe, *One Day in August*, 155.
107 Bassett, *Royal Marine*, 178; Mason, Memoir, 536.
108 Hinsley, *British Intelligence*, Vol 2, 483.
109 NID5 and NID6, 3.
110 War Cabinet, Chiefs of Staff Committee, Minutes, August 5, 1943, CAB/79/27/34, National Archives.
111 Anthony Joseph, "The Painstaking Paper Panorama that Shaped D-Day," *Mail Online*, October 23, 2017. https://www.dailymail.co.uk/news/article-5008511/The-painstaking-paper-panorama-shaped-D-Day.html; "Inter-Services Topographical Department (ISTD), Oxford."
112 Bassett, *Royal Marine*, 210.
113 Bassett, *Royal Marine*, 211–213.
114 Bassett, *Royal Marine*, 214.
115 Hinsley, *British Intelligence*, Vol 3, Part 2, 90–91.
116 Hinsley, *British Intelligence*, Vol 3, Part 2, 754.
117 Bassett, *Royal Marine*, 206.
118 John Greehan and Alexander Nicoll, *The Dieppe Raid: The Allies' Assault upon Hitler's Fortress Europe* (Barnsley: Frontline Books, 2023); O'Keefe, *One Day in August*; and Hinsley, *British Intelligence*, Vol 2, 698.
119 Bassett, *Royal Marine*, 196.
120 Hugh Clout and Cyril Gosme, "The Naval Intelligence Handbooks: A Monument to Geographical Writing," *Progress in Human Geography* 27, no. 2 (2003): 153–173; NID5: Geographical Handbooks, 1946, 6, ADM/223/90, National Archives.
121 NID5: Geographical Handbooks, 1.
122 Rose and Clatworthy, "Specialist Maps," 41.
123 Ralph Bennett, *Behind the Battle: Intelligence in the War with Germany, 1939–1945* (London: Pimlico, 1999), 254.
124 Bassett and Wells, Inter-Service Topographical Department, paragraph 101.
125 Quoted in Mason, 563.
126 David Landes, *The Unbound Prometheus: Technological Change and Industrial Development in Western Europe from 1750 to the Present*, 2nd ed. (Cambridge, UK: Cambridge University Press, 2003), 4; Geoffrey Barraclough, *An Introduction to Contemporary History* (London: C.A. Watts, 1964).

17
THE WARTIME SOCIAL SURVEY AS INFORMATION HISTORY

Henry Irving

Government has always depended on information. As other chapters in this book show, states have used various methods to gather and process data about their citizens. Yet, while the mobilisation of information is as old as civilisation, there have been clear moments of change. The Second World War was one such moment. It encouraged the remarkable expansion of data collection and analysis by states around the world. In Britain, the focus of this chapter, the war led to the unparalleled mobilisation of national life. Britain's war effort was focused on resources and the government used information to align the economy with its military priorities. The expansion of state control over the labour market, raw materials, industrial production, and consumer goods required data. To successfully introduce food rationing, for example, the government needed to know where people lived and shopped, and whether they had children or any dietary requirements.[1]

The Second World War also led to the collection of new forms of information. The interwar period had been marked by speculation about aerial warfare and its implications for the nation's resolve. Military strategists understood that bombing would blur the distinction between home and fighting fronts. Many feared that civilians would lose confidence in the war effort as a result. Civilian morale was arguably "the woolliest and most muddled concept of the war" but it was nevertheless accepted as a precondition of victory.[2] The responsibility for gauging how people felt fell to the Ministry of Information, which was central to the management of information in wartime Britain.[3] It began the war with only a press cutting service to fulfil this part of its role. In time, however, it developed new techniques for capturing opinions. These included the use of observation and testimony to paint a picture of the public mood, and the use of sample surveys to produce detailed reports on individual topics. Together, these activities were described as Home Intelligence.

Wartime surveys are an important source for historians. Social historians use their rich data to consider the impact of the war on ordinary people.[4] Cultural historians explore the way such surveys were constructed, considering what this tells us about dominant social attitudes.[5] Others have placed them within a longer history of ideas: arguing, for example, that their use by officials reflected an increasingly scientific discourse of government.[6] This chapter is concerned with the Wartime Social Survey, which was established by the Ministry of Information in 1940. As we shall see, it was conceived as an integral part of the

Ministry's Home Intelligence machinery, although most of its work was eventually carried out for other parts of government. This outcome was the result of a political storm that encouraged secrecy about the Wartime Social Survey's work and continues to shape the way it is understood. This chapter approaches the Survey as an example of information history, using it as a case study to consider how information was viewed in the 1940s. This approach is inspired by Edward Higgs, who has urged historians of information to match an awareness of general patterns with empirical research.[7] The chapter begins with the scandal that shaped the Wartime Social Survey's history.

Cooper's Snoopers

It is impossible to discuss the Wartime Social Survey without reference to the political storm that threatened to engulf it in summer 1940. The storm centred on the extent to which government should be able to collect and use personal information from its citizens. It broke in late July, when Ritchie Calder, the *Daily Herald's* science writer, revealed the Wartime Social Survey's existence after learning about it from a disgruntled interviewee. He described the Survey as a shadowy "Morale and Social Survey" investigation and warned his readers that:

> A complete stranger is liable to knock at the door and say: "Good morning, Mrs Brown. Do you think Britain ought to go on fighting? And have you any winter underwear?"

Not only did Calder see these as silly questions, he believed the Survey betrayed a negative perception of the British public. In his view, it symbolised an official preoccupation with faltering morale that bore no relation to the way people felt about the war.[8]

The timing of the article was significant. For two months, there had been intense speculation in newspaper offices that government intended to impose stricter censorship rules on the press. These rumours were stoked by the suppression of news about the sinking of the *Lancastria*, which had been bombed in the Bay of Biscay while evacuating British troops and civilians from Nazi-occupied France. The sinking is thought to be one of Britain's worst maritime disasters, although there is no accurate record of how many people lost their lives, with estimates ranging from around two thousand to over six thousand.[9] Newspapers were unable to publish news about the disaster because it was covered by censorship rules that were designed to withhold information about military movements from the enemy. The British media remained gagged even after news of the sinking was broadcast by the Nazi propaganda radio programme "Germany Calling," which was fronted by William Joyce, better known to listeners as Lord Haw-Haw. On July 24, six weeks after the event, the story was broken again by the *New York Sun*. The British ban was finally lifted on the same day Calder's article about the Wartime Social Survey was published.[10]

This spat over censorship coincided with the government's "Silent Column" anti-rumour propaganda campaign. The communication historian Jo Fox explains how this campaign "cast the entire population as potential suspects," undermining the notion of shared endeavour it hoped to promote.[11] It also coincided with a series of contentious prosecutions for spreading "alarm and despondency"—behaviour that was outlawed by Defence Regulations—and the two issues were quickly linked by critics. The press ran a vigorous fight against the "Silent Column," until, under mounting criticism, the government cancelled the campaign less than a fortnight after it began. The *Daily Herald* argued that the government had taken "its own stunt too seriously" and had become fixated on the "hypothetical dangers of a non-existent defeatism."[12] It and other newspapers linked their criticism to the rumours surrounding censorship, arguing that the fight against Nazism could only be won if the government trusted the public. Their argument was aimed squarely at the Ministry of Information, which was the department responsible for press censorship and domestic propaganda campaigns. It was also the department that managed the Wartime Social Survey.

The Ministry's critics seized on Calder's story as further evidence of overreach. Percy Cudlipp, the *Daily Herald's* editor, led the charge in a full page article that called for an immediate end to domestic intelligence gathering.[13] Other newspapers followed suit. Duff Cooper, the Minister of Information, was ridiculed for "snooping" into people's lives. The *Daily Express* said:

> He is wasting his time. British morale is fine. It always has been. What disturbs the public today is people in Whitehall who are always worrying and fretting over public morale, bolstering it up, mollycoddling it, and almost convincing is that there is something wrong with it.[14]

As the days passed, the criticism grew louder, with the Ministry accused of acting like the Gestapo. The matter soon reached the Houses of Parliament. During a three-hour debate on August 1, 1940, Cooper vigorously defended the Ministry's need to understand the public mood and accused the press of acting unfairly.[15] This led to further bad headlines and the resignation of the Ministry's director. Cooper survived the storm, but his authority was badly knocked.

The Development of the Wartime Social Survey

It is unlikely Duff Cooper knew that much about the Wartime Social Survey before the "Cooper's Snoopers" affair broke. The Survey had been sanctioned before he became the Minister of Information and there was said to have been "an almost complete lack of direction from above."[16] The Survey was the brainchild of Mary Adams, the Ministry's Director of Home Intelligence from 1939 to 1941. Her plan for monitoring opinion rested on two separate methodologies. The first involved gathering qualitative reports of behaviour: work which was initially outsourced to Mass Observation but later brought in-house through the recruitment of volunteer Home Intelligence observers. This would be combined with a second, quantitative investigation using standardised questionnaires. Adams envisaged the latter as a longitudinal study that would allow the more idiosyncratic observations to be seen in context. The aim was to use information to produce what she termed a "barometer of morale."[17]

The Wartime Social Survey was designed to collect the information needed to keep track of civilian morale and test the impact of government policy. However, to avoid the pitfall of marking its own homework, the Survey was consciously designed to be semi-autonomous from the Ministry of Information. It was set up by Professor Arnold Plant, an expert in market research at the London School of Economics, and the statistician Frederick Brown, who was at the time working at the Bank of England. Moreover, although it was funded by the Ministry, the Survey initially worked under the auspices of the National Institute of Economic and Social Research and had its own offices. Much to Adams' frustration, its autonomy was reinforced when Ministry officials asked her to prove the Survey's value by focusing on practical investigations before attempting to measure something as ill-defined as civilian resolve. The Survey thus began work carrying out research on the impact of radio broadcasts for the Ministry of Food.[18]

As the war intensified during late spring 1940, Adams repeatedly requested permission to instate her original idea of a barometer of morale. She was finally given the green light at the end of May.[19] This led to a series of experiments where interviewers were armed with questions designed to probe attitudes about the war. It was during these experiments that Calder learned of the Wartime Social Survey and set off the Cooper's Snoopers affair. Adams was not put off by the barrage of criticism his article unleashed. Doubling down, she instead hired ten social psychologists who were asked to analyse their interviewees at the same time as noting their responses.[20]

Yet the Survey was eventually changed. Arnold Plant resigned in protest at Adams' experiments, the National Institute of Economic and Social Research removed its support in the wake of the media storm and Ministry of Information's new director forced Adams to accept a vastly reduced budget. In late September 1940, she reluctantly agreed the Survey should in future be used solely for statistical investigations requested by other government departments.[21] Adams left her post in April 1941 after a further failed attempt to convince her superiors about the need for a barometer of morale. Her departure led to a series of organisational changes, including the appointment of a new director of the Wartime Social Survey and the introduction of new terms of reference. The director's post was filled by Louis Moss, who was recruited from the British Institute of Public Opinion (the London-based offshoot of the Gallup polling and market research company). These changes, which solidified the Survey's shift from tracking morale, upset its original staff, most of whom resigned in protest after a stormy meeting with their new manager.[22]

The mass resignation threatened to revive the Cooper's Snoopers affair, but, in retrospect, it was the start of a new, more stable phase for the Wartime Social Survey.[23] This outcome was made possible by senior Ministry of Information officials who warded off the potential for criticism by inviting the Parliamentary Select Committee for National Expenditure to judge the Survey's value. It was a clever move. The enquiry both drew a line under the Survey's past and gave Moss time to rebuild it from ground up. After weighing up the evidence provided by the Ministry, the committee judged that the Survey had come a long way from 1940 and concluded that "the case against the Survey's work [had been] much exaggerated." The changes made since 1940 convinced the committee that the Wartime Social Survey was "an essential service, performing useful work."[24] *The Times* newspaper reported on this judgement in glowing terms. It greeted the Wartime Social Survey as "one of the most interesting war-time social innovations" and described it as a "quantitative bridge between Central Government Departments ... and the people of this country."[25]

By December 1945, the Wartime Social Survey had completed 120 separate enquiries on subject ranging from consumer shortages to post-war educational policy. Almost all this work was undertaken for other government departments, with only eleven surveys directly commissioned by the Ministry of Information. Notwithstanding Ritchie Calder's criticism in 1940 of silly questions about winter underwear, the list included a large survey for the Board of Trade about the availability of brassieres and corsets because these things really did matter to people on the home front.[26] Nor do such questions appear to have put off interviewees. The wartime enquiries involved interviews with 337,000 members of the public and the Survey calculated there was a 0.5% refusal rate, that is, five refusals for every 1,000 people approached.[27] But how did it operate?

Information Management

The Wartime Social Survey collected, analysed, and disseminated large amounts of information. It did so by adapting techniques developed by academic, commercial, and government bodies. This section describes the steps needed to complete a typical "major report" in the middle part of the Second World War. These processes were formalised in early 1942 and would have stretched across a ten-week period, running simultaneously with other investigations.[28] At this time, the Wartime Social Survey was staffed by two senior researchers, two junior researchers, twenty-four coders and machine operators, and a team of around fifty interviewers.[29]

Research Design

The first stage of the process was to define the scope of the investigation. In line with the September 1940 ruling, most of the Wartime Social Survey's work was completed for other government departments, so this process usually involved a detailed discussion between Survey staff and those from the sponsoring body. Because all investigations had to be approved by the Treasury, these discussions were shaped by the need to complete a formal "Request for Investigation." The pro forma used asked for a summary of specific research questions, a justification of their importance and an explanation of the limitations of existing forms of information.[30]

Once permission had been granted, Survey staff would use the information provided by the sponsoring department to design specific interview questions. Most surveys included a mixture of closed and open questions, which were drawn up with the help of an external panel of advisors (this was transformed into a formal Scientific Advisory Committee in 1944). Surveys typically included between ten and fifteen questions, although some were much more complex. For instance, a 1942 investigation into the effectiveness of the Dig for Victory campaign contained thirty-four generic questions and four supplementary questions specifically for women allotment holders.[31] In most cases, at least one pilot survey was carried out to test the questions before the full investigation began.[32]

As well as writing questions, the Survey staff had to decide the size and make-up of the sample that would be used in the investigation. This was perhaps the most contentious aspects of the Wartime Social Survey's work. The Survey used representative sampling methods, which were relatively well established by the 1940s. Indeed, it had been over twenty-five years since Arthur Bowley showed that samples could be designed to produce data that mirrored that of a larger group during a study of working-class households with Arthur Burnett-Hurst. Sampling methods had been refined during the 1920s and 1930s, most famously by George Gallup's American Institute of Public Opinion in the run-up to the 1936 presidential election.[33] However, the Wartime Social Survey's staff knew they had to balance scientific accuracy with the realities of working to strict deadlines in war conditions. Fully random sampling was, for example, deemed impractical as the chances of finding someone at their registered address was diminished by war work, conscription, evacuation, and bombing.

What emerged was a form of stratified quota sampling, where interviews were carried out with a specified number of people from different social groups. Survey staff would first decide whether an investigation required a national sample or should be limited to specific groups. Where a national sample was required, Survey staff used food rationing registration data to determine the relative population of different areas. Each region would then be stratified by age, sex, and occupation (using employment data from the Ministry of Labour and National Service) to produce quota controls that could be applied to the sample. Once these controls were set, field investigators were responsible for finding respondents to fulfil the quotas. This was usually achieved by their turning up at a place of work or by using local Ministry of Food registrations to select households.[34] Louis Moss later admitted that the results were "some distance from random" but the use of large samples, usually around two thousand, and inclusion of sampling data in Survey reports were seen to offset this weakness.[35] The process was also comparable to that used by the commercial British Institute for Public Opinion during the period.[36]

Data Collection and Processing

After locations had been selected for investigation and sample quotas agreed, staff at the Survey's head office handed over to fieldworkers and notified the relevant local authorities that interviews were being conducted in their area. The Survey operated for most of the war with two teams of fieldworkers. The first was a dispersed group of "fixed" interviewers, who carried out fieldwork in their local region. The second was "mobile" and comprised interviewers who could be dispatched individually or in groups to more remote places. Regardless of their position, all interviewers were trained by established staff and undertook placements in different parts of the Survey to understand how their work fitted into the whole. The training was formalised after the war with the introduction of a training handbook in 1948.[37] This approach was very different to that employed by commercial researchers, where the time and cost of training encouraged the use of untrained, mostly part-time fieldworkers.[38] The Wartime Social Survey justified its method as the best way to ensure consistent approach to asking questions and recording answers.[39]

An emphasis on consistency can also be seen in the design of the questionnaires—or recording schedules—used during the interviews. These included predefined answers for closed questions that could be circled by fieldworkers and spaces to record the response to open questions verbatim. Fieldworkers sent completed interviews to the Wartime Social Survey's head office at the end of each day's work. There, they would be checked for completeness and uniformity, allowing obvious errors to be rectified quickly. For example, in cases where answers appeared to have been recorded differently, editors could ask for clarification from the fieldworker in question. Most Wartime Social Survey reports reproduced the recording schedule as an appendix to show how the investigation had been completed.[40]

The edited questionnaires were processed once the fieldwork was finished. The first stage involved coding the answers so the information they contained could be classified into meaningful categories for analysis. This was a simple task for closed questions as predefined answers could be pre-coded on recording schedules. Responses to open questions were post-coded by grouping together the responses from a random sample of questionnaires. Once these codes were defined and had been tested on a second sample, the responses to each survey were categorised according to the agreed coding frame. Information about the respondent's age, sex, and occupation was also coded although the Survey was only permitted to share anonymised aggregate data in its final reports.[41] At this stage, the information contained in the questionnaires was transferred onto punch cards so that it could be mechanically tabulated. This was one of the most laborious parts of the process as the data had to be punched and verified manually.⁴² One investigation into children's diets for the Ministry of Health involved punching fifty thousand individual cards, one for each item of food eaten by a respondent during the week-long study.⁴³

Interpretation and Analysis

Wartime Social Survey reports usually expressed their results as a series of frequency tables showing the numbers who answered a question in a particular way. These results were computed from the punch cards using a Hollerith machine tabulator, a process which is shown in Fig. 17.1. The machines contained pads of spring-loaded pins which were brought

Figure 17.1 A member of Wartime Social Survey staff feeding punched cards into a tabulating machine in 1944 (photograph D18860), reproduced courtesy of the Imperial War Museum.

down onto the cards. The position of the punched holes determined which pins created an electrical circuit, with different circuits relaying information to different counting dials. Although the results were sometimes presented as percentages or in hand-plotted charts, the Survey claimed "that every effort is made to let the figures speak for themselves, with a minimum of interpretation and comment."[44] This stood in contrast to the qualitative surveys carried out by the likes of Mass Observation and followed an established tradition of official surveys as a form of fact-finding. The way information was framed nevertheless reveals some of the assumptions that underpinned each investigation.[45]

Most reports broke down the results using similar stratifications to those that defined the sample quotas. This allowed the Survey to illustrate difference between regions, those living in urban or rural areas, or according to social characteristics. As Kathleen Box explained: "Analyses by number in family, whether or not there are children in the family, married or single, size of factor, and so on are found to illuminate the results."[46] The reports also included qualitative comments alongside the frequency tables and rarely presented the results in the order that questions were asked. In some cases, the reports also included space for subjective observations. An extreme example of this can be found in a 1943 investigation into the response to a public health campaign about venereal diseases. The final report began with analysis of the public's willingness to answer questions about the campaign's content. This was designed to gauge levels of embarrassment and was based on notes made by fieldworkers at the end of each interview. The report noted that 13% of respondents had shown some signs of discomfort—and that 5% of interviewees were deemed by the fieldworkers to be "dull or ignorant."[47]

Dissemination

The reports produced by the Wartime Social Survey had only a limited distribution. Copies were sent to the sponsoring department for each investigation and to relevant parts of the Ministry of Information, but they were not shared more widely. The statistician Claus Moser (who went onto serve as Director of the Central Statistical Office) believed this was a major weakness as the Survey's information was not available for academic analysis.[48] This secrecy is usually explained as a result of the Official Secrets Act.[49] In practice, it was more likely a legacy of the Coopers' Snoopers affair, to which the Ministry of Information responded by imposing limits on the sharing of Home Intelligence material. The Official Secrets Act certainly did not stop Mass Observation from publishing information gained while it was employed by the Ministry of Information. Whether legally enforced or not, the result was the same: senior officials maintained that "it is not our policy to give any publicity to the work of this organization."[50]

Yet some of the Survey's work did reach wider audiences. Stephen Taylor, who had replaced Mary Adams as the Ministry of Information's Director of Home Intelligence in 1941, was keen to establish the Wartime Social Survey's scientific credentials. He encouraged Louis Moss to present a paper about the Survey to the British Psychological Society in 1943. Later that year, the two men published companion articles about the Survey's value for government in the technical journal *Public Administration*.[51] In mid-1944, a reporter and photographer accompanied interviewers as they carried out investigations for a feature article in the magazine *Illustrated*. Although given the ominous title "They find out what you think," the feature stressed the value of the Survey's work and gave a glowing account of the interviewers themselves.[52]

The most detailed example of sharing the Wartime Social Survey's work came later in 1944. That May, Kathleen Box and Geoffrey Thomas, who had joined the Survey from Mass Observation in 1941, presented a wide-ranging paper about their work to the Royal Statistical Society. The paper included both an account of the Survey's methodology and a series of case studies, included a selection of results covering nutrition, housing, health education, and the impact of different forms of government propaganda.[53] It was followed by a lengthy discussion which drew insights from Moss, the pioneering medical statistician Austin Bradford Hill (who was an advisor to the Wartime Social Survey) and representatives from Mass Observation. The event was significant as the Royal Statistical Society was the largest learned body of its kind and played a key role in popularising sampling methods due to its ability to link academics and practitioners.[54] The next section emulates Box and Thomas's paper by summarising one of the Survey's enquiries.

Case Study: An Investigation into Salvage Habits

In early 1942, the Ministry of Information was asked to devise a national publicity campaign that would encourage households to recycle rubber. The Ministry of Supply had promoted what was then called "salvage" since November 1939 and had run a similar publicity campaign in summer 1940. The request for a new national campaign was the result of worsening military circumstances. Japan had entered the war with a shock offensive against British, Dutch, and American colonial territories in the Asia Pacific region. Japan's rapid advance left 90% of the world's natural rubber supplies under enemy control. This was a serious problem for Britain, which, unlike the United States, did not have a synthetic rubber industry to make up the shortfall.[55] Despite this, the Ministry of Information was wary. It knew that the appeal for recycling in 1940 had ended badly. Its publicity campaign had worked, but disjointed local collection practices had led to confusion and complaints, forcing the campaign to be abandoned.[56] For this reason, the Ministry's advertisers commissioned the Wartime Social Survey to provide a contextual report before it began the new appeal.

The Survey aimed to determine public attitudes towards recycling and the role of different factors in shaping them. It was carried out against the backdrop of an ongoing newspaper campaign designed to increase the collection of wastepaper and a national appeal for volunteers willing to run collection depots. The sample was chosen to reflect different local contexts, with over three thousand people interviewed in a mixture of cities, towns, and rural areas from Dundee in the east of Scotland to Tiverton in the south-west of England. The Survey was clear, however, that this should not be regarded as a representative sample because local differences were thought to render any such sample impossible. The sample was also limited to "housewives," reflecting a belief that recycling was a domestic activity universally undertaken by women. Unlike most other investigations, the Survey team also sought to contextualise their results by interviewing local government officials and refuse collectors in each of the areas under investigation. The recording schedule used for these interviews shows that the Survey hoped to ascertain how much recycling was collected weekly in each area, although this data was not analysed as the information was deemed incomparable and fieldworkers "had the impression that the figures provided were not accurate."[57]

The results still make interesting reading. The interviews began with a series of questions about recycling practices in the home, interspersed with those about consumption habits.

The Wartime Social Survey as Information History

These were followed by a second series of questions about the interviewee's reasons for participating in the salvage effort. Only six interviewees were said to have no knowledge that recycling was wanted and no discernible differences in attitude between different groups was found. Still, the results pointed to marked differences in behaviour. The Survey believed this was a result of variation in collection practices across the country. Their contextual interviews also reinforced the mutual distrust between officials, refuse collectors, and interviewees. These findings offset the more positive conclusion that people were made a special effort when asked to do so. Moreover, in the case of rubber, the Survey cautioned that some 96.8% of the sample said they did not currently recycle the material because they had nothing to put out for collection.[58]

Patchy records make it hard to determine exactly how these findings were used. Louis Moss believed the report convinced the Ministry of Supply to opt for a less intensive publicity campaign than first envisaged.[59] Yet the Wartime Social Survey report is not mentioned in the guidance notes produced for the campaign. These notes also show that the Ministry of Supply pushed ahead regardless of any warnings it received, asking a reluctant Ministry of Information to add paid newspaper advertising about rubber to their plans in April 1942.[60] While this example suggests that information was not always acted upon, it paradoxically shows that information was deemed to be important. Indeed, the Ministry of Supply commissioned a follow-up survey in May 1943, which used some of the same questions to show change over time. This appeared to justify the Ministry of Supply's approach, finding that 32% of people were recycling rubber "regularly" compared to just 3% before the advertising campaign had started.[61]

The most important thing about the second survey, however, is that it was deliberately designed to provide information that would be used to decide how the campaign should be developed. As in the first survey, interviews were cross-referenced with information provided by local officials—or, in some rural areas, representatives from voluntary organisations responsible for collection. Interviewees were told at the outset that the Ministry of Supply wanted to simplify collection practices and an open-ended first question asked all respondents for their suggestions. The answers were clearly wanted: the report noted that "if [the interviewee] found the question too puzzling at the beginning, it was repeated later on." The fact that a similar question had been removed from the recording schedule for the 1942 investigation suggests that information about public attitudes was deemed more important after the survey than before. The objective was not simply to collect up-to-date information, but to marshal the information in a way that could be fed straight into future policy.[62]

After the War

As the war went on, the Survey was increasingly asked to carry out small but detailed enquiries designed to provide data for post-war planning. By 1944–1945, most of its time was spent on surveys of health, diet, housing, industrial design, and road safety. As the historian of the Ministry of Information, Ian McLaine, noted, "Once it had settled down, the WSS became an extremely useful adjunct to government."[63]

This usefulness fed into discussions of the Survey's future. Stephen Taylor pushed for its retention from as early as 1942, arguing that the Survey would play a vital role in ensuring the public's voice was heard during the period of post-war rebuilding. The thrust of his argument was accepted. When the Ministry of Information was wound up in 1946, the

Survey was renamed the Government Social Survey and moved into the new Central Office of Information. Its activities expanded during the late 1940s, with the number of interviews conducted each year rising from 64,000 in 1946 to 110,000 by 1949.[64] Louis Moss believed the "continuous flow of information" it provided smoothed Britain's transition from war to peace. He pointed both to one-off investigations and to longer-term surveys that were designed to support increased government intervention in the economy.[65] The Survey also built up a library of methodological working papers covering the different stages of its work.[66]

The Government Social Survey's decision to position itself as a technocratic guide for policymakers made sense in the immediate post war period. The war had sped the transfer of power from local to national government, while the 1945 General Election had been won by a reforming Labour Party committed to economic planning, a new national welfare system and the planned development of towns and cities.[67] Information was vital currency for a generation of planners who had cut their teeth during the Second World War. As in 1940, however, these matters were open to political criticism. The Conservative Party spent the late 1940s stressing its commitment to individual freedom and reached back on earlier arguments to portray the Survey as an extravagant experiment in state meddling. These criticisms were reflected in a small number of complaints received from disgruntled interviewees, while the Conservatives' election victory in 1951 seemed to threaten the Survey's very existence.[68] Yet, the Survey survived the threat and proved more than able to adapt to changed political landscapes, albeit with a reduced budget. In 1970, after a decade of organisational reshuffling, the Survey was merged with the General Registry Office to become the Office of Population Censuses and Surveys.[69] That body is now the Office for National Statistics and the Survey lives on as ONS Social Surveys.

At various points in its long history, the Survey has been held up as an exemplar in the field of social research. In 1951, for instance, Mark Abrams noted it had become "an integral part of administrative and social planning."[70] Two decades later, Claus Moser and Graham Kalton echoed this sentiment, claiming the Government Social Survey had:

> exerted an unquestionable influence in raising the standard of survey methods and in persuading policy-makers in government to pay attention to survey results.[71]

Raymond Kent similarly praised its "influence in raising the standards of survey research," while Catherine Marsh believed the "the amount and quality of data turned out by the Social Survey [was] quite extraordinary."[72]

Its most feted contribution in the post-war period was the Family Expenditure Survey, which was established in 1957 to capture dynamic information about household income and expenditure. This was designed as a new way to measure inflation by keeping index number under constant review so that data would better reflect changes in living standards. The Family Expenditure Survey inspired other longitudinal studies by demonstrating an ability to carry out continuous fieldwork and process information through time.[73] The use of continuous surveys has been traced back to 1944, when the Ministry of Health commissioned the Wartime Social Survey to conduct a monthly "Survey of Sickness" to keep track of minor illnesses within the civilian population.[74] Of course, that survey drew on practical experiments with repeated questions, such as those asked across the two salvage surveys. It is also worth stressing that continuous surveys were integral to Mary Adams' initial belief that the Wartime Social Survey would provide a "barometer of morale." The main differences between that idea and what was later put into practice were that the Survey had proven its ability to manage information and was working with more clearly defined data.

The influence of the Government Social Survey's approach to information management extends beyond its sponsors in government. Data from the Family Expenditure Survey was, for example, made available to academic researchers at the Social Sciences Research Council (SSRC) archive at the University of Essex. The Government Social Survey also carried out the field for David Glass's influential study of *Social Mobility in Britain*, which involved life-story interviews with around ten thousand British adults. This study was especially significant as it led to the creation of a standardised socio-economic classification system for different occupations. The "Hall-Jones" scale became a key reference point for sociologists working on class in the 1950s, 1960s, and 1970s.[75] The impact of such work should not be underestimated. As Mike Savage has argued, the sample survey, of which the Government Social Survey was a pioneer, became "a crucial technology for defining the modern rational nation." In this view, information did not just provide policymakers with a guide to public attitudes, but instead framed the way that the public was itself conceived.[76]

Conclusion

This chapter has viewed the Wartime Social Survey through the lens of information history. In doing so, it shows how the study of information can add new perspectives to established historiographies. It also provides an example of the importance that was attributed to information during the Second World War. Wars feature prominently in information histories and this chapter complements work on Britain's aircraft detection systems and the indexing techniques employed by codebreakers at Bletchley Park to name but two other 1940s example.[77] It is clear that the scale and scope of the Second World War increased the value attached to information and encouraged innovations in its collection, handling, and use. Yet the history of the Wartime Social Survey shows that the mobilisation of information was not always accepted. As Peter Burke has argued of early modern Europe, "we should not be too quick to assume that our age is the first to take these questions seriously." [78] Just as the implications of surveillance in an otherwise free society that gave rise to information history in the latter part of the twentieth century, the prospect of surveillance was a source of controversy and debate, even in wartime.[79]

The Coopers' Snoopers affair was an important moment in the Wartime Social Survey's information history, but ultimately the Survey moved beyond it. One of the most striking things about the Survey is that it established itself with so little fuss. The Select Committee of National Expenditure noted, for example, that there was "little objection on behalf of the public to being interviewed."[80] The accusations levelled at it in 1940 had fallen wide of the mark. Having been given a clean bill of health, the Survey was able to establish itself as a pioneer in the field of social research and bring policymakers into closer contact with the lives of ordinary people than ever before. These activities expanded far beyond the wartime emergency it was created to meet and have provided government, sociologists, and historians alike with a rich archive of information about life on the British home front.

This same archive reveals much about the way information was conceived. The work of the Wartime Social Survey illustrates the importance that was attached to consistency and scientific processes during the 1940s. It was this that distinguished the Survey from contemporaneous information about public attitudes. And yet, as shown by the belief that some interviewees were "dull" or the decision to ask only women about household recycling, the information produced by the Survey could never be objective. The Wartime Social Survey betrays the attitudes of its fieldworkers, report writers, and sponsors as well as its interviewees. Its history is a reminder, should one be needed, that the social history of information remains important.

Notes

1. Ina Zweiniger-Bargielowska, *Austerity in Britain: Rationing, Controls, and Consumption, 1939–1955* (Oxford: Oxford University Press, 2000), 14–18.
2. Robert Mackay, *The Test of War: Inside Britain 1939–1945* (London: UCL Press, 1999), 138; and Paul Addison, *The Road to 1945* (London: Cape, 1975), 121.
3. Henry Irving, "The Ministry of Information on the British Home Front," in *Allied Communication to the Public during the Second World War*, ed. Simon Eliot and Marc Wiggam (London: Bloomsbury Academic, 2020), 21.
4. Angus Calder pioneered this approach by drawing on material collected by the social research organisation Mass Observation: see Angus Calder, *The People's War: Britain 1939–1945* (London: Cape, 1969).
5. Claire Langhamer, "Who the Hell Are Ordinary People? Ordinariness as a Category of Historical Analysis," *Transactions of the Royal Historical Society* 28 (December 2018): 175–195; Nick Hubble, *Mass Observation and Everyday Life: Culture, History, Theory* (Basingstoke: Palgrave, 2005); and Penny Summerfield, "Mass-Observation: Social Research or Social Movement?," *Journal of Contemporary History* 20, no. 3 (July 1985): 439–452.
6. Mike Savage, *Identities and Social Change in Britain since 1940: The Politics of Method* (Oxford: Oxford University Press, 2010), 195.
7. Edward Higgs, *The Information State in England: The Central Collection of Information on Citizens since 1500* (Basingstoke: Palgrave Macmillan, 2004), vii and 204.
8. *Daily Herald*, "Ministry 'Gossip Column' is Holding an Inquisition on the Doorsteps," July 25, 1940, 3.
9. Jonathan Fenby, *The Sinking of the "Lancastria": Britain's Greatest Maritime Disaster and Churchill's Cover-up* (New York: Simon & Schuster, 2005), 247.
10. *Daily Express*, "Lancastria Sunk – US Report," July 25, 1940, 1.
11. Jo Fox, "Careless Talk: Tensions within British Domestic Propaganda during the Second World War," *Journal of British Studies* 51, no. 4 (October 2012): 937 and 945–949.
12. *Daily Herald*, "No Muzzling," July 22, 1940, 5.
13. *Daily Herald*, "Forget about Morale," July 26, 1940, 2.
14. *Daily Express*, "Prowling and Prying," July 26, 1940, 4.
15. *Parliamentary Debates* (Commons), 5th ser., vol. 363, August 1, 1940, c. 1550. For a fuller account, see Laura Beers, "Whose Opinion? Changing Attitudes towards Opinion Polling in British Politics, 1937–1964," *Twentieth Century British History* 17, no. 2 (2006): 188–191.
16. *Second Report from the Select Committee on National Expenditure, 1941–1942* (London: HMSO, 1942), 4.
17. Mary Adams, "Notes on the Functions of Home Intelligence," February 9, 1940, INF 1/47, The National Archives (TNA), Kew; and Hubble, *Mass Observation and Everyday Life*, 174.
18. James Hinton, *The Mass Observers: A History, 1937–1949* (Oxford: Oxford University Press, 2013), 179–180; and H.G.G. Welch, "Survey of Public Opinion," May 12, 1940, INF 1/263, TNA.
19. Ivison Macadam to H.G.G. Welch, June 4, 1940, RG 40/183, TNA.
20. Hinton, *The Mass Observers*, 181–182.
21. Ian McLaine, *Ministry of Morale: Home Front Morale and the Ministry of Information* (London: Allen and Unwin, 1979), 87–88.
22. R. H. Parker to W. Monckton, September 8, 1941, INF 1/273/A, TNA.
23. Frank Whitehead, "The Government Social Survey," in *Essays on the History of British Sociological Research*, ed. Martin Bulmer (Cambridge, UK: Cambridge University Press, 1985), 84. This chapter wrongly dates the Cooper's Snoopers affair to 1941.
24. *Second Report from the Select Committee on National Expenditure, 1941–1942*, 3 and 5.
25. *The Times*, "War-Time Social Survey," March 28, 1942, 5.

26 Wartime Social Survey, "Foundation Garments," 1941, RG 23/6, TNA.
27 "The (Wartime) Social Survey," November 28, 1945, INF 1/273, TNA; and Kathleen Box and Geoffrey Thomas, "The Wartime Social Survey," *Journal of the Royal Statistical Society* 107, nos. 3–4 (1944): 152.
28 Stephen Taylor, 'Regulations for the Organisation of Individual Surveys,' February 1942, INF 1/263, TNA.
29 Louis Moss, *The Government Social Survey: A History* (London: HMSO, 1991), 5 and 7.
30 "Request for Information," undated, INF 1/263, TNA.
31 Wartime Social Survey, "Dig for Victory," 1942, RG 23/26, TNA.
32 Box and Thomas, "The Wartime Social Survey," 158.
33 Charlotte Greenhalgh, "Social Surveys," in *Reading Primary Sources: The Interpretation of Texts from Nineteenth and Twentieth Century History*, ed. Miriam Dobson and Benjamin Ziemann (London: Routledge, 2020), 120–122; and G. Hoinville, "Methodological Research on Sample Surveys: A Review of Developments in Britain," in *Essays on the History of British Sociological Research*, ed. Martin Bulmer (Cambridge, UK: Cambridge University Press, 1985), 103–107.
34 These processes were determined by established gender conventions: with men interviewed at work and women at home: see Box and Thomas, "Wartime Social Survey," 153–158.
35 Moss, *The Government Social Survey*, 8.
36 Mark Roodhouse, "'Fish-and-Chip Intelligence': Henry Durant and the British Institute of Public Opinion," *Twentieth Century British History* 24, no. 2 (June 2013), 234–237.
37 National Statistics, *60 Years of Social Survey: 1941–2001* (Norwich: HMSO, 2001), 15.
38 Roodhouse, "Fish-and-Chip Intelligence," 238.
39 Box and Thomas, "Wartime Social Survey," 160; and Louis Moss, "The Government Social Survey," *Operational Research Quarterly* 1, no. 4 (December 1950): 64.
40 Box and Thomas, "Wartime Social Survey," 158.
41 *Second Report from the Select Committee on National Expenditure, 1941–1942*, 2.
42 C. A. Moser, *Survey Methods in Social Investigation* (London: William Heinemann, 1958), 282–283.
43 Wartime Social Survey, "Food during the War: Dietary Study,"1943, RG 23/9A, TNA.
44 *Second Report from the Select Committee on National Expenditure, 1941–1942*, 3.
45 Greenhalgh, "Social Surveys," 125.
46 Box and Thomas, "Wartime Social Survey," 161.
47 Wartime Social Survey, "The Campaign against Venereal Diseases," 1943, RG 23/38, TNA.
48 C. A. Moser, "The Use of Sampling in Great Britain," *Journal of the American Statistical Association* 44, no. 246 (June 1949), 235.
49 Greenhalgh, "Social Surveys," 123; and Catherine Marsh, *The Survey Method: The Contribution of Surveys to Sociological Explanation* (London: Allen and Unwin, 1982), 35.
50 Moss, *The Government Social Survey*, 11.
51 Stephen Taylor, "The Study of Public Information: An Aid to Administrative Action," *Public Administration* 21, nos. 3–4 (October–December 1943): 109–119; and Louis Moss, "The War-time Social Survey: Social Research at the Service of the Administrator," *Public Administration* 21, nos. 3–4 (October–December 1943): 119–125.
52 *Illustrated*, "They Find Out What You Think," July 22, 1944, 14–17.
53 Box and Thomas, "Wartime Social Survey."
54 Savage, *Identities and Social Change in Britain*, 199. See also Jennifer Platt, "Anglo-American Contacts in the Development of Social Research Methods," in *The Social Survey in Historical Perspective, 1880–1940*, ed. Martin Bulmer, Kevin Bales, and Kathryn Kish Sklar (Cambridge, UK: Cambridge University Press, 1991), 353.
55 *Statistics Relating to the War Effort in the United Kingdom* (London: HMSO, 1944), 22.
56 Henry Irving, "Paper Salvage in Britain during the Second World War," *Historical Research* 89, no. 244 (May 2016): 383–384.
57 Wartime Social Survey, "Salvage," 1942, RG 23/9B, TNA.
58 Wartime Social Survey, "Salvage," 1942, RG 23/9B, TNA.
59 Moss, "The War-time Social Survey," 122.
60 E. M. I. Buxton, "General Salvage – Proposed Press Advertising Campaign," April 15, 1942, R 34/711/1, BBC Written Archives Centre, Caversham.

61 Wartime Social Survey, "Salvage," 1943, RG 23/41, TNA.
62 Box and Thomas, "Wartime Social Survey," 174.
63 McLaine, *Ministry of Morale*, 260.
64 Savage, *Identities and Social Change in Britain*, 195.
65 Moss, "The Government Social Survey," 56.
66 Hoinville, "Methodological Research on Sample Surveys," 113.
67 Kenneth O. Morgan, *The People's Peace: British History 1945–1989* (Oxford: Oxford University Press, 1990), 30.
68 Daisy Payling, "'The People Who Write to Us Are the People Who Don't Like Us': Class, Gender and Citizenship in the Survey of Sickness," *Journal of British Studies* 59, no. 2 (April 2020): 315–342.
69 Whitehead, "The Government Social Survey," 86–87 and 90–91.
70 Mark Abrams, *Social Surveys and Social Action* (London: Heinemann, 1951), 98–99.
71 Claus A. Moser and Graham Kalton, *Survey Methods in Social Investigation* (London: Heinemann Educational Books, 1971), 13.
72 Raymond Kent, *A History of British Empirical Sociology* (Aldershot: Gower, 1981), 142; and Marsh, *The Survey Method*, 35.
73 Whitehead, "The Government Social Survey," 87–88.
74 Higgs, *The Information State in England*, 159–161.
75 Kent, *A History of British Empirical Sociology*, 126. See also John Hall and D. Caradog Jones, "The Social Grading of Occupations," *British Journal of Sociology* 1, no. 1 (March 1950): 31–55.
76 Savage, *Identities and Social Change in Britain*, 188–189.
77 Alistair Black, "Information History," *Annual Review of Information Science and Technology* 40 (2006): 456; and Daniel Headrick, *When Information Came of Age: Technologies of Knowledge in the Age of Reason and Revolution, 1700–1850* (Oxford: Oxford University Press, 2000).
78 Peter Burke, *A Social History of Knowledge: From Gutenberg to Diderot* (Cambridge, UK: Polity Press, 2000), 1.
79 Toni Weller, "The Information State: An Historical Perspective on Surveillance," in *Routledge Handbook of Surveillance Studies*, ed. David Lyon, Kevin D. Haggerty, and Kirstie Ball (Abingdon: Routledge, 2012), 57.
80 *Second Report from the Select Committee on National Expenditure, 1941–1942*, 3.

18
SENSITIVE INFORMATION
Knowing and Preparing for Nuclear War during the Cold War*

Rosanna Farbøl and Casper Sylvest

Charles Bazerman's classic study of nuclear information, as a rhetorical moment in the construction of the Information Age, demonstrated how an anti-nuclear-test activist group based in St. Louis (Missouri, USA) developed new understandings of the information about nuclear matters that the American public *ought to receive*. Highlighting that "[i]nformation is rhetorical" and that "we need to unpack the entire sets of relations, actions and texts within which information is formed and deployed," Bazerman showed how anti-nuclear enthymemes—a construction of unspoken arguments—issued in demands for a specific kind of information about the effects of nuclear weapons testing, the consequences of nuclear war, and the properties of radioactive fallout.[1] Through its own publications and campaigns, the *Greater St. Louis Citizen's Committee* sought to create the information it demanded—full, independent, transparent, and scientific—and contrasted it to that of "centralized governmental definitions of information."[2] While it is useful to trace the emergence of the Information Age and its central characteristics to social movements and their quest to obtain independent information, it is certainly also a task for information historians to ask what political authorities considered reliable information about nuclear weapons and what deliberations governed the distribution and communication of such information.

For many non-nuclear-weapon states in Western Europe, this was a difficult question during the Cold War, when the arms race gave rise to new kinds of fears, new policies for protecting the civilian population, new forms of activism, and new types of public education. Relying on often incomplete and contested unpublished and published information issued by nuclear powers (allied or not), authorities in these states had to respond to growing demands for information about fallout from nuclear weapons testing and the character of that horrendous unknown lurking in the background: nuclear war. In many of these countries, the responsibility for navigating these treacherous waters fell to civil defence authorities tasked with protecting the civilian population in the event of war. That involved establishing organisations, materially transforming buildings and public spaces,

---

* The authors thank the editors and Aske Hennelund Nielsen for comments and suggestions on draft versions of this chapter.

and installing a culture of preparedness among citizenries. All of these activities required gathering, pondering, assessing, distilling, translating, and packaging information to various audiences using a range of media—from educational materials and technical reports to leaflets, posters, shelters, and films. The types of information aimed at the public were seen as vital education, but several considerations played a role: avoiding panic, controlling and reassuring the population, demonstrating the relevance of civil defence, and, elusively, ensuring national survival in a global conflict beyond immediate control.

This chapter provides a history of information about future nuclear war through a case study of Denmark, a small, Scandinavian welfare state that somewhat reluctantly gave up neutrality and became a founding member of NATO in 1949. Denmark pursued protection—offered in no small part by nuclear weapons—while seeking to balance alliance integration with national priorities designed to avoid confrontation with the Soviet Union. Following a short discussion of the development and transnational character of nuclear information in the post-war decades, the chapter analyses how information about nuclear fallout and thermonuclear war was collected, studied, formed, presented, and communicated to the public during the late 1950s and early 1960s. The first part of the analysis focuses on internal information processing within Danish civil defence as well as on early ideas about dissemination. The second part examines the implementation (and contestation) of these ideas in the public sphere and details some of the considerations that guided public communication. The use of the term "sensitive information" does not refer to secret data or knowledge about nuclear science and technology that malicious actors can exploit to conduct nuclear terror.[3] Instead, the chapter seeks to capture the double sensitivity surrounding questions of information about nuclear weapons, nuclear war, and means of protection and survival. On the one hand, access to information was both restricted *and* viewed as essential to individual and state survival; on the other hand, this information was delicate and required careful phrasing, dosing, and timing. The analysis pays attention to official and unofficial narratives about this information and specifically addresses questions of authority and uncertainty. The chapter ends with a short conclusion that also briefly discusses the return of questions about sensitive nuclear information after Russia's invasion of Ukraine in 2022.

Nuclear Information

In recent decades, the field of nuclear history has detailed the puzzling journey of the atomic bomb from wartime experience to dystopian imagination during the early decades of the Cold War. One aspect of this history concerns how developments in nuclear technologies, especially the weapons technologies that became part and parcel of superpower competition, introduced new conditions of information work.

In the days and weeks after the US bombing of the Japanese cities of Hiroshima and Nagasaki in August 1945, a wide range of reactions could be detected in Western societies—from relief and glee to awe and fear of the long-term consequences of these leaps in atomic science. The underlying science and technology attracted a good deal of attention, and in such presentations, an intense fascination was often imbricated in the dichotomy of utopian or dystopian narratives that soon engulfed everything atomic.[4] These early trends in Western nuclear culture were decidedly transnational, and Denmark was no exception— even if the constant reference to and adoration of the country's foremost scientist and Nobel Prize winner, Niels Bohr, stood out.[5] While this early and intensive post-war preoccupation with atomic technologies built on tropes developed during the early twentieth century, it acquired a distinct temporal quality.[6] Whether it was the prospect of boundless energy provision or a peak into a distant future of suicidal warfare, scientific information typically had a factual orientation, whereas the potential applications of new knowledge were enveloped in speculations about the future.

Indeed, as Western societies recovered from the Second World War and found themselves faced with a new kind of war, a Cold War, the atomic bomb was both seen in the context of the recent war *and* placed in a speculative future. As this chapter demonstrates, this dynamic was evident in relation to the specific problem of protecting the civilian population from the horrors of total war. This was an area of policy that grew in importance after the Second World War and which can be seen as emblematic of an accelerating trend (of modernity) whereby states become more preoccupied with utilising information for specific purposes, especially in the realms of war and security.[7]

The last war had been total and had clearly demonstrated the need for *total defence*, as a Danish white paper on civilian protection put it in 1946.[8] In preparing the ground for the Danish civil defence organisation that was established by law in April 1949—the same month that the country signed the North Atlantic Treaty and took side in the Cold War—the white paper presented the atomic bomb as the latest, regrettable step in the evolution of military weapons. Crucially, however, the bomb was not viewed on its own as a revolution in warfare. Apart from the phenomenon of radioactivity, the atomic bomb was seen to cause damage of a similar nature and on a similar scale to that of strategic bombing during the Second World War. And while the matter-of-fact exclusion of radioactivity from this assessment might appear perilous, the information about the atomic bomb and the threat of atomic warfare that Danish civil defence began issuing was on the whole reassuring. One example was an exhibition on the atomic age in Copenhagen in the late summer of 1949. While artists and intellectuals writing in the exhibition catalogue presented a bleak image of future war—an image used to bolster the case for a world federation—Arthur Dahl, director of the Danish Civil Defence Directorate (CDD), took a different approach. The bomb was clearly terrifying especially in terms of its properties of heat and blast, but radioactivity was by and large manageable. The use of shelters and an orderly response while awaiting the scientific measurements of qualified civil defence personnel made protection and survival realistic.[9]

This type of civil defence information is best understood in three specific contexts: recent experience with protecting the civilian population in war, an American monopoly on atomic bombs, and a widespread expectation that while the future of war appeared bleak, it had not yet arrived. On the eve of the exhibition, however, news broke of the American detection of a Soviet atomic bomb test. The arms race was on and the risk of atomic war a reality.

It was during the 1950s—and especially from the middle of the decade when the threat of a new and essentially unknown phenomenon, thermonuclear warfare, appeared a real possibility—that the themes we have come to associate with nuclear discourse took on particular intensity: mystery, potency, secrecy, and destiny.[10] A crucial event in this development was the political and radioactive fallout from the American *Castle Bravo* test on Bikini Atoll in the Pacific on March 1, 1954. While radioactive fallout was known to scientists and weapons engineers before the *Bravo* test, the explosive power of the hydrogen bomb (H-bomb) produced fallout that was not only local, but regional and global by transporting radioactive particles into both the atmosphere and the stratosphere.[11] The H-bomb raised a series of new questions about the next war: Could it be fought? Would any kind of protection be futile? What would be left?

For civil defence organisations, the thermonuclear age placed new demands on the information they sought, assessed, validated, presented, and distributed. The H-bomb not only heightened the importance of the home front, but also substantially reinforced a belief among authorities that total defence demanded informed and educated publics. Nuclear anxiety, panic, or defeatism threatened individual and state survival. Since the war would be lost if the home front crumbled, keeping up morale was of the essence, and the communication of reassuring and reliable information was key to resilience: "Quick and factual information is the best weapon against hostile propaganda and the rumours the enemy will circulate," as Dahl put it in a memorandum on psychological defence in 1954.[12] With the threat of war inching closer, the demand for information about nuclear weapons, nuclear war, and means of protection grew. As Black and Mak have highlighted, "information— its collection, storage, organization, dissemination, and accessibility—is central to the way power is executed and questioned."[13] This was perhaps especially true in the late 1950s and early 1960s, when the world tethered on the brink of a new kind of war.

Knowledge and the Preparation of Nuclear Information in Denmark

News of *Castle Bravo* reached Denmark in mid-March 1954 and while the American authorities initially sought to reassure international public opinion that everything was under control, confusion soon reigned within Danish civil defence. For some time, the CDD had been preparing a leaflet designed to inform the public about modern warfare and the possibilities of protection, provisionally entitled *What do I do if it Happens?* Work on the leaflet ground to a halt in late 1953 because of a dispute about salaries for two newspaper editors who worked on the project. At that point, two important aspects of the information strategy of Danish civil defence were being established: a concern about the risks of panic and an emphasis on achieving an appropriate tone in communication, one designed to reassure citizens that processing information calmly was the first step towards survival. Reflecting this, a draft depicted a terrified citizen on the front page and stated bluntly on the back of the leaflet: "Read this leaflet - when you know its contents and act on it, you will not have to be as frightened as the man on the cover."[14]

It was all to no avail. The director of the CDD may have been losing his patience with the recalcitrant editors but when he called off the entire project in May 1954, he explained his decision directly with reference to the recent developments in nuclear weapons technology. Already in early April, the director had stated publicly that the CDD lacked knowledge of the H-bomb, which created an entirely new situation for civil defence and civil defence information. He now wrote to the editors that the leaflet was cancelled, because the agency simply did not possess "reliable information about the hydrogen bomb, which is necessary for guiding the public responsibly."[15]

A quest for information about H-bombs and fallout became central to the agency's activities during the ensuing years. In NATO, they asked the United States to release more information and argued for the importance of bolstering public confidence in the idea of civilian protection as a matter of principle.[16] But the CDD also contacted the United Kingdom to request information about H-bombs, radioactive fallout and safe dosages, and it kept up to date with the scientific and political debates that gradually became more intense. The local knowledge base was limited. Denmark was in the early stages of an attempt to exploit the peaceful uses of nuclear energy—an effort heralded by President Eisenhower's Atoms for Peace Program in 1953.[17] Remarkably, the first major assessment of the importance of the H-bomb for Danish civil defence was provided by Dahl himself in a two-volume memorandum completed in March 1956. It reached the reassuring conclusion that Danish civil defence was still relevant and required adjustment rather than wholesale reform in light of the H-bomb. It was a first step in the quest for information, but evidently not a complete analysis of a subject that garnered steadily more public attention.[18] Statements by scientists and public intellectuals about the dangers of nuclear testing also fed uncertainty, especially from the mid-1950s. Inside the CDD, an informal study group, known as the "fallout-trio," tried to follow the complex debate and navigate increasingly diverging scientific assessments of the long-term effects of radioactivity that had consequences for designing protective measures.

Meanwhile, the organisation embarked on a process of assessing and translating this patchwork of information, channelling it into technical analyses outlining the effects of H-bombs in a Danish context. Apart from the information obtained from neutral countries and allies in NATO (an occasionally frustrating quest), engineering studies of blast resilient design and the US Atomic Energy Commission's publication of *The Effects of Nuclear Weapons* in 1957 eventually made such analyses possible. In June 1957, a report on the possibilities of surviving an attack with modern weapons of mass destruction, which focused especially on the role of shelters, deliberately employed the darkest possible scenarios. Analysing H-bomb attacks on Denmark (something especially Dahl regarded as improbable at the time), the report aloofly stipulated the effects of 1 MT, 5 MT, and 20 MT bombs dropped over the country.[19] Tables with columns of total population, dead, and wounded left little doubt about the scale of destruction that would follow—under circumstances that were deemed unlikely. In the bleakest scenario—the dropping of a 20 MT bomb over greater Copenhagen—a table made it plain that 53,700 "unharmed" survivors would be left to take care of 193,600 wounded fellow citizens and bury the more than 1,000,000 dead. A series of accompanying maps projected fallout under varying wind directions and clearly indicated the most lethal path of the fallout by transposing a cigar-shaped figure onto regional or national maps.

The report was not meant for publication, but an underlying rationale was evidently to counter the argument that civil defence was futile. Why then work with the worst possible scenarios? The thought behind "over dimensioning the weapons of attack and working with the most favourable conditions for the attacker" was that "any deviation" from these assumptions would increase the possibilities of survival.[20] Apart from this questionable attempt to boost morale internally, the rest of the report was devoid of any normative remarks.

Having achieved a better understanding of the effects of the new weapons and technologies, CDD resumed work on public information in 1957. It remained a prime concern of the Directorate to supply authoritative information about the possibilities of surviving atomic warfare—something which was also in accordance with NATO priorities with respect to the home front.[21] Armed with new information and aware that its efforts in the early 1950s had been thwarted, the CDD initiated a new project. Relying on expert advice from road safety authorities, the aim was not a leaflet but a poster in every Danish home. In its first approach to the Ministry of the Interior about the new initiative, the CDD stressed both that it was now able to inform the public and that the poster was meant to provide the most basic information. Key aspects of the communication strategy remained intact. To avoid fuelling fears, the introduction stated clearly that there was no acute danger of an atomic attack. It also included the reassuring message that if the guidance was followed, "opportunities for surviving an attack are improved to a significant degree" as well as the ingenious statement that the best protection against nuclear weapons was *not* to be present at the site of the attack. Other advice resembled the duck-and-cover procedure taught to American school kids in the early 1950s.[22] The information about radioactive fallout was anything but detailed. The poster merely stated that radioactive fallout could not be sensed except by specialised equipment, that it was dangerous if ingested and that it was essential to clean food items and discard contaminated clothes.

A short film produced to accompany the distribution of the poster also reflected this approach. Here, the depiction of a post-attack scene was hardly believable; a robust housewife immediately set about wiping radioactive dust of stored food items in a moderately disorganised kitchen. A later evaluation of the film stressed the importance of avoiding such scenes that provoked reactions of incredulity rather than seriousness.[23] While the film made it to the cinemas, national distribution of the poster came to nothing. To the disbelief and disappointment of the CDD, the Finance Committee of the Danish Parliament refused to release the funds needed for printing and distribution. The CDD made sure that the poster and some of its illustrations were published in its internal magazine (mainly aimed at volunteers) and a few national newspapers also publicised the information.

It was hardly a success. Inspired by new peace movements and concerned scientists in the United Kingdom, the Federal Republic of Germany, and the United States, a new form of oppositional activism was emerging among the Old and New Left in politics and within the Danish peace movement. In such circles, people ridiculed the advice not to be present at the site of the attack and questioned the authority and rationale of civil defence even suggesting that this humanitarian organisation contributed to a militarisation of the mind. It was also in this context that peace organisations began publishing their own information. In 1960, the *Committee for Information about Nuclear Armaments* obtained permission from *Greater St. Louis Citizen's Committee for Nuclear Information* to modify and republish a pamphlet detailing the immediate and long-term horrors of nuclear war, a move which testifies to a transnational circulation of unofficial anti-nuclear information. The Danish version was entitled *A City like Copenhagen One Year after a Nuclear Attack* and detailed the grim aftermath of a double H-bomb attack (8 MT and 10 MT) on the Danish capital.[24]

Both civil defence and the anti-nuclear movement considered it crucial to inform the public about the nuclear danger, but they differed in their assessment of what counted as reliable and necessary information. This growing controversy reflected diverging assessments of Danish security and more specifically of relevant threat scenarios. Within the government, alternative scenarios circulated. On the one hand, NATO documents from the late 1950s anticipated that attacks on Denmark would be with atomic (rather than thermonuclear) bombs, and director Dahl repeatedly expressed the view that it was unlikely that Denmark would be targeted with H-bombs. On the other hand, from the mid-1950s, planning in the area of civil protection designed to ensure continuity of government and societal resilience began from the assumption that H-bomb attacks might occur.[25] The powerful chief of staff and later director of the CDD, Erik Schultz, repeatedly if indirectly questioned Dahl's assessment by stressing that H-bomb attacks could not be ruled out, that war was notoriously unpredictable, and that there would always be a task for civil defence *outside* (a possibly extensive) ground zero.[26] Still, the scenarios of apocalyptic thermonuclear war in "information of dissent" contrasted markedly with those that governed civil defence exercises into the early 1960s, where the focus was often on attacks with smaller atomic bombs in the 2–10 KT range.[27]

Specified assumptions about what Danish civil defence should prepare for could go some way towards resolving such disputes. These assumptions were only agreed on in 1959 and stipulated that attacks with conventional weapons or forces in combination with atomic bombs were deemed most likely. The use of H-bombs was seen as possible but unlikely, but the document stressed the need for protection against radioactive fallout. An internal memorandum on this subject was ready in 1960. It tackled a series of difficult questions about exposure, isolation of contaminated individuals and psychological impacts. The memorandum also explicitly acknowledged that it was a difficult subject that required "weighing risks."[28]

Evidently, a period of gathering and digesting information spanning more than half a decade meant that the CDD was now on firmer ground. Still, the issue of public information was by no means resolved. When pressed by the organisation's top advisory council on why the public had still not received such information, CDD director Dahl stressed the complexity of the task. He also admitted that the failed poster project of 1958 had evaded the difficulties and that its short format had not fostered any deeper appreciation of the nature of radioactivity.[29]

Disseminating and Communicating Sensitive Information

By the early 1960s, the CDD thought it long overdue that the public be informed about the character of future war, what preparations the authorities had in place to ease the hardship for civilians and how they could help. If people were sufficiently informed, it was assumed, they would act rationally and contribute to the humanitarian and national objectives that were encapsulated in the quest for individual and national survival. Ironically, when the political and financial support for a public information campaign was finally available, the CDD was initially side-lined. The matter was delegated to a Committee for the Press' Preparedness created by the Prime Minister's Office following pressure from NATO to educate populations and initiate civil emergency planning.[30] The CDD was not originally represented in the new committee, but Schultz was soon headhunted to assist with the preparation of public information. The path to an informed public remained fraught with dilemmas, however: What information could be disclosed? What could be counter-productive? What information was relevant, given the most realistic scenarios, and how were these to be determined? How was information best disseminated?

The information leaflet became a favoured instrument to promote resilience and educate civilians to take (the right) action. A string of leaflets was published in NATO countries, including West Germany, the United Kingdom, and Norway,[31] and in January 1962, the leaflet *If the War Comes* was distributed to all Danish households. The leaflet was inspired by Swedish and Norwegian leaflets as well as based on drafts for the unsuccessful poster of 1958 but, unlike the poster, the leaflet struck a more sinister tone. In the introduction, Prime Minister Viggo Kampmann warned that nuclear war was a possibility, "the modern weapons can strike us, even if the country is not directly attacked, and these weapons do not distinguish between civilian and military targets. War today is total …."[32] Kampmann earnestly stressed the interdependence between individuals and society and appealed to the reader's community spirit: while the nuclear age obliged the individual to prepare for the worst, citizens also assumed responsibility for the survival of the nation. The leaflet described weapon types, fallout, and warning signals, presented the measures already prepared by civil defence such as evacuation and public shelters, and provided instructions and practical advice on precautionary measures to take before or during an attack. The text and illustrations communicated advice and information in an unambiguous, simple, and confident way. The complexities or uncertainties that had characterised the internal preparation phase had vanished.

The authorities pursued an information strategy that sought to adjust civilians to thinking the unthinkable by communicating practical hands-on instructions and simplified technical information. The leaflet was intended to provide facts and build trust; it should avoid trivialising the threat but also communicate hope. While the introduction warned about the risk of nuclear bombs or fallout, the leaflet also claimed that, "We know the effects of these weapons and that in many cases protection is possible. With reasonable precautions, taken by society and everyone, losses among the civilian population can be significantly reduced. If the directions are followed, the possibility of surviving modern war will be enhanced considerably."[33]

To pre-empt criticism from anti-nuclear movements, a single sentence admitted that radiation could cause damage even to future generations.[34] Apart from this, the leaflet made no reference to what would follow the attack or the war, leaving readers to expect that when they emerged from their shelters, everything would soon be back to normal. By defining the threat, explicating protection measures, reassuring that survival was possible and disguising the post-war situation, the leaflet precluded alternative information and scenarios. As information, the leaflet incarnated a specific sociotechnical imaginary that presented the future war as a survivable and manageable parenthesis—if the leaflet's instructions were followed.[35]

Returning to Black and Mak's point about the crucial role of information in the exercise of governance and power, the leaflet also clearly contained an element of population control: keeping up morale was a prerequisite if government was to keep control of the situation. If the civilian population was ensnared by foreign propaganda, paralysed by fear, panicked, or rioted, the government's attempts to fight the war would be undermined. The leaflet should convince the public that survival was possible, perhaps even likely. NATO likewise stressed the importance of information to maintain morale and, as it was put bluntly, get people to "do what they are told."[36] The instructions in the leaflet—keep calm, do not believe in rumours, seek shelter, listen to the radio, obey authorities—were designed to instil in the population the desired behaviour. A film produced by civil defence authorities supported this message by pre-enacting and overcoming the catastrophe.[37]

This official information and the assumptions and scenarios behind it were also contested, however. While the *Campaign against Nuclear Weapons (Kampagnen mod Atomvåben*, KmA)—the Danish version of the new kind of anti-nuclear-grassroots movement emerging in Germany, Britain, and the United States—agreed that information was of the utmost importance, they were sceptical of official information that, overwhelmingly, originated from NATO allies. Tellingly, KmA wrote to the Prime Minister to ask for a copy of the leaflet before it was published in order to suggest changes and additions designed to ensure that the text contained "clear and concrete information about the nuclear danger."[38] KmA's interest in the subject was hardly surprising. It had been a central demand from the movement's founding in 1960 to force the government to supply "clear information about the quantity and consequences of radioactive fallout."[39] The request was turned down, and the government's leaflet fell well short of KmA's expectations. Consequently, the movement published a rival leaflet that questioned the claim that surviving nuclear war was both possible and meaningful.

The two leaflets received roughly the same amount of attention among the public: according to the polling company Gallup, about two-thirds of the population read them. Only 6% of the population felt safer after reading *If the War Comes* and 2% started preparing a shelter. Apart from the anti-nuclear movements' general attacks on the official leaflet's optimism, controversies about specific advice on shelters and canned foods followed. Of all, 22% of the population found the criticism legitimate.[40] Strikingly, the polls were perceived as a victory by the civil defence authorities. Evidently, contestation was expected, but public indifference was a separate fear. Indeed, Schultz found ground for optimism in the attention to the problems of civil defence generated by the leaflet and the critique that followed.[41]

The controversy exemplified the information dilemma authorities faced: on the one hand, they asserted the need to inform and educate the public to ensure that citizens understood the seriousness of the situation and did what they were told; on the other hand, this information risked creating panic, apathy, ridicule, or contestation rather than resilience. The authorities saw this primarily as a question of determining the right dosage of information, neither too little nor too much, but it was also a question of substance and the validity of those imaginaries of nuclear war implied in such information.[42]

The "dialectic between secrecy and disclosure"[43] is characteristic of the genre of public nuclear information and not restricted to the textual medium.[44] Information about nuclear war also took material form, most concretely in the shelters that gave "mass and solidity" to the otherwise imaginary war presented in *If the War Comes*.[45] Denmark embarked on an ambitious shelter programme in the early years of the Cold War—a program only surpassed by the (more or less) non-aligned countries Switzerland, Sweden, and Finland. The official Danish goal was to establish public shelters in urban areas for 25% of the population in addition to private shelters, ensuring in total a 125–200% coverage.[46] The design of this programme and subsequent modifications were influenced by a process of gathering and processing information and calculating and estimating harm.

The shelters' material existence might, however, also be read *as* information: these material structures communicated information from the authorities to the population about the risk of war and about government precaution efforts. In the mid-1960s, public shelters were updated: wooden doors were replaced by steel doors and sand filters and vent pipes were installed. The updates materially communicated the added layer of dangers caused by thermonuclear war and the risk of fallout yet did so in a subtle way. It was not easily intelligible except to people who knew what to look for. General information was printed in *If the War Comes*, civil defence magazines and, later, telephone books, but citizens were only informed that shelters existed; they were not provided information about their specific locations. Shelters were hidden in plain sight: some were covered by grass and shrubs, others were integrated into ordinary buildings, parking garages, locker rooms, schools, and residential buildings, and used for peacetime purposes.[47] Yet, even if this kind of information about the looming nuclear war was easy to ignore, it made a permanent mark upon Danish cityscapes.

The duality in the government's information strategy implied that information should be reassuring and generate interest but not otherwise disturb everyday life by reminding the population too graphically and brutally of the imaginary war that could swiftly upend human existence. Internal memoranda produced at the time made no secret of the fact that no shelter could withstand a direct hit and that decisions about the shelter programme were fundamentally a function of weighing public finances and fatalities under conditions of uncertainty.[48] Authorities nevertheless spent considerable effort assuring people that even if survival could not be guaranteed in the nuclear age, a shelter still offered the best chance.

Conclusions and Contemporary Perspectives

The threat of nuclear war presented a problem of information with which Danish civil defence authorities—and their international counterparts—struggled with for decades. It often involved a deficit in the supply end of the information chain; of certain, detailed and undisputed information, and a surplus on the other end; that of public demand for information. In Dahl's memorandum on psychological defence from 1954, he assumed a near-direct relationship between information and resilience, but as this chapter has demonstrated, constructing and communicating nuclear information were far from straightforward, it was a highly contextualised activity and resilience was no guaranteed outcome.[49]

As a non-nuclear-weapon state, Denmark relied heavily on restricted or incomplete data and knowledge about nuclear weapons' effects, a topic that attracted increasing attention and generated controversy in the public sphere. To some extent, Danish civil defence authorities were groping in the dark during the first decades of the Cold War.[50] That did not prevent them from working with what they had; the organisation's humanitarian ethos and a strong sense of responsibility saw to that. After getting their hands on relevant information, public or restricted, a process followed where this information was translated, processed, and adapted to fit Danish conditions and contexts. The capacity of Danish shelters to resist blast, heat, and radioactivity was meticulously calculated and thermonuclear attacks were turned into statistics and maps projecting fallout patterns. This sense-making process required a technical, emotionally detached approach, and the majority of this nuclear information was not shared with the public.

While the job of procuring and processing nuclear information was characterised by complexity, probing and uncertainty, public communication efforts conveyed reassurance and conviction. Official nuclear information served multiple purposes that spanned several temporalities: it was an honest attempt at responding to a contemporary public demand for information, a contribution to fostering the resilience deemed necessary both before and during a war as well as a more clandestine effort at maintaining social order and controlling the population if the war came. It did not disguise the fact that the total war of the future would likely be a nuclear war and that the goal was no longer, as in previous wars, to save everyone. Rather, "[t]he goal is to make sure the nation as such survives" in accordance with "the terms of the nuclear age," as Dahl's successor, Schultz, bleakly put it in an interview with the civil defence magazine in 1963.[51] Still, the practical information in *If the War Comes* suggested to the public that if they just prepared properly, they stood a fairly good chance to survive, and that there would, indeed, be a functioning post-war state.

Official information was resisted and challenged by alternative or unofficial analyses and scenarios like KmA's leaflet or the hypothetical nuclear attack on Copenhagen/St. Louis. Throughout the Cold War, civil defence authorities and the anti-nuclear movement struggled with keeping up to date with the development of nuclear weapons technologies and the arms race, and their potential impact on peoples and societies. The strategies and purposes that lay behind their information work differed considerably. While unofficial nuclear information was designed to fuel resistance in order to prevent the imaginary war from happening, civil defence information sought to prepare citizens for a war they deemed possible, even likely.

If the War Comes was the first and only leaflet to be distributed to all households in Denmark. Throughout the Cold War, civil defence authorities unsuccessfully tried to turn scattered initiatives into a coherent and extensive information policy. As Schultz later realised, the whole information affair was difficult because "[n]o one knows the situation until it arises."[52] An updated version of *If the War Comes*, eventually titled *About Survival*, was prepared after relations between the Cold War superpowers deteriorated in the early 1980s.[53] It was decided, however, not to distribute it before an urgent situation had created "the right psychological conditions."[54] The leaflet was ready and printed in 1983, but at the request of the Minister of the Interior, Britta Schall Holberg, it was only made available through libraries and public institutions. Holberg's motivations remain unclear, but it is likely that the combination of controversy and indifference towards *If the War Comes* as well as the charged political climate of the 1980s, where peace movements were again strong and vociferous, played a role. Information not only had to be obtained and curated—it also had to be timed.

Following Russia's invasion of Ukraine in 2022, not least President Putin's repeated nuclear threats, a nuclear fear which had prematurely been discarded as a Cold War phenomenon returned. With it followed calls for public information about emergencies, also in Denmark.[55] But what, in a time of misinformation, fake news, and hybrid warfare, counts as reliable information? The Danish Emergency Management Agency, the heir to the CDD, seemed to be caught off guard. While Swedish authorities published the leaflet *If Crisis or War Comes* in 2018, the Danish agency had made no attempts since the end of the Cold War to inform the Danish public about potential disasters of this magnitude. While knowledge about nuclear weapons and radioactivity has expanded, the future remains as unpredictable as the psychology of political decision-makers. The sudden return of demands for information demonstrated that the Agency, like its predecessor, was still caught in the information dilemma: "On the one hand, we have to make sure the citizens are informed. On the other hand, we need to avoid encouraging an uncertainty among the population that is, at the moment, unfounded," said the Agency's head of communications in April 2022.[56]

Six decades after the publication of *If the War Comes,* nuclear information is, then, still considered both necessary and sensitive. It must be carefully dosed, neither too little nor too much, and accurately timed, not too soon and certainly not too late.

Notes

1 Charles Bazerman, "Nuclear Information. One Rhetorical Moment in the Construction of the Information Age," *Written Communication* 18, no. 3 (July 2001): 290–291.
2 Bazerman, "Nuclear Information," 259.
3 For example, Wyn Q. Bowen and Christopher Hobbs, "Sensitive Nuclear Information: Challenges and Options for Control," *Strategic Analysis* 38, no. 2 (2014): 217–229. See also Peter Galison, "Removing Knowledge," *Critical Inquiry* 31 (2004): 229–243.
4 Jonathan Hogg, *British Nuclear Culture: Official and Unofficial Narratives in the Long 20th Century* (London: Bloomsbury, 2016); Spencer Weart, *The Rise of Nuclear Fear* (Cambridge, MA: Harvard University Press, 2012); Dick van Lente, ed. *The Nuclear Age in Popular Media* (New York: Palgrave MacMillan, 2012); Paul Boyer, *By the Bomb's Early Light: American Thought and Culture at the Dawn of the Atomic Age* (New York: Pantheon, 1985).
5 Aske Hennelund Nielsen, *Dansk Atomkultur Fra 1945 til 1963: Forestillinger om Atomenergiens Praktiske Anvendelse i Efterkrigstidens Danmark* (PhD diss., University of Southern Denmark, February 2020).
6 Hogg, *British Nuclear Culture*; Weart, *The Rise*.

7 Alistair Black and Bonnie Mak, "Period, Theme, Event: Locating Information History in History," in *Information and Power in History. Towards a Global Approach*, ed. Ida Nijenhuis et al. (London and New York: Routledge, 2020), 18–36.
8 Indenrigsministeriets Luftværnsudvalg af 1946, *Betænkningen Vedrørende Bygningsmæssige Civilforsvarsforanstaltninger* (København: J.H. Schultz, 1948), 20–21, 40, 46, 213–220.
9 Exhibition catalogue, *Atomalderen: Skandinavisk-Britisk Udstilling*, Charlottenborg (København: September 1–18, 1949), 56.
10 William Kinsella, "One Hundred Years of Nuclear Discourse: Four Master Themes and Their Implications for Environmental Communication," *Environmental Communication Yearbook* 2 (2005): 49–72.
11 Robert Jacobs, *Nuclear Bodies. The Global Hibakusha* (New Haven, CT: Yale University Press, 2022); Toshihiro Higuchi, *Political Fallout. Nuclear Weapons Testing and the Making of a Global Environmental Crisis* (Stanford, CA: Stanford University Press, 2020).
12 Arthur Dahl, memorandum, "Memorandum Vedrørende Psykologisk Forsvar," December 23, 1954, Beredskabsstyrelsen, Civilforsvarsdirektør E. Schultz' embedsarkiv (BES), box 186, The Danish National Archives (DNA).
13 Black and Mak, "Period, Theme, Event," 20.
14 Draft leaflet *Hvad Gør Jeg Hvis det Sker*, undated (September–December 1953), BES, box 171, DNA. In the following, quotes from Danish material are translated by the authors.
15 Dahl, letter to editors Rechendorff and Eriksen, 22/5, 1954, BES, box 171, DNA.
16 Summary and notes "Kortfattet Referat" and "Notater fra Samtale med dr. Taylor, A.E.R.E," BES, box 1, DNA; Civilforsvarsstyrelsen, *Memorandum om de Nucleare Våbens Indflydelse på Civilforsvarets Planlægning* (Copenhagen: Civilforsvarsstyrelsen, March 1956), Appendix 2, BES, box 185, DNA.
17 Henry Nielsen and Henrik Knudsen, "The Troublesome Life of Peaceful Atoms in Denmark," *History and Technology* 26, no. 2 (2010): 91–118.
18 Civilforsvarsstyrelsen, *Memorandum*.
19 Yield is measured either in kilotons (KT, thousand tons TNT) or in megatons (MT, million tons TNT).
20 Research report "En Undersøgelse af Mulighed for Overleven i Tilfælde af Angreb med Moderne Masseødelæggende Våben med Særlig Henblik på Beskyttelsesrums Modstandsdygtighed," June 1957, BES, box 37, DNA.
21 Iben Bjørnsson, "Negotiating Armageddon: Civil Defence in NATO and Denmark 1949–1959," *Cold War History* 23, no. 2 (2023): 217–238.
22 Robert Jacobs, "Atomic Kids: *Duck and Cover* and *Atomic Alert* Teach American Children How to Survive Atomic Attack," *Film & History* 40, no. 1 (2010): 25–44.
23 Civilforsvars-Forbundet, meeting minutes "Møde i Statens Filmcentral Mandag den 26. September, 1960," Statens Filmcentral, Gamle filmsager, folder: "Radioaktivt nedfald," DNA/The Danish Film Institute.
24 Komiteen for Oplysning om Atomfaren, *En by som København et år efter Atombombeangreb* (Copenhagen, 1960).
25 Bodil Frandsen, *Hvis krigen kommer. En undersøgelse af det centrale civile beredskab og Regan Vest under den Kolde Krig (1950–1968)* (Unpublished PhD diss., Aalborg University 2021).
26 Erik Schultz, "Civilforsvaret i en brintbombetid," *Arbejdersamariten* 24, 1955, 3–12; [no author], "Civilforsvar: Nytter det ... i en brintbombetid," *Samvirke* 20 (1957), 18–19; Erik Schultz, "Evakuering og Beskyttelsesrum," *Meddelelser fra Sundhedsstyrelsen, Beredskabsafdelingen*, nr. 66 (1958), 449–452.
27 Casper Sylvest, "Pre-enacting the Next War: The Visual Culture of Danish Civil Defence in the Early Nuclear Age," *Cold War History* 2, no. 1 (2022): 79–102.
28 Civilforsvarsstyrelsen, *Memorandum vedrørende den civilforsvarsmæssige beskyttelse mod radioaktivt nedfald* (Copenhagen: Civilforsvarsstyrelsen, 1960), BES, box 135, DNA.
29 Minutes, Civil Defence Council meeting April 5, 1960, 10. Beredskabsstyrelsen, Civilforsvarsrådets forretningsudvalgs møder, box 2, DNA.
30 Frandsen, *Hvis krigen kommer*, esp. 4–7, 76–82; Iben Bjørnsson, ""Stands tilløb til panik" Civilforsvarspjecer som social kontrol" in *Atomangst og civilt beredskab: Forestillinger om atomkrig i Danmark 1945–1975*, ed. Morten Pedersen og Marianne Rostgaard (Aalborg: Aalborg University Press, 2020), 65–101.

31 Memorandum by Senior Civil Defence Advisor, "Civil Defence Committee. Control of civilian population under attack," September 6, 1956, AC/23(CD)-D/151, NATO online archives; Draft text for *NATO Self-Help Handbook* 1961, BES, box 112, DNA. The West-German leaflet was entitled *Jeder hat eine Chance* (1961), the British *Advising the Householder* (1961).
32 Statsministeriet, *Hvis krigen kommer* (Copenhagen, 1962), 1.
33 Statsministeriet, *Hvis krigen kommer*, 6.
34 Meeting minutes Presseberedskabsudvalget "Foreløbigt referat af udvalgets 2. møde, torsdag d. 6. April 1961," BES, box 112, DNA.
35 Iben Bjørnsson, Rosanna Farbøl and Casper Sylvest, "Hvis krigen kommer. Forestillinger om fremtiden under den kolde krig," *Kulturstudier* 11, no. 1 (2020): 33–61.
36 NATO "Civil Defence Committee."
37 Sylvest, "Pre-enacting the next war."
38 Draft letter by B.G. Toft Nielsen from Viggo Kampmann to Carl Scharnberg September 25, 1961, BES, box 112, DNA.
39 Søren Hein Rasmussen, *Sære Alliancer. Politiske bevægelser i efterkrigstidens Danmark* (Odense: Odense Universitetsforlag, 1997).
40 The Gallup polls are reproduced with comments in *Orientering fra Civilforsvarsstyrelsen* 8, nos. 6 and 7, 1962. See also Marianne Rostgaard, "Kan man overleve en atomkrig," in *Atomangst og civilt beredskab*, 149–153.
41 Letter from Erik Schultz to D. E. H. Wynter, Home Office, Civil Defence Department, March 13, 1962, BES, box 63, DNA.
42 Rosanna Farbøl, "Prepare or Resist? Cold War Civil Defence and Imaginaries of Nuclear War in Britain and Denmark in the 1980s," *Journal of Contemporary History* 57, no. 1 (2021): 136–158.
43 Ida Nijenhuis et al., "Information and Power in History. A New Historiographical Approach?" in *Information and Power in History. Towards a Global Approach*, ed. De Nijenhuis et al. (London: Routledge, 2020), 279; Galison, "Removing."
44 On genre, see Laura Skouvig and Jack Andersen, "Understanding Information History from a Genre-Theoretical Perspective," *Journal of the Association for Information Science and Technology* 66, no. 10 (2015): 2061–2070.
45 Sheila Jasanoff, "Imagined and Invented Worlds," in *Dreamscapes of Modernity: Sociotechnical Imaginaries and the Fabrication of Power*, ed. Sheila Jasanoff and Sang-Huyn Kim (Chicago, IL: Chicago University Press, 2015), 322.
46 Financial restraints and limited political attention in the 1970s put a temporary halt to the programme, but to what extent the ambitious goals were reached remains unclear.
47 Rosanna Farbøl, "Atomkrigens arkitektur. Velfærd og civilforsvar under den Kolde Krig," *Temp – tidsskrift for historie* 11, no. 21 (2020): 101–125.
48 Casper Sylvest, "Atomfrygten og civilforsvaret," *temp - tidsskrift for historie* 16: 16–39; report by Civilforsvarsstyrelsens beskyttelsesrumsudvalg, "En undersøgelse af offentlige beskyttelsesrums evne til at modstå forskellige våbenvirkninger," May 1961, esp. Appendix 9, BES, box 37, DNA.
49 Skouvig and Andersen, "Understanding Information History," 2063. See also Michael Buckland, "Information as Thing," *Journal of the American Society for Information Science* 42, no. 5 (1991): 351–360.
50 Sylvest, "Atomfrygten," 25.
51 "Civilforsvaret må være smidigt i sin opbygning," *Civilforsvarsbladet* May 5, 1963, 14.
52 Letter from Erik Schultz to Palle Simonsen November 4, 1976, BES, box 173, DNA.
53 Note from the CDD to Ministry of the Interior "Civilforsvarets information til befolkningen," April 24, 1981, BES, box 173, DNA; Note "Notat vedrørende civilforsvarets oplysning af befolkningen" no date, (most likely 1981), BES, box 173, DNA.
54 *Folketingstidende* [Danish Parliamentary Records] 1982–1983, question no.1598, 13526–13527; "Befolkningen må informeres grundigt – også i fredstid," *Civilforsvar* 3 1983, 4–5.
55 John Last, "What happened to Europe's public bunkers?," *Foreign Policy* May 8, 2022; "Den almindelige svensker er langt bedre forberedt på krig, end vi danskere er," *Avisen Danmark*, March 5, 2022.
56 Therese Bach Øvlisen and Mette Aaby Andersen, "Trods lav risiko bekymrer fire ud af ti sig om atomkrig," *DR.dk*, April 3, 2022.

19
"MEN ARE ENGINEERS, WOMEN ARE COMPUTERS"
Women and the Information Technology Interregnum

Antony Bryant

In the brief period between the early development of electronic computers in the late 1940s and early 1950s, and the advent of "software engineering" in response to the software crisis of the early 1960s, there was a strict gendered demarcation in organisational deployment of computer technology. Men were assigned to engineering teams, where the key technical decisions and innovations were supposedly taking place. Women were given the secondary status of "computers," regarded merely as a slightly more technical version of the typing pool. This lasted only a short time. By the 1960s, demand for software and the rapid changes in computer technology—faster, cheaper, more reliable hardware; a lack of equally reliable software—produced an interregnum where the old rules did not apply and new ones had not yet been adopted. Several pioneering women took advantage of this, setting up what we would now recognise as the earliest examples of software houses, in several cases using their own homes as their headquarters.[1] In what follows, several contrasting examples will be used to illustrate this development and its aftermath, placing it within the larger context of the ways in which women have been systematically excluded or relegated to secondary roles in a wide variety of practices, disciplines and histories, a phenomenon that has, unfortunately, taken on new guises in recent years.

Introduction

It is now understood that the development of computers from the nineteenth century onwards, a prominent aspect of the history of information in the modern world, involved key contributions by several notable women. Charles Babbage is credited with developing early mechanical computers—The Difference Engine and The Analytical Engine—in the first half of nineteenth century. The former remained incomplete, but the latter, in the form of a sequence of gradually evolving models, was used to perform various mathematical operations, including generating a sequence of Bernoulli numbers. It was able to achieve this using what we would now term an algorithm, devised and implemented by Ada Lovelace, an accomplishment for which she is widely considered to be the first computer programmer, albeit that there was no programming language as such.[2]

The Analytical Engine used punched card technology first implemented by Jacquard on a weaving device. Lovelace thus stated: "[W]e may say most aptly that the Analytical Engine weaves algebraical patterns just as the Jacquard loom weaves flowers and leaves."[3] Babbage's machines did not develop any further, although William Gibson and Bruce Sterling produced a fascinating alternative history, *The Difference Engine*, which imagines that steam-powered computational devices were developed and mass produced, leading to an information revolution similar in many regards to that of our era.[4] Computer technology only developed once valve technology became available in the 1930s and 1940s. Again, however, it was a woman, Grace Hopper, who was responsible for a key advance in the feasibility and spread of the technology, the concept of machine-independent programming languages. In the 1940s, she started working on computers, including UNIVAC I, one of the first general-purpose computers. Her key contribution was the development of an English-language-type programming language—FLOW-MATIC—which formed the basis for the development of COBOL, the first standardised programming language for commercial computers. Hopper eventually rose to become a Rear Admiral in the US Navy, remaining on active service until she was seventy-nine.[5]

The contributions of Lovelace and Hopper are now celebrated, but they are regarded as outliers or anomalies, computing, and technology in general being seen as male domains. This is self-perpetuating; little or no attention is paid to pioneering women in these technical contexts; consequently, the assumption that women are incapable of contributing to these fields gains traction. Enduringly, computing has been structurally gendered. For example, in mid-twentieth-century Britain, as Mar Hicks has shown, the civil service failed dismally to harness the potential of women in its attempts to develop and exploit computer technology, deliberately prioritising instead the labour of "computer men," especially in the area of programming.[6] Similarly, in America, as Nathan Ensmenger explains, the computing industry, especially in specialist areas like programming, proved far less accessible to women than to men, who he terms the "computer boys."[7] These continuing inequalities were, and continued to be, reinforced by training and education programmes, which catered essentially for men and have made little or no attempt to attract women.[8]

We like to think that over the years this situation has changed. Women got the vote in various countries during the twentieth century, often regarded as "the century of women," and in an increasing number of fields, women have overcome outright prohibitions and massive imbalances so that there are now seemingly achievable opportunities for women and other "others." Yet this process has proved far from easy and in many respects, in the past few decades, has not only been stymied but reversed.

Career or Children—But Not Both!

The gendered structuring of computing has been highly visible in popular culture. In the 1957 film *Desk Set*, the computer engineer is predictably a man (Spencer Tracy), who is pitted against Katherine Hepburn's portrayal of an automation-resisting female (though far from passive) corporate librarian.[9] In 2016, the "rediscovery" of the "hidden figures" in Margot Lee Shetterly's eponymous book further stressed the tradition of dichotomous gender roles in computing, additionally incorporating the critical aspect of race/ethnicity.[10] In the film *Hidden Figures* (released in the same year), the office in which Mary Jackson, Katherine Johnson, and Dorothy Vaughan worked bore the sign "Colored Computers."

In her book on which the film is based, Shetterly points out that such a sign was the only one in evidence in the cafeteria at NASA's Langley Research Center:

> ... no other group needed their seating proscribed in the same fashion. The janitors, the laborers, the cafeteria workers themselves did not take lunch in the main cafeteria. The women of West Computing were the only black professionals at the laboratory—not exactly excluded, but not quite included either.[11]

"West Computers" was the term used to refer to the African-American women working as specialised mathematicians at the NASA site. Shetterly notes that:

> ... before a computer became an inanimate object ... before the Supreme Court case *Brown v. Board of Education of Topeka* established that separate was in fact not equal, and before the poetry of Martin Luther King Jr.'s "I Have a Dream" speech rang out over the steps of the Lincoln Memorial, Langley's West Computers were helping America dominate aeronautics, space research, and computer technology, carving out a place for themselves as female mathematicians who were also black, black mathematicians who were also female.[12]

According to the *Oxford English Dictionary* (OED) the term *computer* originally referred to: "[A] person who makes calculations or computations; a calculator, a reckoner." The OED entry goes on to state that this form is: "[N]ow chiefly historical," giving its most recent example from 1943. Yet clearly, it still applied to women well into the 1960s, not only to black women. It was used generically to indicate the way in which roles related to early computer technology were already categorised by gender; men joined engineering teams, while women, in the role of *computers*, were assigned to *computing pools*—a term resonating with the typing pools, staffed exclusively by young unmarried women, found in most large organisations throughout the first seven decades of the twentieth century. This was no accident; it was a clear indication of the ways in which the *superiority* of men over women marked all aspects of working environments, even those which were supposedly dependent upon specific qualifications and emerging areas of expertise. As will be argued below, it provided yet another mechanism for removing women from any role as "creative participants," to borrow Griselda Pollock's insightful term.[13]

It is noteworthy that those classed as West Computers included women who were married with children. The demand at Langley for highly skilled, mathematically proficient workers overshadowed other issues such as race, sex, or family status. Shetterly points out that these opportunities arose from the urgent need for skilled workers in the early 1940s as America prepared to enter WWII. In 1941:

> ... [W]ith two strokes of a pen—Executive Order 8802, ordering the desegregation of the defense industry, and Executive Order 9346, creating the Fair Employment Practices Committee to monitor the national project of economic inclusion—Roosevelt primed the pump for a new source of labor to come into the tight production process.[14]

Elsewhere, this was not the case. In 1957, Elsie Shutt was forced to leave her job at Raytheon when she became pregnant, a stipulation of Massachusetts law at the time.

In response, she started her own company, *Computations Incorporated* (Comp Inc.), offering systems analysis and design services as well as computer programming.[15]

At Raytheon, Shutt had been doing work for Honeywell, a long-established manufacturer of electrical and electronic devices. The company had joined with Raytheon on a computing venture aimed at challenging the dominance of IBM. Having set up Comp Inc., Shutt was given further work by Honeywell, but it was more than she could cope with, and so she enlisted the help of two other women who had also worked at Honeywell until forced to leave in similar circumstances. Her original idea was for the three of them to freelance, but Honeywell found this to be "too much contracting."[16] Shutt therefore opted to set up her own company which can probably claim to be the first software house in the United States. In 1963, it was profiled in *Business Week*, with Shutt and her colleagues labelled "the pregnant programmers." The article included a staged photo of Shutt working at her dining room table, toys in the foreground, with the tag line "mixing math and motherhood."[17]

Shutt deliberately did not let Comp Inc. expand, never employing more than thirteen staff members. In 2001, she pointed out that she saw her company as a way of getting things started, "... and maybe some of these people like Clippinger (her boss at Raytheon) and so forth eventually would leave where they are and want to get a big company started, and this would be the nucleus of it. But I didn't have any ambitions, particularly, to be a wheeler-dealer."[18] Instead, her initiative turned into "a feeling of mission in providing work for women who were talented and did good work and couldn't get part-time jobs. Because you couldn't get them." Clippinger was a man, so Shutt's assumption seems to have been that only a man could get "a big company started."[19]

In an interview with Jane Abbate, a historian of science, technology and society, Shutt stressed that her employees were happy to work when jobs came up and not too bothered when the opportunities dried up. "It was not needing money, because if we had needed a steady income, that wouldn't have been the way to get it."[20]

In 1959, the United Kingdom's first software house, *Vaughan Programming Services* [VPS], was established by Dina St Johnston (née Vaughan). She had previously worked for Elliot Automation, gaining expertise in real-time systems, establishing a formidable reputation for rigour and accuracy in her work. At a time when programmers wrote their code in pencil on coding sheets, since inevitably they would have to revise and correct their work many times before it was sent to be converted into punched cards, it was reputed St Johnston wrote her code in black ink using a Parker fountain pen. Any revisions, and presumably they were few and far between, would have required judicious use of a razor blade.[21]

Dina St Johnston's company focused on systems running on Elliot computers, accounting for more than 90% of their work from the late 1950s to the 1990s. The company gained a reputation for transport signalling and display systems, particularly those for the railways, a speciality for which the company became renowned. In the late 1970s, they branched out into hardware, notably Vaughan's 4M industrial microprocessor equipment which was used in many real-time, online control and communications applications.

It appears that VPS never employed more than one hundred employees, and for most of its existence they numbered around thirty to forty. Most of them were employed as programmers, drawn from a wide variety of backgrounds. A profile of St Johnston written in 2007 noted: "She was ahead of her time in believing that computing could be for everyone—even in the world of intricate machine code and assembly programming."[22] But her general business model was largely similar to those prevailing at the time.

A few years after Shutt and Vaughan had founded their companies, Stephanie Shirley created hers—*Freelance Programmers Limited* [FPL]. Born in Germany in 1933, Vera Buchthal arrived in England on one of the *kindertransports* in 1939, aged 5, together with her older sister, Renate, aged 9, sent by their parents to escape the perils of Nazi Europe. They were taken in by Ruby and Guy Smith and were later reunited with their parents who had managed against the odds to survive. She changed her name to Stephanie Brook in 1951 when she became a British citizen, Stephanie being her middle name, then to Stephanie Shirley when she married Derek in 1959.[23]

Shirley had managed to study maths at what would now be termed A-level, something that her school was unable to offer directly, instead arranging for her to attend lessons at a nearby grammar school. This involved her walking across from one school to the other, often having to arrive late for one lesson or the other as the timetables did not coincide. Shirley recalls this vividly in her memoir:

> The timetables of the two schools had little in common, and so I was always walking out in the middle of lessons and generally falling behind with other subjects. There was also the ordeal of walking into the boys' school: the only young woman among hundreds of drooling young men. I never reconciled myself to the daily gauntlet of leering and catcalls. But the lessons themselves were enjoyable and absorbing, and the sexism was, in retrospect, invaluable preparation for the trials I would later encounter in the workplace.[24]

When she turned eighteen, Shirley took the decision not to go to university, largely because she needed to get a job and earn money; "a decision I have regretted ever since."[25] She was offered two jobs, choosing the one as a junior research assistant at the Post Office Research Station in Dollis Hill in North West London. Although this may sound somewhat prosaic, the research station was at the forefront of many key technical developments of the post-war era.[26] The deciding factor to take this position, says Shirley, was that "the Post Office Research Station was interested in my further development and was prepared to arrange my hours to allow further study."[27]

By the mid-1950s, Shirley had become caught up in the excitement surrounding the introduction of computer technology, glimpsing the possibilities that might be afforded in its wake. This led to a profound change in her self-understanding:

> For years, I had been in the habit of replying, if a man asked me what I did for a living, that I worked for the Post Office—hoping that he would think I sold stamps or something—rather than admitting to working with my brain at the internationally admired Dollis Hill Research Station.[28]

She felt that she had talents that were not being used. She was turned down for several promotions and advancements, her suspicion being that this was because she was a woman.

> No doubt such rejections were largely my fault. I wasn't a great communicator and, on the whole, was better at just getting on with my work than at expressing myself. But it was impossible to avoid the suspicion that, had such suggestions come from a man, they might have caused less offence.[29]

Shirley is being overly modest here. Anyone who has met her immediately understands that she is a highly effective communicator. She does, however, encapsulate the frustrations and feelings of many women at that time, and more generally:

> What shocked me now was the discovery that, the more I became recognised as a serious young woman who was aiming high—whose long-term aspirations went beyond a mere subservient role—the more violently I was resented and the more implacably I was kept in my place.[30]

By the early 1960s, these barriers had grown to the point where Shirley decided to make the "mad leap" of starting her own company, one focused on "selling software."[31] The world's first business computer, the Lyons Electronic Office (LEO), had only started operating for the British firm J. Lyons and Co. in 1951.[32] By the early 1960s, companies such as IBM had developed a market for mainframe machines, but there was no significant market for software as the computers themselves usually came with the software already installed as part of the package:

> Nobody sold software in those days. In so far as it existed, it was given away free. Only the most forward-thinking and well-resourced organisations invested at all in what would now be called information technology, and those that did so would generally have been outraged at the suggestion that, having forked out a hefty sum for a new computer, they should also be asked to pay for the code to make it do what it was supposed to do. They expected that to be thrown in for nothing, as the manual is for a new car.[33]

To add even more risk and uncertainty to this leap of faith, Shirley wanted to create an entirely new way of working, "where I was not hemmed in by prejudice or by other people's preconceived notions of what I could and could not do—a place where, instead, I could exchange ideas freely with like-minded colleagues."[34] In part, this was dictated by her lack of assets at the outset; she had "£6 of capital, a dining room table, a telephone (with a party line shared with a neighbour who, luckily, rarely used it), and one other mad idea: those who worked for me would all be women, employed on a freelance basis and working from home."

In its earliest days, FPL led a precarious existence, generating barely enough work to keep Shirley herself employed. One day she complained to her husband that few, if any, of her letters regarding possible software development projects received replies.

> But still my letters failed to produce a response, until Derek suggested that maybe the problem lay not with the letters themselves but with the signature at the bottom of them. Given my experience with previous employers, it was not unreasonable to speculate that many potential customers, seeing the words "Stephanie Shirley" at the bottom of a letter, would refuse to take its proposals seriously, simply because I was a woman. Derek suggested testing this theory by signing a few letters "Steve Shirley" instead. I did so, and people began to respond. I have been Steve ever since.[35]

FPL later became F International [FI], and by the late 1990s, it had grown into a "truly global business ... with over six thousand employees, including one thousand in India; a market capitalisation of £1.2bn; and forecast sales for 2001–2002 of £515m."[36] In 2001, the company name was changed to Xansa, "a less parochial-sounding name"[37]; then in

2007, the company was acquired by the French software company now known as Sopra Steria. To all intents and purposes, this marked the demise of the company and its pioneering and distinctive characteristics.

Shock and Interregnum

We can mark the introduction of electronic computers to the commercial world with the unveiling of the aforementioned LEO in 1951. This was followed by developments leading to other early office machines, with IBM rapidly becoming the main player in the mainframe market. The use of mainframe computers in commercial companies was limited, and reliant on highly specialised skills. The hardware was extremely costly, not only in terms of initial outlay but also the requirement that a team of operators be available 24/7. It was often said at the time that computers were like babies, in need of constant attention, but babies usually slept for a few hours, whereas computers were on the go all day and all night! Reliability—of computers, not babies—was measured in terms of MTBF (mean time between failure), usually hours rather than days or weeks.

This period was something of a technological *interregnum*, a period where the accepted ideas about the role of technology in commercial organisations were being undermined with the advent of computers. Antonio Gramsci, the Italian political philosopher and activist imprisoned by Mussolini, characterised an interregnum as a period of upheaval and crisis characterised "precisely in the fact that the old is dying and the new cannot be born." He went on to state that in terms of its impact on modes of authority, "a great variety of morbid symptoms appear."[38]

The technological interregnum that began in the 1960s may have been less dramatic in this regard, but in the words of Richard Nolan, writing some ten years later, computer technology "shocked the organization."[39] This was only partially understood with hindsight in the late 1970s, and even then, the magnitude and ramifications of the *shock* were not readily appreciated by many of those at senior organisational levels.

As has already been noted, the field of computing was already *gendered* to some extent, but the massive changes that came about in the 1950s and 1960s—themselves dwarfed by later ones in the next three or four decades—were sufficiently far-reaching to allow significant opportunities to those willing to take risks based on insight into the changes that were occurring.

St Johnson, Shutt, and Shirley all took advantage of this, but in starkly different ways. St Johnson set up a company much like any other, apart from its focus on software development, a novelty for the late 1950s. Shutt was forced to leave her full-time position once she was pregnant. However, her previous employer was keen to engage her on a freelance basis, which she then expanded to include other women in her position, but which she never envisaged as a basis for expansion and a new form of working. When interviewed in 2001, she was at pains to stress how her approach differed from FI, which she referred to as "this group in England."[40] Most of her employees were happy to work when jobs came up and not too bothered when the opportunities dried up: "It was not needing money, because if we had needed a steady income, that wouldn't have been the way to get it."[41] In contrast, she saw FI as:

> ... much more aggressive about finding work—looking for work—than we were. We were really pretty laid-back about it. ... I think for them it was really a business thing more than it was for me. For me it was keeping active in the field, giving work to women who wouldn't otherwise have it.[42]

For Shirley, FI certainly was, to invoke the preceding quote by Shutt, "a business thing." Her hunch that software would prove to be far more important than the hardware was spot on. By the late 1960s, there were conferences to discuss "the software crisis" and in his Turing lecture in 1972, Edsger Djikstra, an early computing luminary, drew attention to the issues as follows:

> The major cause of the software crisis is that the machines have become several orders of magnitude more powerful! To put it quite bluntly: as long as there were no machines, programming was no problem at all; when we had a few weak computers, programming became a mild problem, and now we have gigantic computers, programming has become an equally gigantic problem.[43]

FI was an early and significant actor in this developing context. Signing her letters "Steve Shirley" produced the desired results, but more significantly, the women working for the company were a match for any other programmers. Technically, they may only have been engaged to work twenty or so hours a week, but they often worked more than that for short, intense periods to complete a job. None of them resented this. On the contrary, they extolled the advantages of such a flexible routine. It allowed significant and high-quality family time, together with the chance to exercise and enhance their considerable technical and analytical skills. The overall result was that companies contracting with FI found that software projects were completed within budget, on schedule and to a high standard. This combination of productivity and high quality was so unusual that clients thought that Shirley was "exploiting her women," deliberately under-paying them, forcing them to work extra hours for no further reward. One company threatened not to engage FI for further work since they obviously used "unethical practices," how otherwise could they produce high-quality results at such reasonable costs![44]

It proved to be highly fortuitous that the earliest contract for the company involved developing a set of rigorous standards for the computing division of Urwick Diebold. As Shirley notes in her autobiography, "the brief was to write software standards—in other words, management control protocols—for this group. This wasn't exactly the kind of work I had had in mind for my enterprise, but it would prove immensely valuable in the long run."[45] She goes on to note: "[T]he fact that Freelance Programmers [Limited] could claim to be a source of objective, written standards would ultimately prove to be a major selling point for us, and would help demonstrate to prospective clients that we were no mere fly-by-night operation."[46] This is an understatement; these standards were a key component of the bedrock on which the reputation of FPL and FI were built.

By 1963, further work started to materialise, and this allowed the company to grow through the 1960s. It was given a useful if unexpected boost when in January 1964 *The Guardian* published an article on:

> ... a strange and exotic modern phenomenon: women who worked in the then embryonic computer industry. It was headlined *Computer women* and described how a growing number of women who had decent maths qualifications plus "patience and tenacity, and a common-sense sort of logic" were finding employment opportunities as programmers. "Much of the work is tedious ... requiring great attention to detail, and this is where women usually score." More pertinently it then mentioned a

"Mrs Steve Shirley," of Chesham, Buckinghamshire [who] has found that computer programming ... is a job that can be done at home between feeding the baby and washing nappies. She is hoping to interest other retired programmers in joining her in working on a freelance basis.[47]

This article, plus a brief advert in *The Times* which included the phrase "a wonderful chance, but hopeless for anti-feminists," attracted a host of enquiries.[48] Shirley also took every opportunity to promote her venture with many of her early recruits finding their way to the company in the wake of appearances on *Woman's Hour* and other media outlets, including a slot on *Tomorrow's World*, an enormously popular live TV programme focusing on science and technology.

Shirley established FPL with a founding statement recorded as "Minute Number One." The purpose of the company was "to provide jobs for women with children." This was later changed to "careers for women with children," then subsequently to "careers for women with dependents."[49] But the key motivation remained the same: "[the] company ... would offer opportunities to the kind of women whom traditional male-dominated companies considered unemployable."[50]

A further innovation for the company was common ownership, an idea that had been present at the outset as FPL had initiated a profit-sharing scheme in the mid-1960s, when almost all of those working for the company were independent contractors with limited or no employment rights as such. Shirley was proud of this, but also saw its limitations.

> One of the company's overwhelming strengths was the fact that, in contrast to most companies of the time, its employees felt that they owned the projects they worked on. Yet in legal and financial terms they didn't. The only person who owned the company was me.[51]

The idea of common ownership had been raised early in the company's development by John Stevens, hired by Shirley as their first full-time project manager. Stevens was a passionate advocate of common ownership, and Shirley was receptive to the idea, but with all the challenges the company faced in its earliest days, the idea was set aside. With the prolonged success of the late 1970s, however, there was both time and the necessary resources to progress the idea.

Shirley refers to common ownership in her autobiography, pointing to examples such as the partnership scheme operated by the UK department store John Lewis In typical Steve Shirley fashion, she sought further input, taking advice from all manner of business and academic experts, but found that it was far more complex than she had imagined, particularly as the Inland Revenue had to be placated.[52]

Her first efforts came to fruition, in some regards against the wishes of her senior colleagues, in 1981 with the establishment of the FI Shareholders' Trust. It was only "a small and obscure step," Shirley recalls, but "it marked the beginning of a process that I would come to see as one of the greatest achievements of my life."[53]

By the latter decades of the twentieth century, seemingly all was in place for FI to flourish and spearhead new forms of employment and new opportunities for those all too often cast aside by traditional business models and organisational structures and norms. The company certainly flourished, and The FI Shareholders' Trust provided the basis for many

FI employees to become millionaires. Yet as was noted above, by the end of the first decade of the current century, the company, together with its distinctive philosophy and character, had disappeared. It had become a notable oddity, albeit that the idea of working-from-home would take on other guises in the wake of the COVID pandemic starting in 2020.

Shirley herself remains troubled by this development: "The accepted view of gender equality seems to be that leaders determine who become the leaders of the future. So why in a female dominated company that scaled did the feminine bias get lost? It didn't finish up 50:50 but in fact just like any other corporate: strongly biased to men"; or as she later put it: "Why didn't the imbalance survive as it has done with men?"[54]

Women, Information Technology and Ideology

It may be thought that a key reason behind the move of FI from a distinctive niche to just another male-dominated company was simply the transition from a highly distinctive business and employment model to a more traditional one. Yet many other issues need to be considered to explain the demise and eventual disappearance of the unique character of FI, some internal and some beyond the control of any single organisation.

The development of FI might appear to serve as a model for a reorientation and rectification of the sorts of imbalances and impediments that led Elsie Shutt and Steve Shirley to start their own companies. Clearly, this has not been the case. Across the IT industry, the position of women as a percentage of the workforce, in terms of pay and career prospects, and a host of other key indicators, not only remains poor, but in some cases has deteriorated in comparison to the last decades of twentieth century.[55] Moreover, it is all too easy to find a whole host of initiatives over the past fifty years designed to persuade and support young girls and women wishing to develop technical skills and careers in engineering, computing, and the like. The fact that they are so numerous gives a clear indication that to date they have not been effective. On top of which, in the era of Big Data, a recent report notes that many algorithms and other examples of AI still cannot recognise that male nurses and female historians exist.[56] All of which is indicative of the complexity and potency of the social structures and mores that perpetuate women's secondary role in society.

Although seemingly distinct from the world of computing, historically the world of art offers a striking parallel in terms of the marginalisation of women. In 1981, Rozsika Parker and Griselda Pollock published *Old Mistresses: Women, Art, and Ideology*.[57] The term *Old Mistresses* had been the title of a 1973 exhibition drawing attention to the lack of any feminine equivalent to the reverential epithet *Old Master*. Their book came in the wake of various other feminist writings, such as Linda Nochlin's 1971 essay "Why are there no great women artists?"[58]

Nochlin and others pointed to the discrimination and exclusion prevalent in the artistic realm, in the hope and anticipation that in so doing there would be some form of correction and rebalancing. The exclusion of women in the past was seen as something that could and would now be corrected in the twentieth century, the "century of women." Parker and Pollock's argument was, however, of a different order. They were critical of Nochlin's argument, seeing it as at best partial. Instead, Parker and Pollock exposed the structural sexism and racism in art museums, the art market and academic art history where value and significance was attributed only to what white men had made, said, or created: the prestigious term *artist* being reserved for and colonised by masculinity.

Critically, what Parker and Pollock found was that although there had been some, albeit begrudging recognition of women artists up to and including the nineteenth century, it was only in the twentieth century that women were specifically and effectively removed and erased. They dated this from 1929 and the opening of the first museum of modern art (MoMA) in New York, with few, if any, examples of women's artistic achievements. Previously, women had been pushed to one side, but it was only in the "century of women" that they were effectively erased from cultural memory and removed from any role as "creative participants in culture."[59]

Almost twenty years later, in 1999, Pollock returned to analyse and expose the continuing ubiquity and tenacity of the all-male canon: little or nothing had changed in the interim.[60] Moreover, two decades onwards, in 2020, despite a larger involvement of women in various artistic practices, works of contemporary art by women count for only 2% of the multi-billion-dollar art market.[61] In their conclusion, even in 1981, Parker and Pollock wanted their readers to understand the paradoxes and contradictions in the present situation of women in art, leading to a situation in which "women's practice in art has never been forbidden, discouraged or refused, but rather *what women create has been contained and limited to its function as the means by which masculinity gains and sustains its supremacy in this sphere of cultural production* [author's emphasis]."[62]

Shirley set up her company to offer opportunities to women which otherwise were unavailable. In due course FI became a byword for innovative and pioneering employment models. The wealth of literature on FI and Steve Shirley are ample testimony to this. Yet this repute is associated with its singular nature as an outlier, rather than as the leader in a significant wave of new opportunities for women and others usually excluded from the higher echelons of society.

The history of FI is one of a unique context in which a range of possibilities developed, the exploitation of which required enormous foresight and courage, and some luck. The company from the start offered a range of opportunities, the basis for which was laid by Steve Shirley. The company as potential prospects were seized upon by a small group of redoubtable women working within the generative structure of FPL, including numerous innovations such as working-from-home, flexible working, new opportunities for work and advancement, and the incorporation of new technologies such as email.

Writing in the 1970s, Stafford Beer summarised a range of responses to the initial "shock" of computer technology by considering three questions. Beer believed that the question which asks how to use the computer in the enterprise was the wrong question. A better formulation, he argued, was to ask how the enterprise should be run, given that computers exist. But the best version of all was the question asking: "*what, given computers, the enterprise now is* [emphasis in the original]."[63]

The founding and growth of FI is an example of someone posing and supplying a highly inventive answer to that last question. Shirley understood that there was an opportunity for a company to supply software for computers as a business proposition, not something that was thrown in free of charge with the hardware. She also saw that such an enterprise did not need lavish overheads, offices, expensive equipment, or even full-time employees. Her later move to co-ownership was another organisational innovation to add to the many others she had already put in train.

What happened? Why did the company's unique ethos dissipate and disappear? To an extent, its development from the 1990s onwards is akin to the cartoon character who runs over the edge of a cliff and keeps on running in mid-air, gravity only taking over when the character stops and looks down. In the case of FI, "gravity" took three forms.

The first can be encapsulated in a slight rephrasing of Stafford Beer's third question; the best version of all is the question asking, *what, given computers, the enterprise now is*, but with the proviso that *the question constantly demands new answers and insights*. Some of my respondents thought that the tight-knit group of early FPL women moved from pioneers to traditionalists or conservatives by the 1990s, impervious to some of the technical developments of the time. This "inner circle," "the twinset and pearls division," had been with the company since its earliest days. They were largely responsible for its growth, reputation and determined survival, but later acted as a bulwark against other, younger, newer employees. There is also a generational aspect to this. Born in Germany in 1933, sent by her parents to the United Kingdom on the *kindertransport*, Steve Shirley's background is complex, but she would have shared some experiences with all women drawn from the Silent Generation—born before WWII and growing up in its aftermath. In contrast, those working for the company by the 1990s would be Baby Boomers and early Generation Xers, with very different ideas about work, entitlement, and sex-based roles and responsibilities. The ethos of the company would then have been under scrutiny and challenge from within.[64]

The second form of "gravity" emanates from the strategy for the growth of the company initiated by Hilary Cropper (brought in by Shirley as CEO in 1985) centred around a reorientation of the company ethos—including the appointment of more men in senior positions and on the board—together with various mergers and acquisitions.[65] Given FI's unique character, this inevitably meant that there would be a clash of cultures, but with the company's culture already being somewhat undermined from within. One respondent in my study of FI used the phrase: "[W]e actually bought in the 'male virus,' the 'male infection.'" Mergers and acquisitions always resulted in the FI ethos being challenged and undermined by the attitudes prevalent in whichever company was being acquired or merged. These challenges were always directed towards FI. It was never the case that other companies questioned and challenged their own male-dominated ethos. One very senior woman at FI recalled being asked in an overly aggressive manner to show and verify her CV by someone—a man of course—from a company that FI was acquiring, something that would never have occurred for a man in a similar position.

The third form of "gravity," however, was the most potent, and it remains so. Parker and Pollock have explained this in the context of art and cultural production; Janet Abbate has argued similarly in the context of women and computing. Her book *Recoding Gender* (2012) has the telling subtitle *Women's Changing Participation in Computing*.[66] The common thread running through these books is an explanation of the ways in which women were and are constantly prevented or removed from being "creative participants."

A Further Removal; A Continuing Exclusion

In the early twentieth century, women were removed from art and cultural production, having had a partial and tenuous link to it beforehand. In the 1950s and early 1960s, women's delegated and, by implication, secondary roles as *computers* had similar status, in contrast to men's roles as *engineers*. The rapid expansion of computer technology and the demand for programming skills, however, undermined this arrangement. As Dina St Johnston explained at the time:

> This is an environment where experience is at a premium and must be spread, but job mobility is high with more loyalty given to the programming world at large that (than?) any particular user's business. ... Room, and a demand, for the services of independent programming effort were created.[67]

Steve Shirley was able to take full advantage of this breach in the barriers to women's participation. From 1962 until the early 1990s, FI charted a path for women and others requiring flexible working environments, allowing them to care for children and others.

In mid-2021, Steve Shirley posed the question:

> The accepted view of gender equality seems to be that leaders determine who become the leaders of the future. So why in a female dominated company that scaled did the feminine bias get lost?[68]

Following in the wake of Stafford Beer, this seems to be the wrong question. The real question I would wish to ask to ask is:

> Given the continued and widespread forces that continually prevent or undermine the role of women as creative participants in all aspects of contemporary life, how did F International manage to scale up, make its mark, and last for as long as it did, before succumbing to the exigencies of male-dominated commercial existence?

The term "inclusivity" trips readily off people's tongues, often as part of an institutional promotion of diversity, equality, and inclusion. Unfortunately, the figures regarding women's inclusion in most aspects of organisational life indicate that progress, if any, has been slow, and that in many respects it has gone into reverse. There are no simple remedies for this, but one important aspect is to remind people continually about the roles played by women in the various fields from which they are all too often erased. The few examples given here and the unique case of FI need to become essential components in any history of information and communication technology.

Notes

1 A software house specialises in producing software products, both general-purpose and customer-specific. In the 1950s and early 1960s, these were few and far between, since the dominant hardware manufacturers, such as IBM, bundled the software with the hardware. The market for software as such was very small, but of course, it grew rapidly from the late 1960s onwards in many regards taking over as the key aspect of ICT.
2 For an extended account of the relationship between Lovelace and Babbage, including an explanation of the Bernoulli series, see Thomas Misa, "Charles Babbage, Ada Lovelace, and the Bernoulli Numbers," in *Ada's Legacy: Cultures of Computing from the Victorian to the Digital Age*, ed. Robin Hammerman and Andrew Russell (New York: Association for Computing Machinery, 2015), 11–32.
3 Quoted in Rowan Hooper, "Ada Lovelace: My Brain is More than Merely Mortal," *New Scientist*, October 15, 2012. https://www.newscientist.com/article/dn22385-ada-lovelace-my-brain-is-more-than-merely-mortal/.
4 William Gibson and Bruce Sterling, *The Difference Engine* (London: Gollancz, 1990).
5 Kathleen Williams, *Grace Hopper: Admiral of the Cyber Sea* (Annapolis, MD: Naval Institute Press, 2004). Details of the varied and numerous honours bestowed on Grace Hopper and her work with computers can be found in "Grace Hopper," *Wikipedia*, May 11, 2023. https://en.wikipedia.org/wiki/Grace_Hopper.
6 Mar Hicks, *Programmed Inequality: How Britain Discarded Women Technologists and Lost Its Edge in Computing* (Cambridge, MA: MIT Press, 2017).

7. Nathan Ensmenger, *The Computer Boys Take Over: Computers, Programmers, and the Politics of Technical Expertise* (Cambridge, MA: MIT Press, 2010).
8. Sue Clegg, "Theorizing the Machine: Gender, Education and Computing," *Gender and Education* 13, no. 3 (2001): 307–324.
9. Cheryl Knott Malone, "Imagining Information Retrieval in the Library: 'Desk Set' in Historical Context," *Annals of the History of Computing* 24, no. 3 (July–September 2002): 14–22.
10. Margot Shetterly, *Hidden Figures: The American Dream and the Unknown Story of the Black Women Mathematicians Who Helped Win the Space Race* (London: Harper Collins, 2016). On the intersection of gender and race in the specific area of African-American women, see Evelyn Higginbotham, "African-American Women's History and the Metalanguage of Race," *Signs* 17, no. 2 (1992): 251–274.
11. Shetterly, *Hidden Figures*, 55.
12. Shetterly, *Hidden Figures*, 14.
13. Griselda Pollock, "A Lonely Preface," in Rozsika Parker and Griselda Pollock, *Old Mistresses: Women, Art and Ideology* (London: I.B. Tauris, 2013 [1981]), xxiv.
14. Shetterly, *Hidden Figures*, 20.
15. Elsie Shutt, "Oral-History: Elsie Shutt," *Engineering and Technology History Wiki*, Interview No. 628, conducted by Jane Abbate for the Institute of Electrical and Electronic Engineers (IEEE), February 9, 2001. https://ethw.org/Oral-History:Elsie_Shutt.
16. Shutt, "Oral-History."
17. Shutt, "Oral-History."
18. Shutt, "Oral-History."
19. Shutt, "Oral-History."
20. Shutt, "Oral-History."
21. Simon Lavington, "An Appreciation of Dina St Johnston (1930–2007), Founder of the UK's First Software House," *The Computer Journal* 52, no. 3 (May 2009): 378–387.
22. Lavington, "An Appreciation," 381.
23. Details can be found in Stephanie Shirley, *Let It Go: The Entrepreneurial Ardent Philanthropist* (Luton: Andrews, 2012).
24. Shirley, *Let It Go*, 36.
25. Shirley, *Let It Go*, 45.
26. Rachel Boon, *"Research Is the Doorway to Tomorrow": The Post Office Engineering Research Station, Dollis Hill, 1933–1958* (PhD diss., University of Manchester, 2020); *"To Strive, To Seek, To Find": The Origins and Establishment of the British Post Office Engineering Research Station at Dollis Hill, 1908–1938* (PhD diss., University of Leeds, 2020).
27. Shirley, *Let It Go*, 45.
28. Shirley, *Let It Go*, 56.
29. Shirley, *Let It Go*, 59.
30. Shirley, *Let It Go*, 60.
31. Shirley, *Let It Go*, 60.
32. Georgina Ferry, *A Computer Called LEO: Lyons Teashop and the World's First Office Computer* (London: Fourth Estate, 2003).
33. Shirley, *Let It Go*, 71.
34. Shirley, *Let It Go*, 73.
35. Shirley, *Let It Go*, 77.
36. Shirley, *Let It Go*, 260.
37. Shirley, *Let It Go*, 260.
38. Antonio Gramsci, *Selections from the Prison Notebooks*, ed. and trans. Quentin Hoare and Geoffrey Nowell Smith (London: Lawrence and Wishart, 1971), 276.
39. Richard Nolan, "Managing the Computer Resource: A Stage Hypothesis," *Communications of the ACM* 16 (July 1973): 402.
40. Shutt, "Oral-History."
41. Shutt, "Oral-History."
42. Shutt, "Oral-History."
43. Quoted in "Software Crisis," *Wikipedia*, February 6, 2023. https://en.wikipedia.org/wiki/Software_crisis.

44 These aspects were recounted by former FI employees in a research project carried out by the author, at Steve Shirley's request, in 2021–2022.
45 Shirley, *Let It Go*, 66.
46 Shirley, *Let It Go*, 66.
47 Quoted in Shirley, *Let It Go*, 69.
48 Quoted in Shirley, *Let It Go*, 69.
49 Shirley, *Let It Go*, 70.
50 Shirley, *Let It Go*, 70.
51 Shirley, *Let It Go*, 145.
52 Details can be found in Chapter 8 of Shirley, *Let It Go*.
53 Shirley, *Let It Go*, 159.
54 From an initial exchange of emails and online conversations between Steve and the author in 2021, following which the research was undertaken, funded and supported by Steve Shirley. For a more detailed account of the project see Antony Bryant, "Whatever Happened to F International?," *First Monday* 30, no. 1 (January 6, 2025). https://firstmonday.org/ojs/index.php/fm/article/view/13883
55 Examples of this can be found in numerous reports, including Davina Lynkova, "Women in Technological Statistics: What's New in 2023," *techjury*, April 19, 2023, https://techjury.net/blog/women-in-technology-statistics/; Susanne Hupfer et al., "Women in the Tech Industry: Gaining Ground, but Facing New Headwinds," *Deloitte Insights*, December 1, 2021, https://www2.deloitte.com/content/dam/insights/articles/GLOB164590_Women-tech/DI_Women-tech.pdf; and Jenny Little, "Ten Years On, Why Are There So Few Women in Tech?" *The Guardian*, January 2, 2020, https://www.theguardian.com/careers/2020/jan/02/ten-years-on-why-are-there-still-so-few-women-in-tech.
56 Nicolas Kayser-Bril, "Female Historians and Male Nurses Do Not Exist, Google Translate Tells Its European Users," *Algorithm Watch*, September 17, 2020. https://algorithmwatch.org/en/google-translate-gender-bias/. See also Rosalie Waelen and Michal Wieczorek, "The Struggle for AI's Recognition: Understanding the Normative Implications of Gender Bias in AI with Honneth's Theory of Recognition," *Philosophy & Technology* 35, no. 53 (2022): 1–17.
57 Rozsika Parker and Griselda Pollock, *Old Mistresses: Women, Art and Ideology* (London: I.B. Tauris, 2013 [1981]).
58 Linda Nochlin, "Why Are There No Great Women Artists?" in *Woman in Sexist Society: Studies in Power and Powerlessness*, ed. Vivian Gornick and Barbara Moran (New York: Basic Books, 1971), 145–178. This chapter was revised and retitled with a historical inflection in the journal *Art News*, in January 1971, and has been more recently largely reproduced as Linda Nochlin, "From 1971: Why Have There Been No Great Women Artists?" *ARTnews*, May 30, 2015. https://www.artnews.com/art-news/retrospective/why-have-there-been-no-great-women-artists-4201/.
59 Pollock, "A Lonely Preface," xxiv.
60 Griselda Pollock, *Differencing the Canon: Feminist Desire and the Writing of Art's Histories* (London: Routledge, 1999).
61 Griselda Pollock, "A Lonely Preface," xxiv.
62 Parker and Pollock, *Old Mistresses*, 170.
63 Stafford Beer, *The Brain of the Firm*, 2nd ed. (Chichester: John Wiley, 1981), 16.
64 The issue of the ways in which any generation can be characterised, as well as the complex interrelations between different generations, is well beyond the scope of this brief discussion. Early work by the sociologist Karl Mannheim provides a basis for such discussions: see Karl Mannheim, "The Problem of Generations," in Karl Mannheim, *Essays on the Sociology of Knowledge*, ed. and trans. Paul Kecskemeti (London: Routledge and Kegan Paul, 1952), 351–398. See also John Connolly, "Generational Conflict and the Sociology of Generations: Mannheim and Elias Reconsidered," *Theory, Culture and Society* 36, nos. 7–8 (2019): 1–20.
65 Hilary Cropper was a perfect fit, having studied maths at university. She was initially employed at an engineering company where, amongst other things, she programmed computers in the 1960s.

She then worked at ICL for almost 20 years, including running a home-working software division and latterly heading their Professional Services business: see Shirley, *Let It Go*, Chapter 16.

66 Jane Abbate, *Recoding Gender: Women's Changing Participation in Computing* (Cambridge, MA: MIT Press, 2012).
67 Lavington, "An Appreciation," 379.
68 From initial exchange of emails and online conversations with Steve Shirley in 2021.

20
CENTRAL AND LOCAL
A History of Archives in Twentieth-Century England

Elizabeth Shepherd

Histories of archival and record-keeping practice, one of the core information professions, is an emerging area of interest.[1] An international conference (International Conference on the History of Records and Archives, ICHORA) was set up in 2003 to stimulate, promote, and support research in the history of archives and archival management.[2] It has since been hosted in North America, Australia, and Europe and has uncovered theoretical and historical dimensions of information artefacts across cultures and continents and considered their technologies, juridical, and social values. Records are created by individuals and organisations as recorded evidence of an activity. Archives can be defined as records which have long-term value and are preserved for cultural and social research and for their continuing value for memory purposes and accountability. The relationships between records, archives, data, and information have been extensively examined as part of consideration of a wider information culture in society. Yeo proposes that "records are not merely a variety of information, or a container of information, but have distinct roles in the performance of action and the construction of our social world."[3] Histories of archives study practices, traditions, and standards, shaped by societal forces, legislation and bureaucracy, education and training, and the work of professional societies.[4] This chapter will focus on one jurisdiction (England) and a short period (late nineteenth and early twentieth centuries) to tell the story of how central and local archives and archivists emerged, laying the foundations of the record-keeping profession we see today. In part, the story is one of the dominance of men in establishing national archival institutions and of women historical workers ensuring that local and community archives were preserved for future generations.

A Modern Archival Profession in England

Understanding the history of the modern archival profession in England can be approached from different perspectives. In the nineteenth century, national legislation and regulation followed many official inquiries and reports into archives which shaped the policy framework in England. The Public Record Office (PRO) in London, established by the Public Record Office Act 1838, was one of the first national archives in the world and aimed to secure the preservation of records of the courts of law and of national government. However, other archives and records were largely neglected by legislators. A Royal Commission on Historical Manuscripts was established in 1869, initially for five years, to produce abstracts and catalogues of private manuscripts as a means of access to them for historical research. The separation of public and private archives in legislation, regulation, funding, and archival practice and the lack of a single national policy body for archives and records persists into the twenty-first century. The tension can be characterised as between national, central institutions governed by mandatory legislation, and local, private, and community archives, lacking much legislation or regulation and often organised on an informal or voluntary basis.[5]

Archival history can also be viewed through the lens of the emergence of a distinct occupational group and profession. Although the term "archivist" has been used for centuries to denote someone who worked with and preserved archives, the emergence of an identifiable profession of archivist (as distinct from a librarian, a historian, a record agent, or a registrar) is largely a twentieth-century phenomenon in England. As an occupational group emerged, so too did professional associations developed from historical, archaeological, and local history societies into archival organisations, including the British Records Association (BRA) in 1932 and the first professional body, the Society of Local Archivists in 1947.

Alongside and critical to the development of a modern archival profession came education and training. In England, archival education developed from university teaching in allied disciplines of palaeography, diplomatics, local history and librarianship into the first post-graduate qualifications in archive studies taught at both the University of Liverpool and University College London from 1947. Taken together, an occupational group, a professional association, and a dedicated educational qualification are key markers of a new profession of archivist emerging in England after the Second World War. This chapter will examine this period of formation of the modern profession of archivist and the foundation of the landscape of archives as institutions in England in the twentieth century.[6] In particular, it will examine the pattern of well-established and properly funded central, national archival institutions which emerged by the end of the nineteenth century, and the patchwork of local archives which were established in a piecemeal manner between the two world wars in the early twentieth century in England.

A Short History of National and Central Archival Institutions in England: The Public Record Office

In the nineteenth century across Europe, new national archives were established to preserve and make available archives of government. The Archives Nationale in France, created in 1794, established the idea that citizens had a right to access public archives and hold governments to account, at least for historical purposes. Other national archives followed: the first national archivist in the Netherlands was appointed in 1802, the PRO established in England in 1838; in Spain, the Archivo Historico Nacional was founded in 1866, and the National Archives of Sweden in 1878.[7]

In England, many official reports and inquiries from 1800 onwards made recommendations about archives and records and led to legislation in 1838 to establish proper arrangements for the records of central government and the courts of law. The first of six Commissions was established in 1800, following a Committee Report on public records preservation, and the Royal Commission continued its work until 1837. The Committee and subsequent Commission identified significant defects in the storage of the records of central government and the Courts of law, scattered between sixty buildings and often stored in poor conditions of damp, disarray, lack of access, and general unsuitability. Mindful of costs and the complications of encroaching onto private property, the Committee recommended the establishment of a single central repository for public records but left aside the issue of records in private hands and manuscripts held at the British Museum and elsewhere. The English tradition focused on the historical value of public records and their preservation for legal searches and "literary" scholarly research, requiring their arrangement, publication, and description to be done retrospectively, rather than a seamless administrative system under which records were registered and transferred to a national archive (as in Germany). The Record Commission focused on three issues which would improve access and preservation of records: reform of the unregulated fees systems paid to Keepers to give access or obtain transcripts of records, printing of calendars and indexes of records to improve accessibility, and a recommendation to build a single central record office. The PRO was established under the 1838 Act to centralise responsibility for public records under the Master of the Rolls (the second most senior law lord) and a Deputy Keeper, and a new repository in Chancery Lane, London, was built between 1850 and 1859 to centralise and improve record storage and provide access.[8]

Sir Francis Palgrave, a scholarly publisher and lawyer who had worked on the Royal Commission in the 1820s and was a keeper at the Chapter House from 1834, was appointed as the first Deputy Keeper.[9] Palgrave organised his staff of thirty Assistant Keepers and clerks into distinct departments to deal with the various tasks: the Search Department oversaw access, the Binding Department organised records storage, the Archival Department inventoried and catalogued records, followed later by a Public Records Department to advise ministries. Palgrave also oversaw the building of the central repository in Chancery Lane in the 1850s. The amalgamation of the State Paper Office into the PRO in 1854 facilitated more systematic publication of calendars (abstracts) of records held at the PRO and elsewhere,[10] firmly establishing an academic, historical tradition and orientation among staff, what Levine calls "the first truly professional historians" in England.[11] Palgrave was succeeded by Sir Thomas Hardy in 1861, who was, in turn, succeeded in 1878 by his brother, William Hardy. Thomas Hardy oversaw more building in Chancery Lane, including the opening of a new search room; he continued to develop the publications programme, and improved the reviewing and destruction of public records and the opening of those stored at the PRO as worthy of permanent preservation.

Further legislation was enacted to regulate the flow of public records into the new PRO. The Public Record Office Act 1877 established a system of transfer of records from government departments to the PRO and allowed for the destruction of older records "not of sufficient public value to justify their preservation" (which applied initially to records created after 1715, amended to after 1660 under the 1898 Act). The Act also allowed some public records to be transferred to be held locally, subject to central inspections, although the provision was not much used until the twentieth century.

In 1885, Henry Maxwell Lyte was appointed Deputy Keeper, a role he held until 1926. He oversaw a period of modernisation, such as electric light in the search room which extended the useful opening hours and installation of a lift to improve records production. He introduced Lists and Indexes and the first descriptive Guide to the records which improved access to and understanding of the vast holdings. He established a museum at Chancery Lane and held an exhibition to celebrate eight hundred years of the Domesday Book, one of the most iconic and important records.

In the early twentieth century, a Royal Commission investigated the working of the Public Record Office Acts, producing a series of Reports in 1912, 1914, and 1919.[12] One trigger for the setting up of the Commission in 1910 were calls by Welsh campaigners to return records to the principality. The Commission recommended longer opening hours at the PRO in Chancery Lane and improvements to heating, lighting, and supervision of the reading room and better inventories. A committee of historical scholars was appointed to advise on publications policy and a Committee of Inspecting Officers began to develop rules for the disposal of records judged not to have value for permanent preservation, thus enabling the 1877 and 1898 Acts to be put more fully into effect. The Second Report in 1914 was especially concerned about the inadequate arrangements for the transfer of records from government ministries to the PRO and it recommended intermediate storage for records due for destruction but no longer needed in departments and the appointment of a "properly qualified record keeper with adequate staff" in each ministry to advise on records transfer and destruction, allowing the PRO some authority to inspect records in departments and advise on transfer to the PRO. The Third Report, delayed by the First World War, focused on local records, held outside the PRO. Maxwell Lyte was unhappy with the Commission's work and, since the War largely prevented implementation of its recommendations until the 1920s, retreated into his antiquarian interests. He was succeeded as Deputy Keeper by A. E. Stamp, who had to negotiate complex discussions over Cabinet papers, which were not covered by the PRO Acts but which were to be found at the PRO in departmental files. Stamp also organised a major exhibition and reception to celebrate the PRO's centenary.

Hilary Jenkinson, one of the most well-known English writers on archive theory and practice, served at the PRO from 1906, but his ambition to become Deputy Keeper was not realised until 1947. Jenkinson was a key figure in English archives in the early twentieth century.[13] His foundation text, *A Manual of Archive Administration* published in 1922 partly as a response to the records created during the First World War, was seen as establishing the parameters of the modern archivist's work and approaches.[14] Jenkinson defined archives as being drawn up as part of an administrative transaction and retained by the creator for their use (rather than for "posterity"), exhibiting the qualities of impartiality and authenticity. He set out the "duties of the archivist" which were, first, to safeguard the archives, their innate qualities and their unbroken custody and, only secondly, to provide for the needs of researchers. He wrote about the "physical defence" of archives (that is, their safe preservation) and their "moral defence" (by which he meant maintaining the original order and arrangement and respecting the provenance of the archive through description), and insisted on the neutrality of the work of the archivist. Jenkinson was highly influential well beyond the PRO during his career. For example, he was the Secretary of the newly established BRA from 1932 to 1947 and initiated its work on archival reconstruction after the Second World War which led to the Master of the Rolls Archives Committee, the establishment of a National Register of Archives and better arrangements for local archives. He was the President of the Society of Archivists until his death in 1961. He was also influential across England as an advisor to newly established local archives. He set up the Surrey Record Society in 1913 to develop a series of publications of guides to Surrey records. As a scholar, he published on a wide range of subjects from seals to tally sticks. He held academic posts at Kings College London and at University College London, where he was responsible for the initiation of the Diploma in Archives Administration in 1947 and gave the inaugural lecture. More recently his legacy has been challenged as stultifying of

English archival developments and reappraised through new contextual understandings of his published work.[15]

Between the world wars, little attention was paid by government to public records, in spite of the huge increase in the production of records, partly as a result of war, the creation of the welfare state and its record-keeping implications, and the invention and widespread use of new technologies, the typewriter and the duplicating machine, which facilitated the creation and distribution of records. By 1950, some 120 miles of unreviewed records were in departments awaiting transfer to the PRO, so a Committee was established in 1952, chaired by Sir James Grigg, to "review the arrangements for the preservation of the records of government Departments in the light of the rate at which they are accumulating and of the purposes which they are intended to serve; and to make recommendations as to the changes, if any, in law and practice which are required."[16] It reported in 1954 and led to some significant changes to the law and practice concerning public records in England, many of which were still in place in the early twenty-first century. However, Jenkinson was not invited to sit on the Grigg Committee, disagreed with its recommendations and retired in 1954 before the Report was implemented.

One of the most major changes recommended by the Committee and implemented in the Public Records Act 1958 was in the approach to review and selection of records which were considered to have sufficient value to be permanently retained as archives at the PRO. The two-tier reviewing system recommended that a First Review be undertaken when a file had been closed for five years and was no longer needed for active reference by the administration of the creating department. The Second Review was to be undertaken when a file was twenty-five years old, to consider both continuing administrative need and also historical value for research. Records identified at Second Review for permanent preservation would then be transferred to the PRO during the following five years, that is, before the file was thirty years old. Files would then be opened to public access when they were fifty years old (amended to thirty years under the Public Records Act 1967). The two-stage review cemented the idea in England of a separation between the administrative needs of government for records and the historical value of archives which were accessed for research purposes. However, as staff from the PRO gradually became more involved in providing advice, oversight, and guidance to creating Departments on which records were worthy of preservation as archives, Jenkinson's idea of the neutrality of the archivist was challenged and in time largely overtaken by more complex ideas around archival appraisal, significance, and wider consideration of whose voices and lives were to be represented in archives.[17]

The other key change of the 1958 Act was to alter the governance of the PRO, transferring public records responsibilities to the Lord Chancellor, who appointed a Keeper of Public Records to be responsible for day-to-day selection and preservation of records. The Lord Chancellor was also enabled to appoint places of deposit for public records held locally, bringing some central control and regulation of the preservation of local public records such as records of the courts of quarter and petty sessions, magistrates and coroners' records. Such records were acknowledged as a central government responsibility but were neither stored nor paid for centrally. Although some administrative arrangements were subsequently altered (notably following the Wilson Report of 1981,[18] as a result of the Freedom of Information Act 2000 and following the creation of The National Archives in 2003), at the time of writing sixty-five years later no new public records legislation for England has been enacted.

Central Policy for Private and Local Archives

Private records were also a matter of concern to legislators in the nineteenth century, and in fact, the Royal Commission's work on publishing calendars and indexes included those for some important manuscript collections held at the British Museum, including the Cottonian catalogue (1802) and revised Harleian catalogue (1808–1812). The 1838 legislation, however, did not apply to family or private papers. Historically, the British Museum Department of Manuscripts, the Bodleian Library in Oxford, and other national libraries had acquired archives and manuscripts from antiquarians, dealers, and from private hands during the eighteenth and nineteenth centuries. Originating as part of the British Museum Library, founded in 1753, the Department of Manuscripts acquired many thousands of archives and manuscripts, including the foundation collections of Sir Hans Sloane, Sir Robert Cotton, and Robert and Edward Harley.[19] There was, however, no systematic central programme for private archives or for their preservation. A national survey of private records, proposed in 1857 at the first Congress of the National Association of Social Science, was not funded. In 1869, however, a Royal Commission on Historical Manuscripts was appointed, initially for five years but in fact renewed for more than a century, to enquire about where private manuscripts were held and, with the owner's consent, to make abstracts and catalogues in order to enable some limited access for historical study.[20] Although the Commission was independent of the PRO, it was housed in Chancery Lane and staffed by PRO officers until the middle of the twentieth century.

During the nineteenth century, local archives were not the focus of legislation but some Acts required the creation and keeping of records as a part of their provisions. For example, the Municipal Corporations Act 1835 made major reforms to city administration and elections and required the Treasurer to keep books of accounts; while the Local Government Act 1888 reformed the structures of local government, establishing new county councils and provided for the transfer of some existing buildings and records to the new councils. The Local Government Act 1894 confirmed county responsibilities for records but did not enable or oblige county councils to establish archives. There were moves to put the work of the Royal Commission on Historical Manuscripts on a firmer footing and extend its remit, including a proposal in 1889 by William Phillimore, publisher, antiquarian, and editor of the new British Record Society (BRS), to replace it with a Central Record Board. Phillimore envisaged that the Board, chaired by the Master of the Rolls, would approve the appointment of local Deputy Keepers of Records and enable local record provision to be centrally regulated on the same lines as the PRO. The Board would develop rules for the construction and arrangement of local record offices, and institute an inspection regime, and local archives would hold parish, diocesan, manorial, and land registry records, local public records, and private papers.[21] Without the support of Maxwell Lyte, the proposal did not progress, local archives were not developed in a systematic way, and no central regulation or advice was provided.

The policy and legislative vacuum for local records was filled by inquiries and reports into the arrangements for the collection, custody, and indexing of local records, such as the Treasury Committee set up in 1899, which reported in 1902.[22] This Report noted that while local record societies had published county histories and editions of local records, a few cities had made provision for their archives, and municipal libraries had begun to collect local manuscripts, no systematic provision existed for local records, which were treated unfavourably in comparison with central public records. The Report identified familiar omissions:

no enabling legislation, no funding, no skilled record staff, a lack of catalogues and indexes, and sporadic initiatives with no central direction. The Report recommended that universities be encouraged to establish "schools of palaeography" on a European model in order to create the necessary skilled archivists, that dry, fireproof repositories with a research room should be constructed in localities, and a uniform approach developed to arrangement and indexing to aid researchers, under central supervision with PRO officers inspecting and advising. It recommended that county and borough councils should be responsible for local civil records, which might be combined with ecclesiastical records. Meanwhile, private owners would be encouraged to deposit their records in public custody. Again, the recommendations were not enacted, legislation was not passed and no action was taken.[23]

Local records were again the subject of an inquiry during the First World War, as the focus of the Third Report of the Royal Commission in 1919, discussed above. The Commissioners visited thirty towns to inspect local records and identified thousands of storage places, mainly inadequate, unsatisfactory, and inconvenient, where records had often been lost or improperly disposed. The Commission proposed that local records should be properly housed, properly arranged, and indexed, and reasonably accessible to the public: but yet again no action was taken.

Hilary Jenkinson used his position as the Secretary of the BRA (founded in 1932 to bring together record owners, custodians, and scholars to work on records issues) and as Principal Assistant Keeper at the PRO to write the Report of the Committee on Post-War Dangers to Records in 1943. The Report brought together earlier work by the BRA on the need for a central register of private, ecclesiastical, and local archives, the provision of central inspection and advice, and common approaches to indexing and cataloguing. The BRA report was presented to the Royal Commission on Historical Manuscripts for consideration and the Commissioners asked the Master of the Rolls to appoint an Archives Committee to review the requirements. This time, action would follow and the report shaped much of the post-War development of local archives in England.

The most significant outcome of the Report was the foundation of the National Register of Archives in 1945, overseen by the Historical Manuscripts Commission. The register built on earlier registration activities, including the Manorial Documents Register and the wartime Regional Commissioners List. It was arranged by county area. Local committees gathered information about records, using the BRA's classification scheme, and the work was co-ordinated by a national Registrar, overseen by an expert Directorate, including Jenkinson. George Malet was appointed the first Registrar, with Dr. Kathleen Edwards as an assistant. The vision was to create a "vast Guide to Manuscript Sources covering the needs not only of professional historians but of enquirers seeking information in every field."[24] By 1947, seventeen local committees had been formed and by 1951, forty committees covering most of the country were sending in annual reports on local records. Originally, the Register was expected to complete its work in two years, but it was established on a permanent footing from 1953 as part of the Historical Manuscripts Commission. Gradually the local committees transferred their work to local archives as they became established and they took on the regular reporting of their holdings and catalogues to the central Register.

A second outcome of the BRA report was a further attempt to legislate to require localities to establish local archive services. The opportunity to develop a common model for local archives had been missed at the start of the twentieth century when few existed, and it was now felt to be too difficult to impose a common pattern, reverting instead to proposing that each locality should choose a scheme best suited to its needs. Local inspections were thought to be needed in order to establish the National Register and a proposal for a system of listing and starring archives of national importance held locally was put forward. This immediately faced difficulties around what measure of compulsion could be used, what the rights of private owners might be and whether ecclesiastical authorities or private owners could be required to comply without some form of compensation. However, inspection required legislation, so a Bill was drafted to require county and county borough councils to make provision for archives, to accept private and ecclesiastical archives and to enable the Master of the Rolls to appoint an Inspector General to advise and make rules for archives and to institute a statutory registration and starring system for the protection of archives. The Bill faced all kinds of difficulties, including long-standing objections to legislating for private archives, poor relations between Jenkinson at the PRO and the Treasury, ministerial transfers of responsibilities for local government, and the problem of finding Parliamentary time for "legislation which might be controversial and would involve the expenditure of public money."[25] In spite of further work by a powerful Master of the Rolls Archives Committee between 1949 and 1953, no agreement could be made on the desirable outcome and the work was shelved. Eventually, in 1962, some limited provisions were enacted as part of the Local Government (Records) Act to give local authorities general enabling powers to acquire and preserve local archives and raise funds to do so, along with the power to provide access, index, and catalogue archives and organise exhibitions and other related activities. For the first time, local authorities finally had formal enabling powers to run archive services but were still not compelled to make any local provision.

The Emergence of Local Archives and Record Offices

Private organisations and individuals continued to take an interest in local records, even if central government did not. Many localities, especially cities, valued their archives and records and municipal libraries acquired manuscripts, such as Norwich's City Library founded in 1608 and London's Guildhall Library founded in 1824. The Public Libraries Act 1850 established new libraries in many cities and in the absence of local archive services, many libraries acquired local history collections. Birmingham Reference Library opened in 1866 and acquired local books and manuscripts, which were a particular interest of the City Librarians in the early twentieth century, Walter Powell and H. M. Cashmore.[26] An earlier model had emerged in some areas as the justices and clerk of the peace established storage for county and quarter session records for their judicial and administrative requirements. In some cases, such as in Middlesex, indexes were compiled, storage provided and in the 1880s, records committees appointed to advise the justices, which then became committees to advise the new county councils more generally on records issues. Sometimes, city and borough authorities, proud of their history and heritage, made provision for their archives and records, especially after the administrative reforms of the Municipal Corporations Act 1835. In other areas, antiquarian and historical societies, trusts and museums filled the gap left by public authorities.

The Local Government Act 1888 gave the clerk of the peace responsibility for the records of the new county councils and, although not required to do so, a few of the new county councils established records committees and began to develop archive services. Hertfordshire (in 1895), Bedfordshire and Worcestershire (both in 1898) were the earliest county councils to appoint records committees, and in a few counties these committees led to the foundation of county archive services in the early twentieth century. Bedfordshire is generally credited with being the first county council to establish a local record office for the county, with Hertfordshire following shortly after. In each case, an enthusiastic individual was instrumental in the work. In Bedfordshire, retired zoologist and keen local historian, Dr. George Herbert Fowler, founded Bedfordshire Historical Record Society in 1912 to publish local records, was also elected to the county council and became the chairman of the county Records Committee.[27] In this capacity, Fowler set up a historical archive on the models proposed in the Reports of 1902 and 1919, installing steel shelving in the muniment rooms, devising a records classification scheme as the basis for cataloguing, setting up a repair service, and destruction schedules for the review of current administrative records. Bedfordshire was approved to hold manorial records in 1926 (the first so approved) and as the Diocesan Record Office in 1929, having initiated a survey of local parish records in 1927. Fowler also recognised the lack of a trained workforce for local archives, so he appointed assistants who were interested in historical study and were "orderly, methodical and neat" and trained them in his approach. He produced several of the first generation of county archivists, including F. G. Emmison (who went to Essex), I. P. Collis (to Somerset) and Francis Rowe (to Cheshire). In 1923, Fowler codified his approach to local archives seeking to encourage other county councils to make similar arrangements to preserve their records in his text, *The Care of County Muniments*, appearing just a year after Jenkinson's seminal text.[28]

In Hertfordshire, the firm of record agents, Hardy and Page, based in St Albans, were invited to inspect the county's records by the Records Committee in 1895 and the Committee spent over £2000 in the following decade on storing, binding, calendaring and publishing local records. After the War, in 1919, the Committee reconvened and undertook to develop the record office, approved as a manorial repository in 1927, for diocesan records in 1934 and tithe records in 1936. William Le Hardy, son of the firm's founder W J Hardy, was employed part-time as a record agent to direct the work. Eventually in 1939 a full-time archivist was appointed (Betty Colquhoun, formerly on the staff of Hardy and Page) and after the Second World War the record office was established as a county council department, with Le Hardy as County Record Agent from 1946 and County Archivist from 1957, in which role he continued until his death in 1961. In both cases of Bedfordshire and Hertfordshire, the local archive emerged as a result of local individual connections and enthusiasms, rather than as a result of central policy or legislation. The pattern was repeated around England between the two world wars and it was not until after the Second War that local archives saw consolidation, expansion, and growth, were able to employ trained archivists from the universities and a clearer profile for the modern professional archivist emerged in the localities.

Local Archives and Archivists in Twentieth-Century England: The Role of Women

Archival history, as was common in this period, has tended to be the history of great men and institutional archives, such as the PRO and the Deputy Keepers who ran it. Hubert Hall, a colleague of Jenkinson at the PRO, taught documentary approaches to history, diplomatics, palaeography, and administrative history through seminars at the London School of Economics (LSE) before the First World War. The majority of the LSE seminar participants were women, training "a generation of women historical workers."[29] Although the earliest local archives in England were established by men, drawing on their national and local connections and networks, the role of women is an overlooked and significant part of the story of the development of local archives in England in the twentieth century.

Pioneering women were important in the history of English local archives.[30] Joan Wake (1884–1974), trained at Hubert Hall's LSE seminars, was a record agent, active in the BRS and founder of Northamptonshire Record Society and county archives, was prominent on the Council of the British Records Association in the 1930s and first Vice Chairman of the Society of Local Archivists in 1947.[31] Ethel Stokes (1870–1944), a record agent and a friend of Wake, worked with the BRS to set up a Records Preservation Committee to offer advice, collect and distribute records around the country.[32] Lilian Redstone (1885–1955), also a record agent, was the first archivist for Ipswich and East Suffolk, author of *Local Records: their nature and care*, and succeeded Stokes as Secretary of the Records Preservation Section in 1944.[33] Although not an archivist, Eileen Power (1889–1940), Professor of Economic History at LSE and well-known medieval historian, deserves a mention here both for her role in educating women in historical skills at the LSE, following her tutor Hall's example, and for her proposal for a Committee for the registration, study and preservation of London business archives which led to the foundation of the Council for the Preservation of Business Archives in 1934.[34] Kathleen Major (1906–2000) was an archivist at Lincoln Diocesan record office from 1936 and the Secretary of Lincoln Record Society, Reader in Diplomatic at Oxford University in the 1940s and later the Principal of St Hilda's College Oxford.[35] Ida Darlington (1905–1970) worked for London County Council as a historical researcher on the Survey of London from 1926, was active in the BRA and the Society of Archivists, and was eventually appointed Head Archivist and Librarian to the newly merged London and Middlesex Councils in 1965.[36] These were some of the women who worked on records preservation in the localities between the Wars and made a fundamental, and until now largely unacknowledged, contribution to the development of local archives in England.

Women in the early twentieth century often faced educational barriers, although the Girls Public Day School Trust began to offer grammar school-type education to girls in the 1870s. Few women had the classical education needed for university entrance and few universities admitted women.[37] London University was the first in England to award degrees to women in 1878. When the LSE opened in 1895, women were able to attend lectures and were appointed to academic posts. At Oxford and at Cambridge Universities, women's colleges were established and chaperoned women could attend lectures, but they could not take their degrees at Oxford until 1920, at Cambridge until 1948. By the early twentieth century, educated women with historical interests could not gain employment at national, public cultural and archival institutions: so they carved out new enterprises in the localities.

There is much more work to be done on these women, but to take two examples briefly here: Joan Wake and Ethel Stokes.[38] The two had very different backgrounds. Joan Wake was a daughter of Sir Herewald Wake 12th Baronet whose family seat was at Courteenhall in Northamptonshire. She was educated at home by governesses, was an accomplished organist, and travelled widely around Europe in the early 1910s. She studied at the LSE in 1913 to 1915, attending Hall's seminars and Power's tutorials, developing her skills in Latin, palaeography and diplomatic, and became a Fellow of the Royal Historical Society in 1918. During the War, she volunteered as Secretary of the County Nursing Association. Travelling around Northamptonshire made her realise the wealth of local archives and the danger of their loss and destruction. Determined to take action to preserve local records, she established the Northamptonshire Record Society in 1920, which allowed her to survey and collect local records and to publish editions for study over the next forty years.

Ethel Stokes was born in Holloway in 1870, the daughter of a stockbroker's clerk and a music teacher, and was a student at Notting Hill High School, one of the first founded by the Girls Public Day Schools Trust. She did not attend university but was employed as a copyist for the New South Wales Government Archive at the PRO to trace, transcribe and translate records for publication in Australia. Stokes set up business as an independent record agent, Stokes and Cox, by 1903, with her friend, Mary Cox and was commissioned by private clients to undertake historical enquiries, peerage claims and genealogies, and legal searches at the PRO, the British Museum and in parish, ecclesiastical, municipal and estate records locally. Stokes and Cox also embarked on a project to index local parish registers (baptisms, marriages and burials) from before national registration in 1837. They employed historical record workers (mainly women) around the country to copy parish register entries onto slips of paper, compiled into a General Index. By the 1930s, Stokes and Cox had clients in the United States, Canada, Australia, Argentina, Britain and Europe. Ethel Stokes also edited historical records and wrote for works of reference, including local and BRS volumes, the Victoria County History of England and the Complete Peerage.

In the 1920s, Stokes and Wake together encouraged the BRS to address records preservation issues and began a service to survey records, sort records collected centrally and distribute them to the embryonic local archive services.[39] Wake organised the first Conference of Record Societies at the Archaeological Congress in 1930, which aimed to "formulate a systematic scheme to deal with the practical questions that are daily arising in connection with rescued documents" and to discuss records preservation and "acceptable standards" for record repositories. A Records Preservation Committee was set up in 1929, chaired by the Hertfordshire record agent, William Le Hardy, and run by Ethel Stokes. A Conference of Record and Allied Societies was held in 1930 to formulate a more systematic scheme for the distribution of records locally and to develop some principles and standards. Stokes and Wake were very involved (together with Le Hardy, Jenkinson and others) in the complex negotiations between the Conference, the Committee and new proposals for a separate organisation for records issues, which in 1932 became the BRA. Stokes, as secretary of the Records Preservation Section, established a network of over three hundred volunteers and workers around the country who rescued, registered, sorted, and listed records and she oversaw the collection, sorting and re-distribution of hundreds of archives. A condition of deposit locally was adherence to the standards for record repositories, including secure, fire- and damp-proof storage, proper staffing and provision of access for researchers. Many BRA deposits formed the core of embryonic local collections in the 1930s and 1940s when local archive services were being established.

Joan Wake was very active in national voluntary associations, the BRS, BRA, and Society of Local Archivists, relentlessly advocating for local records. She also exemplified loyalty to the history and records of her native county, Northamptonshire, and was a pioneer in establishing a county record service when there were few models and little guidance, setting a pattern for archivists who followed her in other counties.[40] Adopting the idea of a local record society along the lines of Lincoln Record Society, but extending the typical activities beyond publication of records, to lectures and exhibitions, and to acquiring and preserving archives, Joan Wake in effect established a county record office service and used her position as Honorary Secretary of the Northamptonshire Record Society from 1920 as a proxy for her work as county archivist, long before the county and borough officially created a record office and committee in 1952. Wake believed that there was no real distinction between local and national histories and that local archives such as those in Northamptonshire were of great value. The Record Society, led by Wake, acquired records of landed estates, manors and families, Quarter Sessions, local authorities, and surveyed solicitors. Wake developed a classification scheme for parish records. She visited archives in the Netherlands and Sweden and, inspired by their organisation and training, developed a local archives service initially storing records in County Hall, then at Cosgrove Priory during the War, moving to Lamport Hall, and in due course, after a fund-raising effort, to the refurbished Delapré Abbey in Northampton in 1959, which became both the new County Record Office and the headquarters of the Record Society. Wake had envisaged a future "when all local official archives not in current use will be transferred to County Record Offices under the care of trained archivists and made available for historical study,"[41] and through her efforts, locally and nationally, had worked to bring this to fruition.

Conclusion

This chapter provides an overview of the development of archives in England, centrally and locally, in the nineteenth and early twentieth centuries. In the nineteenth century, government policy and legislation focused on the central provision for records of courts of law and central government ministries, establishing a national PRO in 1838. Led by men, the PRO (fore-runner of the UK National Archives) gradually developed systems for the review and transfer of government records to the PRO building in Chancery Lane, where they were preserved, catalogued and made available for research. Private and local archives were periodically considered by national government, and the Royal Commission on Historical Manuscripts was established (initially on a temporary basis) in 1869 to make private records available through publication. The central policy vacuum for local records was filled by national voluntary associations, such as the BRS and the BRA, especially the BRA's work on records preservation and standards, and by local initiatives and pioneering individuals. Records work in the localities began in earnest after the Local Government Act 1888 when a few county councils set up records committees and, beginning in Bedfordshire in 1914 and Hertfordshire in 1919, established local record offices. In the inter-War period, the development of county record offices was characterised by the individuals who set them up, in the absence of national guidance and standards or archival training. In many areas, these new local archives were run by women, educated in historical skills but excluded from employment in national institutions. Their stories have not been fully told and this chapter has helped to bring some to light. Eventually, after the Second World War, national registration of local and private records began. Universities offered archival education from 1947 and the Society of Local Archivists gave local archivists a chance to work together and learn from each other. By 1948, record services were established in thirty-four English counties, and by 1953, only eight counties did not have a record office. Enabling legislation for local record offices was finally enacted in 1962, confirming the legitimacy of local archives. The local patchwork of services still needed much development, but by the mid-twentieth century, the framework of local and central archives was established in England and the modern profession of archivist was emerging. As with other information professions, the work of women, historically marginalised, was critical to professional development in the twentieth century,[42] and archives are now commonly thought of as "women's work." In 1992, the PRO finally appointed the first female Keeper of public records.

Notes

1. On the core information professions, see Marcia Bates, "The Information Professions: Knowledge, Memory, Heritage," *Information Research* 20, no. 1 (March 2015), http://informationr.net/ir/20-1/paper655.html#.Y0PnEUbMLIU.
2. Barbara Craig, Philip Eppard, and Heather MacNeil, "Exploring Perspectives and Themes for Histories of Records and Archives: The First International Conference on the History of Records and Archives (I-CHORA I)," *Archivaria* 60 (September 2006): 1–10.
3. Geoffrey Yeo, *Records, Information and Data: Exploring the Role of Record-keeping in an Information Culture* (London: Facet Publishing, 2018), 13.
4. See, for example, Geoffrey Yeo, *Record-Making and Record-Keeping in Early Societies* (London: Routledge, 2021); and Ernst Posner, *Archives in the Ancient World* (Boston, MA: Harvard University Press, 1972).
5. For a study of community archives, see Jeannette Bastian, *Archiving Cultures: Heritage, Community and the Making of Records and Memory* (Milton: Taylor & Francis, 2023); and Jeannette Bastian and Ben Alexander, eds., *Community Archives: The Shaping of Memory* (London: Facet, 2009).
6. For a comprehensive treatment, on which this chapter draws, see Elizabeth Shepherd, *Archives and Archivists in 20th Century England* (Aldershot: Ashgate, 2009).
7. Michel Duchein, "The History of European Archives and the Development of the Archival Profession in Europe," *The American Archivist* 55, no. 1 (Winter 1992): 14–25.
8. For details, see Shepherd, *Archives and Archivists*, 21–43.
9. A comprehensive history of the PRO is given in John Cantwell, *The Public Record Office 1838–1958* (London: HMSO, 1991).
10. David Knowles, *Great Historical Enterprises* (London: Thomas Nelson and Sons, 1963), 101–134.
11. Philippa Levine, "History in the Archives: The Public Record Office and Its Staff, 1838–1886," *English Historical Review* 101 (1986): 20–41; and Philippa Levine, *The Amateur and the Professional. Antiquarians, Historians and Archaeologists in Victorian England, 1838–1886* (Cambridge, UK: Cambridge University Press, 1986).
12. Royal Commission on Public Records Appointed to Inquire into and Report on the State of Public Records and Local Records of a Public Nature of England and Wales, *First Report, Second Report, Third Report*, Cmd. 6361, Cmd. 7544, Cmd. 367 (London: HMSO, 1912–1919).
13. James Conway Davis, "Memoir of Sir Hilary Jenkinson," in *Studies Presented to Sir Hilary Jenkinson*, ed. J. Conway Davis (Oxford: Oxford University Press, 1957), v–xxx.
14. Hilary Jenkinson, *A Manual of Archive Administration Including the Problems of War Archives and Archive Making* (Oxford: The Clarendon Press, 1922).
15. Jenny Bunn, "Welcome to This Special Issue on Confronting the Canon," *Archives and Records* 43, no. 2 (2022): 119–124; and Hannah J. M. Ishmael, "Reclaiming History: Arthur Schomburg," *Archives and Manuscripts* 46, no. 3 (2018): 269–288.
16. Committee on Departmental Records, *Report* (London: HMSO, 1954), Cmd. 9163 (The Grigg Report).
17. Terry Cook, "'We Are What We Keep; We Keep What We Are': Archival Appraisal Past, Present and Future," *Journal of the Society of Archivists* 32, no. 2 (2011): 173–189.
18. Committee on Modern Public Records: Selection and Access, *Report* (London: HMSO, 1981), Cmd. 8204 (The Wilson Report).
19. Philip R. Harris, *A History of the British Museum Library, 1753–1973* (London: British Library, 1998).
20. Roger Ellis, "The Historical Manuscripts Commission 1869–1969," *Journal of the Society of Archivists* 2 (1960–1964): 233–242.
21. Jeffery R. Ede, "The Record Office, Central and Local: Evolution of a Relationship," *Journal of the Society of Archivists* 8, no. 40 (1968): 185–192.
22. Committee Appointed to Enquire as to the Existing Arrangements for the Collection and Custody of Local Records, *Report*, Cmd. 1335 (London: HMSO, 1902).
23. Parallels might be drawn with the gradual emergence of the information state, on which, see Edward Higgs, *The Information State in England: The Central Collection of Information on Citizens, 1500–2000* (London: Palgrave, 2004).

24 Dick Sargent, *The National Register of Archives: An International Perspective: Essays in Celebration of the Fiftieth Anniversary of the NRA* (London: Institute of Historical Research, 1995).
25 Cantwell, *PRO 1838–1958*.
26 A series of articles in the journal *Archives* recounting the history of individual archives appeared in the 1950s and 1960s, including A. Andrews, "Local Archives of Great Britain V: The Birmingham Reference Library," *Archives* 1, no. 5 (1951): 11–21.
27 Patricia Bell, and Freddy Stitt, "George Herbert Fowler and County Records," *Journal of the Society of Archivists* 23 (2002): 249–264; and Joyce Godber, "Local Archives of Great Britain I: The County Record Office at Bedford," *Archives* 1, no. 1 (1949): 10–20.
28 G. Herbert Fowler, *The Care of County Muniments* (London: County Councils Association, 1923).
29 Margaret Procter, *Hubert Hall (1857–1944): Archival Endeavour and the Promotion of Historical Enterprise* (PhD diss., University of Liverpool, 2012); and Margaret Procter, "Life before Jenkinson," *Archives* 119 (2008): 140–161.
30 Elizabeth Shepherd, "Hidden Voices in the Archives: Pioneering Women Archivists in Early 20th Century England," in *Engaging with Archives and Records: Histories and Theories*, ed. Fiorella Foscarini et al. (London: Facet, 2017), 83–104.
31 Neil Lyon, *The Best Burglar in the County: Joan Wake and the Northamptonshire Record Society* (Northampton: Northamptonshire Record Society, 2021); and P. I. King, "Obituary: Dr Joan Wake (1884–1974)," *Journal of the Society of Archivists* 5, no. 2 (1974): 144–148.
32 Elizabeth Shepherd, "Pioneering Women Archivists in England: Ethel Stokes (1870–1944), Record Agent," *Archival Science* 17, no. 2 (2017): 175–194.
33 Derek Charman, "Local Archives of Great Britain XVII: The Ipswich and East Suffolk Record Office," *Archives* 4, no. 21 (1959): 18–28; and Lilian J. Redstone and Francis W. Steer, *Local Records: Their Nature and Care* (London: G. Bell and Sons, 1953).
34 Maxine Berg, *A Woman in History, Eileen Power, 1889–1940* (Cambridge, UK: Cambridge University Press, 1996).
35 Donald A. Bullough and Robin L. Storey, eds., *The Study of Medieval Records: Essays in Honour of Kathleen Major* (Oxford: Clarendon Press, 1971); and Geoffrey W. S. Barrow, "Kathleen Major, 1906–2000," *Proceedings of the British Academy* 115 (2002): 318–329.
36 Marie Draper, "Obituary: Ida Darlington 1905–1970," *Journal of the Society of Archivists* 4, no. 2 (1970): 166–168.
37 Mary Spongberg, *Writing Women's History since the Renaissance* (London: Palgrave Macmillan, 2002).
38 Shepherd, "Ethel Stokes," Shepherd, "Hidden Voices," and Shepherd, *Archives and Archivists*.
39 Shepherd, *Archives and Archivists*, 131–136.
40 Peter Gordon, *The Wakes of Northamptonshire: A Family History* (Northampton: Northamptonshire County Council, 1992).
41 Gordon, *The Wakes*, 335.
42 See, for example, Julianne Nyhan, *Hidden and Devalued Feminized Labour in the Digital Humanities: On the Index Thomisticus Project 1954–1967* (London: Routledge, 2023).

21
REPRESENTING INFORMATION IN THE WESTERN WORLD

Classification, Cataloguing, and the Library Context since Industrialisation

Karen Attar

The mid-nineteenth century saw an information explosion, second only perhaps to the "printing revolution" with the coming of moveable type 400 years earlier.[1] In the year 1800, no element of book production was mechanised. By 1850, in the developed world at least, every aspect was, reflecting the developments of industrialisation. Books became cheaper and more readily available to a wider public. Governments made them more accessible to those who could not buy through the establishment of free public libraries. Literacy levels increased. New inventions and discoveries expanded knowledge, which new means of communication further helped to spread.[2] With the increasing demand for, and provision of, information came the need to improve access to it: both by ordering books more precisely by subject matter, in catalogues and, as more commonly seen, on library shelves (classification), and by listing and describing books (cataloguing). "Information" and "knowledge" are here linked: raw facts constitute information, while the same facts when assimilated become knowledge.[3] A book represents knowledge by the author, but information to the reader who has yet to absorb what the author has written. This chapter explores the changing ways in which information was presented and organised within the knowledge institution of the library.

Classification

In the mid-nineteenth century, book classification was largely irrelevant. Books had been divided into broad categories for centuries, as exemplified by Oxford's Bodleian Library's shelfmarks between 1602 and 1789, and then less frequently until about 1840, for the four areas of Art. ("artes," including mathematics, history, philosophy, and literature), Med. ("medicina"), Th. ("theologia"), and Jur. ("jurisprudentia," that is, law).[4] Any further grouping was by size, and in many libraries arrangement was purely by shelfmark: for example, V.e.17 for the seventeenth book on the fifth shelf of case V. Grouping subjects was unnecessary because browsing was not an option: library users requested books from printed catalogues, and the books were brought to them.

Two major changes occurred in the second half of the century. Firstly, institutional libraries became significantly larger. Two national libraries provide the most extreme examples.

The British Museum's holdings rose from about 250,000 volumes to 1.3 million between 1838 and 1884, while the Library of Congress's holdings increased from six thousand books in 1814 to nearly a million by the end of the nineteenth century.[5] Thus, librarians could no longer be expected to have the full overview of their contents that might have been assumed earlier. Secondly, library users began to gain direct access to shelves, which encouraged browsing.[6] Both factors led to the need physically to order information more precisely than hitherto. While the idea of classifying the world around us to make sense of it derives from Aristotle, and had reached new heights with the scientific taxonomies of Carl Linnaeus and the presentation of a structured form of all knowledge in Diderot's *Encyclopédie* in the eighteenth century,[7] classification represented a sea change in book arrangement. The symbol (notation) given to a book no longer referred to its static location within a book case, but to the book's contents and its relative position to other books containing similar information. Thus, for example, all books on classical music would be grouped together, with general overviews preceding books about Mozart, and books about music would be closer to books about visual art than to works of Shakespearean criticism.

The earliest enduring classification scheme is that devised by Melville Dewey, published in 1876.[8] His Decimal Classification is so called because he divided the knowledge of his day into ten broad areas: (0) Generalities; (1) Philosophy, including Psychology; (2) Religion; (3) Social Sciences; (4) Language; (5) Mathematics and natural sciences; (6) Applied sciences and technology; (7) Arts; (8) Literature; and (9) Geography, history, and auxiliary subjects. Each area was subdivided into another ten, which were, in turn, subdivided, for example, within the natural sciences, 520 for Astronomy and 525 for Astronomical observations. Four major schemes followed over the next century: Library of Congress Classification (LCC, 1901–1928); Universal Decimal Classification (UDC, 1905–1907); Colon Classification (CC, 1933); and Henry Evelyn Bliss's Bibliographic Classification (BC, 1935; expanded 1953).[9] Several minor schemes were also devised, most notably Charles Ammi Cutter's Expansive Classification (1882), which influenced the Library of Congress Classification, and James Duff Brown's Subject Classification, designed for British public libraries (SC, 1906).[10]

Placing books on all areas of knowledge in a subject sequence from 1 to 9 or A to Z raised the immediate question of where to begin and how to continue: what is the starting point of knowledge, and how does one subject flow into the next? Kenneth Garside sidestepped the question by devising a classification scheme for University College London in 1954 (and still used there) which enlisted academics from each subject area to ensure internal logic within subjects as they were taught at the College, but which made no attempt to place the main classes in any particular sequence. This was a scheme well suited to the architecture of that specific library, which was divided into a number of discrete rooms, in practice functioning as distinct subject libraries.[11]

Other classification schemes represented diverse world views. The English classificationist James Duff Brown expressed forcefully the vagaries subject order, with each expert favouring his own subject in conflicting interpretations of the world (for example, physics as the genesis of all human activity, or as an annex of general history): "The result of these many claims to sovereignty … is that Classification has become a mere battlefield for theorists."[12]

Intellectually, Dewey's sequence was flawed. Most obviously, the sciences and social sciences divided the humanities subjects from each other, and language was widely separated from literature. An article of 1897 noted briefly "the spatial separation of subjects nearly related."[13] In 1912 (by which time the Decimal Classification was into its seventh edition), an Australian critic writing under the epithet, "a mere librarian," attacked Dewey for such illogicalities as classifying folklore as social science rather than mythology or literature.[14] Just over a century later, a twenty-first-century textbook commented acidly: "[T]here seems hardly to be a single classification that hasn't done better than Dewey."[15] Yet other systems struggled too, providing tangible evidence of the multiplicity of attitudes towards knowledge and how best to access it. LCC (which differed from DDC primarily in its placing of the sciences with respect to the arts) improved upon DDC by collocating language and literature, but it separated a country's geography from its history. Although both Brown and Bliss thought more carefully about logical connections between subjects and saw one growing out of another, neither succeeded fully. Brown placed Generalia first, as universal knowledge pervading all fields of study. Physical sciences followed, in the belief that matter, force, motion, and their application precede life and the mind; biological sciences as arising out of matter; ethnological and medical science as a higher development of animal life; economic biology and domestic arts (like agriculture) as "applications, plant and animal life to human needs"; philosophy and religion as mental attributes following from the physical basis of life; social and political science as succeeding philosophy (mind); language and literature as growing out of the primitive operations of the mind; literary forms as the product of human communication; and finally history, geography, and biography as leftovers which belong together.[16] He distinguished sharply neither between the pure and the applied sciences, nor between theory and practice because: "the old distinction between theoretical and applied science is gradually disappearing from all modern text-books, and it is obvious that, as the systematisation of science and its teaching improve, the separation between physical basis and practical application, hitherto maintained, will no longer be insisted upon."[17] The main criticism was that everything on one term went into one place, disregarding the different aspects of that term: rabbits might function as pets or cookery, but the distinction would not be noted.[18] Brown's view of music purely as sound, and hence as a physical science rather than a performing art, and of mathematics and education as aspects of generalia, also stood out.

Henry Evelyn Bliss, more than anybody else, was concerned with the logical, as opposed to mere pragmatic, ordering of information in the scheme he devised for the New York Public Library, where he spent his professional career.[19] He wanted a scheme that aligned with how subjects were studied and taught ("educational consensus"), opining that it would lack credibility otherwise.[20] For Bliss, philosophy was the ground of all thought, closely followed by mathematics and logic. Physics came next as the science dealing with the most fundamental natural phenomena, then chemistry because it depended partly on the findings of physics, and astronomy as depending on concepts derived from both. There followed the other natural sciences, medicine as their practical application, psychology as an offshoot of medicine, and finally the social sciences and then arts. Bliss separated philosophy from religion, and sociology from applied social science.

All the schemes, especially the twentieth-century ones, toppled theology from its original place as the cornerstone of the world, reflective of secular developments in the world more generally.[21] Beyond that, they demonstrate that there was no one logical arrangement of information, and that perfect logic was unachievable. Within schemes, there was less controversy, with an overall progression from general to specific, and acceptance that the same order could not apply to every subject.

James Hanson and Charles Martel outlined a new system of classification for the Library of Congress in 1898 because they disliked Dewey's hierarchical notation, and felt moreover that DDC made the subject arrangement fit the notation instead of vice versa. But although LCC did not aspire to hierarchy, it resembled DDC in several ways. Both wished in the structure and order of the classes to reflect the thinking process of readers and to be easily understood by them.[22] Both were devised as a practical way to collocate books on shelves in their specific libraries for a particular readership; neither cared about intellectual design. Both followed the principle what Edward Wyndham Hulme made known as "literary warrant": namely, that classification followed what had been written. The existence of a book on a certain subject justified a classmark for that subject; there was no point in having classmarks for subjects in which there were no books, even if the classification of knowledge recognised the theoretical possibility of such classes.[23] Above all, both schemes were initially enumerative, listing every classmark they thought could apply to a subject. They thereby signified a belief that it was possible to impose a universal order on knowledge. Literary warrant and enumeration combined to make both systems were essentially backward-looking, serving contemporaneous knowledge only. Obsolescence of subjects would result in wasted classmarks, while a new subject would either have to be squeezed into a small area, or would necessitate thorough revision. Knowledge overtook them. Thus, for example, the Library of Congress required a fifth edition of the Q schedule (science) in 1950, just two years after the fourth edition, in order to incorporate important changes in nuclear science.[24] DDC was revised constantly, reaching its twenty-third edition in 2018. The enumerative systems lacked the flexibility to cope with such composite subjects as women's studies, Victorian studies, or area studies, which arose later in the twentieth century.

Practical awareness that knowledge is not static was built into classification schemes of the first decade of the twentieth century, James Duff Brown's Subject Classification and above all Paul Otlet and Henri La Fontaine's Universal Decimal Classification (UDC) in 1905–1907.[25] These provided auxiliary tables of notation for form, time, relations, persons, properties, materials, place, and language, which could be applied to any subject (a feature subsequently built into DDC from its seventeenth edition, of 1965). They also allowed for the combination of different subjects with symbols to allow for new connections: composition in Brown, shown through an addition sign (such as "A300+M170" for "Logic and rhetoric"), and several symbols (a colon, a slash, an equals sign, and others) for different relationships in the fully analytico-synthetic, UDC. While DDC and LCC focused on books in specific libraries, Otlet and La Fontaine set their horizons on information produced anywhere in the world in any outlet—newspapers, photographs, patents, and so forth as well as books—and at chapter and paragraph level as well as the entirety of what fell between two covers. Their aspiration automatically improved comprehensiveness, as new topics typically appear on articles before they do in monographs.

The next major change in the perception of information was Colon Classification, introduced by S. R. Ranganathan. In marked divergence from earlier classificationists who had assumed an overview of knowledge, Ranganathan, inspired by the sight of a Meccano set in Selfridges in late 1924, began at the bottom and built classmarks up by combining all the possible elements, in what is called faceted classification. He divided everything into five classes known by the acronym PMEST: Personality (the main subject), Matter (qualification of the main subject: substances, materials, constituents), Energy (processes), Space, and Time. Any element could be combined with any other element to form precise classmarks, and to allow for the fusion of subjects not yet linked and the easy accommodation of new ones. Ranganathan's theory influenced profoundly the development of subsequent theories about arranging information.[26]

This emerged most strongly in the second edition of the Bibliographic Classification (BC2), developed in the United Kingdom in 1977.[27] BC2 took as its basis Bliss's semi-faceted scheme and kept Bliss's outline. Within each class, everything was divided into its smallest components, extending Ranganathan's PMEST to the facets: thing/kind/part; property; material; process/operation; patient; product/by-product; agent; space; time. Terms from different facets were combined, in such a way that shelf arrangement was from the general to the specific with the most important concepts first, and notation increased in length according to the grade of specificity. By taking the building block element to its furthest point, BC2 offered more flexibility, ability to incorporate new concepts ("hospitality"), and future-proofing than any other scheme, and BC2 has been praised as the best general classification scheme intellectually.[28]

The principle of faceted classification avoided biases: for example, building blocks relating to religion could be applied to all faiths. The enumerative and analytico-synthetic systems contained clear biases which reflected their geographic origin. LCC is weak in medicine and agriculture and particularly strong in law, politics, and history (especially pertaining to America), because these were the subjects most important to the members of Congress. DDC, LCC, and Brown all strongly favoured Christianity over other religions, because that reflected contemporary conditions and interests as exemplified in their holdings. All had a strong historical and geographical bias toward the home country.[29] UDC showed a European bias in some classes, for example, reflecting European practice in its social welfare schedules.[30] Unremarkable in their original context, such biases became detrimental when countries with other belief systems and values adopted the schemes, and when, in a twenty-first century, post-colonial world, information perspectives became global. Thus DDC reduced the Christian emphasis in its twenty-first and twenty-second editions, of 1996 and 2003, and the American bias in its section on public administration in its twenty-first edition.[31] The verbal expansion of Library of Congress classmarks in subject headings from 1910 onwards mercilessly exposed cultural and gender biases in such headings as "Women as Judges" and "Illegal Aliens."[32] As social mores and world views changed, the way in which information was presented and classified also changed to reflect this; headings such as "women judges" and "illegal immigration," demonstrated a symbiotic relationship between classification and the real world.[33]

Geographical boundaries remained to an extent, in that LC is used in the United States (mainly in academic libraries) more than it is anywhere else; Brown never extended beyond Britain; and BC2 and CC remained in their countries of origin, the United Kingdom and India, respectively. UDC is particularly strong in Europe. In this sense then, information has borders.

Moreover, practical considerations invariably trumped intellectual ones in the ordering of information. In the bald words of Arthur Maltby and Rita Marcella: "The history of classification shows that if a scheme ever dies, it is on the grounds of poor efficiency (by which is meant administration or finance factors) rather than theoretical effectiveness."[34] The two best intellectual systems, BC2 and CC, are the least used, while DDC and LC, regarded as the worst from an intellectual viewpoint because the most enumerative, have survived best. At least 43 libraries beyond the Library of Congress used its scheme by 1916, 131 (nineteen of which were abroad) by 1930, and over 1,400 by the early 1980s, including close to 200 overseas.[35] In 2014 the Library of Congress claimed it was: "currently one of the most widely used library classification systems in the world."[36] DDC travelled to the British Isles in 1878. One thousand libraries in the United States were using DDC by 1896, and by 2023 in approximately two hundred thousand school, public, and university libraries used it across some 140 countries.[37] These two systems triumphed partly on account of their clear notation, in contrast to the symbols used in CC and UDC and mix of upper and lower case letters in BC1 which did not relate to an intuitive order on shelves—in the 1960s the College of Librarianship in Wales changed from a faceted classification scheme for library science to DDC because junior staff struggled with shelving books in the faceted system.[38]

Consistently, money and power spoke. Intellectually, there may have been little to choose between Brown and Dewey, but Dewey gained strong financial backing to publish and develop his scheme, whereas Brown did not. The Library of Congress added its classmarks and, from 1930 onwards, DDC classmarks to the catalogue cards it distributed to other libraries. This element helped to ensure the use of these two schemes; libraries could save time and money by adopting these classmarks instead of expending effort imposing their own. Intellectual attributes actually mitigated against practical use: Bliss's provision for alternative arrangement increased effort by fragmenting practice. Libraries proved themselves indifferent to his philosophical concerns about the relationships between subject areas and to the perceived benefits of accommodating new information in the most logical place as it came into being, instead of dealing with it retrospectively. DDC's answer to keeping up with new information was to build a plan from the sixteenth edition of 1958 onwards to revise limited sections in each new issue, enabling libraries to reclassify stock gradually, with minimum inconvenience.[39]

Some decisions were at least as personal as they were either academic or pragmatic. Ainsworth Rand Spofford, the former Librarian of Congress, was a principal consultant for a classification scheme at that library; Spofford entertained a strong antipathy to Dewey's Decimal Classification; and Hanson and Martel wanted to placate Spofford.[40] Personalities affected cataloguing decisions too. Antonio Panizzi, Keeper of Printed Books at the British Museum, recommended filing anonymous works by the first word of the title, discounting articles and prepositions. Henry Baber, Henry Francis Cary, and later Sir Henry Ellis argued less logically for placement under a more ambiguous "principal word" and the Trustees supported them.[41] This was, in part, a political issue: Panizzi was an Italian, who faced considerable hostility in the British Museum and England (in part due to the mid-century foreign policy tensions regarding Italian independence and unity), whereas Baber and Ellis were English.[42] When Cambridge University Library moved to computer cataloguing in 1978, it was expected that the guard book used previously would be phased out within the following three years. In fact, retrospective acquisitions continued to be catalogued into the guard book catalogue until 1995 because the University Librarian 1980–1994 was unconvinced of the value of computers in libraries.[43]

Cataloguing

Cataloguing overlapped with classification in its preoccupation with the arrangement of books, albeit in printed catalogues rather than on shelves. When a Royal Commission examined procedures at the British Museum 1834–1836, society at large was interested, with "practically every reader who had ever been inside the Museum ... sending in plans."[44] Debate raged about whether the British Museum should arrange its books by subject or by author (a question sidestepped in America by use of the dictionary catalogue, slotting authors and subjects into a single alphabetical sequence). Opinions were vehement.

Sir Henry Ellis, the principal librarian of the British Museum, wrote that "any intelligent man using the library must be so well up in his subject that he would know the names of all the authors that had written on it, and therefore he would not need a classed catalogue." He further claimed that librarians were living subject catalogues, that a classed catalogue was impossible because it depended on consensus about subjects and their terminology, and "no two people would ever agree as to which heading a book should be assigned." Panizzi added: "the continual discoveries in science make classification ridiculous," and pointed out that subject access was provided in bibliographies, from which one would proceed to the catalogue.[45] Alphabetical arrangement won out. The Bodleian Library faced the same arguments fifty years later, when the classicist Henry William Chandler argued like Panizzi about the impossibility of controlling all knowledge; he added that some books would require several entries, while others, such as poetry books, could not be classed:

> [T]he classed catalogue and all the work that it entails is so much labour thrown away. ... [I]t serves no useful purpose; it is a snare and a delusion. The sciolist, and he alone, thinks how delightful it would be to turn out any given subject and there see all the books that have been written on it. He does not know how impossible the thing is ...[46]

The British Museum rules, rushed out in 1839, represented major progress by codifying practice, realising the importance of consistency when describing, and trying to gain intellectual control over, a large collection.[47] The arrangement of material within the alphabetical catalogue is relevant beyond library catalogues to book indexes and to telephone directories (for example, is "Mc" interfiled with "Mac" and "St" with "Saint"?). The rules also covered descriptive cataloguing. Traditionally this had consisted of the author's name, an abbreviated version of a book's title, its bibliographical format (replaced by size when paper production was mechanised), the edition number if not the first, and the place and date of publication. Catalogues were printed, and information had to be brief to save paper and hence expense, in a further instance of practical considerations dictating practice: Cutter shows the most extreme example by abbreviating the names of common places to single letters, "L." and "P." for London and Paris.[48] The Museum Rules contained instructions for describing "so much of the title page as is necessary" to indicate all parties involved in its intellectual production; the edition statement; the place and date of publication (but not the publisher); the presence of illustrative material "when that information is of interest and is not given on the title page"; and pagination. It gives additional rules for early printed books: the typeface; the material on which the book is printed if vellum; editions on large paper; the name of the publisher; the presence of manuscript notes and the name of their writer, "when of interest." Postnominals are normally to be omitted, and in early printed books, printers' names are to be given "only when important." Other places developed similar rules as basic finding aids for their particular organisations: the newly formed Library Association in 1878, the Bodleian Library (based on the Library Association rules) in 1882 and Cambridge University Library, modelled on the British Museum rules, in 1854 and again in 1879.[49]

In 1862, Harvard introduced catalogue cards.[50] The Library of Congress advanced the concept of shared information when in 1901 it sent its catalogue cards to other organisations, which could add their own shelfmarks to the basic information. Measuring three by five inches, catalogue cards enabled the inclusion of extra details at no additional paper cost.

New cataloguing rules devised in 1908, followed to a large extent in both the United Kingdom and the United States, accordingly gave additional instructions to include a statement of responsibility when transcribing a title, to include the name of publishers, and to state the size of books to the closest half-centimetre. They allowed for notes on the contents, notes to explain the title, "to supply essential information about the author and bibliographical details not given in the title, imprint, or collation," and various other points: bibliographies, authorities, pseudonyms and anonyms, sequels, variations in title, editors and translators, editions, various places, publishers, or dates, reprints, languages of the text, source of the book if first published serially, no more published, imperfections in the copy, and bound with something else.[51] The only restriction was the preference for information to fit on to a single card.

On the whole, libraries are a gateway to information provision. But library descriptions manage information by controlling what they do and do not include. They suppress biographical information about authors by normally excluding descriptions of authors appearing after their name on title pages, like "schoolmaster in Five-Fields-Row, Chelsea" or "M.A. Chaplain to the most Noble Wriothesly Duke of Bedford, and Rector of Newton St. Loe, near Bath in the same county," replacing the information by marks of ellipsis. Sometimes information is omitted without marks of ellipsis. Methods of illustration tend only to be obvious if named on the title page, potentially frustrating the work of those interested in the use of chromolithography or early photographs. Unnumbered sequences of pages are seldom recorded for machine-press books. From the British Museum cataloguing rules onwards, instructions include directions to include a particular feature "if it is considered important", especially concerning early printed books. As J. D. Cowley expressed cogently in 1949 with respect to describing provenance and bindings, "if they are likely to prove of interest": "The immediate response to such a rule is probably: 'Of interest to whom?' This is a question that is often difficult to answer."[52] Researchers depended heavily on the discretion of individual cataloguers, or perusing books systematically on shelves.[53]

Computerised cataloguing rendered decisions intellectual rather than purely practical, by eliminating the three-by-five-inch boundary. It further facilitated the sharing of records across networks, nationally and globally, and facilitated union catalogues (joint catalogues for various libraries). In Britain, the seven largest university libraries in England and Scotland formed the Consortium of University and Research Libraries (CURL) in 1983 to generate the union catalogue Copac. The scheme grew steadily, and in 2023, 202 libraries of all sizes were contributing, sharing information and also misinformation, when libraries duplicated each other's mistakes.[54]

From such schemes, it was a small jump to union catalogues that also functioned as national bibliographies. The idea of the national bibliography was not new, the first edition of *A Short-Title Catalogue of Books Printed in England Scotland & Ireland and of English Books Printed Abroad 1475–1640* having appeared in 1926.[55] International bibliography had begun at approximately the same time with the German-based *Gesamtkatalog der Wiegendrucke* in 1925, a worldwide catalogue of incunabula which stalled at the letter H because of adverse political circumstances, the Second World War and the division of Germany.[56] The Eighteenth Century Short Title Catalogue (ESTC) was proposed in 1975 to record all letterpress books printed either in an English-speaking country or in the English language between 1701 and 1800. It expanded in 1987 to include books going back to the introduction of printing to England in 1476, and "short title" in its revised title, the English Short Title Catalogue, became a misnomer for detailed descriptions.[57] The ESTC inspired the Incunabula Short Title Catalogue (ISTC), begun in 1980, which listed all books which had either been printed by movable type before 1501, or had once been thought to have done so. Its full overview helped to move the field to one of interest not only to incunabulists as printing historians, but to scholars interested in the Renaissance period of any of the subjects represented.[58] Later, in 1992, the ESTC inspired the CERL Handpress Book Database (subsequently renamed the Heritage of the Printed Book Database), to extend coverage to all European books published to 1830 insofar as it could be shown by the online records of the particular contributing libraries. One of its generators claimed that "we have learned to work together, despite the problems of language, politics and traditions."[59]

Full convergence remained a utopian dream. The Incunabula Short Title Catalogue latinised names which appear in the vernacular in most Anglo-American catalogues (for example, Euclid vs Euclides). Vernacular catalogues diverged: for example, the book *Daemonologie* is by King James I according to English-language catalogues, by Jacques I in French catalogues, and by Jakob I in German ones. Yet the aspiration to control information remained in the aim to record all extant books of a certain time period or country, seen especially clearly today through the Universal Short Title Catalogue (USTC) of all books published anyway up to the year 1700.[60]

Such union catalogues moreover transformed the use of catalogues from mere finding aids to research tools themselves. Libraries crunched data to establish their comparative strengths and weaknesses as a guide for future collection development.[61] Researchers conducted catalogue searches to learn about the history of printing. Even before national bibliographies had gone online, H. S. Bennett had relied heavily on the first edition of the printed Short Title Catalogue to examine the subjects and nature of books English people were reading in the early modern period, writing that the researcher would be like "a semi-blind man without it."[62] With human adjustment of the data, similar material online allowed for far more analysis. Scholars used the ESTC to explore questions of book history which catalogues had never been designed to answer, such as the growth of regional printing, the output of printers by the number of sheets, the part reprints played in publishing, the role of women in the book trade, free print distribution, or even the use of the colour red in printing.[63]

The relationship between research and library catalogues was symbiotic. In the above examples, the provision of routinely provided information facilitated research. In other ways, catalogues struggled to keep up with developments in book history as notions of what was of interest broadened. From the early 1980s, book history expanded beyond early printing, fine bindings as art works and the book ownership and reading of intellectual giants like Coleridge or Voltaire.[64] Preoccupation with book ownership and reading widened to encompass women, children, members of particular social classes, and to anonymous owners whose markings indicated what poetic passages most appealed to early audiences, or highlighted polemical arguments.[65] Fascination with bindings extended to plain bindings for their reflection on the social status of owners and owners' opinions of their books.[66] The development of the main standard of descriptive cataloguing rules for early printed books reveals libraries' attempt to keep up. While the *Bibliographic Description of Rare Books* (1981) ignored provenance and binding, a decade later, its successor acknowledged them briefly: "Make notes on any special features or imperfections of the copy being described when they are considered important …. Features that may be brought out here include rubrication, illumination and other hand coloring, manuscript additions, binding and binder, provenance (persons, institutions, bookplates), imperfections and anomalies, and copy number."[67] The third edition did much more, providing two paragraphs about provenance, with examples, and seven instructions about bindings.[68] We see in practice how library catalogues endeavoured to satisfy research in a survey of documents recording provenance, including library catalogues, in David Pearson's *Provenance Research in Book History* (1994): this overview comprised fifty-six pages in the first edition (1994), and seventy-nine pages in the second edition, published quarter of a century later.[69] In the printed sphere, Lotte Hellinga demonstrated the change sharply when introducing the final volume of the catalogue of incunabula in the British Library, declaring the volume's aim to record all annotations, as opposed to practice laid out in the first volume, published a century earlier, of naming former owners selectively.[70]

In some ways, increased detail in catalogues could not meet spiralling demand.[71] The record of an inscription by Alice Malory in 1634 in a copy of *The Recuile of the Histories of Troie* from 1553 tells us that a particular woman owned a second-hand copy of a folio translation into English of a particular popular courtly romance. From there, it is possible to see what else Alice Malory owned, and if enough cataloguers have recorded provenance, it is possible to establish what other women owned the same book. However, even when full provenance information has been provided, technology allows no easy method exists to move from the particular to the general; to generate a list of romances or other books owned by seventeenth-century women from the records of specific books owned by specific women. Researchers must work their own way up from the specific to the general.[72]

Another sea change in the perception of information occurred with the introduction of Resource Description and Access (RDA) for descriptive cataloguing in 2010. While the Anglo-American Cataloguing Rules had made provision for non-print material, RDA actively embraced the multi-formatted nature of information (especially electronic). Its objectives were, like those of classification systems, responsiveness to user needs, cost efficiency, flexibility and continuity.[73] Designed in and for a web environment, its general rules were intended to be applicable for new formats that could arise in the future.[74] Whereas previous rules had been practical and had had a national emphasis, RDA was based on a theoretical framework and was intended to be relevant in an international environment. Just as classification schemes tried to redress cultural biases, so did RDA. Headings for biblical books lost the division by Testament (for example, "Bible. O.T. Psalms" became "Bible. Psalms"), not merely as a concession to decreasing biblical knowledge in a post-Christian world, but to aim for consistent treatment of all sacred scriptures.[75] Some amendments reflected a change in mentality from educating the public to understand library catalogues, to catering to the lowest common denominator of perceived existing user knowledge; from expanding mental horizons, to contraction. RDA avoided square brackets, so that a formula "[4], 100 p." became "4 unnumbered pages, 100 pages." It expanded most standard abbreviations and it eschewed Latin as largely not understood: "sic" and "i.e." as well as bibliographical abbreviations such as "s.n." (replaced by "publisher not identified"). Although the aim was to facilitate access, the substitution of words for symbols and of English words for Latin ones militated against international comprehension, in the balancing of competing claims.

Conclusion

The means to make printed information accessible to library users both physically and intellectually has changed greatly since the information explosion of the mid-nineteenth century. Classification and cataloguing inevitably reflect broader context: —libraries do not exist within a vacuum, and—they have developed to keep pace with society and with such major trends as globalisation and inclusivity. Throughout the modern period, classification and cataloguing have sought to connect people with knowledge—although arguably in so doing, information has been obfuscated as well as provided.

The question of why libraries made the decisions they did yields disappointing answers. Libraries changed as innovations made change possible, for example, as catalogues moved from printed volumes to catalogue cards to computers. These storehouses of information adapted to the world around them as it demanded more expansive world views and as new areas of research developed; reaction was essential for continuing relevance. They consistently followed; they did not lead. Those who enabled libraries to anticipate change, like Ranganathan and the creators of the second edition of the Bliss Bibliographic Classification, remained lone prophets, because their methods lacked mass backing and so were not cost-effective. The order and description of information has always been, and continues to be, imperfect. Personalities and individual strong opinions have played a role, subjectivity frequently rife, and pragmatism has often triumphed over intellectual excellence. Yet these tools remain an important, if imperfect, handle to understand, and make sense of, the vast collections of information throughout the libraries of the world.

Notes

1 The classic English work on the printing revolution is Elizabeth L. Eisenstein, *The Printing Press as an Agent of Change: Communications and Cultural Transformations in Early-Modern Europe* (Cambridge, UK: Cambridge University Press, 1979). Note also advances in a prior desire to control information through scientific classification and taxonomy in the Enlightenment: Roger L. Williams, "Prologue," in *Botanophilia in Eighteenth-Century France: The Spirit of the Enlightenment*, ed. Roger R. Williams (Dordecht: Springer Netherlands, 2001), 1–8.

2 David McKitterick, "Introduction," in *The Cambridge History of the Book in Britain, vol. 6: 1830–1914*, ed. David McKitterick (Cambridge, UK: Cambridge University Press, 2009), 1–74.

3 Author's definition. Scholarly definitions of both "information" and "knowledge" are manifold: see, for example, Toni Weller, "Historians and the Information Turn in History," in *Writing Computer and Information History: Approaches, Reflections, and Connections*, ed. William Aspray (Lanham, MD: Rowman & Littlefield, 2024), 3–26; James W. Cortada, "A Seven Forces Model View of Contemporary Information," *Library & Information History* 39 (2023): 170–204; Peter Burke, *What Is the History of Knowledge?* (Cambridge, UK: Polity, 2016); Aileen Oeberst, Joachim Kimmerle and Ulrike Cress, "What Is Knowledge? Who Creates It? Who Possesses It? The Need for Novel Answers to Old Questions," in *Mass Collaboration and Education*, ed. Ulrike Cress, Johannes Moskalium, and Heisawn Jeong (Cham: Springer, 2016), 105–124; Toni Weller, "An Information History Decade: A Review of the Literature and Concepts, 2000–2009," *Library and Information History* 26 (2010): 83–97.

4 Thomas James, *The First Printed Catalogue of the Bodleian Library 1605: A Facsimile* (Oxford: Clarendon Press, 1986), ix.

5 Philip R. Harris, "British Library," in *International Dictionary of Library Histories*, ed. David H. Stam (London: Fitzroy Dearborn, 2001), 228; Fred Lerner, *The Story of Libraries: From the Invention of Writing to the Computer Age* (New York: Continuum, 2009), 107.

6 America is thought to have introduced open access at Pawtucket Library, Rhode Island, in 1889. England introduced it at Clerkenwell Library, London, in 1894. See Alistair Black, Simon Pepper and Kaye Bagshaw, eds. *Books, Buildings and Social Engineering: Early Public Libraries in Britain from Past to Present* (Farnham: Ashgate, 2009), 211–214.

7 For pre-19th-century classification generally, see Marjorie M. K. Hlava, *The Taxobook: History, Theories and Concepts* (San Rafael, CA: Morgan & Claypool, 2014). Good overviews of Linnaeus and of Diderot, respectively, can be found in Gunnar Broberg, *The Man Who Organized Nature: The Life of Linnaeus*, trans. by Anna Paterson (Princeton, NJ: Princeton University Press, 2023); Martine Groult, *Savoir et Matières: Pensée Scientifique et Théorie de la Connaissance de l'Encyclopédie à l'Encyclopédie Méthodique* (Paris: CNRS, 2019).

8 Melvil Dewey, *A Classification and Subject Index for Cataloguing and Arranging the Books and Pamphlets of a Library* (Amherst, MA: M. Dewey, 1876). The fullest discussion of this scheme is M. P. Satija and Alex Kyrios, *A Handbook of History, Theory and Practice of the Dewey Decimal Classification Scheme* (London: Facet, 2023). For a biography of Dewey, see Wayne A. Wiegand, *Irrepressible Reformer: A Biography of Melvil Dewey* (Chicago, IL; London: American Library Association, 1996); this says very little about classification.
9 Library of Congress Subject Cataloging Division, *Classification: Outline Scheme of Classes* (Washington, DC: United States Government Printing Office, 1904); *Manuel du Répertoire Bibliographique Universel* (Brussels: Institut International de Bibliographie, 1905); S. R. Ranganathan, *Colon Classification* (Madras: Madras Library Association, 1933); Henry Evelyn Bliss, *A System of Bibliographic Classification* (New York: H. J. Wilson, 1935).
10 Charles A. Cutter, *Expansive Classification* (Boston, MA: C. A. Cutter, 1891–1893); James Duff Brown, *Subject Classification: With Tables, Indexes etc. for the Sub-Division of Subjects* (London: Library Supply Co., 1906). Classic textbooks on classification are W. C. Berwick Sayers, *A Manual of Classification for Librarians and Bibliographers* (London: Grafton, 1926 and later editions); A.C. Foskett, *The Subject Approach to Information* (London: Bingley, 1969 and later editions). Excellent modern textbooks are Vanda Broughton, *Essential Classification*, 2nd ed. (London: Facet, 2015); Rita Marcella and Robert Newton, *A New Manual of Classification* (Aldershot: Gower, 1994).
11 Kenneth Garside, "The Basic Principles of the New Library Classification at University College, London," *Journal of Documentation* 10, no. 4 (1954): 169–192.
12 Brown, *Subject Classification*, 7–8.
13 Thomas J. McCormack, "The International Scientific Catalogue, and the Decimal System of Classification," *The Monist* 7, no. 2 (January 1897): 300.
14 Amos William Brazier, *Libraries and Librarianship* (Melbourne: The Author, 1912), para. 13.
15 Broughton, *Essential Classification*, 202.
16 Brown, *Subject Classification*, 12.
17 Brown, *Subject Classification*, 11.
18 See especially W. C. Berwick Sayers, *A Manual of Classification for Librarians*, 4th ed., rev. Arthur Maltby (London: André Deutsch, 1967), 168–170. A more recent discussion of the Subject Classification appears in J. H. Bowman, "Classification in British Public Libraries: A Historical Perspective," *Library History* 21 (2005): 155–159.
19 See Arthur Maltby and Lindy Gill, *The Case for Bliss: Modern Classification Practice and Principles in the Context of the Bibliographical Classification* (London: Clive Bingley, 1979).
20 Maltby and Gill, *Case for Bliss*, 16–20.
21 Archer Taylor, *Book Catalogues: Their Varieties and Uses*, 2nd ed., rev. by William P. Barlow, St Paul's Bibliographies, 16 (London: St Paul's Bibliographies, 1986), 153.
22 For Dewey's consultation of Faculty at Amherst, see Wiegand, *Irrepressible Reformer*, 229.
23 R. K. Olding, ed., *Readings in Library Cataloguing* (London: Crosby Lockwood, 1966), 105–106.
24 Francis Miska, *The Development of Classification at the Library of Congress*, University of Illinois Graduate School of Library and Information Science Occasional Papers, 164 (Chicago, IL: University of Illinois, 1984), 61.
25 See Alex Wright, *Cataloguing the World: Paul Otlet and the Birth of the Information Age* (Oxford: Oxford University Press, 2014); Broughton, *Essential Classification*, 241–248.
26 The longest discussion of Ranganathan and the Colon Classification is M. P. Sattija, *Library Classification and S. R. Ranganathan: A Guide*, ed. Daniel Martínez-Ávila and Rosa San Segunda Manuel (New Delhi: Ess Ess, 2018). See 18–19 for Ranganathan's inspiration by a Meccano set.
27 J. Mills and Vanda Broughton, *Bliss Bibliographic Classification: Introduction and Auxiliary Schedules*, 2nd ed. (London: Butterworth, 1977).
28 For summary of laudatory opinions, see K. E. Attar, "The Practice of Bliss," *Cataloging & Classification Quarterly* 34 (2002): 48.
29 Brown's table of example of places enumerates Edinburghshire, Edinburgh City, Leith, Musselburgh, Dalkeith and so forth; see Brown, *Subject Classification*, 36–37.
30 Broughton, *Essential Classification*, 242.
31 Satija and Kyrios, *Handbook*, 9–10.
32 Library of Congress Catalog Division, *Subject Headings Used in the Dictionary Catalogues of the Library of Congress* (Washington, DC: G.P.O., Library Branch, 1910, 1914–1966).

33 See, for example, Broughton, *Essential Classification*, 115. For recent articles about changes to specific sensitive headings, see Karl Pettitt and Erin Elzi, "Unsettling the Library Catalog: A Case Study in Reducing the Presence of 'Indians of North America' and Similar Subject Headings," *Library Resources & Technical Services* 67 (2023): 4–12; Heather M. Campbell et al., "Improving Subject Headings for Iowa Indigenous Peoples," *Library Resources & Technical Services* 66 (2022): 48–59; Laura M. Hartwell, "On the Linguistic Argument for the Adoption of the Library Subject Heading *Noncitizen*," *International Journal of Legal Information* 50 (2022): 37–42 (specifically about "illegal aliens"); Sara A. Howard and Steven A. Knowlton, "Browsing through Bias: The Library of Congress Classification and Subject Headings for African American Studies and LGBTQIA Studies," *Library Trends* 67 (2018): 74–88.
34 Arthur Maltby and Rita Marcella, "Organizing Knowledge: The Need for System and Unity," in *The Future of Classification*, ed. Rita Marcella and Arthur Maltby (Aldershot: Gower, 2000), 23.
35 Miska, *Development*, 51, 63.
36 Library of Congress, "Library of Congress Classification" (2014). https://www.loc.gov/catdir/cpso/lcc.html.
37 For these figures and the most detailed history of Dewey Decimal Classification, see Satija and Kyrios, *Handbook*.
38 A. C. Foskett, "The Future of Faceted Classification," in Marcella and Maltby, *Future of Classification*, 73.
39 For example, chemistry on the sixteenth edition; psychology in the seventeenth; sociology in the nineteenth. See Satija and Kyrios, *Handbook*, 6–7.
40 Miska, *Development*, 19. The major book about Library of Congress Classification is Lois Mai Chan, Sheila S. Intner, and Jean Weihs, *Guide to the Library of Congress Classification*, 6th ed. (Santa Barbara, CA: Libraries Unlimited, 2016).
41 P. R. Harris, *A History of the British Museum Library, 1753–1973* (London: British Library, 1998), 121; A. H. Chaplin, *GK: 150 Years of the General Catalogue of Printed Books in the British Museum* (Aldershot: Scolar, 1987), 10–11.
42 For hostility towards Panizzi, see Sir Harris Nicolas, *Animadversions on the Library and Catalogue of the British Museum: A Reply to Mr Panizzi's Statement and a Correspondence with that Officer and the Trustees* (London: R. Bentley, 1846), 7; and especially Edward Miller, *Prince of Librarians: The Life and Times of Antonio Panizzi of the British Museum* (London: André Deutsch, 1967; repr. London: British Library, 1988).
43 J. J. Hall, "The Guard-Book Catalogue of Cambridge University Library," *Library History* 13 (1997), 53.
44 Dorothy May Norris, *A History of Cataloguing and Cataloguing Methods 1100–1850, With an Introductory Survey of Ancient Times* (London: Grafton, 1939), 205; see also discussion of the Select Commission of 1847–1850 in David McKitterick, *Readers in a Revolution* (Cambridge, UK: Cambridge University Press, 2022), 80–87.
45 Norris, *History of Cataloguing*, 204–205.
46 H. W. Chandler, *Some Observations on the Bodleian Classed Catalogue* (Oxford: Blackwell, 1888), 5; cited in Norris, *History of Cataloguing*, 157–158.
47 British Museum, *Rules for Compiling the Catalogues in the Department of Printed Books in the British Museum* (London: British Museum, 1900). See Norris, *History of Cataloguing*, 207; Chaplin, *150 Years*, 15.
48 Charles A. Cutter, *Rules for a Dictionary Catalog*, 4th ed. (Washington, DC: Government Printing Office, 1904; repr. London: Library Association, 1962), 259.
49 Library Association, *Cataloguing Rules of the Library Association of the United Kingdom: Reprinted with Corrections for the Use of the Meeting at Cambridge, 1882* (London: Library Association, 1882); *Compendious Cataloguing Rules for the Author-Catalogue of the Bodleian Library* (Oxford: Bodleian Library, 1882). For the dates of Cambridge catalogues, see Hall, "Guard-Book Catalogue," 47; the earliest easily available edition is Cambridge University Library, *Rules for the Catalogues of Printed Books, Maps & Music* (Cambridge, UK: University Press, 1927).
50 On the history of index cards, see Markus Krajewski, *Paper Machines: About Cards and Catalogs, 1548–1929* (Cambridge, MA: MIT Press, 2011).
51 Committees of the Library Association and the American Library Association, *Cataloguing Rules: Authors and Title Entries*, English ed. (London: Library Association, 1963), rules 136–168; see especially "Notes," rule 168.

52 J. D. Cowley, *Bibliographical Description and Cataloguing* (London: Grafton, 1949), 142.
53 For a particularly detailed description of the need to peruse books systematically for annotations unrecorded in catalogue records, see Andrew M. Stauffer, *Book Traces: Nineteenth-Century Readers and the Future of the Library* (Philadelphia, PA: University of Pennsylvania Press, 2021), especially 3–9. Mediation of information applies not only to description of material in cultural repositories of all kinds, but on decisions about what to collect, preserve, digitise and index.
54 Peter Fox, "CURL: Past, Present and Future," *New Review of Academic Librarianship* 5 (1999): 115; Jisc, *Library Hub Discover* (2023). https://discover.libraryhub.jisc.ac.uk. America formed OCLC in 1967, which hosts the union catalogue WorldCat.
55 A. W. Pollard and G. R. Redgrave, *A Short-Title Catalogue of Books Printed in England Scotland & Ireland and of English Books Printed Abroad 1475–1640* (London: Bibliographical Society, 1926).
56 Horst Nickel, "Literature, Kunst und Wissenschaft in den Inkunabeln: 100 Jahre Gesamtkatalog der Wiegendrucke," *Gutenberg-Jahrbuch* 81 (2006): 14.
57 G. Thomas Tanselle, "A Brief History of the English Short-Title Catalogue in North America," in *The English Short-Title Catalogue: Past, Present, Future*, ed. Henry L. Snyder and Michael S. Smith, AMS Studies in the Eighteenth Century 42 (New York: AMS Press, 2003), 3–12.
58 Lotte Hellinga, "Introduction," in *Bibliography and the Study of 15th-Century Civilisation*, British Library Occasional Papers 5 (London: British Library, 1987), 3–4. The database itself is available at British Library, *Incunabula Short Title Catalogue (ISTC)*. https://data.cerl.org/istc/_search.
59 Consortium of European Research Libraries, *Heritage of the Printed Book Database* (2018). https://www.cerl.org/resources/hpb/main. Quotation from: Michael Smethurst, "The ESTC in Practice: A European Perspective," in Snyder and Smith, *The English Short-Title Catalogue*, 99.
60 Universal Short Title Catalogue. https://www.ustc.ac.uk.
61 Copac Collection Management Tools Project in the United Kingdom and GreenGlass in the United States: see Michael Emly, "Informed Decisions: The Copac Collection Management Tools Project" (2012), available at https://blog.ccm.copac.jisc.ac.uk/wp-content/uploads/sites/13/2012/01/Informed-decisions.pdf; OCLC, "Greenglass" (2022). https://help.oclc.org/Library_Management/GreenGlass.
62 H. S. Bennett, *English Books and Readers*, 3, vols. 2nd ed. (Cambridge, UK: Cambridge University Press, 1969–1970), vol. 1, vii.
63 Hugh Amory, "Pseudodoxia Bibliographica, or When is a Book Not a Book? When It's a Record," in *The Scholar and the Database: Papers Presented on November 4, 1999 at the CERL Conference Hosted by the Royal Library Brussels*, ed. Lotte Hellinga, CERL Papers, 2 (London: CERL, 2001), 4–8; David L. Vander Meulen, "The ESTC in Practice: A Bibliographer's Perspective," in Snyder and Smith, *The English Short-Title Catalogue*, 68–71; Michael F. Suarez, "Towards a Bibliometric Analysis of the Surviving Record, 1701–1800," in *The Cambridge History of the Book in Britain*, vol. 5: 1695–1830, ed. Michael F. Suarez and Michael L. Turner (Cambridge, UK: Cambridge University Press, 2009), 39–42.
64 See, for example, James Raven, *What Is the History of the Book?* (Cambridge, UK: Polity Press, 2018), 115; David Finkelstein and Alistair McCleery, *An Introduction to Book History* (Abingdon: Routledge, 2005), 13, 100–117. Seminal contributions to the area are D. F. McKenzie, *Bibliography and the Sociology of Texts* (Cambridge, UK: Cambridge University Press, 1999) and Robert Darnton, "What is the History of Books?" *Daedalus* 111, no. 3 (1982): 65–83.
65 The standard text on marginalia is H. J. Jackson, *Marginalia: Readers Writing in Books* (New Haven, CT; London: Yale University Press, 2001), while an ongoing database about all sorts of readers is *UK RED: The Reading Experience Database*, https://www.open.ac.uk/Arts/Reading/UK; described in Mary Hammond, "'The Reading Experience Database 1450–1945," in *Owners, Annotators and the Signs of Reading*, ed. Robin Myers, Michael Harris and Giles Mandelbrote (New Castle, DE: Oak Knoll; London: British Library, 2005), 175–187. See, for example, Jonathan Rose, ed. *The Edinburgh History of Reading: Common Readers* (Edinburgh: Edinburgh University Press, 2020); M. O. Grenby, *The Child Reader, 1700–1840* (Cambridge, UK: Cambridge University Press, 2011); Heidi Brayman Hackel and Catherine E. Kelly, eds. *Reading Women: Literacy, Authorship and Culture in the Atlantic World, 1500–1800* (Philadelphia, PA: University of Pennsylvania Press, 2008) for reading by particular categories of readers. See Emma Smith,

Shakespeare's First Folio: Four Centuries of an Iconic Book (Oxford: Oxford University Press, 2016) for all sorts of readers reading a particular book.

66 See Mirjam Foot, *The History of Bookbinding as a Mirror of Society* (London: British Library, 1998).
67 Library of Congress, *Bibliographic Description of Rare Books: Rules Formulated under AACR2 and ISBD(A) for the Descriptive Cataloging of Rare Books and Other Special Printed Materials* (Washington, DC: Library of Congress, 1981); Association of College and Research Libraries Rare Books and Manuscripts Section and the Library of Congress, *Descriptive Cataloging of Rare Books* (Washington, DC: Cataloging Distribution Service, Library of Congress, 1991), Rule 7C.18.
68 Association of College and Research Libraries Rare Books and Manuscripts Section and the Library of Congress, *Descriptive Cataloging of Rare Materials (Books)* (Washington, DC: Cataloging Distribution Service, Library of Congress, 2007), Rules 7B19.2 (Provenance) and 7B19.3.1-7 (Bindings).
69 David Pearson, *Provenance Research in Book History: A Handbook*, rev. ed. (Oxford: Bodleian Library, 2019), 247–325; David Pearson, *Provenance Research in Book History: A Handbook* (London: British Library, 1994; repr. 1998), 186–241.
70 *Catalogue of Books Printed in the XVth Century Now in the British Library. BMC pt. 11: England*, ed. Lotte Hellinga ('t Goy-Houten: HES & De Graaf, 2007), 3.
71 See Sarah Lindenbaum, "Hiding in Plain Sight: How Electronic Records Can Lead Us to Early Modern Women Readers," in *Women's Bookscapes in Early Modern Britain: Reading, Ownership, Circulation*, ed. Leah Knight, Micheline White and Elizabeth Sauer (Ann Arbor, MI: University of Michigan Press, 2018): 193–213, 194, 204–210.
72 Cf. searches based on formulaic phraseology: studies of female publishers could be conducted by searching for such terms as "widow of" in various languages in imprints.
73 Chris Oliver, *Introducing RDA: A Guide to the Basics* (London: Facet, 2010), 92.
74 Anne Welsh and Sue Batley, *Practical Cataloguing: AAR, RDA and MARC21* (London: Facet, 2012), 19.
75 Oliver, *Introducing RDA*, 95.

22
THE HISTORY OF COMPUTING
The Development of an Information History Field

William Aspray

The history of computing, when seen as a subfield of information history, is comparable to other subfields such as archival history, library history, book and publishing history, journalism and media history, the history of information management or knowledge management, the history of cybernetics, or the history of information science.[1] There is no ready term that is sufficiently encompassing to describe this subfield. To call it the "history of computing"—the most commonly used phrase—is to give emphasis to the process of calculation. To call it "computer history" is to emphasise the study of the machines that drive these computations. To call it the "history of computer science" is to emphasise the academic study of the organisation, design, and use of these machines. All these topics are elements of this subfield, but none of them denotes it completely. None of these terms point, for example, to the study of the companies that design, manufacture, sell, and maintain the computing machines. Nor do these terms adequately attend to the universality of the computer not only as a stand-alone machine but as a critical element built into our business, manufacturing, communication, and entertainment systems. As historian Michael Mahoney observed, there is not a single history of computing, but instead multiple histories.[2]

This chapter presents an overview of the history of computing by examining its institutionalisation since the 1970s, its various lines of scholarship and how they have changed over time, the relations of history of computing to other historical subfields, exogenous factors that affect the history of computing, and the fact that the history of computing is an emerging discipline with less maturity than some established historical and social science academic disciplines. The multiplicity of uses of the computer places it squarely in the story of the history of information, for example, as part of the studies of surveillance, privacy, information economy, and information age. However, it is beyond the scope of this chapter to explore these various connections between the computer and information history; the focus here is, instead, directly on understanding the history of computing.

The Institutionalisation of the History of Computing

The history of computing began to be studied in the late 1970s.[3] Many of the earliest practitioners, such as John A. N. Lee, Bernard Galler, and Brian Randell were computer scientists.

However, a few established historians of science, such as Bernard Cohen at Harvard and Michael Mahoney at Princeton, took a serious interest and helped make this a legitimate topic for study by historians of science and technology. In the late 1970s and early 1980s, the first few doctorates were awarded—to Martin Campbell-Kelly, Nancy Stern, William Aspray, and Paul Ceruzzi—for dissertations written on computing history.[4]

The American Federation of Information Processing Societies (AFIPS) had a significant role in the early institutionalisation of computing history by subsidising the main journal in the field, *Annals of the History of Computing*, started in 1979, and by holding Pioneer Days events at the annual AFIPS Conference featuring presentations by leading early figures from computing. *Annals* was led from 1979 until 2007 by technically trained academics—computer scientists, information management scholars, and operations research scientists (Bernard Galler, J. A. N. Lee, Michael Williams, Timothy Bergin, and David Grier)—while the next four editors-in-chief were trained as historians (Jeffrey Yost, Lars Heide, Nathan Ensmenger, and Gerardo Con Diaz). When computer professionals began to attend specialty rather than general-purpose conferences, AFIPS's revenue stream dried up and the organisation went out of business in 1990. In more recent years, the computing professional societies have once again taken a significant role in the institutionalisation of the history of computing, with the IEEE Computer Society assuming the sponsorship of *Annals*, ACM organising an active history committee working closely with the Babbage Institute, and SIAM sponsoring systematic oral history and historical writing projects.

AFIPS's demise created a short-term crisis for people interested in the history of computing, but it gave space for the historians of computing to begin to forge their own institutions. The leading book series was begun in 1981, by MIT Press—edited for four decades by three historians: I. Bernard Cohen, William Aspray, and Thomas Misa. While some specialty workshops and conferences on computing history were organised in the 1980s and 1990s by the Charles Babbage Institute and the IEEE History Center in the United States, and by the Deutsches Museum and the Heinz Nixdorf Museum in Germany, the main gathering place of computer historians was the Society for the History of Technology (SHOT), which formed a special interest group in the history of information, computing, and society (SIGCIS) in 1987.[5] During its first five years, the special interest group was a limited affair, with perhaps thirty people meeting around a few lunch tables at the SHOT annual meeting and reporting what each person was working on. When Paul Ceruzzi took over in 1993, he created a listserv and more recently Thomas Haigh and Andrew Russell built up SIGCIS, with an international membership growing into the hundreds, a successful add on-day of talks to the SHOT annual meeting that became a regular event, and new awards for scholarship.[6] Eventually, the historians of computing became the largest special interest group in SHOT.

Museums played an important role in the institutionalisation of the history of computing. Three major national museums, the Deutsches Museum, the Science Museum in London, and the Smithsonian had longstanding interest in computer history. They had collected artefacts and presented permanent exhibits by the 1960s, and each had professional staff members who cared for these computing artefacts and mounted exhibits. By the 1980s, it was becoming increasingly clear that the permanent exhibits needed refreshing; and the museums especially needed to find some way to tell the story of software, which did not have particularly interesting artefacts to display.[7] Each of these museums eventually opened new exhibits. The Smithsonian's *Information Age* exhibit (on display from 1990 to 2006) tracked the parallel histories of computation and communication through the Second

World War and then followed a single, combined path in the postwar years. The centrepiece of the Science Museum of London's new computing exhibition, led by Doron Swade, was a working model of Charles Babbage's difference engine, designed in the 1820s but never built by Babbage and only completed by the museum in 1991.[8] The Deutsches Museum opened a major new exhibit at about the same time, notably exhibiting examples from its superb collection of early mathematical and calculating devices as well as the pioneering computing machines of Konrad Zuse.[9]

The Smithsonian's major computer exhibit was displayed at its National Museum of American History, with intellectual leadership provided over the years by Uta Merzbach, David Allison, and Peggy Kidwell. The Smithsonian held the first major oral history collection on computer history, jointly organised with AFIPS between 1969 and 1977.[10] The Smithsonian also organised major computer history activities (scholarship, exhibits, and artefact collecting) at its National Air and Space Museum—driven for many years by the curator Paul Ceruzzi. Notable was the exhibit *Beyond the Limits: Flight Enters the Computing Age*, opened in 1989.[11]

Two start-up museums also became major forces in the history of computing. One was the Heinz Nixdorf Museum, located in the mid-sized German city of Paderborn.[12] A founding goal was to preserve the history of the computing firm Nixdorf and its founder Heinz Nixdorf, but the museum also aimed to tell the story of the history of computation from antiquity to the present. Especially in the museum's early years, during Ulf Hashagen's term as a principal curator, the museum maintained an active research and research conference programme, regularly bringing together international groups of historians. In more recent years, the museum's science discovery mission has predominated while not entirely eliminating its historical activities.

The other major start-up museum was the Computer History Museum.[13] It was started by the well-known computer scientist Gordon Bell and his geographer and design scholar wife Gwen. First located in the Boston suburbs in 1975, on the campus of Digital Equipment Corporation, it moved in 1984 to Museum Wharf in central Boston where a science discovery mission prevailed. But in the late 1990s it moved again—this time to California. There, it quickly became an important cultural institution within Silicon Valley, with many people visiting its exhibits and attending its public lecture series. The museum's mission resonated with the wealthy technical community in Silicon Valley, and the museum grew much more rapidly than all other institutions devoted to computer history. It first built up a strong collection of machines and devices, and later added important collections of paper records and oral histories. In the early years, the museum focused on building its exhibits and was not as open to use of its collections by outside scholars as the historical community would have liked. In more recent times, the museum has had a closer relationship with the historians.

The Charles Babbage Institute was another major player.[14] Founded in California by computer entrepreneur Erwin Tomash and colleagues in 1978, it moved to the University of Minnesota two years later. It has been the institution most closely tied to the needs of the historical research community. The staff, led in its early years by Arthur Norberg and later by Robert Seidel, Thomas Misa, and Jeffrey Yost, established a major archival collection of paper records and oral histories (but not artefacts), carried out an extensive historical research programme, and participated actively in the national and international life of the history of computing community. Its fellowship programme, running continuously since 1978, has supported the training of many of the leading scholars in the field.[15]

In addition to formal institutions such as the Babbage Institute and the various museums mentioned above, a few individuals have played singular roles in organising the study of the history of computing for individual countries: Brian Randell and Martin Campbell-Kelly in Britain, Gerard Alberts in the Netherlands, and Pierre Mounier-Kuhn in France are good examples. Not only has Mounier-Kuhn, for example, published extensively on the history of computing, he has also organised numerous international conferences and exhibits across France to explore computer history.[16] It is these countries, together with Germany, the Nordic states, and the United States that have had the greatest scholarly activity in the computing history field.

The Scholarship in the History of Computing

The scholarship of the 1970s and 1980s was concentrated mainly on the creation myth stories.[17] Studies typically concerned projects to create one-of-a-kind, large, digital electronic devices during the Second World War and in the Cold War years, used primarily by the military to calculate ballistics firing tables, decode encryptions, and build atomic weapons. These studies focused mostly on the internal developments of the technology—not on the actual uses of the machines or the external issues such as funding or the training of personnel to build, maintain, and use these devices. There was also some scholarship examining links between the creation of the computer and calculating technologies of the 1920s and 1930s.[18]

Detailed, archival-driven historical studies of important topics in nineteenth- and early twentieth-century computing history—for example, of desk calculating machines, punched card tabulating systems, and analogue computing devices—appeared only a decade later, once computer historians began to be interested in the business history of computing and the origins of the computer industry in the business machines and electronics industries.[19] Another topic from pre-1940 computing that has received considerable attention has been the contributions of Charles Babbage and Augusta Ada. [20] Biographies of pioneering individuals such as Alan Turing, Howard Aiken, Vannevar Bush, John von Neumann, and Grace Hopper were also part of the early study of computing history; biography provided a convenient way to chart a path through largely unknown territories.[21]

The writings of James Beniger, Alfred Chandler, and JoAnne Yates were influential in opening the study of the business history of computing; and they were joined by other scholars, including Martin Campbell-Kelly, Steven Usselman, Shane Greenstein, James Cortada, and Jeffrey Yost. The earliest studies were of firm strategy and market structure of the mainframe industry[22]; and, especially through the work of Cortada, were extended back in time to examine the business origins of the computer industry before 1940 and forward in time to examine the diffusion of this technology around the world.[23] IBM, as a dominant player in the computing field, has received strong attention to both its technical and business histories.[24]

The study of later (post-1950s) developments of computing technologies has loosely tracked the advancements in technology and industry themselves, commonly with two decades of lag. Studies of computers—both large mainframe devices and later minicomputers—focused as much on the place of these machines in the offerings of the various computer manufacturers (and on the strategy of firms and structure of the industry) as on the advancements in the technologies themselves. The one major exception to this trend was the study of miniaturisation that came from the infusion of transistors and semiconductor devices into computers, which made possible the creation of both minicomputers and supercomputers. This interest in semiconductors led to connections with both established and young scholars studying the history of electronics, such as Bernard Finn, Frederik Nebeker, Christophe Lecuyer, and Ross Bassett.[25]

Historians have more successfully studied hardware systems and their physical components than the software that runs on them. Although Michael Mahoney, Martin Campbell-Kelly, Tim Bergin, and a few others have studied the histories of programming, software applications, and operating systems, these topics continue to be stubbornly difficult.[26] In more recent years, software has received examination through a philosophical lens from the conferences organised by the Commission for the History and Philosophy of Computing.[27]

The focus of computing history has been more about technology than science. Even today, after almost a half-century of scholarship, there has been no major overarching study published about the development of computer science, and many topics within this area have not been considered by historians. Thomas Haigh has made some initial inroads into the study of databases and numerical analysis; Michael Mahoney studied software and theoretical computer science; and a few other scholars such as Ulf Hashagen, Helena Durnova, Gerard Alberts, Giuseppe Primero, and Liesbeth DeMol have explored relations between the history of mathematics and the history of computing. Despite the great interest in artificial intelligence today, the historical literature on that topic is thin.[28] Some of the studies of computer science build upon the study of the history of mathematics, which is better established in Europe and Canada than in the United States.

One way to understand the evolution in the historical study of computing is to appreciate the ways in which the universality of the computer has amplified the types of usage of the computer. At first, the computer was a calculating machine. Then it served as a business machine used for collecting, organising, and presenting data for business purposes. Later, it was a personal communication and entertainment device. Each of these uses of the computer supplemented rather than supplanted the previous uses. So, the current understanding of computer history, notably as told by Thomas Haigh and Paul Ceruzzi in their recent "master narrative" of computer history, retells the story of the computer many times over: as scientific supertool, data processing device, real-time control system, interactive tool, communications platform, personal plaything, office equipment, graphical tool, universal media device, publishing platform, and network.[29]

A few studies examine the embedding of the computer into other industries, notably including JoAnne Yates's work on the insurance industry, Jon Agar's study of British government bureaucracy, Thomas Misa and Jeffrey Yost's study on use in American government operations, and James Cortada's multi-volume study across many different industries. Thomas Haigh has done important work trying to reconceptualise the story of the 1950s by de-centring the role of the computer and giving more attention to electronics, systems building, and digitisation.[30] But there is still much to be done about the computerisation of society more generally.

The most influential technological changes stimulating a re-setting of the research agenda for computing history were the creation of the microcomputer and the internet. Early studies of these topics examined them from a technology or business perspective,[31] but once these technological innovations became established and spread, a new focus came into historical research about the use by and impact on individuals of these technologies.[32] No longer was the historical scholarship primarily about government or business institutions. Also, the types of uses of these technologies studied changed—to technologies as communication devices, entertainment devices, creativity and self-expression devices, and retail platforms.

Especially stimulated by the phenomenal rise of Silicon Valley, historians of computing have studied regional technological development. There are now strong case studies of California, Minnesota, Boston, and suburban Washington, DC. These range from heroic stories of garage inventors, to profiles of individual companies, to examinations of regional clusters of workers and companies.[33]

The story of the history of the computer as it has been generally told is a male-dominated story. There have been efforts to broaden this story to include pioneering women and provide female role models. These include the stories of Ada Lovelace and Grace Hopper, the women "computers" who carried out scientific calculations on desk calculating machines from the 1920s through the 1940s, and the women working as coders at Bletchley Park and on ENIAC.[34] There is still much to be done in reconceptualising the history of computing with respect to gender, and there has hardly been any historical discussion of race (or intersectionality) and computing, the most notable book being *Hidden Figures*.[35]

The greatest geographical coverage in the history of computing has been on developments in western Europe and the United States. However, there is a growing literature about other parts of the world, especially Japan, Australia, Chile, Canada, India, and northern Europe.[36]

The availability of these new technologies to almost everyone in wealthy societies and selected groups in other societies opened up new threats of harm to individuals, which are now being explored by historians: harms to privacy, risk of loss of control of self-identity, massive spread of misinformation, inequitable access to resources based on race or gender or wealth, ease of access to vices such as pornography and gambling, unrestricted opportunities for excessive material acquisition, and opportunities for enhanced bullying. However, the access to these technologies also enabled individuals to pursue singular interests and connect with small communities of individuals around the world who shared their interests, cultural background, or family ties.[37]

Relations of the History of Computing to Other Historical Subfields

From the 1970s until the early 2000s, the historians of computing were a somewhat insular group, talking mainly to themselves and publishing in specialised journals such as *Annals of the History of Computing*. To the extent they participated in a larger historical community it was primarily in the history of science and technology communities (for example, speaking at the annual meeting of the SHOT on engineering aspects of computing, or at the annual History of Science Society meeting speaking on the history of computer science, the computer as a scientific instrument, or computing as a mathematical discipline)—and to a lesser extent participating in the business history community (for example, speaking at the annual business history conference on mainframe computer firms).

Over time, however, new communities of scholars have become interested in the history of computing. With the movement towards social issues in the history of technology in the late twentieth century, some scholars who self-identified as science and technology scholars began to take an interest in computing history, and we began to see history of computing talks at the annual Society for the Social Study of Science (4S) meeting. As the internet, social media, and gaming became widely practised in society, media studies, communication, and game studies scholars began to take an interest in computing history.[38]

While general historians had written, for many years, about topics that could be identified with computing, or at least with data and information—topics such as government information and disinformation, accounting practices in government and business, or the process of digitalisation in various areas of life—it is only a recent phenomenon to hear general historians identify themselves with computing or information. An example of this is the reader edited by Ann Blair and others.[39] These general historians have a much broader conception of the fields of computing and information history than the computer historians do. Their work includes topics from the Renaissance forward in time, genres that include books and newspapers as well as databases and social media, and professions, including archivists, diplomats, teachers, and spies.

One might expect that there would be strong affinities among the various information history subfields mentioned at the beginning of this chapter, but there has been surprisingly little interaction.[40] Historian Robert Darnton, building on his interests in the history of the book,[41] has done pioneering work on electronic publishing, but this topic has not yet been seriously studied by the computer historians. Digital libraries and computing history both have been of interest to scholars in the digital humanities such as David Anderson, Janet Anderson, and Bernard Geoghegan, but to date there is limited historical research on this topic by mainstream scholars from either library or computer history. Archival and museum scholars, showing an affinity with studies of material culture, such as Patricia Galloway and Lori Emerson, have taken an interest in older computing machinery as physical artefacts,[42] but this work has also not yet connected strongly with mainstream computer history.

Some pioneering scholars are showing ways of connecting computer history with other types of scholarship. The media studies scholar Mara Mills has investigated the connections between computer history and disability studies.[43] Historians of information science and computer history have shared an interest, although with very different perspectives, on the history of information systems.[44] A few scholars, notably Dan Schiller and Richard John, have begun to make deeper connections between computer history and communications history.[45] Game studies scholars such as Ian Bogost and Nick Montfort have made valuable contributions to studies of digital media, using the approach of platform studies, which has been profitably adopted by computer historians.[46] Hallam Stevens and Joseph November have explored the history of computers and data in the biological and medical realms.[47] Gerardo Con Diaz is bringing a strong historical sensitivity to legal issues of computing.[48]

Especially in the early years, most computer historians stayed focused on their subject matter and did not write much about larger issues of computers in society.[49] One indicator of this narrowness is to consider sociologist Frank Webster's *Theories of the Information Society*.[50] It discusses the major scholars who have theorised about the information society, such as Jean Baudrillard, Daniel Bell, Manuel Castells, Anthony Giddens, Jurgen Habermas, Mark Poster, and Herbert Schiller. They represent academic disciplines such as anthropology, sociology, and philosophy, but not a single computer historian is mentioned among these theorists.

Exogenous Factors Affecting the History of Computing

When one studies the history of a topic from recent times, further developments in this topical area may reshape the historical account. This has clearly been true of computing history. As that universal machine, the computer, assumed new roles, not only as a scientific calculator and business machine, but also as a communication tool, business platform, and entertainment device, entirely new historical questions arose.[51] A good example is the change in regulatory environment for computing that came with the technological merger between computing and communications in the form of the internet and social media. Computing, historically, had been mostly unregulated. The only places where a regulatory hand was seen was, first, in the case of the treatment of AT&T as a monopoly, which was not permitted to build upon its technical contributions such as the invention of the transistor to become a strong player in the computer hardware industry; and, second, in cases of blatant antitrust, for example, in consent decrees concerning IBM's actions in the 1950s and Microsoft's actions in the 1970s. There were also short-lived efforts in the 1970s to protect personal privacy from government intrusion. In contrast, the communications industry had been heavily regulated since the 1930s, and it continues to operate under these restraints.

With the rise of the internet and social media, beginning in the 1990s, there were new efforts to regulate, for example, against online pornography and identity theft, as well as to protect national infrastructures against hacking threats. Earlier regulation was directed at business-to-business relations (antitrust) or protection of individuals from government interference (privacy); but beginning in the 1990s, effort was made to protect individuals from business (privacy, pornography, gambling). These regulations have sometimes touched on other information institutions, such as libraries, as in the case of the Children's Internet Protection Act signed into law in 2000. Protection of national security has come in the form of laws to constrain hacking or protect the integrity of electronic voting systems. The computer industry has balked at these recent efforts at government regulation, which they regarded as interference, arguing that the internet had been created to be free. Nevertheless, sometimes the computer industry has sought government protection, for example, over H-1B visa regulation to enhance its workforce to cope with the Y2K problem and the dotcom boom, or to enhance copyright protection in the face of threats from MP3 players and file sharing networks—resulting in the Digital Millennium Copyright Act of 1998. Europe has become more active in recent years, for example, regulating privacy, social media, and market domination by companies such as Apple, but computer historians have yet to weigh in about these issues.

Computing has historically been a practice-driven rather than a theory-driven field. While there is Shannon's heralded Theory of Information, it is not actually central to the computing field. Perhaps more central from an intellectual perspective is automata theory, which characterises those tasks can be computed; but even here, while this topic is of keen interest to theoretical computer scientists trained in mathematics or logic, it is largely ignored by most computer scientists whether they work in academia or industry. A more valuable way of discussing the computer is its capability to represent a wide variety of different situations in the real or abstract world. This representational characteristic goes hand in hand with the notion of the computer as a universal machine, which is a term often used by computer scientists.[52]

Computing work is an unwieldy combination of engineering (for example, computer engineering), mathematics (for example, automata theory), and design (for example, human-computer interaction). This mixture has had a bearing on the nature of training in the computing field. While computer science is a robust academic discipline today, with the topic offered at most colleges and universities, awarding degrees from the associate to the doctoral level, it is a wide tent that provides many different types of education. The core of what to teach students has been disputed for many years; so much so that Georgia Institute of Technology has created its lauded "threads approach" that recognises that the core everyone must know is minimal; and instead allows each student to self-design a curriculum following two narrow threads (for example, the study of devices or of computer architectures) of their own choosing. Despite this well-established formal educational system, fewer than half of the people who programme for a living have formal education in computer science, and there continues to be a belief that people can establish programming careers through informal education and hackathons. This resistance to educational requirements in the professionalisation process represents a stark contrast to another information field, library science, where the profession sought in the decades after the Second World War to make a master's degree a requirement to obtain to work as a librarian.

The reward system for computer scientists is much stronger than it is for most other kinds of information professionals, such as librarians, archivists, and museum curators. Compensation levels for computer scientists are among the highest of any profession in the United States, and high salaries (and, in some cases, valuable stock options) can sometimes be gained without holding even an undergraduate degree. Similarly, the opportunities for research funding through federal grants (primarily from the National Science Foundation, DARPA, and the energy and military departments of the federal government), or through venture capital, are much more readily available, at much higher dollar values, than are available to libraries, archives, and museums through such organisations as NHPRC. This provides a different culture of innovation for computer scientists as compared to librarians, as well as difference in work conditions and attitudes. These differences in compensation are closely tied to both greater opportunities for marketable innovation in the computing field and gendered differences in labour.[53]

Computer History—Still an Emerging Discipline

Two leading scholars in the history of computing have offered harsh assessments of their field. Thirty years ago, Michael Mahoney wrote, "The major problem is that we have lots of answers but very few questions, lots of stories but no history, lots of things to do but no sense of how to do them or in what order. Simply put, we don't yet know what the history of computing is really about."[54] Eighteen years later, Thomas Haigh remained critical: "To be blunt, outsiders from more mature historical subfields are likely to find the bulk of existing scholarship [in the history of computing] narrow, dry, obsessed with details, underconceptualised, and disconnected from broader intellectual currents."[55] It is beyond the scope of this chapter to compare and contrast the history of computing to other subfields of information history. However, one can say that some of these subfields, such as book and publishing history, or library history, have been practiced longer than computer history has, and they each contain a substantial body of scholarship following the guidelines of professional history. For example, *Libraries: Culture, History, and Society*,[56] the official journal of the Library History Round Table of the American Library Association, notes on its web page that the journal "aims to study libraries within their broader historical, humanistic, and social contexts. In addition to Library Science, the journal welcomes contributors from History, English, Literary Studies, Sociology, Education, Gender/Women's Studies, Race/Ethnic Studies, Political Science, Architecture, Anthropology, Philosophy, Geography, Economics, and other disciplines."[57] This statement is probably best read as aspirational. In fact, both library history and computer history are practised by both workers from the information discipline and professionally trained historians, and both literatures contain a mix of literature, written for a variety of goals and in a variety of styles. This is likely to continue into the future.

As the history of computing matures as an academic discipline, the connections to information history are likely to come out more clearly. When greater attention is paid by computer historians to legal and policy issues, for example, more will be understood about the role of computers in important social areas such as privacy, security, and intellectual property. As the business and economic histories of computing mature, we will better understand how computers have driven commerce and built various information economies. As the study of the social history of computing grows stronger, we will better understand the role of computing as part of everyday work and home life in an information society.

Notes

1 Communication history is different from the subfields listed here and is harder to define. Some scholars treat it as a broad catch-all, roughly equivalent to information history. Others tie it partly to other subfields such as journalism history and media history. The field of communication study itself is very broad, with many journals; yet there is no journal that covers all of communication history. See, for example, on the history of the academic study of communication, Peter Simonson and David W. Park, *The International History of Communication Study* (New York: Taylor & Francis, 2015); or on the more general history of communication, see Peter Simonson et al., eds., *The Handbook of Communication History* (New York: Taylor & Francis, 2012).

2 Michael S. Mahoney, "Issues in the History of Computing," paper prepared for the Forum on History of Computing, ACM/SIGPLAN Second History of Programming Languages Conference, Cambridge, MA (April 20–23, 1993). Indeed, one might similarly argue that there are many histories of information, concerning different kinds of information institutions, information disciplines, information professions, and information constructs manifest in various ways in everyday life. Other chapters in this volume give testimony to these many histories of information.

3 The author of this study is not only an American who participated in the development of this field, but also an Americanist in the topics he studies. While many of the key activities in computer history did occur in English-speaking countries and much of the literature appeared in the English language, there are contributions from other nations and in other languages that may be underrepresented inadvertently in this account.

4 The four earliest doctorates in history of computing were awarded by different academic fields: Nancy B. Stern, Ph.D., History Department, SUNY Stony Brook, 1978, "From ENIAC to UNIVAC: A Case Study in the History of Technology," supervisor: Ruth Schwartz Cowan; Martin Campbell-Kelly, Ph.D., Department of Mathematics and Computer Studies, Sunderland Polytechnic, 1980, "Foundations of Computer Programming in Britain (1945–1955)," supervisor: Brian Randell; William Aspray, Ph.D., History of Science Department, University of Wisconsin–Madison, 1980, "From Computability to Computer Science: Alan Turing, John von Neumann, and the Origins of Modern Computing," supervisor: Victor Hilts; and Paul Ceruzzi, Ph.D., American Studies Department, University of Kansas, 1981, "The Prehistory of the Digital Computer, 1936–1946: A Cross-Cultural Study," supervisor: Jerry Stannard.

5 On SIGCIS history, see https://www.sigcis.org/about_history.

6 A *listserv* is an application that distributes messages to subscribers on an electronic mailing list. For example, a list of all the computer science majors at a particular college, so that general announcements can be sent to them as a group. *Listservs* are still commonly used, but the term is not as widely used today as it once was.

7 Hardware, too, but software in particular raised a question about how to study antiquated technologies when there were no working copies of the technology to use in understanding how internal operations worked or how people interacted with the technology as builders, operators, maintainers, or users. Martin Campbell-Kelly has built simulators of some of the early British computers and Raúl Rojas Gonzalez has built a simulator of Konrad Zuse's Z1 computer; Doron

Swade has built a working model of Charles Babbage's Difference Engine; and there have been a few other projects along these lines. Archivists and museum curators, such as Patricia Galloway of University of Texas at Austin, Lori Emerson of University of Colorado Boulder, and Catherine Marshall of Microsoft, have generally been more concerned about this issue than computer historians. See, for example, Martin Campbell-Kelly, Programming the EDSAC: Early Programming Activity at the University of Cambridge, *Annals of the History of Computing* 2, no. 1 (January–March 1980): 7–36; or Raúl Rojas Gonzalez, *Die Rechenmaschinen von Konrad Zuse* [*Konrad Zuse's Calculating Machines*] (Berlin: Springer, 1998). Also see Andrew L. Russell and Lee Vinsel, "After Innovation, Turn to Maintenance," *Technology & Culture* 55, no. 1 (January 2018): 1–25, on the issue of maintenance.

8 Jane Pugh and D. Baxandall, *Calculating Machines and Instruments; Catalogue of the Collections in the Science Museum* (London: Science Museum, 1975).

9 On the Deutsches Museum's computing exhibits, see https://www.deutsches-museum.de/museumsinsel/ausstellung/informatik#c4865.

10 See Walter, M. Carlson, "Why AFIPS Invested in History," *Annals of the History of Computing* 8, no. 3 (1986): 270–274; and Henry S. Tropp, "The Smithsonian Computer History Project and Some Personal Recollections," in *A History of Computing in the Twentieth Century: A Collection of Papers*, ed. Jack Howlett, Nicholas Metropolis, and Gian-Carlo Rota (New York: Academic Press, 1980), 115–124.

11 See the review of this exhibit by M. R. Williams, *Technology & Culture* 31, no. 4 (October 1990): 838–845.

12 On the history of the Heinz Nixdorf Museums Forum, see https://www.hnf.de/en/the-hnf/historical-background.html.

13 On the history of the Computer History Museum, see https://www.computerhistory.org/chmhistory/.

14 On the history of the Charles Babbage Institute, see https://cse.umn.edu/cbi/about.

15 The list of Tomash Fellows can be found at https://cse.umn.edu/cbi/past-tomash-fellows.

16 As an example of his scholarship, see *L'Informatique en France, de la Seconde Guerre mondiale au Plan Calcul. L'Emergence d'une Science* (Paris: Presses de l'Université Paris-Sorbonne, 2010).

17 An excellent literature review is provided in Thomas Haigh, "The History of Information Technology," *Annual Review of Information Science and Technology* 45 (2011): 431–487.

18 William Aspray, ed., *Computing Before Computers* (Ames, IA: Iowa State Press, 1990); Michael R. Williams, *A History of Computing Technology* (Englewood Cliffs, NJ: Prentice-Hall, 1985); and Herman H. Goldstine, *The Computer from Pascal to von Neumann* (Princeton, NJ: Princeton University Press, 1972). In contrast, there are beginning to appear a few more historically sophisticated studies of this era. Notable is Thomas Haigh, Mark Priestley, and Crispin Rope, *ENIAC in Action: Making and Remaking the Modern Computer* (Cambridge, MA: MIT Press, 2018).

19 Matthew L. Jones, *Reckoning with Matter: Calculating Machines, Innovation, and Thinking about Thinking from Pascal to* Babbage (Chicago, IL: University of Chicago Press, 2016); Lars Heide, *Punched-Card Systems and the Early Information Explosion, 1880–1945* (Baltimore, MD: Johns Hopkins University Press, 2009); David Grier, *When Computers Were Human* (Princeton, NJ: Princeton University Press, 2006); and Martin Campbell-Kelly et al., eds., *The History of Mathematical Tables: From Sumer to Spreadsheets* (Oxford: Oxford University Press, 2003).

20 Doron Swade, *The Difference Engine: Charles Babbage and the Quest to Build the First Computer* (New York: Viking Penguin, 2001); and Anthony Hyman, *Charles Babbage: Pioneer of the Computer* (Princeton, NJ: Princeton University Press, 1982). Ada Lovelace has inspired a large popular and children's literature. Perhaps the best more scholarly accounts are Christopher Hollings, Ursula Martin, and Adrian Rice, *Ada Lovelace: The Making of a Computer Scientists* (Oxford: Bodleian Library, University of Oxford, 2018); Robin Hammerman and Andrew Russell, eds., *Ada's Legacy: Cultures of Computing from the Victorian to the Digital Age* (New York: ACM Books, 2015); and Dorothy Stein, *Ada: A Life and a Legacy* (Cambridge, MA: MIT Press, 1985).

21 Kurt W. Beyer, *Grace Hopper and the Invention of the Information Age* (Cambridge, MA: MIT Press, 2009); I. Bernard Cohen, *Howard Aiken: Portrait of a Computer Pioneer* (Cambridge, MA: MIT Press, 1999); G. Pascal Zachary, *The Endless Frontier: Vannever Bush, Engineer of the American Century* (Cambridge, MA: MIT Press, 1999); William Aspray, *John von Neumann and*

the Origins of Modern Computing (Cambridge, MA: MIT Press, 1990); and Andrew Hodges, *Alan Turing: The Enigma of Intelligence* (New York: Simon and Schuster, 1983).
22 Martin Campbell-Kelly, *ICL: A Technical and Business History* (New York: Oxford University Press, 1989). Other examples of excellent studies in the business history of computing include Jeffrey Yost, *Making IT Work: A History of the Computer Services Industry* (Cambridge, MA: MIT Press, 2017); and Martin Campbell-Kelly and Daniel D. Garcia-Swartz, *From Mainframes to Smartphones: A History of the International Computer Industry* (Cambridge, MA: Harvard University Press, 2015).
23 James Cortada, *The Digital Flood: The Diffusion of Information Technology across the U.S., Europe, and Asia* (New York: Oxford University Press, 2012); and James Cortada, *Before the Computer: IBM, Burroughs and Remington Rand and the Industry They Created, 1865–1956* (Princeton, NJ: Princeton University Press, 1993).
24 James Cortada, *The Rise and Fall and Reinvention of a Global Icon* (Cambridge, MA: MIT Press, 2019); and Emerson W. Pugh, *Building IBM: Shaping an Industry and Its Technologies* (Cambridge, MA: MIT Press, 1994).
25 Frederik Nebeker, *Dawn of the Electronic Age: Electrical Technologies in the Shaping of the Modern World, 1914–1945* (New York: Wiley-IEEE Press, 2009); Christopher Lécuyer, *Making Silicon Valley: Innovation and the Growth of High Tech, 1930–1970* (Cambridge, MA: MIT Press, 2006); Ross Knox Bassett, *To the Digital Age: Research Labs, Start-Up Companies, and the Rise of MOS Technology* (Baltimore, MD: Johns Hopkins University Press, 2002); and Bernard S. Finn, ed., *Exposing Electronics* (New York: CRC Press, 2000).
26 Martin Campbell-Kelly, *From Airline Reservations to Sonic the Hedgehog: A History of the Software Industry* (Cambridge, MA: MIT Press, 2003); Thomas J. Bergin and Richard G. Gibson, eds., *History of Programming Languages II* (New York: ACM Press, 1996); and Jean E. Sammet, *Programming Languages: History and Fundamentals* (Eaglewood Cliffs, NJ: Prentice Hall, 1969).
27 https://hapoc.org.
28 Two of the better books on AI history are Ronald R. Kline, *The Cybernetic Connection* (Baltimore, MD: Johns Hopkins University Press, 2015); and Pamela McCorduck, *Machines Who Think* (San Francisco, CA: W.H. Freeman, 1979). There has been a recent effort to more seriously study the history of AI, led by Cambridge historian of science Simon Schaffer and some of his colleagues. A related topic that has received little historical attention so far is big data. The studies of DARPA, discussed below, also have important treatment of AI history.
29 Thomas Haigh and Paul Ceruzzi, *A New History of Modern Computing* (Cambridge, MA: MIT Press, 2021). This book is frequently used in computer science and engineering departments. Its main competitor, used mostly in humanities and social science departments, is Martin Campbell-Kelly et al., *Computer: A History of the Information Machine*, 4th ed. (New York: Routledge, 2023).
30 Thomas Haigh, ed., *Exploring the Early Digital* (Cham: Springer, 2019); Thomas Misa and Jeffrey Yost, *Fastlane: Managing Science in the Internet World* (Baltimore, MD: Johns Hopkins University Press, 2016); JoAnne Yates, *Structuring the Information Age: Life Insurance and Technology in the Twentieth Century* (Baltimore, MD: Johns Hopkins University Press, 2005); Jon Agar, *The Government Machine: A Revolutionary History of the Computer* (Cambridge, MA: MIT Press, 2003); and James Cortada, *The Digital Hand*, 3 vols. (New York: Oxford University Press, 2003, 2005, and 2007).
31 Shane Greenstein, *How the Internet Became Commercial* (Princeton, NJ: Princeton University Press, 2015); William Aspray and Paul Ceruzzi, eds., *The Internet and American Business* (Cambridge, MA: MIT Press, 2008); and Janet Abbate, *Inventing the Internet* (Cambridge, MA: MIT Press, 1999).
32 Examples include Janet Abbate and Stephanie Dick, eds., *Abstractions and Embodiments: New Histories of Computing and Society* (Baltimore, MD: Johns Hopkins University Press, 2022); and Joy Lisi Rankin, *A People's History of Computing in the United States* (Cambridge, MA: Harvard University Press, 2018).
33 Good examples of regional studies include Margaret O'Mara, *The Code: Silicon Valley and the Remaking of America* (New York: Penguin, 2020); Thomas Misa, *Digital State: The Story of Minnesota's Computing Industry* (Minneapolis, MN: University of Minnesota Press, 2013); Paul Ceruzzi, *Internet Alley: High Technology in Tyson's Corner, 1945–2005* (Cambridge, MA: MIT

Press, 2011); and AnnaLee Saxenian, *Regional Advantage: Culture and Competition in Silicon Valley and Route 128* (Cambridge, MA: Harvard University Press, 1994). Edgar Schein, *DEC is Dead, Long Live DEC: The Lasting Legacy of Digital Equipment Corporation* (Oakland, CA: Berrett-Koehler Publishers, 2003); and Michael Hiltzik, *Dealers of Lightning: Xeroc PARC and the Dawn of the Computer Age* (New York: Harper Business, 1999) are examples of histories of organisations that shaped a region. Mitchell Waldrop, *The Dream Machine* [about J.C.R. Licklider], 4th ed. (San Francisco, CA: Stripe Press, 2018); Leslie Berlin, *Troublemakers: Silicon Valley's Coming of Age* (New York: Simon & Schuster, 2017); and Thierry Bardini, *Bootstrapping: Douglas Engelbart, Coevolution, and the Origins of Personal Computing* (Stanford, CA: Stanford University Press, 2000) are good examples of biographies of individuals who shaped a regional computing industry. There are numerous journalistic accounts of computer start-ups such as Apple and Microsoft and their principals, Steve Jobs and Bill Gates, respectively: see, for example, Walter Issacson, *The Innovators* (New York: Simon and Schuster, 2014); and Walter Isaacson, *Steve Jobs* (New York: Simon and Schuster, 2011).

34 Some of the best book-length examples covering gender issues include Janet Abbate, *Recoding Gender: Women's Changing Participation in Computing* (Cambridge, MA: MIT Press, 2017); Mar Hicks, *Programmed Inequality: How Britain Discarded Women Technologists and Lost Its Edge in Computing* (Cambridge, MA: MIT Press, 2017); Thomas Misa, ed., *Gender Codes: Why Women Are Leaving Computing* (New York: Wiley-IEEE Computer Society, 2010); and Grier, *When Computers Were Human*.

35 Margot Lee Shetterly, *Hidden Figures: The American Dream and the Untold Story of the Black Women Mathematicians Who Helped Win the Space Race* (New York: William Morrow, 2016). Much less well known, but covering both race and gender in computing, is William Aspray, *Women and Underrepresented Minorities in Computing: A Historical and Social Study* (Cham: Springer, 2016).

36 There is an excellent bibliography at the end of Cortada, *The Digital Flood*. Both that book and Dick van Lente, *Prophets of Computing* (New York: ACM Books, 2022) provide coverage of computing developments across many different countries. The following is a selection of good studies on specific regions across the globe. On Japan, see Marie Anchordoguy, *Reprogramming Japan: The High Tech Crisis under Communitarian Capitalism* (Ithaca, NY: Cornell University Press, 2005); and Martin Fransman, *Japan's Computer and Communication Industry* (New York: Oxford University Press, 1995). On Australia, see Gerard Goggin, ed., *Virtual Nation: The Internet in Australia* (Sydney: University of New South Wales Press, 2004); and John M. Bennett, ed., *Computing in Australia: The Development of a Profession* (Sydney: Hale and Iremonger, 1994). On South America, see Eden Medina, *Cybernetic Revolutionaries: Technology and Politics in Allende's Chile* (Cambridge, MA: MIT Press, 2011). On Canada, see John Vardalas, *The Computer Revolution in Canada* (Cambridge, MA: MIT Press, 2001). On northern Europe, see the three IFIP Working Conferences on the History of Nordic Computing (Cham: Springer, 2005, 2009, 2010). On India, see Ross Bassett, *The Technological Indian* (Cambridge, MA: Harvard University Press, 2019); and Dinesh Sharma, *The Outsources* (Cambridge, MA: MIT Press, 2015).

37 See, for example, Christina Dunbar-Hester, *Hacking Diversity: The Politics of Inclusion in Open Technology Cultures* (Princeton, NJ: Princeton University Press, 2019); Safiya Noble, *Algorithms of Oppression: How Search Engines Reinforce Racism* (New York: NYU Press, 2018); Cathy O'Neil, *Weapons of Math Destruction: How Bid Data Increases Inequality and Threatens Democracy* (New York: Crown, 2016); Frank Pasquale, *The Black Box Society: The Secret Algorithms That Control Money and Information* (Cambridge, MA: Harvard University Press, 2015); and Virginia Eubanks, *Digital Dead End: Fighting for Social Justice in the Information Age* (Cambridge, MA: MIT Press, 2011).

38 See, for example, Ted Striphas, *Algorithmic Culture Before the Internet* (New York: Columbia University Press, 2023); Jason Steinhauer, *History, Disrupted: How Social Media and the World Wide Web Have Changed the Past* (London: Palgrave Macmillan, 2022); Max Fisher, *The Chaos Machine: The Inside Story of How Social Media Rewired Our Minds and Our Worlds* (Boston, MA: Little, Brown and Company, 2022); Darren Wershler, Lori Emerson, and Jussi Prikka, *The Lab Book: Situated Practices in Media Studies* (Minneapolis, MN: University of Minnesota Press, 2021); and Marshall Poe, *A History of Communications: Media and Society from the Evolution of Speech to the Internet* (Cambridge, UK: Cambridge University Press, 2013).

39 Ann Blair et al., eds., *Information: A Historical Companion* (Princeton, NJ: Princeton University Press, 2021).
40 For an expanded discussion of this point, see William Aspray, "The Many Histories of Information," *Information & Culture* 50, no. 1 (2015): 1–23.
41 See Robert Darnton, *The Case for Books: Past, Present, and Future* (New York: Public Affairs, 2009).
42 See the work of the Goodwill Computer Museum in Austin, TX, as addressed in Virginia Luehrsen and Karen L. Pavelka, "Collaborative Conservation: Sharing Expertise at the Goodwill Computer Museum," *The Electronic Media Review* 2 (2011–2012), https://resources.culturalheritage.org/emg-review/volume-two-2011-2012/collaborative-conservation-sharing-expertise-at-the-goodwill-computer-museum/; or the Media Archeology Lab at the University of Colorado Boulder, https://www.mediaarchaeologylab.com.
43 Mara Mills, *Hearing Loss and the History of Information Theory* (Durham, NC: Duke University Press, forthcoming).
44 The information studies scholars have focused on scientific information databases and services, while the computer historians have focused on the development of technologies of information retrieval. See, for example, and Thomas Haigh, "How Data Got Its Base: Information Storage Software in the 1950s and 1960s," *IEEE Annals of the History of Computing* 31, no. 4 (October–December 2009): 6–25; and Mary Ellen Bowden, Trudi Bellardo Hahn, and Robert V. Williams, eds., *Proceedings of the Conference on the History and Heritage of Science Information Systems* (Medford, NJ: Information Today, 1999).
45 Dan Schiller, *Crossed Wires: The Conflicted History of U.S. Telecommunications from the Post Office to the Internet* (Oxford: Oxford University Press, 2023); and Richard R. John, *Network Nation: Inventing American Telecommunications* (Cambridge, MA: Belknap Press, 2010).
46 See, for example, Ian Bogost and Nick Montfort, *Platform Studies: Frequently Questioned Answers* (UC Irvine, CA: Digital Arts and Culture, 2009). https://escholarship.org/uc/item/01r0k9br.
47 Hallam Stevens, *Life Out of Sequence: A Data-Driven History of Bioinformatics* (Chicago, IL: University of Chicago Press, 2013); and Joseph November, *Biomedical Computing: Digitalizing Life in the United States* (Baltimore, MD: Johns Hopkins University Press, 2012).
48 Gerardo Con Diaz, *Software Rights: How Patent Law Transformed Software Development in America* (New Haven, CT: Yale University Press, 2019).
49 One simple way to see the changing focus in history of computing scholarship is to consider the backlist in the MIT Press series on computer history, which is the oldest and arguably the most prestigious book series in this field. From the series founding in 1981 through the first decade of the 2000s, there were only two books that were not focused primarily on computing technologies, biographies of computer people, or companies that manufactured and sold these technologies: Alex Roland and Philip Shiman, *Strategic Computing: DARPA and the Quest for Machine Intelligence, 1983–1993* (Cambridge, MA: MIT Press, 2002) on the interconnections between external funding for computing research and the American military; and John Hendry, *Innovating for Failure: Government Policy and the Early British Computer Industry* (Cambridge, MA: MIT Press, 1989) about the failed efforts of British policymaking to establish an internationally competitive national computer industry. In contrast, five of the books published since 2010 have been on other topics. Or if one considers the winners of the Computer History Museum Prize (established in 2009, https://www.sigcis.org/chmprize) for the best book in computer history, more than half the winners have been on these broader, more social topics.
50 Frank Webster, *Theories of the Information Society*, 4th ed. (London: Routledge, 2014).
51 This change can be readily seen if one considers, for example, the changes in content of Campbell-Kelly et al., *Computer* over its four editions.
52 Thanks to Clayton Lewis for this observation about the computer's value as a representational device.
53 Peter A. Freeman, W. Richards Adrion, and William Aspray, *Computing and the National Science Foundation, 1950–2016* (New York: ACM Books, 2019); Charles N. Yood, *Hybrid Zone: Computers and Science at Argonne National Laboratory 1946–1992* (Boston, MA: Docent Press, 2013); Alex Roland and Philip Shiman, *Strategic Computing: DARPA and the Quest for Machine Intelligence* (Cambridge, MA: MIT Press, 2002); Arthur L. Norberg, Judy E. O'Neill, and Kerry Freedman, *Transforming Computer Technology: Information Processing for the Pentagon,*

1962–1986 (Baltimore, MD: Johns Hopkins University Press, 1996); and Robert W. Seidel and Roger Meade, *Los Alamos & the Development of the Atomic Bomb* (Santa Fe, NM: Otowi Crossing Press, 1995).

54 Michael S. Mahoney, "Issues in the History of Computing," Paper prepared for the Forum on History of Computing at the ACM/SIGPLAN Second History of Programming Languages Conference, Cambridge, MA, April 20–23, 1993.

55 Haigh, "The History of Information Technology," 53.

56 *Information & Culture* (formerly *Libraries and the Cultural* Record) and *Library and Information History* (formerly *Library History*) are older than *Libraries: Culture, History, and Society* but they lost their "purity" by broadening to include information history and not only library history.

57 https://www.psupress.org/journals/jnls_LCHS.html.

23
SMART CITIES AND INFORMATIC GOVERNANCE
The Management of Information and People in Postcolonial Singapore

Hallam Stevens and Manoj Harjani

Introduction

According to their advocates, smart cities are zones where data from sensors, cameras, financial transactions, health care institutions, government agencies, and other sources are gathered and aggregated into information for managing and improving urban life. Smart cities aim to generate all sorts of benefits for their residents, increasing efficiency, safety, productivity, sustainability, and liveability.[1] There is now a vast literature on smart cities, describing both their potential benefits and their potential drawbacks.[2] Much of this scholarship is focused on how urban data is collected and aggregated from residents. Criticisms of smart cities have also emphasised issues of data privacy, cybersecurity, and equity, noting the close ties between smart cities and "Big Tech" purveyors of surveillance capitalism.[3]

Rather than approaching smart cities merely as sites of intensive data practices, this chapter will examine them as spaces of information management and informatic governance. Alistair Black places the emergence of information management in the nineteenth century when "improvement in the methods and 'machinery' of collecting and communicating information in organisations and in the way that data and documents were controlled—emerged in response to the complex tasks and operational requirements that confronted the burgeoning state bureaucracies and large-scale business enterprises."[4] As this definition suggests, the use of information management for governance—and particularly, in the nineteenth century, for colonial governance—was an important driver in its development. Of course, the notion of the smart city is also a product of longer historical trajectories directed towards ordering, rationalising, and managing cities. These include notions of rational city planning from the nineteenth century, as well as more recent concepts of "wired cities" and "informational cities."[5] While the intensification of data collection in the last two decades—including via mobile devices, Internet of Things, and ubiquitous sensors—has created new possibilities for imagining how information can be used to reorder and govern urban spaces, attention to informatic governance also suggests how the aims and effects of smart cities are continuous with these historical precursors.

In 2014, the city-state of Singapore launched a "Smart Nation" initiative, ushering in adoption of new technologies and practices directed at gathering data about residents and formulating it into information and plans for managing the city. This has amounted to a rebranding and re-imagining of Singapore as a world-leading smart city. As such, Singapore is a useful case study for interrogating the development of smart cities and their effects. But several factors in Singapore also make it an ideal site for investigating how data is put to work. First, Singapore's smart city initiatives are part of a longer history of colonial and postcolonial initiatives to order and reorder the city informatically. This allows us to understand smart city initiatives in the context of longer-term traditions and historical modes of governance. Second, the Singapore state's top-down and integrated approaches to policy allow us to perceive the various ways in which the initiatives ramify through society. Moving from data (more or less unorganised) to information (organised and synthesised in various ways) signals an attempt to focus on how smart cities actually reorganise and reorder individuals and societies. From this point of view, the risks of smart cities become less about privacy, security, and surveillance, and more about trust, community, and governance. In Singapore, we can see not only how data is gathered and aggregated under smart city initiatives, but also how data is transformed into information that is actively deployed to make interventions into the lives of urban residents.

In this chapter, we analyse government documents and reports, policy documents, government web pages, and news media articles to understand the ways in which Singapore has articulated and developed its vision of informatic governance. After providing some brief background about Singapore, the first part of this chapter will provide examples of some of Singapore's longer-term initiatives for information management. In the period of British rule (1819–1959), colonial censuses, racial classification systems, and practices for managing infectious diseases were critical informatic governance systems. Taking two historical examples, the chapter will describe how town planning and efforts towards computerisation aimed to transform Singaporean residents through information management. The second part of the chapter will examine two key elements of Singapore's smart nation plans: its National Digital Identity (NDI) project and its COVID-19 contact tracing systems. This chapter will illustrate how these systems use the opportunity of gathering data to reshape the ways in which urban dwellers interact with the state, with businesses, and with one another.

Understanding these developments as systems for intensified information management suggests the ways in which smart cities are directed not merely towards the passive gathering of data, but also towards active intervention in urban life. In Singapore, intensified information management has become a form of governance, critically shaping relations between state and society. Here we label this form of governance "informatic sanitation." Just as colonial efforts at information gathering were directed towards cleaning and ordering urban spaces, we argue that more recent digital developments, including smart city initiatives, can also be understood as efforts to use information management to order online and physical spaces—cleansing them of unwanted influences or interference that might include hackers, scammers, and sources of misinformation, as well as multi-national corporations with incompatible political values. These efforts are directed not only towards cybersecurity, but also towards controlling information flows. Just as colonial and postcolonial governance sought to create hygienic physical spaces within the city, digital governance under the smart nation likewise seeks to create carefully ordered online and offline spaces.

One of the primary ways that such ordering occurs is through attempts to place the government at the centre of the nation's information networks and enable centralised control over the structure of information exchange. Under such a system, these established patterns and structures determine how residents can participate in and interact with information infrastructures. The informatic interactions of residents are framed by and oriented towards the government, which consequently limits or even precludes other modes of digital and informatic interaction.

Background

The role of information and information management in colonial governance is now well established. The work of Christopher Bayly, to take a prominent example, has described the significance of information gathering networks for British colonial rule in India.[6] Networks of informants, spies, and intermediaries played a critical role in cementing military, social, and political control. Under British rule, Singapore—particularly in its role as a hub for commercial exchange—formed an important node in imperial information management. In the early part of the nineteenth century, Singapore's status as a key port made it a centre for exchange and transmission of information; in the latter part of the century, the city also became a hub for telegraphy.[7] Brenda Yeoh has detailed ways in which information from colonial censuses and surveys were critical to the management of the colony. In particular, the colonial authorities were concerned with racial classification, births and deaths, data about infectious diseases, data about space (including land and dwellings), and sanitation data (such as garbage and night soil disposal).[8] Managing commerce, health, and social harmony in colonial Singapore were information-centred endeavours.

Singapore achieved full independence from the British Crown in 1965. Since then, it has been ruled continuously by the People's Action Party (PAP), which rapidly and successfully implemented a style of governance that places the state at the centre of many aspects of civic, political, and cultural life in the city-state, including the information environment. Although Singapore holds open elections, the dominance of the ruling party has undercut the emergence of liberal democratic political processes.[9] One early aim of the PAP was to attempt to maintain the island's significance as a site of commercial, financial, cultural, and linguistic exchange. This required an investment in infrastructure such as ports, airports, and, later, telecommunications and information technology. Such infrastructure served to increase the role and responsibilities of government in a multitude of aspects of daily life, bolstering the power and legitimacy of the state.

Informatic Past

This section develops two case studies that illustrate how Singapore's laws, platforms, and informatic infrastructures act to place the state at the centre of information networks and facilitate centralised control over the modes and structure of information exchange. In the context of both (colonial) town planning and (postcolonial) computerisation, it is evident that intensified information collection was aimed towards constructing carefully ordered urban spaces in the city-state.

Town Planning in Colonial Singapore

One focus of data collection in colonial Singapore was town planning. As Yeoh has shown, colonial officials in the early twentieth century were particularly concerned with issues of sanitation. Overcrowding, water supplies, the disposal of food and human waste, and inadequate housing were priorities for British officials as they sought to minimise potential sources of disease. In 1918, at the conclusion of World War I, the colonial government appointed a Housing Commission to investigate these problems. Following a model adopted by the colonial government in British India, the Commission recommended the formation of a "Singapore Improvement Trust" (SIT) that would be funded and empowered to gather information to study the problem in depth and initiate improvement works.[10]

In 1921, the Singapore Improvement Trust began an extensive survey of the island, detailing both the topography and human-built structures. Taking four years to complete, the survey showed, "in different colours all permanent structures, all semi-permanent buildings, all attap and squatters huts, with the various uses to which the land is put, i.e. vegetable gardens, fruit trees, rubber and coconut plantations, graveyards, etc."[11] It also included topographic contours at ten foot intervals.[12] Such a survey would prepare the ground for further development of the city, including the improvement of transportation, the development of housing, and the "relief" of slum areas.

But even in 1925, these "four-chain" surveys were considered insufficiently detailed for future planning. "Of about half the area of Singapore, there are no large-scale revenue survey plans in existence," the Deputy Chairman of the Housing Commission complained.[13] Such information would be necessary to create a "General Town Plan" which would assist in the clearance of swamps, the relief of overcrowding in the city, and the rehousing of persons from "insanitary properties." Delays in passing the enabling legislation for the SIT hampered this work. In 1927, the SIT legislation was finally passed under the Singapore Improvement Ordinance, which accelerated the surveying work. The results of this information gathering included efforts to widen roads, zone land, reclaim open spaces, improve existing housing, and develop new housing estates.[14]

Although some new housing developments were completed in the 1930s (including in Tiong Bahru, New Bridge Road, and Banda Street), World War II and the Japanese occupation of Singapore (1942–1945) interrupted the full execution of SIT's plans.[15] Efforts resumed in 1951, with the appointment of Sir George Pepler to carry out a survey of the island once again in order to develop a detailed plan. For Pepler, this plan necessarily included accounting for future economic developments. The expanding population would require new industries and "the requirements of all must be carefully ascertained and studied and the character of the land understood—in effect a diagnostic survey—and an overall plan developed."[16] Pepler's work resulted in the formulation of yet another "Master Plan," initiated in 1952 and completed by 1955.[17] This plan portrayed the city in terms of data indicators such as average residential density (four hundred persons per acre, with some central areas over one thousand persons per acre), open space (which was only 0.84 acres per thousand persons while the desirable level was 4.5 acres per thousand), and peak traffic flow into the city (which was ten thousand vehicles per hour).[18] The aim of future planning would be to increase or reduce these numbers to acceptable values, usually based on prior experience with English or European cities. Although the SIT was disbanded in 1960, many of its plans were taken up by the subsequently-established Housing and Development Board (HDB). In particular, the HDB completed the planning and construction of Singapore's "New Towns," or satellite centres, which would form the nucleus of postcolonial housing plans.

From the 1920s to the 1960s, Singapore's development—the organisation of its land and population—was driven by a series of ongoing and intensive information collection efforts. These surveys attempted to map, enumerate, categorise, and catalogue as much of the physical space of the island as possible, from its trees and gardens to squatters' dwellings and permanent structures. The aim of this detailed gathering of information was to reorganise the city and its inhabitants, "reforming" them through removal, rehousing, and rezoning. While ostensibly directed towards "sanitation" (including managing overcrowding, light, water, and air), the remit of such surveying expanded to include the management of transportation, industry, recreation, and education. Total information about the spatial arrangement of the island, it was imagined, would allow the most effective and efficient governance of all aspects of the lives of its residents.

Computerisation in Postcolonial Singapore

Singapore's nascent postcolonial state moved quickly to adopt the advanced information processing methods made available by the advent of computing. Early public sector adopters of IBM mainframe computers—the dominant player in the 1960s and 1970s—included the Housing and Development Board (responsible for Singapore's public housing), Central Provident Fund (CPF; responsible for Singapore's state-managed retirement fund), Property Tax Board, and Ministry of Finance.[19] The CPF ordered Singapore's first mainframe computer—an IBM 1401—in 1962, and it arrived on the island's shores the following year.[20] Robert Iau, who would eventually become the CPF's general manager from 1971 to 1980, was the data processing manager at the time responsible for getting the computer system set up. He described it as "huge, clumsy, [and] extremely hot."[21]

Nevertheless, the CPF felt a mainframe computer was necessary because the growing number of accounts being managed—over a million at the time—was outpacing the capabilities of the existing mechanical bookkeeping machine that was in use.[22] The CPF would go on to invest heavily in computer systems, upgrading subsequently to IBM's System/360, System/370, and 3031 mainframes.[23] According to Iau, the arrival of computers transformed the culture of the CPF; it was later tasked with projects involving informatic governance for other parts of the Singapore government.

One significant example of these CPF-led computerisation efforts was the Mosque Building Fund, which was launched in 1975.[24] The Mosque Building Fund was a government initiative to raise funds to build mosques in the new towns being developed by the HDB in the 1970s. The state felt that existing fundraising mechanisms for the Muslim community would be insufficient, and there was concern to ensure parity between all religious communities in terms of their ability to build places of worship in new towns.[25] This push for a form of religious equality took on particular significance in postcolonial Singapore, where racial and religious harmony were seen as central to the state's legitimacy and stability. The solution was to use the CPF collection system to source voluntary donations from employed Muslims—in 1975 this amounted to S$0.50, but by 1977 had increased to S$1 due to the rising costs of construction.[26]

The problem was that the state did not know how many Muslims lived in Singapore. The National Registration Identity Card (NRIC), first issued in 1966, did not have data on religion. This lack of detail posed a problem for the CPF when it was tasked to look at operationalising the collection of donations from Muslims for the Mosque Building Fund.[27] Iau and his team had to devise workarounds based on the structure of names associated with particular ethnic groups—a measure that would raise eyebrows today for assuming that someone with a particular kind of name belonged to a certain ethnic or religious community. However, at the time, it was lauded as a "whole new way of looking at data,"[28] given the urgency of addressing fundraising for the Mosque Building Fund.

Following these nascent efforts and beginning in the 1980s, the government embarked on a series of endeavours to augment the city-state's informatic capacities. The Committee on National Computerisation was created by then-Minister for Trade and Industry Goh Chok Tong in 1980. Its first report outlined a plan to enhance computer education, promote an indigenous software industry, and computerise the civil service.[29] These activities were to be overseen by a newly created National Computer Board (NCB). In 1985, to push these efforts further, a subsequent government committee issued a "National IT Plan."[30] This report had two main thrusts. First, it detailed a roadmap for deploying a state-of-the-art information and communications infrastructure for the island. This included plans for a government-operated videotex system known as "Teleview" as well as improved electronic networks connecting Singapore to overseas nodes.[31] Second, the National IT Plan included strategies for preparing residents for the emerging computerised society, creating an "IT culture" that would transform Singapore's society and economy.[32] Information management was, in Singapore, about people and "culture" as well as technology.

These ideals were further articulated in 1992, in the NCB's *A Vision of an Intelligent Island: IT 2000 Report.* Here, the NCB laid out an even more ambitious plan for Singapore's transformation: "In our vision, some fifteen years from now, Singapore, the Intelligent Island, will be among the first countries in the world with an advanced nation-wide information infrastructure. It will interconnect computers in virtually every home, office, school, and factory."[33] As Gregory Clancey has pointed out, the report's linking of IT and "intelligence" signalled the government's ambition to transform Singaporean residents and workers through digitisation, upskilling them into "smarter" and more productive knowledge workers.[34] All these initiatives sought not only to modernise Singapore's information and telecommunications infrastructure, but also to "modernise" its people, reshaping them into new kinds of workers and residents. Information management was about technology strategically directed towards creating particular forms of governance and particular kinds of civic interactions.

The computerisation of postcolonial Singapore was primarily motivated by the prospect of more efficient informatic governance. However, this should not obscure the grander, national-level objective at play—more efficient informatic governance meant a greater presence of the state in day-to-day transactions and activities. The Mosque Building Fund set up in the 1970s not only inserted the state directly into religious affairs, but also served as a means of further "ordering" the population. The government reasoned that by counting Muslims in this way to raise funds for mosque building, religious equity would be preserved and social order maintained. Likewise, subsequent plans to computerise the civil service and to promote information literacy can be seen as efforts to centrally control and manage flows of information in ways that kept the state firmly in the centre of informatic transactions.

Informatic Present

This section will explore examples of more recent informatic governance under Singapore's "Smart Nation" initiative. A clear through line can be traced between the NCB of the 1980s and today's Government Technology Agency (GovTech). Following an initial decade focused on building up the state's computing resources, in the 1990s the NCB turned its attention to using information technology to improve quality of life in Singapore.[35] This was, in part, driven by a "convergence of information technology and telecommunications which transformed the concept of service delivery."[36] It is also possible to trace the origins of the Smart Nation initiative's concept in the Civil Service Computerisation Programme (1980–1999), e-Government action plans (2000–2003 and 2003–2006), and the concept of "integrated government" introduced in the iGov master plan (2006–2010). These plans acted to entrench the state further within digital transactions—and carefully order and sanitise such transactions.

National Digital Identity

One of the key elements of Singapore's Smart Nation initiative is its attempt to create a NDI. Digital identities have grown in importance with increasingly ubiquitous digitalisation. Motivated by the need to prevent unauthorised access, many digital services now typically require some form of user authentication. However, most individuals do not have a single, uniformly applied digital identity—rather they tend to utilise a patchwork of different profiles and credentials created and maintained with a range of digital services. Digital identities also have a feedback loop to the physical world—consider how an individual's professional affiliations or their relationship status is reflected on their social media network profiles, or how membership or usage of a particular social media network signifies that an individual identifies with a particular community or subculture.

This dynamic is similarly at play when it comes to national digital identities. A growing global movement towards "e-government" has pushed states to digitalise their public services, motivated by the potential for greater access and increased efficiency. With growing digitalisation of public services then comes the need for a way to authenticate users' identities. While NDI initiatives could be seen as simply an effort to digitalise something that is already well established—which is the practice of having residents within a state being registered with public authorities and possessing a form of government-issued identification—they also represent a way for governments to further assert their sovereignty over the digital realm.

At the heart of Singapore's NDI initiative is SingPass—short for Singapore Personal Access—an authentication system launched by the Government Technology Agency in 2003 for transacting with government services.[37] Since its inception, SingPass has been periodically updated to incorporate prevailing cybersecurity best practices. For example, two-factor authentication via a one-time password sent via SMS or generated by a hardware token was introduced in 2015.[38] This was followed by the launch of a mobile app in 2018 that allowed users to log in to digital services using SingPass with a six-digit passcode or their fingerprint.[39] In 2020, face verification was introduced for SingPass, adding another option for biometric two-factor authentication.[40]

In addition to SingPass, the NDI also encompasses MyInfo, a "tell-us-once" service launched in 2016 to autofill personal information in online forms for government services.[41] MyInfo is integrated with SingPass, allowing users to authorise automated retrieval of their personal information stored by different public sector agencies with the aim of minimising errors that may arise due to manual form-filling.[42] In 2019, MyInfo was extended to businesses, performing a similar function in terms of information retrieval for form-filling and transacting with government services.[43] This was mirrored by the extension of SingPass to businesses via the introduction of CorpPass—short for Singapore Corporate Access—in 2016.[44]

On the surface, the NDI initiative is a logical infrastructural pillar undergirding Singapore's Smart Nation initiative, as greater digitalisation of government services requires a secure way for users—whether individuals or businesses—to conduct transactions. However, as a "strategic national project" under the Smart Nation initiative, the NDI is viewed by Singapore's government as more than a digital infrastructure enabler and is increasingly being extended for use cases beyond transacting with government services. For example, the financial services sector has been an early adopter of MyInfo. Banks made use of the service to simplify their "know your customer" processes, and by 2018, were even leveraging MyInfo to offer instant approvals for online credit card and loan applications.[45]

In a similar vein, SingPass authentication was extended to businesses and non-government organisations, allowing them to offer users the ability to log into their digital services using SingPass. By 2020, some two hundred organisations had made use of this application programming interface (API), including banks, insurance providers, and even charities.[46] GovTech's ambitions for mass SingPass API adoption are exemplified by a use case where SingPass was adopted to enable the sale of alcohol via vending machines.[47] On its API portal for developers, GovTech markets SingPass to businesses with the selling point that it provides a ready pool of four million users who already make use of the service to transact with the government.[48] This dynamic is not new—Big Tech companies like Alphabet and Meta have for some time understood the value they can play as digital intermediaries, making use of their large global user populations to offer their services as login options to other applications.[49]

The logic behind why the NDI has evolved from simply allowing users to transact with the government to also transact with businesses and non-government organisations is driven by convenience. However, the broader consequences of this are significant. For example, when users transact with the online form of a digital service using MyInfo, they are shown a screen describing the specific personal data fields that they are consenting to share with that digital service. By itself, this feature of the MyInfo user interface is important because it serves to provide users with transparency when providing consent to sharing their personal data with businesses and non-government organisations. But it is unclear how GovTech and other government agencies regulate the data collection practices of MyInfo API adopters.

Singapore's constitution does not include a right to privacy, so in theory there is no legal imperative for data minimisation, such as limiting the collection of personal data only to what is relevant and necessary to accomplish a specific purpose.[50] Moreover, Singapore's Personal Data Protection Act (PDPA) does not mention data minimisation as a guiding principle for collection of personal data, with Personal Data Protection Commission (Singapore's governing body for privacy) only recommending it as a best practice.[51] This stands in contrast to the European Union's GDPR, which has become a model globally for data protection and privacy legislation.[52] Given these circumstances, MyInfo has the potential to be misused for overcollection of personal data. There is a possibility that users may be compelled to consent to non-essential collection of their personal data, such as in the case of opening a bank account or signing up for an insurance policy.

The challenge here is one of trust. Singaporeans have a high degree of trust in government and the digital services it provides.[53] SingPass and MyInfo are used reliably by many users every day and come with the expectation that they are secure. By offering businesses and non-government organisations the ability to use SingPass and MyInfo, GovTech allows them to leverage the broader trust placed in government and its digital services. However, given the limitations of existing regulation regarding data privacy, there is a clear risk of this trust being misappropriated. This risk can only be expected to grow as use of NDI services becomes more pervasive.

The NDI has the effect of organising digital transactions around a centralised platform developed by the state, which then becomes a custodian for ensuring seamless and "healthy" transactions between individuals and businesses. Singapore's NDI infrastructure grants the state the status of a central agent and key node in digital transactions. While this is logical when it comes to public service delivery, it has a broader impact when mediating transactions between residents and businesses. Ultimately, such systems serve to bind residents more closely to the state, making them more reliant on the state and more invested in state-backed digital infrastructure. The risks here are not just to privacy or digital security. Rather, the NDI allows the government to create a kind of monopoly on trust in the digital space, potentially weakening other forms of digital connection.

COVID-19 Contact Tracing

A second contemporary example of Singapore's practices of informatic governance can be taken from the 2020–2022 COVID-19 pandemic. Unlike many other jurisdictions, management of information became one of the primary tools through which the Singapore government sought to both control the pandemic, and to reassure its residents about the successes of their control measures.

During the early stages of the pandemic, the government developed an extensive and powerful system of contact tracing. This involved the use of data from taxis, ATMs, credit cards, and patient interviews. The aim was to achieve knowledge of the "complete graph," linking all known coronavirus cases on the island to other known cases.[54] Unlike Israel and South Korea, Singapore refrained from utilising phone GPS data to track cases or contacts. However, from early in the pandemic, GovTech was developing an alternative contact tracing system that *would* utilise smartphone capabilities. TraceTogether, as it was called when it was released in March 2020, deployed the Bluetooth function of smartphones in order to detect proximity to other phones—and, by extension, to other individuals. If two phones remained proximate to one another for thirty minutes, they would exchange encoded ID numbers. If an individual became infected with COVID-19, this list of encoded IDs could be uploaded to the Ministry of Health which had the ability to connect these IDs with specific phones. The owners of those phones would be considered close contacts and could be subjected to quarantines.[55]

Although Singapore was far from the only nation to roll out Bluetooth-based contact tracing—for example, Australia deployed COVIDSafe and Germany had the "Corona Warn App"—the extent to which the island's government enforced usage of, and relied on, TraceTogether was unique. Although TraceTogether was never made mandatory, the app was required for entry into almost all public places, including shopping centres, supermarkets, public markets, doctors' surgeries, and sometimes even public parks.[56] Non-users were effectively banned from most indoor spaces outside their own homes. Those without access to smartphones (or who preferred not to use them) were issued with wearable "tokens" that performed the same function as the Bluetooth-enabled phone app.[57]

The marketing of TraceTogether by the government attempted to brand the app as both "community-centred" and "privacy-preserving." The release of the TraceTogether code as the open source "Blue Trace," for example, suggested that the government was committed to transparency and sharing.[58] Likewise, the use of Bluetooth tracing rather than GPS was touted as a boon for Singaporeans' privacy. One of the key features of TraceTogether, however, was that it made the Ministry of Health the central node for the management and control of tracing data.[59] The "privacy-preserving" contact tracing apps—developed by Apple and Google—notified close contacts directly, creating a peer-to-peer communication system.[60] TraceTogether, however, required the centralisation of data at the Ministry of Health. Under such a system, trust must be placed first and foremost in the government, not in other residents. Rather than trusting residents to do the right thing, such as voluntarily sending notifications upon falling ill, TraceTogether shifted responsibility to the government to enforce an individual's compliance. In doing so, TraceTogether reorganised the relationships between residents, community, and government.

As some commentators (including one of the present authors) pointed out at the time, any breaches or perceived breaches in government trust could have an adverse effect on compliance with the app and a detrimental effect on contact tracing.[61] Indeed, to stimulate uptake of the app, the government promised that data from TraceTogether would only be used for contact tracing and not shared with other government agencies. This provision was included in the app's terms of service. However, in January 2021, it was revealed that soon after TraceTogether's implementation, data had in fact been shared with law enforcement authorities in Singapore to assist with tracking a suspect.[62] This was a significant breach of public trust, for which the government was forced to apologise.[63] The government's centralisation and redeployment of data for other purposes undermined trust in the app. Such systems require public cooperation to function as intended—for example, they need people to carry their phones or tokens in public and they need people to keep Bluetooth turned on.[64]

When Singapore was struck by large-scale outbreaks of the virus in the second half of 2021, it became clear that TraceTogether data was *not* necessarily being used consistently in all circumstances. While some individuals received TraceTogether-based quarantine orders, many individuals who *knew* that they were close contacts received no notification and no quarantine orders. Indeed, at that stage, using the system as intended would have demanded issuing quarantine orders to a large segment of the population. This proved politically and economically impossible.[65] This, too, acted to undermine trust in the system and created further risk.

Singapore's TraceTogether system brings together the state's concerns with literal and digital hygiene. TraceTogether, of course, was aimed towards preventing the spread of an infectious disease through controlling the movement of the island's residents. However, at the same time, it also imposed a specific organisation of the flows of information around contact tracing—TraceTogether was a dedicated channel created and managed by the state for tracking movement. What is most significant about Singapore's TraceTogether system was the way in which it attempted to make the government the central node in the collection of epidemiological data. Unlike citizen-centric systems like those of Apple or Google, in the case of TraceTogether, the Ministry of Health became the obligatory passage point for all COVID-19 tracing. Interactions between residents were informatically oriented through the government. As with the NDI, such a system relied on significant trust in the government to function effectively. Also, like NDI, any breakdowns or misalignments of this trust led to serious risks. Systems like TraceTogether not only acted to centralise data, but also set the parameters for what was considered *relevant* information during the pandemic. TraceTogether at least partially replaced or substituted for the other forms of data (such as patient interviews) that could provide epidemiologically useful information.[66] The government established control not only over the system itself, but also over the kind of information flowing within that system.

Conclusions

Smart cities are frequently touted as holding great promise for the future. The discourse about smart cities imagines a future city managed by sensors, the Internet of Things, and big data. But in Singapore we can see many aspects of such smart city visions already in action and begin to analyse their consequences. One important finding here is that Singapore's Smart Nation plans do not emerge onto a *tabula rasa*. Rather, these discourses and platforms are grafted onto existing institutional and technological structures, carrying with them significant colonial legacies. Singapore's history of using information technologies and infrastructures to organise how residents may interact with government conditions the ways in which new information systems and practices are developed and utilised. For Singapore, information technologies have long involved interventions into education, work, and family life. Its Smart Nation initiative continues these trends.

One of the most significant critiques of smart cities has been their intensification of data collection by private interests and the intrusion of corporate infrastructure into urban spaces.[67] Here, criticisms of smart cities are linked to critiques of "surveillance capitalism," suggesting that urban sensors will become yet another site for the vacuuming up of user data.[68] This may indeed be true. But what we see in Singapore is something significantly different. Projects such as the NDI show how the government is actively attempting to substitute themselves for corporate actors and services (in this case, acting as a centralised service for identification and authentication). This is not merely a blurring of the lines between the government and the private sector, but an attempt to compete with the private sector in these domains. The government seeks to establish the structure of the interactions on multiple scales: between individual and individual, between individual and government, and between individual and corporation. What is at stake here is not so much the monopolisation of personal data as dominance over the legal, technical, and social infrastructures for collecting that data.

The role that the government wishes to fill in such cases could be described as that of an "honest broker." When a website seeks to verify our identity using our Google or Facebook account, these services and companies are seeking to (honestly) broker a transaction between an individual and a third party, such as an online business. As the Singapore government inserts itself into these transactions, it takes on the brokering role. This has several consequences. First, it means that the government puts itself in a position where it must be trusted. Second, and more importantly, it also means that trust in government comes to *substitute* for other forms of trust. For example, rather than facilitating or building trust between residents, we instead rely on the government to verify their identity or their bona fides. Likewise, rather than trusting a particular business, we can rely on the government to verify its credentials for us.

It may arguably be better to trust the Singapore government than to trust Alphabet or Meta. But such a system has consequences for social and community relations. Singaporeans increasingly need to rely on the state to manage their day-to-day interactions, placing less and less trust in other institutions and individuals. By orienting informatic interactions towards a central node, the Singapore state undermines the possibility of alternative forms of informatic interaction. This intentional disruption of social bonds further demonstrates the necessity of the government's own operations and creates opportunities for the government to consolidate its power and legitimacy.

Framing this in terms of "informatic sanitation" suggests continuity between colonial and postcolonial practices, and also indicates how forms of digital infrastructure become forms of governance. Just as the sciences of hygiene and the modalities of public health and sanitation informed the governance of colonial space, the ordering and cleansing of information have become critical forms of governance under the Smart Nation initiative. This ordering of information not only enshrines the role of the government as the major collector and custodian of data, but also ensures the government's continued monopoly over flows of data between residents, business, and the state. Ezra Ho has argued that Singapore's Smart Nation initiative is likely to entrench existing norms and power structures: "The rollout of such 'smart' interventions aligns with the neoliberal developmental logics of the ruling party. Instead of empowering and transforming practices, these technologies further entrench the pragmatic and depoliticised ethos of Singaporean society, consolidating authoritarian rule."[69]

What we have argued here is that the Smart Nation initiative is also aligned with Singapore's longer-term practices of information management. The ways in which information and its technologies are used to manage people and link people and communities to government in specific (and top-down) ways are reproduced by the Smart Nation initiative. Like Ho, we believe that such practices are unlikely to be transformative. Instead, the monopolisation of informatic flows by the government not only poses risks to privacy and cybersecurity, but also narrows the possibilities for other forms of informatic interaction. Singapore's case suggests how such informatic interactions are vital parameters in establishing, performing, maintaining, or undermining social ties. Who, what, and how we trust—in smart nations and beyond—is shaped by how information is managed and governed.

Notes

1 Carlo Ratti and Matthew Claudel, *The City of Tomorrow: Sensors, Networks, Hackers, and the Future of Urban Life* (New Haven, CT: Yale University Press, 2016).
2 For example, see Anthony Townsend, *Smart Cities: Big Data, Civic Hackers, and the Quest for a New Utopia* (New York: W.W. Norton, 2013).
3 Adam Greenfield, *Against the Smart City* (New York: Verso, 2013).
4 Alistair Black, "Information History," *Annual Review of Information Science and Technology* 40 (Medford, NJ: Information Today, 2006): 441–473, esp. 452.
5 For example, see Manuel Castells, *The Informational City: Information Technology, Economic Restructuring, and the Urban-Regional Process* (New York: John Wiley, 1991).
6 C. A. Bayly, *Information and Empire: Intelligence Gathering and Social Communication in India 1780–1870* (Cambridge, UK: Cambridge University Press, 2009).
7 On the significance of Singapore as a telegraphic hub, for example, see P. M. Kennedy, "Imperial Cable Communications and Strategy, 1870–1914," *The English Historical Review* 86, no. 341 (1971): 728–752.
8 Brenda Yeoh, *Contesting Space in Colonial Singapore: Power Relations and the Urban Built Environment* (Singapore: Singapore University Press, 2003).
9 On the political history of Singapore, see Michael D. Barr, *The Ruling Elite of Singapore: Networks of Power and Influence* (London: I.B. Tauris, 2014).
10 Robert Home, "British Colonial Civic Improvement in the Early Twentieth Century: E. P. Richards in Madras, Calcutta, and Singapore," *Planning Perspectives* 31, no. 4 (2016): 635–644.
11 "Singapore Improvement Trust," *Singapore Free Press and Mercantile Advertiser*, August 19, 1925, 123. For newspaper sources, see the database NewspaperSG, https://eresources.nlb.gov.sg/newspapers.
12 "Improvement Trust," *Straits Times*, October 8, 1923, 11.
13 "Singapore Improvement Trust."
14 "Town-Planning in Singapore," *The Straits Times*, December 14, 1931, 6.

15 "Improvement Trust Flats Occupied," *The Straits Times*, December 2, 1936, 18; and "The Improvement Trust," *Sunday Tribune Singapore*, November 29, 1936, 1.
16 "Need for New Industries in S'pore," *Straits Times*, January 6, 1951, 7.
17 Rolf Jensen, "Planning, Urban Renewal, and Housing in Singapore," *The Town Planning Review* 38, no. 2 (1967): 115–131.
18 "Singapore Improvement Trust. Master Plan Reports," *Tropical Housing and Planning Monthly Bulletin* 1, no. 8 (May 31, 1956): 16–27.
19 "Singapore Chronology," *IBM Archives*, n.d., https://www.ibm.com/history.
20 "Singapore Chronology."
21 Robert Iau, interview by Jason Lim, *The Civil Service - A Retrospective*, National Archives of Singapore, February 1, 2001, 142, https://www.nas.gov.sg/archivesonline/oral_history_interviews/interview/002275.
22 Iau, interview by Jason Lim, 139–140.
23 Iau, interview by Jason Lim, 147.
24 Iau, interview by Jason Lim, 149–155.
25 Iau, interview by Jason Lim, 153.
26 Nurhaizatul Jamila Jamil and Sharon Teng, "Mosque Building and Mendaki Fund," *Singapore Infopedia*, n.d., https://www.nlb.gov.sg/main/article-detail?cmsuuid=28ec75a4-0cd2-401f-bf89-ea0f60bad98d.
27 Iau, interview by Jason Lim, 153.
28 Iau, interview by Jason Lim, 154.
29 Committee on National Computerisation, "Report on the Committee on National Computerisation" (October 1980).
30 National IT Plan Working Committee, "National IT Plan: A Strategic Framework" (November 1985).
31 Hallam Stevens, "Teleview and the Aspirations of the Infrastructural State in Singapore," in *Infrastructure and the Remaking of Asia*, ed. Max Hirsh and Till Mostowlansky (Honolulu, HI: University of Hawaii Press, 2023), 134–154.
32 Tien Chia Liang, Sung Lee Bu, Kiat Yeo Chai, "Information Technology and the Internet: The Singapore Experience," *Information Technology for Development* 8, no. 2 (1998): 101–120.
33 National Computer Board, "Vision of an Intelligent Island: The IT2000 Report" (Singapore: SNP Publishers, 1992), 10.
34 Gregory Clancey, "Intelligent Island to Biopolis: Smart Minds, Sick Bodies, and Millennial Turns in Singapore," *Science, Technology & Society* 17, no. 1 (2012): 13–35.
35 National Computer Board, *Towards an Intelligent Island: NCB 10th Anniversary 1981–1991* (Singapore: National Computer Board, 1991), 20.
36 *iGov2010: From Integrating Services to Integrating Government* (Ministry of Finance Singapore and Infocomm Development Authority Singapore, 2006), 9, https://www.tech.gov.sg/files/media/corporate-publications/2016/01/iGov-2010.pdf.
37 Government of Singapore, "Your Improved Digital ID to Make Life Easy," https://www.singpass.gov.sg/main/.
38 Lester Hio, "New, More Secure SingPass with 2-Step Verification System to Roll out July 5," *Straits Times*, July 2, 2015, https://www.straitstimes.com/singapore/new-more-secure-singpass-with-2-step-verification-system-to-roll-out-on-july-5.
39 Irene Tham, "New SingPass Mobile App Allows Users to Log into Government E-Services by Scanning Fingerprints or Faces," *Straits Times*, October 22, 2018, https://www.straitstimes.com/singapore/new-singpass-mobile-app-allows-users-to-log-into-government-e-services-by-scanning.
40 Cara Wong, "SingPass Users Can Now Verify Identity by Scanning Faces or Sending OTPs to Another User," *Straits Times*, December 16, 2020, https://www.straitstimes.com/singapore/singpass-users-can-now-verify-identity-by-scanning-faces-or-sending-otps-to-another-user.
41 Government of Singapore, "Discover What You Can Do with SingPass," https://www.singpass.gov.sg/main/individuals/.
42 Irene Tham, "New MyInfo Service Cuts Hassle of Filling in Forms for Government Online Services," *Straits Times*, November 1, 2016, https://www.straitstimes.com/singapore/new-myinfo-service-cuts-hassle-of-filling-in-forms-for-online-government-services.

43 Government of Singapore, "Your Corporate Data Platform," https://www.singpass.gov.sg/myinfobusiness.
44 Government Technology Agency, "Introducing CorpPass for Businesses and Other Entities to Transact Online with the Government," Media release, September 1, 2016. https://www.tech.gov.sg/media/media-releases/introducing-corppass-for-businesses-and-other-entities-to-transact-online-with-the-government.
45 Nisha Ramchandani, "DBS, POSB to Give Instant Approvals for Credit Card, Credit Line Applications Made Online," *Straits Times*, October 2, 2018, https://www.straitstimes.com/business/banking/dbs-posb-to-give-instant-approvals-for-credit-card-credit-line-applications-made.
46 Kenny Chee, "Buy Alcohol with SingPass from Vending Machines Soon; App Users Triple in Past Year," *Straits Times*, March 5, 2021, https://www.straitstimes.com/tech/tech-news/singpass-transactions-doubled-in-2020-with-more-people-going-digital-during-pandemic.
47 Chee, "Buy Alcohol."
48 https://api.singpass.gov.sg/library/login/business/introduction.
49 Lily Hay Newman, "Think Twice before Using Facebook, Google, or Apple to Sign in Everywhere," *Wired*, September 21, 2020, https://www.wired.com/story/single-sign-on-facebook-google-apple/.
50 Teo Yi-Ling and Manoj Harjani, "Smart Nation: Privacy Protection and Public Trust," *RSIS Commentaries*, February 2, 2021, https://www.rsis.edu.sg/rsis-publication/cens/smart-nation-privacy-protection-and-public-trust/.
51 Personal Data Protection Commission, "Avoid Overcollection of Personal Data," Media Release, May 25, 2015, https://www.pdpc.gov.sg/news-and-events/press-room/2015/05/avoid-overcollection-of-personal-data.
52 Cedric Ryngaert and Mistale Taylor, "The GDPR as Global Data Protection Regulation?" *AJIL Unbound* 114 (2020): 5–9.
53 Grantly Mailes et al., *The Global Trust Imperative* (Boston Consulting Group and Salesforce, 2021), https://web-assets.bcg.com/bf/de/d2a310054cd8891fd7f8cd95452b/the-global-trust-imperative-salesforce-bcg-whitepaper.pdf.
54 Sean Han Seng Lai et al., "The Experience of Contact Tracing in Singapore in the Control of COVID-19: Highlighting the Use of Digital Technology," *International Orthopaedics* 45, no. 1 (2021): 65–69. See also Yeo Sam Jo, "A Guide to Singapore's Covid-19 Contact-Tracing System." *Straits Times*, March 28, 2020, https://www.straitstimes.com/multimedia/a-guide-to-singapores-covid-19-contact-tracing-system.
55 Government of Singapore, "How TraceTogether Works," https://www.tracetogether.gov.sg/.
56 Jason Fan, "TraceTogether is Now Compulsory for SafeEntry to Public Places. Here are Tips to Make your Life Easier," *Mothership.sg*, May 17, 2021, https://mothership.sg/2021/05/tracetogether-safeentry-tips/.
57 Today Online, "New TraceTogether Token to Have no GPS or Internet Connectivity to Track User's Whereabouts: Vivian Balakrishnan," *Today Online*, June 8, 2020, https://www.todayonline.com/singapore/tracetogether-token-has-no-gps-or-internet-connectivity-track-users-whereabouts-vivian.
58 Government of Singapore, "BlueTrace Protocol," https://www.undp.org/policy-centre/singapore/bluetrace..
59 Hallam Stevens and Monamie Bhadra Haines, "Pandemic Response, Democracy, and Technology," *East Asian Science, Technology and Society* 14, no. 3 (2020): 523–532.
60 Apple/Google, "Privacy-Preserving Contact Tracing," https://covid19.apple.com/contacttracing.
61 Teo Yi-Ling and Manoj Harjani, "Smart Nation: Privacy Protection and Public Trust," RSIS Commentary (CO21018), February 2, 2021, https://www.rsis.edu.sg/rsis-publication/cens/smart-nation-privacy-protection-and-public-trust/.
62 Kirsten Han, "Broken Promises: How Singapore Lost Trust on Contact Tracing Privacy," *MIT Technology Review*, January 11, 2021, https://www.technologyreview.com/2021/01/11/1016004/singapore-tracetogether-contact-tracing-police/.
63 Kenny Chee, "Vivian Balakrishnan Says He 'Deeply Regrets' Mistake on TraceTogether Data," *Straits Times*, February 2, 2021, https://www.straitstimes.com/singapore/vivian-balakrishnan-says-he-deeply-regrets-mistake-on-tracetogether-data-first-realised-it.
64 Mark Findlay, "Commentary: TraceTogether and SafeEntry were Never Foolproof in Averting Fishery Port and KTV Clusters," *Channel News Asia*, July 23, 2021, https://cnalifestyle.channelnewsasia.com/commentary/commentary-tracetogether-and-safeentry-were-never-foolproof-averting-recent-fishery-port-and-ktv-clusters-314066.

65 WHO data shows that by February 2022, Singapore was experiencing approximately 120,000 new COVID-19 cases per week. Assuming each of these cases generated five close contacts, this would result in quarantining almost six hundred thousand individuals (or more than 10% of the population) per week. If a quarantine order lasted for two weeks, then 20% of the population would be quarantined at any one time, See https://covid19.who.int/region/wpro/country/sg.
66 For example, TraceTogether was partially justified on the grounds of being a labour-saving alternative to manual contact tracing. See Sean Han et al., "The Experience of Contact Tracing in Singapore."
67 For example, see Orit Halpern, *Beautiful Data: A History of Vision and Reason Since 1945* (Cambridge, MA: MIT Press, 2015).
68 Shoshana Zuboff, *The Age of Surveillance Capitalism: The Fight for a Human Future at the New Frontier of Power* (London: Profile Books, 2019).
69 Ezra Ho, "Smart Subjects for a Smart Nation? Governing (Smart) Mentalities in Singapore," *Urban Studies* 54, no. 13 (2017): 3101–3118.

PART IV

Circulating, Networking, Controlling

24
THE POLITICS OF COMMUNICATION IN THE EARLY MODERN CITY
Istanbul and Venice*

Filippo de Vivo

Between the fifteenth and eighteenth centuries, Europe experienced a transformation in political information. News about states, wars, famines, rebellions, and other current affairs accelerated and spread like never before to affect government decisions, international relations, and the lives of millions. Historians used to emphasise the role of technology and print in this process, but more recently they have shown that old and new media combined, and that change came from people and institutions more than technology.[1] New resident embassies made diplomatic correspondence more frequent; chancelleries expanded techniques for information management; professionals began writing regular manuscript newsletters; empires, trading companies, and missionary orders exchanged letters between distant parts of the world; meanwhile, paper became cheaper, literacy expanded, and infrastructural improvements in postal systems accelerated long-distance communications. Printed pamphlets and periodicals began fuelling religious and political debate, but orality continued to be decisive: towncriers remained the principal agents of official publication and most people exchanged and discussed the news in face-to-face encounters. But crucial questions remain. Who had access to the news? And did information growth reflect criticism or propaganda, empowerment, or control? To answer, we need to move beyond a history of media to a social and political history of communication practices: who exchanged what news, how, and why.

Two opposite views dominate the history of early modern political communication. In Jürgen Habermas' public sphere, seventeenth-century English coffeehouses and eighteenth-century French salons turned politics into the object of discussion for an increasingly critical bourgeois public. Many early modern historians have exported, expanded, and predated the public sphere, just as many criticise its abstraction, based on an idealised rational and egalitarian public.[2] The other interpretation sees communication essentially as a tool of power, in the vein of Michel Foucault's power-knowledge, whether as part of early

---

* I am deeply grateful to John-Paul Ghobrial and Aslı Niyazioğlu for many conversations on this topic and for their comments on a previous version of this chapter.

DOI: 10.4324/9781003310532-28

modern state centralisation, the expansion of empires, or the rise of capitalism.[3] This view underlines censorship and propaganda, but the risk with it is to overlook information that escaped control, and to ignore the unintended consequences of communication. In countering the rigid one-sidedness of both bottom-up and top-down interpretations, an important inspiration comes from Robert Darnton's communication circuit model, which emphasises people and sees their media-related activities as interacting in a continuous cycle.[4] But those people were not homogeneous. How can we capture their inequalities in accessing information? How do we account for the agency of different groups and for their conflicts? This chapter adopts the view that that communication in the early modern city was itself political because it involved interactions among a plurality of actors with often contrasting views, needs, resources, and desires. These interactions clustered around three poles locked in competition: governments; broader political elites; and large numbers of diverse socio-professional classes too often described as ordinary people. Through this three-way approach, we can question simplistic dichotomies elite-popular while also understanding both dissemination and manipulation, control, and resistance.

While the one-sided models of public sphere and propaganda encapsulate Western ideas of modernisation (whether positive or negative), a multipolar approach to communication politics helps challenge traditional Eurocentric narratives. These include the technological fetishisation of the press as an agent of change; the religio-civilisational dichotomy dear to Max Weber pitting poor political participation in Islamic cities against civic-minded Christian ones; and political stereotypes going back to ideas of 'Oriental despotism' versus 'Western liberties'. This chapter compares Venice and Istanbul, two capitals traditionally regarded as antagonistic and antithetical: the bulwark of Christianity and the residence of the caliph, a republic and an autocracy, a commercial city-state, and the centre of a military behemoth. And yet Venice's republican politics was in the hands of less than 2% of the capital's population, while sultans had to negotiate power with Istanbul's increasingly powerful elites. Demographics differed substantially but not incommensurably: mid-sixteenth-century Istanbul had around 400,000 inhabitants, Venice 150,000, and both grew because of sustained immigration. Istanbul was a multilingual, multi-faith metropolis, but Venice too had important linguistic and religious minorities. Despite huge territorial disparity, both ruled far-stretched composite empires requiring complex information channels. And both were regarded as information hubs at the time.[5] As for their mutual relations, older scholarship emphasised Ottoman-Venetian hostility but, with the years of peace far outweighing those of war, recent historiography has underlined contacts.[6] Istanbul and Venice competed aggressively for intelligence, but they also exchanged information on trade and diplomacy. Finally, besides connections, it is worth exploring comparisons—especially given the imbalance between Venice's thriving publishing industry and Istanbul, where, before the eighteenth century, presses were only established sporadically to serve minorities. Comparing helps us test the impact of technology relative to communication practices by other means. The findings are instructive and may be applied to other case studies.

Secrecy and Communication in Government

Shifting from raw information and media to the processes and practices of communication shows that, even at the centre of government, they made for both power and competition. Firstly, decision-making rested on debating incoming information, where authority derived from eloquence and the accuracy of one's sources. Ruling councils received messengers, letters, petitioners, and foreign ambassadors. In the Venetian republic, this involved several passages. A small cabinet, the Collegio, read incoming letters, then had them summarised and passed on with preliminary decisions to the 250-strong Senate for debate—while the latter retained the final say, the former built its power on information control.[7] For all their supposed despotism, sultans also consulted a council, the Divan, where, as a contemporary of Mehmed II reported, "the sultan begins to talk and everyone answers his questions according to his judgment and in this manner they reach decisions about matters of war and the maintenance of the state."[8] Later, the Divan grew from six to fifteen members and increasingly functioned in the sultan's absence.[9]

Early modern governments were "letterocracies" dealing with masses of correspondence concerning expanding areas of administration with increasingly sophisticated techniques for information management.[10] The Venetian chancellery prepared summaries of incoming information and transcribed outgoing letters in registers with thematic indexes for easy retrieval; its archives increased in time to thousands of volumes.[11] In Istanbul, the Head of the chancery also employed clerks to make summaries of letters for presentation in the Divan.[12] Venetian ambassadors recognised the similarity—moreover, at much the same time in mid-sixteenth century, the Venetians devised sets of registers for sensitive documentation and the Ottomans inaugurated the *Mühimme Defterleri* "Registers of Important Imperial Affairs."[13]

Both governments intensified the collection of information about their capitals, empires, and about foreign countries. Venice systematically collected real-estate and demographic information for censuses. It also required dozens of provincial governors and ambassadors abroad to write regular dispatches and end-of-mission reports about political, military, and economic news. The reading of *relazioni* about the Ottoman Empire in the Venetian Senate attracted crowds of patricians.[14] The Divan, too, ordered tax collectors' reports about every shop in Istanbul, land surveys of the empire's territories, and information about neighbouring countries from the governors of border provinces.[15] Venice pioneered the establishment of permanent embassies. Information and communication were central to the activity of Venetian ambassadors, which one of them described as "listening and advising ... negotiating ... reporting."[16] The Ottomans kept no resident embassies abroad; historians used to regard this as a sign of disinterest, but now underline the variety of Ottoman diplomatic channels, including increasingly frequent interactions with Christian and Muslim states from England to Poland and Morocco to India.[17] In less than two centuries after 1453, they sent 159 missions to Venice: a near-permanent presence.[18] Both were diplomatic centres but, if anything, Istanbul had even more foreign missions (and from further afield) at any given time. The Ottoman equivalents of *relazioni*, s*efaretname*s, date from the eighteenth century, but earlier envoys already reported back orally (as did Venetian ambassadors, alongside submitting written copies). In turn, sultans regularly sent accounts of victorious campaigns, *fetihnames*, to foreign rulers, including to Venice, where they were translated and read out in the Collegio.[19]

Governments were no monoliths, and information growth generated not just power but also tensions. Despite proudly asserting their chancellors' loyalty, the Venetian authorities constantly worried about possible leaks. They enacted bureaucratic reforms intended to both improve information management and protect confidentiality.[20] Just as the Venetians instituted separate chanceries with increasing levels of secrecy, so the Ottomans also had separate rooms, and treasury clerks employed deliberately script incomprehensible to others.[21] Another reason for tension is that information sources were never exclusive: in both capitals, information was subject to competition among branches of government, courtiers or patricians, and their factions. Venetians developed a carefully regulated process empowering the small Council of Ten to acquire the most sensitive information and then select the news they "communicated" (as they called it) onto larger assemblies.[22] But there was frequent rivalry between them, resulting in occasional outright conflict and relentless underlying factionalism. Power was divided in Istanbul too, especially a time of increasing palace struggles and changes in succession rules. Many competed for the "ear" of sultans and grand viziers, who received news and petitions also from the Agha of the Gate, the Steward of the Gatekeepers and others. Selim I dismissed a vizier for daring to ask the grand vizier what he had discussed with the sultan.[23] From the late sixteenth century, the sultans' mothers or *valides* gained growing influence, sponsored large public projects, and played important roles in affairs of state.[24] Murad III's mother, Nur Banu (c. 1530–1583) —from an old Venetian family of Paros though not a patrician as she and Venetian diplomats claimed—corresponded with foreign rulers by way of her own women scribes.[25]

In both polities, the decision-making process was at least in principle covered by secrecy. Secrecy was codified in sultanic law since at least Mehmed II as well as in advice literature for rulers and secretaries.[26] To maintain a façade of unity, trickier in republics than in monarchies, Venetian patricians were sworn to confidentiality not just about the topics they debated, but also about the fact they debated at all; secretaries took no minutes of debates and only recorded outcomes. In 1537, Venice instituted a special magistracy of "State Inquisitors over Disclosures of Secrets." *Arcana Imperii/esrar-ı Saltanat* had both practical and symbolic functions. As Italian reason of state authors put it, "secrecy makes the sovereign similar to God" because "men, ignorant of his thoughts, stand in suspense about his schemes."[27] The Ottoman sultan was also supposed to be omniscient and unknowable, as symbolised in the architecture of his palace. He observed the Divan unseen from behind an internal window—no one could tell whether he was there—while the Palace towers showed he was watching over his subjects.[28] Finally, both republican Venice and imperial Istanbul turned speech limitation into an awe-inspiring sign of splendour. More than two thousand patricians voted silently in Venice's Great Council, deeply impressing eminent visitors invited to attend (but never allowed into the presumably rowdier Senate). Venetian visitors admired the inner court of Topkapı—where servants were mute—"as silent as a sanctuary."[29] But neither government could disguise the fact that politics rested on communication.

Information and Competition in the Political Arena

In both capitals, information leaked out of council chambers to wider political elites. A Janissary overheard the decision to invade Bosnia in 1463 in a private conversation between two viziers in the vault of the Treasury.[30] Venetian patricians gathered daily to discuss state affairs outside the Ducal Palace in a space known as "broglio," a word for intrigue originating from the orchard ("brolo") that once stood there.[31] The informal communication of supposedly secret information served the networks of patronage and partisanship that underpinned formal political advancement in fiercely competitive environments. Sixteenth-century viziers mostly entered the palace as boy-slaves and owed their careers to the sultan, but other Divan members such as judges came from powerful Istanbul families and trained in medreses—they presumably retained connections and continued to discuss their position and other information with their families, old teachers, and classmates. By the seventeenth century, the Istanbulite elite captured even greater power and from the 1650s, the grand vizier began gathering his own Divan in a building next to his home. In Venice too, the boundary between government and the private sphere of statesmen's families was slippery as patricians compiled supposedly confidential information for the use of relatives and friends.[32] Many Venetian diplomatic dispatches, including from the Ottoman Empire, are only preserved because ambassadors kept copies in private archives.

The very expansion of information networks threatened secrecy. Permanent embassies attracted intelligence professionals, agents, spies, and informers.[33] One Venetian ambassador boasted he had entered the Harem, but all his colleagues reported what they heard about Divan meetings. In turn, an Ottoman agent warned that the Venetians could not even "clean their teeth without the spies informing immediately the Sultan."[34] Interpreters serving in Istanbul's Venetian embassy sometimes worked as double agents for the Ottomans, and Venetians regularly complained that the Ottomans knew the secrets of the Senate. Some leaks were intentional, for example, with news from the war front: as a foreign ambassador reported, "there hath been great care to keep all bad news very private & spread false report of good, so it is hard to guess the truth."[35] But the growth of bureaucracy made for unwelcome leaks too as clerks increased in numbers, rotated and owed their career to patron-client relations that escaped institutional communication. In Venice, we know of many cases when one or more of the chancellery's one hundred employees disclosed secrets to allies, betrayed it to foreigners, or sold it under the counter to buyers interested in government information.[36] In the sixteenth century, the Divan grew from sixteen clerks to over fifty: they owed their careers to personal or family connections and no doubt were ready to pass information to their patrons. In 1590, a grand vizier, worried about the forgery of documents in the imperial chancery, believed that some fifty to sixty people may have been involved. He condemned their offence as "sharing the political power."[37]

Sheer numbers undermined confidentiality. Venice is known for its large 2,000–2,500 strong patriciate, and the number of people with positions in Topkapı was probably larger. At any given time, there was a constant movement in and out of republican office or sultanic favour. Insiders had access to power and information, but outsiders could use information to gain or regain power. Minor Venetian patrician and historian Marin Sanudo built a reputation for political knowledge by keeping a massive diary of home and foreign news, including secret information. In the Ottoman Empire too, there were countless bureaucrat-scholars who, like secretary, administrator, historian, and poet Mustafa Ali, elaborated political information in writings for select publics in the hope of obtaining promotion.[38] In Venice, patricians temporarily excluded from councils divulged information as a tool in the political struggle. The former ambassador Ottaviano Bon had associates transcribe and circulate his *relazione* of a recent peace mission to France in order to vindicate his conduct against criticisms and to raise support for his faction's line in foreign policy; the report circulated widely and was even discussed at dinner parties.[39] Figures like Sanudo, Mustafa Ali, and Bon drew from and contributed to a vibrant market for manuscripts of state mysteries—for example, the Venetian *relazioni* became a sought-after genre, avidly bought and read as far as Oxford and likely in Istanbul too.[40]

Despite official secrecy, the production and circulation of intelligence originated in a political arena which overlapped with government but extended far outside it to include prominent locals and their families, foreign ambassadors and their networks, and a host of informal agents. The size of one's household mattered in both courtly and republican capitals.[41] In both, statesmen relied on the services of men of letters, jurists, secretaries, and others who lacked office or power but made political expertise into a semiprofessional skill. Together, they constituted information elites varying in wealth but distinguished by education, knowledge, and connections. They socialised and discussed the news in informal gatherings known in Venice as *ridotti* (from "getting together") and in the Ottoman Empire as *mecalis* (from "sitting"): like the later French *salons*, these words indicated both social occasions and the spaces in which they took place.[42]

Cultural historians have studied the role of these "intelligencers" and their patron-client relations in elaborating knowledge and shaping the literary canon, erudition, or science.[43] Much the same can be said of political ideas concerning government structures, imperial territories, or foreign affairs. Of course, there were specificities; for example, political poetry (*siyaset-name*) was more common in Turkish than in Italian.[44] Dream narratives are rare in Venice, but in Istanbul, they offered ways of reflecting and commenting on important events and individuals.[45] In Venice, however, family chronicles and archives played a crucial role, including transcripts of speeches delivered in government councils and other texts filtering out of the authorities' domain that memorialised the actions of the authors or their relatives and in the process sometimes criticised government policy. But despite these differences, in both cities, intelligence professionals produced a variety of textual genres that turned everyday information into political knowledge: counsels for rulers, political leaders, and minor statesmen; manuals for secretaries; maps, gazetteers, travel accounts; reports about distant provinces or foreign countries. Texts originating from factions in the political arena expressed criticisms about government policy, denounced decline, and offered advice for future corrections. Sometimes, the professionals belonged to the same group, for example, the Christian interpreters known as dragomans who made a living of their ability to act as go-betweens for foreign ambassadors in Istanbul, and in Venice published substantial bodies of writings, reports, or dictionaries that spread knowledge about the Ottoman Empire in the West.[46]

Perhaps the most famous information professionals in Venice were the newswriters who since the sixteenth century picked up information from conversations in the city and from foreign letters, then compiled weekly or bi-weekly newsletters known as *avvisi* which they transcribed in multiple copies for fee-paying correspondents.[47] They made information into a commodity before the periodical press, and in fact printed periodicals regularly drew from manuscript newsletters. Two little-known points need stressing about *avvisi* in the present context. One is that Venetian newswriters participated in networks which extended to Istanbul. *Avvisi* from Venice reached foreign ambassadors there, and, in turn, they almost always featured paragraphs about the Ottoman capital, where other newswriters must have produced regular information.[48] For example, in 1687–1688, an Istanbul-based English intelligencer produced at least thirty.[49] The other point is that periodical newswriting was fully part of the political arena. More than forerunners of neutral journalism, as they are sometimes seen, *reportisti* depended for money and information on foreign ambassadors or leading statesmen, and, in turn, they slanted the news in their patrons' favour. This also explains their survival. In 1571, the Venetian government tried to prohibit their activities but ultimately found them too useful to suppress completely—after all, Venetian ambassadors themselves typically used *avvisi*. Then at a time of crisis around 1606, the government shifted from censoring to manipulating newsletters.[50]

Beyond the professionals, other ramifications of the political arena cast doubt on the binary powerful-powerless in early modern politics. Most women were barred from formal government, but many had access to the informal exchange of political news. In Venice, patrician women played crucial roles as mothers, wives, and sisters in fostering precious political alliances or as hostesses for politically significant social gatherings; they rarely attracted the attention of the Inquisitors of State, but in 1472 Elisabetta Zeno was exiled for passing state secrets to her brother, Pope Paul II.[51] In Istanbul, many women acted as go-betweens in and out of the Imperial Harem. Beatrice Michiel/Fatima Hatun fled an unhappy marriage in Venice to Istanbul and there reported to Venetian ambassadors "that which touches on the interests of Venice."[52] More socially entrenched examples included the women of dragoman families who acted as linchpins between different communities in the capital.[53] Many commoners worked in jobs that gave them professional access to the houses, and secrets, of the powerful. Some Istanbul-based physicians acted as spies; others were instructed to spread rumours against rivals.[54] The Venetian ambassador there had his own resident barber-surgeon but also used local Jewish physicians who treated powerful viziers; in turn, the Spanish ambassador in Venice employed a Portuguese doctor who served in patrician houses.[55] Further down the social scale, intelligencers included musicians— for example, those who moved between the Venetian embassy and the court in London.[56] Artists worked as agents and sometimes as spies, like Velazquez in Venice. From Istanbul, Gentile Bellini brought back not just drawings but also news of the Ottoman court, including about real or imagined conversations with the sultan.[57] Physical proximity to powerful figures gave servants a special role too. In the early seventeenth century, Venice's Inquisitors of State hired the oarsman and waiter of the papal nuncio, who reported about the places the nuncio visited and the people who dined with him.[58] In Istanbul only a few years earlier, a court jester was fired for "associating with people outside the palace." In turn, this was part of a well-publicised campaign by Mehmed III against palace buffoons at a time of military defeats.[59] Thus, the political arena could offer the authorities useful scapegoats for public use.

Discussion, Curiosity, and Criticism in the City

How far did ordinary people participate in the exchange of political information? "Ordinary" is an unsatisfactory tag too often applied to socially and culturally dis-homogeneous social groups. However, in both cities, most of the population shared the double feature of being barred from institutional power and having to work for a living. Information professionals also had these characteristics, but ordinary people worked without direct connections with the world of politics. Venice officially separated patricians and elite citizens serving in government administration from the *popolo*, whom it described as foreigners and only capable of pursuing private profit rather than public interest. Unlike other European cities, Venice assigned no government role to trade guilds. In Istanbul, a similar division separated the *askeri*, serving the empire in military/administrative roles and therefore exempted from taxation, from the *re'aya*: merchants, artisans, workers, whose only perceived contribution to politics was precisely to pay taxes. In both cities, the authorities and the political elites scorned artisans and labourers as incapable of political judgement; whenever they had to confront the fact that ordinary people also engaged in political communication, they belittled it with remarkably similar words as the "idle talk" of "lads" or "mobs" driven only by "pleasure" or "hunger."[60]

In principle, governments assigned workers only one form of political expression: acclamation. Istanbulite and Venetian guilds marched in processions accompanying or celebrating the authorities in public.[61] In practice, however, these were unpredictable moments when some participants could vent discordant ideas and even criticism. In Istanbul, Evliya Çelebi recounts a dispute between butchers and coffeemakers who, vying for ceremonial place in a procession, in fact put forward opposite ideas of the empire's economic priorities.[62] In Venice, people sometimes turned ducal processions into protests against powerful government officers.[63] The potential divisiveness of information made for contradictory attitudes in the authorities. On the one hand, governments sometimes tried to hide or delay news such as the death of a sultan, a confrontation with the papacy, or military defeats.[64] On the other, they knew they had to give people at least *some* information, such as successions or new laws. In Venice, towncriers read out decrees in the main squares, ferry points, and some bridges; printed proclamations were posted on walls and sometimes inscribed in stone, possibly as much for seeing as for reading.[65] The Ottoman government sent *beşaretnames* (literally "letters bringing glad tidings which occasion joy") to governors and judges in the provinces to encourage celebrations.[66] Cannon shots and fireworks saluted the accession of new sultans or the circumcision of princes; following victories, the authorities ordered all shops and houses illuminated for days.[67] As for locations, some proclamations were made to assembled crowds in the Atmeydanı central square, but Evliya Çelebi also mentions towncriers making announcements near coffeeshops.[68]

What kind of news did ordinary people talk about? It is difficult to trace this today, but we can derive indirect glimpses from the communication of authorities and political elites. In both cities, ambassadors and newswriters often referred vaguely to "rumours in the square" or "the wispering of the curious," and newswriters often prefaced reports with "it is said."[69] Such statements cannot be taken literally, because they often were meant to cover individual sources or alternatively disparage undesirable opinions. But other records show that they contained a kernel of truth. In 1611, the English ambassador's secretary in Venice suggested that the authorities keep "a trusted person" at a corner in Rialto where newswriters and "all foreign ambassadors and others meet every morning to discuss the affairs of the world."[70] In fact, Venice's Inquisitors of State had long had informants: they were interested primarily in preventing spying rather than policing dissent, but trailed foreign spies who met with notaries, insurers, apothecaries, barbers, and booksellers. In the early seventeenth century, they began keeping moles in strategic locations like taverns or squares, who by mid-century noted down conversations whenever they overheard critiques of the authorities.[71] The Ottoman government too eavesdropped on popular opinions. Sultans and grand vezirs were said to tour Istanbul in disguise, and Murad IV (r. 1623–1640) planted so many spies in the city that people were afraid that "walls have ears."[72]

Further evidence can be found in sources deriving from members of the elite whose journals and chronicles noted the news they heard in conversations held public spaces. Venetian patrician and diarist Girolamo Priuli disapproved of "rumours" (*voci*) but recorded discussions in piazzas and churches anyway.[73] Istanbul chronicler Mustafa Selaniki reported news of plagues, battles, taxes, public works, ambassadorial visits, palace intrigues, and corruption; his sources included other officials, but also cooks and guards; he recorded seditious talk in coffeehouses and medreses and rumours provoking brawls in taverns.[74] Al-Nahrawali, an envoy from the Sharif of Mecca to Istanbul, kept a journal of his encounters with viziers and pashas, but also their wives and daughters, servants, clerks, teachers, judges, and Sufi leaders. A physician gave him news of the palace and representatives of the Medinese community brought him their complaints. He worried about "envious types wagging their tongues" but praised an imam as "a comrade delightful in banter and conversation, one who consults with viziers and senior-ranking people."[75] Despite their elitism, these sources cannot fail to trace political communication expanding beyond the elites.

Sociability fuelled political communication. In Istanbul, coffee imported from Yemen first thrived in Sufi settings where it facilitated nocturnal ritual—as it did for Venetian Jews a century later.[76] Coffeehouses first opened in the capital in the 1550s and soon became well-known places for conversation, scholars' harangues, singing, storytelling, and the reading of poems, including satirical verses against powerful figures. It must have been difficult to separate entertainment and political information, true or false. Mustafa Ali described soldiers recounting their feats and others bragging about fantasy posts or high-ranking connections; a century later, another witness described customers "smoking, playing chess, and entertaining themselves with the news."[77] Opposition to coffee reflected less Islamic precepts than fear of seditious talk.[78] By the seventeenth century, suspicions shifted onto tobacco, widely consumed in coffeehouses appealing to increasingly popular customers like janissaries, lower-ranking ulema, and workers who found there the space they lacked in cramped homes.[79] The debate spilled into political controversies, with fire-and-brimstone Kadızadeli preachers condemning and other preachers defending tobacco.[80] Katip Çelebi described how the debate spread across places and media, including sermons, written tracts, and fetwas posted on walls.[81] During revolts, coffeehouses became associated with janissaries and other groups protesting against palace and ulema circles.[82] Murad IV briefly closed them down in 1633—yet, this inevitably provoked further discussion, and years later, a chronicler contrasted the prohibition of innocuous smoking with the inability to quench the fuming lamentations of the oppressed.[83]

Coffeehouses only opened in Venice in mid-seventeenth century, but other places long played similar functions for sociability like taverns and inns.[84] Others acquired an indirect reputation for controversial conversations, such as the backroom in a mercers' shop where Paolo Sarpi (1552–1623) met Protestant envoys to discuss European politics.[85] Some establishments turned information exchange into a secondary but open activity. Apothecary shops competed to attract customers keen to exchange the latest news while their medicines were being prepared; they likely provided information about elections or wars as an additional perk, and customers then contributed further news in a self-reinforcing circle. Informers' reports show that apothecaries welcomed people reading out manuscript *avvisi* and exchanging local news, including patricians and embassies' secretaries, as well as physicians, tradebrokers, but also apprentices, shopboys, and female servants—in other words, representatives of all three levels of political communication. Further down the social scale, barbershops were favourite places of male sociability, where customers spent time talking about the latest news.[86] They attracted critiques similar to those of Istanbul coffeehouses: just as Ottoman elites described the latter attracting "pleasure seekers and idlers," so Venetians ones described "the *piazza*'s idle ... spend[ing] their life in the public square ... do[ing] nothing else all day ... sometimes telling false news in barbershops, other times reading newssheets at the stalls."[87] Of course, there were specificities. The circulation of news in Venice's apothecary shops, while common to many Italian cities, is not attested in Istanbul.[88] There were bathhouses in Venice too however, but they played nothing like the role of Istanbul's *hamams* as centres of "chitchat, gossip and political grumbling," including (in Lady Montagu's words) "the women's coffee-houses."[89]

Many questions remain. First, why were ordinary people interested in obtaining political information? Elite sources described them as idle, but in fact talking about the news was a valuable activity. In Venice, news of wars, treaties, shipwrecks, epidemics, or droughts affected the price of commodities.[90] A fifteenth-century manual recommended that merchants seek news from everywhere.[91] In Istanbul too, according to Selaniki, rumours of impending war caused merchants to stockpile in expectation of hikes.[92] Faraway events could have opposite economic and political implications, leading to disagreement. As an English ambassador remarked in Venice: "this *piazza* is full of noise touching the arrival of the Indian fleet in Spain, the merchants glad, the politiques troubled."[93] Secondly, if information was a tool for governments and elites, did it have political uses for ordinary people too? Of course, we have no direct sources about the opinions of those who left no written records, but divergent interpretations like the one just mentioned show that news could serve contrasting worldviews. In the early 1500s, Venetian authorities welcomed news of Safavid advances against the Ottomans, but a doctor returning from Persia preferred to focus on the more socially radical news that Shah Ismail redistributed wealth from the rich to the poor.[94] At the time of the Lepanto battle in 1571, Venice escalated anti-Islamic ceremonial and printed propaganda, but only few months earlier, an anonymous fictional dialogue between Venetian fishermen hailed the Sultan as the liberator of the oppressed.[95] Literary tropes, perhaps—but a few years later, Paduan conspirators also denounced their Venetian overlords as "worse than the Turks"[96] And in both cities, news could attract prophetic interpretations as divine warning about earthly government.[97]

Thirdly, could information fuel open criticism and protest? Again, the sources are biased by their authors' politics. Venetian authorities suppressed records of revolts, which foreign ambassadors were keen to report.[98] In Istanbul too, we need to gage rebels' ideas indirectly from chronicles written within the elites.[99] In both cases, official propaganda—all-powerful sultanic rule upholding Islam and prosperity, or republican concord and fair justice for all—clashed with hostile information, rumours, poems, and satires that denounced elites' extravagance or the squandering of charity funds.[100] Venetians knew about patrician rivalries and gambled on elections, implicitly making a mockery of the myth of the *Serenissima*; anonymous libels posted on walls denounced the corruption of the justice system. In Istanbul, the execution of possible contenders to the throne could provoke discontent, as in the case of sultan Suleyman I's son Mustafa; workers criticised the perceived failings of sultans on the battlefield or grand viziers' unwillingness to live up to Islamic standards of morality.[101] Talk could lead to protest, when ordinary people made themselves amply heard. Stoked at Friday prayers, in ballads and catchy slogans, rumours that the sultan might remove his capital from Istanbul provoked unrest in 1622 and 1703.[102] In the piazza San Marco too, crowds sometimes agitated to pressurise the doge's electors in favour of a particular candidate.[103] As for foreign policy, news of wars caused fear and anger. In the 1650s, reports of Ottoman advances in Crete terrified Venetians and those of the Venetian blockade of the Dardanelles, Istanbulites. With the threat closer to home, the latter unsurprisingly demonstrated against faraway naval campaigns and demanded land defences instead.[104] People did not just hear the news: they realised its implications and were ready to ask for change.

Finally, we have seen that governments and elites recorded ordinary people's rumors, but how far did they care outside isolated moments of rebellion? In other words, did the three levels interact on a regular basis? Consider these examples. In sixteenth-century Istanbul, Hürrem Sultan's letters to her husband Süleyman the Magnificent, away at the front, criticised pashas and warned him about people reeling at contradictory war reports. She asked him to send news and stop the rumours, assuring him "don't think that it is just for myself that I am asking."[105] In seventeenth-century Venice, uncertain reports of naval battles provoked fears in some and hopes in others: the government at first censored the news but soon had to contrast the negative spin of foreign ambassadors; each newswriter toed his patron's line; merchants and ordinary people reeled and quarrelled over the truth, including Ottoman merchants, who elicited formal protests from the sultan. Manipulated yet uncontrollable, information reverberated across Europe and the Mediterranean.[106] These examples demonstrate a three-way competition among the authorities, a plurality of elites, and broader urban societies who also had a stake in the news. Each tried to secure the news and realised that it was risky to neglect what the others were discussing. Secrecy was not an option.

Conclusion

Political communication both connected Venice and Istanbul and also made them commensurable. The similarities outweighed the differences in the ways information circulated, and the latter had to do with socio-cultural specificities at the time and on the ground rather than with essentialising Eurocentric narratives about politics, religion, or technology. As for politics, once we abandon one-sided models of propaganda or public sphere to look at practices, we can understand the pervasiveness of political communication. In both republican and sultanic capitals, the discussion of political news engaged men and to some extent women at three socio-political levels: authorities, elites, and broader urban society. And it also constantly connected them—not in a seamless cycle (as for Darnton), but in tense, at times creative interactions ranging from exchange to competition to outright opposition. Communication almost invariably frustrated government secrecy, with news leaking because of rivalries among elites. In both cities, information attracted, entertained, and enraged ordinary, working people, and fed criticism against their social and political superiors. The three-way model helps us read the sources produced by governments and elites against the grain, and see how, despite their conceit, both eavesdropped on popular rumours and recorded them in letters, chronicles, and diaries. Governments sought legitimation, but even celebratory moments could turn confrontational, and rumours mobilised people to exercise pressure on government. In fact, official proclamations and ceremonies were less top-down propaganda than defensive responses to fiercely competitive communication outside the authorities' control.

Neither is there evidence of a stark Muslim-Christian dichotomy affecting political communication. First, in these large metropolises, religious minorities played important roles in the political arena, and both also allowed them a degree of self-administration. In fact, Venice's non-Catholics were barred from (formal) politics, while the Ottoman *devshirme* opened imperial governance to Christian converts.[107] Scholars of Venice or other European countries would refuse to reduce political communication to Christianity, but the same and more can be said of the Ottoman Empire to Islam. Of course, confessional politics mattered, but diversity mattered as much. Moreover, even if we restrict ourselves to the dominant faith, Christian and Muslim religious institutions and beliefs similarly provided a framework for rituals, motivated many people's reactions to the news, and offered channels for communication. In both cities, preaching fuelled debate, and religious establishments turned into hotbeds of political discussion, from Sufi brotherhoods to convents. Finally, both governments occasionally clashed with religious authorities, provoking heated debates like Venice with the papacy in 1606–1607 and Osman II with leading ulema in 1618–1622. This divided elites and people inside and outside government institutions. If anything, though Osman lost his head in a rebellion, it was Venice that suffered the heaviest offensive against its legitimacy and had to respond through a vast campaign of pamphleteering.[108]

This brings us to print. It is hard to underestimate the imbalance between early modern Venice, a leading centre of publishing, and Istanbul where presses were few until the eighteenth century. When the pope excommunicated the republic in 1606, Venetians defended themselves with printed pamphlets. However, the government did so reluctantly, after trying to censor news of the conflict; only the dissemination of information through manuscript and word of mouth by people outside the authorities forced Venice to enter the printed fray. And eventually, it was the interaction between texts (printed or in manuscript) and orality that proved resolutive. The comparison between Venice and Istanbul shows that, as far as political communication is concerned, we need to avoid technological determinism. Printing multiplied books cut their costs and fed debate in the political arena and wider publics. But, due to strict ecclesiastical and secular censorship, it hardly turned into an agent of political change by itself. Historians of Venice's information have shown that scribal publication continued to dominate the production of newsletters into the seventeenth century because it avoided control and catered to individual customers. In other words, a market for political news developed outside, and to some extent to the detriment of, print.[109] In similar fashion, historians of the Ottoman book in the last twenty years have overturned old Orientalising ideas about the Ottoman "ban" on printing and underlined the proliferation of texts by means of manuscript.[110] In fact, if anything, early modern Ottoman authors formulated greater criticism of their government than Venetian ones, whose printed books were overwhelmingly celebratory (not least because they had to undergo press censorship). Manuscript and orality dominated decision-making in both governments, and in both cities, manuscript ensured the circulation of news, chronicles, and texts of advice and criticism. Finally, in both cities, it was orality that dominated the *use* of all media—visual, performative, manuscript, as well as printed—and ultimately it was in orally dominated contexts that political communication turned into action.

This chapter has made the case for a comparison between Istanbul and Venice. Only further research can tell how, in turn, they compare with other early modern cities. Do they constitute a Mediterranean model of port cities' entanglement?[111] Or can similar arrangements be found in, say, early modern London or Paris? Do differences in size, religion, or political arrangements between them and, say, Isfahan, Agra, or Beijing undermine commensurability? And can the comparison be extended beyond capitals, to imperial centres like Damascus or Mexico City? In different ways, cities attracted both greater demand for and greater supply of information through the concentration of actors, spaces, and practices of communication. For all their singularity, Istanbul and Venice were not alone as seats of government, arenas for factionalism, centres of commercial and informational routes, or intermediaries of information across countries. The degree of communication inside and across social groups made them special—but not unique. To overcome the mono-directional models illustrated at the beginning of this chapter, comparison shows that the defining development of the age was neither triumphant propaganda nor the rise of the press and unfettered public sphere. The real transformation in early modern political communication was the increasing competition for information among different political and social groups, with inevitably unintended consequences.

Notes

1. Paul M. Dover, *The Information Revolution in Early Modern Europe* (Cambridge, UK: Cambridge University Press, 2021); Andrew Pettegree, *The Invention of News: How the World Came to Know about Itself* (New Haven, CT; London: Yale University Press, 2014); Brendan Dooley, *The Dissemination of News and the Emergence of Contemporaneity in Early Modern Europe* (Farnham and Burlington: Ashgate, 2010).
2. Massimo Rospocher, ed., *Beyond the Public Sphere: Opinions, Publics, Spaces in Early Modern Europe* (Bologna: Il Mulino, 2012); Peter Lake and Steven Pincus, *The Politics of the Public Sphere in Early Modern England* (Manchester: Manchester University Press, 2007); Roger Chartier, *The Cultural Origins of the French Revolution* (Durham, NC: Duke University Press, 1991).
3. For example: Anna Maria Forssberg, *The Story of War: Church and Propaganda in France and Sweden 1610–1710* (Lund: Nordic, 2016); Jason Peacey, *Politicians and Pamphleteers: Propaganda during the English Civil Wars and Interregnum* (Aldershot: Ashgate, 2004). See also the recent exhibition catalogue *Propaganda: Power and Persuasion*, ed. David Welch (London: The British Library, 2013).
4. Robert Darnton, *The Forbidden Best-Sellers of Pre-Revolutionary France* (London: Harper Collins, 1996).
5. John-Paul Ghobrial, *The Whispers of Cities: Information Flows in Istanbul, London, and Paris in the Age of William Trumbull* (Oxford: Oxford University Press, 2013); Filippo de Vivo, *Information and Communication in Venice: Rethinking Early Modern Politics* (Oxford: Oxford University Press, 2007).
6. Maria Pia Pedani, *Venezia Porta d'Oriente* (Bologna: Il Mulino, 2010).
7. De Vivo, *Information*, 18–40.
8. Gulru Necipoğlu, *Architecture, Ceremonial, and Power: The Topkapı Palace in the Fifteenth and Sixteenth Centuries* (New York; Cambridge, MA: MIT Press, 1991), 77.
9. Colin Imber, *The Ottoman Empire, 1300–1650: The Structure of Power* (Basingstoke: Palgrave Macmillan, 2002), 154–176.
10. Dover, *The Information Revolution*, 20.
11. De Vivo, "Archival Intelligence: Diplomatic Correspondence and Information Management in Italy, 1450–1650," in *Archives & Information in the Early Modern World*, ed. Liesbeth Corens, Kate Peters and Alexandra Walsham (Oxford: Oxford University Press, 2018), 53–85.
12. J. Deny, "Re'īs ül-Küttāb," in *Encyclopaedia of Islam*, 1st ed., ed. C. E. Bosworth et al. (Leiden: Brill, 1995), 481–483.
13. Suraiya Faroqhi, "Mühimme Defterleri," in *Encyclopaedia of Islam*, 2nd ed. online, ed. P. Bearman et al (Leiden: Brill, 2006).
14. De Vivo, "How to Read Venetian Relazioni," *Renaissance and Reformation* 34 (2012): 25–59.
15. For example, Eunjeong Yi, *Guild Dynamics in Seventeenth-Century Istanbul* (Leiden: Brill, 2003), 28; Gábor Kármán, ed. *The Correspondence of the Beylerbeys of Buda 1617–1630* (Szeged: Faculty of Humanities and Social Sciences, 2022).
16. Dover, *The Information Revolution*, 112.
17. Tracey Sowerby and Christopher Markiewicz, eds., *Diplomatic Cultures at the Ottoman Court, c.1500–1630* (London: Routledge, 2021); A. Nuri Yurdusev, ed. *Ottoman Diplomacy: Conventional or Unconventional?* (Basingstoke: Palgrave Macmillan, 2004).
18. Maria Pia Pedani, *In Nome del Gran Signore: Inviati Ottomani a Venezia Dalla Caduta di Costantinopoli alla Guerra di Candia* (Venezia: Deputazione di Storia Patria, 1994), 195–202.
19. Pedani, "Ottoman Fetihnames: The Imperial Letters Announcing a Victory," *Tarih İncelemeleri Dergisi* 13 (1998): 181–192.
20. De Vivo, "Cœur de l'État, Lieu de Tension: Le Tournant Archivistique vu de Venise," *Annales: HSS* 68 (2013): 699–728.
21. Imber, *The Ottoman Empire*, 170; Necipoğlu, *Architecture*, 77.
22. De Vivo, *Information*, 32–40.
23. Imber, *The Ottoman Empire*, 173–174; Douglas Howard, *A History of the Ottoman Empire* (Cambridge, UK: Cambridge University Press, 2017), 119; Gábor Ágoston, "Information, Ideology, and Limits of Imperial Policy: Ottoman Grand Strategy in the Context of Ottoman-Habsburg

Rivalry," in *The Early Modern Ottomans: Remapping the Empire*, ed. Virginia H. Aksan and Daniel Goffman (Cambridge, UK: Cambridge University Press, 2007).
24 Leslie P. Peirce, *The Imperial Harem: Women and Sovereignty in the Ottoman Empire* (Oxford: Oxford University Press, 1993).
25 Susan Skilliter, "The Letters of the 'Venetian Sultana' Nur Banu and Her Kira to Venice," in *Studia Turcologica Memoriae Alexii Bombaci Dicata*, ed. A. Gallotta and U. Marazzi (Naples: Istituto Universitario Orientale, 1982), 515–536.
26 Sefik Peksevgen, "Secrecy, Information Control and Power Building in the Ottoman Empire, 1566–1603," (Unpublished PhD, McGill University, 2005).
27 De Vivo, *Information*, 40–45.
28 Necipoğlu, *Architecture*, 33, 85.
29 Necipoğlu, *Architecture*, 50, 64.
30 Imber, *The Ottoman Empire*, 154.
31 Donald Queller, *The Venetian Patriciate: Reality versus Myth* (Urbana, IL: Illinois University Press, 1986), 57–75, 95–101.
32 Dorit Raines, "Office Seeking, Broglio, and the Pocket Political Guidebooks in Cinquecento and Seicento Venice," *Studi Veneziani* 22 (1991): 137–194.
33 Preto, *I Servizi Segreti di Venezia* (Milano: Il Saggiatore, 1994). See also Emrah Safa Gürkan, *Spies for the Sultan* (Washington, DC: Georgetown University Press, 2024).
34 Theoharis Stavrides, *The Sultan of Vezirs: The Life and Times of the Ottoman Grand Vezir Mahmud Pasha Angelović (1453–1474)* (Leiden: Brill, 2001), 233n, 402–408.
35 Ghobrial, *Whispers of Cities*, 139. See also Emrah Safa Gürkan, "Hile ü Hud'a: Deception, Dissimulation and Manipulation of Information in 16th-century Ottoman Empire," *Acta Orientalia Academiae Scientiarum Hungaricae* 72 (2019): 437–454.
36 Preto, *Servizi Segreti*, 75–76; Raines, "Office Seeking."
37 Pál Fodor, "How to Forge Documents? A Case of Corruption within the Ottoman Bureaucracy around 1590," *Acta Orientalia Academiae Scientiarum Hungaricae* 48 (1995): 386–387; Christine Woodhead, "Research on the Ottoman Scribal Service," in *Festgabe an Josef Matuz*, ed. Christa Fragner and Klaus Schwarz (Berlin: Klaus Schwarz Verlag, 1992), 311–328.
38 Fleischer, *Bureaucrat and Intellectual in the Ottoman Empire: The Historian Mustafa Ali (1541–1600)* (Princeton, NJ: Princeton University Press, 1986).
39 De Vivo, *Information*, 63–70.
40 De Vivo, "How to Read Venetian Relazioni," *Renaissance and Reformation* 34 (2011): 25–59.
41 Imber, *The Ottoman Empire*, 168; Jonathan Walker, "Bravi and Venetian Nobles, c.1550–1650," *Studi Veneziani* 36 (1998): 85–114.
42 Helen Pfeifer, *Empire of Salons: Conquest and Community in Early Modern Ottoman Lands* (Princeton, NJ: Princeton University Press, 2022); Ghobrial, *Whispers of Cities*, 65–87. A study of *ridotti/mezzà* is still awaited in Venice, but for politics in literary academies, see Simone Testa, *Italian Academies and Their Networks, 1525–1700* (New York: Palgrave Macmillan, 2015).
43 Peter Burke, *A Social History of Knowledge from Gutenberg to Diderot* (Cambridge, UK: Polity, 2000); Simon Schaffer et al. eds., *The Brokered World: Go-Betweens and Global Intelligence, 1770–1820* (Sagamore Beach, MA: Science History Publications, 2009); Alain Viala, *Naissance de l'Écrivain. Sociologie de la Littérature à l'âge Classique* (Paris: Minuit, 1985).
44 Osman Horata, "Didactic Poetry, Ottoman and Modern Turkish," in *Encyclopaedia of Islam*, 3rd ed. online, ed. Kate Fleet, Gudrun Krämer, Denis Matringe, John Nawas, and Devin J. Stewart (Leiden: Brill, 2021).
45 Aslı Niyazioğlu, *Dreams and Lives in Ottoman Istanbul: A Seventeenth-Century Biographer's Perspective* (London: Routledge, 2017).
46 Natalie Rothman, *The Dragoman Renaissance: Diplomatic Interpreters and the Routes of Orientalism* (Ithaca, NY: Cornell University Press, 2021).
47 Mario Infelise, *Prima dei Giornali: Alle Origini della Pubblica Informazione, secoli XVI e XVII* (Rome: Laterza, 2002).
48 A study of the Fugger collection (1568–1605) mentions 285 newsletters about Istanbul, https://fuggerzeitungen.univie.ac.at/en/orte/istanbul-konstantinopel. Examples of *avvisi* in *The Negotiations of Sir Thomas Roe, in his Embassy to the Ottoman Porte, from the Year 1621 to 1628* (London: Samuel Richardson, 1740), 494, 775.

49 Ghobrial, *Whispers of Cities*, 125–136.
50 De Vivo, *Information*, 185–186.
51 Queller, *Venetian Patriciate*, 213–214; Preto, *Servizi Segreti*, 479–481.
52 Eric Dursteler, "Fatima Hatun née Beatrice Michiel: Renegade Women in the Early Modern Mediterranean," *The Medieval History Journal* 12 (2009): 368.
53 Rothman, 66–67.
54 Giancarlo Casale, *The Ottoman Age of Exploration* (Oxford: Oxford University Press, 2010), 87; Benjamin Arbel, *Trading Nations: Jews and Venetians in the Early Modern Eastern Mediterranean* (Leiden: Brill, 1995) chapter 4; Giancarlo Casale, *The Ottoman Age of Exploration* (Oxford: Oxford University Press, 2010), 87.
55 De Vivo, *Information*, 78–79; Francesca Lucchetta, "Il Medico del Bailaggio di Costantinopoli: Fra Terapie e Politica (secc. XV-XVI)," *Quaderni di Studi Arabi* 15 (1997): 5–50.
56 Alana Mailes, "'Much to Deliver in your Honour's Ear.' Angelo Notari's Work in Intelligence, 1616–1623," *Early Music History* 39 (2020): 219–252.
57 Donado da Lezze, attr., *Historia Turchesca 1300–1514*, ed. I. Ursu (Bucharest: Institut Français d'Études Byzantines, 1909), 119–121.
58 De Vivo, *Information*, 76.
59 Hakan Karateke and Helga Anetshofer, eds., *The Ottoman World: A Cultural History Reader, 1450–1700* (Oakland, CA: University of California Press, 2021), 168.
60 De Vivo, *Information*, 87–88; Marinos Sariyannis, "'Mob,' 'Scamps' andRebels in Seventeenth-Century Istanbul: Some Re-marks on Ottoman Social Vocabulary," *International Journal of Turkish Studies* 11 (2005): 1–15.
61 Zeynep Yelçe, "Palace and City Ceremonials," in *A Companion to Early Modern Istanbul*, ed. Shirine Hamadeh and Çiğdem Kafescioğlu (Leiden; Boston, MA: Brill, 2022), 143–168; Iain Fenlon, *The Ceremonial City: History, Memory and Myth in Renaissance Venice* (New Haven, CT; London: Yale University Press, 2007).
62 Evliya Çelebi, *An Ottoman Traveller, Selections from the Book of Travels of Evliya Çelebi*, ed. Robert Dankoff and Sooyong Kim (London: Eland, 2011), 24–26. For earlier examples, Çiğdem Kafescioğlu, "Picturing the Square, Streets, and Denizens of Early Modern Istanbul: Practices in Urban Space and Shifts in Visuality," *Muqarnas* 37 (2020): 139–177.
63 Maartje van Gelder, "Ducal Display and the Contested Use of Space in Late Sixteenth-Century Venetian Coronation Festivals," in *Occasions of State*, ed. J. R. Mulryne (London: Routledge, 2018), 167–195.
64 Filippo de Vivo, "Microhistories of Long-Distance Information: Space, Movement and Agency in the Early Modern News," *Past and Present* 242, Suppl. 14 (2019), "Global History and Microhistory," ed. J.-P. Ghobrial, 179–214; Ebru Boyar and Kate Fleet, *A Social History of Ottoman Istanbul* (Cambridge, UK: Cambridge University Press, 2010), 44–45; De Vivo, *Information*, 160–176; Richard Blackburn, ed., *Journey to the Sublime Porte: The Arabic Memoir of a Sharifian Agent's Diplomatic Mission to the Ottoman Imperial Court in the Era of Suleyman the Magnificent* (Beirut: Würzburg: Orient-Institut, 2005), 194.
65 De Vivo, *Information*, 127–136.
66 Christine Woodhead, "Fctihname," in *Encyclopaedia of Islam*, 3rd ed. online. Kate Fleet, Gudrun Krämer, Denis Matringe, John Nawas, and Devin J. Stewart (Leiden: Brill, 2021).
67 Karateke and Anetshofer, eds., *The Ottoman World*, 118. On cannons see, Boyar and Fleet, *A Social History*, 48–50.
68 Evliya, *Selections*, 393; Mustafa Naima, *Annals of the Turkish Empire from 1591 to 1659 of the Christian Era* (London: John Murray, 1832), 220–221.
69 De Vivo, *Information*, 81–82; Ghobrial, *Whispers of Cities*, 137–140.
70 De Vivo, *Information*, 89–90.
71 Federico Barbierato, *The Inquisitor in the Hat Shop: Inquisition, Forbidden Books and Unbelief in Early Modern Venice* (Farnham: Ashgate, 2012); De Vivo, *Information*.
72 Boyar and Fleet, *A Social History*, 39–41.
73 Massimo Rospocher and Rosa Salzberg, "'El Vulgo Zanza': Spazi Pubblici, Voci a Venezia Durante le Guerre d'Italia," *Storica* 16 (2010): 83–120.
74 Karateke and Anetshofer, eds., *The Ottoman World*, 162–172.
75 Blackburn, *Journey*, 158–210.

76 Elliott Horowitz, "Coffee, Coffeehouses, and the Nocturnal Rituals of Early Modern Jewry," *American Jewish Studies Review* 14 (1989): 17–46.
77 Mustafa Ali, *The Ottoman Gentleman of the Sixteenth Century*, ed. D. S. Brook (Cambridge, MA: Harvard University Press, 2003), 130; Mouradgea D'Ohsson, *Tableau Général de l'Empire Othoman*, vol. 4 (Paris: De l'Imprimerie de Monsieur, 1791), 80, 82.
78 Ralph S. Hattox, *Coffee and Coffeehouses: The Origins of a Social Beverage in the Medieval Near East* (Seattle, WA: University of Washington Press, 1985).
79 Sariyannis, "Sociability, Public Life, and Decorum," in *A Companion to Early Modern Istanbul*, ed. Shirine Hamadeh and Çiğdem Kafescioğlu (Leiden; Boston, MA: Brill, 2022), 82.
80 Howard, *Ottoman Empire*, 150–155, 162–163, 170.
81 Kâtip Çelebi, *The Balance of Truth*, ed. Geoffrey Lewis (London: Allen and Unwin, 1957), 51
82 Gülay Yılmaz, "Urban Protests, Rebellions, and Revolts," *A Companion to Early Modern Istanbul*, ed. Shirine Hamadeh and Çiğdem Kafescioğlu (Leiden; Boston, MA: Brill, 2022), 570.
83 Ayşe Saraçgil, "Generi Voluttuari e Ragion di Stato: Politiche Repressive del Consumo di Vino, Caffè e Tabacco Nell'Impero Ottomano nei Secc. XVI e XVII," *Turcica* 28 (1996): 187–188.
84 Rosa Salzberg, "Little Worlds in Motion: Mobility and Space in the Osterie of Early Modern Venice," *Journal of Early Modern History* 25 (2021): 96–117.
85 Van Gelder, *Trading Places: The Netherlandish Merchants in Early Modern Venice* (Leiden: Brill, 2009), 123–124.
86 Sariyannis, "Sociability," 482; De Vivo, *Information*, 98–106.
87 Bernard Lewis, *Istanbul and the Civilization of the Ottoman Empire* (Norman, OK: University of Oklahoma Press, 1963), 132. See also De Vivo, *Information*, 107.
88 De Vivo, "La Farmacia Come Luogo di Cultura: Le Spezierie di Medicina in Italia," in *Interpretare e Curare. Medicina e Salute nel Rinascimento*, ed. M. Conforti, A. Carlino and A. Clericuzio (Rome: Carocci, 2013), 129–142.
89 Boyar and Fleet, *A Social History*, 249.
90 Pierre Sardella, *Nouvelles et Spéculations à Venise au Débuts du XVIe Siècle* (Paris: Colin, 1947).
91 Benedetto Cotrugli, *The Book of the Art of Trade*, ed. Carlo Carraro and Giovanni Favero (London: Palgrave, 2016), 62, 75.
92 Boyar and Fleet, *A Social History*, 44.
93 Smith, *The Life and Letters*, vol. 1, 246, 439–440.
94 Margaret Meserve, "The Sophy: News of Shah Ismail Safavi in Renaissance Europe," *Journal of Early Modern History* 18 (2014): 579–608.
95 Paolo Preto, *Venezia e i Turchi* (Florence: Sansoni, 1975), 268.
96 Marino Berengo, "Padova e Venezia alla Vigilia di Lepanto," in *Tra Latino e Volgare: Per Carlo Dionisotti*, ed. G. Bernardoni Trezzini et al., vol. 1 (Padua: Antenore, 1974), 27–65.
97 Fleischer, "A Mediterranean Apocalypse: Prophecies of Empire in the Fifteenth and Sixteenth Centuries," *Journal of the Economic and Social History of the Orient* 61 (2018): 18–90; Ottavia Niccoli, *Prophecy and People in Renaissance Italy* (Princeton, NJ: Princeton University Press, 1990).
98 Van Gelder and De Vivo, "Papering over Protest: Contentious Politics and Archival Suppression in Early Modern Venice," *Past & Present* 258 (2023): 44–78.
99 Gabriel Piterberg, *An Ottoman Tragedy: History and Historiography at Play* (Berkeley, CA: University of California Press, 2003).
100 Boyar and Fleet, *A Social History*, 33; David Chambers and Brian Pullan, eds., *Venice. A Documentary History, 1450–1630* (Oxford: Blackwell, 1992), 213–221.
101 Yi, *Guild Dynamics*; Boyar and Fleet, *A Social History*, 28.
102 Yılmaz, "Urban Protests," 567.
103 Van Gelder and Claire Judde de Larivière, eds., *Popular Politics in an Aristocratic Republic: Political Conflict and Social Contestation in Late Medieval and Early Modern Venice* (London: Routledge, 2020); Van Gelder, "The People's Prince: Popular Politics in Early Modern Venice," *The Journal of Modern History* 90 (2018): 249–291.
104 Anastasia Stouraiti, *War, Communication, and the Politics of Culture in Early Modern Venice* (Cambridge, UK: Cambridge University Press, 2023); Marc Baer, *Honored by the Glory of Islam: Conversion and Conquest in Ottoman Europe* (Oxford: Oxford University Press, 2008), 56–58.

105 Peirce, *The Imperial Harem*, 64–65.
106 De Vivo, "Microhistories."
107 Tobias Graf, *The Sultan's Renegades: Christian-European Converts to Islam and the Making of the Ottoman Elite, 1575–1610* (Oxford: Oxford University Press, 2017).
108 Baki Tezcan, *The Second Ottoman Empire: Political and Social Transformation in the Early Modern World* (Cambridge, UK: Cambridge University Press, 2010); De Vivo, *Information*, 157–248.
109 Infelise, *Prima dei Giornali*.
110 K. A. Schwartz, "Did Ottoman Sultans Ban Print?" *Book History* 20 (2017): 1–39; Ghobrial, "Printing," in Gábor Ágoston and Bruce Masters, ed., *The Encyclopaedia of the Ottoman Empire* (New York: Facts on File, 2008), 471–474.
111 Giovanni Tarantino and Paola von Wyss-Giacosa, eds., *Twelve Cities – One Sea: Early Modern Mediterranean Port Cities and their Inhabitants* (Napoli: Edizioni Scientifiche Italiane, 2023).

25
RECIPES, GOLD, AND INFORMATION EXCHANGE

Workshop Cultures in the Early Modern Metropolis

Jasmine Kilburn-Toppin

Introduction

"Take the bones of the Legges of sheepe or else the feete of them [...] and burne them tyll they be all whit burnt both w[i]thin and w[i]thout, then stampe them in a morter of Iron or of Brasse tyll they be very small then seive them." So instructed artisan-author Thomas Aunsham in his early sixteenth-century manuscript of workshop recipes, secrets, and know-how. This scrap of information on preparing animal bones was part of a recipe for making a bone-ash vessel to refine silver "after the manner used in the mint w[i]thin the Towre of London in ano. 1508."[1] In the early sixteenth century, "information" connoted "the communication of instructive knowledge," "a teaching, an instruction, a piece of advice."[2] As Deputy to the Comptroller of the Mint, Aunsham's metallurgical expertise was crucial for the refining and testing of precious metals at the Tower of London, the international site of coin production.[3] And yet, like most early modern artisans, we know very little about his life circumstances or personal history. Aunsham's modest account does, however, reveal a real enthusiasm to communicate instructive knowledge about his workshop experiences in London and those continental centres of minting where he had been trained up in his art. This metropolitan artisan shared an eagerness for information exchange with contemporary craftsmen across Europe, a small minority of whom authored manuscripts and printed texts on recipes and workshop knowledge. Alistair Black and Bonnie Mak have argued that "information history offers an avenue to explore people, systems, and events at the micro-level—and especially those that continue to be over-looked in favour of leading personalities and major technical advances."[4] This chapter uses a forgotten practitioner's largely unknown manuscript as a lens to explore broader themes in early modern artisanal writing and to consider the significance of information in craft and institutional cultures.

Early modern Europe witnessed a swell of manuscripts and later printed texts on the techniques and recipes—the "secrets"—of artisanal workshops. Crafts ranged widely, from sausage-making to ink production, shipbuilding to pottery. Information was disseminated on ingredients and raw materials, production processes, ideal working and environmental conditions for production, the design and materials of tools, and the ideal characteristics of the artisan. Typically, first-hand experiential knowledge was blended with inherited wisdom. Many authors borrowed liberally from ancient and contemporary authorities already in print.[5]

The focus here is upon metallurgy, the art of working metals, which included techniques such as smelting, separating, refining, and testing the purity of alloys. This was a significant genre of workshop writing, clearly of relevance to artisans working with metals (such as blacksmiths and pewterers) but also to those engaged in the extraction of ores, the testing of metals, and the production of coinage. Patrons and governors of mines and mints were also an audience for such literature.[6] In their investigations into the natural world, an amorphous group we might term natural philosophers were also interested in the generation, manipulation, and purification of precious metals.[7] This trend for authorship of workshop secrets has certainly not gone unnoticed by historians, especially scholars of early modern science and technology.[8] However, artisans have not featured prominently in publications within the broad remit of information history—unlike merchants, natural philosophers, humanists, and archivists. This chapter explores the cultural valency of information for artisans, and how craftsmen were central agents in the communication and exchange of information about the natural world.

At surface value, manuscripts like that authored by Thomas Aunsham in the Tower look to be relatively straightforward compilations of notes concerning ingredients, measurements, methods, and workshop practices. Closer examination and contextualisation, however, reveal deeper cultural and political significance. Communication of recipe information, especially relating to the investigation and transformation of precious metals, could impact profoundly on social, political, and epistemological status among goldsmiths. Recording, preserving, and sharing workshop information was a means of enhancing social standing and competing for coveted institutional roles in the early modern city. Moreover, against the backdrop of metropolitan experimental science—which encouraged active exploration into matter and nature—close observation and note-taking in workshops had heightened epistemological worth.

Taking Thomas Aunsham as our guide, this chapter first considers the working and professional contexts of this artisan-author and his manuscript production. We then consider what information was recorded in his text and, crucially, why skilled artisans might have communicated know-how about workshop processes. Next, we turn to the afterlife of Aunsham's manuscript and explore how information shared, borrowed, and adapted across generations of goldsmiths and assayers worked to shape an institutional or professional community. Finally, the conclusion brings together ideas about the value of metallurgical information in sixteenth- and seventeenth-century England and Europe.

Thomas Aunsham and Metallurgy at the Tower of London

In the early sixteenth century, when Thomas Aunsham was authoring his informative guide on work with silver and gold, the Royal Mint at the Tower of London was the most significant national site for coin production. The Tower Mint, as it was known, consisted of a series of workshops for weighing, melting, refining and assaying precious metals, and for producing dies and coin.[9] These artisanal workplaces were located within the curtain (inner and outer) walls of the Tower, a narrow horse-shoe-shaped space which also housed domestic residences, stables, taverns, and gardens. Merchants and goldsmiths brought precious metals to the Tower and collected their coin by passing through a series of gates manned by guards and porters.[10]

Though we know the names and career trajectories of those holding the most prominent and authoritative posts at the Tower Mint—the roles of Master, Warden, and Comptroller—the lives and working practices of the labourers, technicians, and artisans who manned the Mint workshops are much more obscure. They are seldom named in the public records.[11] Notably, it was these craftspeople who had the skills and expertise to test metals and produce coin. Named postholders often held the Mint roles as sinecures and employed knowledgeable deputies, usually goldsmiths, to do the work.[12] Aunsham, who gave "daily attendance" at the Tower workshops from c.1509 to c.1520, was just such a deputy to the Comptroller and Assay-Master, Sir Henry Wyatt. The Comptroller maintained oversight of the Mint Master on behalf of the Crown and kept a monthly account of all bullion melted and money coined.[13] Aunsham routinely presented the Comptroller's accounts to the Exchequer.[14] The role of the assay-master was fundamental to the operation and reputation of the Mint, for it was this skilled practitioner who ensured that coin was of the appropriate standard. As a contemporary metallurgist wrote, no one can "know for sure what virtues or evilness" metals may contain "unless the light of the assay itself shows them."[15] Assay was carried out by sight when a practitioner compared the streak left by a metal sample on a (black) touchstone to that made by a needle of known purity. There was also cupellation (or the "fire assay"), a more complicated process, involving precision instruments for weighing a sample which was melted down multiple times in a cupel, and chemical solutions such as aqua fortis (nitric acid) for the separation of precious and base metals.[16] A late thirteenth-century London Mint treatise stressed how "a sure knowledge of gold and silver can be obtained by testing, but among a great variety of tests, examination by assay is considered the most certain and hardly anyone can know its certain signs unless he has learned it from practice in the art."[17] Assayers were typically apprenticed in the workshops of goldsmiths who were expert in this specialism. However, knowledge of assay was relatively rare among goldsmiths in general.[18] Bullion was tested (assayed) when it entered the Tower Mint, and batches of completed coins were also tried before they entered general circulation. A grand ceremonial testing process at the court of Star Chamber at Westminster, usually held on an annual basis and known as the Trial of the Pyx, was overseen by a jury of goldsmiths. This was a semi-public means of examining the work of the Mint and checking coin was up to standard.[19]

Official information about institutional supplies and outputs, penned by Tower clerks, is plentiful.[20] However, communication by Mint workers about their working practices and knowledge cultures is exceptionally rare. Aunsham's manuscript is significant because it allows us to glimpse what information a skilled worker thought worthy of mention, and how he framed the networks and value of his instructive knowledge. Aunsham's original manuscript, dating from the first decade of the sixteenth century, has not been found; the earliest copy survives from the early seventeenth century in a wider compilation of metallurgical information transcribed by archivist and merchant Ralph Starkey, "an avid collector of old deeds, manuscripts, and coins."[21] As we will see, Aunsham's instructive information had rich afterlives.

Compiling and Recording Workshop Information

What information was deemed worthy of record by assayer Thomas Aunsham? How did he organise his information? And where did his information come from? Aunsham's text cannot be neatly categorised. In essence, it contains a comparison of weights and recipes tried and tested in various European minting workshops, and by the author himself in the assay house at the Tower of London. These recipes relate to the assaying (testing of gold and silver), the cementing and refining (purifying) of metals, and techniques to alter the colour of gold. Recipes usually include information such as ingredients, tools, methods, and timings. For example, a recipe for cementing gold called for various quantities of "salte peeter sall armonak vitreall Roman or whit," "Spanish greene," and "allome de plum." These ingredients were to be ground together upon a stone, mixed with "the strongest redd vinegar that ye can gett."[22] The bodily fluids of the artisan might also be required, Aunsham advised: "wash it in hott or warme pisse, the staller or older that it is the better collor will it give vnto yo[u]r gould."[23] Elsewhere in the manuscript "moyste your gould with the moysture of yo[u]r mouth."[24] Such an intimate bodily engagement with labour was typical.[25] Twelfth-century metalworker Theophilus suggested in his manuscript that one polished blackened silver by "rubbing it all over with saliva and then to 'take some wax from your earhole and after wiping the niello [silver] smear the wax all over it.'"[26]

In Aunsham's Tower manuscript a broad range of methods for working metals are recorded, often within a single entry. A recipe to separate gold and silver instructs the artisan to "beate it very thin," "stirre it faste … rounde about," to "hold it strongly a yard high," and pour "w[i]th as smale a stream as is possible." Timings are measured "by the space of an avemary."[27] Information on methodology or technique focuses especially upon the strength used during a particular process. Aunsham instructs practitioners to "poure softely," "softlely take the s[aid] peece of copper out of the bottom of yo[u]r panne," or "washe out yo[u]r cemente softely by litle and litle."[28] Softly meant undertaking an activity gently or in an unhurried way.[29] Elsewhere, greater force was needed: "blowe thereunto right sore [with great force; strongly] untyll it have a convenyent heate w[hi]ch will cause it to drive and worke."[30] Vigour in these recipes also relates to elements, so the strength of the fire, or degree of heat applied to the precious metals. Aunsham differentiates between "a very softe fyre" a "somwhat better fyre, and then a meetley [moderately] good fyre."[31] Even ingredients themselves are described in terms of their active potency: "that the stronge water may have his strength to worke through them" [the molten metals].[32] Overall, an artisan is required to be attentive in the workshop: "ye muste be right well ware," as Aunsham puts it. He cautions against distraction when undertaking a lengthy procedure: "take ye good heede ther vnto for this pointe desceaveth many a man and especially at the latter ende of their worke."[33] Similarly, in one of the first printed works on metallurgy, the Italian Vannoccio Biringuccio warned how when parting gold from silver using acid "this art … requires continual working night and day with extreme watchfulness and care."[34] The broader workshop environment, including organisation and cleanliness, also matters to Aunsham: "it is to be noted that leade, tynne and the pisse of cattes and rats amonge yo[u]r meltynge coles, and also unclean tonges and ingotes … all thes things will cause yo[u]r goulde to be eger [sic]," meaning brittle.[35]

The recipes vary in length, some being relatively substantial, covering a couple of manuscript pages, others are only a few lines long. Each new recipe is clearly indicated with a sub-heading. Some of these titles are simply listed as "an other good waye to make [gold] malliable."[36] In other instances (less commonly), the source of the recipe information and the timing of the method are mentioned: "An other cement to affine w[i]th any man[n]er of gould at xii hours as John Leonard … useth."[37] In the ordering and the comparison of the recipes, Aunsham explicitly presents a compendium of contemporary knowledgeable practice that is superior to former times. Old masters at the Tower Mint were said to have "had no p[er]fecte sight or knowledge of partyng or makynge of assaye by water for that is best and moste sureste as herafter more playnly is written."[38] Aunsham is keen to highlight his own metallurgical skill, and it is notable that when he talks about his own recipes and practices in the manuscript, he explicitly enters a first-person narrative: "this manner may be good but I doe in this manner followinge being better and lesse labore."[39] The trial-and-error nature of workshop knowledge also comes to the fore, such as the instruction to take especial care with your instruments during a procedure to cement or affine any manner of gold: carry this out "w[i]thout puttyng of yo[u]r tonges in to yo[u]r [molten pot of] goulde" (the implication being that Aunsham has learnt from experience how to manage his instruments at this point in the recipe).[40] He establishes his personal mastery over particular recipes with the phrase: "proved trewe by Thomas Aunsam."[41] To prove was to "make trial of; to try, test."[42] In the later sixteenth and seventeenth centuries, this language of proof would be used widely in medicinal and food recipes, manuscript and print, "to signal experiential knowledge, hands-on trials, and personal endorsement and approval."[43] Through the placement of his workshop techniques and recipes at the end of thematic sections, Aunsham recommends his particular expertise and methods—"a trew proued waye … w[i]the the leaste losse."[44]

Recipe information did not simply originate from Aunsham's own experiences as an employee at the Tower Mint. A narrative is also constructed over the course of the manuscript about technical expertise and method in different European centres of metalwork and minting.[45] Aunsham refers to practices in Brabant, Flanders, Paris, and workshops "in the borders of Spayne." He records information on a recipe "to make an assaye … approved and used w[i]th all the minte m[aste]rs at Lisbon and in Portugall." Elsewhere in the text a recipe to purify gold used by master "Jacob Uncerlemig of Antwerp."[46] There is also a clear sense of Aunsham having been trained, perhaps as an apprentice, in continental workshops. He speaks of "ye master and wardens of the mints beyond the sea w[i]th whom I was brought up and learned."[47] John Leonard and Joyce Powle are mentioned recurrently as masters during his training. We get an impression in a handful of the recipes of Aunsham's experiential, observational learning processes as a young man, how "my master did counsel me" on various aspects of the method of cementation.[48] Perhaps most of these recipes came from Aunsham's observations of more experienced and respected artisans, or from word of mouth during his training. At least one recipe, in this case for brightening the appearance of base gold, is also explicitly listed as "being in print" and used by "mint masteres"; maybe this information came from printed technical literature Aunsham encountered once he was himself an established master in London.[49] Intriguingly, this Mint worker also accessed archival information which was deposited within the Tower of London. In a discussion of weights used in the assayer's work, he writes of how "it doth shewe in the Recordes of the Minte: But I saye that wrott this booke […]." Elsewhere, in a dialogue concerning the legal checks on the Master of the Mint, Aunsham refers to specific documentation in the Exchequer archives (stored in the Tower): "the Indenture made between the kynge and them as appeareth in the booke called *Domus Dei* and in the Redd book in the kings exchequer."[50]

In his Tower manuscript, Thomas Aunsham references information from a wide variety of sources—archival, printed, word of mouth, observed (when he was training and working in European workshops), and experiential (as proved in his own London Mint workspace). The written word, spoken utterance, and witnessed or performed action are all fonts of information about valuable methods of separating, testing, and evaluating precious metals. These channels of information are not discreetly organised but jostle alongside each other on Aunsham's folios. From our modern logocentric perspective, we might suppose that written information was the most esteemed source of authority, especially within the medium of a manuscript. And yet, this would be a problematic assumption. For Aunsham as a practitioner, information derived from his own experience was the most privileged form of knowledge.

The Value of Notes on Silver and Gold

We have established how Aunsham recorded detailed information on metallurgical workshop processes, including those taking place contemporaneously in the Tower, and activities "beyond the sea."[51] It was rare for a practitioner to translate tacit information into the written word. Most craftsmen were not literate, and, in any case, knowledge was passed down through word of mouth or imitation in the workshop. Reading a text would never give you the full embodied knowledge required for carrying out a recipe, which depended upon observation, repeated trials, and experience.[52] Aunsham himself acknowledged that "there is no man that can do this by the te[a]chinge of any man but onely by experience of proofe and of exercise, not w[i]thstandinge he may faile some tymes ... that doth make him full expert and cunnynge therein."[53] Trial and error gradually led to expertise. This was a typical attitude for an artisan-author. German metallurgist and assayer Lazarus Ercker wrote in his *Treatise on Ores and Assaying* from 1580 how "reading shows you the way, but the work of your own hands gives you the experience."[54]

What motivated the authorship of Thomas Aunsham's manuscript? Artisan-authors were rarely explicit in their reasons for writing, but Aunsham's text does provide clues. It is evident that the work was intended to be instructive, particularly for men in the higher echelons of the Tower Mint hierarchy. The opening dedication to the text is suggestive:

In this present volume is declared many proper and notable Instructions very nessesary and convenient to be hade of all estates and specially to those w[hi]ch wilbe a m[aste]r or wardene or any other minestr[ie] w[i]thin the kinge Mintes.[55]

As the roles of Mint master or warden could be sinecures, a manuscript detailing procedures and practices might have been very welcome for men with institutional authority but without specific expertise in metallurgy. We can imagine how it would be useful for Mint post holders to be able to speak knowledgeably about assaying and metallurgical regulation, even if they could not carry out the processes themselves. Manuscripts and later printed texts on mining and metallurgy originating from Central Europe were often dedicated to rulers, investors, and those with institutional authority. Information on the mining, processing, and minting of metals was hugely valuable, especially as the demand for ores and coinage grew in the fifteenth and sixteenth centuries.[56] The anonymous author of one of the first printed books on assaying of precious metals—the *Probierbüchlein*—compiled their work "with great care for the benefit of all mintmasters, assay-masters, goldsmiths, miners, and dealers in metals."[57] In his 1540 *De la Pirotechnia*, metallurgist Biringuccio on "how to operate a mint honestly and with profit" framed his advice for "if you should need to practice it or even to talk about it and if you find yourself in this activity it may not be new to you."[58] Biringuccio had many powerful patrons, including the governing Petrucci family of Sienna, and he held numerous institutional posts, including head of the Sienese armoury and mint.[59] Information was a form of currency in these contexts as artisan-authors frequently sought patronage of some description. For example, Pamela Smith has written of Michalli da Rhuodo, or Michael of Rhodes who "joined the Venetian navy as a lowly galley oarsman in 1401, taking part in more than forty voyages in as many years across the Mediterranean and to Flanders, rising to a high position." His professional ascent appears to have been partly enabled by a written account of his voyages, "which contains an unusual level of detail about seafaring life." In the context of fierce competition for the position of nonnoble office, Michael's manuscript likely came to the attention of Venetian patricians, with very little direct personal experience of life at sea.[60] Perhaps Thomas Aunsham had ambitions for his career within the Tower Mint and hoped to catch the attention of powerful patrons through composing a presentational manuscript of useful workshop information.

Recording workshop information through the medium of a manuscript was also related to social status. As James Amelang writes of artisan autobiography, "writing was often (though not always) a transformative strategy, enabling authors to cross social as well as cultural boundaries."[61] As discussed, writing of any form was an unusual activity for early modern artisans. Those craft workers who did record their experiences frequently omitted detail concerning their working lives.[62] The impression, though, from reading Aunsham's Tower manuscript is of an author having compiled a great deal of collective craft information from a skilled network of masters. The manuscript establishes this worker as part of a European network of minting professionals. As Michelle DiMeo and Sara Pennell have argued, in the case of early modern recipe collections "for the manuscript compiler ... the acts of collecting, collating and circulating the compiled text were a means of self-formation and self-presentation."[63] For Aunsham and his metallurgical manuscript, we see how this process of authorship and collation was about his "self-presentation" as an institutional expert. A detailed recording of information about testing and weighing precious metals was a means of asserting status and expertise.[64] The repeated phrase "proved trewe by Thomas Aunsam" next to recipes trialled in his Tower workshop elevated both the body of knowledge and the standing of the practitioner.[65]

This brings us to the final probable motivation for Aunsham's authorship of his manuscript. Articulating information about workshop practices through the written word was a means of raising the status of the craft. In Aunsham's world, knowledge of the "mind" and work of the "hand" were often seen to be distinct practices. "Doing was knowledge of 'how to' rather than of 'why,'" observes Pamela Smith, and therefore was understood "as goal-oriented 'know-how' involving specific practices, while 'knowing' was regarded as generalizable, abstract knowledge expressed in propositions, general theories, and proofs."[66] Texts like Aunsham's that translated and formalised embodied exercises into discreet written recipes worked to bridge the perceived gap between the manual and the cerebral. Recording information on metallurgy was a way of elevating the art. As Pamela Long writes, "authorship created disciplines of knowledge out of practices formerly based primarily on craft skill."[67] It is notable that Aunsham refers to assaying practitioners as "masters of this science."[68] As we have seen, the organising of information about testing and measuring processes was also a way of making comparisons between recipes. Articulating information through the written word uniquely allowed for such evaluations. In Aunsham's case, contrasts were made both between the present (how he managed processes and techniques) and the past (how things had been done historically at the Tower Mint), and between Aunsham's institutional workshop and his contemporaries in Continental Europe. Organising information in this way—"here after followeth the most assured way ...," "an other good way ..."—encouraged repeated trials and experimentation.[69]

Information on techniques for testing, separating, and refining precious metals was valuable material in sixteenth-century London. The recording of metallurgical methods and recipes was a possible means of gaining patronage, raising social standing, and elevating the epistemological status of the craft. Hitherto, Thomas Aunsham's Tower Mint manuscript has been largely unknown as an example of a master artisan recording and ordering information. However, in thinking through motivations for authorship, common trends between Aunsham and European artisan-authors have emerged. In the penultimate section, we consider the afterlives of Aunsham's information.

Information Afterlives

Thomas Aunsham had hoped that institutional authorities would pay attention to the information documented in his 1508 manuscript. He wrote how: "yf that ye will keepe a exchange or be the assayer, or warden or comptroller of any mynte, the firste thing that ye muste surely knowe is the verye true reconinge [reckoning] of the assay and it to be surely and trewly made."[70] A handful of seventeenth-century manuscripts authored by London goldsmiths and institutional officials demonstrate how his instructive knowledge in fact had much longer legacies. Across multiple generations of practitioners and Mint officers, Aunsham's information was copied, adapted, and re-recorded for new audiences.

We do not know how many copies of Aunsham's Tower manuscript were circulating among interested parties in the sixteenth and early seventeenth centuries. And yet, it evidently caught the attention of London goldsmiths and other metallurgical specialists. In 1604, Hannibal Gamon the Younger presented a manuscript to the Goldsmiths' Company for which he "had taken great pains in translat[i]on."[71] The text was entitled *The Gouldesmythes' Storehowse. Wherein is Layd up Many Hidden Secrets of that Ingenious Mysterie*. Thematically, it focuses on assaying, refining, and coinage. Gamon had the Goldsmiths' guild to thank for funding his BA and MA studies at Oxford University, and he dedicated the copy to the livery company (drawing the company's arms on the title page).[72] Gamon had experienced scholarly culture, but, notably, he came from a dynasty of working goldsmiths: he had a foot in both academic and artisanal environments. Gamon was a member of the Goldsmiths' Company; so, too, his father, Hannibal Gamon senior. The latter was a practising goldsmith with many apprentices and a busy commercial premises on Cheapside, the main ceremonial and shopping route through the City of London, and the heart of the goldsmiths' trade.[73] In *The Gouldesmythes' Storehowse*, his written metallurgical masterpiece, Hannibal Gamon the Younger drew on many sources, including ancient authorities, like Pliny the Elder, and sixteenth-century metallurgical writers, such as Georgius Agricola. Markedly, Gamon had also read Aunsham's early sixteenth-century manuscript, though Aunsham's name was not mentioned along with the information he supplied.[74]

At the time that Gamon was writing, scholars were becoming increasingly interested in information about the natural world, and investigations into workshop practices were a significant part of this. Metallurgy, including the work of assayers like Aunsham, was of great interest to gentlemen natural philosophers. The assay workshop at the Tower of London, where metals were transformed and trials (or experiments) performed, was a site of particular attention. In 1622, merchant and writer on economics Gerard Malynes wrote of how "coming to the Assay-house [within the Tower liberties], there we found diuers gentlemen desirous to see the manner of making of Assayes of Gold and Siluer, as also diuers Goldsmiths which brought some Ingots of Gold."[75] In February 1660/1, Fellows of the Royal Society conducted experiments "on the weight of bodies increased in the fire"—heating cupels containing lead and copper—using Tower furnaces.[76] Against this backdrop of, broadly speaking, metropolitan "scientific" curiosity, we can imagine how Aunsham's metallurgical instructions and recipes found receptive audiences.[77]

Towards the end of the seventeenth century, an unknown official at the Tower Mint composed an elaborate presentational manuscript entitled *Mint and Moneta* (Mint and Money).[78] Though we have no compelling evidence for who compiled this impressive document, it is reasonable to speculate that, like Aunsham and Gamon, the author was trying to impress those above him in the institutional or corporate hierarchy. Consisting of two parts, the "first book" focuses on London weights, assay, and the Trial of the Pyx; the "second book" is a historical narrative of (significant legislation and events pertaining to) the London Mint, beginning with the establishment of the institution.[79] The first section is what concerns us here, as it is heavily focused on recipes for testing and evaluating precious metals. A close read reveals how substantial sections have been copied directly from Thomas Aunsham's 1509 Tower manuscript and *The Gouldesmythes' Storehowse*, sometimes with extra details added. For example, Aunsham's recipe on preparing animal bones for making a cupel to refine silver (used at the opening of this chapter) was copied verbatim; so too were Aunsham's instructions for a cementation "to make fine a course gold" and how to part gold from silver using aqua fortis.[80]

Aunsham's carefully recorded discussion of weights and recipes at the Tower Mint was of interest for centuries after his death. Through the scribal afterlives of Aunsham's Tower manuscript we can see how information on the testing and regulation of precious metals linked metallurgical specialists and officials across the generations. Over time, information about workshop practices at the Tower Mint, and Continental mints, shifted cultural and social registers. Evidence about regulating and evaluating metals moved from the experiential artisanal realm of Thomas Aunsham to that of the youthful scholar Hannibal Gamon with a first-hand knowledge of the goldsmith's trade, to the unknown institutional official, perhaps with limited direct experience of furnaces and molten metals. Nevertheless, the recording of "information expertise" shaped a sense of collective identity and practice across two centuries of institutional history.[81]

Conclusion

Thomas Aunsham was a small cog in the vast institutional machine that was the early sixteenth-century Tower of London. Though of minor rank in his own time, and of little interest to historians since, this chapter has argued that Aunsham's written presentation of instructive knowledge is highly revealing of the value of information for early modern artisans and urban inhabitants more broadly. The recording and careful ordering of detailed information on metallurgical recipes, and their presentation to his institutional betters, was an attempt to claim cultural, social, and epistemological status. These instructions on managing, manipulating, and appraising precious metals proved both that metallurgy could be theorised and categorised as an art, and that Aunsham himself was one of the "masters of this science."[82] In a recent book on the early modern "information revolution," Paul M. Dover has written of how information or *informatio* for early moderns "was typically employed to describe a process of shaping or forming, and often carried didactic connotations." Information "was something gathered, collated and then 'informed' for the recipient: the delivery of information served to help knowledge take 'form' within the recipient."[83] Aunsham hoped that having mastered the shaping and separation of metals in the Tower, his expertise on these matters might be delivered to those with authority, and deepen their knowledge of what actually occurred in Mint workshops.

Information in any context is rarely inert or static, nor can its routes or reworkings be controlled by the originator of knowledge or intelligence. Aunsham's workshop know-how was incorporated and adapted in seventeenth-century manuscripts composed by goldsmiths, scholars, and institutional officials, even as his name was excised from the information that he had hoped to impart. His manuscript was the backbone of a scribal tradition which linked goldsmiths, guildsmen, and administrators working and living generations apart. In the early sixteenth century, Aunsham's contemporaries might have found his "many proper and notable Instructions" useful.[84] A century later, as a fascination for experimental science gripped many Londoners, his advice and knowledge on molten metals and handling instruments and furnaces had a revitalised appeal, forming part of the vast reservoir of codified information on the natural world.

Notes

1 Harley MS 38, fos 237r-283v, *A Work on Coinage Attributed to Thomas Aunsham*, British Library, London. Fos 280 r-v.
2 *Oxford Online English Dictionary*, s.v. "information, n., sense I.1.a" (July 2023); *Oxford Online English Dictionary*, s.v. "information, n., sense I.1.b" (July 2023).
3 Christopher E. Challis, *The Tudor Coinage* (Manchester: Manchester University Press, 1978), 38.
4 Alistair Black and Bonnie Mak, "Period, Theme, Event: Locating Information History in History," in *Information and Power in History: Towards a Global Approach*, ed. Ida Nijenhuis et al. (Abingdon: Routledge, 2020), 29.
5 William Eamon, *Science and the Secrets of Nature: Books of Secrets in Medieval and Early Modern Culture* (Princeton, NJ: Princeton University Press, 1994); Pamela H. Smith, *From Lived Experience to the Written Word: Reconstructing Practical Knowledge in the Early Modern World* (Chicago, IL: The University of Chicago Press, 2022), 139–150.
6 Thomas Morel, *Underground Mathematics: Craft Culture and Knowledge Production in Early Modern Europe* (Cambridge, UK: Cambridge University Press, 2022), 20–49; Pamela Long, *Openness, Secrecy, Authority: Technical Arts and the Culture of Knowledge from Antiquity to the Renaissance* (Baltimore, MD: John Hopkins University Press, 2001), 175–209.
7 On the value of metallurgical knowledge in sixteenth-century London, see Deborah E. Harkness, *The Jewel House: Elizabethan London and the Scientific Revolution* (New Haven, CT; London: Yale University Press, 2007), chapter 4.
8 Elaine Leong and Alisha Rankin, eds., *Secrets and Knowledge in Medicine and Science, 1500–1800* (Farnham; Burlington, VT: Ashgate, 2011); Alison Kavey, *Books of Secrets: Natural Philosophy in England, 1550–1600* (Urbana, IL: University of Illinois Press, 2007); Eamon, *Science and the Secrets of Nature*.
9 Martin Allen, *Mints and Money in Medieval England* (Cambridge, UK: Cambridge University Press, 2012), 104–105.
10 Christopher E. Challis, *A New History of the Royal Mint* (Cambridge, UK: Cambridge University Press, 1991), 1–3, 268, 286.
11 Allen, *Mints and Money*, 92; Christopher E. Challis, "Hackney, Shoreditch and Moneyers in the Mint in Later-Medieval and Early-Modern London," *Hackney History* 16 (November 2010): 6.
12 Allen, *Mints and Money*, 90–91.
13 Challis, *A New History*, 401.
14 Steven Gunn, *Henry VII's New Men and the Making of Tudor England* (Oxford: Oxford University Press, 2016), 74.
15 *The Pirotechnia of Vannoccio Biringuccio*, trans. Cyril Stanley Smith and Martha Teach Gnudi (New York: Dover; London: Constable, 1990), 136.
16 J. S. Forbes, *Hallmark: A History of the London Assay Office* (London: Unicorn, 1999), 20–21.

411

17 Charles Johnson, *The De Moneta of Nicholas Oresme and English Mint Documents* (London: Thomas Nelson and Sons Ltd., 1956), 67.
18 For more on the training and knowledge cultures of assayers, see Jasmine Kilburn-Toppin, "'A Place of Great Trust to be Supplied by Men of Skill and Integrity.' Assayers and Knowledge Cultures in Late Sixteenth- and Seventeenth-Century London," *British Journal for the History of Science* 52, no. 2 (June 2019): 197–223.
19 Simon Wortham, "Sovereign Counterfeits: The Trial of the Pyx," *Renaissance Quarterly* 49, no. 2 (1996): 334–359.
20 The most comprehensive institutional histories of the Tower Mint focused on bullion supplies and coinage outputs include Allen, *Mints and Money*; Challis, *A New History*; John Craig, *The Mint: A History of the London Mint from A.D. 287 to 1948* (Cambridge, UK: Cambridge University Press, 1953).
21 Harley MS 38; Knafla, Louis A. "Starkey, Ralph (d. 1628), Archivist and Merchant," *Oxford Online Dictionary of National Biography* (September 23, 2004).
22 Harley MS 38, fo. 267r.
23 Harley MS 38, fo. 267v.
24 Harley MS 38, fo. 276r.
25 Pamela H. Smith, *The Body of the Artisan: Art and Experience in the Scientific Revolution* (Chicago, IL; London: The University of Chicago Press, 2004): "bodily labor in the workshop was more than just hard work; it also involved bodily fluids and processes," 112.
26 Smith, *The Body of the Artisan*, 112.
27 Harley MS 38, fos 263r-v, 274r.
28 Harley MS 38, fos 262r, 264v, 266r.
29 *Oxford Online English Dictionary*, s.v. "softly, adv., sense 8.b" (July 2023).
30 Harley MS 38, fo. 275r. *Oxford Online English Dictionary*, s.v. "sore, adv., sense 7.b" (July 2023).
31 Harley MS 38, fo. 266v.
32 Harley MS 38, fo. 263v.
33 Harley MS 38, fos 262r, 265r.
34 *The Pirotechnia of Vannoccio Biringuccio*, 201. Pamela H. Smith has similarly observed in other artisanal writings the call to be alert in the workshop: see "Why Write a Book? From Lived Experience to the Written Word in Early Modern Europe," *Bulletin of the German Historical Institute* 47 (2010): 45.
35 Harley MS 38, fo. 274v. *Oxford Online English Dictionary*, s.v. "eager, adj., sense II.6" (July 2023).
36 Harley MS 38, fo. 274r.
37 Harley MS 38, fo. 273r.
38 Harley MS 38, fo. 247r.
39 Harley MS 38, fo. 271v.
40 Harley MS 38, fo. 272r.
41 Harley MS 38, fo. 275v.
42 *Oxford Online English Dictionary*, s.v. "prove, v., sense I.1.a" (July 2023).
43 Elaine Leong, *Recipes and Everyday Knowledge: Medicine, Science and the Household in Early Modern England* (Chicago, IL; London: The University of Chicago Press, 2018), 101.
44 Harley MS 38, fo. 263r.
45 Harley MS 38, fos 263r, 271v.
46 Harley MS 38, fos 252r, 265v, 273r.
47 Harley MS 38, fo. 252r.
48 Harley MS 38, fo. 269v.
49 Harley MS 38, fo. 278r.
50 Harley MS 38, fos 260v, 249r.
51 Harley MS 38, fo. 252r.
52 Pamela Smith, "In the Workshop of History: Making, Writing and Meaning," *West 86th: A Journal of Decorative Arts, Design History, and Material Culture* 19, no. 1 (Spring–Summer 2012): 4–8.
53 Harley MS 38, fo. 246v.
54 Lazarus Ercker, *Treatise on Ores and Assaying*, trans. Annelise Grünhaldt Sisco and Cyril Stanley Smith (Chicago, IL: The University of Chicago Press, 1951), 194.

55 Harley MS 38, fo. 237r.
56 Long, *Openness, Secrecy, Authorship*, 175–177.
57 *Bergwerk- und Probierbüchlein: A Translation from the German of the Bergbüchlein, a Sixteenth-Century Book on Mineral Geology*, by Anneliese Grünhaldt Sisco, and of the *Probierbüchlein, a Sixteenth-Century Work on Assaying*, by Anneliese Grünhaldt Sisco and Cyril Stanley Smith, with Technical Annotations and Historical Notes (New York: American Institute of Mining and Metallurgical Engineers, 1949), 70.
58 *The Pirotechnia of Vannoccio Biringuccio*, 358.
59 Long, *Openness, Secrecy, Authorship*, 178–179.
60 Smith, *From Lived Experience*, 29, 32–33.
61 James S. Amelang, *The Flight of Icarus: Artisan Autobiography in Early Modern Europe* (Stanford, CA: Stanford University Press, 1998), 48.
62 Amelang, *The Flight of Icarus*, 119–120.
63 Michelle DiMeo and Sara Pennell, "Introduction," in *Reading and Writing Recipe Books, 1550–1800*, ed. Michelle DiMeo and Sara Pennell (Manchester: Manchester University Press, 2013), 11.
64 Smith, *From Lived Experience*, 33.
65 Harley MS 38, fo. 275v.
66 Smith, "Why Write a Book," 28.
67 Long, *Openness, Secrecy, Authorship*, 176.
68 Harley MS 38, fos. 247r, 270r.
69 Harley MS 38, fos. 262r, 272r. See also Smith, "Why Write a Book," 36.
70 Harley MS 38, fo. 249v.
71 Wardens' Accounts and Court Minutes, O3, fo. 454, Goldsmiths' Hall Archive, London (hereafter GHA).
72 MS C II.2.1., GHA.
73 Hannibal Gamon the Younger went on to become a Church of England clergyman. Anne Duffin, "Gamon, Hannibal (bap. 1582, d. 1650/51), Church of England clergyman," *Oxford Online Dictionary of National Biography* (September 23, 2004).
74 MS C II.2.1., fos 6v-8r.
75 Gerard de Malynes, *Consuetudo, vel, Lex Mercatoria; or, The Ancient-Law Merchant*, vol. 1 (London, 1622), 284.
76 Thomas Birch, *The History of the Royal Society of London*, vol. 1 (London, 1756), 16.
77 On Robert Hooke's interest in experiments on gold, see Rob Iliffe, "Material Doubts: Hooke, Artisan Culture and the Exchange of Information in 1670s London," *The British Journal for the History of Science* 28, no. 3 (September 1995): 306. For a detailed study of natural knowledge and artificial practice in London see Rebekah Higgitt and Jasmine Kilburn-Toppin, *Metropolitan Science: London Sites and Cultures of Knowledge and Practice, c.1600–1800* (London: Bloomsbury Academic, 2024).
78 T 48/92, The National Archives, Kew, London, UK.
79 For a more detailed exploration of the historical dimension, see Jasmine Kilburn-Toppin, "Writing Knowledge, Forging Histories: Metallurgical Recipes, Artisan-Authors and Institutional Cultures in Early Modern London," *Cultural and Social History* 18, no. 3 (2021): 305–309.
80 T 48/92, fos. 4r, 23v, 24r.
81 I've taken the phrase "information expertise" from Ida Nijenhuis et al., "Information and Power in History. A New Historiographical Approach?" in *Information and Power in History*, ed. Ida Nijenhuis et al. (London: Routledge, 2020), 278.
82 Harley MS 38, fos. 247r, 270r.
83 Paul M. Dover, *The Information Revolution in Early Modern Europe* (Cambridge, UK: Cambridge University Press, 2021), 18.
84 Harley MS 38, fo. 237r.

26
COLONIAL POLITICAL ECONOMIES OF INFORMATION

The East India Company and the Growth of Science in Britain

Jessica Ratcliff

Introduction

Global economic historians often classify the period of c. 1750–1850 as that of the "Great Divergence": the period in which the wealth of certain parts of Western Europe, particularly Great Britain and France, began to rapidly outpace the wealth of other large economies, particularly India and China. Part of this major shift in the global economy also involved a "Great *Data* Divergence," an acceleration in the differential growth of the accumulation of information in Britain, France, Germany, and other areas of Europe—and, increasingly, North America.[1] This chapter explores the place of colonial expansion as a driver of both, and a main link connecting economic and scientific change.[2] It does so by analysing the history of the British East India Company's (1601–1858) role in shaping the history of museums and collections-based sciences in Britain.[3]

Historians have long recognised that the history of science in Europe is connected in complex ways to European colonial expansion. During the period covered here, c. 1600–1860, one of the major developments was the emergence of the ideas of "science" and "empire" (and "company" and "state") in distinctly modern terms.[4] The historical coproduction of modern forms of science and modern forms of empire has been explored from many different angles. There is wide agreement that colonial expansion coincided, in particular, with an unprecedented information boom in Europe.[5] Connected to this was a marked acceleration in the growth and spread of information management institutions such as libraries, museums, observatories, and zoological and botanical gardens. Many hallmarks of the so-called "second scientific revolution" of this period were a consequence of these material and institutional developments: the rise of statistical science, the expansion of research devoted to classification, growing disciplinary specialisation, and revolutionary theoretical changes in geology, astronomy, and the biological sciences. It was only after around 1840, for example, that natural philosophy began to reorganise into specialised disciplines, and as part of this, the cultural and professional identity of the "scientist" was established.

One common way of understanding these remarkable aspects of the growth of science in Britain between roughly 1750 and 1850 has been to situate it as a consequence of earlier

Colonial Political Economies of Information

intellectual and social developments of the eighteenth century, specifically in connection to the Enlightenment, in which a new culture of empirical enquiry flourished.[6] While the new cultures of enquiry that emerged in the Enlightenment are undoubtedly critically important to our understanding of the history of modern Europe, other causes of the second scientific revolution remain unexamined. It may be especially useful to consider in more detail the question of the relationship between economic change and scientific-intellectual change. The present chapter explores this relationship by focusing on information practices, or, as Lissa Roberts might put it, the "concept, processes and management of accumulation" as a way into the colonial political economy of science.[7] Roberts has argued that, in order to understand and explain the interconnections between the growth of modern science and the growth of modern empires, historians must find a way avoid "dividing up the cloth we want seamless," that is, avoid applying present-day categorical distinctions, which tend to obscure the very subject we are trying to study.[8] "Accumulation," she argues, is the fundamental historical process that needs to be analysed. But the current problem, according to Roberts, is that accumulation still tends to be "investigated separately within the fields of political economy and history of science" when in fact accumulation is a key point of coextension across information, capital, and many other sources of value.[9]

In what follows, I use the term "information resources" (or sometimes "knowledge resources"—for my purposes, these terms are interchangeable) to refer to the material from Asia being accumulated and managed first in personal collections and later in corporate or semi-public libraries and museums. The term encompasses a huge variety of stuff, from manuscripts and books to specimens and samples to coins and jewellery to manufactures and crafts to works of art and antiquities. The stuff accumulated was sometimes never used for anything, remaining packed in warehouses or cellars. Sometimes it was used for purposes other than research or scholarly production, such as being given as a gift (some would say bribe), or even simply sold for cash. But, as we will see, the library and museum was often presented by contemporaries as having the purpose of contributing to the preservation, production, and distribution of what was considered to be, from the imperial metropole, "useful knowledge."

Many recent studies have explored in detail the changing place of the sciences and information practices more broadly within Europe's colonial arms of states, either trading corporations or colonial offices.[10] Despite all this work, the central importance of the Company as the administrative and legal entity regulating (whether intentionally or not) the circulation of information resources between Britain and India has yet to be fully explored. This chapter focuses in particular on the Company's monopoly rights, and on the related issues of ownership of and access to information resources. The East India Company held, with some key gaps, from 1600 until 1813, a Crown-granted monopoly—one laid out in charter agreements between the Crown and the Company—on all British trade east of the Cape of Good Hope. In effect, this monopoly on *trade* also gave the Company a near-total monopoly on *access* to Asia and its cultural and natural resources, including information resources. In practice, the Company's control over access and movement and information between Britain and Asia was far from complete. But it was formidable, and it played a significant role in shaping cultures and practices of science in both Britain and the colonies. Especially after around 1800, a particular information order between the Company and its colonies would be established: though funded with tax revenue from Asia, and though museums and libraries were also rapidly growing in some colonial regions, a resource hierarchy within the Company territories would crystallise with the library and museum in

415

London at the top, to the benefit of the growth of many sciences in Britain.[11] Towards the end of the nineteenth century, the imperial information order between Britain and its colonies would become entrenched, with lasting repercussions for the global political economy of information. In 1858, the Company was abolished, and the British government took over direct rule of the Company's colonies in Asia. Thereafter, its library and museum was absorbed into Britain's national libraries and museums. Those collections are now dispersed across the British Museum, British Library, UK Natural History Museum, and the Victoria and Albert Museum, as well as smaller collections in both the United Kingdom and India.

Before 1757: Contracting Out Information Accumulation and Management

In many ways, the origins of Britain's empire began in libraries. Compared to her European neighbours, England came late to overseas trade and colonisation. England's early attempts at transoceanic trade thus began in large part as a process of capturing and translating sources from Iberian and Dutch trading rivals. When assessing the opportunities and dangers in investing in trade to the East or the Americas, early investors turned to the encyclopaedic and compiling "cosmographers" such as the sixteenth-century chaplain and geographer Richard Hakluyt, and astrologer-mathematician and antiquary John Dee. Hakluyt had managed to acquire rare and valuable Portuguese, Spanish, and Dutch travel accounts, and in 1601 was appointed an advisor to the newly formed East India Company.[12] Hakluyt produced an English translation of a Portuguese manuscript compendium of "the different and astounding routes by which in times gone pepper and spice came from India to our parts ... up to the year 1555."[13] In seeking material to translate and compile, Hakluyt sometimes turned to the library of John Dee. Dee was a great "informer" of his day, an advisor to the Crown and colonial adventurers, and his library was rumoured to be one of the largest in England, especially rich in accounts of travel and exploration.[14] From the 1570s onwards, Dee had been drawing on his library to promote English economic and territorial expansion, using his antiquarian collections to make various arguments for British extraterritorial claims. His most ambitious work, *The Brytysh Monarchy*, was the first to use the term "British Impire," and also made the argument (based on Welsh folklore about transatlantic voyages) for Elizabeth to be titled "Queen of the New World."[15] In these and other ways, the collecting, translating, copying, and publishing work of antiquarian geographers such as Dee and Hakluyt were the routes through which the would-be English colonists and adventurers gathered both critical intelligence and an ideological-legal justification for their projects in the earliest years of English colonialism.[16]

While profiting greatly from their private collections, Dee and Hakluyt also argued that the English nation desperately needed its own repository. Hakluyt had argued in 1587, for example, that the English Crown should also "collect in orderly fashion the maritime records of our own countrymen, now lying scattered and neglected, and ... bring them to the light of day in a worthy guise, to the end that posterity ... may at last be inspired to seize the opportunity offered to them of playing a worthy part."[17] But, as we will see, neither the English Crown nor the Companies themselves attempted to form a centralised repository for information until nearly two hundred years later. Instead, as the colonial companies—the Virginia Company, the East India Company, the Hudson's Bay Company, to name a few—expanded their operations over the next century, this basic model of relying on the information resources of independent advisors would remain.

From its earliest days, Company servants (that is to say, employees) were engaged in a wide range of early modern sciences, but they tended to collect and (sometimes) publish as individuals, not for the Company. Wherever Company-hired ships landed, captains and crew voraciously sought information that might help them get home with a profitable cargo, or provide future advantage over their European trading rivals. At India House, the Company's headquarters in the City of London, day-to-day operations of the joint-stock company were managed by a group of directors elected by stockholders. The directors managed committees in charge of finance, trade, transport military engagement, and the constant, all-important correspondence between headquarters and the Company's governments in Asia. All of these committees produced huge amounts of written records. But, with the key exception of requiring a ship journal of each voyage to be deposited at India House, the Company itself did not directly engage in collecting or natural knowledge resource storage and handling. Instead, until the late eighteenth century, the Directors "outsourced," or contracted out, much of the sciences required for long-distance trade.[18] Cartography and geography, for example, was managed not by any Company office but by the ship owners and, even more, by the captains hired separately for each voyage. Generally, it was the ship captains who maintained their own chart collections as part of their set of navigational instruments. Captains, in turn, relied upon London's thriving commercial market in navigational knowledge throughout the seventeenth century and well into the 1750s. The Thameside Chartmakers, a branch of the Draper's Company, supplied the captains hired by the Company and those of the Royal Navy with many of the charts, maps, and plans used in commercial exploration and navigation.[19] Until well into the eighteenth century in Britain, hydrographical information, like charts and maps in general, was not produced, managed, or controlled by the state. London was also a leading European centre for the manufacture of the practical mathematical instruments depended upon by astronomers, navigators, and surveyors hired by the Company.[20] The same outsourcing pattern held for the Company's surgeons and naturalists, who were required to purchase their own medicines, books, instruments, and other supplies. It was not until 1773 that the Company established a board in London to review candidates for assistant surgeon posts (and a similar review board was established in Madras in 1775).[21] Company writers (administrators) or factors (traders) wishing to learn the foreign languages or other skills useful for trade and diplomacy were on their own until the late eighteenth century, when outgoing writers were granted a "munshi's allowance" to hire tutors once in India.

None of the Company's imperial rivals contracted out so much of their information management. The medical, nautical, commercial, cartographic, and archival information in the Iberian empires were highly centralised. In Portugal, for example, navigational knowledge was directed by the *cosmógrafo-mor* (chief cosmographer) and a group of pilots and scholars. The chief cosmographer's duties, according to a 1592 *Regiment*, included examining and rating makers of nautical instruments and charts, and "authenticating" all charts, globes, and maps. His office was also in charge of training future pilots in mathematics, astronomy, and cosmography. All navigational information was kept in strictest secrecy, including the officially sanctioned map for use by the pilots, the *Padrão Real*.[22] In Spain, the *Casa de Contratación* (House of Trade) in Seville had since the early 1500s been the centre of administration and information collection and production, including navigational, medical, and natural philosophical works.[23] France, whose empire was second in size only to Spain during the seventeenth century, had begun to organise many branches of science and medicine hierarchically under the state from the time of Louis XIV. France's "colonial machine" as James McClellan and François Regourd have called it became, during the eighteenth century, inseparable from the state's institutions of science.[24]

The flipside of the East India Company's outsourcing of knowledge management was that those whom the Company hired were largely free to profit from knowledge or information that they gained while under the employ of the Company. By the early decades of the eighteenth century, there was a robust market in travel accounts and histories of English (and increasingly Scottish) seamen and traders. Captains regularly published accounts of voyages, including diaries, routes, and charts, hoping to defray some of the costs of their voyages in this way.[25] For the same reason, returned surgeons printed herbals, natural histories, or their own travel accounts. Often the Company, or a group of directors, would contribute to the publication by agreeing in advance to purchase (subscribe for) a certain number of books. It was also through individual employee trading, not the Company's official imports and exports, that collections of specimens, *naturalia*, manuscripts, and other material for libraries and cabinets of curiosity would pass. Underneath the umbrella of the East India Company's monopoly on all trade east of the Cape of Good Hope, there was a vibrant ecosystem of private trade conducted by individuals for their own profit. Some were illegal "interlopers," that is, British individuals conducting trade between Britain and Asia without the permission of the Company. But the bulk of the private trade was legal and under licence from the Company. Ship captains and other officers were a great beneficiary of the legal private trade, or as Emily Erikson calls it, the "internal free trade market" under the Company monopoly.[26] Unlike textiles, spices, raw materials, and other commodities, manuscripts, books, works of art, and curiosities were *not* sold directly by the Company at the auction rooms within India House. Instead, this material passed directly between private hands. In the period before territorial and wartime expansion under the Company, much of this collecting would be conducted on a small scale, as piece-by-piece sale or barter, or—in the cities and towns in the East—by visiting the local markets or bazaars. It was thus *under* the Company, but not *at* the Company, that the voracious culture of collecting and natural history grew in Britain and its colonies in Asia in the seventeenth and eighteenth centuries. Erikson has argued that it was this decentralised organisation of the Company that fostered a robust information exchange in general: "When the English Company had a decentralised organisational structure, which is to say that significant autonomy lay in the hands of employees, social networks encouraged the transmission of local information and led to the incorporation of more ports and goods into the English trade network."[27]

1757–1800: The Asian Roots of EIC Accumulation and Management

Into the early eighteenth century, the Company managed to establish a more solid presence in Asia. Although still only maintaining control of a string of fortified ports on the subcontinent and in the Malay Archipelago, the Company's expansion was backed by a growing military. As the political and economic stakes of the Company's monopoly trade continued to grow, the Company became more deeply entangled in domains of knowledge upon which its operations had always depended. For this, the foreigners had to forge relationships with knowledgeable locals. Informants (such as local doctors, teachers, translators, and guides) were sought, as were collections of manuscripts and other records. These knowledge resources were copied, appropriated, hybridised, and sometimes repressed by the foreigners. Meanwhile, local rulers were also seeking European informants for similar purposes. Beyond the British-ruled territories, some native kingdoms actively extended their patronage to European naturalists, surgeons, and engineers who had managed to gain a reputation in the subcontinent. In the northeast, gardens and cabinets of curiosity were flourishing in Lucknow, capital of Awadh (Oudh), under the rule of nawab Asaf-ud-Daula, who ruled between 1775 and 1795.[28] The Oudh royal library was particularly famous.[29] The Serampore gardens started out in 1771 as a public gardens supported by local rulers.[30] In the south, the Nawab of Arcot in the Carnatic (in which Madras was situated) employed in the late 1760s the first of Linnaeus' "disciples" in the subcontinent.[31] And, adjacent to the Carnatic, in the southern kingdom of Mysore, Sultan Hyder Ali was investing heavily in the growth of engineering, arts, and sciences.

After a series of wars in 1757, the Company became a dominant territorial power, stepping in to take the reins of the Mughal Empire's centuries-old systems of governance. It was now a mammoth task of both appropriation and invention for Company servants to gain even a partial understanding of the land, languages, laws, finances, and religious and civil structures in the societies that it was purportedly now governing. A vast paper trail of colonial expansion was growing continuously within the headquarters at India House. In these changes, too, were the roots of a new colonial information order in which India House was becoming increasingly important.

The appointment of Warren Hastings as the first Governor General of Bengal in 1775 is often taken as a turning point in colonial science in British India under the Company. Hastings promoted a version of imperial rule according to the "native" or "natural" laws of the region, according to which, as Hastings sometimes argued, the route to prosperous Company governance of Bengal was a matter of increasing knowledge of the history, laws, and resources of the region, by way of the work of orientalists, surveyors, and naturalists. In this mode, Hastings positioned himself as a translator of India for the British, and as a "liberal" (that is, generous) protector and promoter of the arts and culture of Asia.[32] With various forms of encouragement from Hastings, a new generation of Company servants also took on the collection and study of Indian language, history, geography, and natural resources.

Such changes should not be read, as it sometimes has been, as primarily the result of Hastings' own qualities, or of "Enlightenment values" reaching British India by way of Hastings' patronage. Equally if not more important were the wider transformations in the Company's political economic position in Bengal, which opened new opportunities for knowledge exchange, collecting, and scholarship. For one thing, the new offices and administrative positions created in response to expanding British control over territorial revenue also created new sites and situations for British interaction with local scholars and administrators of the Mughal courts. Furthermore, Hastings' generation of scholars were perfectly poised take advantage of the radical cultural and economic upheaval produced in the wake of the Company's takeover of revenue collection in Bengal, in particular a devastating famine in 1770. It is that conjunction of genuine *amateur* orientalism with the brutality of the Company's expansion at the time that is critical to understanding the growth of British collecting and scholarship in Asia in the period. Before 1757, it had been common for Company servants to complain that the local administrative and learned elite were uninterested in sharing their knowledge. Hastings claimed there had long been a "jealous prejudice," against interlocution with the British, which led them to "guard" their knowledge from foreigners.[33] By the early 1770s, however, with many formerly wealthy patrons now unable to support them, the local intellectual elite increasingly turned to the British for employment.[34] Native experts on local laws and religions were also increasingly hired directly by the India-based Company administration (such as the Presidency governments in Calcutta and Madras) to compile and translate the existing laws and statues in practice in different regions. This relatively large-scale integration of the local scholarly elite into the Company's administration in the Presidencies marked a new shift in the way information was being accumulated by the British. The orientalist and judge William Jones, for example, worked closely with Sanskrit tutors such as Ramlochan, *munshis* such as Bahaman, and when on the bench as a judge, depended on the advice of the court *pandits* Goberdhan Kaul and Ramcharan.[35]

Thirty years after the Company's first major military victory on the subcontinent, the British now enjoyed much greater ease of access to, and usage of, the natural and cultural resources of the region. Whereas it had once been very difficult and expensive for Europeans to gain even minimal acquaintance with the "science, arts and literature of Asia," now, as the nineteenth century approached, the situation was very different. While foreigners in India had always engaged in collecting, both wartime plundering and the Company's new position relative to the Mughal Empire would open up many new avenues of access for Britons intent on acquiring manuscripts, curiosities, and other knowledge resources. As Jones optimistically put it in a speech at the newly founded Asiatic Society of Bengal (est. 1787), all that the aspiring scholars and collectors at the Company now needed was *more time*: "'Give me a place to stand on,' said the great mathematician [Archimedes] 'and I will move the whole earth.' Give us time, we may say, for our investigators, and we will transfer to Europe all the sciences, arts, and literature of Asia."[36]

Even the barrier of time was also beginning to fall, as the Company now began to create positions and offices devoted to information management and production. Between the end of the Seven Years' War and the beginning of the Napoleonic Wars, the Company was beginning to engage much more directly in the organisation and management of the sciences upon which its trade and governance depended. Kapil Raj calls this period "the first step in the transformation of the study of exotic peoples from an individual activity—mainly European missionaries—into a massive and institutionalised activity … [and] the first step in the transformation of the emerging British empire from one held by force of arms to one held—at least in theory—by information."[37] In this period, the Company too began to engage more directly with the organisation and production of information in new ways. Virtually, all of these new developments were happening in the colonies: the ambitious new terrestrial surveys, which deployed state-of-the-art techniques, the generously funded botanical gardens at Calcutta, and the wider, more formalised employment of *pandits, munshis*, and other native educators and scholars. These new spaces for information production and management within the Company represent some of the many changes that accompanied the Company's structural transformation during the late eighteenth century from a relatively marginal militarised maritime trading company to the subcontinent's dominant territorial imperial power. As we will see, however, within a few short years, pressures from both the subcontinent and the home country would lead the Company to increase investment sharply in institutions of information management back in Britain.

Monopolies and Networks: The Leadenhall Street Library-Museum and the Growth of Science in Britain after 1800

In 1798, the same year the Company first broke ground on an ambitious expansion of India House, the Directors announced their plan for a new "public repository." The Directors' decision to establish—after nearly two hundred years of operation—a library and museum at its headquarters was enmeshed to the rapidly changing geography of knowledge resource accumulation within the empire. These changes spurred the Directors to intervene in and take more direct control over the increasingly significant information resource trade between Britain and colonial India.

It was the damage being done by the voracious collecting of their own servants that was given as the motivation for finally establishing, after two hundred years, a dedicated library and museum at India House. The directors noted that private collecting and exportation of oriental manuscripts by Company servants was now "thinning" the stock of original works in India. This, however, was not in itself a problem, since the Directors also argued that materials remaining in India were always at risk of damage by heat, humidity, and lack of care. The real problem was that all of these materials were disappearing into *private* libraries, likely to be forgotten or unused, and "not greatly enriching Britain" as a whole. Thus, so it was proposed, a safe harbour was needed *in Britain* for the literary and scientific material of the subcontinent. The new library and museum was thus presented as a stately move to preserve an endangered "oriental literature" from the now flourishing commercial trade in manuscripts, antiquities, and specimens. In this way, the Directors' first vision of the repository was *not*, like that of the botanical gardens or the surveyor's offices on the subcontinent, as a new arm of an "improving" mission. And it was also, in expecting to grow at "no great expence" and by way of donations, not much of a departure from the old outsourcing model of knowledge management. It was merely a signal of a willingness to take "public," but, in effect, corporate, ownership of some portion of the knowledge resources flowing out of Asia and into Britain. But in that little shift was the making of what would become an important new institutional space for the accumulation and management of information in Britain.

A year later, this modest idea had been spun into a plan for a small British Museum-like library and museum at India House. This new proposal was the work of Warren Hastings and the orientalist Charles Wilkins, both of whom had returned to London in the mid-1780s. Wilkins' proposal described a repository-like archive of "maps, charts, plans, views, manuscripts, printed books, coins, medals, statues and inscriptions" as well as three "cabinets": "natural productions," "artificial productions," and "miscellaneous articles." Importantly, the establishment *in London* of a new Company repository was also tied to political infighting—and an invaluable library captured from Mysore—within the Company over the relative autonomy and authority of the Presidency governments in comparison to India House. After a successful war against the Kingdom of Mysore, the new Governor General of Bengal, Richard Wellesley, had announced in 1801—without first seeking permission from the Directors in London—an ambitious plan for a new complex of libraries and colleges in Calcutta, which would be built symbolically around Tipu Sultan's famous library that was now in the hands of Wellesley. In response, the Directors in London ordered the Calcutta colleges closed and demanded that Tipu Sultan's library be shipped back to India House, where it added a major boost to the fledgling library in London.

As part of a major expansion of India House, the new dedicated space for a library and museum opened in 1801. The collections occupied two large sky-lit rooms on the second floor, overlooking the grand neoclassical entrance to India House. The walls were lined with custom-built book cases to accommodate many textual formats from massive folio volumes of natural history to tiny portable religious texts, from scrolls to folding bamboo plates. Glazed cases were specially built for incoming collections, such as stuffed birds from Java or jade sculptures from China. At several long tables, visiting orientalists and naturalists would consult the materials (and sometimes bring things home). The library and museum was described as free and open to the public, although, until the 1830s, opening times were limited and visitors had to obtain a card of admission from a member of the court of directors (although it was rumoured that access could also be gained through a small bribe to one of the guards).[38] Still, the curators would sometimes complain about the noise and disruption caused by tours and curious sightseers, who might test out some of the Javanese instruments or crank up the automaton known as "Tipu's Tiger": a wooden mechanical organ in the shape of a tiger savaging a European, which would emit growls and squeals.

Aside from the large deposit of plunder from the last Anglo-Mysore War, the Company's repository initially grew slowly. But grow it eventually did, and the rate of accumulation at India House would continue to accelerate over the next half-century. Most important to the acceleration of accumulation was the Company's ongoing territorial wars, which expanded during the French Revolutionary and Napoleonic Wars of 1798–1815, when France threatened Britain's position on the subcontinent. The upheavals of the Napoleonic Wars as they played out in Asia would result in another wave of materials captured through looting and plundering. Before 1800, semi-sanctioned practices of individual looting, collecting, and personal enrichment were the norm. Such norms were beginning to change during and after the Napoleonic Wars.[39] By the early nineteenth century, the plunder-based system of payment to soldiers—where plunder would be gathered by designated "prize officers," sold at auction, and only the proceeds distributed—was targeted for reform. But even after such laws were in place, and after wartime looting had generally come to be seen as unethical in Europe, even greater material flowed into Europe.[40] Perhaps even more important for the growth of the Company's own collections, starting in the early nineteenth century, advancing armies were now followed by a much more organised and official form of collecting: the territorial survey, such as those conducted by Francis Buchanan in Mysore and the surveyor General Colin Mackenzie in Mysore and Java. For the first time in the Company's history, these collections were formed for the Company's own repositories, and the India House library and museum was now considered at the top of a hierarchy of smaller libraries and museums across the Company's territories. The result was that even as collections were also growing all across Asia, such as those at the Calcutta Botanical Gardens and the Asiatic Society of Bengal, the cultural and scientific capital held at India House grew at an even faster pace during the last phases of the Napoleonic Wars and in the "little wars" of border aggression that followed.

Between 1813 and 1858, as the collections grew more rapidly, and as the Company's monopoly privileges and trading activities were curtailed, more and more rooms within India House were transformed into rooms for collection storage and display. An additional room on the second floor—formerly the building surveyor's office—became the de facto natural history room. One of the largest rooms on the ground floor—formerly the pay office—was turned into a gallery for especially heavy or large objects, and in the 1840s this was filled with fossils from the Siwalik Hills. In the late 1850s, with a mass of new objects acquired during the of the Great Exhibition of 1851, the grandest of the spaces within India House—the old tea sale and auction hall—was renovated into a mosque-like "new museum" for art and antiquities, and another wing of the building was devoted to an industrial museum focusing on manufactures and raw materials. Books and manuscripts were stored in an ever-expanding section of the attic. In the damp and rat-infested basement, vaults were housed hundreds of unopened cases of botanical and natural history specimens. Ancient sculptures from central India were sometimes stored in the open courtyard.

Well beyond the confines of Leadenhall Street, Company science was in this period shaping the material available for knowledge production in Britain. Out of the information extracted from India and gathered at India House and elsewhere would be built an increasingly profitable web of what would now be called intellectual property resources, generally owned and traded by Europe-based actors. The folding of information about Asia into Britain's provincial systems of ordering and classification would contribute to the growth of European sciences at the time while also generating social, intellectual, and financial capital for the authors. This systematic possession of Asia in Europe was the stuff by which not only careers and intellectual property but also whole disciplines and institutions could be made.

By 1830, the material impact of the collections was felt well beyond India House. Company collections were also feeding into the new professions, societies, and intellectual networks of Britain's so-called second scientific revolution. Between 1820 and 1840, the social organisation of what was once called natural philosophy began to take on new disciplinary distinctions. In London alone, some of the new societies included the Royal Horticultural Society (founded 1804, chartered 1861), the Geological Society (f. 1807, c. 1825), the Royal Astronomical Society (f. 1820, c. 1831), the Society for the Diffusion of Useful Knowledge (f. 1826), the Zoological Society (f. 1829), the Geographical Society (f. 1830, c. 1859), the British Association for the Advancement of Science (f. 1831), the Entomological Society (f. 1833), the Ethnological Society (f. 1843), and the Hakluyt Society (f. 1846).

These new subject-specific societies often formed around a perceived need to manage an accumulation of information specific to their domains. Specialised collections were part of the institutional structure of every one of these new societies. The Company's museum supplied materials to many of the new society collections. For example, it had long been the practice to share so-called "duplicate" specimens with other collectors, as when, in 1828, for example, the Directors permitted members of the Medico-Botanical Society of London to visit "the Herbarium of the Company ... and [take] duplicates of such medical plants as are therein contained."[41] By 1830, the Company was sending duplicate specimens to the British Museum as well as other institutions such as at Oxford, Cambridge, the Zoological Society, and the University Museum in Geneva.[42] It was also donating manuscripts and books to literary societies. In general, and like other museums at the time, the Company's museum often operated less as a final resting place for inflows from the empire, and more as a sorting house or sieve.[43] While Kew, the British Museum, and then, usually, Cambridge and Oxford were the first in line within a hierarchy of outflow recipients, a surprisingly broad number and type of institutions were also in line to receive the Museum's donations.[44] The Company thus became a prominent participant in an economy of barter, exchange, purchase, and donation of material among hundreds of repositories across the world.

The Company's Library-Museum in the Age of Reform: From a Formal to a Natural Monopoly on Information?

The 1830s and 1840s were a transformative period in British culture. A push came from many directions to upend old orders and replace them with new foundations. The reformist Whig party had come into power in 1830. The Reform Act of 1832 significantly expanded voting rights (though not to women or working-class men). By the Slave Emancipation Act of 1833, slavery had become illegal throughout the British Empire. Agitation to repeal import laws—such as the Corn Laws—that favoured agricultural landholders was growing, and the Chartist and other working-class movements were on the rise.

Discourse and practices of knowledge production were also reshaped during the so-called Age of Reform. With liberalism came a push for increasing access to, and state support of, science and education. Cheap and informative periodicals such as those produced by the Society for the Diffusion of Useful Knowledge (SDUK) (with which Company administrator James Mill was very involved) were seen to be key to facilitating the self-improvement and self-determination of the "middle ranks" at the centre of Bentham's and Mill's utilitarian social philosophy. The opening of the secular University of London in 1836 sought to break the hold of the Anglican Oxbridge colleges. The British Association for the Advancement of Science (1831) was established as an antidote to the perceived aristocratic elitism of the Royal Society. And attention was also turned to exhibitions, museums, and galleries, and the British Museum in particular, and a Parliamentary inquiry scrutinised the public utility of that institution.

The political rise of liberalism, and particularly liberal utilitarianism, also brought with it the end to the Company's ancient monopoly privileges. When the Company's charter renewal came up in 1813, the Company narrowly retained its monopoly and trading privileges, and then only for the case of trade with China, while the India monopoly was abolished. The charter of 1833 dealt a much more severe blow to the Company's corporate sovereignty and monopoly privileges. Under the conditions set out in 1833, the Company was to cease *all* trading activities, and all Company property was formally transferred to the Crown, to be held in trust by the Company for the purposes of governance in India only. In other words, the Company was stripped of all commercial activities but retained its role as administrator of the government of British India. But the Company's entire colonial infrastructure, from the Presidencies to the Company ports to India House itself and everything within it—including the Company's library and museum—was now, on paper at least, property of the British government.

Immediately after the completion of the new charter, both defenders and critics of the Company turned to the question of what would happen to the Company's library-museum, which was caught up in those same movement for increased public access and public utility. But the valence of both "public access" and "public utility" would become complicated in the context of this newly realigned set of colonial institutions. While the legal and political status of the Company could be changed with a passage of laws, what was now in effect the Company's *natural* monopoly—not legally granted but gained via market dominance—on access to information about Asia was harder to undo or transfer into a public information resource. Furthermore, even the conceptualisation of the Company's collections as a public resource had its own problems: despite many assertions that the Company's collections were now public *just like* the British Museum, it remained unclear whether these knowledge resources could (or should) both serve the interests of the Government of India *and* the British public, to say nothing of the question of use and access for the people of British India whose taxes funded the India House operations.

However, although ownership of the library and museum was formally transferred to the British state after 1833, some free trade progressives would argue that the Company continued to enjoy an insidious form of information monopoly via its control of access to, and management of, the library and museum.[45] Even some shareholders argued that the Company's library and museum was, in effect, largely inaccessible to all but a few curators, scientists, and scholars. During the charter debate season in 1832, some shareholders, criticising the public utility of the Company's library and museum, proposed that it should be merged with the British Museum. A Parliamentary Report on the operations of the British Museum in the same year had examined in detail both the question of the usefulness of a "public" museum and the extent to which the British Museum was meeting those goals of utility. A museum's utility was here judged largely according to *accessibility*. The British Museum report paid a great deal of attention to things like the availability of catalogues, guides, clear and informative labels, opening times, and cost of admission. Now questions were being asked about the status of the Company's printed catalogues and guides—two things it turned out the British Museum was doing very well at, and which visitors voraciously consumed—but which the Company had not yet produced.

In response to such criticism, the Directors argued against the idea that the Company collections should be considered a public resource in the first place. Instead, it defended the relatively closed nature of its collections as a necessity. In short, the Directors regarded the knowledge produced by "scholarly" orientalist work as coextensive with the useful knowledge required in governance: history, languages, literature, natural history, etc. In this way, as the Directors claimed, no matter its ownership status, the India House library and museum is *not* like the British Museum in that it is very closely tied in some ways into actual work of state; the collections are somewhere on a continuum between state archive (which themselves were only just then beginning to become organised into standalone institutions, let alone with conventions of public access) and scholarly or public collection. Therefore, access is arguably different.[46]

These debates also invoked the tricky question of how "public" is defined in an imperial polity. The argument suggests that ultimately these collections belong more to the public of British India than to the public of Britain. From first plans for the India House library and museum back in 1798, it had always been discussed as a set of institutions intended to serve the interests of the people of India (believe it or not). Obviously serving the interests of the people of India had, in this case, always been understood as having *nothing to do* with providing the Indian public physical access (or even virtually in the form of catalogues or guides) to the India House collections. This is ironic, given that during the Parliamentary inquiry into the British Museum in 1832, reformers worried about the inaccessibility of those resources to the typical worker living outside London.[47] In the case of the India House library and museum, the resources were to be put to use *for* the good of the Indian public, without being able to be used *by* them.

Importantly, critics of the library-museum at India House were not just focused on the conduct of the Company but also that of the British state. Critics argued not only for the Company to improve its opening times, produce catalogues and guides, and so on, but *also* for the government to treat the collections more like a national (or actually imperial) collection. For example, *Alexander's* complained bitterly that the recently established Public Records Commission did not include a survey of the records of India House. Why, it asked, isn't the British government treating the Company's library and museum as the "national" collection that it is? The Public Records Commission, so it was argued, should both include in its study the India House archives and records, and the libraries and archives in all of British India, and, even further the Commission Reports should be sent throughout the empire, just as the commission has done for the recently completed survey of UK records. Ultimately, it was neglect and inefficient organisation and management at the hands of both the Company and Government that allows this monopoly to continue.[48]

At a time when a coherent British imperial identity was only just beginning to crystallise, the extremely convoluted property relations for the library-museum (held in trust by the Company for the Crown, which, in turn, held it in trust for the people of British India) raised awkward questions about the very coherence of the idea of an imperial public. That idea would begin to cohere much more rapidly in the wake of the Indian Mutiny of 1857 and the subsequent abolition of the Company in 1858. In the early 1860s, all of the Company's collections were first transferred to offices near the new India Office at Whitehall, but by the 1880s they were being distributed across the British Museum (and its library, the future British Library), Kew Gardens, and the South Kensington museums (the future UK Natural History Museum and Victoria and Albert Museum). The orientalist training and scholarship that had been the domain of the Company's college at Haileybury would be largely taken over by the Oxford India Institute. Now located in universities and public museums in Britain, the Company's old colonial information order was eventually recast, on a global scale, as a part of a new international information order.[49]

The imperial centres of accumulation that had emerged by the start of the twentieth century were not so much the result of the growth of states in themselves, or of science in itself (more scientists calling for more data) but coextensive with larger political and economic changes, of which the changing information order was just one part. From the beginning, and in different ways at different times, the Company's monopoly on trade and communication between Asia and Britain had allowed it to accumulate an unrivalled collection of knowledge resources and expertise, which then became folded into Britain's state-owned science, which, in its turn, fed into Britain's global dominance in science. Britain alone cannot be said to have had anything like a *global* monopoly on science, but it could be argued that, *within the British Empire*, London, Oxbridge, and a few other cities in Britain did achieve, for a time, and out of a foundation laid by the Company, something with a similar effect.

Notes

1 Jessica Ratcliff, "The Great (Data) Divergence: Global History of Science within Global Economic History," in *Global Scientific Practice in an Age of Revolutions, 1750–1850*, ed. Patrick Manning and Daniel Rood (Pittsburgh, PA: University of Pittsburgh Press, 2016), 237–254.
2 For a more in-depth study of the subject of this chapter, see Jessica Ratcliff, *Monopolizing Knowledge: The East India Company and Britain's Second Scientific Revolution* (Cambridge, UK: Cambridge University Press, 2025).
3 The history of the Company's collection and management of information related to trade, administration, taxation, and other corporate and financial records is connected but distinct. See H. V. Bowen, *The Business of Empire: The East India Company and Imperial Britain, 1756–1833* (Cambridge, UK: Cambridge University Press, 2006).
4 See Mark Harrison, "Science and the British Empire," *Isis* 96, no. 1 (March 2005): 56–63, esp. 56. For two sustained arguments about the interdependence of states and corporations in the making of modern science, see Sven Beckert, *Empire of Cotton: A Global History* (New York: Vintage Books, 2015); and Mariana Mazzucato, *The Entrepreneurial State: Debunking Public vs. Private Sector Myths* (New York: Public Affairs, 2015). On the entanglements of corporations and states in the early modern period, see Philip J. Stern, *Empire, Incorporated: The Corporations That Built British Colonialism* (Cambridge, MA: Belknap, 2023).
5 For example, Peter Burke concludes that "The amount of new knowledge gathered or collected in … 1750–1850, was staggering, especially the knowledge collected by Europeans about the fauna, flora, geography and history of other parts of the world," in Burke, *A Social History of Knowledge II: From the Encyclopaedia to Wikipedia* (Cambridge, UK: Polity Press, 2012), 12.
6 See, for example, Joel Mokyr, *The Gifts of Athena: Historical Origins of the Knowledge Economy* (Princeton, NJ: Princeton University Press, 2004).

7 Lissa Roberts, "Accumulation and Management in Global Historical Perspective: An Introduction," *History of Science*, 52, no. 3 (September 2014): 227–246, esp. 228.
8 Bruno Latour, *Science in Action: How to Follow Scientists and Engineers through Society* (Cambridge, MA: Harvard University Press, 1987), 223.
9 Roberts, "Accumulation," 228.
10 An excellent overview summary is in Anna Winterbottom, "Science," in *The Corporation as a Protagonist in Global History, c. 1550–1750*, ed. William A. Pettigrew and David Veevers (Boston, MA: Brill, 2019), 232–254.
11 On colonial information orders, see C. A. Bayly, *Empire and Information Intelligence Gathering and Social Communication in India, 1780–1870* (Cambridge, UK: Cambridge University Press, 1996).
12 On Hakluyt, see Daniel Carey and Claire Jowitt, eds., *Richard Hakluyt and Travel Writing in Early Modern Europe* (London: Routledge, 2016).
13 Richard Hakluyt, *The Discoveries of the World [...]*, 1601. Recent reprint: António Galvano, *Discoveries of the World: From Their First Original unto the Year of Our Lord 1555* (Cambridge, UK: Cambridge University Press, 2010).
14 Christopher Hill, *Intellectual Origins of the English Revolution Revisited* (Oxford: Clarendon Press, 1997), 18.
15 On Dee, see E. G. R. Taylor, *Tudor Geography, 1485–1583* (London: Methuen, 1930).
16 David Armitage argues that it is this reconstruction of a British history that created ideological space for an expanding imperial strategy in David Armitage, *The Ideological Origins of the British Empire* (Cambridge, UK: Cambridge University Press, 2000).
17 Oxford Dictionary of National Biography. "Hakluyt, Richard (1552?–1616), Geographer."
18 The Company was also itself the most important "contractee," of the Crown; in effect, the Company's monopoly was a way for the Crown to contract out the project of long-distance trade and colonisation. See John Brewer, *The Sinews of Power: War, Money, and the English State, 1688–1783* (New York: Knopf, 1989).
19 See Mary Sponberg Pedley, *The Commerce of Cartography: Making and Marketing Maps in Eighteenth-Century France and England* (Chicago, IL: University of Chicago Press, 2005).
20 See, for example, Gloria Clifton, *Directory of British Scientific Instrument Makers, 1550–1851* (London: Zwemmer, 1995); and E. G. R. Taylor, *The Mathematical Practitioners of Tudor & Stuart England* (Cambridge, UK: Institute of Navigation at the Cambridge University Press, 1954). More recently, studies have focused on the urban context for London makers: Jim Bennett and Rebekah Higgitt, "London 1600–1800: Communities of Natural Knowledge and Artificial Practice," *The British Journal for the History of Science* 52, no. 2 (June 2019): 183–196; and Alexi Baker, "'Scientific' Instruments and Networks of Craft and Commerce in Early Modern London," in *Cities and Solidarities: Urban Communities in Pre-Modern Europe*, ed. Justin Colson and Arie Steensel (London: Taylor & Francis, 2017), 245–274.
21 Dirom Grey Crawford, *A History of the Indian Medical Service: 1600–1913* (London: W. Thacker, 1914), 496–497.
22 Palmira Fontes da Costa and Henrique Leitão, "Portuguese Imperial Science, 1450–1800: A Historiographical Review," in *Science in the Spanish and Portuguese Empires, 1500–1800*, ed. Daniela Bleichmar, Paula De Vos, Kristin Huffine, and Kevin Sheehan (Stanford, CA: Stanford University Press, 2008), 35–54, esp. 39–40.
23 See Antonio Barrera-Osorio, *Experiencing Nature the Spanish American Empire and the Early Scientific Revolution* (Austin, TX: University of Texas Press, 2006). Also see Antonio Barrera, "Local Herbs, Global Medicines: Commerce, Knowledge, and Commodities in Spanish America," in *Merchants & Marvels: Commerce, Science, and Art in Early Modern Europe*, ed. Pamela H. Smith and Paula Findlen (London: Routledge, 2002), 163–181.
24 James Edward McClellan, III, and François Regourd, *The Colonial Machine: French Science and Overseas Expansion in the Old Regime* (Turnhout: Brepols, 2011). A useful summary of their argument for the "colonial machine" metaphor is in McClellan and Regourd, "The Colonial Machine: French Science and Colonization in the *Ancien Regime*," *Osiris* 15 (2000): 31–50.
25 Anne M. Thell, *Minds in Motion: Imagining Empiricism in Eighteenth-Century British Travel Literature* (Lewisburg, PA: Bucknell University Press, 2017); Mary Louise Pratt, *Imperial Eyes: Travel Writing and Transculturation* (London: Routledge, 2008); and Felix Driver and Luciana Martins, *Tropical Visions in an Age of Empire* (Chicago, IL: University of Chicago Press, 2005).

26 See Emily Erikson, *Between Monopoly and Free Trade: The English East India Company, 1600–1757* (Princeton, NJ: Princeton University Press, 2014).
27 Erikson, *Between Monopoly*, 107. See also Erikson and Sampsa Samila, "Networks, Institutions, and Uncertainty: Information Exchange in Early-Modern Markets," *The Journal of Economic History* 78, no. 4 (December 2018): 1034–1067.
28 Maya Jasanoff, "Collectors of Empire: Objects, Conquests and Imperial Self-Fashioning," *Past & Present* 184, no. 1 (August 2004): 109–135.
29 Aloys Sprenger, *A Catalogue of the Arabic, Persian and Hindu'sta'ny Manuscripts, of the Libraries of the King of Oudh* (Calcutta: Thomas, 1854).
30 Sujit Sivasundaram, "'A Christian Benares': Orientalism, Science and the Serampore Mission of Bengal," *The Indian Economic & Social History Review* 44, no. 2 (April 2007): 111–145.
31 Minakshi Menon, "Medicine, Money, and the Making of the East India Company State: William Roxburgh in Madras, c. 1790," in *Histories of Medicine and Healing in the Indian Ocean World: The Medieval and Early Modern Period*, ed. Anna Winterbottom and Facil Tesfaye (New York: Palgrave Macmillan, 2016), 151–178.
32 P. J. Marshall, "The Making of an Imperial Icon: The Case of Warren Hastings," *The Journal of Imperial and Commonwealth History* 27, no. 3 (September 1999): 1–16.
33 Charles Wilkins and Charles Anthon, eds., *The Bhăgavăt-Gēētā, or, Dialogues of Krĕĕshnă and Ărjŏŏn: In Eighteen Lectures, with Notes* (London: Printed for C. Nourse, 1785), 24.
34 John Bowen, "The East India Company's Education of Its Own Servants," *Journal of the Royal Asiatic Society of Great Britain and Ireland* 3/4 (October 1955): 105–123. On South India in particular, see Bhavani Raman, *Document Raj: Writing and Scribes in Early Colonial South India* (Chicago, IL: University of Chicago Press, 2012); and T. R. Trautmann, ed., *The Madras School of Orientalism: Producing Knowledge in Colonial South India* (New Delhi: Oxford University Press, 2009).
35 Kapil Raj, *Relocating Modern Science: Circulation and the Construction of Knowledge in South Asia and Europe, 1650–1900* (New York: Palgrave Macmillan, 2007), 100.
36 William Jones, "The Design of a Treatise on the Plants of India," in *The Works of Sir William Jones with the Life of the Author*, ed. Lord Teignmouth (London: J. Stockdale and J. Walker, 1807), 5:1.
37 Raj, *Relocating*, 109.
38 Arthur MacGregor, *Company Curiosities: Nature, Culture and the East India Company, 1600–1874* (London: Reaktion Books, 2018); and Ray Desmond, *The India Museum, 1801–1879* (London: HMSO, 1982).
39 See Elise S. Lipkowitz, "Seized Natural-History Collections and the Redefinition of Scientific Cosmopolitanism in the Era of the French Revolution," *The British Journal for the History of Science* 47, no. 1 (March 2014): 15–41.
40 Wayne Sandholtz, *Prohibiting Plunder: How Norms Change* (New York: Oxford University Press, 2007).
41 For this and the following section, see Ratcliff, *Monopolizing Knowledge*, part II.
42 Ratcliff, *Monopolizing Knowledge*, 125.
43 A private French collection is described as a "centre of distribution" in Thierry Hoquet, "Botanical Authority: Benjamin Delessert's Collections between Travelers and Candolle's Natural Method (1803–1847)," *Isis* 105, no. 3 (September 2014): 508–539.
44 Ray Desmond counts sixty-four receiving institutions. Desmond, *India Museum*, 53.
45 See Ratcliff, *Monopolizing Knowledge*, chap. 7.
46 Ratcliff, *Monopolizing Knowledge*, 188.
47 The reformer William Cobbett worried that "the man who worked in the field, at a distance from London, could not come up to view it." Quoted in Gordon McOuat, "Cataloguing Power: Delineating 'Competent Naturalists' and the Meaning of Species in the British Museum," *British Journal for the History of Science* 34, no. 1 (March 2001): 1–28, at 14.
48 Ratcliff, *Monopolizing Knowledge*, 190–195.
49 Ratcliff, *Monopolizing Knowledge*, 259.

27

IN-BETWEEN WRITING AND ORALITY

The Circulation of Information in the Black Spanish Caribbean during the Age of Revolutions, 1789–1808

Cristina Soriano

Introduction

July 1797 was an eventful month in La Guaira, one of Venezuela's most important ports during the seventeenth and eighteenth centuries. On July 13, the captain-general of Venezuela, Don Pedro Carbonell, first heard rumours of an emerging republican movement that allegedly involved dozens of people from Venezuela's capital, Caracas, and from the port of La Guaira. Immediately after receiving the news, the captain-general formed a commission composed of judges and colonial authorities. The inquiry led them to the conclusion that the movement—which they called the "conspiracy of Gual and España," after two of its most important leaders—had begun in La Guaira, a mixed-race town where free people of African descent made up approximately 55% of the population; a little more than 20% were Black slaves; around 10% were Indigenous peoples; and about 15% were whites (Spanish and Creoles).[1]

Although concerned, colonial authorities were not particularly surprised by this discovery. For months, many of them had suspected that the Venezuelan coast had been ideologically "contaminated" by the constant flow of people, papers, and ideas into Venezuela's ports and coastal towns. In fact, members of the commission placed particular blame on the significant presence of French Caribbean individuals (soldiers, army officials, prisoners, and travellers) who had visited the said port between 1793 and 1796. They claimed that these French men spread ideas of liberty and equality, thereby fostering a permissive and liberal environment in which revolutionary principles were frequently debated on public spaces shared by diverse socio-racial groups. Furthermore, they claimed that written texts from France and Saint Domingue had also helped to spread these "false seeds of equality and liberty ... introducing anarchy."[2] For colonial authorities, it was clear that the flexible and liberal atmosphere of La Guaira was fertile ground for the emergence of a movement that followed the French model and that, as a white creole priest put it, "went against the monarchical system, slavery, and the harmony and order of society."[3] Colonial authorities also recognised the effectiveness and permeability of different media of information (oral and written) among local Black communities; these were mostly illiterate groups of people who nonetheless found creative ways to access information, disseminate, and produce their own political ideas. This chapter will offer an analysis of the different media that allowed communities of mixed-race and Black people in the Spanish Caribbean to access information about political events and social movements during the Age of Revolutions. Its main argument is that literacy and printing presses were not central to the development of effective communication networks, as these diverse communities had access to information through a myriad of media that went from newspapers, broadside, and manuscripts, to oral enunciations and rumours that kept them well informed about the unfolding events.

With the exception of Havana and Santo Domingo, which had operating printing presses since the early decades of the eighteenth century, many cities and ports in the Spanish Caribbean, such as Cartagena or Mompox in New Granada, Puerto España in Trinidad, San Juan in Puerto Rico, and Cumaná, Caracas, La Guaira, and Maracaibo in Venezuela did not possess printing technology until the early nineteenth century. Prior to that date, all printed materials (including books, pamphlets, and newspapers) circulating in these towns came from Europe, North America, or other Spanish-American provinces, like Mexico and Peru. The lack of a printing press, however, did not prevent the publics of these port-towns from exchanging and sharing ideas during the age of the Atlantic Revolutions. The strategically located, frequently visited, and poorly controlled ports of the Spanish Caribbean, where numerous ships loaded with both goods and information stopped daily, allowed many individuals to collect foreign newspapers, books, and broadsides, and to disseminate these materials orally or through handwritten copies to circles of both foreign and local readers/listeners. During the Age of Revolutions, inhabitants of Spanish Caribbean towns of diverse social and racial backgrounds actively participated in the networks of information-sharing that connected these ports to both the British and French Antilles and Europe, creating a vibrant and defiant political environment.[4]

Several historical studies have analysed the crucial role that the printing press, newspapers, and printers played during the revolutionary years of the United States (1763–1783) and France (1789–1798). In the British colonies of North America, for example, newspapers accounted for almost 80% of all late colonial imprints, and printers became a crucial force in shaping the communication networks of the nascent Republic.[5] In the case of the French Revolution, the surge of newspapers, broadsheets, and pamphlets in France was also impressive. According to historian Andrew Pettegree, by 1788, for example, printers of the French capital published half a dozen of journals; by 1790, more than 300 newspapers were being published. The great majority of these papers were entirely devoted to political topics.[6] For decades, historians have been dedicated to analysing the connection between the Atlantic Revolutions and the operation of the printing press and the social spaces where print materials circulated, but these connections are less evident in those societies that—like most of the ones in the Spanish Caribbean—lacked the technology. The bicentennial commemorations of the Haitian Revolution (1791–1804) and the increasing interests in the last twenty years on studying the Atlantic Revolutions from a Caribbean perspective have created an important historiographical shift that put Caribbean Black communities' agency and political participation at the centre, revealing the communication networks and information strategies these semi-literate communities creatively employed.[7]

In the 1980s, an emerging Atlantic World historiography paid close attention to commercial relations and trade between Europe, Africa, and the Americas during the seventeenth and eighteenth centuries, and to the ways in which traders and smugglers shaped this world through the exchange of commodities and services. These studies offered important insights into how commercial dynamics linked four continents beyond imperial decisions and diplomatic agreements.[8] However, these histories overlooked a crucial medium of exchange: information. Historian Julius Scott was one of the first scholars to analyse the Caribbean region from the perspective of information and communication networks. Based on his widely read 1986's dissertation, Scott's pioneering book *The Common Wind: Afro-American Currents in the Age of the Haitian Revolution*[9] exposed how the rebellious events in Saint-Domingue and the political turbulence of other Caribbean islands catalysed political movements and insurgencies. According to Scott, communities of African descent in the Atlantic Basin were bound together by a network of communication that gave momentum to the cause of emancipation. Enslaved and free Black people moved easily across the Caribbean basin, spreading news of liberation and brewing political unrest throughout the eighteenth-century Atlantic world. Scott's ground-breaking study of Caribbean communication networks allowed historians of the Atlantic World to recognise the relevance of the circulation of information in the configuration of the complex commercial, social, and political webs that linked Spanish, French, British, Dutch, and US port towns and cities during the Age of Revolutions.

The increasing scholarly attention to information networks in the Caribbean has been transformative for the field. Today most scholars of the seventeenth and eighteenth centuries Caribbean characterise the region as a transimperial and plural space that encompassed both islands and continental coasts – a space that was linked by communication threads that blurred imperial boundaries. Recent studies have shown, for example, that the constant movement of free and enslaved Black people, mixed-race dwellers, and white European subjects to exchange goods, technology, ideas, and information across imperial frontiers created a tangled transimperial space that challenged colonial authorities and imperial control.[10]

Between 1789 and 1808, the circulation of texts and rumours from the Atlantic Revolutions increased in the Spanish Caribbean; this expansion of media and information not only stimulated the curiosity of a growing number of mixed-race and Black communities, but also heightened fears of racial confrontation and political conflict among white elites and colonial authorities in different regions. Colonial officials and white elites in Cuba, Venezuela, coastal New Granada, Santo Domingo, and Puerto Rico began to pay more attention to the words and the actions of communities of mixed-race, free Black, and enslaved people, and to reconsider their own relationships with these subordinated groups, while at the same time increasing their vigilance and trying to isolate them from external sources of information.[11] These official efforts created an abundant historical record that have allowed historians to study the different practices and strategies that subordinated groups of colour used to stay informed and shape their political decisions.

The controlling actions, however, were challenging as news of the revolutions spread through a variety of written and oral media that escaped the control of the colonial agents. Mixed-race and Black communities of the Spanish Caribbean were at the centre of a "media crossroads" that included the circulation of newspapers, the wide dissemination of pamphlets and manuscripts, the operation of itinerant (and even unauthorised) printing presses, and the overflow of rumours and oral messages. Divided into three parts, each corresponding to a different media, this chapter analyses the diverse written and oral media that successfully connected Black communities in the Spanish Caribbean during the Age of

Revolutions to show that formal printing presses and books were not essential for them, and that these diverse media gave place to an effective information network that allowed Black communities to engage and participate in the politics of the time.

The Circulation of Dangerous Newspapers in the Spanish Caribbean

In 1804, the captain-general of Cuba, Marquis of Someruelos, complained to the Spanish Minister of the State, Don Pedro Ceballos, about the lack of attention and care in the editing and circulation of the official Spanish newspaper *La Gaceta de Madrid*. According to Someruelos, the said newspaper offered excessive information about events developing in French Saint-Domingue, including intimate accounts of Black leaders such as Toussaint Louverture and Henri Christophe, and details of the confrontations between Black and French troops since the arrival of Leclerc's expedition in Saint-Domingue in 1802. As historian Ada Ferrer explains, Someruelos was concerned not only about the "dangerous" content of the official newspaper—which even reproduced verbatim the political proclamations of Haitian Black leaders—but also about the popularity of a newspaper that was "sold to the public, and everyone buys it, and it circulates well among the blacks."[12] It seems clear that the Black population in Cuba had found ways to access newspapers and use them as a source of information.

What exactly did communities of the Spanish Caribbean learn about the Atlantic Revolutions from newspapers? And what effects could this information bring into the Spanish Caribbean? As we will see here, newspapers were accessible to different socio-racial groups and played an important role in the complex network of media and information that expanded in the Spanish Caribbean during the Age of Revolutions. It is interesting to note, for instance, that despite the efforts of colonial authorities to contain revolutionary information that could spread sedition and insurrection in the Spanish Caribbean, official newspapers—such as *La Gaceta de Madrid*—were widely distributed and read in the region, offering critical views on the Atlantic Revolutions.

Beginning in the 1750s, King Charles III of Spain had enthusiastically favoured the spread of newspapers throughout the Spanish territories, seeing them as important vehicles for the rational thought that the Spanish enlightened reformism promoted. In fact, many Spanish writers, editors, and publishers believed that newspapers, gazettes, and periodicals offered several benefits for the expansion of knowledge: they were inexpensive, they were produced quickly and regularly, and their subjects were presented clearly. However, the Spanish Crown, aware of the danger of "excessive enlightenment," also encouraged the Council of Castile to monitor the content of periodicals printed in Spain; since "false information" could easily promote anti-monarchical or seditious ideas, and confuse innocent readers. Nevertheless, reformist intellectuals agreed that newspapers and periodical publications favoured the development of more flexible and extensive circuits of communication between Europe and the Americas, and that they were likely to benefit both Spain and the American possessions.[13]

Substantial evidence shows that readers in various Spanish Caribbean towns such as Caracas, La Guaira, Havana, Cartagena, and Santo Domingo had access to a wide array of newspapers and periodicals from Spain and Spanish America. Periodicals such as *El Semanario Erudito* (Madrid), *El Semanario Económico* (Madrid), *El Mercurio Histórico-Político* (Madrid), *El Semanario de Agricultura* (Madrid), *La Gaceta de Madrid* (Madrid), and *La Gaceta de México* (México City), among others, were frequently found in local private libraries and in the personal belongings of travellers arriving in Havana, Cartagena, and La Guaira.[14] In fact, a detailed historical study of Spanish newspapers' subscriptions during the last decade of the eighteenth century shows that Spanish Caribbean residents were avid readers of Spanish newspapers. Residents of Havana, Cartagena, Santo Domingo, and Puerto Rico regularly paid subscriptions to *El Semanario Erudito* (Madrid), *Correo de Ciegos* (Madrid), *Correo Mercantil de España e Indias* (Madrid), and the literary journal *Memorial Literario*.[15] In addition, foreign newspapers, such as the *London Gazette*, the *London Journal*, the *Pennsylvania Gazette*, and various French periodicals, were also found during government searches of luggage and homes in the province.[16] Many of these newspapers provided Spanish Caribbean readers with detailed information about international politics during the Age of Revolutions.

La Gaceta de Madrid, the newspaper that became the official journal of Spain in 1661, had turned particularly popular in the Spanish Caribbean. *La Gaceta* was a weekly newspaper until 1778, when it became biweekly. The Spanish government had assigned a team of officials to edit, produce, and economically manage this popular newspaper that covered a great variety of topics from court affairs, political news, information about wars (with special attention to those won by Spain), as well as the life of the members of the royal family.[17] By the 1780s, around twenty-thousand copies of the official newspaper were published and distributed each week in Spain and its American possessions. By the said decade, more than 75% of the copies of *La Gaceta de Madrid* to Spanish America were destined for the Spanish Caribbean.[18]

Like many other European journals, *La Gaceta* published several news items about the events of the Atlantic Revolutions. For example, in several issues published in the 1780s *La Gaceta* reported on the American Revolution and the political climate of the young republic. By the end of 1792, *La Gaceta* also began to offer some news of the growing conflict in France, with details of the king's mounting difficulties and the possible eruption of a new political order, but there was no direct mention to the Revolution. On 8 February 1793, however, *La Gaceta* published the last will and testament of Louis XVI, opening a new phase in the way that information about the Revolution was presented to the readers. The editors adopted a decidedly negative view of the Revolution in France, but still provided accurate information about the main political debates, events, and protagonists of the time.[19] *La Gaceta de Madrid* also provided detailed information about the events unfolding in the French colony of Saint-Domingue and the massive enslaved-people rebellions that erupted in the summer of 1791.[20]

According to official records produced by extremely concerned colonial agents in Cuba, Venezuela, and Santo Domingo, the residents of the Spanish Caribbean, including mixed-race pardos, free Black and enslaved people, learned about the events of the Atlantic Revolutions through the pages of newspapers like *La Gaceta*. Even if they could not read the news directly, they found people who read for them or joined conversations in public and semi-public spaces such as barbershops, and bodegas (popular shops) where the news was discussed and debated. By the end of the eighteenth century, it became very clear to colonial officials in the Spanish Caribbean that this tangled region was not an extension of Iberian Spain and that its socio-racial complexity, its large presence of Black free and enslaved people, and its open exposure to the revolutionary theatre required extreme measures of control and new strategies for managing public information. In turbulent circumstances, Spanish American vassals could not be trusted, so it was extremely important to limit their access to newspapers, even those printed in Spain.[21]

Ephemeral Pamphlets and Peripheral Presses in the Spanish Caribbean

Official and foreign newspapers were not the only sources of information residents of the Spanish Caribbean had access to, as "ephemeral papers" such as broadsides, pamphlets, and "loose papers" (*papeles sueltos*) were also smuggled into various ports of the Spanish Caribbean. For example, several written texts from France, Saint Domingue, and Trinidad—in printed or in manuscript form—were collected by colonial officials in different coastal towns of Venezuela and New Granada. From 1793 to 1808, officials in La Guaira, Cumaná, Cartagena, and Havana continuously reported the ease with which these ephemeral papers circulated in the region. Among the texts that circulated in the coastal towns, there were political proclamations and letters, Spanish translations of papers published by the French National Assembly, and texts written by French agents appointed to Spanish Santo Domingo after the Treaty of Basel in 1795.[22] In fact, several copies of crucial political texts such as *The Social Contract* (1762), *The Declaration of Independence of the United States* (1776), *The Rights of Man and Citizen* (1790), *The Last Will of Louis XVI, the King of France* (1792), and *The Declaration of Independence of Haiti* (1804) found their way to the Spanish Caribbean, where they even suffered discursive and narrative adaptations to make them more comprehensible to the general population.[23] These ephemeral texts arrived in ports and cities in different ways: either in the cargo of Spanish and foreign visitors who brought books, gazettes, and newspapers with them or thanks to smugglers who included printed matter among their goods.[24]

In December 1789, for example, Venezuela's captain-general reported to the authorities in Madrid that since the month of August "gazettes, dailies, and supplements from or about France, providing news about current events in Paris, have entered Venezuela." According to him, the "evil designs" of these texts represented a great danger to the captaincy. As a result, he was ready to use all possible means to protect the province from the "revolutionary contagion that has shaken the world," and issued an order to the governors of the six provinces under his jurisdiction, to collect all the potentially dangerous papers that are found in their territories.[25] The geographical location of these port-towns made it relatively easy for foreign written texts to enter, either smuggled in by visitors, merchants, and sailors, or brought in from urban centres like Bogotá, where residents enjoyed the operations of the printing press. For example, *The Declaration of the Rights of Man and Citizen,* illegally translated by the *bogotano* Antonio Nariño in 1793, widely circulated in Mompox and Cartagena. As historian Aline Helg points out, "Momposinos and cartageneros had more access than residents of other cities to revolutionary news from Bogotá, the Caribbean, and Europe, reported by free and slaves, sailors, and merchants ...."[26]

As shown in previous research by the author, the lack of printing presses in Venezuela's coastal towns did not prevent the general public from exchanging ideas and participating in an incipient public sphere that was fed by the vibrant and dynamic circulation of papers, pamphlets, and newspapers within Caribbean networks. However, there were also occasions when small itinerant printing presses were set up in coastal towns, where they operated illegally, producing brief printed materials accessible to all, including local Black communities. As Vanessa Mongey has explained, "portable printing presses, which could be easily carried on board ship or across tracts of land, played an important role in the revolutionary Caribbean."[27] In many cases, these presses passed unnoticed by the authorities, allowing information and ideas to spread from one locality to another, connecting the Caribbean communities at critical moments of confrontation and change.

In-Between Writing and Orality

Although the operation of a printing press was not allowed in Venezuela until 1808, historical records show that a small printing press operated in Puerto España, on the island of Trinidad in 1786. At that time, the island of Trinidad was one of the seven provinces of the Captaincy of Venezuela, to which it was annexed by Royal Decree in 1777. Therefore, we can safely assert that the first Venezuelan printing press operated illegally (or at least in disguise) on the peripheral island of Trinidad. But how did this printing press get there in the first place? How did it pass unnoticed? And what did it mean that the, an apparently insignificant, province of Trinidad had a printing press in the Age of Revolutions?

When the Governor of the island of Trinidad, José María Chacón received royal orders from Venezuela's captain-general on the need to control the circulation of information and to ensure that seditious papers were not circulated on the island, Chacón took drastic steps. In January 1790, he decided to condemn to exile the French writer and printer of the *Gaceta de Trinidad,* Jean Bautiste Viloux, for having "copied and printed diverse articles of public foreign newspapers about the current Revolution in France, in which were published many subversive phrases, contrary to the good order of our Constitution, to spread dissension, corrupt the true faith, and disturb the good order of our rule."[28] Apparently, the printer had not foreseen the consequences of his actions, but the fact that Trinidad even had a printing press was even more concerning. As mentioned earlier, Caracas, La Guaira, and many other important coastal cities in Venezuela, New Granada, and Puerto Rico had no printing presses, yet the small island of Trinidad possessed a press that produced brief papers containing news of current events.[29] How and why Trinidad obtained this printing press is still not entirely clear, but it was certainly operating illegally.

Trinidad's minor importance and peripheral nature probably allowed for the entry and operation of a printing press, and the creation of the *Gaceta de Trinidad* was an event that went unnoticed by the Venezuelan and Spanish authorities. Although Spanish Governor Chacón never explained why there was a printing press in Trinidad in the first place, he did confirm that he had gotten rid of it. He explained: "It was my intention to prevent the evil or to eliminate it at its origins, without alarming the public or provoking its curiosity about the reasons for my decision … Different news would make people talk about themes that are better left in silence."[30] On an island with a majority of Black French inhabitants—free and enslaved—he preferred to avoid public announcements and deliberately chose silence. It is possible that Chacón chose silence also because he could not provide a sound explanation for why he allowed the press to operate without the proper official authorisation.

According to historian Roderick Cave, "Juan Viloux" was a pseudonym under which the real editor remained anonymous. Viloux was in fact a man named F. J. Willox de Douay, a printer and editor who moved around the Caribbean islands, especially between Martinica and Dominica, where he published a variety of newspapers. In Dominica, Willox de Douay became the editor of the periodical publication *Le Furet Colonial*. In one of his issues, published in 1791, he confessed that he had been the editor of the "Courier de la Trinité Espagnole" or *Gaceta de Trinidad* and that he had been arbitrarily expelled from the island. Later, in 1793, Willox reappeared as "Imprimeur du Government" in Saint Pierre, Martinique, in 1793.[31]

More intriguing, however, is the discovery that this itinerant French editor and printer was not the first one to operate an itinerant printing press in Trinidad. The historian José Toribio Medina found a 12-page booklet entitled "Ordenanza publicada en el Puerto de España, el 11 de Agosto 1786" printed in Puerto España in the house of Don Juan Cassan. Juan Cassan was probably the French printer Jean Cassan, who in 1779 had been the

435

printer of the *Gazette Royale de la Grenade* at Fort Royal in Grenada.[32] The close ties between the people of Grenada and Trinidad, probably allowed the latter to move to Trinidad with a printing press that was used to published new laws and regulations created by the Governor of Trinidad. Thus, although Trinidad had not received royal permission to have a printing press, the Governor himself had authorised the establishment of a printing press that he used to support his government and keep Trinidadians informed of his decisions.

Since the beginning of the 1780s, Trinidad had undergone a significant demographic transformation as hundreds of white and free Black French families, along with enslaved workers, moved from Grenada to the Spanish island.[33] According to Chacón, these French colonists brought not only experience and knowledge to the island, but also "tools, products, furniture, provisions and slaves who are very valuable"[34] for the island's "economic development." Among those valuable "tools" brought by Grenadian colonists was the printing press that printer Jean Cassan carried with him. The events of the French Revolution and the rebellions of Saint-Domingue, however, altered Chacón's original plan for the local press and prompted the printer to begin publishing information about the unfolding events to satisfy the curiosity of the Trinidadian residents, increasingly thirsty for news.

Despite of officials' willingness to be vigilant about the circulation of written news, historical records show that the situation was very difficult to control. Governor Chacón, for example, insisted that he was guarding against the entry of seditious texts, but he was concerned that these could easily enter Trinidad from the French Windward islands or the mainland directly from Saint-Domingue because the administration simply lacked the capacity to monitor the Venezuelan coast and its islands.[35] For Chacón, it was not only logistically impossible but contradictory to investigate French residents or to control their actions and words. The only promise Chacón could make was to keep a close eye on the new families from Grenada and to reject the introduction of potentially dangerous individuals. In a letter to the Spanish Minister in 1791, he mentioned that although he was trying to control the circulation of news about the revolution on the island, it was an almost impossible task. For this reason, he was urged to abruptly expel the printer from the island. Although the printing press that operated in Trinidad around 1786 was originally established with the purpose of communicating the government decisions and new regulations, the revolutionary wave that swept the Caribbean in the last decade of the eighteenth century, transformed it into an instrument in which hundreds of pamphlets and papers about the revolution were printed.

Rumours and Stories of Revolutions: Oral Communication Networks

Written texts were not the only sources of information about the Atlantic Revolutions the Black communities in the Caribbean had access to during the tumultuous decade of the 1790s. Waves of refugees, soldiers and prisoners, Black corsairs, and maritime maroons visited coastal towns and shared their revolutionary experiences with curious locals. Notwithstanding the various mechanisms of control that the colonial state had put in place during this last decade in order to prevent communication between locals and foreigners, the rebellions and wars in the French colonies produced an important movement of people of different social statuses, races, and political tendencies across the Atlantic world. This mobilisation, in turn, changed the social compositions and dynamics, the geopolitical perceptions, and even the economies of those regions affected by the increased flow of people and information.

In-Between Writing and Orality

In Cuba, Ada Ferrer argues, French refugees "became critical conduits of stories and sentiments associated with the revolution in Saint-Domingue"; their stories and testimonies of their experiences in Saint-Domingue were told and retold among the island's communities. "Cuba," Ferrer explains, "received 35,000 refuges," but also many French officers and soldiers, ship captains and crew members who spread the news in the ports and coastal towns.[36] In 1792, for example, the captain-general of Venezuela ordered local governors and regional lieutenants to investigate foreigners living in their jurisdictions. They were instructed to find out "who they are, the lifestyle and customs of each one of them, their occupation or profession, and the reasons for their presence in the province."[37] The lieutenants were also instructed to determine whether these foreigners, especially Frenchmen, had made any suspicious verbal statements.[38] Immediately, information about the presence of suspicious Frenchmen began to circulate throughout official channels. Several French people living in Venezuelan towns were interrogated by colonial agents about their presence and occupation, and they became the centre of paranoid suspicions of revolutionary contagion. On several occasions, colonial authorities arrested some of these French suspects and sent them to Spain. They often portrayed them as people who challenged both colonial authorities and the Church, and who had no problem in spreading false news and dangerous ideas.[39]

But French visitors did not monopolise the attention of colonial agents. Enslaved visitors and maritime maroons were also an important source of information. Throughout the eighteenth century, slaves had fled from the Antilles to Spanish Caribbean islands such as Cuba and Puerto Rico, and to the vast and unpatrolled coasts of Venezuela, New Granada, and Florida. A royal decree in 1750 freed all slaves fleeing foreign colonies who agreed to convert to Roman Catholicism. From that point onwards, hundreds of maritime maroons from the Caribbean felt compelled to flee to Spanish territories to gain their freedom.[40] The policy changed abruptly when, in May 1790, the king issued a royal decree forbidding the entry of foreign slaves into his American territories; almost a week later the king extended the decree and forbid the entry of all French slaves, including those who were legally purchased in the French colonies.[41] As Ada Ferrer explains: "That such people were coloured and French served as sufficient evidence of their propensity to circulate dangerous notions."[42]

Although the Viceroy of New Granada, the captain-generals of Venezuela and Cuba, and the provincial governors restricted the entry of fugitive slaves, the clandestine immigration of fugitive Black people from the Caribbean continued along the northern coast of South America and the Spanish Caribbean islands. For example, enslaved people from Dutch Essequibo entered the Spanish province of Guayana; slaves from English and French colonies such as Grenada and Trinidad entered the eastern coast of Venezuela; and slave ships from Saint-Domingue continued to arrive in Cuba. In the case of New Granada, most of these maritime slaves arrived on the northern coast and settled in ports and towns such as Riohacha, Barranquilla, and Cartagena.[43] In the Coro region in Venezuela, the presence of maritime maroons from Curaçao was so important that they formed their own communities, commonly known as *luangos*, *minas*, or *curazaos*. These communities became important to the economic development of the region as their presence helped to alleviate the region's chronic labour shortage, but the fear of revolutionary contagion continued to be a concern among white elites and colonial officials.[44]

As military conflict escalated in French colonies such as Guadeloupe and Saint-Domingue in 1792 and 1793, increasing numbers of refugees, prisoners of war, soldiers, and slaves were sent to other Spanish American destinations by the Spanish governor of Santo Domingo. In the case of Venezuela, more than one thousand French militiamen, prisoners, and slaves from Saint-Domingue, Martinique, and Guadeloupe reached the towns of Puerto Cabello, La Guaira, Cumaná, and Puerto de España in Trinidad.[45] New Granada did not receive a comparable number of officially captured prisoners, but its coastal towns were subjected to frequent visits by Black corsairs. In fact, between 1797 and 1800, military commanders and governors of Venezuela's western provinces and New Granada frequently reported the presence of French corsairs near the coast and requested military reinforcements. In some cases, they even provided the exact number of ships captained by "French blacks" that had been seen "visiting" their communities and detailed their suspicious practices; others reported large-scale attacks on coastal towns. For Spanish colonial authorities, it seemed evident that these black corsairs, imbued with revolutionary ideas, were trying to incite sedition and destabilise the region.[46]

As Scott argued in the *Common Wind*, these Franco-Caribbean visitors created an important network of communication, and providing local Black communities with contrasting stories of republicanism, Black insurrection, emancipation, and equality. Black communities in Cuba, Puerto Rico, Venezuela, and New Granada were receptive to this new wave of oral information and did not hesitate to disseminate it locally. In many cases, Black communities were able to read the fears of colonial officials and white elites and use their knowledge they had acquired in processes of negotiation.

Conclusion

On January 1, 1804, the Haitian Black general Jean-Jacques Dessalines proclaimed the Declaration of Independence of Haiti, the first Black republic of the western world. The document was signed by thirty-seven Black military officers, many of whom, only fifteen years earlier, had been enslaved workers in plantations. Although most of these officers were illiterate, they were very aware of the content of the document, the political significance of the moment, and the crucial implications that declaring equality among the races and the definitive abolition of slavery had in the Atlantic world. Copies of *The Declaration of Independence of Haiti* circulated throughout the Caribbean, sparking the curiosity of Black communities and awakening deep concerns among Spanish, British, and French colonial agents who feared ideological contagion and the political chaos in the colony. Haiti's status as independent republic had become a point of no return: Black communities were attuned with the new times and were ready to appropriate and adapt the revolutionary language to their realities. The news of Haiti spread like fire throughout the Caribbean region giving place to communities of information.[47]

As we have seen through this chapter, illiteracy and the lack of a printing press among Black communities in the Spanish Caribbean did not represent significant obstacles to their members' access to news and shared dynamic information networks during the turbulent period of the Atlantic Revolutions. A variety of information media, such as newspapers, pamphlets, manuscripts, and letters, as well as oral communication in the form of stories and rumours were accessible to a large number of Black and mixed-race people who lived in the ports and coastal towns of the Spanish Caribbean, and who did not hesitate to follow the unfolding political events. The variety of media they had access to and the practices they designed to access and disseminate information gave shape to a socially diverse platform for the circulation of political knowledge that escaped the control of colonial institutions, and that allowed Black communities to become producers of information and political actors in a changing world.

Notes

1. Alí Enrique López Bohorquez, ed., *Manuel Gual y José María España: Valoración Múltiple de la Conspiración de La Guaira de 1797* (Caracas: Comisión Presidencial del Bicentenario de Gual y España, 1997); Juan Carlos Rey et al., eds., *Gual y España, La Independencia Frustrada* (Caracas: Colección Bicentenario de la Independencia, Fundación Polar, 2007); Cristina Soriano, *Tides of Revolution. Information, Insurgencies, and the Crisis of Colonial Rule in Venezuela* (Albuquerque: University of New Mexico Press, 2018), 149–183.
2. "Report by the Real Audiencia in Caracas about the insurgency movement uncovered in the city, August 18, 1797," AGI (Archivo General de Indians- Seville), Caracas, 434, no. 232.
3. "Observaciones de un Ciudadano Sobre la Conspiración Descubierta en Caracas el día 13 de Julio del Presente Año y de los Medios a qué Podrá Ocurrir el Gobierno para Asegurar en lo Sucesivo a sus Habitantes de Iguales Insultos by José Ignacio Moreno" AGI, Caracas, 434, folio 798.
4. For an interesting analysis on the multiple media through which revolutionary ideas circulated in the Atlantic World, see Janet Polasky, *Revolutions without Borders, The Call to Liberty in the Atlantic World* (New Haven, CT: Yale University Press, 2015). See also Soriano, *Tides of Revolution*.
5. See Carol Sue Humphrey, *"This Popular Engine": New England Newspapers during the American Revolution, 1775–1789* (Newark, DE: University of Delaware Press, 1992); Richard D. Brown, *Knowledge Is Power: The Diffusion of Information in Early America, 1700–1865* (New York: Oxford University Press, 1989); and Bernard Bailyn and John B. Hench, eds., *The Press and the American Revolution* (Worcester, MA: American Antiquarian Society, 1980). On the crucial role of printers in the American Revolution, see Joseph Adelman, *Revolutionary Networks. The Business and Politics of Printing the News, 1763–1789* (Baltimore, MD: John Hopkins University Press, 2019).
6. See Andrew Pettegree, *The Invention of News, How the World Came to Know about Itself* (New Haven, CT: Yale University Press, 2014), 326–346. See also Jeremy Popkin, *Revolutionary News: The Press in France, 1789–1799* (Durham, NC: Duke University Press, 1990); and Robert Darnton and Daniel Roche, eds., *Revolution in Print: The Press in France, 1775–1800* (Berkeley, CA: University of California Press, 1989).
7. For example, José A. Piqueras, ed., *Las Antillas en la Era de las Luces y la Revolución* (Madrid: Siglo XXI, 2005); David P. Geggus, ed., *The Impact of the Haitian Revolution in the Atlantic World* (Columbia, SC: University of South Carolina Press, 2001); David Barry Gaspar and David P. Geggus, eds. *A Turbulent Time: The French Revolution and the Greater Caribbean* (Bloomington, IN: Indiana University Press, 1997); Michel Trouillot, *Silencing the Past: Power and the Production of History* (Boston, MA: Beacon, 1995).
8. See, for example, John Fischer, *Commercial Relations between Spain and Spanish America in the Era of Free Trade, 1778–1796* (Liverpool: Centre for Latin American Studies, 1985), and Peggy Liss, *Atlantic Empires: The Network of the Trade and Revolution, 1713–1826* (Baltimore, MD: Johns Hopkins University Press, 1983).
9. Julius Scott, *The Common Wind. Afro-American Currents in the Age of the Haitian Revolution* (New York: Verso, 2018).
10. For example, Ernesto Bassi, *An Aqueous Territory* (Durham, NC: Duke University Press, 2016); Julia Gaffield, *Haitian Connections in the Atlantic World. Recognition after Revolution* (Chapel Hill, NC: University of North Carolina Press, 2015); Ada Ferrer, *Freedom's Mirror, Cuba and Haiti in the Age of Revolution* (Cambridge, UK: Cambridge University Press, 2014); Aline Helg, *Liberty and Equality in Caribbean Colombia* (Chapel Hill, NC: University of North Carolina Press, 2004). Also Soriano, *Tides of Revolution;* and Scott, *The Common Wind*.
11. Several historical works have analysed the impact of revolutionary information in the Spanish Caribbean during the Age of Revolutions; see Soriano, *Tides of Revolution*; Alejandro E. Gómez, *Le Spectre de la Révolution Noire: L'Impact de la Révolution Haïtienne dans le Monde Atlantique, 1790–1886* (Rennes: Presses Universitaires de Rennes, 2013); Helg, *Liberty and Equality in Caribbean Colombia*; Maria Dolores González-Ripoll et al., eds., *El Rumor de Haití en Cuba: Temor, Raza y Rebeldía, 1789–1844* (Madrid: Consejo Superior de Investigaciones Científicas, 2004); and Ada Ferrer, "Noticias de Haití en Cuba," *Revista de Indias* LXIII, no. 229 (2003): 675–694.
12. Ferrer, *Freedom's Mirror*, 184–185.

13 Cristina Soriano, "Newspapers and the Atlantic Revolutions: The Circulation of the *Gaceta de Madrid* in the Spanish Caribbean," *Global Exchange of Knowledge in the Long Eighteenth Century: Ideas and Materialities, 1650–1850* ed. James Raven (London: Boydell and Brewer, 2024), 217–239.
14 Soriano, "Newspapers and the Atlantic Revolutions."
15 Elisabel Larriba, *El Público de la Prensa de España, El Público de la Prensa en España a Finales del Siglo XVIII (1781–1808)* (Zaragoza: Prensas de la Universidad de Zaragoza, 2013), 192–193.
16 "Informe de la Real Audiencia Sobre Lectura de Libros y Papeles Sediciosos Relacionados con la Sublevacion de la Guaira, 1797," AGI, Caracas, 432, 434 and 436; AGN (Archivo General de la Nación-Caracas, Venezuela), Testamentarías 1770–1810.
17 Ivy Lilian McClelland, "Disturbing Effects of the Periodical Press," in *Ideological Hesitancy in Spain, 1700–1750* (Liverpool: Liverpool University Press, 1991), 138–147; and Arthur Hamilton, "The Journals of the Eighteenth Century in Spain," *Hispania* 21, no. 3 (1938): 161–172.
18 Larriba, *El Público de la Prensa de España*, 200–201.
19 *Gaceta de Madrid*, no. 11, February 17, 1793, 86–87; and *Gaceta de Madrid*, no. 53, June 28, 1793, 619.
20 *Gaceta de Madrid*, no. 94, November 25, 1791, 856–857.
21 Soriano, "Newspapers and the Atlantic Revolutions."
22 For example, the pamphlet "Instrucciones que Debe Servir de Regla al Agente Interino Francés Destinado a la Parte Española de Santo Domingo," AGI, Estado 58, no. 8, and AGI, Caracas, 169, no. 86.
23 Soriano, *Tides of Revolution*, 47–77 and Cristina Soriano "The Unruly Caribbean: Reverberations of Saint Domingue's Rebellions in the Caribbean Coast of New Granada and Venezuela," in *The Cambridge History of the Age of Atlantic Revolutions*, vol. 2 *The Global French Revolution. France, Europe, and Haiti*, ed. Wim Klooster (Cambridge, UK: Cambridge University Press, 2023), 715–738.
24 On many occasions in which Venezuelans were accused of reading prohibited books or papers, they defended themselves by saying that these were brought to their attention by foreigners who encouraged them to read these texts and even left copies at their homes. See "Cuadernillo de Denuncias al Secretario del Santo Oficio," AAC, Santo Oficio, Carpeta II. See also Soriano, *Tides of Revolution*, 1–77.
25 "Expediente de la Intendencia Relativo a Asuntos de Francia," AGN, Diversos, LXVI, 290–295.
26 Helg, *Liberty and Equality*, 89.
27 Vanessa Mongey, "The Pen and the Sword: Print in the Revolutionary Caribbean," in *L'Atlantique Révolutionnaire. Une Perspective Ibéro-Américaine*, ed. Clément Thibaud et al. (Rennes: Les Perséides Éditions, 2013), 49–69, quote from 49.
28 "Sobre Destierro del Redactor de la Gaceta o Papel Publico de Ocurrencias Semanales de la Ysla de Trinidad," AGI, Caracas, 153, no. 10, and "Noticias sobre Introducción de papeles extranjeros," AGI, Caracas, 115.
29 Agustín Millares Carlo, *La Imprenta y el Periodismo en Venezuela, Desde sus Orígenes Hasta Mediados del Siglo XIX* (Caracas: Monteávila, 1969); and Soriano, *Tides of Revolution*.
30 "Sobre Destierro del Redactor de la Gaceta."
31 Roderick Cave, *Printing and the Book Trade in the West Indies* (London: The Pindar Press, 1987). See also Douglas C. McMurtrie. *Notes of the Beginning of Printing on the Island of Trinidad* (Fort Worth, TX: National Association for Printing Education, 1943).
32 Roderick Cave, "Early Printing and the Book Trade in the West Indies," *The Library Quarterly: Information, Community, Policy* 48, no. 2 (April 1978): 163–192; and McMurtrie, *Notes of the Beginning*, 3–4.
33 Cristina Soriano, "A Spanish Colony Made of Foreigners: Transimperial Trinidad during the Age of Revolutions," *Atlantic Studies: Global Currents* 21, no. 1 (2024): 115–138; Carl Campbell, "The Rise of a Free Coloured Plantocracy in Trinidad, 1783–1813," *Boletin de Estudios Latinoamericanos y del Caribe* no. 29 (December 1980): 33–54; and Jesse A. Noel, *Trinidad, Provincia de Venezuela. Historia de la Administración Española de Trinidad* (Caracas: Academia Nacional de la Historia, 1972).
34 "Carta del Gobernador de Trinidad al Gobernador de Caracas, Comunicándole que Pondrá en Ejercicio su Orden de Recoger y Remitir Papeles que se Introduzcan por la via de Santo Domingo," AGN, Gobernación y Capitanía General, LIX, 258.

In-Between Writing and Orality

35 "Carta del Gobernador de Trinidad," 258.
36 Ferrer, *Freedom's Mirror*, 49–51.
37 "Orden a los Tenientes Justicias Mayores de Coro," AGN, Gobernación y Capitanía General, XLVII, 68.
38 "Orden a los Tenientes Justicias Mayores de Coro," 69.
39 In 1794, for example, Francisco Combret, a Frenchman who worked as a tobacconist in the city of Maracay, was accused by his workmates of expressing subversive ideas in public. Combret was arrested "along with all his books and papers," and sent to Cádiz in 1795. Accompanying Combret in the same ship was a Basque merchant, Santiago Albi, who was accused by his neighbours of celebrating the fall of the port of San Sebastián to the French during the War of the Pyrenees with fireworks and joyful cries. In an official report, Albi was described as "an insolent, vain, and atheistic young man, capable of inspiring others with the project that the National Assembly of Paris has spread." See "El Gobernador a Juan N. Pedroza, Noviembre de 1794," AGN, Gobernación y Capitanía General, LIII, 30.
40 Ramón Aizpurua, "Coro y Curazao en el Siglo XVIII," *Tierra Firme* 14 (1986): 229–240. See also "Real Cédula de Su Majestad Sobre Declarar por Libres a los Negros que Viniesen de los Ingleses u Holandeses a los Reinos de España Buscando el Agua del Bautismo. Buen Retiro, September 24, 1750," AGN, Caracas, Reales Cédulas, X, 332.
41 "Real Orden Reservada del 21 de Mayo de 1790," AGI, Caracas, 115.
42 Ferrer, *Freedom's Mirror*, 61.
43 Marixa Lasso, *Myths of Harmony: Race and Republicanism during the Age of Revolutions, 1795–1831* (Pittsburgh, PA: University of Pittsburgh Press, 2007), 16–34.
44 In a report written to the Spanish King in 1794, the Captain of Venezuela warned about the danger that the proximity between Curaçao and Coro represented for the Province: "the closeness of that Province [Coro] to the Island of Curaçao is such that one might estimate that it is almost a Dutch possession on the coast." See "Captain General of Venezuela to King Charles IV, March 13, 1794," AGI, Caracas, 95. See also Ferrer, *Freedom's Mirror*, 63–66; and Linda Rupert, *Creolization and Contraband, Curaçao in the Early Modern Atlantic World* (Athens, GA: Georgia University Press, 2012).
45 See Alejandro Gómez, *Fidelidad Bajo el Viento: Revolución y Contrarrevolución en las Antillas Francesas en la Experiencia de Algunos Oficiales Emigrados a Tierra Firme 1790–1795* (México: Siglo XXI, 2004); and Ángel Sanz Tapia, "Refugiados de la Revolución Francesa en Venezuela (1793–1795)," *Revista de Indias* XLVII, no. 181 (1987): 833–867; See also Soriano, *Tides of Revolution*, 77–117.
46 The list of denunciations of the presence of French corsairs in the coasts of Venezuela and New Granada between 1798 and 1801 is extensive. See "Informe del Comandante de Coro, Andrés Boggiero al Capitán General, enero 1801," AGI, Estado, no. 60; "Comunicación del Gobernador de Maracaibo para el Capitán General Sobre Presencia de Corsarios con 120 Franceses de Color, Julio 1800," AGN, Gobernación y Capitanía General, LXXXVIII, 7; "Comunicación del Capitán General de Venezuela al Virrey de Santa Fé Sobre Presencia de Corsarios Franceses en las Costas, Octubre 1799," AGN, Gobernación y Capitanía General, LXXXI, 287; "Expediente Sobre Negros y Mulatos Franceses Dejados en la Península Goajira, 1799," AGI, Estado, no. 60; "Comunicación del Gobernador de Maracaibo Sobre Presencia de Corsarios Franceses en Río de Hacha, Mayo 1799," AGN, Gobernación y Capitanía General, LXXVII, 76; and "Comunicación de Fernando Mijares al Capitán General, Sobre Presencia de Corsarios Franceses, J 1799," AGN, Gobernación y Capitanía General, LXXIX, 223–227.
47 Julia Gaffield, ed., *The Haitian Declaration of Independence: Creation, Context, and Legacy* (Charlottesville, VA: University of Virginia Press, 2016); and Cristina Soriano, "The Unruly Caribbean."

28
INFORMATION AND MOBILITY
Migrants and Roma as Historical Cases*

Eve Rosenhaft

This chapter explores the existing scholarship on and some open questions about the relationship between information and geographical mobility in the past. Mobility and information have shared histories. One of the key innovations of the "first information revolution" during the late seventeenth and early eighteenth centuries was the notion and institution of the intelligence office. Intelligence offices were clearing houses for information about things lost and found, employment and housing opportunities and the like. Their principal function became the editing and printing of early newspapers (intelligencers), but their utility was initially seen as answering the needs of an increasingly mobile and urban society: providing local knowledge for travellers who, arriving from outside, could not rely on personal or occupational networks to help them find their way in the city. In turn, cameralist thinkers argued, a network of such information hubs could promote the circulation of people, ideas, and wealth necessary for a flourishing economy.[1]

European society was never static, however. In the early modern period, the services imagined for the new intelligence offices were already being provided for travelling artisans by institutions of their own making. Set on the road by the terms of their training which dictated that apprenticeship should be followed by a period of tramping (as "journeymen") from one master to another and/or by the shortage of local employment, they joined together to establish inns and hostels (*Trinkstuben, Herbergen, logis,* houses of call) where they could learn about local job opportunities and gather intelligence about prospective employers. Sixteenth-century German journeymen swore an oath that they would themselves pass on any such information that they gained. And even in nineteenth-century England, it has been argued, "tramping had a powerful ancillary benefit in the dissemination of news."[2] This reminds us that one of the defining features of information is that whether it is disseminated by word of mouth or in print on paper or in digital form, it has to move.

---

* Research for this chapter was supported by a grant from the Arts and Humanities Research Council (AH/W010658/1) for the AHRC-Deutsche Forschungsgemeinschaft collaborative development project Romani Migration between Germany and Britain (1880s–1914): Spaces of Informal Business, Media Spectacle, and Racial Policing (2022–2026).

Information and Mobility

Knowledge becomes information in the process of being communicated. And so the history of information is closely bound up with the history of technologies of communication, transport, and travel. It is thus also the history of how people engage with those technologies when they are planning to move or are already on the road.

Continuing this focus on Europe, this chapter looks at two groups of historical actors whose history has been written in terms of their mobility.[3] The larger and more extensively studied group is that of migrants, those millions of individuals and families who have left their homes and crossed geographical and political borders with the intention of settling in a new territory. In European history, the late nineteenth century is seen as the age of mass migration; this vision reflects in particular the transatlantic movement of between fifty-five and fifty-eight million Europeans between 1850 and 1940, but the pace of social and economic change during the first and second industrial revolutions also set large numbers of people in motion within Europe itself.[4] In the context of European colonialism, however, the option of seeking a new home, career, or identity across the ocean was already opening up to ordinary people as early as the seventeenth century. Historians of migration have (largely) followed scholars interested in contemporary migration experiences in asking about the role that information of various kinds plays in migrant lives and decision-making: the decision to move, the choice of destinations and the continuing relations with friends and family back home. The first part of this chapter outlines the current state of knowledge about how migrants in the past made use of a variety of information sources and technologies to find their way to and in new worlds.

In the second part of the chapter, the focus shifts to another form of mobility, one which has received less attention from historians of modern societies: that of groups who built their social and economic existence on regular travel over relatively long distances, their purpose not to find a new home but to pursue temporary opportunities for making a living. Sometimes moving as whole families, commonly on a seasonal basis, they travelled over relatively familiar routes under normal circumstances—although a change of circumstances could mean that they had to seek out new opportunities or extend the distances travelled. Those changes could even mean that they became migrants "proper," losing the labels that were historically attached to them: nomads, travellers, or itinerants. Recent scholarship has introduced the term peripatetic to apply to these groups, since it is more descriptive and less value-laden in the European context than the older terms.[5]

Among these peripatetic groups, the most significant in Europe is certainly the Roma,[6] and the second part of the chapter explores the evidence for Romani information practices and experiences. As important as it is simply to note that not all "movers" are "migrants," the history of the Roma offers a particular kind of counterpoint to migration narratives because of their status as outsider-insiders to European economic and social life. As such, they have only recently been acknowledged as people with a history worthy of critical research.[7] The case of nineteenth- and early twentieth-century European Roma, surrounded by a rich press landscape but often illiterate, socially marginalised but also embedded in highly articulated cross-border networks, pursuing economic opportunities not as individual labourers but as family units operating in largely informal economies, raises in particularly acute terms the question of how formal and informal sources of information interacted in facilitating both the peripatetic lifestyle and, in some cases, long-distance migration. More generally, the way in which they have been positioned (and often positioned themselves) as but occasional visitors to forms of modernity in which citizenship depends on being literate and having a fixed address means that their ways of gathering and sharing intelligence can be seen as forms equally of appropriation and exploitation and evasion and subversion of modern information regimes. As will become clear, Roma have also been among the victims of those regimes—or rather of state practices of information-gathering (on the one hand) and of persecution facilitated by that information on the other.

Migrants

The emergence in the early years of the twenty-first century of a perceived "migration crisis" in the Global North (in fact the outcome of global population movements driven by conflict and environmental change) prompted a wave of new research in migration studies. Questions of why and in particular *how* people decide to leave home, of how they plan and execute their journeys and of the role that social and family networks play in the migration process have been at the centre of this research, which often draws explicitly on the language of information studies.[8] The fact that contemporary migrants and refugees have had computers (the ubiquitous internet café) and more recently mobile phones at their disposal at nearly all points in their journey, dramatically even at the most hazardous moments of crossing land and sea barriers, means that the ways in which migrants use digital technologies have led to a convergence of scholarship in migration and information and media studies. (To the objects of interest in this case, we might also add the use of sophisticated technologies like facial recognition by the authorities seeking to control migration.)[9]

The scholarly interest sparked by new population movements has also given new impulses to the study of migration in the past. Here, too, a focus on the agency and qualitative experience of individual migrants that reflects wider trends in social history has led to questions being posed about how what people wanted and the choices they made were informed by what they knew and how that knowledge was communicated. This is where information history meets migration history. To a considerable extent, this involves interrogating long-standing concepts and observations to ask how they "worked" at a human level. One of these is "chain migration," the process by which one cohort of migrants is followed to the same destination by family members or other associates. This can be linked to "step migration," in which an individual or family moves in successive stages to a final place of settlement; one way the two combine is when family businesses set up a series of outposts as they extend their business activities abroad.[10] These do not happen automatically. Flows of people are (and were) motivated and facilitated by flows of information transmitted between home countries and countries of settlement through family, business, and friendship networks.[11] Another key concept in migration studies has been "push and pull factors"—the conditions which move people to emigrate and those which attract them to particular destinations.[12] "Push factors" are likely to be all too familiar, experienced as fear, hunger, or distress. "Pull factors"—the qualities of a potential new home—need to be learned, and are associated with elements of uncertainty and risk that create a demand for credible information. In asking how people in the European past decided when, how, and where to move, historians have explored a range of information sources.

Migrant Letters

Letters written by emigrants to friends and family back home are among the oldest forms in which people received information about the conditions of travel and settlement, and they have been explored by migration historians with increasing intensity since the 1990s. The information they conveyed about the circumstances of migrants might be characterised by gaps, inaccuracies, and misrepresentations, but they offer important insights into what people "back home" knew or imagined they knew—details that might have informed their own decision to emigrate.[13] The analysis of correspondence networks can reveal the power of circulating information, as when Dutch men writing home from the United States in search of spouses effectively generated a virtual marriage market.[14] Moreover, in their very subjective and discursive qualities, migrant letters yield insights into the changes wrought by the migration experience on the migrants themselves, their shifting identities, sense of self and others and affiliation to their home culture, which are themselves important questions for historians of migration and diaspora.[15]

By the late nineteenth century, relatively rapid land and sea transport and well-developed postal systems meant that such letters could be exchanged at a quick pace, so that there exist substantial archives of continuous chains of correspondence for the period of mass migration. For the seventeenth and eighteenth centuries, a new body of manuscript sources began to open up in 2018 with the project to sort and digitise the Prize Papers held by the British National Archives. This collection comprises documents captured from enemy vessels by the Royal Navy between 1652 and 1815, and includes 160,000 undelivered letters.[16] Early studies of German migrants based on these letters confirm the function of the letters themselves in sustaining and deploying family connections and communicating information; the letters also provide new insights into the ways in which travellers collected information themselves before departure.[17]

Of course, there is a paradox embodied in the Prize Papers: never delivered, they are a reminder that material chains of information can be fragile. In the late nineteenth and twentieth centuries, the kind of person-to-person communication originally enabled by letter-writing was facilitated by the telegraph and then the telephone. However, such evidence as we have for forms of communication that left little or no physical trace suggests that until the middle of the twentieth century, they were used rarely and mainly in emergencies or to pass on news of events like births and deaths.[18]

Print Media

Among the details that the Prize Papers afford about pre-departure information-gathering by eighteenth-century migrants is the purchase of dictionaries, and this is a reminder that since the early modern period print culture has been an important source of information for migrants. Migrant letters themselves entered into the printed circulation of knowledge about distant lands at a very early stage. By the late nineteenth century, such letters from abroad were a regular feature of newspapers in European hometowns, and they were also published in travel handbooks and emigrant guides.[19] But as early as 1720, propaganda about Louisiana, the new French territory in America, which was designed to spark the interest both of potential investors and of possible colonists, took the form of enthusiastic (and fabricated) "letters home" from new immigrants.[20] In addition to what could be gleaned from newspapers from the eighteenth century onwards, printed prospectuses and books of advice for emigrants proliferated in the nineteenth. Their titles often betrayed particular advertising and recruitment purposes—for example, the 1852 London publication.

> Cassell's Emigrants' Handbook: Being a Guide to the Various Fields of Emigration in All of the Globe. With an Introductory Essay, on the Importance of Emigration,

and the Danger to Which Emigrants are Exposed. To Which is Added, a Guide to the Gold Fields of Parts Australia, With Copious Instruction, Government Regulations, etc., Accompanied by a Map of Australia, in Which the Gold Regions are Clearly Indicated.

An example of a conventional tourist guidebook re-purposed for migrants (in the broad sense) is the volume on German-occupied Poland published in the well-known Baedeker series during the Second World War, which was primarily aimed at the occupying military forces and German civilian colonists who were expected to follow them.[21] Reader annotations in early modern English almanacs provide some evidence of how people used them as guides when travelling locally.[22] For modern travel guidebooks and handbooks, there is still research to be done on the specific, material ways in which they circulated among prospective migrants to be mined for useful information.

To the printed sources of information available to and used by long-distance travellers, including migrants, may be added railway and shipping timetables. By the twenty-first century, printed timetables of this kind were increasingly obsolete, and at the same time their format and use continues to be taken for granted. But railway timetables were a novelty in the nineteenth century; the first tabular one was published in 1838. They had to be invented and designed and re-designed, and recent research on the ways in which people used them has emphasised how understanding them was a learned skill.[23]

Other People

At the beginning and end of a migrant journey, there were nearly always human agents and face-to-face conversations. Word of mouth, in conversations with others who had returned from a period of migration or with the families that were in contact with those abroad, was always an element in the information mix, with local points of encounter—the tavern, the grocery store, the barber shop—key nodes in an information network.

Once they had decided to leave, long-distance migrants might rely on the knowledge and advice of the agents of the shipping lines, paid employees, or more often sub-contracted brokers, who sold tickets for oceanic journeys. The Holland America Line had more than two thousand agents spread across Europe by 1890, and they were part of a network of middlemen which included agents of various kinds at the point of departure and lodging house owners at transfer points and ports of call. It was in their interest to offer prospective migrants a vision of their destination and the nature of the journey that would prompt them to move, but also as far as possible to keep them safe. Moreover, it was in the interest of the shipping lines to ensure that if passengers were allowed to board their ships, they would not be turned back at their destination; they needed to be in conformity with the relevant immigration regulations. In the 1900s, for example, emigrants travelling from Russia to America via German ports had to have purchased their tickets before they crossed the Russian border to be allowed through German territory. The brokers would have made sure the travellers were aware of that while encouraging them on their journey with the posters and brochures placed at their disposal by the shipping firms. What migrants could expect from those in the pay of the shipping firms, then, was a fairly standard combination of useful information, guidance in filling out the necessary documentation and propaganda.[24] It was the job of the broker to be persuasive, and that of the migrant to identify her or his relative advantage in weighing up what was said and what was offered. Called to testify at an 1889 trial of Jewish travel agents in Poland, which the Habsburg authorities staged in a drive to stop emigration, Anna Fujarkos and Marjanna Gnapp insisted that the agents had not swindled or misled them; they had only needed the agents' help and advice to fulfil their own reasons for emigrating to the United States: Anna to meet her fiancé, Marjanna to escape poverty.[25]

The Roma

Mobility has played a series of distinct but related roles in the history of the Roma. They have a migration history in the sense outlined above, having left northwest India as a group and moved westward as early as the fifth century C.E. After spending time in Persia and Armenia, they settled in the Greek-speaking parts of the Byzantine Empire (the Balkans), where the first records of their presence date from the thirteenth century. In the early fifteenth century, a new wave of migration set in, and a hundred years later Roma groups were appearing in Britain and Scandinavia, having already established a presence on the European continent. Often described (and describing themselves) as Egyptians (hence the term Gypsy), they were recognisable everywhere by their distinctive appearance, dress and language (Romanes, derived from Sanskrit), and by the fact that they travelled in extended families and earned their living as entertainers. A second wave of westward migration was touched off in the middle of the nineteenth century, when Roma who had been enslaved in Wallachia and Transylvania (today's Romania) were emancipated and moved to Western Europe in large numbers.[26]

Mobility of a different kind became a feature of the Romani way of life in many parts of Europe once their initial migrations had ended. Among the many stereotypes that were applied to Roma in the modern period was that of the "nomad"—a romantic misnomer. In fact, significant numbers of Roma were settled in rural communities and did not travel at all. Those who did travel generally followed fixed circuits which took them to towns and villages, fairs and markets, where they dealt in horses, provided services like sharpening knives and mending pots, sold their own artisanal wares like metalwares, pottery and baskets, peddled small manufactured goods and textiles, or offered musical entertainments and acrobatic displays. Roma also operated travelling shows, including (by the twentieth century) travelling cinemas. These travels were seasonal; during the winter months, Romani families rested in safe spaces.

Among the different Romani groups that were on the move, it is possible to distinguish different patterns of mobility. The Sinti who had settled in Germany in the fifteenth century and the French Manouche tended to travel on relatively closed circuits in their national territories and borderlands, while the Lovara (whose name denoted their horse-dealing traditions) and Kalderash (coppersmiths), having arrived in Western Europe relatively late along with other Eastern European Roma, seem to have been more ambitious, ranging from Belgium and France to the Balkans on their seasonal travels. Lovara and Kalderash were also prominent among the Romani groups who took part in the wave of transoceanic migration around 1900, often by way of British ports. Groups of Continental Roma visited England and Scotland on several well-recorded occasions between 1886 and 1913. Some families travelled on to and across the Americas; these include the Kalderash Ciurons (also Tschorons), who established a global network of "branch families" that extended to North and South America and Australia. Others looked to Asia, forming communities as far East as Shanghai. And those who paused or abandoned their travels to form permanent communities in European and American cities maintained ties to family members still on the move or far away.[27]

An important driver of mobility for European Roma was the hostility of state authorities. From the sixteenth to the eighteenth centuries, they were identified as "heathens" and vagabonds. They fell under bans in most parts of Europe and were subject to penal sanctions and even massacre. Starting in the eighteenth century, there were repeated attempts to force them to settle down and lose their cultural distinctness. The westward migration after the 1880s coincided with and was likely driven by a Europe-wide panic about the "Gypsy menace," leading to a reinforcement of police measures that amounted to continuous harassment and systematic criminalisation. This modern antigypsyism culminated in the genocidal violence that Roma suffered all over Europe at the hands of the Nazis and their allies between 1933 and 1945. Historians explain the nineteenth-century intensification of public hostility to the Roma as a consequence of the consolidation of nation states, which called for the policing of borders and meant that people who travelled and communicated across borders and were typically multilingual were inherently suspect. Geographical mobility and cultural flexibility (including having a "secret" language of their own) laid Roma open to the charge of being spies.[28]

Under these circumstances, information-gathering had two main functions for travelling Roma. The first was to sustain productive relationships within and among Romani families. When Lovara or Kalderash went on the road, they typically formed a *kumpania*, a group of households which travelled together for reasons of both pragmatism and affinity. The households within a *kumpania* were not necessarily related by blood, and different households from the same family group could travel with different *kumpanji*. In a single season, a *kumpania* might dissolve and re-form several times, as the group was forced apart by police action or one household needed to split off for family reasons, but the value of critical mass for mutual support, protection, and sociability brought them back together again, sometimes incorporating new households. Under these circumstances, it was important to know where other members of one's *kumpania* or family were.[29] More generally, the extended family was the site of socialsation, the guarantor of survival, and the point of reference for personal and group identity for Roma. The tie of family was critical, even if it was geographically elastic. Accordingly, getting the news about one's family members—communicating with or about them—was critical even if one didn't know where they were. As the migrant experience shows, sharing news and gossip with family and friends is an inherent part of social life and can be crucial for getting along in a new place; the special challenge for travelling Roma was that both parties to a conversation were likely to be in motion.

The second purpose of information-gathering was to provide knowledge of where and where not to go and of the conditions that awaited travellers at their destination. Information of this kind included intelligence about the local police force and other authorities—their numbers and attitudes—and more broadly about how receptive a particular community would be to the presence and needs of the Roma. Would shopkeepers welcome their custom or lock their doors? Would farmers be willing to sell or trade food or livestock, or even to exercise charity to hungry travellers? Was there a demand for the goods the Roma had to peddle or the services they had to offer? Was there someone—a farmer or an innkeeper—who would allow them to camp on his land?[30] These are mainly questions about opportunities for earning a living, and when Roma routes took them beyond regional circuits with which they were relatively familiar, the questions that needed answering were more specific: horse dealers wanted to know where the nearest horse fairs were. Performers and musicians had to learn where to find an audience, and what would draw the crowds. But Roma were also particularly alert to news of unanticipated opportunities. Historians Ilsen About and Adèle Sutre have written of the dialectics of information in the peculiar knowledge economy of the Roma: "Each journey feeds on encounters and received bits of information which inform their decisions, leading them onto new trajectories which were never planned but which seem to answer their hope of being *baxtalo*—lucky—a fundamental concept in the Romani world."[31] And families whose hope led them across oceans and prairies needed markers and signposts in genuinely unknown territories.

Romani Technologies: "Vurma" and "Patrin"

A long-standing practice of spatial communication among Roma travelling in the countryside was to place objects by the road to let those who were following know what direction to follow. Among Lovara Roma, such a message was known as *vurma* (Lovara Romanes for track or trace). In the interwar period, Burgenland (Austrian) Lovara marked their trajectories at crossroads with such things as two stones tied together with horsehair, or a forked twig with the middle twig pointing in the direction of travel. Signs could also be made of pig's bristles, dog's hairs, pumpkin seeds, cuts in tree trunks, scorched twigs, tears in pieces of cloth or marks made with coal on walls. Each family had its own set of markers.[32] In his account of travelling with Lovara families mainly in the Low Countries and France in the 1930s, Jan Yoors reports that a route might be indicated by a branch broken or with a scrap of textile tied to it at the eye-level of a wagon driver, or else by objects placed at the side of the road of the kind "that did not seem too out of place and therefore obvious."[33] Among British Romanies, the standard term for a trail marker is *patrin*, variations of which mean "leaf" in many European Romani dialects.[34] Thus, the English Romani poet David Morley writes: "PATRIN/or *pateran*, *pyaytrin*, or *sikaimasko*./The marker used by Roma/that tell others of their direction,/often grids of branches or leaf-twists or/bark-binds. Used for passing on news/using prearranged forms, patterns/or permutations of these. Yet/it also means a leaf or,/simply, a page."[35]

The information communicated by these signs went beyond the purely directional, as Yoors reports: "There are special signs indicating such specific messages as: 'speed up travel and join us'; 'follow us'; 'assembling for *Kris* [the periodic meeting of households to resolve disputes]'; 'Rom died, burial ahead'; 'do not stop around here: local police and population hostile to Gypsies'; 'turn back and tread softly,' etc. The leaving of such trails of information covers whole territories with an effective intelligence network."[36] According to Yoors, failure to furnish such information to other Roma, and especially to warn them of hazards, was a punishable offence in the internal code of justice of the Lovara.

Appropriating Technologies to Keep in Touch: Letters and Telephones, Literacy and Orality

Travelling Roma also made use of the technologies made available by the wider culture. The oldest of those technologies was of course the writing and exchange of letters. But this called for some specific adaptations on the part of Romani families as they engaged with the business of writing letters and of making sure they came into the hands of their intended recipients.

Romani culture is traditionally an oral culture. Knowledge of the past, at whose centre was always the history of the extended family, was communicated by word of mouth and in particular through a rich storytelling practice, and in the twenty-first century, the preference for oral over written communication persists within Romani communities. By extension, before the Second World War, many if not most travelling Roma were formally illiterate (as signalled at least by the inability to write their names), and this persisted in the older generations even as formal schooling became available for their children. Non-literacy was only partly the consequence of schooling avoided or interrupted. Rather, it can be understood as a strategic choice, a conscious rejection of the terms of non-Romani culture based on the conviction that the written word detached from the person who had issued it was inherently untrustworthy. But while word of mouth (what has been called the "Romani post") played an important role (for example) in helping scattered families to find each other after the Second World War,[37] in practice people who needed to communicate over distance could not avoid engaging with the written word.

The strategic character of Roma orality is emphasised by the anthropologist Patrick Williams in his observations about mid-twentieth-century French Roma. He argues that just as Roma live inside of their respective societies while preserving their own way of life at a distance from non-Roma (*gadje*, in Romanes), they "define their relationship to the written word from 'inside writing'"—while engaging with the written and spoken word in a variety of different combinations. One of the examples he offers dates from the 1960s: a Rom declares that he will "write a letter" to his cousin, selects the letter paper, and proceeds to dictate to a *gadjo* scribe. His wording has the form neither of speech nor of formal writing, but it has a conventional declarative shape and rhythm of its own, dictated in part by the fact that news and greetings from various other members of the family are communicated in successive sentences. The scribe is not expected to offer editorial interventions, and the author makes no changes to the text once it is on paper.[38] Letters (and postcards) that show evidence of this kind of dictation can be encountered elsewhere among the surviving traces of European Romani life in the nineteenth and early twentieth centuries, and this suggests that the practice that Williams describes was characteristic of many Roma groups. In their travels through Britain and across the Atlantic, the Ciurons employed a *gadjo* "secretary," and also engaged local gypsiologists to read, write, and translate letters for them.[39]

As long as they chose not to (literally) write, then, Roma relied on *gadje* to receive and transmit information wherever they were, and this reliance—usually informal and based on trust—extended to Romani engagement with postal systems. The most conventional of these was the use of the *poste restante* or General Delivery facility in urban post offices. One Lovara family head said he could recognise the sender of a letter from the surname to which it was addressed (he used several different names).[40] Under other circumstances, and probably more often, Roma used informal "drop points," usually in businesses managed by *gadje*. In Europe, these were often the premises of sympathetic innkeepers or restaurateurs, who could hope to benefit from the custom of the large groups of travellers when they called in for their mail and by the public attention their presence would attract. In the United States between the wars, the proprietress of a drug store in Fort Smith Arkansas "handled the mail" for Romani families from all over the country.[41]

Travelling Roma also routinely used the newer communication technologies to exchange information on their journeys. Long-distance phone calls made and received—again—on the premises of friendly *gadje* were an important element of their information economy in the twentieth century. Jan Yoors' Lovara companion used several different premises and distinguished callers by the telephone number at which they contacted him. Yoors' description of the characteristic way in which he engaged physically with the technology anticipates Williams' account of "writing" a letter: "He was ill at ease, stiff, and his speech became declamatory. Finally, he handed me the telephone receiver, asking me to hold it up to him like a microphone. Pulika stepped a little to the side, and using both free hands to gesture in emphasis of his words, he spoke to the telephone rather than into it."[42]

Seizing Opportunities: Communications and Transport Technologies, Non-Romani Intermediaries, and Self-Advertisement

A micro-study of one episode in the history of Romani mobility further underlines the range and complexity of practices and media that constituted their information economy. In the spring of 1906, some two hundred Roma travelled from Germany to Britain fleeing intensified police harassment and seeking new business opportunities (specifically, by their own account, as horse traders and performers).[43] When the last of them, a group of 112, was forcibly returned to Hamburg in November of that year, it was observed that they were organising their onward journeys by telephone and telegraph. This strategic engagement with technological modernity is in keeping with the fact that the Romani families made their way to and from the ports by train and used scheduled ferries for their crossings, and these steps involved relatively complex negotiations about transporting the horses and caravans with which they travelled.

In this particular episode, if we ask how the travellers were informed about how to get to Britain and what awaited them there, we find some evidence that they relied in the first instance on the same public actors as other migrants—ticket sellers and travel agents. More particularly, it was presumably the officers of the shipping lines who gave the travellers the critical information that they would not be denied entry at British ports if they travelled in groups of less than 20. It is also clear that intra-community word of mouth was in action as different groups of travellers communicated their experiences to one another, even across the North Sea (as some groups of travellers returned before others had set off): Scotland was a more welcoming place than England, Ireland might be even better.

On their first arrival at a new place in Britain, the travellers clearly depended on local *gadje* for information about opportunities: where and how they could earn money. They rapidly learned where the key horse fairs were, for example. Their progress through the country also brings home the interactions between the performance culture that many of them belonged to and an informal information economy. Romani musicians in Germany generally played either on the street or in country inns where their stock in trade was current hits.[44] The few records we have of their performances in Europe show that they were quick to adopt the latest dance music into their repertoire. By the time they left Britain, members of these groups of travellers were performing not only the globally popular cakewalk, but also versions of the Lambeth Walk; when challenged by the police to move on, one group burst into a rendition of "I Wouldn't Leave My Little Wooden Hut for You"—a music-hall song which had only come out in the previous year.[45] These Roma had clearly benefited from contact with locals. Like some friendly innkeepers back home, there were people in Britain ready to assist the visitors in exploiting their capacity for spectacle— the public fascination with exotic others. These included pastors who encouraged public "Gypsy weddings," farmers on whose land they were allowed to camp, and professional theatre managers and promoters, some of whom had come to specialise in collaborating with visiting Roma. The travellers learned from these people what kind of show and what tunes would draw a paying audience.

What they did not need to learn was how to promote themselves, and in communicating information about themselves they made their own use of the opportunities afforded by the press. The Romani travellers in Britain sold picture postcards of themselves, a practice which also appears in the Netherlands at the same time. How they managed the trade in postcards, for example whether they commissioned their own or acquired stock from printers serving the large market in circulating images of "Gypsies," remains an open research question. Similarly, Roma engaged in artisanal trades and repair services who travelled in Europe left a trail of newspaper advertisements and trade cards which were clearly of their own initiative.[46]

Counter-Information: Resistance and Subversion

A discussion of the role of information in Romani history would not be complete without a consideration of the ways in which Roma have historically evaded and subverted modern information regimes. Managing information and developing complex systems for that purpose are recognised by historians as one of the central functions of the modern state, and in this context the surveillance and control of the mobility of populations is a key application of information technologies. These include systems of personal identification (passports) and of registering and recording individuals and their whereabouts (certification of birth, death, and marriage; address registers; censuses). The securing of national borders is one of the principal uses of these systems, and to this end states can be inventive in projecting as well as processing information. In 2020s Britain, the immigration authorities justified changes to the treatment of migrants and refugees after their arrival not in terms of what the migrants themselves might or might not deserve, but as a way of sending a message to others who might be contemplating an attempted border breach and/or their traffickers—informing them that a journey was pointless.[47]

As noted above, the historical harassment and persecution of Roma was predicated on their mobility as well as on their cultural non-conformity. Official information systems were deployed specifically to keep them under surveillance: as early as 1899, the Bavarian police began systematically compiling a database on Roma; it included more than thirty thousand individuals at the point when the files were transferred to the new Reich Central Office for Combatting the Gypsy Nuisance in 1938. The French authorities introduced a compulsory anthropometric identification document for all itinerants in 1912, with a particular emphasis on Romani travellers. And by 1930, Roma in two-thirds of German territories were similarly required to carry identification papers designed specifically for them.[48]

Roma thus had good reasons to be suspicious of police systems. James C. Scott, one of the most influential of contemporary scholars to argue that modern states require space and people to be "legible" (and by extension recordable), numbers the Roma among those who have historically practised "the art of not being governed." He argues that orality, the resistance to literacy and to written records, is itself an effective strategy for evading governance.[49]

A Romani practice that commonly frustrated police and researchers alike was the use of dual naming systems: typically, Romani individuals had both a Romani name by which they were known to family and friends, and which was rarely if ever written down, and given names and surnames characteristic of the wider community in which they lived. In official contexts, these latter names were used. But in everyday life, it was the Romani name that had a fixed association with the person, while the use of non-Romani "civil" names was strategic and flexible. Families or individuals might adopt a regional surname and use it over several generations, but choose a new one (or choose to let the authorities record a different one) as circumstances changed. While the use of non-Romani names was approached largely as a matter of convenience, Roma marriage and child-raising practices meant that they sometimes had to be deployed strategically. Roma generally started their families very young, and registering a baby under the name of another adult could screen families against the kinds of questions that might be raised where the natural mother was still legally underage. Among German Sinti in the 1920s and 1930s, it was common for women to take the "German" surnames of their husbands in public and official contexts and for their children also to be registered under the father's surname, even when they were married according to Romani custom rather than before the law.

The utility of this practice for the Romani subjects is obvious, though it continues to complicate the study of Romani history. Under the Nazis, it was answered by the grotesque policy of forcing two generations of people born to such couples to adopt their mothers' surnames. The National Socialist drive to make the Roma legible once and for all was the first step in a process that led to forced registration, violent and physically invasive measures to determine people's family background and "racial" status, immobilisation, and internment, and finally to genocide. Compounded by the failures of official acknowledgement and compensation after 1945, this experience left many survivor communities even more sceptical than before of letting the *gadje* know who they were and where to find them.[50]

Conclusion: Moving Targets

Information history operates at the intersection of social and cultural history and the history of technology. It involves the study both of the material media which moved information and of the ways in which people have used those media. But while we see information as inherently in motion, historians of the Global North have often pictured its human subjects as static. Attention to the information needs and practices of users who are themselves mobile—among them migrants and peripatetic groups such as Roma—highlights the very wide range of media (human and material, formal and informal) that may constitute particular information economies. At the same time, the lens that brings moving subjects into focus should sharpen the historian's awareness of how far modern civic norms of settledness, traceability, and legibility have been contested. Information regimes have been designed to facilitate and enforce a system of bordered nation states, and people who need to move have developed inventive strategies for appropriation, evasion, and disruption—though often at a heavy cost.

Notes

1 Anton Tantner, "Intelligence Offices in the Habsburg Monarchy," in *News Networks in Early Modern Europe*, ed. Joad Raymond and Noah Moxham (Leiden: Brill, 2016), 443–464; and Eve Rosenhaft, "Hands and Minds: Clerical Work in the First 'Information Society'," *International Review of Social History* 48, no. S11 (2003): 20–21. On the "first information revolution," see Paul M. Dover, *The Information Revolution in Early Modern Europe* (Cambridge, UK: Cambridge University Press, 2021); and Daniel R. Headrick, *When Information Came of Age*.

Technologies of Knowledge in the Age of Reason and Revolution, 1700–1850 (Oxford: Oxford University Press, 2000).
2 Malcolm Chase, *Early Trade Unionism. Fraternity, Skill and the Politics of Labour* (London: Routledge, 2000), 62. Compare (for France) Michael Sonenscher, "Journeymen's Migrations and Workshop Organization in Eighteenth-Century France," in *Work in France*, ed. Steven Laurence Kaplan and Cynthia J. Koepp (Ithaca, NY: Cornell University Press, 2019), 74–96; and (for Germany) Knut Schulz, "Gesellentrinkstuben und Gesellenherbergen im 14./15. Und 16. Jahrhundert," in *Gastfreundschaft, Taverne und Gasthaus im Mittelalter*, ed. Hans Conrad Peyer (Munich: Oldenburg, 1983), 221–242.
3 The subjects of the chapter are people who move by choice (however much their choice may be forced or constrained by circumstance), rather than forced migrants or trafficked or enslaved people.
4 Adam McKeown, "Global Migration, 1846–1940," *Journal of World History* 15 (2004): 155–189.
5 On "peripatetic," see Daniele Viktor Leggio and Yaron Matras, "How Open Borders Can Unlock Cultures. Concepts, Methods, and Procedures," in *Open Borders, Unlocked Cultures. Romanian Roma Migrants in Western Europe*, ed. Daniele Viktor Leggio and Yaron Matras (London: Routledge, 2018), 1–25; and Aparna Rau, ed., *The Other Nomads: Peripatetic Minorities in Cross-Cultural Perspective* (Cologne: Böhlau, 1987). See also the critical discussion of the distinction between "migrants" and "movers" in Jan Lucassen and Leo Lucassen, "Measuring and Quantifying Cross-Cultural Migrations: An Introduction," in *Globalising Migration History: The Eurasian Experience (16th–21st Centuries)*, ed. Jan Lucassen and Leo Lucassen (Leiden: Brill, 2014), 5–11.
6 I use the endonym Roma (adjective Romani) to designate historical subjects. The discriminatory exonym "Gypsy" is used only where it is necessary to reproduce the language current in contemporary official and public usage.
7 Cf. Jodie Matthews, "Where Are the Romanies? An Absent Presence in Narratives of Britishness," *Identity Papers: A Journal of British and Irish Studies* 1, no. 1 (2015): 79–90.
8 For recent examples, see Paola Campana and Loraine Gelsthorpe, "Choosing a Smuggler: Decision-Making amongst Migrants Smuggled to Europe," *European Journal on Criminal Policy and Research* 27 (2021): 5–21; Elizabeth Koomson-Yalley, "Information Sharing and Decision-Making: Attempts by Ghanaian Return Migrants to Enter through Libya," *Social Inclusion* 9 (2021): 226–234; and Fang Wang, "Social Capital or Non-human Sources? A Cross-context Study on Information Source Selection of Migrant Farmer Workers," *Journal of Information Science* 49, no. 5 (2021): 1–17.
9 See, for example, "Precarious Migrants, Migration Regimes and Digital Technologies: The Empowerment-Control Nexus," *Journal of Ethnic and Migration Studies* 48, no. 8 (2022) (Special Issue), ed. Mihaela Nedelcu and Ibrahim Soysüren; and Athina Karatzogianni, Dennis Nguyen, and Elisa Serafinelli, eds., *The Digital Transformation of the Public Sphere: Conflict, Migration, Crisis and Culture in Digital Networks* (London: Palgrave Macmillan, 2016). On digital media use by other mobile groups, see Allison Hailey Hahn, *Media Culture in Nomadic Communities* (Amsterdam: Amsterdam University Press, 2021).
10 See, for example, Margrit Schulte Beerbühl, *The Forgotten Majority. German Merchants in London, Naturalization and Global Trade 1660–1815*, trans. Cynthia Klor (New York: Berghahn, 2015).
11 For relevant historical approaches, see Annemarie Steidl, "The 'Relatives and Friends Effect': Migration Networks of Transatlantic Migrants from the Late Habsburg Monarchy," in *Maritime Transport and Migration: The Connections between Maritime and Migration Networks*, ed. Torsten Feys et al. (St. John's: IMEHA, 2007), 75–95; and Simone A. Wegge, "Chain Migration and Information Networks: Evidence from Nineteenth-Century Hesse Cassel," *Journal of Economic History* 58 (1998): 957–986 (a broadly quantitative study).
12 See, for example, Michael John, "Push and Pull Factors for Overseas Migrants from Austria-Hungary in the 19th and 20th Centuries," in *Austrian Immigration to Canada: Selected Essays*, ed. Franz A. J. Szabo (Ottawa: Carleton University Press, 1996), 59–60.
13 For an introduction to the field, see Bruce S. Elliott, David A. Gerber, and Suzanne M. Sinke, eds., *Letters across Borders: The Epistolary Practices of International Migrants* (Cham: Palgrave Macmillan, 2006).

14 Suzanne M. Sinke, "Marriage through the Mail: North American Correspondence Marriage from Early Print to the Web," in *Letters across Borders: The Epistolary Practices of International Migrants*, ed. Bruce S. Elliott, David A. Gerber, and Suzanne M. Sinke (Cham: Palgrave Macmillan, 2006), 75–94.

15 Kathleen A. de Haan, "Negotiating the Transnational Moment: Immigrant Letters as Performance of a Diasporic Identity," *National Identities* 12 (2010): 107–131.

16 The Prize Papers Project, https://www.prizepapers.de/the-project/the-prize-papers-collection.

17 See, for example, Francisca Hoyer, *Relations of Absence: Germans in the East Indies and Their Families c. 1750–1820* (Uppsala: Acta Universitatis Uppsaliensis, 2020).

18 Colin Pooley, *Mobility, Migration and Transport: Historical Perspectives* (Cham: Palgrave Macmillan, 2017), 66–67.

19 William D. Jones, "'Going into Print': Published Immigrant Letters, Webs of Personal Relations, and the Emergence of the Welsh Public Sphere," in *Letters across Borders: The Epistolary Practices of International Migrants*, ed. Bruce S. Elliott, David A. Gerber, and Suzanne M. Sinke (Cham: Palgrave Macmillan, 2006), 175–199.

20 May Rush Gwin Waggoner, ed., *Le Plus Beau Païs du Monde: Completing the Picture of Proprietary Louisiana, 1699–1722* (Lafayette, LA: Center for Louisiana Studies, 2005).

21 Jane Caplan, *"Jetzt Judenfrei": Writing Tourism in Nazi-Occupied Poland* (London: German Historical Institute, 2012).

22 Laura Williamson Ambrose, "Travel in Time. Local Travel Writing and Seventeenth-Century English Almanacs," *Journal of Medieval and Early Modern Studies* 43 (2013): 419–433.

23 Mike Esbester, "Nineteenth-Century Timetables and the History of Reading," *Book History* 12 (2009): 156–185.

24 Torsten Feys, *The Battle for the Migrants: The Introduction of Steamshipping on the North Atlantic and Its Impact on the European Exodus* (Liverpool: Liverpool University Press, 2013), 71–118.

25 Tara Zahra, "Travel Agents on Trial: Policing Mobility in East Central Europe, 1889–1989," *Past & Present* 223 (May 2014): 176.

26 For a recent general account, see Lev Tcherenkov and Stephane Laederich, *The Rroma*, 2 vols. (Basel: Schwab, 2004).

27 Ilsen About and Adèle Sutre, "Circulations Raisonnées: Consciences et Discours du Voyage dans les Sociétés Romani-Tsiganes au Début du XXe Siècle," in *L'Expérience de la Mobilité de l'Antiquité à nos Jours, Entre PréCarité et Confiance*, ed. Claudia Moatti and Emmanuelle Chevreau (Mayenne: Ausonius, 2021), 319–333; and Adèle Sutre, "They Give a History of Wandering All Over the World: A Romani Clan's Transnational Movement in the Early 20th Century," *Quaderni Historici* 49 (2014): 471–498.

28 Jennifer Illuzzi, *Gypsies in Germany and Italy, 1861–1914: Lives Outside the Law* (Basingstoke: Palgrave Macmillan, 2014); and Leo Lucassen, Wim Willems, and Anne-Marie Cottaar, *Gypsies and Other Itinerant Groups: A Socio-Historical Approach* (Cologne: Böhlau, 1996).

29 For the 1930s, see Jan Yoors, *The Gypsies* (Prospect Heights, NY: Waveland Press, 1967). For contemporary France, see Lise Foisneau, "Former une *Kumpania*: Composition et recomposition des Collectifs Roms de Provence," *Ethnologie Française* 48 (2018): 635–644.

30 On the ambivalent relations between traveling Roma and rural communities, see Simon Constantine, *Sinti and Roma in Germany (1871–1933): Gypsy Policy in the Second Empire and Weimar Republic* (London: Routledge, 2020), 103–105; and Angelika Albrecht, *Zigeuner in Altbayern 1871–1914: Eine Sozial-, Wirtschafts- und Verwaltungsgeschichtliche Untersuchung der Bayerischen Zigeunerpolitik* (Munich: Kommission für Bayerische Landesgeschichte, 2002), 258–285.

31 About and Sutre, "Circulations Raisonnées," 320.

32 Claudia Mayerhofer, *Dorfzigeuner: Kultur und Geschichte der Burgenland-Roma von der Ersten Republik bis zur Gegenwart* (Vienna: Picus, 1987), 119.

33 Yoors, *The Gypsies*, 126.

34 Current usage is recorded in the Romani lexical database RomLex, http://romani.uni-graz.at/romlex/. *Patrin* was also the title of a web journal of Romani studies between 1996 and 2002.

35 David Morley, "Patrin," in *The Invisible Kings* (Manchester: Carcanet Press, 2007), 8. The lexical root of *sikaimasko* means point, direct and teach.

36 Jan Yoors, "O Drom le Lowarengo: Recollections of Life and Travel with the Lovara [Part II]," *Journal of the Gypsy Lore Society*, 3rd series, 38 (1959): 96.

37 On the "Romani post": Volha Bartash, "The Joy and Burden of Living: Roma Communities in the Western Borderlands of the Postwar Soviet Union," in *No Neighbors' Land. Postwar Europe in a New Comparative Perspective*, ed. Anna Wylegała, Sabine Rutar, and Małgorzata Łukianov (Cham: Palgrave Macmillan, 2022), 170.
38 Patrick Williams, "L'Écriture entre l'Oral et l' Écrit. Six Scènes de la Vie Tsigane en France," in *Par Écrit: Ethnologie des Écritures Quotidiennes*, ed. Daniel Fabre, Martin de La Soudière and Claudie Voisenat (Paris: Editions de la Maison des Sciences de l'Homme, 1997), 59–78.
39 About and Sutre, "Circulations Raisonnées," 325.
40 Yoors, *The Gypsies*, 210–212.
41 About and Sutre, 325, citing E. P. Hicks, "She handled the mail for Gypsies all over the world. The passing of 'Mother Cole' leaves vacant the unique post which made this Arkansas woman the one stationary factor in the lives of all the Romany tribes," *The Journal of the Fort Smith Historical Society* 7, no. 1 (1983): 9–11.
42 Yoors, *The Gypsies*, 52, 212–213.
43 For the following account, see Eve Rosenhaft and Tamara West, "'Invaders': Mobility and Economy in the Lives of the Laubinger Family," in *European Roma: Lives Beyond Stereotypes*, ed. Eve Rosenhaft and María Sierra (Liverpool: Liverpool University Press, 2022), 127–147, and continuing research into this episode in the context of the AHRC-Deutsche Forschungsgemeinschaft collaborative development project Romani Migration between Germany and Britain (1880s–1914): Spaces of Informal Business, Media Spectacle, and Racial Policing (2022–2026).
44 Bernard Gilliat-Smith, "The Gypsies of the Rhine Provinz in 1902–1903," *Journal of the Gypsy Lore Society*, New series, 1 (1907–1908), 129.
45 "Visit of the German Gipsies to Langholm," *Eskdale and Liddesdale Advertiser*, November 21, 1906.
46 About and Sutre, "Circulations Raisonnées," 326.
47 UK Home Office, "World First Partnership to Tackle Global Migration Crisis," April 14, 2022, https://www.gov.uk/government/news/world-first-partnership-to-tackle-global-migration-crisis.
48 Rainer Hehemann, *Die "Bekämpfung des Zigeunerunwesens" im Wilhelminischen Deutschland und in der Weimarer Republik* (Frankfurt a.M.: Haag + Herchen, 1987); and Emmanuel Filhol and Marie-Christine Hubert, *Les Tsiganes en France: Un Sort à Part (1939–1946)* (Paris: Perrin, 2009), 87–93.
49 James C. Scott, *The Art of Not Being Governed: An Anarchist History of Upland Southeast Asia* (New Haven, CT: Yale University Press, 2009), 226–237. Cf. James C. Scott, *Seeing Like a State: How Certain Schemes to Improve the Human Condition Have Failed* (New Haven, CT: Yale University Press, 1998).
50 Julia von dem Knesebeck, *The Roma Struggle for Compensation in Post-War Germany* (Hatfield: University of Hertfordshire Press, 2011); Eve Rosenhaft, "Wissenschaft als Herrschaftsakt: Die Forschungspraxis der Ritterschen Forschungsstelle und das Wissen über 'Zigeuner'," in *Zwischen Erziehung und Vernichtung. Zigeunerforschung und Zigeunerpolitik im Europa des 20. Jahrhunderts*, ed. Michael Zimmermann (Stuttgart: Steiner, 2007), 329–353; Heike Krokowsi, *Die Last der Vergangenheit: Auswirkungen nationalsozialistischer Verfolgung auf Deutsche Sinti* (Frankfurt a.M.: Campus, 2001); and Michael Zimmermann, *Rassenutopie und Genozid: Die Nationalsozialistische "Lösung der Zigeunerfrage"* (Hamburg: Christians, 1996).

29
EMOTIONS AS COMMODITIES
Street Ballads and the Commercialisation of Information

Laura Skouvig

Introduction

"She admits the last eight days to have cried ballads and pleads that she cannot sell any when she does not cry or sing them."[1] This vivid testimony in a police report about the arrest of a balladmonger in the streets of Copenhagen in March 1807 gives us a glimpse of how information was for sale in the streets. Penny prints containing street ballads and pieces in prose were commercialised genres for the lower classes in society.[2] The ballads themselves were often poetic disasters and of poor aesthetic quality. Sensationalism was a commercial hallmark and the content often propagated libels and rumours. Consequently, street ballads have been disregarded as trustworthy sources of past events. It is, however, precisely the mix of commercial strategies such as horrifying, gory depictions of homicides and catastrophes together with factual information about the same events that makes them interesting from the perspective of information history.

Penny prints and street ballads are just one example of how information was a commercial product far earlier than the advent of the digital information society. Peter Burke argues that there is a need to broaden the horizon of the information society by acknowledging the fact that information has always been for sale.[3] Modern, and now late modern, commercial practices of selling and buying information are far from new. However, the main question to pursue is not when information became a commodity, but rather, what were the contexts—social or ideological, political, economic, and so forth—in which information was commodified in the past.

Stating that information has always been a commodity—or at least always for sale—entails the risk of identifying commercialisation only when it is identical to that of our present age. What is particularly interesting when discussing the commercialisation of information are the fluctuations of the kinds of information that were considered relevant as commodities: what was the information about; why was it worth selling; and who were the interested parties? As a commodity, information is almost inseparable from its material forms or genres such as newspapers, snippets of secret information, or books.[4] Information has also been exchanged for other kinds of information, but more frequently, as Burke

DOI: 10.4324/9781003310532-33

457

argues, information as a commodity has been exchanged for money, and as Will Slauter stresses, the very commodification of information has been as "a *product* that can be sold."[5]

This chapter discusses street ballads as commercialised information at the turn of the nineteenth century in Denmark. It first introduces a historiographic overview of the literature on information as a commodity in early modern Europe in order to situate ballads as a distinct form of commercialised information. One main aspect of this overview is the fact that information as a commodity has not always supported reasoning or reflected a factual representation of reality. Though street ballads circulated information about crucial events, the information often did not represent the event in a factually correct way. This, it is argued, is inherent in their function as communicative actions. As genres, street ballads had the function of promoting a "true" interpretation of events through the presentation of factual but also emotional information. The truth presented by street ballads should not be evaluated according to epistemic norms but rather as an offer of navigation through a complicated information landscape. This is illustrated in a case study which dates from two catastrophic events in Danish history: the two battles of Copenhagen between Danish and British forces on April 2, 1801, and September 2–7, 1807. This case study shows how the street ballads presented patriotism as a lens for making information about the two battles comprehensible. In this way, the ballads supported loyalty towards the monarchy despite there being critical voices against the government.

Commercialised Information in Early Modern Europe, 1500–1800

Information as an attractive and valued commodity has a long history which crosses geographical borders and cultures.[6] This initial contextual overview focuses mainly on early modern Europe, with Denmark as a specific case. The history of information as a commodity does not imply that there have been no changes to how information has been commodified and commercialised. Slauter and Burke point to the seventeenth and eighteenth centuries as a period of increasing awareness of information as a commercial product.[7] Burke, as well as Andrew Pettegree, distinguishes between a medieval information culture and an early modern information culture of the seventeenth and eighteenth centuries. Burke argues that the medieval culture relied on an understanding of knowledge as divine and hence not for sale—an understanding paralleled by the Classical Greek tradition where Plato criticises the Sophists for commercialising knowledge.[8] Pettegree, along with Paul Dover, also points to an outspoken suspicion towards written, and later printed, news as another characteristic of medieval information culture. Trust in information was ascribed to the messenger delivering it.[9] This trust might have been influenced by Plato's critique of writing as technology but does also reflect that information was carried and communicated in person.[10]

Information was a valuable commodity in numerous contexts, especially in politics, commerce, and for military purposes, but also in personal, as well as societal and cultural, contexts. In the political and military realm, information took the shape of intelligence that was sometimes unearthed by spies in the service of governments or rulers.[11] Information about commerce, industry, and trade took on many different forms and statuses such as publicly available information about trade, and information about prices, goods, and trade routes.[12] Trade secrets also constituted commercialised information in the context of the tension between inward openness in a guild and outward secrecy.[13] Finally, on a societal and personal level, information about events—either on a large national or international scale or on a personal level such as information about family matters, deaths, births, and so on—brought information as news to the forefront. Often used slightly synonymously, information in the form of news has been widely researched and discussed.[14] Nevertheless, not all news seems to reflect factual information and the idea of a rational mind.[15] As Paul Goring argues, the early modern period witnessed how practices and methodologies were established to make printed information trustworthy. Identification of the sources of information as part of establishing the trustworthiness of information became crucial when selling it.[16] Heidi Tworek has discussed how the obfuscation of provenance might also have helped sell information in the much later period of the 1920s.[17] Street ballads failed as factual conduits of information that spoke to a rational mind. In fact, they were often of an opposite character: emotional, and focused on anxiety and grief, as well as faith.[18]

Information circulated and was constantly subject to transformation. As a commodity it was produced under specific circumstances and with specific intentions which changed as it moved through different geographical places.[19] The following section will focus on places and their topography, genres and media, actors, and practices of information, using Copenhagen in the period 1770–1815 as an example, before turning to the concrete cases of penny prints and street ballads.

Topographies of Information

Historians use an overall conceptual understanding to discuss the market for information: who was interested in obtaining and paying for information; who was willing (or perhaps not so willing) to sell information; and who was willing to pay to keep information secret. But on a much more practical level, information was for sale in marketplaces in cities (and elsewhere). In seventeenth-century Venice, information was a desired commodity for merchants as well as for inhabitants in general, and the Rialto was one of its marketplaces.[20] Other marketplaces included offices of the scribes, print shops, booksellers, taverns, and barber shops.[21] Coffee houses became pivotal during the eighteenth century as places of information and news exchange.[22] Hubs of information outside the larger cities included roadside inns and travellers' stables, where couriers changed horses. Information in the shape of news in letters, newsletters, or newspapers transgressed borders and circulated between countries.[23] For instance, the mail arrived in Copenhagen twice a week from Hamburg. Being close to Denmark, Hamburg was a central news hub providing Copenhagen with news via the aforementioned newsletters, letters, and newspapers from the European continent and beyond.[24]

Recently, research has emphasised the need to understand the public sphere less in an idealistic Habermasian sense but rather by favouring the broader commercial and sociological scopes of the public sphere that include the streets, as Robert Darnton did when he investigated the information networks of Paris in the 1740s.[25] In recent Danish and Norwegian research about freedom of speech and of the public sphere in the eighteenth century, the focus has been on the topography of printers, writers, and authors.[26]

The topography of information reveals that the market for information in Copenhagen had a much more complex character than merely consisting of elite readers who bought books, newspapers, and periodicals and who met in literary salons and clubs to discuss and read the latest newspapers and periodicals. The astonishing information production during the years of freedom of the press (1770–1772) came in the forms of penny prints and pamphlets and illustrated an increasing demand for information that at the time was considered unhealthy.[27] The "written word as commodity" and the increasing demand for news made the commercial circuit of authors, publishers, printers, bookshops, and readers all the more visible.[28] Despite the cascade of prints the information market was still characterised by presence based on the circulation of information by word of mouth in the streets, exchanged over wine or coffee in pubs, around the bookshops at Børsen (the Stock Exchange Building), or at Adressekontoret (The Address Office). This office was modelled over the bureau d'adresse et de rencontre (The Address Office) established by Théophraste Renaudot in Paris in 1630. The Danish version linked employers with employees and sellers with buyers but did not include the medical services later offered by Renaudot.[29] The printers' shops were located around Kgs. Nytorv or in the Latin Quarter.

Besides the permanent sales opportunities, the "sales guerrilla,"[30] in the shape of the balladmonger, roamed the streets with their noisy advertisements of new ballads or pamphlets. The commercialisation of information was in general met with dislike amongst Copenhagen's intellectuals, and an undesired exposure to rumours and libels from the balladmongers was a common complaint.[31]

Information Actors and Practices of Information

The actors involved in the production of information about news also covered a broad spectrum. Princes, merchants, and ordinary people consumed information of all sorts, and especially about news. But princes and merchants were also producers of information that could be deemed worthy of selling. In the shape of state secrets in the *arcana imperii* tradition, such information had a certain value, and chancellors and secretaries often had a sideline business selling such secret information.[32]

Journalism as a profession came much later, but incidents of people who proactively searched for (news) stories are known.[33] In short, a broad variety of people could be identified as information brokers or retailers, working in many different occupations: innkeepers, couriers, barbers, and of course the newsmongers in the streets.[34]

Each of these actors took part in many kinds of information practices such as sorting, storing, writing, digesting, selecting, printing, and circulating information. They enquired about and exchanged information. Newspaper editors picked from a news "commons." The newspapers recirculated, remediated, and reproduced information from other sources, but no one proactively engaged in finding, or rather creating, information as news.[35] At the beginning of the nineteenth century, a failed theologian, Johan Christian Brestrup, strolled the streets of Copenhagen, listening to gossip and rumours, and intercepting information about missing persons or whatever might have been of interest to the people in the streets. He digested the court proceedings of criminal offences and turned this into verses about war, thieves, murderers, and other events that attracted local attention. Ruth Andersen points out that in many ways Brestrup's production was journalistic in the modern understanding of the term since he depicted everyday lives and wrote about major events.[36]

Censorship was a crucial information practice of the state. The control of information helped define the state in the eyes of the citizens as it clearly categorised those who had access to information (including state secrets) and those who did not.[37] In Denmark, censorship rules originated during the Reformation in 1536. These rules were substantially reiterated in the large legal work of absolutism, the Danish Code of 1683, but changes in the media landscape soon made further revisions necessary.

Censorship was part and parcel of Danish writing culture. As Ellen Krefting argues, despite their negative consequences, censorship regulations also resulted in creative efforts to circumvent the regulations.[38] Especially for authors of street ballads, creativity was in high demand. Following instructions given to the police chief constable in Copenhagen in 1701, a distinction between reasoning and commenting on the one hand and the factual representation of events on the other was introduced. According to Krefting, this led to different roles for newspapers and periodicals in Denmark-Norway: the periodicals commented, reasoned, and speculated, whereas newspapers merely reported events.[39] Street ballads fitted into this distinction, as penny prints often consisted of the factual reporting of events but also commentaries on these events through verse. Though preventive censorship had been formally abolished in 1770, it was explicitly defined that critique of religion, government, and the royal familiy were off-limits for authors and commentators.[40] Street ballads and especially the balladmongers were explicitly targeted in 1805 with a police bill which prohibited balladmongers from crying or singing (hand)written or printed ballads, as it was prohibited for newspapers or other media to circulate rumours about citizens' private lives.[41] Yet however much the government tried to control what could be published, these measures did not prevent information from remaining a commercial asset that was produced, sold, advertised, and consumed in Copenhagen as in the rest of the country.

Genres and Media

Genres of commercialised information were manifold. Having grown out of correspondence and handwritten newsletters and later printed reports, the commercialisation of information was tightly associated with the development of diplomatic and merchants' correspondence.[42] Most commonly known are the Venetian *avvisi* and *relazione*. Maps became an asset for merchants as well as for princes as part of merchant capitalism.[43] Newspapers, mainly identified as a product of the printing press, emerged throughout the seventeenth century. In Denmark, the first newspaper was published in the 1660s, but while Mendle illustrates how the political crises in England in the 1640s resulted in a proliferation of newsletters and other prints, the political upheavals in Denmark in the late 1650s and the new form of government in 1660 were not reflected in newspapers, yet still in a flood of other kinds of publications.[44] Newspapers largely relayed information about international and even global events, whereas street ballads focused on the local area and circulated news that was already known.[45]

An important characteristic of early modern information culture was that it was cross-medial, comprising orality, writing, and print.[46] This becomes particularly visible when it comes to street ballads.[47] Print influenced information as a commodity and reified and itemised information as pieces of (printed) paper for sale.[48] The cross-medial character of early modern information and the fact that street ballads were meant to be sung indicates that it was not just the pamphlet that was sold. The performance—the singing—was also for sale. This is particularly the phenomenon of the German Bänkelsänger.[49]

Street Ballads as Genre

Street ballads were a commercial medium and hence the preferences of the audience influenced their content. According to Brandtzæg, ballads played specific and several concrete functions for the audience, offering comfort, entertainment, and moral knowledge.[50]

One of the main functions was to communicate news of events to ordinary people, but it is important not to over-interpret news ballads as the only news source for ordinary people. McShane Jones points out how the inclusion of the news ballads as forerunners of a democratic press was an attempt to make these ballads more respectable despite their lasting reputation as unreliable tabloids, wallowing in gory stories about catastrophes and murders.[51] The news ballads, as Jones claims, did not have the function of informing the audience about news because the audience already knew about it. Their function would have been different. Brandtzæg describes some of the ballads as "docudramas" or even as true crime that re-enacted the dramatic events.[52] News ballads had the function of teaching, satirising, and commenting on news, which is emphasised when their transmedial position between orality and print is considered.[53]

The function of the ballads relies on their transmedial position, where the singing stressed the affective, panegyric side of the ballads and their function of making the world comprehensible, whereas the printed broadsheet stressed factual information in the form of documentation in footnotes or short memoranda explaining the concrete event.[54] In order to understand the function of the ballad it is worth abandoning the moral evaluation of them as dubious entertainment in favour of an approach that addresses why they existed. For this purpose, it is rewarding to see the ballads as communicative actions and to look at what kind(s) of situation(s) generated their existence.[55]

One way of doing this is to understand street ballads as rhetorical genres, which is a different genre approach compared to traditional literary genres which are often defined by form. Genres are not merely form but social actions which connect texts with contexts. Like communicative actions, a genre is understood as "typified actions in response to recurring social contexts."[56] The field of rhetorical genre studies see the genres as everyday phenomena and as gateways for people to participate in the actions of a community.[57] This also has implications for how information is understood. Rhetorical genre studies stress information as a rhetorical construct evoked by a perceived social need for information. Charles Bazerman introduced the term "informational landscape" with reference to Bakhtin's chronotope as a way of addressing the relation between texts, their information, and their function.[58] Genres help people navigate through texts and contexts as readers and writers of texts.[59] When texts and genres are forms of social action, it implies that people create and read texts within particular social contexts. Street ballads as genres are contextually embedded in a commercial regime that shapes and forms the information landscape of each ballad in certain ways. Besides the commercial context, the ballads are characterised by an orientation towards the superficiality of the contemporary world.

The tight relationship with the passing events of the day has also resulted in the oblivion of ballads: old news does not sell.[60] The commercial interests behind the ballads were defined by newness, as expressed in the title of many ballads: "a new ballad about ..." This indicates a close relationship with actual events. Such events did not normally have a political scope but represented aspects of people's everyday life: unhappy love stories, adultery, infanticides. Yet ballads on these topics could also be purely fictitious. Events such as adultery were perpetually topical and thus not related to a new event.[61] This flexible relation to real events has probably emphasised the status of ballads as unreliable sources. However, the prominent Danish historian of folklore, Iørn Piø, argues that the reliability of the fictional ballads relied on how they created acceptance of, and emotions related to, reality and topicality through their poetic form. In this way, street ballads are valuable sources of information concerning the imaginations and popular ideas of ordinary people.[62]

However, it is argued here that street ballads were much more than that. As communicative actions street ballads did not necessarily reflect a desire for factual news that supported rational reasoning about the world. They addressed the fictional part of reality with the function of helping the audience to navigate through complicated events—or the dreariness of everyday life.[63] This means that street ballads responded to a specific socially constructed need for information and formed this information in certain ways.

Denmark 1770–1815: "An All-New Ballad about the British Brigands"[64]

The Danish conglomerate state had an absolutist system of government, and from 1784 the government was in the hands of the crown prince (from 1808 ruling as King Frederik VI) because the king, Christian VII, was mentally ill.[65]

At the turn of the century, problems were looming over the Danish-Norwegian monarchy as the British government questioned Danish allegiances.[66] This led Britain to attack the Danish fleet twice in 1801 and 1807. While the citizens of Copenhagen had been in high spirits after the 1801 encounters, their optimism waned in the wake of the 1807 encounter.[67] After the Second Battle of Copenhagen in 1807, attitudes in Copenhagen turned critical towards the crown prince, and in 1814 he was estranged from the general population of Copenhagen.[68] In 1801, the citizens of the capital were spectators to the battle that took place outside the Copenhagen harbour. Despite patriots in Copenhagen claiming a partial Danish victory, the battle was a defeat for Denmark.[69] In 1807 Copenhagen was surrounded and surrendered after a three-day-long bombardment of the city. The navy surrendered to the British—a resounding defeat that sparked patriotic sentiments against the British troops in Copenhagen.[70]

In an atmosphere of crisis, war, and total devastation, the writers of street ballads thrived. Penny prints and ballads became vital means for people to understand the emotions of the day through the selection and framing of available information. In this respect they remain important sources of the world of ordinary people. The intricate developments of the two battles of Copenhagen were events of a character that evoked a need for interpretation to make them comprehensible. In both situations a broad variety of news sources provided factual information as well as navigation through a broad variety of different emotions. The following section will discuss how factual, and what one might call emotional, information circulating in Copenhagen was formed and shaped by different genres and how ballads in particular, as a commercialized genre, established patriotism as the framework for understanding and interpreting the battles.[71] Patriotism is understood here as a feeling of love towards the state (not towards the nation or the people as an imagined community, as in the case of nationalism). Patriotism towards the state was a central concept for the bourgeois elite in the multicultural Danish monarchy and formed their identity in opposition to the cosmopolitan nobility.[72]

1801: From Official Account to the Streets

The broadsheets and the ballads discussed here mainly stem from two different collections in the Royal Library in Copenhagen. The first consists of pamphlets relating to the Napoleonic wars, the materials examined reflecting the course and character of the two battles. The second collection comprises street ballads printed by the printer Mathias Seest. Only few exist from the period immediately after the bombardment in 1807.[73] Several ballads that had been confiscated were additionally found located in the police archives.

The collection of pamphlets at the Royal Library also contains a supplement to the newspaper *Handels- og Industrie-Tidenden*.[74] It is unclear why this supplement has been preserved in the collection since its audience would have been the bourgeois middle class of merchants and civil servants. It might have been posted on the city walls to make the official account accessible to all inhabitants. The supplement contained two accounts of the events of March and April 1801: an editorial summary of the events from late March, when the British navy approached Copenhagen, and the official account by the commander of the Danish navy, Olfert Fischer, to Crown Prince Frederik.

The two accounts in the newspaper present an informational landscape defined by patriotic information. Olfert Fischer's account addressed Crown Prince Frederik as the recipient, which stresses that this was the official account. Using a first-person narrative served two purposes: it was a guarantee of trustworthiness, but also a narrative technique that invited the reader on board the ships to catch a glimpse of the battle from the inside as a means of explaining the Danish defeat in front of the crown prince and the citizens of Copenhagen who watched from the landside. Fischer directly evoked the audience as witnesses to what he described as a "highly unequal combat":

> When I merely historically report what Your Royal Highness, the crown prince, has seen with your own eyes, and with you a large part of the Danish and European citizens …[75]

In this way, the commander relied on witnesses as potent actors in supplying a moral verdict. This verdict stressed the battle as an example of the cruelty of war more than as a military event. The audience witnessed heroism on the Danish side in the uneven engagement with British superiority. In the final paragraphs, Fischer praised the courage of the officers but also of the enlisted sailors, which indicated a rank-less, non-hierarchical society which, however, did not exist at the time. The commander's appraisal of the courage of the sailors that he compared with sea warriors as an age-old glorious Danish tradition constituted a formative narrative of the battle: Denmark won against a huge and strong British navy if not militarily, then morally.

Handels- og Industrie-Tidende, as well as *Collegial-Tidende*, were targeted at the cultivated and educated citizens – not the masses in the streets of Copenhagen. Nevertheless, two penny prints addressed the battle and its outcome in detail through two fictional conversations: one between a burgher and a farmer and the other between Admiral Parker and Vice-admiral Nelson.[76] In the fictional conversation between a burgher and a farmer (or a farm hand), the events were interpreted for the wider population. The events were first summarised by the burgher with reference to the official account that he had from the *Collegial-Tidende* for the benefit of the farmer. Since the farmer allegedly served on the Holstein (one of the ships), the burgher enquired about the events from a first-hand perspective. The following summary by the farmer is based on the official account but takes the form of a personalised and appealing narrative targeting the lower classes in Copenhagen. The informational landscape is centred around the actors in the form of the ships, the crown prince, and the metaphoric invocations of the entire state. The characters of the burgher and farmer addressed the different ranks of society and stressed an imaginary idea of how the rest of Denmark came to defend Copenhagen. The burgher called the farmer "brother," emphasising the absolutist idea of the king as the father and his subjects as his children. The names of the ships *Holstein*, *Aggershus*, and *Jutland* are explicitly mentioned not merely to stress the factual background, but also because the names referred to the other provinces

Emotions as Commodities

in the conglomerate Danish state. The notion of the king as a fatherly, loving, rewarding, and caring rallying point is concisely demonstrated at the end, where the burgher rejects the worries of the farmer concerning the fate of the dead and the wounded, and their relatives. The crown prince would take care of them as a caring father would for his family.

This image of the state with the king as father and the provinces and subjects as children was a recurring theme in patriotic sentiments at the turn of the nineteenth century. In the second fictional conversation between Admiral Parker and Vice-admiral Nelson, they are found complimenting each other with their success in Copenhagen. They both express admiration for the courage of the Danes which originated in the fact that it was "the children of the country who fought for their own country," unlike Nelson's easy victory in Aboukir which, according to the author J. C. Brestrup, was left in the hands of "some foreigners" who had nothing to fight for.[77] The national origin of the defenders was seen to have had an impact on their will to fight for the glory of king and country.

The official account and the two fictional conversations cultivated patriotism, but in two different ways. The evocation of the past glories of sea warriors, as well as the idea of defending one's own country, point towards a national patriotism defined by a nation's needs and history. However, the conversation between the burgher and the farmer illustrated a patriotism directed towards the (conglomerate) state with the king as a central figure.[78] Together they formed and sold a David-and-Goliath-style myth attached to the Danish defenders which incorporated and communicated patriotism and loyalty towards the king (crown prince), state, and government.

1807: Hatred and Revenge for Sale

The second battle of Copenhagen in September 1807 followed a Danish balancing act between the great powers in Europe. In 1807, it eventually became impossible to insist on neutrality. This time the city was besieged and surrounded. The citizens in the city followed the preparations for a coming attack, as well as Danish counter-attacks, through penny prints.[79] The bombardment of the city took place between September 4 and 7 and left the inner city in ruins. Patriotism suffered greatly in the ruins of the devastated—and now also occupied—city.

After the prohibition of 1805, the police archive slowly reflected the crime of singing, with files on women arrested and charged with crying ballads in the streets. To the benefit of the later historian, some of the ballads were seized and used as evidence in the court proceedings. From the police files, it is possible to get a glimpse of the commercial aspects behind the ballads. In one case, forty copies of a ballad were confiscated. Another balladmonger stated that she had bought twenty-four, while another had bought twenty-five and sold ten. In other cases, the balladmonger claimed to have bought the ballads in well-known print shops. Some of the women admitted knowing that it was illegal to cry the ballads, but as the quote in the introduction to this chapter illustrates, most of them considered it necessary as a way of advertising their commodities.[80]

After the bombardment, sentiments of revenge against, and hatred of, the British found expression in the ballads. These emotions were reflected in the titles of some ballads which discriminated against the British king, George III; the foreign secretary at that time, George Canning; and William Congreve, the inventor of the devastating Congreve rocket.[81] The central actor in the ballads was George Canning. In a penny print with the telling title *Epitaph over the King of England George's Government with his Dismissed Office, in Addition a Conversation in the Other World Between the Incendiary Congreve and his*

Brother Canning the verses described a conflict between George III and his government which persuaded him to attack Copenhagen, to the resentment of the English people. According to the text, King George had stepped down, and the people elected the Prince of Wales as the new king. However, this accession did not happen in 1807, and it is also questionable whether the description of the British political situation is factual. Though the verses seem to raise a critique against the British government, it is reasonable to read the verses as a disguised critique of the advisors surrounding Crown Prince Frederik. It also adds to the non-factual description of events that the conversation between Congreve and Canning took place in hell and in the future. Since both Canning and Congreve were alive in 1807, the fictional character of the conversation was only supported by time and place. The conversation between the two reveals that Congreve was remorseful, but Canning not, and in this way the Danish view of the British population as civilised was given emphasis. Another of the confiscated ballads presented Canning as the architect behind the attack that led to the infamy of Britain.[82] Emotions of anger and hate dominated, with visions of revenge and the destruction of Britain. The British were (as elsewhere) described as a gang of robbers, and in the future "rats, lizards and foxes" would replace the ministers as a sign of the moral decay that followed Canning's deed.[83]

The critique in these two examples accused the British government of the attack and excused the Danish king, thereby stressing an intact loyalty towards the monarchy. Though it was still illegal to criticise the king and his government according to the censorship regulations of 1799, it is reasonable to read the critique of the British government as a disguised critique of the Danish government—or of the increasingly unpopular advisors of the crown prince. It reflects a consistent trend during absolutism to exempt the king from critique and accuse the people around the king (advisors, the court, and so forth) of misleading him.[84] The tense situation in Copenhagen, however, made it hazardous to criticise the British too. The two 1807 ballads offered ways of coming to terms with the emotions of hatred and anger and imagining vengeful attacks on the British Isles. While the British people were also excused for any involvement in the bombardment in the first example, the second ballad revealed the unappealing face of a nationalist desire for construing an entire nation as the enemy. In this way, the street ballads were not merely commercialised genres for factual information;, they also facilitated interpretations of the disastrous events as emotional information.

The Urge to Cry Ballads

In Copenhagen, as elsewhere, street ballads were part of a larger information network of commercialised information. Street ballads were commodities—commercialised genres written by authors and printed by printers who knew their audience, its interests, and its sentiments in every detail. Different genres were adapted to different kinds of audience and street ballads found theirs amongst the less literate and educated part of the population in Copenhagen. During times of distress and anxiety, when the enemy stood in front of the city gates, ballads framed information in a patriotic guise. They were not merely providers of sensational and unreliable information about actual events during the battles highlighted here but also crucial ways of negotiating emotions and establishing interpretations of the events amongst the people. The patriotic sentiments in the penny prints and ballads oscillated between a state and a national patriotism. In this way, the ballads both supported—loyally—the existing regime and state structure while also pointing to a future, more nationalistic and visceral characteristic of the Danish mentality.

Notes

1 Case 775/189: DC-013. Københavns Politiret, 1. Protokol 1791–1814. Behandlede Sager ved 1. Protokol 1807, 101–200 (løbenr. 12–118). All quotes from Danish are translated by author.
2 There are various ways to translate the Danish "skillingsvise" into English. A direct translation would be "penny ballad"; yet, this does not seem to be in use in English. The Danish ballads were not single sheet-prints, as indicated by the English term "broadside," but were often included in pamphlets with explanatory notes in prose. Hence, the term "penny print" is used here to indicate the pamphlet of both verse and prose.
3 Peter Burke, *A Social History of Knowledge: From Gutenberg to Diderot* (Cambridge, UK: Polity Press, 2013), 149–150.
4 Jack W. Chen et al., "Introduction for a History of Literary Information in China," in *Literary Information in China: A History*, ed. Jack W. Chen et al. (New York: Columbia University Press, 2021), xxiii–xxv.
5 Will Slauter, "Periodicals and the Commercialization of Information in the Early Modern Era," in *Information: A Historical Companion*, ed. Ann Blair et al. (Princeton, NJ: Princeton University Press, 2021), 128–152, 128; italics added by author; Burke, *A Social History*, 176.
6 Anthony Grafton, "Premodern Regimes and Practices," in *Information: A Historical Companion*, ed. Ann Blair et al. (Princeton, NJ: Princeton University Press, 2021), 3–21.
7 Slauter, "Periodicals and the Commercialization of Information." See also Burke, *A Social History*.
8 Burke, *A Social History*, 150.
9 Paul M. Dover, *The Information Revolution in Early Modern Europe: New Approaches to European History* (Cambridge, UK: Cambridge University Press, 2021), 11; Andrew Pettegree, *The Invention of News: How the World Came to Know about Itself* (New Haven, CT: Yale University Press, 2014), 2.
10 Olesen-Bagneux Ole, "Alexandria og Internettet: En Undersøgelse af Bibliotekets to Dimensioner" (PhD diss., Københavns Universitet, 2015), 39–40.
11 Andreas Marklund, *Overvågningens Historie: Fra Sorte Kabinetter til Digital Masseovervågning* (København: Gads Forlag, 2020), 34ff.
12 Grafton, "Premodern Regimes." See also Alistair Black and Dan Schiller, "Systems of Information: The Long View," *Library Trends* 62, no. 3 (2014): 628–662.
13 Elaine Leong and Alisha Michelle Rankin, *Secrets and Knowledge in Medicine and Science, 1500–1800: The History of Medicine in Context* (Burlington, VT: Ashgate, 2011), 8.
14 Heidi J. S. Tworek, *News from Germany: The Competition to Control World Communications, 1900–1945*, Harvard Historical Studies (Cambridge, MA: Harvard University Press, 2019), 190; Pettegree, *The Invention of News*; Joop W. Koopman, ed., *News and Politics of Early Modern Europe (1500–1800)* (Leuven: Peeters, 2005).
15 Brendan Dooley, "Introduction," in *The Dissemination of News and the Emergence of Contemporaneity in Early Modern Europe*, ed. Brendan Dooley (London: Ashgate, 2010), 1–19, 18.
16 Paul Goring, "A Network of Networks: Spreading the News in an Expanding World of Information," in *Travelling Chronicles: News and Newspapers from the Early Modern Period to the Eighteenth Century*, ed. Siv Gøril Brandtzæg, Paul Goring, and Christine Watson, Library of the Written Word - The Handpress World (Leiden: Koninklijke Brill NV, 2018), 3–23, 8.
17 Tworek, *News from Germany*, 141–169. See also Goring, "A Network of Networks," 14–15.
18 Bjarne Markussen, "Skillingsviser om Død og Sorg," in *Skillingsvisene i Norge 1550–1950: Studier i en Forsømt Kulturarv*, ed. Siv Gøril Brandtzæg and Karin Strand (Oslo: Scandinavian Academic Press, 2021), 95–145; Sarah Dahle Hermanstad, "Menneskets Møte med Overmakten: Skillingsviser om Forlis i Norge på 1800-Tallet," in Brandtzæg and Strand, *Skillingsvisene i Norge 1550–1950*, 145–183.
19 Filippo de Vivo, "Microhistories of Long-Distance Information: Space, Movement and Agency in the Early Modern News," *Past and Present* 14 (2019): 179–214.
20 Filippo de Vivo, *Information and Communication in Venice: Rethinking Early Modern Politics* (Oxford: Oxford University Press, 2007), 89–94.
21 Mario Infelise, "News Network between Italy and Europe," in *The Dissemination of News and the Emergence of Contemporaneity in Early Modern Europe*, ed. Brendan Dooley (London: Ashgate, 2010), 51–67, 53.

22 Jürgen Habermas, *Strukturwandel der Öffentlichkeit: Untersuchungen zu Einer Kategorie der Bürgerlichen Gesellschaft* (Frankfurt am Main: Suhrkamp Taschenbuch, 1990).
23 De Vivo, "Microhistories."
24 Laura Skouvig, "Genres of War: Informing a City," in *Genre Theory in Information Studies*, ed. Jack Andersen (Bingley: Emerald Group Publishing Limited, 2015), 133–154, 139; Jørgen Mührmann-Lund, "Private News: Private Letters as a Source of News in Eighteenth-Century Copenhagen Newspapers," in *Private/Public in 18th-Century Scandinavia*, ed. Sari Naumann and Helle Vogt, Cultures of Early Modern Europe (London: Bloomsbury Academic, 2021), 87–88.
25 Robert Darnton, *Poetry and the Police: Communication Networks in Eighteenth-Century Paris* (Cambridge, MA: Harvard University Press, 2010), 13.
26 Henrik Horstbøll, Frederik Stjernfelt, and Ulrik Langen, *Grov Konfækt: Tre Vilde År med Trykkefrihed 1770–1773* (København: Gyldendal, 2020), 2:416; see also Ellen Krefting, Aina Nøding, and Mona Renate Ringvej, *En Pokkers Skrivesyge: 1700-Tallets Dansk-Norske Tidsskrifter mellom Sensur og Ytringsfrihet* (Oslo: Scandinavian Academic Press, 2014). Jakob Malik argues for the existence of a much longer history of the public sphere in Denmark-Norway; see Jakob Maliks, "Vilkår for Offentlighet: Sensur, Økonomi og Transformasjonen av det Offentlige Rom i Danmark-Norge 1730–1770" (PhD diss., Norges teknisk-naturvitenskapelige universitet, 2011).
27 Horstbøll, Stjernfelt, and Langen, *Grov Konfækt*, 2:73.
28 Horstbøll, Stjernfelt, and Langen, *Grov Konfækt*, 2:73.
29 Horstbøll, Stjernfelt, and Langen, *Grov Konfækt*, 2:74
30 Horstbøll, Stjernfelt, and Langen, *Grov Konfækt*, 2:74.
31 Horstbøll, Stjernfelt, and Langen, *Grov Konfækt*, 2:74.
32 Zsuzsa Barbarics-Hermanik, "Handwritten Newsletters as Interregional Information Sources in Central and Southeastern Europe," in *The Dissemination of News and the Emergence of Contemporaneity in Early Modern Europe*, ed. Brendan Dooley (London: Routledge, 2010), 155–178, 176.
33 Michael Mendle, "News and the Pamphlet Culture of Mid-Seventeenth-Century England," in *The Politics of Information in Early Modern Europe*, ed. Brendan Dooley and Sabrina Alcorn Baron (London: Routledge, 2001), 57–79, 58.
34 De Vivo, "Microhistories."
35 Goring, "A Network of Networks," 7.
36 Ruth Andersen, "Bogtrykker Matthias Seest og Hans Produktion især af Skillingsviser," *Fund og Forskning i det Kongelige Biblioteks Samlinger* 33 (1994): 116.
37 Jacob Soll, *The Information Master: Jean-Baptiste Colbert's Secret State Intelligence System* (Ann Arbor, MI: University of Michigan Press, 2009); De Vivo, *Information and Communication*.
38 Krefting, Nøding, and Ringvei, *En Pokkers Skrivesyge*.
39 Ulrik Langen, "Reportage, Rumours, and Conversation: Curating News during Political Upheaval in Eighteenth Century Copenhagen," *Media History* 29, no. 2 (2022): 149–162, 2.
40 The repeal of censorship rules in 1770 was initiated by J.F. Struensee (1737–1772), the Cabinet Secretary of King Christian VII. Struensee had used the illness of the king to gain powers to rule and was removed from power in 1772. The new rulers soon tightened the meshes of public debate with sharper control over the freedom of the press (October 1772). Following the coup of 1784, where the crown prince claimed power, he allowed a moderate liberal tone of the press as long as it was in his favour. Growing suspicions and fears of revolutions led to the euphemistically named "Trykkefrihedsforordning" (Freedom of the Press) in 1799 that, despite its name, in practice strictly defined what themes were legitimate to write about, to publish, and to print.
41 "Placat Angaaende Forbud mod Rygters Indførelse i Offentlige Tidender og Falholdelse af Viser, Bøger, Almanakker m.v. ved Udraab paa Gaden," in *Kong Christian den Syvendes Allernådigste Forordninger og åbne Breve for 1805* (Copenhagen: Johan Frederik Schultz).
42 Mührmann-Lund, "Private News."
43 Black and Schiller, "Systems of Information." See also Daniel R. Headrick, *When Information Came of Age: Technologies of Knowledge in the Age of Reason and Revolution, 1700–1850* (New York: Oxford University Press, 2000).
44 Paul Ries, "The Politics of Information in Seventeenth-Century Denmark," in *The Politics of Information in Early Modern Europe*, ed. Brendan Dooley and Sabrina A. Baron (London; New York: Routledge, 2001), 237–272, 247. Also Mendle, "News and the Pamphlet Culture."

45 Goring, "A Network of Networks"; Andersen, "Bogtrykker Matthias Seest," 105.
46 Dover, *The Information Revolution*, 17.
47 Siv Gøril Brandtzæg, "Dommedag og Skøyteløp. Skillingstrykk som Kulturarv og Studieobjekt," in *Skillingsvisene i Norge 1550–1950: Studier i en Forsømt Kulturarv*, ed. Siv Gøril Brandtzæg and Karin Strand (Oslo: SAP Scandinavian Academic Press, 2021), 9–47.
48 Robert Darnton argues for the existence of an information network in Paris with the circulation of snippets of information and handwritten libelous verses; see Darnton, *Poetry and the Police*, 11.
49 Una McIlvenna, *Singing the News of Death: Execution Ballads in Europe 1500–1900* (Oxford: Oxford University Press, 2022), 12–13.
50 Brandtzæg, "Dommedag og Skøyteløp," 23–24, 9.
51 Angela McShane Jones, "The Gazet in Metre; or the Rhiming Newsmonger: The English Broadside Ballad as Intelligencer. A New Narrative," in *News and Politics in Early Modern Europe (1500–1800)*, ed. Joop W. Koopmans (Leuven: Peeters, 2005), 131–151.
52 Brandtzæg, "Dommedag og Skøyteløp," 38.
53 Jones, "The Gazet in Metre," 131.
54 Brandtzæg, "Dommedag og Skøyteløp," 13–15; Jones, "The Gazet in Metre," 142.
55 Laura Skouvig, "Technik der Aufklärung: Die Vermittlung von Information im Dänischen 'Almanak' 1782–1842," in *Volksbildung durch Lesestoffe im 18. und 19. Jahrhundert: Voraussetzungen, Medien, Topographie*, ed. Reinhart Siegert, Peter Hoare, and Peter Vodosek (Bremen: edition lumiére, 2012), 223–240, 226.
56 Kristin Asdal et al., *Tekst og Historie: å Lese Tekster Historisk* (Oslo: Universitetsforlaget, 2008), 193-194.
57 Carolyn R. Miller, "Genre as Social Action," *The Quarterly Journal of Speech* 70, no. 2 (1984): 151–167.
58 Charles Bazerman, Joseph Little, and Teri Chavkin, "The Production of Information for Genred Activity Spaces: Informational Motives and Consequences of the Environmental Impact Statement," *Written Communication* 20, no. 4 (2003): 455–477.
59 Charles Bazerman, "The Orders of Documents, the Orders of Activity, and the Orders of Information," *Archival Science* 12, no. 4 (2012): 377–388.
60 Brandtzæg, "Dommedag og Skøyteløp," 16.
61 Iørn Piø, *Produktionen af Danske Skillingsviser mellem 1770 og 1821 og Samtidens Syn på Genren* (København: Institut for Folkemindevidenskab, 1969), 48–55.
62 Piø, *Produktionen af Danske Skillingsviser*, 48–49.
63 Jack Andersen and Sille Obelitz Søe, "Communicative Actions We Live by: The Problem with Fact-Checking, Tagging or Flagging Fake News – the Case of Facebook," *European Journal of Communication* 35, no. 2 (2020): 126–139.
64 The quotation comes from a ballad that was confiscated by the police. National Archive: DC-013. Københavns Politiret, 1. Protokol 1791–1814. Behandlede Sager ved 1. Protokol 1808, 101–200 (løbenr. 12–128), file 158/657.
65 Ole Feldbæk, *Den Lange Fred, 1700–1800*, ed. Olaf Olsen, vol. 9, Gyldendal og Politikens Danmarkshistorie (København: Gyldendal, 1990), 235.
66 Ole Feldbæk, *Tiden 1730–1814*, ed. Aksel E. Christensen et al., vol. 4, Danmarks Historie (København: Gyldendal, 1982), 284–285.
67 Jens Engberg, *Den Standhaftige Tinsoldat: En Biografi om Frederik 6* (København: Politiken, 2009).
68 Rasmus Glenthøj, *Skilsmissen: Dansk og Norsk Identitet før og efter 1814* (Odense: Syddansk Universitetsforlag, 2012), 79; Engberg, *Den Standhaftige Tinsoldat*.
69 Glenthøj, *Skilsmissen*, 68.
70 Skouvig, "Genres of War," 148.
71 The author has previously discussed street ballads and information networks of this period; see Laura Skouvig, "Produktivitet og Moral: Almanakkens Anmærkninger og Skillingsviser omkring 1800," *Fund og Forskning i det Kongelige Biblioteks Samlinger* 51 (2015): 337–365. See also Skouvig, "Genres of War."
72 Glenthøj, *Skilsmissen*, 65–67.
73 Andersen, "Bogtrykker Matthias Seest," 107; Bordings Skillingsvisesamling DA-småtryk 8°, The Royal Library, Copenhagen.

74 Krigssange o. Lign, Collection of Pamphlets, The Royal Library, Copenhagen. The exact issue was from 1801, no. 27. *Handels- og Industrie-Tidende* was published between 1782 and 1841 by the Royal Department of Commerce (Det kongelige Land-Oekonomie og Commerce-Collegium), whereas the *Collegial-Tidende* was published by civil servants of the Royal Chancellery.
75 *Handels- og Industrie-Tidende*, 1801, 117.
76 J.C. Brestrup, Samtale imellem Admiralerne Parker og Nelson ombord paa Skibet London den 4de April (København: Matthias Seest, 1801); Sange om 2. April, Collection of Pamphlets, The Royal Library, Copenhagen: Sange om 2. April (37–122); C. A. Borgen, Samtale mellem Bonde og en Borger om Slaget den 2den April, den Engelske Admiral Nelsons Landbesøg og hvad mere Dagens Historie kunde give Anledning til (København: Matthias Seest, 1801); and Krigssange o. Lign, Collection of Pamphlets, The Royal Library, Copenhagen.
77 Brestrup, Samtale imellem Admiralerne.
78 Glenthøj, *Skilsmissen*, 28.
79 Skouvig, "Genres of War."
80 National Archive: DC-013. Københavns Politiret, 1. Protokol 1791–1814. Behandlede Sager ved 1. Protokol 1807 (løbenr. 12–118), file 137/557; National Archive: DC-013. Københavns Politiret, 1. Protokol 1791–1814. Behandlede Sager ved 1. Protokol 1807 (løbenr. 12–124), file 824/3756.
81 National Archive: DC-013. Københavns Politiret, 4. Protokol 1801–1805. Behandlede Sager ved 4. Protokol 1807, August–December, Pådømte (løbenr. 34–57), file 942/4309.
82 National Archive: DC-013. Københavns Politiret, 4. Protokol 1801–1805. Behandlede Sager ved 4. Protokol 1807, August–December, Pådømte (løbenr. 34–57), file 938/4293.
83 National Archive: DC-013. Københavns Politiret, 4. Protokol 1801–1805. Behandlede Sager ved 4. Protokol 1807, August–December, Pådømte (løbenr. 34–57), file 938/4293.
84 Ulrik Langen, *Den Afmægtige: En Biografi om Christian 7* (København: Jyllands-Posten, 2008), 17.

30
HOW INFORMATION CHANGED BETWEEN THE LATE NINETEENTH CENTURY AND WORLD WAR II

James W. Cortada

Historians are in almost universal agreement that more changed in the human condition since the mid-nineteenth century than in any earlier historical period.[1] Economic historians have long defined the Second Industrial Revolution as beginning in the 1840s or 1850s, with many advocating for the 1870s, and most extending to World War I, or more broadly to at least the end of World War II. Others, including the author, wonder if the "Third" or "Fourth" Industrial Revolutions are so new as to warrant distinguishing these years as different from the "Second." Economists, cultural anthropologists, demographers, sociologists, and others have joined historians in recognising that much transformed in the humanities and social sciences.[2] Increasingly, the 1880s to the early days of World War II proved seminal, creating new practices, behaviours, social structures, institutions, and attitudes that continued to evolve in the post war period.[3] It would be difficult to exaggerate how much the world changed; transforming from a largely agricultural economy and rural society to a more industrialised urban one. The Second Industrial Revolution was an economic and social phenomenon located in the Northern Hemisphere around the world, from England across Europe through western Russia, parts of China and, of course, Japan and North America. One of the fundamental causes of these transitions was the emergence and use of new bodies of information.[4]

While why and how all that occurred remains the subject of much debate, it has become increasingly obvious that underpinning these activities has been a new and growing collective body of information that included economics, business, public administration, and myriad academic disciplines. The results were dramatic: approximately 1.5 billion people lived in 1900 but, by 1950, that population had grown to 2.5 billion—the fastest growth in human population in recorded history up to that time.[5] Measured by national economic output per capita, in the most advanced economies, it hovered at just over $1,400 in 1860, but climbed to over $5,200 in 1950—over three-fold in barely a century. Even poor economies were swept along from $768 to $945.[6] Average lifespans in Europe rose from thirty-three to forty-five years in the 1800s, in the Americas thirty-five to forty-one; averaging around forty by 1900. By 1950, the average on both sides of the Atlantic had jumped to around sixty years and to the present of over seventy-two years; in that near century once again almost doubling. To put these estimates into some perspective, just in England, where the First Industrial Revolution kicked off the great transformations of modern times in the mid-1700s, life expectancies ranged from twenty-five to forty years, but were closer to twenty-seven to thirty in continental Europe in the late 1700s to the early decades of the 1800s.[7] Information was one ingredient in the changes that occurred in the human condition.

To make all this possible, fundamental transformations occurred quickly based on the application of new information—much of it scientific and technological—resulting in new jobs, industries, and products. These included innovations in steel, chemicals, electricity, transportation (ships, trains, automobiles, aircraft), manufacturing of all types, agriculture and food processing, human welfare, hygiene, medical practices, lethal weapons (machine guns), and water purification, among others. All were made possible by the discovery, production, and then application of new information. The pace and activities involved took time, operated at different paces depending on what industry, technology, or scientific process was involved, but occurred in an evolutionary manner as new data and insights became available. Because economic and business historians have studied the use of new information to shape the Second Industrial Revolution, we will dispense with a lengthy rehearsal of their ideas. The key thought offered here is that the evolution of industries and society using information were the consequence of an information ecosystem which enveloped economies experiencing this industrial revolution. Six features of the role of information characterise, and help, the information ecosystem that proved so crucial to the shaping of the Second Industrial Revolution.[8]

Depending on one's discipline—or perspective—information can fall under a general heading of data, facts, knowledge, wisdom, and so forth.[9] Regardless of the definitions one might posit, humanity collected, organised, and used new and ever-larger collections of information, which escalated rapidly in the nineteenth century. That recognition is one of the fundamental rationales for this *Handbook*.

As academic disciplines formed (themselves components of the new information ecosystem and pillars of the new industrial revolution), and about which more is said below, new perspectives emerged to help describe this information and its features.[10] For example, historians linked economic and business transformation, and creation of large corporations and "big government," to humanity's ability to collect, communicate, and use information in greater and more diverse forms than in prior centuries. Cultural anthropologists showed how to view information as comprising ecosystems of their own on which people depend, while the telecommunications experts and computer scientists saw these as information infrastructures that permitted the movement—flow—of information among individuals and their institutions.[11] Biologists are now pointing out that humans do not have a monopoly on information and its use; that animals, fauna, even entire planets, have it too, and have been at the business of collecting and applying information for a longer time than residents of the Second Industrial Revolution. As one scholar of this process has put it: "Cognition and information are intimately entwined."[12] So, students of information have much to learn from many disciplines. One can build a strong case that looking at the variety of information that exists and how it is used is more effectively understood as part of an integrated reality—what I refer to as information ecosystems—that makes increasingly good sense as scholars borrow frameworks, theories, and empirical findings from each other.[13]

This chapter argues that the emergence and use of such a massive increase in information since the mid- to late 1800s was due to six forces at work that continue to affect the role of information today. But a caveat is in order: historians recognise that all human civilisations relied on information with which to function. Paul M. Dover has used language in his study of the role of information in the centuries following the end of the Middle Ages that one might read about our times: "The early modern Information Revolution forced people and institutions to generate new taxonomies in which to slot the abundance of information."[14] His era of interest, too, has an underlying new fundamental technology: paper supported later by printing. Today, our underlying technology is digital in the form of computers, telecommunications, and the internet. Biologists would add that one should understand that above all activities in any historic period were the actions of chromosomes in our DNA and in all living creatures and chemically based communications in fauna.[15] Research on the emergence and use of information today by humans indicates that six forces were simultaneously—and continuously—at work. They are better understood as elements of the crucial information ecosystem that provided an umbrella over the entire Second Industrial Revolution. This is so much the case that to understand today's "Information Age" dialogue one will need to keep such an ecosystem in mind, if for no other reason than historians may increasingly view the evolution of societies and cultural norms through the lens of information ecosystems.[16]

The list of six is, admittedly, biased by your author's positivist view of information and decades of working in the world of computing. One could argue that over time, this list of six can be countered by the increased availability of less structured, less organised information now available to anyone using such tools as Google. That reality is compounded, too, by the increased availability of oral forms, such as mediated by YouTube and the ongoing access to content through television and radio.

The List of Six: Modern Information Ecosystems and Their Infrastructures

Information in the Second Industrial Revolution changed in part because of the emergence of new, or more complicated, nuanced information ecosystems and their infrastructures. The notion of people living in an information ecosystem has circulated for decades under the guise of different names extracted from the terminology of various disciplines. The essential concept is simple to conjure by using the metaphor of a jungle. Bugs, animals, trees, and other fauna all live at the same time in a jungle—an environment also affected by the availability of water and, of course, the weather. Every living resident learns about how to survive, thrive, and adapt to changes in that ecosystem; their jungle. Their work is about understanding what is happening, that is to say, collecting and processing information needed to make decisions. An information infrastructure is that which supports these activities, such as having trees in which some mammals and birds can live and find food, bugs, and worms needing rich soil with nutrients and sources of protection, and so forth. These decisions govern how well they eat, procreate, and avoid becoming some other resident's dinner. Societies, information within communities, even whole continents, can be understood as information ecosystems for people.[17]

Because ecosystems require inclusion of all components—think, members or participants—in order to sustain life and activity, by inference and later due to *de facto* realities, so too scholars studying information from most academic disciplines have to take into account the thinking of colleagues outside their own home disciplines. Sociologists, economists, cultural anthropologists, political scientists, and librarians may have been the first to think in terms of ecosystems, but by the end of the twentieth century, others did too; in the hard and social sciences, history, and today in such humanities as comparative literature, languages, and communications arts.[18] As one team commenting about such late arrivals to the notion that information plays a pervasive role in all human activity put it, "there is no place for the human outside or beyond information. There is no human without information."[19] That is about as affirmative a blunt comment as one can find endorsing the underlying idea of an information ecosystem. The debate, then, is about how that jungle operates, its features, and so forth, a dialogue reinforced by research findings and how various disciplines shape discussion. Much of what the debates look like has been explained elsewhere, but what is important to point out is that these emerged out of massive increases in information created and identified by the activities of the Second Industrial Revolution. Recognition of information's role came out from behind the shadows of academic discourse into public view, which is largely why so many commentators and public leaders could use such phrases as the "Information Highway" or "Information Society."[20]

While information systems have existed since before the dawn of civilisations, and more contemporaneously with the arrival of the Second Industrial Revolution, historians have only recently begun to describe these environments. They are learning a great deal. Features of such ecosystems and their infrastructures are worth calling out. The list can be criticised as too short, but it is a start.

First, that information ecosystems exist only if they have supporting infrastructures. Whether scholars use these two terms or not, their case studies include descriptions of the realities surrounding what information people use, how they do so, and what means they rely upon. Thus, priests needed monasteries; professors, university libraries; large corporations, research laboratories; the military, training academies; public schools, libraries and newspaper, and book publishers. Today it seems most people in all walks of life rely on Google, Amazon, and Apple products, their producers, and electronic networks (such as the internet). During the Second Industrial Revolution many new infrastructures emerged: telegraph and telephone networks, fast moving steam ships and trains, academic societies, expanded school systems and universities, and scholarly societies complete with their publishing outlets, most important of which for many disciplines were discipline-specific, peer-reviewed journals.

Second, that combined, ecosystems and infrastructures can be seen almost as an x-ray of society. As sociologists and scholars in the humanities and social sciences point out, all features of a society hang on the flesh of ecosystems and the bones of infrastructures.[21] Physics and biology add to the growing embrace of ecosystems; their components are integral and essential for understanding the world as it is and how it functions.[22] One can think of these as building blocks of society. The hard sciences did this first, by identifying and then studying atoms in physics and cells in biology, and social scientists seeking similar components of society, beginning largely in the late 1800s.[23] The diversity and number of professions that emerged for the first time in the past two centuries, along with the organisations that funded these jobs, included new government agencies (such as economic data collection bureaus) and technology-dependent corporations (for example in steel, pharmaceuticals, chemistry, and office appliances). These became the major components of modern society.[24]

Third, that labels used to describe the nature and role of information carry within them embedded meanings and implications. To say indigenous people live in the Brazilian jungle is also to say that the local residents know a great deal about how to thrive there, even before the cultural anthropologist spends chapters or entire books explaining that indigenous information.[25] So, words and cultural contexts serve as shorthand collections of information, too, known to experts within a field, such as in the language and understandings common to economists, or to sociologists. However, because of the inclusionary nature of the concept of information ecosystems in modern times, scholars are learning how others in different disciplines view information. This goes far to explain, for example, why multidisciplinary publications are appearing at a rapid pace, including the volume in which this chapter appears.[26] Over the course of the late 1800s, and extending to the start of World War II, many communities of specialised experts emerged who, by dint of their interests and needs, developed their own set of concepts, theories, and frameworks as intellectual infrastructures. These were buttressed with such other components as societies, academic departments, and specialised journals. Consequently, they developed highly specialised descriptors—think language—which became difficult for those not part of their ecosystems to understand. By the end of the twentieth century, students of information were having to cross over boundaries of well-established groups of experts to benefit from the latter's findings, such as happens now with political scientists and historians learning enough economics to understand what economic historians are discovering.[27] That process had been less necessary prior to the mid-1800s, because so few subgroups of experts existed, but that has all changed.

Fourth, that features of information infrastructures are being described in more eclectic ways than in prior decades. There was a time, for example, when scholars might write about books, libraries, and archives as discrete topics. Or about the history of technologies such as the telegraph, telephone, radio, movies, television, and, most recently, computers and then the internet, all as if separate topics with little or no relation to each other. Today, one must account for the interactions of one with another, because enough crossover appreciation about information learned from one discipline to another set the expectation that the next wave of understanding was expected to include findings from multiple disciplines.[28] Tapping into multiple disciplines to discuss what otherwise might have been discrete topics apart from each other increased after World War II. For example, when studying the information infrastructure of nineteenth-century diplomats or American farm wives of the late twentieth century, we learn that both depended on information infrastructures that included postal systems, newsletters, written notes shared with one another, manuals, and cookbooks written and published for local use; spaces in which information could be collected, stored, and used, from embassy offices to school and church buildings.[29] During the Second Industrial Revolution other components became essential, among which were the use of electricity (in the home, office, manufacturing facility, in telecommunications) and transportation (new and more roads, automobiles and trucks, aeroplanes). These were worldwide developments. The activities considered here are those so evident in the daily lives of people living through the Second Industrial Revolution, made even more evident as they became what later came to be known as the jobs of "knowledge workers."[30]

Fifth, that both ecosystems and their infrastructures are often unseen until uncovered. It began with sociologists, economists, and historians pointing out what humans could see with the naked eye. Then, with the use of ever-more effective microscopes, germs, later DNA and chromosomes, and, most recently, telescopes probing deeply into space.[31] We now know that animals have information and communicate with each other; physicists argue that even non-living objects do too (such as rocks, entire planets, or solar systems). Notions of *systems*—recognition that processes, bodies of relevant information for such processes, and recognition of a larger cohort of participants all interacting with one another—have been around for centuries. But those that argue that information interacts with many things made the idea of systems more appealing to scholars over the past half-century as a way to uncover new insights. With extensive appropriation of that notion came new possibilities. For example, in computing, multiple specialised machines could collaborate to collect, process, and display results when they were caused to work together as systems, leading to the invention of necessary collaborative tools called software.[32] Physicists spent the past half-century breaking down into ever-more finite components what makes up the physical universe. They identified ever-smaller units of information, often simply called data or facts. It is not clear yet if they have identified the smallest possible sized objects, or units of information, let alone how they work. So, while televised documentaries show bugs on a full screen, or tiny plants in sped-up motion going about their business, there may yet be organised substrata of ecosystems and infrastructures still to be identified.[33] Here is yet another example of how technologies in one discipline affect knowledge in another, computing affecting photography, which, in turn, influences the biologist's appreciation of reality. One can begin reading that the universe is composed of matter, energy, and now information; before World War II, it was just energy and matter.[34] But the key observation is that the creation of information ecosystems over the past two centuries made it possible for entire specialties to collaborate and appropriate from each other their own findings and insights.

Sixth, that standardising on a few widely used common languages facilitated the communication of information. Such standardisation was normal practice for centuries: in Europe, Greek was used before the Roman Empire; Latin right through the Middle Ages; French and German in the Early Modern Period; then beginning at the end of the 1800s, and clearly by the start of World War II, English.[35] The latter became the language of choice worldwide among scholars, with German and French to a lesser extent. By the end of the twentieth century, English dominated overwhelmingly. Extant scholarship on the dominance of English can be largely explained by the massive infusion of research and publications by the English in the 1800s, more so by North Americans after World War II. The latter could most afford the costs of research and infrastructures among the wealthiest economies, both economic and academic.[36] German and French speaking academics bent to the reality that the key journals, publishers, and markets for their work had to be presented in English. Today, it is expected that students of any type of information must have a working knowledge of English, whereas in the early 1800s, German, French, or Italian were more essential than perhaps even English.[37] Other forms of standardisation became important during the Second Industrial Revolution and that spilled over into information ecosystems, such as in the manner in which information was uncovered, created, and presented.[38]

Thus, a major change in modern information involves viewing the subject as both discrete bodies of facts and as an integrative whole. The amount of it increased dramatically, so too its increased flow through entire societies. These observations become more obvious when one looks at how people organised these ever growing bodies of information.

Organisation of the New Information

The ability for people to create, and use, ever-larger quantities of new information became possible through its organisation into topics with the typologies and catalogues, academic disciplines, professions, and infrastructures needed to support it. New academic disciplines (and sub-disciplines within these), professions and industries created bodies of information that had not existed previously, such as how to make steel or cure a disease. In every period from the Ancient Greeks to the present, people complained that there was too much information to consult to get things done or to be understood. Historians have documented these complaints for centuries.[39] In the nineteenth and twentieth centuries, neuroscientists, biologists, and later brain experts and sociologists, worked to explain the human mind's need to organise information, most notably in recent decades by those studying how the brain works, and how people deal with its assimilation.[40] What they came to was the idea that one cannot remember everything that they need to know, that is to say, memorisation is a limited tool and humans are not very good at using it. What we think we know keeps changing.[41] Writing things down on clay tablets, later parchment, then on paper and in books and journals, helped enormously, but by the mid-1800s, were themselves too voluminous, and so needed further organisation. Librarians led the way in the 1800s and became crucial, indeed powerful, in organising information from the mid-1800s to the late 1900s, or at least until computer scientists could develop such tools as databases, search engines, and the mighty Google.

An early initiative in response to the growing variety and volume of new information were innovative cataloguing systems that made it easier and more practical for people to access information, that were implemented broadly and quickly, and that mapped topics that made sense to users of information in the late 1800s. For most Americans, the Dewey Decimal Classification system was, and continues to be, the most familiar, followed by the Library of Congress Classification system now used by most large libraries around the world in one form or another. This was a precursor to computerised Google-like system called the Universal Decimal Classification developed in Europe in the early twentieth century.[42] The Dewey system divided all information into ten categories: general works, philosophy, religion, social sciences, language, pure science, technology, arts, literature, and history. These could then be subdivided, such as within science into mathematics, algebra, and so forth. The Library of Congress system, introduced at the start of the twentieth century, was even designed to include additional topics, including more categories for science and engineering subfields, because of the enormous growth in the variety and quantity of new information appearing about them. It also recognised the concept of information in hierarches of relationships to each other. This system continues to evolve today to reflect still emerging new collections of information.

The least deployed, but perhaps the most interesting to library historians, is the Universal Decimal Classification system, because it spawned what came to be known as the Documentation Movement in Europe. It was an attempt to create a universal encyclopaedia, rather than simply a catalogue of publications, diving deeper into these to provide the actual information stored on cards. Think paper-based Google.[43] This third cataloguing initiative demonstrated that information could be located via bibliographic means and that information about information could be collected and used; concepts that in the era of computers became central to the development of databases and search engines.

Bibliographies published between the late 1800s and the present also appeared by subject (best literature, on books and articles dealing with history, specific subfields of science, and so forth). Perhaps the most important one focusing on scientific literature was that published by the Royal Society of London, *The International Catalogue of Scientific Literature,* which appeared between 1902 and 1914. It highlighted the importance of scientific papers as crucial to the presentation and acceptance of new scientific findings underway by the late 1800s.[44]

A second infrastructure feature of information was the emergence of many new academic disciplines that included professors at colleges and universities (later also researchers working in government and large commercial enterprises), national and international associations dedicated to the development, promotion, and communication of specialised bodies of information. Their institutions promoted codification of research practices, accepted canons of beliefs, typologies, and theories, including acceptance and use of theories with which to apply scientific methods of research and presentation of findings. They published what came to be known as "journals of record," in which creators and discoverers of new information presented their findings in articles vetted by peers, which, in turn, were accepted as factual by the rest of their discipline-centric community. It would be difficult to exaggerate the importance of information disciplines and their institutions. They came into existence in embryonic forms in the Early Modern Period (1600s–1700s), largely as royal societies, with the British and French leading the way, but in evidence all over Europe. In the last half of the nineteenth century, and extending down to the present, it seemed that every category of information (such as the Dewey categories) created their own associations, often with such names as, for instance, the American Historical Association (founded 1884).[45]

Even subfields did this, beginning in the early 1900s. With history, for example, societies devoted to specific national historical investigations in Great Britain, France, economic history, social history (the French *Annals*, although a journal, in 1929, instead of an association), among others. The American Medical Association (founded in 1847 but professionalising late in the century) became instrumental in reforming the appalling American medical profession of pre-Civil War United States into what became a disciplined, structured profession, based on scientific medical practices by the 1920s. Similar developments occurred in all other industrialised countries. By the start of World War II, professors and other researchers were expected to (a) conduct empirically based research in their discipline, (b) write up their results in a standardised way published in respected journals and by reputable book publishers, and (c) be studied by professors, professionals (engineers, medical doctors, and so forth) and applied. Information had, through such processes, become objects, tools that could be trusted.[46]

A parallel development already in evidence during the early 1800s, but that expanded rapidly beginning in the last three decades of the nineteenth century, was the emergence of new professions based on new bodies of information. Examples included electricians, plumbers, cost accounting accountants, business managers, chemists working in German chemical companies, agricultural scientists, professional corporate managers, cancer experts, automotive mechanics, aeroplane aeronautical engineers and pilots, and manufacturing process consultants. Still others included office clerical employees and file clerks, data processing staffs, industrial researchers who invented light bulbs in Europe and the United States, nylon stockings, dyes, hundreds of chemical and pharmaceutical products (largely in Germany), others that developed plate glass manufacturing and steel—the list ran into the many hundreds of new professions. Most were developed by the 1920s and remain familiar today; all were outgrowths of the application of new collections of scientific information and new bodies of information leading to new products and services.[47] These new professions also created their own disciplines and infrastructures paralleling academic ones. Large corporations that sold complex products established their own research laboratories, most famously exemplified by Bell Laboratories in the United States starting in the late 1800s, but expanding as a movement across many industries following the end of World War I. They formed their own associations, codified credentialing processes, launched trade magazines often by industry or topic, and held annual conventions to present their own work and to interact with other vendors and rivals much as the academics did within their own. Some blended the two—academics and professionals, such as the IEEE (Institute of Electrical and

Electronics Engineers)—that became a composite of both specialised communities and associations. Today it has over four hundred thousand members in 160 countries.[48]

While these developments took place in all industrialised countries, before World War I they centred in Western Europe and the United States, but because of the massive devastation to the economies, infrastructures, and societies in Europe resulting from this war, initiatives in their further development shifted to the United States, which had not been damaged by the fighting. In the 1930s, researchers and academics, many that were Jewish, evacuated to Great Britain and the United States, embedding their own work into the local information ecosystems. Albert Einstein is the poster child of that activity, even though he had done his seminal work while living in Europe prior to the 1930s, while others did their most significant after coming to the United States, such as economist Joseph A. Schumpeter and business consultant Peter Drucker. Schumpeter captured the essence of what academics and professionals did to shape information in the twentieth century when he commented in 1939 that:

> Even that amount of information which we have been able to derive so far was as much due to the application of our common-sense understanding of the modus operandi of our facts as it was to the facts themselves. The consequence of this is that we must now try, with a view of acquiring a more powerful apparatus of analysis, to refine upon our common-sense methods exactly as we must try to increase our stock of facts and to improve upon our statistical methods.[49]

All of these activities were core to what occurred during the Second Industrial Revolution and could be more clearly observed as part of the information ecosystem of the day. These also demonstrated that there was not a smooth inevitable march towards new information—although much was new—rather there were bumps on the road, such as wars and economic depressions, but those generated new bodies of information and institutions, such as grater insights into how to deal with battlefield injuries or use of aeroplanes.

Emerging Features of Modern Information

It is an axiom of today's studies about information that discussions are held within the context of their development and use—a socially constructed sociological approach. Thus, to know what are the features of information as they developed between the late 1800s and World War II, one is urged to appreciate the discovery (or creation) of new findings and applied research, and the emergence of new professions, disciplines, and their intellectual infrastructures. Features of information changed a great deal in that sixty- to eighty-year period, and not simply becoming more voluminous, or in that new information, or new uses of it, essentially led to the Second Industrial Revolution and its attendant profound changes in societies. Holding to our metaphor of an ecosystem, features evolved incrementally over time as residents of such an environment responded to changing conditions. It is how information features evolved. The specifics of those incremental changes remain to be uncovered by historians of information, but at least at this time worthy of recognising as a subject for future investigation. Such behaviour is also consistent with how biologists describe the way humans learn about new circumstances and how to respond to these.[50]

While one could argue that features of new collections of information were in evidence in earlier historical periods, they were profoundly evident in use and diffusion in modern societies. Several stand out as essential to not ignore in future discussions of the history of information. Each offered below originated in one form or another prior to the late nineteenth century. What changed is that they were enhanced, used for more diverse purposes, and morphed as new information emerged.

Begin with the acceptance made in this period that information was not some ethereal construct, "just" knowledge, wisdom, or experience. Increasingly, information—facts, data—were seen as objects, as "things."[51] If we are to continue embracing the concept that information is an object: physical, ephemeral, intellectual, or conceptual) it must have features that can be identified and studied. Avatars of information have long been described, notably parchment, paper, books, newspapers, magazines, radio, television, computers, telegraphy, telephones, and most recently, the internet. Since its physical embodiments, too, have a history that evolved, so it was also the evolution of information. Its features from the mid-nineteenth century to World War II did so quickly and massively, suggesting features that solidified in that period before the mid-twentieth century.

Information was still paper-based, if more diverse. New formats included inexpensive paperbacks, newspapers, magazines, and included publications that had photographs and other illustrations. Costs of paper and printing declined all through this period, and became more attractive as ephemera to read. But the key transformation that the variety of physical formats made possible was increased modularity of ever-larger amounts of more specialised information. Thus, scientists could have their own bodies of information presented to them in formats and quantities that they needed, while historians had their own too, accountants and business managers yet their own, and so forth. Because of the expansion of specialised information ecosystems, information within one discipline, for example, could be moved from one format to another, such as from scholarly journal articles to full-length books on the same topic, to lectures at a university and to consulting in business and government. Information could be transported from one discipline to another, as happened in all industrialised countries where government agencies collected demographic and economic data, then made these available across a society. Census reports come to mind as a good example, so too social and economic data used, for instance, in determining public policies regarding education of children and establishing pension programmes.[52]

But perhaps the most obvious transformation in the nature of information was the increased reliance made by many disciplines and professions in using numbers—normally called numeracy—and the language of mathematics with which to apply and understand numeric data. From mid-nineteenth century to World War II, certain disciplines intensified their use of mathematics, notably in physics—think of Albert Einstein and his work, largely mathematical in explaining his general theory of relativity (1905, 1907). Much happened, such as the formal construction of real numbers explained (1872), introduction of partial differential equations (1873), use of Venn diagrams for use in set theory (1881), expanded use of statistics, differential equations, and calculus (1880s–1930s), Henri Poincaré describing algebraic topology (1890s), introduction of Fourier series (1900), probability analysis (1921), and Allen Turing on computable numbers (1936).[53] A similar list could be offered for statistics.[54] To manage the enormous increase in the collection, organisation, analysis, and presentation of numeric data across industrialised societies tables, charts, and graphs were introduced into research, measurements, and presentations of information. Narrative explanations of anything in the 1700s and early 1800s now competed with numbers calculated and presented in new ways by the 1890s.

Mentioned earlier but worth repeating is that as information became more specialised; to understand it required greater appreciation of the context in which it was sheltered

How Information Changed

then used. For example, one needed to know physics and mathematics to understand what Einstein was explaining. Mathematically oriented economists in the 1920s and 1930s could advocate for their way of using numeracy in their field in part because their audiences were already familiar with much basic economics.[55]

Information became more routinely grounded in the development and testing of theories within disciplines. Scientific methods of research, which became universalised across disciplines, led to articulation of hypotheses to be tested, thereby generating new findings and observations, while simultaneously encouraging use of such information to make predictions (as in weather reports or economic possibilities), and all using models of optional scenarios. With the arrival of computers after World War II, these features of information—from hypotheses and theories to predictive models—became major features of modern information handling. A byproduct of that process was that in this era organisations and experts developed, in J. Bradford DeLong's telling, "the systematic invention of how to invent" and that process was about discovering or creating new information.[56]

As these long-term developments happened, even in the years after, say, the 1870s, standardisation of work practices was articulated and enforced in academia, the military, engineering, construction, manufacturing, and large businesses in general, government policies and in law. It is why, for example, Japanese manufacturing or military equipment (such as ships and guns) looked like what the French, British, and Germans used, why consumer products and even fashions mimicked one to the other in multiple industries. The key idea was the use of information to standardise work, the way information was presented, and how it was used.[57] By the 1920s, cooking recipes had been standardised in many countries that continue to use the same format (aka grammar) today, also in the chemical and pharmaceutical industries for the manufacture of industrial chemicals that do not change over time. All of these features of information emerged as part of myriad conditions, such as the desire for control of business practices,[58] discovery of new scientific and medical facts and solutions to problems,[59] and to improve the economic and social quality of life while simultaneously the lethality of the weapons of war (the machine gun by the 1890s or deadly gas during World War I).

As a result of the ecosystems, infrastructures, and disciplines, coupled to the capabilities that made possible changes in the industrialising economies of the world, and alongside improvements in health and safety, as well as the capability of massive losses of human life in wars and pogroms, information changed in form and content.

Conclusions

Information became a highly prized feature of modern society in the decades preceding World War II. As one student of Victorian times put it when commenting on the British experience, people believed, "the best and most certain kind of knowledge was the fact" and it "was thought of as raw knowledge, knowledge awaiting ordering." Users "were desperate for these manageable pieces of knowledge," which "were light and moveable."[60] The types of information and their broad availability profoundly affected the nature of life during the Second Industrial Revolution. Its influence proved so ubiquitous that, beginning in the 1950s, much of the nature and appropriation of information after World War II mimicked that of the prior era, with the exception of much being digitised. But to this day, paper ephemera and the features of information established in the earlier period remain essentially the same. As in earlier centuries, too, the transition of information's forms and uses take generations to evolve. Our contemporary experience is proving to be no exception.

All of this became possible not just because new information became available, but also because that information helped people and extant institutions to expand or be created, in turn, facilitating the development and use of more of it. That process of creating supportive institutions and practices that, consequently, stimulated demand for ever-more information, was the core activities of an information ecosystem. The human behaviour of creating an ecosystem mimicked what living creatures had developed for their survival and success for millions of years. This practice is a reminder that viewing life during the Second Industrial Revolution, and even in our own time, as the activities of information ecosystems is a reasonable approach for understanding an "Information Age."

Notes

1 Economic historians have provided the most specific empirical evidence in support of this observation. For recent examples, see J. Bradford DeLong, *Slouching towards Utopia: An Economic History of the Twentieth Century* (New York: Basic Books, 2022); Robert Gordon, *The Rise and Fall of American Growth: The U.S. Standard of Living since the Civil War* (Princeton, NJ: Princeton University Press, 2016).
2 For a detailed discussion of the literature from multiple disciplines, see James W. Cortada, *The Birth of Modern Facts: How the Information Revolution Transformed Academic Research, Governments and Businesses* (Lanham, MD: Rowman & Littlefield, 2023), 395–400.
3 Gordon, *The Rise and Fall of American Growth*.
4 Peter N. Stearns, ed., *The Industrial Revolution in World History* (New York: Routledge, 2020); Joel Mokyr, *A Culture of Growth: The Origins of the Modern Economy* (Princeton, NJ: Princeton University Press, 2016); Toni Weller, ed., *Information History in the Modern World: Histories of the Information Age* (New York: Palgrave Macmillan, 2011); David S. Landes, *The Unbound Prometheus: Technological Change and Industrial Development in Western Europe from 1750 to the Present* (Cambridge, UK: Cambridge University Press, 1969, 2003).
5 Angus Maddison, *The World Economy: Historical Statistics*, vol. 2 (Paris: OECD, 2008).
6 Paul Bairoch, *Economics and World History: Myths and Paradoxes* (Chicago, IL: University of Chicago Press, 1993), 95.
7 These are estimates due to the quality of the data. However, demographers and economists are in agreement on the general findings that life expectancies increased substantially in the period discussed here.
8 The evidence for this paragraph's comments is described more thoroughly in Cortada, *Birth of Modern Facts*; James W. Cortada, *All the Facts: A History of Information in the United States since 1870* (New York: Oxford University Press, 2016); and James W. Cortada, *The Digital Hand*, 3 vols. (New York: Oxford University Press, 2004–2008).
9 For a detailed discussion of these definitions, see Cortada, *All the Facts*, 1–22.
10 Cortada, *Birth of Modern Facts*.
11 For an extensive discussion of this literature, see Cortada, *Birth of Modern Facts*, 397–421.
12 N. Katherine Hayles, "Cognition," in *Information: Keywords*, ed. Michele Kennerly, Samuel Frederick, and Jonathan E. Abel (New York: Columbia University Press, 2021): quote 72, but see full article, 72–88.
13 This concept is explained in greater detail in James W. Cortada, *Building Blocks of Society: History, Information Ecosystems, and Infrastructures* (Lanham, MD: Rowman & Littlefield, 2021).
14 Paul M. Dover, *The Information Revolution in Early Modern Europe* (Cambridge, UK: Cambridge University Press, 2021), 32.
15 Marcello Barbierdi, ed., *An Introduction to Biosemiotics: The New Biological Synthesis* (Dordrecht: Springer, 2008); Jan Sapp, *Genesis: The Evolution of Biology* (New York: Oxford University Press, 2003).
16 For a discussion of the logic and historiographical sources, see Cortada, *Building Blocks of Society*, 3–32.
17 Cortada, *Building Blocks of Society*, 13–18.

18 Cortada, *Birth of Modern Facts*; Anthony Grafton, *Worlds Made by Words: Scholarship and Community in the Modern West* (Cambridge, MA: Harvard University Press, 2009).
19 Michele Kennerly, Samuel Frederick, and Jonathan E. Abel, "Introduction," in *Information: Keywords*, ed. Kennerly et al. (New York: Columbia University Press, 2021), 7.
20 Cortada, *Birth of Modern Facts*; Cortada, *Building Blocks of Society*.
21 For discussion of this rich literature, see Cortada, *Birth of Modern Facts*.
22 Jim Al-Khalili, *The World According to Physics* (Princeton, NJ: Princeton University Press, 2020); Jon Agar, *Science in the Twentieth Century and Beyond* (Cambridge, UK: Polity Press, 2012); Jan Sapp, *Genesis: The Evolution of Biology* (New York: Oxford University Press, 2003).
23 Two collections of essays open windows into the engagement with information issues in the social sciences and humanities; Eric Hayot, Anatoly Detwyler, and Lea Pao, eds., *Information: A Reader* (New York: Columbia University Press, 2022) and Kennerly et al., *Information: Keywords*.
24 DeLong, *Slouching towards Utopia*, 3–12, 17–19.
25 It all began in modern times with the work of Claude Lévi-Strauss, *The Savage Mind* (London: Trafalgar Square, 1966), but also available in multiple subsequent editions.
26 Hayot et al., *Information: A Reader*; Kennerly et al., *Information: Keywords*; and Ann Blair, Paul Duguid, Anja-Goeing, and Anthony Grafton, eds., *Information: A Historical Companion* (Princeton, NJ: Princeton University Press, 2021).
27 Hans-Dieter Kingermann, ed., *The State of Political Science in Western Europe* (Opladen: Barbara Budrich Publishers, 2007); S. F. Schramm and B. Caterino, eds., *Making Political Science Matter: Debating Knowledge, Research, and Methods* (New York: New York University Press, 2006); David E. McNabb, *Research Methods for Political Science: Quantitative and Qualitative Methods* (Armonk, NY: M.E. Sharpe, 2004).
28 For an example of the more inclusive approach, see Thomas J. Misa, *Leonardo to the Internet: Technology and Culture from the Renaissance to the Present* (Baltimore, MD: Johns Hopkins University Press, 2022).
29 Cortada, *Building Blocks of Society*, 91–180.
30 This perspective came into its own by the end of the 1950s and extended to the present. The first scholar to describe such an information ecosystem emerging over the previous century was Fritz Machlup, *The Production and Distribution of Knowledge in the United States* (Princeton, NJ: Princeton University Press, 1962).
31 The central issue discussed in Cortada, *Birth of Modern Facts*.
32 Thomas Haigh and Paul E. Ceruzzi, *A New History of Modern Computing* (Cambridge, MA: MIT Press, 2021).
33 David Attenborough produced a series of documentaries about the Earth's environment, "David Attenborough," *Wikipedia*, accessed August 12, 2022, https://en.wikipedia.org/wiki/David_Attenborough.
34 Bruce Clarke, "Information," in *Critical Terms for Media Studies*, ed. W. J. T. Mitchell and Mark B. N. Hansen (Chicago, IL: University of Chicago Press, 2020), 131–144.
35 Arabic was the scientific language of choice for centuries during the Early Middle Ages of Europe, while various dialects of Chinese were widely used, but only in the Chinese empires for several millenia.
36 Discussed in greater detail in Cortada, *All the Facts*.
37 Michael D. Gordin, "Introduction: Hegemonic Languages and Science," *ISIS* 108, no. 3 (2017): 606–611.
38 For details as to how this happened during the Second Industrial Revolution and that also describes many of the other features described in our article, see JoAnne Yates and Craig N. Murphy, *Engineering Rules: Global Standard Setting since 1880* (Baltimore, MD: Johns Hopkins University Press, 2019), but see also Yates, *Control through Communication: The Rise of System in American Management* (Baltimore, MD: Johns Hopkins University Press, 1989).
39 For an excellent introduction to the issue, Damien Smith Pfister, "Abundance," in *Information: Keywords*, ed. Kennerly et al., 17–30; Richard Gartner, *Metadata: Shaping Knowledge from Antiquity to the Semantic Web* (Berlin: Springer-Verlag, 2016); now often discussed as "Big Data"; David Bollier, *The Promise and Peril of Big Data* (Washington, DC: Aspen Institute, 2010); an old problem, Ann Blair, *Too Much to Know: Managing Scholarly Information Before the Modern Age* (New Haven, CT: Yale University Press, 2010).

40 Brain studies are the most recent wave of new research, Bob Garrett and Gerald Hough, *Brain & Behavior: An Introduction to Behavioral Neuroscience*, 5th ed. (Thousand Oaks, CA: SAGE, 2018); Steven Sloman and Philip Fernbach, *The Knowledge Illusion: Why We Never Think Alone* (New York: Riverhead/Penguin, 2017); Howard Gardner, *Multiple Intelligences* (New York: Basic Books, 1993, 2006) and *Frames of Mind: The Theory of Multiple Intelligences* (New York: Basic Books, 1983, 2004, 2001).

41 Rudiger F. Pohl, *Cognitive Illusions: A Handbook on Fallacies and Biases in Thinking, Judgement and Memory* (Hove, UK: Psychology Press, 2005) and the very approachable Daniel L. Schacter, *The Seven Sins of Memory: How the Mind Forgets and Remembers* (New York: Houghton Mifflin Harcourt, 2001).

42 These three systems have been analysed in Cortada, *The Birth of Modern Facts*, 57–87.

43 Alex Wright, *Cataloging the World: Paul Otlet and the Birth of the Information Age* (New York: Oxford University Press, 2014).

44 Alex Csiszar, *The Scientific Journal: Authorship and the Politics of Knowledge in the Nineteenth Century* (Chicago, IL: University of Chicago Press, 2018), but see also his, "How Lives Became Lists and Scientific Papers Became Data: Cataloging Authorship during the Nineteenth Century," *British Journal for the History of Science, Norwich* 50, no. 1 (March 2017): 23–60.

45 Cortada, *Birth of Modern Facts* and Cortada, *All the Facts*.

46 Andrew Abbott, *The System of Professions: An Essay on the Division of Expert Labor* (Chicago, IL: University of Chicago Press, 1988); Eliot Freidson, *Professional Powers: A Study of the Institutionalization of Formal Knowledge* (Chicago, IL: University of Chicago Press, 1986).

47 Cortada, *All the Facts;* the subject often also coached in the language of innovation, Jan Fagerberg, David C. Mowery, and Richard R. Nelson, eds., *The Oxford Handbook of Innovation* (New York: Oxford University Press, 2005).

48 IEEE, accessed August 12, 2022, https://www.ieee.org/membership-catalog/productdetail/showProductDetailPage.html?product=MEMIEEE500#:~:text=IEEE%20is%20the%20leading%20professional,world's%20largest%20technical%20professional%20society.

49 Joseph A. Schumpeter, *Business Cycles: A Theoretical, Historical, and Statistical Analysis of the Capitalist Process*, vol. 1 (New York: McGraw-Hill, 1939), 30.

50 Thomas Suddendorf, Jonathan Redshaw, and Adam Bulley, *The Invention of Tomorrow: A Natural History of Foresight* (New York: Basic Books, 2022), 30.

51 Information as objects and tools is discussed more thoroughly in Cortada, *All the Facts*.

52 For an excellent study of how all this happened, see Paul M. Dover, *The Information Revolution in Early Modern Europe* (Cambridge, UK: Cambridge University Press, 2021) which aligns nicely with discussions in Cortada, *All the Facts*.

53 Ron Larson and Bruce H. Edwards, *Calculus: Early Transcendental Functions*, 6th ed. (Boston, MA: Cengage Learning, 2014) and Steven Strogatz, *Infinite Powers: How Calculus Reveals the Secrets of the Universe* (New York: Houghton Mifflin Harcourt, 2019).

54 Stephen M. Stigler, *The History of Statistics: The Measurement of Uncertainty before 1900* (Cambridge, MA: Harvard University Press; 1986) also his, *Statistics on the Table: The History of Statistical Concepts and Methods* (Cambridge, MA: Harvard University Press, 2002).

55 Mary S. Morgan, *The History of Econometric Ideas* (New York: Cambridge University Press, 1990), 1–14; Francisco Louçã, *The Years of High Econometrics: A Short History of the Generation That Reinvented Economics* (New York: Routledge, 2007).

56 DeLong, *Slouching towards Utopia*, 62.

57 JoAnne Yates and Craig N. Murphy, *Engineering Rules: Global Standard Setting since 1880* (Baltimore, MD: Johns Hopkins University Press, 2019); Andrew L. Russell, *Open Standards and the Digital Age: History, Ideology and Networks* (Cambridge, UK: Cambridge University Press, 2014).

58 James R. Beniger, *The Control Revolution: Technological and Economic Origins of the Information Society* (Cambridge, MA: Harvard University Press, 1986).

59 Harvey J. Graff, *Undisciplining Knowledge: Interdisciplinarity in the Twentieth Century* (Baltimore, MD: Johns Hopkins University Press, 2015); R. S. Ledley, *Use of Computers in Biology and Medicine* (New York: McGraw-Hill, 1965).

60 Reprinted in Thomas Richards, "From *The Imperial Archives: Knowledge and the Fantasy of Empire* (1994)," in Hayot, Detwyler, and Pao, *Information: A Reader*, 122–123.

31
FACTUAL FICTIONS AND FICTIONALISED FACTS IN THE REPORTS OF THE ROMANIAN SECRET POLICE

Valentina Glajar and Corina L. Petrescu

The secret police forces of the former Eastern Bloc countries have left behind kilometres of files built on information that adds up to snippets of life stories slanted and contorted to fit politically motivated agendas. Romania's infamous Securitate was no exception.[1] The voluminous paper trail it left behind allows us to trace the covert process of recruiting informers, gathering information about them, and translating that data into knowledge and the power to turn an unsuspecting individual into a collaborator with the secret police. The elaborate steps in vetting, approaching, and convincing selected Romanian citizens to agree to collaborate and inform on others are all recorded in the various informer files. They also reveal so-called "legends"—fictional scenarios that recruiting officers concocted to attract their potential candidates. These "legends" are what we term "factual fictions," consisting of compromising information the officers had gathered about their prospects' vulnerabilities. By weaving these factual pieces of information into fictional narratives, the officers created a credible narrative that was designed to ensure the success of their operation. The first two parts of this chapter examine the various stages of the recruitment process and how the information obtained gave rise to "factual fictions" as deceptive tools of entrapment. It presents the file case of source MOGA MIRCEA, the code name of the German Romanian writer Claus Stephani, born in 1938, as an exemplary for the Securitate's recruiting techniques, which in the 1960s still drew on historical and political events that circled back to World War II (Fig. 31.1).[2]

Access to files also sheds light on the information transfer that took place between the Securitate and unrecruited sources, that is, persons who did not have an individualised—either official or unofficial—relation to the secret police, but by virtue of their professional positions had to write reports that made their way to the Securitate. The third part of the chapter investigates how this type of source could capitalise on their knowledge, submitting factual information to state authorities, that would both benefit the state and address their own concerns. Unlike factual fictions, this information was embellished and fictionalised to create accounts meant to incentivise the authorities to further pursue interests that aligned with those of the source. Franz Auerbach, the manager of the Jewish State Theatre in Bucharest (Teatrul Evreiesc de Stat—TES), fabricated fictionalised facts in his reports that

DOI: 10.4324/9781003310532-35

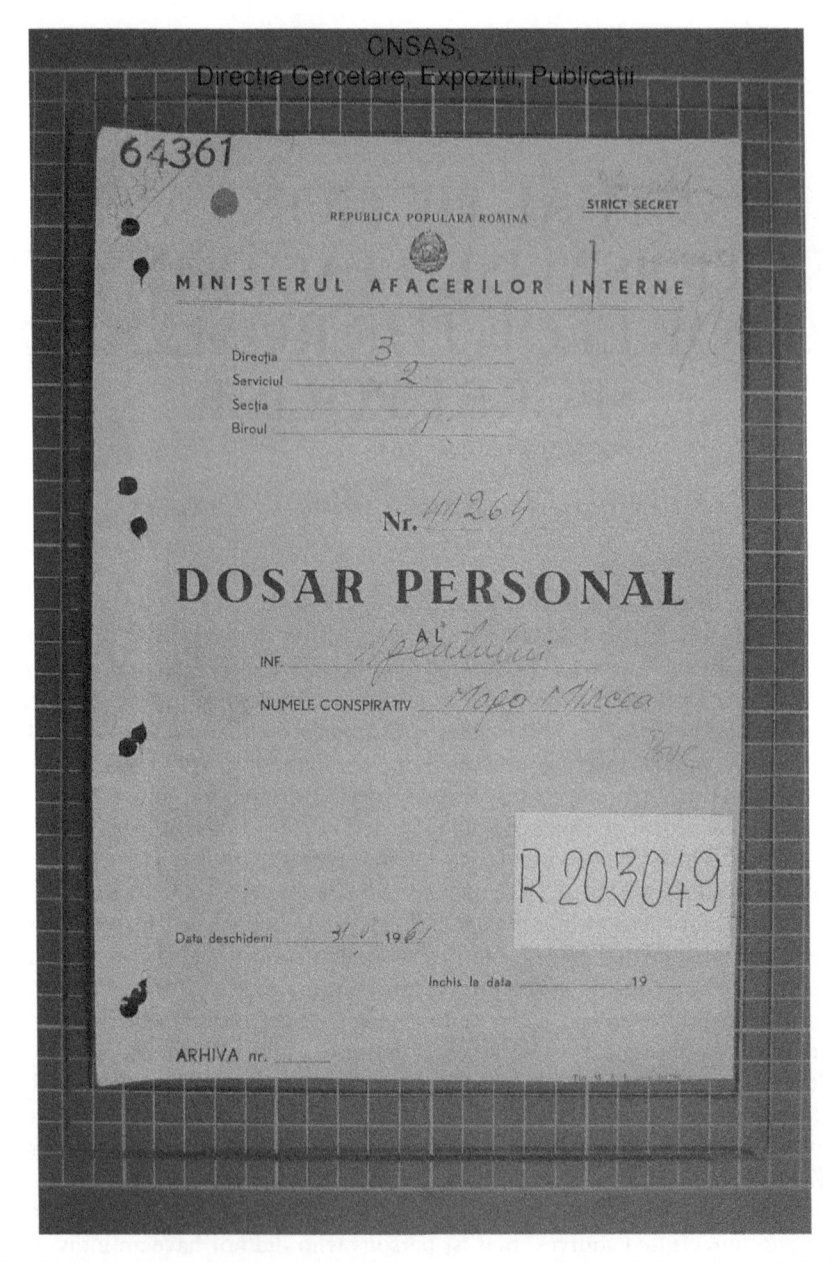

Figure 31.1 Cover page of Claus Stephani's informer file, code-named MOGA MIRCEA. Image from ACNSAS, Bucharest, Romania. ACNSAS, FR, File 203049.

allowed him to obtain concessions for the institution he led and ensure its survival under the most unlikely circumstances.[3]

The Stuff "Legends" Are Made Of

"Information means knowledge."[4] This is the title and the first sentence of an educational publication for Securitate officers. This manual of sorts is in fact a translation of material obtained from the US secret services that Lt. Ioan Rotar ably translated for his fellow officers in 1971. This publication exposes the strategic and operational procedures of the United States in its quest for intelligence, and thus knowledge, about other countries and their vulnerabilities. The main operations outlined in this text, surveillance and reconnaissance, have a unique goal: that of supplying information. This publication not only shows the Securitate's interest and means to obtain such materials from the US secret services during the Cold War, but also a clear departure from its initial training methods by Soviet secret service officers. It constitutes one in a series of organised educational materials in a professionalisation era of the new generation of secret police officers in the 1970s.[5]

Obtaining this valuable information began with recruiting the right people equipped to carry out a spying job. Towards this end, in 1976, the Securitate compiled a recruiting manual as elaborate and detailed as the US secret service material pertaining to gathering intel about various countries.[6] This manual highlights the so-called "informative network" (rețea informativă)—the sources—as the principal means of achieving the intelligence officers' goals in their line of work. The same "best practices" existed before as well, as evidenced by pre-1976 recruitment stories, but inexperienced officer trainees must have learned them on the job. The anonymous authors of this top-secret manual approached recruitment as a complex goal-oriented process of selecting informers or collaborators who had opportunities to obtain information, exhibited the correct kinds of personality traits, and were guaranteed to maintain a sincere attitude towards the Securitate. The intel the Securitate officers received from this network of informers allowed them to learn about what they perceived as potential hostile activities, and to work towards the prevention, uncovering, and, ultimately, the termination of these activities. Informers had to possess aptitudes commensurate with the tasks of the officers, to infiltrate certain hostile groups and get close to the surveilled targets. Working in tandem with their case officers, informers were expected to provide the requested intelligence but also to recognise and analyse unforeseen yet useful information.[7]

A year before the Securitate manual appeared in a top-secret, in-house publication designed to recruit unsuspecting Romanian citizens, Michel Foucault published his arguably most famous book, *Discipline and Punish*.[8] Foucault himself was no stranger to the tactics of East bloc secret services; he had spent a year in Poland in 1958–1959, fell into the honey trap of the Polish Służba Bezpieczeństwa and had to leave Poland abruptly.[9] Thus, perhaps unsurprisingly, many of the Foucauldian tenets can be recognised, albeit in a simplistic and unsophisticated way, in this target-oriented manual that was based on psychological studies from the 1970s.[10] Yet, the manual and the practices it outlines refer to disciplining and training those who eventually became instruments of the ultimate discipliners. The importance of these informers to the Securitate surveillance system cannot be overstated, and thus the recruitment process and its several prescribed steps were dutifully recorded: observing, approaching, and persuading its candidates to agree to collaborate. These steps were all filed in the various informers' dossiers and expose the fictional scenarios, internally referred to as "legends," that the recruiting officers concocted to attract their prospective candidates. The officers' reports expose fascinating scenarios in which they exploited any shred of compromising intel they had gathered about their candidates' vulnerabilities. Thus, while these candidates were eventually selected to observe and spy on others, they themselves became targets of observation in the first step of the recruitment process.

Every informer file includes materials gathered during the observation phase; a detailed recruitment proposal, the recruitment report, and the ultimate prize: the collaboration agreement. In the Foucauldian understanding of surveillance, observation, the first step in the process of accumulating information, is a mechanism of coercion obtained through "eyes that must see without being seen."[11] In the context of the Securitate, these eyes were not some sophisticated panopticons.[12] The recruiting officers employed what Alison Lewis calls "para-panoptical" means, that is, they relied on other informers, colleagues, friends, acquaintances, neighbours, and even unsuspecting family members.[13] The veil of secrecy that obscured these eyes was the glue that kept the network of officers and informers working and intact. Thus, each of the recruitment proposals details the initial information recruiting officers obtained from their sources in the observation phase. The officers relied mostly on incriminatory intelligence that exposed the candidates' vulnerabilities and potential for blackmail. In the case of the German Romanian communities in the 1950s and early 1960s, the candidates' past involvement in the Waffen-SS, the post-World War II political trials in Romania, or any critique of the Soviet Union and its forced labor camps afforded the recruiting officers sufficient compromising material to proceed with the recruitment process.[14]

The observation and information-gathering phase thus followed what the recruiting manual calls the biographical and observational methods that could single out the optimal contenders or exclude less optimal ones from the pool of candidates.[15] While the biographical method also included data about the candidate's family members and their own vulnerabilities, the observation method placed the potential informers in a field of surveillance akin to that of their future targets. This method focused on the candidates' position in society, their entourage, their work place, and most importantly, the character traits that would allow them to become the "James Bonds" of the Romanian Securitate. Viable candidates had to be sincere, objective, courageous, intelligent, and discreet sociable types that inspired trust among their peers and friends. They needed to be observant and exhibiting a visual and auditive memory that allowed them to render facts accurately.[16] Both the biographical and the observation methods were documented in some detail in the files of the selected prospects.

An examination and analysis of the obtained intel would then situate the candidates in a field of surveillance and, as Foucault explains, the "normalizing gaze" in a network of writing.[17] These prospective informers, similar to their future targets, themselves became cases.[18] The information accumulated in their files—references from various sources, the officer reports, the recruitment proposal, and agreement—remained fixed in their files and suspended in time. Documenting every step in these loquacious files, describing, judging, classifying, accepting, or excluding these individuals turned their lives into written documents affixed or sown between the covers of their informer files. Thus, "the existence of these men and women reduces itself to exactly what has been said about them: nothing subsists of who they were or what they did, except in a few sentences."[19] This information in the hands of the officers became knowledge that translated into power.

Yet, officers accumulated this precious intel with the clear purpose of exercising this power to convince the candidates to collaborate in the process of turning the lives of others into filed cases. Once the phases of gathering and examining intel concluded, the recruiting officers needed a plan to approach the candidates who had shown promise and the desired traits and skills. This too was documented in their network files, first as a recruitment proposal, then as a report outlining the meeting with the candidate, and finally, the candidate's handwritten and signed collaboration agreement.

The recruitment proposal, based on the gathered intel, allowed the recruiting officers to shine and impress their superiors with their own analytical skills. They sifted the obtained information for the vulnerable aspects in a candidate's life, and addressed the scope, area of influence, and the necessity of infiltrating the prospective informer among groups of trusting, but potentially hostile, colleagues or friends. The officers' recruiting proposal thus became a power exercise in weaponising certain aspects of a particular candidate's life. The officers used these factual elements and created a fictional scenario around them—a plausible tale that would successfully lure the candidate into their trap. In the Securitate lingo, they were the "legends" meant to deceive the candidate into believing the officers' factual yet fictional stories.

How to Lose an Informer in Two Years: The File Case of "Agent MOGA MIRCEA"[20]

On May 30, 1961, two Securitate officers, Captain Alex Munteanu and Major Ion Gr. Popa, used a "legend contact" to persuade Claus Stephani, a freshman at the University of Bucharest at that time, to meet with them. By the end of this fateful meeting, the officers had convinced him to join their network system. Yet this meeting and the officers' persuasion techniques, forged and finessed through repetition and experience, were part of a carefully orchestrated process. He had been selected as the most viable prospect from a pool of worthy German Romanian students and entrusted to spy on his fellow students, who apparently exhibited nationalist and antisemitic tendencies.

Four days earlier, the same Maj. Popa had submitted a detailed, typed, textbook proposal for recruiting Stephani, in which he analysed his profile according to the biographical, political, cultural, and personal information obtained during the observational vetting phase in order to justify the Securitate's interest in him. Stephani, born in the Transylvanian city of Brașov, appeared to have the perfect credentials for the job. Unlike many Transylvanian Saxons who had adhered to the Nazi ideology and had enrolled in the German Army during World War II, Stephani's parents had declined to participate in local fascist organisations. According to the officers' information compiled in Stephani's informer file, his father had gone to a Deutsche Mannschaft meeting[21]; because he had refused to greet the attendees with the "German salute," he had been thrown out, and later demoted and persecuted. Stephani himself had a proletarian résumé that spoke to the officers, as he had worked from the age of fourteen as an electrician, while also attending classes at a trade school for electricians for two years. He had then taken an exam to transfer to a local lycée, and after graduation, he had worked for three years as a stock boy in a warehouse. A year before his recruitment, he had passed the entrance examination at the University of Bucharest, where he was studying *Germanistik*. Politically, Stephani's profile was a perfect fit as well, as he was an active propagandist of the Workers' Youth Union (Uniunea Tineretului Muncitoresc—UTM). He was sociable and made friends easily. He was also a published writer whose poems and short prose pieces had already appeared in Romania and East Germany. The editors of various German-language publications in both Brașov and Bucharest appreciated his talent.

Stephani's prospective sphere of influence was the group of forty-four students studying *Germanistik* at the University of Bucharest, mainly those whose parents had already been under surveillance for their past fascist involvement. Most of these students apparently had relatives in capitalist countries, mainly West Germany and Austria, with whom they often corresponded. Due to the education received at home and the negative influence of their capitalist relatives, these students, especially those in their first year of study, needed the "normalizing gaze" of an observant informer.[22] Three young women in particular were singled out as prospective targets: Renate S. who had exhibited antisemitic sentiments; Ursula B. who was suspected of a "tendentious" attitude; and Alida S. whose father was a Lutheran priest. One of the students, presumably Renate S., had refused to read assigned poems by Christian Morgenstern claiming erroneously that he was Jewish.[23]

Having ascertained that the *Germanistik* students constituted a hotbed of antisemitic and nationalist ethnic Germans in dire need of disciplining, and that Stephani was one of the few, or the only one, who could steer them away from capitalist views and towards more communist attitudes and ideals, Maj. Popa seemed to have checked every box in his proposal. What remained were the deceptive "legend" and the exit strategy.[24] The "legend" Maj. Popa concocted was not up to par, and definitely not up to the glowing characterisation of his chosen candidate. He suggested for both the "legend" and the exit strategy to have Stephani summoned to a police station to clarify a simple clerical error in his personal data record—certainly not a creative story but straightforward enough as to sound credible and not raise any suspicions in the candidate's mind. His superior, Maj. I. Andronic, though, must have found it tedious and missing any personalised factual elements that could have attracted Stephani into their trap. An inspired Andronic suggested in a handwritten comment two "legends" for the recruitment meeting. First, the officers were to pretend to represent the Department of Education or another cultural organisation in order to lure him to the meeting place. Second, once they revealed their identity to him, they should resort to another fictional fact: to inquire about a person from Stephani's hometown of Brașov. Presumably, the third step, the test of sincerity he had to pass, would finally allow the officers to get to the stringent and non-fictionalised point: the collaboration agreement.

Diligently following regulations, Maj. Popa wrote a new report about how the recruitment meeting unfolded.[25] Readers are left to assume that Maj. Andronic's two "legends" were applied and had the desired effect; the officer does not offer any details other than that bringing the candidate to the recruitment place went according to plan. Maj. Popa and Cpt. Alex Munteanu approached the candidate from an ideological angle, along party lines, and applied the principle of "free consent."[26] Stephani passed the sincerity test as well by corroborating the officers' information about his parents, who had applied for emigration because his father had not been allowed to visit his relatives in West Germany. At the end of the meeting, the candidate Stephani assumed the new identity of agent MOGA MIRCEA by writing and signing a collaboration agreement.[27] Yet, according to Stephani's recollections from 2010, when his file became accessible, the recruitment meeting had elements of serious spy craft. In a *FAZ* article titled *Schwester Lüge, Bruder Schmerz* (*Sister Lie, Brother Pain*), Stephani recalls that during the recruitment meeting, he was served a cup of delicious coffee, and then a refill. At that time, or perhaps after reflecting on the incident, he suspected that the coffee was laced—a farfetched story in its own right, as there is no evidence in the file that would suggest that the recruiting officers resorted to such methods.[28]

As Popa's report outlines, Stephani was asked about his future targets, the three students in question, who allegedly tried to influence a canon change in the German department according to capitalist and Aryan principles. Apparently, as per Popa's report, the three had refused to read a certain progressive author named "BRECHNER."[29] Popa and Munteanu were evidently neither speakers of German nor readers of German literature, and as such what might have been Bertolt Brecht (1898–1956), or possibly the German politician and writer Johannes Robert Becher (1891–1958) became "Brechner." The irony continued, as the three women seemingly preferred Heinrich Heine (1797–1856) and other bourgeois writers to the elusive "Brechner." It is not clear whether Stephani did not mention, or did not know, that Heine was in fact born to assimilated Jewish parents. Clearly, the clueless officers missed the ironic twist in the three students' proposed literary cannon at the University of Bucharest.

The informing activity of MOGA MIRCEA was short-lived and his file does not include an annexed folder (mapă anexă), which would typically include his own reports on his targets.[30] While in the *FAZ* article Stephani mentions that his file includes three handwritten reports, those reports must have since been removed, since none of them exist in either his informer or his surveillance files. Instead, several reports by source SILVIU, a university lecturer in the 1960s, inform about Stephani, SILVIU's student, who after one year was expelled from the university.[31] Stephani took advantage of this opportunity and disappeared from the Securitate's radar. He moved from his Bucharest address on file and was successful in deceiving the Bucharest Securitate, who was not able to find him for an entire year. His third assigned handler had lost him in October 1962,[32] and Maj. Popa, his original recruiter and handler, was finally able to track him down on September 11, 1963.[33] They had looked for him in Brașov,[34] while all the while Stephani had been hiding in plain sight at a new address in Bucharest.[35] When the officers finally got hold of him and convinced him to attend another meeting at a police station, Stephani categorically refused to continue any collaboration and they were forced to abandon him.[36] While they insisted that he sign a nondisclosure agreement of sorts, he firmly refused to sign that either, but promised to safeguard the secrecy of his collaboration.[37]

And so Stephani apparently did until 2010, when he addressed this brief collaboration in the aforementioned *FAZ* article. Clearly, the Securitate's procedures for recruiting sources were not an exact science, although based on true and tried experiences. While in the beginning of the recruitment process Stephani seemed like a candidate with perfect credentials, he turned out to be a source who tried to escape this signed collaboration. It might have been the element of surprise, fear, and the superior persuasive attributes of his well-versed recruiting officers that convinced him to write and sign the agreement. By October 1963, however, that fear had dissipated, and Stephani mustered the courage to stop any cooperation. And yet, fragments of his and his targets' lives remained fixed in these archival files. In fact, one document reveals that less than four months after his recruitment, the Securitate was in the process of approaching MOGA MIRCEA's target Renate S. for recruitment.[38] Once candidates like Stephani or Renate S. were selected, and under duress or of their own free will accepted to become sources, they too were trained and pushed to exercise their power on unsuspecting targets. They were expected to both gather and examine information and do their part in chronicling and fixing their targets' lives in informer reports. They became an essential tool in the chain of command that encapsulated a hierarchy of knowledge and power.

Spilling Ink to Play for Keeps with the State Authorities

Franz Auerbach, the manager of TES, was not an informer; yet in his capacity as an administrator of a state institution, he delivered information on the Theatre's activities to various bodies from 1955 until 1985. On November 22, 1972, for example, he signed and submitted a report addressed to the Romanian Agency for Artistic Representation and Promotion (Agenția Română de Impresariat Artistic—ARIA; Fig. 31.2). Auerbach elaborated on

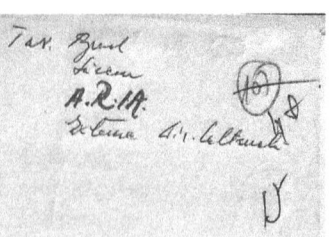

Figure 31.2 First page of Franz Auerbach's report to ARIA. Image from ACNSAS, Bucharest, ACNSAS, FD, File 137, Volume 10, Page 15.

TES's artistic and PR activities and his own interactions during the Theatre's international tour to the United States and Canada between September 15 and November 7, 1972. This report was noteworthy to the Securitate because it contained potentially valuable information about Romania's ideological enemies during the Cold War. It also provided the authorities with Auerbach's suggestions on how best to use this information to benefit the Romanian state.

TES was the only minority cultural institution in Romania's capital, Bucharest. The Securitate surveilled its activities, not least because the authorities used the Theatre to showcase to foreign visitors the country's supposed liberal minority policies.[39] TES was also allowed to go on international tours (Israel 1968, and United States and Canada 1972) and to give guest performances (East Berlin 1977 and Vienna 1979) to promote this fabricated progressive image of the country. After each trip abroad and each visit to the Theatre by a foreign national, TES's leadership had to submit reports to the authorities about the exchanges that had taken place between the hosts and their visitors, and some of these reports—as was the case with Auerbach's—ended up in the surveillance file, which the Securitate compiled about TES.[40] In fact, Auerbach built on his knowledge about the international ambitions of the Romanian regime to advocate for the specific needs of the institution he led by intentionally fictionalising facts to its advantage.

In a lecture he gave to the American Society of Political and Legal Philosophy in 1958, J. L. Austin showed that speech acts denote not only intention, but also deliberation and purposiveness.[41] An intentional operation merely presupposes the existence of an idea "to [be] put into effect," while deliberation entails "weigh[ing] up" an action's "pros and cons" even if rudimentarily before proceeding, and to act for or on purpose implies the existence of a clear "objective" that guides one's actions until it is achieved.[42] Applying Austin's ideas to Auerbach's account helps understand the leverage of a report in which it was not only the facts that were essential, but also their elaboration through a careful interplay of admission and omission of details. Strategically, Auerbach conceived his report as an "illocutionary speech act," in which he amassed "intentional utterances about facts, people, and opinions" expecting them to carry "considerable perlocutionary force, i.e., the power to convince and persuade and hence to bring about real-world impacts."[43] By taking advantage of Romania's fixation on positive publicity abroad, Auerbach managed to feed the authorities fictional facts in order to serve his institution and community.

TES's North American tour included performances in the United States in New York, Hartford, Philadelphia, San Francisco, Los Angeles, and Seattle, and in Canada in Vancouver, Ottawa, and Montreal.[44] Upon his return to Bucharest, Auerbach submitted his mandatory report to ARIA on TES's activities while overseas. Addressed to comrade Brad Săceanu from the agency's branch for culture abroad, the report follows prompts provided by ARIA. It details that thirty-five people took part in the tour, which was organised and financed by the American impresario company Pacific World Artists of New York City. TES staged forty performances of its two shows—An-sky's *Der dibek* (*The Dybbuk*) twenty-five and Israil Bercovici's *A shnirl perl* (*A Pearl Necklace*) fifteen times—which enjoyed success with both the public and the press. To stress the impact of TES's art, Auerbach indicated that in New York, "prof[essor] Lifson" had translated the shows into English, a fact that had attracted numerous new-Jewish spectators. Auerbach did not explain who the professor was, yet, the stress on his academic title and the fact that his involvement with TES could draw non-Jewish audiences to the theatre hall shows Auerbach's knowledge about the type of information that reflected well on TES, and made the authorities take it seriously.[45]

Throughout his report, Auerbach employed this strategy of emphasising TES's relevance for Romania's international reputation by playing up the cultural, social, or potentially political capital of international notables with whom the company came into contact. In this sense, he indicated that the Romanian Library (Biblioteca Româna) in New York offered a reception for TES at which "President Nixon's brother-in-law, Mr. Knox" was in attendance. Richard Nixon did not have a brother-in-law by that name so the person who could have been present was at best his son-in-law, Edward F. Cox, husband to Nixon's oldest daughter Patricia. But the information's accuracy seems secondary to the fact that somebody close to President Nixon showed interest in TES's presence in the United States. Similarly, the fact that Nixon himself sent a message to the troupe was more important than the detail that the message reached the troupe after it had left the United States. Other figures whose interaction with TES Auerbach noted were "the famous actor and professor" Paul Mann, who wanted to return to Romania for a professional exchange, and "the rabbi Schneier," who discussed with Auerbach the possibility of a special show for "political and financial notables from New York City."[46] Although that performance did not occur due to "material difficulties," Auerbach's mention illustrates his efforts on behalf of and TES's diplomatic potential for the Romanian state. He emphasised the latter further by pointing out that the diplomatic personnel at Romania's embassies in the two countries appreciated TES's tour as "helpful in their work."

Auerbach also indicated that he had given five interviews to newspapers and that he had been on the air with a New York-based broadcasting company three times, all in the interest of heightened publicity for Romania and its political regime. Auerbach based his reporting on these facts, but fictionalised specific aspects about them so as to feed the authorities desired and anticipated information. For each of the media outlets he included details such as their names and the dates when the interviews had been conducted, but left out particulars that could have undermined the impression of TES's profile-raising actions. Of the five newspapers—*New York Times*, *Forverts/The Yiddish Forward*, *Morgn frayhayt (Morning Freedom)*, *Tribune Juive (Jewish Tribune)*, and *Montreal Star*—only two were mainstream publications—*New York Times* and *Montreal Star*. The others were journals that addressed the Jewish community in their respective countries, and they did so in a language other than the country's primary idiom. Similarly, WEVD was a Yiddish-language radio station established by the Socialist Party of America in 1927, so its PR value was limited in scope not only to those who understood Yiddish, but also to those on the same political spectrum as the Romanian authorities.[47] By leaving these specifics out, Auerbach did not provide falsehoods or tall tales to the authorities, but he finessed the reality behind the facts to meet the authorities' expectations and the long-term goals he had for TES.

Auerbach also reported about the interactions between the members of TES's ensemble and their North American hosts that came about during official or private gatherings. The official welcome reception for TES took place at the Brooklyn Academy of Music following the Theatre's opening night in New York, while the Organisation of Romanian Jews (Asociația Evreilor Români) and the Romanian Library hosted functions for the ensemble. Independently, there were private parties which the actors attended "in groups" and in which Auerbach did not always participate on account of their late hours and his being tired.[48] The specification about the group attendance of private parties was not random. On the one hand, it signalled that the individual members of the company did their jobs well in gaining the admiration of their hosts, who were eager also to interact with them outside of official settings. On the other hand, it offered cover to all those who interacted with their hosts in a less supervised fashion by stressing that none of them had ever been completely unobserved. With respect to himself, Auerbach underlined that the gatherings presented him with the opportunity to socialise with people drawn not only to Jewish culture, but also to Romania and its social and political realities in general. This, in turn, afforded him the chance to learn about American and Canadian attitudes vis-à-vis Romania and its foreign policies, which he unsurprisingly deemed positive.

In light of the generally well-received activities of TES during its North American tour and its accomplished propaganda mission, Auerbach took the liberty of building on the information he had gathered and making several suggestions to his addressees that would further improve Romania's standing overseas. First, he deplored the absence of Romanian merchandise in American and Canadian stores the ensemble had visited and urged the authorities to partner up with serious local business people to remedy the situation. To his mind, such export-import ventures could yield profits for both parties in two to three years.[49]

Secondly, he encouraged the authorities to intensify their efforts of cultural diplomacy by sending more artists abroad to showcase their talents, which were a credit to the state's care for its artistes. He opined that establishing or strengthening contacts to the Romanian diaspora, whose members enjoyed participating in cultural events related to their country of birth, would, in turn, result in more positive publicity for Romania's accomplishments. He also advised that future tours be organised at least a year in advance so as to yield the best publicity value for Romania.[50] That had not been the case with TES's tour and, consequently, the Theatre had not been able to perform "in the heart" of New York and "exploit its success politically" to the best.[51] Yet, the North American tour had served as a learning experience for all parties involved, and Auerbach was optimistic about future cultural exchanges between Romania and the United States and Canada. To facilitate further tours, he endorsed the female impresario who had attended to TES's needs and recommended her as a long-term partner for ARIA.

Thirdly, Auerbach commented on the good nature of TES's hosts throughout the tour and on their genuine curiosity about Romania. Paired with the desire of Jewish Romanian émigrés in North America to revisit and explore their country of birth, Auerbach proclaimed this disposition the best premise to promote tourism to Romania among Americans and Canadians. Such business considerations reveal Auerbach's shrewd understanding of the regime's efforts to curry favor in North America and expose him as an adept foil of the Romanian establishment. As with his earlier points, his pitch was pragmatic and utilitarian: for an effective influx of tourists, the Romanian authorities had to establish direct air connections to the North American continent and operate high-performance aircrafts "under the Romanian flag," as the Czech planes in use at that time no longer corresponded to contemporary demands.[52] Auerbach seems to have known exactly what information the authorities wanted and offered it in a way that allowed him to raise concerns with them that affected his institution and the community at large.

The year 1976 marked the centennial of professional Yiddish theatre worldwide, and Auerbach aspired to commemorate it in style. Not only was TES one of only two Jewish state theatres in the world, but the city of Iași in Romania counted as the birthplace of modern Yiddish stagecraft. Emboldened by TES's success during the tour and the invitations for the company to return to the United States in the following years, Auerbach proposed that the occasion be marked in Romania with a year-long programme of "international resonance."⁵³ Yet, to be able to rise to the occasion and also to ensure Yiddish theatre's continued existence in Romania, TES needed a new studio to train between five and eight young actors to join its troupe. Auerbach's concrete demand, compared to the persuasive suggestions beforehand, signals that the studio was the concession that TES needed and Auerbach sought to obtain from the authorities for having delivered on its PR mission abroad.⁵⁴ Having built up his case progressively throughout the report, Auerbach identified his ensemble's need, coated it in a discourse that underlined its significance for Romania's efforts to project a positive image abroad, and offered a solution. To strengthen his case, he educated his readers about Iași's status, insisting that the city's standing was a well-known fact "everywhere" and documented in encyclopedias.⁵⁵ A grand celebration would also attract numerous Jewish tourists from abroad, Auerbach further insisted, changing the perspective from his interest to that of the authorities, in a renewed effort to demonstrate how ably TES served the Romanian state. For the festivities, TES would prepare a special repertoire and Auerbach even suggested making a feature or documentary film about Yiddish theatre's evolution in Romania and distributing it internationally.⁵⁶

Auerbach did not write his account for the Securitate per se, but he knew that the institution was informed—after all, Securitate practices, not unlike those of other Eastern bloc secret services, were a "public secret," to use Michael Taussig's term.⁵⁷ Moreover, he was aware of earlier efforts on part of the Executive Council at Bucharest's City Hall to shut down TES in 1966 after its sister institution in Iași had been closed at the end of its 1962 season for insufficient audiences and loss of cultural relevance.⁵⁸ TES Bucharest nearly escaped Iași's fate because the Ministry of Foreign Affairs had intervened and opposed the measure as "unbefitting the current conjuncture."⁵⁹ During its début international tour to Israel in 1968, in the aftermath of the so-called Six Day War of 1967, but also at a time when Israelis were beginning to accept Yiddish culture as part of their overall cultural heritage, TES had had to prove its worth and it had done so.⁶⁰ Israeli audiences had reacted positively to TES's performances, even if their enthusiasm had not just been a reflection on TES's artistic merits but also an expression of *shtetl*-nostalgia and—most importantly—gratitude for the political course of Nicolae Ceaușescu's regime during and after the aforementioned war.⁶¹ Bearing this in mind, Auerbach's report was intentional, deliberate, and purposeful, to return to Austin's theory. He knew what he was doing, had most likely weighed the pros and cons of embellishing TES's role for Romania's international image, and had a clear objective that guided him in his decision to pursue the chosen course of action.

Moreover, Auerbach's report was post-factum textual evidence of relevant events and encounters of the Theatre ensemble during its first ever presence on the North American continent. In a specific, bureaucratic jargon the text informed the authorities about the people who participated in specific events. In writing the report, Auerbach followed the prescribed protocols of the Romanian authorities and thus affirmed his compliance with the state's requirements. Yet, he also funnelled information and suggestions to the authorities that could benefit his institution. As manager of a state institution, he collaborated with the regime, but also reclaimed—even if only partly—his agency vis-à-vis the authorities by devising strategies that allowed him to safeguard the existence of the institution and the well-being of the people he led. His report informed about events, people and places but also prompted the authorities to assist TES, so TES in return could continue to serve the Romanian state. His focus on the state's interests allowed him to equate what was profitable for Ceauşescu's regime with what was beneficial for the Theatre, and thus ensure TES's survival for some time longer.

Conclusion

The two-way flow of information between the Romanian secret police and willing, reluctant, or unrecruited sources was uneven and based on attempted trickery and deception. Both sides could claim an information filter through which they monitored what information they delivered and possibly to what end. As in the case of MOGA MIRCEA and per the detailed recruitment manual, officers created "legends" to trap potential candidates for recruitment—a process that relied on observational and biographical methods. SILVIU gathered and tendered information through his own filter and with a clear agenda in mind: to expose and inform about any hostile events at his university. Auerbach, apparently the most thoughtful of them all, processed, filtered, and embellished the information before submitting it, with the goal of gaining concessions for TES and ensuring its survival as an institution. However, informers were rarely able to fool their handlers who periodically tested their loyalty and sincerity. Whether Auerbach obtained the privileges he sought by writing reports or by other means remains a matter of debate. Initially, officers provided their potential confidential informers with just enough information to persuade them to cooperate. Through the ensuing initiation ritual and the tasks assigned to the informers, handlers allowed informers a glimpse into the repository of intelligence they so closely guarded. They sold them the illusion that informers and collaborators too could gain access to this repository and thus participate and rise in the hierarchy of knowledge and power. Their goal was to gain and keep the informers' trust, and paradoxically, this uneven power relation between handler and informer often translated into a peculiar closeness. Securitate officers had a bird's-eye view and the discretionary power to evaluate and analyse information from all these sources, to detect the targets' weaknesses and exploit them. Like Foucauldian "cases" filed and fixed in this unusual archive of life fragments, the paper trail the Securitate left behind exposes the collection and manipulation of information as an effective and fear-inducing instrument of power.

Notes

1 Officially called the General Directorate for the Security of the People in 1948 and the Department of State Security until 1989, the Securitate was Romania's secret political police after the country became a people's republic on December 30, 1947. The agency was established by Decree 221 of August 28, 1948, under the direction of the Soviet Union's NKVD counterintelligence service. Its main tasks were to eliminate opponents of the regime in order to consolidate power, to ensure compliance with the regime and its leaders, and to influence public opinion to ensure support for public policies. The Securitate's methods, goals, and personnel changed over the course of the two political regimes that made up Romania's experiment with state socialism. During the rule of Gheorghe Gheorghiu-Dej (1948–1965), the Securitate relied on untrained and brutal personnel and engaged in summary executions, illegal house arrests, imprisonment, and deportations. During the years of Nicolae Ceauşescu (1965–1989), specially trained and educated officers engaged in more sophisticated methods of control and surveillance, which also relied on the proper functioning of an extensive network of informers. Ten years after the end of the Ceauşescu regime, Romania enacted Law 187 of December 7, 1999, which led to the establishment of the National Council for the Study of the Securitate Archives (Consiliul Naţional pentru Studierea Arhivelor Securităţii, or CNSAS), the authority that manages the archives of the former secret police. CNSAS exposes former informers, grants former victims and informers access to their own files, and gives

scholars permission to conduct research in its holdings. It also develops programmes, materials, and exhibitions that educate about the history of the Securitate in a way that also preserves the memory of its victims. See Florian Banu and Liviu Țăranu, ed. *Securitatea (1948–1989): Monografie* (Târgoviște: Cetatea de Scaun: 2016) and "Misiunea CNSAS" (The Mission of CNSAS), http://www.cnsas.ro/.
2 Claus Stephani (b. 1938, Brașov, Romania) is a German Romanian writer who emigrated to Germany in 1990. He received his doctorate in ethnology from the Ludwig-Maximilian University in Munich in 1995. His ethnological work focuses on various German and Jewish communities, legends, and fairy tales from the German-speaking regions of Romania. In 2010, he was accused of having collaborated with the Securitate under three code names (MOGA MIRCEA; MOGA; and MARIN), but he adamantly insisted that his only short-lived involvement was the one discussed in this chapter and archived in his informer file housed at the CNSAS. To clear his name, Stephani sued the late German Romanian writer Richard Wagner, the target of MOGA and MARIN, for defamation in 2011 and won in the German court.
3 ACNSAS, FD, file 137, vols. 10 and 11.
4 Consiliul Securității Statului (The State Security Council), *Culegerea și Exploatarea Informațiilor* (Collecting and Exploiting Information), 1971, file D 008712, vol. P31, ACNSAS, Bucharest, 5.
5 As part of the secret Cold War West German-Romanian ransoming operation of ethnic Germans, West Germany supplied communist Romania with surveillance equipment in 1971 and twice in 1972. See Florica Dobre et al., eds., *Acțiunea "Recuperarea": Securitatea și Emigrarea Germanilor din România (1962–1989)* (The Operation "Retrieval": The Securitate and the Emigration of Germans from Romania; Bucharest: Editura Enciclopedică, 2011), LI–LII.
6 Ministerul de Interne (Ministry of the Interior), *Criterii privind recrutarea de informatori și colaboratori pentru munca de securitate* (Criteria Regarding the Recruitment of Informers and Collaborators for Securitate Work), 1976, file D 008712, vol. P19, ACNSAS, Bucharest.
7 File D 008712, vol. P19, 3.
8 Michel Foucault, *Discipline and Punish*, trans. Alan Sheridan (New York: Vintage Books, 1995).
9 See Anna Krakus and Cristina Vatulescu, "Foucault in Poland: A Silent Archive," *Diacritics* 47, no. 2 (2019): 73.
10 Ana Tucicov-Bogdan, *Psihologia Generală și Psihologia Specială* (The General Psychology and the Specific Psychology; Bucharest: Editura Didactică și Pedagogică, 1973), and A. Cosmovici et al., *Metode Pentru Cunoașterea Personalității* (Methods for Knowing the Personality; Bucharest: Editura Didactică și Pedagogică, 1972).
11 Foucault, *Discipline and Punish*, 170.
12 Alison Lewis advances the notion of a "communist panopticon" in her study on East German informers. See Alison Lewis, *A State of Secrecy* (Lincoln, NE: Potomac Books, 2019).
13 Lewis, *A State of Secrecy*, IV.
14 Two trials involving German Romanians took place in Brașov (then Orașul Stalin—Stalin Town): The Black Church Trial in 1958 and the Writers' Trial in 1959. For information about these trials, see Corneliu Pintilescu, *Procesul Biserica Neagră 1958* (The Black Church Trial 1958; Brașov: Aldus, 2008). For post-1989 testimonies regarding the Writers Trial, see Peter Motzan, Stefan Sienerth, and Andreas Heuberger, eds., *Worte als Gefahr und Gefährdung: Fünf Deutsche Schriftsteller vor Gericht* (Dangerous and Endangering Words: Five German Writers on Trial; Munich: Südostdeutsches Kulturwerk, 1993).
15 File D 008712, vol. P19, 15.
16 File D 008712, vol. P19, 17.
17 Foucault, *Discipline and Punish*, 189.
18 Foucault, *Discipline and Punish*, 191.
19 Michel Foucault, "The Life of Infamous Men," in *Michel Foucault: Power, Truth, Strategy*, ed. Meaghan Morris and Paul Patton (Sydney: Feral Publications, 1979), 80.
20 File R 203049 (MOGA MIRCEA–Claus Stephani), ACNSAS, Bucharest; hereafter MOGA MIRCEA. For reasons of readability, we have kept Stephani's and other code names in all caps, as they appear in the files.
21 Deutsche Mannschaft was a militant fascist organisation in Romania. For information on the Nazi involvement of German Romanians, see Paul Milata's comprehensive study *Zwischen Hitler,*

Stalin und Antonescu (Between Hitler, Stalin, and Antonescu; Göttingen: Vandenhoeck & Ruprecht, 2009).
22 Foucault, *Discipline and Punish*, 189.
23 The Securitate source SILVIU had reported this incident to his handler, claiming that Stephani had complained to him about his fellow classmates (MOGA MIRCEA, 39). It was most likely this remark by SILVIU that brought Stephani to the acute attention of the Securitate. According to Stefan Sienerth's extensive research, the code name SILVIU belonged to the literary critic Heinz Stănescu. See Stefan Sienerth, *Bespitzelt und Bedrängt—Verhaftet und Verstrickt* (Spied on and Harassed—Arrested and Entangled; Berlin: Frank & Timme, 2023), 26, n.4.
24 In his study *Informatorul* (The Informer), Mihai Albu insists that invoking fear of repercussions for justifying one's collaboration with the Securitate was not reasonable since recruiting officers always counted on and prepared for a candidate's refusal. In hindsight, this might sound like a valid argument, but those who accepted to collaborate were evidently unaware of the officers' exit strategy. See Mihai Albu, *Informatorul: Studii Asupra Colaborării cu Securitatea* (The Informer: Studies on the Collaboration with the Securitate; Iași: Polirom, 2008), 29–30.
25 MOGA MIRCEA, 5–8.
26 MOGA MIRCEA, 5.
27 MOGA MIRCEA, 9–10.
28 Claus Stephani, "Schwester Lüge, Bruder Schmerz" (Sister Lie, Brother Pain), *Frankfurter Allgemeine Zeitung*, November 20, 2010, https://www.faz.net/-grb-xpnp.
29 MOGA MIRCEA, 5.
30 Albu, *Informatorul*, 26–27.
31 In a document dated November 27, 1965 filed in Stephani's surveillance dossier, Stănescu is identified as a former Securitate officer who had the rank of Major in 1953. See Report, November 27, 1965, file I 211829, vol. 1, ACNSAS, Bucharest, folio 38.
32 MOGA MIRCEA, 31.
33 MOGA MIRCEA, 101.
34 MOGA MIRCEA, 97–98.
35 MOGA MIRCEA, 100.
36 MOGA MIRCEA, 105.
37 MOGA MIRCEA, 107.
38 MOGA MIRCEA, 38.
39 The official status of the Jewish community in Romania during the Cold War was that of a religious and not an ethnic minority; see "Decree 589 from June 1, 1949," in *Evreii din România. Mărturii Documentare (1945–1965)* [The Jews from Romania. Documentary Testimonies, 1945–1965], ed. Andreea Andreescu, Lucian Nastasă, and Andrea Varga (Cluj-Napoca: Centrul de Resurse pentru Diversitate Etnoculturală, 2002), 423–429.
40 ACNSAS, FD, file 137 has twenty-five volumes covering the timespan 1952–1989 and refers to the religious life of Jews, Armenians, and Bulgarians in Romania. Volumes 1 through 12 cover the Jewish community identified as "the Mosaic cult," whereby volumes 10 and 11 focus on TES as its cultural mouthpiece between 1978 and 1989. Auerbach's 1972 report is in volume 10.
41 J. L. Austin, "Three Ways of Spilling Ink," *The Philosophical Review* 75, no. 4 (1966): 427–440.
42 Austin, "Three Ways," 437, 439.
43 Alison Lewis, "'Man Habe Niemandem Geschadet': Towards a Typology of Secret Police Informer Reports and Their Impact," talk delivered at the German Studies Association Conference 2021 (virtual mode). See also Glajar's discussion of Austin's tenets in her analysis of the Nobel laureate Herta Müller's unusual rapport with her case officer in Valentina Glajar, *The Secret Police Dossier of Herta Müller: A "File Story" of Cold War Surveillance* (Rochester, NY: Camden House, 2023), 81–82.
44 Franz Auerbach, "Informare" [Report], November 22, 1972, file D 137, vol. 10, 15–23, ACNSAS. Subsequent information comes from this report unless otherwise noted.
45 David S. Lifson, taught English and Theatre at Jersey City State College, the Pratt Institute and Monmouth College of New Jersey, but was best known as the author of the pioneering work *The Yiddish Theatre in America* (1965), see [n. a.], "David S. Lifton, Author and Teacher, 87," *New York Times*, November 11, 1996, https://www.nytimes.com/1996/11/11/arts/david-s-lifson-author-and-teacher-87.html.

46 For details on the actor and acting coach Paul Mann, see [n. a.], "Paul Mann, 71, Dead; An Actor and Teacher," *New York Times*, September 25, 1985, https://www.nytimes.com/1985/09/25/arts/paul-mann-71-dead-an-actor-and-teacher.html; For details about Rabbi Arthur Schneier and his activism during the Cold War, see his biography on Park East Synagogue's website. https://parkeastsynagogue.org/about-us/clergy/rabbi-arthur-schneier/.
47 For information on the radio station WEVD, see Naom, "WEVD: Yiddish Radio in New York," *Mapping Yiddish New York*, October 9, 2017, http://jewishstudiescolumbia.com/myny/arts/wevd-yiddish-radio-in-new-york/.
48 Auerbach, 17.
49 Auerbach, 19.
50 Auerbach, 20.
51 Auerbach, 21.
52 Auerbach, 20.
53 Auerbach, 21.
54 Auerbach's strategy paid off in that TES hosted an international celebration of professional Yiddish theatre's centennial in 1976 and published a two-volume commemorative tome in Romanian, English and Yiddish—*Teatrul Evreiesc de Stat București în Anul Jubiliar 100, 1876–1976/ Bukareshter yidisher melukhe-teater in yuval-yor 100, 1876–1976* (TES in the Jubilee Year 100: 1876–1976; Bucharest: December 13, 1918, 1976). However, neither before not after this event was TES allowed to organise a studio to train new actors for its troupe, although Auerbach brought up the issue with the authorities in charge periodically.
55 Auerbach, 21.
56 Auerbach, 21.
57 In Michael Taussig's definition, the "public secret" is "that which is generally known but cannot be articulated" for one reason or another; see Michael Taussig, *Defacement: Public Secrecy and the Labor of the Negative* (Stanford, CA: Stanford University Press, 1999), 5.
58 According to a letter from Pompiliu Macovei, President of the State Committee for Culture and Art to President of the Council of Ministers, Ion Gheorghe Maurer, from October 25, 1966, the Executive Council at Bucharest's City Hall had asked for approval to close TES at that time. Macovei cited as reasons for this action the "massive" and "continuous" decrease in TES's audiences, the "exaggerated" increase in the price per spectator that the City Council contributed to the Theatre's budget, the lack of interest for shows in Yiddish, and the ensemble's chronic loss of members—due to emigration, although the document did not name the phenomenon explicitly. See Macovei to Maurer, October 25, 1966, reproduced in *Istoria Comunismului din România* [The History of Romanian Communism], Vol. II: *Documente Nicolae Ceaușescu (1965–1971)* [Documents Nicolae Ceaușescu, 1965–1971], ed. Mihnea Berindei, Dorin Dobrincu and Armand Goșu (Iași: Polirom, 2012), 213–214.
59 Berindei et al., 214.
60 For Yiddish theatre's return to the public sphere in Israel in the 1960s, see Rachel Rojanski, *Yiddish in Israel* (Bloomington, IN: Indiana University Press, 2020), 225–249. For an analysis of TES's tour and its political implications, see Corina L. Petrescu, "The Penetrable Iron Curtain: The Bucharest Jewish State Theatre's Tour to Israel in 1968," in *Socialist Yiddishlands Language Politics and Transnational Entanglements between 1941 and 1991*, ed. Miriam Chorley-Schulz and Alexander Walther (Berlin; Boston, MA: Walther De Gruyter, 2024), 355–376.
61 *Shtetl* is the Yiddish word for a small town with a predominantly Ashkenazi Jewish population as it existed in Eastern Europe prior to the Shoah. However, literature and other arts both before and more so after the destruction of the European Jewry transformed the concept into an imagined construct, a substitute for a bygone worldview and way of life built on values such as community, piety, belonging, and Ashkenazi authenticity. Consequently, Yohanan Petrovsky-Shtern has defined it for contemporary times as "nothing but a cultural artifact, a caprice of collective memory." "[S]trip[ed] of its corporeality" and with "its imaginary residue sugarcoat[ed]," it "signifies a vanished Jewish Atlantis, a yearning for a distant and utopian national culture and for the redeeming values of East European Jerusalem." See Petrovsky-Shtern, *The Golden Age Shtetl: A New History of Jewish Life in East Europe* (Princeton, NJ: Princeton University Press, 2014), 27.

32
FAMILIES AS COMMUNITIES OF INFORMATION

Or: The Importance of Knowing Your Relatives

Markus Friedrich

I have no accurate knowledge of my age, never having seen any authentic record containing it. By far the larger part of the slaves know as little of their ages as horses know of theirs [...]. I was not allowed to make any inquiries of my master concerning it. [...] The opinion was also whispered that my master was my father; but of the correctness of this opinion, I know nothing; the means of knowing was withheld from me. My mother and I were separated when I was but an infant—before I knew her as my mother. [...] I never saw my mother, to know her as such, more than four or five times in my life [...]. I do not recollect of ever seeing my mother by the light of day. [...] Very little communication ever took place between us. [...] She was gone long before I knew anything about it.[1]

These words come from the first chapter of one of the most famous autobiographies of the nineteenth century, Frederick Douglass's *Narrative* of his own life as a slave and a freedman. The excerpt is notable for the prevalence of epistemic vocabulary, as Douglass highlights the near-total lack of information about even the most basic facts of kinship and family. He describes the wilful and systematic enforcement of almost absolute ignorance in family-related matters as one of the most potent, and demeaning, elements of slavery. Depriving enslaved people of any kind of information about their relatives, as Douglass describes, was a key strategy of the masters to subdue Black individuals by denying them the comfort, protection, and support of family networks. The "want of information concerning my own was a source of unhappiness to me even during childhood," as the author poignantly recalls.[2]

As slavery thus brutally demonstrates, the question of how families produce, share, maintain, and curate knowledge about themselves (or not) is a very important one. Examining Douglass's words, we may say that families exist in meaningful ways only when enough relevant information about family members, including oneself, is readily available and may be shared among relatives. Therefore, as this chapter argues, families must be understood as communities of information. To identify family members, and to connect with them in meaningful ways, specific pieces of information about the individuals under consideration must be available. A family member about whom we have no information is not familiar to us and is effectively non-existent. "(K)information," to use Maren Klotz's fortuitous formula, is foundational for the existence of kinship, relatedness, and family.[3]

Even in less oppressive circumstances than those of Douglass's youth, however, the availability and circulation of (k)information are highly contextual. Across time and space, humans have established numerous practices to learn about family members, to discover and share relevant information about relatives, and to curate what should or should not be known about those people whom we consider family. Families, thus, exist and thrive not least through changing sets of intra-familial knowledge and information practices. The first section of this chapter establishes the notion of families as communities of information, while the reminder examines historical applications of this idea by looking at select examples from the early modern and modern European bourgeois and noble classes.

(K)information: Families as Communities of Information

For our purposes here, we can distinguish two epistemic approaches to kin and kinship: one conceptual or abstract, the other empirical or concrete. On a conceptual level, kinship relies on abstract understandings of specific social structures. What is an uncle? What is a father? What is a lineage? What is a family? Such abstract forms of family knowledge are usually the domain of (classical forms of) ethnography and anthropology, which attempted, from the nineteenth century onwards, to discover "abstract models and classificatory types" of relatedness, positing, and inventorying generalised kinship "systems."[4]

Everyday family life, however, additionally depends strongly on a more empirical type of information, concerned with identifying human individuals. For families to function as meaningful social units, individuals need (to be able) to identify particular men and women as being their father, mother, or aunt, as Frederik Douglass's words implied. They need to know: Who is my uncle? Who is my father? Who belongs to my lineage? Who is family for me? Answering such questions hinges on positive identification of specific individuals as being *my* great-great-aunt or *my* paternal uncle. Families, therefore, are based on shared familiarity with non-abstract, circumstantial, and contingent biographical facts about individual relatives that include names, dates, and important life events—from birth to marriage to death. This may be called "family-related who-is-who information," and it is this kind of empirical information that is at the centre of this chapter.

This kind of specific and detailed information about individuals and their kinship relationships to other family members is sometimes colloquially called "genealogy." Genealogy, narrowly defined, may be understood as (the collecting and sharing of) explicit sets of biographical facts that allow individuals to be arranged into larger social groups called "families" by connecting them through descent and other propositions of relatedness. In practice, this type of family-constituting genealogical data often comes in the form of stemmata, family trees, or ancestor lists. Despite genealogy's enormous global prominence, the following paragraphs insist that it is necessarily surrounded by additional layers of (k)information. This chapter will highlight, for instance, the relevance of more extensive biographical narratives in constituting families and placing individuals within them. Even more broadly, genealogical (k)information, in order to fulfil its family-constituting function, often requires embedding in family-specific rituals or performances, including for instance regular visits or carefully planned meetings. Finally, the sharing of (k)information, genealogical and other, is regularly linked with material objects (heirlooms) and immaterial traditions, including specific values and habits that are considered to be, and shared as, family-specific. (K)information is therefore highly multi-faceted and occurs in numerous forms. It ranges from bare genealogical facts, perhaps transmitted within broader narratives of family history, to self-consciously maintained family traditions that are profoundly connected to a rich array of material manifestations. Accordingly, the chapter situates the narrowly defined genealogical who-is-who-(k)information within these additional layers of family-related information and knowledge.[5] In doing so, it also highlights that there is no fixed boundary between individual bits of information and broader conceptualisations or narratives ("knowledge") of families. (K)information comprises both isolated facts and nuanced assessments of larger familial realities.[6]

Traditional ethnographic research was not uninterested in this kind of concrete information. In fact, applying instructions from William Rivers's 1910 landmark methodological essay on *The Genealogical Method of Anthropological Inquiry*, generations of ethnographers and anthropologists working in the field habitually questioned indigenous informants about their relatives, thus compiling vast stores of data about the kinfolk of these individuals. However, scholars did so with the explicit intent to distil "general laws" about abstract kinship systems from the empirical data.[7] This chapter proposes a different perspective on family-related who-is-who information. It relies on a newer brand of kinship studies that focuses less on abstract kinship structures and more on the analyses of "practices […] by which relationships are constructed in everyday social life."[8] It is argued here that among the practices of everyday kinship-construction those related to the circulation of familial who-is-who information are particularly relevant. Thus, one can incorporate approaches from the rapidly growing body of scholarship that is commonly referred to as the history of information into the cultural analysis of kinship more thoroughly than is customary.[9] One important lesson to draw from the history of information is that information is never simply "there." Similarly, who-is-who information about family members—what Rivers called the "facts about each person"[10]—is by no means always easily available. Familiarity even with "close" kinship groups is not to be taken for granted. Information about relatives is not an *explanans*, but an *explanandum* of kinship studies. As this chapter argues, families rely on historically changing internal knowledge regimes that are dedicated to creating, circulating, and curating such information. Knowing each other and sharing relevant personal information are key practices that constitute families.

Questions about how families know about themselves have not, by and large, attracted much attention thus far. Among the exceptions are several studies that have used the amount of select individuals' "kinship knowledge" as indicators of class and social standing.[11] These concluded that family-related who-is-who information is more extensive among the powerful, rich, or influential. These studies also point to the somewhat opportunistic motives behind the conscious cultivation of who-is-who information: "those who benefit […] from kin association are more likely to be knowledgeable about their kin."[12] Other publications highlight that "kinship knowledge" advances an individual's "sense of connectedness," thereby influencing a person's "sense of identity."[13] Janet Carsten, for example, finds strong links "between knowing and being in personhood and relatedness."[14] Marilyn Strathern, finally, has frequently pointed out that empirical identification of family members is more than just an external accessory to family life. Rather, empirical (k)information is "constitutive" for family: "Because of its cultural coupling with identity, kinship knowledge is a particular kind of knowledge: the information (and verification on which it draws) is constitutive in its consequences."[15] That is, empirically verifying that this or that person actually fits the culturally specific concept of my "father" or "uncle" immediately changes my entire social relationship to that individual. By being identified as a father through empirical information, the person in question immediately also becomes a father, whether we like it or not. Opportunities for acquiring empirical (k)information, thus, not only mirror or deepen kinship relations—they create them. The remaining sections of this chapter sketch a few examples of intra-familial information practices to illustrate the richness of topics that a comprehensive history of (k)information could address.

Learning about Relatives: (K)information as a Subject of Education

Frederick Douglass's drastic experiences notwithstanding, basic information about immediate relatives is usually acquired in the process of ordinary socialisation from early childhood. Yet even in the most family-friendly circumstances, the number of relatives casually encountered through everyday socialisation remains limited and is determined by ever-changing class- and context-specific habits and customs.

The deeply family-conscious European nobility provides a case in point. Nobles are generally assumed to be particularly dedicated to knowing about past and present family members.[16] Yet an advanced level of informedness does not come naturally even in this social group; it is the result of carefully crafted processes of transmitting such information to new generations and new family members, such as in-marrying women. How are young nobles to learn about those relatives they cannot meet in person, either because they are long dead or reside as separate family branches elsewhere? In some of the more prominent families, including the royal and princely dynasties of France or Germany, the transmission of information about forbears was at least semi-institutionalised. When, in 1693, the sons of Louis XIV were found wanting in their knowledge even of the most important aristocrats at court—many of whom furthermore had genealogical connections to the royal family—Pierre Clairambault, the king's official genealogist, was brought in three times a week for two years to remedy the situation.[17] A little genealogy was also taught to the young Dukes of Mecklenburg.[18]

In many other families, however, especially those of the middle and lower nobility, children would often have learned about more distant relatives, whether past or present, through presumably rather unsystematic "storytelling" about past events and important relatives.[19] Some of these stories about the family's past may have been put into writing for educational purposes. One wealthy late medieval Nuremberg patrician composed a brief "book of remembrance" (*Gedenkbuch*) about the family and "read it to his children."[20] Julius von Bülow, a prominent nobleman from Mecklenburg, also penned a brief essay on his family in 1635 "so that you [children] may be informed about the family you come from."[21]

While these examples highlight the paramount role of a dominant male figure, the family senior or paterfamilias, in the process of transmitting family information, there may in fact often have been other figures more centrally involved. There is no reason that the politically and legally dominant individual should automatically also have been a key figure in familial knowledge practices. On the contrary, future research should explore more in depth the relevance of otherwise "minor" family members, such as women or representatives of collateral branches, as family-focused information hubs. Some nobles, when reminiscing about their youth, highlight the role of "old aunts" in this context.[22] Elsewhere, the role of family historian fell to otherwise relatively obscure individuals.[23]

Oral and textual representations of the family past may have been substituted or complemented by visual media. Many palaces featured painted representations of family history, including, most prominently, displays of family trees and genealogies. We may imagine that such depictions could have been used as a prop to improve the beholders' information base. German Prince Christian II of Anhalt, for instance, remarked in his diary that he attentively inspected painted genealogies on his visits to the residences of German sovereigns during the Thirty Years' War.[24] Sometimes, and not least for pedagogical purposes, influential families ordered manuscript copies of genealogical wall paintings so that these representative illustrations of dynastic glory could circulate more widely among family members.[25] Yet visual representations of (k)information could also include portraits of important individual family members or group-portraits. Other material representations of family history, including, for instance, coins or church decorations, could also serve as prompts for genealogical knowledge transfers.[26] Collections of heirlooms, often transmitted carefully from generation to generation, helped the sharing of (k)information and served to crystallise memory. Family archives deserve particular mention here, for they influence the nobility's self-centred information regimes in two connected ways. On the one hand, once the nobility had started to build up a solid system of recordkeeping, their archives equipped them with highly sophisticated tools to create and verify relevant information. On the other hand, family archives, independently of their informational content, also served as material tokens and symbols of the nobility's antiquity.[27] Well into the twentieth century, the combination of (fragmentary) written narratives, oral storytelling, and material objects served as key media for an unsystematic, though nevertheless often intense, process of providing new arrivals with necessary information about past and present family members.[28]

Rituals of Sharing Information: Visits and Family Reunions

Not only the objects and media used for circulating (k)information, but also the rituals serving the same purpose provide a rich field for scholars to investigate. Family visits and reunions are cases in point. Both activities certainly serve a plethora of functions, as they provide occasions for enjoying the emotional comfort of family and kin while also providing opportunities for relaxed socialising. In addition, however, these social practices were—and still are—crucial for the cultivation of family bonds by providing a forum for the exchange of family news and for introducing hitherto unknown or new family members to one another.

In pre-modern and modern Europe, planned family visits are second in importance only to regular letter-writing among family members as tools for creating and maintaining family bonds. On the one hand, visiting and writing both fulfil a strong performative role. The unusually frequent visits of Prussian king Frederick the Great in the second half of the eighteenth century to (some of) his more distant family branches and members, for instance, appear to have been a powerful means of establishing and maintaining intra-familial hierarchies of power.[29] On the other hand, such routines also help to exchange news. This was a highly important feature, for intra-familial familiarity, that special status of shared lives that clearly transcended mere politeness or courtesy was, among many other things, also predicated upon and expressed by "degrees of knowledge."[30] The sharing of information about relevant recent family events such as births, marriages, or deaths, but also of family-related stories and news in general, both marked and, at the same time, produced intra-familial social proximity and coherence.

While families may always have come together to celebrate prominent life events, such as marriage or death, family reunions became a distinctive social ritual through the nineteenth and twentieth centuries. Elite families staged lavishly orchestrated gatherings, organised for the sole purpose of family members' meeting and publicly sharing the presentation of the glory, wealth, and power of the family. Family reunions also helped individuals expand their family-related information base. Sometimes, planning included concerted efforts to learn and share knowledge about family history.[31]

Family reunions became a key part of (elite) bourgeois life. One impressive reunion of the patrician Burckhardt family in Basel, Switzerland in 1890 brought together more than 260 relatives.[32] Although the reunion was organised primarily for celebrating the basic fact of "belonging together" as one family, the family's rich history was also celebrated and discussed. Elsewhere, such gatherings served to familiarise the family with new members. In 1937, the Peissel family came together in Saxony: "Buses and cars kept arriving, unloading their precious passengers and triggering constant questions and speculation—'Who is this?' and 'Does he belong, too?'—since several blood relatives and in-laws were participating for the first time."[33] Clearly, then, family reunions were crucially important for acquiring and circulating (k)information.

The nobility, too, took up the practice. Based on a small number of early modern cases and an intensifying tradition of such meetings in the nineteenth century, family reunions became key features of the (minor) nobility in Europe after World War I and even more so after 1945.[34] As aristocratic legal privileges continued to erode after 1919, family identity centred increasingly on tradition and shared knowledge. While the nobility had always been an imagined community, this state of existence came into its own in the twentieth century, when more "genuine" markers of identity were under continuous stress. In this context, family reunions became a key means "for younger generations to get to know their older cousins," as the von Bülows claimed in 1937.[35] A generation later, in the 1960s, their peers still agreed: regular meetings not only ensured "a sense of togetherness" but also created possibilities to "personally get to know" relatives.[36] In addition, such meetings very frequently aimed to familiarise the attendees with their family's past, whether through public lectures, cultural excursions to family sites, or visits to historical monuments in general. German noble families exiled after World War II from formerly German territories in Eastern Europe—among them, Mecklenburg, Pomerania, Prussia, Silesia—often used such occasions to conjure memories of their erstwhile homes. In recent years, families from formerly German lands in today's Poland use their regular meetings to collect and circulate stories and knowledge about their displacement in 1945, intentionally preserving such information in the hope of maintaining emotional ties to the original homeland.[37]

Such meetings were often enhanced and recorded for posterity by the circulation of family-internal news media, so-called "Familiennachrichten."[38] In modern times, digital media is used increasingly as an additional tool. The current website of one German noble family, for instance, specifies explicitly that its sophisticated online page is meant to "enhance knowledge about the family among family members and the broader public." A family-internal, password-protected sub-page is designed to "provide opportunities for family members to inform themselves about the clan."[39] While such intra-familial information exchange has certainly changed over time, family-focused information regimes remain essential for families to thrive.

Genealogy

Among the many social practices of creating and circulating (k)information, perhaps none has become more powerful and prominent than genealogy. While not to be considered the gold standard of family knowledge, genealogy nevertheless throws a particularly bright light onto many features of (k)information regimes. Producing and sharing genealogical family histories was considered a powerful weapon against "the darkness of oblivion or forgetfulness" of family ties, and, as such, functioned as a "token of coherence," as one nineteenth-century German nobleman claimed.[40]

Genealogy, however, also highlights the difficulties and complexities of family-related information management. Sources demonstrate repeatedly that there never existed a uniform standard of genealogical information among the nobility. Some nobles cultivated relevant information much more eagerly than others, such as the Marquis de Pomponne, who was characterised by contemporaries as "the man most knowledgeable about genealogy in all of Europe."[41] Henri-Louis Chasteigner de la Rochepozay, too, was an expert in genealogical matters.[42] Other nobles, while perhaps not as fluent in genealogy, were at least interested and found it to be a joyful pastime. In the 1620s, Prince Christian II of Anhalt once spent two entire days reading a genealogical publication—presumably Antonio Albizzi's *Principum Christianorum Stemmata* of 1612.[43] Others, however, were much less interested. For instance, according to a contemporary voice, only one family member of the illustrious Orsini family from Rome, Cardinal Pietro Francesco Orsini (elected Pope Benedict XIII in 1724), was knowledgeable enough to answer detailed questions, while his brother Domenico, Duke of Gravina, "does not dabble in genealogies or family trees."[44] Or: "It is a very strange thing to note that princes and nobles do not have their kinship tables [*Stammregister*] ready at hand and in their archives," the seventeenth-century German genealogist Nicolaus Rittershusius once complained.[45]

Genealogical information about past family members was not only unevenly distributed, but also by no means easy to acquire and store. Learning about past generations had a high threshold of requirements. In the European context, it usually implied literacy, as (k)information was stored to a significant degree in writing, and written evidence was generally considered the most reliable basis. Finding and analysing relevant written documents, moreover, inevitably involved historical research; the study of such archival sources required palaeographic and linguistic skills. Perhaps most importantly, investigation of family history required significant time and money.[46] Every amateur genealogist can testify to these challenges. Family members intent on learning more about their ancestors and relatives must adopt specific genealogical "information-seeking behaviour."[47]

Similarly, the acquisition and circulation of information about contemporary generations was often not without difficulty. Long-distance separation of relatives often prevented easy transmission and investigation of news, not to mention the fact that spatial separation might have led to families' splitting into self-contained branches. And knowledge about distant branches—whether geographical or genealogical—often evaporates more quickly than information about closer relations. Instances of forced migration or violent displacement, including pre-modern and modern slavery, as well as some of the most recent conflicts and ensuing refugee crises, frequently go hand-in-hand with the severing of established information ties among family members, which thereby threatens the survival of functional kinship ties.[48]

Family Secrets as "Difficult Information"

In addition to the basic biographical facts primarily associated with genealogy, families need to share additional forms of (k)information that we may call "operative."[49] Family members also need to be informed about their relatives' specific familial functions and social roles, especially any accompanying challenges, problems, or unspoken secrets. Many families, in fact, have a proverbial skeleton in the closet. Families develop practices of managing such problematic episodes, either by explicitly curating information about them, trying to suppress information, or by limiting access to relevant stories. Who-is-who information about family members often contains material that falls into the broad category of "difficult knowledge," a term designed by psychologists and educators to indicate bodies of information that are painful, disadvantageous, or connected to trauma, shame, and guilt.[50] The category is named for the difficulties involved in making traumatic experiences explicit, whether by actively remembering them or by speaking out about them. Not only the relevant events themselves may be difficult, but also the sharing and cultivating of information about them. Reconceptualising families as communities of information thus also requires consideration of intentional non-knowledge and collaborative silence.

This resonates powerfully with a small, but significant body of scholarship on "family secrets," a key topic for any history of family-related information.[51] Family secrets "require the constant management of information, both inside and outside the family," as Deborah Cohen notes.[52] Yet the practices of hiding and the categories of defining secrets change over time and according to social context. Family secrets, and the forms of managing relevant information about them, have a history, as notions of family, privacy, intimacy, and morality evolve and shift, often in connection with wider-ranging national, religious, or political taboos and preferences.[53] While the Victorian Age was, according to Cohen, characterised by a straightforward equation of familial privacy with near-absolute secrecy about difficult information, recent decades have turned this almost entirely upside down. Today, a confessional culture prevails, shaped by constant public discussion of problematic episodes. Explicitness and "coming out of the closet" now count as admirable, viable strategies of dealing with familial nonconformity.

Sometimes the information itself is vague enough so as to mitigate any risk of exposure. Stories about secrets are often full of confusion, indicating that in these cases only inadequate means are available within a family to clarify details, verify data, and corroborate accounts.[54] If difficult facts are, by contrast, well-known and clear, families often resort to collusion to manage the potential fallout. This implies the careful management of access to relevant information and the meticulous curation of all occasions for speaking out about such topics. Only some family members may talk at all about difficult things, and only at select, and appropriate, occasions. Some early modern noble families explicitly obliged their members to maintain secrecy about internal affairs.[55]

Scholars have identified different types of family secrets, distinguishing, for instance, between within-family secrets and family-wide secrets, the first being known only to a small select minority even of family members, while the second are known to the entire family but not divulged to the outside. Family-wide secrets, while widely shared, are nevertheless often shrouded in silence—they are known, but not talked about, like the proverbial "elephant in the room." Shared marginalisation of certain difficult facts may, in itself, have been a socially integrative act. When, in 1937, the respected German noble family von Bernstorff marked their seven hundredth family jubilee by, among other things, publishing a celebratory brochure about their past, they simply left out the most shameful recent event, though it must clearly have been on everyone's minds: in 1932, they had lost their most prestigious piece of property, Wedendorf. While the loss must have shaken the family, it simply went unmentioned.[56]

Even as families faced with difficult (k)information were often keen on controlling it, there was always the risk that such secrets could be publicised. Sometimes, secrets were simply broken and problematic behaviour was too widely known to warrant further restraint. A complex affair that tore apart the Portuguese royal family in the final third of the seventeenth century, for instance, was general knowledge in the European reading public: King Alfonso VI, a man of diminished physical and mental capacities, had not only behaved "wildly" against his wife, but also (allegedly) attempted to force a favourite onto her to father the desired heir. Moreover, Alfonso was eventually pushed out of office by his more capable brother, future king Pedro II. Only with a papal dispensation did Pedro later marry Alfonso's wife, with whom he had previously had an affair. All these scandals circulated publicly throughout Europe.[57]

Other family secrets, however, had to remain under control. Observers of (noble) families often calibrated their attitude towards unbecoming information very carefully. Jakob Wilhelm Imhoff, born in 1651 and later a prominent author of books on the nobility, once received the following bit of information in an informal handwritten note:

> In his youth, Prince Ludwig of Baden was enamoured with one Amalia von Löwenstein, and made a promise to her concerning the future [to marry her]. When he forgot her, though, once he came of age and the Princess of Neuburg came to his attention, she [Löwenstein] entered a convent. His cousins, the two sons of Markgraf Leopold, are badly disabled: the older one is mute, and the other is not much better off.[58]

This piece of gossip not only highlights the role of (presumably wilful) "forgetting" of inconvenient facts, but also serves to indicate an outsider's nuanced reaction. Imhoff used only part of this information in print. He never published the report about the seventeenth-century affair of Prince Ludwig Wilhelm, who was, by then, a powerful man. Imhoff also failed to mention the younger of the two cousins (presumably Karl Friedrich Ferdinand, who only lived for twelve years). Imhoff *did*, however, mention in print the other cousin, Leopold Wilhelm and the fact that he "lacked the ability to speak."[59] While physical (and mental) ailments of ruling families were obviously not beyond public mentioning, as they were probably widely known anyway, the secret of Prince Ludwig's amorous youth remained better hidden. There was always a context-specific and ever-changing, yet nevertheless highly functional consensus about the limits of public exposure, whether from within a family or outside.

The urge to uncover family secrets and divulge them publicly emerged as a key element of Europe's information culture. Investigating family secrets became a prominent aspect not only of many journalistic and political media,[60] but also as a major plot line in European literature. Fictional as well as non-fictional works throughout the centuries abound with stories of family secrets, their management, and their exposure to either uninitiated family members or the wider public. Scholars of the nineteenth century have pointed out the crucial role of servants in uncovering secrets for an interested public that revelled in juicy gossip about scandalous behaviour, distributed widely by the penny press.[61] Accordingly, Victorian (crime) novels, too, are replete with instances of servants spying on their masters.

Clearly reflecting a growing anxiety among upper social classes about privacy, these plots also testify to increasingly elaborate attempts to control family-internal information. Many nineteenth- and twentieth-century detective stories, too, involve outsiders probing family secrets and acquiring difficult information against the family's will.[62] In a very different context, the investigative exposure of family secrets also became a defining feature for younger Germans from the 1960s. Uncovering, and reporting, the potential involvement of their parents in National Socialist policies emerged as a major issue for a new generation.[63] As all these examples indicate, "non-knowing," and especially "not wanting to know," recently highlighted as important objects of historical study, should also figure prominently in future historical studies of (k)information.[64]

Who-Is-Who Information in the Twenty-First Century

In the ever-changing history of (k)information regimes, recent decades have seen the evolution of at least three important new developments: advances in reproductive medicine, internet-based computer genealogy, and ancestral DNA testing. Dramatic innovations in reproductive medicine since the 1980s have brought the importance of knowledge and information ecologies for kinship into sharper focus than ever before.[65] Technological advances have raised numerous unprecedented questions: Should information about biological fathers be shared in the case of sperm donors? Should information about potential half-siblings be shared? Who should control access to such information? How should information about biological descent be handled in the case of same-sex couples, where only one biological parent is present, if at all? While the new bio-medical technologies highlight the epistemic implications of family structures in particularly radical ways—much like the brutal example of slavery—they in fact only illustrate a feature of every family in whatever cultural context: we need to know who those individuals are that we may identify as kin; yet this kind of who-is-who information is rarely simply available in unproblematic or uncontested ways.

No less important is the influence of digital technologies on family-related who-is-who information.[66] Internet-based collaboration of individuals, together with mass digitisation of records, has amplified the possibilities for genealogical research. It is much easier today to know much more about one's ancestors than ever before. With web services such as Ancestry.com, finding ancestors and learning about family connections has not only become more efficient, but also less cumbersome than previously. (K)information has also become more commodified than ever before, as multi-national corporations sell such services at a substantial profit. While these new digital resources should be seen in continuity with earlier, analogue technologies of genealogical information-sharing, they nevertheless pose entirely new questions. Ancestry.com's policy of making millions of digitised public records accessible through their web portals often overrides concerns for privacy, especially regarding sensitive information obtained from vulnerable minorities.[67]

DNA testing, finally, is a third recently invented information technology that has significantly affected our understanding of who-is-who information.[68] It claims to go back far deeper into history than the written record, thereby altering the temporalities of (k)information-based identities.[69] Moreover, while sometimes actually linking specific historical individuals—such as, potentially, Thomas Jefferson and Sally Hemings—most of its power is derived from linking individuals to broader collectivities, determining otherwise unspecific

"African" or "European" or "Jewish" ancestral backgrounds.[70] The shift of ancestral information away from historic individuals to broader ethnic groups not only influences how genealogical identities are constructed, but also allows for new forms of abuse. Several First Nations, for instance, have opposed DNA testing as a criterion for tribal identities, following white racists' usage of DNA testing to support "white claims to indigenous identity" for purely opportunistic reasons.[71]

Internal and External (K)information Regimes: The State and the Family

These examples from very recent developments in (k)information regimes, not least because of their often highly emotional and deeply political implications, already indicate that the shape and limits of family-internal information practices are often very closely related to external forces. Frequently, the "formation of families and the formation of states were [...] implicated in each other."[72] It is, for instance, government legislation that determines whether or not the names of sperm donors must be made available. On a different note, early modern ecclesiastical institutions often required quite detailed genealogical information before partners were allowed to marry, thereby requiring couples to maintain, and present, relevant who-is-who information in externally imposed formats.[73] Administrative routines, as well, frequently require processes of (k)information-gathering and enforce specific styles of documenting and memorising kinship. External moral, legal, and political criteria, moreover, often determine what is considered as "difficult" (k)information—an obvious example, well-known and brutal, would be the Nazi-era requirement to document "Aryan" ancestry, which led not only to wide-ranging research activities, but also to complex strategies of evasion in the event that "non-Aryan" forebears were discovered.[74] In fact, the Nazis' obsession with race put in place a vast machinery of genealogical research that also came to be used by genealogists for other and often private research projects. There is thus often no clear-cut boundary between the inside and outside of families when it comes to (k)information history. What needs to be pointed out, rather, is the interdependence of external and internal ways of knowing family. States and other bureaucracies may impose (k)information regimes on families; yet the families are often well equipped to not just evade, but proactively instrumentalise external information routines for their own purposes.[75]

Conclusion

Departing from Frederick Douglass's passage about slavery's wilful denial even of basic (k)information to the enslaved, this chapter has explored some of the media, rituals, challenges, and implications of intra-familial information regimes. In addition to being structured by regimes of power, economy, religion, or politics, families must also be considered as depending on, and institutionalising, specific information practices. Families not only coalesce as communities of social ties, wealth, or patronage, but also exist as communities of information. For families to take shape, individuals must be identified as actually being related by a set of personal data. These basic items of family-related who-is-who information usually include names, dates, and biographical facts, such as birth, marriage, and offspring. Usually, these basic pieces of genealogical (k)information are closely intertwined with broader narratives about family history and traditions, often emotionally connected to material objects and heirlooms. Sometimes, these bodies of knowledge might contain difficult information, requiring special handling. To provide, and manage, relevant (k)information, families enact distinctive information regimes—without this, as Douglass's drastic experience shows, families can hardly exist. In any given family, individual family members may, of course, still cultivate distinct and personal attitudes towards intra-familial information habits. They may accommodate these knowledge regimes to various degrees, thereby expressing individual standpoints and feelings towards their families—not every relative participates in family-internal information-sharing with equal gusto. As individuals' commitment to family varies, so does their family-related information base.

Further development of this epistemic perspective on family and kinship will be beneficial for several scholarly fields. The History of the Family, a distinctive and tradition-rich part of historiography, can benefit from further expanding ongoing work on intra-familial memory practices. Sharing (k)information via storytelling was and is a major form of creating sociability, and deserves to be fully integrated into that historiography.[76] Moreover, a focus on (k)information will draw attention to intra-familial information media, including oral and written forms as well as textual and visual objects, and their production processes. The growing sub-discipline of information history, in turn, could use the family as a case study to explore its topics beyond the fields of state and science (or scholarship), the two currently dominant empirical areas of investigation. Families have received some attention as collective producers of scientific knowledge, including discussions of women's roles in scholarly research. Yet the family itself, as a basic social unit, has hardly been subjected to a history-of-information approach.

Notes

1 Frederick Douglass, *Narrative of the Life of Frederick Douglass, an American Slave* (Boston, MA: The Anti-Slavery Office, 1845), 1–3.
2 Douglass, *Narrative*, 3.
3 Maren Klotz, *(K)information. Gamete Donation and Kinship Knowledge in Germany and Britain* (Frankfurt: Campus Verlag, 2014).
4 Susan D. Gillespie, "Beyond Kinship. An Introduction," in *Beyond Kinship. Social and Material Reproduction in House Societies*, ed. Rosemary A. Joyce and Susan D. Gillespie (Philadelphia, PA: University of Pennsylvania Press, 2000), 1–21, esp. 1. Also, Maurice Godelier, *The Metamorphoses of Kinship* (London: Verso Books, 2020); Sandra Bamford, ed., *The Cambridge Handbook of Kinship* (Cambridge, UK: Cambridge University Press, 2019); and Laurent Barry, *La Parenté* (Paris: Gallimard, 2008), folio essays, 498.
5 One prominent field of historical investigation which could be fruitfully connected to the approach suggested here is the study of funerary practices and rituals, including the maintenance of cemeteries; for a wide-ranging discussion, see, for example, Thomas W. Laqueur, *The Work of the Dead. A Cultural History of Mortal Remains* (Princeton, NJ: Princeton University Press, 2015).
6 The distinction between "information" and "knowledge" is a vexed one. This chapter prefers a low-key, pragmatic distinction as suggested by Peter Burke who (borrowing from Claude Levi-Strauss) famously called "information," the "raw," and "knowledge," the "cooked," epistemic forms of representing the world in, Peter Burke, *A Social History of Knowledge. From Gutenberg to Diderot* (Cambridge, UK: Polity, 2002). Of course, this is a question of scale and perspective: if genealogical data may constitute raw "information" for an elaborate autobiographical memoir, a complex genealogical family tree may be already considered sophisticated "knowledge" as opposed to its disjointed and fragmented sources. For this reason, this chapter does not maintain a strict conceptual distinction; the usage of the two terms rather indicates where on that scale from "raw" to "cooked" individual forms of (k)information are situated. Furthermore, there is considerable semantic drift through time. As Douglass's quote above shows, much of what one would call "information" in the context of this chapter—bare information about when he was born or who his father was—was conceptualised as "knowledge" in earlier times.

7 Quotation from William H. Rivers, *Kinship and Social Organization* (London: Athlone Press, 1968), 107. For a book-length, highly critical re-evaluation of Rivers's foundational contribution, see Sandra Bamford and James Leach, eds., *Kinship and Beyond. The Genealogical Model Reconsidered* (New York: Berghahn Books, 2009).
8 Gillespie, *Beyond Kinship*, 1.
9 For the state of the art, see Ann Blair, Anthony Grafton, Paul Duguid, and Anja-Silvia Goeing, eds., *Information: A Historical Companion* (Princeton, NJ: Princeton University Press, 2020). See also Paul Dover, *The Information Revolution in Early Modern Europe* (Cambridge, UK: Cambridge University Press, 2021). None of these books, however, include "family" or "kinship" as relevant topics.
10 Rivers, *Kinship*, 99.
11 Michael Gordon, "Kinship Boundaries and Kinship Knowledge in Urban Ireland," *International Journal of Sociology of the Family* 7 (1977): 1–14.
12 Gordon, *Kinship Boundaries*, 5f.
13 Janet Carsten, "Constitutive Knowledge: Tracing Trajectories of Information in New Contexts of Relatedness," *Anthropological Quarterly* 80 (2007): 403–426, 404.
14 Carsten, "Constitutive Knowledge," 404.
15 Marilyn Strathern, *Property, Substance, and Effect. Anthropological Essays on Persons and Things* (London: Athlone Press, 1999), 68.
16 For a powerful summary, see Eric Mension-Rigau, *L'enfance au château. L'éducation familiale des élites françaises au vingtième siècle* (Paris: Rivages, 1990), 193–214.
17 Pascale Mormiche, *Devenir prince. L'école du pouvoir en France, XVIIe–XVIIIe siècles* (Paris: CNRS Éditions, 2009), 399–401.
18 Antje Stannek, *Telemachs Brüder: Die höfische Bildungsreise des 17. Jahrhunderts* (Frankfurt/Main, New York: Campus, 2001), 138, with n. 302.
19 Silvio Jacobs, *Familie, Stand und Vaterland. Der niedere Adel im frühneuzeitlichen Mecklenburg* (Cologne: Quellen und Studien aus den Landesarchiven Mecklenburg-Vorpommerns 15, 2013), 62, 70.
20 Barbara Schmid, *Schreiben für Status und Herrschaft. Deutsche Autobiographik in Spätmittelalter und früher Neuzeit* (Zürich: Chronos Verlag, 2006), 74: "den[en] ich das zu letzte las."
21 Jacobs, *Familie, Stand und Vaterland*, 70.
22 Mension-Rigau, *Enfance*, 198.
23 This was the case, for instance, in the semi-noble Imhoff family from Nuremberg. See Markus Friedrich, *Maker of Pedigrees. Jakob Wilhelm Imhoff and the Meanings of Genealogy in Early Modern Europe* (Baltimore, MD: Johns Hopkins University Press, 2023), 71.
24 Arndt Schreiber, Alexander Zirr, Andreas Herz, and Antoine Odier, eds., *Digitale Edition und Kommentierung der Tagebücher des Fürsten Christian II. von Anhalt-Bernburg (1599–1656)* (Wolfenbüttel: Herzog August Bibliothek, 2013), http://diglib.hab.de/wdb.php?q=genealog*&dir=edoc%2Fed000228&qurl=wdb%2Fsearch%2Fsearch.xql&distype=results-transcript.
25 For a relevant example, see Kamil Boldan, "Eine unbekannte Handschrift mit einer Porträtgalerie der Wettiner," *Studie o rukopisech* 47 (2017): 49–69.
26 For one example of family history told exclusively via coins, see Christoph Andreas von Imhoff, *Sammlung eines Nürnbergischen Münz-Cabinets*, Band 1, Abtheilung 2 (Nürnberg: Felsecker, 1782). This is a major theme in Mension-Rigau's above-quoted chapter.
27 Imogen Peck, "'Of no Sort of Use'? Manuscripts, Memory, and the Family Archive in Eighteenth Century England," *Cultural and Social History* 20 (2022): 1–22.
28 For the twentieth century, see Eckart Conze, *Von deutschem Adel. Die Grafen von Bernstorff im zwanzigsten Jahrhundert* (Stuttgart: DVA, 2000), 345.
29 Thomas Biskup, "Four Weddings and Five Funerals. Dynastic Integration and Cultural Transfer between the Houses of Braunschweig and Brandenburg in the Eighteenth Century," in *Queens Consort, Cultural Transfer and European Politics, c. 1500–1800*, ed. Helen Watanabe-O'Kelly and Adam Morton (Abingdon: Routledge, 2017), 202–229, esp. 209–215.
30 Sarah M. S. Pearsall, *Atlantic Families. Lives and Letters in the Later Eighteenth Century* (Oxford: Oxford University Press, 2008), 58.
31 Robert M. Taylor, "Summoning the Wandering Tribes: Genealogy and Family Reunions in American History," *Journal of Social History* 16 (1982): 21–37.

32 Fiona Vicent, "Abstammung zelebrieren. Das 'Erinnerungsfest' zum 400-jährigen Geburtstag des Stammvaters der Familie Burckhardt am 14. September 1890," in *Genealogie in der Moderne. Akteure – Praktiken – Perspektiven*, ed. Michael Hecht and Elisabeth Timm (Berlin: de Gruyter Oldenbourg, 2022), 129–157.
33 Staatsarchiv Leipzig, 22179, no. 2235 (Mitteilungsblätter des Familienverbandes Peissel, 1936–1944), here no. 5, 1938, reporting on the previous year, n.p.
34 On early modern examples, see Vicky Rothe, "Geschlechts- und Familienordnungen," in *Adlige Lebenswelten in Sachsen. Kommentierte Bild- und Schriftquellen*, ed. Martina Schattkowsky (Cologne: Böhlau, 2013), 85–95.
35 Quoted in Daniel Menning, *Standesgemäße Ordnung in der Moderne. Adlige Familienstrategien und Gesellschaftsentwürfe in Deutschland 1840–1945* (Munich: Oldenbourg, 2014), 376.
36 Michael Seelig, *Alltagsadel. Der ehemalige ostelbische Adel in der Bundesrepublik Deutschland 1945/49–1975* (Cologne: Böhlau Verlag, 2015), 387–406, esp. 388.
37 For interesting sources from oral history, see Simon Donig, *Adel ohne Land – Land ohne Adel? Lebenswelt, Gedächtnis und materielle Kultur des schlesischen Adels nach 1945* (Berlin: de Gruyter Oldenbourg, 2019), 231f.
38 Seelig, *Alltagsadel*, 382–387. Menning, *Standesgemäße Ordnung*, 380f.
39 Familie von Bülow website, https://familievonbuelow.de/.
40 Werner von Bernstorff-Wedendorf, 1880s, quoted in Conze, *Von deutschem Adel*, 342f.
41 Saint-Simon, *Mémoires. Vol. IV (1711–1714)*, ed. Yves Coirault (Paris: Gallimard, 1985), x, 9.
42 Hilary J. Bernstein, "La Rochepozay, Ghost-Writer: Noble Genealogy, Historical Erudition, and Political Engagement in Seventeenth-Century France," *Proceedings of the Western Society for French History* 37 (2009): 1–20.
43 October 27 and 28, 1626, "Lectio in Principum Christianorum stemmatis. etc(etera)"; see http://diglib.hab.de/wdb.php?q=stammb*&dir=edoc%2Fed000228&qurl=wdb%2Fsearch%2Fsearch.xql&distype=results-transcript.
44 Andrea Gittio to Imhoff, February 14, 1690, in Germanisches Nationalmuseum, Nachlass Imhoff VII, vol. 1, unpaginated. Cf. also Elisabetta Mori, *L'Archivio Orsini. La famiglia, la storia, l'inventario* (Rome: Viella, 2016), 174–176, 185, and passim.
45 Ritterhusen to ?, Staats- und Universitätsbibliothek Göttingen, Ms Phil 94, Nr 68 (n.d., n.p.). Many more examples appear in Friedrich, *Maker of Pedigrees*, passim.
46 Markus Friedrich, "Genealogy as Archive-Driven Research Enterprise in Early Modern Europe," *Osiris* 32 (2017): 65–84.
47 Wendy Duff and Catherine Johnson, "Where Is the List with All the Names? Information-Seeking Behavior of Genealogists," *The American Archivist* 66 (2003): 79–95.
48 Charlie Knight, "'I Beg You Again from My Heart to Help Me Find My Sister': RELICO and the Need for Knowledge," *History of Knowledge*, December 13, 2022, https://historyofknowledge.net/2022/12/13/relico-and-the-need-for-knowledge/.
49 For a useful distinction between "genealogy" and "operative kinship," made in the very different context of a section on Arab genealogy, see Aziz Al-Azmeh, *The Emergence of Islam in Late Antiquity. Allah and His People* (Cambridge, UK: Cambridge University Press, 2014), 126f.
50 George Steiner, *On Difficulty and Other Essays* (Oxford: Oxford University Press, 1978); and Alice Pitt and Deborah Britzman, "Speculations on Qualities of Difficult Knowledge in Teaching and Learning: An Experiment in Psychoanalytic Research," *International Journal of Qualitative Studies in Education* 16, no. 6 (2003): 755–776.
51 Annette Kuhn, *Family Secrets: Acts of Memory and Imagination*, new edition (New York: Verso, 2002); and Carol Smart, "Families, Secrets and Memories," *Sociology* 45 (2011): 539–553.
52 Deborah Cohen, *Family Secrets. The Things We Tried to Hide* (London: Viking, 2014), xvi.
53 For a distinctive focus on the "interconnection of family practices and national memory," see Ashley Barnwell, "Hidden Heirlooms: Keeping Family Secrets across Generations," *Journal of Sociology* 54 (2018): 446–460.
54 For this, and the following, see, with its rich additional bibliography, Robyn Fivush, Helena McAnally, and Elaine Reese, "Family Stories and Family Secrets," *The Journal of New Zealand Studies* 29 (2019): 20–36.
55 Rothe, *Familienordnungen*, 92.
56 Conze, *Von deutschem Adel*, 352–354.

57 For example, in Samuel Pufendorf, *An Introduction to the History of the Principal Kingdoms and States of Europe*, trans. Jodocus Crull (1695), ed. and with an introduction by Michael J. Seidler (Indianapolis, IN: Liberty Fund, Natural Law and Enlightenment Classics Ser, 2013), 108f.
58 Germanisches Nationalmuseum, Nuremberg, Nachlass Imhoff VII, vol. 7, unpaginated (Baden).
59 Jakob Wilhelm Imhoff, *S. Rom. Germanici Notitia Procerum* (Tübingen: Cotta, ³1693), 187 (no. 22).
60 See, for example, Rebecca Bullard and Rachel Carnell, eds., *The Secret History in Literature, 1660–1820* (Cambridge, UK: Cambridge University Press, 2017), esp. 166–171, 244f.
61 Cohen, *Family Secrets*, 56.
62 Anthea Trodd, "Household Spies. The Servant and the Plot in Victorian Fiction," *Literature and History* 13 (1987): 175–187.
63 Norbert Lebert and Stephan Lebert, *Denn Du trägst meinen Namen. Das schwere Erbe der prominenten Nazi-Kinder*, 3rd ed. (Munich: Blessing, 2000); and Lars Reichardt, "'Monster sind nicht charmant, oder?' Bettina Göring ist die Großnichte der Nazi-Größe Hermann Göring," *Süddeutsche Zeitung Magazin*, 7/2017 (online: https://sz-magazin.sueddeutsche.de/geschichte/monster-sind-nicht-charmant-oder-83327).
64 Renate Dürr, ed., *Threatened Knowledge: Practices of Knowing and Ignoring from the Middle Ages to the Twentieth Century* (Aldershot: Routledge, 2022).
65 Klotz, *(K)information*. Andreas Bernard, *Kinder machen. Neue Reproduktionstechnologien und die Ordnung der Familie* (Frankfurt: S. Fischer, 2014). See also Carles Salazar and Jeanette Edwards, eds., *European Kinship in the Age of Biotechnology* (New York: Berghahn Books, 2009).
66 See, for example, Francesca Morgan, *A Nation of Descendants. Politics and the Practice of Genealogy in U.S. History* (Chapel Hill, NC: University of North Carolina Press, 2021); and Julia Creet, *The Genealogical Sublime* (Amherst, MA: University of Massachusetts Press, 2020).
67 A case study in Katharina Hering, "The Representation of NARA's INS Records in Ancestry's Database Portal," *Archival Science* 23, no. 1 (2023): 29–44, esp. 39–41.
68 Creet, *Genealogical Sublime*; and Elisabeth Timm, "Populäre Familienforschung und DNA-Genealogie in Deutschland: Ausprägungen und Akteure im Überblick," *Mitteilungen der Berliner Gesellschaft für Anthropologie, Ethnologie und Urgeschichte* 43 (2022): 141–166.
69 Hallam Stevens, "Genetimes and Lifetimes: DNA, New Media, and History," *Memory Studies* 8 (2015): 390–406.
70 Stevens, "Genetimes."
71 Darryl Leroux, *Distorted Descent. White Claims to Indigenous Identity* (Winnipeg: University of Manitoba Press, 2019); and Kim TallBear, *Native American DNA. Tribal Belonging and the False Promise of Genetic Science* (Minneapolis, MN: University of Minnesota Press, 2013).
72 Nandini Chatterjee, *Negotiating Mughal Law. A Family of Landlords across Three Indian Empires* (Cambridge, UK: Cambridge University Press, 2020), 24, here quoting earlier work by Sumit Guha.
73 Jasmin Hauck, *Ehen mit Hindernissen. Verwandtschaft, Recht und genealogisches Erinnern im Florenz der Renaissance* (Tübingen: Mohr Siebeck, 2022).
74 Eric Ehrenreich, *The Nazi Ancestral Proof. Genealogy, Racial Science, and the Final Solution* (Bloomington, IN: Indiana University Press, 2007).
75 Michael Szonyi, *The Art of Being Governed. Everyday Politics in Late Imperial China* (Princeton, NJ: Princeton University Press, 2017); André Burguière, "L'etat monarchique et la famille," *Annales. Histoire, Sciences Sociales* 56 (2001): 313–335; and Burguière, "La centralisation monarchique et la naissance des sciences sociales: voyageurs et statisticiens," *Annales. Histoire, Sciences Sociales* 55 (2000): 199–218.
76 For a recent contribution, see, for example, Tanya Evans, *Family History, Historical Consciousness and Citizenship. A New Social History* (London: Bloomsbury Academic, 2023).

33
FEATHERS AND FORMATS
Information, Technology, and Homing Pigeons in War*

Frank A. Blazich, Jr.

Homing pigeons have aided the transmission of critical information during times of war for more than two millennia. They could be relied upon as a one-way method of information delivery when more traditional methods of communication failed. Over the years, the birds have carried information in different formats—from small scraps of paper to map overlays to film. Although developments in communication technologies threatened to make military homing pigeons obsolete in the mid-twentieth century, these same developments may also have provided an opportunity for the return of the birds to action. On the twenty-first-century battlefield, wireless transmission is vulnerable to sophisticated cyberattacks; pigeons are not. Furthermore, the advent of miniaturised digital storage devices has enabled much more information to be moved by a single pigeon. By combining digital and pigeon technologies, large amounts of encrypted data can be transmitted beyond the reach of existing electronic countermeasures. This chapter will explore how homing pigeons were used as a technology of transmission that evolved with—and could be adapted to—changes in the information formats that are characteristic of military operations.

Understanding the Feathered Messenger

Homing pigeons are the genetic relatives of the rock dove, *Columba livia*, yet are more akin to racehorses in that they are not only bred but also trained for speed, endurance, and navigational prowess.[1] As detailed in a 1918 US Army manual, the birds are "the result of several centuries of intelligent crossbreeding…[which] has produced an amalgam: the Homing pigeon of today, a variety of the pigeon family noted for its superior intelligence and physique."[2] Individual pigeons typically weigh one pound. They can fly uninterrupted for twelve to fifteen hours—to distances up to seven hundred miles—and at speeds between thirty and sixty miles per hour. Champion birds can now sprint at speeds exceeding ninety miles per hour.[3]

---

* The author thanks Lucy Betteridge-Dyson, Katie Borcuk, Laurence Burke II, Justin Craig, Susan Dawson, Bonnie Mak, Susan Thompson, and the anonymous reviewers for their editorial and intellectual support.

The science behind the skill of homing is unclear, but it is likely that pigeons navigate using several abilities. There is evidence that pigeons visually navigate by natural or man-made landmarks, such as roads or railroad tracks. Other theories suggest that pigeons use the angle and position of the sun to orient themselves or detect Earth's magnetic fields to navigate with a natural compass. They may also use smell to find their way home. Pigeons might even use low-frequency infrasound waves to navigate. It is possible that homing pigeons rely on some or all these powers when travelling from a new, unknown location to their home loft.[4] But why do pigeons reliably home to a *specific* location? The desire to return over great distance is linked to food and sex; home is where pigeons find food and reproduce. Because pigeons mate for life and both hens and cocks care for the young, the innate desire to return home can therefore be controlled and enhanced by the removal of a bird from its loft. Meanwhile, hunger is managed in training by acclimating a bird to return to a specific location to feed.[5]

Ancient Use to 1800s

The earliest recorded references to the use of pigeons for communication purposes suggest that the birds themselves operated as symbolic indicators of information. Surviving archaeological ruins and records indicate that pigeons (sometimes referred to as "doves") were understood as symbols of reverence in Sumerian, Egyptian, Greek, Roman, Hebrew, Hindu, Assyrian, Persian, and Phoenician culture and religious beliefs beginning in at least 5000 BCE.[6] There is an account in the Book of Genesis of Noah sending forth a dove to see if waters had receded from the Earth. On the bird's second flight, it returned to Noah clutching an olive leaf in its beak, proving that the water had receded.[7]

Greek and Roman references to pigeons in pre-Biblical times offer further clues about the use of pigeons for sending messages. In the sixth century BCE, the Greek lyric poet Anacreon composed an ode wherein the dove (likely a pigeon) carries his letters.[8] Around 200 CE, Roman author Claudius Aelianus (Aelian) wrote about the Greek wrestler Taurosthenes and his victory at Olympia. Some said that the wrestler had brought a pigeon with him, taken from her squabs, to send news of the outcome to his father on the island of Ægina. Upon his victory, Taurosthenes tied a piece of something purple around the bird and released her to the sky, returning to her nest from Pisa to Ægina in a day, a trip of approximately one hundred miles.[9] Although the message may have been a simple one, the use of colour to convey meaning proved effective when paired with a pigeon messenger.

Roman author and naturalist Pliny the Elder provides the earliest recorded evidence of military use of homing pigeons. During the War of Mutina (contemporary Modena, Italy) in the first century BCE, Mark Antony's forces attempted to seize Cisalpine Gaul from the governor and Roman general, Decimus Junius Brutus Albinus. Because Antony's forces could block human messengers who travelled on foot, Brutus had to find another way to communicate with his Roman consuls and the Senate forces.[10] According to Pliny, despatches were fastened to the feet of pigeons; the birds carried the messages from inside the city to the camp of the consuls.[11] Frontinus references how Hirtius kept his birds isolated and hungry during the siege, then fastened notes to the necks of the pigeons with hair. Once released from confinement, the birds flew to Brutus, specifically to locations where he had trained them to alight and feed.[12] This use of the birds to overcome ground defences by Brutus is one of the earliest recorded uses of air power for transmitting information on the battlefield.

The recorded history of using pigeons as messengers for military purposes in the Western world is scarce for the next millennium. Two references to pigeons in war are found in the Levant. During the Siege of Acre in the Third Crusade (1189–1191 CE), communication between the Muslim forces inside the city continued with Yusuf ibn Ayyub ibn Shadhi (Saladin) by means of pigeons. These birds had been trained as part of a pigeon post established previously by Sultan Noureddin Mahmoud.[13] Writing in the mid-1300s, Sir John Mandeville notes that in Syria in the kingdom of Judea, when forces were under siege in a city or castle, pigeons—rather than human messengers—would be utilised, with messages bound around their necks (Fig. 33.1). The bird would be trained to home back to locations with food.[14]

Crusaders learned from the Muslims and began to use the birds as messengers in Europe. Chroniclers from the eleventh through thirteenth centuries describe the technique of attaching messages to the necks, feet, wings, and tails of the pigeons.[15] The first documented use of pigeons in western Europe for military purposes was at the sieges of the Dutch cities of Haarlem and Leiden by Spanish forces during the Eighty Years' War. During the siege of Haarlem, from December 1572 to July 1573, William the Silent, Prince of Orange, used pigeons as messengers to communicate with leadership inside the city. This method was effective until a pigeon was captured and found to be carrying a message; thereafter, the Spanish forces attempted to kill every pigeon flying over their encampment. During the siege of Leiden, from October 1573 to October 1574, the Prince of Orange again used pigeons for

Figure 33.1 Pigeon post as described by Sir John Mandeville, depicted in a 1488 woodcut published by Johann Prüss.

Source: Jean de Mandeville and Otto von Diemeringen, *Johannes Von Moneuilla, Ritter* (Straßburg: Johann Prüss der Ältere, 1488).

communication with the besieged Dutch. His messages on small pieces of paper urged the city's residents to persevere until relief arrived.[16]

Following the conclusion of the Eighty Years' War, some European civilians used homing pigeons specifically for expedience. Beginning in 1824, the Rothschild brothers began employing pigeons to transport important correspondence and financial information—sometimes in code—from France to England, and faster than their competitors. The birds carried the messages in small tubes attached to their legs.[17] In 1845, Paul Julius Reuter, founder of the Reuters news agency, tasked forty-five pigeons with transmitting the prices of stocks, bonds, and news between Aachen, Germany and Brussels, Belgium. The information was recorded on thin sheets of paper and placed in silk bags that were secured around the necks of the birds.[18] Conflict in 1849 found pigeons impressed into service again; during the Austrian siege of the Venetian Republic, residents of the city used the famed Piazza San Marco pigeons to carry messages outside the city.[19] Although merely a footnote in pigeon history, this siege foretold a far more significant event that would occur two decades later.

The Siege of Paris, 1870–1871

The Siege of Paris marked the beginning of the modern, mass military use of homing pigeons. After the French Emperor Napoleon III and his army surrendered to Prussian forces on September 2, 1870, leading to the collapse of the French Second Republic, Prussian forces encircled Paris by September 20, severing all lines of communication. Balloons became the only option to transport people and messages out of the city. Pigeons taken out by balloon were released to communicate with Parisians, carrying tightly rolled messages tied to their tail feathers to indicate successful escapes. The Parisian racing pigeon club, Société Colombophile L'Espérance, advocated for the birds' value, leading to their increased use.

On November 4, a pigeon post in Tours allowed individuals to send messages to Paris, limited to twenty words. Messages were copied onto thin paper, attached to cardboard, photographed, and reduced to carry 150 messages on a small piece of paper. One bird could transmit six "pigeongrams," or nine hundred messages, which were rolled tightly and inserted into a goose quill tied to the pigeon's tail feather. By December, René Dagron's microphotography techniques improved the process, reducing images by more than forty diameters and printing them on lightweight collodion films. Each film carried twenty-five hundred letters, and a pigeon could carry up to twenty films, representing thirty thousand to forty thousand despatches. Multiple copies were sent with successive birds to ensure delivery. Upon arrival, the films were unrolled in water, placed between glass sheets, projected onto a wall, and copied onto telegraph forms for delivery.

Of the 363 pigeons taken out of Paris by balloon, fewer than 200 were released over the six-month siege. Only 59 arrived safely, owing to poor winter weather, but successfully conveyed 95,581 private messages and newspaper reproductions.[20] Paris surrendered on January 28, 1871, with the last message-carrying pigeon arriving on February 6.

Refinement of Military Pigeon Operations, 1872–1913

Recognising the utility of the birds for transmitting information under certain constraints, several European militaries began to develop their own capabilities with pigeon message operations. The first military pigeon system emerged in Russian Poland in April 1871 with a series of stations and regular pigeon posts operating between major cities. Germany likewise established a military pigeon system in its empire in May 1872. By the end of the decade, an extensive system of pigeon lofts and messenger posts were used whenever opportunity allowed. The Imperial German Navy also experimented with pigeons to enable cruisers at sea to communicate with shore stations. Argentina, Austria, Brazil, Bulgaria, Italy, Portugal, Spain, Switzerland, and Uruguay all established military pigeon operations. France did not take concrete steps towards a military pigeon service until 1877, but soon thereafter created an extensive operation for fortress, cavalry, coastal defence, and naval service.[21]

During this period, the United States also explored the use of pigeons for military purposes. In 1878, the US Army Signal Corps (ASC) shipped a dozen pigeons to Colonel Nelson Miles in Montana, who declared that the birds could "be made useful for military service."[22] However, General William T. Sherman, Commanding General of the US Army, disagreed. Citing concerns about the one-way limitations of homing pigeons, he concluded that "for military use they are worthless."[23] In 1888, ASC established a small pigeon loft at Key West, Florida, but closed the operation in 1892. The birds were subsequently transferred to the US Naval Academy, where Academy Assistant Professor of French Henri Marion built up the flock and experimented with the birds as a ship-to-shore communication method.[24] He patented a leg-mounted message holder, an improvement over earlier methods of attaching notes to birds. With this innovation, Navy homing pigeons transported messages from ship to shore for East Coast vessels during the brief Spanish-American War. The advent of wireless telegraphy, however, soon made the Navy's pigeons obsolete.[25] In 1916, the ASC experimented with homing pigeons in the Mexican Expedition but found fault with personnel inexperienced at handling the birds, and pigeons insufficiently acclimated to the environment.[26]

Great Britain likewise experimented with, but never committed to, pigeons for military communications. In 1899, during the siege of Ladysmith, Natal (South Africa) in the Second Boer War, a pigeon post operated between Ladysmith and Durban, two cities separated by a distance of 120 miles. From November 4 to December 1, seventeen of twenty-eight birds made the journey, carrying messages that had been written on special paper and secured by silk thread under a rubber ring on the leg. Among these messages were two maps for use by British Army intelligence. The maps, hand-drawn and depicting enemy Boer military positions around Ladysmith, were photographed at scale and divided into two. Each half was flown out by a separate bird.[27] The communication of military maps by pigeon represents a first in military warfare: the birds were able to deliver valuable intelligence on enemy positions, the details of which could not be sent by other signalling methods such as the telegraph, semaphore, or heliograph.

Across Europe, military training exercises that incorporated pigeon messengers resulted in a greater familiarisation with the birds as a communication technology. Soldiers became increasingly acquainted with transporting and handling birds with Marion's message holder adapted to suit their needs. In the Russo-Japanese War (1904–1905), both combatants used pigeons for communication. The Imperial Japanese Army (IJA) adopted pigeons in 1899 and began experimenting with them for army and naval purposes. It succeeded in developing mobile lofts that could advance and manoeuvre with the military force. Scouts on horseback or bicycle could then carry birds from the mobile loft to the front lines, with the birds flying messages back in celluloid leg capsules.[28]

Complementing their long-standing ability to *transmit* information, pigeons also began to *collect* information with the aid of new technologies—specifically, the miniaturised camera. In 1908, German apothecary Julius G. Neubronner received a patent for a camera that was designed to be attached to a pigeon's breast.[29] It could automatically take photographs during flight. The shutter was operated by a pneumatic device or clockwork mechanism, at intervals of thirty seconds per exposure. At only 2.5 ounces, the camera offered the capability of aerial reconnaissance by pigeon. Bird and camera technologies together could be used to gather intelligence on enemy military operations.

Birds of War, 1914–1918

World War I witnessed the first mass use of pigeons for communication in recorded history. Tens of thousands of birds were used by both sides as part of a broader system of information technologies. Innovations such as the message capsule and mobile loft increased the effectiveness of the birds. In addition, microphotography and the carrying of complete or partial maps to and from the battlefield allowed the birds to transmit information in ways that were not possible with electronic means. Developments in technology meant that pigeons equipped with cameras could conduct surveillance by collecting strategic and tactical battlefield intelligence.

Along the static lines of the Western Front, wired communications were vulnerable to disruption by massed artillery fires. Human message runners made enticing targets for enemy snipers or poison gas. When these forms of communication could not be relied upon, birds were used to transmit information from either stationary or mobile lofts—from the trenches or advancing forces. Partially coded messages were inscribed onto small pieces of paper from a special message pad; these were attached to the pigeon's leg, either held in place by two rubber rings or placed in an aluminium capsule (Fig. 33.2). Once a pigeon and its message had arrived back at its home loft, the message would be transmitted electronically or via human runner to the appropriate addressee. Compared to other methods

Figure 33.2 Pigeon after arrival at Fort Lucy, France, carrying a message about a gas attack at Toul, October 1918. Note the aluminium message holder still attached to its leg, a refinement of Marion's original design.

Source: RG 111, NARA.

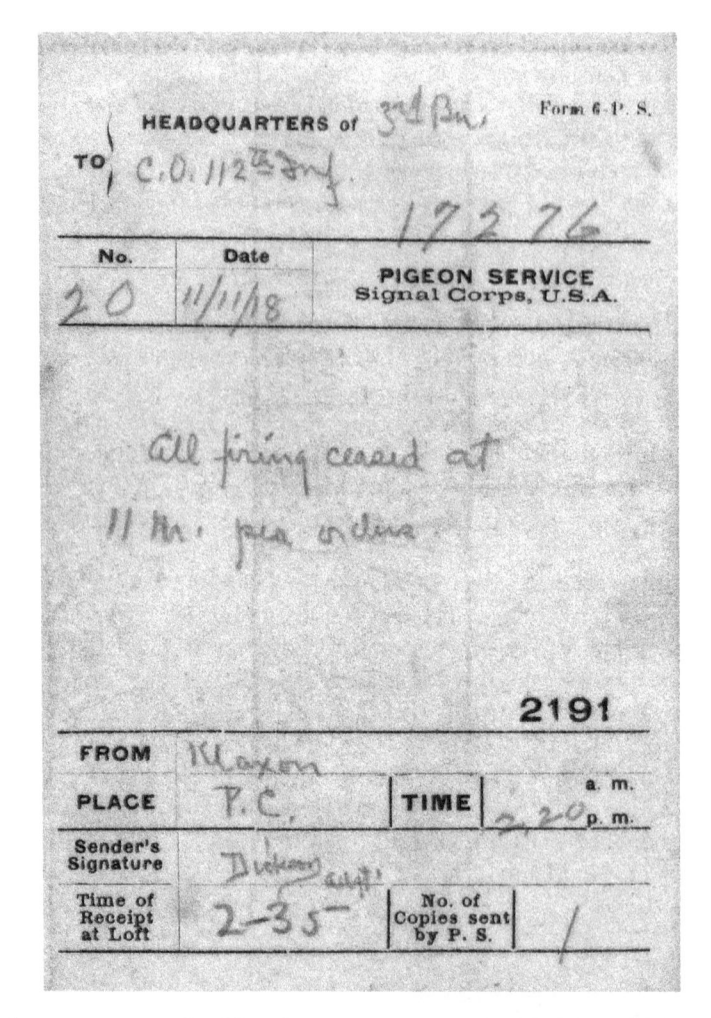

Figure 33.3 A message transmitted by pigeon, announcing the Armistice of November 11, 1918. The message reads "All firing ceased at 11 hr. per orders." The bird with leg band number 17276 took fifteen minutes to fly the message from the post of command (PC) to the commanding officer of the Third Battalion, 112th Infantry Regiment.

Source: Pennsylvania National Guard Military Museum, Fort Indiantown Gap, Pennsylvania.

of signalling—such as with flares, rockets, or aerial signals—pigeons could transmit longer and more detailed messages, either encoded or in plain text (Fig. 33.3).[30]

France began the war with an extensive system of twenty-eight pigeon houses and thirty thousand birds along the eastern frontier. Of the Allied powers, the French possessed the most refined and developed military homing pigeon service, having acquired decades of specialised knowledge in the operational use of the birds. The French service provided the model for other Allied nations.[31] On September 11, 1914, the French military gave fifteen pigeons to the British Intelligence Corps; these were the first birds the British Army would employ in the war.[32] In late October, the British Admiralty—having previously cancelled its pigeon programme in 1908—launched a Naval Pigeon Service to provide birds to small auxiliary ships and boats serving as minesweepers in the North Sea that lacked wireless communication technologies.[33] The pigeons were a reliable means of communicating with bases that were 70–150 miles distant. For example, pigeons brought news of an attack by a German Zeppelin on the minesweeping fleet, the first time a Zeppelin attempted an attack on British targets. Despite the rough conditions at sea, the birds sustained courier operations.[34]

On land, the British Expeditionary Force (BEF) began to field birds in France in 1915. In the Second Battle of Ypres from April to May—when the battlefield saw the first use of poison gas that threatened the safety of human couriers—the BEF used pigeons that skirted above the noxious fumes, transmitting situation reports and requests for artillery fire support.[35] Civilian pigeon fanciers who engaged in the ongoing breeding of birds were essential to the BEF's pigeon force, as they donated tens of thousands of feathered recruits for service to king and country.[36]

Germany initially did not employ its twenty-one thousand homing pigeons in their advance in 1914. Once mobile warfare became confined to trenches, however, German pigeons came into use, with approximately 120,000 birds employed over the course of the war. Over 70% of these pigeons were supplied from private lofts (Fig. 33.4). By law, all homing pigeons had to be used exclusively for military purposes, and the government banned the shooting of pigeons in Germany or occupied territories.[37]

The French, British, and German armies made considerable use of pigeons during the battles at the Somme and Verdun. At the former, the French managed communications with

Figure 33.4 German soldiers writing a report to be delivered by homing pigeon, March 1917.
Source: RG 165, NARA.

over five thousand pigeons; only 2% of those released with messages failed to return.[38] At Verdun, French officials noted how "pigeons only, can work regularly, and in spite of bombardments, dust, smoke or fog, can bring accurate details concerning the situation of the troops in action within a relatively short space of time."[39] As the operation on the Somme progressed, the British recognised the need for even more pigeons. The birds became the primary means of communication for advancing forces. The number of birds at the front increased with the use of mobile lofts that were predominantly horse-drawn. When the British Army introduced tanks at the Somme in September 1916, pigeons accompanied them as means of communication. As more tanks were deployed in 1917, pigeons became standard issue for every vehicle and adapted to the oil, grease, smoke, and noise inside the armoured "lofts."[40] That year, pigeons delivered 75% of all British communication received from the frontline.[41]

In mid-July 1917, the fledgling American Expeditionary Forces (AEF) requested pigeon personnel and birds. Field operations with pigeons began in late January 1918, with equipment and procedures copied from or directly influenced by French and British experience. The Americans appropriated the French technique of deploying pigeons to transmit sketches and map overlay tracings. As a "useful means of showing the situation concisely," sketches and map overlays offered precision for the spatial orientation of forces, especially for directing artillery fires.[42] In over forty-seven continuous days of fighting in the Meuse-Argonne Offensive from September 26 to November 11, the Pigeon Service provided communications to AEF forces in the field. Not a single pigeon carrying an important message is known to have gone astray during the offensive. Postwar, the ASC estimated that no more than 10% of the AEF pigeons failed to return to their lofts.[43]

Pigeons also found their way into air warfare. In April 1918, the Royal Air Force (RAF) took over pigeon operations from the British Admiralty. The RAF Pigeon Service placed pigeons aboard aircraft, with the birds transporting messages that reported the location of forced landings at sea, non-urgent information from airships reporting engine or wireless failure, and reconnaissance observations over uninhabited areas.[44] The US Army Air Service and US Navy (USN) also carried pigeons that would relay intelligence information or aid in the rescue of aircraft downed at sea (Fig. 33.5).[45] Throughout 1917 and into 1918, the British General Headquarters Intelligence Section arranged to have agents parachute behind enemy lines with pigeons to use for clandestine communications. Other operations used aircraft or small balloons to transport pigeons over the trenches to occupied French and Belgian territory. Finders of the pigeons would discover questionnaires requesting specific information on German movements and units. The written responses would be encapsulated and attached to the birds for return to friendly forces.[46] Pigeons were also involved in activities that might now be called disinformation; aircraft dropped dead pigeons with false messages behind German lines to deceive enemy operations.

Interwar and World War II, 1919–1945

Homing pigeons were used in World War II as they were in World War I, but in greater number—still carrying paper documents that were enclosed in leg or tail capsules.[47] Although electronic communications continued to improve, pigeons remained an important information technology for both Allied and Axis powers.

Because the British Army Pigeon Service had been completely disbanded after World War I, the volunteer National Pigeon Service (NPS) was established in mid-1939 under the

Figure 33.5 Homing pigeon being released from an aircraft in flight, US Naval Air Station Anacostia, Washington, DC.

Source: Naval History and Heritage Command, Washington, DC (NHHC), undated photograph.

Air Ministry with the support of racing pigeon experts to register and organise Britain's civilian pigeon lofts for the use of pigeons by the British Army, RAF, and civil departments of the government.[48] NPS served as the source for supply of pigeons and suitable technical personnel for British pigeon services.[49] From 1939 to 1945, NPS members donated almost two hundred thousand pigeons to the RAF, British Army, and British Secret Intelligence Service (SIS). In 1940, RAF Coastal and Bomber Command aircraft began carrying pigeons for air/sea rescue purposes or as emergency communication equipment. The birds could be released should the aircraft ditch in the ocean. Messages placed in watertight, plastic leg capsules would alert rescuers where to find airmen who were bobbing about in the water. For those aircrews that ditched, 80% of the pigeons released homed; no bird released fit and dry within three hundred miles of its base failed to home; and 14% of the location and rescue of downed aircrews resulted from pigeon SOS messages.[50] A Middle East Pigeon Service sprang up in January 1942 in Cairo, Egypt, providing secure communications for the British 8th Army and later operations in Italy and the Mediterranean. Other pigeons served with the British Army during the invasion of German-occupied France in June 1944.[51]

British intelligence employed pigeons for active intelligence gathering and deception operations. SIS parachuted pigeons into German-occupied Northern Europe with instructions and questionnaires for finders to provide information on German forces and occupation activities. Of 16,554 pigeons employed, only 1,842 made the return flight to Great Britain—but the valuable intelligence received compensating for the losses.[52] Under MI5's "Pigeon Service Special Section, B3C," British pigeons were equipped with counterfeit German wing stampings and leg bands. As part of the grand deception operation for the invasion of Nazi-occupied Western Europe, the British airdropped 350 of these "double-agent" pigeons hoping they would enter enemy lofts and be discovered by German attendants. But the deception was too convincing. Because the Germans considered it impossible to attach a one-piece metal leg band to a grown bird, the "bogus" pigeons were not exposed as planned.[53]

The IJA initially disbanded its pigeon operations in 1909 owing to the advent of radio communications. However, after learning about the successful use of pigeons by the British and French during World War I, the IJA decided to revive its military pigeon programme in 1919. They hired three French instructors and purchased one thousand birds to develop the new programme. The Japanese adopted equipment and messaging techniques that closely resembled those used by the French, British, and American pigeon operations. During the interwar period, the IJA incorporated pigeons into their military communication operations. One notable instance of their use was during the Great Kanto Earthquake of 1923, where pigeons were used to coordinate information among government officials.

IJA pigeons successfully operated as backup communications during the Second Sino-Japanese War and the Pacific War. The birds proved valuable for reliable and clandestine communications in various terrains, from the Manchurian steppe to the South Pacific islands and the jungles of Burma. Some pigeons even became national heroes for delivering messages despite being mortally wounded by bullets. On the home front, members of the Greater East Asia Carrier Pigeon Federation sold top racing pigeons to the IJA for fifteen yen, which was more than the monthly salary of an average Japanese soldier.[54] As American submarine operations and aerial bombing devastated the Japanese home islands, military pigeons, like their human counterparts, faced reduced rations. They nevertheless served as vital communication links for military and civil officials in heavily damaged urban areas.[55]

The Wehrmacht of Nazi Germany used pigeons in both the Heer and Waffen-SS as a backup communication method, alongside radio equipment and messenger dogs. Birds were assigned to stationary lofts in fortifications, shelters, outposts, and reconnaissance platoons. Signal intelligence platoons relied on pigeons to transmit important time-sensitive information on enemy activities, while defensive forces used them for communication under heavy fire.[56] German-bred birds served Army units, but soldiers also confiscated Belgian pigeons and entire lofts when needed.

Messages were typically enclosed in aluminium leg capsules, but the Germans devised additional methods of transmitting information with pigeons. Two to four birds with different feathering would be sent at once, their colours communicating different messages. Intelligence agents behind Allied lines used various techniques, including soluble message capsules that were ingested by birds (requiring the pigeon to be killed for recovery), encrypted messages clipped into wing feathers, invisible ink on wing feathers, or message papers inside main feather quills.[57]

The ASC operated a small Pigeon Section throughout the interwar period and began to build up its operation in June 1941. Pigeoneers relearned and perfected mobile loft operations, and new airborne paratroopers and other soldiers were introduced to the use of pigeons.[58] The training manoeuvres allowed for the testing of new message capsules made of celluloid which were lighter and had three times the carrying capacity of the aluminium capsules of World War I. The improved capsules enabled pigeons to carry larger map overlays and messages. Moreover, a capsule could be attached to each leg in emergencies, doubling the transmitting potential of each pigeon.[59]

After the United States entered the war in December 1941, the Pigeon Section grew dramatically; by 1943, it numbered 135 officers, 2,250 enlisted men, and 70,000 birds. Voluntary donations of forty thousand birds from civilian racing pigeon owners from 1941 to 1943 helped sire twenty-three thousand birds for ASC use in the war.[60] Demand for pigeons and pigeoneers, particularly in Europe, necessitated the expansion of the ASC's pigeon operations. From 1941 to 1944, the Army activated eleven signal pigeon companies and several detachments that used fifty-four thousand pigeons—thirty-six thousand of these birds served overseas.[61] During the war, the Army experimented with using pigeons to transport undeveloped photographic films or ethyl cellulose film belts, each with eighteen thousand words of recorded audio.[62]

From December 1942 until the end of hostilities in August 1945, American pigeons and pigeoneers participated in combat communication in Europe and the Pacific. The experiences gained during the interwar period with breeding and training culminated in superior performances compared to those of World War I. The Army reported a pigeon casualty rate of less than 0.5% in operations; one Army publication listed a 99% reliability for tactical pigeon messages.[63] More importantly, the use of pigeons increased within the Army in tandem with their improved performance and as communications personnel became more familiar with their capabilities.[64] In combat operations in Italy, pigeons proved the only means of communication available to ground forces on at least twenty different occasions. Birds saved lives and could have saved more if they had been available for other emergency communication exigencies. Armoured patrols, night patrols behind enemy lines, Rangers, and airborne units all used pigeons with considerable success.[65]

Nevertheless, the birds remained an auxiliary communications method. Radio communication remained a priority for the Army—over one hundred American companies manufactured radios during the war, with the Crosley Corporation producing 150,000 units of the SCR-284 radio model alone.[66] In 1944, the supplemental system of pigeons became essential for American and British airborne units fighting behind German lines in Normandy, France, and Arnhem, the Netherlands: radios had failed, and several pigeons managed flights of hundreds of miles over open sea to deliver critical information.[67]

Taking a cue from the RAF, the US Army Air Forces (AAF) organised a pigeon service in February 1943. By October 1944, the AAF Pigeon Service maintained a force of over twenty thousand homing pigeons for emergency communication purposes. The birds could survive drops from four-engine aircraft at speeds up to 350 miles per hour at altitudes of thirty-five thousand feet. Wrapping a split paper bag gently around a bird, airmen would release the pigeons in flight. Once falling at terminal velocity, the bird could escape the bag and fly to its home loft. Notably, the bomber waist gunners, who handled the pigeons, flew with oxygen masks and heated flight suits. Meanwhile, the pigeons endured sub-zero temperatures and limited oxygen in the confines of a small box.[68]

The USN, having dispensed its pigeons in 1929, brought the birds back in 1942 to send messages under radio silence, avoiding any electronic transmission that might reveal the position of the Americans. During the Battle of the Atlantic, pigeons went aloft in blimps operating on antisubmarine patrol or convoy escort. Reporting a suspected submarine by radio would risk electronic detection and provide a chance for the enemy to escape; a pigeon could instead deliver the information covertly and preserve the element of surprise.[69]

In Burma, the Office of Strategic Services (OSS) found pigeons to be a suitable method of communication for forces operating behind Japanese lines. Pigeons readily carried maps, diagrams, or other documents which could not be transmitted by radio. They demonstrated marathon-like abilities, flying distances of 230 miles during the monsoon season. In another instance, a bird flew 275 miles over high mountains in seven hours, while another, dropped from an aircraft, flew 325 miles back to its loft the same day.[70] Agents also employed birds that had no homing training to conduct exercises in disinformation. These birds carried propaganda that was intentionally released to fall into Japanese hands. In such cases, the pigeons were not expected to return home.

1946 to the Present

After World War II, the use of military pigeons declined significantly. By early 1947, the US Army had only seven enlisted pigeoneers, two civilian specialists, and around one thousand birds in operation.[71] During the Israeli War of Independence in May 1948, imported Belgian pigeons working with the Haganah paramilitary organisation maintained crucial communication links between Jerusalem, Tel Aviv, and Kibbutz Givat Brenner when other forms of communication were impractical or impossible. The Israel Defence Forces maintained a unit of 700 birds and nine handlers until 1954.[72]

In 1951, the US Eighth Army shipped out to Korea with around one hundred pigeons for operational use, providing a clandestine, mobile means of communication between small infantry patrols and special operations.[73] Advances in electronic communications, however, soon led to the disestablishment of the Pigeon Service in late 1956. The ASC donated fifteen distinguished World War II hero pigeons to zoological parks across the nation and sold the remaining one thousand birds.[74]

During the Cold War, the American Central Intelligence Agency (CIA) researched a system for high-resolution photography over denied areas, particularly Leningrad in the Soviet Union, using homing pigeons as both collectors and transmitters of information. From 1976 to 1977, the CIA tested a film camera weighing 43 g with a shutter speed of 1/2400 of a second. A pigeon flying at one hundred feet in altitude could capture images covering a 90 by 90 foot area with a resolution of less than one inch, equaling or surpassing the image quality of the then-state-of-the-art KH-8 reconnaissance satellite (Fig. 33.6). Much of this initiative remains classified, and it is unknown if pigeons ever entered service as operational intelligence gatherers for the CIA.[75]

Military operations in the twenty-first century are conducted in the invisible electromagnetic spectrum, with electronic-based systems enabling attacks and blocking counterattacks. For example, Russian electronic warfare operations caused significant difficulties for Ukrainian forces, intercepting and decrypting communications at a cost of up to ten thousand drones a month in 2023.[76] American forces also faced challenges against Russian electronic warfare technologies and tactics in Syria, finding themselves at a disadvantage.[77] Those who control the electromagnetic space dominate the battlefield and restrict the options of their adversaries.[78] But vulnerabilities in electronic communications persist despite technological advancements. Pigeons offer an alternative way to transmit information amidst the escalation of cyber and electronic warfare, and currently serve as the only non-electronic backup communications network available to militaries.[79] The homing

Figure 33.6 A refinement of Neubronner's efforts at the turn of the twentieth century, the American Central Intelligence Agency developed a miniaturised film camera for pigeons in the late 1970s which provided a remarkable resolution of less than one inch, enabling the gathering of detailed photographic information.

Source: The CIA Museum.

pigeon's small size, reliability, and hardiness provide frontline forces with a low-observable method to transport information over considerable distances, with zero electromagnetic emissions and minimal detectability to radar.[80] During periods of radio silence or emissions control (EMCOM), pigeons can transmit vital information without exposing the positions of friendly forces.

The increasing inverse relationship between information volume and mass could make homing pigeons even more effective. MicroSD memory cards with a capacity of two terabytes (TB) weigh half a gram, and pigeons can carry weights of around 15–20 g for optimal health and speed.[81] A pigeon can theoretically transport 80 TB of encrypted data up to several hundred miles a day, offering faster and more secure transmission than some US Army radios, as there is no electromagnetic signature or dependence on local infrastructure.[82] Research in the 1980s found that homing pigeons are unaffected by electromagnetic pulse (EMP) exposure.[83] Although falcons remain a threat, the loss of pigeons is generally low. The birds travel within predominantly friendly territory and can blend into local populations in urban environments.

Miniaturised electronics offer new possibilities for homing pigeons in information gathering. Scientists and environmentalists have used pigeons with sensors to gather air pollution data.[84] In a military context, aerial reconnaissance of sensitive sites and monitoring airborne materials, such as radionuclide emissions, have limited but relevant applications. Lightweight cameras and digital technology have improved image resolution, and GPS tracking leg bands weighing less than 5 g allow owners to select the fastest navigating birds. In the future, pigeons may travel with surgically embedded data storage. Sensors could upload and download data wirelessly, eliminating the need to handle the birds physically.

As demonstrated, homing pigeons remain a viable military communications resource. In the twenty-first century and beyond, battlefield conditions, network security, and information format will determine the reactivation of military pigeon operations. Pigeons are versatile, capable of transmitting and circulating information or misinformation, depending on circumstances and equipment provided. Technology and techniques for transmitting or collecting information, not the birds themselves, will be the limiting factors should countries attempt to re-establish such operations.

Notes

1 William D. Lea Rayner, *The Creation of a Strain (Tracing the Evolution of the Racing Pigeon from the Earliest Times to the Present Day)* (Teddington: All-British Pigeon Racing, 1955), 1–8.
2 War Department, Office of the Chief Signal Officer, "Instructions on the Use of Carrier Pigeons in War – U.S. Signal Corps," Confidential, April 1918, 1, Box 502, Entry NM-95 2051, Record Group (RG) 120, National Archives and Records Administration (NARA), College Park, MD. Hereinafter cited as "Instructions."
3 "Instructions," 5; American Racing Pigeon Union, *AU Yearbook 2018* (Oklahoma City, OK: American Racing Pigeon Union, 2018), 63.
4 Elizabeth G. Macalaster, *War Pigeons: Winged Couriers in the U.S. Military, 1878–1957* (Jefferson, NC: McFarland, 2020), 4–5; and Wendell Mitchell Levi, *The Pigeon* (Columbia, SC: Levi Pub. Co., 1963), 377–380.
5 War Department, *Technical Manual TM 11-410, The Homing Pigeon* (Washington, DC: Government Printing Office [GPO], January 1945), 1. See also Levi, *Pigeon*, 364–369.
6 Sian Lewis and Lloyd Llewellyn-Jones, *The Culture of Animals in Antiquity: A Sourcebook with Commentaries* (New York: Routledge, 2018), 245–263; Jean Hansell, *The Pigeon in History or The Dove's Tale* (Bath: Antony Rowe, 1998), 14–78; Levi, *Pigeon*, 1–5.
7 Genesis 8:6–12.
8 Anacreon, *The Odes of Anacreon, the Teian Bard, Literally Translated into English Prose*, trans. T. W. C. Edwards (London: W. Simpkin and R. Marshall, 1830), 29–33. See also Hansell, *History*, 129.
9 Claudius Aelianus, *His Various History*, trans. Stanley Thomas (London: Thomas Dring, 1666), 171.
10 Elizabeth Rawson, "The Aftermath of the Ides," in *The Cambridge Ancient History Vol. 9: The Last Age of the Roman Republic, 146–43 B.C.*, 2nd ed., ed. J. A. Crook, Andrew Lintott, and Rawson (Cambridge, UK: Cambridge University Press, 1992), 468–490, esp. 478–490.
11 Pliny, *The Natural History*, Vol. II, trans. John Bostock and H. T. Riley (London: Henry G. Bohn, 1855), 519–520.

12 Frontinus, *The Stratagems and the Aqueducts of Rome, with an English Translation by Charles E. Bennett* (New York: G.P. Putnam's Sons, 1925), 249.
13 John D. Hosler, *The Siege of Acre, 1189–1191: Saladin, Richard the Lionheart, and the Battle that Decided the Third Crusade* (New Haven: Yale University Press, 2018), 77, 200 n. 27, 213 n. 7; Marius Kociejowski, *The Pigeon Wars of Damascus* (Detroit, MI: Biblioasis, 2011), 207–208; Edgar Chamberlain, *The Homing Pigeon: A Complete Text Book on the Subject of Pigeon Breeding, Rearing, Feeding and Racing* (Manchester: Homing Pigeon Pub. Co., 1907), 18–19; and H. T. W. Allatt, "The Use of Pigeons as Messengers in War and the Military Pigeon Systems of Europe," *The Journal of the Royal United Service Institution* 30, no. 133 (1886): 107–148, esp. 111–112.
14 Sir John Mandeville, *The Travels of Sir John Mandeville: The Version of the Cotton Manuscript in Modern Spelling* (London: Macmillan and Co., 1915), 79. Also Hansell, *History*, 135.
15 Susan B. Edgington, "The Doves of War: The Part Played by Carrier Pigeons in the Crusades," in *Autour de la Première Croisade: Actes du Colloque de la Society for the Study of the Crusades and the Latin East: Clermont-Ferrand, 22–25 Juin 1995*, ed. Michel Balard (Paris: Publications de la Sorbonne, 1996), 167–175.
16 Chamberlain, *Homing Pigeon*, 20–21; Allatt, "Use of Pigeons," 112; and War Department, Signal Service Notes No. II, William E. Birkhimer, *Memoir on the Use of Homing Pigeons for Military Purposes* (Washington, DC: Office of the Chief Signal Officer, 1882), 4; and John Lothrop Motley, *The Rise of the Dutch Republic: A History* (London: Routledge and Sons, 1880), 507–512.
17 Niall Ferguson, *The House of Rothschild, Vol. 1, Money's Prophets: 1798–1848* (New York: Penguin Putnam, 1998), 234.
18 Roy S. Freedman, *Introduction to Financial Technology* (New York: Elsevier, 2006), 13; and Gilbert Mant, "The Romantic Story of Reuters," *Australian Quarterly* 11, no. 3 (September 1939): 83–87, esp. 83.
19 Victor La Perre de Roo, *Monographie des pigeons domestiques* (Paris: au bureau du journal "l'Acclimatation", 1884), 286.
20 Michèle Martin and Christopher Bodnar, "The Illustrated Press under Siege: Technological Imagination in the Paris Siege, 1870–1871," *Urban History* 36, no. 1 (May 2009): 67–85; John D. Hayhurst, *The Pigeon Post into Paris, 1870–1871* (Ashford: J.H. Hayhurst, 1970); John Fisher, *Airlift 1870: The Balloons and Pigeons in the Siege of Paris* (London: Max Parrish, 1965); and Charles de Lafollye, *Dépêches par pigeons voyageurs pendant le siège de Paris. Mémoire sur la section photographique et administrative du service de ces dépêches* (Tours: Alfred Mame et fils, 1871).
21 War Department, Adjutant General's Office, Military Information Division, *Notes of Military Interest for 1901* (Washington, DC: GPO, January 1902), 231–241. Also Allatt, "Use of Pigeons," 107–148.
22 Birkhimer, *Memoir*, 8, 10; *Report of the Secretary of War*, Vol. 1, 44th Cong., 1st sess. 1875, Ex. Doc 1, Part 2, 84.
23 William T. Sherman, Headquarters of the Army, December 26, 1882, 1882 – File No. 5360, RG 94, NARA.
24 Rebecca Robbins Raines, *Getting the Message Through: A Branch History of the U.S. Army Signal Corps* (Washington, DC: Center of Military History [CMH], 2011), 68; and Department of War, *Annual Report of the Chief Signal Officer of the Army to the Secretary of War for the Year 1888* (Washington, DC: GPO, 1889), 47–48.
25 Macalaster, *War*, 22–64; Henri Marion, "Message Holder for Use with Homing Pigeons," United States of America, patent 569,111 filed June 6, 1896, and issued October 6, 1896. See Wendy Arevalo, "The Navy's Use of Carrier Pigeons," *Naval History and Heritage Command*, October 13, 2023, https://www.history.navy.mil/browse-by-topic/exploration-and-innovation/navy-pigeons.html.
26 Evan D. Cameron, Jr., "The Development and Use of Homing Pigeons for Military Purposes," Box 9, Entry UD 1025, RG 111, NARA.
27 E. A. Altham, "The Ladysmith Pigeon Post," *The Journal of the Royal United Service Institution* 44, no. 273 (November 1900): 1231–1236.
28 Army Ministry of Communications Office, "The Mission and Current Status of Military Pigeons (November 1943)," *Kyokōsha Bulletin Special Issue*, no. 830 (November 1943); H. C. Howden,

"War Pigeons," *The Boy's Own Paper* 26, no. 1334 (August 6, 1904): 731–734; and "Pigeons in the War: Japanese and Russian," *Black and White* 27, no. 698 (June 18, 1904): 914–915.
29 Nicolò Degiorgis and Audrey Salomon, *The Pigeon Photographer* (Berlin: Rorhof, 2019); and Berlin Correspondent, "Carrier Pigeons as Photographers," *Scientific American* 100, no. 1 (January 2, 1909): 4.
30 Gervase Phillips, "Pigeons in the Trenches: Animals, Communications Technologies and the British Expeditionary Force, 1914–1918," *British Journal for Military History* 4, no. 3 (September 21, 2018): 60–80, esp. 70; General Staff, *C.B./305T. Notes on the Use of Carrier Pigeons in France (Revised Edition)* (London: Army Printing and Stationery Services, August 1917), 1–12; Intelligence Section, General Staff, General Headquarters, Home Forces, 40/W.O./4044. *Instructions on the Use of Carrier Pigeons in War* (London: His Majesty's Stationery Office, May 1917), 5–21; and Carrier Pigeon Service, General Headquarters, Director of Army Signals, "Organization of a Carrier Pigeon Service for the Armies in France" (London: War Office, General Headquarters, August 28, 1915).
31 Ernest Harold Baynes, *Animal Heroes of the Great War* (New York: Macmillan Co., 1925), 221; and Lucien Fournier, "Carrier Pigeons in the French Army," *Scientific American* 109, no. 2 (July 12, 1913): 32–33.
32 Brian N. Hall, *Communications and British Operations on the Western Front, 1914–1918* (Cambridge, UK: Cambridge University Press, 2017), 113; and R. E. Priestley, *Work of the Royal Engineers in the European War, 1914–19: The Signal Service (France)* (Chatham: W & J Mackay and Co., 1921), 53.
33 Naval Staff, Intelligence Department, *C.B. 1512. Report on Administration and Procedure of the Government Pigeon Service* (London: Admiralty, November 1918), 6; "Naval Pigeons Abolished," *Forest and Stream*, March 7, 1908, 362; and "The Navy's Pigeons," *The Observer* (London), May 31, 1908, 8.
34 Alfred H. Osman, *Pigeons in the Great War: A Complete History of the Carrier-Pigeon Service during the Great War, 1914 to 1918* (London: The Race Pigeon Pub. Co., 1928), 18–21.
35 Phillips, "Trenches," 68–71; and Priestley, *Engineers*, 89–92.
36 Phillips, "Trenches," 67; and Osman, *Great War*, 6.
37 Rainer Pöppinghege and Tammy Proctor, "Außerordentlich hoher Bedarf an Gebrauchstauben für das Feldheer–Brieftauben Weltkrieg," in *Tiere im Krieg: von der Antike bis zur Gegenwart*, ed. Pöppinghege (Paderborn: Ferdinand Schöningh, 2009), 103–118, esp. 107–110; and Johannes Theuerkauff, ed., *Tiere im Krieg* (Berlin: W. Kolk, 1932), 77–82.
38 Osman, *Great War*, 29.
39 Grand Quartier Général, État-Major, Service Colombophile, "Exploitation des pigeons voyageurs: résultats obtenus par ce mode de liaison pendant les batailles de Verdun et de la Somme," October 1, 1916.
40 Phillips, "Trenches," 73–74; and Priestley, *Engineers*, 142–143, 247–248.
41 Phillips, "Trenches," 75–77; and Priestley, *Engineers*, 221–222.
42 "Instructions," 32–33.
43 Frank A. Blazich, Jr., "Feathers of Honor: The U.S. Army Signal Corps Pigeon Service in World War I, 1917–1918," *Army History* 38, no. 4 (Fall 2020): 32–51.
44 Air Ministry Weekly Orders, No. 624 – R.A.F. Pigeon Service, July 10, 1918, AIR 1-619-16-15-348, National Archives, Kew, London, United Kingdom (NA-Kew); Naval Staff, *C.B. 1512.*, 7.
45 Macalaster, *War*, 76–94.
46 Various correspondence and memorandum in file WO 208-3508, NA-Kew. See also Gordon Corera, *Operation Columba: The Secret Pigeon Service* (New York: HarperCollins, 2018), 19–22; Jim Beach, *Haig's Intelligence: GHQ and the German Army, 1916–1918* (Cambridge, UK: Cambridge University Press, 2013), 123–125; Osman, *Great War*, 46–50; and Walter Nicolai, *The German Secret Service* (London: Stanley Paul & Co. Ltd., 1924), 152–161.
47 For examples, see Ministère de la guerre, École des transmissions, *Tome IV: Colombophilie* (Paris: Imprimerie Nationale, 1930), 30–33; Reichswehr, *Heeresbrieftauben, December 19, 1925* (Berlin: Druck und Verlag de Reichsdruckerei, 1926), 54–60; and US Army, Training Manual No. 32, *The Pigeoneer* (Washington, DC: GPO, 1925), 42–53.
48 Corera, *Columba*, 17–18; Levi, *Pigeon*, 7; W. H. Osman, ed., *Pigeons in World War II: The Official Records of the Performances of Racing Pigeons with the Armed Forces* (London: Racing

Pigeon Pub. Co. Ltd., 1950), v; Committee of Imperial Defence, Carrier Pigeons Sub-Committee, Report, March 29, 1939, CAB 21-1149, NA-Kew. Following World War I, the British Army had a single loft in Singapore for emergency communication purposes; in 1934, RAF established a voluntary pigeon service with lofts in Singapore, Malta, and Calshot, UK.

49 Air Ministry, Directorate General of Signals, Directorate of Telecommunications, Tels. 1(c), "Particulars of Royal Air Force Pigeon Service, for Information of Interested Dominions or Allied Air Forces," July 24, 1942, AIR 20-1569, NA-Kew.

50 William D. Lea Rayner to Headquarters, Bomber Command, Coastal Command, Flying Training Command, memorandum, subject: R.A.F. Pigeon Service – Home Commands, June 1, 1943, AIR 14-1582, NA-Kew.

51 Garry McCafferty, *They Had No Choice: Racing Pigeons at War* (Charleston: Tempus, 2002), 33–47, 52–56, 65–81, 93–95.

52 Osman, *World War*, 1. For a detailed history of this work, see Corera, *Columba*.

53 Ben Macintyre, *Double Cross: The True Story of the D-Day Spies* (New York: Crown, 2012), 118–121, 180–183, 329.

54 Some Japanese officers referred to conscripted soldiers as *issen gorin* ("penny postcard") referring to the cost to mail a draft notice, meaning a conscript was less valuable than a pigeon or horse. Saburō Ienaga, *The Pacific War, 1931–1945*, trans. Frank Baldwin (New York: Random House, 1978), 52. The monthly salary for a Japanese private was 5 yen and 50 sen. See Edward J. Drea, *In the Service of the Emperor: Essays on the Imperial Japanese Army* (Lincoln, NE: University of Nebraska Press, 1998), 85.

55 Fujimoto Yasuhisa, *Showa Edition 2 China Affairs, vol. 5*, and *Showa Edition 3 Greater East Asia War, vol. 6, Chronology of Japanese Military Pigeons* (Middletown: Kijibato, 2021); Army Ministry of Communications Office, "The Mission and Current Status of Military Pigeons (November 1943)," *Kyokōsha Bulletin Special Issue*, no. 830 (November 1943).

56 Military Intelligence Division, *German Doctrine of the Stabilized Front* (August 1943), 34–39; and Military Intelligence Division, *German Tactical Doctrine* (Washington, DC: War Department General Staff, December 1942), 24.

57 Great Britain War Office, Combined Services Detailed Interrogation Centre, "Carrier Pigeon Service – German Army," 1944, https://cgsc.contentdm.oclc.org/digital/collection/p4013coll8/id/4608/rec/1; War Department, *Intelligence Bulletin* 3, no. 6 (February 1945): 21–22.

58 Robert B. Folson, "A History of 280th Signal Pigeon Company," November 1944, 2–7, Box 16, Entry UD 1025, RG 111, NARA; John K. Shawvan to Robert E. Meeds, memorandum, subject: Monthly Report, January 16, 1942, Box 7, Entry ID 1025, RG 111, NARA; "Cloud Writing and Carrier Pigeons Used in Maneuvers," *Leader-Telegram* (Eau Claire, WI), November 25, 1941, 2; "'Pigeon' Troops Join Maneuvers in Carolinas," *Pittsburgh Press*, November 2, 1941, 64; "Pigeoneers Join First Army for Maneuvers," *The Town Talk* (Alexandria, LA), October 20, 1941, 8; and "Pigeons Used in Maneuvers in Louisiana," *Washington C.H. Record-Herald* (Washington Court House, OH), September 11, 1941, 9.

59 Tim Scherrer, *War Pigeon! The Operations and Gear of the US Army Pigeon Corps* (Columbia, SC: Tim Allen Scherrer, 2021), 154–155; and John K. Shawvan, "Report on Service Test of PG-52, PG-53, PG-54," February 25, 1942, Box 7, Entry UD 1025, RG 111, NARA; *TM 11-410*, 42–44.

60 Dulaney Terrett, *The Technical Services: The Signal Corps: The Emergency (to December 1941)* (Washington, DC: CMH, 1994), 223; and Army Service Forces, "Historical Data of the Pigeon Service," March 17, 1944, Box 16, Entry UD 1025, RG 111, NARA.

61 US Army Signal Corps Board, Fort Monmouth, NJ, Report on Study No. 67: Status of Pigeon Service, February 28, 1951, 9–10, Box 10, Documents and other Paper Related Materials Related to Pigeons, US Army Communications-Electronics Command Historical Office, Aberdeen Proving Grounds, MD (CECOM).

62 Otto Meyer to Commanding Officer, 2nd Platoon, 280th Pigeon Signal Company, memorandum and attachment, subject: Spoken Messages by Film, May 4, 1945, Box 8, Entry UD 1025, RG 111, NARA; and Otto Meyer to Chief, Military Training Branch, memorandum and attachment, subject: Transportation of Films by Pigeons, January 8, 1945.

63 Otto Meyer thru Chief, Military Training Branch, memorandum, subject: Transmittal of Information Concerning Pigeon Service, September 26, 1944, Box 2, Entry UD 1025, RG 111, NARA;

War Department, *Field Manual FM 11-80, Signal Pigeon Company* (Washington, DC: GPO, September 14, 1944), 4.
64 Otto Meyer to Chief, Military Training Branch, memorandum, subject: Pigeon Communication – World War II, November 26, 1945, Box 10, UD 1025, RG 111, NARA.
65 H. V. Roberts to Adjutant General, memorandum, subject: Use of Homing Pigeons in Combat Operations, January 10, 1944, WO 204-3930, NA-Kew.
66 Alice Shackelford Clifton-Morekis, "Front-line Fowl: Messenger Pigeons as Communications Technology in the U.S. Army," *History and Technology* 37, no. 2 (June 2021): 203–246, esp. 223.
67 Thomas H. Spencer to Signal Officer, Twelfth Army Group, APO 655, US Army, memorandum, subject: Transmittal of Pigeon Report with attachment, "Use of Pigeons in the Invasion of France," July 27, 1944, Box 16, Entry UD 1024, RG 111, NARA; Osman, *World War*, 22, 25, 33; Corera, *Columba*, 268–271.
68 "Our Pigeon Air Force," *Air Force: The Official Service Journal of the U.S. Army Air Forces* 27, no. 10 (October 1944): 36–37.
69 Laurence M. Burke II, "The First 'Naval Aviators,'" *Naval History Magazine*, October 2022, https://www.usni.org/magazines/naval-history-magazine/2022/october/first-naval-aviators.
70 Office of Strategic Services, Pigeon Activities – OSS-SU Detachment 101, June 1945, Box 16, Entry UD 1025, RG 111, NARA.
71 Otto Meyer, "Unit History of the Pigeon Breeding and Training Center, 1946 thru 1947," December 31, 1947, Box 5, CECOM.
72 David Harvey, "Military Mail: Same Day Delivery," *IDF Journal* 18 (Fall 1989), 56.
73 Macalaster, *War*, 153–157; "Carrier Pigeons Serving Again in Korea," *SIGNAL* 6, no. 5 (May–June 1952): 31–32.
74 Press release, Headquarters, Fort Monmouth, NJ Information Office, November 1959, Box 10, CECOM; Headquarters, US Army Signal School, General Orders No. 6: Discontinuance of Pigeon Breeding and Training Branch, Academic Services Department, US Army Signal School, April 29, 1957; "15 Pigeon Heroes to Go to New Roosts; Army Closing Their Monmouth Center," *NYT*, April 7, 1957, 120; J. P. Hoffman to Chief of Staff, memorandum, subject: Army Homing Pigeons, February 13, 1957; Jack Raymond, "Army's Pigeons to Turn in Wings," *New York Times (NYT)*, December 5, 1956, 1; and J. D. O'Connell to Commanding General, Fort Monmouth, NJ, memorandum, subject: Discontinuance of Pigeon Breeding and Training Facilities, November 30, 1956.
75 Charles N. Adkins, "Feasibility Research on a System to Provide High Resolution Photography Over Denied Areas," Office of Research and Development, Central Intelligence Agency, April 1978, https://www.cia.gov/readingroom/document/06527327; Artifacts – Pigeon Camera, Central Intelligence Agency, February 5, 2024, https://www.cia.gov/legacy/museum/artifact/pigeon-camera/.
76 Jack Walting and Nick Reynolds, *Meatgrinder: Russian Tactics in the Second Year of Its Invasion of Ukraine* (London: Royal United Services Institute for Defence and Security Studies, May 19, 2023), 18.
77 Jared Keller, "After Experiencing Russian Jamming up Close in Syria, the Pentagon is Scrambling to Catch up," *Business Insider*, June 3, 2019; and Anna Varfolomeeva, "Signaling Strength: Russia's Real Syria Success is Electronic Warfare against the US," *The Defense Post*, May 1, 2018.
78 Frank Blazich, "In the Era of Electronic Warfare, Bring Back Pigeons," *War on the Rocks*, January 16, 2019, https://warontherocks.com/2019/01/in-the-era-of-electronic-warfare-bring-back-pigeons/.
79 Katie N. Borcuk, "More than Flights of Fancy: The Critical Need for a United States Pigeon Messenger Service in the Age of Electronic Warfare" (MA thesis, Air Command and Staff College, Air University, October 2021), 2.
80 Andrew D. Blechman, *Pigeons: The Fascinating Saga of the World's Most Revered and Reviled Bird* (New York: Grove Press, 2006), 4–5.
81 James A. Gessaman and Kenneth A. Nagy, "Transmitter Loads Affect the Flight Speed and Metabolism of Homing Pigeons," *The Condor* 90, no. 3 (August 1988): 662–668; and Martin C. Michener and Charles Walcott, "Homing Pigeons – Analysis of Tracks," *Journal of Experimental Biology* 47 (1967): 99–131.

82 Devlin Winkelstein, F100 Essay-Staff Group 15A, November 4, 2018, 4, US Army Command and General Staff Officers Course, Fort Leavenworth, KS.
83 T. E. Aldrich, C. E. Easterly, P. C. Gailey, and C. B. Hamilton, *Bioelectromagnetic Effects of EMP: Preliminary Findings* (Oak Ridge, TN: Oak Ridge National Laboratory, June 1988), A-10.
84 Annalisa Di Bernardino, Valeria Jennings, and Giacomo Dell'Omo, "Bird-Borne Samplers for Monitoring CO_2 and Atmospheric Physical Parameters" *Remote Sensing* 14, no. 4876 (September 2022): 1–15; Eleanor Beardsley, "Pigeons are London's Newest Pollution Fighters," *NPR*, March 17, 2016.

34
INFORMATION AND COMMUNICATION THEORIES
A Global History of the (Con)fusion

Gabriele Balbi, Gianluigi Negro, Maria Rikitianskaia,
Carlos A. Scolari, and Dominique Trudel

Introduction

Information and communication theories are often intertwined, making the boundaries between them blurry. The most quoted and relevant paper at the crossroads of the two is Claude Shannon's *A Mathematical Theory of Communication* (1948), which is widely recognised as the founding text of what we call *information* theory.[1] But Shannon himself, in a dialogue with his wife captured in a 1987 interview, denied that he had ever fathered anything called "information theory":

"In the first place, you called it a theory *of communication*" Betty Shannon reminded her husband. "You didn't call it a theory of information." "Yes, I thought that *communication is a matter of getting bits from here to here*, whether they're part of the Bible or just which way a coin is tossed," Shannon confirmed. [...] Betty testified to Shannon's distress when scientists far removed *from the field of communication engineering jumped on the information "bandwagon,"* as he called it, and Shannon watched his work career out of proportion to the technical theory he had propounded.[2]

In the same year, 1948, Norbert Wiener published *Cybernetics: Or Control and Communication in the Animal and the Machine*, which is considered another milestone in the history of information. Wiener was interested in studying the forms of communication (that is, the messages) exchanged "between man and machines, between machines and man, and between machine and machine."[3] These two champions of information theory, Shannon and Wiener, are, as Colin Koopman has argued, actually champions of communication theory:

The misappellation "information theory" carries as its unfortunate residue the implication that Shannon and Wiener's theories were primarily focused on information itself. Yet, the central focus of their work was not information at all, but rather communication. Both writers, of course, conceptualized information. But those conceptions were not so much full-blown theories of information as *they were limited technical models of information for the purpose of resolving problems endogenous to communication theory*. If information theory is a theory of information at all, then it is a theory of information only for the limited purposes of communication.[4]

Consistent and clear definitions on information and communication theory are also lacking in contemporary discourse. According to the Encyclopedia Britannica,

> "*Information theory overlaps heavily with communication theory*, but it is more oriented towards the fundamental limitations on the processing and communication of information and less oriented towards the detailed operation of particular devices."[5]

Handbooks of information theory quite frequently use information and communication as synonyms, or devote a chapter to discuss the differences between information and communication and the relationships between the two.[6] Inversely, in handbooks of communication theory, Shannon and cybernetics are often quoted as the most relevant starting points to theorise about communication and the media. Robert Craig, in his famous paper on communication theory as a field, reminds us that among the seven most relevant "traditions," cybernetics is crucial:

> Modern communication theory originated with the cybernetic tradition and the work of such mid-20th-century thinkers as *Shannon, Wiener,* von Neumann, and Turing. [...]. *Communication in the cybernetic tradition is theorized as information processing* and explains how all kinds of complex systems, whether living or nonliving, macro or micro, are able to function, and why they often malfunction.[7]

Disciplinarily, we tend to consider communication theory as being closer to the social sciences and media studies, with information theory closer to hard sciences. But, again, this is debatable. When Alistair Black and Bonnie Mak locate information theory within history, they mainly focus on different media which fundamentally changed the quantity and accessibility of information over time: poetry, books, telecommunications, broadcasting, and the internet, for example, which changed human relationships with information.[8] Similarly, communication theory can be easily applied to non-mediated forms of communication, as the long-term traditions in linguistics, pragmatics, and rhetoric in communication studies make clear: the focus of communication theory could be in the human, face-to-face, and non-mediated exchanges. Conversely, this is also true, that a great deal of communication studies has been conducted in the realm of media studies, as several histories of the field have shown.[9]

The historiography of information and communication theory (and their connections to media studies) are fairly consistent in focusing on the United States, American scholars, and American perspectives. Not by chance, the two champions of information (or communication?) theory, Shannon and Wiener, both American scholars, worked for powerful American stakeholders of Bell Labs and MIT. And, with few exceptions, the history of communication and information theories has tended to be reconstructed in the United States, or by American scholars.[10]

This chapter is an attempt to de-Americanise the history of information and communication theories by focusing on four traditions of scholarship in this field: Chinese, Latin American, French, and Soviet/Russian. These four case studies aim to answer the following research questions: How were, or are, information and communication theories combined in the region? What were the most relevant concepts about information and communication and who suggested them? What are the main connections with other disciplines and other theorists all over the world—and, specifically, with American theorists of information?

The Chinese Tradition

The US academic influence on Chinese information theory can be considered crucial. Indeed, the introduction of information theory in China was possible mainly through experiences of Chinese scholars in the United States, along with seminars and conferences of US communication scholars in China. All these activities contributed to reduce the differences between Chinese and American communication studies, but also had the consequence of partially losing Chinese identity in the field; between 1911 and 1979, there were no publications in the Chinese language which focused on information theory (信息论).[11]

An analysis of Chinese periodicals dates the first references to information theory to 1979, with the start of China "Reform and Opening-up" (改革开放) period. Angela Xiao Wu argues that, after Mao, during the Reform period, the Chinese media appropriated information theory and the "cybernetic notion of ontology and control."[12] Information theory was functional to CCP to distance itself from Maoism, but it was also to legitimate a process of media marketisation managed by the state.

The role of cybernetics is also crucial in the case communication theory. According to the *Chinese Dictionary of Propaganda and Public Opinion* (宣传舆论学大辞典), the term was imported in China from the United States mediated by Harvard professor Karl Deutsch, who referred to the principles of cybernetics to explain social and political phenomena.[13]

From an academic perspective, first attempts to define information theory in China date back to the mid-1960s; however, it is between the end of the 1970s and the beginning of the 1980s that the idea of "information fever" (信息热) begun to circulate also among the general public, after a systematic media reform took place.[14] From that moment onwards, the Chinese media system was not only asked to support propaganda activities but also national economic development.[15] This idea is evidenced in the official narrative, according to which China moved from a highly politicised media environment to a neoliberal model.[16]

Using the China National Knowledge Information (CNKI) database, it is possible to identify the contributions of Cai Changnian as one of the most relevant authors in the field, who is considered one of the "founders of the information theory in China."[17] Cai published a book titled *Information theory* (信息论) in 1962, and his research is considered one of the first contributions on the topic in China.[18] However, it is worth mentioning that Cai's academic background in mathematics and applied sciences benefited from his experience in the United States, where he was based at Cornell University between 1944 and 1947. After his return to China, he was appointed as head of the Department of Telecommunication Engineering at the Beijing University of Post and Telecommunications. Cai's major influence came from the studies of Claude Shannon with reference to the aforementioned *A Mathematical Theory of Communication*. Cai argued that "information theory is a basic applied science that studies the general laws of information transmission, storage and processing."[19] Cai also opened the first academic course on information theory in China at the Beijing University of Post and Telecommunications in 1956, which further contributed to the field's development within China.

The interest on information theory in China was not only driven by Chinese scholars who had an experience abroad, but was also supported by US scholars who visited China during its "Reform and Opening-up" period. One of the most significant contributions in this sense came by the visit of Wilbur Schramm to China in 1982. The general media reform that started to take place during that period, as well as the necessity to reconfigure the role of political propaganda in support of a more liberal journalistic environment, facilitated the circulation of technical definitions of *information* and *feedback*. These were two key concepts that justified the idea of *news value*, a turning point in the history of the media system in contemporary China.[20]

According to Angela Xiao Wu, during his series of lectures at the Chinese Academy of Social Sciences, Schramm claimed that Claude Shannon and Warren Weaver established information theory to "study the feedback phenomenon in the communication on human society."[21] Schramm also stated that "information theory has migrated from natural sciences to social sciences" and that Shannon and Weaver's goal was to "scientifically measure the circulation of information among people."[22] Wu herself notes how Schramm's interpretation on Shannon and Weaver must be considered wrong and biased.[23] Indeed, compared to Schramm's vision that mainly focused on the social dimension, Shannon clearly highlighted the limitations of information theory on technical communication because of the lack of semiotic dimension. Likewise, Weaver never explicitly theorised on concrete impact of information theory on a social dimension; he only expressed a wish that information theory would be expanded also in the domain of human communication.[24]

The concrete attempt to develop a theory of human communications through information theory was launched by Schramm. Shannon's model, based on the prototype of a phone call, focused on the technical features of communication; it explains the transmission of the message from its source to the destination, it elaborates the role of the signal and the action of converting back the signal into the message upon reception. All in all, Shannon's mathematical theory of communication emphasises the channel capacity of a technical system. Whereas Schramm's approach focused on the *effects* of communication with an emphasis on audience's opinion. A further step that enriched Schramm's information theory in the field of communication studies as it was eventually introduced to China was the application of *feedback*, a concept which was originally developed by Norbert Wiener in his cybernetic theory.

Importing, adopting, and applying information theory in China were especially functional to Chinese journalistic norms. The reference to "information" in the sense of Wiener and Shannon supported the shift from a dimension almost uniquely dominated by propaganda to a new liberal environment in which the quality of journalism was defined by "news value" (新闻价值).[25] Indeed, during the Reform period the CCP's conservative wing expressed concerns on the possible spread and impact of Western liberal ideas on the centrality of the CCP. Specifically, communication and media studies were believed to "negate class struggle." The reference to "news value" inspired by the imported definitions of information and feedback were functional to leverage journalism from propaganda. At the same time, considering news as information supported the idea that news can, and should, be non-ideological. Furthermore, Chinese scholars, following Shannon's theory, developed a series of mathematical formulas to identify "news information content." The relevance of information theory in this period was made clear by the decision of the State Science and Technology commission in 1987 to list the media sector as "information industries."

Information theory and concepts such as information value and feedback were supported by a broader political vision, but they also had academic consequences. Indeed, according to Liu and Qin, one of the main characteristics of Chinese communication studies was the importance addressed to audience research and the consequences of research.[26]

The role played by audience research particularly has been and is still useful nowadays at least for two reasons. On the one hand, it contributed to support the economic turn of the Chinese media sector, after the "Reform and Opening up" was more subjected to market dynamics compared to the Mao period. On the other hand, audience research was considered a new tool from the Chinese government to monitor its own propaganda activities.

The Latin American Tradition

In Latin America, the effects of information theory were felt across different disciplines. This part of the chapter focuses on the central role played by the concept of *information* in communication studies. Latin America and communication theory went through three stages, throughout which the modifications in the definition of *information* (and the tensions with the concept of *communication*) were constant. The first stage, which could be placed in the years 1950–1970, corresponds to the entry and diffusion of mass communication research as a key component of the development policies promoted by the United States, especially after the Cuban Revolution of 1953–1959. An institution like CIESPAL (Centro Internacional de Estudios Superiores de Comunicación para América Latina) in Quito, Ecuador, played a key role in that dissemination. The work of some authors were translated and adopted by the nascent Schools of communication.[27] The second phase, roughly 1960–1980, was characterised by the adoption of critical European models, halfway between French semiotics (such as Roland Barthes and Christian Metz) and the Frankfurt School (Max Horkheimer, Theodor Adorno, Herbert Marcuse). The theoretical contributions of Mattelart are quintessential examples of this theoretical approach.[28] Finally, starting in the 1980s, a Latin American-born culturalist paradigm took shape at the hands of researchers such as Martín-Barbero, García Canclini, or Reguillo.[29]

Shannon and Weaver's classic text *A Mathematical Theory of Communication* was only translated into Spanish in 1981, but the model had been in circulation since the early 1960s, such as in the texts of Wilbur Schramm, translated into Spanish by CIESPAL.[30] Unlike the cases of China and of France (see below), in Latin America the concept of *information* was radically opposed to *communication*. This theoretical exchange started in the early 1960s and went through the three research phases. In this context, the publication of *Comunicación y Cultura de Masas* by Antonio Pasquali in 1963 should be considered a milestone in the history of Latin American media and communication research.[31] Published before Eco's *Apocalittici e Integrati* (1964), Marcuse's *One-Dimensional Man* (1964), McLuhan's *Understanding Media* (1964), and Enzensberger's *Constituents of a Theory of the Media* (1970), Pasquali's ideas anticipated many of the philosophical discussions about mass media that dominated the 1960s and beyond.[32]

To understand *information*, it is first important to define *communication*. For Pasquali a "communicational relationship" is a dialogic liaison that "produces (and supposes at the same time) a biunivocal interaction of the type of knowing."[33] Communication is an activity exclusive and limited to human beings; they are the "only entities capable of provoking authentically communicational and social types of behavior."[34]

Pasquali proposes "reserving the term *information* both for the *process* of unilateral transmission of knowledge between an institutionalised transmitter and a mass receiver, as well as for its *contents*, and whatever the language or medium used."[35] For Pasquali, this predominance of "communicational unilateralism (information)" determines a "massification of receivers."[36] In this framework, the expression *mass communication* should be avoided:

it would be better to call them *broadcast media, mass media,* or *mass information channels* because the receiver "is in the impossibility of becoming directly or indirectly a transmitter of a dialogic replica, favouring in the transmitter the progressive sterilisation of his receptive potentiality."[37] In the unilateral information relationship, "the control, selection and use of the information media become absolute prerogatives of the transmitting agent."[38]

The opposition between *information* and *communication* is fundamental in Latin American media and communication studies. Pasquali's opposition was enhanced by another basic opposition between *extension* and *communication*, promoted by Paulo Freire. The concept of (rural) *extension* was broadly used in Latin America to define the informal educational strategies directed towards the rural population, including instructions to increase the production and the efficiency of farms. In extension processes there is a *unilateral transmission of information* from an active subject (the rural extensionist) to a passive one (the farmer). Freire's *extension* is therefore close to Pasquali's *information*. According to the Brazilian educator, "only through communication can human life hold meaning (...) Authentic thinking, thinking that is concerned about *reality*, does not take place in ivory tower isolation, but only in communication."[39]

The opposition between *information* (understood as a unilateral transmission of information) and *communication* (understood as a dialogic exchange) led in Latin America to a proliferation of experiences and theories of "alternative communication" (*comunicación alternativa*) inspired by Pasquali and Freire's semantic oppositions.[40] Those experiences—from local radios to video productions and theatre performances—differed from the traditional ones at the level of organisation, source of financing, management, content, or relationship with the audiences. The 1970s were the "golden age" of alternative communication in Latin America.

As can be seen, Pasquali's philosophical opposition between *information* and *communication* was also appropriated by Freire and applied to the lived reality of the popular classes, rendering it operational within the framework of a critical educational praxis. For Freire, traditional "banking education" consisted in filling the students "by making deposits of information."[41] On the other side, dialogic and liberating education "consists in acts of cognition, not transferals of information."[42] The experiences and theories of "alternative communication" of the 1970s were fed from the same sources.

On a theoretical level, the decline of the radical opposition between *information* and *communication* ran parallel to the emergence of a new culturalist theoretical paradigm in Latin America (although in some areas—like media activism—it is still very much in force). According to Martín-Barbero, alternative communication cannot be built outside of the tensions and hybridisations between traditional media and popular cultures:

> Communication will be alternative to the extent that it assumes the complexity of these processes, if the language of the medium is investigated alongside its perception and recognition codes and the enunciation devices of the popular, the codes and devices in which they materialize and express entangled with popular memory and mass imaginary.[43]

While it may have been useful at the time, for the new generation of Latin American researchers that emerged in the 1980s and 1990s a basic opposition such as *information* versus *communication* was not the best theoretical tool for understanding the complexities of contemporary cultural and media life. New concepts and oppositions, like Martín-Barbero's displacement from *media* to *mediations,* set the course for theoretical discussion. Rather than perceiving media merely as a one-way conduit for disseminating information, he advocated for understanding it as a dynamic space of mediation, where diverse and sometimes conflicting cultural meanings are negotiated and exchanged.[44]

The French Tradition

The history of information and communication theories in France is complex, full of paradoxes, and in many ways unique. In France, the field that is commonly associated with media and communication research in the English-speaking world is labelled *Sciences de l'Information et de la Communication.* Colloquially known as "SIC" or "infocom" by French speaking researchers, it can be translated as "information and communication sciences." In this context, "information" loosely refers to library and information science and is associated with specific French or francophone research traditions such as "bibliologie," "documentologie," and "médiologie." In this respect, the field covers a very specific ground, quite different from the mainstream American tradition which has so often been imitated in other countries like China. This history is not well-known and yet to be written since only a handful of works have attempted to map the history of the field, or some aspects of it.[45] Through the lens of the twin concepts of information and communication, which were alternatively opposed and articulated and whose definitions shifted, the field reveals some of its distinctive features and singularities.

Among the first generation of researchers in *SIC,* the tendency was often to draw a theoretical framework encompassing both information and communication. Among these, the voices of Robert Escarpit and Jean Meyriat were possibly the most important. Escarpit and Meyriat are widely recognised as the twin founders of the field in France. In the mid-1970s, they were at the forefront of the campaign for the official administrative recognition of *SIC* by the French *Conseil Consultatif des Universités,* which was attained in 1975. In this context, institutional recognition and theoretical developments both supported and justified each other.

Escarpit began developing *infocom* at the Université de Bordeaux in the mid-1960s, securing the creation of a local *Unité Plurisdisciplinaire des Sciences de l'Information et de la Communication* in 1968. At the time, many similar professional training programmes revolving around "information"—an all-encompassing buzzword meaning journalism, organisational communication, and library science, among other things—were being developed in France. In parallel with his activities aimed at further institutionalising his home-cooked formula, Escarpit was ambitioning a general theory of information and communication. In his 1976 seminal *Théorie Générale de l'Information et de la Communication,* Escarpit drew heavily on the work of Claude Shannon and very broadly construed communication as the transmission of information.[46]

At the time, in the context of the official recognition of *infocom* by the French *Conseil Consultatif des Universités,* similar efforts at developing a general theory of information and communication were common. In November 1975, the first meeting of the newly formed French Society for Information and Communication Sciences (*Société Française des Sciences de l'Information et de la Communication,* or *SFSIC*) had as its theme the convergence of information and communication sciences. More than any other theoretical approaches—and there were plenty of them—it was cybernetics that provided the theoretical cornerstone needed to articulate information and communication.[47]

That information was the content of communication was then consensual among the founders of the field.[48] But information, in this context, was much more associated with arts and literature than mathematics and engineering. Escarpit was a literary scholar. Building on previous work by Abraham Moles and Umberto Eco, he was investigating readers and the various meanings they associated with literary material.[49] In a word, he approached literature as a problem of communication.[50] Meyriat was also a literary scholar whose intellectual trajectory also leans towards political science and history. As the head of the research library of the *Fondation Nationale des Sciences Politiques*, he developed an expertise in information science and wrote extensively about "information." "Information," Meyriat wrote, "is the cognitive content of an actual or possible communication."[51] In this respect, information implies active reception and the development of personal knowledge. It is radically different from data as objective, finite elements, or as information defined by cybernetics. Meyriat was much more explicit with regard to the heritage of cybernetics and its limits. In *SIC*, information has meaning, and in this respect, the concept differs from Shannon's. Despite this criticism, a cybernetic impetus remains: information is a content, and communication a process. Information was the key concept for Meyriat, who thought that communication was of second importance.[52] He later recognised that the union of information and communication was much more opportunistic and related to institutional and political realities than it was theoretically and epistemologically driven.[53]

Soon enough, cybernetics and information theory associated with the work of Claude Shannon became much less important. In 1978, the second meeting of the *SFSIC* made clear that a generational shift was already in place among information and communication researchers.[54] Institutionally robust, the field was not in need of a unified general theory of information and communication, and theorisation efforts similar to those of Escarpit and Meyriat seemed to belong to another era. Most scholars who contributed to the institutionalisation of the field in the early 1970s did not attend the second SFSIC meeting, but their former PhD students did. Bernard Miège, who eventually succeeded Meyriat as the President of the *SFSIC*, was among those who thought that a general theory was impossible.[55] In other words, the idea was no longer to articulate information and communication in a coherent theory, but as Dominique Wolton puts it, "to clearly distinguish the logic of information from that of communication."[56] Nevertheless, the question of the relationship between information and communication remains a sensitive one, and is regularly the subject of debate.[57]

This distancing from cybernetics and the mathematical theory of communication certainly echoes other factors. In France, the frenzy around cybernetics was intense and much longer lasting than in the United States.[58] Writing in the mid-1970s, Escarpit was still in the long tail of the cybernetic mania. Google Books NGram Viewer shows that in the mid-1970s, *cybernétique* was as often used than in the mid-1950s.[59] By the early 1980s, the frenzy was over and cybernetics was mostly the object of a radical political criticism by some of the heavyweight of French intellectual life, including, among others, Gilles Deleuze and Cornelius Castoriadis.[60]

The Soviet and Russian Tradition

In Russian, the word "media" has been widely adopted only in the last couple of decades. Throughout the Soviet era, and up until today, a more prevalent expression to describe media is "средства массовой информации" (abbreviated to СМИ), or the means of mass information. In Russian, media do not mediate communication – they are the means, tools, instruments to spread information to the masses. Dubin and Reitblat suggest that the difference in "media" and "means of mass information" is also linked to the different historical trajectories of their formation.[61] The European press developed as one of the mechanisms to express opinions of social groups, institutions, organisations, and parties—so, as an element of the nascent public sphere.[62] In Russia, however, the publication of newspapers (and the Soviet radio and television development later) was primarily a state affair for a long time. Thus, in Russian media, asymmetrical power relation is in their name, and information is in the essence of their asymmetry.

The concept of information has been covered in some depth in Russian scholarship, although not within media and communications studies. The media and communication field in Russia began to emerge only in recent decades. In 2021, Benjamin Peters drew attention to the absence of a Russian media theory despite the broad Slavic intellectual tradition.[63] Yet some Russian theoretical insights into media and communications developed sporadically in the realms of other disciplines, and consequently now contribute to Russia's media and communication scholarship. Having a regional advantage of learning from the best practices and schools in media and communication, simultaneously paired with the solid intellectual legacy of philosophy, semiotics, and linguistics, Russian scholars are now focused more on communication and media than before. New areas of scholarship are developing and trying to define their borders: journalism theory, media theory, and even *communicativistics*, meaning communication theories as a separate field.[64]

As in other countries, the distinction between the concepts of information and communication is as paramount as it is complicated to define. Media scholars Ilya Kiria and Anna Novikova define information as "the content we exchange in the process of communication."[65] They point out that the concept of information differs from discipline to discipline, so we should differentiate between the terms according to different schools of thought. It is thus essential to consider how scholarship progressed in the fields, adjacent to Russian media studies, such as computer science, mathematics, informatics, philosophy, journalism, and linguistics. These differ in understanding information as something more objective and neutral, to being more subjective and socially constructed.

Mathematics and computer sciences are fundamental to understanding the concept of information. Scientific articles before the 1980s mainly concerned themselves with information theory and its application to the mathematical and applied sciences. In addition to American scientists Ralph Hartley and Claude Shannon, Russian mathematician Andrei Kolmogorov is considered one of the founders of information theory.[66] In the 1990s, he developed the *Algorithmic Theory of Information* (which was later elaborated by Gregory John Chaitin, an Argentine-American mathematician), where the concept of information can be seen as similar to data; the information is a signal encoded in a certain way for transmission by electronic media. In this sense, information for such sciences is unambiguous and differs only in coding. Machine systems thus see information as unambiguous data—decoding the message makes it possible to obtain identical information encoded. Therefore, information as such is not a problematic concept for machine systems. To this end, the development of scientific thought has mainly focused on systems for collecting, processing, and accumulating information.

This brings us to the further development of the information as a concept. Since the 1960s, scholars have tried to understand the value of "information." In management and sociology, the role of information was explicitly seen through its value for achieving of goals.[67] Thus, with this practical oriented approach, *measuring* the value of information was important and Aleksandr Kharkevich was one of the first to draw attention to the possibility of measuring it in terms of the incremental probability of achieving a goal before, and after, the cybernetic system obtains information. In 1960, he founded an *Institute for Information Transmission Problems* of the Russian Academy of Sciences (also known as Kharkevich Institute). He also postulated a theory: "The amount of information is growing at least in proportion to the square of the country's industrial capacity."[68] With Kharkevich's method, the concept of information is again seen as objective and neutral, and only the quantity of information is an important variable for effective communication. Only later, scholars such as Michail Bongard, Ruslan Stratonovich, and Boris Grishanin, using game theory, algorithm theory, and optimal control theory, developed further the study of the information value, where it could be negative and dependent on the subject (recipient of the information) and the goals of communication.[69]

From the 1970s, information as a concept was put into a new critical perspective. Arkady Ursul critically reflected on the concept of information and its impact on society.[70] At first, his understanding of information was influenced by Marxism-Leninism: for example, whether information is a property of matter. Then, the reflection acquired a broader social scope, which gave rise to a new scientific discipline—informatics.[71] Informatics, in this case, is understood as a broad meta-reflection on the meaning and notion of information. Informatics is distinct from the computer sciences because it is not specifically concerned with the storage and transmission of information in the computer systems. Instead, informatics focuses on the information at large within a broader social scope. An even narrower branch within this field is social informatics, which focuses on the importance of information in the development of society and within the computer revolution.[72]

Journalism is probably the academic field which has been the most critical towards information in Russia. In journalism, one of the stumbling blocks is the problem of objectivity and subjectivity. Information is, therefore, a central concept for this problem. The theories of journalism emphasise that information is objective and, in contrast to information, communication is a product of social processes and can thus become propaganda.[73] Overall, Soviet thought on information confronted and problematised the ideas of propaganda and ideological confrontation.[74] Russian theory of journalism, being normative in its essence, asserted that the spread of information, as objective and neutral as it is, is the goal of any mass media. This tendency to refer to the concept of information as purely accurate, neutral, and reliable data, details, or facts is evident in many publications, even in other fields. Information, again, appears as objective data. Scholars in journalism questioned information only through the lens of the lack or excess of information, overload or scarcity. This is mainly associated with the development of communication technologies as they multiply the amount of the surrounding information and allow access to the previously unreachable information.[75]

Russian philosophers and sociologists elaborated more on media and communications from the late 1980s, influenced heavily by the linguistic school of semiotics and Western media and cultural studies, such as the Birmingham and Frankfurt Schools. One of the key aspects was the intensification of the information flow. Instead of just measuring value of information, the philosophers enquired *why* information has value. Kurennoj suggested two mechanisms of the information function of media: first, semantically, media stories set up a way of giving a subject or fact; the second notion of meaning we can use in relation to news media is the hermeneutic notion of giving meaningfulness.[76] In this sense, the philosophy of information was also an object of interest for Russian scholars. There are even some claims that the philosophy of information was developed by Russian scholars before the works of Luciano Floridi in the 1990s; for instance, Konstantin Kolin attributes the birth of philosophy of information to Ursul's works of the 1960s–1970s.[77] The philosophy of information challenges notions of artificial intelligence, navigates the computational turn, and raises issues of computational ethics. More scholarly works on information technology are being published now that concern how information is processed, biased, and can also be problematic for technology.[78]

Overall, these scientific branches have continued to develop at their own pace in parallel, so that significant names, concepts, and theoretical frameworks can be found in each area. Despite many points of overlap, these sectors remain distinct branches of scientific knowledge. For example, between 2010 and 2015, the work of Kolin and Ursul in the field of social informatics led to the formation of a new scientific trend in the field of cultural studies—called informational cultural studies.[79] Cultural studies in Russia, which grew from philosophy and followed Western schools of thought, have done similar work.[80] However, despite the apparent similarities, the two fields' conceptual apparatus and theoretical foundations remain different, affecting different ideas about information. Overall, this brief overview of Russian scholarship on information and its reflection in the various scientific fields demonstrated that while the concept of information is entangled in a constellation of different notions, such as communications, media, and data, it is heavily loaded with the idea of objectivity, as opposed to communication as subjective and potentially biased.

Conclusions

The four case studies analysed above demonstrate how information and communication are, and have been, conceptualised and interpreted in various ways in different geographic regions. Consequently, the first, and most interesting finding, is the fact that a history of information and communication theory (or theories) is mostly impossible to tell. We should instead talk about histories and different periods inside the same region, as we can clearly see from the evolutions in the Latin America and French traditions, for example. What counts as "information" and "communication" differs as each of the national and transnational communities of researchers domesticated information and communication theories in specific ways.

Second, all the histories of information and communication theories in the four different regions are linked to American scholarship. By linked, it means that they were often inspired by the US model and, even if we are trying to recount a non-US history, the starting point and the founding fathers are nevertheless Shannon and Wiener in most of the cases. That being said, they were a starting point only for further evolution of ideas. There are of course heralds of the American development of information theory, establishing a clear lineage: for example, the communication scholar Wilbur Schramm acted as an information and communication theory evangelist both in China and in Latin America. Where the American champions were not directly imported or referred, other national scholars seemed to play a key role in importing or translating their theories, as Escarpit did in France for Shannon. But there are also cases where the American legacy was rejected or limited, and we have seen some attempts to build "autochthonous" information and communication theories which are explicitly or implicitly original compared to American ones. The cases of Pasquali in Latin America and Cai in China are quite symbolic of non-Western founding fathers of contemporary information/communication/media theory, not yet acknowledged historically.

A third useful insight towards a new history of information and communication theory(ies) deals with the variety of fields where these theories can be placed in the different regions. In the French tradition, information (and communication) theory has emerged in the field of literary studies. In the Latin American and Chinese ones, it has emerged mainly in conjunction with communication and media theory. Whereas in the Soviet and Russian arena, there is a wide spectrum of fields reflecting on similar issues but not interacting or collaborating: from mathematics to computer science, from (social) informatics to social sciences. Where is the place, or better, the field of "information theory"? The answer perhaps is both everywhere and nowhere. The place changes in the same region according to the time period and time frame: think about the French case, where the project of a general theory of information and communication has been slowly abandoned over time. Apparently, information and communication theories (together or separate and despite the disapproval of Shannon himself) have been broadly applied in the twentieth and twenty-first centuries; their success can be explained in part due to this flexibility. This is one of the cases when the uncertainty of names, definitions, and disciplines contribute to the popularity of concepts and ideas.

Finally, focusing on the key aspect of this chapter, how have the relationships between information and communication theories developed in the four regions? The *con-fusion* of the two fields, already discussed in the introduction, clearly emerges in the French case, where the labels "*Sciences de l'Information et de la Communication*," "SIC," and "infocom" all underline the fact that information and communication are profoundly intertwined and occupy a common ground. But, as already mentioned, this combination changed over time. In other traditions and regions, several unquestioned differences among the two fields are discussed, but drawing a clear line between the two is mostly impossible, and its value questionable. In some places and traditions, information theory seems to deal more with hard sciences and communication theory than with the social sciences. Information theory seems to operate more with the quantity of information, while communication theory with its quality. And in the Russian case, this also brings up related issues such as understanding information as objective, and communication as subjective and potentially biased. Information theory seems to be more concerned with the mechanical and technical aspects of information transmission, while communication theory with the social effects of this transfer, with a specific interest on the receiver/the audience. Similarly, information theory deals more with one flow, while communication theory looks more dialogic. This is clear in the Latin American tradition, where communication is seen as the exchange of messages, the interactivity between the actors, while information has a "low coefficient of communicability," of interactivity. This idea has also become popular in Brazil thanks to the work of Freire. According to him, information is an extension, meaning passive, one-to-many, asymmetrical, and with negative connotation; communication is the opposite and therefore has a positive connotation. But these are not fixed categories. In the Russian case, information is considered as "the content we exchange in the process of communication" or, reversely, communication is the act of transmitting pieces of information; in this sense, information looks like as something static and given and communication something more processual. At the opposite side, in French, according to Meyriat, information is the cognitive content of an actual or possible communication. So, information in this case implies active reception and the development of personal knowledge, in a sense which is radically different from data as objective, finite elements, or as information defined by cybernetics. Of course, information and communication theories deal with power, even political power: governments have often defined them and, through definitions, classified them with related consequences.[81] If the Chinese State

Science and Technology Commission list the media sector as "information industries," this has consequences on the media themselves. If powerful French academics decide to create a unique sector collecting all the studies in information and communication theory, this has an impact on the academia, on other disciplines, but also at political level.

The history of information and communication theory has been stabilised over time, and with the impact of digitalisation and of convergence between traditional media and information and communication technologies, the two fields and the two theories are merging more and more. Digital media as a research object in a broad sense seems to dissolve and challenge traditional disciplinary boundaries between information studies and communication studies. For example, many media and communication publications cover topics such as search, archiving and the management of information and data by platforms and media, topics that historically have been seen as the core of information studies. And vice versa, information studies can no longer avoid discussion about media, content, audiences, and other media-related topics. In this process of stabilisation, the classic vulgate of American scholarship, trying to draw a line between the fields and often quoting the same Western scholars, has gained more visibility. We hope this chapter can help contest the one-dimensional history of information and communication theory, while it may also add to its complexities, reciprocal connections, and tensions.

Notes

1. Claude E. Shannon, "A Mathematical Theory of Communication," *Bell System Technical Journal* 27, no. 3 (1948): 379–423.
2. Quoted in Flo Conway and Jim Siegelman, *Dark Hero of the Information Age: In Search of Norbert Wiener, the Father of Cybernetics* (New York: Basic Books, 2005), 189–190. Italics added by the authors.
3. Norbert Wiener, *Cybernetics, or Control and Communication in the Animal and the Machine* (Cambridge, MA: MIT Press, 1948).
4. Colin Koopman, "Information Before Information Theory: The Politics of Data Beyond the Perspective of Communication," *New Media and Society* 21, no. 6 (2019): 1326–1343, quote at 1329–1330. Italics added by the authors.
5. See https://www.britannica.com/science/information-theory. Italics added by the authors.
6. See, for example, Stefan Host, *Information and Communication Theory* (Newark, NJ: Wiley, 2019).
7. Robert T. Craig, "Communication Theory as a Field," *Communication Theory* 9, no. 2 (1999): 119–161, quote at 141. Italics added by the authors.
8. Alistair Black and Bonnie Mak, "Period, Theme, Event. Locating Information History in History," In *Information and Power in History. Towards a Global Approach*, ed. Ida Nijenhuis, Marijke van Faassen, Ronald Sluijter, Joris Gijsenbergh, and Wim de Jong (Abingdon, Oxon; New York: Routledge, 2020), 18–36.
9. See, for example, David W. Park and Jefferson Pooley, *The History of Media and Communication Research: Contested Memories* (New York: Peter Lang, 2008).
10. For the exceptions, see, for example, Peter Simonson and David W. Park, *The International History of Communication Study* (New York: Routledge, 2016), with several case studies building national histories of communication studies; Ronald R. Kline, *The Cybernetics Moment, or, Why We Call Our Age the Information Age* (Baltimore, MD: Johns Hopkins University Press, 2015), where the American theorists of information are confronted with the British ones.
11. Wang Wenjuan (王文娟), 改革开放第一个十年信息论在我国新闻界的引入——对中国期刊全文数据库 1979 年-1989 年相关文献的考察), 新闻传播, 3 (2012): 202–204. ["The Introduction of Information Theory in China Journalism in the First Decade of Reform and Opening Up——A Survey of Related Documents in China Periodicals Full-text Database from 1979 to 1989"].

12 Angela Xiao Wu, "Journalism via Systems Cybernetics: The Birth of the Chinese Communication Discipline and Post-Mao Press Reforms," *History in Media Studies* 2 (2022): 1–31. The reform period began between the end of the 1970s and the beginning of the 1980s and is characterised by the economic reforms of Deng Xiaoping which contributed to the restoration of international business and international relations extremely limited during the Mao era.
13 Wu, "Journalism via Systems Cybernetics."
14 Wu, "Journalism via Systems Cybernetics."
15 Yuezhi Zhao, *Communication in China: Political Economy, Power, and Conflict* (Plymouth: Rowman & Littlefield Publishers, 2008).
16 Zhao, *Communication in China*.
17 Bei You (北邮), 中国信息论研究的先行者——记全国劳模、北京邮电大学教授蔡长年), ["The Forerunner of China's Information Theory Research——Cai Changnian, a National Model Worker and Professor of Beijing University of Posts and Telecommunications,"] 工会博览 9 (2020): 43–45. According to the results of the database, Cai Changnian was the first Chinese author to publish in Chinese and in PRC on "information theory."
18 Cai Changnian (蔡长年) "Information Theory" (信息论) (Beijing, Post and Telecom Press 人民邮电出版社, 1962).
19 Bei, "The Forerunner of China's Information Theory Research," 44.
20 Zhengrong Hu and Deqiang Ji, "Retrospection, Prospection and the Pursuit of an Integrated Approach for China's Communication and Journalism Studies," *Javnost - The Public* 20, no. 4 (2013): 5–16.
21 Wu, "Journalism via Systems Cybernetics," 8.
22 Wilmer Schramm, 传学与新闻及其它,["Communication Study and Journalism, and Other Issues"] 新闻学会通讯 14 (1982): 19–22.
23 Wu, "Journalism via Systems Cybernetics."
24 Everett M. Rogers and Thomas W. Valente, "A History of Information Theory in Communication Research," in *Between Communication and Information*, ed. Brent D. Ruben and Jorge R. Schement (London: Routledge, 2017), 35–56.
25 Wu, "Journalism via Systems Cybernetics."
26 Hailong Liu and Yidan Qin, "Toward a New Media Study in China: History and Approach," *History in Media Studies* 1 (2021): 1–8.
27 Wilbur Schramm, *Media and National Development: The Role of Information in the Developing Countries* (Redwood, CA: Stanford University Press, 1964); Daniel Lerner, *The Passing of Traditional Society: Modernizing the Middle East* (New York: Free Press, 1958); Everett M. Rogers, *Diffusion of Innovations* (New York: Free Press, 1962).
28 See Armand Mattelart, *Agresión Desde el Espacio. Cultura y Napalm en la Era de los Satélites* (Mexico: Siglo xxi, 1972); Armand Mattelart, *La Comunicación Masiva en el Proceso de Liberación* (Buenos Aires: Siglo xxi, 1973).
29 The most known books of these authors are Jesús Martín-Barbero, *De los Medios a las Mediaciones* (Barcelona: Gustavo Gili, 1987); Néstor García Canclini, *Culturas Híbridas: Estrategias Para Entrar y Salir de la Modernidad* (México: Grijalbo, 1989); Rossana Reguillo, *En la Calle Otra Vez. Las Bandas Juveniles. Identidad Urbana y Usos de la Comunicación* (Guadalajara: ITESO, 1991); Rossana Reguillo, *La Construcción Simbólica de la Ciudad. Sociedad, Desastre, Comunicación* (Guadalajara: Universidad Iberoamericana/ITESO, 1996).
30 Claude Shannon and Warren Weaver, *Teoría Matemática de la Comunicación* (Madrid: Forja, 1981).
31 Antonio Pasquali, *Comunicación y Cultura de Masas* (Caracas: Colección Bicentenario Carabobo, 2021). First edition published in 1963.
32 Umberto Eco, *Apocalittici e integrati* (Milan: Bompiani, 1964); Herbert Marcuse, *One-Dimensional Man* (Boston, MA: Beacon Press, 1964); Marshall McLuhan, *Understanding Media: The Extensions of Man* (New York: McGraw Hill, 1964); Hans M. Enzensberger, "Constituents of a Theory of the Media," *New Left Review* 64 (1970): 13–36.
33 Pasquali, *Comunicación*, 61.
34 Pasquali, *Comunicación*, 62.
35 Pasquali, *Comunicación*, 75.
36 Pasquali, *Comunicación*, 90.

37 Pasquali, *Comunicación*, 78.
38 Pasquali, *Comunicación*, 75. Pasquali also anticipated information overload: because through the "quantitative explosion" of information, the consumer "is forced to believe that the apparent information surplus automatically equals good 'information', and that this 'knowledge', ingested in elephantine doses, can only improve it automatically. The current use of the information media by the cultural industry must be denied, therefore, as a matter of priority" (Pasquali, *Comunicación*, 40).
39 Paulo Freire, *¿Extensión o Comunicación? La Concientización en el Medio Rural* (Mexico: Siglo xxi, 1973), 70.
40 See Fernando Reyes Matta, *Comunicación Alternativa y Búsquedas Democráticas* (Mexico: ILET, 1983); Alejandro Barranquero and Emiliano Treré, "Comunicación Alternativa y Comunitaria. La Conformación del Campo en Europa y el Diálogo con América Latina," *Chasqui* 146 (2021): 159–182.
41 Paulo Freire, *Pedagogy of the Oppressed* (New York: Bloomsbury, 2000), 76. First edition published 1970.
42 Freire, *Pedagogy*, 79.
43 Jesús Martín-Barbero, "Retos a la Investigación de Comunicación en América Latina," in *Comunicación y Teoría Social*, ed. Fátima Fernández Christlieb and M. Yépez Hernández (Mexico: UNAM, 1984), 61.
44 Martín-Barbero, *De los Medios a las Mediaciones*.
45 See Robert Boure, ed., *Les Origines des Sciences de l'Information et de la Communication. Regards Croisés* (Villeneuve d'Ascq: Presses Universitaires du Septentrion, 2002); Dominique Trudel, Olivier Le Deuff and Stefanie Averbeck-Lietz, "L'Histoire Digitale et la Recherche en Communication," *Communication* 40, no. 1 (2023), https://doi.org/10.4000/communication.17010.
46 Robert Escarpit, *Théorie Générale de l'Information et de la Communication* (Paris: Hachette, 1976), 7; 14–15.
47 Regarding theoretical approaches, Daniel Bougnoux argues that French "sciences de l'information et de la communication" have been built on five theoretical pillars: semiology, pragmatics, *médiologie*, psychoanalysis, and cybernetics. See Daniel Bougnoux, *La communication par la bande: Introduction aux sciences de l'information et de la communication* (Paris: La Découverte, 1991), 8. On the first scientific event organised by the SFSIC, see Jean-François Têtu, "Sur les origines littéraires des sciences de l'information et de la communication," in *Les Origines des Sciences de l'Information et de la Communication. Regards Croisés*, ed. Robert Boure (Villeneuve d'Ascq: Presses Universitaires du Septentrion, 2002), 71–93. For cybernetics as the theoretical cornerstone, see Bernard Miège, "Les Apports à la Recherche des Sciences de l'Information et de la Communication," *Réseaux* 18, no. 100 (2000), 555.
48 Frank Renucci and Maud Pélissier, "L'Esprit d'Aventure, le Trésor Perdu des SIC," *Hermès* 3, no. 7 (2013): 113–121.
49 Abraham Moles, *Théorie de l'Information et de la Perception Esthétique* (Paris: Flammarion, 1965); Umberto Eco, *L'Oeuvre Ouverte* (Paris: Seuil, 1965).
50 Têtu, "Les Origines Littéraires," 75.
51 Jean Meyriat, "De la Science de l'Information aux Métiers de l'Information," *Schéma et Schématisation* 19 (1983), 66.
52 Anne-Marie Laulan, "Jean Meyriat (1921–2010). Le Paradoxe de la Discrétion," *Hermès* 1, no. 59 (2011): 199–200.
53 Renucci and Pélissier, "L'Esprit d'Aventure," 116.
54 Têtu, "Les Origines Littéraires."
55 See Robert Estivals, *Théorie Générale de la Schématisation 3* (Paris: L'Harmattan, 2003), 22–23.
56 Dominique Wolton, "Communication," *Hermès* 1, no. 80 (2018), 103–113, 110.
57 Philippe Dumas, Eric Boutin, Daphné Duvernay, and Gabriel Gallezot, "Is Communication Separable from Information?" First European Communication Conference, Amsterdam (January 2006).
58 Dominique Trudel, "L'Abandon du Projet de Construction de la Tour Lumière Cybernétique de La Défense," *Le Temps des Médias* 1, no. 28 (2017): 235–250.
59 Google Books NGram Viewer is a tool for exploring the usage of words over time, based on their occurrence in the Google Books digitised collection. According to the tool, the occurrence of "cybernétique" in French books, which peaked in 1966–1967, was the same in 1956 and 1977.

60 See Dominique Trudel, "La Philosophie de Cornélius Castoriadis: Pour une Critique des Conceptions Cybernétiques/Informationnelles de la Subjectivité," *Commposite* 9, no. 1 (2006): 153–173.

61 Boris Dubin and Abram Reitblat "Государственная Информация и Массовая Коммуникация" [State information and mass communication], *Отечественные Записки* 4 (2023): 237–248.

62 As widely argued by Jürgen Habermas, *The Structural Transformation of the Public Sphere* (Cambridge, MA: MIT Press, 1989).

63 Benjamin Peters, "Russian Media Theory: Is There Any? Should There Be? How About These?" *Media Theory* 5, no. 2 (2021): 223–246.

64 Denis Dunas and Anna Gureeva, "Медиаисследования в России: к определению научного статуса" [Media Studies in Russia: Defining Its Academic Status] *Theoretical and Practical Issues of Journalism* 8, no. 1 (2019): 20–35, https://doi.org/10.17150/2308-6203.2019.8(1).20-35; Е. Н. Пенска, "О Характере Наших Дискуссий Вообще и Образовательных в Частности. Обсуждение Журналистского Образования Как Универсалии и Ремесла" [On the nature of our debates in general and educational debates in particular. Discussing journalism education as a universalism and a craft], *Вопросы Образования* 4 (2010): 150–159.

65 Ilya Kiria and Anna Novikova, *История и Теория Медиа: Учебник Для Вузов* [Media History and Theory: Handbook for Universities] (Москва: Изд. дом Высшей школы экономики, 2017), 20.

66 Andrei Kolmogorov "Three Approaches to the Definition of the Notion of Amount of Information," in *Selected Works of A.N. Kolmogorov. Volume III: Information Theory and the Theory of Algorithms*, ed. A. N. Shiryayev (Dordrecht: Springer, 1993), 184–193.

67 G. G. Vorobyov, "Информационная культура управленческого труда" [The Information Culture of Managerial Work] (Москва: Экономика, 1979).

68 Aleksandr Kharkevich, "Информация и Техника" [Information and Technology], *Коммунист*, 12 (1962).

69 Vadim Goncharov, "Концепции Информации в Современной Науке" [The Concepts of Information in the Contemporary Sciences], *Наука и Современность*, 2010, 22–27.

70 Arkady Ursul, *Информация. Методологические Аспекты* [Information: Methodology Aspects] (Москва: Наука, 1971).

71 Arkady Ursul, *Природа Информации: Философский Очерк* [The Nature of Information: Philosophical Reflection] (Челябинск: Челяб. гос. акад. культуры и искусств, 2010), 218.

72 Arkady Sokolov and A. Majkevich, "Социальная Информатика и Библиотеко-Библиографические Дисциплины," [Social informatics and Library-Bibliographic Disciplines], in *Социальные Проблемы Информатики: Сб. Статей ЛГИК Им. Н.К. Крупской* (Ленинград, 1974).

73 Kiria and Novikova, *История и Теория Медиа*, 22.

74 A. Poklad and N. Yudina, *Массовая Информация: Международное Общение Или Подрывная Пропаганда* [Mass Information: International Communication or Subversive Propaganda] (Москва: Междунар. отношения, 1987).

75 П.П. Гайденко, "Информация и Знание," *Философия Науки* 3 (1997), 189.

76 Vitaly Kurennoy, "Медиа: Средства в Поисках Целей" [Media: Means in Search for Aims], *Отечественные Записки* 4 (2003): 1–21.

77 Luciano Floridi, *The Philosophy of Information* (Oxford: Oxford University Press, 2011); Konstantin Kolin, Философия информации и фундаментальные проблемы современной информатики [Philosophy of Information and Fundamental Issues of the Contemporary Informatics], Alma mater (Вестник высшей школы [Journal of higher school] 2010, 1: 29–35.

78 Konstantin Glazkov, Lily Zemnukhova et al., *Приключения Технологий. Барьеры Цифровизации в России* [Adventures of technologies: Barriers of digitalization in Russia]. (Санкт-Петербург: Федеральный научно-исследовательский социологический центр РАН, 2020).

79 Konstanin Kolin and Arkady Ursul, *Информационная Культурология: Предмет и Задачи Нового Научного Направления* [Informational Cultural Studies: Subject and Objectives of a New Scientific Direction] (Saarbruchen, 2011).

80 See, for example, mentioned above Ilya Kiria and Anna Novikova, *История и Теория Медиа*; and Kurennoj, Медиа: Средства в Поисках Целей.

81 As Bowker and Star have pointed out, every classification has consequences: see Geoffrey C. Bowker and Susan Leigh Star, *Sorting Things Out: Classification and Its Consequences* (Cambridge, MA: MIT Press, 1999).

35
DECOLONISATION AND INFORMATION IN POSTCOLONIAL EGYPT, 1952–1967

Zoe LeBlanc

Introduction: Decolonising Information and Contextualising the Arab Spring

In 2011, a series of mass anti-government protests erupted across the Middle East and North Africa, collectively known as the Arab Spring. Sparked by decades of authoritarian rule, the protests demanded democratic reforms to institutionalise the protection of political freedoms and civil liberties. Although those hopes have yet to be fully realised, the Arab Spring continues to cast a long shadow, particularly in Egypt, one of the epicentres of the movement, where many of the gains of the protests have subsequently been rolled back under the government of Abdel Fattah Al-Sisi. While we are only beginning to understand the legacies of the Arab Spring, initial scholarly assessments have explored how the protesters leveraged new social media platforms to counter and circumvent the massive censorship regimes that existed in many of these states, developing innovative information practices and networks.[1] However, as Miriyam Aouragh and Paula Chakravartty have argued, this scholarship often fails to consider historical antecedents, resulting in an uncritical treatment of the Arab Spring as "a vindication for the universal appeal of Western liberal democracy delivered through the gift of the Internet, social media as manifestation of the 'technologies of freedom' long promised by Cold War social science."[2] Such a critique is especially apt for Egypt, which had been an information powerhouse in the Mediterranean region since at least the Mamluk and Ottoman periods. Understanding Egypt's role in the Arab Spring requires contextualising it in this longer history. Accordingly, the present chapter focuses on the mid-twentieth century, when Egypt first gained political independence through decolonisation. In this era, radio, printed materials, and—increasingly—television were the dominant information technologies, rather than tweets or social media posts. This chapter explores how Egypt transformed different media into tools for political liberation, contributing to the rising winds of decolonisation and offering an alternative to the Western-centric vision of information that remains ascendant.[3]

While decolonisation has become a popular and widely deployed term today—some scholars have argued to its detriment—it was also a historical process that emerged after the Second World War and gained momentum in the late 1950s and early 1960s, as European colonies used new international institutions like the United Nations to advocate and achieve national sovereignty.[4] Egypt was one of these colonies. Although Egypt gained nominal independence in 1922 and technically had a monarchy, the British continued to exert significant political and economic control over the country. Mounting frustrations over this colonial influence, coupled with widespread corruption under the Egyptian King, led a group of Egyptian military officers to seize power through a peaceful coup in July 1952 that is now known as the Free Officers revolution.[5] The leader of this group was Gamal Abdel Nasser, who would go on to serve as President of Egypt until his death in 1970. Nasser's impact on modern Egypt would be difficult to overstate; his influence extended far beyond Egypt's borders through what scholars have termed Nasserism, a revolutionary political ideology that promoted pan-Arab unity, anti-imperialism, and socialism.[6] Nasserism also resonated with other postcolonial leaders of the era, such as Kwame Nkrumah of Ghana, who championed Pan-Africanism, and Jawaharlal Nehru of India, who promoted non-alignment. Their shared anti-colonial ideology fostered an internationalist coalition, reinforced by well-founded fears that their revolutions were in danger of being reversed, whether through resurgent colonialism or more covert means. For example, a year after the Egyptian Revolution in 1953, the United States fomented a coup in Iran to overthrow its democratically elected leader, who threatened American oil interests. Given their need to protect decolonisation from Cold War and imperial machinations, newly independent states eventually coalesced into the Third World movement. Unlike today, when the term Third World tends to be used pejoratively, at the time it symbolised a new hope for most of the world's population, comprising countries across Asia, Africa, and Latin America that sought to forge a "non-aligned" path beyond the Cold War binary of Western capitalism or Soviet communism.

Recent work on the Third World movement has emphasised the importance of looking beyond high diplomacy and elite figures like Nasser to understand how anti-colonial solidarity was experienced across different scales and communities.[7] Central to this broader perspective has been renewed interest in what scholars have termed "hubs of decolonisation"—that is, anti-colonial capitals where national liberation revolutionaries and leftist intellectuals could meet and share resources, effectively building an information network for decolonisation.[8] This chapter draws on this research but also remains focused on these elite spaces and state institutions since they were central to making decolonisation into more than just an ideology. Case in point: Nasser's support for liberation was instrumental in establishing Cairo as one of these early hubs. The city also enjoyed an advantageous geographic location at the crossroads of the African, Asian, and Arab worlds, making it relatively accessible for revolutionaries travelling from these regions. Scholars have begun to investigate Third World movements and hubs in relation to mid-twentieth-century information histories, adding to earlier studies of postcolonial cybernetics and Cold War information politics.[9] However, much of this work has yet to fully explore how the internationalism of the Third World movement shaped information itself, often continuing to treat it as a source rather than a subject of historical inquiry.[10]

The present chapter seeks to address this gap by examining how Cairo became a hub for decolonisation *and* information in the 1950s and 1960s. The new Egyptian revolutionary government's commitment to preserving independence and dismantling colonialism led them to conceive of their liberation as a global project. To exert such expansive influence, they built and developed new information platforms and practices. This effort not only cemented Cairo's leadership among anti-colonial movements but also transformed information into more than mere propaganda. As the Third World movement evolved, so too did Egypt's conceptualisation of the relationship between decolonisation and information. While information helped circulate the ideologies of decolonisation, this chapter highlights how decolonisation, in turn, redefined what information could be, making them co-constitutive processes that together advanced the cause of liberation.

Although decolonisation efforts were in some ways more successful than the later Arab Spring, they also faced enormous difficulties and produced a similarly mixed legacy, especially with regard to information. On the one hand, they were relatively successful in using information to further decolonisation and challenge the international information order which favoured European empires and Cold War superpowers. On the other hand, they struggled to make that international information order more equitable or to balance spreading decolonisation globally with ensuring that information would foster liberation locally. Studying these contradictions in the case of Egypt is crucial because Cairo's information infrastructure became a model for other decolonising states. Moreover, this era laid the groundwork for many of the problems that sparked the Arab Spring. In returning to this earlier history, we can start to more fully understand the potential for making information—an idea that often seems neutral or technical—into a means for liberation, a struggle that is far from over.

Revolutionary Information: Radio Cairo and Spreading Liberation

Long before social media platforms such as Twitter and Facebook became instrumental for organising anti-government protests during the Arab Spring, radio served as the primary medium for disseminating revolutionary information. Radio technology had been in use well before the Egyptian revolution. First developed in the late nineteenth century and utilised extensively during the First World War, it began to flourish in Egypt and other colonies during the 1920s, starting with amateur radio hobbyists and eventually private commercial broadcasters. From the outset, the proliferation of private broadcasting often led to the overcrowding of frequencies, as too many broadcasters using the same radio frequencies caused interference and poor signal quality. However, its potential for spreading anti-colonial or anti-monarchical content posed the greatest threat to Britain's colonial rule in Egypt, prompting the centralisation and consolidation of radio in 1934 with the creation of the Egyptian State Broadcasting (ESB). The British replicated this model across the Middle East, establishing the Palestine Broadcasting Service (PBS) in 1936 and the Near East Broadcasting Service (NEBS) in 1944—all part of a broader imperial communication strategy.[11] This centralisation not only reduced the variety of programming but also imposed strict control over cultural narratives, in order to align them with colonial interests.[12] Despite these colonial restrictions, early radio broadcasting in Egypt incubated many of the nationalist ideas that became the foundation for the 1952 revolution.

Indeed, radio played a pivotal role in the revolution's success, with the initial cadre of military officers announcing their takeover via broadcast, foreshadowing its central role in the new regime. Since radio was already state-run, the new government continued to utilise the ESB as its primary broadcasting institution. However, in 1952, the ESB was still a relatively modest operation with a small staff and no shortwave capabilities, limiting its broadcasts to Egypt and its immediate neighbours. This reach quickly expanded as the new state prioritised radio capacity, with Nasser describing it as "one of the revolution's weapons for the realisation of Egyptian and Arab independence[, and] one of the most important weapons of the future."[13] The first shortwave broadcasts began on July 4, 1953, with the inaugural half hour transmission of the Voice of the Arabs (VOA). This was a significant development, as shortwave radio could transmit signals over far greater distances than medium wave transmitters, and Egypt would continue to invest in both capacities over the next two decades.[14]

VOA or *Sawt*, as it was known in Arabic, became synonymous with the Nasser regime, serving as one of its primary vehicles for propagating Cairo's message of liberation. Like Egypt's growing radio infrastructure, the content of this message was also evolving in the early years of the revolution, as Nasser increasingly argued that Egypt's destiny was intertwined with the fates of what he termed the three circles: the Arab, African, and Islamic worlds.[15] Protecting the revolution in Egypt, therefore, required uniting and uplifting these regions through a shared struggle against imperialism. This international and expansive vision had profound implications for Egyptian radio broadcasts, which gradually focused on not only developing a revolutionary Egyptian national consciousness but also fostering a broader sense of shared anti-colonial struggle across Arab states. For example, after the exiling of the Moroccan King Muhammad V in August 1953, VOA advocated for North African liberation, with Ahmed Ben Bella officially launching the Algerian Revolution on November 1, 1954, through a VOA broadcast.[16]

This spirit of anti-colonial liberation also gained momentum beyond the Middle East and North Africa. In April 1955, the first-ever Afro-Asian Conference, commonly known as the Bandung Conference, was held in Indonesia. Bringing together postcolonial officials and anti-colonial activists from across the decolonised world, the conference fostered a sense of solidarity and shared ethos among the participants.[17] For Egypt, Bandung marked more than just Nasser's debut on the world stage; it affirmed the possibility of extending Pan-Arabism to include Afro-Asian solidarity. This era, later known as the "Bandung Period" in histories of Egypt, became a turning point for Cairo's information strategy, accelerating the expansion of its broadcast infrastructure and anti-colonial messaging, both of which now needed to engage new international audiences beyond the Arab world.[18]

The drive to build international coalitions and promote anti-colonial liberation was a response not only to the growing number of decolonised states, but also to heightened fears over Cold War polarisation, which made radio even more essential. As Egypt built its radio infrastructure, Nasser had also sought Western support for the construction of the Aswan High Dam, a project central to Egypt's economic modernisation. However, in July 1956, the United States abruptly withdrew its offer of funding, a move widely interpreted as intending to curtail Nasser's influence that had been amplified in no small part due to the success of Radio Cairo. In response, on July 26, 1956, Nasser took to the airwaves to announce the surprise nationalisation of the Suez Canal to finance the dam, seizing control of one of the world's most lucrative waterways, which had previously been under British and French authority. In retaliation, Britain and France colluded with Israel to launch a covert military attack in late October 1956, initiating the Suez Crisis.[19] While this moment is one of the most studied in modern Egyptian history, what stands out, in particular, is the critical role of radio in mobilising public support and securing an eventual Egyptian victory.

Such a victory was far from guaranteed, however. Prior to the outbreak of the crisis, Britain had established secret radio broadcasting facilities and requisitioned the NEBS, the latter of which had moved to Cyprus and was lagging in popularity compared to Cairo's broadcasts. Renamed the Voice of Britain during the crisis, it was apparently "among the most heavily criticised of Britain's propaganda initiatives during the entire crisis," largely failing to articulate a compelling or coherent message capable of undermining Nasser's support.[20] Consequently, radio remained a primary target throughout the crisis, with British and French bombers repeatedly attacking broadcast facilities across Egypt. In response, the Egyptian government organised "information caravans," which were mobile broadcasting units that transmitted news updates, political commentary, and even music, throughout Egypt.[21] Although the Suez Crisis ended relatively quickly, the battle over airwaves would only intensify in the aftermath.

Beyond the nationalisation of the canal, British and French officials were also alarmed by the perceived threat that Cairo's popular broadcasts posed to imperial rule in the still-colonised world. In July 1954, Cairo had launched a new Swahili programme, *Sauti Ya Cairo*, that promoted "a powerful vision of an emerging Afro-Asian world that would assist Britain's East African colonies in throwing off the chains of Western colonialism."[22] This messaging was further bolstered in April 1957 by the creation of the Egyptian "pseudo-clandestine" Voice of Free Africa station. These broadcasts eventually inspired a riot in Dar-es-Salaam in 1958, leading Cairo to tone down its anti-colonial rhetoric to some degree.[23] By the end of the year, the ESB was considered a major operation, with a professional staff, larger budget, and more powerful radio transmitters imported from Czechoslovakia. This new infrastructure enabled broadcasts to reach as far as Latin America and facilitated Egypt's continued "clandestine radio warfare" against the more conservative Arab states, eventually contributing to the overthrow of the Iraqi monarchy that year.[24]

The potency of Radio Cairo lay partially in its broadcasters, like Ahmed Saïd, the voice behind VOA. He was often vilified in the Western press for his shows, which included segments such as "Truth and Lies" and "Do Not Forget," that countered foreign newspaper coverage and explicated the history of imperialism in Arab states.[25] Cairo also utilised African revolutionaries in their broadcasts, enabling them to broadcast in multiple languages and, as Reem Abou-El-Fadl argues, to "constitute its listeners as members of national fighting fronts, but also of a wider African public, in which Egyptians featured by their side."[26] This strategy helped transform radio into an "infrastructure of solidarity" that resonated with audiences across the globe. Cairo's model was so influential that it was mimicked, with varying degrees of success, by stations from Radio Moscow and Radio Peking to Voice of America and the BBC to Ghana's Radio Accra and Tanzania's Radio Tanzania.[27] While Radio Cairo continued to broadcast into the 1960s, one of its most lasting impacts was in how it cemented the Egyptian revolution and connected it to the burgeoning Third World movement. This internationalist anti-colonialism rationalised a massive expansion in radio infrastructure and the postcolonial state's power, which, in turn, re-envisioned radio from a tool for colonialism to one for spreading decolonisation.

Non-Aligned Information: Print Media and Networking Anti-Colonialism

Although radio remained a primary platform for Egypt's anti-colonial messaging, it was not the only one. The new revolutionary government was also deeply concerned with the power of print media, recognising that it could either advance liberation or undermine it, especially if it remained privately owned. In the immediate aftermath of the revolution, the government moved swiftly to found new publishing houses and publications. However, unlike radio, which rapidly expanded to broadcast in multiple languages, these early print media efforts were primarily intended for Arabic-speaking audiences.[28]

The development of print media into an international platform followed a similar trajectory to that of radio, as both were accelerated by Cairo's transformation into a hub of decolonisation, which required not only information infrastructure but also personnel. The government turned to members of African national liberation movements who were converging in Cairo. These groups were attracted to Cairo's strategic location on the African continent and its support for anti-colonialism, as well as the material resources provided by the government, including a monthly salary and offices at the newly created state-funded African Association.[29] This association enabled members to utilise Egypt's burgeoning information infrastructure to disseminate their message, organise press conferences, and network with ambassadors—all of which helped legitimise these movements. In total, twenty-one distinct liberation movements from seventeen different African states operated in Cairo, producing twenty-three new publications.[30] The ability to circulate their nationalist message both domestically and abroad was vital to these movements, given the censorship of news media by their respective colonial governments and the imbalances of international news flows. But it was also useful to Egypt, which was looking to expand its information platforms into what scholars have termed the Cultural Cold War. Although the Cold War was initially conceived as primarily a political and military confrontation, it also involved a struggle for ideological influence, with culture and information serving as key battlegrounds for superpowers who were competing to win hearts and minds.[31] Recent research has explored how this Cultural Cold War impacted the Third World and, in the case of Egypt, it reinforced the sense of decolonisation under siege.[32]

As the Cultural Cold War intensified, 1960 was also heralded as the "Year of Africa," with seventeen formerly colonised African nations gaining independence—a sign of the rising "winds of decolonisation." But this progress was soon overshadowed by the outbreak of the Congo Crisis in July 1960, when the sudden secession of the mineral-rich province of Katanga threatened Congo's newly won independence from Belgium and rapidly escalated into an international crisis.[33] Nasser began coordinating with other African leaders like Kwame Nkrumah to find a peaceful solution to the conflict.[34] In Cairo, the crisis was of immediate and grave concern, frequently becoming front-page news. At the same time, however, the press itself had also been recently reconfigured to ensure that it furthered the state's socialist mission in response to these threats.

Since the revolution, the government had fluctuated through periods of press liberalisation and censorship, at times even preventing African nationalists from circulating their messages.[35] This culminated in May 1960, when the government moved decisively to nationalise the press, safeguarding its socialist ideals and preventing what it considered subversive critiques. As part of this transformation, the government also created the National Publications House (Dar al-Nasharat al-Qawmiyya or NPH), which became a clearinghouse for all state-funded publications.[36] Unlike earlier efforts, these new publications were explicitly designed to reach Third World audiences, with magazines printed not just in Arabic but also in English, French, Italian, Spanish, and German. The coverage varied by audience, blending news coverage of global decolonisation with in-depth articles on Egypt. The magazines were available through subscriptions and new information centres, which were often located in hotels and Egyptian embassies of major cities. These centres were part of an evolving international information campaign strategy, aimed at making Egyptian information, though political in content, seem mundane and accessible. The magazines also experimented with how to engage readers, from printing letters to the editor to including tear-away pages of key resolutions and events. One notable experiment was in the magazine, *The Scribe*, which opened each issue with an editorial entitled "Under the Probing Lens of Truth." The magazine also aimed to establish an "Army of Truth" through a write-in campaign, encouraging readers to sign up to receive official government pamphlets and books. While the success of this particular initiative is unknown, many of these magazines boasted a monthly circulation in the tens of thousands, all promoting Egypt's version of anti-colonialism.[37]

For instance, one of these new NPH magazines, the *Arab Observer*, reflected this anti-colonial solidarity in its prominent billing of the Congo Crisis. Its July 17, 1960 issue and featured a cover image of the deposed Congolese leader Patrice Lumumba with the headline, "Cairo Prepared to Help Congo."[38] Coverage of the crisis remained consistent in these magazines, and in the Egyptian press, as the situation worsened through the autumn and culminated in February 1961 with Lumumba's assassination. Scholars have argued that his murder became "a common reference point for Third World left-wing forces' fury toward superpower intervention in decolonisation."[39] Such fury was palpable in Cairo, but even more urgent was the realisation that the United Nations' failure to resolve the conflict signalled that decolonisation was neither inevitable nor secure. Instead, it underscored the threat of resurgent imperialism—eventually termed neo-colonialism—which could jeopardise the progress of the Egyptian revolution and its plans for global liberation.

To prevent this reversal, Nasser not only leveraged Cairo's information infrastructure but also deepened international alliances to fortify anti-colonial networks. Some of these efforts predated the Congo Crisis, including the creation of the Afro-Asian People's Solidarity Organisation in 1958, but the crisis sharpened their urgency. This momentum led to the formation of the Casablanca group of states in January 1961—a coalition of progressive African states promoting unity and liberation. That March, Egypt hosted the third All African Peoples' Conference, where Nasser stressed the significance of anti-colonial unity and cautioned against assuming imperialism was in retreat.[40] Following the conference, Nasser and Yugoslavia's leader Broz Tito corresponded on the necessity of a meeting between non-aligned countries to discuss global tensions.[41] Despite being somewhat eclipsed by Soviet nuclear testing, the Belgrade Conference in September later that year successfully formalised the Non-Aligned Movement (NAM).[42] Composed of most decolonised states—although they often disagreed on tactics—NAM would eventually become one of the primary platforms for advancing anti-colonial solidarity and independence.

While this new non-aligned form of anti-colonialism was evident in Egyptian rhetoric, it also shaped the production of these magazines. The *Arab Observer*, for instance, changed its tagline from "The Weekly Middle East News Magazine" to "The Non-Aligned Weekly." The magazine also increasingly employed activists drawn to these non-aligned and anti-colonial ideals, including well-known figures like David Graham Du Bois and Maya Angelou.

Du Bois had arrived in Cairo in the summer of 1960, initially working intermittently for various newspapers, including the *Egyptian Gazette* and *Egyptian Mail*, while also developing a radio programme, entitled "Africa Marches Together," which promoted pan-African unity.[43] His first article appeared in one of the newly created NPH magazines, *The Arab Review*, in February 1960, followed by a six-part series in the October and November issues of the *Arab Observer*.[44] In letters to his mother, Du Bois described the magazine as "Egypt's *Time* Magazine" and "the most important weekly news magazine published in English by the UAR Information Office."[45] He eventually became instrumental in relaunching and rebranding the magazine, although he noted that his prominent position as a foreigner provoked jealousy among some of his Egyptian colleagues.[46] Angelou encountered similar challenges at the *Arab Observer*, where Du Bois had helped her secure a job as the Africa Editor after moving to Cairo in 1961. Angelou credited the magazine with developing her skills as a journalist, but she also faced obstacles due to her gender and nationality. Her work was often misattributed to her husband, the South African activist Vusumzi Make, and after the Cuban Missile Crisis in October 1962, like many Americans, she was increasingly viewed with suspicion in Cairo.[47] Yet both Du Bois and Angelou spoke highly of their time in Egypt, with Du Bois describing Cairo as "situated at the crossroads of the three continents" and "rapidly becoming the capital of Africa, defender of African freedom and the freedom of the oppressed [...] everywhere in the world."[48]

Taking their positive assertions at face value may be problematic given the challenges that Du Bois and Angelou faced, as well as their reliance on the Egyptian state through their employment at the *Arab Observer*. Nonetheless, their experiences, along with those of African nationalists in Cairo, demonstrate Egypt's success in transforming Cairo into a hub of decolonisation and highlight the integral role of information to this process. The Congo Crisis, however, exposed the fragility of this success, further justifying the continued expansion of these information platforms—although not without trade-offs. The commitment to spreading liberation led to the proliferation of new information platforms, like print media, but also tightened the state's control over information. Meanwhile, the emerging anti-colonial community in Cairo began to challenge which vision of liberation should take precedence within the messaging of this global information infrastructure. As Egypt positioned itself as a leader in NAM and the Cultural Cold War, the lines between information and propaganda became progressively blurred. This tension was evident even in smaller initiatives like the *Arab Observer*. As Angelou noted, the magazine "was not strictly speaking an official organ of the Egyptian government; that is, it did not come directly under the heading of the Ministry of Information. Its editorial position, however, would be identical with the national politics."[49] Such dynamics were increasingly common across the Third World, where aspirations for liberation confronted the limits of state-centric information politics. As more colonies gained independence and joined NAM, the goalposts for global liberation continued to shift, but so did the boundaries between the state and information, further eroding as these decolonising states struggled to overcome the challenges of colonialism.

Third World Information: Postcolonial Television and Coordinating Solidarity

While radio and print media were the most well-known pillars of Egypt's information infrastructure, other initiatives were also accelerated by the country's rising international stature. Specifically, in February 1958, the Egyptian state's information infrastructure was abruptly extended to serve more than one country. Following the Suez Crisis, Nasser and Egypt were lauded as the vanguard of pan-Arabism, and Syrian military officers, seeking a solution to continued domestic political instability, saw Nasser as the answer. The result was an unexpected and hastily arranged union between the two states, forming the United Arab Republic (UAR). Egypt, as the senior member in the partnership, absorbed Syria's information infrastructure, consolidating control over radio and the press, while also extending its influence into new information technologies—foremost among them, television.[50]

Much like radio, which took decades to transition from invention to mass adoption, television was first invented in the 1920s, but only became widespread in the 1950s. As a medium that combined both sound and moving images, it revolutionised mass communication by reaching audiences on an unprecedented scale. Even though Egypt had somewhat strained relations with the United States, in December 1959, the United States extended a loan to construct Egypt's first television broadcasting stations, along with manufacturing facilities for electronics and communications equipment with the help of the Radio Corporation of America (RCA). Initially, five stations were planned, three in Egypt and two in Syria, connected by microwave links, with the first television broadcast beamed on July 21, 1960, coinciding with the eighth anniversary of the Egyptian revolution.[51]

Television, initially managed under Egypt's radio infrastructure, rapidly grew from a single channel to multiple channels and broadcasting over 150 hours weekly by 1963. Egypt's television capacity quickly became a model for other Arab and African countries, with Egyptian television experts assisting in the development of television in these regions.[52] Although primarily intended for Arab audiences, television was also integrated into Egypt's anti-colonial information infrastructure. For instance, Cairo's television broadcast a film on Patrice Lumumba after his assassination in 1961.[53] That April, Cairo also hosted the first African Broadcasting and Television Conference, where representatives from fourteen decolonised states discussed how television could enable Pan-African connections. Proposals included establishing an African radio and television training centre, as well as a technical centre in Cairo to monitor African stations and prevent frequency interference. Emphasising the necessity of the conference, one Egyptian official remarked, "Africa's battle for liberation from colonialism and foreign domination is being fought today more with the spoken word and the news item than with the gun and the bomb."[54]

This focus on Pan-Africanism was also motivated by the breakup of the UAR, which had collapsed in late 1961, as well as the intensifying competition between Egypt and Saudi Arabia in the Yemeni Civil War. It also signalled the growing institutionalisation of the Third World movement. In May 1963, the Organization of African Unity (OAU) was founded to promote solidarity among African states, support ongoing national liberation struggles across the continent, and foster more coordination with anti-colonial information activities.[55] A month earlier, Egypt had attended the UNESCO-sponsored "Meeting of Experts on the Development of News Agencies in Africa" in Tunis, which sought to facilitate the sharing of information infrastructure across the continent. The meeting brought together twenty-eight news agency directors and other press experts from some twenty-five African countries to discuss the obstacles to developing domestic African news agencies and enhancing regional and continental exchanges, which at the time remained limited in scale. Egypt, one of the first decolonised states to establish a news agency, the Middle East News Agency (MENA), offered to provide training to African journalists at the meeting. This initiative eventually led to the creation of the Union of African News Agencies and the proposal for a Pan-African News Agency.[56] The push for a shared continental and anti-colonial news network stemmed from the fact that, even after decolonisation, the big four news—Reuters, AP, UPI, and AFP—continued to dominate global news flows. These agencies' coverage often sidelined events in African countries unless there was a crisis, presenting an obstacle to both national development and the sharing of information and news between decolonised states.

This imbalance reinforced Egypt's rationale for building its anti-colonial information infrastructure as well as international collaborations, thereby necessitating and justifying further centralisation of information governance. Throughout the 1950s, information management was fragmented across multiple departments and ministries, including the Information Department, founded in 1952 and later upgraded to a Ministry of Information in the early 1960s. This new ministry was initially responsible for all radio and television broadcasting, MENA, and the NPH and its magazines. By 1962, its responsibilities extended to include oversight of the Ministry of Culture, and in 1964, it further absorbed the Ministry of Tourism and Antiquities.[57] Consequently, almost all cultural production was not only nationalised as part of Nasser's Arab socialist agenda, but also integrated into the state's information infrastructure, ensuring a consistent anti-colonial message was spread across the globe.

Since the founding of Egypt's Information Department, other Arab states had adopted its model of information governance. In 1964, Cairo hosted the Conference of Arab Information Ministers. Similar to the UNESCO and African Broadcasting conferences, the primary goal was to coordinate information activities across the Arab world. Proposals included establishing a unified Arab broadcasting network, developing a cohesive Arab information service, standardising tourism advertising, coordinating international information campaigns, funding Arab scholars to promote the Arab cause abroad, creating an Arab publishing clearinghouse, and organising a regional film organisation.[58] Egyptian news coverage of the conference echoed the need to enhance Arab information efforts, highlighting Cairo's lagging printing standards and advocating for more information offices, particularly in the United States, in order to reach larger audiences more effectively.[59]

While not all proposals at these meetings were implemented, many were realised over the late 1960s and 1970s through the OAU, UNESCO, and the Arab League, eventually contributing to the rise of the New World Information and Communication Order (NWICO), which represented the ideological culmination of Egyptian efforts to address global information imbalances.[60] The groundwork for these later achievements was laid by the consolidation of the Third World through these institutions in the early 1960s, as the struggle for anti-colonial liberation shifted from formal decolonisation to arenas like the Cultural Cold War. This institutionalisation fostered greater unity and collaboration among decolonised states. However, it also drew criticism for the growing bureaucratisation of liberation efforts, which often limited more radical forms of support for national liberation movements. For instance, the creation of the OAU's Coordination Committee for Liberation, despite its radical aims, ultimately reflected a shift towards more structured and less militant forms of support.[61] Such a transformation was paralleled in Cairo, where the centralisation of the production and distribution of information had expanded the very definition of information. While this process facilitated a coherent anti-colonial message, it also positioned the state as the sole arbiter of this message. As information governance became more bureaucratised, it risked stifling the very radical impulses that had driven the liberation movements it sought to support.

Conclusion: Postcolonial Information and Liberation Ideologies

A series of coups in the mid-1960s across the Third World, along with the outbreak of the Six-Day War with Israel, ultimately reshaped and curtailed Cairo's international position as a hub for decolonisation and information. Nevertheless, despite its brevity, this period remains necessary for understanding how Egypt's vision for anti-colonial liberation became internationalised through information. At the same time, understanding this vision is equally crucial for tracing the foundations of Egypt's postcolonial information infrastructures, practices, and ideologies.

The impact of these information platforms in spreading decolonisation cannot be overstated, especially at a time when the idea of liberation seemed more a dream than a reality. These platforms provided anti-colonial activists with opportunities to network and share their message, and fostered a sense of global solidarity that contributed to the success of many liberation movements across Africa, Asia, and Latin America. The information strategies developed by Egypt, particularly in radio, print media, television, and information governance, became a blueprint for other decolonising states seeking to harness information for political and social change. The integration of information into the broader decolonisation project not only redefined the role of information but also expanded what constituted information, encompassing a much greater range of activities than those initially conceived during the early stages of the Egyptian revolution. The expansion of Egypt's information infrastructure, while facilitating a coherent anti-colonial message, also produced friction between centralisation and the revolutionary ideals it aimed to promote. Future research will explore how these tensions shaped not only Egyptian efforts but also those across the decolonised world, while also considering how these information strategies were adopted, adapted, and contested beyond elite circles and state institutions. Such work will help bridge these early efforts with later Third World information policy debates and activism, particularly the NWICO movement of the 1970s.

Revisiting this history is important not only because it became a model for many other states but also because many of these institutions remain intact today and thus played a role in the repression that led to the Arab Spring. Although we have yet to fully delve into how this liberationist ideal also contributed to restricting individual liberties—through the creation of and challenges against what Egyptian officials at the time termed the "information machine"—we can nonetheless see in this moment a vision for how information could further justice. This history will hopefully serve as an inspiration, as this mission remains unfinished and urgent today, both in Egypt and across the world.

Notes

1 For examples, see Joe F. Khalil et al., eds., *The Handbook of Media and Culture in the Middle East* (Hoboken, NJ: Wiley & Sons, 2023); and Miriyam Aouragh, *The Arab Spring a Decade On: Revolution, Counter-Revolution and the Transformation of a Region* (Amsterdam: Transnational Institute Amsterdam, 2022).
2 Miriyam Aouragh and Paula Chakravartty, "Infrastructures of Empire: Towards a Critical Geopolitics of Media and Information Studies," *Media, Culture & Society* 38, no. 4 (May 1, 2016): 559–575, esp. 560. There are exceptions to this trend, such as Limor Lavie and Bosmat Yefet, "The Relationship between the State and the New Media in Egypt: A Dynamic of Openness, Adaptation, and Narrowing," *Contemporary Review of the Middle East* 9, no. 2 (June 1, 2022): 138–157, but the majority of this work focuses on media rather than the broader category of information.
3 This chapter is not a comprehensive assessment of every information technology or activity in Egypt, but rather focuses on these three and the institutions that supported them owing to their central role in Egypt's anti-colonialism.
4 Eve Tuck and K. Wayne Yang, "Decolonization Is Not a Metaphor," *Decolonization: Indigeneity, Education & Society* 1, no. 1 (2012): 1–40.
5 For more, see Joel Gordon, *Nasser's Blessed Movement: Egypt's Free Officers and the July Revolution* (Oxford: Oxford University Press, 1992).
6 Sara Salem, *Anticolonial Afterlives in Egypt: The Politics of Hegemony* (Cambridge, UK: Cambridge University Press, 2020).
7 Carolien Stolte and Su Lin Lewis, eds., *The Lives of Cold War Afro-Asianism, The Lives of Cold War Afro-Asianism* (Amsterdam: Amsterdam University Press, 2022). While the present chapter primarily focuses on Nasser, future work will explore some of the officials involved in these information activities, looking at what Jeffrey Byrne has described as "revolutionaries with briefcases."
8 Eric Burton, "Hubs of Decolonization. African Liberation Movements and 'Eastern' Connections in Cairo, Accra, and Dar Es Salaam," in *Southern African Liberation Movements and the Global*

Cold War "East," ed. Lena Dallywater, Chris Saunders, and Helder Adegar Fonseca (Berlin: De Gruyter Oldenbourg, 2019), 25–56.

9 For examples of early work, see Benjamin Peters, *How Not to Network a Nation: The Uneasy History of the Soviet Internet* (Cambridge, MA: MIT Press, 2016); and Eden Medina, *Cybernetic Revolutionaries: Technology and Politics in Allende's Chile* (Cambridge, MA: MIT Press, 2011). For examples of this new approach, see Ismay Milford, *African Activists in a Decolonising World: The Making of an Anticolonial Culture, 1952–1966* (Cambridge, UK: Cambridge University Press, 2023); and Liesbeth Rosen Jacobson, "Carved in Stone? The Role of Written and Unwritten Information in Solving the Eurasian Question after 1945," in *Information and Power in History: Towards a Global Approach*, ed. Ida Nijenhuis et al. (London: Routledge, 2020), 238–253.

10 For examples of excellent research on Third World, but that still continues to focus on media over information, see Rasmus C. Elling and Sune Haugbolle, *The Fate of Third Worldism in the Middle East: Iran, Palestine and Beyond* (London: Simon and Schuster, 2024); and Sorcha Thomson and Pelle Valentin Olsen, *Palestine in the World: International Solidarity with the Palestinian Liberation Movement* (London: I.B. Tauris, 2023).

11 Andrea Stanton, "Part of Imperial Communications: British-Governed Radio in the Middle East, 1934–1949," *Media History* 19, no. 4 (November 1, 2013): 421–435; and Stanton, "Can Imperial Radio Be Transnational? British-Affiliated Arabic Radio Broadcasting in the Interwar Period," *History Compass* 18, no. 1 (2020): 1–8.

12 Ziad Fahmy, "Media-Capitalism: Colloquial Mass Culture and Nationalism in Egypt, 1908–18," *International Journal of Middle East Studies* 42, no. 1 (February 2010): 83–103.

13 Reem Abou-El-Fadl, *Foreign Policy as Nation Making: Turkey and Egypt in the Cold War* (Cambridge, UK: Cambridge University Press, 2018), 170.

14 Douglas A. Boyd, "Egyptian Radio: Tool of Political and National Development," *Journalism Monographs* 48 (February 1, 1977): 1–34.

15 Gamal Abdel Nasser, *The Philosophy of the Revolution* (Cairo: Dar al-Maaref, 1955).

16 Abou-El-Fadl, *Foreign Policy*, 172. For more information on North African revolutionaries in Cairo, see Jeffrey James Byrne, *Mecca of Revolution: Algeria, Decolonization, and the Third World Order* (Oxford, UK: Oxford University Press, 2016); and David Stenner, "'Bitterness towards Egypt' – the Moroccan Nationalist Movement, Revolutionary Cairo and the Limits of Anti-Colonial Solidarity," *Cold War History* 16, no. 2 (April 2, 2016): 159–175.

17 Christopher Lee, ed., *Making a World after Empire: The Bandung Moment and Its Political Afterlives* (Athens, OH: Ohio University Press, 2010).

18 Anouar Abdel-Malek, *Egypt: Military Society; the Army Regime, the Left, and Social Change under Nasser* (New York: Random House, 1968), 116.

19 Laura M. James, *Nasser at War* (London: Palgrave Macmillan, 2006); and Salim Yaqub, *Containing Arab Nationalism: The Eisenhower Doctrine and the Middle East* (Chapel Hill, NC: University of North Carolina Press, 2004).

20 Simon M. W. Collier, "Countering Communist and Nasserite Propaganda: The Foreign Office Information Research Department in the Middle East and Africa, 1954–1963" (PhD diss., University of Hertfordshire, 2014), 87; and James R. Vaughan, *The Failure of American and British Propaganda in the Arab Middle East, 1945–1957: Unconquerable Minds* (London: Palgrave Macmillan, 2005), 35–36, 210.

21 Douglas A. Boyd, "Development of Egypt's Radio: 'Voice of the Arabs' under Nasser," *Journalism Quarterly* 52, no. 4 (Winter 1975): 645–653, esp. 649; and M. Abdel-Kader Hatem, *Information and the Arab Cause* (London: Longman Group Ltd., 1974), 198–199.

22 James R. Brennan, "Radio Cairo and the Decolonization of East Africa, 1953–64," in *Making a World after Empire*, ed. Lee (Athens, OH: Ohio University Press, 2010), 173–195, esp. 174–177.

23 Brennan, "Radio Cairo," 177–183; and Boyd, "Egyptian Radio," 25.

24 "Egyptian Propaganda Activities – 1958," Record Group (hereafter RG) 306, USIA Office of Research and Intelligence, Research Note RN-34-59, February 25, 1959, 5–6. National Archives and Records Administration (hereafter NARA). See discussion in Cyrus Schayegh, "1958 Reconsidered: State Formation and the Cold War in the Early Postcolonial Arab Middle East," *International Journal of Middle East Studies* 45, no. 3 (2013): 421–443, esp. 422; and Owen L. Sirrs, *A History of the Egyptian Intelligence Service: A History of the Mukhabarat, 1910–2009* (London: Routledge, 2010), 46.

25 James, *Nasser at War*, 47–48; and Laura James, "Whose Voice? Nasser, the Arabs, and 'Sawt al-Arab' Radio," *Arab Media & Society*, June 1, 2006, https://www.arabmediasociety.com/whose-voice-nasser-the-arabs-and-sawt-al-arab-radio/.
26 Reem Abou-El-Fadl, "Building Egypt's Afro-Asian Hub: Infrastructures of Solidarity and the 1957 Cairo Conference," *Journal of World History* 30, no. 1 (2019): 157–192, esp. 169.
27 Abou-El-Fadl, "Building," 158; K. Roth-Ey, "How Do You Listen to Radio Moscow? Moscow's Broadcasters, 'Third World' Listeners, and the Space of the Airwaves in the Cold War," *Slavonic and East European Review* 98, no. 4 (October 1, 2020): 712–741. See also Alex White's forthcoming work on the impact of Radio Cairo on British colonial administration in Africa.
28 Ahmad Hamroush, *Qissat Thawrat 23 Yulyu*, vol. 2 (Cairo: Madbouli, 1983), 94–95; Khaled Mohieddin, *Memories of a Revolution* (Cairo: American University of Cairo Press, 1995), 145.
29 For the most in-depth study of the association, see Abou-El-Fadl, "Building," 163–169; Helmi Sharawy, "Memories on African Liberation (1956–1975): A Personal Experience from Egypt, Part I," *Pamvazuka News* 530 (May 19, 2011), https://www.pambazuka.org/pan-africanism/memories-african-liberation-1956-1975; and Marthe Moumié, *Victime du Colonialisme: Mon Mari Félix Moumié* (Paris: Duboiris, 2006), 99.
30 Ankush B. Sawant, *Egypt's Africa Policy* (New Delhi: National Publishing House, 1981), 64–66.
31 Frances Stonor Saunders, *The Cultural Cold War: The CIA and the World of Arts and Letters* (New York: New Press, 2000).
32 Kerry Bystrom, Monica Popescu, and Katherine Zien, eds., *The Cultural Cold War and the Global South: Sites of Contest and Communitas* (New York: Routledge, 2021).
33 Alanna O'Malley, *The Diplomacy of Decolonization: America, Britain and the United Nations During the Congo Crisis 1960–1964* (Manchester: Manchester University Press, 2018); and Lise Namikas, *Battleground Africa: Cold War in the Congo, 1960–1965* (Washington, DC: Wilson Center, 2013).
34 Mohamed Heikal, *Nasser: The Cairo Documents* (London: New English Library, 1973), 175–176; and "The UAR and the Congo," RG 84, Folder 320, UAR-Congo, NARA.
35 "Transmitting Letter and Note of Protest from Cameroonian Nationalists," August 20, 1959, RG 84, Egypt Embassy General Classified Records, 1959–1961, Box 9, Folder UAR-Communism, NARA; and Sonia Dabbous, "Nasser and the Egyptian Press," in *Contemporary Egypt through Egyptian Eyes*, ed. Charles Tripp (London: Routledge, 1993), 100–121, esp. 100–101.
36 Menachem Klein, "Egypt's Revolutionary Publishing Culture, 1952–62," *Middle Eastern Studies* 39, no. 2 (April 2003): 149–178; and Dabbous, "Nasser and the Egyptian Press," 107–108.
37 USIA, "External Information and Cultural Relations Programs: The Arab Republic of Egypt," 1973, 84.
38 *Arab Observer*, July 17, 1960, 8.
39 Taomo Zhou, "Global Reporting from the Third World: The Afro-Asian Journalists' Association, 1963–1974," *Critical Asian Studies* 51, no. 2 (April 3, 2019): 166–197, esp. 175.
40 Tareq Y. Ismael, *The U.A.R. in Africa: Egypt's Policy under Nasser* (Evanston, IL: Northwestern University Press, 1971), 61; and *Arab Observer*, April 2, 1961, 13–15.
41 CG-968 Washington to American Embassy Cairo, May 10, 1961. RG 84, 320 Non-Aligned Peoples Conference Preparatory Meeting, 1. NARA.
42 Heikal, *Nasser*, 263–264.
43 David Graham Du Bois (hereafter DGD) to Shirley Graham Du Bois (hereafter SGD), June 29, 1961, Shirley Graham Du Bois Papers (hereafter SGD Papers), Box 12, Folder 23, 1; DGD to SGD, November 5, 1961, SGD Papers, Box 12, Folder 23, 1.
44 DGD "Africa as Seen by Negro Scholars Part 6," *Arab Observer*, November 27, 1961, 24; DGD "Impressions of Cairo," *The Arab Review*, February 1960, 38–39.
45 DGD to SGD, November 5, 1961, SGD Papers, Box 12, Folder 23, 1–3.
46 DGD to SGD, July 31, 1962. SGD Papers, Box 12, Folder 23, 1; DGD to SGD, August 13, 1962, SGD Papers, Box 12, Folder 23, 1. See Keith Feldman, *Shadow over Palestine: The Imperial Life of Race in America* (Minneapolis, MN: University of Minnesota Press, 2015), 90.
47 Maya Angelou, *The Heart of a Woman* (New York: Random House, 2009), 231–234. See also Alex White, "The Caged Bird Sings of Freedom: Maya Angelou's Anti-Colonial Journalism in the United Arab Republic and Ghana, 1961–1965," *Journal of Global History* 19, no. 3 (January 22, 2024): 9–11.

48 DGD, "Impressions of Cairo," 40.
49 Angelou, *The Heart of a Woman*, 223–224.
50 Mohammed Abdel Kader Hatem and Ibrahim Abdel Aziz, *Mudhakkirāt 'Abd al-Qādir Ḥātim, ra'īs Hukūmat Harb Uktūbir* [Memoirs of Abdel Kader Hatem, Leader of the October War] (Cairo: al-Hay'ah al-'Āmmah li-Quṣūr al-Thaqāfah, 2016), 66.
51 "United Arab Republic Television and Facsimile Transmissions, 1960–1962," NARA via ProQuest History Vault, File 003109_015_0896, 1–48.
52 Gehan Rachty and Khalil Sabat, "Importation of Films for Cinema and Television in Egypt - UNESCO Digital Library," 1980, https://unesdoc.unesco.org/ark:/48223/pf0000043411.
53 "Television's First Birthday," *Arab Observer*, July 23, 1961, 10; and "Arabic Press Roundup," February 14, 1961, RG 84, 350 Congo, Box 10, 1959–1961, Egypt US Embassy Cairo General Records, NARA, 1.
54 "Broadcasting in the Service of Africa," *Arab Observer*, April 30, 1961, 24–25.
55 Helmi Sharawy, "Memories on African Liberation (1956–1975): A Personal Experience from Egypt, Part II," *Pamvazuka News* 531 (May 25, 2011), https://www.pambazuka.org/pan-africanism/memories-african-liberation-1956-1975-part-2; and Ismael, *The U.A.R. in Africa*, 67.
56 "Present Status of News Agencies in Africa," UNESCO Meeting of Experts on the Development of News Agencies in Africa, Paris, March 11, 1963, 1–2; and "Report of the Meeting," UNESCO Meeting of Experts on the Development of News Agencies in Africa, Paris, May 27, 1963, 16. See William A. Hachten, *Muffled Drums: The News Media in Africa* (Ames, IA: Iowa State University Press, 1971), 71.
57 Hatem, *Mudhakkirāt*, 64, 68.
58 *Arab Observer*, March 16, 1964, 22–23.
59 Joint Weekly No. 10, March 25, 1964. RG 59, Central Foreign Policy Files, 1964–1966, POL 2-1, 4. NARA; and Joint Weekly No. 11, April 13, 1964. RG 59, Central Foreign Policy Files, 1964–1966, POL 2-1, 3. NARA.
60 Ulla Carlsson, "The Rise and Fall of NWICO: From a Vision of International Regulation to a Reality of Multilevel Governance," *Nordicom Review* 24, no. 2 (2003): 31–67.
61 Sharawy, "Memories, Part II."

36
DYNAMICS OF THE HUMAN ELEMENT IN SOUTH AFRICA'S INFORMATION HISTORY

Archie L. Dick

Introduction

Information historians explain that the shift from pre-modern to modern understandings of information was not the same everywhere, and that time and place matter. They contend too that transnational perspectives reinforce the universal ideals of freedom of access to information, and freedom of expression.[1] Technologies that raised the global profile of information rightly deserve scholarly investigation. Its "social and cultural drivers" call attention however to the "potency of the human element"—the importance of individual agency—and so warrant further enquiry with possibilities for a new research agenda.[2]

Using archival evidence in four case studies, Toni Weller and David Bawden have shown how certain individuals in Victorian-era England (1837–1901) understood information.[3] They discovered that research focused on this historical period emphasises its technological developments. A more significant finding was that, for Victorians themselves, matters of access, use, influence, as well as social and economic values, placed on information could be just as powerful then as they are in England today. For Arthur Wellesley, the Duke of Wellington, Napoleon's nemesis at the Battle of Waterloo (1815), information was a fluid concept tied up with politics and social class. Eleanor Sidgwick, who advocated women's rights to university education, considered it as fluid too but its semantic meaning had to operate "within the existing framework of what was acceptable." For Florence Nightingale, the founder of modern nursing, information meant "facts with a function," and that it was "fixed and scientific." Yet for Paul Julius Reuter, the pioneer of telegraphy and news reporting, it could be "packaged and processed," as well as "bought and sold." Weller and Bawden conclude that perceptions of information were "tied up with Victorian values and wider concerns" than just its technologies.[4]

Weller has widened that information lens to examine also, as noted above, the "potency of the human element," with a focus on power in history.[5] She identifies areas of research that could include marginalised groups; ideas about the exchange of power; information hegemony by the state; and, information disclosure and control.[6] Engaging and expanding these and other themes, while adopting the case-study method also, this chapter discusses *dynamics of the human element* in South Africa's information history. They include personal values and social dynamics that include determination, identity, integrity, and sharing across historical periods in South Africa.

The chapter examines ways in which these values and dynamics featured when three South Africans collected, repurposed, shared, and disclosed information. They are:

A *slave in the first Dutch colonial period* (1652–1795) who collected information that included Tamil-language medical recipes, and became a teacher and healer in the Cape Slave Lodge;

A *printer in the apartheid period* (1948–1994) whose focus on producing anti-apartheid information shifted in the "new" South Africa to repurposing heritage information for "restorative memory," and "restorative justice"; and

A *whistleblower in the "new" South Africa* who shared and disclosed information about a global management consultancy's corruption and fraud in South Africa's public sector, including its organs of state.

Their stories reveal aspects of South Africa's long and ongoing struggle for freedom of access to information and freedom of expression. They signal the need for a more inclusive approach that locates its information history in South African history. That information history should emphasise the human element, with a sharp focus on the social identities and information networks of South Africa's forgotten and marginalised communities. It will contribute to the wider view of information as an important theme in "cultural, intellectual, political, social and economic history," and a "key ... to understanding major cultural phenomena and historical processes."[7]

Johannes Smiesing: Collecting Medical Information in a Cape Slave Lodge

Travellers' and explorers' reports about the early eighteenth-century Cape of Good Hope's[8] indigenous plant species attracted scientific attention that "fed the European imagination."[9] A Cape slave's notebook in the same period identified exogenous plant species in a list of Tamil-language cures.[10] This notebook revealed medical information that still feeds the South African imagination.[11] In the first period of Dutch colonialism (1652–1795) a Slave Lodge, built in the port city of Cape Town in 1679, housed the Dutch East India Company (VOC) slaves brought from Mozambique, Madagascar, and trading posts in South-East Asia.

The VOC was founded in 1602, having incorporated several competing Dutch spice-trading firms that emerged in the 1590s into a single trading company. The Dutch government granted it authority in the trade zone between the Cape and the East "to erect fortifications, appoint governors, keep a standing army, and conclude treaties in its name."[12] For most of the VOC's life-span a special committee decided what information should be sent to its supreme board, the *Gentlemen Seventeen*, which took key decisions for the company.[13] In order to control the trade and to support the VOC's business operations, an extensive network accumulated information to exercise its power.[14] A Company slave would access that information network to assume a new identity. The 1714 Slave Lodge Census lists seventeen-year-old Johannes (Jan) Smiesing as a third generation creole "half-caste" slave.

His Dutch father, a "second medical master," had returned to Amsterdam. His slave mother became the matron in charge of the Slave Lodge School for girls and women.[15] Johannes was manumitted in 1731, and the VOC's Council of Policy Resolutions described him as a "Company Slave" and a "School Master." His notebook however introduces him as "Writing and Reading Master in Service of the Honourable East Indian Company."[16] It is a kind of commonplace book with blank bound pages that Johannes used for writing his entries using the VOC's quill pens. Whether he had learned how to keep a notebook as a pupil in the Slave Lodge School is uncertain. He was however following the practices, already common in early modern Europe, of note-taking and of making notebooks at school, as well as collecting and recording potentially useful information.[17]

These notebooks were designed not only to store information but, as "specialized paper tools," they became a kind of "information recovery machine" also to process it.[18] The notebook includes family-related information, letter types for writing and reading, examples of arithmetic, and a morning hymn. Johannes recorded the arrival, inauguration, death, and burial of Pieter Gysbert Noodt who was the governor at the Cape from 1727 to 1729. Across two pages, and in a different handwriting, there is the intriguing list of medical recipes written in the Tamil language. This list confirms Johannes' other identity as a healer or "doctor." He had aspired to his father's medical occupation, and may have worked briefly in the Slave hospital in the Lodge.

It was separated from the Company hospital that was just across the road. In 1713, more than half of the Slave Lodge's population died as a result of a smallpox epidemic at the Cape. That may have triggered his search for medical information. One paragraph is repeated in the list, suggesting that either Johannes or a Lodge slave from Ceylon (Sri Lanka today) may have copied the Tamil medical recipes into his notebook. Nicolaas Ondaatje, an exile to the Cape, is however the most likely source of this information sent to him by his family. They became acquainted through relatives of Johannes. Nicolaas was from Colombo in Ceylon, which the VOC occupied from 1640 to 1796. He had been well educated as an interpreter, and could speak and write fluently in Tamil, Sinhalese, Portuguese, and Dutch.[19]

Responding to a request in a letter, Nicolaas' family had sent him two books with medical recipes, as well as roots and pills indigenous to the Ceylon region from which he came.[20] These were very likely traditional family recipes that represented the *Siddha* tradition, a South Indian variant of Vedic medicine that Nicolaas' family practised at that time. Confirming the early modern practices of collecting, circulating, and copying medical recipes, Elaine Leong explains how householders in England too collected and treasured health-related information to make recipe books.[21] Many recipes came from friends and family when plague had destroyed entire communities and this practice led households to develop private collections. They applied "information management technologies" for caring, nursing, diagnosing, and prescribing, as well as cultivating medicinal herbs and making medicines. Reading and writing practices were central to these activities.

The Tamil-language list in Johannes' notebook includes recipes with active ingredients to cure common ailments such as fever, indigestion, coughs, and tooth infection. Alternative Dutch medical traditions, as well as Malay and Khoisan indigenous folk systems at the early Cape, are documented in greater detail than this *Siddha* tradition. Little is known about how it related to the medicine practised in both the Slave Lodge and Company hospitals. Neither is it yet fully understood how the information about ingredients listed in these recipes was used or adapted to local conditions, nor how indigenous substitutes were applied. The Slave Lodge served Company soldiers and sailors as a brothel for one hour every night, which may explain why there are three recipes for venereal diseases in Johannes' notebook. This information was crucial for women in the Slave Lodge, and one remedy required *Evolvulus Alsinoides* (Dwarf Morning Glory) to reduce infection.[22]

A second remedy required *Acacia Nilotica*, a species of Acacia or thorn mimosa tree, native to both Africa and the Indian subcontinent. The Zulu people in South Africa still use the bark of this tree to treat tuberculosis.[23] As in Ceylon it was common at the Cape, and along with the roots shipped to Nicolaas, these plants and trees were cultivated in the Company Garden in front of the Slave Lodge. The VOC is regarded as a pioneer in ethnopharmacology for the early modern Cape. Its Garden represented an impressive source of Khoi and San ethnomedical information.[24] There is still a gap however in the VOC archives for the Ceylon roots and possibly other exogenous plant information that Nicolaas had shared with Johannes. Tended and worked by over fifty male and female slaves from different countries, a visitor called it an "African Mother-Garden." He marvelled at its international character and "rare trees from all four parts of the world."[25] Besides the sections for vegetable and fruit trees, there were sections too for medicinal plants and trees, with special sections for Indian trees.

Another source of alternative medical information was the visiting ships carrying exotic spices and drugs. All Asian trade from India and the Indonesian archipelago passed through the Cape, and morphine and opium were available there already in the early eighteenth century.[26] In that way, the VOC slaves and manumitted slaves (or *Free Blacks*) also participated in local and transnational trading networks that facilitated the flow of information and goods, and they experimented too with imported plants. This alternative medical information system connected with the larger networks of Dutch, Portuguese, and other trading companies whose ships frequented the early Cape. Indigenous communities, slaves, and *Free Blacks* exploited these visits and bartered in unexpected ways. Alette Fleischer argues that:

> Commerce and cultivation ... went hand in hand with a growing understanding and possession of the Cape's natural and geographical knowledge, and simultaneously allowed for an exchange of information and goods between the networks of the settlers and the locals.[27]

Her implied reference to the Khoi, San, and other Cape indigenous people overlooks the exogenous information networks of imported slaves and exiles like Johannes and Nicolaas. Fiona Vernal maintains however that "Slaves accessed informal and formal information networks to accrue useful knowledge, and to envision different horizons for themselves, their kin, and their peers."[28] Preferring the phrase "discourse network," she explains how slaves collected, interpreted, and disseminated information at the Cape. Using their own information and discourse networks as grapevines that included "rumour, socialisation, and alternative sites of discourse," they circulated useful information to other slaves.[29] This even included information about how to use mercury to poison their masters, and how to lodge complaints with local government officials.

The Cape Slaves and Free Blacks used these rudimentary networks to access, assess, share, and act on information. Some remedies listed in Johannes' notebook had to rely on indigenous substitutes. As a result, he developed an alternative medical information system in the Slave Lodge, substituting local active ingredients for those copied into his notebook. These medical remedies, and the other categories of information in the notebook, may well have been re-copied and circulated more widely in the Lodge, and subsequently among the Cape's underclasses after Johannes was manumitted in 1731. But the Slave Lodge was a "demographic sinkhole" with a constant mortality that Johannes witnessed, sometimes daily. Staying healthy and alive until manumission was both a priority and a challenge that required reliable medical information. The death notices of Company slaves included the names and age of children, which affected Johannes' work and personal relations with those whom he taught.

His role also as a "barefoot doctor" necessitated the kind of information vital to the protection of his scholars' health, well-being, and educational progress. The recipes listed in his notebook against fever, dropsy, vomiting, inflammation, and tooth infection were essential in the unsanitary conditions of captivity. In both its oral and recorded forms, this kind of curative information was life-saving and reassuring to the Slave Lodge's "unfree" inhabitants, as well as the Cape's lower classes. It was in these distressing circumstances that access to both indigenous and exogenous sources of medical information sustained Johannes' journey, and that of his fellow slaves, to personal freedom and to successful careers after manumission. Equipped with this information, the Lodge and the manumitted slaves could negotiate improvements in their status and livelihoods at the early Cape. They re-fashioned their social identities away from the legal categories of "slave," "convict," and "unfree."[30] For Johannes, the kinds of information collected in the notebook had affirmed his identity as a "Reading and Writing Master" for a multinational company, and as a respected "physician" in his community.

Patric Mellet: Information for Political and Identity Freedom

Remarkably, in South Africa's apartheid period (1948–1994), similar information themes characterised the life and work of a distant relative of Johannes Smiesing. It was only in the "new" (post-apartheid) South Africa that Patric Tariq Mellet, a political activist and an African National Congress (ANC) printer in South Africa's "liberation struggle," discovered family connections with Johannes on his mother's side.[31] The apartheid government had classified both his grandmothers as "Coloured," and Patric grew up in Cape Town's working-class districts not far from the Slave Lodge. Parallels with his slave ancestor started early, when he was placed in foster care, in what he describes as:

> a very cruel Dickensian Children's Home where hard labour, beatings and other abuse and deprivations were the order of the day. While there for over three years I saw my mother once every two months.[32]

He then attended the Catholic Salesian Institute, a residential industrial trade school. Here, in a more respectful environment, he learned the basics of lead compositing at its printing press. He also received basic training in political and trade union literacy, read many "socialist" books that the censor board had overlooked, and commenced work in a factory when he turned fifteen.[33] As in the case of Johannes' assigned "creole" and "half-caste" identity in the Slave Lodge, the apartheid government racially classified Patric as "Other Coloured" when he applied for an identity document as a sixteen-year-old. He rejected that imposed classification, as well as the ascribed "White" category that the official completing the application insisted on, based on his fair complexion.

He later insisted about identity and heritage that "People need information, and the fractured approach to looking at sub-identity as South Africans does not help anyone."[34] The "lie" about his family name, and the lies of both the apartheid and ANC governments, drove his long search for information and for truth.[35] Access to information was a critical element in South Africa's liberation struggle, and for many like Patric it implicated political themes of power and propaganda, as well as cultural themes of identity and heritage. As one of the ANC's printers', Patric had committed himself to producing and distributing information about non-racialism. But he now deplores the ANC's "ridiculous and regressive approach" of promoting tribalism and still labelling people as "Coloured." At the same time, he laments that today "many, if not most people so labelled, self-identify as 'Coloured'."[36]

His life-story from political activist to heritage activist emphasises themes of access to information, and of information freedom as endlessly relevant. Based on his fair complexion, and a letter from his mother to the South African Defence Force about him keeping bad company and needing discipline, Patric was drafted against his will into compulsory military service for "White" boys. He resisted fiercely, and for this defiance he was beaten severely and humiliated. On six occasions, he was arrested and interrogated by the military, as well as the security police, and he explains his response at that time as "complete non-cooperative resistance."[37] He was even accused of using radio equipment to transmit information to the ANC, as well as other enemies such as SWAPO (the South West African People's Organisation), which was an independence movement in neighbouring Namibia.[38]

Whether that may be true or not, some scholars confirm that SWAPO's war against South Africa was much more "a clash of information-related activities directed at hearts and minds than it was of guns and bombs."[39] After release from the South African army in May 1976, Patric earned a certificate in mechanical engineering, and trained as a maintenance fitter at a printing and packaging company. Despite an awareness of surveillance by the Security Police he joined the ANC, determined to take up arms against the apartheid regime and to work underground. He successfully avoided arrest, and was able to establish a secret ANC cell in Cape Town. Patric moved through several youth organisations, some of which changed their names for security reasons.

It was as a member of the Southern Socialist Working Youth that he bought an untraceable Remington typewriter and printing equipment at second-hand stalls on Cape Town's *Grand Parade*. He used it to edit and produce an "underground" anti-apartheid newspaper, *Young Voice*, and when it was banned he re-published it as *New Voice*. But the government banned that as well. By then Patric had joined *Umkhonto we Sizwe* (Spear of the Nation), the military wing of the ANC. In 1978, he and his family went into exile in Botswana where he trained with the ANC's political ally, the South African Communist Party (SACP). Determined to engage in the "information struggle" against apartheid, his training included basic agitational propaganda ("agitprop") journalism, graphic layout and design, photographic darkroom work, and lithographic printing.[40]

With this basic printing and editing experience, the ANC deployed him to Zambia at the end of 1979 to establish a "liberation press" at its headquarters just outside Lusaka. With scant supplies and deficient equipment he helped to produce the ANC and Communist Party journals and magazines *Mayibuye, Dawn, Umsebenzi*, and *VOW* (*Voice of Women*).[41] The ANC's Department of Information and Publicity and its Radio Freedom, where he also worked, contradicted the propaganda of the apartheid government's own Department of Information. That government department had stemmed in 1972 already from a supposed "highly organised and generously funded international propaganda offensive against South Africa."[42] The Prime Minister, John Vorster, had been advised to mount a counter-offensive against this "invented threat" using covert means, if necessary. The result was the Department of Information, initiated by the Military Intelligence section of the government's National Intelligence Service.

By the late 1970s, the apartheid regime "had gained a reputation as one of the most dreaded information-gathering machines in the world."[43] The Department of Information used clandestine government funding, sourced from public money, for propaganda schemes and to buy the South African Associated Newspapers (SAAN) Company that owned several of the country's newspapers. One of its ill-fated schemes was the launch in 1976 of a daily newspaper, *The Citizen*.[44] The boast that it was selling ninety thousand copies per day was soon exposed as a lie. In fact, up to thirty thousand newspapers were dumped daily on a farm belonging to a financial backer and staunch supporter of the apartheid government.[45] Growing more sensitive to criticism, the government also banned several Black newspapers, and imprisoned editors and journalists under its detention-without-trial laws of October 19, 1977, which became known as "Black Wednesday."[46]

A less well-known scheme was its purchase of half the shares in UPITN (United Press International Television News), which was the world's second-largest television news agency at that time. The money was provided too by the South African government in "an attempt to influence television news reporting at a global level."[47] These information scandals eventually brought down the "Vorster government" in 1978.[48] In further efforts to discredit apartheid disinformation schemes and projects, Patric studied and graduated from the London College of Printing. From 1985 to 1990, he worked full-time for the ANC's Department of Information and Publicity Press and served on the editorial boards of its journals committed to exposing apartheid propaganda. His identity at that time was "totally wrapped up with being the liberation movement printer."[49]

The Companero Printing Press produced literature that circulated internationally, and "underground" in South Africa. Patric saw it as a champion for information freedom, and as a strategic centre for the liberation of all oppressed South Africans. Disillusioned however in the "new" South Africa by the ANC's same disparaging approach as that of the apartheid regime in separating out and labelling people as "Coloured," Patric launched a "new" information struggle for "restorative memory." He now firmly maintains that "restorative memory" informs projects that can bring "restorative justice," reparation, and restitution. Acting on discussions with political stalwarts, he spearheaded a group of "heritage activists" that founded the Camissa Museum and Centre for Restorative Memory.

Located in the iconic Castle of Good Hope in Cape Town since April 2021, when it officially opened to the public, the museum affords physical access and "open source" information. It takes its name from the Camissa River (place of sweet waters), which was what the indigenous *Khoi* named Cape Town. It symbolises several rivers, including the Camissa River and thirty-six springs of Table Mountain, all of which were channelled underground and drained into the ocean as the city grew. The museum symbolises the "heritage tributaries" of the Cape's peoples, brought together in different ways and from many roots or origins. A Camissa Museum Online[50] is now publicly accessible too as a teaching and learning resource, and it includes the story of Patric's distant relative, Johannes Smiesing. Patric argues that agency is a feature of "living documents" to produce certain effects, and that Smiesing's notebook could play a "restorative memory" role in the online museum.

It is in fact the "agency" quality of the information in the notebook as a "living document" that should be enriched and visualised in this online museum to effect and achieve "restorative memory." A film clip produced by the late slave historian, Robert Shell, is already an example of how to restore memory of the early eighteenth-century Slave Lodge classroom atmosphere. Its music and scenes with water paintings of learners with educational tools, and their caring teacher, help to generate this atmosphere for restoring memory.

These information-based elements combine in one of Johannes' lessons to recover and reveal emotions of hope in captivity.[51] The clip dramatises some of his notebook's text that could play "restorative memory" and "restorative justice" roles both to repair the harm committed against victims and their community, and to consider the perpetrators. That approach to criminal justice already characterised the ethos of the "new" South Africa's Truth and Reconciliation Commission in 1995 to investigate human rights violations by the apartheid regime.[52]

The online museum's technologically and historically enriched information would also challenge what Patric labels as "ethno-nationalism, singular ethnicities, tribalism, and notions of race or ethnic purity."[53] The film clip should be added to the online museum's envisaged "high-tech IT Memory Well." Visitors would "draw from," or retrieve, its information formatted as text narratives, photographs, the spoken word, imagery, music, poetry, and video clips projected onto a large overhead screen. This heritage information would support the museum's and Patric's quest for restorative memory and restorative justice.

Athol Williams: Whistleblowing in the "New" South Africa

One of the Camissa online museum's editorial consultants and financial backers, Athol Williams, explains that: "The more I know my ancestors, the more I know myself." He learned more about himself when he uncovered the insidious information strategies of his employer. And, like Patric, he emphasises the importance of information for restorative memory, and for restorative justice. In October 2019, in the "new" South Africa, Athol blew the whistle on the global management consultancy firm, Bain & Company, based in Boston, Massachusetts in the United States. Whistleblowing can be considered to be a form of information practice, being the act of informing on a person or organisation which the informer believes has acted unlawfully or unethically. It can occur in a variety of information channels, from internal organisational processes to external communication pathways via the police, government, or the media.

Athol has qualifications in engineering, management, and politics, and is an award-winning poet. He co-founded the non-government organisation, Read to Rise which promotes literacy in the Western Cape's working-class townships. Having previously worked for them, Bain & Company contracted Athol to help mend relations with the South African government after the Nugent Commission of Inquiry into Tax Administration and Governance at SARS (South African Revenue Service) found in 2018 that it had been involved in "state capture." The presiding judge had described the relationship between the company and a former Commissioner of SARS as "deep collusion" to damage the tax collection authority.[54] "State capture" can be defined as "a type of systemic political corruption in which private interests significantly influence a state's decision-making processes to their own advantage."[55] Drawing on his own experience, Athol elaborates that: "Full-on state capture occurs when corporations influence governmental processes, and political actors allow them to do so for private gain."[56]

Because he had already worked for Bain & Company, Athol believed that it was his good standing with the company that led to his selection for this task. He understood his new involvement not as defending Bain & Company, but as "acting in the interests of South Africa" to bring remedy for harms the company had caused.[57] By 2009 already, the "new" South Africa was experiencing a take-over by corrupt politicians and officials that

Bain & Company would begin to exploit. This had occurred through "a collaborative effort to repurpose" some of the country's public institutions, and "redirect public resources for private gain."[58] In 2010, for example, the Head of the Government Communications and Information System (GCIS), Themba Maseko, was pressured by a member of a wealthy and influential business family to divert the government's entire advertising budget to its media company. Despite pressure from the country's president to comply, Maseko refused and courageously blew the whistle on their corrupt activities.

This government spokesperson was hounded out of his job and subsequently shunned, slandered, and threatened. It was one of the earliest acts of state capture, and was quickly followed by Bain & Company's irregular contracts with the public institutions responsible for transport and electricity.[59] Bain & Company would eventually charge and earn exorbitant consulting fees that ran into billions of South African Rands. For this to be achieved, it was necessary first to "capture" SARS as the main source of funding for the country's public institutions, and its government projects. It was also a whistleblower who had initially uncovered and exposed evidence of corruption at the tax agency, as preparation for full-blown state capture. Johann van Loggerenberg, a former SARS group executive, had headed its elite crime-busting unit. It had an impeccable record for apprehending high-level fraudsters and tax criminals.[60]

In 2014, as a result of a disinformation campaign involving the country's largest Sunday newspaper, van Loggerenberg's unit was falsely branded as a "rogue unit," and accused of involvement in criminal activities. That led to several senior *SARS* officials having their reputations tarnished, and resulted in a "mass exodus" with the entire top management tier losing their jobs. The South African tax agency had in effect been set up for state capture as a result of collusion between a corrupt SARS commissioner, a former President of the country and the global management consultancy firm, Bain & Company. The effect on SARS was devastating, and had led by 2019 to a "tax collection shortfall .... estimated at R100 billion."[61] The overall cost of state capture to South African society according to the current President, Cyril Ramaphosa, was between R500 billion and R1 trillion.[62]

Frustrated by his efforts with Bain & Company and its legal team (Baker McKenzie) to obtain information from relevant reports and documents, Athol reported the company in October 2019 to the Zondo Commission for withholding information about its complicity in state capture. In March 2021, he was summoned to testify as a witness, and disclosed information at this Judicial Commission of Inquiry into Allegations of State Capture, Corruption and Fraud in the Public Sector, Including Organs of State. Athol explained that he had insisted on seeing Bain & Company's final report in order to fulfil the task it had assigned to him. Without this information he could not in good conscience report to the commission and to South Africans that the company had made amends for damaging SARS and other state or public institutions in the country. But Bain & Company had never intended to make a full disclosure, and the reason was that it feared a more comprehensive investigation and possible prosecution by the US Department of Justice. The Zondo Commission concluded that *Bain & Company* and its South African branch had colluded with the former president of South Africa, and with its Revenue Service chief executive officer, to "capture" the tax agency.[63] As a result, *SARS* and other state institutions were damaged as public funds were siphoned off into private pockets.

Athol's account is a dark and unfinished chapter in South Africa's information history as a "new" democracy. For its criminal dealings, the South African and the UK governments banned Bain & Company for ten years in August 2022. But the UK government had already lifted that ban by March 2023 after the company had admitted to "making mistakes," yet maintained that its motives had never been intentional. Of greater concern was that Athol Williams remained in hiding without income or guarantees for his safety. Trusted friends cautioned him following the assassination of Babita Deokaran in August 2021 and, without protection or support from the government, Athol fled the country.

Babita had been the chief director for financial accounting when she blew the whistle on corruption at the Gauteng Province's Department of Health. The connection of violence with whistleblowers still resonates with the label of *impimpi* as traitors during the anti-apartheid "struggle." Branded as informants for the South African police and its security structures, *impimpis* were often "necklaced," or, publicly burnt to death using a gasoline-soaked tyre placed around their shoulders. Tina Uys explains, however, that while apartheid informants were "lackeys of the powerful," whistleblowers in the "new" South Africa "place limits on the abuse of power by power holders."[64] Commenting on American and British attitudes towards whistleblowers in a period that overlaps both the "old" and "new" South Africa, Joris Gijsenbergh maintains too that whistleblowers have affected the power balance between the rulers and the ruled by wresting control over the information flow.[65]

Reversing Bain & Company's abuse of deliberately withholding relevant information from the South African public, Athol had also assumed control of the information flow by publicly disclosing information about its attempt to protect corrupt interests. He explains how *Bain & Company* had used the labels "commercially confidential" and "non-public" to withhold and effectively hide information about tampering with a tender process at South Africa's telecommunications company (Telkom). That subterfuge had won it a contract that "would run into the billions, and their collaborators could go on to loot the country's public finances at will."[66] *Bain & Company*'s effort to make amends was to reveal to him only the information it wanted to reveal instead of the information he needed for the task it had assigned to him. Athol labels this deception as *Baintruth* in the sense of only revealing information if and when asked, or of invoking legal privilege not to reveal information. It was not the truth to which Athol was committed to pursuing and finding.

Bain & Company's "information" was instead about showing "mistakes" that it had made, but not that it had done anything morally wrong or caused any injustice.[67] Athol, however, committed himself to sharing his own information about Bain & Company with South Africa's Zondo Commission, as well as with the Federal Bureau of Investigation (FBI) in the United States. In doing so, he had also exposed himself to the vulnerable situation of other South African whistleblowers. The Protected Disclosures Act No. 26 of 2000 is the key piece of legislation governing whistleblowing in South Africa, and Section 159 of the Companies Act No. 71 (2008) contains provisions dealing with the protection of whistleblowers. These measures do not work for most of them because of "significant flaws and gaps." A recent report calls instead for strengthening protection through collaboration between the public and private sectors.

An important recommendation is an independently administered legal fund to ease the financial burden on whistleblowers, and enabling them to access and secure legal advice, protection, representation, and financial support.[68] Equally important is changing the public perception of whistleblowers. Wim Vandekerckhove explains that although whistleblower protection was initially framed in terms of protecting freedom of expression as a human right, the whistleblower laws that subsequently emerged are instead the result of "an anti-corruption agenda, not a human-rights one."[69] In South Africa, he adds, whistleblower protection legislation was enacted as part of the democratisation process to deal with "the historical weight of the apartheid regime." But it seems that freedom of expression has become the "broken promise" of whistleblower protection.[70] In the "new" South Africa it is therefore necessary for a culture change. As Mandy Wiener explains: "we must alter how we think about them, how we perceive them and how we respond to them," and "they must be brought into the light and be celebrated."[71]

Athol was deeply disappointed however that the President of South Africa made no mention of protection for whistleblowers in his State of the Nation address on February 9, 2023. Although their stories are well documented they still have no effective protection and support, and remain in a precarious and vulnerable position.[72] Assassinations, as well as government and public indifference, are among their main fears and worries. The media have also been ineffective, and sometimes bad experiences for whistleblowers. Another serious concern is that many perpetrators of corruption have not yet been prosecuted. Nor is the amended legislation, as recommended by the Zondo Commission, in place yet. It identifies channels for disclosure; rewards whistleblowers for providing credible information; and immunises them from criminal or civil liability.

Conclusion

This chapter discusses some dynamics of the human element with a view to connecting aspects of South African history with its information history. The "information lives" of Johannes Smiesing, Patric Mellet, and Athol Williams afford rich insights into personal and collective experiences of surviving slavery, challenging identity, and defending integrity. The medical and other categories of information collected in Johannes' notebook affirmed his social identity following manumission. In Cape Town's free black community in the early 1730s, he was addressed as "Meester" (Master) Jan, and recognised as a respected teacher and healer. In the "new" South Africa, Patric moved on from the "golf-ball" typewriter that he used in the anti-apartheid "struggle." Active in another "struggle" involving identity, and "restorative memory" for "restorative justice," he helped to develop a high-tech memory well for navigating heritage information searches. Athol remained in hiding abroad, with an uncertain future and without effective support. For whistleblowers, a collective effort led by business and political leaders may be the most promising path to a solution. The stories of Johannes, Patric, and Athol reveal the changing roles of information in this country's past, and present possibilities for a wider understanding of information in history.

Notes

1 Ida Nijenhuis et al., eds. *Information and Power in History: Towards a Global Approach* (London: Routledge, 2020); W. Boyd Rayward, ed., *Information Beyond Borders: International, Cultural, and Intellectual Exchange in the Belle Époque* (London: Routledge, 2014); Toni Weller, ed., *Information History in the Modern World: Histories of the Information Age* (London: Palgrave Macmillan, 2011); and Toni Weller, *Information History – An Introduction: Exploring an Emerging Field* (Oxford, UK: Chandos, 2008).
2 Toni Weller, "The Potency of the Human Element: Information and Power in History," in *Information and Power in History: Towards a Global Approach*, ed. Ida Nijenhuis et al. (London: Routledge, 2020), 1–17.
3 Toni Weller and David Bawden, "Individual Perceptions: A New Chapter on Victorian Information History," *Library History* 22, no. 2 (2006): 137–156.
4 Weller and Bawden, "Individual Perceptions," 143, 151, 145, 148, and 152.

5 Weller, "The Potency of the Human Element."
6 Weller, "The Potency of the Human Element."
7 Simon Franklin, "Introduction," in *Information and Empire: Mechanisms of Communication in Russia, 1600–1850*, ed. Katherine Bowers and Simon Franklin (Cambridge, UK: Open Book Publishers, 2017), 8; and Jeremy Black, *The Power of Knowledge: How Information and Technology Made the Modern World* (New Haven, CT: Yale University Press, 2014), ix.
8 Jacob P. Brits, *Concise Dictionary of Historical and Political Terms* (London: Penguin, 1995), 42. Named as the Cape of Good Hope by Portuguese explorers in the fifteenth century, and known also as the Cape.
9 William Beinart and Saul Dubow, *The Scientific Imagination in South Africa: 1700 to the Present* (Cambridge, UK: Cambridge University Press, 2021), 1.
10 Notebook of Johannes Smiesing, Western Cape Archives and Records Service, KAB, A1414.
11 Helena Liebenberg, *People of the Early Cape: What VOC Documents Reveal* (Cape Town: University of Cape Town, 2020), http://www.tracinghistorytrust.co.za/files/People%20of%20the%20early%20Cape.pdf; Herman Tieken, "Letters Dealing with the Slave Trade from Ceylon: The Ondaatje Correspondence, 1728 to 1737," *Quarterly Bulletin of the National Library of South Africa* 67, no. 3 (July–September 2013): 113–122.
12 Memory of the World Register. Nomination Form (2002), 1, http://www.nationalarchives.gov.za/sites/default/files/u64/Nomination%20Form%20VOC.pdf.
13 Michiel Idema, *Revolution in the Dutch Republic and Resoluties in Batavia: A Quantitative Approach to the Perspective of the VOC in Batavia between 1790 and 1806* (Master's diss., University of Leiden, 2019), 23.
14 Gerrit Knaap, "Communication, Information, and Power in the Dutch Colonial Empire: The Case of the Dutch East India Company, c. 1760," in *Information and Power in History: Towards a Global Approach*, ed. Ida Nijenhuis et al. (London: Routledge, 2020), 122–137; Djoeke van Netten, "Sailing and Secrecy: Information Control and Power in Dutch Overseas Companies in the Late Sixteenth - Early Seventeenth Century," in *Information and Power in History: Towards a Global Approach*, ed. Ida Nijenhuis et al. (London: Routledge, 2020), 157–171.
15 Robert Shell and Archie Dick, "Jan Smiesing, Slave Lodge Schoolmaster and Healer, 1697–1734," in *Cape Town Between East and West: Social Identities in a Dutch Colonial Town*, ed. Nigel Worden (Auckland Park: Jacana, 2012), 142.
16 Archie Dick, "The Notebook of Johannes Smiesing (1697–1734), Writing and Reading Master in the Cape Slave Lodge," *Quarterly Bulletin of the National Library of South Africa* 64, no. 4 (2010), 159.
17 Ann Blair, "The Rise of Note-taking in Early Modern Europe," *Intellectual History Review* 20, no. 3 (2010): 303–316.
18 Anthony Grafton, *Inky Fingers: The Making of Books in Early Modern Europe* (Cambridge, MA: Belknap Press of Harvard University Press, 2020), 158 and 255.
19 Herman Tieken, "Letters Dealing with the Slave Trade from Ceylon: The Ondaatje Correspondence, 1728 to 1737," *Quarterly Bulletin of the National Library of South Africa* 67, no. 3 (July–September 2013): 113–122.
20 Tieken, "Letters Dealing with the Slave Trade from Ceylon."
21 Elaine Leong, *Recipes and Everyday Knowledge: Medicine, Science, and the Household in Early Modern England* (Chicago, IL: University of Chicago Press, 2018); and Elaine Leong, *Note-taking for Health: Medical Notebooks in the Early Modern Household* (2013), https://notebooks.hypotheses.org/workshops/notebooks-medicine-and-the-sciences-in-early-modern-europe/abstracts/elaine-leong.
22 Dick, "The Notebook," 168.
23 Ian Cock and Sandy van Vuuren, "The Traditional Use of Southern African Medicinal Plants for the Treatment of Bacterial Respiratory Diseases: A Review of the Ethnobotany and Scientific Evaluations," *Journal of Ethnopharmacology* 263 (2020): 1–26.
24 Gill Scott and Margaret Hewett, "Pioneers in Ethnopharmacology: The Dutch East India Company (VOC) at the Cape from 1650 to 1800," *Journal of Ethnopharmacology* 115 (2008): 339–360.
25 Robert Shell, *From Diaspora to Diorama: A Guide to the Old Slave Lodge CD* (Cape Town: NagsPro, 2013), 1938.
26 Shell and Dick, "Jan Smiesing, Slave Lodge Schoolmaster," 142.

27 Alette Fleischer, "(Ex)changing Knowledge and Nature at the Cape of Good Hope, Circa 1652–1700," in *The Dutch Trading Companies as Knowledge Networks*, ed. Siegfried Huigen, Jan De Jongh, and Elmin Kolfin (Leiden: Brill, 2010), 245.
28 Fiona Vernal, "Discourse Networks in South African Slave Society," *African Historical Review* 43, no. 2 (2011): 3.
29 Vernal, "Discourse Networks in South African Slave Society," 4.
30 Nigel Worden, *Cape Town between East and West: Social Identities in a Dutch Colonial Town* (Auckland Park: Jacana, 2012), xxii.
31 "The Slave and Khoena Ancestors in my Family Tree," *Camissa People: Cape Slavery and Indigene Heritage* (March 9, 2016), https://camissapeople.wordpress.com/2016/03/09/the-slave-and-khoena-ancestors-in-my-family-tree/. Armozijn Claas, or Armozijn de Groote van der Kaap, was Johannes' maternal grandmother, and Patric's ninth great aunt (Slave Cape Creole).
32 Patric Tariq Mellet, "The Camissa Museum – A Decolonial Camissa African Centre of Memory and Understanding @ the Castle of Good Hope" (2023), https://herri.org.za/6/patric-tariq-mellet/.
33 Patric Tariq Mellet, *Cleaner's Boy: A Resistance Road to a Liberated Life* (Cape Town: Tafelberg, 2022), 55–56.
34 Patric Tariq Mellet, "Noem My Skollie," *Facebook*, October 19, 2016, https://www.facebook.com/NoemMySkollieFilm/posts/patric-tariq-mellet-was-asked-what-it-means-to-be-coloured-and-other-questions-h/354762814863428/.
35 Patric Tariq Mellet, *The Lie of 1652: A Decolonised History of Land* (Cape Town: Tafelberg, 2020).
36 Patric Tariq Mellet, "Noem My Skollie," *Facebook*, October 19, 2016, https://www.facebook.com/NoemMySkollieFilm/posts/patric-tariq-mellet-was-asked-what-it-means-to-be-coloured-and-other-questions-h/354762814863428/.
37 Patric Tariq Mellet, "The Camissa Museum."
38 Mellet, *Cleaner's Boy*, 85.
39 Paul Sturges, Mbenae Katjihingua, and Kingo Mchombu, "Information in the National Liberation Struggle: Modelling the Case of Namibia (1966–1990)," *Journal of Documentation* 61, no. 6 (2005): 749.
40 Mellet, *Cleaner's Boy*, 106.
41 Mellet, *Cleaner's Boy*, 123.
42 Siyasanga Tyali, "Re-reading the Propaganda and Counter-Propaganda History of South Africa: On the African National Congress' (ANC) Anti-Apartheid Radio Freedom," *Critical Arts* 34, no. 4 (2020): 61–75; and Allister Sparks, *The Sword and the Pen: Six Decades on the Political Frontier* (Johannesburg: Jonathan Ball, 2016), 360.
43 Paul Erasmus, *Confessions of a Stratcom Hitman* (Auckland Park: Jacana, 2021), 18.
44 Mervyn Rees and Chris Day, *Muldergate: The Story of the Info Scandal* (Johannesburg: Macmillan South Africa, 1980).
45 Sparks, *The Sword and the Pen*, 361.
46 Sparks, *The Sword and the Pen*, 354.
47 Chris Paterson and Vanessa Malila, "Beyond the Information Scandal: When South Africa Bought into Global News," *Ecquid Novi: African Journalism Studies* 34, no. 2 (2013): 1–14.
48 Eschel Rhoodie, *The Real Information Scandal* (Pretoria: Orbis, 1983).
49 Mellet, *Cleaner's Boy*, 163.
50 *Camissa Museum: A Camisa African Centre for Restorative Memory* (2021–2023), https://camissamuseum.co.za/.
51 Shell, *From Diaspora to Diorama*.
52 Christian Gade, "Restorative Justice and the South African Truth and Reconciliation Process," *South African Journal of Philosophy* 32, no. 1 (2013): 10–35; and Lucy Allais, "Restorative Justice, Retributive Justice, and the South African Truth and Reconciliation Commission," *Philosophy & Public Affairs* 39, no. 4 (2011): 331–363.
53 Mellet, "The Camissa Museum."
54 Athol Williams, *Deep Collusion: Bain and the Capture of South Africa* (Cape Town: Tafelberg, 2021), 9.
55 "State Capture," *Wikipedia*, May 23, 2023, https://en.wikipedia.org/wiki/State_capture.
56 Williams, *Deep Collusion*, 208.

57 Williams, *Deep Collusion*, 29.
58 Williams, *Deep Collusion*, 11.
59 Themba Maseko, *For My Country: Why I Blew the Whistle on Zuma and the Guptas* (Jeppestown: Jonathan Ball, 2021).
60 Johann Van Loggerenberg, *Rogue: The Inside Story of SARS's Elite Crime-busting Unit* (Johannesburg: Jonathan Ball, 2016).
61 Williams, *Deep Collusion*, 55.
62 Williams, *Deep Collusion*, 211.
63 Williams, *Deep Collusion*, 195.
64 Tina Uys, "Whistleblowing: The South African Experience," in *Whistleblowing: In Defense of Proper Action – Praxiology: The International Annual of Practical Philosophy and Methodology*, ed. Marek Arszulowicz and Wojciech W. Gasparski (London: Routledge, 2011), 165.
65 Joris Gijsenbergh, "Struggling for the 'Right to Know': American and British Attitudes towards Whistle-Blowers (1966–2005)," in *Information and Power in History: Towards a Global Approach*, ed. Ida Nijenhuis et al. (London: Routledge, 2020), 185.
66 Williams, *Deep Collusion*, 11.
67 Williams, *Deep Collusion*, 13–14.
68 Whistleblower Protection in South Africa: Where to From Here, *Future Growth: Asset Management* (2022), https://justshare.org.za/wp-content/uploads/2022/11/Just-Share-Whistleblower-protection-in-South-Africa-Report_May-2022.pdf.
69 Wim Vandekeckhove, "Freedom of Expression as the 'Broken Promise' of Whistleblower Protection," *La Revue DesTroits de L'Homme* 10 (2016), 3.
70 Vandekeckhove, "Freedom of Expression," 2.
71 Mandy Wiener, *The Whistleblowers* (Johannesburg: Pan Macmillan, 2020), 438.
72 Maseko, *For My Country*; and *Heroes under Fire: South African Whistleblower Stories* (Open Democracy Advice Centre, 2015), https://opendemocracy.org.za/images/docs/publications/HeroesUnderFire.pdf.

PART V
Afterword

37
WHAT IS INFORMATION HISTORY FOR?

Bonnie Mak

"Information" has begun to be tilled by scholars across the disciplines as fertile ground for enquiry, with many hoping that cultivation of the area will yield a richer understanding of our contemporary world. But efforts to establish a footing for the study of information may have paradoxically suppressed the emergence of critical initiatives. Contributing to the intellectual quagmire are the radically divergent senses of "information," each having engendered its own particular body of scholarship on a topic that is ostensibly shared.[1] Although information is considered a regular companion in the general exchange of knowledge, the word can also be used in a more limited way to describe the non-semantic parts of a message. This mathematical sense of the term is rooted in twentieth-century studies of telecommunication signals and now flourishes in many fields under the designation of information theory.[2] In some contexts, then, "information" is understood to be devoid of meaning. In others, it is a unit of meaning that can be communicated in any form. But "information" can signify a unique embodiment of form, format, and content—or even designate anything that has the potential to be informative.[3]

Where to begin, then, if the proposed object of study is a thing that has been characterised alternately by the presence and privation of meaning? Some might prefer a retreat to more familiar territory in search of intellectual comradeship. Yet by accounting for—rather than avoiding—the diversity of attitudes and cultural practices related to information, we campaign toward a better understanding. Guidance might be found in the work of philosopher Rafael Capurro, who suggested that the main concept in the study of information is not information, but humanity: "When we say: 'we store, retrieve, exchange etc. information' we act as if (!) information were something *out there*. But it is, on the contrary, we who are *there*."[4]

If the study of information is the study of the human condition, then the humanities—and history in particular—have much to offer. Indeed, a historical perspective on the question of information transfixes attention on the human endeavour. What comes into focus is a particular grouping of intellectual efforts that are manifested in different practices across time.[5] Most prominent among such activities are those of collecting, organising, and disseminating. The interpretation and analysis of these practices and the "information-ising" impulses that motivate them is the task of information history. The primary object

DOI: 10.4324/9781003310532-42

of investigation in information history is not that which is informative, but the conditions in which something may come to be informative.[6] In other words, information history is a humanistic exploration of "how information becomes information."[7]

But in its pursuit of the becoming and being of information, the historical approach eschews narratives of simple causation. Indeed, "history seeks for causal wave-trains and is not afraid, since life shows them to be so, to find them multiple."[8] Not preoccupied with assigning a single cause, nor satisfied with an easy one, the work of history helps to develop "clearer ideas both of the *explananda* and of possible explanations."[9] Information history seeks to render intelligible the manifold workings of information through an examination of particular attitudes and activities. With a heightened appreciation of the diverse conditions in which information becomes information, we can begin to contend with the concept and our relation to it.

Why Hasn't History Been Used (Much) to Study Information?

Although a historical approach is by no means unusual, it has yet to be broadly adopted in studies of information.[10] One obstacle is the nature of the topic itself. Information is often understood in ways that impede or even undermine attempts at historicisation.[11] When defended as an unavoidable necessity of contemporary life, it can be construed as incompatible with the project of history. But information and its practices become mundane through practice. Ubiquity is the winding-sheet that shrouds their contingent nature.

If, as some claim, information is a distinguishing feature of modernity, a critical analysis of information must also entail a critical analysis of modernity. As Bruno Latour and others have observed, it was we who deliberately hewed time asunder, marking our difference from the past by adopting transcendental, unchanging laws that would organise the present and future.[12] This contrived estrangement obscures the fact that the digital techniques by which we make sense of the world today are the issue of rationalities that themselves only became settled after much negotiation. None of these approaches are entirely new; none of them are immutable certainties. Historians of science have shown how the codification of select practices in the early modern period would eventually determine what kind of objects should be "seen"; which of their properties should be described; and the manner in which both would be done.[13] By following standardised procedures, various and varied data points could be made to seem commensurable. How else to capture a world of infinite change, except by agreeing upon a set of rules by which dynamic phenomena could be stabilised for study? Endorsed by institutional bodies and repeated over centuries, these logics became widely accepted, habitual, and even obligatory.

It is with such an apparatus that we have draughted our present understanding of information and erected its technologies. Our modern information infrastructures are configured to retrain uncertainty. Controlled vocabularies and classification systems tolerate neither incommensurability nor imagination well. Every "null" in a relational database indicates an absent value that arrests attention; every blank space of a spreadsheet must be addressed. A species needs a genus. And it is according to these rules that we play. Because such principles now discipline our interactions with the world, ways of knowing and doing that are less amenable to their routines—and indeed *because* they are less amenable—have been located in uncertain territory. It is the work of information history to remap this terrain.

What Would a Historical Approach to Information Be?

Deciphering inscriptions, interpreting medieval relics, and running queries against datasets are performed by experts in many fields—such activity might be described as "getting" or "extracting" information. But information history must go further if it is to shed light on the human condition. The endeavour of information history therefore cannot limit itself to the hermeneutics of information, or, at least, not in the sense that refers to the reading of sources. In its study of information, its practices, and technologies, information history may draw upon the same sources that others might, but seeks to gain purchase on an information-ising attitude, that is, "what lies behind the act."[14] Information history would therefore explore how and why medieval relics were classified or by what means and for what purposes corporeal bodies are transformed for management in a database.[15] Such practices produce, situate, and sustain information in the role of information.

In searching out information-ising impulses, information history sensitises us to customs that include not only the organisation of notches on a wooden stick or scholarly commentary on a manuscript page but also the online collection of consumer data.[16] These practices are cross-fertilised in the home, school, marketplace, and bureaucracies in both the public and private sectors; they are expressed in the special arrangement of sounds, objects, graphic notations, and more. Paper devices, such as inventories, ledgers, or spreadsheets, can be taken as evidence of an information-ising attitude, and there are also counterparts made of clay, wood, wax, papyrus, parchment, string, and sand that have been worked methodically by hand, machine, or both.[17] Hand and machine often work hand-in-hand: Morse code, developed to transmit natural language with electrical pulses, has been used to encrypt messages destined to be knitted by hand into clothing for onward communication; documents continue to be marked up by hand before being rewritten or typeset by hand and machine. A historical directive can marshal such heterogeneous examples in the study of information as a human condition.

But modern notions of information cannot simply be retrojected and assigned a historical reality if we hope to discern the complexities of the past and the present. Looking for origins in an effort to reaffirm a particular position should be avoided. Even as we examine the practices and technologies of information, we must also consider such categories to be "contextual, contested, and contingent."[18] Anything that appears to operate as a foundation—including the notion of information—is open to interrogation. In this way, we "fold back" conceptions and preconceptions that are associated with the object of study as well as our act of enquiry.[19] This nonfoundational approach historicises both sides of the analytic frame. In refiguring the past, we likewise refigure our own authoritative status. Such a strategy is especially appropriate because the project of devising categories with which to assess the world is itself an information practice. Information history may then perform a "double fold": it sets its analytical sights on a past practice as well as the present category of historical interpretation, scrutinising the logics of each in relation to the ways that information is now understood. Because our understanding of the past is always implicated in contemporary concerns, the pursuit of history is also a pursuit of the present.[20]

Why Use "Information" as an Organising Principle?

Using "information" as an organising principle helps distinguish an area of investigation within a broader history of cultural practices. "Information" offers a coherent strategy for charting a route through time and space that need not demonstrate allegiance to any particular material or intellectual domain. Such an itinerary easily traverses the boundaries of form, format, and location, as well as the divisions separating the study of scientific and scholarly activity, and those from explorations of daily life. With an expansive scope that is trained on "information," actors and activities that are not commonly in evidence, as well as the reasons for their omission, come into sight. Although the most familiar characteristics of information may not be present in all instances, it would be difficult for even the most sceptical reader to deny that something very much like a tradition of arranging data had already coalesced in ancient Babylon, or that activities bearing a resemblance to search and retrieval were conducted routinely in medieval Europe and Qing China. Despite the diverse recipients of their application—whether ideas or livestock or financial data—what becomes visible are shared strategies of management and control. We can then begin to track the multiple conceptions of information as political, examining how the formulation and rhetoric of each have been designed to realise particular ambitions. By seizing on the manoeuvres of information practice, we capture and make available for analysis the stakes of sameness and commensurability; claims of precision or repeatability; or tactics by which trust is established, expressed, and communicated over time and distance. However, the debates are not situated in isolation in the distant past. What also becomes apparent are the trajectories by which certain notions of information, seeded in certain kinds of historical consciousness, have come to be naturalised and are now orienting not only present scholarship but also future enquiry.

What if, for instance, we suppose that the hand that traces the beads of a *lukasa* also sketches algorithms and trains artificial intelligence? The lukasa is a device associated with the Bambudye society of the Kingdom of Luba, a pre-colonial central African state in the Congo Basin. A curved and carved wooden board, it represents the female body, the Luba kingdom, and the social and spiritual landscape of Luba culture. The lukasa is incised with striations or other patterns; it is also studded with beads, shells, and pieces of metal that have been arranged to stimulate recitation, imagination, and movement. The designs have the capacity to engender different narratives, but are nevertheless understood to record and transmit particular kinds of information. Indeed, some characters and relationships of events appear in the interpretations of a single lukasa with regularity. Beads organised in a circle frequently refer to centres of administrative power; straight lines generally refer to travel, an activity that is often related to the cultivation of political ties.[21]

In the double-fold of information history, the lukasa provides an occasion to revisit prevailing assumptions about information. Although sameness, repeatability, and universal accessibility are frequently invoked in the twenty-first century as ideal or even necessary conditions of information, the lukasa is suggestive of a practice that demands in its interpreter the skills of adaptability, judgement, and restraint. The lukasa is "multireferential and polysemic" in nature and cannot be deciphered without "an extensive body of knowledge that includes royal history, genealogies, and initiation procedures."[22] This is a far cry from being intellectually accessible to all; potential narratives are instead purposely delimited by a series of material and cultural controls.

Interpreters are required not only to perceive variations in shading and texture, but also to construe such distinctions as prompts for memory and music.[23] Colour and pattern recognition, hardly the exclusive realm of machine learning, is a response elicited in a particular narrator by the materiality of the lukasa. In the encounter, the lukasa reminds members of the Bambudye of their obligations to each other and their ancestral spirits.[24]

What Is Information History for?

The lukasa constitutes one aspect of a complex information practice that is situated in a specific cultural and geographical landscape; it regulates, and is regulated through, the secret society of the Bambudye. In its provision of information—perhaps better characterised as an evocation—the lukasa also organises, manages, and even conceals.

Does our current understanding of information and its technologies accommodate the fact that the same set of material elements of a lukasa can generate and withhold different stories? Repeatability and accessibility, it seems, are not necessarily key features of a successful exchange of information. We may then be inspired to imagine that sameness resides elsewhere or behaves elsewise, and we may conclude that "access" is not a suitable vehicle for calling on the diversity of information practices around the world and across time. In other words, by admitting into consideration the sensorial aspects of information transmission, we claim the grounds for reassessing the putative entitlements of reproducibility and what it means to call something the same. The foundations for the principle of accessibility are also exposed for closer inspection. Pursued in this way, a historical approach to information helps "unsettle present certainties and thereby enlarge our sense of the thinkable."[25] The anomalous, unintelligible, or even unimaginable might suddenly emerge as central to understanding. In so doing, history can provide impetus for revising how we comprehend the becoming and being of information.

Hasn't Someone Else Done This?

The investigation of activities related to the management of information has traditionally been the province of so-called auxiliary disciplines. For example, scholars of palaeography examine scribal practices, often discussing the intellectual and social implications of the particular contouring of pen-strokes and letter-shapes, word spacing, ruling patterns, headings, section divisions, systems of referencing and cross-referencing, and other ways of organising information on the manuscript page.[26] Meanwhile, diplomatists, legal theorists, and others explore the performativity of documents and the repositories in which such materials are held.[27] Special insights into the curatorial challenges of facilitating the reuse of sources of all types have long been offered by those in archival science, library and information science, and museum studies.[28] Some aspects of information-ising customs, such as recordkeeping and the idea of the archive, have piqued scholarly curiosity more broadly.[29] The influence of bibliographic forms and genres of information upon the cultural imaginary has likewise stimulated interest across the humanities; other scholarship tests the heuristic possibilities of information theory.[30] Not all explorations are analytical or historical in nature, and many are not conceived in relation to the study of information. But they are nonetheless useful in illuminating the work of different agents, and how the provision of information continues to be shaped by material, institutional, and other constraints.

Different theories of information and informing have been proposed by philosophy, some taking the aforementioned mathematical understanding of information as a starting point, and others concerning themselves with how information in its general sense is involved in the processes of coming to be informed about something.[31] The distinction between the act of informing and the state of being informed became a particular matter of interest for R. A. Fairthorne and others in the middle of the twentieth century as they contemplated how automation could be deployed to improve the provision of information to users in the library and beyond. Attention to acts of informing in the context of library and documentary services would clarify the priorities of these information scientists, especially as regards the questions of technical, semantic, and interpretive effectiveness that had been identified in earlier discussions of communication systems.[32] In a cognate field, Margaret E. Egan and Jesse H. Shera acknowledged that any such system—because it organises information *for people* and delivers information *to people*—is necessarily shaped by the society in which it is produced. They devised a framework of "social epistemology" to support considerations of how society comes to be informed.[33] In contrast to traditional epistemology which focuses on the intellectual processes of an individual, social epistemology should study such dynamics in an aggregate context. Investigating the production, distribution, and use of information in society was to give rise to a theory of how information is to be made useful.

Analyses of information infrastructures have been conducted in such fields as communication, media studies, media archaeology, as well as business and labour history. From the ambitions of Google, Apple, and Alibaba to the role of office equipment and its operators, these studies locate the various agents, materials, and systems in the global landscape, and draw out their relationships.[34] Added to histories of computing that also reveal how information technologies are entangled with the political economy, such scholarship casts a different light on some of the challenges that face society today.[35] The genealogies that they develop can be brought to bear on a consideration of the cultural influences that continue to shape information and its practices.

Our understanding of information practices is also aided in no small part by histories of scientific and scholarly activity, in which note-taking, classifying, and similar efforts have lately been explored.[36] For example, examinations of Carl Linnaeus's use of word, image, and dried specimen—on paper slips, the page, and in cabinets—elucidate the techniques by which descriptions of the natural world were created, ordered, and "fixed" on the page, thereby vivifying at least one early modern attitude toward the management of information.[37] Emerging from the traditions of intellectual history and the history of ideas, such enquiries seek to account for the sociomaterial circumstances of the production of knowledge. This broader context might include the role of paper and printing technologies, as well as the significance of heated debate, quiet conversation, and the cultivation of friendships. Studies often converge on particular actors and certain kinds of knowledge, having been influenced "either implicitly or explicitly by anachronistic criteria as to what counts as scientific" or scholarly activity.[38] Recently characterised as the history of knowledge, this burgeoning area of research has the potential to spread beyond the borders of the history of science, books, and learning, but proponents have yet to address concerns about focus and the question of "anything goes."[39]

What Is Information History For?

As a cultural history of information practices, information history offers a distinctive rationale for the constitution and analysis of a particular group of intellectual challenges. These challenges are of interest to many scholars, and especially those who work on topics related to the formation of knowledge and the dissemination of ideas. Although it is within the remit of information history to explore how acts of collecting, organising, and sharing have profoundly influenced knowledge-making, such information-ising practices are not always rehearsed in support of the creation or management of *knowledge* in an obviously immediate way. An emphasis on *information* obliges us to pause over a consequential intellectual move that can too readily be overlooked by scholars in the haste to cross the finish line of knowledge production. Material evidence of an information-ising attitude is often discarded, contributing to the obfuscation of its own role and process. For instance, notes inscribed on strips of paper or the backs of playing cards were used to aid the rearrangement of ideas before they were committed to a particular order.[40] But once the details had been copied out in the desired sequence in a ledger or register, perhaps in tabular form, the slips were often considered to have fulfilled their function. These waypoints are common across different domains and perdure even after the advent of digital technologies; they therefore deserve close attention if we hope to catch sight of—and engage with—the ghostly armatures of management and control.

The taxonomic systems developed by Linnaeus and his contemporaries in the eighteenth century are important developments in information practice and have had critical outcomes in the history of knowledge. But further inspection of these exercises might reveal that the relationship between information-ising and knowing is not a direct one. Distinguishing one plant from another—or grouping two plants together—are activities that may be taken to have some relationship with knowing, but they are nevertheless distinct from it. Although the aim of such practices appears at first glance to be the production of something that is later called knowledge, it is not an inevitable teleology. The particular configuration of the outcome is not guaranteed. It behooves us to understand for what purposes and according to what constraints these systems were devised, and furthermore compare them with other possible approaches. As Staffan Müller-Wille has observed, "Division, definition, and classification do not represent timeless conceptual structures …. Changes in such practices can therefore not be appreciated by conceptual analysis alone."[41] Today's debates about metadata demonstrate a similar collapsing of information-ising efforts and knowing. Descriptive practices in libraries and archives were promulgated to aid search and retrieval—that is, to facilitate navigation within the context of the respective collections.[42] For this reason, the resulting descriptions might be better understood as expressive of institutional mandates which depend on a specific mode of seeing. Yet such metadata has often been taken by some as if it were a product of direct observation that could record what the objects are "about" or what they simply "are."[43] As a linguistic convenience, this imprecision may occasionally be excused. As an account of reality, however, it can have disastrous consequences. Because metadata is now frequently used in machine learning, it can be and has been constituted as evidence for assertions about not only the content of the objects represented, but also various states of affairs related to knowing and knowledge. Information practice once again slips away into the murky shadows.

In *The Historian's Craft*, Marc Bloch describes one of the special attractions of the discipline of history: "The spectacle of human activity which forms its particular object is, more than any other, designed to seduce the imagination—above all when, thanks to its remoteness in time or space, it is adorned with the subtle enchantment of the unfamiliar."[44] For those who are unmoved by its aesthetic appeal or insist on a value beyond disciplinary merit, a case for the pursuit of history may be made that is situated in its use of creativity to aid understanding. History explains by representing; history represents by interpreting. Using language and imagination, history harnesses the unfamiliar to traverse improbable ground. Such intellectual exertions make us more cognisant of the contingencies of our present situation, which, in turn, make us better able to transcend them. Good history illuminates life. Although "information" seems to have taken centre stage in our engagements with the world, it is information history that will help direct the unfolding drama that is the human condition.

Information History Remembers Our Future

As the historian of science George Sarton explained in 1924 in his vision of a "new humanism," technological advances can be understood as among the most remarkable of human activities.[45] Humanistic study must therefore include an account of creative achievements across the arts and the sciences, through time and across cultures—from the development of writing, music, and metaphor to the formulation of elegant algorithms and artificial intelligence. With a panoramic prospect across domains and technologies, information history can recognise meaningful particularities while remaining on guard against superficial resemblances and false distinctions.[46] Correspondences between the practices of philologists in the nineteenth century and those of bioinformaticians in the twenty-first are then brought into full relief. By scrutinising the usage of tree-like diagrams in earlier studies of textual transmission, we may come to a different understanding of the role played by computational phylogenetics in literary scholarship today. We may also see how the practice of bookkeeping, with its logic and language of productivity, was honed by diverse agents, used for colonial regulation, and continues to apportion society.[47] The study of attempts to "tame" chance in the eighteenth and nineteenth centuries by adopting statistical thinking and its accompanying apparatus of mechanical objectivity can provide ways to articulate contemporary concerns about the entrenchment of data science, the methods of which likewise operate according to particular rules of probability and invoke similar apparitions of impartiality.[48]

Because of its peculiar techniques, history constitutes an unexpected arena for grappling with the questions of explainability, accountability, and trustworthiness that have been major preoccupations of those who seek to understand the cultural effects of artificial intelligence. Past, present, and future are part of the same time span that the historian folds and stitches together to "imagine the past and remember the future."[49] For this reason, the historical enterprise has the potential to offer new and unusual insights that elucidate even the most recent developments in the information sector, making intelligible not only the circumstances of their emergence but also their consequences for society. The current manifestation of artificial intelligence is undergirded by specific practices of description, classification, and statistical reckoning that are themselves expressions of a narrow set of rationalities; it is according to attendant senses of certainty and efficiency that society has aligned its values.[50] Without humanistic examinations of the kinds of logics that underpin today's version of AI, we cannot hope to understand—let alone resolve—the ongoing challenges to racial equity, truth, and civil rights. These problems are not technical ones; they were not brought on by the arrival of a new information technology. A satisfactory and sustained resolution will not be exclusively technical in nature. Artificial intelligence may be one of the most significant cultural events of our time. But information and its technologies are expressions of humanity, and it is therefore to the humanities that we must turn for their interpretation and, indeed, stewardship.

With a global perspective that is cross-disciplinary and transhistorical, information history demonstrates how regard for the patterns, colours, and textures in a lukasa adds dimension to our understanding of the workings of information—from information-ising attitudes, practices, and technologies, to the broader concept that continues to evolve. Most importantly, however, such explorations enhance our sense of the human condition. Enlisting the ingenuity of both humanity and the humanities, information history offers ways to navigate society in the present. As the former president of the American Historical

Association and medieval historian Edward Muir has characterised it, "Life offers not the certainty of grace or mathematical precision but rather the responsibility to make decisions based on partial or conflicting evidence."[51] In a world adrift in a sea of uncertainty and buffeted by questions about the future, we can find direction by charting a historical course, with our heading set on the becoming and being of information.

Notes

1 See, for example, Luciano Floridi, ed., *The Routledge Handbook of Philosophy of Information* (London: Routledge, 2016); James W. Cortada, "Shaping Information History as an Intellectual Discipline," *Information & Culture* 47, no. 2 (2012): 119–144; Marcia J. Bates, "Fundamental Forms of Information," *Journal of the American Society of Information Science and Technology* 57, no. 9 (June 2006): 1033–1045; Rafael Capurro and Birger Hjørland, "The Concept of Information," *Annual Review of Information Science and Technology* 37, no. 1 (2003): 343–411; and Fritz Machlup and Una Mansfield, eds., *The Study of Information: Interdisciplinary Messages* (New York: Wiley, 1983). Recent attempts at clarification as well as demurrals in Eric Hayot, "Information: A Reader. An Introduction," in *Information: A Reader*, ed. Hayot, Anatoly Detwyler, and Lea Pao (New York: Columbia University Press, 2022), 1–14; Jack W. Chen, Anatoly Detwyler, Christopher M. B. Nugent, Xiao Liu, and Bruce Rusk, "Introduction for a History of Literary Information in China," in *Literary Information in China: A History*, ed. Chen, Detwyler, Nugent, Liu, and Rusk (New York: Columbia University Press, 2021), xxi–xxxii; Paul Duiguid, "Introduction," in *Information: A Historical Companion*, ed. Ann Blair, Duiguid, Anja-Silvia Goeing, and Anthony Grafton (Princeton, NJ: Princeton University Press, 2021), vii–xi; and Michele Kennerly, Samuel Frederic, and Jonathan E. Abel, "Introduction: Information + Humanities," in *Information: Keywords*, ed. Kennerly, Frederic, and Abel (New York: Columbia University Press, 2021), 1–16.
2 The seminal work is C. E. Shannon, "A Mathematical Theory of Communication," *Bell System Technical Journal* 27, no. 3 (July 1948): 379–423 and no. 4 (October 1948): 623–656. See also R. V. L. Hartley, "Transmission of Information," *Bell System Technical Journal* 7, no. 3 (July 1928): 535–563; and Harry Nyquist, "Certain Factors Affecting Telegraph Speed," *Bell System Technical Journal* 3, no. 2 (April 1924): 324–346. Warren Weaver underscored the difference between the ordinary usage of the word, which entails semantic meaning, and Shannon's technical notion of information, which does not: "The word *information*, in this theory, is used in a special sense that must not be confused with its ordinary usage. In particular, *information* [in this theory] must not be confused with meaning," in Shannon and Weaver, *The Mathematical Theory of Communication* (1949; repr., Urbana, IL: University of Illinois Press, 1964), 8.
3 Michael K. Buckland, "Information as Thing," *JASIST* 42, no. 5 (June 1991): 351–360. See the subsequent debate between A. Neil Yerkey and Buckland in the Letters to the Editor in *JASIST* 42, no. 10 (December 1991): 758. An important discussion in Robert A. Fairthorne, "'Use' and 'Mention' in the Information Sciences," in *Proceedings of the Symposium on Education for Information Science, Warrenton, Virginia, September 7–10, 1965* (Washington, DC: Spartan Books, 1965), 9–12.
4 Rafael Capurro, "What Is Information Science for? A Philosophical Reflection," in *Conceptions of Library and Information Science. Historical, Empirical and Theoretical Perspectives*, ed. Pertti Vakkari and Blaise Cronin (London: Taylor Graham, 1992), 82–98, esp. 83, 90. Emphasis in the original.
5 For a similar discussion about the use of the term "science" in the history of science, see, for example, Alexander Jones and Liba Taub, "Introduction," in *The Cambridge History of Science, Volume 1: Ancient Science*, ed. Jones and Taub (New York: Cambridge University Press, 2018), 1–4; Michael H. Shank and David C. Lindberg, "Introduction," in *The Cambridge History of Science, Volume 2: Medieval Science*, ed. Lindberg and Shank (New York: Cambridge University Press, 2013), 1–26; Pamela H. Smith, "Science on the Move: Recent Trends in the History of Early Modern Science," *Renaissance Quarterly* 62, no. 2 (2009): 345–375; Peter Dear, "What Is the History of Science the History *Of*? Early Modern Roots of the Ideology of Modern Science,"

Isis 96, no. 3 (September 2005): 390–406; and David Pingree, "Hellenophilia versus the History of Science," *Isis* 83, no. 4 (December 1992): 554–563.

6 See the seminal work, Suzanne Briet, *Qu'est-ce que la documentation?* (Paris: EDIT, 1951).

7 Bonnie Mak and Allen H. Renear, "What Is Information History?" *Isis* 114, no. 4 (December 2023): 747–768, esp. 761.

8 Marc Bloch, *The Historian's Craft*, trans. Peter Putnam (1953; repr., New York: Vintage, 1964), 194.

9 G. E. R. Lloyd, "Methods and Problems in the History of Ancient Science. The Greek Case," *Isis* 83, no. 4 (December 1992): 564–577, esp. 576–577.

10 Efforts to articulate such an approach in, among others, William Aspray, ed., *Writing Computer and Information History: Approaches, Connections, and Reflections* (London: Rowman & Littlefield, 2024); James Evans and Adrian Johns, "Introduction: How and Why to Historicize Algorithmic Cultures," *Osiris* 38 (2023): 1–15; Soraya de Chadarevian and Theodore M. Porter, "Introduction: Scrutinizing the Data World," *Historical Studies in the Natural Sciences* 48, no. 5 (November 2018): 549–556; Elena Aronova, Christine von Oertzen, and David Sepkoski, "Introduction: Historicizing Big Data," *Osiris* 32 (2017): 1–17; William Aspray, "The Many Histories of Information," *Information & Culture* 50, no. 1 (2015): 1–23; Alistair Black and Dan Schiller, "Systems of Information: The Long View," *Library Trends* 62, no. 3 (Winter 2014): 628–662; Antony Bryant, Alistair Black, Frank Land, and Jaana Porra, "Information Systems History: What Is History? What Is IS History? What IS History? ... and Why Even Bother with History?" *Journal of Information Technology* 28, no. 1 (March 2013): 1–17; Arndt Brendecke, Markus Friedrich, and Susanne Friedrich, eds., *Information in der Frühen Neuzeit. Status, Bestände, Strategien* (Berlin: LIT, 2008); Toni Weller, *Information History—An Introduction* (Oxford: Chandos, 2008); Alistair Black, "Information History," *ARIST* 40, no. 1 (2007): 441–473; and Norman Stevens, "The History of Information," *Advances in Librarianship* 14 (1986): 1–48. Also see note 1.

11 See the discussion in Evans and Johns, "Introduction: How and Why," esp. 5–6; Laura Skouvig, "Present and Past: The Relevance of Information History," *Information & Culture* 58, no. 1 (2023): 1–16; and John Durham Peters, "*Information*: Notes towards a Critical History," *Journal of Communication Inquiry* 12, no. 2 (1988): 9–23.

12 Bruno Latour, *We Have Never Been Modern*, trans. Catherine Porter (Cambridge, MA: Harvard University Press), 72.

13 For example, Lorraine Daston and Elizabeth Lunbeck, eds., *Histories of Scientific Observation* (Chicago, IL: University of Chicago Press, 2011); Brian W. Ogilvie, *The Science of Describing: Natural History in Renaissance Europe* (Chicago, IL: University of Chicago Press, 2006); and Patrick Singy, "Huber's Eyes: The Art of Scientific Observation before the Emergence of Positivism," *Representations* 95, no. 1 (Summer 2006): 54–75.

14 E. H. Carr, *What Is History?* 2nd ed. (1986; repr., Houndmills: Palgrave, 2001), 46.

15 Examples may be found in Colin Koopman, *How We Became Our Data: A Genealogy of the Informational Person* (Chicago, IL: University of Chicago Press, 2019); Hallam Stevens, *Life Out of Sequence: A Data-Driven History of Bioinformatics* (Chicago, IL: University of Chicago Press, 2013); Geoffrey C. Bowker and Susan Leigh Star, *Sorting Things Out: Classification and Its Consequences* (Cambridge, MA: MIT Press, 1999); and Patrick J. Geary, *Living with the Dead in the Middle Ages* (Ithaca, NY: Cornell University Press, 1994).

16 On "practices" as a framework for investigation, see Lorraine Daston and Glenn W. Most, "Focus: History of Science and History of Philologies," *Isis* 106, no. 2 (June 2015): 378–390, esp. 389–390.

17 In addition to the chapters in this volume, see also, among others, Dominique Charpin, *Reading and Writing in Babylon*, trans. Jane Marie Todd (Cambridge, MA: Harvard University Press, 2010); Lars Heide, *Punched-Card Systems and the Early Information Explosion, 1880–1945* (Baltimore, MD: Johns Hopkins University Press, 2009); Martin Campbell-Kelly, Mary Croarken, Raymond Flood, and Eleanor Robson, eds., *The History of Mathematical Tables: From Sumer to Spreadsheets* (New York: Oxford University Press, 2003); and Jocelyn Penny Small, *Wax Tablets of the Mind: Cognitive Studies of Memory and Literacy in Classical Antiquity* (New York: Routledge, 1997).

18 Joan W. Scott, "The Evidence of Experience," *Critical Inquiry* 17, no. 4 (1991): 773–797, esp. 796. See also Gabrielle M. Spiegel, "Revising the Past/Revisiting the Present: How Change Happens in Historiography," *History and Theory* 46, no. 4 (December 2007): 1–19.

19 Kathleen Biddick, *The Shock of Medievalism* (Durham, NC: Duke University Press, 1998), esp. 187; and Peter de Bolla, "Disfiguring History," *diacritics* (Winter 1986): 49–58, esp. 57.
20 Benedetto Croce, *History as the Story of Liberty*, trans. Sylvia Sprigge (New York: W.W. Norton, 1941), 19.
21 Mary Nooter Roberts, "The King Is a Woman: Shaping Power in Luba Royal Arts," *African Arts* 46, no. 3 (2013): 68–81; and Roberts, "Locating History in a Labyrinth of Memory," *Journal of the Iris & B. Gerald Cantor Center for Visual Arts at Stanford University* 3 (2002–2003): 73–82, esp. 77.
22 Mary Nooter Roberts, "Luba Memory Theater," in *Memory: Luba Art and the Making of History*, ed. M. N. Roberts and Allen F. Roberts (New York: Museum for African Art, 1996), 116–149, esp. 134–136. For "multireferential and polysemic," see Roberts, "Locating History," 76. In general, see Mary Nooter Roberts, "Memory and Identity at the Threshold in Gregory Maqoma's *Beautiful Me*," *African Arts* 44, no. 4 (December 2011): 76–81; and Christine Mullen Kreamer, M. N. Roberts, Elizabeth Harney, Allyson Purpura, eds., *Inscribing Meaning: Writing and Graphic Systems in African Art* (Washington, DC: Smithsonian National Museum of African Art, 2007).
23 Roberts, "Luba Memory Theater," 114.
24 Thomas Q. Reefe, "Lukasa: A Luba Memory Device," *African Arts* 10, no. 4 (1977): 49–50+88, esp. 50.
25 Lorraine Daston, *Rules: A Short History of What We Live By* (Princeton, NJ: Princeton University Press, 2022), 22.
26 For instance, Bonnie Mak, "Manuscript," in *Cambridge Critical Concepts: Technology and Literature*, ed. Adam Hammond (Cambridge, UK: Cambridge University Press, 2023), 45–68; Ayelet Even-Ezra, *Lines of Thought: Branching Diagrams and the Medieval Mind* (Chicago, IL: University of Chicago Press, 2021); Erik Kwakkel, "Decoding the Material Book: Cultural Residue in Medieval Manuscripts," in *The Medieval Manuscript Book: Cultural Approaches*, ed. Michael Van Dussen and Michael Johnson (Cambridge, UK: Cambridge University Press, 2015), 60–76; Paul Saenger, *Space Between Words: The Origins of Silent Reading* (Stanford, CA: Stanford University Press, 1997); Richard Sharpe, "Accession, Classification, Location: Shelfmarks in Medieval Libraries," *Scriptorium* 50 (1996): 279–287; Armando Petrucci, *Writers and Readers in Medieval Italy: Studies in the History of Written Culture*, trans. Charles Radding (New Haven, CT: Yale University Press, 1995); M. B. Parkes, *Pause and Effect: An Introduction to the History of Punctuation in the West* (Berkeley, CA: University of California Press, 1993); Christopher de Hamel, *Glossed Books of the Bible and the Origins of the Paris Booktrade* (Woodbridge: D.S. Brewer, 1984); Richard H. Rouse and Mary A. Rouse, "*Statim Invenire*: Schools, Preachers, and New Attitudes to the Page," in *Renaissance and Renewal in the Twelfth Century*, ed. Robert L. Benson and Giles Constable with Carol Lanham (Cambridge, MA: Harvard University Press, 1982), 201–225; Parkes, "The Influence of the Concepts of *Ordinatio* and *Compilatio* on the Development of the Book," in *Medieval Learning and Literature. Essays Presented to Richard William Hunt*, ed. J. J. G. Alexander and M. T. Gibson (Oxford: Clarendon Press, 1976), 115–141; Stanley Morison, *Politics and Script: Aspects of Authority and Freedom in the Development of Graeco-Latin Script from the Sixth Century B.C. to the Twentieth Century A.D.* (Oxford: Clarendon Press, 1972); Jean Irigoin, "Pour un étude des centres de copie byzantins," *Scriptorium* 12 (1958): 208–227 and 13 (1959): 177–209; and F. Masai, "Paléographie et codicologie," *Scriptorium* 4 (1950): 279–293.
27 Among others, Trish Luker, "Sovereign Signatures: Australian First Nations Petitions," in *The Routledge Handbook of Cultural Legal Studies*, ed. Karen Crawley, Thomas Giddens, and Timothy D. Peters (London: Routledge, 2024), 333–351; Katherine Biber, Trish Luker, and Priya Vaughan, eds., *Law's Documents: Authority, Materiality, Aesthetics* (London: Routledge, 2021); Brigitte Bedos-Rezak, *When Ego Was Imago: Signs of Identity in the Middle Ages* (Leiden: Brill, 2011); Laurie Nussdorfer, *Brokers of Public Trust: Notaries in Early Modern Rome* (Baltimore, MD: Johns Hopkins University Press, 2009); Cornelia Vismann, *Files: Law and Media Technology*, trans. Geoffrey Winthrop-Young (Stanford, CA: Stanford University Press, 2008); Adam J. Kosto and Anders Winroth, eds., *Charters, Cartularies and Archives: The Preservation and Transmission of Documents in the Medieval West. Proceedings of a Colloquium of the Commission Internationale de Diplomatique (Princeton and New York, September 16–18, 1999)* (Toronto: Pontifical Institute of Mediaeval Studies, 2002); and M. T. Clanchy, *From Memory to Written*

Record, England 1066–1307, 2nd ed. (Oxford: Blackwell, 1993). In general, see Georges Tessier, *La diplomatique*, 2nd ed. (Paris: Presses universitaires de France, 1962).

28 For example, Geoffrey Yeo, *Record-Making and Record-Keeping in Early Societies* (London: Routledge, 2021); David A. Wallace, Wendy M. Duff, Renée Saucie, and Andrew Finn, eds., *Archives, Recordkeeping, and Social Justice* (London: Routledge, 2020); Jennifer Douglas, "Origins and Beyond: The Ongoing Evolution of Archival Ideas about Provenance," in *Currents of Archival Thinking*, ed. Heather MacNeil and Terry Eastwood, 2nd ed. (Santa Barbara, CA: Libraries Unlimited, 2017), 25–52; Francis X. Blouin and William G. Rosenberg, eds. *Archives, Documentation, and Institutions of Social Memory: Essays from the Sawyer Seminar* (Ann Arbor, MI: University of Michigan Press, 2006); Heather MacNeil, "Picking Our Text: Archival Description, Authenticity, and the Archivist as Editor," *The American Archivist*, 68 (Fall/Winter 2005): 264–278; Laura Millar, "The Death of the Fonds and the Resurrection of Provenance: Archival Context in Space and Time," *Archivaria* 53 (2002): 1–15; Bowker and Star, *Sorting Things Out*; James M. O'Toole, ed., *The Records of American Business* (Chicago, IL: Society of American Archivists, 1997); Susan M. Pearce, *Museums, Objects, and Collections: A Cultural Study* (Washington, DC: Smithsonian Institution Press, 1993); and Ernst Posner, *Archives in the Ancient World* (Cambridge, MA: Harvard University Press, 1972).

29 For instance, Laura E. Helton, *Scattered and Fugitive Things: How Black Collectors Created Archives and Remade History* (New York: Columbia University Press, 2024); Maryanne Dever, ed., *Archives and New Modes of Feminist Research* (London: Routledge, 2019); Angus Vine, *Miscellaneous Order: Manuscript Culture and the Early Modern Organization of Knowledge* (Oxford: Oxford University Press, 2019); Randolph Head, *Making Archives in Early Modern Europe: Proof, Information, and Political Record-Keeping, 1400–1700* (Cambridge, UK: Cambridge University Press, 2018); Alexandra Walsham, Liesbeth Corens, and Kate Peters, eds., *Archives and Information in the Early Modern World* (Oxford: Oxford University Press, 2018); Jacob Soll, *The Information Master: Jean-Baptiste Colbert's Secret State Intelligence System* (Ann Arbor, MI: University of Michigan Press, 2009); Antoinette Burton, ed., *Archive Stories: Facts, Fictions, and the Writing of History* (Durham, NC: Duke University Press, 2005); and Carolyn Steedman, *Dust: The Archive and Cultural History* (New Brunswick, NJ: Rutgers University Press, 2002).

30 Among others, Nicholas Danes, *The Chapter: A Segmented History from Antiquity to the Twenty-First Century* (Princeton, NJ: Princeton University Press, 2023); Dennis Duncan, *Index, A History of The* (New York: W.W. Norton, 2022); Chen et al., eds., *Literary Information in China*; Anatoly Detwyler, "'Distant Reading' and the Pull of Literary Abstraction in New Culture China," *Modern Chinese Literature and Culture* 33, no. 2 (2021): 1–48; Hoyt Long, Anatoly Detwyler, and Yuancheng Zhu, "Self-Repetition and East Asian Literary Modernity, 1900–1930," *Journal of Cultural Analytics* May 21, 2018; Arthur Bahr, *Fragments and Assemblages: Forming Compilations of Medieval London* (Chicago, IL: University of Chicago Press, 2013); and John Guillory, "The Memo and Modernity," *Critical Inquiry* 31, no. 1 (August 2004): 108–132.

31 Relevant work may be found in epistemology as well as the philosophies of mind, language, and information. Among others, Chris Meyns, ed., *Information and the History of Philosophy* (London: Routledge, 2021); Luciano Floridi, *The Philosophy of Information* (New York: Oxford University Press, 2011); Peter Janich, *What Is Information?* trans. Eric Hayot and Lea Pao (Minneapolis, MN: University of Minnesota Press, 2018); Fred Dretske, *Knowledge and the Flow of Information* (Cambridge, MA: MIT Press, 1981); Jon Barwise and John Perry, *Situations and Attitudes* (Cambridge, MA: MIT Press, 1983); and Rudolf Carnap and Yehoshua Bar-Hillel, "An Outline of a Theory of Semantic Information," *Technical Report (Massachusetts Institute of Technology. Research Laboratory of Electronics)* 247 (1952). See Floridi, "On Defining Library and information Science as Applied Philosophy of Information," *Social Epistemology* 16, no. 1 (2002): 37–49.

32 For example, Robert A. Fairthorne, "Repartee: The Limits of Information Retrieval," *The Journal of Library History (1966–1972)* 3, no. 4 (1968): 363–369, followed by the reply by Joseph Z. Nitecki, 369–374; and Fairthorne, "Morphology of 'Information Flow,'" *Journal of the ACM* 14, no. 4 (October 1967): 710–719. See Shannon and Weaver, *The Mathematical Theory of Communication*, 4–6.

33 Margaret E. Egan and Jesse H. Shera, "Foundations of a Theory of Bibliography," *The Library Quarterly* 22, no. 2 (April 1952): 125–137. See also Jonathan Furner, "'A Brilliant Mind': Margaret Egan and Social Epistemology," *Library Trends* 52, no. 4 (Spring 2004): 792–809.

34 For instance, Dan Schiller, *Crossed Wires: The Conflicted History of US Telecommunications, From the Post Office to the Internet* (New York: Oxford University Press, 2023); ShinJoung Yeo, *Behind the Search Box: Google and the Global Internet Industry* (Urbana, IL: University of Illinois, 2023); Hong Shen, *Alibaba: Infrastructuring Global China* (London: Routledge, 2022); Craig Robertson, *The Filing Cabinet: A Vertical History of Information* (Minneapolis, MN: University of Minnesota Press, 2021); Geoffrey C. Bowker, Stefan Timmermans, Adele E. Clarke, and Ellen Balka, eds., *Boundary Objects and Beyond: Working with Leigh Star* (Cambridge, MA: MIT Press, 2016); Jack Linchuan Qiu, *Goodbye iSlave: A Manifesto for Digital Abolition* (Urbana, IL: University of Illinois Press, 2016); Nicole Starosielski, *The Undersea Network* (Durham, NC: Duke University Press, 2015); Lisa Gitelman, *Paper Knowledge: Toward a Media History of Documents* (Durham, NC: Duke University Press, 2014); Lisa Nakamura, "Indigenous Circuits: Navajo Women and the Racialization of Early Electronic Manufacture," *American Quarterly* 66, no. 4 (December 2014): 919–941; Markus Krajewski, *Paper Machines: About Cards & Catalogs, 1548–1929*, trans. Peter Krapp (Cambridge, MA: MIT Press, 2011); Gregory J. Downey, *Telegraph Messenger Boys: Labor, Technology, and Geography, 1850–1950* (London: Routledge, 2002); Delphine Gardey, *La dactylographe et l'expéditionnaire. Histoire des employés de bureau (1890–1930)* (Paris: Belin, 2001); James C. Scott, *Seeing Like a State: How Certain Schemes to Improve the Human Condition Have Failed* (New Haven, CT: Yale University Press, 1998); and JoAnne Yates, *Control through Communication: The Rise of System in American Management* (Baltimore, MD: Johns Hopkins University Press, 1989).

35 In the history of computing, among others, Janet Abbate and Stephanie Dick, eds., *Abstractions and Embodiments: New Histories of Computing and Society* (Baltimore, MD: Johns Hopkins University Press, 2022); Matthew L. Jones, *Reckoning with Matter: Calculating Machines, Innovation, and Thinking about Thinking from Pascal to Babbage* (Chicago, IL: University of Chicago Press, 2016); Nathan Ensmenger, *The Computer Boys Take Over: Computers, Programmers, and the Politics of Technical Expertise* (Cambridge, MA: MIT Press, 2010); and Donald E. Knuth, "Ancient Babylonian Algorithms," *Communications of the Association for Computing Machinery* 15, no. 7 (July 1972): 671–677. See discussion in Thomas Haigh, "The History of Information Technology," *Annual Review of Information Science and Technology* 45, no. 1 (January 2011): 431–487.

36 Among them, Lorraine Daston, "Cloud Physiognomy," *Representations* 135 (Summer 2016): 45–71; Blair, *Too Much to Know*; Frank Büttner, Markus Friedrich, and Helmut Zedelmeier, eds., *Sammeln, Ordnen, Veranschaulichen. Zur Wissenskompilatorik in der Frühen Neuzeit* (Münster: LIT, 2003); Peter Becker and William Clark, eds., *Little Tools of Knowledge: Historical Essays on Academic and Bureaucratic Practices* (Ann Arbor, MI: University of Michigan Press, 2001); H. J. Jackson, *Marginalia: Readers Writing in Books* (New Haven, CT: Yale University Press, 2001); Anthony Grafton, *The Footnote: A Curious History* (Cambridge, MA: Harvard University Press, 1997); and Lisa Jardine and Anthony Grafton, "'Studied for Action': How Gabriel Harvey Read His Livy," *Past & Present* 129 (November 1990): 30–78. On paper tools, see, for example, Carla Bittel, Elaine Leong, and Christine von Oertzen, eds., *Working with Paper: Gendered Practices in the History of Knowledge* (Pittsburgh, PA: University of Pittsburgh Press, 2019); Boris Jardine, "State of the Field: Paper Tools," *Studies in History and Philosophy of Science* 64 (2017): 53–63; Volker Hess and J. Andrew Mendelsohn, "*Paper Technology* und Wissenschaftsgeshichte," *N.T.M.* 21 (2013): 1–10; and Anke te Heesen, "The Notebook. A Paper-Technology," in *Making Things Public. Atmospheres of Democracy*, ed. Bruno Latour and Peter Weibel (Cambridge, MA: MIT Press, 2005), 582–589.

37 For instance, Gunnar Broberg, *The Man Who Organized Nature: The Life of Linnaeus* (Princeton, NJ: Princeton University Press, 2023); Staffan Müller-Wille and Sara Scharf, "Indexing Nature: Carl Linnaeus (1707–1778) and His Fact-Gathering Strategies," *Yearbook of the Swedish Linnaeus Society* 2011 (2012): 31–60; M. D. Eddy, "Tools for Reordering: Commonplacing and the Space of Words in Linnaeus's *Philosophia Botanica*," *Intellectual History Review* 20, no. 2 (June 2010): 227–252; Dániel Margócsy, "'Refer to Folio and Number': Encyclopedias, the Exchange of Curiosities, and Practices of Identification before Linnaeus," *Journal of the History of Ideas*, 71, no. 1 (2009): 63–89; Müller-Wille, "Linnaeus' Herbarium Cabinet: A Piece of Furniture and Its Function," *Endeavour* 30, no. 2 (June 2006): 60–64; Müller-Wille, "Systems and How Linnaeus Looked at Them in Retrospect," *Annals of Science* 70, no. 3 (July 2013): 305–317; Isabelle

Charmantier, "Carl Linnaeus and the Visual Representation of Nature," *Historical Studies in the Natural Sciences* 41, no. 4 (2011): 365–404; Charmantier and Müller-Wille, "Carl Linnaeus's Botanical Paper Slips (1767–1773)," *Intellectual History Review* 24, no. 2 (April 2014): 215–238; Lisbet Koerner, *Linnaeus: Nature and Nation* (Cambridge, MA: Harvard University Press, 1999); and Gunnar Eriksson, "The Botanical Success of Linnaeus: The Aspect of Organization and Publicity," *Yearbook of the Swedish Linnaeus Society* (1979): 57–66.

38 Lorraine Daston and Glenn W. Most, "History of Science and History of Philologies," *Isis* 106, no. 2 (June 2015): 378–390, esp. 385.

39 Christan Joas, Fabien Krämer, and Kärin Nikelsen, "Introduction: History of Science or History of Knowledge?" *Berichte zur Wissenschaftsgeschichte* 42, nos. 2–3 (September 2019): 117–125, esp. 118. See also Suzanne Marchand, "How Much Knowledge Is Worth Knowing? An American Intellectual Historian's Thoughts on the *Geschichte des Wissens*," *Berichte zur Wissenschaftsgeschichte* 42, nos. 2–3 (September 2019): 126–149, esp. 149; Lorraine Daston, "The History of Science and the History of Knowledge," *KNOW: A Journal on the Formation of Knowledge* 1, no. 1 (Spring 2017): 131–154; and Peter Burke, "The Cultural History of Intellectual Practices: An Overview," in *Political Concepts and Time: New Approaches to Conceptual History*, ed. Javier Fernández Sebastián (Santander: Cantabria University Press: McGraw-Hill Interamericana de España, 2011), 103–128, esp. 119. More generally, Johan Östling, David Larsson Heidenblad, and Anna Nilsson Hammar, eds., *Forms of Knowledge: Developing the History of Knowledge* (Lund: Nordic Academic Press, 2020); Sven Dupré and Geert Somsen, "The History of Knowledge and the Future of Knowledge Societies," *Berichte zur Wissenschaftsgeschichte* 42, nos. 2–3: 186–199; Lorraine Daston and Martin Muslow, "History of Knowledge," in *Debating New Approaches to History*, ed. Marek Tamm and Peter Burke (London: Bloomsbury, 2019), 159–187; Peter Burke, *What Is the History of Knowledge?* (Cambridge, UK: Polity, 2016); and Simone Lässig, "The History of Knowledge and the Expansion of the Historical Research Agenda," trans. David B. Lazar, *Bulletin of the German Historical Institute* 59 (Fall 2016): 29–58.

40 For example, Markus Friedrich, "How to Make an Archival Inventory in Early Modern Europe: Carrying Documents, Gluing Paper and Transforming Archival Chaos into Well-Ordered Knowledge," *Manuscript Cultures* 10 (2017): 160–173; John Considine, "Cutting and Pasting Slips: Early Modern Compilation and Information Management," *Journal of Medieval and Early Modern Studies* 45, no. 3 (2015): 487–504; Krajewski, *Paper Machines*; Blair, *Too Much to Know*; and Judith Hopkins, "The 1791 French Cataloging Code and the Origins of the Card Catalog," *Libraries & Culture* 27, no. 4 (Fall 1992): 378–404.

41 Müller-Wille, "Systems," 316.

42 Elaine Svenonius, *The Intellectual Foundation of Information Organization* (Cambridge, MA: MIT Press, 2000), esp. chap. 2 on "Bibliographic Objectives." Also see MacNeil and Eastwood, eds., *Currents of Archival Thinking*; MacNeil, "Metadata Strategies and Archival Description: Comparing Apples to Oranges," *Archivaria* 39 (1995): 22–32; and Patrick Wilson, *Two Kinds of Power: An Essay on Bibliographical Control* (Berkeley, CA: University of California Press, 1968).

43 See discussion about techniques of observation above, esp. note 13.

44 Bloch, *The Historian's Craft*, 8.

45 George Sarton, "The New Humanism," *Isis* 6, no. 1 (February 1924): 9–42. An earlier iteration in Sarton, "Le nouvel humanisme," *Scientia* 23 (1918): 161–175.

46 See "analogie superficielle" in Marc Bloch, "Pour une histoire comparée des sociétés européennes," *Revue de synthèse historique* 46, nos. 136–138 (December 1928): 15–50, esp. 32.

47 Among others, Caitlin Rosenthal, *Accounting for Slavery: Masters and Management* (Cambridge, MA: Harvard University Press, 2018); Miranda Joseph, *Debt to Society: Accounting for Life under Capitalism* (Minneapolis, MN: University of Minnesota Press, 2014); and Mary Poovey, *A History of the Modern Fact: Problems of Knowledge in the Sciences of Wealth and Society* (Chicago, IL: University of Chicago Press, 1998).

48 For instance, Iris Clever, "Biometry against Fascism: Geoffrey Morant, Race, and Anti-Racism in Twentieth-Century Physical Anthropology," *Isis* 114, no. 1 (March 2023): 25–49; Alex Csiszar, "Bibliography as Anthropometry: Dreaming of Scientific Order at the Fin de Siècle," *Library Trends* 62, no. 2 (2013): 442–455; Ian Hacking, *The Taming of Chance* (New York: Cambridge University Press, 1990); Lorenz Krüger, Lorraine J. Daston, and Michael Heidelberger, eds., *The Probabilistic Revolution Volume I: Ideas in History* (Cambridge, MA: MIT Press, 1987);

Theodore Porter, *The Rise of Statistical Thinking, 1820–1900* (Princeton, NJ: Princeton University Press, 1986); and Stephen M. Stigler, *The History of Statistics: The Measurement of Uncertainty before 1900* (Cambridge, MA: Harvard University Press, 1986).

49 Lewis B. Namier, "Symmetry and Repetition," in *Conflicts: Studies in Contemporary History* (London: Macmillan, 1942), 70.

50 Brian Cantwell Smith, *The Promise of Artificial Intelligence: Reckoning and Judgment* (Cambridge, MA: MIT Press, 2019).

51 Edward Muir, "On Ideological Litmus Tests," *Perspectives on History* 61, no. 7 (October 2023): 6.

INDEX

Pages in *italics* refer to figures.

Abbate, Janet 319
Abrams, Lynn 258
academic discipline and information history 545, 587; communication theory 537; journals of record 478; sociology 17, 544. *See also* information and communication theory
academic disciplines and information history: academic societies 140, 269, 270, 324, 334, 354, 423, 430, 474, 475, 478; affects one's perspectives on information 472; anthropology 359, 361, 502, 503; associations 12, 134, 256, 325, 329, 333, 334, 335, 344, 361, 423, 424, 477–479, 557; biology 340, 414, 472, 473, 474, 476, 477, 479; chemistry 141, 258, 340, 472, 473, 478, 481; cultural anthropology 472, 473–474; digital humanities 359; discipline of history 4, 584, 589; emergence of new fields of knowledge 423, 477–478; emergence of new professions 325, 423, 478–479; the humanities 188, 339, 473–474, 583–584, 587, 590–591; information and communication sciences 11–12, 542, 543, 547; and information ecosystems 472, 473–474; information society studies 18; information theory 540; library and information science (LIS) 11–12, 18–19, 542; literary studies 547; media and communication studies 544; media studies 537; migration history 442–443, 444; multidisciplinarity 474–475; organisation of new disciplines' information 476–479; physics 475, 476, 480; psychology 190, 192, 283, 287, 301, 304, 305, 339, 340, 487, 508; *Sciences de l'Information et de la Communication (SIC)* 542, 547, 553; standardisation of work practices 481; and technologies 476; women's studies 341. *See also* information history

accessibility: of archives 326, 330, 334; browsing in libraries 338–339; censorship rules in the press 281–282; as criterion for an institution's utility 425; of encyclopaedias 130, 131, 132, 134; of foreign news in Spanish Caribbean 433–434; of information by the state 204; of information in ancient Rome 38, 39, 42, 47, 51n63; to information in apartheid South Africa 567, 570–577; of information in Denmark 460–461; and literacy 430; of personal information 490; population data collected by the state 209; and the requirement of extensive knowledge 90, 586–587

Africa 10, 556, 560, 586–587, 590. *See also* Cameroon; Chad; Congo; Egypt; enslaved people; slavery; South Africa

age of information 13–14, 17–18. *See also* information age

Alim, H. Samy 106
Alphabet (company) 375, 378
Amelang, James 408
ancient Rome: accessibility of information in 38, 39, 42, 47, 51n63; census-taking in 44, 46; collection of personal identity information 44–46, 47, 48; collections in public libraries 46–47; the economy of 40–41, 44; instruction on practical tasks in

Index

41–42, 47; legal information 42–43; literacy in 38, 46, 49; recordkeeping 45–46, 47, 48; way-finding in 43–44; writing media in 38–39. *See also* class; Egypt; maps; slavery; visual information; women
Andersen, Ruth 460
anthropometrics: collection of children's 256; connection to eugenics 249; facial AIs 195–196; and the female body 248, 250–254, *252*; identification documents in France 452; and science 248; standardisation in 195; and working-class women 254. *See also* class; Galton, Francis
anticolonialism 553–554, *555*, 556–559, 560–562
antiracism 104
Aouragh, Miriyam 552
archives: accessibility of 326, 330, 334; and cartularies 67, 67–69, *68, 69*; definitions 324, 327; family archives and chronicles 390, 505; and information-ising attitudes 587. *See also* archives in England; Dutch East India Company (VOC); police archives; storage; specific countries
archives in England: administrative system of the national 326; British National Archives 445; Deputy Keepers 326–327; destruction compared to permanent preservation of 326, 327, 328, 332; education/training 325, 327, 330, 332, 333, 334, 335; Jenkinson 327–328, 331; Keepers and Deputy Keepers 328, 335; legislation regarding 325, 326, 327, 328, 329–330; libraries' acquisition of 329; local archives and record offices 331–332; London School of Economics 332, 333; Lyte 326, 327, 329; National Register of Archives (England) 330–331; Newnham College (Cambridge University) 251; as profession 324–325; Public Record Office (PRO) 324–325, 326–328, 329–330, 331, 335; public records compared to local 329–330; public records compared to private 325–326; role of women in 332–335; Royal Commission on Historical Manuscripts 329, 330, 335; Stokes 333, 334; Wake 333–335. *See also* accessibility
Argentina 195–196, 334, 520
Aristotle: *Metaphysics* 216; *Organon* 224; origin of classification 339; *Physiognomonica* 190–191; *Politics* 249. *See also Categories* (Aristotle)
artificial intelligence (AI): affect technologies 187, 188, 190; and civil rights and racial equity 590; and humanistic examinations of history 590; and the philosophy of information 545–546; recognition of gender in the workplace 317; scholarship on 357; systems 182, 188; training of 586. *See also* facial AIs
artisans/trades 403–409, 442–443. *See also* Japan; secrecy
Aspray, William 5
attack journalism: Cobbett 164–165; debates of public spheres 159–161; as editorial strategy 158; and emotions 22; and homophobia 167–168; Junius 162; newsbooks 159–161, *160*, 161–163; nineteenth-century radical popular press 163–165; public body shaming 162, 167, 169; public shaming 158, 167, 170; as representational culture 169–170; rhetorical criminalisation 161–163; rise of daily news 159–161; and tabloidism 166–169; viewer society 168
Auerbach, Franz 485–486, 491–493, *492*, 493–497
Austin, J. L. 493
Australia 165, 324, 334, 339–340, 446
autochthonous information theories 546
avvisi (newsletters) 390, 393, 461

Babbage, Charles 308, 355, 356
Baillet, Adrien 13
bans: Bain & Company 574–575; by the Catholic Church 89; and COVID-19 pandemic 376; in historical China 237; and newspapers 281, 571, 572; and pigeons 523; on printing 396; *Rights of Man* (Paine) 163; and the Roma 448. *See also* censorship
Barthes, Roland 161
Bawden, David 566
Bayly, Christopher 370
Bazerman, Charles 295, 462
Beard, Mary 253
Belgium: Institut International de Bibliographie 11–12, 140, 149; Mundaneum (Palais Mondial) 140, 141, *143*, *144*; and the Roma 447; use of homing pigeons for military purposes 519, 524, 526, 528
Bell, Daniel 17, 359
Bentham, Jeremy 164, 424
Berners-Lee, Tim 150, 151, 152
Bertillon, Alphonse 195
bibliographies. *See* cataloguing; classification systems; Otlet, Paul
biology. *See* academic disciplines and information history
Black, Alistair 298, 302, 368, 402, 537
Blair, Ann 13, 359
Bletchley Park 291, 358
Bloch, Marc 589
Bodleian Library 266, 269, 270, *271*, 329, 338, 344

599

Index

Bogost, Ian 359
books: authority status of 124; *Bibliographic Description of Rare Books* 346–347; Book of Kells 66; and the British East India Company 418, 422–423; and the codex 30n113, 39; effect of industrialisation on 338; Eighteenth Century Short Title Catalogue (ESTC) 345–346; history of 16; Incunabula Short Title Catalogue (ISTC) 345–346; substitutes for 141–142, 146–147, *148*, *149*; writing *codices* 61. *See also* attack journalism; cataloguing; class; the codex; Darnton, Robert; encyclopaedias; museums
Borgman, Albert 4
botanical gardens 414, 420, 422, 423
Box, Kathleen 287
Brandtzæg, Siv Gøril 461–462
Brazil: categorisation of enslaved people of 97–98, 102, 103, 104, 105; and communication theories 547; military pigeon operations of 520
Brendecke, Arndt 4
Brestrup, J. C. 465
Brezine, Carrie 84
Briggs, Asa 17, 255
Britain: anti-nuclear-grassroots movement 302; Association of Special Libraries and Information Bureaux (ASLIB) 12; attacks on Denmark by 458, 463–464; decentralised employment in 10–11; effect of Radio Cairo in 556; and Egypt 553, 554, 555–556; expansion of the Empire 414, 415, 416, 420; the Family Expenditure Survey 290–291; first social media election in 168–169; and the history of computing 354; informatic governance of the empire 369; Ministry of Information 280, 282, 283; Navy Wrens 270, *271*; Office of Population Censuses and Surveys 290; Public Records Commission 425; and the Roma 447; slavery in 424; treatment of migrants and refugees 452; use of pigeons for military purposes 520, 522–525; women in computer technology 309. *See also* archives in England; British East India Company; British Museum; Inter-Service Topographical Department (ISTD); museums; the Wartime Social Survey
British East India Company: and the British Library 416; donation of material 423; information accumulation and management 418–420; library and museum of 415–416, 424–425; monopolies of 22, 415–416, 418, 423–426; storage and display 420–423. *See also* colonialism; Dutch East India Company (VOC)

British Museum: archives and manuscript collections at 326, 329; and the British East India Company 416, 426; cataloguing practices at 343–345; growth in holdings of 339; printed catalogues and guides 425; public utility of 424; sharing duplicate specimens 423
Brokaw, Galen 82, 89
Buckland, Michael 204; "Information as Thing" 120
Burke, Peter 7, 17, 291, 457, 458
Burma 526, 528
Bush, Vannevar 173, 356

Cai Changnian 538, 546
calendars 17, 80, 326, 329
Cameroon 195
Campbell-Kelly, Martin 354, 356, 357
capitalism: communication as power 385–386; criticisms of surveillance capitalism 378; and decolonisation 553; and demarcation 183; and journalism 159; merchant capitalism 9; and the normalising gaze 490; private/public domains 249; and Romanian surveillance 490; and rupture 8. *See also* colonial capitalism; economics; merchant capitalism
Capurro, Rafael 583
Carey, Jane 256
cargo manifests 239, 242
cataloguing: the Bible 347; bibliographies 477; Bodleian Library practices 344; British Museum practices 343–345; changing to meet the audience 347; computerised 345; the dictionary catalogue 343; Eighteenth Century Short Title Catalogue (ESTC) 345–346; introduction of cards 344; national and international bibliographies 345–346; new rules in 1980 345; overlaps with classification 343–344; Répertoire Bibliographique Universel 140, 141; Resource Description and Access (RDA) 347; serving researchers 346–347
Categories (Aristotle): *Categoriae decem* 216, 217–221, 223, 224; *Commentary on the Categories* (Boethius) 216; *De dialectica* (Alcuin) 217; Göttweig, Benediktinerstift, Cod. 33/14 227–228; and the Isidorean phrase 215, 216–218, 219–221, 220, 221, 224; *Liber contra Eutychen et Nestorium* (Boethius) 221, 222; and Priscian's classes of the noun 222–223; significance of 216; type of categories 216, 217
categorisation: devising categories as practice 585; types of 216, 217
Catholicism and the Catholic Church 161; banning khipus 89; and slavery 437; tracking parishioners 90. *See also* recordkeeping

Index

Cave, Roderick 435
Çelebi, Evliya 392
censorship: banned publications 281, 571, 572; in Denmark 460–461, 466; of the news 394–395, 396; rules on the press 281–282; in Venice 390, 396. *See also* bans
censuses: in ancient Rome 44, 46; collection in Venice 387; colonial informatic governance 369, 370; and determining public policy 480; of the free and enslaved 118–119, 121; Inka Empire 83; Office of Population Censuses and Surveys (Britain) 290; as surveillance mechanism 10, 452; withholding personal information 257, *257*
certainty: and data 115. *See also* uncertainty
Chad 194–195
Chakravartty, Paula 552
charters in the medieval West: charters 52–53, *53*, *54*, *55*, *56*, 56–58, *57*, 61; chirographic duplication 64, *65*, *66*; diplomas 53, 57, 58, 61, 63; documentation production as information 61–63; graphic signs *54*, *55*, *62*–*63*; *manu propria* 53, *54*, *55*, 61, *62*; seals 38, 46, *56*, 56–57, *57*, *59*, 60, 71–72, 210, 327; and subscriptions 61–62. *See also* archives
Chile 81, 90, 358
China 8–9, 548; *Book of Lord Shang* 208–212; Shang Yang 204; and British East India Company 424; information theory in 538–540, 546, 547; the *Mozi* 204, 206–208, 211–212; Radio Peking 556; role of collection in governance 203–204, 206; VOC trade 237. *See also* Taiwan
Christensson, Jakob 128
Christianity: *Categories* (Aristotle) 217; and *Commentary on the Categories* (Boethius) 216; and dragomans 390; Great Offa (or Ceolfrith) Bible 70; and homing pigeons 517; salvation 64–66, *65*, 70; and soul and body as distinct 190; in Venice 386, 395–396; visual representation of partnership with the divine *53*, *58*, 63–64. *See also* cataloguing; Catholicism and the Catholic Church
circulation of information 432–433; in ancient Rome 42–43; of medical recipes 568–569; and the political arena 389–390; and race 437; and slavery 437
Clancey, Gregory 373
class: anthropometric information 250–251, 254; and book ownership 346; and Christianity in Venice 395–396; and Cobbett 163–164; and communication as political 386; concerns about privacy 510; and confidential information 388–389; and corruption 574; and documentary practices in the medieval West 56–57; and eugenics 255–256; and family reunions 506; and genealogical information 504–505, 507; the Hall-Jones scale 291; hysteria in women 253; and information in ancient Rome 46, 51n63; personal identity information 44; intellectual elite in India as knowledge resource 419–420; and journalism 163, 164, 168–169; and khipus 89; and literacy in South Africa 573; the market for and sale of information 459, 460; media studies in China 539; mortality statistics of women 257–258; and newspapers: of newspapers' audiences 164, 464; and pacificism 204; and penny prints 457; and political change 164–165; and political communication 391, 392–393, 395; and preservation of material 464; and radicalised othering 159; and rumours 394; and sharing medical remedies 569, 570; and skin colour 103–104; the specific library compared to the universal 339, 340, 341; and taxonomy 110; and tobacco 393; Victorian perceptions of information 248, 566
classification: and anthropology 502; connection to the growth of science 414, 423; and contextual information 589; Cordonnier 149–150; as declaration 120; documents compared to UDC 142; Ellis on 343, 344; and ethnography 502; and flexibility 153; on ImageNet 191; impulse to engage in 9–10; of ISTD information in WWII 270; and literary warrant 341; method of, in *Encyclopédie* (Diderot) 123n63; National Register of Archives (England) 330–331; obsolescence and new subjects 341; overlap with cataloguing 343–344; and parish records 329, 332, 334, 335; of population data 209; and religion 342; and the Renaissance episteme 187; trees of knowledge and limits in 149–150; vital statistics 370. *See also Categories* (Aristotle); categorisation; classification systems; libraries; Linnaeus, Carl; taxonomy
classification systems: bias in 342, 347; Bibliographic Classification (Bliss) 339, 340, 342, 343; Bodleian Library's shelfmarks 338; Colon Classification 149–150, 341, 342, 343; criticisms of 110–111; Dewey Decimal Classification (DDC) 110–111, 140, 142, 339–341, 342–343, 477; efficiency compared to practical considerations 342–343; filing anonymous works 343; and geographical boundaries 342; Library of Congress Classification (CC) 339, 340–341, 342, 343, 344, 477; need for precise order

in libraries 339; notation/symbols of 339, 340–341, 342, 343; obsolescence and new subjects 341; PMEST 341–342; for race 369, 370; Ranganathan 149–150; sharing catalogue cards with other organisations 344; sharing catalogue cards with other organisations 343; Subject Classification (Brown) 339, 340, 341; and uncertainty 584; Universal Decimal Classification (UDC) 12, 139, 142–144, 145–146, 149, 150, *151*, 153, 173, 339, 341, 342, 343, 477; used in libraries 339–340. *See also Categories* (Aristotle); classification; libraries; Linnaeus, Carl; taxonomy
Clindaniel, Jon 85, 87
the codex 30n113, 39, 70, 218–219, 225
Cohen, Deborah 508
Cold War: collecting information during 493; and decolonisation 553; effect on decolonisation in Egypt 555; NATO 296, 298, 299, 300, 301, 302; use of homing pigeons 528; US training publications 487. *See also* Cultural Cold War; Denmark; nuclear information; Soviet Union
collection 42, 44–46, 47, 48; of anthropometric information of children 256; of anthropometric information of women 251, 252; by British East India Company servants 421; centralised 256–257; curiosities 418, 419, 420; of emigrants' pre-departure information 445–446; impulse to engage in 9–10; of Indian information 420; from individuals 241–242; of information in notebooks 567–568, 572–573, 576; intentional withholding information 257, 574–575; by the ISTD 268–269; of local information by British East India Company 237–239, 240, 419; looting and plundering in wars 422; of medical recipes 568–569; objectification of women through 247–248; people as knowledge resources 237–239, 418–420; of personal data 248, 375, 421; to provide useful knowledge for the future 448; questionnaires to identify material for 271; registering refugee aliens 268–269, 270; role in governance 203–204; role of, for the Roma 448–449; in Singapore 370–373; by the state 203–204, 206–212, 250; and state expansion 208–209; statistical information 249; survey method 250; by teachers at colleges 251–252; via radio and appeals 269, 270. *See also* censuses; data collection; homing pigeons; informants
colonial capitalism 111
colonial governance: and information management 368; role of information in 370

colonialism 11, 21–22, 97, 112, 120, 369, 430, 435–436, 443, 445, 556. *See also* Britain; British East India Company; Singapore; South Africa
colonisation: centuriation in ancient Rome 44, 48
colour 79, 80–81, 86–89, 222, 526, 586, 590
commercial data: prices/supply etc 239
commodification of information: commercialised information in Europe 1500–1800 458–459; information brokers 460, 461; markets for 389, 390, 418, 459–460; as public cultural commodity 10–11; street ballads 461–466; value in different contexts 14, 457–458. *See also* economics
communication: cognition compared to transfer of information 541; and cybernetics 542; discussion 391–395; in governance 386–388; and information 547; is the act of transmitting information 547; mathematical theory of 543; opposition to extension 541; as political 386; as power 385–386; propaganda 545; and silence 388; as the transmission of information 542
communication and media theory 547
communication circuit model 386
communication history 362n1
communication networks 430, 431, 436–438. *See also* British East India Company
communication systems: social epistemology 587–588
communication theory: *Comunicación y Cultura de Masas* (Pasquali) 540; and cybernetics 536–537, 538; as a field 537; information theory as 536–537; *A Mathematical Theory of Communication* (Shannon) 536; quality of information 547. *See also* Escarpit, Robert; Shannon, Claude
computerisation: to order people 372–374
computer science 472, 545
computing history: Beer 318–319; common ownership 316; Dijkstra 315; external factors affecting 359–362; *Freelance Programmers Limited* [FPL] 312, 313–317, 318–319, 320; the growth of programming as a problem 315; Hopper 309, 356, 358; IBM 313, 356, 360, 372; identity theft 360; institutionalisation of 353–356; Lovelace 308–309, 358; Nolan 314; punch card technology 285–287, *286*, 309, 311; quality of women's work 315; and racial segregation 309–310; relationship to other historical subfields 358–359, 361–362, 362n4; role of American Federation of Information Processing Societies (AFIPS) 354; scholarship in 356–358; scope of 353, 361–362; selling

Index

software 313; and Shannon's Theory of Information 360; Shirley 312–314, 315–316, 318–319, 320; Shutt 310–311, 314; Vaughn (St Johnston) 311, 314, 319; women in 310–311, 312–314, 315, 358, 359. *See also* Babbage, Charles; gender
Conboy, Martin 159
concealing information: *lukasa* 10, 586–587
Congo 103, 557, 558, 559
controlled vocabularies 584
Cornips, Leonie M. E. A. 106
Corrias, Anna 227–228
Cortada, James 356, 357
COVID-19 pandemic 90, 317, 369, 376–377
Cowley, J. D. 345
Craig, Robert 537
Cukier, Kenneth 111
Cultural Cold War 557, 559, 561
Cutter, Charles 344
cybernetics 537, 538, 539, 542, 543, 547, 553
Cybernetics: Or Control and Communication in the Animal and the Machine (Wiener) 536–537
cybersecurity 368, 369, 374, 379, 516

Darnton, Robert 6, 359, 386, 395, 459, 469n48
Darwin, Charles 191, 250
Daston, Lorraine 16–17
data: about infection diseases 370; and certainty 115; and conjecture 114, 116, 118; and decision-making 113–114, 117–118; encryption of 516; numeracy 480; as objective 547; as term 112–113; as unit of information 476. *See also* metadata
databases and search engines 477
data collection 15, 280, 285–286, 368, 370–371, 375, 378
datafication 21, 110, 111–112, *112*, 121
data protection 375
Davies, Bethan 194
Day, Ronald E. 120
D-Day planning 268, 269
dealing with an abundance of information: generating taxonomies 473
decolonisation 512–513, 554, 557–558, 559
DeLong, J. Bradford 481
Denmark: battles with Britain 458, 463–464; censorship in 460–461, 466; dissemination and communication of sensitive information 301–304, 305; encyclopaedias of 125, 128, 129, 130, 131, 132, 133, 134; freedom of the press 459–460, 468n40; information strategy of nuclear information 298–301; internal nuclear information processing and dissemination 296–298; market for information as commodity 459–460; and nuclear energy 298–299; nuclear shelters in 303–304; and nuclear weapons 296, 300–301; racial slurs in 104–105; *Rigsarkiv* 97
De Rooij, Vincent A. 106
Descartes, René 190
diagrams: ancient Roman maps 44; carried by pigeons 528; of *Categoriae decem* 219; in manuscripts 220; in the Naval Intelligence Handbook 275; related to *Categories* (Aristotle) 224–226, *226, 227*, 228; tree-like 590; Venn diagrams 480. *See also* Otlet, Paul
Dickens, Charles: *Hard Times* 14; *Little Dorrit* 5
dictionaries: compared to encyclopaedias 125; in *Etymologia* 126; and migrants 445; of nautical terms 270; in Norway 134; in Venice 390. *See also* encyclopaedias
Diderot, Denis: *Encyclopédie, ou Dictionnaire Raisonné* 123n63, 124, 125, 127, 128, 173, 339
digital libraries: scholarship on 359
digital media: as research object 548
digital physiognomy 187
Dikant, Thomas 119
diplomatic correspondences 385
disinformation 3, 359, 524, 528, 572, 574. *See also* fake news; misinformation
dissemination 300; of crucial political texts 434; "linked liability" system 210; models 274–275; Radio Cairo 554–556; by smugglers 434; social epistemology 588; tramping artisans 442–443
Dobrescu, Caius 174
documentation 18; *docére* 120; production as information 61–63. see also information science 11–12
Douglass, Frederick 501
Dover, Paul 14–15, 410, 458, 473
Dubin, Boris 544
Dubois, Laurent 97
Dutch East India Company (VOC): administrative structure of 243; in Ceylon 568; decision-making on limited information 237–239, 567; ethnopharmacology in the archives 569; in the Far East 235–237, *236*; information and shipping schedules 239–241; personal information of enslaved people 567. *See also* British East India Company
Duyvis, Frits Donker 142–144, 145, 153

East India Company. *See* British East India Company; Dutch East India Company (VOC)
economics: amount of information in relation to a country's industrial capacity 545; effect of information technology 11; extension

processes 541; the information ecosystem 472; national economic output of nations 471; numeracy 480, 481; peripatetic migrants 443; and political information 393–394; propaganda about foreign places 445–446; and the Roma 443–444; state capture 573–574; transmission of information by pigeon 519; using data to determine public policy 480. *See also* capitalism; commodification of information

Egan, Margaret 588

Egypt: ancient recordkeeping in 39, 40–41; Cairo as hub for decolonisation 557–558, 561; census in antiquity 44; Du Bois 558–559; model of information governance 560–561; Nasser 553, 554–555, 557, 558, 559; radio in 552, 554–556; state funded publications 557–559

emerging features of modern information 479–481

encyclopaedias: alternate terms for 125–126; amount of space for a subject 176; the book club encyclopaedia 131–132; *Brockhaus Enzyklopädie* 124, 128, 133; in the changing information societies 134–135; compared to dictionaries 125; cross-references in 127, 129; as cultural carriers of information 124–135; digital solutions in Norway 134; *Encyclopaedia Britannica* 124, 127, 133; *Encyclopedia Synthetica Schematica* 145; *Encyclopédie, ou Dictionnaire Raisonné* 123n63, 124, 125, 127, 128, 173, 339; *Etymologiae* (Isidore) 126, 215; *Grosses Vollständiges Universal-Lexicon* 126; organisation of 125–126, 127, 129; Raunkjær 131; *Salmonsens Store Illustrerede Konversationsleksikon* 125, 129–130; Scandinavian tradition 128–131; for social conversations 126–128; *Speculum Majus* 126; strategies to address updating 127; use of images in 129, 130, 131, 132, 134. *See also* dictionaries; Diderot, Denis; Wikipedia

England: police use of facial AIs in London 194; printed matter and political crises 461; the Tower Mint 403–404, 406, 410. *See also* archives in England; artisans/trades; museums

enslaved people: advertisements about 98–102; apartheid parallels treatment of 570; as collectors of information 567; denied information about relatives 501; in the Dutch Republic 97, 98; as important source of information 437; language used to describe 97–98, 99, 100, 102, 103, 104; manumission of 445, 567, 569–570, 576; medical treatment of 569–570; personal information of 98, 567; recognition of, through advertisements 95–96; in South Africa 567–70. *See also* Douglass, Frederick; slavery

Ensmenger, Nathan 309

Erikson, Emily 418

Escarpit, Robert 542–543, 546

eugenics 103, 193, 248, 249, 254–256, 258–259

facial AIs: analogue precursors of 191–194; anthropometrics 195–196; Basic Emotion Theory (BET) 190–191; and bias 194, 196; blended memory 193–194; to determine sexuality 189; fingerprinting 193, 195, 196; human body as site of datafication 21; to identify the criminal face 192–194; and infringement of human rights 194; Lombroso 192–193; market for 188; and phenomenology 191–194, 196; and physiognomy 187, 188–190; and racism 189, 191; recognition systems 187, 444

facts: the concept of information as 545; and information 338; and knowledge 338; and street ballads 458, 461, 465–466; and truth 116–117; type of knowledge 481; as unit of information 476; and Wikipedia 177, 178, 183. *See also* fictionalised facts

Fairthorne, R. A. 587

fake news 3, 8, 152, 183, 184. *See also* disinformation; misinformation

families. *See* (k)information

Fara, Patricia 250, 257

Farradane, Jason 150

feminism 248, 249

Ferrer, Ada 432, 437

fictionalised facts: Auerbach and cultural diplomacy 485–486, 491–493, 492, 493–497; "legends" of the Romanian secret police 485, 487–488, 489, 490, 497; role of 489

Flanders, Judith 8

Fleischer, Alette 569

Floridi, Luciano 546

Foucault, Michel 182, 385–386, 487, 488

Fox, Jo 281

France: an information network in historical Paris 469n48; anthropometric identification documents in 452; Archives nationales 325; Bureau d'adresse et de rencontre (The Address Office) 460; and cybernetics 543; information theory in 542–543, 546, 547; intelligence in preparation for D-Day 274–275; and the ISTD 267, 268; last will of Louis XVI 433, 434; Louis XIV 417, 504; military

pigeon service 520, 522; reporting on the Revolution 433; Sciences de l'Information et de la Communication 542, 547, 550n47; Siege of Paris 519; use of anthropometrics 195–196; use of pigeons for military purposes 522; World Congress of Universal Documentation (Paris) 12. *See also* Diderot, Denis
Franklin, Bob 163
Freire, Paulo 541, 547
Friedrich, Susanne 4
Fussey, Pete 194, 196

Galton, Francis 53, 193–194, 249, 250, 251, 255, 258
game theory 545
gender: in advertisements about runaway enslaved people 99; AI's inability to recognise 317; anthropometrics 250; and attack journalism 169–170; and deployment of computer technology 308; and documentary practices in the medieval West 56; engagement with political news 395; and the establishment of archives 332–335; and eugenics 256; and the history of computing 358; and journalism's ideological baggage 163; *Man and Woman* (Ellis) 255; private/public domains 249; and the Wartime Social Survey 288, 291–292. *See also* women
gender equality 249, 317–318, 319, 320
gender identity: and equality 167
Germany: anti-nuclear-grassroots movement 302; Bernstorff family secret 508–509; COVID-19 contact tracing in 376; encyclopaedias of 124, 126, 127, 128, 129; Familiennachrichten 506; and the history of computing 354; informants 510; museums and the history of computing 354, 355; national archives of 326; and the Roma 447, 452, 453; use of pigeons for military purposes 519–520, *523*, 523–524, 526. *See also* West Germany
Gessner, Conrad 13
Gijsenbergh, Joris 575
Giles, Judy 257–258
Gjörwell, Carl Christopher 128
Gleick, James 5
glossaries 218–219, 221, 222
Goldman, Lawrence 255, 256
Google: and classification 111, 191, 477; and the information ecosystem 124, 473, 474, 477, 588; privacy 377, 378
Google Books NGram Viewer 112, 543
Goring, Paul 459
gossip: as circuit of information 6, 393; as daily news 159; and the free press 162–163;

information brokers of 460; and the Roma 448; and tabloidism 166; and wilful forgetting 509. *See also* rumours; tabloids
Gramsci, Antonio 314
Griffin, Michael 216
Grotans, Anna 223–224

Habermas, Jurgen 161–162, 359, 385, 459
Hagoort, Lydia 98
Haigh, Thomas 3–4, 357
handwriting: clay tablets 8, 477, 585; to copy printed material 218, 222, 430; diaries 140, 233–234, 389, 392, 418, 505; indicating more than one writer 218, 219, 225, 568; khipus as 78, 80, 81; in the medieval West 52; of newsletters 461; notes as information 251, 490, 509; origins and early history of 6, 8–9, 16; papyrus 8, 38–39, 585; parchment prepared for 225; of reports 491; the scriptorium 61; signing agreements 489; stone and bronze 38; wax tablets 38, 39, 585; by women 39. *See also* books; charters in the medieval West; manuscripts; parchment
Harambam, Jason 183, 184
Headrick, Daniel 125
Hecht, Gabrielle 8
Helg, Aline 434
Hewitt, Martin 15
Heywood, Linda 102–103
Hicks, Mar 309
Higgs, Edward 256–257, 281
high modernism 194
history: viewing the information ecosystem 472, 473
Ho, Ezra 379
Hobhouse, L. T. 13
homing pigeons: attaching the message 519, 520, 521, *521*, 522, 524, 526; casualties 526, 527, 530; to collect information 528–529, *529*; Germany military pigeon system 519–520, *523*, 523–524, 526; and human message runners 521; long distance flying 528; navigation skills 517; pigeongrams 519; pigeon post 517, 518, *518*; reliability rates 527; return rates 523–524, 526; security of 529–530; speed of 516, *522*; to transmit information 517–520, 528; use before 1800s 517–519; use in Russian Poland 519
Hondius, Dienke 98
Hopper, Grace 356, 358
human body: as analytical category 21; as document 120–121; as informational and passive 120; physical limits of 47;

relationship to objects: tactility and materiality 21; as site of datafication 21; traces of the body on charters 52, 56–58, 59, 60. *See also* anthropometrics; women
humanistic study 590
human-object interaction systems 47
Husserl, Edmund 191
Hyland, Sabine 86–87, 91
hypertext 139, 150–151, *151*, 173

imperialism 11, 431, 553, 556, 558
Indonesia 189–190
informants 43, 206–208, 211, 370, 392, 418–419, 503, 510, 575
informatic governance: authentication systems 374; to control 376; digitisation of the government 374–375; face verification 374; government as a broker 378; to reassure 376; sanitation 369, 370–371, 372, 378–379
informatics 544, 545, 546, 547
information: and accumulation 415; *Algorithmic Theory of Information* (Kolmogorov) 544; of animals 472, 473, 475; animals as resource of 120; becoming more specialised 480–481; benefit of focussing on 588–589; cognitive content of communication 543; and communication 547; as a concept 17, 544–545; as contaminated 429; as content of communication 543; contents regardless of medium 540–541; and cybernetics 542. 547, 543; and decision-making 386–387; defining 3–4, 13–14, 117–118, 204–205, 410–411, 472, 539, 540, 547, 554, 583–584; and demarcation 183, 184; as extension 547; feedback (concept) 539; as field of study 583–584; as the history of knowledge 588; intelligence offices 442; and knowledge 7, 15, 338, 512n6; as knowledge 206, 207; Latin American approach to 540, 541; leaks 388; and machine systems 544; and mathematics and computer sciences 544; as neutral 545, 547; news as a tool of instruction and 158–159; as object/thing 205, 480; as physical in nature 5–6; as political 586; for political and identity freedom 570–573; privileged forms of 407; process of unilateral transmission 540–541; relationship to knowledge 5, 488; relationship to power 488; relationship with resilience 304; reliable data 545; and resistance 304–305; and restorative memory and justice 567, 572–573, 576; as rhetorical 295, 462; role in adapting to new environment 234–235; and rupture 13; and SIC 542, 543;

similarity to data 544; state uses of 12, 82, 163–164, 289–291, 302; suppression of, by government 394; as a tool 22, 394, 570–572; Victorian perceptions of 566. *See also* Meyriat, Jean
information age: Buckland's use of information 204–205; and collection by state agents 203; and computers 12–13, 204, 353, 354–355; and the information ecosystem 473; nuclear information and the 295; phenomenon of antiquity and modernity 19; and Shannon 13. *See also* age of information
informational landscape 462, 464
information and communication theory 536, 537, 546–547; in China 538–540; and cybernetics 536–537, 538; in France 542–543; in Latin America 540–542; in Russia 542–546
information control: *The Book of the Courtier (Il Libro del Cortegiano)* (Castiglione) 11; and power 575; whistleblowing 575
information dilemma: informing without causing panic 303, 305
information ecosystems 472–476
information exchange 10–11; about the economy in ancient Rome 40; and colonialism 21–22; communication of instructive knowledge 402, 403–409; decentralised organisation 418; through smuggling 430–431, 434. *See also* knowledge exchange
information history: *Cybernetics: Or Control and Communication in the Animal and the Machine* (Wiener) 536–537; definition and context 3–5; development as a field 16–19; a historical approach to 585; how information becomes information 583–584; information as organisation principle 585–587; information-ising impulses 585; interdisciplinarity of 3, 16; maximalist/ minimalist views of 37; and the over-looked 402; and periodisation 8; rupture talk 8, 19; and the Second World War 291; and uncertainty 584. *See also* Wiener, Norbert
information-ising attitudes 587, 589, 590
information management in WWII: by Churchill 265–266; and D-Day 268, 269, 270, 274; deficiencies in topographical intelligence start of WWII 264–265; Inter-Service Intelligence Study (ISIS) 273; in the Naval Intelligence Handbooks 272–273, 275; and Oxford 266, 269, 270, 271, 271, 272–273; and Oxford University Press (OUP) 273–274; of the Wartime Social Survey 284–288. *See also* Inter-Service Topographical Department (ISTD)

information networks 142, *143*, 369–370, 389, 469n48, 487, 553
information overload 13, 14–15, 545, 550n38
information society: computopia 13; and information as thing 205; and information history 19; and information management practices 267–268; Masuda 13; relationship to industrial society 17
the information state 248
information structures: analyses of 588
information studies: study of the human condition 583–584
information theory: in China 538–540; in France 542–543, 547; *infocom* 542; in Latin America 540–542; *A Mathematical Theory of Communication* (Shannon) 536, 538, 540; move from natural sciences to social sciences 539; quantity of information 547; in Russia 543–546. *See also* Shannon, Claude
Inka Empire. *See* khipus
Innes, Martin 194
intellectual property 362, 423
intellectual property resources 423
intelligencers 389–390
intentional leaks 389
International Institute of Bibliography. *See* Otlet, Paul
Inter-Service Topographical Department (ISTD) 264–275; analysis by 272–273; Bassett 266–268, 270, 271–273; Battle of Culloden 264; and centralisation 265; collection of intelligence 268–269; and D-Day 268, 269, 270, 274; deficiencies in topographical intelligence start of WWII 264–265; dissemination 273–275; formation of 265–266; information-management system 267–275; infrastructure of 266–267; Naval Intelligence Division (NID) 266, 272, 275; processing and organisation 270–271, *271*; use of models 274–275; in WWI 265
Ireland 184
the Isidorean phrase: and *Categories* (Aristotle) 215, 216–218, 219–221, *220*, 221, 224, 227–228; and dialectic 217, 218, 222–223; as a grammatical aid 222–224; in the Laon Greek-Latin glossary 218–219, 222, 223; and philanthropic nomenclature 221–222; recollection and storage of 215
Islam 386, 393, 394, 518
Istanbul: collection of information 387; confidentiality in 388–391; information and decision-making in 387; and Islam 386; political expression in 391–395; secrecy and decision-making 388; women and the informal exchange of political news 390–391

Japan 9; and Dutch East India Company (VOC) 235–237, *236*; shipping and maritime conditions 239–240; silver trade in 238, 239, 241–242; use of pigeons for military purposes 520, 526. *See also* Dutch East India Company (VOC)
Jasanoff, Sheila 184
Jefferson, Thomas: classificatory decisions 120; and datafication 111–112; *Declaration of Independence* 110, 116–117, 118, 121; *Notes on the State of Virginia* 110, 113, 115–116, 118–120, 121; use of data, fact and other terms 112, *112*; use of data as term 112–116; use of fact as term 116–117; use of information as term 118–119
John, Richard 359
journalism 545; agitprop 571; bias in 390; criticism towards information 460; and information theory 539
journalism theory 544
Judaism 391, 393, 446–447, 479, 510–511. *See also* Auerbach, Franz

Kalton, Graham 290
Kent, Raymond 290
Kharkevich, Aleksandr 545
khipus: about 78, 82–83; colonial and republican khipus 89–90; colour and materiality 86–89, *88*; as court evidence 89; early modern to modern encounters with 80–81; ethnographic khipus 90–91; Inka khipus 83–84; Lockean decimal system 79, 86, 88; pachacamac khipus 83–84; purpose of 78, 80; radiocarbon dating and chronology 84–85; as recordkeeping system 9, 80–81, 82, 83–84; structure of 78, *79*; subject markers and the "flow chart" theory *88*, 88–89; types of 90
(k)information: DNA testing 510–511; families as communities of information 502–504; family reunions 506; family visits 505; genealogy 502, 507; Klotz 502; material representations of family history 505
Kiria, Ilya 544
Klotz, Maren 502
knowledge: authority of the expert 15, 17, 41, 153, 176, 177, 183–184, 339, 389–390, 475; Bacon's division of 123n63; becomes information through communication 443; datafication and production of 112; facts as foundation of 117; facts compared to opinions 177, 178; imposing order on 341; impossibility of controlling 344; and information 338, 512n6; interpreting the epistemological foundation of Wikipedia 174; relationship to power 488; Répertoire

Bibliographique Universel 140, 141, 142–144; statistics as 211. *See also* information; Wikipedia
knowledge exchange 241–242, 423. *See also* information exchange
knowledge management: outsourcing of 416–418
Kohsla, Ashok 85
Kolin, Konstasntin 546
Kolmogorov, Andrei 544
Koopman, Colin 536–537
Krefting, Ellen 461
Kristeller, Paul Oskar 227
Krotz, Elke 223
Kühl, Sarah 249
Kurennoy, Vitaly 545

La Fontaine, Henri 139, 140, 142–143, 341
Latin America: information theory in 540–542, 546, 547. *See also* Argentina
Latour, Bruno 8, 117, 584
law enforcement: information networks (sources) 487; police report writing 485–486; and public trust 377. *See also* surveillance
Lessig, Lawrence 152
Levine, Philippa 326
Lewis, Alison 488
Lewis, Norman 6
libraries: acquisition of archives and manuscripts 329, 331; automation and providing information 587–588; and the British East India Company 418; browsing in 338–339; classification schemes of 339–340; computer cataloguing and the guard book 343; educational requirements for librarians 361; Ellis 344; information resources (knowledge resources) 415; informing compared to state of being informed 587–588; Library of Congress 339; as living subject catalogues 344; the monastery of St Gall 221; need for librarians to organise 477; Oudh royal library 419; private 432–433; private v public 416, 424–425; public domain information 269; public utility of 424–425; roles during wartime 269, 270; Royal Library (Copenhagen) 463–464; storage and display 420–423. *See also* Bodleian Library; British East India Company; classification; classification systems; digital libraries
life expectancy data 471–472
Linnaeus, Carl 119, 339, 419, 588, 589
literacy: and accessibility 430; in ancient Rome 38, 39, 46; and Andean elites 89; in Denmark 130; effect on capitalism 9; expansion of 385; and genealogy 507; graphic pluralism 89–90; and oral transmission of information 52, 58; origins and early history of writing 6, 8–9, 16; of the Roma 430, 443–444, 452; and slavery 438; in South Africa 573; and street ballads 466
Liu, Hailong 539
Locke, John 13
Locke, Leland 86
Loveland, Jeff 126
Lowe, Lisa 111
Loza, Carmen Beatriz 89–90
Luhtala, Anneli 223

Mahoney, Michael 353, 354, 357
Mai, Jens-Erik 174
Mak, Bonnie 298, 302, 402, 537
Maltby, Arthur 342
management of information / handling of information 9–10, 38–39, 40–42, 44–45, 47, 52, 345; authentication systems 374; in the British East India Company 418–420; the codex 39; and colonial governance 368; connection to growth of science 414; to control 376; ephemerality of material evidence 589; forecasting 243; government as a broker 378; gov't collected information 209–210; historical precursors to Wikipedia 173; and the histories of scientific and scholarly activity 588; informatic governance 368–379; information retrieval in ancient Rome 46, 47; the *lukasa* 10, 586–587; origins of /emergence of 368; outsourcing of 416–418; roles of personnel in 233; software protocols 315; strategies of control 586; systematic management method 11
Mandeville, John 518, *518*
manuscripts: acquisition of, by libraries 329, 331; annotations in 218–219, 220, 224; and the British East India Company 418; in the British Museum 326, 329; chirographic duplication 64, 65, 66; collecting 420; *Consuetudines Fructuarienses* 225; digitisation of Prize Papers 445–446; diplomas 53, 57, *58*, 61, 63; documentation production as information 61–63; graphic signs *54, 55,* 62–63; as information 585, 587; layouts of 218–222, *220, 224, 225, 226, 227; manu propria* 53, *54, 55,* 61, 62; market for selling 389; on metallurgy 407–409, 410–411; Royal Commission on Historical Manuscripts 329, 330, 335; seals 38, 46, *56,* 56–57, *57, 59, 60,* 71–72, 210, 327; storage and display 422–423; and subscriptions 61–62; technology 16; trade in 421; on workshop knowledge 402, 408–409.

See also archives; charters in the medieval West; diagrams; handwriting; the Isidorean phrase

maps: in ancient Rome 43–44; of Australia 446; in Boer War 520; in *Lademanns Leksikon* 132; and merchant capitalism 461; for oceanic navigation 417, 421; production in Venice and Istanbul 390; projecting nuclear fallout 299, 304; and racial difference 121; sea charts 418m 243; of Singapore 371–372; and social knowledge 15; of trading around Japan 236; use of, in WWI 521, 524; use of, in WWII 269, 270, 272, 274, 275, 527, 528

Marcella, Rita 342
Marenbon, John 218, 219–221
Marland, Hilary 250–251, 256
Marsh, Catherine 290
Martin-Barbero, Jésus 541–542
masculinity: attack journalism 169
mass communication 540–541
mass media 540, 545. *See also* Pasquali, Antonio
Matei, Sorin Adam 174
mathematical theory of communication 543
mathematics 538, 539, 543, 587
Maudsley, Henry 254
Mayer Schonberger, Viktor 111
McLaine, Ian 289
McLellan, James 417–418
McLuhan, Marshall 17–18, 540
McShane Jones, Angela 462
media: censorship rules on the press 281–282; definitions in Russia 543–544
media theory: absent in Russia 544
Mendle, Michael 461
merchant capitalism 461
Meta 375, 378
metadata: and knowledge 589
methodology of the book 6–7, 21–22
Meyriat, Jean 542, 543, 547
Miège, Bernard 543
migrants. *See* mobility
Miles, Rosaline 250
Mill, John Stuart 164, 424
Mills, Mara 359
Misa, Thomas 357
mis/dis-information 183
misinformation 3, 23, 182, 305, 345, 358, 369, 526, 530. *See also* disinformation; fake news
mobility 446–447; antigypsism 448; chain and step migration 444; of enslaved people seeking freedom 101; immigration regulations 446, 451; informatic movement tracking 376–377; information caravans (mobile broadcasting units) 556; intelligence offices 442; mass migration 443; migrants 443, 444–447, 452; migration and kinship ties 507; pre-departure information gathering 445–447; push and pull factors 444; of refugees 436, 444; and the Roma 447–453. *See also* refugees

modernisation 10, 158, 386
modernism 194
modernity 8, 111, 443–444, 584
Mongey, Vanessa 434
Montfort, Nick 359
Moser, Claus 290
Muir, Edward 591
Müller-Wille, Staffan 589
Mumford, Lewis 12
Murdoch, Rupert 166–167, 168
Murra, John 83
museums: Camissa Museum and Centre for Restorative Memory 572; exhibiting the Doomsday Book 326; and the history of computing 354–356, 359; information resources (knowledge resources) 415; public utility of 424–425; role in recordkeeping of local histories 331; Smithsonian 354–355; storage and display 420–423; structural sexism and racism 317–318; UK National History Museum 416; Victoria and Albert Museum 416. *See also* British East India Company; British Museum
Mutch, Alistair 4

national bibliographies 345–346
natural philosophy 403, 409, 414, 417, 423
Nelson, Ted 150–151, 173
neoliberalism 379, 538
the Netherlands: and Britain's ISTD 267, 272; first national archivist of 325; and the history of computing 356; and military use of pigeons 527; Romani travellers in 452; and Wake 335. *See also* Dutch East India Company (VOC)
newsletters: market for international news 459; in Venice 390
Noble, Safiya Umoja 111, 191
Norway: and Britain's ISTD 267, 268, 272, 275; encyclopaedias 128, 129, 130, 131, 132, 134; and nuclear information 301
Novikova, Anna 544
nuclear information: an informed public 298; Denmark's internal processing and dissemination 296–298; dissemination and communication sensitive information 301–304, 305; Greater St. Louis Citizen's Committee 295, 300; information

distribution stopped 300; information strategy for 298–301; and morale 298, 299. *See also* Denmark
nuclear shelters: as information 303
Nunberg, Geoffrey 118, 121

obsolescence 133, 341, 446, 516, 520
Olson, Hope 110–111
orality: in ancient Rome 39; and communication networks 436–438; and early modern information culture 461; ephemerality and value of 52; and the information ecosystem 473; and literacy 52, 58, 429–430; and news ballads 462; and political communication 396; reporting transgressions of others 207–208; of the Roma 450; strategy to evade governance 452; towncriers 385, 392; and the VOC 234. *See also* gossip; informants; rumours
organisation: Central Office of International Institutions 140; of channels of information 406–407; determined through questionnaires 271; handling the problem of too much information 141–142; and hypertext 150–151; the *lukasa* 10, 586–587; maritime traffic 239–240; of new information 476–479; of recipes 405; rise in taxonomy 10; the tree structure 139, 147, 149–150; use of colours 79, 80–81, 86–89, 222. *See also* recordkeeping
Otlet, Paul: document-instrument 139, 154; Hyperdocumentation 154; idea of documentation 140; International Institute of Bibliography 11–12 140; interrelated strategies for information as action 141–145; Mondothèque (multimedia desk) 142, *144*; Mundaneum (Palais Mondial) 140, 141, *143*, *144*; Répertoire Bibliographique Universel 140, 141; les schèmes fondamentaux (fundamental schemas of knowledge) 139, 144–148, *146*, *147*, *148*, *149*; substitutes for the book 141–142; trees of knowledge 139, 149–150; Universal Decimal Classification (UDC) 12, 139, 142–144, 145–146, 149, 150, *151*, 153, 173, 339, 341, 342, 343, 477; Universal Documentary Repertory 141

Paine, Thomas 163, 168–169
parchment: as avatar of information 480; binding of a single leaf into a manuscript 224–225, 226; and change 477; and the codex 39, 70, 225; and information practices 20, 57; in manuscripts 226; preparations of 225; relationship to scholarship 8; as valued 225
Parker, Geoffrey 14

Pasquali, Antonio 540–541, 546
passports 194, 197, 210, 452
patriotism 458, 463, 464, 465, 466
Pearson, Karl 256
Peru 80, 81–82, 84, 88, 89–91, 430
Peters, Benjamin 544
Peters, John Durham 19, 211
Pettegree, Andrew 430, 458
philosophical liberalism 161
philosophy of evidence: and documentarity 120
philosophy of information 545–546
physical space 371–372
physics. *See* academic disciplines and information history
pigeons. *See* homing pigeons
Piø, Iørn 462
Plato 458
pluralism 89–90, 184
police archives 463, 465
political communication: early modern views of 385–386
Pollock, Griselda 310, 317–318, 319
Ponte, Marc 98
population 471; as informants used to keep the peace 206–208; registration cards 372
population data 204, 208–211
Portugal 235–237
positivism 140, 183
postal systems. *See* technologies of information
Postman, Neil 14
power 385–386, 547–548, 566, 571, 575
pre-modernity: and rupture 8
printed information 96, 432–434, 442, 445–446, 459, 461, 464, 558–559; about anti-apartheid 567; bans 396, 572; in Copenhagen 460; costs of 480; networking anticolonialism 556–559; and news ballads 462; newspapers 164, 281, 432–433, 464, 556, 571, 572; penny prints 457, 459–460, 462, 464; and the political crises in England 461; price lists 39; recipes 402, 404–406, 568–569; role in political communication 396; Seest 463; trustworthiness of 459, 464; of workshop knowledge 402, 406. *See also* books; Britain; British Museum; handwriting; maps; United States; Venice
printing presses 8–9, 16, 141, 430, 431, 434–436, 570, 571
privacy: attack journalism 162–163; computing history 360; and data in smart cities 368; genealogical information 511; and Google 377, 378; of personal information 510; and smart cities 369; and telephone GPS data tracking 376
propaganda: about foreign places 445–446; and audience research 539–540; and the

Chinese media system 538–540; in early modern Istanbul and Venice 394, 395, 396; in Egypt 553–554, 555–556; information as 161, 553–554, 559, 571; and modern state centralisation 385–386; and nuclear information 298, 302; and Soviet thought on information 545; in wartime Britain 281–282, 288, 528

Qin, Yidan 539
Quebec 96, 98–100, 103

race: and attack journalism 169–170; and banned newspapers 572; Black corsairs 436, 438; colonial classification systems 369, 370; and computing technology 309–310; Declaration of Independence of Haiti 438; desegregation of the defense industry 310; and DNA testing 511; ethnic purity/assigned identities 96–97, 99–106, 567, 570, 571, 572, 573; and eugenics 254; and of foreign news in Spanish Caribbean 434; and the history of computing 358; and information circulation 437; and journalism's ideological baggage 163; *Man and Woman* (Ellis) 255; maroons 100, 436, 437; in *Notes on the State of Virginia* 118–119; and printing 571; and the Roma 453; "simianisation" by Google 191; and taxonomies 110, 119, 120–121, 189; universalisation of the white male subject 110–111, 121; use of terms for the colour black 98, 102–104, 106; and Victorian perspective 248; and women's hysteria 255. *See also* enslaved people; slavery
racial equity: and artificial intelligence (AI) 590
racism 121, 189, 191, 317–318
radio: in Egypt 552, 554–556; information and communication theory 541; information caravans (mobile broadcasting units) 556; in information ecosystems 473, 475, 480; media gags 281; medium for governmental appeals for information 269, 270; and military operations 526, 527–528, 529–530; and nuclear information 302; and Otlet 141, 142; primary medium for disseminating revolutionary information 554; as public information technology 12, 17–18, 552; Radio Cairo 554–556; Radio Freedom (South Africa) 571; in Russia 544, 556; and tabloidism 166; Voice of Free Africa 556; and the Wartime Social Survey 283; WEVD 494. *See also* secrecy
railway and shipping timetables 446
Ranganathan, S. R. 341–342
Raymond, Joad 159

Rayward, W. Boyd 140, 150
Reagle, Joseph 173
recordkeeping 9, 10, 80–81, 82–84, 86; accounting (checks and balance) 84; in ancient Rome 44–45, 48; bookkeeping 8, 38, 590; and cemetery records 98; judicial records 97; mass digitisation of genealogical records 510; parish records 89, 90, 268, 329, 332, 334, 335; Public Records Commission 425. *See also* archives in England; registration
refugees: communication networks of 437–438; mobility of 436, 444; registration of 268–269, 270; as result of conflict 507; treatment in Britain 452. *See also* mobility
registration: birth records 9, 44–45, 370, 452; death records 9, 45, 370, 452, 568, 570; marriages 9, 45, 98, 334, 452; military discharge records 45; of the movement of people 209–211; subversion of system 452–453. *See also* recordkeeping
Regourd, François 417–418
Reitblat, Abram 544
religion: and attack journalism 169–170; and classification 342; and education 424; and genealogical information 511; and homing pigeons 517; Mosque Building Fund (Singapore) 372, 373; parish records 89, 90, 268, 329, 332, 334, 335; and political communication 395; and registration cards 372; and secrecy 388. *See also* Sufism
retrieval: cross-references 127, 129, 219; glosses 218, 219–221, 223–224; the Isidorean phrase 215, 218–219; multi-codex reference 218–219; notebooks as information recovery machines 568; and search 586, 589
Ribeiro, Djamila 103, 104
Richardson, Angelique 255, 256
Ritchie, Sheila 6
Rivero, Mariano Eduardo de 87, 88, 89
Roberts, John 19
Roberts, Lissa 415
Robins, Kevin 12
Rodrigues, Aldair 97–98
the Roma: information practices of 443–444, 448–451; literacy of 430, 443–444, 452; orality of 450; resistance and subversion 452–453; *vurma* and *patrin* technologies 449; word of mouth 451
Romanian secret police: the collaboration agreement 490; information-gathering phase 488; information in files 487–489, 491; "legends" of the Romanian secret police 485, 487–488, 489, 490, 497; MOGA MIRCEA (Stephan), *486* 485, 489–491, 497, 499n23;

observational phase 488, 489; recruiting informer and collaborators 485, 487–489
Rosenberg, Daniel 111, 115, 118
rumours 392, 394, 395, 457, 460, 569
Russia 305, 547; information theory in 543–546; radio in 544, 556

Salomon, Frank 82–83
Sanger, Margaret 254
Sarton, George 590
Savage, Mike 291
Schiller, Dan 359
Schramm, Wilbur 46, 539, 540
Schumpter, Joseph A. 479
science: anthropometrics 248; growth of 414–415, 420–423, 474; importance of scientific papers 477; mind/body connection 248–249; new societies and professions 423, 474; relationship to economic change 415; scientific methods of research 481. *See also* academic disciplines and information history
scientific management: as information revolution 12
scientific racism: and datafication 121
Scotland: encyclopaedias 127, 288
Scott, James C. 194, 452
Scott, Julius 431, 438
secrecy: Bambudye secret society 586–587; and communication in governance 386–388; and confidentiality in the political arena 388–391; family secrets 508–510; implications of having a secret language 448; impossibility of 395; and leaks 395; and the market for information 459; nondisclosure agreements with collaborators 491; public secrets 496; radio broadcasting facilities 555; relationship to amount of information held 241; role of servants in uncovering 509–510; secret missives during rebellions 90; selling of state secrets 460; and subterfuge 575; and trade secrets 402–403, 409, 458; underground activism 571; wilful "forgetting" 508–509. *See also* fictionalised facts; law enforcement; spying; surveillance
security: and smart cities 369. *See also* cybersecurity
Semantic Web: addition of provenance 153; Berners-Lee's dream of the web 151; and document-instrument 139, 154; and Hyperdocumentation 154; Lessig's invisible hand 152; and Otlet 153–154; Resource Description Framework (RDF) 152–153; social tags and UDC 153
Serampore gardens 419
settler colonial statistics 119
sex 167, 169–170
sexism 312–313, 317–318
sexuality 163, 167–168, 169
Shannon, Claude 360, 536–537, 538, 539, 540, 542, 546, 547
Shera, Jesse 150, 588
Simmet, Hilton 184
Simonsen, Gunvor 97
Singapore: COVID-19 contact tracing 369, 376–377; the informatic present times 373–377; National Digital Identity (NDI) project 369, 374–376, 377, 378; postcolonial computerisation 372–374; town planning in colonial times 370–372
Slauter, Will 458
slavery 41, 47; in Britain 424; and Catholicism and the Catholic Church 437; Declaration of Independence of Haiti 438; and information circulation 437; Jefferson's census of the free and enslaved 118–119; and kinship ties 507; lack of family information 501; *Letters of the Late Ignatius Sancho* (Santo) 119–120; and literacy 438; maroons 100, 436, 437; reporting on rebellions 433; Spanish conquistadors and the Inka 80; Trinidad 436. *See also* Douglass, Frederick; enslaved people; race
smart cities: criticisms of 368, 378
Smith, Pamela 408
Smitherman, Geneva 105, 106
social media 552
South Africa: collecting medical information 567–570; Department of Information 571–572; information as tool of liberation 22, 570–572; Mellet 570–573; Smiesing 567–570; use of pigeons for military communications 520; William 573–576. *See also* enslaved people; radio
South America: Andes 9. *See also* Argentina; Brazil; Chile; Peru
Soviet Union 296. *See also* Russia
Spain 235–237, 241, 242, 325
Spanish Caribbean 431, 432–436, 437
specimens 421, 423
Spencer, Herbert 140, 145, 149
spying 370, 389, 391, 392, 448, 458, 487, 488, 489–490, 509
Standage, Tom 11
standardisation: in anthropometrics 195; and classification systems 291; COBOL 309; and colonialism 21–22; and communications 11; and information practice 16; and the ISTD 273; and khipus 78, 82
statistical science 414, 479, 480
statistics 253, 255
Stevens, Norman 19

storage: and the gloss 218, 219–221, 223–224; of the Isidorean phrase through description 215; Lockean decimal system 78, 79, 86, 88; notebooks as information recovery machines 568; standards for archives 334

street ballads: circumventing censorship 461; during crisis or war 463; failure as factual conduits 457, 458, 459; sensationalism of 457; subjects of 461

Sufism 393

surveillance: and abscondence 209–210; application of information technology 452; censuses as mechanism of 10, 452; eavesdropping 392, 395; Foucauldian 487, 488; goals of 487; human and imaginary intelligences (HUMINT) (IMINT) 268; intentionally fictionalised facts in reports 493–497; mechanisms as antecedents to information policy 10, 15, 44; panopticism 158, 164; para-panoptical means 488; of the Roma 452; and secret services 487, 496; and smart cities 368, 369. *See also* law enforcement; Romanian secret police; spying

surveillance capitalism, criticisms of 378

surveying land: as data 114, 116

surveys 370, 371, 420, 422; as method of collection 250. *See also* censuses; the Wartime Social Survey

Sweden 128–131, 132–133, 301, 305, 325

Syria 559, 560

tabloids 462

Taiwan 184, 242

Taussig, Michael 496

taxonomy: dealing with an abundance of information: generating taxonomies 473; and racial difference 110, 111, 119, 120–121, 189; relationship to information-ising and knowledge 589. *See also* Linnaeus, Carl

technologies of information: and academic disciplines 476; appropriation of, to keep in touch 449–451; change from people as opposed to 385; ferry schedules 451; finding new strategies to analyse new media 141; letters 45, 80, 81, 112, 113, 114, 115–116, 119–120, 122n15, 444–445, 449–450, 505, 557, 558, 568, 571; notebooks 568; pamphlets 385, 430, 459–460; postal systems 10, 385, 445, 450, 459, 475, 517, 518, *518*, 533n54; printing presses 8–9, 16, 141, 430, 431, 434–436, 570, 571; shipping schedules 239–241; telegraph 4, 8, 11, 14, 17, 195, 370, 445, 451, 474, 475, 480, 519, 520, 566; television 141, 142, 556, 559, 560, 572; trade routes 458; *vurma* and *patrin* of the Roma 449. *See also* artificial intelligence (AI); books; diagrams; facial AIs; handwriting; homing pigeons; human body; informants; manuscripts; maps; printed information; radio

telecommunications 376, 472

telephones 450–451

terminology: importance of distinctions in 112, *112*

Third World movement 553–554

Thornton, John 102–103

Toffler, Alvin 17

Touraine, Alain 17

transmission of information. *See* homing pigeons

travel agents 446–447, 451

Trinidad 435–436

trust: and informatic governance 376, 377, 378; in printed information 459, 464; of the public in law enforcement 377; and smart cities 369

Turing, Alan 480

Turits, Richard 97

Tworek, Heidi 459

uncertainty: and classification systems 584; and controlled vocabularies 584; as factor in popularity of ideas 547; and information 591; information as that which reduces 205; and information history 584; minimising 96; and need for reliable information 444; and public communications 296, 299, 302, 303–304, 305

United Arab Republic 559

United Kingdom: British National Archives 445; computing technology commencement in 13; IPSO and OFCOM codes of practice 169–170; Murdoch 166–167; and nuclear information 298, 301; software houses 311, 314; and South Africa 574–575. *See also* Britain; Ireland; Scotland

United Nations Sustainable Development Goal 16.9 188

United States 166, 167; African-American terminology in 105; American Documentation Institute (ADI) 12; American Medical Association 478; American Revolution 112, 163, 433; anti-nuclear-grassroots movement 302; and the atomic bomb 296, 297; and Britain's ISTD 267, 272, 274; cataloguing practices in libraries 343; cybernetics in 543; *The Declaration of Independence* 434; Dewey Decimal Classification (DDC) 477; effect of Radio Cairo in 556; effect of the postal system and telegraphic messages 10; and Egypt

559–560; fingerprinting in New York 196; Graber photographic reproduction machines 270, 274; and the H-bomb 297–298; history of computing scholarship 358; influence on information theory 537, 538–539, 546; influx of international academics after WWI 479; Jefferson's censuses 118–119, 121; library and information science (LIS) 18–19; Library of Congress Classification (CC) 477; mail of the Roma 450; propaganda about Louisiana 445; radio of 560; release of nuclear information 298, 299; role of printing in 430; secret services materials 487; software houses 311; tabloidism in 168; use of affect AIs 190; use of homing pigeons for military purposes 516, 520, 524, 525, 527–528; women in computer technology 309. *See also* Jefferson, Thomas; museums; nuclear information

universal control of information 11–12, 140, 149

Universal Decimal Classification (UDC). *See* classification systems

Ursul, Arkady 546

Vandekerckhove, Wim 575

Venezuela 429, 434–438

Venice: and Christianity 386, 395–396; coffeehouses 393; confidentiality in 388–391; marketplaces for information 459–460; newswriters of 390, 392; political expression in 391–395; *relazioni* 387, 389, 461; secrecy and decision-making 388; women and the informal exchange of political news 390–391

Vernal, Fiona 569

visual information: aerial photographs in WWII 269; in ancient Rome 39–40, 43–44; in descriptive cataloguing 345; diagrams related to *Categories* (Aristotle) 220, 224–226, 226, 227; in *Encyclopedia Synthetica Schematica* 145; and institutional mandates 589; preparing for D-Day 269, 270, 274; in reports 273; reproduction machines in WWII 270; and tabloidism 166. *See also* Christianity; diagrams; encyclopaedias; maps; Otlet, Paul

Wahl-Jorgensen, Karin 163

the Wartime Social Survey: accuracy of 288; and civilian morale 280, 282–283, 290; Cooper 282; data collection and processing 285–286; development of 282–283; dissemination of 287–288; effect of, on survey methods 290–292; effect on post-war policy 289–291;

interpretation and analysis 286, 286–287; methodology of 282, 288; Moss 283; recycling habits of the public 288–289; research design 284–285; use of punch cards 285–287, 286

Weaver, Warren 539, 540

Weber, Max 386

Webster, Frank 12; *Theories of the Information Society* 359

Weller, Toni 112, 211, 566

Wells, H. G. 12

West Germany: and nuclear information 301

whistleblowing as information practice 567, 573–576

Wiener, Mandy 576

Wiener, Norbert 536, 537, 539, 546

Wikipedia, pluralism and 184

Wikipedia's Neutral Point of View: and bias 180, 181, 182–184; first draft of NPOV policy 175–177; hierarchy of information 173–185; lack of bibliographic imagination 176, 178, 179, 180, 183; minority views 176, 177, 179, 180–181, 182; philosophy of 133; POV fork 179, 182; pseudoscience in 175, 177, 178, 179–180, 182; and religion 175–176, 178, 182; Sanger 133, 173, 175–176; undue weight 178–179, 180–181, 182; use of the term fundamentalism 178, 180, 182; Wales 133, 173, 175, 179, 180–181

Williams, Patrick 450, 451

Wolfe, Patrick 110, 111

Wolton, Dominique 543

women 44–45; anthropometrics and the female body 250–254, 252; assisting in processing information in WWII 270, 271; and the census in ancient Rome 42; collecting one's personal information 248; in computing history 308–309, 310–311, 312–314, 315–316, 318–319, 320, 356, 358; education and training 248, 249, 309, 312, 317, 333; excluded from systems of registration in ancient Rome 45–46; handwritten examples by 39; hysteria in 248–249, 253, 255, 258; influence of *valides* 388; and the informal exchange of political news 390–391; Nochlin 317; recipes to treat venereal disease 568–569; and representational othering 163; and reproductive issues 99, 248, 250–251, 253–256, 257, 258, 310–311, 314; role in England's archives 332–335; and street ballad singing 465. *See also* computing history; gender

women's studies: and the Dewey Decimal Classification 341

word of mouth 158, 396, 406, 407, 442, 446, 450, 451, 460
Wu, Angela Xiao 538, 539
WWW: and hypertext 139, 150–151, *151*, 173; and the limits of universal classification 150; *Linked. How Everything is…Everyday Life* (Barabási) 152; and loss of control of personal data 152; and Otlet 139, 140; as result of a gradual design process 150–152; self-organising growth of, due to collective human behaviour 152. *See also* Semantic Web

Yeo, Geoffrey 324
Yeoh, Brenda 370
Yoors, Jan 450–451
Yost, Jeffrey 35, 354, 355, 356

For Product Safety Concerns and Information please contact our EU representative GPSR@taylorandfrancis.com
Taylor & Francis Verlag GmbH, Kaufingerstraße 24, 80331 München, Germany